1,000,000 Books

are available to read at

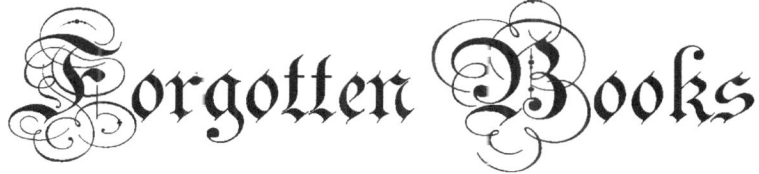

www.ForgottenBooks.com

Read online
Download PDF
Purchase in print

ISBN 978-0-259-83850-0
PIBN 10829004

This book is a reproduction of an important historical work. Forgotten Books uses
state-of-the-art technology to digitally reconstruct the work, preserving the original format
whilst repairing imperfections present in the aged copy. In rare cases, an imperfection in
the original, such as a blemish or missing page, may be replicated in our edition. We do,
however, repair the vast majority of imperfections successfully; any imperfections that
remain are intentionally left to preserve the state of such historical works.

Forgotten Books is a registered trademark of FB &c Ltd.
Copyright © 2018 FB &c Ltd.
FB &c Ltd, Dalton House, 60 Windsor Avenue, London, SW19 2RR.
Company number 08720141. Registered in England and Wales.

For support please visit www.forgottenbooks.com

1 MONTH OF FREE READING

at

www.ForgottenBooks.com

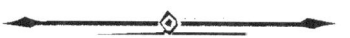

By purchasing this book you are eligible for one month membership to ForgottenBooks.com, giving you unlimited access to our entire collection of over 1,000,000 titles via our web site and mobile apps.

To claim your free month visit: www.forgottenbooks.com/free829004

* Offer is valid for 45 days from date of purchase. Terms and conditions apply.

English
Français
Deutsche
Italiano
Español
Português

www.forgottenbooks.com

Mythology Photography **Fiction** Fishing Christianity **Art** Cooking Essays Buddhism Freemasonry Medicine **Biology** Music **Ancient Egypt** Evolution Carpentry Physics Dance Geology **Mathematics** Fitness Shakespeare **Folklore** Yoga Marketing **Confidence** Immortality Biographies Poetry **Psychology** Witchcraft Electronics Chemistry History **Law** Accounting **Philosophy** Anthropology Alchemy Drama Quantum Mechanics Atheism Sexual Health **Ancient History Entrepreneurship** Languages Sport Paleontology Needlework Islam **Metaphysics** Investment Archaeology Parenting Statistics Criminology **Motivational**

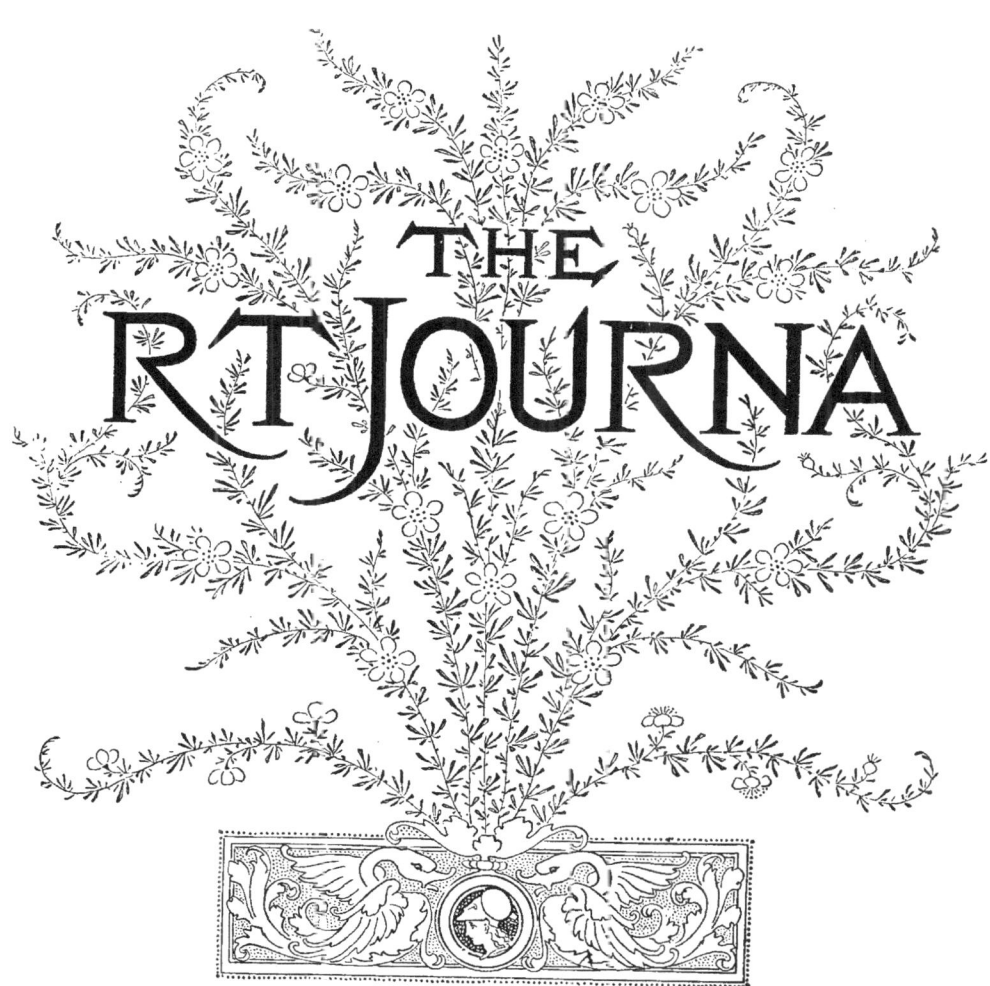

THE ART JOURNAL

NEW SERIES

LONDON: J.S. VIRTUE & CO. L^{IMTD.}
56 1894

[The right of Translation and Re...

THE ART JOURNAL, 1894.

LIST OF PLATE ILLUSTRATIONS.

ETCHINGS.

1. "A SILENT GREETING" . . . . C. O. MURRAY, after L. ALMA TADEMA, R.A. . *Frontispiece.*
   Described on p. 4.
2. "IN THE FOREST OF ARDEN" . . . . . . C. O. MURRAY, after JOHN COLLIER . . . . *To face p.* 68
   Described on p. 68.
3. "ON THE RIVER" . . . . *Original Etching by* JOSEPH PENNELL . . . . ,, 100
4. A SURREY LANDSCAPE . . . . CLOUGH BROMLEY, *after* VICAT COLE, R.A. . ,, 194
   Described on p. 195.
5. AN IDYLL . . . . J. DOBIE, *after* M. GREIFFENHAGEN . . . . ,, 226
   Described on p. 226.
6. A SHEPHERD ON SALISBURY PLAIN . . . *Original Etching by* EDGAR BARCLAY . . . . ,, 266
   Described on p. 266.
7. HOME WITH THE TIDE . . . . R. SPINELLI, *after* J. C. HOOK, R.A. . . . . ,, 318
   Described on p. 318.
8. THE BILLET DOUX . . . . LÉON LAMBERT, *after* T. ROBERT-FLEURY . . ,, 324
   Described on p. 325.

PHOTOGRAVURES.

1. "HER MOTHER'S VOICE" . . . . *From the Picture by* W. Q. ORCHARDSON, R.A. . . *To face p.* 34
   Described on p. 34.
2. WEAVING THE WREATH . . . . *From the Picture by* SIR FREDERIC LEIGHTON, P.R.A. ,, 136
   Described on p. 136.
3. THE REVOLUTIONIST'S BRIDE, 1799 . . *From the Picture by* F. H. KAEMMERER . . . . ,, 164
   Described on p. 164.
4. LITTLE MISS MUFFIT . . . . *From the Picture by* SIR JOHN EVERETT MILLAIS, R.A. ,, 376
   Described on p. 375.

CHROMOTYPOGRAVURES.

1. FLORA IN JANUARY . . . . *Sonnet by* WILLIAM SHARP . . . . *To face p.* 16
2. VESPER . . . . *Sonnet by* WILLIAM SHARP . . . . ,, 114
3. THE PEACE OF SUMMER . . . . . . *Sonnet by* WILLIAM SHARP . . . . ,, 208
4. AFTERMATH . . . . *Sonnet by* WILLIAM SHARP . . . . ,, 312
   Reproduced in colours from drawings by C. BERNAMONT.

TINTED PLATES.

1. NAPOLEON DICTATING HIS MEMOIRS
   Described on p. 60. *From the Picture by* W. Q. ORCHARDSON, R.A. *To face p.* 58
2. ARIADNE . . . . *Described on p.* 78. *From the Picture by* JOHN LAVERY, A.R.S.A. . ,, 78
3. ATHLETE STRANGLING A PYTHON
   Described on p. 180. *From the Statue by* SIR FREDERIC LEIGHTON, P.R.A. ,, 140
4. RUNNING THE BLOCKADE . *Described on p.* 180. *From the Picture by* BRITON RIVIÈRE, R.A. . . . . ,, 180
5. DORA . . . . *Described on p.* 244. *From the Picture by* WILLIAM MCTAGGART, R.S.A. . ,, 244
6. LE PÊCHEUR D'ÉCREVISSES *Described on p.* 260. *From the Picture by* J. B. COROT . . . . ,, 260
7. THE VIOLINIST . . . . . *Described on p.* 335. *From the Picture by* G. A. STOREY, A.R.A. . . . . ,, 336
8. LES BÉBÉS DU LUXEMBOURG . . . . *Original Lithograph by* JAMES MCNEILL WHISTLER ,, 362

THE ART JOURNAL, 1894.

GENERAL INDEX TO ARTICLES AND TEXT ILLUSTRATIONS.

À VERSAILLES. By V. C. Prinsep, 221
Absinthe, L'. By Degas, 206
Academy (see Royal)
Achilles. By T. Woolner, 83
Adam Bede. By J. H. Henshall, 123
Adams, Mrs. J. By J. Tassie, 96
Adelaide Art Gallery, 344
After a Storm. By W. H. Bartlett, 247
Alum Bay. By J. B. Pyne, 177
American Tariff Bill, The, 351
Amsterdam by Night. By Breitner, 88
Ancestor on the Tapestry, The. By J. Haynes-Williams, 289
Ancient Cambodian Art, 364
Ancient and Modern Dancing, 338, 360
'And ye shall walk in Silk Attire.' By T. Faed, 194
Angel of Death, The. By G. J. Frampton, 303
Anglers, The. By J. Linnell, 179
Annunciation. By Raphael, 121
Antwerp Exhibition, Furnishings at the, 252
Appledram. By G. L. Little, 171
Architecture at the Academy, 213
Architecture (Domestic) in Norfolk, 274
Ariel. By H. H. Armstead, 202
Armourer's Shop, The. By W. Gay, 4
Art and Mr. Whistler, 358
Art Association of Montreal, 95
Art at Bradford, 157
Art Criticism and Bribery, 60
Art, German. By Sir F. Leighton, 2
Art at Glasgow, 30
Art at Guildhall, 302, 335
Art Publications—
  Art Union, 64, 380
  Dott, 380
  Elkin Matthews and John Lane, 192
  Gardner, W. B., Wood Engraving, 192
  Librairie de l'Art, 160
  Sedelmeyer, 96
  Swan Electric Engraving Co., 288
Art in the Shop Windows, 52
Art in the Transvaal, 28
Artemis. By H. Thornycroft, 141
Arthur and Hubert, Prince. By W. F. Yeames, 36
Artistic Discovery, An (Pinelli Engravings), 284
Arts and Crafts at Sheffield, 158
Astarte Syriaca. By D. G. Rossetti, 35
At the Bridge. By J. Maris, 288
Athlete putting the Stone. By H. Thornycroft, 200
Autumn Leaves. By Sir J. E. Millais, 37

BAISER Suprême, Le. By Christophe, 45
Ball under a Colonnade. By Watteau, 363
Banks of the Rhine, The, 293
Banquet at Guildhall. By W. Daniell, 302
Baptism of the Eunuch. By Rembrandt, 24
Bass Rock, The. By A. W. Henley, 262
Bayerthurm, The, Cologne. By F. Williamson, 295
Bear Inn, The, Rickmansworth. By F. G. Kitton, 330
Beaux-Arts, Acquisitions at the, 285
Before the Procession. By V. Chevilliard, 346
Belfry Tower, The, Ghent. By Sir J. Gilbert, 335
Belle, The. By W. McTaggart, 245
Bench Bill Water. By J. E. Mitchell, 233
Bequests to Scottish Artists, 69
Berwick. About North, 261
Bettws-y-Coed, 267
Birmingham Brass Work, 313
Birmingham Jewellers, 112, 256
Birmingham Silversmiths, 217

Bismarck Monument at Berlin, 285
Bitumen and Varnish. Sir J. C. Robinson on, 326
Black Poplar, The. By A. Parsons, 319
Blanchisseuse, La. By Degas, 204
Blossoms. By A. Moore, 89
Bosham. By G. L. Little, 174
Boston Gallery, Gifts to the, 286
Boy catching Crab. By H. Montalba, 217
Bradford, Art at, 157
Bradlaugh Statue, The. By G. Tinworth, 286
British Art Gallery, The, 373
British Painting in 1893, 1
Browning, R. By H. Montalba, 216
Bull Inn, The, Harpenden. By F. G. Kitton, 108
Burne-Jones, Sir Edward, 94, and Art Annual
Burning Kelp. By W. H. Bartlett, 251
Bury, The, Rickmansworth. By F. G. Kitton, 330

CAMBODIAN Art, Ancient, 364
Cape of Good Hope Art Gallery, 298, 378
Carisbrooke Castle, 160
Castles of the Channel Islands, 238
Causerie. By Meissonier, 59
Changing Pasture. By A. Mauve, 260
Chantrey Bequest Purchases, 191, 221
Chapu. By himself, 320
Cheltham Hospital, Manchester, 147
Chicago, British Fine Art Section at, 124
Children in Paradise. By T. Woolner, 82
Chloe. By E. J. Poynter, 369
Christ Ch., Turnham Green, Altarpiece at, 286
Christophe. E. L. A., 40
Church St., Rickmansworth. F. G. Kitton, 334
Cinque-Cento Jewelry, 152
Circe. By J. Collier, 65
Clair Bois. By Th. Rousseau, 257
Clement de Jonghe. By Rembrandt, 188
Cleopatra. By G. A. Lawson, 140
Cleopatra, Death of. By J. Collier, 67
Cleopatra's Needle. By J. Pennell, 100
Clock. By H. Mason, 317
Clyte. By Chapu, 320
Clytie. By G. F. Watts, R.A., 138
Coast Life in Connemara, 247
Coblenz. By F. Williamson, 295
Cook, Captain. By T. Woolner, 82
Copyright and "Living Pictures," 124, 242
Corday, Charlotte. By T. R. Fleury, 323
Collier, John, 65
Cologne. By F. Williamson, 294
Colour, Theory of Sensation of, 328
Conquerors. By E. Mullins, 199
Contemplation. By J. Linnell, 179
Constantinople at Olympia, 94
Conway Falls. By H. C. Whaite, 268
Cook, Captain. By T. Woolner, 82
Copyright and "Living Pictures," 124, 242
Corinth, the Last Day of. By T. R. Fleury, 325
Cornet Castle, Guernsey. By J. A. Symington, 238
Correspondence—
  Dr. Blatherwick, 222
  Chatto and Linton, 28
  G. C. Haité, 378
Courage (David and the Lion). By H. H. Armstead, 203
Critics and Criticism, 327
Critics and Bribery, 60
Croquet. By J. Lavery, 79
Crossing the Brook. By E. Gardner, 186
Cupid's Spell. By H. Woods, 2
Customs Duties, American, 351

DA VINCI, L. (see Leonardo)
Danseuse, La première. By Degas, 205

Dante and Virgil. By E. Delacroix, 353
David and the Lion. By H. H. Armstead, 203
Dawn of Womanhood. By T. S. Lee, 277
Death and the Prisoner. By A. H. Pegram, 280
Decorative Art in London, French, 5
Degas. By T. Duret, 204
Déjeuner sur l'herbe. By P. Outin, 187
Delacroix, Eugène, 353
Dellquay. By G. L. Little, 174
Depression of Trade, 60
Descent from the Cross. By J. V. Krämer, 345
Dick-Lauder, Sir T. By W. Crombie, 272
Dionysius. By F. Pomeroy, 310
Dispute, The. By F. K. Kaemmerer, 165
Dochart, The. By J. E. Mitchell, 236
Donald Collection, The, 257
Drawbridge, The. By J. Maris, 258
Driving Home the Flock. By D. Cox, 38
Dunkeld Church. By J. E. Mitchell, 234

EAST BARSHAM, Remains at, 275
École des Beaux-Arts, 61
Edinburgh. By J. Kinnear, 11
Electric Push. By H. Mason, 316
Electrolier. By Best & Lloyd, 314
Electrolier. By Messenger, 316
Elizabeth Castle, Jersey. By J. A. Symington, 238
Elsi, Lake. By H. C. Whaite, 271
Eve. By M. Greiffenhagen, 225
Evening. By A. Mauve, 104
Evening Shadows. By H. J. Johnstone, 346
Exhibitions—
  Agnew's, 31
  Antwerp Exhibition, The, 61, 252
  Birmingham Royal Soc. of Artists, 31, 158
  Blacksmith's Exhibition, 223
  Boussod, Valadon & Co. 31, 95, 285
  British Artists, Society of, 31, 377
  Burlington Fine Arts Club. 124, 255
  Deaf and Dumb Artists at Munich, 158
  Dowdeswell's, 285
  Dunthorne, 377
  Earl's Court Industrial Exhibition, 351
  Eland's, Exeter, 125
  English Silk Exhibition, 222
  Fair Women, 255
  Ferrarese and Bolognese Pictures, 255
  Fine Art Society, 31, 285
  French Decorative Art, 5
  Glasgow Institute, 125
  Grafton Gallery, The, 5, 88, 255
  Graves, 377
  Haddon, Trevor, 318
  Hanover Gallery, The, 191
  Home Arts and Industries Association, 285
  Jeffrey & Co., 193
  Liverpool Exhibition, 60, 285
  McLean's, 377
  Mendoza's, 31
  New English Art Club, 31, 191
  New Gallery, The, 62, 120, 191
  Oil Painters, Institute of, 31, 377
  Oil Painters, Royal Society of, 31
  Portrait Painters' Society, 377
  Royal Academy, The, 62, 191
  Royal Scottish Academy, 124
  St. George's Gallery, 285
  Salons, The Paris, 185
  San Francisco Exhibition, 31
  Tooth's, 95, 377
  Water-Colour Society, Royal, 191

CONTENTS.

Farmer and Son. By A. J. Gaskin, 32
Fatalité, La. By Christophe, 41
Faults on both Sides. By T. Faed, 371
Favourites of Honorius, The. By J. W. Waterhouse, 346
Felpham. By G. L. Little, 173
Field Flowers. By J. W. Waterhouse, 210
First Cloud, The. By W. Q. Orchardson, 33
First-born, The. By F. H. Kaemmerer, 163
Firth of Forth, The. By A. W. Henley, 266
Fishbourne Mill. By G. L. Little, 173
Fleury, Tony Robert, 321
Flirtation. By S. Lucas, 337
Flock Returning, The. By A. Mauve, 105
Folly. By E. O. Ford, 306
For Whom and from Whom? By J. Haynes-Williams, 293
France, Picture Sales in, 347
French Decorative Art in London, 5
Furnishings at the Antwerp Exhibition, 252

Gardner, W. B., Wood Engraving by, 192
Garnier, H., Reported Suicide of, 286
Genius of Poetry, The. By T. Brock, 309
Gentleman of Louis XII. By Meissonier, 31
German Art. By Sir F. Leighton, 29
Girl's Head. By A. Roche, 78
Girl I left behind Me, The. By R. Caldecott, 36
Gladstone, Mr. (Laughing at Labby.) By H. Furniss, 192
Glasgow, Art at, 30, 222
Glasgow School, The, 75
Going to Church. By F. H. Kaemmerer, 161
Going to Labour. By J. F. Millet, 257
Going to Market. By Troyon, 259
Good Neighbours. By J. Israels, 347
Good Story, A. By W. D. Sadler, 195
Great Hautbois Farmhouse, 275
Great Master, The. (Rembrandt), 23
Greek Dances, 338
Greek Vase Painting, 208
Greenwich Hospital. By J. Pennell, 97, 100
Greiffenhagen, Maurice, 225
Guildhall, Art at, 133, 302, 335

Haden, Sir F. S., 222
Harp, The. By F. H. Kaemmerer, 162
Harpenden, 107
Haynes-Williams, J. M., 289
Healing Shrine, A. By W. H. Bartlett, 250
Helmingham Park. By J. Constable, 57
Herod's Birthday Feast. By E. Armytage, 134
Herring Market at Sea. By C. Hunter, 35
Highland Mother, The. By T. Faed, 372
Hill, D. O., 272
Hill Legacy, The, to South Kensington Museum, 317, 377
Hobart (Tasmania) Art Gallery, 368
Holland, Picture Sales in, 347
Housekeeper, The. By A. Neuhuys, 348
Housemaid, The. By T. Woolner, 85
Howard, John. Memorial by A. Gilbert, 191
Huntly, Marquis of, 30

Illustrators, Society of, 60, 378
Industry and Prudence. By R. Smirke, 303
Inn, The. By S. Bough, 59
Irish Fair, An. By E. Nicol, 58
Irish National Gallery, Grants for the, 350
Irving as Hamlet. By E. O. Ford, 201
Israels, Josef, 95
Italian Art, Early, 120

Jaguar with Young. By J. M. Swan, 17, 21
Japanese Coloured Prints, 342
Jewellers, Birmingham, 112
Jewelry, Cinque Cento, 152
Jewelry, The Setting of Stones, 182
Johnson, C. E., School of Animal Painting by, 125

Kaemmerer, F. H., 161
Keiller Collection, The, 54
Kenmore Village. By J. E. Mitchell, 233
King's Lynn Almshouses, 276
King's Lynn Vicarage, 276

King William Range. By W. C. Piguenit, 368
Knocker. By H. E. & L. Fontaine, 6
Knucklebone Vase, The, 339
Knysna Heads. By A. De Smidt, 298

Lady (Our). *See* 'Our Lady of the Rocks'
Land's End. By F. R. Lee, 299
Lansdowne, Marquis of, 349
Laren, Near. By A. Mauve, 102
Last Brief Voyage, The. By W. H. Bartlett, 249
Last of the Struggle, The. By J. E. Mitchell, 235
Laughing at Labby. By H. Furniss, 192
Leather Bottle, The, Harpenden. By F. G. Kilton, 108
Leçon de Danse, La. By Degas, 207
Lectern. By J. Powell, 313
Leighton, Sir F. By T. Brock, 281
Leonardo da Vinci, 166, 229, 300
Lime Trees, Under the. By Bernier, 85
Linos. By E. O. Ford, 280
Lion Drinking. By J. M. Swan, 17
Lion and Lioness. By J. M. Swan, 18, 20, 22
Lion, Study of a. By Rembrandt, 26
Little White Girl, The. By J. M. Whistler, 259
Loan Collection at Guildhall, 133
Loch Tay. By J. E. Mitchell, 237
Lock. By A. L. M. Charpentier, 5
Lock Plate. By H. Mason, 316
London Bridge, Old. By J. Scott, 335
London. By Canaletto, 129
London County Council and Art Study, 60
Lord Mayor going to Westminster. By F. Wheatley and R. Paton, 303
Lord St. Vincent. By Sir W. Beechey, 304
Losing. By J. Haynes-Williams, 291
Louis XIV. By Chapu, 320
Louvre, Old View of the, 51
Low Tide. By H. W. Mesdag, 188
Luxembourg at Paris, The, 60

MacEwan Hall, Edinburgh, 126
McTaggart, William, 243
Manchester City Art Gallery, 35
Marooned. By E. J. Gregory,
Masque, Le. By Christophe, 43
Massacre of Scio. By E. Delacroix, 315
Match Girl, The Little. By A. J. Gaskin, 32
Mauve, Anton, 101
Meissonier's House, 318
Meissonier's Last Wishes, 351
Mellon, Miss. By G. Romney, 135
Mermaid, The. By M. Greiffenhagen, 226
Mermaid, The. By F. Stuck, 90
Mesquinez, Woman of. By G. Montbard, 209
Middleton Towers, 274
Milking Time. By W. Maris, 348
Mill at the Canal. By J. Maris, 347
Mind and Muscle. By H. S. Marks, 123
Minuet, The. By Sir J. E. Millais, 362
Minuet, A Long. By H. Bunbury, 363
Moel Siabod. By F. H. C. Whaite, 267
Mont Orgueil Castle. By J. A. Symington, 2, 1
Montalba, Henrietta, 215
Montesquieu, Comte de. By J. M. Whistler, 361
Montreal, Art Association of, 95
Mower, The. By H. Thornycroft, 279
Munich Exhibition Awards, 318
Murder, The. By F. Stuck, 91
Murillo, Early Career of. By J. Phillip, 55
Murillo's St. Clara, 318
My Few Things, 6, 70

Nakhon Wat, Temple of, 364
Nasmyth Bequest, The, 69
Nasty Weather. By G. Montbard, 209
National Competition Awards, 1894, 350
National Gallery, Critical Sketches at the, 166
National Gallery, New Director of the, 191
National Gallery, New Trustees at, 349
National Gallery, Parliamentary Grants for, 350
National Gallery of Ireland, 350
National Gallery for Wales, Demand for a, 350
Neilson, Miss J. By J. Collier, 66
New Forest, The. By P. Nasmyth, 299

New Sculpture, The, 138, 197, 277, 306
Newlands, Cape Town. By C. Rowlands, 300
Niederbreisig. By F. Williamson, 296
Noblesse oblige. By F. Haynes-Williams, 290
Norfolk Domestic Architecture, 274
North Berwick, About, 261
North-West Passage, The. By Sir J. E. Millais, 3
Nude at Glasgow, The, 191, 222

Oberwesel. By F. Williamson, 297
Obituary—
  Bodmer, Karl, 31
  Boussod, Léon, 61
  Buckler, J. C., 125
  Cain, A., 352
  Combe, Mrs. M., 125
  Destailleur, H., 61
  Fontana, G., 61
  Gray, J. M., 158
  Hamerton, P. G., 377
  Hart, W., 286
  Holyoake, W., 95
  Loustau, J. L., 286
  Madrazo, F., 286
  Marshall, W. C., 286
  Matejko, J., 61
  Millet, Madame J. F., 125
  Mousset, P. J., 286
  Newcombe, F. C., 125
  Papworth, W., 351
  Raemakers, J. A., 192
  Rossetti, Lucy, 192
  Satchell, Mrs. S., 125
  Steel, Gourlay, 125
  Vannutelli, S., 286
  Woodington, W. F., 61
On the River, 97
Ophelia. By M. Greiffenhagen, 227
Orchardson as a Dramatist, 33
Our Lady of the Rocks, 167, 229, 300
Our River. By W. L. Wyllie, 344
Oxburgh Hall, 274

Paddy's Love-Letter. By E. Nicol, 196
Painter-Etchers, R. Soc. of, 60, 222
Painting, British, in 1893, 1
Pancakes, The. By J. Israels, 56
Pandora. By D. G. Rossetti, 136
Panther and Bull. By J. M. Swan, 21
Paris (Ile de la Cité). By J. M. Whistler, 9
Parliamentary Votes for Art, 350
Parting, The. By W. G. John, 308
Pasture, Going to. By C. Troyon, 92
Peace. By E. O. Ford, 277
Peacock's Feather, The. By F. Stuck, 93
Perseus rescuing Andromeda. By H. C. Fehr, 212
Phillip IV. By Velasquez, 258
Pianoforte, The, 142
Picture Sales of 1894, 311
Picture Sales in France and Holland, 347
Picture, Ups and Downs of a, 271
Pigeonswick. By F. G. Kitton, 107
Pinch of Poverty, The. By T. B. Kennington, 344
Pinelli, B., Discovery of Engravings by, 284
Pont-au-Change. By Méryon, 72
Pont-de-l'Estacade, Le. By L. Luigi, 191
Pont-y-Pair. By H. C. Whaite, 267
Poppies. By G. Henry, 80
Portrait. By M. Greiffenhagen, 228
Portrait. By J. Guthrie, 76
Portrait. By E. A. Walton, 77
Poynter, E. J., 191
Preservation of Ancient Buildings, 156
Printemps, Le. By Fragonard, 170
Prints, Japanese, 321
Puck. By T. Woolner, 82

Queen's Park, Edinburgh, 11
Queen of Swords, The. By W. Q. Orchardson, 34
Quilter, Henry, 94

Racecourse, On the. By Degas, 208
Racing Day, A. By P. Graham, 180
Red Riding Hood. By A. J. Gaskin, 380
Rehearsal, The. By Degas, 204

Rembrandt, 23
Rembrandt, Brother of, 26
Rembrandt, First Wife of, 25
Rembrandt, House of, 25
Returning from the Fair. By W. H. Bartlett, 248
Reverie. By F. Stead, 157
Reviews—
  Ancient Arms and Armour, 128
  Andersen's Fairy Tales, 32
  Anglo-Saxons, Industrial Arts of, 160
  Antoinette, Marie, Life of, 127
  Archæologia Oxoniensis, 352
  Architecture, History of, 224
  Art, Contemporary, Examples of, 93
  Art, Egyptian, 64
  Art and Handicraft, Women's, at Chicago, 64
  Art of Illustration, 287
  Art, Japanese, 128
  Art of the World, 320
  Art, The Year's, 1894, 32
  Biarritz, Etchings of, 287
  Birmingham Gallery Catalogue, 224
  Bookbindings in Nat. Art Library, 352
  Book Plate Annual, 128
  Botticelli, Sandro, 93
  Burns' Chloris, 32
  Canaletto, 224
  Celtic Ornament, Examples of, 160
  Céramique Chinoise, La, 92
  Céramique, Dictionnaire de la, 92
  Chapu, 320
  Christmas Books, 380
  Chronology of French Cathedrals, 288
  Churches of Shropshire, 319
  Colours, Handbook on, 32
  Columbian Exposition, History of, 320
  Days in Clover, 160
  Delacroix, Journal of, 90
  Design, Elementary, 64
  Design, Theory and Practice of, 287
  Dictionary, Funk & Wagnall's, 287
  Drawing and Design, 64
  Drawing Room Duologues, 224
  Dress, English History of, 32
  Egyptian Art, 64
  Fables, Iconographie des, 94
  Fans and Fanleaves, 127
  Fans of Japan, 181
  Faulkner's Publications, 32
  Fine Arts, Books on the, 128
  Flowers, Wild, in Art and Nature, 288
  Flushing, Vià, 224
  France, Artistique et Monumentale, 51
  Gardening, Landscape, in Japan, 224
  Genius and Art, 224
  Grand Old Mystery Unravelled, The, 192
  Graphic Atlas, 128
  Greek Vase Painting, 208
  Greek Vases in the Ashmolean Museum, 64
  Greeks, Ancient, Home Life of the, 128
  Handicraft and Design, 64
  Hanging of the Crane, The, 32
  Heaton's Record of Work, 128
  Illustration, Art of, 287
  In the Footsteps of the Poets, 32
  Japan Society, Transactions of, 128
  Japonais, Documents Décoratifs, 128
  Jeffries, Richard, 128
  Joan of Arc, 32
  Jones, Inigo, & Wren, 32
  Landscape Gardening in Japan, 224
  Lathes, Turning, 352
  Leadwork, Old and Ornamental, 64
  Living Memories of an Octogenarian, 224
  Louvre, The (Lafenestre), 352
  Manchester Gallery Catalogue, 224
  Manchester Water-Colour Drawings, 319
  Méditerranée, Autour de la, 94
  Miereveit, Michael van, 224
  Modern Painting, 64
  Moors, Among the, 209
  Mountain, Moor, and Loch, 320
  New South Wales Gallery Catalogue, 159
  Northcote, Conversations of, 127

Reviews—continued.
  Ornament, Handbook of, 128
  Ornament, Theory and Analysis of, 160
  Peinture, Histoire de la (École Française), 92
  Photography, Books on, 127
  Pierres Gravées Décrites, 320
  Poker Work, Designs for, 318
  Pottery of United States, 93
  Reeves' Easel and Colour-box, 288
  Rembrandt, 23
  Rembrandts, Two New, 94
  Reproductions d'Orfèvrerie Hollandaise, 92
  Reynolds, Sir J., 127
  St. Louis Gallery Catalogue, 224
  Salome, 159
  Schalekamp's Catalogue, 288
  Studies for Artists, 352
  Studio, The, 128
  Stuck, Franz, 90
  Sylvia's Annual, 128
  Tassie, J. and W., 96
  Tennyson and His Illustrators, 127
  Turnbull's Carton, 318
  Venetian Painters of Renaissance, 224
  Vorsterman, Lucas, 91
  Wight, Isle of, 160
  Wild Garden, The, 319
  Yemen, Journey through the, 64
  Zeichnungen Deutscher Kunstler, 160
Rhine, The Banks of the, 294
Rhinoceros. By R. Stark, 311
Rickmansworth, 329
River, On the, 97
River Scene. School of Van Goyen, 336
Riverside Inn, The. By F. H. Kaemmerer, 164
Robinson, Sir J. C., on Bitumen and Varnish, 326
Rothamsted Manor House. By F. G. Kitton, 110
Royal Academy, The, 1894, 211
Royal Academy, Architecture at the, 213
Royal Academy, Elections at the, 60, 94, 221
Royal Academy in Parliament, 222
Royal Association for Promoting Fine Arts in Scotland, 94
Royal Scottish Academy, 30, 273
Royal Scottish Water-Colour Society, 94
Rubens, Discovery of Letters by, 95

SACRO MONTE at Varalla, The (Poem), 122
St. Aubyn's Castle, Jersey. By J. A. Symington, 242
St. Clara, Death of. By Murillo, 318
St. Helenius' Rock, Jersey. By J. A. Symington, 239
St. Paul's by Night. By J. Pennell, 98
Salons, The Paris, 60, 95, 185
Salmon Pools o' Tay, By the, 233
Sanctuary Lamp. By Hardman, 315
Sanderson, Prof. B. By J. Collier, 68
Sardanapalus, Death of. By E. Delacroix, 356
Scotland for ever! By Lady Butler, 137
Scottish Architecture. A new piece of, 126
Scottish Art, A Phase of, 75
Scottish Artists, Bequest to, 69
Scottish Artists, Society of, 30
Scottish Collection, A Representative, 257
Scottish Impressionist, A (W. McTaggart), 243
Sculpture, The New, 138, 197, 277, 306
Seal Diving. By W. H. Bartlett, 247
Seaweed Gatherer, The. By J. C. Hook, 3
Secession Verein Bildender Künstler, Munich, 61
Selsey Peninsula, The, 171
Sensation of Colour, Theory of the, 328
Sergeant Tanviray. By P. Grolleron, 189
Setting of Stones, The, 182
'1789.' By T. R. Fleury, 321
Sforza, Caterina, 115
Sheep entering a Barn. By A. Mauve, 106
Sheffield Arts and Crafts, 158
Silversmiths, Birmingham, 217
Singer, The. By E. O. Ford, 307
Sluggard, The. By Sir F. Leighton, 278
Snowdon. By H. C. Whaite, 269

Snowdon. By E. M. Wimperis, 368
Society of Illustrators, The, 60, 378
Socrates. By H. Bates, 278
Solomon and the Queen of Sheba. By E. J. Poynter, 159
Son of Pan, A. By W. Padgett, 287
Souper de Beaucaire, Le. By L. de Nouy, 185
South Kensington Expenditure, 196
Spring's Delay. By J. Paterson, 77
Stevenson, Macaulay, 222
Stewart, Prof. D. By J. Tassie, 96
Stothard, Thomas, 86
Studies at the National Gallery. Leonardo da Vinci, 166
Summer. By E. A. Hornel, 78
Summer Breezes. By W. McTaggart, 243
Summertime. By H. W. B. Davis, 64
Sunny Hours. By K. Halswelle, 195
Sunset. By M. Dignam, 352
Surprise Pendant, The, 314
Swallow Waterfall, The. By H. C. Whaite, 268
Swan Hotel, Rickmansworth. By F. G. Kitton, 331
Swan, J. M., 17
Swedish Peasant. By H. Montalba, 216

TANTALLON CASTLE. By A. W. Henley, 263
Tassie, W. By Hagbolt, 96
Tate Collection, The, 1, 33, 177, 193, 285, 318, 370
Temptation, In. By Bright-Morris, 283
Ten Virgins, The. By J. M. Smith, 127
Tennant, Sir Charles, 349
Tennyson. By T. Woolner, 84
Teucer. By H. Thornycroft, 199
Tholinx, Dr. A. By Rembrandt, 23
Throne of J. de Medici. By D'Agnolo, 121
Through Wind and Rain. By W. McTaggart, 246
Tigers by Moonrise. By J. M. Swan, 19
Tlemçen, 46
Tomb in Montmartre Cemetery. By Rude and Christophe, 43
Tomkins, T. By Sir J. Reynolds, 305
Topaz. By A. Moore, 88
Tower Bridge, The. By J. Pennell, 97
Toy, The. By J. Israels, 260
Tragedy. By T. N. MacLean, 139
Transvaal, Art in the, 28
Triumph of Spring, The. By G. P. Jacomb-Hood, 159
Trustees, New, of the National Gallery, 348
Turning the Plough. By G. Clausen, 211
Twilight (Poem). By J. Fullwood, 39

UNDER the Trees. By A. Mauve, 103
Ups and Downs of a Picture, The, 271
Utamaro, Portrait of, 343

VAN STRY. By Himself, 378
Varsovie. By T. R. Fleury, 322
Venetian Council of War, A. By S. J. Gilbert, 38
Venice. By J. M. W. Turner, 54
Vinci, A. See Leonardo
Virago of the Renaissance, A, 115
Virgin, The. By Bartolomeo, 63
Virgin and Child (Panel), 120
Virgin with St. Catharine. By Van Dyck, 86
Virgin of the Rocks. See 'Our Lady,' &c.

WAITING to Cross. By A. Hagborg, 190
Warrior carrying Wounded Youth. By H. Thornycroft, 139
Watering Cows. By H. H. La Thangue, 157
Waterloo Bridge. By J. Pennell, 99
Watts, G. F. Gift of 'Love and Life,' 158
Wayside Prayer. By E. Nicol, 370
Wellington Shield, The. By T. Stothard, 87
Welsh National Gallery, Demand for a, 350
West Pans. By A. W. Henley, 99
Westminster Bridge. By Canaletto, 130
Whistler, Mr., and Art, 358
Windsor. By A. Hunt, 177
Winter. By A. Mauve, 104
Woolner, Thomas, R.A., 80
Woolner. (A Correction), 158
Word with My Critics, A., 256

ZENOBIO, San. By Botticelli, 62

THE ART JOURNAL, 1894.

LIST OF ARTISTS WHOSE WORK IS REPRODUCED IN THIS VOLUME.

ALLEYNE, E. H., 286
Alma Tadema, L., R.A. (*See Frontispiece*)
Armitage, E., R.A., 134
Armstead, H. H., R.A., 202

BARCLAY, Edgar, 266
Bartlett, W. H., 247
Bartolomeo, Fra, 63
Beechey, Sir W., R.A., 304
Bernamont, C., 16, 114, 208, 312
Bernier, 185
Botticelli, 62
Bough, Samuel, R.S.A., 59
Breitner, 88
Bright-Morris, 283
Brock, T., R.A., 281, 309
Bunbury, H., 363
Butler, Lady, 137

CALDECOTT, Randolph, 36
Canaletto, 129
Chapu, 320
Chevilliard, V., 346
Christophe, E., 41
Clausen, Geo., 211
Cole, Vicat, R.A., 191
Collier, John, 65
Constable, John, R.A., 57
Corot, J. B. C., 260
Cox, David, 38
Crombie, B. W., 272

D'AGNOLO, Baccio, 121
Daniell, W., R.A., 302
Davis, H. W. B., R.A., 64
De Smidt, A., 298
Degas, E., 204
Delacroix, E., 90, 92, 353
Dignam, M., 352

FAED, T., R.A., 194, 371
Fehr, H. C., 212
Fleury, T. R., 321
Fontaine, H. E. and L., 5, 6
Ford, E. Onslow, A.R.A., 201, 277, 280, 306, 307
Ford, H. J., 379
Fragonard, 170
Frampton, G. J., A.R.A., 308
Fullwood, John, 39
Furniss, Harry, 192

GARDNER, Elizabeth, 186
Gaskin, A. J., 32, 380
Gay, Walter, 4
Gilbert, Alf., R.A., 191
Gilbert, Sir John, R.A., 38, 335
Graham, Peter, R.A., 180
Gregory, E. J., A.R.A., 1
Greiffenhagen, M., 2
Grolleron, P., 189
Guthrie, James, 76

HAGBOLT, 96
Hagborg, A., 190
Haynes-Williams, J., 289

Henley, A. W., 262
Henry, George, A.R.S.A., 80
Henshall, J. Henry, 123
Hook, J. C., R.A., 3, 318
Hornell, E. A., 78
Hunt, Alf., R.W.S., 177
Hunter, Colin, A.R.A., 35

ISRAELS, Josef, 56, 260, 347

JACOMB-HOOD, J. P., 159
John, W. Goscombe, 308
Johnstone, H. J., 346
Jong, J. de, 95

KAEMMERER, F. H., 161
Kennington, T. B., 344
Kinnear, James, 11
Kitton, F. G., 107, 329
Krämer, J. V., 346

LA THANGUE, H. H., 157
Lavery, John, A.R.S.A., 79
Lawson, Geo. A., 140
Lee, F. R., R.A., 299
Lee, T. Stirling, 277
Leighton, Sir F., P.R.A., 136, 140, 278
Leonardo da Vinci, 166, 231
Linnell, John, 179
Little, G. Léon, 171
Lucas, Seymour, A.R.A., 337
Luigi, Loir, 191

McTAGGART, W., 243
Maris, James, 258, 288, 347
Maris, William, 348
Marks, H. Stacy, R.A., 193, 379
Mason, H., 315
Mauve, Anton, 101, 260
Meissonier, 31, 59
Méryon, 72
Mesdag, H. W., 188
Millais, Sir J. E., R.A., 3, 37, 362, 376
Millet, J. F., 257
Mitchell, J. E., 233
Montalba, H., 216
Montbard, G., 209
Moore, Albert, 88
Mullins, E. Roscoe, 199

NASMYTH, P., 299
Neuhuys, A., 348
Nicol, Erskine, A.R.A., 58, 196, 370, 372
Nouy, Le Comte de, 185

ORCHARDSON, W. Q., R.A., 33, 34, 55
Outin, Pierre, 187

PADGETT, W., 287
Parsons, Alfred, 319
Paterson, James, R.S.W., 77

Pennell, Joseph, 97
Phillip, John, R.A., 55
Piguenit, W. C., 368
Pinelli, 283
Pomeroy, F., 310
Powell, W., 313
Poynter, E. J., R.A., 159, 369
Prinsep, V. C., R.A., 221
Pyne, J. B., 177

RAPHAEL, 121
Rembrandt, 8, 23, 71
Reynolds, Sir J., P.R.A., 305
Riviere, Briton, R.A., 180
Roche, Alex., A.R.S.A., 78
Rolando, C., 300
Romney, 135
Rossetti, D. G., 35, 136
Rousseau, Th., 257

SADLER, W. D., 195
Scott, Samuel, 335
Smirke, Robt., R.A., 303
Smith, J. Moyr, 127
Smith, Sidney, F.R.I.B.A., 373
Spall, M., 220
Stark, Robt., 311
Stead, Fred., 157
Storey, G. A., A.R.A., 336
Stothard, Thos., R.A., 87
Stuck, Franz, 90, 91, 93
Swan, J. M., A.R.A., 17
Symington, J. Ayton, 238

TASSIE, James, 96
Thornycroft, Hamo, R.A., 139, 141, 199, 200, 279
Tidmarsh, H. E., 147
Tinworth, G., 286
Troyon, C., 92, 259
Turner, J. M. W., R.A., 54

UTAMARO, 342

VAN DYCK, 96
Van Goyen, School of, 336
Van Stry, 378
Velasquez, 258
Vinci, Leonardo da, 166, 231

WALTON, E.A., A.R.S.A., 77
Waterhouse, J. W., A.R.A., 210, 346
Watteau, 70, 363
Watts, G. F., R.A., 138
Whaite, H. C., P.R.C.A., 267
Wheatley, F., R.A., and R. Paton, 303
Whistler, J. McNeill, 9, 359, 361
Williamson, F., 294
Willms, M., 218
Wimperis, E. M., 368
Woods, Henry, A.R.A., 2
Woolner, Thomas, R.A., 82
Wyllie, W. L., A.R.A., 344

YEAMES, W. F., R.A., 36

THE ART JOURNAL, 1894.

LIST OF CONTRIBUTORS
OF SIGNED ARTICLES TO THIS VOLUME.

ARMSTRONG, WALTER, 1, 33, 177, 193, 370
ASHBEE, C. R., 152, 156, 182
AUBER, EUGÈNE, 284

BALDRY, A. L., 327
BARTLETT, W. H., 247
BENN, R. DAVIES, 252
BERNAC, JEAN, 161, 321
BROWN, Prof. G. B., 126
BROWNE, W. T., 147

CARTWRIGHT, JULIA (MRS. H. ADY), 115, and
    Art Annual
CAW, JAMES L., 75, 243
COOKE, MRS. E. T. (Poem), 122
CROAL, J. P., 11
CUNDALL, H. M., 35

DAY, L. F., 5, 52, 120
DILKE, LADY, 40
DURET, THEODORE, 204, 342

FULLWOOD, J. (Poem), 39

GOSSE, EDMUND, 138, 199, 277, 306
GRAHAM, D. S., 233

HEPWORTH-DIXON, M., 215
HOLMES, R. R., 129

KITTON, F. G., 107, 329

LITTLE, JAS. STANLEY, 171
LOFFELT, A. C., 101
LORD, FREWEN, 298, 344, 368

MIDDLETON, G. A. T., 213

O'FALLON, J. M., 112, 217, 256, 313

PENNELL, MRS. J., 97
PHILLIPS, CLAUDE, 353
POLLOCK, W. H., 65
POYNTER, E. J., R.A., 229

RICHTER, DR. J. P., 62, 166, 255, 300
ROOK, CLARENCE, 238
RUNCIMAN, J. F., 142

SHARP, W., 46, 185, and Sonnets facing pages
    16, 114, 208, 312
STEPHENS, F. G., 80
STEVENSON, R. A. M., 17, 54, 208, 210, 257
STORY, A. T., 86

TEMPLE, A. G., 133, 302, 335
THOMSON, JOHN, 364

WARD, T. HUMPHRY, 23
WATT, FRANCIS, 261
WEDMORE, FREDERICK, 6, 70, 289
WILLIAMSON, F., 294

The Rights of Translation and Reproduction are reserved.

THE ART JOURNAL,
1894.

NOTES ON BRITISH PAINTING IN 1893.

THE confusion into which British painting has been thrown by the movements of the last forty years came to what may very well turn out to be its climax in the summer of 1893. Never before, I should think, have so many notions of what Art should be, been illustrated together on our exhibition walls. All the fallacies—and all theories in Art are fallacious when they pretend to be strictly *à priori*—all the fallacies, I say, had their chance. The old-fashioned painters—sentimentalists, if you like—the neo-Botticellis, the Newlynites, the "Glasgow Lads," the symbolist-impressionists of the New English Art Club, of all these, and of other groups besides, the exhibition-haunter can now plead no involuntary ignorance. Each is with us, and the studio-world of London has become, in Art, very much what the French Chamber is in politics. The ordinary man is to be excused if he feels some bewilderment at the variety of the groups between which he is peremptorily, if tacitly, invited to choose. The worst of it is that all are right, and all wrong. The proportions between rightness and wrongness vary, no doubt, but each creed in painting, even that of the sentimentalists, holds some article for which the strictest logic can find no condemnation.

It is a matter of course that painters themselves should be narrow in their sympathies. Their lives are spent in developing such gifts as nature may have endowed them with for the expression of their own ideas. Their craft is long and arduous, so long and so arduous that it has scarcely ever been practised with full success until middle age. The painter looks in pictures for the quality he is aiming at himself. A pupil of

JANUARY, 1894.

Carolus Duran passes a Raphael with a shrug; while one of Ingres might do the like with a Velazquez. Each believes that the artistic notions he has imbibed are right, and that the other man's are wrong. Neither understands that the constituents which give his craft a value above any other handicraft are the pictorial conceptions of which it is the servant. To a real artist these pictorial conceptions come so easily, so spontaneously, that he is almost unconscious of them, and nine times out of ten denies their capital importance. What is a pictorial conception? Simply an idea fitted to be expressed in line and colour just as a dramatic conception is one fitted to be told by *doing*. When Van Eyck conceived the 'Jan Arnolfini and his Wife,' or the 'Man with a Red Turban,' he did so in the light of the manner in which he was going to express himself. The beauty of those pictures depends on the perfect harmony between their conception, in all its details, and their execution. A second harmony, that with the time in which they were created, might, of course, be added. But about that we can only get true ideas through a very deep historical perspective. A large, in fact by far the largest, school of young painters just now would define a pictorial conception as one fitted to be told in opaque colour put on thick and square. They do not understand what they are about when they say so. They think they are insisting upon the best way to paint. As a fact they are insisting that nothing shall be painted except things which lend themselves to one of many possible forms of treatment. They are making the same blunder as was made after the 1851 exhibition, when our teachers declared

"MAROONED."
FROM THE PICTURE IN THE HENRY TATE COLLECTION. BY E. J GREGORY, A.R.A.

B

that all sorts of things—natural forms in decoration, the graining of wood, the masking of structure, etc., etc.—were in themselves *anathema*. These things led to atrocious results because they were atrociously used. Grain a piece of wood well enough and put it in the right place, and you may defy the critics to find an artistic reason for blaming you. They will have to fall back upon a fantastic view of morality. It is the same with picture-painting. Express a truly pictorial notion in any way you please, and, if you express it thoroughly, with point and without irrelevance, posterity will admire what you do. You may use the dialect of Van Eyck, or of Holbein, or of Velazquez, or of Constable, or of John Sargent, or of Burne-Jones. It is all one, so long as the dialect fits the theme and the theme is right. A hundred years hence no one will ask whether it is *vieux jeu*. They will take it for what it is, for its harmony and its unity, and on those lines they will judge.

All of which means nothing more than that we must not test by formulas, that we must not allow the notion of the day, however imposing it may seem, to get between us and the one perennial touchstone of Fine Art, the touchstone of unity in harmony.

"CUPID'S SPELL." FROM THE PAINTING IN THE HENRY TATE COLLECTION. BY HENRY WOODS, A.R.A.

The best picture exhibited in 1893 in London was probably Mr. John Sargent's 'Mrs. Hugh Hammersley.' The only criticism one feels tempted to apply to it is the most difficult to justify of all, I mean the sort which would make the artist go farther than he wishes. Mr. Sargent's conception, down to the details of handling, was so thoroughly at peace with itself that our cry for more depth, more richness, more force, dies away on our lips, and we are reduced to believing that if he could only have enjoyed the direct inspiration of Velazquez, instead of having it filtered through Carolus-Duran, he would have hit the very bull's-eye. As it is, the portrait stimulates rather than satisfies, and makes us look to the Sargent of four or five years hence rather than be content with the Sargent of to-day. Technically the 'Lady Agnew' was even finer, and the 'Lady Lewis' almost as fine, but as pictorial creations neither can be mentioned in the same breath as the 'Mrs. Hammersley.' In England, putting aside the tomfooleries of a few impertinents who shall be nameless, Mr. Sargent's picture is so far the last word of what is supposed to be the modern spirit. By its demand upon our intelligence, upon our imagination, upon our dexterity, as it were, of wit; by its quick selection of essentials and contempt for surplusage; by its disregard, in a word, for the Philistine and its trust in his opposite, it stimulates all appreciations, and makes everyone feel before it as if he were himself on trial.

To jump from Mr. Sargent to Mr. Orchardson may seem bold, but truly both men obey one principle, different although the conclusions may be at which they arrive. Both are artists. To both nature has given the creative faculty, which includes not only the power to conceive in unity, but the perhaps rarer gift of insight into the limitations of material. To those who pin an exclusive faith to cool, high tones in colour, Mr. Orchardson's work may seem too hot and yellow. The stickler for actual relations may quarrel with his values. The symbolist may dislike his common-sense. But no one of them can deny his power to draw, to design, to make colour sing in tune, to grasp character—in a word, to create. His 'Lord Rookwood' was the best portrait he has done since his 'Mr. Walter Gilbey.' I wonder why Sir George Reid's work has been seen so little in London. It is only two years since he became P.R.S.A., but he has long been one of the most competent and scholarly—to use two very chilly adjectives —of Scottish painters. The 'Lord Trayner' of the last Academy, good as it was, was by no means up to his highest level. Perhaps the R.A.'s had never heard of him till he won the handle to his name. George Paul Chalmers, a greater man than Reid, only fought his way into the present "Old Masters" through the insistance of Mr. Horsley, who had met some of his work in Scotland. In manner the Scottish president has more in common with some of the older French painters, notably with J. P. Laurens, than with his own colleagues. His colour is peculiar; but has a certain family likeness to that of his predecessor, Sir William Fettes Douglas. His handling is broad, incisive, and square. In this, I should fancy, he has kept Raeburn in his eye more than any one else. The final combination reminds one rather of Paris twenty years ago than of Edinburgh.

The last few years have been disastrous for English portrait painters. They have seen the death of Frank Holl, whose reputation, kept up by his vigorous masculinity, will never sink below a certain respectable level. They have seen, too, a great falling off in the work of some of our older men, as well as much unfulfilled promise in the cases of two or three younger ones. The rapid rise of Mr. Sargent and the quieter advance of such men as Mr. Lavery, Mr. Mouat Loudan, Mr. Gotch and a few more, are all we have to put on the credit side of the account. If Sir Frederick Leighton had only followed up the success he won so long

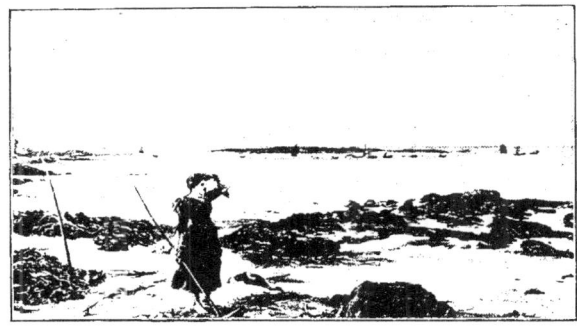

THE SEAWEED GATHERER. FROM THE PAINTING IN THE HENRY TATE COLLECTION. BY J. C. HOOK, R.A.

ago with his 'Captain Burton,' and gone on painting male portraits the retrospect would have been more satisfactory. Turning to a class of Art which is generally supposed to require more imagination than the painting of portraits, Mr. J.W. Waterhouse's 'La Belle Dame sans Merci' and Mr. Hacker's 'Circe' were good, each in its own way. The fascination of Mr. Waterhouse's picture lay in the echo it gave to Keats' verse. It had a touch of the mystical suggestiveness which makes the poem unique in modern English literature. The painter's colour and the poet's music strike the same chord, and the result on our senses is to be measured rather by quantity than quality. Mr. Hacker's performance is more matter of fact. His 'Circe' depends upon the witch's contours and upon the force with which her naked flesh tells against the shadowy background for its charm. The only touch of invention is in the combination of pigs and men, which gets over more than one difficulty in a sufficiently happy way. Pictures like these are an answer to the theory that would banish subjects—in the conventional sense —from painting. A good French critic asks what can be more horrible than a subject? He should have said, what can be more horrible than a picture painted for the subject. If a picture is painted for a good pictorial reason, and the pictorial reason is kept in command of the situation, the subject—the illustrative side — will do no more harm than a good story does to a novel. In Sir John Millais' 'North-West Passage,'

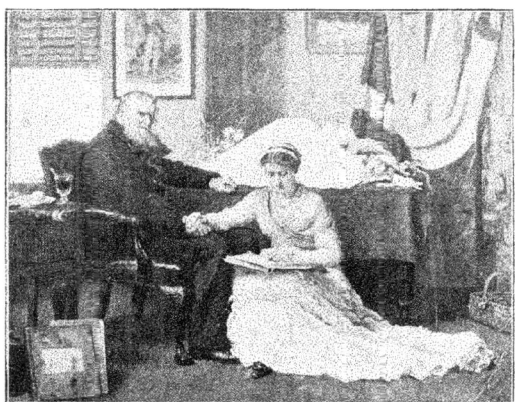

THE NORTH-WEST PASSAGE. BY SIR J. E. MILLAIS, R.A. FROM THE PAINTING IN THE HENRY TATE COLLECTION.

here reproduced, the subject is embarrassing because it controls the distribution of the masses, and, moreover, does not explain itself without a glance at the catalogue. Another Millais in the Henry Tate collection, the 'Knight-Errant,' was open to neither objection in anything like the same degree. Its motive was entirely pictorial, and as for its subject, the meaning of that was clear at a glance.

It is strange how tantalising a dramatic touch in which there is any ambiguity may be in a picture. In the Alma Tadema etched in the frontispiece by Mr. C. O. Murray a young soldier is laying a bunch of flowers in the lap of a sleeping girl. The only doubtful point is the relation of the man to the woman, and yet that is enough to distract our attention from the purely artistic qualities, and to set us half consciously guessing about irrelevant things. Look at 'Cupid's Spell' (page 2), by Mr. Henry Woods. The idea is of the same kind as Mr. Alma Tadema's, but it lends itself far better to painting, and so we have nothing to do before this canvas but to appreciate the Art. An example of the same felicity on a much more important scale was Mr. Frank Bramley's 'After Fifty Years.' Like the 'Wedding' of Mr. Stanhope Forbes (see *The Art Journal* for 1893, p. 299), Mr. Bramley's picture pretended to deal with an event in village life, and, in fact, did deal with it, and yet all the time it was working out a legitimate pictorial problem, a problem both of line and colour, and one that was never sacrificed for a moment to any illustrative necessity. Even now people are so unaccustomed to the realistic treatment of outdoor effects that they do not see the truthfulness of such a performance as Mr. Bramley's, but the remarks made about it showed that even among the uneducated—in an artistic sense —there was a consciousness that 'After Fifty Years' was not merely the report of a village function.

THE ARMOURER'S SHOP. FROM THE PAINTING BY WALTER GAY IN THE HENRY TATE COLLECTION.

Mr. Forbes himself was less happy than usual in the design of his chief picture. 'The Lighthouse' is now in the Corporation Gallery at Manchester. So far as painting goes, it represents a year's advance upon what he did in 1892. But it has no reason for existing, or rather for existing as it does. Its parts have only a fortuitous relation to each other. If you take a detail here and a detail there you can see why they are as they are, but there is no governing idea, no ruling line, to blend them all together, and to make the most widely separated parts necessary to each other and to the scheme. The designs of the 'Health of the Bride' and of the 'Fish Sale on a Cornish Beach'—the two best things he has done so far, to my mind—show that Mr. Forbes can hit upon first-rate conceptions when he tries. 'The Armourer's Shop,' by Mr. Walter Gay, 'The Seaweed Gatherer,' by Mr. J. C. Hook, and 'Marooned,' by Mr. E. J. Gregory, belong to the same class as Mr. Alma Tadema's, 'A Silent Greeting,' but they explain themselves better, and leave us more completely to the quiet enjoyment of their technique.

The Glasgow pictures at the Grafton Gallery, and Mr. Brangwyn's *éclaireur* in the same interest at the Academy, seem to aim at something that shall be neither decoration nor description. It would be waste of time, however, to talk about their classification, to discuss whether they should call themselves symbolist or impressionist, or some new "ist" altogether. The principle upon which they seem to go differs from that of the impressionist in this—that their selection of material is governed by a decorative idea, while the impressionists obey a principle which comes nearer to science. Both are within their rights, but both sometimes might learn a useful lesson from the faculty. In a doctor's prescription you will often see six or seven ingredients. Only one, probably, has any active therapeutic value; the others are to control it, to make it palatable, to promote its absorption. If the drug alone were given the patient either would not take it, or, if he did, it wouldn't do him any good. It is just the same with a picture; if you strip it to its naked theme you reduce your public to the narrow circle of those whose sympathies are already yours and whose knowledge is equal to your own. Perhaps you may say that is just what you want—very well, then don't appeal to Cæsar.

WALTER ARMSTRONG.

'A SILENT GREETING.'

From the Picture by L. ALMA TADEMA, R.A. Etched by C. O. MURRAY.

SHINING marbles and crowds of flowers, blue skies and exquisite stuffs—in a world made up of these do Mr. Tadema's graceful Romans move. And who can equal him in the rendering of cool, translucent, white marble, on which pink and crimson petals lie, a carpet for the dainty feet of some beautiful woman? Who can equal the delicate touch with which he weaves those marvellous garlands of flowers, pressed and crowded close together, that crown his maidens' heads, and wreath their necks, and fill their arms at feast or procession—each tiny floweret absolutely distinct and true to nature in form and colour.

Mr. Alma Tadema, though a much younger man, has a close affinity to the group of artists who arose on the Continent after 1848, and under whose hand the every-day life of Greece and Rome—especially of Rome—lives again; the men who in France went by the name—they are always giving names in France—of Neo-Greeks or Pompéists. But while Hamon paints adorable babies, chains butterflies and cages Loves in a hencoop, while Coomans gives us the graceful difficulties of the Roman nursery, while M. Gérôme dwells on the great dramas of later Greece and Rome, Mr. Alma Tadema revels in actual detail.

An accomplished antiquarian, an impeccable draughtsman, a superb colourist, he loves to dwell on the seductive outward seeming of things—the subject matters little. It is but an opportunity for the painting of rare and strangely coloured fabrics that cling to the olive or tender pink limbs of those beauties of the Roman Decadence, with the blue-black or tawny-red hair, in the penumbra of some rich interior, where, over white and coloured marbles, through close-set blossoms of rose and oleander, we catch glimpses of blue sky and yet bluer sea. Mr. Alma Tadema delights in the effect of cool half-shade, while the hot sun beats on sea and land outside, and reflected lights play on the marble seats beneath the trees, on the balustrade under the open portico of some patrician's house, on the jewels upon the women's arms, on the flowers in their hair. This coolness and freshness, within sight of the hot sunlight, is a subtle touch which adds to the general sense of idle luxury, in which nothing is of importance unless it ministers to sensuous enjoyment.

In the 'Silent Greeting,' one of the pictures in the Henry Tate Collection, published by the consent of Mr. Stephen T. Gooden, the owner of the copyright, so admirably rendered in Mr. C. O. Murray's etching, we get this effect of a cool, luxurious, half-shaded interior. Outside the curtain, held back by the discreet slave, the vestibule glows with hot light; and the lazy beauty, overcome by the heat, sleeps so profoundly on her soft-cushioned seat that even her soldier lover's 'Silent Greeting' of half-open rosebuds fails to rouse her.

ROSE G. KINGSLEY.

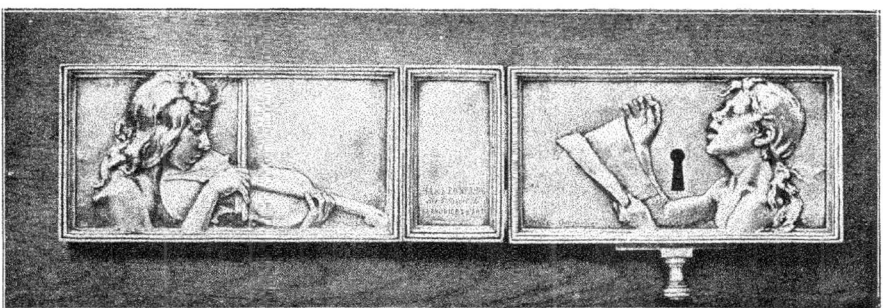

The Violin and the Song. Lock designed by A. L. M. Charpentier. Executed by H. E. and L. Fontaine.

FRENCH DECORATIVE ART IN LONDON.

IT is impossible not to couple in one's mind the two exhibitions now being held in London, one at Grafton Street, the other, the Arts and Crafts at the New Gallery. M. de Fourcaud, in his preface to the catalogue of the first, traces back to the exhibition of 1851 all recent evolution of decorative art; he might with equal truth have mentioned the Arts and Crafts as the starting point of this new departure made by the French. Like the English exhibition, it is initiated by a body of artists, who engage the gallery for the time being, and conduct the show; it also professes to deal exclusively with decorative art, and, as was the case with the earlier London exhibitions, its catalogue is prefaced by short introductory essays on the industrial arts. But there the likeness ends.

The one exhibition is little more than a protest by artists and workmen against mere trade manufacture; the other is a display of artistic production, claiming, indeed, to represent the flower of French-grown decorative art. The two series of essays are pitched in quite different keys. The British workman, when he is not actually pessimistic, preaches, as one may say, the theory of his Art, in the hope of quickening or awakening some just appreciation of it. The French expert proclaims the perfection of modern practice, and sees in the resources of modern industry nothing but promise for art.

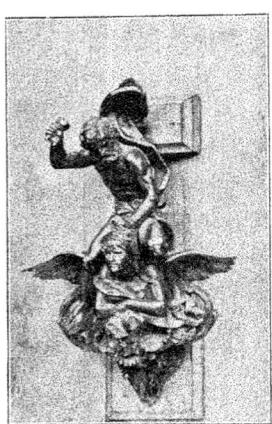

KNOCKER IN BRONZE. BY H. E. AND L. FONTAINE.

When we come to compare the two exhibitions the contrast is quite startling. The French are strong where we are weak, and weak where our strength lies. If the exhibitors at the Grafton Gallery do not always justify the high opinion pronounced upon them by their introducers, they reach frequently a standard of execution high above the level of British workmanship. This may be seen in their reliefs, like the knocker here illustrated, in bronze, pewter, and silver, but it is most apparent in their pottery. Even when the French porcelain is not at all to our liking—when it is finikin in detail, as in the case of many of the tea services; or commonplace in design, as in the case of some of the plates shown; where it is aggressively realistic, as in the soup tureen by Madame Sarah Bernhardt, and the other Palissy-inspired productions of M. Lachenal; or merely eccentric in shape, as with some of the *grès*—there is no mistake about the consummate skill of the potter. Whether he is modelling semi-impressionistic vase shapes, or painting them with enamel or with slip; whether he is glazing his ware with juicy colour, or finishing it with a surface like the peel of a fruit; whether he is carrying execution to the extreme of precision, or seeking unexpected effects of "splashing"—it is clear that he is always master of his material, and that, even in the happy "flukes" he makes, it was not quite independent of his control.

To descend from the general to the particular, the names of Messrs. Deck, Delaherche, and Dalpayrat deserve particular mention: the last mentioned having been extraordinarily successful in the texture of his ware, which is almost as tempting to the hand as to the eye of the connoisseur; for beautiful low-toned colour, exquisite surface, and fanciful —if sometimes too fantastic—form, his *grès flammé* is unsurpassed.

The cut glass of M. Leveillé, although of rather unequal merit, also deserves mention. Bright colours appear to be beyond his management; at all events, he is not happy with them; but his jade-like and agate tints are sometimes very beautiful.

In the way of furniture, there is one quaint and amusing little bit of carpentry in the form of a baby's linen-chest, inlaid with symbols in pewter, by M. Charpentier, who is also responsible for the lock in our headpiece, and one sumptuous piece of inlay executed by M. Gallé de Nancy, from a design by Comte R. de Montesquiou. This is what might be called "painters' inlay" as distinguished from marquetry in the old sense; one may doubt what will be the effect of time upon its delicate colour, but of its beauty, as we see it, there is no doubt.

Two further thoughts occur to the critic on his way home— one is, the very strong influence upon modern French design which is still exercised by Japanese art (what was with us a passing fashion, appears to be, on the other side of the Channel, an abiding impression); the other is, what an artist the Frenchman is—in a sense; and yet how little one can rely upon him for what we call taste.

LEWIS F. DAY.

"MY FEW THINGS."

"MY few things!" In the very title there is conveyed, I hope, some apology for writing about them. If I accept the invitation to do so it is partly because I must needs know more of what they are—they are "but poor few," in Shakespeare's phrase—than anyone else can know; partly again because, as I am pleasantly informed, it may be interesting to certain readers to be told, for a change, not what can be amassed—amassed and perhaps neglected—by a millionaire who gives several thousand guineas for a modern painting, but what can be got together with merely "joyful trouble,"—with pains, and waiting, and love of the things, and only a little money—by a simple man of Letters, who happens to have been concerned, to some extent, with other arts than his own; and partly also because, connected with the few things that one has, there are associations, not few but many.

A little blue-grey drawing—an early drawing of Varley's, which has nothing but the lasting virtues of Economy and Style—was the first artistic thing that ever belonged to me. It came to me—like a Morland mezzotint, some years later,— indirectly from the portfolio of a great-grandfather, who was, as I am told, a friend of Turner's Dr. Monro. But it is prints, not drawings, that, since I began to collect a little, I have brought together for the most part.

In a collection of prints there is something less indefinite, something more systematic, than in a collection of drawings. The things, if they are good, have the advantage of being known, of being more or less recognised — not, indeed, by the large public, but at least by the people with whom, on matters of Art it is most interesting to come into contact. Prints are classed and catalogued. Each print by a particular master has, in the collector's mind, a direct bearing on the component parts of that master's work. Again, fine drawings, although cheap in relation to the prices paid for modern paintings, are dear in comparison with many prints to which the adjective "fine" could scarcely be denied; for, while here and there an 'Adam and Eve' of Dürer is sold under the hammer for many hundred pounds, that is the exception absolutely; and while, at Sotheby's or Christie's, on eventful sale days, two thousand pounds may be the ransom of a Rembrandt etching, that is not because it is fine, but because that particular etching — or that particular "state" of it — is excessively rare. It has been chronicled; it has been read of; it has profited by the existence of the accurate catalogue of the work of the Master — it is a certified thing. But, with knowledge gradually acquired, with diligence exercised in the right place, a print extremely fine, extremely desirable, may still be bought for a few pounds. It will be much fuller of Art than any drawing which ordinary good fortune is to enable you to get for the same outlay. And I say this as one who loves drawings — as one who, notwithstanding his theories, even ventures to live with a few of them; but, if I have a preference in the matter of collecting — well, I suppose it is for prints. About a print, every point is interesting. Apart from subject, apart too from technical treatment of the copper, there is the delightful question, How does your own impression compare with other people's? And, again, the paper. The true print-lover can talk about different papers — old French, old Dutch, old English, Japanese — as the connoisseur of clarets talks of Pontet Canets and Pichon Longuevilles. . . . But my Solander-box is all this time unopened!

I suppose the first print that I ever bought was a "Liber" print of Turner's. The Burlington Fine Arts Club had held a wonderfully important exhibition of them — there were Mr. J. E. Taylor's, Mr. Henry Vaughan's, Mr. Gambier Parry's finest impressions; Illustrative, thoroughly, of that which Turner meant to do; of the means, to some extent, by which he did it. And having by that time discovered what I most cared for in the set, and made, no doubt, the politic compromise — learning to bring my needs within the limits of a lean purse — I got Mr. Stopford Brooke to kindly choose from amongst several impressions of the 'Hind Head Hill,' that happened then to

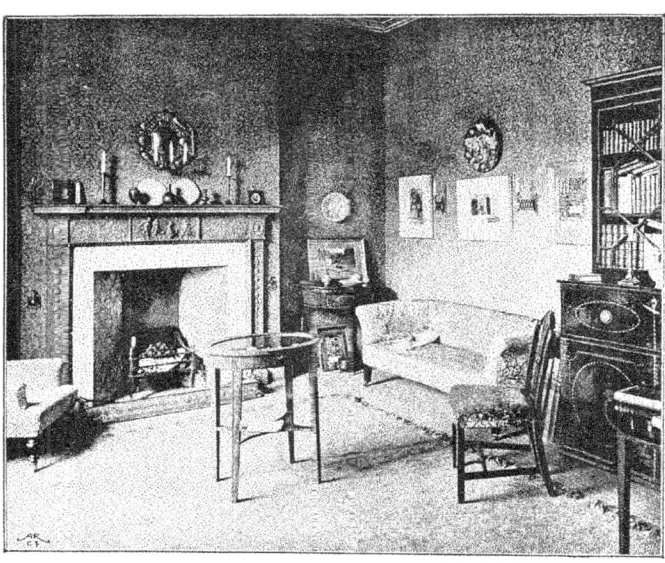

THE DRAWING-ROOM.

be at Colnaghi's, the one he thought the best; and from amongst an equal number of impressions of the 'Severn and Wye,' that happened to be at Mrs. Noseda's, similarly, the best. "And chose well that day," said Mr. Brooke, many years afterwards, noticing the prints on my wall. No such opportunities of choice, as existed then, are likely again to be afforded.

Those were the days when, if I bought at all, it was — at first at least — "for the wall" and not "for the folio" — to use a phrase of Halsted's. Halsted meant by it to distinguish between the buyer who, from the very nature of things, must promptly be satisfied (since you can neither multiply "walls" nor enlarge them), and the buyer to whom the infinite was open — that infinite in which Solander-box succeeds Solander-box, folio succeeds folio, and drawer succeeds drawer. His, perhaps, is the more dangerous case; but the collector who can display on his walls the whole of his possessions — who can stop buying when the mere purposes of furnishing are answered — is simply *not* a collector. Halsted scorned him. The mention of this aged dealer's name brings back to me other recollections. I saw Mr. Halsted in almost the latest

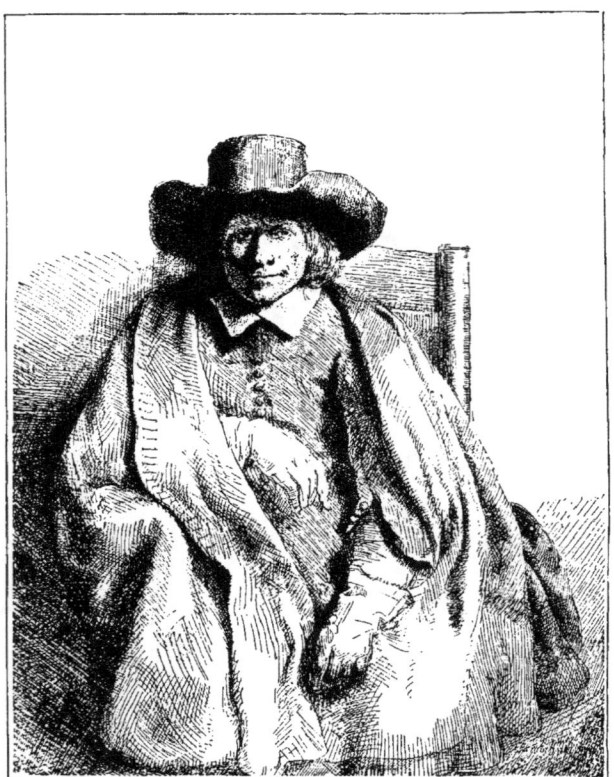

CLEMENT DE JONGHE. FROM A FIRST STATE OF REMBRANDT'S PLATE.

of his days, when he was a less prominent, but probably a more interesting figure in the world of art and connoisseurship, than he had been in his prime. In his prime his shop was in Bond Street; but when it was my privilege to go, a humble learner, sitting at the feet of a dealer who had known Mr. Turner, and had been for at least one generation surrounded by his work, Halsted, elderly, deliberate of speech, slow and almost halting of movement, large, angular—a craft somewhat difficult to "bring round" or "change the course" of, within the scanty waters of his back shop—had his abode—his mart at all events —in Rathbone Place, by the French *blanchisseuse de fin* and a little Swiss *café*. He was half retired; and there in the back shop he would cause you to sit down, in a perfect light under the window, and would show you what you had asked for, if he had it—for, in those days, he bought nothing; he was engaged merely in selling, in the most leisurely of manners, and at prices which were never open to any suggestion of abatement, the remains of his old stock. Standing over you—a little away from you—with something of a soldierly sternness, like a sergeant in a barrack-yard, he rolled out, slowly, story after story of Mr. Turner, of Sir John Hippesley, whom he had influenced to admire the "Liber," by placing before his eyes a 'Severn and Wye,' at breakfast-time, and then of Mr. Turner again. You bought something, of course, but the best of it is, you never were sorry for it afterwards, for Halsted's eye was faultless; his knowledge, though he was old, was in advance of his day. I cherish as impressions which had received his *imprimatur*—if one may use the word of things he had thought worthy to buy and to sell—an 'Oakhampton Castle,' a 'Hindoo Worshippers,' and I forget for the moment what else. These two, I remember, bear the stamp of passage through the collection of the famous Mr. Stokes—the first "Liber" collector—and of his niece, Miss Constance Clarke.

One thing amusing about a visit to Halsted's was the occasional presence of his brother. You went to the shop perhaps once by chance, and Halsted was away. In his place was an inferior sort of person, courteous and good-natured, but entirely conscious of his own inferiority. You could do no business with him. If I remember rightly, he was not even permitted to have the keys. The fine prints were inaccessible. Yet this was, after all, but one of the inferior brother's manifestations. He had another phase—another facet. Chancing, one summer evening, to walk northwards, through Camden Town, I suddenly beheld the brother, standing on what proved to be his own doorstep, free of heart and with no one to say him nay. He, too, had a shop, it appeared, and here it was, come upon unexpectedly: a print shop of the third order—you wondered who they were, in Camden Town or anywhere else, who bought the cheap things which alone it contained.

Only one other of the old-fashioned dealers, the dealers of another generation, did I ever see. That was the aged Mr. Tiffen, once busy in the Strand, but, when I called upon him to inspect the remains of his possessions, living chiefly retired, slow and deaf, in the small bourgeois comfort of a villa at Canonbury. There—not to much practical purpose—I once sought him out. He too was a figure of the elder world, and as such he dwells in the memory.

But I have wandered from the prints of the "Liber Studiorum," of which indeed, though one of the warmest admirers of them, I possess but a handful. Amongst them I greatly cherish one impression—the gift of a friend whose benefactions to the National collections are remarkable, and whose knowledge of Turner is profound. It is an early "state" of the subject known as 'Inverary Pier, Loch Fyne, Morning'—one of those plates engraved from end to end by Turner's own hand. This impression was given by the Master to Lupton, the mezzotint engraver of the 'Solway Moss,' and, a generation ago, my friend had bought it from him. Another kindly student of Turner's art sent me once more than one of those etchings which, in Turner's case, are the interesting preparations for

No one who appreciates Turner can quite confine himself to the "Liber," though the "Liber" is the most comprehensive expression of that artist's infinite genius. Accordingly, in my drawers, there may be found, no doubt, pieces from one or other of his engraved publications: something, it may be, from the "Rivers of England"—amongst them the 'York' and the 'Ripon,' which are not his indeed, but his friend Girtin's—something from the "Southern Coast;" and, from the "England and Wales," that exquisite 'Yarmouth,' which, like the 'Clovelly' and the 'Portsmouth' (both of them in the "Southern Coast") exemplifies old William Miller's quite marvellous faculty of rendering the sky effects, the aerial

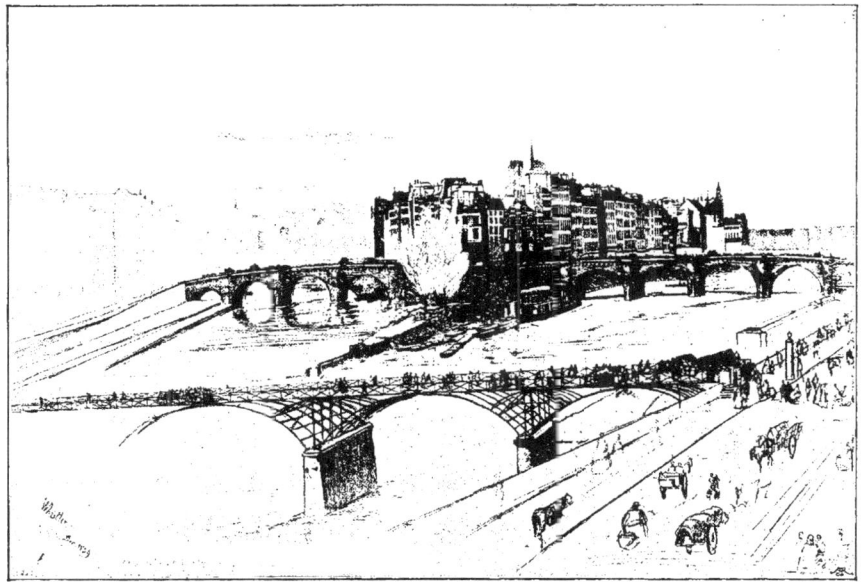

PARIS: THE ISLE DE LA CITÉ. FROM A RARE ETCHING BY WHISTLER.

the finished "Liber" plate. The rare 'Isis' is amongst them. Amongst the Turner prints that I have bought, I have always been guided rather by fineness of impression than by priority of "state." Thus, side by side with a First State of the 'London from Greenwich' I do not fear to place a late one of 'The Frontispiece, with the Rape of Europa.' The impression must have been printed the moment the plate had profited by Turner's retouch. As for the costly curiosities known as "Engraver's proofs"—working proofs in fine, struck off to see how the plate was progressing—speaking broadly, I do not believe in them. They have their own interest, of course, as illustrating the means by which the effect was obtained; but, in quality, yield to an impression taken when the effect had just been got, or, in the case of a fine Second or later State, to an impression taken when the effect, lost in the interval by wear, had just been regained.

1894.

perspective, of Turner's maturest art. One has heard of Turner's compliments to John Pye, over 'Pope's Villa,' and they were not undeserved; but how great should his recognition have been of the Scottish Quaker, simple of nature, subtle of gift, for whom no passage of Turner's brush-work was too intricate or too baffling! But let us turn to earlier Masters.

Only well-to-do people can buy, in any large numbers and in those fine impressions which alone rightly represent their subjects, the etchings of Rembrandt; but it is a wonder, and almost a shame, that so few well-to-do English people take advantage of their opportunities, for, as a result of their not doing so, or doing so at the best in so scanty a measure, a most undue proportion of the fine Rembrandts which have been the ornaments of English collections have within the last few years crossed the seas, and are now lodged—where they are justly appreciated—in Paris, Berlin, Vienna, Baltimore,

New York. Where, amongst us in England, are the successors of Dr. Wellesley, of Sir Abraham Hume, of Mr. Holford, of Richard Fisher? We want a new race of collectors of the highest class of ancient prints: the old is dying out: the young is too modest or too timid: it is afraid to spend its money, though its money could hardly be spent more economically. Looked at even from the commercial point of view—as the great auctions prove to us—nothing is better justified than the investment of considerable sums in the prints by the Masters. Rembrandt is for all Time. Every year—taking the wide world over—there is an increase in the number of people sensible enough to desire and determine to possess themselves of some representation of his work.

Nothing but small means has prevented my buying in abundance Rembrandt's incomparable landscapes, so well aware am I that Landscape Art reaches its topmost level in the best of his work—in his 'Cottage with Dutch Hay Barn,' and in his 'Landscape with a Tower.' His Sacred Subjects, with all their virtues of "sincerity and inwardness," commend themselves less to us. His Portraiture, upon the other hand, combines every artistic charm with every human interest.

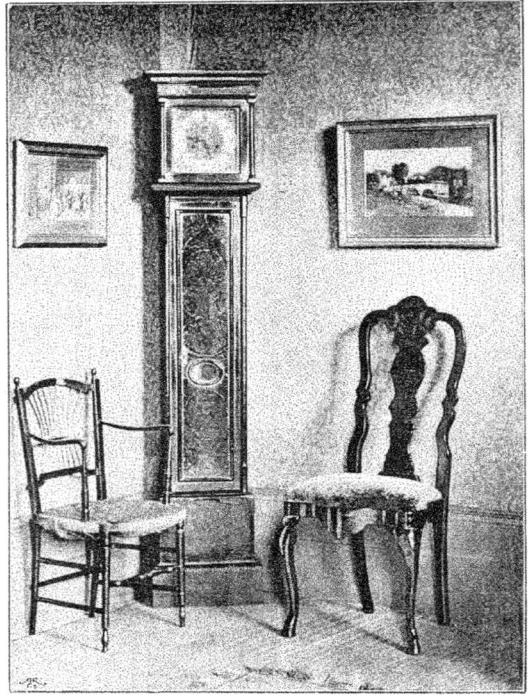

A CORNER, WITH COTMAN'S 'BISHOPGATE BRIDGE.'

A few examples I have—a mere handful, but good impressions they must always be; and the two which, from their subjects, are least unworthy of mention are, I suppose, a First State of the 'Clement de Jonghe,' the Amsterdam print-seller, which has a picturesqueness less obvious, but a character more subtle, than in the plate's later states; and an early and fortunate impression from that group of studies, executed, I am convinced, in different years, and containing as its chiefest and latest ornament an energetically-sketched portrait of Rembrandt himself, in that advanced middle life of his, which gave us, perhaps, the greatest number of the fine fruits of his genius. To certain of the commentators on Rembrandt, this rare little plate—a masterly collection of *croquis* and nothing besides —is not, I fancy, quite sufficiently known, though our admirable English amateur, Wilson—who wrote in 1836—and the latest deceased of the great French collectors and commentators, Monsieur Dutuit, of Rouen, do it conspicuous justice. My impression belonged, a generation or two ago, to the Arozarena collection. I got it, with some other things, at that fascinating shop in Paris, whose outside is so simple and so unassuming, whose inside is stuffed with treasures—the shop a door or two from the Quai Malaquais, up the dark and narrow "Rue des Saint-Pères," at which, from the morning to the evening hours, sits placidly at his desk the learned "Marchand d'Estampes de la Bibliothèque Nationale."

Even the smallest of collectors may have a "speciality"—and I suppose my speciality to be the comparatively humble one of Méryon and of Whistler—or, perhaps, of modern etchings generally—but (let me say it for myself as well as for others) it is at one's peril that one is specialist alone. Things are seen then out of all proportion; bias and prejudice take the place of judgment—a mere fanaticism flourishes where there ought to be a growing critical capacity, alert and lively. On that account, in my small cabinet, a Whistler or a Méryon is liable to be confronted with an Italian of the Renaissance, a German of the day of Dürer. Zoan Andrea's 'Dance of Damsels,' after a design of Mantegna's, a Coat of Arms of Beham's, an ornament of Aldegrevers's, instructively remind me of a delicacy earlier than Whistler's, and of a "*burin sobre et mâle*" that was wielded three hundred years before Méryon's. But while in collecting I venture to discountenance the exclusive devotion to a particular master, I am almost as strongly against the acquisition of merely isolated examples of many men. If a man is worth representing at all, represent him at the least by a little handful of his works. Collect one or two masters largely, and obtain of others small but characteristic groups.   FREDERICK WEDMORE.

(*The sequel in another article.*)

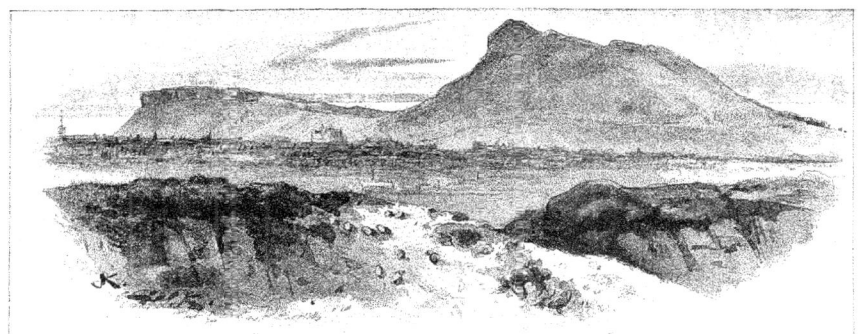

ARTHUR'S SEAT AND SALISBURY CRAGS FROM THE BRAID HILLS. FROM A DRAWING BY JAMES KINNEAR

THE QUEEN'S PARK.

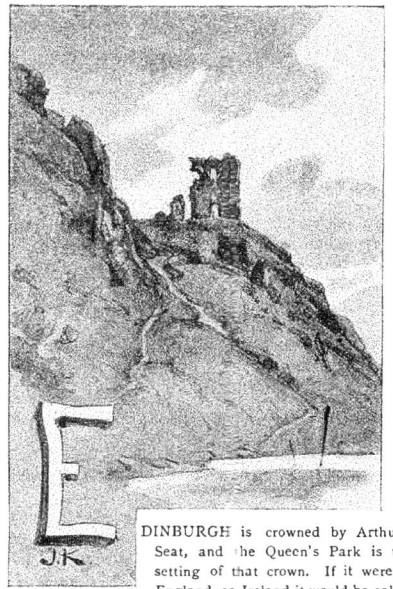

ST. ANTHONY'S CHAPEL.

EDINBURGH is crowned by Arthur's Seat, and the Queen's Park is the setting of that crown. If it were in England or Ireland it would be called a mountain. It is in fact no common hill. Its height alone makes it bulk largely in the prospect, for it goes up more than 800 feet, and in days of trailing mist and cloud it hides its head in quite a mysterious Alpine way. But it is its conformation rather than its altitude that gives it an unquestioned air of grandeur. There are many hills of more than double its height that would lose character and impressiveness beside it; its fine majestic lines give it something of a proud and imperious aspect. Its leonine form is matter of everyday observation. The old lion, crouching in its sentinel watch over the city, is the familiar friend of every Edinburgh citizen; no stranger is allowed to pass along the London road without his guide pointing out to him how nature has moulded the hill, so that at every point from the crest of the noble head to the curl of the tail, it shall recall the lion at rest, and that on a scale which even Landseer could not have conceived.

Edinburgh is indeed a highly favoured city. The Firth of Forth sends up sea breezes to invigorate her people; Arthur's Seat brings to them the fresh breath of the mountains. What others have to travel miles in search of, lies within reach of her citizens in an easy afternoon stroll. The Queen's Park is not an ordinary pleasure ground. Other cities make glad when a wealthy neighbour presents them with a park of thirty or forty acres; if there chance to be a few old trees in the ground the admiration of them becomes almost pathetic. But here is a park which is really a royal demesne, associated with the proud if somewhat sad history of the palace of the Stuart kings, and happily bearing the stamp of nature as fresh as when it was first enclosed early in the sixteenth century. It was the fifth James who, fortunately for the generations that came after, discovered that he required a hunting ground convenient to his palace. He enclosed a large area of ground more than four miles in circumference, and the enclosure remains pretty much as it was in his time; a few roads have been made: that is all. The gloom of Salisbury Crags which sit on the rising crest of the Park has forbidden the landscape gardener to enter; the park and the hill remain as they were in the Stuart time, except that "deaes" and the hares have been 'survived only by their friends the "cones." Kincaid, who wrote in 1807, tells us that between Salisbury Crags and the town "is a deep valley,' and on the other side, "between Arthur's Seat and the Crags, there is a valley so romantic and sequestered that scarce

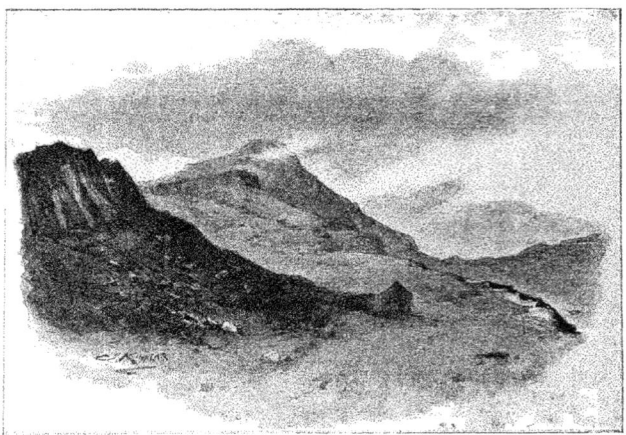

ARTHUR'S SEAT FROM THE HAGGIS KNOWE. BY JAMES KINNEAR.

hand shall bear the title of an English enemy. Yet that is so. The legend has it that these rocks are in a sense the monument of English aggression and of Scotland's humiliation, for it is said that they take their name from the Earl of Salisbury, who, in the reign of Edward III., accompanied the Prince on an expedition against Scotland. Surely some patriotic scholar ought to be able to wipe away this reproach from the city of the Stuarts.

But it is time to enter the Park and look around. It may best be approached at two points, either from Holyrood or St. Leonard's. At the former gate the visitor finds himself at once face to face with the rugged grandeur of the Park, but not its most enticing beauty. The Crags rise right opposite to him, crowning a gradually ascending ridge which sweeps away round till it touches the line of Arthur's Seat; from which, however, it is separated by a lonely glen, known as the Hunter's Bog. Mr. Kinnear has depicted admirably the picturesque setting of this chain of rocks and hill, as seen from the Braids, on the opposite side of the

any one who has not seen it could believe that such a place existed in the neighbourhood of a great and populous city. Edinburgh is now much more of "a great and populous city" than it was a century ago, but Kincaid's description of the park can still be quoted as tolerably accurate. Mr. Kinnear's drawings might have been made to illustrate this old book. In another early work the writer describes the Park in simple words, which, however, in a sentence, group all the outstanding features as effectively in a way as the artist's skilful pencil. "The King's Park," he says, "is of a very singular nature to be in the immediate vicinity of a populous city, for it is little else than an assembly of hills, rocks, precipices, morasses, and lakes."

Naturally the visitor asks how the hill came by its name, and how the huge coronet of rocks that leads the eye down from the summit to Holyrood have been associated in nomenclature with Salisbury. The answer he gets may be one of several; as usual there are conflicting traditions. There are archæologists who think with Maitland that Arthur's Seat owes its name to Gaelic lore. The words are, they say, a corruption of Ard-na-said, which, being interpreted, has some reference to the flight of herons. This, however, seems a straining of Celtic ingenuity. There is the less occasion for this severe exercise of archæological acumen, seeing that fairly well-authenticated history supplies a much more likely explanation. Whitaker suggests, and most people accept the suggestion, that the hill commemorates by its name the British Prince Arthur, who, in the end of the sixth century, defeated the Saxons in this part of the country. The popular belief regarding Salisbury Crags is more curious. It is an odd freak of fate that has decreed that here, in the capital of Scotland, where the Campbells and the Douglases made history, the most notable imprint of Nature's wonder-working

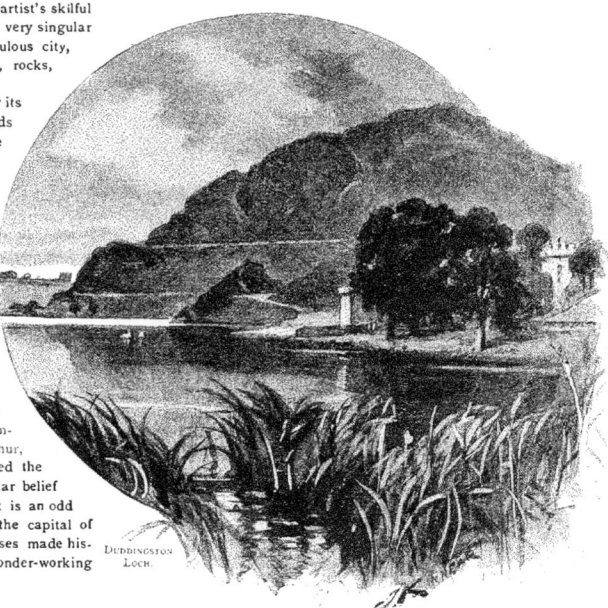

DUDDINGSTON LOCH.

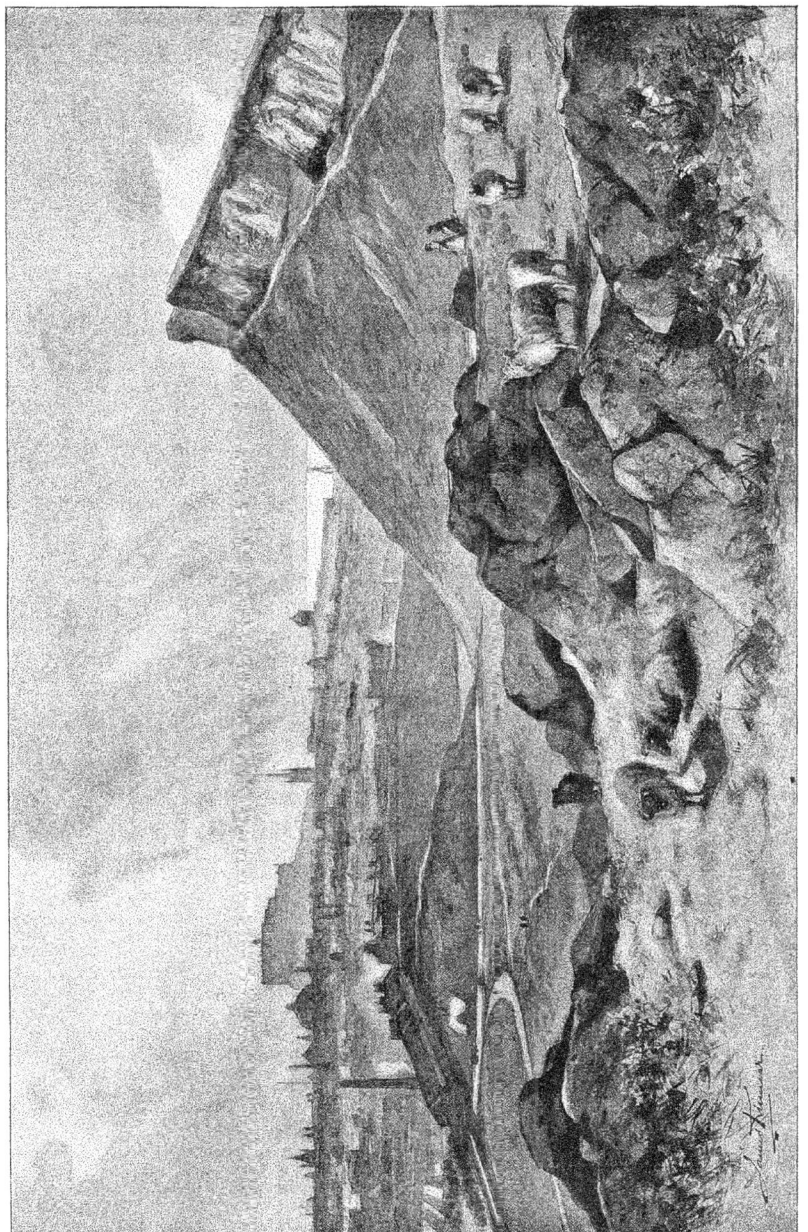

Edinburgh from the Top of Samson's Ribs, showing the Castle, St. Leonard's and Salisbury Crags. From a Drawing by James Kinnear.

city. The Crags are great greenstone upheavals, interspersed with layers of sandstone. They are as rugged and wild as the granite cliffs of Sutherland. Where, for example, could a finer rock study be found than in the "Cat Nick," by which Mr. Kinnear has wisely sampled the Crags? This is a cleft in the mountain, to which an Alpine climber might without condescension address himself. The boys of Edinburgh have given it its name. It is dear to them, for it reminds them in later years of an adventurous youth, when they scaled its dangerous and precipitous face with feline agility. There have been accidents here, many of them serious enough. The place has long been under the maternal bann; but the urchins of the Canongate are just as plucky to-day as they were a generation since, when one of them met his death here; and the climbing of the Cat Nick will long continue to be a test of juvenile hardihood and daring. Not one in a thousand among the holiday-seekers who talk at Chamounix *table d'hôtes* of the sensations of crossing *le mauvais pas* would find his head strong enough or his feet sure enough to carry him half-way up the "Nick." The path along the foot of the Crags was a favourite resort of Scott. He has said that to it he used to go morning and evening when engaged with a favourite author or a new subject of study. It is, however, not the place to which an earnest and close-reading student can be recommended. Scott, in all probability, studied the scene much more than he did his book. He has himself described the entrancing prospect that spreads itself out over the

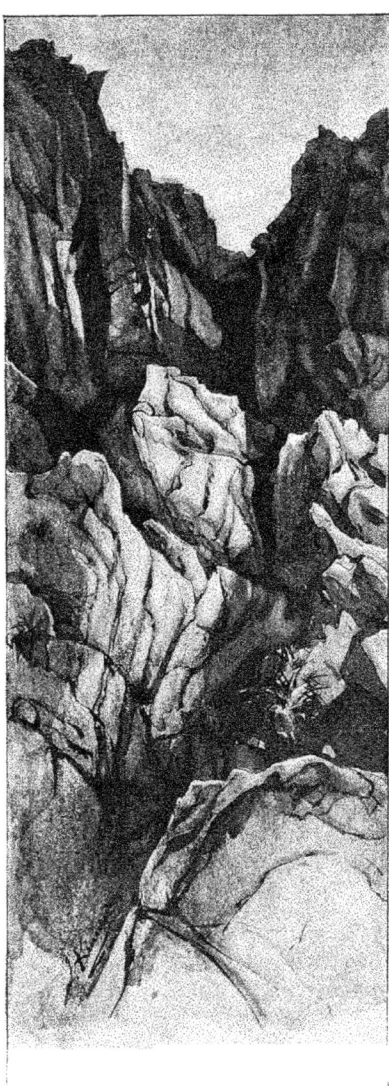

THE CAT NICK, SALISBURY CRAGS. FROM A DRAWING BY JAMES KINNEAR.

city and away to the north — from the glittering Forth to the misty peaks of Perthshire. The path that now runs along the foot of the cliff is not the same as was trodden by the great romancer. In Scott's time it fell into an impassable condition, but his writings called attention to the wonderful beauty of the place, and before his death he had the satisfaction of knowing that what he rightly described as a "beautiful and solid pathway" had been formed. It is known as the Radical Road, because of its having been made by hand-loom weavers who had been thrown out of employment. Here is a promenade of which Edinburgh may well be envied. In the "Heart of Midlothian" it has been described in an eloquent passage which has since done duty in numberless guide-books. The city lies at our feet, its castle mounting guard over the many spires of this highly ecclesiastical town, and the Calton Hill asserting itself on an opposite ridge with the classic ruins which one would fain believe to be genuine. The sea stretches its broad arm, carrying with it glistening light, far up past the home of Lord Rosebery towards the rival castle of Stirling. Fife rises from the shore to its prim but beautifully proportioned uplands, and on the south the eye ranges over fertile plains until it is caught and held by the bold outline of the Pentlands and the more distant and receding heights of Lammermoor. Scott said that the effect upon him of this scene approached near to enchantment. And yet may it be whispered that there are thousands of worthy Edinburgh citizens who know nothing of it. The Radical

Road is as lonely to-day as it was when the Waverley Novels were still unwritten.

The visitor, who puts himself in the hands of a guide, drives round the Park, a circuit of five miles. It is a drive such as no other city in Europe can match. Let us enter at Holyrood, a palace by which one is tempted to linger, so enticing is its aroma of the romance and tragedy of history. The Park here wears, as has been already said, its least pleasing aspect. The plateau at the foot of the Crags, lying between them and the Dumbiedykes—the latter recalling fearsome juvenile traditions pointing to the days of Burke and Hare, when the "Dumbie Doctors" used to prowl abroad seeking whom they might devour—this plateau serves as a somewhat barely-furnished entrance hall. But in a few minutes St. Leonard's Hill is reached. Here the colour which the park takes from the "Heart of Midlothian" at once suggests itself. It was close by here, on the outskirts of the city, in a lonely spot overlooking this part of the Park, that Davie Deans came to live; it was from this corner that Jeannie set out in the awesome night to keep her tryst at Muschat's Cairn. And now we are at the base of Arthur's Seat. It is from this point that the ascent is most frequently undertaken. To the top is a pleasant clamber. The lion looks a little more terrible than he really is. Come here on May morning, and you will hear the echoes of the hills ringing with musical laughter. It is the merriment of lads and lasses who are mounting blithely to the summit to test the virtues of the morning dew. For a time this pleasing fancy seemed to be dying out; latterly it has happily come in fashion again.

Near the base of the hill the carriage-road sends off a branch, past Samson's Ribs, alongside Duddingston Loch, and through the pleasant little hamlet where Thomson, the painter, lived in the manse which belonged to him as parish minister. Mr. Kinnear has made it easy to realise the impressiveness and the beauty of the scene as it unfolds itself along this road. Samson's Ribs are great basaltic columns chiselled by nature in regular pentagonal or hexagonal form, rising some eighty or ninety feet sheer from the road. They look as if they had been brought and set there from the wildest part of the Western Highlands. The road, too, at this point reminds one of a Highland pass. Narrow and overhung by cliffs, it is often called the "Windy Gowl"—a gorge through which the winter blast sweeps with roaring bitterness. There beyond is the placid stretch of Duddingston Loch, a piece of water that is worthy of its picturesque surroundings. Mr. Kinnear lets it be seen how finely Arthur's Seat rises when looked at from the other side across the Loch.

Duddingston Loch is at this end the boundary of the Park. From it a path ascends to Dunsappie, a lesser loch, but in its way not less picturesque. We are now at a considerable altitude; we are in the very heart of the Park; all around the prospect moves to

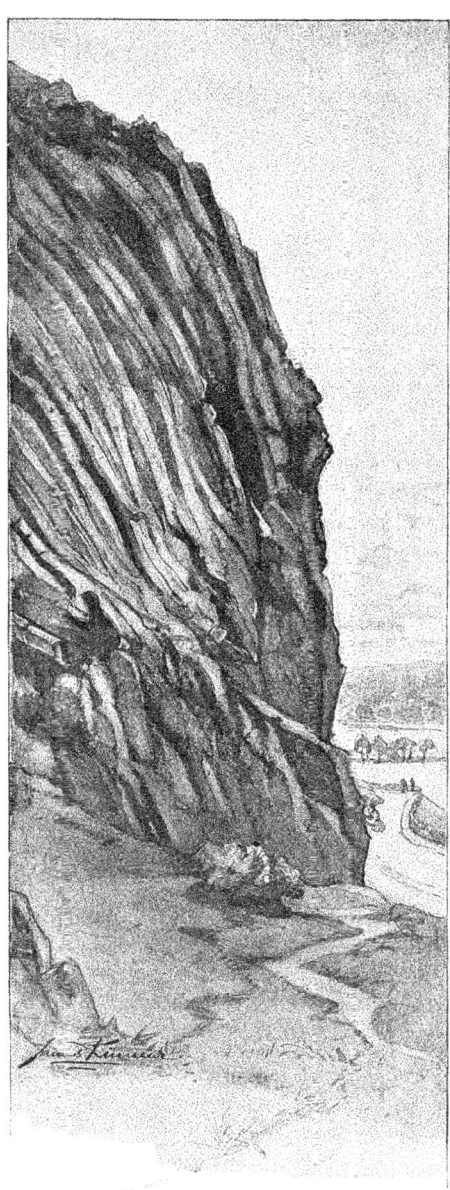

SAMSON'S RIBS FROM THE WEST. FROM A DRAWING BY JAMES KINNEAR.

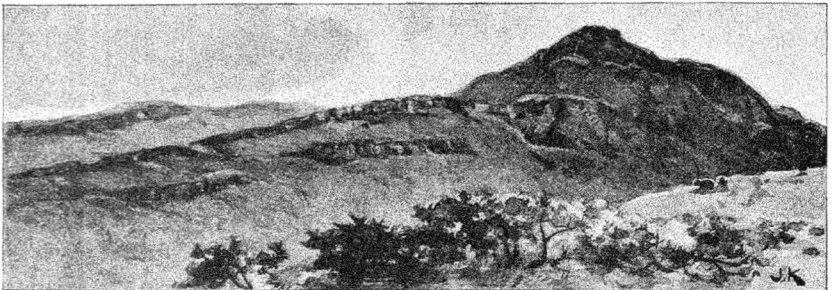

ARTHUR'S SEAT FROM BACK OF QUARRY IN THE HUNTER'S BOG. FROM A DRAWING BY JAMES KINNEAR.

admiration. In one direction lies the Port of Leith, far enough off for its lines to be softened in a dreamy impressionist way. Beyond is the Firth of Forth, passing far inland. The beauty of this prospect attends the visitor as he drives along, till dipping down on the north side, the road leads round to St. Margaret's Loch, and runs between it and the parade-ground on which the troops of the garrison are exercised. The loch itself is not so large as the other two sheets of water, but its surroundings are even more romantic. On a knoll stand the classic ruins of St. Anthony's Chapel. Before the days when ancient buildings became objects of reverence, the chapel walls had almost disappeared. Now they are only an interesting relic; forming, however, a connecting link with the distant Stuart time, for the chapel was founded by the queen of James the Fourth, and formed a hermitage attached to the monastery of South Leith, a place to which holy fathers retired to brood amid the loneliness of what was then a wild heath. Just over against this ruin is another relic, as unhallowed in its memory as the other is venerable. It is " Muschat's Cairn," known to every one as the place of the midnight meeting between Jeannie Deans and the lover and undoer of her sister Effie. The Cairn perpetuates the memory of a terrible murder which, foul and diabolical as it was, would probably long ago have been forgotten, but for the use Scott made of the place in the " Heart of Midlothian." The pile had, indeed, almost entirely disappeared at one time owing to the making of a new road. Now it remains, but chiefly as a landmark in the story of the unhappy Effie. The circuit of the " Queen's Drive " has now been made. It turns off near St. Anthony's Well—a spring which figured in old ballads—and sweeps back into the court of Holyrood Palace.

But if one wishes to enjoy the inmost charm of the Park he must explore it on foot. Away up through the Hunter's Bog, the geologist and the naturalist will find fresh fields of study, the lover of the picturesque will find the climb a perpetual soul-gladdening delight. Mr. Kinnear has made two sketches of Arthur's Seat from points which reveal the true mountain character that belongs to the place. At the back of the hill one feels as if he might be at the back of Schiehallion, so lonely and secluded is the spot. The sheep and the whins are beside him. They and the hillside make up all the picture. The Edinburgh citizen is indeed favoured. He lives in a great town, yet here in half an hour he finds the repose, the refreshing solitude, the poetic beauty of a Highland glen.

JOHN PETTIGREW CROAL.

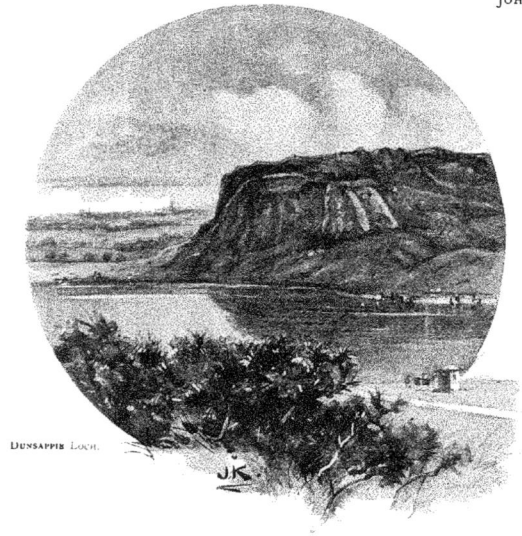

DUNSAPPIE LOCH.

'FLORA' IN JANUARY.

The goddess slept. About her where she lay,
  Dead pansies, fragrant still, and the myriad rose:
Adream 'mid the fallen drift, to wake one day
  And the blooms stirred, seeing her eyes unclose.

The oaks and beeches stood in disarray,
  Gaunt, spectral, dark, in dismal phantom rows:
She smiled, and there was a shimmer mid the grey,
  And sudden fall of the first winter-snows.

But when, tired with the icy blossoms of the air,
  She slept once more, and all the snow was over,
  She dreamed of Spring, and saw his sunlit hair,

And heard the whisper of her laughing lover;
  But, while she dreamed, the dead blooms had grown
    fair,
  And Christmas-roses made a veil above her.

WILLIAM SHARP

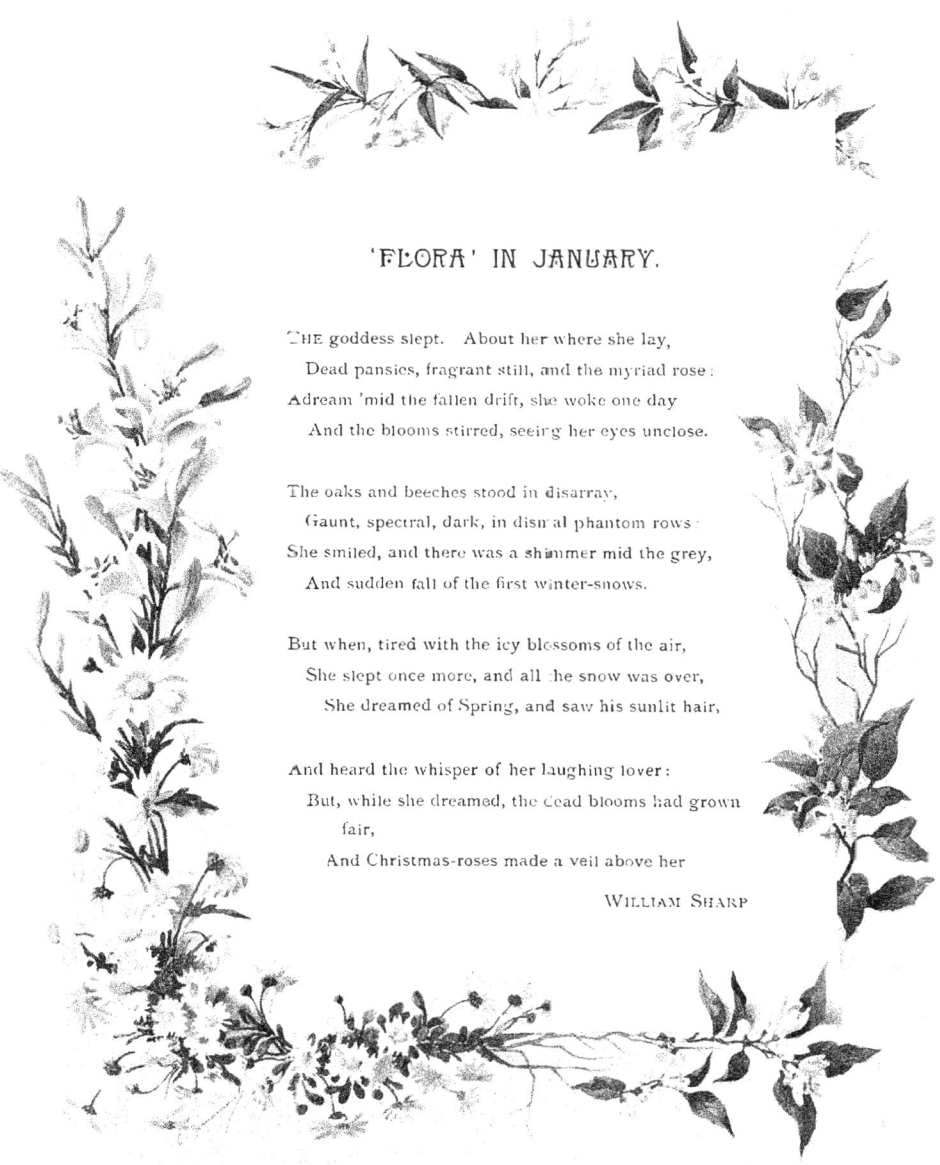

'FLORA' IN JANUARY.

THE goddess slept. About her where she lay,
   Dead pansies, fragrant still, and the myriad rose :
Adream 'mid the fallen drift, she woke one day
   And the blooms stirred, seeing her eyes unclose.

The oaks and beeches stood in disarray,
   Gaunt, spectral, dark, in dismal phantom rows :
She smiled, and there was a shimmer mid the grey,
   And sudden fall of the first winter-snows.

But when, tired with the icy blossoms of the air,
   She slept once more, and all the snow was over,
     She dreamed of Spring, and saw his sunlit hair,

And heard the whisper of her laughing lover :
   But, while she dreamed, the dead blooms had grown fair,
     And Christmas-roses made a veil above her

WILLIAM SHARP

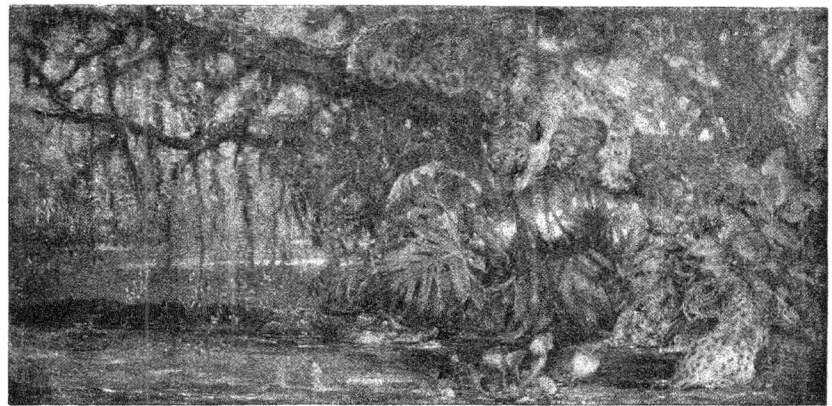

JAGUAR WITH YOUNG, AND ALLIGATOR. BY J. M. SWAN. FROM THE PAINTING IN THE COLLECTION OF J. G. JOHNSON, ESQ., OF PHILADELPHIA.

J. M. SWAN.

MEN of note are so often reported to have foreseen their future eminence that youthful self-appreciation is considered almost a characteristic of ability. In this respect Mr. John Macallan Swan cannot be said to have belied popular opinion. Early in life he was possessed with that firm conviction of talent, which not unfrequently becomes a main incentive to its cultivation. I remember Mr. Swan in the seventies as a prominent figure in the Latin Quarter Club. His own certainty of success then seemed unsupported by any evidence of efforts towards a speedy realisation. Many said that he did nothing to justify his belief in himself. Indeed, his ambition came less from a desire for popular success than from a thorough appreciation of the rare qualities of good work which he felt assured he both could and would attain. Perhaps, in the face of many illustrious examples offered in French Art it would have been folly to expect fame or money as the immediate

or necessary consequence of good work. And so Mr. Swan's self-assurance never led him to attempt an immature assertion of his powers, or to neglect a steady and laborious preparation of the basement works of his ambition. His life when I knew him as a student was given to unusually severe and solid study, which a dogged disposition of mind and great physical strength enabled him to take cheerfully. He never burst out in exuberant production and seldom deserted his appointed paths for those premature, and often futile if heroic excur-

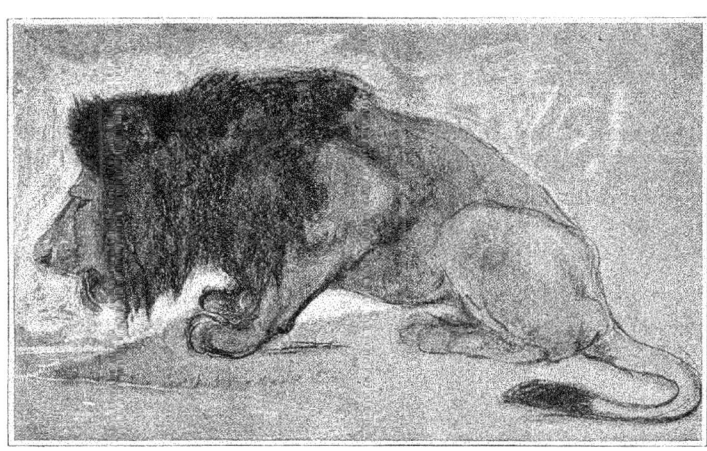

LION DRINKING. FROM A STUDY BY J. M. SWAN.

1894.

sions, into the unexplored country of imagination. In plain words Mr. Swan, as a student, suppressed rather than encouraged that faculty of working from *chic* which in later years he has developed with such advantage to his art.

Here it is well to touch slightly on Mr. Swan's education as an artist, his advantages and his surroundings as a student, and to speak afterwards of his later work and his present position. His first lessons were taken in the Lambeth School

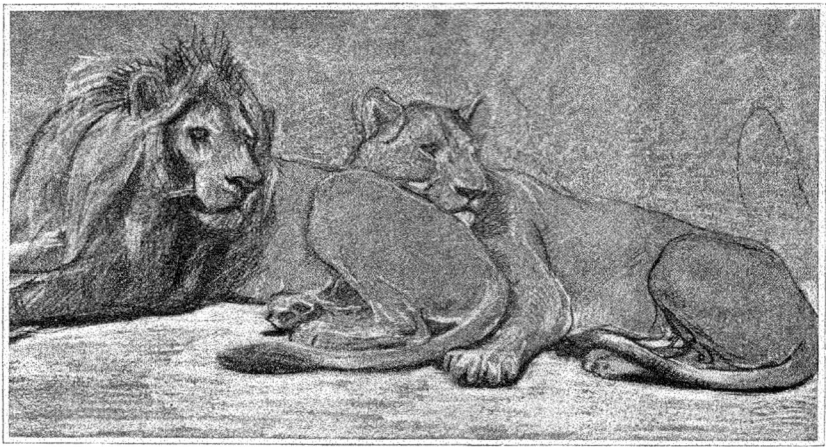

LION AND LIONESS. FROM A STUDY BY J. M. SWAN.

I do not wish to draw any comparison between the value of different turns of mind in the arts, and most certainly I do not wish to forget Keats, Coleridge, Shelley, Byron, or to underrate the rare incandescent quality of early genius. But painters differ from writers. They bear the burden of a *métier* learnt tolerably late in life, while language, on the other hand, is sucked in unbeknown by the child. Therefore, a painter's mental equipment contains a larger proportion of technical acquisition than a writer's. I should say rather that a painter's use of technique is bound to be more conscious than the writer's; and, in youth at least, his indulgence of fancy less absolved from considerations of his medium. When we speak of Velasquez, Rembrandt, Corot, etc., it is their later work that we praise for unconscious poetry, miraculous suggestion, and the spontaneous graces of free Art. It would have been well if many men of genius (to name but Rossetti) could have exchanged some of their exuberance of conception for an artist's love of his material. Imagination gains when judiciously robbed in the interest of knowledge, and the well balanced artist distributes his energy equally between what is called ideas and what is called drudgery. In fact there is no such thing as separation of technique and imagination in real Art. There is good expression of feeling and bad expression of feeling; expression by which the idea gains, and expression by which the idea loses. Mr. Swan, partly by himself, partly by education, rightly estimated the importance of knowing nature and Art profoundly. For a long time he studied Art as a science, a tendency of our day which undoubtedly may be pushed too far. He determined to give his imagination a really finished weapon, and, after heavy preliminary preparation, he entered the field about as well equipped as any man of his time.

of Art; then he attended the classes of the Royal Academy. Hardly satisfied with the Academy teaching of that time, and thinking it particularly unsuited to him, he became desirous of going to France. His wishes were kindly forwarded by several artists who gave him their services and advice. He received a letter to the English Embassy in Paris from Sir Francis Grant, as well as useful introductions from Sir F. Leighton and Messrs. Armitage, Yeames, and others of the Academy. At the Beaux-Arts his drawings gained him immediate permission to paint from the life. To say nothing of the advantages of direct teaching this meant association with some of the best of the younger men. Bastien Lepage and Dagnan-Bouveret, men already beginning to attract attention, were those among his fellow-students who most readily influenced the young Englishman. As the study of form was at this time his chief object, he was fortunate in having such a careful and accurate master as J. L. Gérome. Modelling, however, has been much used in France along with drawing for the study of form. Gérome, therefore, introduced Swan to Fremiet, the sculptor, you may say, of the realistic movement, and the successor of Barye.

Many of my readers doubtless know equally well both Fremiet and Barye as sculptors of animals. Painters of the present day as well as sculptors feel a real admiration for Fremiet's use of animals in his art; for his close study of their structure and his sympathetic interest in their characteristic action. If we think of the revolution this man was effecting quietly in his own branch of work, and of its relation to the general movement in all provinces of Art, we shall understand the fascination he exercised on the mind of a student who was to become famous as a painter of wild beasts. Mr. Swan's natural love for animals easily became an artistic

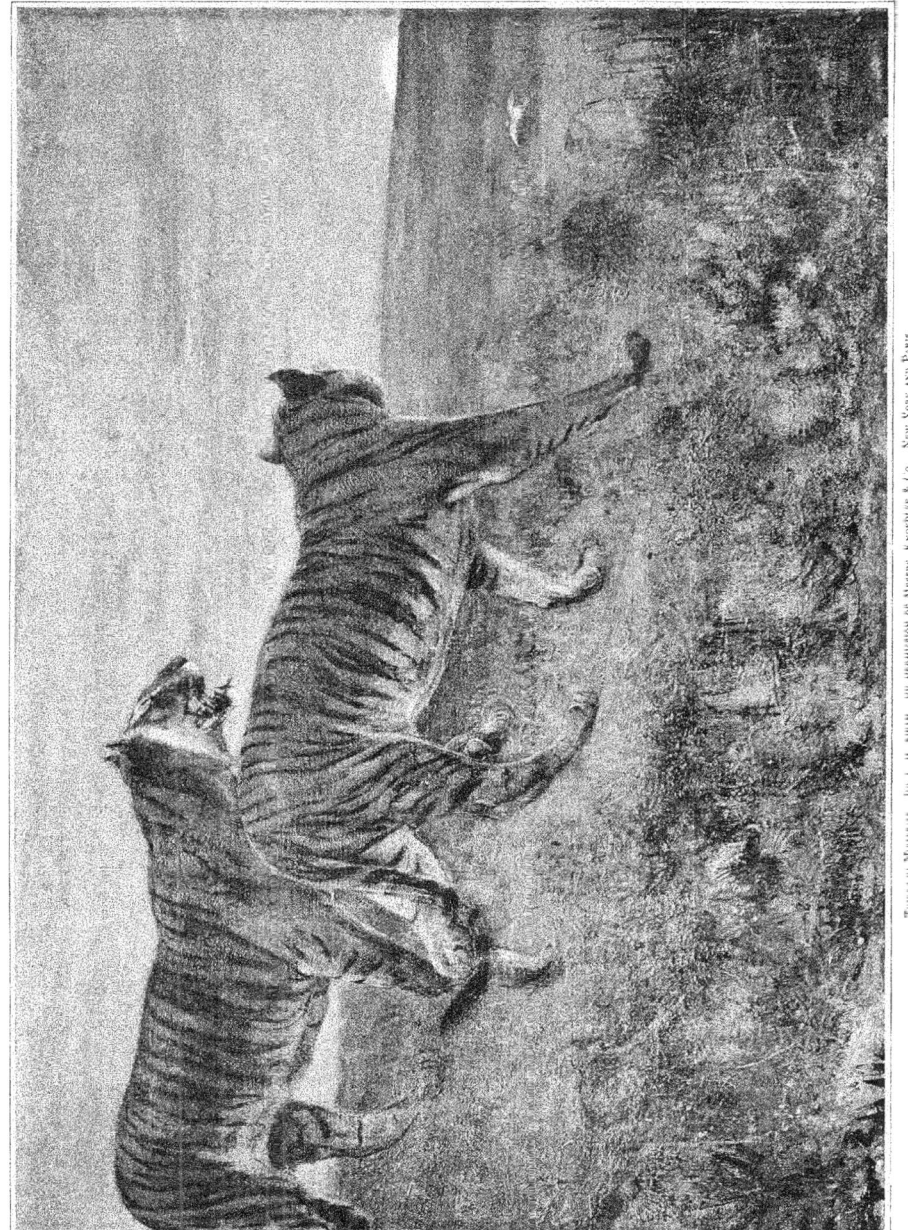

TIGERS IN MOORAGE. BY J. M. SWAN. BY PERMISSION OF MESSRS. KNOEDLER & CO., NEW YORK AND PARIS.

purpose under the counsels of the author of 'The Centaur and Bear,' 'The Gaulish Chieftain,' 'The Knight Errant,' 'Joan of Arc,' 'The Gorilla and Woman,' and many other illustrious groups in which animals play a principal part. Practice from nature under Fremiet's guidance in the Jardin des Plantes followed on this acquaintance. The master noted, explained, and lauded nature and natural movements. He praised and criticised the pupil's work; he directed his study, but encouraged him to teach himself. The complaint that French teaching of those days stifled individuality once met with some entertainment in England. It was never justified; and cannot now be sustained in the face of the originality and exuberance of the rich crop which has sprung from this admirably tilled field of instruction.

Fremiet was certainly one of those excellent teachers who have done so much honour to France by sowing amongst the artists of all lands the seed of the great French Renaissance. He imposed no dodge of the trade, inculcated no mannerism of his own, refused indeed to teach modelling as a trick, but rather pointed to nature, to anatomy, to the example of good work, and left the young man to develop himself—left him, however, walking in the right path and not uninspired by enthusiasm. Swan, as it happened, wanted little spurring to make him face the so-called drudgeries of his profession. He took to anatomy and dissection with alacrity; and as to the patient following, pencil in hand, of the animal-model through constant change of light and movement, that could never disgust a born animal painter. If anything, Swan grubbed too scientifically and too profoundly into the mysteries of structure and anatomy. In a weaker man this might have imperilled the artistic growth of the mind; and doubtless, in Swan as in others, this sort of study has tended to delay artistic maturity. Fremiet, indeed, sometimes accused him of pertinacity and obstinacy, and pointed out the dangers of too much knowledge, warning him that deliberation may waste away the power of conception. Once when Swan had worried over a skeleton as if he were a professional anatomist, Fremiet, to wake him up and remind him that Art is not science, set him to model a jaguar *écorché* in twenty-four hours. Forced to sum up his previously acquired knowledge and fuse it in the heat of rapid conception, the pupil put in such a good eighteen hours' work that Fremiet bade him touch it no more. These details of education may possibly be called trivial; but they will perhaps enlighten people unfamiliar with such a course of study and its effects on the artist's mind.

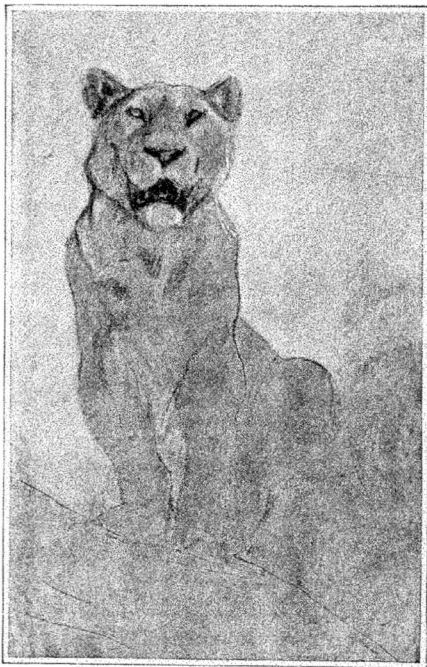

STUDY OF A LIONESS FOR BRONZE. BY J. M. SWAN.

At this juncture Swan fell upon the works of the sculptor Barye, about whom all Paris was talking. This is not the place to examine Barye's claims to poetry, to realistic truth, to classicism, or to romanticism. He had enough of all that for the purpose. There will always be contention on such points. Some will hold him more beautiful, even more true (because broader), than Fremiet. Others will prefer Fremiet's closer pursuit of truth. Any way, Barye was one of the men who helped to remind the extreme realists of the century that their work was of necessity incomplete. The realistic revolt against convention was justified by previous carelessness about truth, one of the two great elements in Art. People were sick of worn-out poetical mannerisms reposing on observations that had become staled by second-hand repetition. But it was not long permitted to the avenging realist to rob Art of her other element, style. It is only when the basis of truth, that must underlie and give a meaning to style, is forgotten, that the brutal realist becomes a necessary evil. In common with many of his day, Mr. Swan felt Barye's art as a reconciliation between sincerity on one side and style and beauty on the other. Such was Corot's work in landscape. This effort to express nature in a classic style, which was the main tendency during his younger days, Mr. Swan compares with that attraction towards the purely decorative side of Art due to the more recent impulse of Japanese work. It is a hopeful combination. There can be no doubt that the great Greek ideal arose under the double influence of an interest in nature and the heritage of the oriental spirit of ornament. At this period of his life Mr. Swan spent considerable time in working from Barye's *écorchés* in the collection of the Beaux-Arts. His Paris studies also included comparative anatomy under Gervais, and the anatomy of the human figure under Duval, whom many of my readers will know from Mr. Fenton's translation of his book, "Artistic Anatomy."

To sum up the motive power of Paris life on this artist, as well as the work or direct teaching of Gérome, Fremiet, Barye, Duval, and Gervais, we must mention the example of

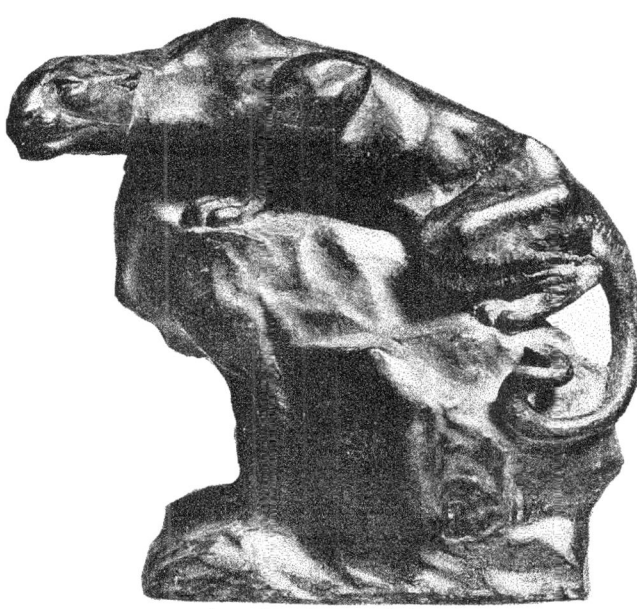

JAGUAR. FROM A BRONZE BY J. M. SWAN.

fellow-students, especially Dagnan-Bouveret, Bastien Lepage, and Wencker. To complete the account of educating influences, if they can ever be said to end, there remain a visit to Rome, where Swan consorted chiefly with the French artists of the Villa Medici, and his subsequent life in England, where he saw something of the brothers Maris, and where he continued his studies in anatomy at Bartholomew's and St. Thomas's hospitals; and lastly, his study of the life at the Zoological Gardens. During all this period, for the most part, Mr. Swan made no exertions to push himself before the public in exhibitions. Indeed, it is but in the last two or three years that he has become at all widely known, through his appearance at the Goupil galleries, and at the Academy, where his 'Prodigal Son' was bought by the trustees of the Chantrey Bequest, and in New York at Messrs. Knoedler's.

From what I have said it will be clear that such a man is slow of growth; that he is one who will spare no experiment; who will long maintain his interest in a motive; who will not soon run through his stock of ideas. Therefore, long as Mr. Swan may have been in manifesting himself, he has shown even now only a little corner of his art. From this man the public need not expect equality of style or the slickness of a success too cheaply earned. He is one who will pitilessly spoil the surface of many well-started canvases in pursuit of an ever-growing ideal; who will not easily permit himself to be tied down to the formal repetition of a subject that has lost significance to him, but who, nevertheless, will not readily abandon it as incapable of further perfection. Preferring the gain of new thoughts to increased mechanical dexterity, technical ease, or mere pretty smoothness, he may be expected to push on after further knowledge and fresh artistic experiment. So to the casual observer he may sometimes seem to be going back when he is only gathering for a fresh spring. I know the man, and of this, at least, I have hope, that he will maintain a sincere, courageous self-criticism, although with so many painters success relaxes the fibres of effort.

In the 'Prodigal Son,' to take a picture which all know,—it can be seen at the South Kensington Museum—we can trace the influences I have mentioned. The broad poetic presentment of the scene is kindred to the romantic conceptions of the century, to the spirit of Millet, Courbet, and the Marises. The advanced hour of the day by a large convention suggests this rich wrapping of warmth. Everything answers to the general tone as to a key-note. To pursue the image, a fertile invention makes good use of grand and simple elements of tonality. In fact, Mr. Swan has revelled in exquisite but well-restrained quality in his treatment of the black swine and the foreground flowers

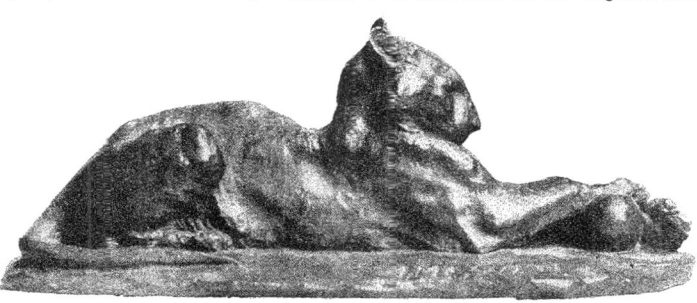

YOUNG PANTHER AND BALL. FROM A BRONZE BY J. M. SWAN.

and rocks. When again we inquire into what is given firmly, like the man's back, or even indicated like the swine, we find a profound study of structure and a mastery of modelling form that allies the picture to the revival of thorough research which we see in Frémiet, Gerôme, Bonnat, Duran and so many others of the century. It would be a mistake to suppose the setting of this picture a merely fanciful background, introduced decoratively without consideration of nature. To me it recalls the bare limestone plateaux of the Ardennes, a favourite place of study with Mr. Swan. Nor is Mr. Swan limited to the dark romantic tones of this canvas. He has full command over other schemes of colour. He delights in the sharp realistic contrasts of fresh greens, nude rosy flesh, blue skies and water. His 'Piping Boy and Fishes' shows a third and quite another vein of colour; blue, but dreamy, and closely kept to one key of feeling. In spite of the beauty of his landscape settings of figures of animals, in spite of his love of colour and of a handling that tends to fine qualities of paint, Mr. Swan continues to delight chiefly in the form of objects. No wonder, then, that many of his ideas are derived from modelling, and that numerous statuettes in his studio show the first realisation of the movements of figures and animals in his pictures. His ideal of modelling lies somewhere between those of Fremiet and Barye.

Perhaps the accompanying illustration from a bronze statuette which was shown in the Salon Champ de Mars will explain, better than any words, the use which Mr. Swan makes of modelling. Something like the movement of the crouching animal on the rock appears in Mr. Swan's pictorial treatment of the larger beasts of prey. Another bronze, ' Young Panther and Ball,' also illustrated in these pages, shows a noble and imposing silhouette from most points of view. Of Mr. Swan's many studies in black and white, chiefly in crayons, we reproduce four. One is a simple massive sketch from nature of a lion in repose. Firm and thorough rendering of the form in no way militates against the proud majestic aspect of the beast. The drawing shows no uneasy pursuit of anatomical lines. Mr. Swan's art enables him to trust entirely to the subtler and more decorative language of truthful and suggestive breadth. Another illustration is a more complicated affair; it is a picture of jaguars in the wild state in their natural forest habitat. A big one crouches in a characteristic attitude on a large branch which crosses the picture diagonally. Two young ones may be seen below in the ferns and undergrowths, crawling hurriedly out of the reach of the crocodile which half hidden silently approaches the cubs. The large illustration, ' Tigers by Moonrise,' reproduces a fine canvas recently painted, in which a couple of tigers go out on an evening prowl. The relation of the animals to the landscape is admirable. It is by no means easy to adjust these huge near hand forms with long undulating backs so as to secure decorative dignity and some sense of natural space and proportion. The management of the stripes, moreover, deserves attention; far from producing an irritable pattern they fall into the general arrangement and follow the form with agreeable suavity.

R. A. M. STEVENSON.

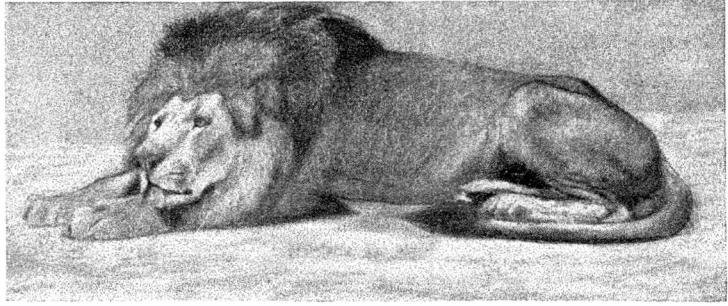

STUDY OF A LION. BY J. M. SWAN.

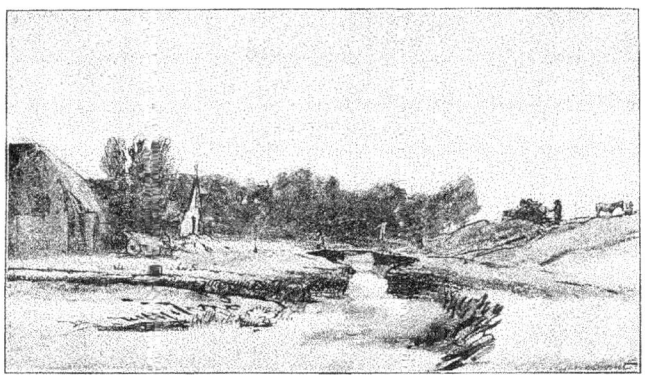

LANDSCAPE STUDY, FROM A PEN AND WASH DRAWING BY REMBRANDT. IN THE BRITISH MUSEUM.

THE GREAT MASTER.

OF the Old Masters, the one that excites the greatest interest at the moment is undoubtedly Rembrandt. Our fathers and grandfathers were taught to put Raffaelle and Michelangelo on thrones by themselves; to give the second place to the Venetians, and to assign the next rank to Guido and the Bolognese. Our own generation in England was brought up on Mr. Ruskin's revised version of these views, and though we saw the Carracci ousted in favour of the Primitives, and Michelangelo bidden to take a lower place than Tintoret, the honours remained with the Italians. With them they still remain, in the minds of that large class of persons to whom the ideal in art is everything, and to whom classical rhythm and harmony count for more than that "utterance of all that life contains," which, as the latest historian of Æsthetic declares, is the essence of the modern conception of beauty. To accept this latter position is to explain at once why the drift of modern opinion in art has set so definitely towards the great Dutch painters. "We are all realists now," if one may so vary a statesman's celebrated sentence; and though we assign the highest formal honours to the great men of the Re-

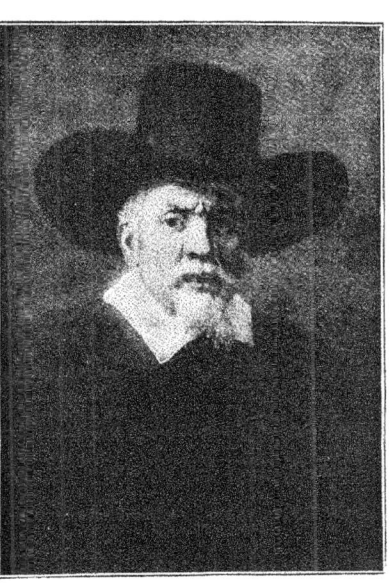

DR. ARNOLD THOLINX. BY REMBRANDT, 1656.

naissance and give them the loftiest pedestals and the finest shrine in our Pantheon, we reserve our human admiration for the men who have painted with the broadest sympathy, the subtlest insight, and the strongest mastery, the complex facts of human life. To say this is to explain the fascination which Rembrandt, the head of the Dutch School, and yet so unlike any other member of it, exercises over the modern mind. A year or two ago the literary event of the season in Germany was the appearance of a book in which bureaucracy-ridden Prussia was bidden to find salvation in contemplating the freedom, the unconventionality, the spontaneousness of Rembrandt's genius. Rembrandt was to be taken as the *Erzieher*, the educator, in all departments of life. It is not so that the professed students look at him; but the presence of this element in him goes far to account for the initial push that sends them—for they too are modern—on their search after all that can be known of his life and work. The latest of those students' books is before us to-day; the remarkable book which M. Emile Michel has written in French, and which Miss Florence Simmonds—writing now for the first time, we believe, under her own name—has translated into good and simple English. To call attention to it, and to the enterprise of Mr. Heinemann who has published the English version in so sumptuous a form, is a task that is at once a pleasure and almost a duty.

M. Michel, who is not to be confused with his namesake, the Art critic of the *Débats*, has long been well known to all students of Dutch painting as a careful and learned writer, who has worked with and after Dr. Bode and Dr. Bredius, and has performed the task which none can do so well as a Frenchman: that of giving form and currency to the dry results of their researches. He reads Dutch and German; he has *Oud Holland* and the *Preussische Jahrbücher* at his fingers' ends, and he knows the Amsterdam of the seventeenth century almost as he knows the Paris· of to-day. It would be unjust, however, to say no more than this, for M. Michel has studied with his own eyes in all the great European galleries, and does not describe what he has not seen. Hence, though in all his books, his little "Ruysdael" and "Hobbima," his "Les Cuyp" and "Les Van de Velde," as well as in this great "Rembrandt," there is a great deal of firsthand judgment, his habitual deference to the authority of his two friends sometimes gives the impression that his work is less first-hand than it really is. In one respect we are conscious of a certain shortcoming: M. Michel does not know England and the English collections nearly as well as he knows the Continental galleries. That terrible Channel has barred his way. Even for the sake of becoming acquainted with the collections which still, after all that has been sold from them, contain such unnumbered examples of the great Dutch masters, he has not often been here. Perhaps now that his chief work has been naturalised among us, he will feel less unwilling to make pilgrimages among the English collections, still, as far as Dutch art goes, the richest private collections in the world.

The immense success of the French edition of M. Michel's work is a proof that the time was ripe for a complete book on Rembrandt. Research has been busy since Scheltema, the Dutch archivist, published his brief rectification of the vulgar errors that had grown and clustered round the life of the great man, and even since Vosmaer wrote his, in its day, very excellent Life. Dr. Bode, a fine judge and a mighty and an indefatigable hunter after the master's works, has been everywhere and remembered everything and his "Studien," published in 1883, with some supplemental lists issued since, have gone far beyond Vosmaer. Our own Old Masters' Exhibitions have also done much in the way of bringing to light new Rembrandts; witness the great show in 1889, when Lord Ilchester's splendid 'Portrait of the Artist' (1658)—reproduced in the English but not in the French version of M. Michel's book—was seen for the first time since 1815, and last year, when Captain Holford exhibited three uncatalogued works, one of them, the portrait of an old lady (the wife of the preacher Sylvius), a picture of the highest importance. But most of all have the zealous researches of Dr. Bredius in the archives of Amsterdam and Leyden served to throw light upon the life and work of Rembrandt, as upon that of hundreds of other artists. The world thinks little of this poring over musty records; it prefers to such patient zeal the cheap talent of the rhetorician who can turn a phrase

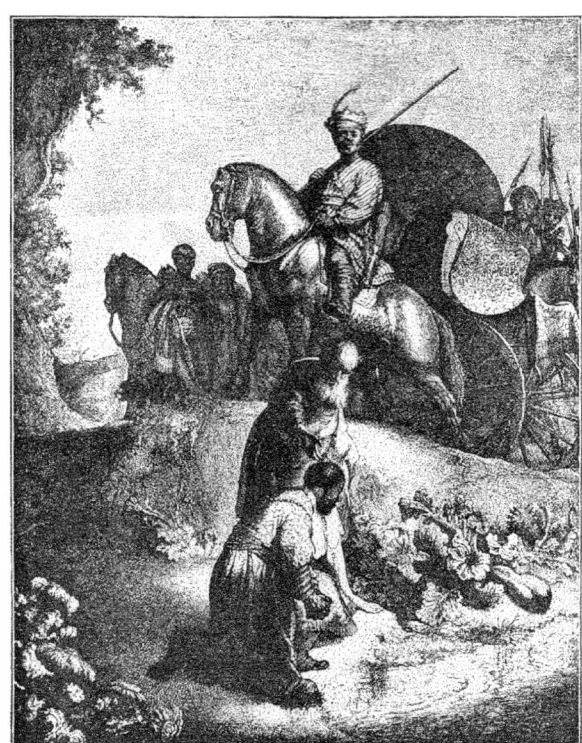

The Baptism of the Eunuch. Engraved by J. Van Vliet, in 1631, after a Picture by Rembrandt.

effectively; but to those who can feel and know, is there not

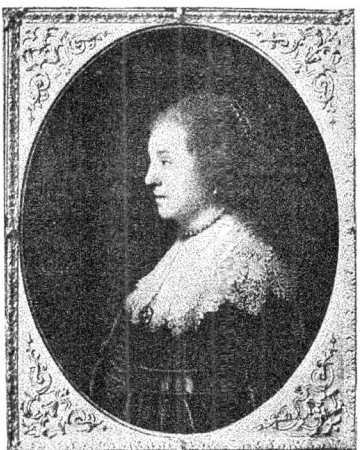

PORTRAIT OF SASKIA, REMBRANDT'S FIRST WIFE. BY REMBRANDT, 1632.

something almost heroic in this lifelong devotion to the memory of those whose work has made humanity illustrious, and brought a glory upon one's country? The search is long, the labour intense, and the results often insignificant; and yet the seeker goes on his way undaunted, till the discovery of a date, or a name, or a signature rewards him. It seems little, but it tells. The grain of truth may be but a grain, but it helps to make the heap, and in due time comes the sowing, and the growing, and the crop—the crop of knowledge which the man of letters gathers together, as M. Michel has done, and which from henceforth all the world may call their own.

M. Michel's plan is, in brief, to gather up all that is positively known of Rembrandt, his *milieu*, and his work; to trace step by step the story of his life—artistic and personal; and to accompany the narrative with descriptions of large numbers of pictures, especially those which are not very generally known, or which are of special importance in the master's development. It is only in the descriptions that we have to complain of any *longueurs*—probably M. Michel would have done better had he allowed his readers to take the colours and forms for granted, since after a little while minute descriptions of a number of pictures in succession are sure to become wearisome. For the rest, the story moves well, and the life of Rembrandt, as full of pathetic contrasts of light and shade as one of his own pictures, is told in a way that carries on the reader, even though he be not a professed student or collector. We shall make no attempt here to tell the story over again, but in what remains of this article may dwell on some incidents which are more or less new in Rembrandt's life, and speak of some of the less-known pictures and their history, especially the portraits of his family and friends. It may be that these details, together with the illustrations which we reproduce, will be found interesting enough to send readers to the book itself. As to the illustrations, they are very numerous—beautiful examples of modern "process" work.

1894.

and, on the whole, selected with much care and skill. In the main, though not entirely, the arrangement of them is chronological, so that the reader can follow at his ease the development of the master from the days of the Hague 'Presentation in the Temple,' and the so-called 'Oriental Heads,' down to those of the Brunswick 'Family Piece' and 'The Syndics.' The advantage of such accompaniments to the text is obvious; and it is the first time that a biographer has been found able—and a publisher willing—to provide it on an adequate scale. From this point of view the book is not likely to be superseded; though, of course, it will not stop the way for the gigantic work which Dr. Bode is now engaged upon, and which M. Sedelmeyer is to publish—a series of folio photogravures of every known picture by the master, with descriptions and comments by the eminent German critic.

Among the new discoveries, one that deserves notice is the interesting "find" of Dr. Worp, of Groningen, in the library of the Academy of Sciences at Amsterdam. In examining a MS. of the poems of Constantine Huygens, he lately came upon an unknown autobiography of that author, written in the scholarly and somewhat over-subtle Latin of the day, and in it the earliest existing criticism of the young painter, then (about 1630) only twenty-three years old. It is an elaborate comparison between "two adolescents, one the son of a simple artisan, a tapestry weaver, and the other of a miller,"—Jan Levens and Rembrandt van Rijn. Huygens thinks

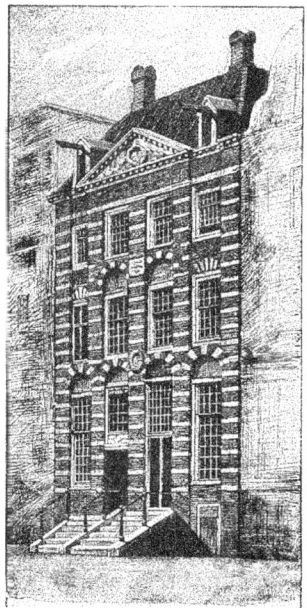

REMBRANDT'S HOUSE IN THE BREESTRAAT, AMSTERDAM. (IN ITS PRESENT STATE.)

that "Rembrandt surpasses Lievens in intelligence and in

H

vivacity of impression; but Lievens, on the other hand, is superior in dignity and in amplitude of form. The latter, in his youthful impulsiveness, will have nothing that is not grandiose, and he loves to paint objects on a scale even larger than life. But Rembrandt, although he chooses to paint pictures of small dimensions, attains by the force of his talent a concentrated power for which you look in vain in the vast pictures of his companions." And then the critic proves his point by quoting a small picture of Judas bringing back the pieces of silver, and speaks with enthusiasm of the tremendous power of tragic expression displayed by the painter.

M. Michel claims to have discovered this picture of Judas in the possession of M. Haro, the well-known dealer in Paris; but another one, attributed to Salomon Koninck, was exhibited at Berlin in 1890, and we believe that another—unless it was the same picture and came afterwards to M. Haro—was sold many years ago in the collection of Lord Charlemont. It would be rather surprising, indeed, if Rembrandt had not painted it more than once; for few New Testament subjects could be found to give greater scope to his special talents than this scene of tragic passion in the midst of the very surroundings which he best loved to paint.

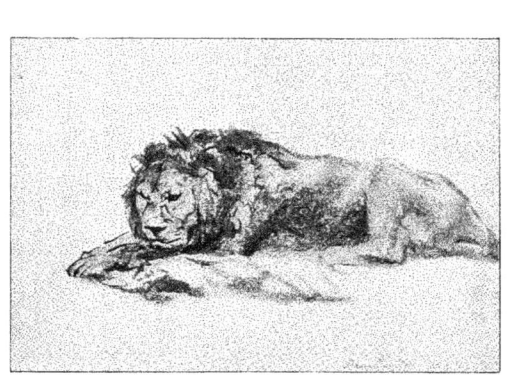

REMBRANDT'S BROTHER, 1650. IN THE HAGUE MUSEUM.

Another matter of interest that M. Michel brings into prominence for the first time, is the degree to which Rembrandt drew for his materials upon himself, his family, and his immediate surroundings. To the self-portraits, of which the book produces a great number, we need not refer except to point out that the epochs in Rembrandt's life when they were most frequent are two: the period of his first great activity (1630-6), when he was most restless in his search after the subtleties of light and shade, and when he treated himself as frankly the best,

the most useful, and the most complaisant of models; and next, the period of his ruin and the years that followed, when the world had deserted him, when clients were few, and when, if he was to paint at all, he must either paint any old mendicant or Jew *chiffonnier* who would sit to him, or himself. Of such a type are the Louvre picture of 1662, the National Gallery undated picture, Lord Ilchester's of 1658, and that which was mezzotinted by Earlom in 1767, when it was described as " in the collection of the Duke of Montagu." There is a pathetic personal interest about them all, when one compares them with the works of the Saskia epoch, and contrasts the wrinkled, melancholy Rembrandt of the later date, clothed in the plainest and roughest dress, with the brilliant creature of 1630-1640, brave to look upon, and decked with velvets and with armour. The master's passion for fine things had helped to ruin him; his young wife died, his affairs went to pieces; creditors pressed, overthrew and overwhelmed him, and adieu the jewels, the pictures of Old Masters, the portfolios of their drawings, the house in the Breestraat and all; except his love for his art, his genius that ripened with misfortune and with age, and his affection for that home circle upon which Death was to make, as the master's years declined, so cruel a succession of inroads.

Of the other portraits of the home circle, we may notice the very frequent pictures and etchings of the painter's father and mother; the numerous pictures and etchings of Saskia his wife; the several known paintings of Titus his son; those after Hendrickje, the master's faithful companion in his later years, and the fine study of Rembrandt's brother Adrian, which Dr. Bredins lately bought

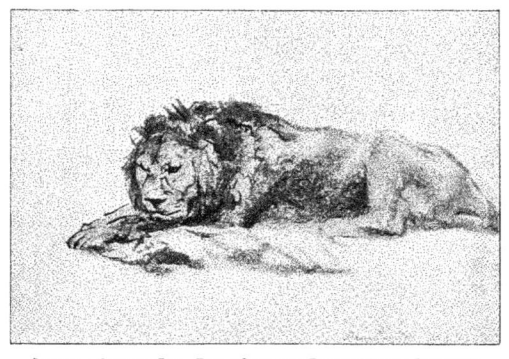

STUDY OF A CROUCHING LION. FROM A DRAWING IN PEN AND WASH BY REMBRANDT. IN LORD BROWNLOW'S COLLECTION.

in England for the Hague gallery. As to the portraits of old Harmen van Rijn, the painter's father, it is only quite recently that he has been identified as the original of the etching of the so-called 'Oriental head,' retouched in 1635, and of the portraits by Rembrandt at the Hague, and by G. Dou at Cassel. We may add to those mentioned by M. Michel a very highly-finished and beautiful little portrait of the mother, and a larger portrait of the father, in the collection of the Marquis of Exeter at Burleigh House. The portraits of the painter's father are highly interesting; this keen, weak face, with the staring eyes and the excitable, nervous look, proclaims just the man who might have done his business as a miller very badly, and been the father of a great artist. Of Saskia the book gives us more than have ever been grouped together before, though one or two of them are thought by Dr. Bode to be of Rembrandt's sister Lysbeth, rather than of the fair creature who became the painter's wife. Besides the famous Cassel profile and the ' Saskia on Rembrandt's knees' at Dresden, we have illustrations of the so-called 'Burgomaster Pancras and his Wife' at Buckingham Palace—certainly Rembrandt and Saskia in masquerade costume ; we have M. Haro's fine profile portrait, now the property of M. Edouard André; we have Mr. Samuel Joseph's rather similar picture; and we have two works from Prince Lichtenstein's wonderful gallery at Vienna. One of these, of Saskia at her toilette, is a most characteristic work of this period, about 1633 or 1634, and is among the best examples of Rembrandt's fondness, in those early happy days of his, for decking out his favourite models in splendid costumes, that he might have the joy of painting jewels and rich tissues. The picture came from that wonderful sale in 1885, the like of which we shall hardly see again, when Sir William Knighton's capital pictures by Rembrandt, Gainsborough and others, were literally given away at Christie's. Buyers are wiser and keener now, at all events where Rembrandt is concerned; though, to be sure, it is never quite certain that the sale of a quite unknown collection will not prove to be a "frost." Another of the home group of portraits came from the same sale, the 'Painter's Brother,' now at the Hague, a strong, expressive face, rapidly painted, in which we find a type so often repeated by Rembrandt that the presumption in favour of its being the portrait of a relation is strong. It is interesting to note that a fine and very similar head, but wearing a black cap, was in the late Lord Ely's collection, from which it passed into the possession of Mr. Martin Colnaghi. It was one of a pair; the woman is painted with surprising mastery, and an excellent type of the humble class from which Adrian van Rijn, a shoemaker and afterwards an unsuccessful miller, would doubtless have chosen his wife.

The known portraits of Titus, the painter's son, are fairly numerous: of them one of the best is a picture of which the history can be traced, we believe, to 1699; it now belongs to Mr. R. Kann, of Paris, one of the most fastidious and successful of modern collectors. Another, painted several years later, was shown by Captain Holford in the last Old Master's Exhibition; and a third, at the age of ten or twelve, representing the lad looking out of the window and holding a book and inkhorn, is known to us through an interesting old copy. All are charming as pictures, and to lovers of Rembrandt they have a pathetic interest from the history of the boy, whose services to his poor broken father were so invaluable, and who died just after his own marriage in 1668. As to Hendrickje—the subject of the splendid portrait in the Louvre, and of the Edinburgh picture—who has so long been thought to have been lawfully married to Rembrandt, it seems that that idea must be definitely laid aside. But she provided for him in his age, she nursed him till she herself died, and, for many years after their first association had begun, she was his ready and constant model. One child was born of this union, Cornelia, who after the death of Hendrickje was the chief consolation of Rembrandt's age, and who at some later date married one Suythoff, went to Batavia, and became the mother of two sons, Rembrandt and Hendrick.

Such details as these have only now been put together for the first time, by M. Michel, on the authority of the Dutch students and archivists, whose patient labours are now at last placing the history of their great school on a sound footing. But this is only one part of his work, and the least important. What Vosmaer did in the way of chronologically classifying Rembrandt's work and following out the productions of each year from the beginnings at Leyden to the days of weariness and eclipse at Amsterdam, M. Michel does once more, with greater fulness, and with the advantage of the much wider knowledge that has been accumulated since Vosmaer's day. The increase of our knowledge is in all directions. The etchings have been re-catalogued—laboriously, but a little too speculatively—by Mr. Middleton-Wake, and again criticised in the dry, definitive German manner by Herr von Seidlitz, of Dresden. The study of Rembrandt's drawings, of which new examples are constantly coming to light, has received a fresh impulse from the publication of the beautiful portfolios of fac-similes under the direction of Dr. Lippmann, of Berlin. As to the pictures, they are becoming better known in two ways ; by the labour that is being expended on the question of their origin, and by the eager search of collectors, especially in London and Paris, which has of late years brought so many of the lost, back into the fold.

Of the former, the most remarkable instance is the immense and mysterious canvas called 'The Conspiracy of Claudius Civilis,' which is now in the museum at Stockholm—a picture measuring nine feet by six feet, and yet only a fragment. It represents a dark night scene—a group of persons in strange dress seated round a table ; in the midst the figure of a man, evidently the principal personage, about whom all that can be asserted positively is that he is one-eyed and that he holds a broad, drawn sword. Since the picture came to the Stockholm Academy in 1798, as a bequest from a lady of Dutch origin settled in Sweden - Madame Peill—it has borne many fancy titles : it has been called 'The Oath of John Ziska,' 'Judas Macabeus and his Brethren,' and 'The God Odin, Founder of the Swedish Kingdom.' At last the key to the mystery has been found by M. De Roever, one of the joint editors of *Oud Holland*, who in Fokkens's "Description of Amsterdam," 1662, and in various other records, has discovered that Rembrandt, before that year, painted for the Town Hall of Amsterdam, a picture representing the oath of Claudius Civilis in leading the revolt of the Batavi against the Romans. Readers of Tacitus will remember that earliest of the Dutch patriots was one-eyed. The picture appears to have been never placed in the Town Hall, but to have lain *perdu* for an unknown period, when the centre was cut out and passed into Madame Peill's possession. There is a drawing of the whole composition in the Munich Collection.

Other cases of the re-discovery of smaller pictures are the two studies of Rembrandt's brother, to which we have referred ; at least ten or twelve true Rembrandts sold in minor sales at Christie's and other English auction rooms during the last fifteen years ; and one very fine picture, 'The Pilgrim at Prayer,' figured in M. Michel's book.

This last now belongs to Consul Weber, at Hamburg, the owner of a choice collection. M. Michel says that he gave one hundred thousand francs for it, but this may be an exaggeration. Anyhow, we believe that the picture " turned up " at a furniture sale in London some three years ago, and was bought for nothing by a lucky connoisseur who chanced to be present. Of course, this *chasse* and its great rewards have their unfortunate side; many discoveries prove to be no discoveries; many a swan's nest is found which proves to be filled with the eggs of a goose. And generally this happens when the noise made about the discovery is most resounding; witness the case of the " Rembrandt du Pecq," in Paris two or three years ago. A picture came to light at a little suburban sale; the reporters and the interviewers got hold of it, and the world was invited to believe that it was one of the most important of existing Rembrandts. Alas! like Charles Lamb's Raphael, which gradually subsided into a Carlo Maratti, the Rembrandt du Pecq declined, in due course, into an Arnold de Gelder.

To conclude this somewhat unsystematic notice of M. Michel's book it may be mentioned that the English version appears under the supervision of Mr. F. Wedmore, who has written an introduction, who has greatly improved the catalogue of pictures, which appears, defaced by a good many mistakes, in the original French edition, and who has added three or four illustrations, taken from pictures in this country.

HUMPHRY WARD.

ART IN THE TRANSVAAL.

FINE Art out in the Transvaal is a thing of the future, although the way in which any stray illustrated paper from the Old Country is appreciated, and the eager demand for the sight of anything better, seems to show that there is a taste for the refining influences of life lying dormant which only needs opportunity and leisure to develop itself. It is interesting to compare the advancement in respect of the Fine Arts of the various races which are represented in the Transvaal. Just as the towns are in advance of the country in this respect, so do the British seem in advance of the Boers. Among the natives, Art, if it can be so called, is of the rudest and most primitive description; but this is not to be wondered at so much as the fact that amongst the descendants of the early Dutch settlers not a single instance has occurred, where even a spark of the grand old ancestral school has shown itself in its migrated progeny.

The average Transvaal Boer is one of the most hopeless Philistines imaginable. While generally of good physique, his countenance is plain, and his clothing patched, ill-fitting, and greasy. He wears heavy hob-nailed boots, a dirty shirt, and an antiquated slouch hat. Truly there is plenty of scope for the refining influences of Art to work upon him. Moreover, it is by no means lack of wealth which necessitates his appearing thus, for as a rule the richer he grows the meaner he becomes. In his house one finds nothing more artistic than the eternal portraits of Oom Paul, or Piet Joubert, just as in cottages at home one finds the inevitable chromo-lithograph of Mr. Gladstone or the late Lord Beaconsfield.

But it is not so much the absence of anything artistic about him, as the want of Art in his life, that makes the Boer's condition so hopeless. It seems impossible to believe as one contemplates him that he comes from the stock which has produced some of the world's greatest masters, so utterly extinct in him seems all refined taste or artistic fancy. Even the highest developments of Dutch Art and culture were somewhat mundane, and the race, transplanted from its old home, and separated from the influences of the slowly built-up civilisation of centuries, seems to have lost any idealism their fathers may have once possessed, together with their undoubted love of the beautiful and the harmonious.

With the British population things are not so bad, and some efforts towards taste and culture are constantly being made. Not very long ago an exhibition was got up in Johannesberg, which, though only a children's one, gave some promise of better to come. We believe there is an artist with a studio either in that town or in Pretoria. Doubtless when the necessities of life have been satisfied, and wealth and leisure afford opportunities for its luxuries and refinements, attention will be paid to the Fine Arts.

A PIONEER.

CHATTO AND LINTON.

To the Editor of THE ART JOURNAL.

SIR,—Acknowledging the very kindly notice of my book, "The Masters of Wood Engraving," in your October number, may I be allowed to make some brief remarks in justice to both Mr. Chatto and myself? My critic speaks of " a terrible note upon poor Chatto," at the foot of my page 24, of which " the inference seems intended that Chatto had no authority for describing the graver with a handle rounded at the top."

My note at page 24 was only this:—" Chatto, translating Sach's verses under this cut of 'The Formschneider,' gives him a *graver*, and writes also that the wood engravers of that period used 'a tool with a handle rounded at the top similar to the graver used at the present day.' I know not of the handle, but a graver cannot be used on a plank."

Chatto does so mistranslate Sach's words under the cut of 'The Formschneider,' giving the line as:—" I with my *graver* cut so neat." Sach's word is *tool*, and not *graver*. Chatto also is wrong in the remark that the wood engraver of that period "used a tool similar to the modern graver with a handle rounded at the top." The tool they used is not similar, either with or without the handle, to the modern or the ancient *graver*; but a knife, the very opposite in its action; the graver *drives*, the knife is *pulled*. In giving the *C. S.* figures Chatto is again in error, calling them " wo gravers of different kinds." The figures are a knife and a graver; probably, as my critic observed, indicating that *C. S.* engraved in wood (in which case only the knife could be used) and also in metal (for which he would use the graver). The object of my note was simply to show that Chatto misused the word *graver* as the tool of the plant-cutting ' Formschneider.'

But more important than any insufficiency of my note is my critic's remark that "Chatto is evidently one of Mr. Linton's pet aversions." I hope I have neither pet nor petty aversions. If I had, certainly Mr. Chatto is not one. I knew him personally and in a friendly way; and have always respected him as a very earnest student, a thoroughly conscientious writer, and an excellent bibliographer. This is the statement in the very opening of the preface to my book :—

"Chatto, to whom I owe a large indebtedness, for without him my work had been hardly possible, was only a most conscientious and excellent bibliographer, not by any means qualified, even with such help as he had from Jackson, to criticise and judge the works which he chronicled and described." It was the special object of my book to show where, in their judgment of engraving in wood, Chatto, Sotheby, Otley, Conway and others, erred through their want of an engraver's technical knowledge. Have I in any one instance expressed any aversion to the men, however averse to their untechnical conclusions?   W. J. LINTON.
New Haven, Conn., U.S.A.
October, 1893.

*** Of course it was not suggested that Mr. Linton's frequent and stringent criticisms on the hapless Chatto were due to aversion to that writer personally. The less important element of Mr. Linton's remarks speaks for itself.

SIR FREDERIC LEIGHTON ON GERMAN ART.

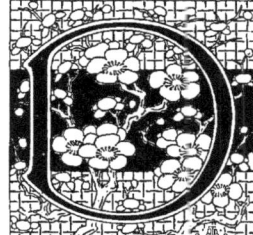

DISTINGUISHED as the official head of Art in England, Sir Frederic Leighton every second year devotes himself to deliver to the students of the Royal Academy an address on the Art of neighbouring nations. Some day, perhaps, Sir Frederic will tell the world his own ideas of the present condition of Art in his own country; but this, of course, might include the direct or indirect censure of some of his own colleagues. Meanwhile, avoiding any too pronounced views on the most difficult problem he could discuss, the President gave, on December 9th, a survey on German Art, with a few words on the paintings of Albert Dürer and Holbein.

Of German Art in general Sir Frederic said :—

"In considering the subject of German Art we find ourselves confronted with a strangely perplexing phenomenon; for we are brought face to face with a people possessed during many centuries with a strong craving for artistic expression, and reaching on occasions to achievement of a very high order, and yet, as a whole, wanting, it seems to me, in qualities which we connect with the artistic temper—a people which, through the exceptional fruitfulness of its æsthetic impulses, or, more accurately, perhaps, of its desire for expression through form and colour, and in virtue of the power, the thoroughness, and the masculine sincerity which stamp its handiwork, establishes a just claim to a prominent place in the wide republic of the arts, and has, nevertheless, put upon the world, by the side of many and noble masterpieces, a quite curious amount of ungainly and at times all but repellent, work. It is impossible, indeed, to survey, however cursorily, the immense field of German activity in Art without being powerfully impressed by the high qualities revealed in every part of it; nevertheless, the final impression left by such a survey is of a people amongst which the ethic sense is constantly predominant over the æsthetic impulse, and we are made conscious that if we have been frequently moved to respectful appreciation and admiring wonder, it is but seldom that we have been conscious of that sweet, that enveloping, that sufficing sense which has its springs only in the æsthetically beautiful."

Of the two painters to which the President made special reference, he said : "Albert Durer may be regarded as *par excellence* the typical German artist. He was a man of a strong and upright nature, bent on pure and high ideals, a man ever seeking, if I may use his own characteristic expression, to make known through his work the mysterious treasure that was laid up in his heart; he was a thinker, a theorist, and, as you know, a writer; like many of the great artists of the Renaissance, he was steeped also in the love of science. In his colour he was rich and vivid, not always unerring as to his harmonies, not alluring in his execution—withal a giant. In Holbein we have a complete contrast to the great Franconian of whom I have just spoken; a man not prone to theorise, not steeped in speculation, a dreamer of no dreams; without passion, but full of joyous fancies he looked out with serene eyes upon the world around him; accepting nature without preoccupation or afterthought, but with a keen sense of all her subtle beauties, loving her simply and for herself. As a draughtsman he displayed a flow, a fulness of form, and an almost classic restraint, which are wanting in the work of Dürer, and are, indeed, not found elsewhere in German Art. As a colourist, he had a keen sense of the value of tone relations, a sense in which Durer again was lacking. A less powerful personality than Dürer, he was a far superior painter. Proud indeed may that country be that counts two names so great in Art."

1894.

SCOTTISH ART AND ARTISTS.

THE Society of Scottish Artists was originated in 1891 to encourage artistic endeavour among the younger men north of the Tweed. There was a feeling that in the Exhibition of the Royal Scottish Academy the bulk of the space on and about the line was monopolised by pictures by Academicians and Associates, and that, in consequence, good work by younger artists could not receive that consideration its merit deserved. The Scottish Academy, it is only fair to say, warmly denied the impeachment, and the Society does not necessarily involve antagonism to the older institution; but it was sufficiently believed outside to give strength to the formation of this Society, which now numbers 470 members, and embraces on its professional side many clever young artists of the East and North of Scotland, and on its lay side many prominent citizens. The members were fortunate in securing as President the Marquis of Huntly, who, deeply interested in Art and the personal friend of many artists, has taken the liveliest concern in all the affairs of the Society, to its great advantage. The second Exhibition, which was held in the autumn in the Edinburgh National Galleries, has given great satisfaction. In selecting pictures for it, the two leading aims of the Society were steadily kept in view. By hanging good pictures in good places, the Society seeks to stimulate the younger artists to produce "more original and important works," and there has also been procured on loan many educative examples of various schools of Modern Art. In particular the Council has been deeply indebted to Mr. J. S. Forbes, the well-known Scotsman, residing in London, for allowing them to exhibit many of the gems of his collection. Among these may be mentioned the 'Beppino' of M. Carolus-Duran, several beautiful Corots, a lovely Daubigny ('Noonday'), a masterly forest scene by Diaz, and several delightful pastels by Millet. Major Thorburn lent a splendid Mauve and a James Maris.

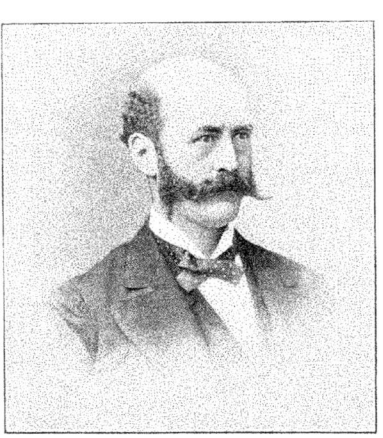

THE MARQUIS OF HUNTLY.

The Royal Scottish Academy has just passed through an acute crisis. In September last Sir George Reid, the President, intimated to the Council that he proposed to resign office at the annual meeting in November unless certain important questions of policy were taken up and settled. The chief of these had reference to what is called the "unlimited Associateship," and to the institution of an order of Honorary Retired Academicians. At the meeting held in November the President withdrew his resignation on a pledge being given by the Academy that no more Associates should be elected until the questions raised by him have been settled. It may be mentioned that in two years, under the new charter, twenty-two new Associates have been added to the roll of the Scottish Academy, so that at the present time there are more Associates than Academicians. Sir George Reid has acted wisely and with a moral bravery few could command in calling serious attention to the dangers of the position, and public sympathy is entirely with him. If the younger artists of Scotland were a little more far-seeing, they would not hesitate to rally to the defence of their President, who seeks only to defend the best interests of the Academy, and who, moreover, is one of the best of Scottish painters.

Artistic life in Glasgow is just now full of vigour, and on every side evidence may be found of the interest taken in the works and ways of artists. Mr. Robert Walker, the popular secretary of the Fine Art Institute, is as successful as ever, and rejoices in the sum of £5,000 recently left to his gallery. Under the efficient guidance of Mr. Paton the municipal collection—whose *chef-d'œuvre* is Mr. Whistler's 'Carlyle'—will, in due course, have a new and magnificent home. Mr. Lavery has just closed a successful exhibition at Messrs. Lawrie's, and Mr. James Paterson has opened at Mr. W. B. Paterson's charming little rooms, a remarkably interesting collection of water-colours. Mr. James Paterson has also just published through Messrs. Maclehose a series of drawings of 'Nithsdale,' reproduced in aquatint with great strength by Messrs. Annan, wherein the artists' effects are rendered with the power of a mezzotint and the fidelity of a sun picture. Messrs. Connell, in their house in Redfield Street, have been exhibiting some representative English pictures, notably some of Sir Frederic Leighton's; and Messrs. Van Baerle will enter a new gallery in a short time. The Art Club Exhibition, just closed, was the best ever held; certainly this exhibition surpasses the New English Art Club, now open in London. Lastly, Mr. Newberry at the Art School is the centre of a training organization which, though a branch of South Kensington, has aspirations far beyond the effete routine of that establishment. The artistic expression of some of the advanced pupils appears full of promise.

ART NOTES AND REVIEWS.

OF the usual autumn exhibitions in London little need be said; they show the utmost content of their contributors to paint by tradition, and they have their patrons. The Society of British Artists is still hampered with the flight into Impressionism, and its eras date from that point. The Institute of Oil Painters has soberly respectable exhibitions where enthusiasm is seldom seen. The Royal Society's winter collection of sketches and studies is always more unconventional than the "finished" drawings. Sir Francis Powell, the President of the Scottish Water-Colourists, has developed a new and broad style individual to himself, but sympathetic with Mollinger and others of the best side of the Dutch School.

The exhibition of the New English Art Club shows that it is still the day of small things with our most advanced artists. Content with schemes of colour and composition which contain no superlative difficulties, the newer ideas which these artists strive for have very little chance of expansion and of acceptation by any but a small section of the community. At the same time, there are several pieces of excellent artistic work. Professor Fred. Brown's 'At the Piano,' Mr. Steer's 'Miss Emma Freude,' and Mr. Strang's 'Bathers,' are works which are worthy to class with the best.

One of the most successful exhibitions held during the autumn has been Mr. Albert Goodwin's collection in the rooms of The Fine Art Society. Messrs. Agnew have also found an attraction in Mr. Wilfrid Ball's Drawings of Egypt; and Mr. D. S. MacColl's water-colours, in the new gallery of Messrs. Boussod, Valadon & Co., have been much discussed, for it is not often that a critic will submit his own work to be publicly exhibited.

That Mr. Mendoza has reached his eleventh annual "Black and White" Exhibition shows that patronage is not exclusively given to colour. Many of those in the present collection are pleasing pictures, and several are high-class works of Art, such as Meissonier's 'Gentleman of the Time of Louis XIII.'—of which we give a reproduction—L'Hermitte's 'Plucking Geese,' and various other drawings by G. C. Haité and H. Marr.

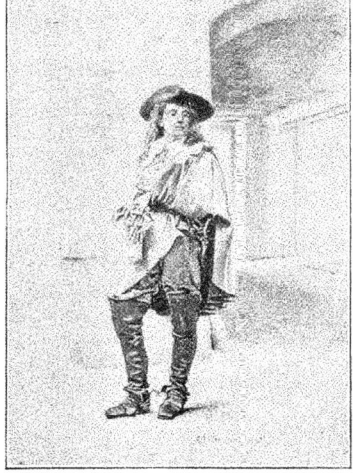

GENTLEMAN OF THE TIME OF LOUIS XIII. BY MEISSONIER.

The Royal Society of Artists' Autumn Exhibition in Birmingham is likely to prove very successful, as the sales are considerably in excess of those of last year. Mr. J. W. North's large oil picture, 'Sweet Water Meadows of the West,' has been purchased by Mr. W. Kenrick, M.P., and presented to the Corporation Art Gallery. A very fine oil study by Sir F. Leighton, of 'The Sea giving up its Dead,' has also found a purchaser, and we hear this also is likely to be presented to the Art Gallery.

The Birmingham Society is arranging, for their next Spring Exhibition, a loan collection of the works of the late Frederick Walker, combined with those of J. W. North. Professor Herkomer will deliver a presidential address on the works of these artists, whose genius is not at present sufficiently recognised in the provinces; Mr. Agnew's recent gift to the National Gallery of Walker's 'Harbour of Refuge,' and Mr. Kenrick's gift to the Birmingham Gallery, having created a strong desire among the people of the Midlands to become better acquainted with their works.

It has been arranged to hold an International Exhibition at San Francisco from January to June, 1894, but as the notices have reached this country from Chicago undated and illegibly signed, it is not likely that the Art Commissioner for Great Britain has received many replies to his request to send on pictures to him from the World's Fair. A number of the pictures from Chicago have, however, been promised for the annual exhibition of the Pennsylvanian Art Society in Philadelphia In this connection it may be mentioned that the duty on Fine Art work entering the United States will probably be abolished in the course of 1894. At present the duty is fifteen per cent. on paintings and twenty-five per cent. on engravings and books.

OBITUARY.

Karl Bodmer, who has just died at Paris in his eighty-fifth year, was one of the minor lights of the Barbizon School. He was a Swiss, but became a naturalised Frenchman. He went to Barbizon to study the forest of Fontainebleau about 1845, and became acquainted with Millet, Diaz, and Rousseau. He is represented in the Luxembourg by a scene in the forest. He was also an engraver of some merit.

The excellence of children's books becomes more marked every season. Messrs. C. W. Faulkner enter the field with a collection well suited for juveniles, and, at the same time, full of good artistic work. Confessedly they are of the "pretty" order, but in many parents' eyes this is a failing in the right direction. The late Alice Havers made her drawings for "Love and Sleep," by Lewis Morris, daintily attractive, and the most successful book of the series is "The Love of Christ," by an unnamed artist, where several are worthy of enlargement and separate publication. Messrs. Faulkner's calendars and Christmas cards are also successful, the best designs being by Miss H. M. Bennett.

The choicest book for children this season is, however, "HANS ANDERSEN'S FAIRY TALES" (G. Allen, Orpington), with many charming illustrations by A. J. Gaskin, of the Birmingham School of Art. Combining, without too great subservience, some of the qualities of Mr. Burne-Jones with the quaintness of Bewick, the drawings are complete works of Art in themselves. 'The Little Match Girl' is not an unworthy following of the modern master, and the 'Farmer and his Son' is a legitimate rendering of a landscape after the fashion of the Father of English wood engraving. "Pictured Carols" (G. Allen), illustrated under the direction of Mr. Gaskin, is hardly so successful, but the designs by Miss Manly, Miss Rudland, and Mr. F. Mason show more than ordinary talent.

THE LITTLE MATCH GIRL. BY A. J. GASKIN. FROM "ANDERSEN'S FAIRY TALES."

Lord Ronald Gower has compiled an interesting volume in "JOAN OF ARC" (J. C. Nimmo), and the publisher has taken care to set it forth with admirable print and paper. The story of the Maid of Orleans is rendered in a simple and sympathetic way, and the reasons for her rehabilitation are given without bias. Had the author expressed more of his personal conclusions the reading would be more satisfactory; but this is still possible for him to do in a companion volume. With illustrations such as Bastien Lepage's 'Jeanne d'Arc' and Fremiet's well-known Parisian statue, there would be more interest than in the somewhat feeble plates in this book, although two of the photogravures are successful.

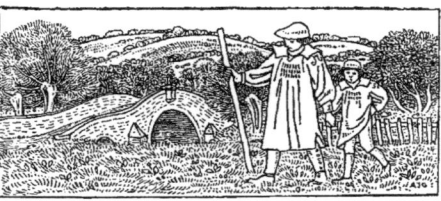

FARMER AND SON. BY A. J. GASKIN. FROM "ANDERSEN'S FAIRY TALES."

With all possible respect to feminine susceptibilities, it may be said that it is seldom a lady writer is business-like enough to write such a systematic and clearly expressed work as "A HISTORY OF ENGLISH DRESS," by Miss Georgiana Hill (Bentley). Only a woman can write on dress with the necessary authority, and diffuseness might reasonably have been occasionally expected. Touching gracefully on the earliest dresses in England, the authoress gives a vivid picture of the scantiness of household furniture in the days of the first Plantagenets, and speaks of the astonishment caused by Eleanor of Castile, wife of Edward I., when she had her rooms covered with carpet. She points out that although our fashions come from France they are not always French, but often Italian or Spanish, diluted by Parisian taste. To a costume painter or an actor, these two volumes are almost necessary, while to the ordinary reader the theme is well rendered and readable throughout:

For painters and students, Mr. W. J. Muckley's "Handbook on Colours" (Baillière) is invaluable. It has reached a fourth edition: its success is well deserved, for it is practical and trustworthy.—For architects, and perhaps even more for persons about to engage an architect, Mr. W. J. Loftie's "Inigo Jones and Wren" (Rivington) is a book to be pondered over. Mr. Loftie brings evidence to bear on the superior quality of the Palladian or Renaissance style, but he spoils himself by his hatred of Mr. Waterhouse and all his works. The author's contention that "this style is about 400 years old, yet its admirers are not obliged to build after a 400-years-old pattern," is however worthy of serious consideration.

"In the Footsteps of the Poets" (Isbister), with biographical sketches by Professor Masson and others, is thoroughly readable and appropriately illustrated. The essay on James Thomson gives a living portrait of the poet of the Seasons.— "The Hanging of the Crane" (Longmans), and other Home poems by Longfellow, is a delightful little book, and it is surprising that the illustrators' names are not given with the pretty vignettes.—Another singularly charming book is "Burns' 'Chloris,'" by Dr. Adams (Glasgow, Morison Brothers), carefully printed, and, although not illustrated, full of word pictures of "The Lassie wi' the Lint-white Locks."

"The Year's Art, 1894" (J. S. Virtue & Co.) offers to artists, art-students, and all who have pleasure in Art, or business in its production, a volume of greater variety and interest than ever. One of the new features is a series of portraits of the editors of illustrated and artistic periodicals.

NOTE ON MR. ORCHARDSON AS A DRAMATIST.

THE irrelevance of the words printed above to anything that should concern a painter, will no doubt be the first idea to strike some of those who may condescend to glance over these lines. In England, they may think, we have too much dislocation of the arts already—too much drama on canvas, too many pictures on the stage—and they may go on to declare that a painter has no right to be dramatic at all. But in these days it is possible, by good luck, to appeal from the craftsman whose vision is bounded by his own easel and the easels of his own particular clique, to the man who understands, to the artist with what I may call a classical education—an education based on familiarity with what was done in years too distant to be affected by the passions of to-day. In a recent number of this journal Mr. Humphry Ward was able to say, with perfect truth, that "of the old masters, the one that excites the greatest interest at the moment is undoubtedly Rembrandt," and Rembrandt's popularity is by no means confined to connoisseurs; although, with their wider experience and greater catholicity, the best amateurs see deeper into his genius than a painter can be expected to see. Well, Rembrandt was a great dramatist. Even his portraits are dramatic. They show us more than a man's quiescent possibilities. In those painted after 1640, or thereabouts, we see not only living men, but men with their characters in action. His sitters are quick; they are barely arrested for the sitting. In spite of his own despotic personality he shows them as they pass from one act of their lives to the next. Even in those fantastic portraits of himself in which his individuality is overlaid with exotic decoration, this movement of life, this unbroken passage of thought and action, is never lost; and if this be so with his portraits, still more completely is it so with his subject pictures. He was, of course, a painter first and above all. As soon as he became an artist, which was none too early, even with Rembrandt, the pictorial idea always governed his proceedings. His theme might be given, as, for instance, in the 'Lesson in Anatomy,' but his treatment stood on its own base. It was decided by consideration for his own artistic vernacular, by his desire for a unity to be won by light and colour. And yet his instinct for the dramatic was so great that any one

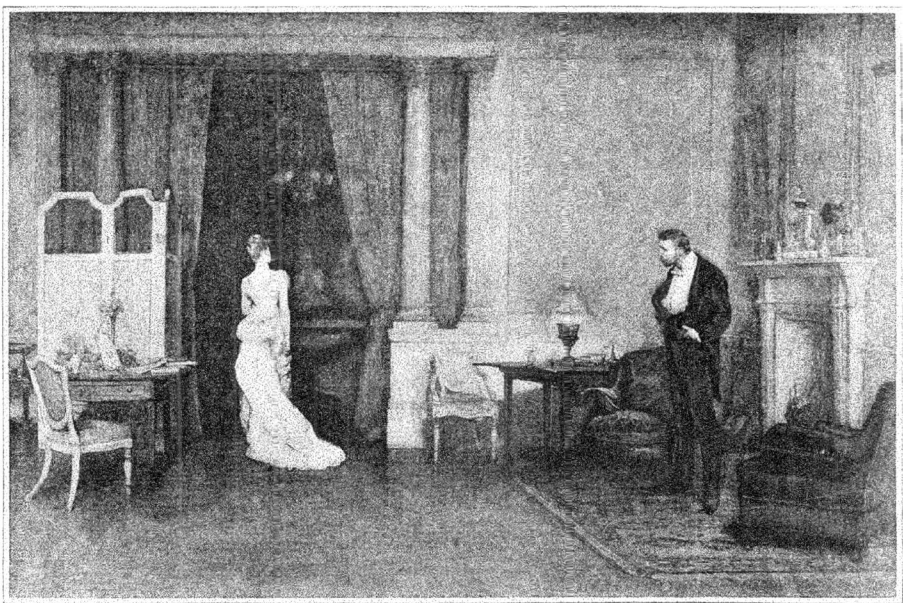

THE FIRST CLOUD. BY W. Q. ORCHARDSON, R.A. FROM THE PICTURE IN THE HENRY TATE COLLECTION.

with an eye for action and none for more narrowly pictorial qualities, might conscientiously argue that he was a dramatist first and a painter afterwards.

FEBRUARY, 1894.

Now there is a good deal of Rembrandt in Orchardson. The portrait of Mr. Walter Gilbey, which was at the Academy in 1892, although not in the least "Rembrandtesque," was conceived on the same lines as a Rembrandt. It showed character in action plus the painter's own predilections in colour, chiaroscuro, and design. By its momentariness, by the vigour of its grip, we were irresistibly reminded of such things as the so-called 'John Sobieski,' at St. Petersburg, the 'Rembrandt in a Yellow Gaberdine,' at Lord Ilchester's, or the 'Hendrikje Stoffels,' of the Berlin Museum. And, without pushing the comparison too far, I may repeat it in connection with Mr. Orchardson's work as an illustrator, as a painter of what one is compelled to call subject pictures. He first caught the eye of the crowd with his 'Napoleon on the *Bellerophon*,' which was at the Academy in 1880, was published in *The Art Journal* for February, 1885, and now hangs with the other Chantrey things at South Kensington. No one, except those who have never heard of Napoleon, could fail to understand the drama at a glance, no one trained in Art could fail to see that the picture's æsthetic reason for existing, the motive which led to its being painted at all, was not dramatic but pictorial. And so with Orchardson's next venture into the same field, the 'Voltaire,' now at Hamburg. Dramatically, the conception is not so self-contained. One requires to know more exactly what has and what is about to happen. The *Bellerophon* episode was not an incident in the Emperor's career, it was the end of the Napoleonic pageant, it was the catastrophe to which the six years' captivity in the South Atlantic was an anti-climax. When, after some twelve years, Orchardson turned to the General Buonaparte of St. Helena, and painted him dictating to his secretary, it was a postscript he gave us, the sort of tag which, in an old-fashioned novel, used to show us the hero and heroine playing with their babies. The last look at the French coast was the death of the Emperor Napoleon. The picture might have been named in a word. With the 'Voltaire' it was different. The incident was not even characteristic, and so the picture built upon it was less of an epic. Pictorially, I think it the finer of the two. The essential contrast between the raging little quill-driver on the one hand, and the *société* of bored and apathetic *ducs* and *vicomtes* on the other, and the luxurious setting of it all, gave a better opportunity than the deck of a man-of-war and groups united by sympathy.

The 'Mariage de Convenance' (1884), 'After' (1886), 'The First Cloud' (1887), and 'Her Mother's Voice' (1888), illustrate the experiment of marriage from different but always real points of view. They are all dramatic. In each the action moves. In each are we face to face with a past and a future, as well as with a present, and yet pictorial fitness, the signs of a pictorial origin, are dominant all through. If we could see them only with our senses, if for the moment we could narcotize the thinking sides of our brains, our satisfaction would still be complete. Mr. Orchardson does not cover so much ground as Hogarth, he does not hit so hard a blow as Rembrandt, but the mantles of both touched him as they fell, and it would be hard to name a painter of our time who more happily unites the dramatic with the pictorial instinct.

WALTER ARMSTRONG.

*** 'Her Mother's Voice,' which forms the frontispiece to this number of *The Art Journal*, represents the widower and father thinking of the "sound of a voice that is still," and is from the Henry Tate collection. 'The First Cloud' comes from the same gallery. 'The Queen of Swords' belongs to Mr. James Keiller's collection in Dundee, which is described a few pages further on.

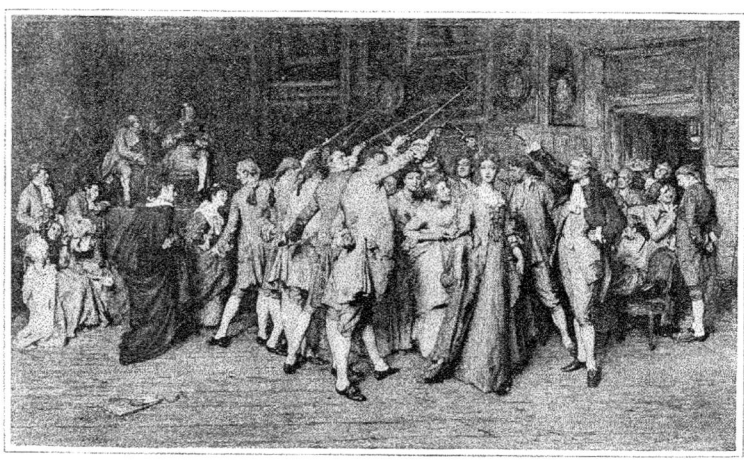

THE QUEEN OF SWORDS. BY W. Q. ORCHARDSON, R.A. FROM THE PICTURE IN MR. KEILLER'S COLLECTION, DUNDEE.
(SEE PAGE 59.) BY PERMISSION OF THE FINE ART SOCIETY, THE OWNERS OF THE COPYRIGHT

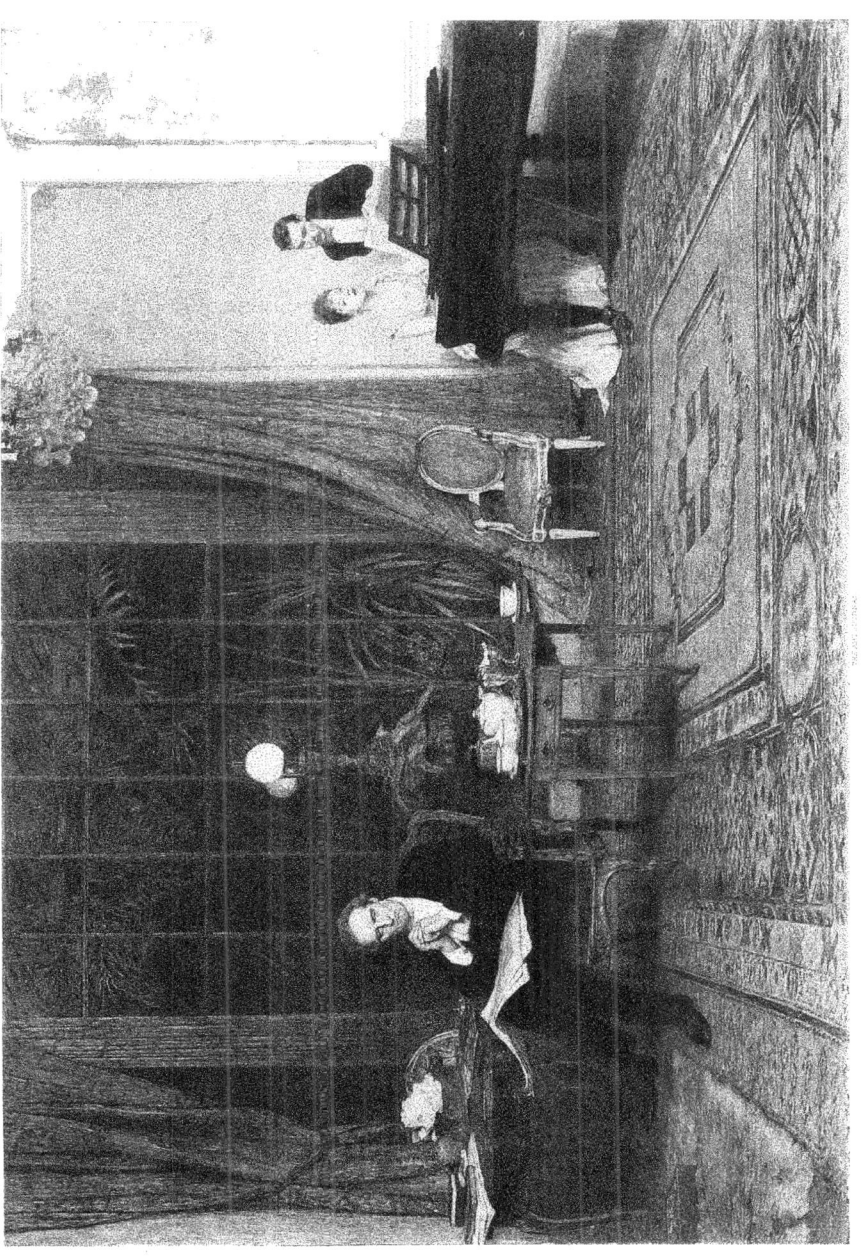

THE MOTHER'S VOW.

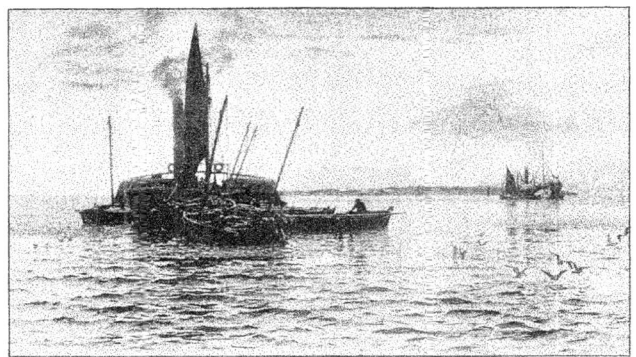

HERRING MARKET AT SEA. BY COLIN HUNTER, A.R.A.

MANCHESTER CITY ART GALLERY.

IN the year 1823 a meeting of the principal merchants and other influential inhabitants of Manchester was held in the Royal Exchange, to take into consideration a suggestion of the establishment of an institution for the encouragement of the Fine Arts. The scheme met with warm approbation, and a large sum of money—about thirty thousand pounds —was raised towards carrying it out. A temporary gallery was acquired in Market Street, and the subscribers became governors of it. Two years later the eminent architect, Sir, then Mr., Charles Barry, was engaged to erect the present building, which was completed from his designs in 1830.

The Royal Manchester Institution, as it was originally called, is situated in the centre of the city at the corner of Mosley Street and Princess Street. It is a classic building, and the entrance-hall is decorated with plaster casts of the Parthenon frieze, built into the wall. They were presented by King George IV. On the first floor were originally seven galleries, but recently the building has been thoroughly renovated and some structural alterations have been made under the directions of Mr. Allison, city surveyor, whereby two new rooms have been added. The top lighting of the galleries has also been materially improved, and electric incandescent lamps substituted for gas throughout.

The Royal Institution from the first was invested in a board of management selected from the governors, and from its completion down to the year 1882, exhibitions of pictures were held annually under their direction. As a voluntary association of persons interested

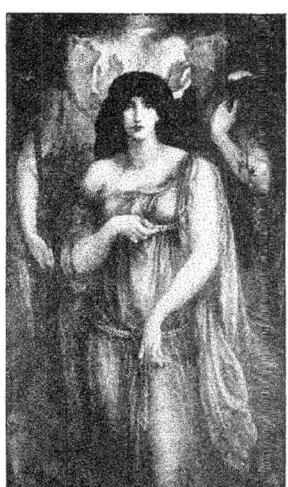

ASTARTE SYRIACA. BY D. G. ROSSETTI.

in art, literature and science, it doubtless contributed largely to foster the taste for Art in the district. It was felt, however, that these galleries and the works of Art contained in them, which had been obtained both by gift and purchase, might become of greater utility to the public by being placed directly under the control of the Corporation. Accordingly, by an Act of Parliament, which received royal assent in 1882, effect was given to an agreement, between the governors of the Royal Manchester Institution and the Municipal Authorities, by which the building and its contents were transferred to the town, and the management of the whole was placed under an Art Gallery Committee, a body consisting of twenty-one members, of whom fourteen are selected by the Corporation, and seven nominated by the governors of the Royal Manchester Institution. The special Act provides for the perpetuation of the personal privileges of the governors and for the annual expenditure, for twenty years, of not less than £2,000 a year by the Corporation, together with all profits derived from exhibitions, in the purchase of works of Art.

On August 31st, 1883, the building was formally handed over to the Corporation, and the first exhibition held under their direction was opened by Lord Carlingford, at that time the Lord President of the Council.

During the ten years the Art Gallery has been under the control of the Corporation the sum of £31,000 has been expended upon pictures for the permanent collection, which is always on view daily to the public free of charge, whilst an exhibition of works by living artists has been held annually every autumn. The permanent collection has also been materially increased by numerous and important gifts of oil paintings and water-colour drawings.

It is impossible to enumerate all the valuable works belonging to the City of Manchester contained in these galleries, but it will suffice to mention the more important of them. Amongst the principal paintings in possession of the Royal Manchester Institution when the buildings were transferred to the Corporation in 1883, are 'Ulysses and the Syrens,' by William Etty, R.A., a fine painting which the artist in his autobiography considered one of his greatest works; it was presented to the institution by Mr. William Grant in 1838. 'Pope Leo IV. anointing Alfred the Great,' by Richard Westall, R.A., the gift of Mr. S. Green in 1840. 'John Baliol surrendering his crown to Edward I. of England, A.D. 1296,' by James Northcote, R.A., presented by Mr. J. W. Barton in 1845. These two latter belonged to a set of pictures styled the "Historic Gallery," which was collected by Bowyer and engraved by him to illustrate his edition of "Hume's History of England." 'The Chase,' by Richard Ansdell, R.A., a large work representing a deer being worried by two hounds, purchased in 1847. 'Samson Betrayed,' by F. R. Pickersgill, R.A., purchased in 1851; 'The Good Samaritan,' by G. F. Watts, R.A.; this work was presented by the artist in 1852 to the citizens of Manchester as an expression of admiration for Thomas Wright, the prison philanthropist. 'Maréchal Ney supporting the Rearguard during the retreat from Moscow,' by the French artist, Adolphe Ivon, who died on the 11th September, 1893; it is a fine painting of its kind and it was purchased in 1858.

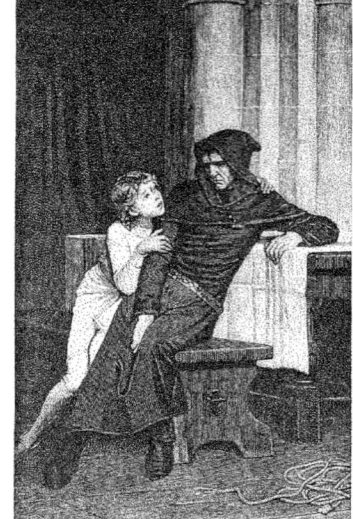

PRINCE ARTHUR AND HUBERT. BY W. F. YEAMES, R.A.

In 1882, Sir Joseph Whitworth, Bart., presented to the Corporation four works by William Etty, R.A., including the artist's own portrait. In commemoration of the transfer of the galleries to the city, the late Mr. Thomas, and Mr. William Agnew, presented the valuable painting, 'The Shadow of Death,' by W. Holman Hunt. "This picture," says the artist, "was painted in the conviction that Art, as one of its uses, may be employed to realise facts of importance in the history of human thought and faith." Our Lord is represented "just risen from the plank on which He has been working, and is portrayed as throwing up His arms, to realise that pleasant sensation of repose and relaxation caused by the inverse action of the tired and stiffened muscles of arms and body."

As described in the ART ANNUAL for 1893, Mr. Holman Hunt executed it in Palestine. The original design on a canvas of portable size was actually painted in a carpenter's shop, at Bethlehem,—"because the people there, in their complexion at least, most perfectly represent the son and the daughter of the House of David." The larger work was afterwards executed at Jerusalem; all the details of the picture were carefully carried out from models of those which it is believed existed in our Lord's time; for instance, the trestle on which the plank has been sawn is of a shape peculiar to the East, the saw is the form of the oriental implement, and the tools on the rack behind are from a collection of ancient carpenter's implements bought at Bethlehem. At the same time the late Mr. W. A. Turner, then chairman of the Art Gallery sub-committee, also presented 'At the Golden Gate,' by Val C. Prinsep, A.R.A., portraying one of the foolish virgins shut out through neglecting oil for her lamp. From the Autumn Exhibition of

THE GIRL I LEFT BEHIND ME. BY RANDOLPH CALDECOTT.

this year (1883) the Corporation obtained, amongst their first purchases, 'The Ides of March,' by E J. Poynter, R.A., which represents Act ii., Scene 2, of Shakespeare's play of *Julius Cæsar;* the wife of the great general is showing him the comet, and is trying to dissuade him from going to the senate.

"When beggars die, there are no comets seen;
The heavens themselves blaze forth the death of princes."

'Prince Arthur and Hubert,' by W. F. Yeames, R.A., another subject selected from Shakespeare, and of which we give an illustration:

"Well, see to live: I
will not touch thine
eyes
For all the treasure
that thine uncle
owns;
Yet am I sworn, and
I did purpose, boy,
With this same very
iron to burn them
out."
King John,
Act iv., Scene 1.

And the 'Minister's Garden,' by the late Cecil G. Lawson, a wide expanse of landscape seen from a garden in the foreground. In the following year (1884) four paintings were purchased, 'Work' by the late Ford Madox Brown, who died 6th October, 1893. It is a busy scene in the main street of Hampstead, painted in 1852, in very bright colours under the effect of hot July sunlight. The centre of the picture is filled with navvies making extensive excavations in the roadway, whilst numerous persons representing various kinds of work are standing about, and in one corner, as an example of a brain-worker, is the portrait of the late Thomas Carlyle. Madox Brown will always be associated with Manchester, on account of the historical mural decorations in the Town Hall, representing various incidents connected with the city, from the building of the Roman fort of Mancunium down to the invention of the fly-shuttle by John Kay, in 1753. 'The Herring Market at Sea,' by Colin Hunter, A.R.A., a good representative of the artist's seascapes. It was painted on Loch Pyne, and as may be seen from our illustration, it shows some steamers in early morning fetching the herrings from the fishing boats. 'Lifting Mist,' by Joseph Knight a Welsh mountain scene near Capel Curig; and 'The Girl I left behind me,' also illustrated, by the late Randolph Caldecott, a charming little picture of a cavalry soldier who, before mounting his horse, is kissing his hand to a young girl who is being led away from the garden gate by her parents. Caldecott's works have special interest to Manchester people, for he gained his livelihood in the city from 1867 to 1872 before he definitely devoted himself to Art.

In 1885 the principal works acquired were the 'Venetians,' by Luke Fildes, R.A., a bright scene by the side of a canal with gaily dressed figures, and as a contrast, it may be presumed, 'Hard Times,' by Hubert Herkomer, R.A.; also a sunny seascape, entitled 'The Norman Archipelago,' by John Brett, A.R.A. In the next year (1886) 'Sibylla Delphica,' by E. Burne-Jones, A.R.A., was purchased, and in the following year (1887) the Corporation acquired their first work by Sir Frederic Leighton, Bart., P.R.A., 'The last Watch of Hero'; the pictrue represents the maiden waiting in vain for Leander, whilst in the predella is the lifeless body of the youth washed up on the shore of the Hellespont.

"With aching heart she
scanned the sea face
dim.
Lo! at the turret's foot
his body lay,
Rolled on the stones,
and washed with
breaking spray."

AUTUMN LEAVES. BY SIR J. E. MILLAIS, BART., R.A.

'Abandoned,' by Adolphe Schreyer, was obtained at the sale of the Marston Hall collection in 1888. It is a work full of pathetic sentiment, representing a starving horse attached to an army waggon struggling in vain to release itself, whilst another horse and the driver have already succumbed. In the same year was purchased from the Autumn Exhibition, 'Britannia's Anchor,' by David Murray, A.R.A., a view on the River Dart with the old *Britannia,* to which joined by a gangway is the *Hindostan*—the training ships for England's future naval officers. In the foreground is an old rusty anchor of the ship embedded in the sand.

After the Corporation of Liverpool had refused to confirm

the recommendation of the committee of the Walker Art Gallery, to purchase the large work by Sir Frederic Leighton, 'Captive Andromache,' it was acquired in 1889 by the Manchester Corporation, and now hangs in the place of honour in the galleries. In the following year a Sussex landscape by James Aumonier entitled 'The Silver Lining of the Cloud' was presented by Mr. F. Smallman.

'Astarte Syriaca,' by Dante Gabriel Rossetti, was acquired in 1891. Of this work, which we illustrate, Mr. A. M. Rossetti says, "I think my brother was always wont to regard this as his most exalted performance, ranking it, in a certain proportionate scale, with 'Dante's Dream.' The latter hangs in the Walker Art Gallery at Liverpool. Two other works purchased in the same year are 'A Flood,' by Sir John E. Millais, Bart., R.A., a babe in a cradle floating away upon a swollen stream ; and 'From under the Sea,' by J. C. Hook, R.A., painted in 1864. One of the latest acquisitions to the gallery is another picture by Sir John Millais, styled 'Autumn Leaves,' painted in 1856, at a time when he was still a member of the pre-Raphaelite brotherhood, together with Rossetti, Holman Hunt, and others. It represents, as may be seen from the illustration, four girls in the twilight standing round a heap of fallen leaves which they are burning. It is a work full of poetic feeling, but we do not imagine that the artist himself ever sought to convey any of the mystic meanings with which the admiring critics of the pre-Raphaelite School, at that time, endeavoured to surround it.

The work selected for purchase from the last Autumn Exhibition was 'The Lighthouse,' by Stanhope A. Forbes, A.R.A.; and 'The Rising of the Nile,' by F. Goodall, R.A., in the same Exhibition, was presented to the gallery by Mr. F. Smallman, making the second gift by this gentleman. An excellent example of W. W. Ouless, R.A.'s, painting hangs in the galleries. It is the portrait of the late Alderman Philip Goldschmidt, twice Mayor of Manchester. It was presented in acknowledgment of his public services.

Besides pictures in oil, there is a fair representation of the English School of water-colour painting, consisting of fifty-eight drawings presented by Mr. Roger R. Ross. The collection comprises works by David Cox, John Varley, Copley Fielding, Samuel Prout, Peter De Wint, Cotman, Müller, Cattermole, and Samuel Palmer. They are for the most part small. Two important works, however, by David Cox, were purchased by the Corporation at the sale of the Allan collection last year—one, 'Peat Gatherers,' and the other, 'Driving Home the Flock,' of which an illustration is here given, and at the same time a fine drawing of 'Glen Falloch,' by Copley Fielding, was acquired.

Among the latest gifts to the galleries are thirteen valuable works, five oil paintings and eight water-colour drawings by Sir John Gilbert, R.A. They have been presented by the artist himself, and are a good representation of this gifted painter's work. 'A Venetian Council of War,' of which an illustration is printed below, was exhibited at the Royal Academy in 1892.

The permanent collection at the present time consists of one hundred and seventy paintings and drawings, in addition to which there are a few pieces of sculpture.

An illustrated catalogue of the entire collection is now in the course of preparation, under the able supervision of Mr. William Stanfield, who has been for many years the curator of the Art gallery, and this work will shortly be published.

It may safely be predicted that if the galleries continue to be enriched in like manner during the next decade, the city of Manchester will possess at the end of that period a collection

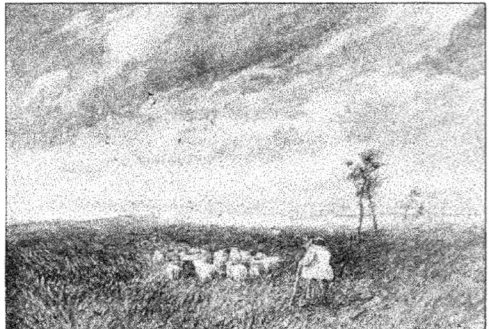

Driving Home the Flock. By David Cox.

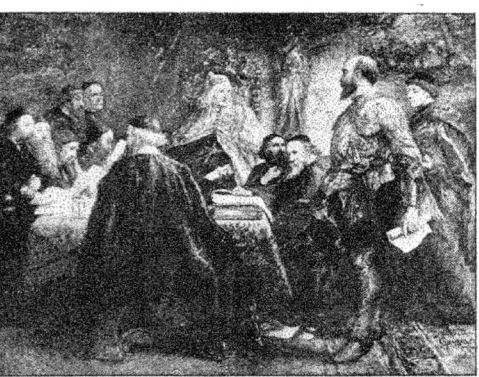

A Venetian Council of War. By Sir John Gilbert, R.A.

of modern works of British Art which will possibly be unrivalled by any other city in the United Kingdom.

H. M. CUNDALL.

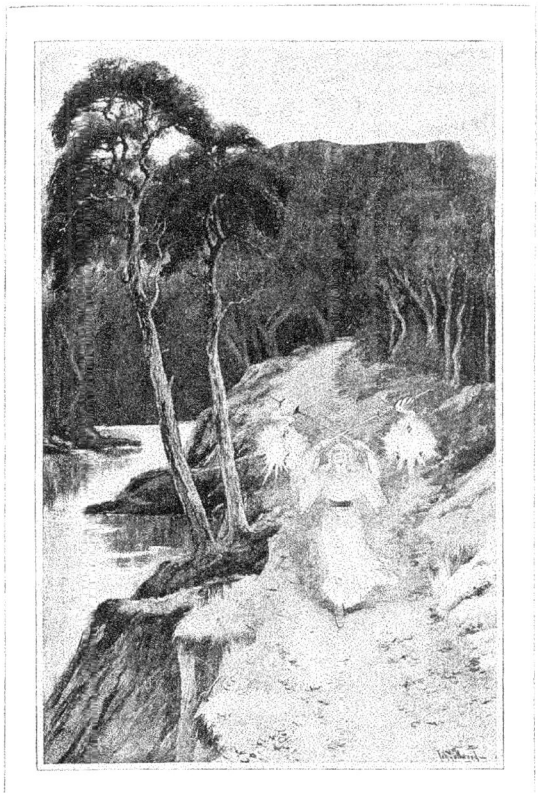

TWILIGHT. FROM A PAINTING BY JOHN FULLWOOD, R.B.A.

TWILIGHT.
BY JOHN FULLWOOD.

GAY Twilight is tripping downhill,
    The Echoes are silent and sleeping,
And the tarn and the pines are still,
    And Slumber comes soundlessly creeping
With his mantle tightly holding,
    Swiftly unfolding,
Now Twilight is far down the hill.

Ah! Twilight will soon quit the hill,
    And Slumber has finished his weaving
In the deep dim gorge at his mill;
    He is folding, circling, now leaving;
And already in the dark'ning
    My soul is hark'ning
To his soothing whisper, "Be still."

"Soul, weary soul, rest at the hill,
    The Echoes are silent and sleeping;
In the folds of my shawl I will,
    Unconsciously, bear in safe keeping
Over the dark jagged mountains,
    To star-lit fountains,
For Twilight has gone from the hill."

As I pace by the deep, deep mere
    I can ne'er hear my own feet falling,
Behind me, beside me comes Fear,
    And he leers as he croaks, "Appalling";
But Slumber is now descending,
    Over me bending,
To carry me safely, is here.

CHRISTOPHE.[*]

AT four o'clock one hot September afternoon in the autumn of 1876, I went with my old friend, M. Victor Pollet, to the studio of 4, Square Malesherbes, to make M. Christophe's acquaintance. He had exhibited, in the May Salon of that year, his colossal statue 'Le Masque,' some one had translated to him a short criticism of the work which had appeared above my signature in *The Academy*, and he, having pronounced it to be "pas tout à fait aussi imbécile que les autres," had expressed a wish to see me. At that date, I had already heard enough of the gossip of Paris to know that M. Christophe was reckoned as one completely outside the prevailing current of thought and feeling. Sometimes this was lamented by men who had a high opinion of his talent but disliked its eccentricity, and declared that in striving to render conceptions of a lofty nature, he imposed on himself tasks for the successful accomplishment of which his powers were insufficient. They asserted that his talent was distinguished but incomplete, and regretted that he had taken a road along which no one could follow him. By those who knew him very intimately, a totally different explanation was given of the alleged insufficient character of his execution. "There is no lack of stuff in Christophe," said M. Pollet; "unfortunately he is not a poor man, and can afford to dally with his work."

There was certainly no sign of poverty about the small *hôtel* in which M. Christophe lived. The handsome Pyrenean wolf-hound which came bounding to the door, the entrance-hall with its groups of statuary and the broad white stairs which led to the upper floors, seemed to show at once that the master was at liberty to choose his own surroundings, and that his taste did not incline towards toys and bric-à-brac. A door on the left-hand opened into a large well-lighted studio, in which the only striking object of furniture was a big carved cabinet of walnut-wood, full of sketches and tools, which looked as if it had been brought up from M. Christophe's native Touraine, and might once have graced the walls of Chambord or Chenonceaux.

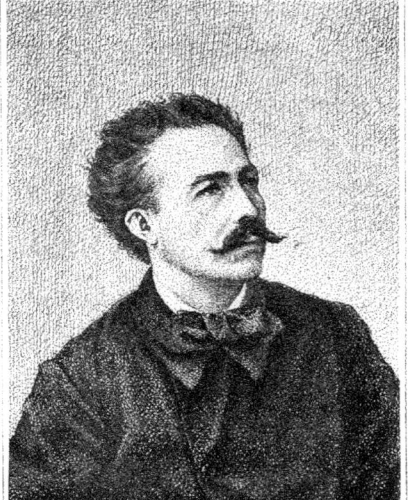

ERNEST LOUIS AQUILAS CHRISTOPHE.

[*] Christophe (Ernest Louis Aquilas), Chevalier de la Légion d'Honneur. Né à Loches, 15 Jan. 1827 ; mort à Paris, 14 Jan., 1892.

We were early; the model—who had been posing for the clay sketch of a group, afterwards worked out as 'La Fatalité'—finished her hasty toilet and went. M. Christophe threw open the doors which led into a second room full of unfinished studies, and there came to us a fresh and welcome air from across the little green lawn, visible through further doors wide open to the garden. The only complete thing in the studio that day happened to be the bust of Henri Regnault's *fiancée*, a remarkable, not beautiful, head, which the sculptor had endowed with extraordinary vitality, whilst indicating the minutest signs of individual character. The work had, in fact, been carried out whilst the impressions of the deadly struggle round Paris—in which Christophe himself had taken an active part, and in which Regnault fell—were yet fresh in the sculptor's mind.

A close examination of this bust was the point of departure for an eager, almost passionate dispute between Christophe and my old friend, as to the methods and tendencies of the Art of the day. Christophe, who had seemed languid and bored when we came—as in after-times I often found him after an unsuccessful day's work—was roused at once. All trace of heaviness disappeared as he began to talk. The lines of power knit together the drooping muscles of the dark face, the loose blouse lent itself to every strong and nervous gesture, as with the clay still sticking to his fingers, he launched paradox after paradox, interwoven with trenchant criticisms on works which our common friend—*premier grand prix de Rome pour la gravure* in the days of M. Ingres—chose to defend or admire.

M. Pollet had an extraordinary gift of ready receptivity for the most varied impressions, which, whilst it gave charm and delightful freshness to his enthusiasms, fortunately did not obscure the faculty of judgment; yet this judgment became instinctively relative to the point of view taken by the artist whose work was before him—so sincere was his sympathy with all work that showed signs of life or intention. He would seize another man's point of view unconsciously, make it his own for a moment, and look only for the measure in which it had been attained. M. Christophe, on the other hand, had a creed. The "something new" which is often more than half the reason for the success of a Paris salon, found no grace in his eyes, whilst the performance of perfect executants like M. Guillaume left him contemptuously cool. And, indeed, it may be said of him, as of his old master Rude, "Il s'est montré dans tout le cours de son existence bien supérieur aux illustres pédants et à la plupart des artistes libres qui ont pris pour l'exaltation de l'art le désordre de leurs esprits." A talk between M. Christophe and M. Pollet, therefore, soon resembled one of those great disputes which, as Thoré reminds us in his charming articles on the Salon of 1844, used to deprive artists and critics alike of their senses; it took one back to the days when men crossed swords over Delacroix's 'Massacre de Scio' or the 'Hernani' of Victor Hugo, to the days when the sentiment of beauty, the love of colour and form had their apostles and their martyrs, when fanatics were plenty, and the indifferent few.

As I write, there stands by me a reduction of 'Le Masque,' the work which had been the means of my introduction, and the possession of which I owe to the sculptor's kindness. The original now stands in the Tuileries Gardens; at first we used to call it 'La Comédie Humaine,' too literary a title for the public. Something in the pose of this colossal figure and the writhe backwards of the suffering body recalls the anguish of the famous 'Slaves' of Michael Angelo, and reminds one of the sculptor's close study of that great master's works; but 'Le Masque,' though it in nowise lacks that nobility of purpose ever present in Christophe's art, is not completely effective. The enormous woman who stands before us (see overleaf) firmly planted on her right leg, lifts to her face the mask which she holds in her left hand, whilst with the right she grips the serpent which has fastened on her breast. If we turn to the left, we see only the smiling mask and not the head which breathes out agony from behind it; and this mask always seems to me to have scarcely sufficient importance and size, to crown with adequate dignity the bulky form beneath. In its present position, the look of squatness, which provoked much criticism when the work was exhibited at the Salon of 1876, disappears, but the proportions still convey the impression of heaviness rather

1894.

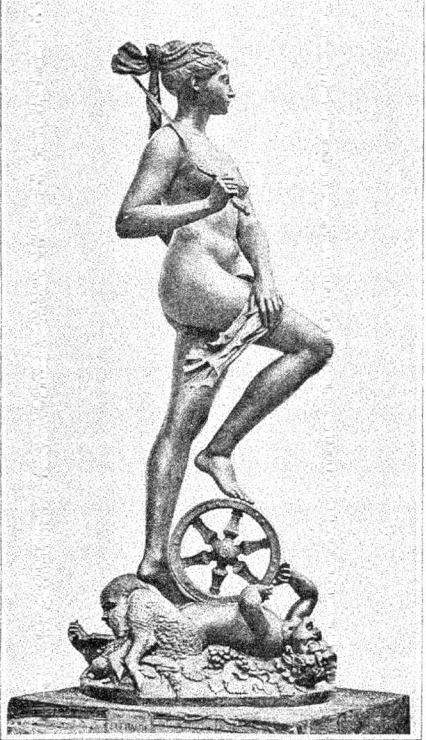

LA FATALITÉ. FROM THE GROUP BY CHRISTOPHE.

than strength. This is due to the fact that whilst infinite devotion and care have been spent on the surface modelling, the larger forms, taken as a whole, have not been sufficiently accentuated, not accentuated duly in relation to the vast size of the figure: the consequence is that even where passages are full of the most lovely undulations, the lines which enclose them look empty and much that should seem great fails of its effect. Say what we will, however, we must still confess that 'Le Masque' was the outcome of a high and serious ambition, the offspring of aims not common to the crowd of men.

'La Douleur' (1855); 'Le Masque' (1876); 'La Fatalité' (1890); and 'Le Sphinx' (1892); these are the four works which stand as landmarks in Christophe's life:—Sorrow; The Agony of Life; The Irony of Life; and The Secret of Death; and these works honestly embody the ideas by which their author was constantly preoccupied. "Le sens de l'art, la vision de la beauté, l'amour de la nature, l'enthousiasme de la vie sont bien rares;" and of these four rare things the rarest is perhaps "l'enthousiasme de la vie." This enthusiasm, of which dear old Pollet had an abundance, was, when I knew him, entirely lacking in M. Christophe; and I can well believe that when serious illness overtook him he made no fight against it, but welcomed the end like so many other noble artists whose life has been compact of unsatisfied ambitions and baulked achievements.

When we were talking one day over the first sketch of the work eventually carried out as 'Le Sphinx,' he said, by way of letting me see his thought, "Le secret de la vie, l'homme ne le trouve que dans la mort. Le secret de l'immortalité, il le veut à tout prix. Il a l'amour, la passion du Sphinx, elle cède enfin à ses désirs, elle lui donne le baiser suprême et il meurt dans ses bras." The large rough sketch in clay was really executed before he seriously took up and began to work out his statue-group of Fortune. As this sketch originally stood it was instinct with deep poetic feeling, and was extraordinarily dramatic in conception, but it could never have been carried out as an independent composition, though it might have been treated as a mural monument—the figures lying right and left above the entrance to a tomb, after the fashion of the "gigantic shapes of Night and Day" created by Michael Angelo in the Medici Chapel. I suggested this one day, when he was considering the means of bringing the two figures together, and he admitted that it was feasible, but, said he, "Les Médicis d'aujourd'hui sont tous Juifs."

I was always too busy, having much work in hand during my brief visits to Paris, ever to give M. Christophe sittings for the bust which he had wished to carry out, but I saw a good deal of him and of his methods of work one autumn when I had a little leisure and he found that "une bouche de femme ironique" was necessary to 'La Fatalité.' It seemed to me that he overworked in the clay to a degree which was injurious to the class of ideas which he sought to render. A conception such as that of 'Le Sphinx' rarely if ever is brought to take a definite form without losing something of its first impressiveness, and final failure is perhaps ensured by the very nature of the methods employed. The clay, long-caressed, submits itself to incessant rehandling, and the artist may pause in the labour of completely realising his conception, sure of being able to attack it again and again in detail; he thus works out preliminary modifications and changes, in that which is actually destined to be the final form of his thought. For the embodiment of a certain order of ideas this process offers advantages easily recognised; but when the expression of energy, of passion, of fire is necessary much is risked. Whence comes it, it has been asked, that the rough-hewn sketches of Michael Angelo produce an impression of majestic force and character? Whence comes it that the mere blocking out of the marble, which according to our daily practice is allotted to the workman, yields in his hands an unmeaning performance, whereas every blow from the chisel of the great master gave life, gave movement, gave a meaning which can rouse us to the liveliest emotion? Michael Angelo made no clay model; he assured himself of his own intimate possession of his own thought, and of his complete knowledge and mastery of the form in which it should take ultimate shape, by long premeditation, the results of which were noted on the paper with a firm hand, and a fixed intention; finally, he recorded in a little wax model the form and proportions now definitely fixed. With this wax model at his side and the living figure before his eyes, he then attacked the marble, with the zeal of his first resolve, as it would seem, fresh upon him. It may be urged that the dangers of this procedure are such as can be faced only by a genius, a force and a courage equal to his; and the blocks which he left in a hopeless state bear witness that not even he was always victorious in the struggle; yet perhaps it is the only way by which his conceptions or those of a like order could find adequate expression. To ideas of an eminently rational order, which embody themselves in calm and dignity, the modern method is plainly a good servant; but where the passions of the heart or the weird dreams of the spirit evoke their own image, they seem to demand a different kind of toil for their realisation—not less labour nor less strenuous preparation, but labour and preparation of a different order.

For a pupil of Rude any approach to methods such as these was out of the question. *Le père Rude*, who used to define man as "un squelette dont les muscles sont l'ornement," worked by the strictest rules and put in practice, when using the living model, much the same system of geometrical measurements as are in use by sculptors' assistants when blocking out and preparing stone and marble from the clay. "Armé du compas et du fil à plomb en face du modèle vivant, il prenait ses 'trois points de ronde bosse' entre les clavicules, au milieu de l'os pubien, à la malléole interne; réglait les parties comprises entre ces grandes divisions, marquait les têtes d'os, les éminences musculaires, et levait, pour ainsi dire, le plan topographique du corps humain." Christophe, who had entered Rude's *atelier* as a lad of eighteen, and who had received from him the most generous and liberal recognition of his talent, never shook off the influence of the methods in which he had been trained, although his own character, the order of the ideas in which he moved, and the nature of the subjects which he inclined to treat, differed in every respect from the character, ideas, and subjects proper to Rude. Rude was, however, always "mon cher maître," and at the Salon of 1890 M. Christophe exhibited the wax model of the monument to Rude, showing him at work on the reliefs of the Arc de Triomphe, which was afterwards cast in bronze for the Musée of Dijon. To the last Christophe spoke with the strongest sentiments of gratitude and respect of his old master. I happened to say before him, one day, that I was going out to Montmartre to look at the tomb

ERNEST CHRISTOPHE. FROM A DRAWING BY LOUIS LELOIR.

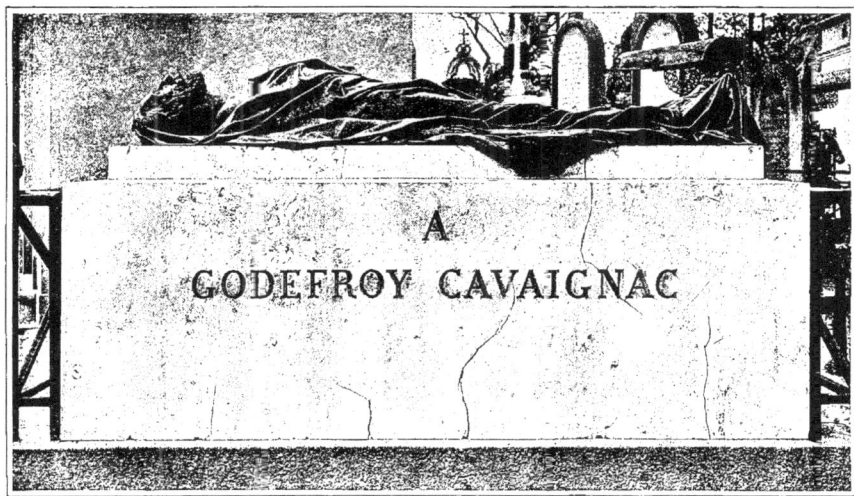

TOMB IN MONTMARTRE CEMETERY—"WHERE THE BIRDS COME TO DIE." BY RUDE AND CHRISTOPHE.

of Godefroy Cavaignac—the tomb on or near which all the birds of the cemetery come to die—a mystery simply explained by the fact that the water, lying in the folds of the shroud, becomes impregnated with oxide of copper, from the bronze in which the statue is cast, and the birds who drink of it, drink death. The tomb itself was one of Rude's most successful and celebrated works, and, as soon as I mentioned it, "Il faut regarder," said Christophe, "le côté où le maitre a signé, vous y verrez mon nom!" and then he told me the story of his first triumph, of how Rude had thought so well of him as to give him the chance of distinguishing himself, by setting him to work with him on this monument, and how he had acquitted himself so well in the eyes of his master that Rude had insisted on his signing the unknown name of "son jeune élève Christophe" beside the illustrious one of "Rude."

The affectionate pride with which he related this incident was all the more touching on account of the contrast between master and pupil. Rude, to the day of his death, remained the peasant that he was born, with the tastes, the virtues, the naïve enthusiasm, and the limited horizon of a peasant. Christophe, on the other hand, was a man of wide culture, with tastes of exquisite distinction, held in check by a certain native severity of requirement and robustness of character. Every volume in his little library was beautifully bound; the panels on the walls of his dining-room were of old Coromandel lacquer; in the drawing-room was a perfect set of fine Louis-Seize furniture, chairs and couches, all backed

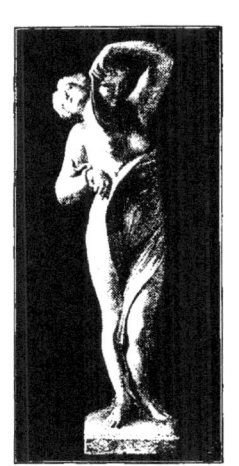

"LE MASQUE." FROM THE REDUCTION BY CHRISTOPHE IN THE POSSESSION OF LADY DILKE.

and seated with graceful Gobelins tapestry. I believe that set was found by him in Touraine, or was actually transferred to Paris from his old home, whence he brought also the fittings of his bed-chamber, which was always shown with the other rooms, because of the exquisite needlework with which its white satin hangings were flowered.

How Christophe found time for the amount of reading he got through puzzled me much till he explained that the months which he spent at La Cigogne, his little manor-house near Loches, were chiefly occupied in reading. There, in the winter of 1875, Darwin's theory of evolution took strong hold of his imagination, and affected if it did not suggest the motive of his group 'La Fatalité,' or as it was first entitled, 'La Fortune—*rapax fortuna*.' The graceful woman (see page 41) who withdraws the veil in which her features have been shrouded, reveals herself in unusual fashion, as the goddess pictured by Horace—she who was dreaded of tyrants, the Fortune who thrusts them from their high estate, calling, "To arms! to arms!" Bearing in her right hand an uplifted sword, she crushes beneath her wheel one of two sleeping children, whilst the other is left smiling and unhurt. The end of the veil, floating from her head, is gathered from behind into her left hand, which rests on the raised right knee; her head turned over her shoulder to the left is boldly lifted, and the features wear an expression of indifference which contrasts with the menace of the naked blade. There is some lovely ornament on the hilt of this sword, and I remember how the perfection of the workmanship delighted the small group of distinguished artists whom I met in the studio in 1882, the day before the group went off to be cast in bronze. Gustave Moreau was amongst them—he had not then entirely shut himself up from the outer world, and before I knew who he was I noted the keenness of his interest, and the odd, burning light in the depths of his strange, brown eyes, as he listened to Christophe's account of the method of casting *à cire perdue*, which spurred me to hunt out, some months later, the workshop, in some obscure street behind the Invalides, where this work was carried out.

It had become an established custom that M. Christophe I did guide in the English section, and we came to Sir Frederic Leighton's 'Athlete and Python,' which was then by way of being our great boast, Christophe looked and passed rather rapidly with, "Merci, pas de ça! Montrez-moi autre chose ; nous faisons ça ici, et mieux!"

Once, and once only, I recollect having myself unwittingly provoked one of those extraordinary displays of eloquent paradox, by which he would cover his unwilling agreement with judgments which coincided with that of his own reason, but which were repellent to his feelings. I was talking with M. Marcille at the posthumous exhibition of Fromentin's works, when Christophe joined us. I did not know then how

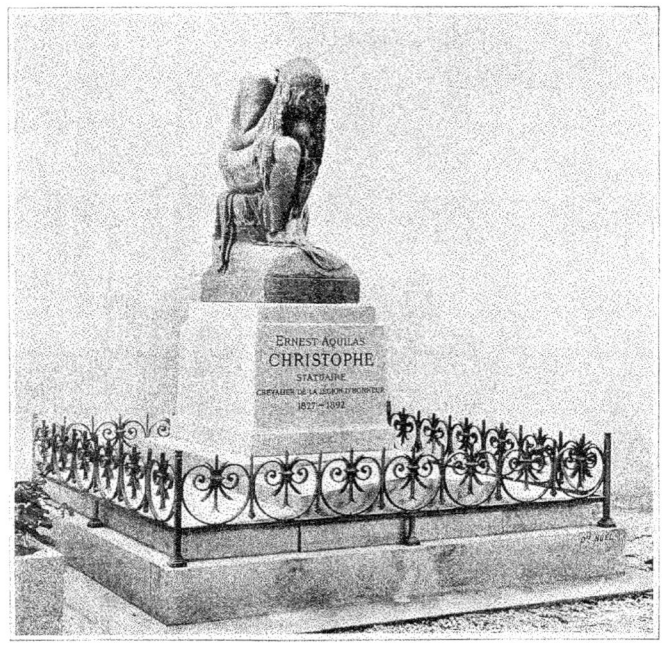

MONUMENT TO CHRISTOPHE IN BATIGNOLLES CEMETERY.

should give me at least one day at the Salon, when I came through Paris in the spring. Generally most of the time was spent amongst the sculpture, but sometimes the paintings came in for a share of attention. His quick, short criticisms were always valuable, and impressed themselves on my mind, because they usually went much farther than the work to which they immediately applied, and characterized sharply the whole class to which it belonged,—as, for example, one day when I pointed out a small Bastien-Lepage, with "N'est-ce pas, il y a quelque chose là?" and his quick "Si,—un peu bestial, vu d'un homme sensible,"—gave me not only the measure of the particular work, but placed it in a large category which might even include Holbein. In the same way, when once, at the International Exhibition of 1878, where close had been the tie of friendship which had united him with Fromentin, of whom he had executed a fine medallion portrait, and to whose memory he had designed a monument, so when he asked what we thought of the collection, as a whole, I replied lightly, "M. Marcille est tout à fait de mon avis,—bien de belles choses, mais cela ne fait pas un œuvre." To this Christophe, with some heat, instantly opposed the theory that a man who had succeeded in expressing himself through various forms of energy, had accomplished as great, or a greater achievement, than he who had put his whole life into one such form ; that in estimating Fromentin the painter, we had to take into account the author of " Dominique " ; the critic of "Les Maitres d'Autrefois"; the delightful narrator of " Un Eté dans le Sahara," and " Une Année dans le Sahel." In the warmth of his appreciation of "Dominique," Christophe seemed to me exaggerated. The average reader of that long-drawn romance is inclined to say with Sainte-Beuve, "Les morceaux parfaits abondent, mais l'ensemble manque d'unité, la fin languit, le dénouement est plus curieux que naturel;" and I cannot help thinking that the passionate admiration which the book aroused amongst those to whom Fromentin was personally known, was due really, as in M. Christophe's case, to the belief that they were reading what was, to a great extent, an autobiography—that Dominique, in short, was Fromentin.

"Pas un œuvre;" that is a criticism which cannot be justly applied to that which has been left us by Christophe. After his first work, 'La Douleur'—the colossal statue intended for the highest point at Père Lachaise, of which a reduction in red granite has been placed by the care of his friends above his grave at the Batignolles—we get a series completed by the 'Sphinx' or 'Le Baiser Suprême,' which was exhibited at the Salon in the very year of the sculptor's death. Of this conception, as it struck me in its first shape, I wrote in *The Athenæum* at the time, "The man has striven with the Sphinx for her secret to his sorrow. He has conquered, and in the final grapple tears from her head the veil which hides the awful mysteries of her eyes. He gazes and dies, for, as she takes him to her breast, her cruel claws are unsheathed and bury themselves in his heart." In this rough sketch there is not only a terrible pathos, which instantly appeals to the imagination, but there are also passages of execution which are nobly expressive; the curve of the body of the Sphinx is so energetic that it almost seems to writhe along the rocks on which she rests, and the despairing triumph of the man who knows and dies is finely suggested by the action in which, abandoning all defence, he grasps the veil in both hands and gazes passionately on that which is at last revealed. As, bent wholly on the attainment of his end, he yields his life in price of victory, the Sphinx watches him with a cold smile playing upon her face; no set grimace, but a smile which haunts the memory with a dreadful fascination. When, at last, the group found its way to the Salon (1892) Christophe was lying in his grave at the Batignolles.

Of this group as ultimately worked out, I have no need to speak further. It stands, as does his statue of 'La Fatalité,' or 'Fortune,' in a prominent position in the Museum of the Luxembourg, and if, as has been said, "C'est à l'originalité personnelle que se mesure le talent" then, in face of this group we must accord to Christophe a high meed of honour.

It is difficult for the most competent critic to name the authors of the innumerable works which crowd our yearly exhibitions. A sculptor, a painter, may be a trained and skilful craftsman, yet have no real or distinct existence. Unless he himself has a temperament powerful enough to react against his training and enable him to affirm his own fashion of being and seeing, he will remain for ever indistinguishable from the dozens of others who may have issued from the same school. As to the authorship of Christophe's work there never would be a doubt. Not from his studies with Rude did he get his singular vein of thought, nor that strange mingling of romantic and classical feeling which gives peculiar character to his execution. In

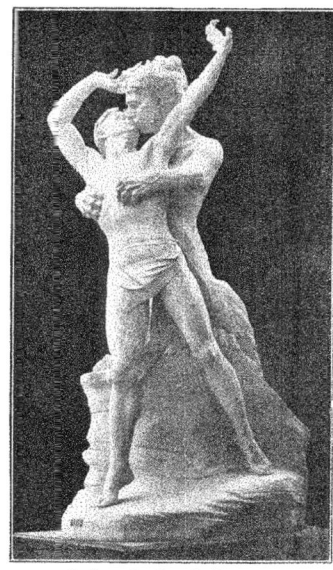

LE BAISER SUPRÊME. BY CHRISTOPHE.

his case once more was fulfilled the universal rule—"Le principe de tout talent est un caractère particulier."

An admirable reproduction of the 'Sphinx' has been executed by the distinguished engraver M. Monziès, which deserves to be in the hands of all who care for perfect workmanship; one or two copies have come to London, and may, doubtless, be obtained from the print-sellers. Until I saw this plate I had no idea that there was any one now alive capable of etching from the round with the same accuracy, brilliance, and distinction. It is at M. Monziès' request, and by the wish of other old friends of M. Christophe —to five or six of whom, after full provisions for his faithful *praticiens*, he left his fortune—that I write these lines in memory of one dear to us; a friend whom neither absence nor neglect could alter, nor any jest of fortune change.

EMILIA F. S. DILKE.

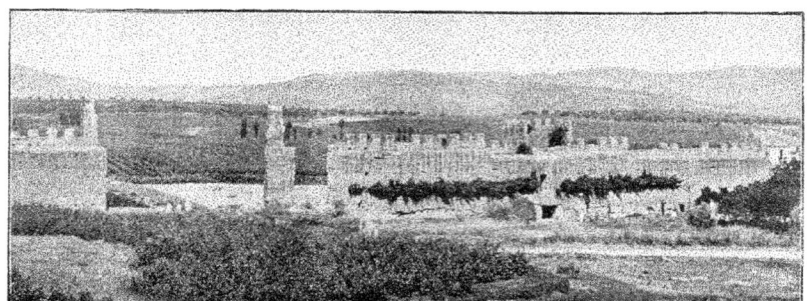

RUINS OF MANSOURAH, TLEMÇEN.

TLEMÇEN,
AND ITS VICINAGE.

TLEMÇEN, the former capital of Mauritania, should be the true goal, in the Barbary States, of the student of Moorish history, and, in particular, Moorish art. In the period of the Arabic ascendancy it was Tlemçen the Superb, and was to Western Islam what mediæval Florence was to Italy. The magnificent efflorescence of the Moorish genius in Spain had its real fount in this hill-city, which has known so many vicissitudes since the days when Rome planted her eagles there and made of Pomaria one of her most important occidental stations.

Of the several ways to reach the Queen of Orania, as the great western province of French Africa is often, though non-officially, called, the easiest is by the recently opened railway from Oran, or by rail from Algiers (or any place along the Algiers-Oran line) to Sidi-bel-Abbés and Ste. Barbe du Tlélat, and thence, in two or three hours, to Tlemçen. These, naturally, are the two common lines of approach so far as foreign visitors are concerned. But I would strongly recommend any one who does not object to a little discomfort and fatigue to start from Nemours, and drive thence by Nedrôma, and thence almost along the frontier of Morocco, to Lalla Marnia, and thence again to Tlemçen through a district of Mauritania that has scarcely, if at all, changed in appearance since the days of the Barbary pirates.

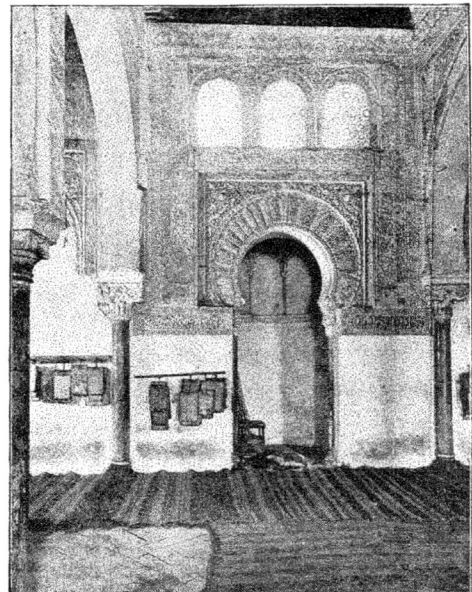

INTERIOR OF THE MÉDERSA, TLEMÇEN.

Nemours can easily be reached from the south of Spain, or by one of the Compagnie Transatlantique steamers from Gibraltar. It is not a place of any particular interest, except for those who have never been in Mauritania before, and to whom there is charm in even the slightest glimpse of the East. The traveller from Spain should take heed to sail either on a fine day or when the wind is not very strong from the north, otherwise the steamer will keep away beyond "Les Deux Frères" ("The Brothers," in the Itinerary of Antonine), as the picturesque rocks outside the harbour are called, and the *voyageur* be carried elsewhere. It is a clean, healthy place, and the Hôtel de France is comfortable.

It is only some nine miles inland to Nedrôma. The route is picturesque, but otherwise has no particular attraction, though to Frenchmen it has a keen historical interest. A short drive from the coast brings one within sight of a pyramid girt by an iron railing—a cairn over the remains of the French troops who perished in the disastrous combat of Sidi Brahim, a few miles to the east. In Algeria "the heroism of Sidi Brahim" is still a charm to conjure with, though it is just fifty years ago since Colonel Montagnac, with his cavalry and infantry, was enticed into an ambuscade and saw his small army almost

rising throughout the West, not so much in the hope of driving the Christians out of Algiers, or even Algeria (the province), but of making an independent state of Orania, with Tlemçen as a capital and Oran as a sea-port. Even when this dream promised to result in failure, it was clear that the Moors had been captivated by the idea, and that endless danger lay in passive indifference to its spread.

It was at this juncture, in 1845, when the French were galled by the taunting of an enemy whom they could easily crush, and yet who held them at bay and menaced them with innumerable perils, that Colonel Montagnac, the commandant at Nemours, believed he had an opportunity of giving the Emir such a lesson as would make even the patriots of Tlemçen see

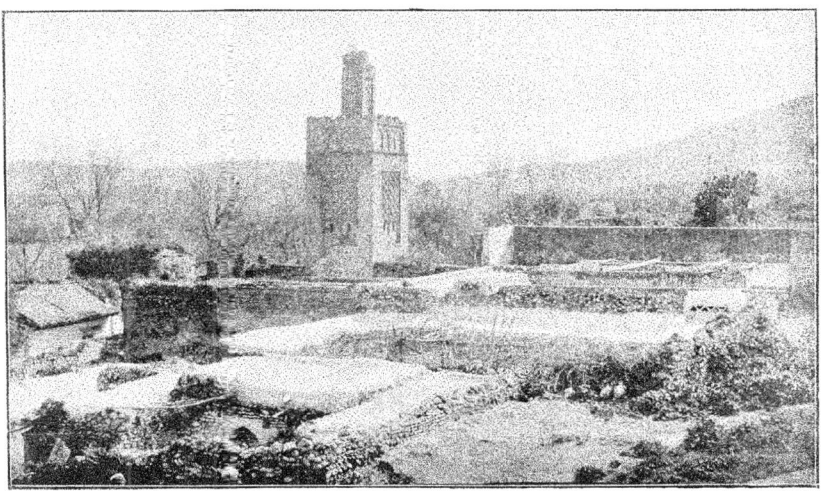

MOSQUE OF SIDI-BEN-HALAOUI, BEYOND THE ROOFS OF THE NEGRO VILLAGE OUTSIDE TLEMÇEN.

annihilated before he, too, was slain. The name, moreover, recalls a double event—the later one of triumph for the *colon*: for it was at this very place of his signal victory that the great Emir, Abd-el-Kadr, at a subsequent date, surrendered. This episode is, though so dear to the French, so little known, that I may give it here.

While French Barbary, and particularly the Oranian portion of it, was still either unconquered or but partially subdued, it seemed, early in the 'forties, as though Abd-el-Kadr were likely to become a powerful autocrat. His word was law among the Arabs, the Kabyles, and even the great mass of the town-Moors. He was urged to make Tlemçen the capital of a new and independent Mauritania, and to enter into a close offensive and defensive alliance with the Sultan of Morocco. In the east of Barbary the power of the Bey of Constantine had disappeared, and the tricolour waved over ancient Cirta in place of the green standard of the Prophet. But, in any case, Abd-el-Kadr knew that there was no hope from the East, whether as near as Constantine, or Tunisia, or Tripoli, or as far as Stamboul. The French believed that he intended a general

that the downfall of the Arab dominion was an accomplished fact. Already the French had an important military station at Lalla Marnia, close to the Morocco frontier—to this day their most occidental garrison-post, and, at this moment, of vital importance owing to the ferment among the border tribes and Kabyles, consequent on the Spanish-Mauresque struggle at Melilla, a short distance to the north. Colonel de Barral had sent word that he needed immediate reinforcements, and Colonel Montagnac was just about to despatch a battalion of infantry and a squadron of cavalry, when the sheik of a friendly tribe, the Soualia, appealed for protection against Abd-el-Kadr, who, he said, intended to castigate the Soualia, though he had really only a handful of cavalry at his disposal. It is likely that this information was an act of treachery, though it is possible that the sheik himself had been purposely deceived. At any rate, Colonel Montagnac not only considered it his duty to protect the Soualia, but believed that he could entrap the Emir, probably capture him, and disperse his already small and disheartened following. He set forth at once with 350 infantry and 60 hussars, though not so incautiously, despite the sheik's reassuring news, but that he kept to positions where, if attacked, he would not be taken at a disadvantage. He chose to go as far as and to camp at the marabout of Sidi Brahim—or, as some say, was enticed thither. Next morning, while making a reconnaissance, he was surrounded by masses of mounted Arabs, who hitherto had remained hidden among the adjacent ravines. At the first onset the commandant of the cavalry was wounded, and Captain Gentil Saint-Alphonse killed. The enemy was not only led by the "invincible" Abd-el-Kadr, but was ten times superior in strength to the belated force it attacked. The infantry now came upon the scene, and a severe engagement seemed inevitable, though the French were still confident. Just then Colonel Montagnac was mortally wounded. He refused, however, to waive his command, and said that since he must die he would die in the fulfilment of his duty. He now sent for the second squadron of hussars to hurry forward, and ordered his battalion of chasseurs (save a company of carabineers) to guard the stores and other war material, which he supposed the Emir wished to capture both for his own use and to thwart the garrison at Lalla Marnia. But the entrapped infantry could not evade or prevent the fire of the enemy, and fell man by man. Commandant Fromont Corti arrived with his relief column, but was straightway killed, and with him nearly all his company. So dire was the loss among the reserve that both cavalry and infantry broke up. A number of men hastily ran across the open and rejoined the company of carabineers, commanded now by Captain de Géraux.

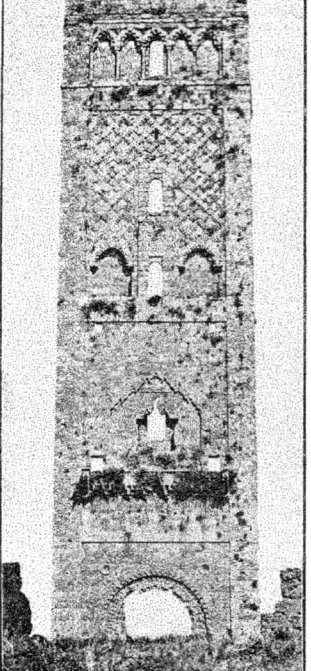

MINARET OF MANSOURAH, TLEMÇEN.

This officer realised what had actually happened, and also recognised that it would be impracticable to make a rapid retreat on Nemours: so he decided to occupy the marabout of Sidi Brahim itself, and then to fight to the last in order to keep Abd-el-Kadr at bay. Before the enemy could understand his purpose, he managed to despatch two friendly Arabs in his following to General Cavaignac at Nemours and to Colonel de Barral at Lalla Marnia. His first difficulty was with ammunition. Promptly, he ordered every rifle-ball to be cut in two, and ultimately in four. In vain Abd-el-Kadr tempted him to surrender by pointing out that he was caught in a trap and could not escape, and, at last, by the promise to spare the lives of him and his company. On Captain de Géraux's definite refusal, the Emir stooped to one of the few inexcusable acts in his brilliant and noble career. Among his prisoners was a wounded infantry officer, Captain Dutertre—the hero of Sidi Brahim, as he came to be called by many of his countrymen. This officer he bade go within hail of the marabout; and, at peril of his life, and those of his friends, persuade De Géraux to surrender. Then, says a chronicler, "Alors on vit un de ces traits d'héroïsme que l'histoire enregistre pour l'enseignement des races futures." Captain Dutertre listened in frigid silence to the commands of the Emir, and then, escorted by four watchful mounted Arabs who understood French, and who had orders to shoot the prisoner if he did not urge the garrison to surrender, slowly approached the marabout. When within hail, he cried in a loud voice: "Géraux, and all of you, my comrades of the brave Eighth, I am sent to call upon you to surrender; but I conjure you in the name of honour to resist until death. *Vive le Roi, vive la France!*" With this cry actually upon his lips the brave Dutertre fell, shot dead by his Arab convoy. This splendid heroism animated the garrison with dauntless courage, and for three days, amid frightful sufferings from wounds and hunger, and above all from thirst, they held their improvised fort. On the fourth they made a desperate sally, and at first managed to evade death. The fugitives actually saw Nemours in the distance, but they also saw a limpid stream, and in their agony threw down their weapons and quenched their raging thirst. The delay and disorganization proved fatal. A fresh detachment of two thousand Kabyles had come up to join Abd-el-Kadr, and the fire of the whole body converged upon the doomed troops. Captain de Géraux, Lieutenant Chapdelaine, and the whole company, in a word, except twelve men, were shot down like entrapped wolves. Of the twelve exhausted and wounded fugitives who managed to gain Nemours, only one man still carried arms.

No wonder, when Abd-el-Kadr surrendered at a subsequent date at Sidi Brahim, that the French, and particularly the Oranian colonists, looked upon the coincidence as little, if at all, less than a direct sign from heaven.

Except for the beauty or strangeness of the country there is nothing of note after the crossing of the Oued Tafna, one of the most important of Oranian rivers, till the ruined towers and walls of Mansourah come into view—and Mansourah is now but an annexe of Tlemçen.

One might well wax enthusiastic about the majesty of these ruins. In magnificence and beauty they are unequalled of their kind even in Italy, though they have not the Cyclopean vastness of Volterra.

The coming into existence of Mansourah has perhaps no

parallel in history. That a superb town, famous for its civilisation and splendour, should spring up over against a besieged city, while originally but a fortified camp, is an astonishing thing; and scarce less so, that it should so soon have lapsed from its high place among Moorish towns.

The famous Mansourah minaret, being of hewn stone, has survived to this day—a rare thing in the history of ancient Moorish buildings, built as these were of cement and concrete. Sir Lambert Playfair speaks of it as by far the most beautiful architectural monument of Moorish times in Algeria. "The thickness of the walls," he adds, "is about 1½ mètres, and the separate stones 36 cent. in height, and usually, at least, twice that length. Instead of an interior staircase it had a series of inclined planes, or ramps, up which a horse could mount to the summit. Æsthetically, the tower can hardly be too highly praised. The proportions are perfect, the decoration rich and original, or, at least, unlike anything else in the neighbourhood. The arches are either circular or pointed, and never horse-shoe. The height is nearly 40 mètres." This absence of the characteristic Moorish horse-shoe arch is interesting, though it is to be noted that the beautiful Bab-el-Khamis, the gateway in the wall by which Abou Yakoob invested Tlemçen, has the horse-shoe shape.

The present writer visited Mansourah again and again, and each time found it more and more impressive — in the vastness of its area, the cyclopean majesty of its ruined walls, and in its gigantic minaret, solitary among the desolation which now environs it.

In beauty — at once grand, picturesque, and lovely —Tlemçen and its immediate vicinage is too unique to permit of its comparison with any other locality. If, however, any comparison be instituted, that with Florence most naturally suggests itself. Florence is, perhaps, lovelier, though it is certainly not so picturesque; while even the superb view from Fiesole is surpassed by that from the north-eastern wall of the chief square in the African city. Tlemçen stands on the slope of the mountain Lalla Setta, one of the innumerable spurs of the Atlas, at an elevation of 2,500 feet. The views all around comprise

1894

mountains and hills, valleys and plains, an unsurpassable verdure and orchard loveliness, and lovely perspective far northward to the African littoral—westward to Nemours, more easterly towards Oran. And just as one could not possibly enter into detail, much less adequately describe, in a brief article, all that is worth seeing in Florence, so is it out of the question to attempt to set forth the innumerable attractions of the "Flower of the West," as the Moors called this favourite city of old.

Although in a sense Tlemçen is the modern equivalent of the ancient Roman town of Pomaria, it is doubtful if the Romans had any buildings on the actual site of the present city. Arab historians allude vaguely to an aboriginal Berber town, before Cæsarine Pomaria came into existence, but not even the oldest record gives any clue to its name. Indeed it was by an accident that even the Roman name survived, for after that obliterating Vandal invasion which swept over North Africa on the collapse of the Roman dominion, even the imperial designation was utterly forgotten. In the year 174 of the Hegira (A.D. 790), an Arab prince, Idris ben Idris ben Abd-Allah, bought the site from the Berbers, who had ownership of that part of the country, and built a great mosque round which a town soon collected. Aghadir, as the new town was called for the next hundred and forty years, was, however, rather Pomaria raised again in Moorish guise than Tlemçen as we know it. The real origin of the latter was a rival town almost a stone's throw from Aghadir — a town called Tagrart, which became the greatest city of commerce and civilisation and the arts in western Mauritania, and really that to which, as mentioned above, the merchants of the Mediterranean and Adriatic ports came as traders.

In this "City of Soldiers," as the royal town was called, there was even at one period a guard of several thousand Christians; and it is a very suggestive commentary upon civilisation in Christian Spain or France that in this Moorish capital all foreigners, whether Jews or Christians, had exemption from either insult or indignity or interference of any kind; indeed, there was in Tagrart even a Christian church. What is to this day the

THE MIHRAB OF THE GREAT MOSQUE, TLEMÇEN.

barracks of the Spahis at Tlemçen were the ancient Kissaria, or Bazaar of the Franks, and here the law of the foreign consuls was practically paramount over their particular fellow-

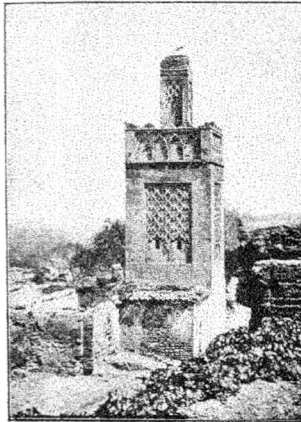

THE MINARET OF SIDI-BEN-HALAOUI.

countrymen. It is not quite certain when the name Tlemçen was given to the united towns of Aghadir and Tagrart, but it was some time early in the twelfth century. Under divers dynasties and with varying fortunes Tlemçen remained an important city—"as a Moorish prince of Spain who preferred to remain in his own sovereign land," to paraphrase the proud words of an Arabic historian—till the sixteenth century, when, having succumbed to the Spaniards, it began to wane in all respects. Its ruin, however, was still far off, or might never have become irremediable, when, in the middle of the sixteenth century (1553), the Turks, under the Pasha of Algiers, brought about its utter collapse. For nearly three hundred years the glory of Tlemçen was a thing of the past. Early in the thirties of the present century the town was claimed by the Sultan of Morocco, but was held by the Turkish soldiery in the pay of the French. In 1834 the patriot Emir, Abd-el-Kadr, appeared before it and demanded it as his own "in the name of the Prophet." His was a short sovereignty, for in his absence the French troops entered the city early in 1836. Abd-el-Kadr besieged it, but the small garrison made a heroic defence against the whole army of the Emir, and maintained it for months, till General Bugeaud appeared in June with reinforcements. True, in 1839 Tlemçen was formally ceded to Abd-el-Kadr, when it became his capital; but on the renewal of hostilities his sovereignty definitively lapsed, and in 1842 the town became a French city. It is now one of the most prosperous, delightful, and beautiful of French-African possessions, and has a future of singular promise; in fact, it is even spoken of as the possible capital of a possible United States of North Africa.

Inside the city there is enough of interest, apart from the singularly picturesque Moorish, Arab, and Berber native life of the streets, to occupy one for some days. Guides generally speak of the Mechouar, or citadel, as the first place it is fitting to see; but as a matter of fact this ruined mass of building has neither history nor artistic attraction for the foreigner. Then the so-called museum is a "frost"; what is really of interest is to be discovered only by the intelligent and industrious antiquarian, and often not even by him. Probably the only object of general interest is the onyx slab with its Arabic inscription setting forth that it is the tombstone of Bou Abdulla, that last king of Granada, who, after he had bowed before Ferdinand and Isabella, left that Moorish-Spain which he and his ancestors had made so beautiful, and died here a forlorn exile. There are several fine mosques, but little else of ancient Tlemçen, for even of the once-famous Medrassa, or college, where the once-celebrated historian Ibn Khaldoun taught, nothing now remains. The Art-lover should visit the mosque of Sidi Ibrahim, for its lovely arabesques, though these are unimportant compared with the exquisite mihrab-arabesques in the ancient mosque of Sidi Ahmed Bel Hassen el-Ghomari, now a school. These arabesques and other Moorish Art here enshrined date from the end of the thirteenth century (A.H. 696), and are unsurpassed in grace, variety and beauty, and perhaps not equalled even in Granada or in the whole of Mauritania.

But the paramount attraction in Tlemçen is the chief mosque, the Djamaa-el-Kebir. Its beautiful mihrab (corresponding to our altar in point of importance, though actually simply the Holy of Holies for Prayer) is the delight and despair of those who love Moorish architectural decoration. The building itself is internally vast and impressive, though it is actually the mid-twelfth century successor of the great mosque which Ibn Khaldoun tells us was built towards the end of the eighth century. Another mosque that should be visited, not only for its beautiful mosaics and arabesques and columns of Algerian onyx, but also for the architectural beauty of the minaret and for the picturesqueness of the site, is that of Sidi-el-Halawi, or Halaoui, just outside the walls of Tlemçen to the north, and adjacent to the small negro village (with, too, a mosque of its own) which is well worth a visit on the part of those who are eager to see as much as possible of native life "in the rough." The summit of the minaret of this lovely Djamàa-ed-Abou Abdulla esh-Shaudi, as its proper name is, has long been frequented in the due season by a family of building storks—the legend on one hand being that Father Stork comes to Tlemçen annually to bring Christianity in its train; and, on the other, that it is a Moslem missionary who annually goes north to promulgate the truths of Islamism.

Tlemçen is environed by three places of fascinating interest —Mansourah, Aghadir, and the village and famous sanctuary and mosque of Sidi Bou Medine. The fine tower of Aghadir has the added interest that its lower part is constructed of large blocks that were once part of Roman Pomaria; but, in the main, Aghadir is now interesting only for its beauty and fertility, and its lovely views. As for Sidi Bou Medine, almost as much might be written about it as concerning Tlemçen itself. It has been called the Fiesole of Tlemçen, but it is more than Fiesole to Florence; for while El Eubbad was once as flourishing and intellectually and artistically as important as the neighbour of Florence, it has, in its shrine and mosque of the patron saint of Tlemçen, Shoaïb ibn Hoosein el-Andalousi, commonly known as Sidi Bou Medine, an attraction of a highly sacred and venerated character in Moorish eyes. The tomb itself, though shown to the scrupulously respectful (unshoed) visitor as though it were surpassingly impressive, is really anything but impressive to others than the Moslem. The real glory of the place is neither the Koubba of the Saint nor the ruined palace of "Our Lord the Sultan Abou el Hassan Abdulla Ali," famous in Moorish history as "The Black Sultan," but the superb mosque, one of the greatest triumphs of Moorish art, entered by bronze gates of surpassing decorative beauty. "A journey of a thousand miles is more than repaid by an hour in the great mosque of Sidi Bou Medine," says an Arab enthusiast, and many visitors will be inclined to agree with him.

One word more : let the would-be visitor to Tlemçen not delay overlong. The Berber, the Arab, even the Moor, are all giving way before the French (and perhaps more emphatically the Jews), and in a few years, great as French Tlemçen may become, Moorish Tlemçen will only be a memory.

WILLIAM SHARP

LA FRANCE ARTISTIQUE ET MONUMENTALE.

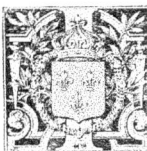

IN his preface to the first of the three portly quarto volumes already issued, M. Henry Havard sets forth their *raison d'être*. He speaks as a Frenchman should of the architectural glories of his country; and, as a writer of repute, as an Inspecteur des Beaux-Arts, and as editor of the work before us, he is entitled to a respectful hearing. Under the apprehension that there was a decline in the productivity of France in books of beauty and worth, and that her supremacy in the Art world was thereby at stake, a body of amateurs enrolled themselves under the title of the Société de l'Art Français, each devoting a sum of money, not in the ordinary spirit of trade, but with the generous and patriotic resolve to abide by the complete absorption of his quota, provided only some tangible result were obtained—some real effort made to keep the foreigner at a distance. The result is this series of monographs on churches, palaces, picture galleries, museums, monuments, etc., and, as foreshadowed in the preface, it is likely to be "de longue haleine." M. Havard contends that many of the Art treasures of France being practically unknown, thousands of his countrymen wander yearly abroad, while within a reasonable distance of their own homes they have the wherewithal to satisfy any ordinary student or sightseer. (The argument holds good everywhere, for the failing is not peculiarly French.) M. Havard asks : What town in Italy can vie with Nimes and its environs and show a finer Roman aqueduct than the Pont du Gard, a grander amphitheatre, or a temple that is more perfect in form than the Maison Carrée? He is equally confident, and justly so, of the many mediæval and Renaissance examples ; for the former referring to well-known cathedrals, the Abbey of Mont St. Michel, and Aiguesmortes, and for the latter pointing with effect to the grand châteaux along the Loire and Seine.

The first article is on the "Religious Monuments of Rheims," from the pen of M. Louis Gonse. In so ancient a city—the capital of Remi in the days of Julius Cæsar, and the scene of the coronation of a long line of kings with little interruption for thirteen hundred years, from Clovis to Charles X.—there should be, and there is, much to interest the visitor ; but time, fire and revolution, and the necessities of the Grand Monarque, who consigned many of the gold and silver ornaments of the Cathedral to the Mint, have deprived us of many of the heirlooms of the old royalty of France.

In such a work, where each writer treats of his own special subject, one should not look for continuous dovetailing or the stereotyped form of an itinerary ; still, a more systematic arrangement under which each volume might have related to a definite district of France, and the insertion of a corresponding sectional map, would, we venture to think, have rendered the work more complete, and more readily available to Frenchmen and foreigners. As it is, in the first volume we go from Rheims to Versailles and Brou, and then with enormous bounds we are transported to the south to Pau and Avignon. The main idea of the work is, nevertheless, admirable, and might be followed with success in an analogous survey of the British Isles.

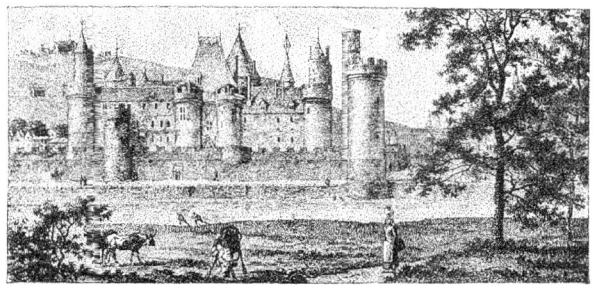

LE LOUVRE AU TEMPS DE PHILLIPPE-AUGUSTE.

ART IN THE SHOP WINDOWS.

TO review in a short space the recent course of Decorative Art would be out of the question; but at least a survey of the shop windows is possible; and a walk through the main streets of the West End of London should be enough to give one a very fair idea as to where we stand with regard to the progress of industrial design.

The very best work may not, it is true, there be displayed; some of the best is certainly not to be seen there; it is made to special order, and goes direct from the workshop to the place for which it is destined. There are doubtless, also, makers and vendors who, for reasons not difficult to imagine, carefully abstain from exhibiting in their windows the best, and especially the newest, things they have imported or produced; but it takes nowadays a very short time for even novelties in design to find their way into the open market; and, at any rate, the shop windows in fashionable quarters of the town may fairly be taken to represent the average of the better class of work done, and to reflect the taste of—one hardly knows whose taste it is, the taste of the public or of those who purvey to it, or whether to call it taste at all. One cannot, either, safely call it liking—for it is impossible to suppose that any one really cares in the least for some of the things which appear to be "the thing." Perhaps it is the average carelessness in matters of taste which is everywhere displayed: that would account for much.

The fear, expressed in a former article dealing more especially with design in furniture, that we were drifting in the direction of the stereotyped French styles, is more than confirmed by a very careful scrutiny of the shop windows. The one fact which there asserts itself, which stares us persistently in the face, is that French fashion, after a period of banishment, has reasserted itself. One may hope that its supremacy is not to be for long; one may see in the incompatibility of eighteenth-century French art with nineteenth-century English life the impossibility of its permanence; one may argue from the violence of this fever of imitation that it must work itself out before long; but meanwhile there is no sort of doubt as to which way the fashion tends. The fashion is French, Louis Quinze, or at best Louis Seize. Those who regulate their taste according to the shop, and to the ruling of the shopman, may rest secure of that; and it is the loosest and most riotous form of French art that is for the moment uppermost.

Sobriety in decoration, symmetry in design, restraint in ornament, are at present out of date. The furniture which is offered to us might all have been imported from France, but that much of it costs more, and is less worth the money, than genuine French work would be; the very clocks chime in, and strike the hour of the Regency or of the Empire; the silks are largely from French looms, delicate in colour often enough, but without form and void of design; and the wall-papers which are not absolutely foreign, are reproductions of old French silks, wanting of course the charm of texture which redeems the original fabric from dreariness, and obviously less adapted to be spread out flat on a wall than to fall in folds of drapery. The French themselves, by the way, when they show such papers in shop windows, do actually drape them in folds, so much more pleasing are they in that foolish form.

In the windows of the more important silversmiths the fashion pronounces itself very emphatically. The larger portion of plate, and that which almost invariably occupies the most conspicuous position, is in the manner of the first half of the eighteenth century. In one case it is genuine Georgian work which is shown. There is a certain historic interest in that, dull as it may be artistically, to which no mere reproduction can lay claim, but it argues little for the progress of the silversmith's art, or for the enterprise of the silversmith, that these should be the things he shows in his window. In most cases the design is not English at all. The best of it might have been designed by Pierre Germain, and is probably copied from him; but the greater part of it is in imitation of the more popular, because more extravagant style of Meissonier, in which curves run riot, where the very notion of symmetry is abolished, and never a line is allowed to go straight about its business. One hardly knows which is the more hopelessly astray from the right path in design, this orgy of licentious form, or the quasi-picturesque productions which still hold their own even in the most fashionable shop windows. There is still to be found the presentation vase with most uncomfortably horned stags' heads by way of handles. There the epergne of our childhood still survives and flourishes. The silver pointer points, the silver setter sets, the realistic silver huntsman holds high above the silver hounds a realistic silver fox, all under the boughs of a would-be rustic but quite impossible oak-tree, spreading out to receive a glass dish cut in the mechanical and commonplace pattern which has bored us from our youth.

It is refreshing to find here and there instances of cut glass designed more on the lines of old crystal, lacking indeed somewhat in the matter of breadth and boldness of treatment, but comparatively fresh and tasteful, and promising to develop into a form of cut glass of which we need not be ashamed. Side by side with this, however, and in places of at least equal honour, we find the familiar prism patterns in all their inevitable rigidity. It would seem indeed that this kind of thing is most in favour. So at least it proved in the case of the king who last year gave to London what is said to be the largest order ever given for table glass. There were shown in the British court at the last Paris exhibition some glass bowls, decorated with waves and fishes cut cameo-fashion out of green and white glass, which a king might well aspire to possess. But it was not for the sake of work of this kind that he passed over the beautiful industry of his own country. He came to us for work devoid altogether of design (unless the cutting of cross-lines on glass can be called design) and loaded his tables with glass, such as perhaps could not be made out of this country, but notable only for the chemical perfection of the material and the mechanical precision of its facetting. One lays the blame upon the royal taste rather than suppose that the firm who furnished this ordinary ware would not have greatly preferred to supply some of the really beautiful glass to be found in their show-rooms.

The bronzes in the lamp shops one may fairly suspect of being for the most part French. Some of the quasi-classical figures are designed with distinction if with no great originality, and modelled with knowledge; but they are not so much designed for lamps as degraded to the office of lamp-bearing, the undignified office one may say, when the lamp itself is lost in the folds of what looks like a huge lace parasol.

The contriver of lamp shades seems to have scarcely an idea above millinery. Perhaps the newest of his devices is where he has evolved from his imagination, or borrowed from a scene in a ballet, a monster rose several feet in circumference, which hangs inverted over the light, trimmed (as though it were a hat) with a rose of natural size. He could scarcely have hit upon a clearer way of demonstrating the monstrosity of the thing.

Among the duplex and other lamps displayed are some very beautiful vases, used to form the bowl, but the lamp proper is usually something of an excrescence upon the vase; it is seldom that the vase has been designed as a receptacle for the oil, and shaped so as to *want* the lamp to complete it. Prominent among the exceptions to the rule are certain lamps in copper, or in copper and silver, which have obviously been designed from first to last with a view to the purpose and function of an oil lamp. These are distinctly a step in the right direction, but there would be no harm in going a step or two beyond the somewhat rigid simplicity which is at present characteristic of this new departure.

The spread of electric lightning has called forth a certain amount of ingenuity in the design of fittings. The fact that the old devices would not do, has compelled the makers to try all manner of expedients, some of them ingenious enough; but the difficult problem of designing fittings for incandescent lamps remains yet to be solved. Certainly it is not met by the device of a silver column, with capital supporting no entablature but a porcelain candle, surmounted in its turn by an electric lamp. Let us hope that by the end of 1894 we shall have got past that stage of incompetence.

For any new thing in the way of pottery we must look rather to processes of technique than to design. The potter may have perfected a method of painting between two glazes, which results in a certain artistic softness of effect; he may have invented a kind of marquetry in clay, which is at all events a curiosity in manufacture, capable perhaps of some artistic development; but in the way of design he has not brought out anything very fresh. M. Solon's plaques, for example, at the Arts and Crafts, some of which are certainly not of the last year's painting, are the most delightful things in the way of pottery that have been seen in London for some time past.

A few years ago we had a revival of lustre painting. The industry may, for all one knows, still flourish; but there is scarce a sign of it in the shop windows. One is led to suspect that the initiation of the amateur into the mysteries of underglaze and overglaze, and barbotine painting, must have been fatal to the pottery industry. Folk had for a while so many feebly painted and half-baked plates upon their walls and everywhere about them, that they grew sick of the very sight of pottery, and so has come a lull on the demand. The supply has often an air of "old stock" about it, as in the case of the rather costly imitation of ivory, which loses its charm when one realises that it is porcelain. Importations of miniature arm-chairs, settees, and windmills in blue and white Delft, do not witness to our progress; nor does the white Dresden ware, nor even the services of Sèvres, or imitation Sèvres, which, admirably as they are painted, never rise above insignificance of design. When it comes to dessert plates representing "'Arry out for a holiday," and suchlike graceful and appropriate subjects, it is not to be wondered at if persons of taste prefer the wares of China or Japan at half the price.

One observes, by the way, that the rage for the Japanese is already almost a thing of the past. Collectors of course will continue to value old work for its rarity, and artists to appreciate it for its character, and especially for its consummate workmanship; to some of us the lesson it has taught remains part of us so long as we shall live; but the Anglo-Japanese manner is happily dead. We continue indeed to import from Japan, but it is becoming more and more the custom to send out there designs to be executed in leather—paper or what not. It is a pity that we should, so to speak, debauch the native art of Japan; but, on the other hand, it is clear that traditional Japanese design is out of time with our life and surroundings; and if Orientals can do our work for us better than we can get it done at home, no free-trader, at all events, can consistently complain. The ugly side of the question is, that some of the work goes to them, not because they can do it better, but because they will do it at a cheaper rate.

There are signs of vitality in the booksellers' windows, and notably in the book-bindings. This is not apparent in the tooling of costly leather bindings, which continue, with rare and familiar exceptions, to be executed as if for the library of Henri Deux or Louis Treize, nor yet very markedly in the more work-a-day "half binding," although even here there is some departure from the too familiar, and as it seemed inevitable, marble paper at the sides of the book. The patterns which take its place may not be all the heart could desire, but one is grateful for any sign of coming-to-life in a craft that has so long lain torpid.

The change for the good is apparent chiefly in cloth binding, which your dilettanti does not recognise as worthy of the name of binding at all. In this less pretentious, but more important, because more popular, branch of industry, it appears to be much less the fashion than it was, to take some illustration out of the book itself, stamp it in gold upon the cloth (where all its detail is to the bad) and imagine that, without more ado, the cover is decorated. The better class of publishers appear to be often content to use a serviceable cloth, without torturing it all over with ornament, but they leave something to be desired in the choice of colour to which they needlessly limit themselves. Some few of the younger generation of publishers go farther, and have actually ventured upon a style of enrichment in gold, which owes, one is inclined to suspect, something to American influence. The design is not altogether devoid of affectation, but it is appropriate in treatment, broad in effect, and sometimes refreshingly original.

Among other trades which, judging always by the shop windows, are not without vitality, is brass- and copper-smithing. There is a good deal of immature repoussé work, the output, it may be assumed, of what are called "village industries"; but there is also some very characteristic work of the kind; and in the matter of pots and kettles it is not difficult to find well-shaped vessels which are not ashamed to own themselves beaten.

The carpet trade appears to languish. The "seamless" carpet is the only kind which lends itself to the style in vogue. There are rumours afloat of American importations flooding the British market. It is possible to nourish the pious hope that the worst one sees in the way of would-be French Brussels and Wilton pile may not be home-made.

Of curtain fabrics it may be said that it is easier than it was a short while ago, to find heavy and comparatively rich-looking, and yet not very costly material, both of British and foreign make; and this tapestry, or whatever else it may call itself, is becomingly broad and large in treatment, and sometimes modern in design. But it is in dress fabrics that one finds the greatest novelty in texture, and the most delicate and beautiful variety of colour. Even in mere trimmings and such-like frivolities, there are signs of taste; they are often fanciful, if sometimes extravagant. One may not be prepared to admit that a lace butterfly makes a very adequate bonnet; but it may make a very becoming ornament to a lady's hair, and it is long since a bonnet really fulfilled the purpose of a substantial head covering.

Compared with the slippers which ladies are invited to work, spotted over with chessmen, or with an airy combination of horse-shoes and swallows, the butterfly bonnet is a miracle of taste and fancy. One lived in the happy faith that Berlin-wool work was no more! Is this a survival (of the least fit), or is it a revival? Let us hope that the turn of worsted-work has not come round again.

It is more than possible that the reviewer, looking in at the shop windows, may see too much the reflection of himself and of his own prejudice. He can but declare that he did not realise, until he began to look into them, how generally they reflect French taste, a degraded taste very often, a poor one at the best. That is certainly not a subject of congratulation either for the British artist, or for the British manufacturer, or for any one who cares for the growth of our art and manufacture. Among this latter class it is rarely that one can include the proprietor of the shop window. He tells us there only too plainly the lines on which he acts.

It is a curious commentary upon the Frenchification of our British design, that both French and German manufacturers have within the last few months been asking Englishmen to design for them. They at all events have some faith in our native art, and believe, as the British tradesmen appears not to do, in its commercial value. There seems some hope in that.

LEWIS F. DAY.

MR. KEILLER'S COLLECTION IN DUNDEE.

SIR WALTER SCOTT thought his country a fitting nurse for the poetic and artistic mind. Energic, formative, visited by the throes of sprouting life, Scotland, though active in the subterranean preparations of growth, lay long bound like a land in winter under the frost of Puritanic discipline snatched this early season for commercial enterprise. If not the first, the fairest of the blossoms of an early spring, Burns gave promise of what we may expect when mid-summer visits a soil so rich in all that favours poetic-eclosion. Already Scotland has been remarked in the art of painting;

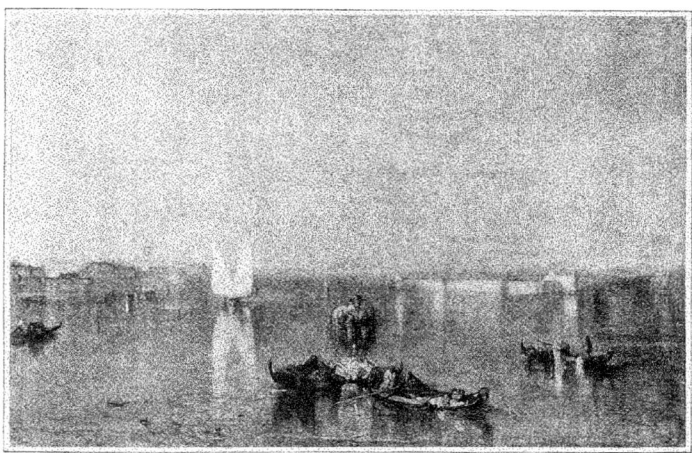

VENICE. BY J. M. W. TURNER, R.A. IN MR. KEILLER'S COLLECTION.

and its cloaking snows of hypocrisy. It is but lately that the genial breath of toleration has thawed the sterner virtues of rude and forcible times, and, naturally, Scotsmen have many an impulse for good or bad has come from beyond the Tweed. Not to speak of old names, Raeburn, Wilkie, John Thomson, Nasmyth, and many more, one may note at the

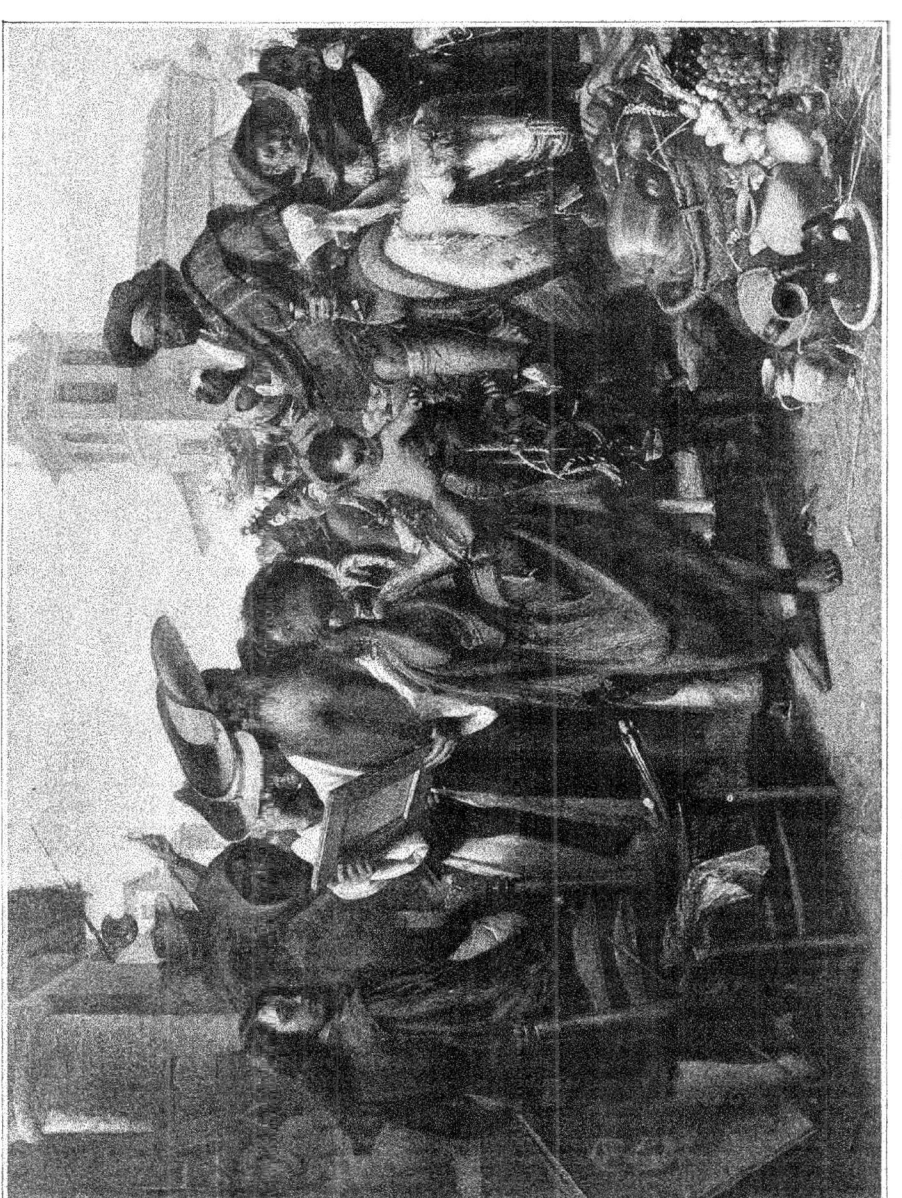

The Early Career of Murillo. By John Phillip, R.A. In Mr. Kehler's Collection in Dundee.

present day various original schools of painting, some just beginning, others near the end of their course. With energy in the production of the Fine Arts public appreciation goes almost exclusively from the Art of this century and at the whim of the moment. If a tendency of any sort directs the choice of canvases it is towards the figure-picture with an

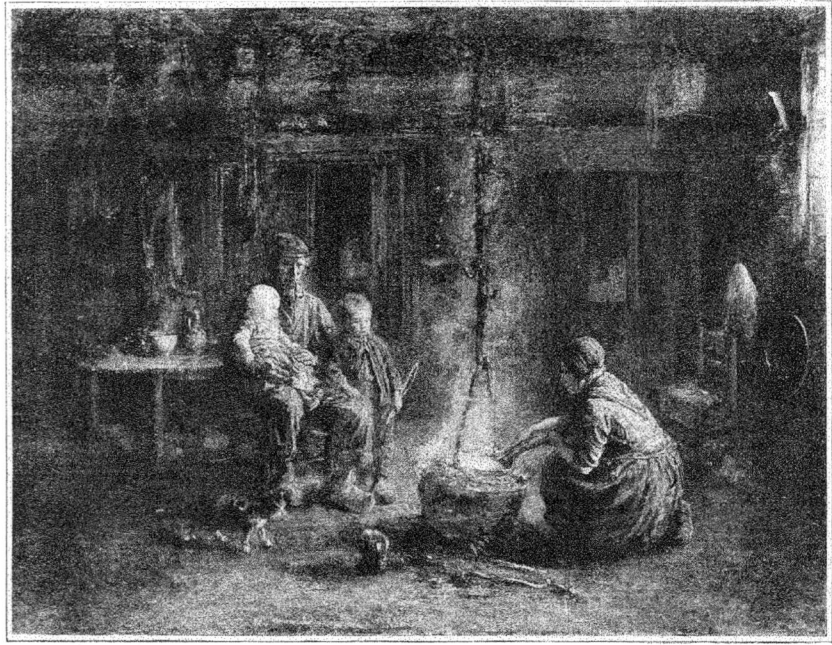

THE PANCAKES. BY JOSEF ISRAELS. IN MR. KEILLER'S COLLECTION.

hand in hand, and, as Scotland gets richer, private collections multiply and become larger. In Edinburgh, Glasgow, Aberdeen, Dundee, many houses, unpretentious save for their fine material or good proportions, contain at the present day fair collections of pictures.

Mr. Keiller, of Dundee, possesses a considerable number of pictures in oil or water-colour, as well as some original etchings and proofs from various kinds of reproductive plates. His billiard-room, made extremely high in the roof and top-lit, serves as a veritable picture-gallery, and shows his best pictures in an equable light. His collection, however, far exceeds its boundaries and occupies the greater part of his house. From this introduction do not suppose Mr. Keiller's collection a Scottish one, except that, made in Scotland, it may represent the tastes of an ordinary citizen of a Scottish commercial town. It contains, it is true, many pictures by Scotsmen, none of them by the older painters, yet it cannot be called a representative gathering of Scottish Art, or, indeed, of any Art in particular. It illustrates no principle in painting and points to no definite taste for schools or methods. Its elements, however, would appear to have been collected incident; and Scotland, England, and Holland have been called upon indifferently to supply such subjects.

What has been said above, though true of the bulk of the gallery, by no means applies to that which constitutes its main interest. For Mr. Keiller's is a collection with a great landscape picture—one, in fact, which stands away from its surroundings upon a different platform. There is no comparing work, however clever, or however sincere, by a painter of the illustrative and popular view of life with something which has been seen grandly by the eyes of a great poet. Although of the same century and equally concerned to express its feelings, Thackeray and Wordsworth are divided by the gulf between the every-day and the exceptional, between particular truth and general truth, between prose and poetry. So the wide-sweeping vision of Constable reveals an exalted state of mind about the world which awakes a quite different order of feelings from the prose creations of John Phillip, Pettie, Sir J. Millais, Mr. Orchardson, Mr. Alma Tadema, Mr. Colin Hunter, and Mr. Riviere. It is difficult in words to mark such a distinction without impropriety.

Prose possibly is not the right word, although it would in

MR KEILLER'S COLLECTION IN DUNDEE.

no way deny a certain sort of artistic merit in the pictures to which it was applied. Let us say that one feels it possible to conceive things as these painters have conceived them, even though one could never hope to render the conception with their ability. Indeed, it is difficult to avoid seeing the world as the anecdotic painter sees it, that is to say, as a collection of separate objects. Often pictures consist of studies and sketches made separately, and then united in a false *ensemble*, which represents no one of the points of view under which the objects were originally studied. Rather it represents no real point of view at all, but merely an arbitrary illustrative gathering and grouping of detail. This practice merely deifies the common unesthetic vision distracted by the cares of business, pleasure, or science, and uninformed by the spirit of artistic reverie.

tricks of convention, and, at times, leant more to knowledge than to beauty. Nevertheless, we say of him as of Wordsworth, that he entertained some absolutely new sentiments, and that he rose occasionally to the emphatic expression of a great artist. Art with Constable was never attained as an added grace of communication. When he aimed consciously at style then he fell into poor trickiness unworthy of his views, as, for instance, in his treatment of the near-hand corner of 'The Cornfield.' It was when he clearly meant to carry an impression by assault that he triumphed all along the line. Then everything went together—style and impression became fused into Art. Mr. Keiller's 'View in Helmingdale Park,' here reproduced, shows the virtue of that nobility in the eyesight which the painter himself perhaps scarcely felt as conscious artistry. Probably this work was, as it were, an inspired rush made

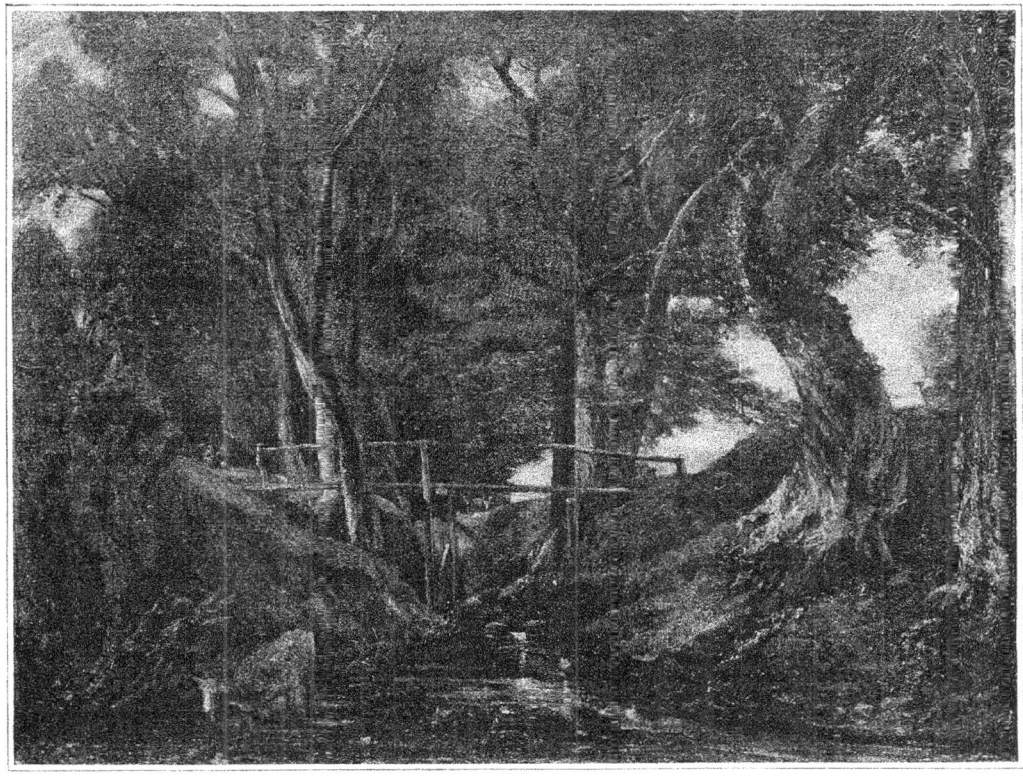

VIEW IN HELMINGDALE PARK. BY JOHN CONSTABLE, R.A. IN MR. KEILLER'S COLLECTION.

We often speak of Constable as a more original observer than other men, inclining, perhaps, to overlook him as an artist in expression. He fell at times, it is true, into bad old

at prey that had long been stalked, rather than a deliberate strategic siege of the beautiful. The picture, having been hung in a winter show at Burlington House, is well known—our illustration will recall it. If you feel a profound depth and solemnity in these trees, it is because Constable was never more alive than at this moment to the broad shapes and majestical beauties of foliage. As he painted each bit he saw the whole, and felt the spring of trunk and branch, the droop or wave of bough as part of a larger pattern. No mere expense of labour, no compilation of careful studies could have produced this picture. It is one of the best preserved and most complete of Constable's works. Its style is as grand as that of the two large sketches in South Kensington, but more assured; as finished as that of 'The Hay Wain,' but less sacrificed to detail. If ever Constable showed himself an impressionist in a large finished work it was in painting 'Helmingdale Park,' when he would seem to have lost all fear of those who look at the minute touches of a canvas and have no eyes for the explanatory *ensemble*. Mr. Keiller's picture could stand the neighbourhood of the best work of Constable's successors —Diaz and Rousseau. Here, indeed, the great romantic impulse which ran through the century is seen as thoroughly expressed as it ever was, wanting neither the initial breadth of view nor the matured grandeur of style necessary to preserve the conception.

Next to 'Helmingdale Park' hangs one of Josef Israel's most notable efforts, 'The Pancakes,' of which we also give an illustration. The large and vigorous style of this canvas fits it rather than any other in the room to support such a neighbourhood. A woman cooking a family supper in a peasant's cottage, a man with a baby on his knee, are familiar sights, not provocative, to the ordinary mind, of this solemn mood of colour, this broad, telling summary of the action of light. In such a case most English painters have annoyed us with a sham forced lighting used to make everything look bright, clean, and snug. They have not been sparing of the still-life glitter on bottles or fire-irons, the shelves set with cups and glasses, the fair chubby children and that favourite harmony of pink and brown. It was Rembrandt who found that the natural source of dignity in simple subjects is in the pathos and mystery of real light.

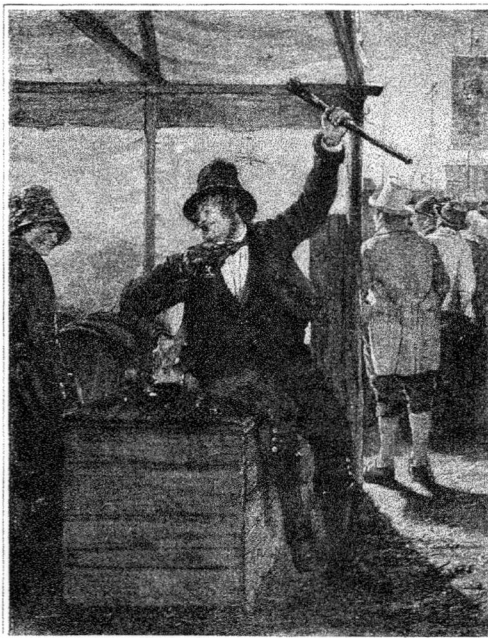

An IRISH FAIR. BY ERSKINE NICOL, A.R.A. IN MR. KEILLER'S COLLECTION.

Another large figure canvas is the work of John Phillip, who was born in 1817, the same year as Herbert and Daubigny, and died like Rousseau in 1867. Thus he worked level with a fine passage of French, and through a poor period of English Art. He was one of the most robust and human of the English figure painters of his time. In large works his art was a modern study of older models. Of Nature and of Phillip's feelings there is more to be seen in smaller pictures, but he never felt the inspiring fervour that now and again swept Constable or Delacroix into a passion of grandeur. Perhaps the most interesting relic of Phillip's talent is the unfinished "lay-in" at the Edinburgh National Gallery, of Spanish boys playing at a bull-fight. Here and there he shows a finer temper, as in Mr. Keiller's 'Farewell of a Spanish Soldier,' a small picture whose strength is somewhat flouted by a pink handkerchief on the girl's shoulders, in disagreeable contrast with her deep red skirt and the man's orange head-covering. A Spanish priest talking to several women is pleasanter decoratively, and has all the vivacity of a De Blaas with a much soberer and more dignified colouring. One of Phillip's largest pictures, 'The Early Career of Murillo,' belongs to the billiard-room, but it is at present in the first room of the Old Masters Exhibition at the Royal Academy; the scene, which we reproduce, shows a crowded market-place: connoisseurs examine a canvas by Murillo in the open-air, or, at least, in Phillip's open-air, which is scarcely the same thing. The picture is composed well in the old piled-up style, and abounds in still-life arranged artificially, and painted from sketches made at all sorts of different focusses. It places us at the back of Murillo's canvas; the handling and realisation are powerful but not consistent, the general effect is unconvincing, and the colour plentiful but not rich. Still no one would deny the picture a certain sumptuousness of conception and robustness of brushing which lift it far above the work of E. M. Ward, Leslie, Mulready, Maclise, Landseer, and other contemporary painters.

Of Mr. Keiller's Turner it is difficult to speak decidedly, for the picture could only be seen in a bad light. The canvas gives a panoramic view of Venice; and owing to its fine state of preservation, it is indicative beyond most Turners of the great painter's views of colour. Less fanciful, too, than the generality of his mature work, this large oil gives

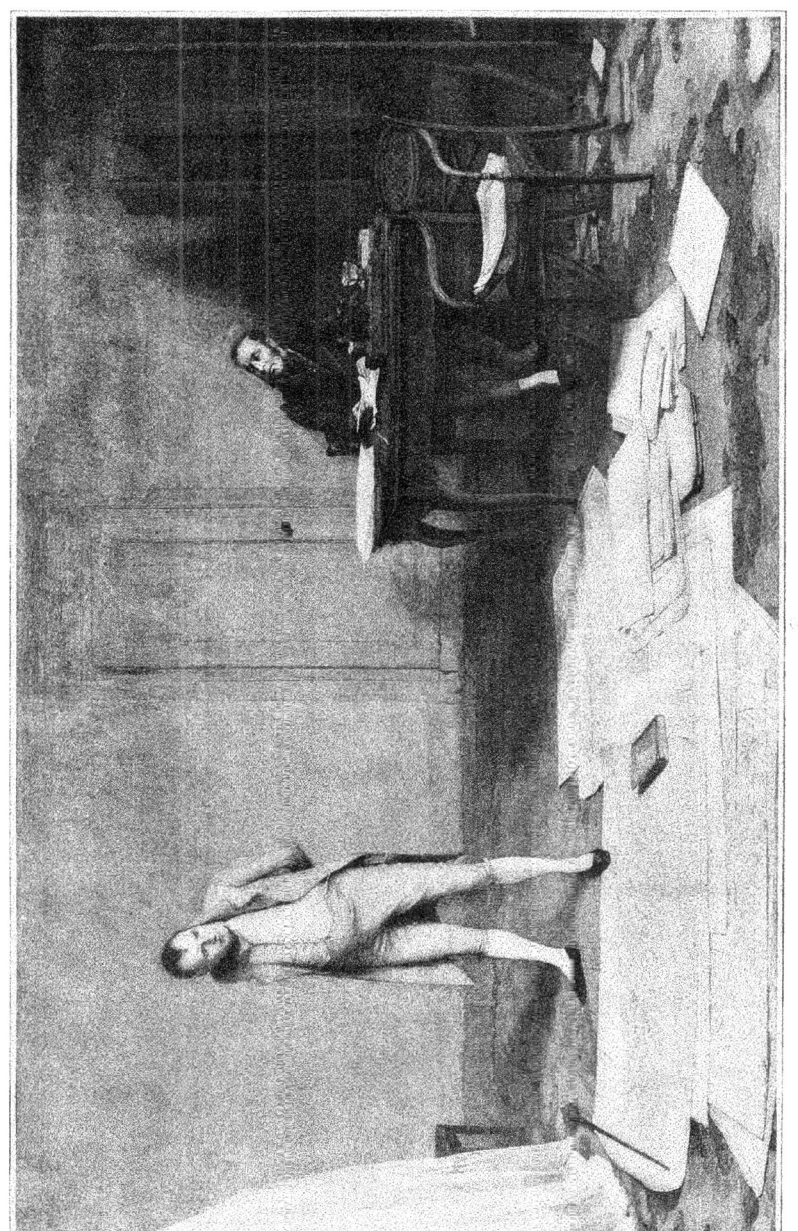

NAPOLEON DICTATING HIS MEMOIRS.—ST. HELENA, 1816.
BY W. Q. ORCHARDSON, R.A.
From the picture in the Collection of James Keiller, Esq., Dundee,
By special permission of the artist.

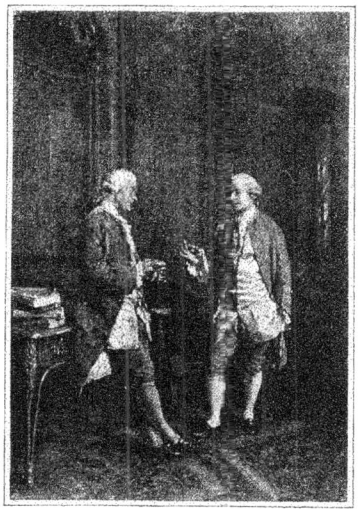

CAUSERIE. BY MEISSONIER. IN MR. KEILLER'S COLLECTION.

their savour or practised realism on cheap terms, treating as motifs for canvases popular subjects suitable enough for slight drawings in children's journals or the comic papers. In spite of his openly expressed contempt for those who sacrificed dignity to domestic incident and character to prettiness, Bough was not altogether uninjured in his own art by their example. His intentions and his choice of subject defied contamination, though his technique suffered. By nature he saw broadly, but his mental growth was cramped so that he rarely expresses essential facts with the unhampered directness of great art. Yet Sam Bough was a man of genius and his faults were rather extraneous and due to his time and place than native to his talent. During many years his pictures were remarkable in the Royal Scottish Academy for the vigour and honesty of their treatment. He was very successful in water-colour, and our illustration comes from a specimen of his work in that medium, representing a coach about to change horses at an old English inn. The composition is natural, well arranged, and free from trivialities. Sam Bough was born in Cumberland, but having spent most of his life in Edinburgh, he is usually classed among Scottish painters.

'An Irish Fair' is a particularly good example of Nicol, who was rarely so refined in his practice of realism. The scene takes place inside a tented booth, and the effect of the light, both that transmitted and that direct from the open door, is very well shown. The treatment reminds one of Dutch work in the amount and quality of detail, in the rendering of the light, and in the painting of the figures and their costumes.

Mr. Keiller owns several large and well-known works by Mr. Orchardson—'The Queen of Swords,' 'Napoleon dictating his Memoirs,' and the last scene of 'Le Mariage de Convenance.' 'The Queen of Swords' (illustrated on page 34) represents a country dance in past days at the moment when a couple come down the avenue of uplifted

some idea of Venice as Turner really saw it. Doubtless much of his apparent wildness and his arbitrary departure from reality must be charged to the evanescence of his pigments. Not the least charming feature of this picture is the distant range of Alps rising behind Venice viewed from the sea. On the whole we may call Mr. Keiller's Turner a singularly fresh and natural canvas.

Amongst work by foreigners we noted a Meissonier, entitled 'Causerie,' which shows the Frenchman's skilful arrangement of figures to illustrate a subject, and his conscientious and workmanlike realisation of his somewhat commonplace conception of things. This is one of the most celebrated of the smaller Meissoniers, and it was one of the gems of the Secrétan Collections. Our three remaining illustrations are drawn from the work of well-known Scotsmen —Sam Bough, Erskine Nicol, and Mr. Orchardson. Sam Bough was deservedly popular as a man and as a painter. His eyes were his own, if one may so put it, but he was surrounded by men who trifled with old conventions that had lost

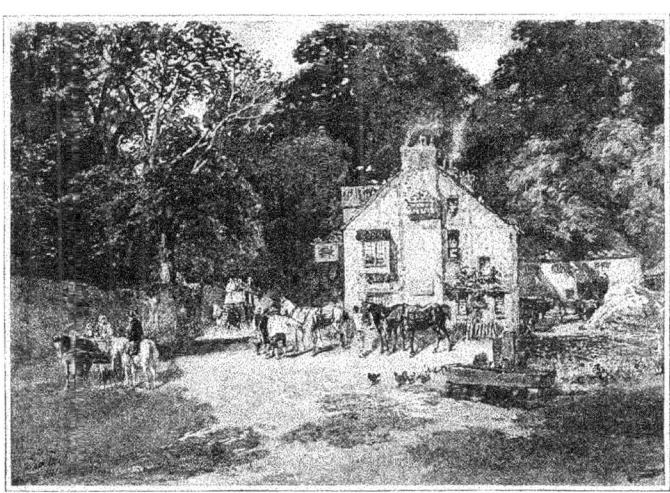

THE INN. FROM A WATER-COLOUR BY SAM BOUGH, R.S.A. IN MR. KEILLER'S COLLECTION.

swords. The citron dress of the chief figure is pleasing, and the figures abound with action. The aspect of the canvas is a little flat, and drier and harder than Mr. Orchardson's later work. His representation of Napoleon and Las Casas at St. Helena—the subject is a matter of history—see our large illustration—surpasses 'The Queen of Swords' in workmanship, but the canvas looks a little empty. It is not necessarily disparagement of a painter to call him conventional, for art implies some measure of convention. Mr. Orchardson's convention, though clever and original, stands in overwhelming proportion to his sentiment for nature. He is connected with truth by drawing chiefly; his colour, tone, air, and light are many degrees removed from an interest in reality. He arranges all his pictorial elements, however, with unquestionable taste, and he always stamps his work with an unmistakable individuality

R. A. M. STEVENSON.

ART NOTES.

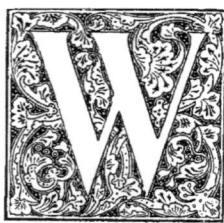

WITHOUT doubt the general depression in commercial affairs has been telling with exceptional severity on the artistic community. Artists, even of assured position, find that they are coming to the end of their commissions, and it is painful to learn the straits to which many are reduced. Unfortunately, this state of things is not confined to this country, although so far the artists of France have not suffered so much as their brethren in England. Italian painters, who look on London as an unfailing gold mine, are still turning their eyes in that direction, but the encouragement they have recently received must be but small. Architects are also not finding it easy to keep themselves employed, and they cannot but think with envy of their American colleagues, who have just arrived to commence work on the large hotel to be erected "on American lines" in Pall Mall and Haymarket.

Mr. John S. Sargent, Mr. Frank Bramley (painters), and Mr. G. Frampton (sculptor) were elected Associates of the Royal Academy on January 9th, and Mr. John M. Swan and Mr. A. Hacker (painters) on January 16th.

The London County Council has issued an elaborate statement setting forth that the Council will, in June next, award twenty Art scholarships, and a hundred sums of £5, to enable qualified students to study Art at certain selected schools in London, in the evening.

A good deal of discussion has taken place amongst Art critics with regard to a letter a firm of art publishers sent to *The Times* on Christmas Day. This letter showed, that while the vast majority of critics were influenced only by their opinions, there was at least one—a lady—who did not scruple to ask for bribes in return for criticism. It is very satisfactory to know that it is possible for a publishing house to receive over one thousand notices per annum, without being more often importuned for something tangible in return.

An effort is being made to found a Society of Illustrators, and the President of the Royal Academy, Mr. R. W. Macbeth, and Mr. Joseph Pennell have lent aid to the movement. The idea is not to form a trade union for the maintenance of prices, but to form an association which will assist the younger illustrators to find a market for their wares for reasonable remuneration. We think the society will be useful also in other directions.

The president and council of the Royal Society of Painter-Etchers have decided to hold their next exhibition from March 12th to April 7th, 1894. A selection of the engraved work of Marc Antonio will be a feature of the exhibition.

The Liverpool Autumn Exhibition of Pictures, held at the Walker Art Gallery, was closed on Saturday, December 16th, after what may be justly considered a very successful season, both as regards the attendance and the number of pictures sold, notwithstanding the great depression in commercial matters. Since the opening of the Exhibition, early last September, the galleries were visited by upwards of eighty thousand persons, including nearly ten thousand pupils of schools, admitted by invitation of the Committee. During the season several soirées were given to the season-ticket holders, which added considerably to the popularity of the Exhibition. One hundred and thirty pictures were sold, realising a little over £5,000, this amount being smaller than usual. The Arts Committee purchased the following works out of the Exhibition for the permanent collection, viz.:—'Meadow Sweet' (David Murray, A.R.A.); 'The Punishment of Luxury' (Signor G. Segantini); 'A Man Overboard' (Thomas Somerscales); 'The Old Hero' (J. B. Burgess, R.A.); 'An Eastern Tale' (T. M. Rooke, R.W.S.); 'The Mere' (John Finnie); 'Spells' (Henry M. Rheam); and a bronze statuette, 'Love, the Conqueror,' by F. W. Pomeroy.

The Salon of the Champs-Elysées will open, as usual, on the 1st of May, and close on the 30th of June. The following are the dates for sending in works for exhibition:—*For paintings*, from the 14th to the 20th of March; *for sculpture*, from the 1st to the 5th of April; *for architecture*, from the 2nd to the 5th of April. Sketches, water-colours, pastels, and miniatures, must be sent in between the 14th and 16th of March, and engravings and lithographs between the 2nd and 5th of April. All the dates mentioned are inclusive.

The Luxembourg Gallery, at Paris, was re-opened on the 1st of January, after cleaning and repairs. Several new acquisitions for the National Collection are now to be seen on the walls for the first time. The most important, perhaps, are some of Meissonier's studies recently bought by the Government, and the picture by Mr. G. F. Watts, R.A., called 'Love and Life,' which he presented to the State under circumstances which greatly gratified the French national feeling. Two years ago there were no English works in the Luxembourg, but now there are two by Sir Frederic Leighton, three drawings by Mr. Burne-Jones, and a picture by Edward Calvert, besides Mr. G. F. Watts' work. Paintings by Mr. Alex. Harrison, and Mr. Dannat, both Americans, and by Herr Von Uhde, German, have also been acquired. It is satisfactory to find the authorities at the Luxembourg relaxing the rigid exclusiveness which they have long maintained. For a considerable time Mr. Whistler's 'Portrait of My Mother'—probably the most serious picture in the collection—was the only important work, not French, upon its walls.

The chair of Æsthetics and the History of Art at the École des Beaux-Arts in Paris, rendered vacant by the death of H. A. Taine, has been recently filled by the appointment of M. de Fourcaud. M. Taine held this professorship from October, 1864, until his death, and it was in connection with it that he put forth his well-known works on the Philosophy of Art, the Ideal in Art, and the Philosophy of Art in Italy, in Greece, and in the Netherlands. After his election to Loménie's chair in the French Academy, in 1878, he ceased to discharge the active duties attaching to the Professorship, his advancing age and numerous occupations preventing his doing so.

In the official announcement of the International Exhibition of Fine Arts, which is to be held at Antwerp from May to November under the patronage of H.M. the King of the Belgians, invitations are made to foreign governments to appoint commissions to facilitate the collection and despatch of works of Art from their respective countries. Exhibits must be the work of artists, either Belgian or foreign, who were alive on the 1st of August, 1885, and are restricted to the usual classes —oil paintings, sculpture, architecture, etchings, engravings, drawings, pastels, water colours, or miniatures. Belgian artists will have the advantage of free carriage both ways for their exhibits over the State railways while foreign artists will have free carriage for the return journey only, and must pay the carriage in both directions outside the Belgian frontier. Arrangements are made for the appointment of juries to judge the works sent in by each section, and the inevitable State Lottery will also be a feature of the Exhibition.

We have received from Munich a copy of a petition which the "Secession" Verein Bildender Kunstler has addressed to the Bavarian Parliament. In it they state that their aim is to encourage the holding of frequent select exhibitions rather than those of indiscriminate extent, and they express the hope that the State will in future recognise their existence, that the works of their members may be considered eligible for purchase by the Government, and that they may also be considered in the distribution of State commissions. Movement in Art is, we think, always worthy of encouragement, and doubtless the Bavarian Government will give this application its earnest consideration.

OBITUARY.

We have to record the death, at Brixton Hill, on the 24th of December, 1893, of William Frederick Woodington, Honorary Retired Associate of the Royal Academy. He was born at Sutton Coldfield, near Birmingham, in 1806, and first learned drawing under Robert W. Sievier, the engraver, to whom he was articled at the age of twelve. Four years afterwards, Sievier
1894.

took up sculpture, and Woodington's attention was also turned to that branch of the arts; and it was by his sculpture that he became chiefly known, although he was also a painter, studying painting at the Academy Schools, where he was a contemporary and associate of Etty, Scott-Lauder, and others. The following are some of his public works in London and elsewhere :—The bronze bas-reliefs of the Battle of the Nile, on the pedestal of the Nelson Column; the marble bas-reliefs decorating the chapel in St. Paul's Cathedral, which contained until recent y the Wellington Monument; statues for the House of Lords, the Royal Exchange at Liverpool, the town of Carlisle, and also the colossal bust of Sir Joseph Paxton, so familiar to visitors to the Crystal Palace. His works were marked by much dignity and refinement. He has been an Associate of the Academy since 1876.

Mr. Léon Boussod, the senior partner of the house of Boussod, Valladon and Co., died on December 20th, 1893, at the age of sixty-eight. M. Boussod was a partner with M. Adolphe Goupil for forty years, and his amiable disposition and strict business integrity rendered him loved and respected by every one with whom he had dealings. He chiefly interested himself in illustrated books and publications, such as "Les Lettres et les Arts," a sumptuous periodical, which, however, was found too bulky for most libraries; "Les Aquarellistes Français and L'Armée Française," "L'Abbé Constantin," and "Flirt," with illustrations by Madeleine Lemaire.

On the 17th of November, 1893, died at Paris, Hippolyte A. G. W. Destailleur, best known in this country as the architect employed by the Empress Eugénie in the construction of the chapel at Farnborough which contains the ashes of Napoleon III. and the Prince Imperial. In addition to executing many important commissions in France and elsewhere, he found time to make a valuable collection of prints and books upon Art, and also to publish one or two works of his own upon kindred subjects. He died in his seventy-first year.

Giovanni Giuseppe Fontana, who died in December last in his seventy-second year, was a sculptor who was responsible for several important works in this country and in the colonies. He was born at Carrara, in Italy, and came of an artistic stock. While a youth he gained the gold medal at the Carrara Academy, and later, a scholarship at Rome. He threw himself into the movement led by Garibaldi, and being exiled in 1848, came to this country, where he became a naturalised Englishman, and remained until his death. He received commissions from the Corporation of Liverpool, the Government of Sydney, and the Government of New South Wales. Many of his works, such as 'The Prisoner of Love,' 'Jephthah and his Daughter,' 'Baffled,' &c., were exhibited at the Royal Academy, and were marked with a certain sense of beauty.

Jean Matejko, Polish historical painter and foreign Associate of the French Academy of Arts, died at his native town of Cracow on the 1st November last, aged fifty-five years. He occupied his artistic life with themes chosen from his country's stirring history. He was medalled in the Paris Salon in 1865, and received the Cross of the Legion of Honour for his picture exhibited there in 1870. He also published a series of etchings.

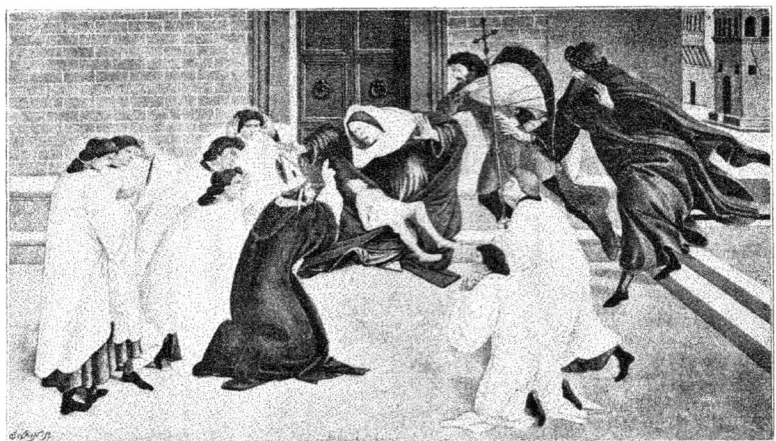

SAN ZENOBIO BRINGING BACK A CHILD TO LIFE. BY BOTTICELLI. IN THE COLLECTION OF LUDWIG MOND, ESQ.

ITALIAN PICTURES AT THE NEW GALLERY AND AT BURLINGTON HOUSE.

THE display of Italian pictures at the New Gallery is certainly, so far as London is concerned, without a precedent among the exhibitions of this kind. In fact, within its limits of time and territory—for all works later than 1550 and all pictures by Venetian artists have purposely been excluded —it may justly be regarded as the best possible supplement to the National Gallery that Art students could require. In the first place a whole room, containing about eighty pictures, has been devoted to the Trecento Art, that is the Art of Giotto, his pupils and followers, and the quaint and naive productions of the Sienese. In this group we find several pictures bearing the great name of Giotto; but students who have made themselves acquainted with the grand works of this artist on the walls of churches at Florence, Assisi, and Padua will probably find it rather difficult to reconcile their impression with the effect produced by these so-called Giottos, even when old inscriptions, such as 'Opus Iocti' and the like, are attached to them. The only pictures of small dimensions, which form an exception to this rule, are a set of predella panels in the Stanza Capitolare of S. Pietro in Vaticano at Rome, and the picture marked No. 24 in this exhibition lent by Mr. H. Willett. The subject is the presentation of the Infant Christ in the Temple, and the treatment is marked by that grandeur and simplicity which always predominates in the works of the master himself, but which none of his followers were able to attain. Abundant proof of this is afforded not only by several of the pictures here, but also by examples in the National Gallery. The followers of Giotto are very profuse in the display of ornamentation, so that the effect of their pictures generally depends more on details and accessories than on their intrinsic merits of drawing and composition. The small triptych No. 68 (lent by Mr. W. Fuller Maitland) dated 1338, and ascribed to Taddeo Gaddi, is one of the best specimens of this class.

The juxtaposition of early Florentine and Sienese pictures affords the student a unique opportunity of studying the differences of artistic tendency in the two schools. Duccio di Buoninsegna, the head of the Sienese School, is here represented by five pictures, one of which, namely, the Crucifixion (No. 21, lent by the Earl of Crawford), I believe to be superior to the replica in the centrepiece of the artist's famous 'Majestas' in the Duomo of Siena. The picture is in the best possible state of preservation, which cannot be said either of the four others by him in this exhibition, or of Mr. Willett's Giotto hung close by. It is evident that, unlike Giotto, Duccio never abandoned the traditions of Byzantine Art. On the contrary he appears to me to have aimed at bringing about a Renaissance, as it were, of the established traditional types and modes of drawing and composition. In this he is closely followed by Ugolino, another Sienese master, as may be seen in his 'Descent from the Cross' (No. 26, lent by Mr. H. Wagner). A similar style prevails in the Diptych with the Crucifixion and the Pieta (No. 30, lent by Mr. R. H. Benson), to which the name of another great Sienese master of very different tendencies, namely, Ambrogio Lorenzetti, is attached. However, the heads of four nuns in the National Gallery are, it appears, all that England can claim to possess by the hand of Ambrogio.

We also find a good many pictures by the later Sienese painters, such as Sano di Pietro, Giovanni di Paolo, Benvenuto di Giovanni, Matteo di Giovanni, Cozzarelli, Fungai, Pacchiarotto, Girolamo del Pacchia and Sodoma, but of these only a few have been correctly named by their respective owners, and space does not allow us to discuss them here.

Of far greater interest are the pictures by the contemporary Florentine artists, hung on the walls of the West Gallery. To begin with, there is a large altar-piece by Bicci di Lorenzo, representing the Assumption of the Virgin (No. 94, lent by Mr. W. Drax). This little-known painter, who was the son of Lorenzo di Bicci, evidently worked under the influence of Masaccio and Masolino, the two leading artists of the Florentine School, who in this exhibition, however, are not represented by genuine works. Several figures in the altarpiece recall the fresco paintings by Masaccio in the Brancacci Chapel. Of the pictures ascribed to Fra Filippo there is none which calls for special attention, all of them being inferior productions, but his pupil Pesellino is represented by several works of the first order and interest. Signor Morelli-Lermolieff has said of this great poet among the early Florentine painters, that nowadays not more than twelve pictures can be ascribed to him. I propose to add two to this meagre list, namely, the beautiful Cassone pieces representing the Triumph of Fame, Time and Religion (No. 129) and the Triumph of Love, Chastity and Death (No. 139), which are erroneously ascribed here to Pier di Cosimo.

The same Gallery contains a number of pictures which originally adorned the fronts of Cassoni, with quaint representations of mythological, historical and similar subjects. Few pictures of this class are now to be found in Italy. The exhibition at Burlington House also contains several examples, and among these the two by Sandro Botticelli, lent by Mr. Ludwig Mond (Nos. 158 and 164), call for special notice as being the best-preserved genuine works of the master among the very many ascribed to him in these exhibitions. They represent a succession of scenes from the life of San Zenobio, a patron saint of the town of Florence. In one of them (see our illustration) we see the bishop bring back to life the child of a French lady, who had fallen out of a window in the Via degli Albizzi. Another genuine Botticelli is the death of Lucretia in the New Gallery (No. 160, lent by the Earl of Ashburnham); but here unfortunately nearly all the faces have been painted over.

There is no genuine Leonardo da Vinci in either of the exhibitions, though at the New Gallery we have several fine drawings by him, lent by Her Majesty the Queen. But the other chiefs of the Florentine School namely Fra Bartolomeo and Andrea del Sarto, are represented at the New Gallery by one or two works of the first importance. Mr. Mond's large Madonna (No. 239), by the former artist, belongs to the time when Raphael came under Bartolomeo's influence. The accompanying illustration reproduces the very fine head of the Virgin who is kneeling before the infant Christ. In the background the artist has introduced himself with two of his assistants engaged in preparing a fresco painting on the wall over a gateway.

None of the pictures ascribed to Raphael can be accepted as having been executed by him, but of the works bearing his name, one of the finest is undoubtedly the portrait of Carondelet, with his secretary (No. 243, lent by the Duke of Grafton). It is by the hand of Sebastiano del Piombo, the great Venetian painter, who during his lifetime did everything he could to discredit and depreciate Raphael in the eyes of the public; but the irony of fate, working unconsciously, no doubt, and without malice, obliterated his own name from some of the very choicest of his works and substituted that of Raphael. One of the chief features of the Exhibition at the New Gallery is the rich display of Lombard pictures, most of which naturally reveal the influence of Leonardo da Vinci.

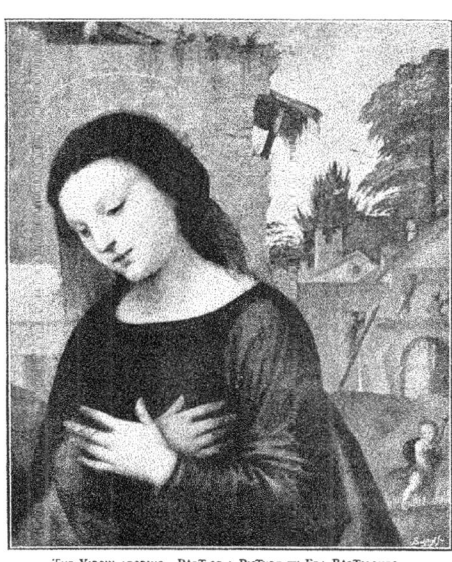

THE VIRGIN ADORING. PART OF A PICTURE BY FRA BARTOLOMEO. IN THE COLLECTION OF LUDWIG MOND, ESQ.

Turning now to Burlington House we find several Venetian masters represented by works of special interest. First, the two Madonna pictures by Giovanni Bellini, Nos. 142 and 143, hung side by side, one of which is in the artist's early manner of about 1470, and recalls a similar composition by Bartolomeo Vivarini, while the other is in his latest style, and seems to have been executed about the year 1510 by his pupil Bissolo, which may account for the marked difference in style between the two. Of all the pupils of Bellini the most original and most fanciful is undoubtedly Vincenzo Catena, whose works, however, are mostly ascribed to Bellini himself (as we see in the National Gallery), or to Giorgione, as in the last winter exhibition. No. 149, 'The Virgin, with Saints and Donors,' in the present exhibition, is an early signed production by this master; the other, No. 151, representing 'Christ with St. Peter, surrounded by Faith, Hope, and Charity,' is richer in colour and more finished, as well as more subtle and poetic in conception. In the Gallery at Madrid there may be seen an old copy of it. The Duke of Abercorn's 'Portrait of a Senator,' No. 115, ascribed to Raphael, is evidently by the hand of Parmigiano.

Among the signed pictures there is a fine 'Flute-Player,' by Saveldo (No. 117), and the large canvas from the Tiepolo Palace, representing 'Christ among the Doctors.' It is by Paris Bordone, and belongs to the ripest period of the master.

JEAN PAUL RICHTER.

ART PUBLICATIONS.

MR. GEORGE MOORE on "MODERN PAINTING" (W. Scott) is intensely interesting. As an artist trained, and now a critic of the most living and advanced ideas, the writer knows too well to be misled by the work of initialled artists. Deeply, and with a freedom which many will call by a stronger name, he analyses the work of contemporaries. Mr. Moore is most suggestive when he praises, for this he always does with discrimination, whilst his condemnations are too sweeping to be entirely just. His passages on Corot, Whistler, Rembrandt, and on Sir Frederic Leighton's 'Garden of the Hesperides,' are specially remarkable.

The Catalogue of the Greek Vases in the Ashmolean Museum, by Percy Gardner (Clarendon Press), which is the first of a series designed to illustrate the Oxford University collections, forms a valuable addition to the literature of a subject of ever-increasing popularity, the growth of which is due, to no small extent, to the labours of the late Miss Jane Harrison. Professor Gardner had, in producing it, to consider whether he should deal with Greek vase-form and painting as a whole, illustrating it as far as possible from the somewhat incomplete collection at Oxford, or merely content himself with describing the specimens contained therein, and with the limits of treatment they imposed. Although the adoption of the latter course deprives us—let us hope, only for the present—of a valuable history of this branch of Ceramics, we are bound to admit that he has chosen the wiser course, the catalogue being, consequently, much more detailed and exact in its information, and, so far as it goes, all the more reliable—an important consideration when we consider how slight the differences which may make or mar a hitherto accepted theory.

A little book on popular lines, "DRAWING AND DESIGN" (Macmillan), by E. R. Taylor, the well-known Birmingham teacher, will be found of great use for children beginning to draw. As the author says, any child who can write can also be taught to draw; and following out this idea, the designs to be copied are headed with written words, and underneath these letters are adaptations of the same forms to simple ornament. It is the most common-sense text-book in the market. Another excellent elementary handbook is Mr. C. Ryan's "EGYPTIAN ART" (Chapman and Hall), well written and fairly illustrated, giving a concise account of the Pyramids and the best art of the country of the Pharaohs. The same publishers' "TEXT BOOK OF ELEMENTARY DESIGN," by R. G. Hatton, is specially of service to students attending weekly classes, and could indeed stand in place of the lectures themselves. Another capital teacher's book is "ELEMENTS OF HANDICRAFT AND DESIGN" (Macmillan), by W. A. S. Benson. "LEADWORK, OLD AND ORNAMENTAL," by W. R. Lethaby (Macmillan), treats of Old English Leadwork, and pleads for a revival of the artistic uses of lead as may be found in most of the old cathedrals in this country.

Of recent books of travel, "A JOURNEY THROUGH THE YEMEN," by W. B. Harris (Blackwood), is one of the most interesting. As a part of Arabia almost entirely unknown, "The Yemen" has attractions for the pioneer and the archæologist. "Coins, gems, inscriptions, sculptures, old Persian and Arab antiquities, embroideries, arms, brass and pottery work, manuscripts, carpets, Oriental pottery and glass—the Yemen is full of these, and as yet her treasures are almost untouched." It is evident, therefore, that this part of Arabia, whence Mr. Theodore Bent has gone, almost within reach of Aden, is a country to which the collector may with the greatest advantage turn his attention.

The first of the illustrated books on the Chicago Exhibition has appeared—to the Women's Section belongs the honour. "ART AND HANDICRAFT IN THE WOMAN'S BUILDING, CHICAGO, 1893" (Boussod, Valadon & Co., New York and London), is the title of a handsome and profusely illustrated volume on this section, combining articles by ladies of all countries, and reproductions of everything of permanent interest.

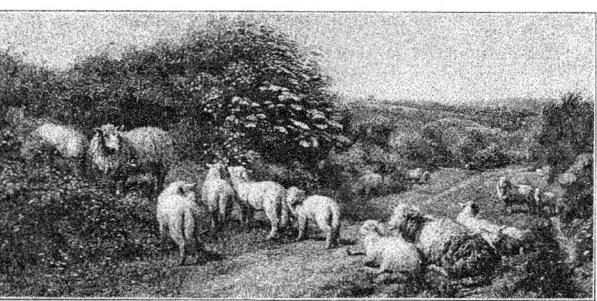

SUMMER-TIME. BY H. W. B. DAVIS, R.A.

The Art Union of London, under its new Secretary, is becoming once more an organization of popular interest 'Summer-time,' by H. W. B. Davis, R.A., of which we give a small reproduction, is etched by R. W. Macbeth, A.R.A., and being of important size, it will probably be sought after by those who like a decorative engraving, as well as the chance of an original painting.

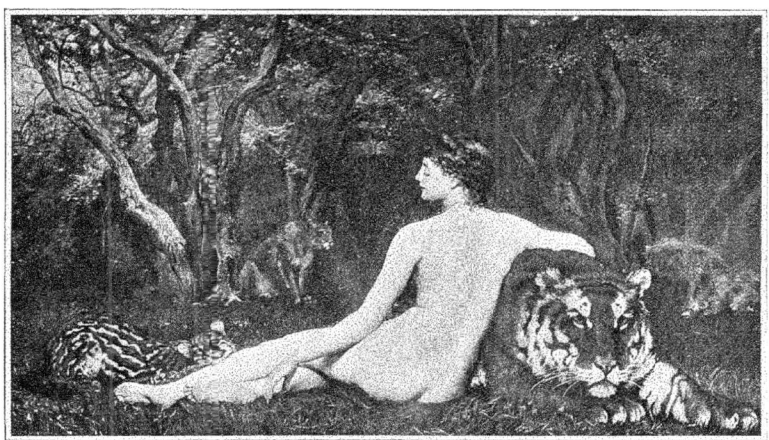

CIRCE. FROM THE PAINTING BY THE HONBLE. JOHN COLLIER.

JOHN COLLIER.

THE Hon. John Collier, second son of the late Lord Monkswell, who was in some ways better known by his former title of Sir Robert Collier, Barrister, Solicitor-General, Attorney-General, Judge, and Member of the Judicial Committee of the Privy Council, was born in 1850. *Il chasse de race*— that is, if his father had not been a great lawyer he would have been a great painter.

The first Lord Monkswell, indeed, was perhaps more brilliant as a so-called amateur painter than as a professional advocate.

In other words, the first Lord Monkswell sought and found in painting precisely the qualities which, with the wisdom which belonged to him, he is said to have avoided in his career at the Bar—to wit, dash, brilliancy, and individuality. Compare, for instance, any one of Sir Robert Collier's Alpine pictures with any one of Mr. Loppé's and note the difference. Mr. Loppé gives you a portrait—and a very dull one—of the glacier, the ice, the moraine, and the snowfields. Sir Robert painted these things with the eye not only of the painter, but of one who knew them and felt the poetry of their beauty. Under his brush they became so

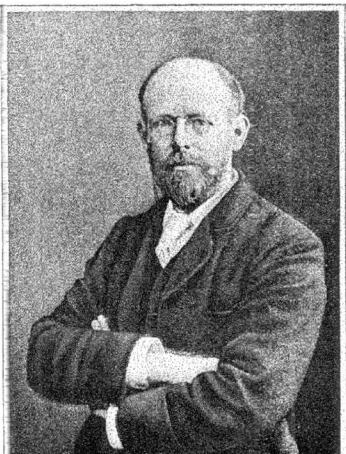

THE HONBLE. JOHN COLLIER.

alive, so picturesque, that any one who had ever felt the Alpine fever, looking at Sir Robert's pictures, could not but fancy he was going over old ground again, old excitements, old risks, old joys. I mention this because one of Mr. John Collier's earliest efforts in landscape was a portrait of a moraine, a portrait so accurate that there were those who said that it showed a want of imagination. That they who said this were strangely mistaken is amply proved by the true as opposed to meretricious imagination displayed in much, if indeed not in all, of Mr. Collier's recent works. I imagine that when Mr. Collier painted this and other pictures to which the same objection has been taken, he was, so to speak, trying his wings. He started with the idea that the painter's mission is to be true to nature, and to this idea, whether it is modified or not, I believe he still clings.

He thought, and for aught I know still thinks, that the painter's mission is absolute truth to nature; that is, to paint nature as it appears to him without any attempt at improving on God's handiwork. Without the least Zolaesque desire to celebrate the ugly, he

MARCH, 1894

thought it right not to make any attempt to improve what he saw with his own eyes before him—to put in or to take out a cloud, a tree, or an effect of sunlight was to him the one obnoxious thing—in fact, he applied to landscape the truth of vision and record which has served him so admirably in portraiture, a branch of Art in which he has few rivals. But in this very branch of Art he has amply shown that those who once accused him of want of imagination and poetic feeling are mistaken. In his portraits he not only faithfully delineates the features and the colouring, but also the characteristics of his sitter. Take, for instance, his well-known portrait of Mr. Rudyard Kipling, which, while absolutely exact as a portrait, brings out in the indefinable way known only to the true artist, the character and the poetic force lying behind the features of a man painted in modern habit as he lives. Take also the portraits of Mr. Irving and Mr. Toole, in each of which the strongly marked individuality is brought out with a not too common knowledge of mankind and discernment of character; in short, Mr. Collier is one of those gifted painters who study their sitters, not with a mere view of catching one, perhaps individual, expression, but with the intention of calling out and collecting, as he who would crystallise carbon, every mood and every expression that combine together to make an *Ich*. He lets his sitters walk, he lets them talk, he never bullies them, he watches them intently, he studies them intently, and the result of his studies is very seldom far from the idealised reality that he aims at.

It is, in fact, the quality of sympathy, a quality that belongs to imagination and poetry, which makes Mr. Collier's portraits at once so lifelike and so pleasant—a quality which involves on the part of the painter the capacity of calling out absolute confidence on the part of the sitter, the half-unconscious response to a call which cannot be resisted. This is, indeed, the great portrait-painter's great art, that, against Hotspur's imputation on Glendower, the spirits *do* come when he does call for them. And for examples of this we cannot do better than consider the portraits of Professor Huxley, the late Mr. Darwin, and Professor Burdon Sanderson. In each the dominant feeling, not unlike in either of the three, and yet individual in each, is brought out with delicate, strong insistence. In each the mere portraiture is admirable, and in each the marked personality of the man is conveyed with a skill as fine as it is incisive. Mr. Burdon Sanderson is represented engaged on a labour connected with the science that he loves, and the enthusiasm, no less than the strength of the attitude and the expression of the face, are represented as no one less than a master of the study of mankind—and what is a portrait-painter without that?—could represent them.

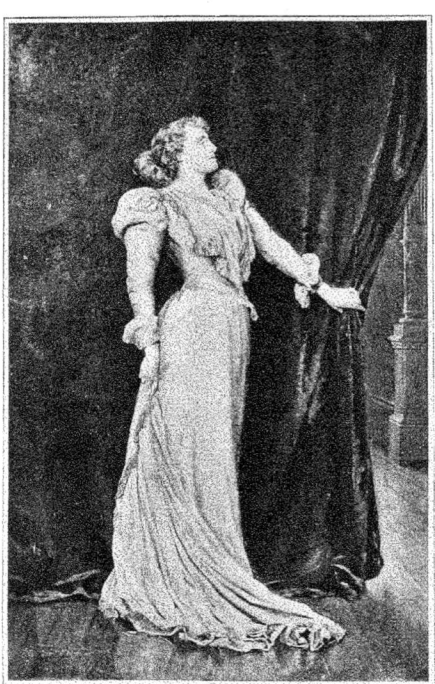

PORTRAIT OF MISS JULIA NEILSON (MRS. F. TERRY).
BY THE HONBLE. JOHN COLLIER.

As I have already said, it is not possible for a man without imagination to paint portraits with so fine a touch and difference, therefore it is not surprising that at a certain period of his career Mr. Collier, as if to give the lie to the critics who were presumptuous enough to accuse him of want of imagination, launched out into a field of imaginative painting exemplified by what are known as figure pictures. One would like to face such a critic with the 'Cleopatra,' a picture on a large scale, compact of study, feeling, imagination, sense of colour and composition—a picture which should have given, had time and circumstances suited, the frontispiece to Mr. Rider Haggard's brilliant, mystical, and entrancing romance concerning the "Serpent of Old Nile." This picture did not perhaps attract "the general" so much as a less intellectual picture might have done, and this for the very reason that Mr. Collier always paints, to paraphrase an old saying, not only with his palette, but also with brains and two other things which do not always go with brains, intellect and research. There is no detail in this fine work that is incorrect, no matter, however seemingly trifling, that has been neglected or for which the painter had not some good authority.

Following in the track of his master in England, Mr. Alma Tadema, Mr. Collier took with excellent result excellent pains as to the pillars, the hangings, the fans—in fact, all the decorations he had to depict. Great art, be it in painting, in writing, in acting, is made up in its absorbing influence by attention to such details as these. But such attention is powerless to command either crowd or critics without what a great Frenchman

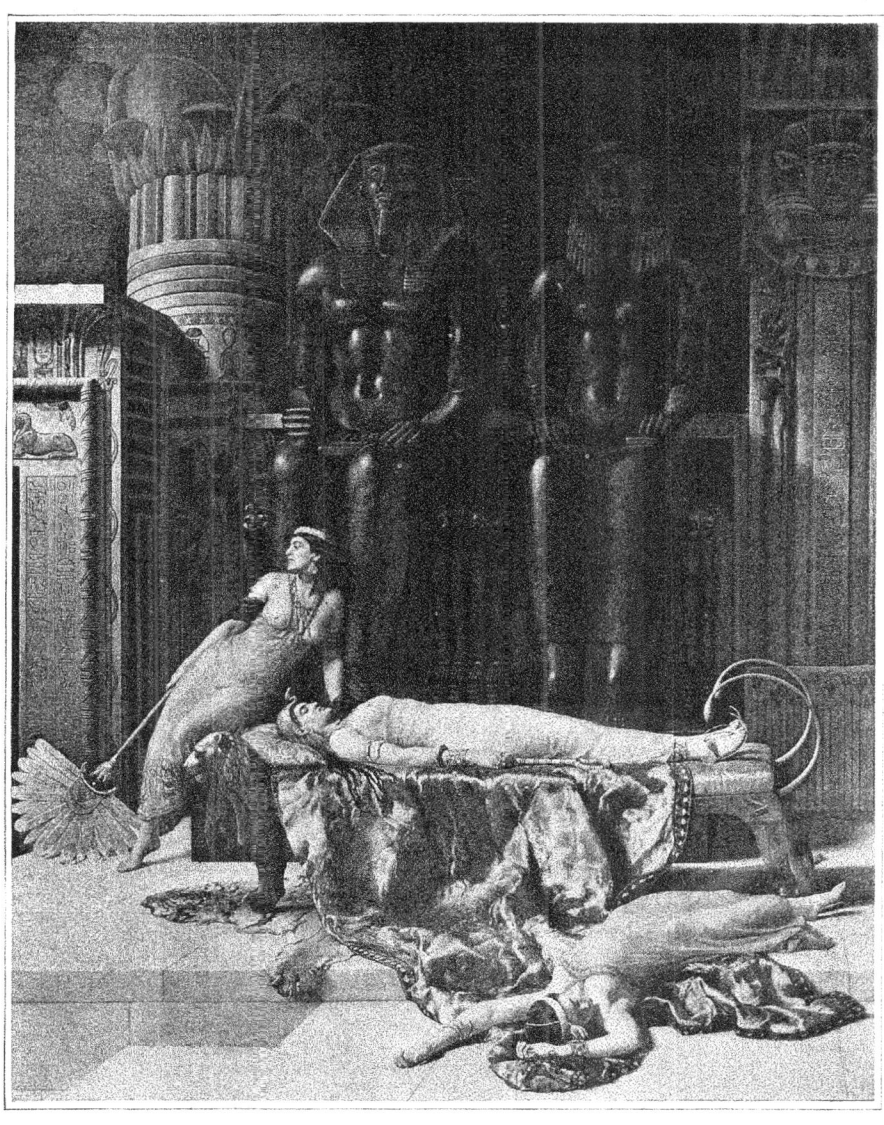

THE DEATH OF CLEOPATRA. FROM THE PAINTING BY THE HONBLE. JOHN COLLIER.

called "that little word *genius*," and that little word is, to my thinking, a very big one in Mr. Collier's dictionary. Genius, indeed, is the only thing which can lightly turn a boy leaving Eton for a mercantile career into the arms of that most jealous mistress, Art. To Art Mr. Collier has been ever faithful. Even when he was an Eton boy his talent for drawing was discovered by those who were in his Tutor's house. When he left the career of commerce he devoted himself with incessant ardour and study to draughtsmanship and to painting, and if ever a man was justified by results for changing his career, that man was Mr. John Collier.

There are some who even yet—and I am sometimes among them—find fault with his scheme of colour in this picture or in that, but no one who has gone through the most elementary studies in what is, in some ways, the noblest of arts, will find it easy to pierce a crevice in the armour of his drawing. And when you compare his first charcoal sketch with his finished picture of the same subject, you will find that the light, firm touch of the first essay has undergone very few changes before taking on the complete canopy of paint. 'Circe' offers a remarkable tribute to the justice of this remark. I happen to have before me the first painted sketch of one of the most characteristic animals in this fine picture, and the only difference between the admirable characterisation of this sketch and that shown in the completed picture lies in the difference of size. For the character of animals Mr. Collier, who loves them as they love him, has an exceptionally keen eye, and in the 'Circe' his knowledge in this regard, cultivated carefully by many visits to the Zoological Gardens, is here as remarkable as the knowledge of flesh colour and its varying tints displayed in the treatment of the figure of Circe herself. This comes out finely in the expression of the huge tiger lying at Circe's right hand—in the mixture of fawning and would-be insolence in the puma at her feet, and in the downright sulks of the panther squatting under the trees in the background, to whom I have already referred. The composition of the picture is not less remarkable than the excellence of the colour-scheme, with which it would be difficult to find any fault. I have just said that I do not always agree with Mr. Collier's colour, and I think the picture in which I like it least is the finely-drawn portrait of Miss Julia Neilson. In this the contrast between the pink of the dress and the red of the background was most daringly imagined, but I must confess that it seemed to me to be rather the vaulting ambition which o'erleaped itself. The colours, as I thought, "swore" horribly, but evidently the artist did not think so, or he would not have used them. And who shall say which of us two is slightly colour-blind? Apart from any difference of opinion as to the colour, there is no room for doubt as to the excellence of the portraiture and the skill of the brushwork. As to another portrait in red, there is likely to be less difference in opinion between critics. I refer to the portrait of the late Mr. Edwin Booth, in the character of Richelieu, a portrait intensely characteristic both of the actor and of the part which he represented. Here, again, the quality of sympathy in Mr. Collier's work plays an important part. He shows you not only the Cardinal, as played by Mr. Booth, but he also gives you an insight into the reasons why Mr. Booth's impersonation was so fine and so commanding.

In another instance Mr. Collier has gone to the drama, but not to the actor, for inspiration. This is in the 'Forest of Arden,' where we have Audrey with Touchstone sitting on a log in the foreground, with a perfectly delightful landscape behind them. To my thinking, however, the landscape is so very much more agreeable and lifelike than the people, that I could heartily wish they had never been put there. Audrey, to be sure, may pass well enough, although she is commonplace, but there was certainly more wit and wisdom in Touchstone than Mr. Collier has chosen to give to this well-painted puppet.

PORTRAIT OF PROF. BURDON SANDERSON. BY THE HONBLE. JOHN COLLIER.

The same qualities of insight, observation, and command, on which I have dwelt, are, as will be seen, noteworthy in the 'Wood Nymph.' This picture is instinct with imagination and grace, and if anyone objects to the expression of the smile, the answer is simple enough—a wood nymph is an elf, and though an elf's smiles are always fascinating, they are not apt to be, in a human sense, agreeable. As to the careless grace and air of life in the figure, they are beyond praise. The same lifelike air, I may note in passing, is constant in Mr. Collier's work, and is especially to be observed in his fine contribution to the last year's Academy, a scene at Cæsar Borgia's table, in which the pictorial and the dramatic perceptions are mixed with admirable effect. The artist's portrait of himself is not a little remarkable. There are many self-portraits, as Mark Twain's delightful

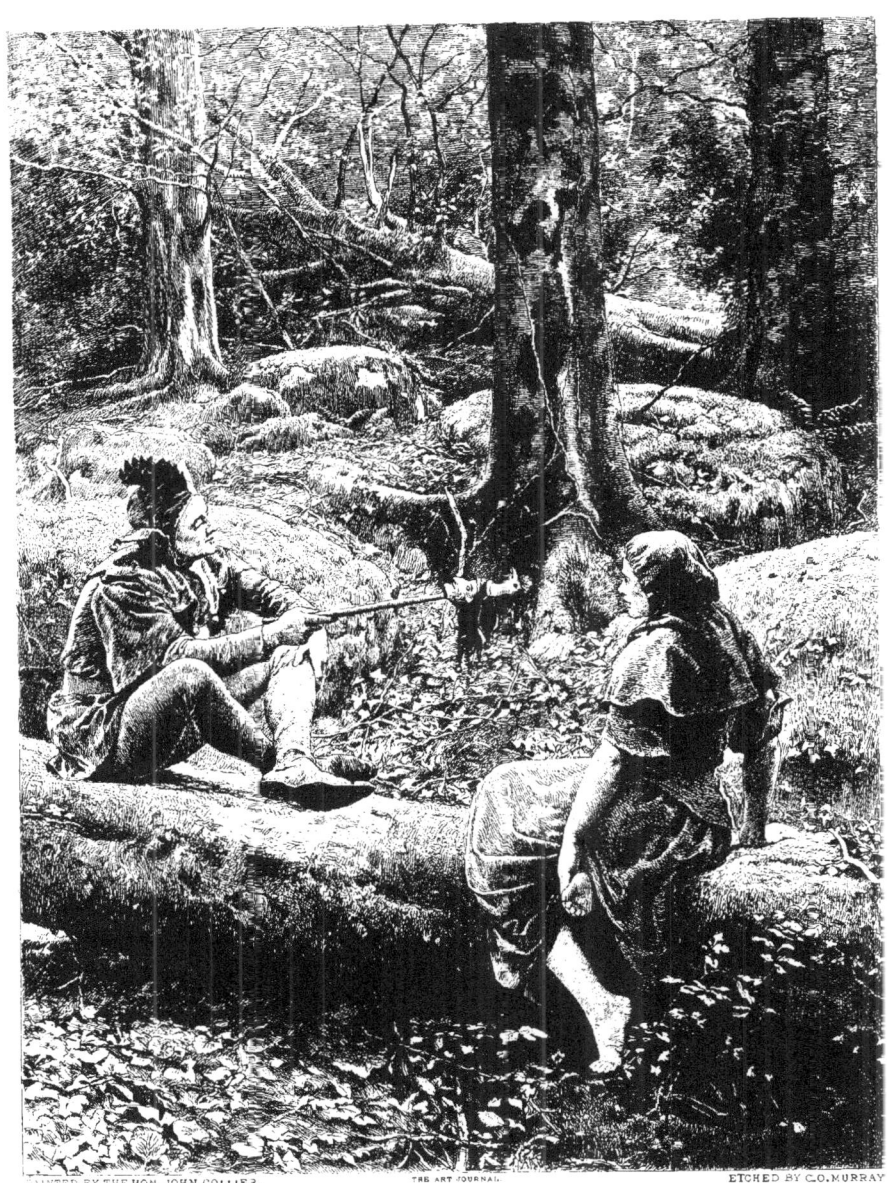

IN THE FOREST OF ARDEN.

catalogue has it, by artists of distinction, but it is not too often that a painter portraying himself hits so truly upon his own liking and seeming, and in doing this Mr. Collier has conferred a favour upon all who know him and his work.

WALTER HERRIES POLLOCK.

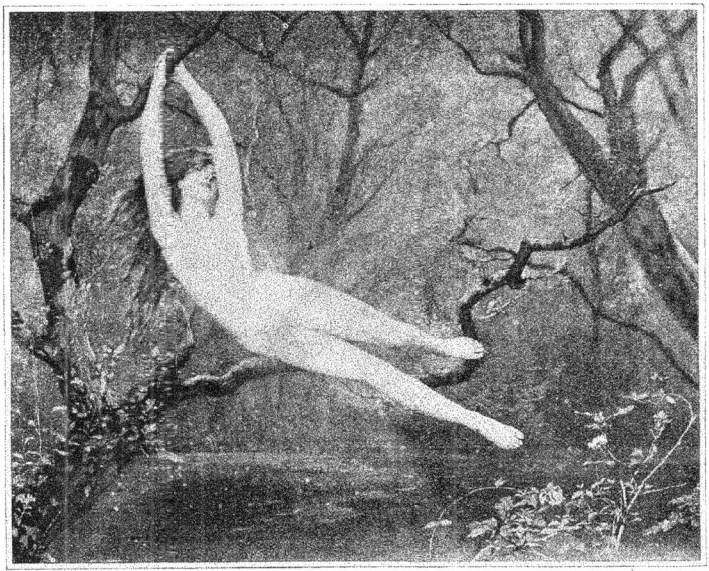

A WOOD NYMPH. FROM A PAINTING BY THE HONBLE. JOHN COLLIER.

IMPORTANT BEQUEST TO SCOTTISH ARTISTS.

BENEFACTIONS on behalf of artists as a class are so few that the munificent bequest to the Royal Scottish Academy, under the title "The Alexander Nasmyth Fund," made by the late Mr. James Nasmyth, the great engineer and inventor of the steam-hammer, deserves special notice. Mr. James Nasmyth was youngest son of Alexander Nasmyth, an artist who was correctly designated in the Scottish Academy's report for 1890 as "the father of Scottish landscape painting." It was from filial affection that the donor at his death, in 1890, left a considerable portion of his estate "for the benefit of decayed Scottish artists," putting the duty of framing rules and administering the fund on the Royal Scottish Academy. The value of the bequest is not yet, we believe, fully realised, as the death of Mr. Nasmyth's widow only took place in October last. But enough has become known of the value of the "sixteen hundredth parts" of his estate bequeathed by Mr. Nasmyth for this object, to show that a most valuable fund has been opened up. Already, under an admirable code of rules framed by the Scottish Academy in 1892, a number of calls have

been considered, and substantial benefit has accrued in necessitous cases. By the rules, those admissible to the benefits must be professional artists, Scotsmen by birth and Art education, or artists who, " by a reasonable length of domicile and practice of their profession in Scotland," shall be considered by the committee to be Scottish artists. Full provision is made for ascertaining the *bonâ-fides* of applicants, one rule laying down that examples of their work must be submitted if desired. The committee administering the fund consists of the President, two Academicians, and two Associates of the Royal Scottish Academy, one of the four selected members retiring each year, while the secretary and treasurer to the Academy act in the same capacities to the Nasmyth Fund. It may be of interest to mention that a handsome monument, from Mr. James Nasmyth's design, forms a conspicuous object in the Dean Cemetery, at Edinburgh, commemorating his mother and his brother, Patrick Nasmyth, the distinguished artist. A monument also adorns his father's burial place in St. Cuthbert's churchyard, Edinburgh.

1894

"MY FEW THINGS."[*]

PART II.

I AM fond of my few French prints of the Eighteenth Century. It is very easy to dispose of them (a common way in England)—the works, I mean, of all that Eighteenth Century School—by calling them light, trifling, even indiscreet in certain of their revelations of a life that seldom aimed to be austere; but, in reality, the prints of the "*Dix-Huitième*" represent all phases of the thoughts and ways of French society—its deeds and its ideals—from the childhood of Louis Quinze to the Revolution; and, if you read French *contes* and comedy, memoir and criticism, these things, from Watteau to Chardin, from Chardin to Fragonard, are their true illustrations. For myself I do but mourn that I have so few of them: not a single Moreau, for instance—not the 'Sortie de l'Opéra,' with the love-letter conveyed in the nosegay, nor 'C'est un Fils, Monsieur!' in which a well-favoured young woman bounces into the library of the fortunate collector, with the news that he is also, as it seems, a parent. The insular pre-Raphaelite speaks of the French Eighteenth Century as "the bad period." Yes, it is "the bad period" to people who are too rigid to grasp its grace. The narrowly learned, as Walter Savage Landor reminds us—"the generality of the learned," he is even severe enough to say—"are apt to conceive that in easy movement there is a want of solidity and strength." Now, "easy movement," a spontaneous elegance, is the very characteristic of the Art of France, as it is of its delightful people; and not to recognise, not to enjoy that, is merely to be under the sway of pedantry, antiquarian or academic. French Eighteenth-Century Art, like Dutch Art of the Seventeenth Century, like the Art of Titian and of Velasquez, reflected Life—much of the charm of Life—and unless it be that Life itself and Beauty have no interest for us, we cannot afford to pass that Art superciliously by.

[* Continued from page 10.]

Wonderfully small, however, is the amount of sympathy that I am privileged to expect from English collectors of the older type in my enjoyment of a sometimes faulty, but an often bewitching, school. A score of French prints, some of them recording the high elegance of Watteau, the pleasant gallantry of Baudouin or Lavreince, the sober homeliness and the grave truth of Chardin (whose lessons were wellnigh Wordsworthian in their way)—these things, which I shall still venture to cherish, are wont to be "sat upon" by the antiquary; much as a certain little table-case of Battersea enamels, dainty and aglow with colour, like flowers on a wintry day (puce and gold and *rose du Barry*, that no time and no winter fades), is "sat upon" by some of my friends who behold indescribable virtues in every product of Japanese design. We have all of us got our limits, I suppose—I remember, though, that in France, two of the men most prominent and influential in their love for the work of their own country in its famous *Dix-Huitième*, had been almost the first to welcome the inventions of the Japanese. These men were Philippe Burty and Edmond de Goncourt — but then, they ignored Rembrandt and Dürer, as far as any practical interest in them was concerned.

The mention of the men brings me once more face to face with two striking personalities. Burty was a critic in journalism and an *Inspecteur des Beaux Arts* besides —an enthusiast, a connoisseur, a real *curieux*. When I knew him he had already done much in France for the popular recognition of Etching. His flat upon an outer boulevard — the Boulevard des Batignolles — told charmingly of the refinement and variety of his tastes. Some *kakemonos* and *tsubas* hung on the walls; but here there was an etching, and there an ivory. And he had a little "*coin de tapisserie*," as he smilingly said, "like Erasmus at the Louvre"—he was thinking of Holbein's picture. In his deep French bookcases, well-bound volumes

SHEET OF STUDIES BY WATTEAU.

were ranged, one row behind and her, and when the glass doors were opened and a few vacant places discovered, his favourite cat—the cat of the literary man, moving with quietude, treading with grace—curved about in the bookcase, sleek and smooth, harmless, careful, and almost appreciative.

One Sunday afternoon, when, I remember, as the result of an accident, we had failed to see Monsieur Zola, Philippe Burty drove me down to Auteuil — to the Villa Montmorency—to spend a couple of hours with Edmond de Goncourt and his treasures. Jules, the beloved brother, was already dead, and Edmond, surrounded by his collections, lived lonely at Auteuil, in the house that had been arranged for both. Stately and distinguished, melancholy, and yet interested, a descendant of the old *noblesse*, with many memories in the dark brown eyes that lay under his silver-grey hair, Edmond de Goncourt moved about amongst his portfolios, saying a word here, and there directing a glance. The history of his life surrounded him—the charming treasures he and his brother had amassed and studied, before the *Dix-Huitième* was fashionable, and very much as a recreation from those "*noires études de la vie contemporaine*"—the words are his own—which had given us *Germinie Lacerteux* and *Manette Salomon*. No such collection of that fascinating French *Dix-Huitième* as belongs to Edmond de Goncourt has ever been made. His *Maison d'un Artiste* is a book which is written for the most part about it, and in comparison with its treasures my humble score of chosen prints—chiefly, after all, by the Eighteenth Century's more serious masters—becomes absolutely insignificant. Still they remind me pleasantly enough of a delightful period, a delightful people, and of an art that was masterly when it was Watteau's, more lightly gracious when it was Pater's, and, when it was Chardin's, was sedate and simple and almost austere.

Sketches in oil or water-colour by Cotman and James Ward, by Thomas Collier and Charles Green, Edwin Hayes and Alfred East, Linton, Fulleylove, Carl Haag and Francis James— I need not finish the list and it would be foreign to the present purpose to enlarge on the men—do something, one may hope,

REMBRANDT'S HEAD AND OTHER STUDIES. ETCHING BY REMBRANDT.

to prevent one's bowing the knee at only a single shrine. But is that indeed my danger?—I, who confess to have felt at times the force of quite another temptation—the temptation to be busy at last in getting together things with which the pictorial Art that I love has nothing to do. A comely little piece or so of "Blue and White," a bit of Worcester with the square mark, a Nantgarw plate, with its 'Billingsley rose,' a plate of Frankenthal—bought in the Corratorie at Geneva, at a shop where, two generations ago, they had sold things of that same fabric to none other than Balzac (who declared, through his *Cousin Pons*, that Frankenthal would one day be as much sought after as Sèvres)— these things, I say, the thin end of the wedge, things that are nothing by themselves, remind me that, in gathering china, Man may be happy. And so a few books — the earliest obtained being the *Lyrical Ballads* of 1798, *relieuse Janséniste*, a green coat by Riviere, and the Rogers with the Turner illustrations, in "original boards," now, alas! disposed to crack—assure me of the charm that must lurk for my luckier brethren in the seriously gathering together of First Editions or of famous ones.

Let us pass to the examples of the Revival of Etching. About forty Méryons, about eighty Whistlers, are mine. The one artist has been much more prolific than the other, and thus, while, as regards Méryon, the possession of even 'forty" prints allows the collector to be fairly well provided for, as regards Whistler, the "eighty" represent scarcely more than a third part of that etcher's catalogued work.* Mr. H. S. Theobald, I think, has more Whistlers than I have; Mr. B. B. Macgeorge, of Glasgow, has, I know, more Méryons; while, of both these masters, distinctly larger collections than my own rest in the hands

---

* Two hundred and fourteen plates had been etched by Mr. Whistler when I compiled my *Whistler's Etchings, a Study and a Catalogue*—in 1886—and Mr. Whistler has been at work since then. It is well, however, to remember that of all these, some are insignificant and many unobtainable. In my *Méryon*—of which Messrs. Deprez and Gutekunst published the Second Edition in 189—I was able to chronicle but ninety-five plates; more than half of which are, from one cause or another, quite unimportant. Thus it will be seen that while a possessor of forty carefully-chosen Méryons has practically finished collecting, a possessor of eighty Whistlers has still some Future—may it even be an eventful one!—of research and acquisition.

of Mr. Samuel P. Avery and of Mr. Howard Mansfield, of New York.

Nearly all the finer plates of Méryon—those in which, to use his own phrase, he "engraved Paris," with a fidelity so affectionate, yet with an imagination so tragic—were wrought between the year 1850 and the year 1854. Bracquemond was the only important figure in the group to whom the Revival of Etching is due, who was working at that time. Whistler, Seymour Haden, Jules Jacquemart, and Legros, were all of them a little later; Whistler's first dated plate—and he was quite among the earliest of these artists—being of the year 1857.

In looking through my Méryons, it interests me to find that a good many that are in my Solander box to-day belonged, long since, to distinguished Frenchmen who were Méryon's contemporaries. Thus a First State of the 'Saint-Etienne-du-Mont' was given by Méryon to Bracquemond. My impressions of the 'Abside' and the 'Stryge' belonged to Aglaüs Bouvenne, who catalogued Bonington, appreciated Méryon, and, in comparatively recent years, wrote some reminiscences of him. A 'Rue des Toiles, à Bourges' has on it Méryon's dedicatory inscription addressed to Hillemacher the painter. A curious proof of the 'Partie de la Cité de Paris,' before the introduction of the towers, which were never really in the actual view, though Méryon chose to see them there, came from the friend of Méryon's youth, a friend who spoke over his grave—M. de Salicis. Some others of the prints have been Philippe Burty's. The final trial proof of the 'Tourelle, dite "de Marat,"' and one or two other subjects, of which I spare the reader the details, were originally bought of Méryon by M. Wasser, a man the public wots not of, but a collector full of character: the "Cousin Pons," I dare to call him, of my own earlier day.

Let me, in a paragraph devoted to himself alone, recall M. Wasset to my memory. An employé—*secrétaire*, it may be—at the Ministry of War, he lived, when I mounted to his flat, one winter's night (how many years ago!) in a dark, winding, narrow street, of the Rive Gauche, between the Seine and St. Sulpice—the Rue Jacob. The Cousin Pons, did I say, this gentleman resembled? But Pons was *gourmet* as well as connoisseur—M. Wasset knew no passion but the collector's. He dined modestly—by subscription, it was understood—at the Café Procope, in the Quarter—was *abonné* for repasts taken there, in a haunt once classic, now dull and cheap. His rooms in the Rue Jacob, low and small, were stuffed full with his collections. *Bric-à-brac* he had, even more than prints: strange beings who dredged in the River brought him ancient jewellery, and Seventeenth-Century watches, that had slept their Rip Van Winkle sleep in the mud of the Seine. I see the venerable collector now, his sombre and crowded rooms lit with a single lamp, and he, passing about, spare, eager, and trembling, with bowed figure; garrulous, excited as with wine, by the mere sight and handling of his accumulated possessions. A few years afterwards—urged thereto by the greatest of Parisian print-sellers, M. Clément, who is now no more—he had a sale, in the Rue Drouot, of his hundreds of prints, of which the Méryons, of course, formed but a small part. Other treasures—then ardently desired—he was to purchase with the proceeds. Is his heart, one wonders, with those treasures now—in the dark Paris street? Or, the hands that trembled so, fifteen years since—have they relaxed their hold, for ever, of the things that were meat and drink, that were wife and child to him?

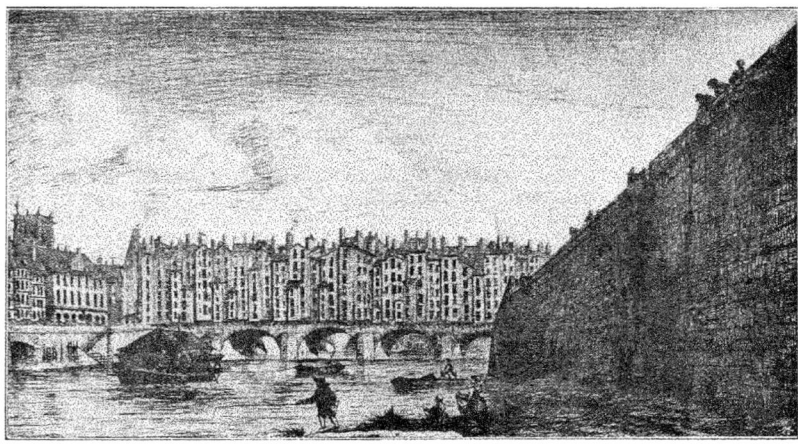

Méryon's 'Pont-au-Change vers 1784.' From a Proof 'before the Great Rope.'

Méryon, I remember, took me by storm as a great artistic personality, and, since he conquered me immediately, I have always been faithful to him. In that there is no sort of virtue; for has he not become, thus early, almost everywhere, where prints are loved, an accepted classic? To appreciate Whistler

—even at all to enjoy him—requires a longer education. There are even some things that at first one resents. A touch of charlatanry lurks, one at first supposes, in the Bond Street "arrangement in yellow and white," and in the *velarium* under which we were invited to gather when the master held in the work of both. But by what different measures has it been maintained! Whistler, in so much of his work, has shown himself the flexible, vivacious, and consummate sketcher, the artist whose choice of economical and telling "line" is faultless and perhaps well-nigh immediate. Méryon, upon the

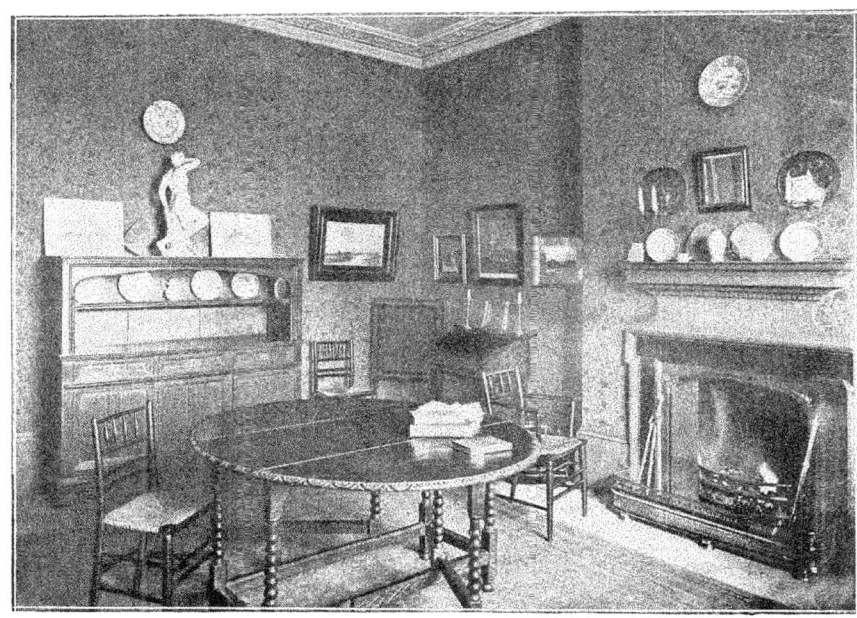

THE DINING ROOM.

sway in Suffolk Street. But, in time, that impression passes. Then, one accepts the man whole—takes him as he is—genius like his has a certain license to be abnormal. And though it pleases Mr. Whistler, or sundry catalogues and joyous little books about "the art of making enemies," to represent from time to time that I, among a hundred others, do not appreciate him, that is only because he would have us believe he is a victim to the interesting monomania of persecution, and I, forsooth, when this is his mood, am called upon to figure as one of those who would pursue him. Peace! peace! Now that he has "done battering at England" (I will not vouch precisely for the phrase), I am, it seems, an "enemy" no more. So much the better!

I take it, he and Méryon are quite the greatest of the etchers this century has seen, and if so (since of great true etchers, the Eighteenth Century was barren), they are the greatest since the days of Claude and Rembrandt. To no one who has studied any group of their plates for a single quarter of an hour, can it be necessary to insist upon the essential unlikeness of these two remarkable men. Unity of impression —almost a test of excellence, the one note dominant, the rest subordinated—that is found, I know, and found almost equally,

1894

other hand, has been remarkable for building up, with learned patience worthy of Albert Dürer, little by little his effects, so that when the thing is done, and that sombre vision of his has become a realised performance, he has not so much made a drawing upon a plate as erected a monument (for so it strikes one) from base to coping-stone. Such work has at least the permanence of the very monuments it records. An "*œuvre de longue haleine*"—a task severe and protracted—is each one of his important coppers. Yet all the length of Méryon's labour witnesses to no relaxing hold of his first thought, and in the great complexity of ordered line there is revealed no superfluous, no irrsignificant stroke.

Each mar is discovered in his work. In Méryon's 'Abside' say, in the 'Pont Neuf,' in the 'Saint-Etienne-du-Mont,' is his brooding spirit, his patient craftsmanship, his temperament intense and profound.* He was poor, he was often weary, he spent himself on his work. In Whistler's

---

* I choose fo sole illustration of his work, in this place, one of the smaller of his plates, and a plate not original. I choose it for two reasons—first because i is less known than many of the others, even to people not wholly without interes in Méryon's work; and, again, because it shows that even when working professedly from an old-world drawing, he was bound to put into any record of Pari something of the spirit that was his own. But of course I am not under the impression that it can represent adequately his noble vision.

U

'Garden,' in his 'Piazzetta,' in his 'Florence Leyland,' in the 'Large Pool,' in that wonderful tiny thing, 'The Fruit Shop,' there is the boyish freshness, the spirit of enjoyment which he has known how to preserve till the present time. Whistler has never been tired, or, if he has, he and his work have parted company at the very moment. Wonderful as is his gift of observation and handling, his plates are a lark's song. As you see the man before you, elastic, joyous, slim, and *débonnair*, having never known the heavy and sad wisdom of our modern youth, nor the cares of our middle age, his appearance almost persuades you that all his exquisite craftsmanship, practised now for nearly forty years, is but the blameless re-creation of an hour snatched from life's severer tasks—the task of sipping duly, *à l'heure de l'absinthe*, one's *aperitif* on the Boulevard; of pulling on the River in the long June days; of condensing every rule of life into perhaps three epigrams effective at a London dinner-party. Who would not envy this possessor of a craft fantastic, airy, and immortal! Though Mr. Whistler may entertainingly insinuate that long life has been denied to his friendships, he will agree with me, I know, when I assert that it is secured to his etchings.

That my print-drawers contain but four or five etchings by Mr. Seymour Haden is at once my misfortune and my reproach. As one looks at them one conjures up visions of byegone sales at Sotheby's, when as yet Mr. Wilkinson, benign and aged, sat in the chair to wield the ivory hammer—what opportunities neglected, of which the more diligent have availed themselves! For I cannot accept Mr. Haden's too modest estimate of the value of his own work. Labour so energetic and decisive is not destined to be prized by one generation alone, and in estimating it comparatively lightly, his connoisseurship, accurate enough when it is concerned with Claude and Rembrandt, Méryon and Whistler—all of whom, in his time, he has collected seriously—is for once at fault.

I am somewhat poor again in those etchings which are the creation of the austere genius of Legros. Popular they will never be, for Mr. Legros is almost alone among men of genius in not belonging to his own day—in receiving well-nigh no influence from the actual hour. He is a belated Old Master—but a "master" always: never an affected copyist, who pranks "in faded antique dress." Had he but humoured the affectations of the time, it is quite possible that the time would at all events have talked about him, and, denied actual popularity, he might yet have been solaced by an æsthetic coterie's hysterical admiration. But that has not been for Legros. As it is, with his gravely whispered message, his general reticence, his overmastering sense of Style, his indifference to attractive truths of detail, his scorn of the merely clever, he is placed at a disadvantage. But his work remains; not only the etchings, of which Messieurs Thibaudeau and Poulet-Malassis catalogued a hundred and sixty-eight as long ago as 1877, but the grave pictures in which the peasant of the Boulognais devoutly worships, or in which the painted landscape is as the landscape of a dream, and the vigorous oil portraits—not one of which, perhaps, reaches the nobility of his etched portrait of Watts—and the pencil drawings of the nude, several of which Legros has given to the Museum of his birthplace, Dijon, where the stray Englishman who stays to look at them finds that they are just as finely severe as are the pencil drawings of Ingres. I have his one big etching, 'La Mort du Vagabond'—the scale too large to be effective generally, but, *pace* Mr. Whistler, I do not, in this case, find it "an offence,"*—and amongst others, two that have, it may be, no particular rarity, but that are worthily, and I think even exceptionally, characteristic. The one is 'La Communion dans l'Eglise Saint-Medard:' in line and in feeling an instance of the most dignified treatment of ecclesiastical function or religious office. And the other is 'Les Chantres Espagnols,' the singers, aged and decayed, eight of them, in a darkened choir—was ever a vision of narrow and of saddened lives more serious or more penetrating!

From these it is sometimes a relief to turn to Jacquemart's etchings of still-life. The man himself had troubles: not difficulties about money, nor, like Méryon, the knowledge that he was little appreciated—for appreciation came to him early—but lack of health during years that should have been vigorous, and a compulsory flight towards the sunshine, which yet did not appreciably lessen the distance that divided him from Death. But his work, from end to end, in its serene and deliberate accomplishment, suggests no chances and changes, no personal emotion, and even no actual experience of human life. One says at first, it might have been done at any period; then one recognises perhaps what one may call a modern feeling for the object portrayed; then one thinks of Hollar's 'Five Muffs,' and of Rembrandt's 'Shell,' and remembers that both have a freedom, a delicate skill, akin, after all, to the skill and the freedom in the etchings of Jacquemart. Of Jacquemart's two great series, the prints for his father's 'Histoire de la Porcelaine' and those of the 'Gemmes et Joyaux de la Couronne,' I possess only the first, and these in book form, as they were sent me by Madame Techener, the widow of Jacquemart's publisher and friend. In a simple russet-coloured half-binding, done afterwards by Zaehnsdorf, they stand on a shelf I often go to. Elsewhere are such proofs of Jacquemart etchings as the occasional good fortune of auction rooms—snatched in a spare half-hour—has brought to a life-long lover of engravings. There is a certain plate of sword-handles and daggers—things, some of them, that "rend and rip"—

"Gash rough, slash smooth, help Hate so many ways,
Yet ever keep a beauty that betrays
Love still at work with the artificer, through all his quaint devising—"

as Mr. Browning wrote, describing weapons that lay, as one remembers, at peace at last, on his own drawing-room table. How Jacquemart etched such blades! By this there is another plate of a Seventeenth-Century watch—just such a one as I said used to be fished for old Monsieur Wasset from the bed of the Seine—and with it a Renaissance jewel; and elsewhere, perhaps, a carved mirror, or a bit of Valenciennes porcelain.

Allow me a reflection. The cheapest way of enjoying *objets d'art* is to enjoy them in etchings, and it is often the easiest way, since you have but to sit in your chair and look, and it is often not the least true, since the etcher himself has seen with a trained eye before the trained hand came to draw. Well, to enjoy *objets d'art* in that fashion with tolerable completeness and extreme satisfaction, the intelligent poor man has really but to get the two chief series of Jacquemarts (those that are still lacking to me, the 'Gemmes et Joyaux de la Couronne,' are, I know Seymour Haden would tell me, the bigger, broader, richer, more spontaneous of the two), and those fifty plates by different etchers, of whom Courtry, Greux, and Le Rat were among the principal, which Holloway's

---

* ", The huge plate," writes Mr. Whistler—on the whole truthfully—'the huge plate is an offence: its undertaking an unbecoming display of determination and ignorance, its accomplishment a triumph of unthinking earnestness and controlled energy."

published about a score of years since, "Works of Art in the Collections of England." In that excellent volume in folio, the men who have just been mentioned, and several others, followed hard on Jacquemart's heels. What a treatment of jade in some of those plates! Mr. Addington's vase in particular. What a treatment of *cristal de roche!* Desgoffe's painted panel at the Luxembourg is only a little finer. What a treatment of ivory!—that extraordinary Moorish casket, I mean, that was Malcolm of Foltalloch's.

But this is only copyist's etching, some people may say. "Copyists"—No! You would not enjoy it so much were it merely servile imitation. It is interpretation, significant and spirited.

Of the original etchers of the younger school in England, Frank Short and William Strang have long seemed to me the most interesting, notwithstanding the as yet somewhat marked limitations of theme of the one, and that possessing "devil" of the love of ugliness which I have now almost ceased to hope may be exorcised from the other. Strang, for all the presence of that which is repulsive to many, is a man of great qualities. A Celt to the depths of him, he is even wildly imaginative. He is dramatic, and his prints are dramatic, however much he may profess to be busy with line and tone. Besides, there are moments in which he confesses to being a poet. He has the instinct of tragedy. Technically, his etchings are almost invariably good; nor is it, to my mind, a sin in them that so many of them set you thinking. I have but a few of Mr. Strang's prints; of Frank Short's I have more, and when he can interpret a Dewint like that 'Road in Yorkshire,' and a Constable like that sketch of Mr. Vaughan's, I see no reason for not putting those mezzotints—interpretations so brilliant, translations so faithful yet so free—by the side of his work in Etching, inspired not by familiarity with the art of another, but by the presence of charming line or charming vista in Nature. Short in his original work is a most delicate draughtsman of form in landscape; 'Evening, Bosham,' and 'Sleeping till the Flood,' sufficiently show it.

Of another good man, Mr. C. J. Watson, I have not enough to judge him quite at my case; but he is a sterling etcher, distinctly gifted, and quite without artifice and trick. An actually imaginative vision one may not perhaps ask of him, but mental flexibility—can he but cultivate it—will enable him to go far and to last long. 'Profil de Jeune Fille,' a somewhat rare dry-point by M. Helleu, has, it seems to me, like much of the work by that most modern of Parisian pastellists and etchers, a delightful spontaneity, and force and freedom. My gossip stops. Grant me only the grace of one more line in which to avow the satisfaction with which, even after having enjoyed the companionship of at least some little work that is admittedly classic, I can look upon the prints of Mr. Charles Holroyd, the young etcher of our latest day. In them so much of what is generally, and often even rightly, seductive, is frankly abandoned, that they may keep unimpaired at least the distinction and reticence which are the very soul of Style.

FREDERICK WEDMORE.

A PHASE OF SCOTTISH ART.

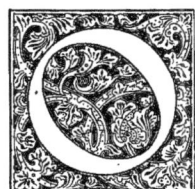

ONE of the most interesting phases of contemporary Art in this country has been the gathering together, in groups, of artists in whose work some special æsthetic motive predominates. England has given us the Newlyn men and the London Impressionists, Scotland the Glasgow School; and widely separated as are the places from which they have taken or been given their distinctive names, their art found for some time common meeting-ground in the rooms of the New English Art Club. First, the Newlyners, finding acceptance at the Academy, deserted, and now the Scots, to whom other channels of exhibition have opened, do not contribute so largely as is desirable; for the club, despite many an affectation, was the rallying point for not a few of the most talented of the younger men. Of these three groups the so-called Glasgow School, because of the greater complexity of its artistic motive, has been least understood and most misrepresented.

The Newlyn picture is but the lineal descendant of the anecdotal picture that has been the delight of the British public for so many generations; the problems of values and of technique are tackled in the modern manner, and with the greater power a more thorough training gives, but the point of view is essentially that of the popular genre painter, and easily understood, the sentiment is cheap, the material familiar, and the manner meretriciously inoffensive. The London Impressionists, on the other hand, are frankly at war with convention, and exceeding anxious to prove themselves original; a serious error, when the past has left so much accomplished and glorious achievement on which to build. Too often it results in the eccentric rather than the beautiful, but there is a freshness in the standpoint—although it be influenced by Manet and Monet—and a striving after more adequate and suggestive means of expression, that are refreshing in an atmosphere of smug respectability and effete convention.

In France the term "Impressionism" includes both a point of view and a method of expression; it means the impersonal record of visual impression, the effect of light and the movement of coloured masses rendered in the strongest, most concise, and expressive terms. In this country the method is usually confounded with the point of view, for like every method the impressionistic may be used for the expression of widely different artistic motives. The London Impressionists are so in the French sense, but the Glasgow men, to whom the term is also applied, are not. They use the method, which they need not have left their own country to acquire, for Mr. McTaggart, before impressionism as a thing *per se* was even heard of in Scotland, had evolved a style for the expression of his individual and very beautiful conception of nature, which exceeds in vividness and suggestion that formed by the French masters, but they use it as he does for the manifestation of personal feeling. In Art it is the personal and imaginative idea of facts that we desire and prize, the cataloguing of them is the province of science; the function of Art is the transfiguration of material by temperament, and the special temperament of the artist is the atmosphere through which we see nature transfigured. Mr. McTaggart's art has not, however, been without influence, although, owing to the

the groundwork for their more realistic and impressionistic art.

Decorative treatment, such as is appropriate to a panel, is not always suitable for a canvas encircled by a frame, and hung on *any* wall. A picture, like Mr. Hornel's 'Summer,' lately bought after "an artistic storm in a tea-cup" by the Liverpool Corporation, and reproduced over-leaf, is hardly on the great high-road of art, in the line of the great achievements in oil-paint; it holds much the same relation to these that exotic verse, the ballad or rondeau, bears to the greater forms of poetry. But looking on it as a decorative panel, having 'Summer' for subject, it yields a great deal of pleasure. The wealth of colour alone would justify its existence, and when we add to that, charm of rhythmic line, fanciful invention, and a certain element of fun and frolic, we are almost willing to forgive the mosaic-like surface and the somewhat archaic design. The fonts of inspiration from which Messrs. Henry and Hornel have drawn are not difficult to trace, but it is in the blending of them that the personality of the artists appears. In an age so complex as ours, Art cannot fail to be eclectic. The impulse from the East is clear, but the convention and the material are used not with the reticence and frugality of the Japanese, but with the profusion of the Gothic temper, to which the grotesqueness of the figures is also due; a certain element of mysticism is, perhaps, traceable to the influence of Matthew Maris, while the colour is reminiscent of the far subtler harmonies of Monticelli. A

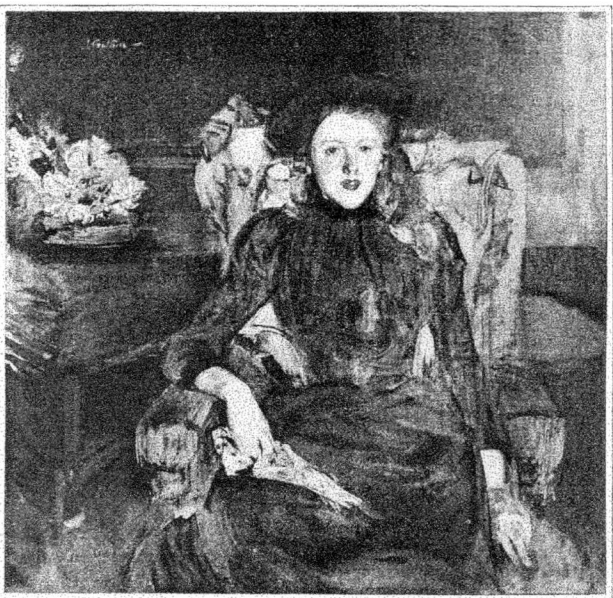

PORTRAIT. BY JAMES GUTHRIE, R.S.A.

preference for low tone that is characteristic of the school, and not always used with discretion, it is not apparent on the surface. But the most powerful individual factor in the formation of their artistic aims and technical methods has been the genius of Mr. Whistler. Through it they are linked to what is greatest in the Art of the past, and most beautiful in the decorations of the East. Happy, too, was the inspiration that early turned the eyes of these young painters toward the wonderful work of the Barbizon School.

The public with customary exaggeration has seized on the pictures of Messrs. Henry and Hornel as typical of the group, and to a certain extent it is right, for a frank acceptance of decoration as the basis of picture-making is the distinctive feature of the Glasgow School. This preoccupation with decorative effect is most obvious in the work of the two painters named, but all the others use it, more or less, as

later picture by Mr. Hornel, 'Springtime,' has similar faults and good qualities, and confirms the impression that he has not yet fully assimilated the influences under which he is working. In this larger canvas, too, one may notice, what was not quite so much in evidence in the other, a want of agreement in the treatment of the figures and the landscape; for while the latter has been rendered with the flatness appropriate to decoration, the former are modelled as if in atmosphere.

Mr. George Henry's best-known picture is the much-discussed 'Galloway Landscape.' To judge this landscape from the usual pictorial standpoint is to do violence to the liberty of the artist and to his intention, which evidently has not been to reproduce Nature, but to use her as material for the decoration of a space; and as a decoration it seems to me very successful indeed. All the elements in it, the fields, the cattle, and the sky, have alike undergone transformation in the painter's mind, and appear upon the canvas with the unity and charm of a clear, poetic conception. Mr. Henry is not always so successful; in an 'Ayrshire Landscape,' painted the following year, he fell, like his fellow, between the stools of pure decoration and realism. A very striking portrait, 'Mademoiselle,' shown in the last Glasgow Institute, marks a considerable departure in style, being much more realistic than any of his previous work. It is splendidly, almost brutally, strong in handling and colour, a little bizarre, perhaps, and certainly a trifle vulgar; but had the drawing been better, and the treatment more restrained, it would have been a triumph; as it is, it is a *tour de force*. But of all Mr. Henry's work, 'Poppies,' a little canvas on which he had painted four rosy children's heads above a bank of scarlet poppies, lingers in my memory as the most fascinating. Messrs. Henry and Hornel have gone for a lengthened stay in Japan, and it will be interesting to watch the effect of their visit in their pictures.

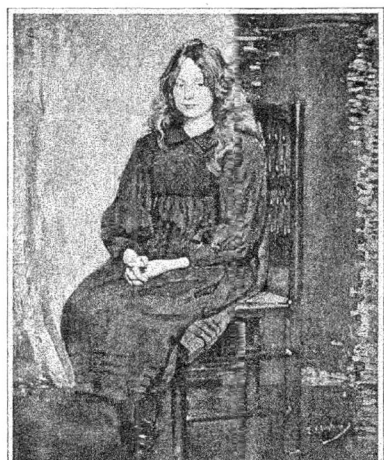

PORTRAIT. By E. A. WALTON, A.R.S A.
IN THE POSSESSION OF MR. ROWAT, PAISLEY.

Greater spontaneity and artistic reserve, a more distinguished and refined sense of style, and a more dignified conception of art and life, are the qualities that separate the pictures of Mr. Guthrie, Mr. Walton, and some others from those we have been considering. Even in this second portion of the School there is difference, one section inclining to impressionism, the other toward more personal revelation; but underlying all there is the ever-present preoccupation with decoration, with the arrangement of the selected material in such a way as to fill the space beautifully and give the greatest pleasure to the eye.

Mr. James Guthrie's diploma picture, 'Midsummer,' is an admirable example of the impressionistic inclination. Embowered in the cool greenness of wavering tree shadows, three girls sit drinking afternoon tea; the sunshine filters through the leaves, and falls in flickering flakes of light upon them, and farther off floods the lawn with light. Mr. John Sargent has painted kindred themes, but never with such mastery as Mr. Guthrie here displays; the American painter's handling is thin, his colour crude, when compared with this. Some of Mr. Guthrie's finest pictures have been of children, but beautiful though they are in delicate and just observation, there is a lack of that intense personal sympathy which gives such charm to a Mason or a McTaggart. This note of impersonality is rarely present in his portraits, which, as a rule, display a fine grasp of character; the portrait of Dr. Gardiner remains to me a notable achievement; but his later work, the Miss Spencer, the Miss Wilson, or the Mr. Ritchie, has an exquisiteness not to be found in his earlier pictures. They are decorative in the same sense that Velasquez and Rembrandt are so, not because the painter used his sitter as material for a decoration, but

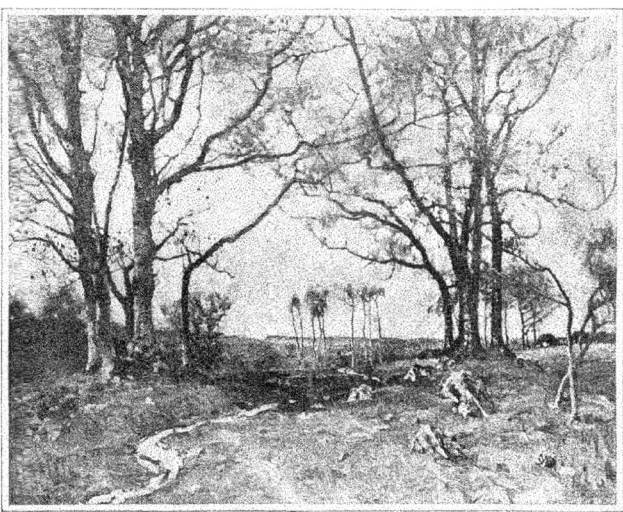

SPRING'S DELAY. BY JAMES PATERSON, R.S.W.

because, being a true artist, he could not fail to place his subject so as to decorate the canvas beautifully. In addition to his work in oils Mr. Guthrie has produced a number of pastels, which display a wonderful sense of the possibilities and limitations of the medium. A very delightful characteristic is the frugality with which the material of expression is used; in some of them more of the ground is left untouched than what is worked on; but this is half the battle, and only to be won by the rarest taste and judgment. There is something exceedingly fascinating in many of these studies of every-day life; it may be some navvies at their work, a group of people on Helensburgh Esplanade at sunset time, or a girl in the latest fashion; but each is vital in virtue of fine technique and keen observation. No Glasgow painter has had so many successes as Mr. Guthrie; his technique is always admirable, and often masterly, his sense of what goes to make the picture unfailing, and his colour almost invariably fine.

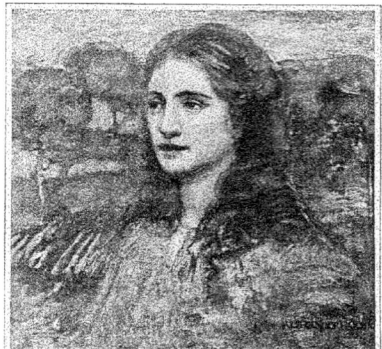

GIRL'S HEAD. BY ALEXANDER ROCHE, A.R.S.A.

Mr. John Lavery, like Mr. Guthrie, has painted contemporary life; he has given us his impressions of 'Croquet' (illustrated on the page opposite), of a 'Tennis Match,' and of a day on the river, recorded his observations at that popular resort, an international exhibition, commemorated a great regal and municipal ceremony, and painted many good portraits. The realism of some of these pictures is very great, and gives a vivid impression of nature uncoloured by personal interpretation; but charming though they are in perfect modernity of treatment and subject, Mr. Lavery's most beautiful work has had far different inspiration. The 'Ariadne,' which we reproduce, is a lovely decoration founded on an old-world story; the 'Queen Mary' picture stirred visions of twilight woods and mysterious dawn, and awakened memories of the fateful story of the fair unfortunate, with its glamour of beauty and romance of war. Mr. Lavery has a facile technique; he seems to paint without difficulty, and his colour has often an exquisite quality of tender grey; but occasionally the facility comes perilously near flimsiness, and the colour is then apt to be a little unsympathetic.

In Mr. Walton's, Mr. Roche's, and Mr. Paterson's pictures the personal element fully reappears. Some of Mr. Walton's finest work has been portraiture, and no one who saw his 'Girl in Brown' can have forgotten its dignified design, subtle modelling, rich colour, and masterly workmanship, or the sweetness and naiveté of girlhood expressed in face and figure. A very noticeable thing in this artist's portraits is the beautiful way in which the hands are treated; they are drawn and modelled as if he loved to paint them, and often add very considerably to the character expression. In landscape Mr. Walton's favourite colour scheme appears to be green and blue; do the names not suggest summer and the country? One of them often comes back to me; I do not remember what he called it—indeed, it never occurred to me to ask. It was not so much the recorded beauty of a particular spot, as an epitome of the charms of meadow landscape, the luxurious softness of green grass, the quiver and shiver of willows, the overarching blue sky, the perfect calm and serene silence of a summer day, unbroken save by the munching of the red and white cattle lying in the shade. At another time into such a scene he will introduce two children, girl and boy, day-dreaming, and one feels that they too live in "one of those heavenly days" that Wordsworth immortalised in "Nutting." In such a mood the artist seems to be absorbed by nature, to pass into her secret being, whence emerging he is able to give us a more beautiful, significant, and inclusive record of her

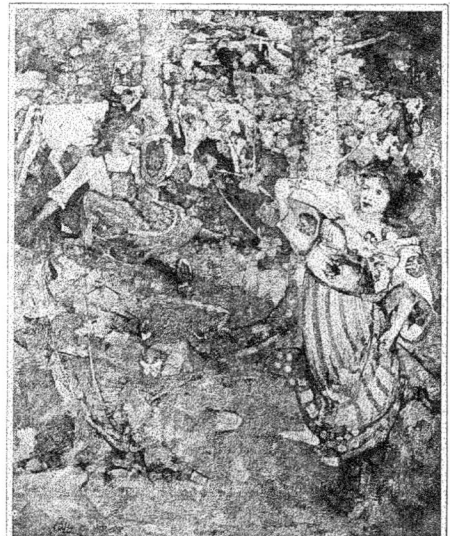

SUMMER. BY E. A. HORNEL. IN THE POSSESSION OF THE CORPORATION OF LIVERPOOL.

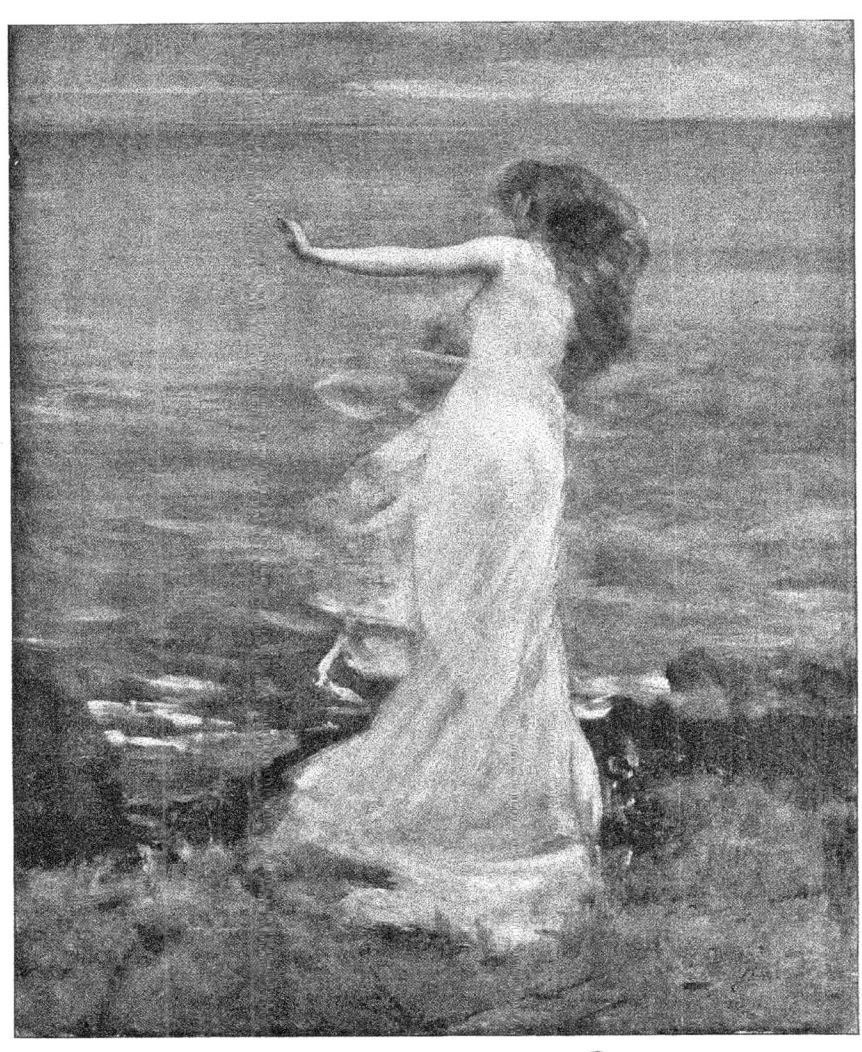

ARIADNE
BY JOHN LAVERY, A.R.S.A.
From the picture in the Collection of R. Strathearn, Esq., W.S., Edinburgh.

charms. If it is not always so with Mr. Walton, it is not infrequent, and the mood may be said to be habitual to his work in water-colour. The subjects of these drawings are often of the slightest, but they are conceived so poetically, and chosen with so fine a regard for the qualities of the medium, that they possess an unfailing note of distinction. The most striking qualities in Mr. Alexander Roche's pictures are a quaint and decidedly romantic element in the informing sentiment, an exceptional grasp of the material aspects of nature, and technically an exquisiteness of handling and of surface that are very delightful. The spirit of the woodland has been imprisoned in some, the charms of the riverside in others; now and then we are given a glimpse of girls in a garden, and occasionally of some charming interior; but in all there is a genuinely poetic strain, a combination of the sensuous beauty and colour that pervade the verse of Keats, and the fervid earth-worship that inspires Mr. Meredith's

tender melancholy. He leads you by shallow streamlets, fringed with alders and mirroring the blue sky in tranquil pools, to quiet woodland places where he reveals the beauty of 'Spring's Delay,' of which we give an illustration, or in more gladsome mood carries you to some happy valley amongst the green sheep-hills of Nithsdale. Many of his most beautiful pictures are in water-colour, of which Mr. Paterson has wonderful command, but in both mediums there is sometimes a tendency to vagueness without compensating suggestion.

Much of Mr. W. Y. Macgregor's finest work has also been in water-colour. In his pictures justness of tone, delicacy and breadth of handling, and a charming quality of pensive colour are conspicuous. The misfortune of delicate health, which has often sent him abroad, has had one compensating feature, in that it has enabled him to give us stay-at-homes vivid and suggestive glimpses of foreign lands and strange

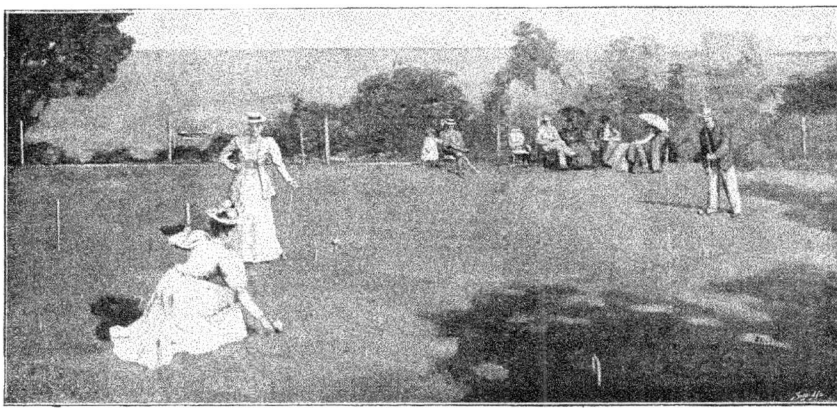

CROQUET. FROM THE PORTRAIT-PICTURE BY JOHN LAVERY, A.R.S.A. NOW IN THE GRAFTON GALLERY.

nature poetry, joined in his best work to a quaintness that is quite mediæval in flavour. Such is the feeling in that picture of the 'Shepherdess' kneeling at the foot of a tree-clad bank on which her sheep are feeding, whilst the moon rises solemnly behind the stems, and nature seems to listen with the child to the moon's wondrous story. In 'Springtime' the measure is sprightlier, the pensiveness of autumn and coming night are exchanged for the promise of the opening year, pictured in the freshness and beauty of the girl with the handful of blossoms, and mirrored in the landscape beyond. Both Mr. Walton's and Mr. Roche's pictures give expression to the joy of life, the delight in beauty, the pleasure in work and fine craftsmanship, and in both poetic conception is wedded to essential truth to nature.

Mr. James Paterson's work is always notable for marked individuality, distinguished style, and charming decorative effect; sylvan and pastoral scenery are his themes, autumn or early spring ere the delicate green begins to appear his chosen season, for his best-loved colour is a harmony of blue and brown, of a tone sombre but never sad, only touched with

peoples. But Mr. Macgregor has other claims to attention than the undoubted merit of his work, for, from the very inception of the movement, he has exercised a stimulating and formative influence on his fellows, which has determined in no small degree the course of art development in the West of Scotland.

Amongst more recent recruits Mr. D. Y. Cameron is certainly the ablest. He is already known as an etcher whose work possesses fine technical and artistic qualities. Always appreciative of the value and beauty of the acid-bitten line, his work, at first somewhat hard and wiry, has gradually acquired greater freedom, and in his latest plates, a series of Dutch subjects, it is characterized by great charm and variety of expressive power. As a painter Mr. Cameron has also made great progress, several portraits of girls exhibited at a recent Institute being very charming indeed.

Of Mr. Millie Dow's decorative floral pictures, of Mr. William Kennedy's vivid records of military life, of Mr. Macaulay Stevenson's twilights, of Mr. David Gauld's comparatively little known but very beautiful designs and pictures, and of other work by other men I should have liked to have written, but enough has been said to show the leading characteristics of the picture that comes from the city on the Clyde. Several names, Mr. Crawhall's and Mr. Arthur Melville's amongst others, have been closely associated with the group, but for various reasons their work hardly comes within the scope of this article. Of the host of imitators that the recognition of the school has called into existence the less said the better. They follow but do not understand, they imitate (very badly) the manner, and miss the matter altogether, but this harm they have done; it is not small, but time shall surely mend it: their work has perhaps hindered the appreciation and acceptance of the really fine qualities of the school, as it has formed the ground from which the Philistine might make his mud-pellets.

One is doubtful if any body of painters, whose work exhibits so great a variety of moods, can properly be called a "School"; still, as I have pointed out, certain characteristics are common to all, and when we for convenience speak of the "Glasgow School," let it be understood that it is because the common ground of its art is personal emotion, expressed in impressionistic manner and on a decorative basis. As a rule they are fine colourists, the colour glows through sober tone, like sacred fire amid a cloud of incense, and in the best of their pictures technique and conception seem inseparable; the painting is unconsciously fine rather than finely conscious, and rarely exists for mere idle display.

I have refrained from writing of them as men; I have even abstained from entering into the history of their technical training, for with these the critic has very little concern, his business being with the achievement, and not with the circumstances under which it has been produced. Much that seems at present most novel and interesting in the work of the Glasgow School may prove of ephemeral value, but there will still remain in many of the pictures these two qualities that alone give art work enduring charm, vitality of thought and beauty of expression.

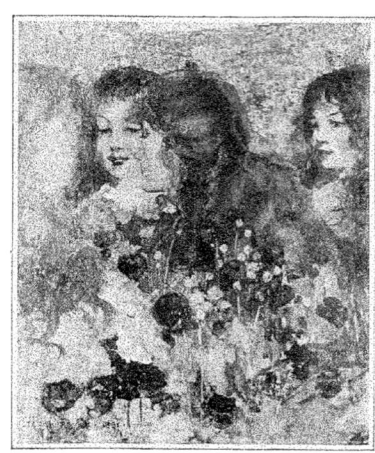

POPPIES. BY GEORGE HENRY, A.R.S.A.
IN THE POSSESSION OF WILLIAM WILSON, ESQ., PAISLEY.

JAMES L. CAW.

THOMAS WOOLNER, R A.

A<small>T</small> Hadley, in Suffolk—a comely little, but now somewhat decayed town upon the Bret, which is a branch of the Stour, and from King Edward's time until the Civil War had half ruined all manufactures of the sort in that region an important centre of wool-growing and the wool-weavers' craft, —was born, on the 17th of December, 1825, the sculptor who produced a very considerable proportion of the finest statues and busts we English can be proud of. It is an artistic region, well known to admirers of Gainsborough, Constable, Stark, and Crome; rich in streams and noble trees, and, in the Middle Ages, hardly less renowned for its wood-carving of misereres, roofs and panels of exquisite device, than for its wool and dealings with that material which, not more than a century ago, was the staple of the province. For centuries, ere civil dissensions and religious contests drove out of the Low Countries a host of artisans, the wide and shallow valleys of Suffolk exported all their wool to Flanders, to be woven at Bruges and other cities of that great plain. It was Edward III. who encouraged the troubled Flemings to settle in East Anglia, and there weave or spin the raw material into kerseys, lindseys, lindsey-woolseys, worsted, and other fabrics, each of which took its name from a village where the craftsmen of the fourteenth century settled, and as hand-workers flourished until the quicker streams and more docile population of the West enabled manufacturers of cloth, with huge water-wheels and immense ranges of buildings—the ruins of which still encumber Somersetshire riversides—to outbid the East Anglians with cheaper goods, much as the West itself has, in turn, been outbidden by the coal and steam of Yorkshire and Lancashire, and Suffolk wool-working followed Sussex iron-forging out of the markets.

The name Woolner sufficiently indicates an ancestor of our sculptor not as working, but as dealing, in the ancient staple, exactly as its analogue "vintner" means a dealer in, not a grower of, wine. What Thomas Woolner's modern forefathers were is not recorded, but it is certain that when the boy was about ten years old he quitted the school at Ipswich, which, till then, he had attended, and was brought to London by his father, who settled in the metropolis and held some sort of an appointment in the Post Office. While little more than a child our subject had occupied himself in modelling in clay, carving and drawing, and did this so successfully that his father, who was not over-burthened with wealth, and quite aware that an artist had better begin early if he means to succeed—mere "schooling" of the ordinary sort not going for much before the easel or the modeller's bench—willingly consented that the boy, who was then barely thirteen years old, should be apprenticed to William Behnes, a well-known sculptor of that day, *i.e.* 1838, for not less than four years. The promise of the pupil was so great that Behnes, although he was accustomed to accept round sums for training less capable youngsters, took him without any premium, only stipulating that, when the lad was sufficiently advanced in skill, he should, for a short time, work for him without wages, and afterwards, during his term, for somewhat less than the ordinary rate of pay. This was an excellent and honourable arrangement for Woolner, because the master had a very large practice in sculpturing figures and busts in marble, bronze, and stone, while, so far as the workmanship of these objects went in modelling and carving, he could not possibly, at least in London, have had a better teacher than the thoroughly skilful, but rather inert and dull man, who was, it is said, not a little exacting withal, yet who most honourably fulfilled his part of the compact. Behnes made Woolner an admirable executant, or, as the technical phrase is, "a carver" of the highest skill. The pupil always warmly acknowledged the abundance of his teacher's somewhat rough kindness and zeal; and, during his apprenticeship, worked hard and faithfully in helping to carry out the commissions which then filled the large atelier at No. 13, Osnaburgh Street, Regent's Park, where Foley afterwards had his shops, and which are now occupied by Mr. Thomas Brock, R.A.

When the four years had expired, and Woolner was already an accomplished pupil, it was at Behnes's instigation that, on December 16th, 1842, he, having passed the probationary six months in the School of Sculpture, entered the Royal Academy as a Student. This school was then held, not as now in a special part of the modern building devoted to its purpose all the year, but in that dismal, cavernous annexe to the old Academy in Trafalgar Square where, during the summer months, rows of ghastly busts were ranged in tiers on shelves along the walls, and portentous statues grouped in the middle of the floor added depression to the scene. Woolner worked there with characteristic energy and diligence, and during the exhibition season as well as at odd times returned to Osnaburgh Street, and served Behnes at a by no means high salary for about two years more, improving himself with every effort, and gaining a high place in the opinions of those excellent judges, his fellow-students. He was just nineteen years of age when he sent to the Academy exhibition of 1843 a bas-relief of moderate size, which the catalogue described as "No. 1442. Model of Eleanora sucking the Poison from the Wound of Prince Edward." This, his first effort, is still in existence, and, with an excellent composition and thoroughly good execution, illustrates a good design and conception of the subject. The British Institution of those days often re-exhibited works from the Academy of a previous year, and such in 1844 was 'Eleanora's' fate.

His family being quite unable to help Woolner, the young sculptor had to shift as well as he could upon Behnes's stipend while he worked for him as a carver, and upon a few independent commissions of small amounts. The time was a hard one, but the robust spirit of the Englishman held him up in spite of short commons and such privations as healthy young men make light of. Before 1844 he contrived to obtain means sufficient for the execution of an ambitious group of life-size figures representing 'The Death of Boadicea.' This, as No. 154, occupied a conspicuous place in the great national contest of that year, which was held in Westminster Hall, for commissions to decorate the Houses of Parliament, then building. It stood quite close to Foley's famous and beautiful 'Youth at a Stream,' and even in that neighbourhood did not suffer. This bold venture did not help Woolner to a commission at Westminster or elsewhere, but it affirmed his fellow-students' opinions of him, and drew the attention of wealthier amateurs, who, nevertheless, bought nothing, and all the while the future remained very cloudy indeed. During the remainder of 1844 and all the next year Woolner continued working for Behnes, and at intervals, I believe, for another sculptor of less distinction, but upon almost equally hard terms; but practice was developing his handicraft, stern discipline adding force to his will, and knowledge of nature improving his resources

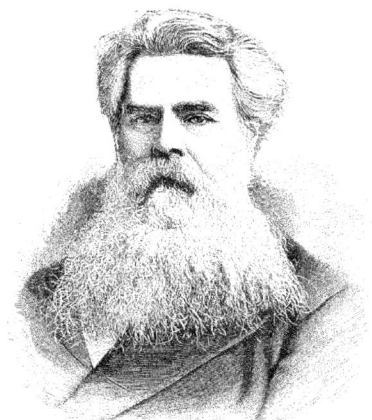

THOMAS WOOLNER, R.A.

and that feeling for style which thereafter distinguished the artist; but, as might be expected, the fruitlessness of his labours as regards 'Boadicea' told upon Woolner, and despite the noble and guarded mood which nature gave, did not in after-life make him less tolerant of injustice.

Thus two years passed, and left the sculptor's strong spirit chafing and distressed, gave him bare bread and butter, and no better opportunities than sufficed for the modelling of a graceful little bas-relief of 'Alastor,' dead and recumbent upon the poet's grave:—

"An image, silent, cold, and motionless,"

which, to those who saw it in the corner at the Academy, adequately represented Woolner's ideas of Shelley—he was then in the "Shelley stage"—but brought the sculptor no commissions, although it is probable a 'Medallion of E. A. Ashford, Esq.,' which, in 1846, accompanied it at Trafalgar Square, was more auspicious. 1847 came, and the horizon did not lighten for Woolner, although the Academy found room for a bas-relief of 'Feeding the Hungry,' a boy and chickens, and the British Institution exhibited the statuette in plaster of 'Puck,' one view of which is before the reader, a brilliant and original design that was, some years afterwards, cast in bronze for Lady Ashburton, a version now in hiding somewhere. 'Puck' represents the goblin elf, having folded his bat's wings, and from his airy path alighted upon a monstrous mushroom, which lay beneath him, because he saw an ususpicious frog, resting there, in peril of the serpent sliding nearer and nearer to its prey. Deftly the laughing sprite touched the batrachian with his foot, and the baffled reptile slid away among the herbage. 'Puck' is, as the reader will see, the very type of the rough and muscular urchin who toiled for maids and matrons in the shed and on the hearth; "the merry wanderer of the night" who knocked louts' heads together, and pulled out of bed the sluts that left the dairies foul.

It was late in 1847 that, Rossetti taking me to the huge, dusty, barn-like studio at 15, Mary Street, Hampstead Road, where, amid casts of antiques, fragments moulded from "the life," and more or less unfinished models, the sculptor was, so to say, encamped like a Bedouin in the desert, I first knew our subject, and the painter-poet said, "This is our friend Woolner, whom you wished to know!" Our host thereupon rose from the creaking seat (I think it had three castors on four feet), welcomed us, put chairs near the cindery iron stove which gave heat to the dusky air, handed us pipes, and, with that half-sardonic earnestness and force, half grave, half jest, which always distinguished him, began to talk of men we knew and things about us. 'Puck' had come back from Pall Mall, and stood high on a pedestal at the side, so that, when I turned to look at the masculine little gem of art and thought, its inventor's eye changed and his lips twitched a little because he remembered that, for two or three years gone by, it had been in hand, and fruitlessly. He was then twenty-two years of age, broad-chested, square-shouldered, rather more set in form than usual at that time of a man's life, robust, active, muscular, and with remarkably fine hands; his square-featured and noble face was set in roughly-cut, thick masses of brownish auburn hair, and under his full eyebrows vigorous, resolute, and penetrating eyes glowed steadfastly while he looked at you. His talk was a little bitter, and, as in later days more so, somewhat angry in denouncing shams and knaves, nor spared denunciations for fools.

PUCK. BY THOMAS WOOLNER, R.A., 1847.

Woolner's 'Eros and Euphrosyne,' and a spirited and elegant figure in bas-relief of 'The Rainbow,' "The Airy Child of Vapour and the Sun," attracted attention at the Academy in 1848, while 'Titania caressing the Indian Boy' was at the British Institution. In the conception and execution of such specimens as these, the young sculptor found whatever compensations there are possible for the dreariness of carving other people's marble.

It was in the latter part of 1848 the Pre-Raphaelite Brotherhood, our subject being the sculptor-member, was founded, and in it he soon took an eminent position; but he exhibited nothing for some years. Meanwhile, small medallions and unrecognised tasks alternated with carving marble for a living, but his works were, as it has been said elsewhere, not less thorough, learned, and accomplished than they could be made by the diligent and studious hands in which the experience of ten years had already accumulated. At the end of 1849 *The Germ* was getting under weigh with contributions and etchings by the Brotherhood and their friends. To Woolner was given the first place in No. 1 of that then hapless monthly periodical which nobody would buy, though it now sells for about its

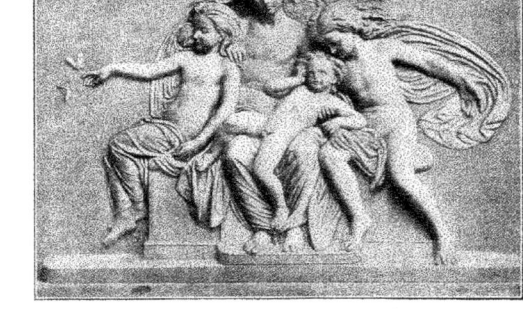

FOUR CHILDREN IN PARADISE. BY THOMAS WOOLNER, R.A., 1870.

weight in gold. That place our sculptor filled with the first version of "My Beautiful Lady," a poem of which two other extended versions have since appeared. It was published in January, 1850; the fifth number never came forth, and Woolner lost the money he had put into the venture. He contributed two other less important pieces, and no more, to the magazine. Woolner struggled on, but neither fortune nor *The Germ* could help him, and a disappointment of another sort, such as most men undergo, did not raise his hopes of life. In 1852 he sent to the Academy a 'Design for a Medal,' 'Sketch for a Monument to William Wordsworth,' * and the medallions of Carlyle, Wordsworth, and 'A Lady.'

Fortune still turned her face from him, and Woolner, half weary of struggling for her favours, determined, the "gold fever" being then at its height, to try his luck as a "digger" in Australia, for which region he sailed in July, 1852. Not only the Pre-Raphaelite Brotherhood, but Carlyle, Browning, Tennyson, Coventry Patmore, David Masson, Madox Brown, and a score of other friends of note deplored the departure they could not prevent. As it turned out, gold-digging did not "pay," and, after a few months, Woolner left the "fields" for Melbourne, where Fortune seemed to relent and many successful colonists sat to him for medallion portraits in bold relief, which furnished means for his return to England early in 1857. † I return for a moment to record that it was while accompanying Woolner to Gravesend on board the *Kent*, then bound for Melbourne, that Madox Brown observed the tragic incident of his masterpiece, 'The Last of England,' which, engraved in THE ART JOURNAL for 1870, is now in the gallery at Birmingham. In 1856 Woolner contrived to

* This was not executed, but later, in 1858, Woolner sculptured the medallion portrait which is over the poet's grave in Grasmere Church.

† It was during this absence of about four years an incident occurred which has been so grossly misrepresented that the truth of it demands to be told. By correspondence, early in 1853, it was arranged between Woolner and his friend and companion, Bernard Smith, and the brethren whom they left behind, that, on a given day and hour, the artistic members of each party should, at opposite sides of the earth, make sketches of each other's likenesses and exchange them as souvenirs athwart the seas. This was done in England so far as all but one brother, who was at the time very ill and in sore distress, were concerned; this defaulter's portrait was taken by Sir John (then Mr. .E.) Millais, and sent to Australia, but he, naturally, drew none. It has been alleged that the sketches were dispatched from England in order, by means of the distinctions of the eminent brethren, to give a sort of *cachet* to Woolner in Australia. The facts are that, these worthies being then martyrs to press critics and with every man's hand against them, their patronage would have been of no good in Melbourne, where, indeed, their fame had not yet reached; while, so far Tom Woolner needing patronage from this side, it is certain he took with him ample introductions to William Howitt, then settled in honour at Melbourne, and many other notabilities, while his bosom Companion of the time was Mr. Latrobe Bateman, the Governor's nephew, an engineer. The portraits were gifts of affection, not dues of meaner patronage.

send to the Academy the charming half-nude female figure in marble of 'Love,' or 'Un Rêve d'Amour,' a lovely piece of finished modelling and chaste, dreamy expression, which has never been engraved, as well as medallions of Mr. C. E. Howitt, two Australian gentlemen (the statesman, W. C. Wentworth, and another), and 'Thomas Carlyle, Esq.'

With his return a new phase seemed to open in Woolner's life. In 1857 another 'Thomas Carlyle,' 'Robert Browning,' 'A Lady,' and 'Tennyson' the medallion — engraved in Moxon's illustrated edition of the late Laureate's "Poems " — were still at the Academy ; and in that year he carved in Caen stone the expressive statue of Lord Bacon—his face "beaming" with a persuasive smile, touching the palm of one hand with the forefinger of the other, and thus adding point to a demonstration—which is in the New Museum at Oxford. A better known example of great merit and the choicest execution is the bust, without the beard, of Tennyson, now in the Library of Trinity College, Cambridge. Next year came four striking bas-reliefs of 'Moses,' 'David,' 'St. John the Baptist,' and 'St. Paul,' for the pulpit of Llandaff Cathedral. Then appeared, besides minor examples, medallions of Mrs. Tennyson, Mr. Vernon Lushington, and Sir F. Palgrave ; busts of Prof. Sedgwick (in Trin. Coll., Cam.), The Rev. F. D. Maurice, Sir W. Hooker, Prof. Henslow, Archdeacon Hare, A. H. Clough, Thomas Combe, and others, until 1863. 1862 was, meanwhile, signalised in Woolner's annals by the striking marble group of Sir J. Fairbairn's deaf and dumb children, which, as 'Brother and Sister,' were conspicuous in the International Exhibition. A statue of Prince Albert was executed for Oxford in 1864 ; in 1865, for Sir Walter Trevelyan, and now at Wellington, an important marble group of 'A Mother and Child,' and a bronze statue of Robert Godley for Christ Church, New Zealand ; in 1866 'Lord Macaulay,' statue in marble for Trin. Coll., Cam. ; a bust of J. H. Newman, and a third medallion (in three-quarters view) of Tennyson, engraved with the 'Enoch Arden' of 1866. Very beautiful indeed is the thorough execution of the large monument, in alto-relief of marble, that is set in Wrexham Church to commemorate the deaths of Mrs. Archibald Peel and her infant son. The design is intensely pathetic, and the composition very fine and lovely. The boy died in 1860, and the panel represents a stately angel with the child in her arms advancing to meet at Heaven's gate the soul of his mother, who died three years later. It belongs to Woolner's work of 1867, and is called 'Heavenly Welcome.' A bust of R. Cobden of the Corn Law League agitation was pro-

ACHILLES SHOUTING FROM THE TRENCHES. BY THOMAS WOOLNER, R.A., 1868.

duced in this year. 1868 saw the marble figure of 'Elaine,' instinct of girlish chastity and tender beauty, leaning against the shield of Lancelot; the statue of William III. for Westminster Hall, where Woolner's 'Boadicea' made an early mark in his honour; and a marble bust of Carlyle.

In 1858 Woolner had attained so much of the popular voice that Mr. Gladstone, never behindhand in recognising that element of renown, sat to him for the vigorous bust which is now in the Bodleian Library. This work is signalised to lovers of modern sculpture by the transcendent merit and splendid energy of the bas-relief, one of three inserted in the pedestal, and called, 'Achilles shouting from the Trenches,' which a block overleaf represents better than most of such things. The panel speaks for itself. The sculptor gathered

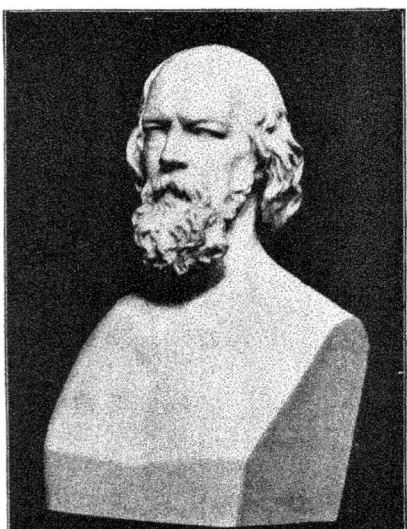

ALFRED TENNYSON. BY THOMAS WOOLNER, R.A., 1876.

inspiration from Leigh Hunt's brilliant and passionate translation of the Homeric text:—

"Thrice did great Hector drag him by the feet
Backward, and loudly shouted to the Trojans;
And thrice did the Ajaces, springy-strength'd,
Thrust him away; yet still he kept his ground,
Sure of his strength; and now and then rushed on
into the thick, and now and then stood still,
Shouting great shouts;—and not an inch gave he."

Juno sent Iris to command Achilles to deliver the body of his friend, thus beset; but "the Swift of Foot," demurring, desired to wait till Thetis, in his behoof, brought new armour from the Vulcanian forge. The "glorious Messenger of Jove," nevertheless, bade the sulking hero wait no longer, but, mounting the trenches, show himself unarmoured and shout his cry of war.

Woolner, who was elected an A.R.A. in 1871, and in 1875 an R.A., in 1875 gave as his diploma-work anent the later event, a replica of 'Achilles shouting from the Trenches.' The original is in the Bodleian, with corresponding bas-reliefs, representing ' Thetis and Zeus'—distinguished by the exquisite coquetry of the naked goddess, who, with both palms under the beard of Jove, petitions him on her son's behalf—and ' Thetis and Achilles.' In 1869 Woolner, besides the bust of Mr. Gladstone and its fine reliefs, produced a bust of Sir Bartle Frere, two other busts, and the beautiful marble figure of ' Ophelia,' which remains in the studio of the deceased artist. In the same year he completed an heroic size statue of Mr. David Sassoon, in Parsee robes, a noble cast of drapery carved with unusual skill, and the peculiar cap of his people: this work was exhibited at South Kensington ere being sent to Bombay, where it now stands.

The beautiful monumental composition of four children in Paradise, of which, entitled 'In Memoriam,' a block accompanies this essay, was never carried out in marble according to the commission it was designed for, but remains in plaster. I have selected it to illustrate Woolner's skill in composing groups of figures in alto-relief, his rare knowledge of the naked form, and the charm of his faces of children. It was executed in 1870, a year during which the sculptor, besides other works then in hand, added to his already numerous busts of famous men that of Charles Darwin. Their category was, in the next year, increased by busts of Bishop Temple and Sir Hope Grant. This marble company of the illustrious is so remarkable that it can be compared with the body of portraits of celebrities painted by Mr. Watts, and the two groups of likenesses include so many worthies that the artists may be said to have combined their skill for the benefit of posterity. A more important composition than 'In Memoriam' followed it in 1871, and was at the Academy of that year, being 'Virgilia, wife of Coriolanus, bewailing his Banishment.' This work, which is in marble, shows, with noble intensity and spirit, Virgilia seated on a bench, leaning against its back and weeping; her face is instinct with a stately, passionate grief, very patrician and beautiful; while her drapery, an element of his works on which Woolner always expended the most exquisite care, takes a place among modern triumphs of studious grace, learning, and finish.

Tennyson was so deeply in love with Woolner's marble statue of Guinevere—a simple and elegant figure of Arthur's queen, standing coronetted, holding a rose, and to her feet draped in a simple robe, through which the stately fulness of her form is seen—that he caused the statue to be engraved for "The Idylls of the King." It was No. 1503 at the Academy in 1872. Of the same year is 'In Memoriam, G—— B——,' a sculpture of great and simple pathos, of which I regret there is not room here for a cut, which expressed the very original and poetic idea of a boy, who died young and was accepted in Heaven, seated close to the gate of that high region and leaning there while he listened intently for the steps of his parents on their way to him. A blossoming jasmine extends behind the child and athwart the celestial wall. The modelling of the flesh, imparting life's *morbidezza*, and the firm contours of youth, is of the first order. A marble statue of Sir Bartle Frere, for Bombay, belongs likewise to 1872, together with a capital bust of Charles Dickens. 1873 was signalised by the completion of the fine seated statue of Dr. Whewell, which is now at Trinity College, Cambridge, and gives us an energetic record of the famous scholar seated in his Master's gown and cassock, and with outstretched hand holding before him upon the seat a large book, while, gravely and full of thought, he looks forwards, a type of earnest meditation in the act of judgment. Here, again, Woolner sculptured his best in drapery. The marble bust of Prof. de Morgan belongs to this time and the above-mentioned category of the famous. In 1874 Woolner carved the bust of John Hunter, which is in Leicester Square. A number of works succeeded this humble one and they comprised the marble monument of Mrs. J. A. Froude, in S. Lawrence's Church, Ramsgate; the noble bronze statue of Lord Lawrence, now at Calcutta, which, when it was exhibited in Waterloo Place, thoroughly impressed us all by its vigour and masculine conception, so different from modern portrait-sculpture at large, and a masterpiece in every respect; a marble statue of Sir Cowasjee Jehangheer Readimoney, for Bombay; the bronze standing figure of Lord Palmerson, now in Parliament Square; a whole-length marble portrait of Mr. Edwin Field, now in the Law Courts, London; a similar work representing Sir Thomas White, now at Merchant Taylors' Hall; and J. S. Mill, in bronze on the Northern Embankment; besides busts of Lord Sandon, Charles Kingsley (in Westminster Abbey), Edmund Lushington, W. Fuller Maitland, Prof. Key, John Simon (at the College of Surgeons), Sir W. Gull, Prof. Huxley, Sir William Hooker, Rajah Brooke, Sir T. Fairbairn, and Sir F. Palgrave. All these followed each other in rapid succession till 1879.

The period thus concluded gave us, in addition to the above, of which the 'Lawrence' alone would have made the fortune of a master—three specially important sculptures, being poetic, masculine, and beautiful in the highest degree, and, in their execution, *chefs-d'œuvre* of Woolner, nor inferior to any in modern art. They are the superb bearded bust of Tennyson, executed in 1876, and the last portrait of the Laureate taken while all his vigour was intact. A block of it now before the reader inevitably gives but a general impression of this capital piece, and, of course, entirely fails to represent the inexhaustible fineness of the modelling which, with exquisite research, retains consummate breadth, simplicity, and severe purity of style—that rarest merit of modern work in marble, and gives, as to the life, every element of the flesh, such as the elastic skin here stretched and tense over the slightly covered bone, there half hiding the subtly moulded vein that lies close below the surface, elsewhere covering the pressed muscles and pulpy softer substances of the form. It is proposed to buy this masterpiece of art and thoroughly interesting portrait, and, in honour of the Laureate and his life-long friend the sculptor, present it to a National Collection.

The second of the three great pieces I have named is the colossal statue in bronze of Captain Cook (see the block on the next page) which Woolner produced for the Sydney Government, and is now placed in the public park there, so that, from its elevated pedestal, it overlooks the finest harbour in the world; and, with one hand upraised, a telescope in the other, seems, as in the great discoverer's vision of prophecy, to hail the future of that Australia which he gave to the world. Its simplicity, dignity, and energy, not less than its noble reserve and incomparable execution, can only

speak for themselves in an adequate representation. They are qualities of the first order and, when the bronze was exhibited in Waterloo Place before it crossed the sea, commanded universal admiration, and proved the sculptor to be worthy of the highest honours of his art.

The third work of this group of masterpieces—which, after all, are only types of a much greater number of fine things I can barely find room for the names of—is the stately and beautiful statue in marble of Godiva disrobing, letting the last

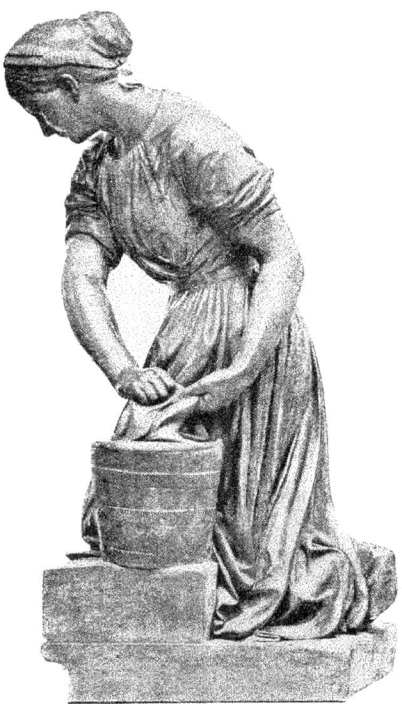

THE HOUSEMAID. BY THOMAS WOOLNER, R.A.

white garment of her sacrifice slide downwards to her feet, and, with her noble face held high, looking out as to the blind distance and empty echoing streets of the city that, so to say, turned its eyes away to let go unseen the sumptuous peeress, as "She rode forth, clothed on with chastity"; and, having returned, "Built herself an everlasting name."

It has always seemed to me that Woolner's ideal Countess, so gravely passionate and intensely pure as the statue is, and as becomes a piece of sculpture, is much nobler and more masculine than Tennyson's. The marble figure, because her very nakedness is armour like that of Britomart, has no "rippled ringlets" showered to her knee, and there is no need for coverings where the very nudity is, because of its completeness, heroic.

The cheek of this Godiva will not "flame," and no "light horrors" will stir the pulses of that grand matron, who, fair as a virgin, and, with lips and eyelids all composed, with not the least self-consciousness to move them, thinks less of her

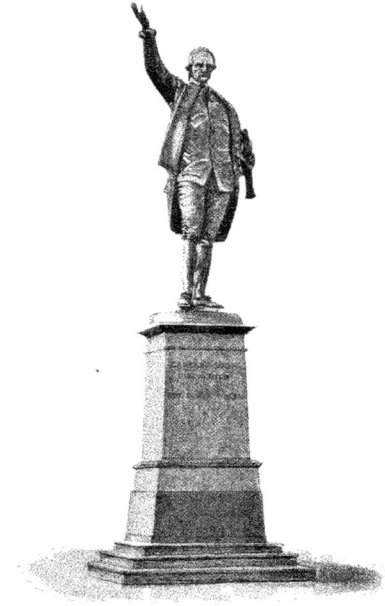

CAPTAIN COOK. BY THOMAS WOOLNER, R.A. IN SYDNEY.

nakedness than of her reward. It is thus easy to slide the full and rounded strong arms out of the armholes of the last garment which had to go, and, uncovering both breast and thigh, to push it down.

I have barely space left for naming Woolner's more important sculptures, which include a medallion of James Spedding, at Trinity College, Cambridge; busts of E. M. Barry, at Westminster Palace; the Earl of Clanwilliam and Lord Lawrence, in the Abbey; a very fine statue of the Queen, at Birmingham; a bust of Mr. W. E. Gladstone, for the City; the nude 'Water Lily,' an alto-relief in bronze; Lord Frederick Cavendish, the murdered Minister, recumbent on his tomb at Cartmel; the like of Bishop Jackson, in St. Paul's; Sir Stamford Raffles, a statue in bronze, for Singapore; and Bishop Fraser, statue, bronze, at Manchester

Woolner's last important work, illustrated overleaf, the very admirable life-size statue in bronze called 'The Housemaid,' which, while it attests the originality and resources of the artist, marks a new departure in sculpture, because it applies to a subject of common life the canons of the noblest style. It had, in the style of all his works, and, most of all, in such ideal ones as I have named, been part of Woolner's ambition to embody something of Phidian dignity, simplicity, and naturalness to his achievements, combined with exhaustive representation of details, such as we saw in the bearded bust of Tennyson. It was this view of the potentialities of sculpture which, in 1848, induced him, who, as an artist, was then the most advanced of the friends, to join the Pre-Raphaelite Brotherhood, and while that body retained its original features to join heartily in its efforts. In carrying out his ideal he obtained for his works that choice breadth and repose, as well as *morbidezza* of a very noble, and, in modern sculpture, very rare kind, which is so distinct in all he did as to be characteristic of, and easily recognisable in, every one of them.

Of Woolner's literary efforts I have already in "My Beautiful Lady" mentioned the first: to this, at long intervals, succeeded "Silenus," "Tiresias," "Nelly Dale," and "Pygmalion." Towards the end of September last our artist had been confined to his room for a week or two by an internal disorder, from which, after an operation of no unusual severity, he was apparently recovering satisfactorily when, with an acute spasm, the end came suddenly on the 7th of October, 1893. A few days later he was buried in Hendon Churchyard.

So passed to the majority one of the most powerful, earnest and best equipped of our artists; one of the most sincere and outspoken men of our time, and a man whose friendships were without a flaw.

F. G. STEPHENS.

THOMAS STOTHARD, R.A.

ALTHOUGH the collection of drawings and paintings by Thomas Stothard now at the Royal Academy is in some respects disappointing, it must be acknowledged to be highly representative of the genius of the man, and well worth the trouble it has taken to get them together. It has often been remarked that nothing tries and tests a man's art so much as to have numerous specimens of it placed side by side in one room. This is abundantly exemplified in the case before us; but in passing judgment upon Stothard we must not forget he flourished a century ago, and that, considering the rapid development of the English school, he must be regarded as one of the earliest of the "Old Masters," for, born in 1755, he was an Associate in 1785 and an Academician in 1794.

Although the son of a Long Acre innkeeper, Stothard, on account of his delicacy, spent the greater part of his childhood at Acomb, in the county of York. Here it was that his attention was first turned to Art. In his country home were some heads by Houbraken, and an engraving of Strange's

Blind Belisarius, also a number of religious subjects by the same artist; and these had so deep an impression upon his mind that he soon began to use the pencil himself, showing therewith not a little aptitude.

After some time spent at a school at Ilford, Essex, he was apprenticed to a designer of patterns for brocaded silks, and in the evenings he amused himself by making drawings—washing them in with Indian ink and sepia to give them some degree of effect—to illustrate scenes in the Iliad and "The Faery Queen"; thus unconsciously striking into the line of Art that was to prove his chief source of income. For Harrison, editor of the *Novelists' Magazine*, having seen some of his designs, gave him a commission; this was followed by others, not only for that but for the *Poetical Magazine*, and other illustrated works

Some of these early efforts are to be seen in the collection, and one cannot wonder at the admiration they evoked at the time of their production. To a colouring that is always delicate and pure, and to a line that is never wanting in grace, he added a facility and a felicity of composition which could only have been acquired by long and patient study of the best models. He designed for all the leading authors of his period—Gray, Collins, Rogers, Campbell, and for most of those whose works were republished in his time, including Chaucer, Shakespeare, Milton, Cervantes, and Richardson. Some of his Milton illustrations are exceptionally fine in their way, tender and poetic; but they lack "character." For not one writer in the wide range of literature he illustrated did Stothard effect what Leslie did for the Uncle Toby of Stern, or Cruickshank for the Fagin of Dickens. In all his work we behold him as the wielder of the facile pencil, nowhere as a man of insight and originality.

This criticism is still more true of his paintings than of his illustrations. Here again we may admire the richness of his colouring, his composition, and his clever—if often slight—handling; but, alas, for any individuality of characterization! while, as to his drawing, especially when he gets beyond the human figure, his faults become painfully conspicuous. Take, for instance, the horses in the 'Canterbury Pilgrims' in the National Gallery: were ever such horses seen except in the Noah's Ark of our childhood? This is his best known and most celebrated picture; but it is inferior to many of the other oil paintings in the collection. It does not even come up to his usual standard of excellence as regards colour, being spotty and suggestive of illumination more than of harmonious painting.

One of the best of the larger pictures is 'Calypso with her Nymphs crowning Cupid': it exhibits good feeling, while the landscape background is very poetic. Similar commendation may be given to the 'Seven Ages of Man,' about which there is a noble simplicity and charm which make one forget its obvious faults of drawing. A touch of nobility too makes itself felt in his 'Jacob's Dream,' although the work is more or less a copy of a well-known "old master." But this is one of Stothard's great weaknesses: everywhere his original shines through.

The 'Battle Scene,' which formed the study for one of his mural decorations at "Burleigh House by Stamford town" is a thoroughly vigorous piece of work, full of the fire and turmoil of war, and a good specimen of his inventiveness of design. It constitutes almost the one exception to his noted inability to rise to the heroic and tragic. He is at his best in subjects of a domestic or gracefully ideal description, as in his Watteau-like *fêtes champêtres*—and even thus when more or less sketchy in handling.

The work that best exhibits Stothard in his strength, apart from his weaknesses, is undoubtedly the one from which we have chosen our illustration, namely, the Wellington Shield. This shield (3 ft. 4 in. in diam.) was executed in silver-gilt, and presented to the Duke by the merchants and bankers of London. It was designed after the Peninsular campaign and before Waterloo. The work was competed for by the London goldsmiths, all of whom are said to have applied to Stothard for a design. He gave it to Ward and Green, who were accordingly successful in the competition. The artist not only made the sketches and carefully finished drawings, but himself modelled all the compartments in clay for the guidance of the silversmiths. These, however, were so bad that to safeguard his reputation he afterwards etched the entire work with his own hand and published it as an authentic record of his design. The finished shield, the centre of which is here shown, differs materially from the original sketch in sepia, which is in the collection of Mr. James Knowles of *The Nineteenth Century*. In the latter the central compartment shows a somewhat weak figure of Britannia awarding a crown to Valour: this was at the last moment changed by the artist into the equestrian group of the Duke and his generals, with Victory about to place the laurel on Wellington's head, while Anarchy, Discord, and Tyranny lie beneath his horse's feet.

THE WELLINGTON SHIELD.
BY THOMAS STOTHARD, R.A.

A. T. STORY.

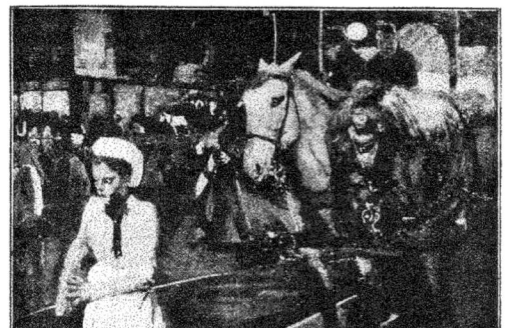

AMSTERDAM BY NIGHT. BY BREITNER. BY PERMISSION OF MESSRS. VAN WISSELINGH, LONDON AND AMSTERDAM.

THE GRAFTON GALLERY COLLECTION.

THE fourth exhibition at the Grafton Gallery will be long memorable on account of the opportunity it has afforded to the Art world of doing homage to the genius of the late Albert Moore. It has given to those who believe in him as an artist, of whom this country may well feel proud, a chance of strengthening first impressions and of renewing early acquaintances; while to those who knew little of his work before, or who had studied him unintelligently, it has made possible fuller knowledge and juster appreciation. It cannot, of course, be pretended that the hundred or so of his pictures and drawings, which fill one of the rooms in Grafton Street, include all the best things which he produced in nearly forty years of steady endeavour; but as a memorial collection they have the great advantage of showing the way in which he worked and the manner in which his power developed and matured.

From this collection it may be gathered that the two salient characteristics of Albert Moore's art were its sensitiveness and intelligence. It left nothing to chance, and needed the closest preliminary study and the most devoted application. It had its foundations in a peculiar temperament, an exceptional individuality, and it was carried through by the influence of a strong will, aided by a determined conviction. It was, in a word, a matter of sincere belief, and owed nothing to the impulse of the moment nor to any half-considered suggestion. By inclination the artist was a student of dramatic expression, but by instinct he was led irresistibly into the pursuit of pure decoration. At first he tried, as we see in his superbly emotional 'Elijah,' and to a less extent in the 'Shunamite Woman,' to combine the two motives, incidental and decorative; but he soon realised how impossible such a partnership would be, and set himself thenceforward to eliminate from his painting everything but the expression of the one belief that dominated his life—decoration. In each successive picture we find him progressively sacrificing all the external interests which in pictorial art make for popularity, and adopting more and more the technical method which his instinct taught him to accept. At first he was content to simplify emotion into gentle human interest, into a placid recognition of an existence which was conscious of no passion and of no jarring note. This stage is represented in the exhibition by such canvases as 'The Marble Seat,' 'The Quartette,' 'A Musician,' 'Pomegranates,' 'Battledore,' 'Shuttlecock,' and 'A Garden,' in all of which there is the hint of activity, the idea of intention, and of actual interest taken in their occupations by the types of humanity that he was illustrating. His pictures during this period told no story, it is true, but they certainly contained the suggestion of incident, and dealt under a veil of classicism with minor occurrences of everyday life.

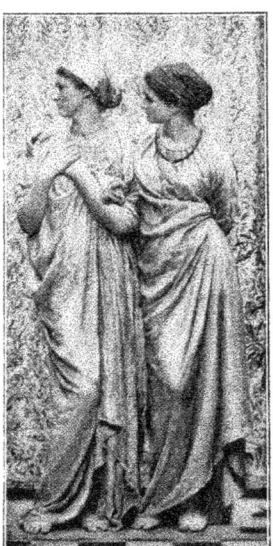

TOPAZ. BY ALBERT MOORE.
FROM THE PICTURE IN THE COLLECTION OF HUMPHREY ROBERTS, ESQ., THE OWNER OF THE COPYRIGHT.

Towards the end of the seventies, however, he rid himself completely of

THE GRAFTON GALLERY COLLECTION.

the taint of emotion, and then for about ten years he was occupied solely with the frankest assertion of beauty for its own sake. Humanity ceased to interest him except as a pattern, as a superlatively composed arrangement of lines and masses; and was useful to him in his artistic methods simply on account of its decorative appropriateness. With this logical development of his conviction came also the perfecting of his technical system. His best work was done during the decade that ended in 1888, a period that provides the Grafton Gallery with the exquisite 'Blossoms,' first shown at the Grosvenor in 1881, from the Henry Tate collection, and of which we give an illustration, and with 'Jasmine,' 'Acacias,' 'Companions' 'An Alcove,' 'A Decorator,' 'The Toilet,' 'Topaz,' another of our illustrations, 'Anemones,' and 'Waiting to Cross.' The large canvas, 'A Summer Night,' which has been lent by the Liverpool Corporation, was at the Academy in 1890, and marks the commencement of the final stage of his career. For some months previously to the completion of this picture his health had been affected, and the first symptoms of the illness which ultimately caused his death had made themselves perceptible. Strangely enough, with the increase of physical suffering came a modifying of the definiteness of his artistic belief, and a partial reversion to the emotional motives of his earlier works. The 'Summer Night' was an awakening from the sublime unconsciousness of the dozen years immediately preceding; and this was followed, in 1892, by the picture 'Lightning and Light,' in which human interest was once again as active as in the 'Marble Seat' or 'The Quartette.' In 1893 he was represented by a love scene—the sketch for which, called 'Lovers,' is on view—which went a step further towards passion; and in the same year he completed his last work, 'The Loves of the Winds and the Seasons,' the loan of which the directors of the Gallery have been fortunate in securing from Mr. MacCulloch, the owner of the picture. This important canvas is unlike anything else that Albert Moore ever painted. It is an allegory, a poetic personification of Nature's changes, and tells its story through the medium of dramatic action and the most human emotions. It is astonishing, as the last production of a man who had been occupied for more than thirty years in subordinating to the rules of Art the very passions that give all its meaning to this picture. It is, as it were, a note of interrogation at the end of the artist's life, and

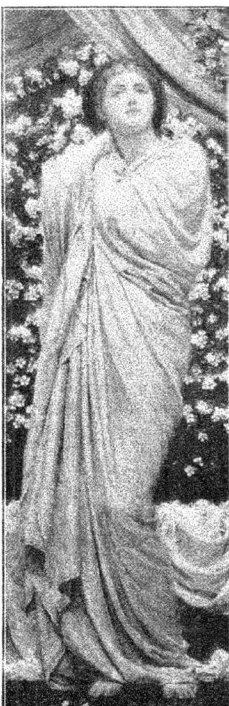

BLOSSOMS. BY ALBERT MOORE.
FROM THE HENRY TATE COLLECTION.

leaves us seeking the cause of his departure from the æsthetic principles which we had all come to regard as part of his nature and as essential to his art. It adds, beyond question, by its presence on the walls of the Gallery, to the historical interest of the exhibition; but its real significance cannot now be explained. We can only regard it as an experiment and as a sign of transition, marking a change to the new series of motives with which, had a longer life been possible for him, Albert Moore would have busied himself during years to come.

Of the contents of the remaining three rooms which are filled with a general collection of British and foreign works it is scarcely necessary to write at great length. The feature of this part of the show is variety of a somewhat exaggerated kind. There are three exquisite sea pieces by Mr. Whistler, delightful in colour and in strong suggestion of movement, which were painted last autumn on the coast of Normandy; the colour in 'Violet and Blue; among the Rollers,' being a veritable *tour de force;* the excellent landscapes by James Maris, Emile Claus, and Pierre Lagarde are the most worthy of note. The panel by Mr. Weldon Hawkins is remarkable as an ingenious and intelligent attempt to revive a type of imaginative design which was at one time widely popular, but which has succumbed to the matter-of-fact realism of our times. Mr. Alexander's two portraits, though very far from faultless, show a certain distinction of arrangement, and a sense of large style, which are convincing so far as they go; and Mr. Shannon's pretty pictures of children have the lightness of touch and brightness of subject which appeal most vividly to the public taste. But for artistic quality there is nothing better than Mr. Lavery's beautiful women. In M. Breitner's 'Street in Amsterdam by Night' popularity is sought through sensationalism, through the expression of strong effects, and through the use of familiar motives; of this powerful piece of work we give an illustration. There is good work from Mr. Greiffenhagen and Mr. Theodore Roussel and a portrait by J. M. Swan; there is real capacity in the contributions of MM. Alfred Stevens, Muhrmann, and Ary Renan, and in such a picture as Mr. William Stott's 'Nymph,' which is none the less welcome because it has been seen before, and there is plenty of work quite as much worthy of attention in many other canvases.

1894.

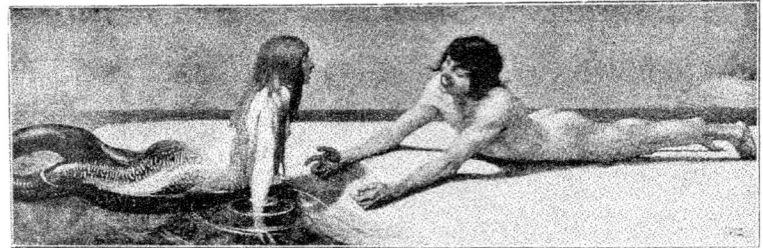

THE MERMAID. BY FRANZ STUCK.

RECENT FOREIGN ART BOOKS.

SO many books on artistic subjects are continually being published that it is not an easy matter for the public to keep pace with them. In addition to the large number from British presses, there are numerous works issued in France, Germany, Belgium and Holland, a certain number of which are directly interesting to the British buyer of Fine Art books. We have therefore thought it best to group the chief of these foreign books under one heading, only premising that all the works noticed are worthy the serious attention of connoisseurs.

The most fascinating book recently published on the continent is "FRANZ STUCK" (E. Albert, Munich), containing over one hundred reproductions with text from the competent pen of Otto J. Bierbaum. The illustrations here printed will give an idea of the power of the extraordinary painter whose faculty for depicting the weird is unsurpassed, yet whose facility in suggesting the beautiful is occasionally supremely great. He is sternly impressed with the reality of the fall of Eve, and he treats the subject in a way no other artist has dared or cared to do. As a young artist, Franz Stuck seeks by novelty of subject to obtain the attention demanded by every prophet; when he is accepted as the splendid artist he really is, he will certainly modify his ideas and paint pictures that will only satisfy and please, and not as at present repel almost as much as they attract. Franz Stuck is a young artist about whom we hope to speak in detail some day, and he is a friend of Lenbach, the well-known German painter.

The "JOURNAL DE EUGÈNE DELACROIX" (Plon, Paris) is a work concerning an artist of more established renown, but the book is really of somewhat less actual interest. Delacroix' journal has for forty years been a matter of public discussion, and occasional fragments of it have appeared. It has been very jealously guarded as a whole, and it was only about two years ago that it became possible to print it completely so far as it exists. Delacroix, when he died in 1863, left his journal in the hands of his friend and pupil Pierre Audrieu, who refused to let it be published, although he is said to have read and re-read it continually. In 1892 Audrieu died, and his widow has permitted the work to be printed. Delacroix was greatly influenced by his visit to England in 1826, and he was a particular admirer of Constable and Lawrence. To English readers therefore, the journal for that visit would have been very interesting, but unfortunately it is at the most interesting points that the journal fails. From 1825 to 1832 is missing, and the portion for 1848—the revolution time—is also gone. But, notwithstanding these gaps, the journal of Delacroix, who knew every one worth knowing in Paris for many years, is a most interesting study. Twice the name of Constable appears, but without any opinion of his pictures being expressed. On June 19th, 1824, he writes, "Vu les Constable. C'était trop de choses dans un jour. Ce Constable me fait un grand bien," and on the 25th following "Revu les Constable." As it was at the Salon of 1824 that Constable won the medal with 'The Hay Wain,' now in the National Gallery, a picture which is said to have caused Delacroix to modify the colour of his picture, the 'Massacre de Scio,' it would have been interesting to hear what he really thought of the English master he so much admired. These volumes contain, however, the 'Voyage au Maroc,' a portion

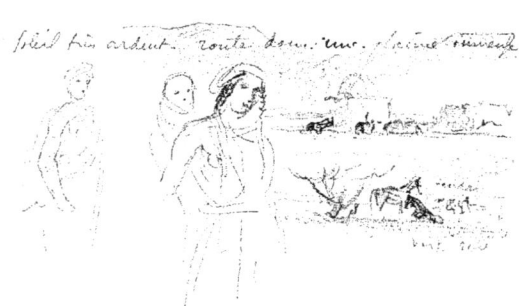

SKETCHES FROM THE JOURNAL OF EUGÈNE DELACROIX.

of the journal which was believed to have been lost. From this we give two facsimile sketches. The work is published in three volumes, of which the first two only are ready.

engravings He employed the graver only, and his plates are masterpieces of the art. M. Hymans gives a complete list of all Vorsterman's works, together with a biography,

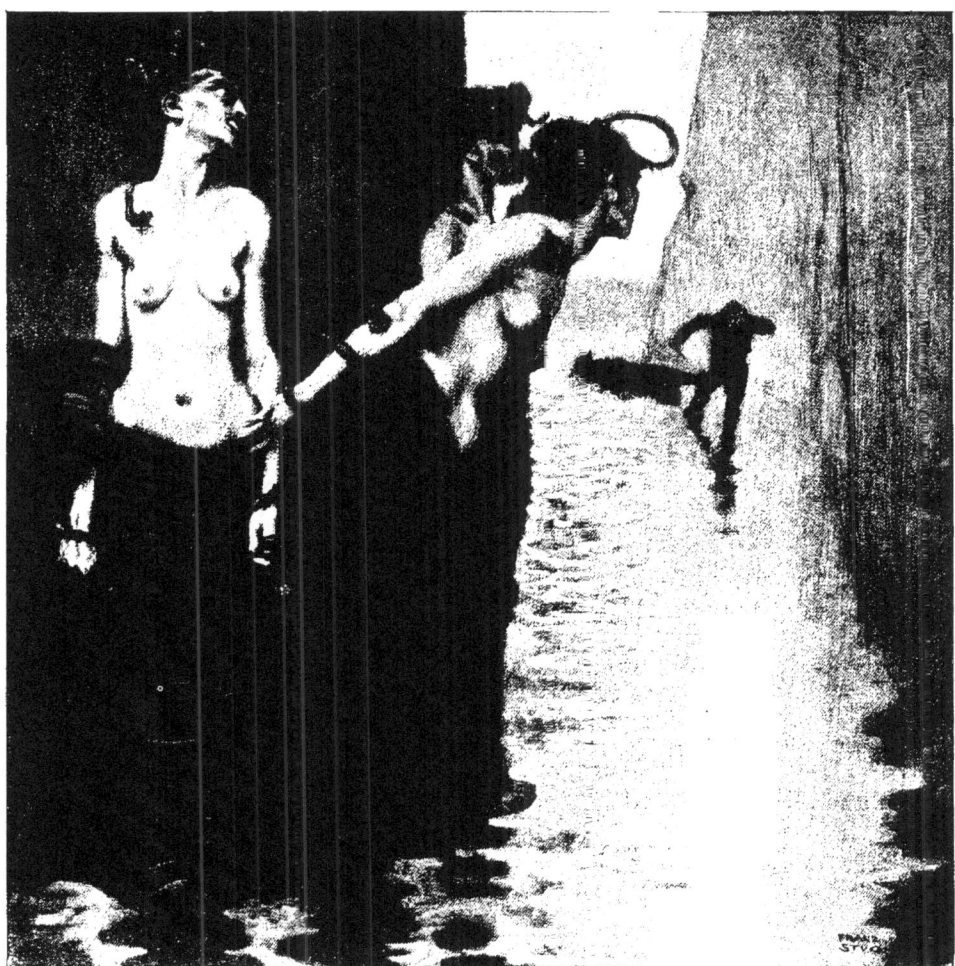

THE MURDER. BY FRANZ STUCK. (E. ALBERT, MUNICH.)

From Belgium we have a learned and painstaking volume by Henri Hymans, royal librarian, on " LUCAS VORSTERMAN" (Emile Bruylant, Bruxelles), the celebrated engraver of the works of Van Dyck and Rubens. Born at Antwerp in 1595 (not 1578, as is generally said), he lived for over seventy years —passing eight in England—and executed many important illustrated with a few plates, which are not so interesting as a reduction of the 'Adoration of the Magi,' after Rubens, or one of Van Dyck's English portraits would have been. There is, however, an excellent reproduction of M. Heseltine's portrait of Vorsterman, by Van Dyck, and also of Vorsterman's own plate from the same.

From Holland come two folio volumes on modern gold and

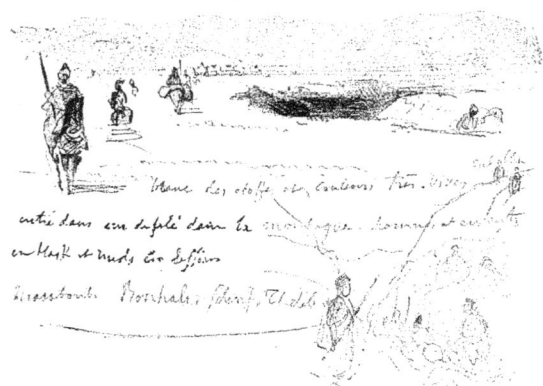

SKETCHES FROM THE JOURNAL OF EUGÈNE DELACROIX.

silversmith's work. This kind of work has sunk to such a depth of degradation, and there are so few signs of any revival of really artistic work, that we are disposed to welcome with great satisfaction "RÉPRODUCTIONS D'ANCIENNES GRAVURES D'ORFÈVRERIE HOLLANDAISE:" I. Adam van Vianen; II. Balthasar Sylvius (Martinus Nijhoff, La Haye), a series having for its object the reproduction of designs and drawings by goldsmiths of an earlier epoch. It affects the value of the publications before us very little, that the two craftsmen whose work is recalled therein were neither the greatest nor the most interesting of their school; the important matter is that they belonged to a school at all, had a great measure of skill and individuality, and each left a considerable number of designs for the use and instruction of posterity. Of Balthasar Sylvius nothing is known except his work, and that he lived, perhaps at Antwerp, about 1560. The best of his productions are arabesques, "quas vulgo Marusias vocant," for knife or sword-handles and blades, armour, etc., and these are of much beauty and delicacy. Adam van Vianen, who worked in Utrecht about 1610-30, also produced many designs for cups and vases, which, although overloaded with the bad ornament of the seventeenth century, are also worthy of study; there is, by the way, an excellent tazza by this master in the South Kensington Museum. We have no hesitation in recommending these works. The reproductions are well done, on good hand-made paper, and, both for their historical and intrinsic value, they ought to find a place in the library of every institution concerned with the teaching of practical art.

Returning to France, we have Edward Garnier's "DICTIONNAIRE DE LA CERAMIQUE" (Librairie de L'Art,) wherein the indefatigable guardian of the Museum at Sèvres brings together all the most useful information for collectors of "Faïences, Grés, et Poteries," in all parts of the world. This is probably the most authoritative work in French on the subject of Ceramics. The details on French ware and its manufacturers are very complete; the volume is illustrated with a dozen well-executed coloured plates, and a series of marks and monograms in alphabetical order.

In these days of specialism it is not easy to grasp the whole history of painting in one country, and it is likely, therefore, that those who wish to have a survey of painting in France will find Arsène Alexandre's "HISTOIRE POPULAIRE DE LA PEINTURE—ECOLE FRANÇAISE" (Paris, Laurens) useful to English readers. Like all histories of Art, it has to begin with the primitive, and somewhat dry-as-dust, details. The latter half of the volume, which has in all two hundred and fifty illustrations, is, however, lively enough. It deals with Delacroix, Corot, Millet, Courbet, and Manet in a sympathetic way, which shows how thoroughly the impressionist movement has been accepted by our neighbours, even in the preparation of a popular history of Art.

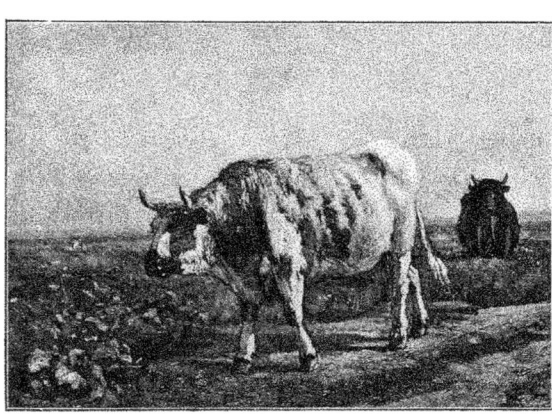

GOING TO PASTURE. BY TROYON.

"LA CERAMIQUE CHINOISE," by Ernest Grandidier (Paris, Firmin-Didot; 50 francs), is an important work by one of the first authorities on Chinese ceramics, and it is illustrated

RECENT FOREIGN ART BOOKS.

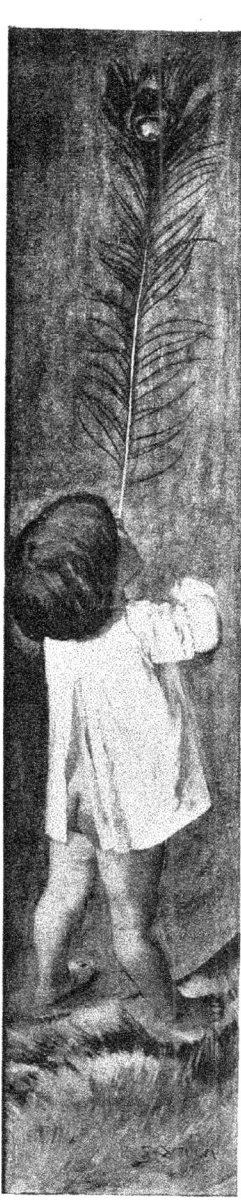

THE PEACOCK'S FEATHER.
BY FRANZ STUCK.
1894.

by forty-two photogravures from beautiful examples of the best types. The author is no follower of preceding critics' systems, but boldly takes a line of his own. In place of classing the works by families, M. Grandidier has received a hint from the Chinese method, and he groups the art in three great categories, "le décor Ming, le décor Khang-hi, le décor Yung-tching." By further dividing the manufacture of Chinese porcelain into five periods of time, and again classing these epochs in two divisions, "monochromes" and "polychromes," M. Grandidier inaugurates a system which is simple, correct, and easily recognised, and one we believe that will come to be adopted everywhere. After these observations it is almost needless to say that we think this a work of far more than ordinary excellence. The illustrations are themselves very valuable.

The "ALBUMS OF EXAMPLES OF CONTEMPORARY ART" are continued in two series, "Animaliers" and "Sculpteurs" (L'Art, Paris), in each of these being one hundred drawings and sketches by masters of all countries. Another interesting French publication from the same house is "Constant Troyon," by A. Hustin. This is the first attempt to make a systematic account of the great animal-painter's career, and there does not seem to be much material for a story. The illustrations are, however, well chosen, although not well printed. We give a specimen of Troyon's work in the accompanying illustration. "Méthode Pratique de Dessin," for teaching drawing in schools, is another of this firm's recent publications; and Alphonse Wauters, of Brussels, writes learnedly for the same on "Bernard van Orley," the Flemish master who flourished at the beginning of the sixteenth century.

The influence of Sandro Botticelli on modern British decorative art has been so far-reaching, and its effects are still so widely felt, that we receive with interest "SANDRO BOTTICELLI," by Hermann Ulmann (Bruckmann, Munich). The work before us is in the form of a biographical study and description of the artist's life-work, with the addition of numerous illustrations. The subject is carefully and scientifically treated, Herr Ulmann having evidently spared no pains to gather the best available information; and he is, moreover, perfectly honest in the matter, giving numerous but not too copious references to his authorities wherever at all necessary, a matter in which many biographers are nowadays somewhat lax. This book gives the latest theories on the career of Botticelli, and is a serious addition to the literature of the subject.

The history of the artistic crafts of the United States is necessarily very limited, and in many sections almost non-existent; but records of its pottery reach well back into the early seventeenth century, a period which covers much of the history of our own wares. It is unfortunate that this epoch should have been one of such bad taste—we have even yet scarcely recovered from its effects—and also that home influence was so strong that the American colonies could not grow so as to entitle their craftsmen to rank as a school apart. Nevertheless, in recording the early struggles of the craft, and the gradual steps by which an important industry, if not an art, has been built up, Mr. E. A. Barber, in "THE POTTERY AND PORCELAIN OF THE UNITED STATES: An Historical Review of American Ceramic Art, from the Earliest Times to the Present Day" (Putnam), had an opportunity of producing a valuable and interesting work, and of rendering a distinct service to the Art history of his country. We fear he cannot be said to have achieved a success. He has undoubtedly collected a considerable amount of information, which will be of use to his successors, and, in some cases, this is both valuable and complete. But a serious fault is the presence of the commercial element to a very great degree. The book is brought absolutely up to date in such matters as the manufacture (with full style and title of the firms concerned) of door-knobs and drain-pipes. Mr. Barber has nothing to say of William Osborne, the first maker of "Danvers Ware," early in the seventeenth century, a pottery which continued for over two hundred years to produce a somewhat coarse glazed earthenware which is well known to American collectors. And there is no mention as such of the numerous patriotic and topical pieces produced from about 1770 to 1820.

Collectors of Fable Books, and there is nothing more delightful and less costly than forming a collection of such works, will be glad to hear of the "ICONOGRAPHIE DES FABLES DE LA FONTAINE, LA MOTTE, DORAT, ET FLORIAN" (Flammarion, Paris), by Eugène Lévêque. This, containing over a hundred fac-similes "en sanguine" from these French fables, is an accurate account of their illustrations and illustrators, and might readily form the basis of a collection of Fables, hand in hand with the Bewick, and other Fable Books of which a large number were issued in England about a century ago.

A series of volumes which ought to be as popular in Britain as in France has been commenced under the title of "AUTOUR DE LA MÉDITERRANÉE." The series is divided into nine not too bulky volumes, of which two have already appeared, "Tripoli à Tunis" and "Tunis à Alger" (Henri Laurens, Paris). The illustrations, of which there are many, are by A. Chapon, are freely treated yet drawn in detail, and are interesting as well as artistic. The letterpress, by Marius Bernard, is more or less an account of personal experiences, but it takes in the opinions of others also, and while it is a book for home reading, it intelligently takes note of every point of interest in the various localities, and it is by no means a simple guide. Each winter a volume will be published on the coasts of the great inland sea, so that several years will elapse before the project is completely carried out.

Herr Ludwig Keim, of Vienna, believes he has discovered two early works by Rembrandt, and he has published a brochure (Spielhagen & Schurich, Wien) thereon, with reproductions from the picture in question. One is 'A Descent from the Cross,' the suggestion being that it was painted when Rembrandt was about sixteen, and the other 'A Monk reading,' set down at about two years later.

ART NOTES.

THE recent elections of five Associates of the Royal Academy indicate in their result the strength of the newer school of painting. That it should be possible for Mr. Sargent to be the first to be chosen of the five, reveals how quickly the older methods of work are now being passed by. Mr. Sargent is to the present generation what Mr. Whistler was before him. The great master of Impressionism would never enter the Academy, but thirty years ago he too was an exhibitor at the annual exhibition. Mr. Sargent has more fortunately been caught earlier, and besides he has had the powerful influence of *The Times* on his behalf for a good many years, and, after all, such influence counts for something. Mr. Swan, about whom also THE ART JOURNAL has frequently favourably written, has a reputation of the highest kind in France, Holland, and America. Two years ago one of his bronzes was the sole exhibit in one of the *Salons* of the Champ de Mars collection. His chief pictures are in Philadelphia, and his works are better known in Canada than in London. A good modern Dutch collection is not thought complete unless an example of his work is found therein, and Scotland emulates the example of the Netherlands. It is certain that until an artist has a living reputation in several countries, he is now only a comparatively local painter. Mr. Arthur Hacker, another new Associate, was trained in the Academy Schools, and under Bonnat in Paris. This, in conjunction with the election of Mr. Frank Bramley, is satisfactory to the lover of subject pictures, and Mr. George Frampton, who is only thirty-three, is a decorative sculptor from whom the greatest things may be expected. It is only a few years since he was an Academy student, for in 1887 he won the £200 travelling studentship for sculpture.

We heartily congratulate Sir Edward Burne-Jones on his baronetcy. Mr. Gladstone has been well advised in his selection of the artist, and it now only remains for Her Majesty the Queen to give Sir Edward an important commission to show the reality of the royal appreciation of English talent. Mr. G. F. Watts was also offered a baronetcy, but he "respectfully declined."

Outside the Society of Lady Artists there has not hitherto been any official recognition of ladies as members, but the Royal Scottish Society of Painters in Water Colours has recently resolved to admit ladies to equal privileges with the masculine element. This Society, under the able presidentship of Sir Francis Powell, is in a very healthy condition.

Mr. Henry Quilter has collected his works in painting for the past ten years, and has exhibited them in the Dudley Gallery. They may be interesting as showing that this writer on Art has strenuously endeavoured to acquire knowledge of practical painting; but as artistic productions, giving evidence of originality or power, we fear they have no value whatever.

"Constantinople," as produced at Olympia, in the West End of London, is far more than an ordinary entertainment. The display of colour throughout stamps the designer, Mr. Bolossy Kiralfy, as an artist of considerable power. Strongly imbued with the brilliant colouring of the Impressionists, he has rendered the various scenes highly impressionistic in effect. His scheme of tones and values rises occasionally to a high artistic level.

The Royal Association for the Promotion of the Fine Arts in Scotland—an Art Union for subscribers—has for several years left the old-fashioned way of distributing an out-of-date engraving, and has issued for 1893, and will also do so for 1894, a valuable artistic rendering of a famous picture. For last year, Mr. William Hole, R.S.A., one of the few first-rate living etchers, produced a remarkable plate of the portrait, by Velasquez, of Don Adrian Pulido-Pareja, Admiral of the Fleet of New Spain, formerly in the possession of the Earl of Radnor, and recently added to the National Gallery in London. For this year Mr. Hole is preparing an equally-important etching of the famous equestrian portrait, by Velasquez, in the possession of the Earl of Elgin, of the statesman, Don Gaspar de Guzman, Conde Duque d'Olivarez, minister to Philip IV., and patron of Velasquez.

It appears, however, that this Association meets with no popular support, and that notice has been given by the committee of management of their resolution to wind it up.

The Société National des Beaux-Arts, which holds its exhibition at the Champs de Mars, known as the New Salon, is running in close rivalry to the Salon of the Champs Elysées. For the coming year the exhibition will open on April 25th, one week before the opening of the Old Salon. Hitherto it has opened a fortnight later. At a general meeting the treasurer announced that at the end of its fourth year the Society found itself in an assured position. The public support received has been large and steady, the balance in hand on the year's working is nearly £400; a new lease at practically half their old rent has been granted by their landlords, the Municipal Council of Paris; the portions of the Palais sublet by the Society are estimated to produce nearly double in 1894 the amount realised in the previous year; and there is a satisfactory prospect of the speedy extinction of the original debt of the Society. A new section devoted to architecture has been added. The receiving days for the Salon Champs de Mars will be, for paintings and engravings, March 18th to 22nd, and sculpture, 25th to 27th.

JOSEF ISRAELS. BY JOSSELIN DE JONG.

Some new and important letters written by Rubens have recently been discovered at Ghent, in Belgium, and have been acquired by the Royal Library at Brussels. They are four in number, and bear the dates 1619, 1620, and 1622, which was about the most productive period of Rubens' artistic career. Their importance lies in the subject with which they deal, and in the fact that they give light upon several points which had hitherto been obscure. They are addressed to Peter Van Veen, advocate at La Haye, who was a brother of Rubens' old master, Otto Van Veen. They concern themselves with the question of the licence which it was necessary to obtain in Holland for the sale of engravings after the works of artists. In Sir Philip Thicknesse's "Journey through the Pays-Bas," London, 1786, there are three letters by Rubens which are very little known.

The Art Association of Montreal runs a successful Loan Collection annually, and the seventeenth exhibition held at the end of the year was specially varied. Corot and Constable, Romney and Rembrandt, Daubigny and David Cox were contributed by such prominent citizens of Montreal as the Hon. G. A. Drummond, Mr. Van Horne, Sir Donald Smith, and Mr. Popham.

In announcing the awards to exhibitors of oil paintings at the Chicago Exhibition last year (p. 306, 1893), we erroneously gave the name of Edward Goodall instead of that of Mr. T. F. Goodall, to whom the medal was awarded.

It was seventy years on the 27th of January since Josef Israels, the Dutch artist, was born. Preparations had been made to mark the date by a "fête du maitre," and artists in all countries to the number of three hundred joined in signing their names in an album presented by the Haagsche Kunstring. The Queen Regent of Holland named Israels Commander of the Order of Orange Nassau; and when he entered his studio on January 27th he found his easel decorated with a magnificent crown of laurels. But all these congratulations were unhappily overcast by the death of the artist's wife only a few days before the anniversary. Israels, true to the brave spirit he is known to possess, received the deputations and the homage of his brother artists on his birthday, pathetically trying to save disappointment in others, while his heart was buried with the devoted partner of his long and busy life.

The water-colour art of Israels may be studied with advantage in the collection of Dutch drawings now on exhibition at Messrs. Tooth's Gallery. There are also some unsurpassed examples of the art of Mauve and James Maris. It is remarkable that Paris as well as London has a Dutch water-colour collection on public view. Messrs. Boussod, Valadon & Co., at their new galleries, 24, Boulevard des Capucines, are showing a large series, mostly on loan. Sir John Day, the eminent English judge, contributes nearly a score, these being amongst the best in the Parisian exhibition.

OBITUARY.

Among the best-known works of the late Mr. William Holyoake, who died on the 17th of January, are 'The Sanctuary,' which now hangs in one of the chapels of Westminster Abbey, 'The Home at Nazareth,' and 'The Broken Vow.' Mr. Holyoake was twice the curator of one of the Academy schools, and was very popular amongst the students. A little later we hope to give an account of his career.

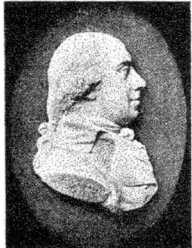
Prof. Dugald Stewart.
Medallion by James Tassie.

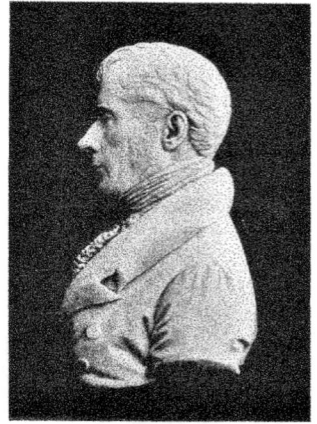
William Tassie.
Wax Medallion by Hagbolt.

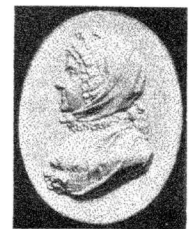
Mrs. Jean Adams.
Medallion by James Tassie.

NEW ART PUBLICATIONS.

ALTHOUGH it may directly appeal to only a small number of connoisseurs, we think the biographical and critical sketch of James and William Tassie, by John M. Gray (W. G. Patterson, Edinburgh), deserves more than ordinary attention. The Tassies were artists in medallions and reproducers of antique gems, who flourished, the elder from 1735 to 1799, and the nephew, William, from 1777 to 1860. James Tassie, the greater of the two artists, was a native of Glasgow, and many of the medallion portraits he produced were Scottish ladies and gentlemen. Over one hundred and fifty of his medallions were left to an institution in Edinburgh, and these with other enamels and plaster casts are now deposited under Mr. Gray's care in the Scottish National Portrait Gallery. We give two examples of his work, Mrs. Adams, a medallion dated 1791, and Professor Dugald Stewart, the metaphysician, dated a few years later. William Tassie, whose portrait is from a wax medallion, by Hagbolt, was more commercial in his instincts.

The thorough practical knowledge of how best to produce a book of this kind displays the author's conspicuous aptitude for still more important productions in the future.

The house of M. Ch. Sedelmeyer is not very well known in this country, although on the Continent it is recognised as the origin of many of the finest etchings in the market. M. Sedelmeyer is an expert of the best kind, quiet and unassuming, yet full of the knowledge which comes only from great experience and continual study. He has published during the past few years the splendid plates of Koepping and Laguillermie after Rembrandt, Hals, and Van Dyck; as well as Waltner's and Mathey-Doret's etchings after Munkacsy.

Under the same guidance Dr. William Bode is preparing a great work in eight volumes on Rembrandt, about which we hope to say something later. M. Sedelmeyer's last publication is 'The Virgin, Child, and St. Catherine,' etched by A. Mathey-Doret from a painting by Van Dyck, now in the possession of Mr. A. A. Sprague, a Chicago magnate. Painted for the family of the Marquis Cambiasso by the master during his sojourn in Geneva, it remained with them until 1840. Then it passed to Count Cornelission, of Brussels, and was sold at his sale a few years ago. It is a most beautiful picture, and the etching by M. Mathey-Doret is well worthy of the masterpiece it represents.

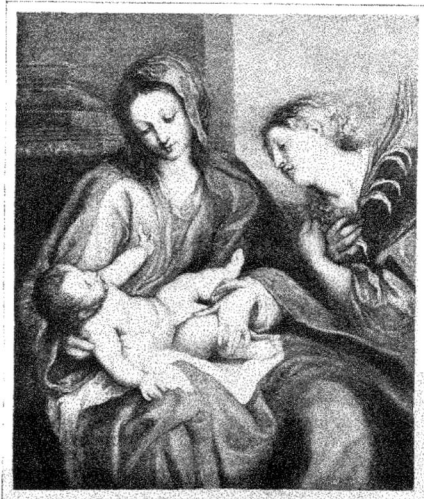
The Virgin, Child, and St. Catherine. By Van Dyck.

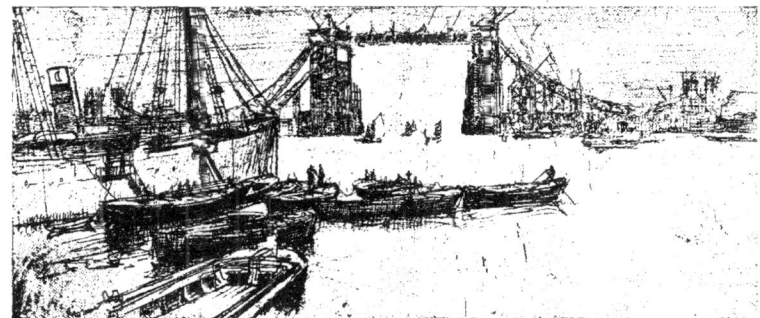

THE TOWER BRIDGE. FROM AN ETCHING BY JOSEPH PENNELL.

ON THE RIVER.

IT is easier to admit than to explain the charm of the Thames. For me it is not one of "the rivers of home," which, Mr. Stevenson says, are "dear in particular to all men." And yet my fancy lingers, as I do myself, on its banks rather than on the shores of the broad Delaware, or the Schuylkill, with its pretty Indian name, where more than half my life was spent. In historic dignity alone the reason may not lie; here, the Seine and the Rhine are its rivals, while the Tiber far outstrips it in whatever attraction history may give. Nor can daily familiarity be held responsible: for many weeks I lived with the Danube hurrying past beneath my window, but it never stirred admiration into the warmer sentiment aroused by the first journey on a Thames penny steamboat.

It is ten years since that first journey was made, but I remember it in all its details: first impressions are ever the strongest. From Westminster to Greenwich was the distance covered, so that the trip to the cockney would have seemed an ordinary half-day outing. But I had been in England not quite a week; the faces and speech of my fellow passengers were still foreign to me; the quiet, unassuming little steamer still astonished by contrast with the big, blustering ferryboats of the Delaware; and before we had pushed from the pier the excursion savoured of an adventure. But once out upon the river, I was, in a measure, at home. The big pile of Westminster we were leaving behind, the great dome we were fast approaching, the Monument, the Tower—these I knew only less well than the State House preserving its old-fashioned calm amidst the bustle of Chestnut Street, than the spire of St. Peter's rising sedately from the red brick and white marble of Pine Street, than the Pennsylvania Hospital, with the statue of Penn, that gets down from its pedestal and walks when it *hears* the clock strike midnight. And when we stopped at other piers the names were pleasantly familiar: Charing Cross and the Temple, Rotherhithe and Wapping. In these was nothing new; they sounded in my ears like the music of a well known refrain. Memories and associations, some vague, some vivid, clustered about them: memories, not learnedly historical but tenderly intimate, not of kings and Lord Mayors and pomps processional, but of old and tried friends, of Johnson and "the Club," of Pendennis and Warrington, of Lizzie and Roger Hexham. And this, it may be, helps to account for at least a part of the Thames' charm, for one's love of its waters and its shores even before one sees them. I am not sure, after all, that it is not the "river of home" for all English-speaking people. In a word, it first attracts, as London itself does, by an indefinable homelike quality: that quality, literary in inspiration, which makes the shabby Strand dearer far than more imposing avenue or gayer boulevard, which gives the Mall precedence over the fair glades of St. Cloud or the stately walks of the Borghese. In books one has ever been on terms the most intimate with London and its river.

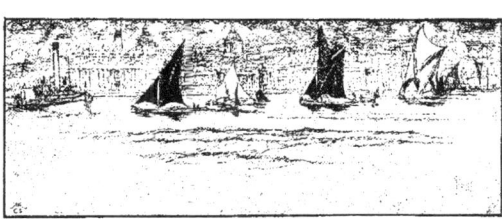

GREENWICH HOSPITAL. FROM AN ETCHING BY JOSEPH PENNELL.

It comes as the surprise that one expected to find the Thames in every way so worthy a background for these old and friendly memories. More than any other stream, it has its special sound and colour. There is a distinct character in its very stillness after the roar of London town, so much louder and more terrible than the voice of lesser cities. And the waters seem to swish and splash with a music all their own against the big black coal-lighters and the barges piled high with hay. The very whistle of the passing tug or steamboat invites with more urgent summons to the world of romance, to the long wanderings by sea.

But, above all, it is the colour that enchants. I do not mean in the "social, athletic, and idyllic." reaches above Richmond, whither, on slightest pretext, the Londoner escapes to make holiday. In the pastoral Thames there is colour enough, and to spare, in the rich blue distances, the lilied waters, the mass of brilliant blazers and blouses. But it is the commercial Thames, from Hammersmith or Chelsea seaward, where the traffic and movement by day, and the stationary and shifting lights in the blue night, present that incomparable series of colour schemes and harmonies that enrapture the painter and inspire the poet. It is here you must look for its glimmer and glitter, for the endless play of smoke and sunshine, of mist and fog; here that stately and squalid banks vie with each other in the majesty and mystery of their august and solemn shapes. For if it be true, as Mr. Henry James thinks—and the truth I dispute—that no European city

elegance to the fairest prospect, and clothes with beauty the most sordid details.

But to dismiss the river's front with wholesale condemnation is to mislead. Mean and shabby warehouses there may be, strange rookeries—too many of these, alas! fast disappearing—black and squalid wharfs. Factories and breweries, perhaps, are to be deplored; London may have no Louvre to turn a faultless façade upon the Thames, whose waters, throughout their windings from source to sea, flow beneath; nought so imposing as the Palace that, at Avignon, looks down upon the Rhone, nor between banks so picturesque as those with which the City of Lilies lines the Arno. But it has its compensations. Beauty there is, though of another kind, in the pleasant pile, red in the old brick, grey in the church tower, at Lambeth; in the Houses of Parliament, assuming their most commanding aspect when seen from the river, and the many towers of Westminster arranging themselves in effective and fantastic groups, loveliest when they rise, purple and shadowy, against London's lurid sunsets; in the great mass of Whitehall Court and the National Liberal Club, distance softening vulgar detail and disguising abortive ornament. Serene and stately is the long, classical line of Somerset

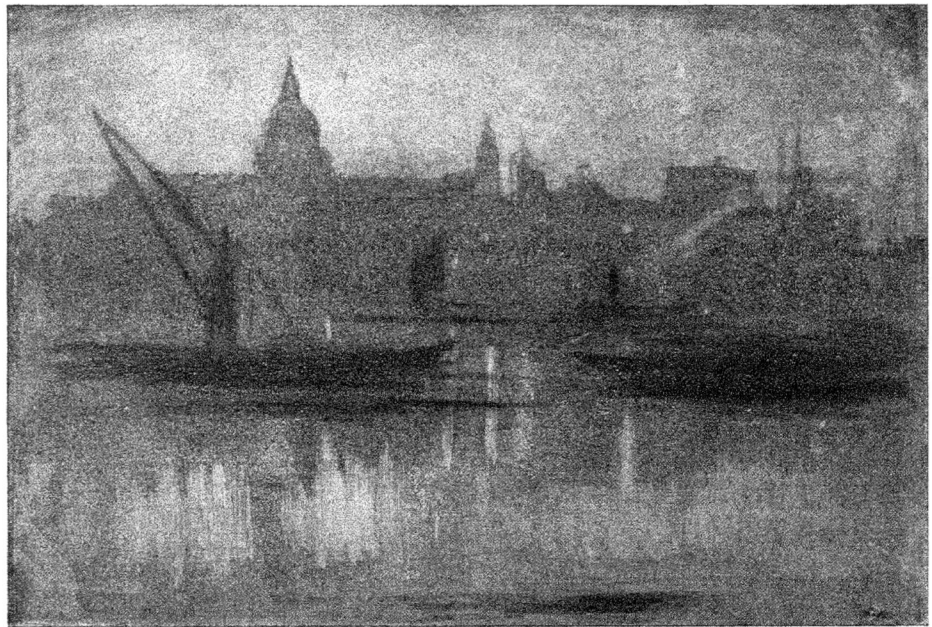

COMING UP IN THE EVENING. ST. PAUL'S BY NIGHT. FROM AN ETCHING BY JOSEPH PENNELL.

has expended more ingenuity than London in producing an ugly river front, still more certain is it that no other town in the world rejoices in an atmosphere that lends new grace and

House, pictorial the Temple group; and who shall say that either is not a fitting adornment here, where the river curves in graceful sweep toward the great dome that would redeem ugliness more uncompromising than that of Bankside? To be sure—if I except the Tower—after this, one passes little save the warehouses. But, thanks to the atmosphere, each be- be so harmonious. But in colour, in the solidity which is London's prevailing characteristic, they excel. I heard once of a country woman who, when she came to London for her

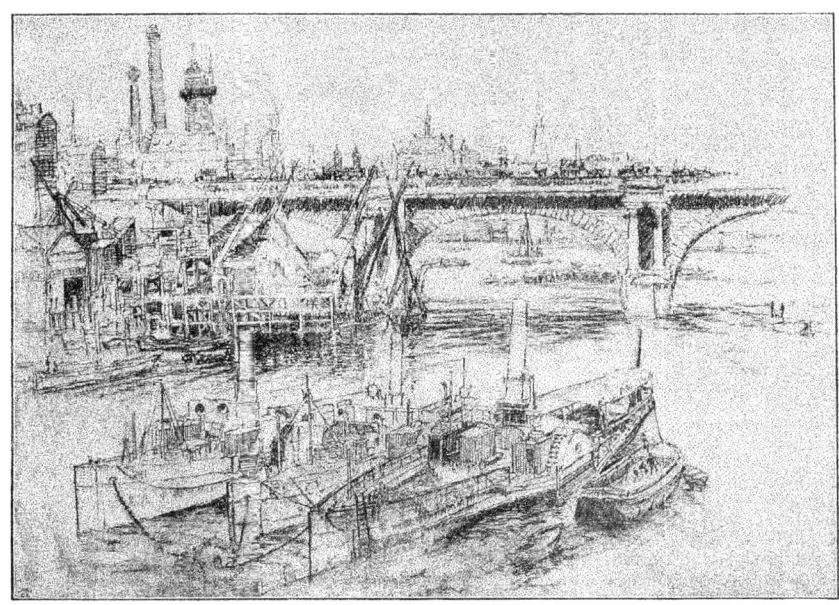

COALING AT WATERLOO BRIDGE. FROM AN ETCHING BY JOSEPH PENNELL.

comes palatial in its vagueness, while every shot-tower might have had a Giotto for its architect.

The atmosphere, however, will not always work this kindly spell. On days of rare sunshine, the bare griminess of commercial shores stands out unabashed and undisguised. But he must have a feeble imagination, upon whom the signs of London's greatness will not make a corresponding impression. For it is this which distinguishes London from all other towns: its industry, its importance, its colossal commerce. And as one goes farther down the river, these signs ever increase. The warehouses form an unbroken front. On each side a forest of masts rises before them. Big steamers lie at anchor or move majestically out to sea. The barges impress by numbers rather than size, for, large as they seem about Charing Cross, here they are dwarfed by the giant sea-going ships. Probably nowhere does the world's work beat with such feverish pulse. It may be the new contrast which gives to Greenwich, with its long, low-fronted hospital and the lovely wooded hill above, so rural and peaceful an aspect after the ceaseless activity in the Pool, which helps to make it seem so quiet and retired a haunt for the long hot summer afternoon, when town becomes unbearable.

But, before coming to Greenwich, the river has borrowed no little of its beauty and grandeur from the bridges. These are not so many as in Paris; their proportions may not always first visit, cared to see nothing but London Bridge : this was the summit of her ambition. Here, she thought, was the pivot upon which the world turns, and in so thinking she showed a nice sense for traditional importance and actual pre-eminence. Had her sympathies been a little broader, they would have gone out as fondly to old Battersea Bridge, with its memories of Whistler and Turner; to Westminster, from which Wordsworth watched the river gliding at its own sweet will ; to Waterloo, suggesting Constable; to Blackfriars, where Rossetti's Magdalen was "Found"; to each, indeed, that spans the muddy, turbid waters of the Thames. Even where railroads cross the stream in dull, prosaic lines, the smoke, in long white trails, decorates the mean architecture with rare devices ; even the Tower Bridge, though it still looks to the future for its associations, though it all but ruins a broad, beautiful reach of the river, has on a misty day a majesty unparalleled on the Thames, as its great piers shoot high up above barges and steamers and clustered masts.

If the river were a big spectacle, shut in by jealous walls, to which an admission fee was charged, all London would rush to see it, and "Constantinople" lose half its visitors ; so long as a thing is called a show, and is guarded by turnstile and booking office, it runs a chance of popularity. As it is, the river, except on Sunday and Saturday afternoons, is monopolised by business; it becomes a mere adjunct to the Underground, and the Strand: the highway it was in Pepys'

Nowadays, the Thames lies practically at my door; a little pier is within a five minutes' walk. I am always pro-

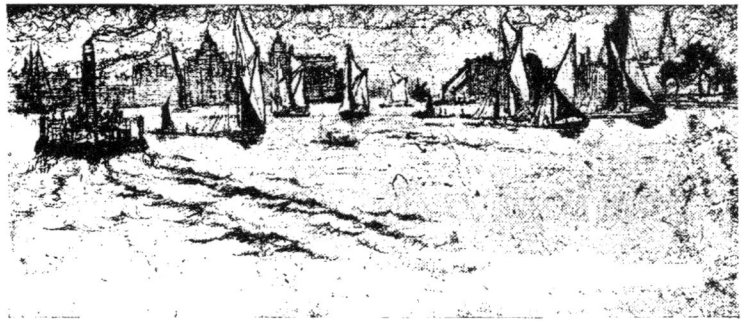

GREENWICH. FROM AN ETCHING BY JOSEPH PENNELL.

time; the little steamboat is a pleasant exchange from railway carriage or omnibus. It is too near, too easy of access. The average Londoner thinks nothing of the early morning flight to Paddington or Waterloo in time to catch the first train that will carry him and his hamper to Taplow or to Moulsey; his holiday is the more prized if he has worked hard for it. To walk down to the Embankment and board a penny steamboat would be all too tame an undertaking, too simple an enterprise for pleasure. On Sundays and holidays the boats might, like popular theatres, hang out the sign "Standing room only!" But they are filled with a very different crowd to that which passes elegantly through Boulter's Lock, and drinks tea in the willowed backwaters about Clieveden. It is a crowd which does not run to

mising myself—that is, in summer, when steamboats are running—new and strange adventures. There is one in particular that, in fancy, never fails to fascinate: the excursion to Clacton-on-Sea. No sooner does summer come than I begin to think of the delight of steaming down to this delectable spot, and here breathing a breath of sea air to serve as tonic, and send me back, with braver heart, to London and to work. The very name has a magical sound in my ears, so many are the pleasures it represents. When I hear it, already, in imagination, I look out upon the sea and the ships, "adventurous and fair," sailing away for the dim lands of romance, I smell the salt air, and wander along the beach. But to Clacton-on-Sea, as yet, I have never been. The expedition is too preposterously simple. It necessitates no preparation, no

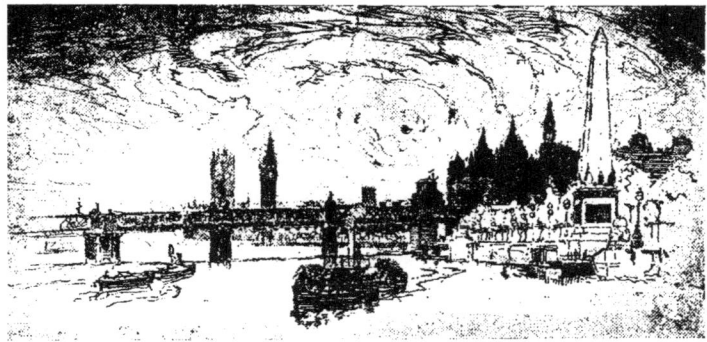

CLEOPATRA'S NEEDLE. FROM AN ETCHING BY JOSEPH PENNELL.

blazers and blouses, relying chiefly upon Tommy Atkins to give it a dash of colour and vivacity. But with it lies wisdom. For the upper river has no pleasanter, no more pictorial journey than that from Charing Cross to Westminster. Long experience has but confirmed my first impressions.

planning. Besides, to go might be to discover that there is no beach; and, after all, even at Charing Cross, the incoming tide brings with it the smell of the sea. It is best not to chance adding one more to one's stock of lost illusions, already all too large.

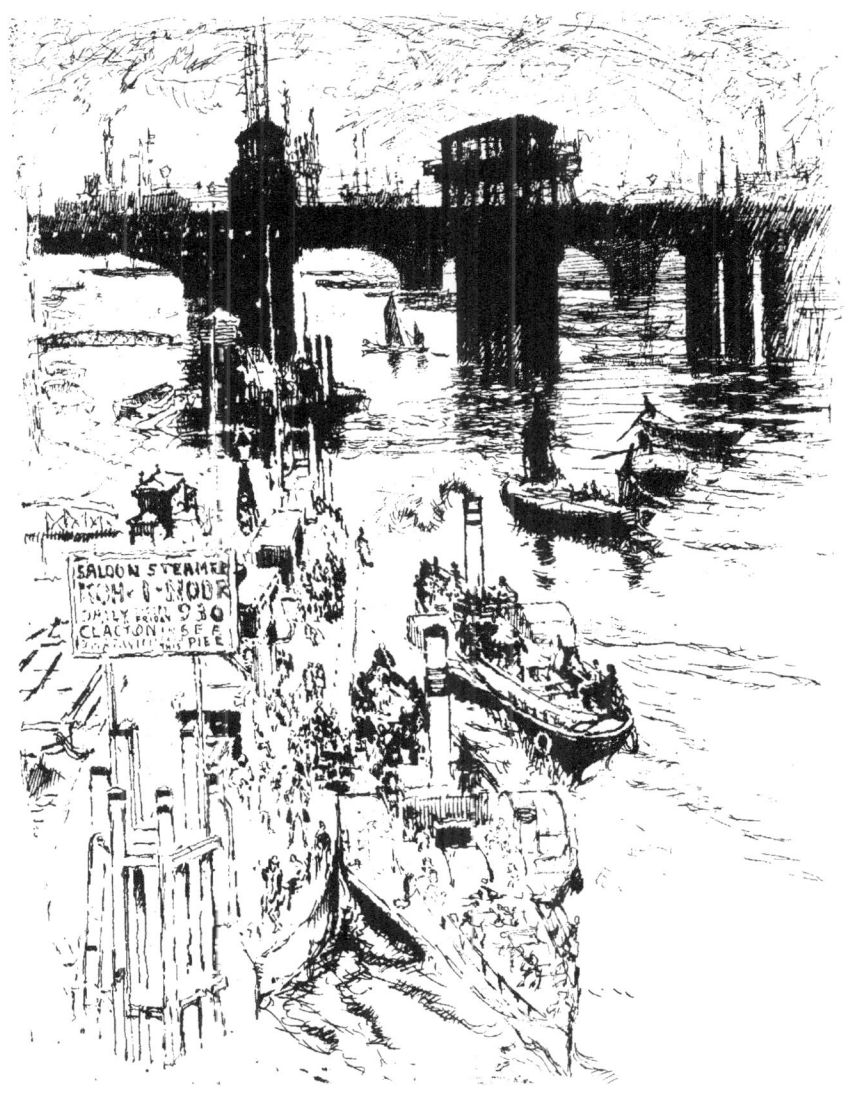

ON THE RIVER.

ORIGINAL ETCHING BY JOSEPH PENNELL

LONDON, J.S. VIRTUE & CO. LIMITED

And so, it has come about that my longest adventure has ever followed the track of the first; that I have ever been content with the same goal. And Greenwich may well suffice: nowhere could there be a lovelier place to waste the long summer evening than its hill-top, looking down upon the broad reaches of the Thames, and the red-sailed barges and black ships that sail sea and townward.

ELIZABETH ROBINS PENNELL.

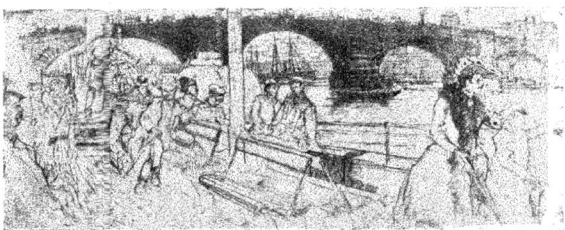

ON THE RIVER. FROM AN ETCHING BY JOSEPH PENNELL.

ANTON MAUVE.

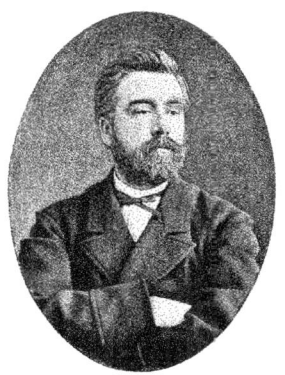

THE 5th of February, 1889, was the first anniversary of Mauve's death. His friends and admirers met that day at the burial-place near the Canal—which runs from The Hague to Scheveningen—to unveil a monumental stone, erected by the painter's brother-artists and friends. It was just such a fine silvery and slightly hazy day as the painter himself used to love, and one which exquisitely harmonized with his mind and art. On the day of his burial, almost a year before, it had also been noticed that nature seemed to bestow a last proof of her affection for the sympathetic artist who had adored her in this calm and transparent mood, rather than in her moments of dramatic display. The slab is a simple granite stone, polished only on the side which bears the name, "ANTON MAUVE, 1838-1888," and roughly hewn on the top. It stands erect, because the painter's loving wife preferred to have only turf and wild flowers over the resting-place. A slender birch-tree and a fir had been transplanted from Laren, where the painter spent the last and happiest years of his life. They had been chosen from a group growing not far from his homely cottage, which has been memorized in some of those last superb water-colours, which show the painter at the highest level of his charming art.

The sheep painter, Ter Meulen, Mauve's most fervent admirer, and one might almost say his truest disciple, delivered a short oration full of feeling and that classic simplicity which the master had always loved. He thanked Mauve's brother-in-law, Mr. Le Comte, painter and professor at the Delft Polytechnical Academy, for his sympathetic project of the monument, and made over Mauve's last resting-place to his widow and children. These scattered flowers on the grave and deposited funeral wreaths. On the turf now grow the daisies and dandelions with which the master often embellished his silvery foregrounds. The simple solemnity of this occasion was not so imposing as that of the burial a year before, but it had a rural charm of its own.

Mauve had died quite unexpectedly at Arnhem, in the Dutch district of Gelderland, at the house of his brother, the "sub-rector" of the gymnasium or high school there. For some days he had been suffering of melancholia or depression of spirits; "my head is weary, I cannot work," he had complained. But this depression often came over him; every three or four years almost; and sometimes such a period would last for weeks. So the physician advised him to get about a little; and he made a trip to visit some friends and relations in the east of Holland. Aneurism, or some disease of the heart, was the immediate cause of his death.

When the painter was in one of his dejected moods, he felt unable to finish the work he might have in hand, and could only sketch his plans. If the attack were severe he was not even equal to that. It did him good at such times to see some friends, though the effort required to entertain society was distasteful. His wife, however, encouraged such visits, and a few of his quiet, more intimate friends would penetrate to his studio, a roomy, well-lighted wooden construction. Thus, stand at the same spot to admire the simple beauty of nature unmanipulated by the art of composition.

Some time after his death, Mr. Tersteeg, representative

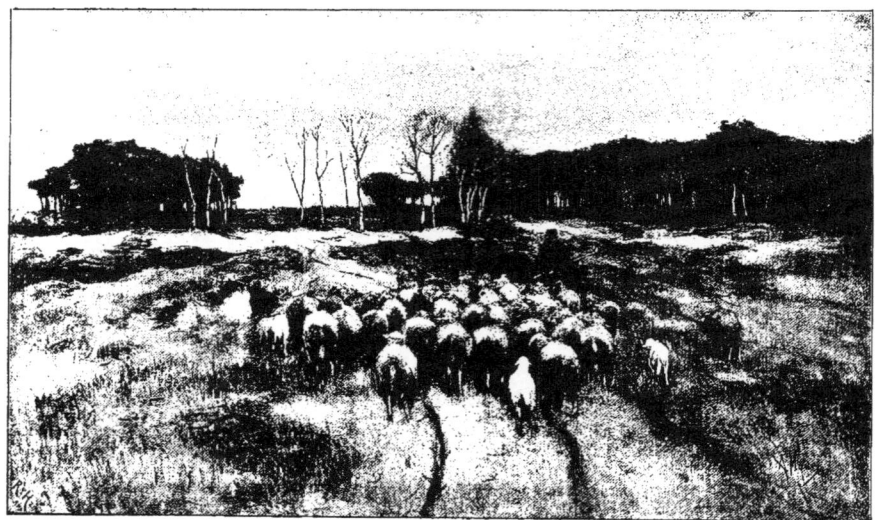

NEAR LAREN. FROM THE PICTURE BY ANTON MAUVE.

in his garden, I often saw him, leaning his head on his hand, gazing into blankness with gloomy brow and heavily-wrinkled forehead, looking the picture of melancholy. He invariably reminded me of a frontispiece I once saw in an American edition of Burton's "Anatomy of Melancholy."

To rummage among old studies and sketches, to talk about rambles in search of beautiful rustic scenery among the downs or near Oosterbeek and Wolfhezen—two very picturesque Geldrian spots, where Mauve had sojourned for some time in his younger years, and where he made the acquaintance of the Bilders, father and son, and William Maris—sometimes smoothed away the wrinkles from his gloomy brow. When the veil which hung over his mind was lifted more or less, a game of dominoes in the afternoon, and a quiet rubber in the evening, would bring him some solace. Then at last would arrive the moment when he could be induced to take a walk along the canal of Scheveningen, or by the rustic paths of Clingendaal, where the downs gleam so beautifully under the light blue sky of our coasts. Sometimes, the sketch-book still being at home, he could not resist the temptation of a cheerful moment and make a memorandum on one of his cuffs, which afterwards developed into a characteristic oil-painting or water-colour.

When he was entirely his real self again, he would often tear a page out of his pocket-book to show me how he found complete pictures in nature. He would cut a little aperture in the paper and look through the opening at a piece of landscape which had struck him, and he would then make me

of the firm Goupil (Boussod, Valadon & Co.), organized both at The Hague and in London, an exhibition of work selected from the sketch-books in the possession of Mdme. Mauve, and there could be seen in this exhibition quite a collection of such unpretentious rural pieces, which the painter had apparently discovered through the medium of his paper "peep glass." Every one who is familiar with Mauve's work will remember having been attracted by his classic purity of composition. Not Mauve, but Nature herself, composed the greatest part of that goodly array of noble works, which is now dispersed all over the world. For simplicity and purity of style, Mauve was hardly equalled by Corot. There may be more fantasy in Corot, who appeared sometimes to look through the eyes of Claude.

After Mauve had suffered for some time from one of his fits of melancholy, it would seem at last as if the veil were entirely withdrawn, and then a wonderful mental energy and clearness would come, enabling the painter to finish or to produce an immense amount of intensely conscientious work. Once, when I had been to see him in his studio, he told me, with beaming eyes and flushed face, that in one week he had painted eight pictures and fourteen water-colours. Of course there were among that number some which had been partly sketched before, but which he had only now found the power to finish. The spirit of inspiration returned to him, and the sudden rekindling of genius enabled him to transfuse into his work that spiritual life of nature which he prized so highly, and without which Art is but a dumb show.

The news of Mauve's death created a profound impression in Holland, and especially at the Hague, where the painter had lived so many years, and where he had many friends. Yet, strange to say, alas for Holland! few of his works are to be found in Dutch homes or Dutch collections. When Mauve had become sufficiently appreciated here, he had already attained considerable popularity in Scotland, England, and America, consequently the prices of his pictures were too high for Dutch purses. There are few genuine lovers of nature in Holland, and those few are, as a rule, scantily blessed with the *nervus rerum* which makes buying pictures a possibility. The Dutch merchant spends most of his life at his desk or on the exchange, and has more taste for Swiss and German mountain landscape, than for the quiet familiar poetry of Dutch rural scenery. M. Mauve's countrymen mostly judge modern landscape art from the conventional point of view, such as they see in the pictures of one or two preceding generations, and not from nature herself.

It is remarkable that during his last three or four years Mauve strove much more after plastic beauty and anatomical correctness than before. I believe this is due to the influence of Millet, whose works he admired and closely studied from

The grandest and the most exquisite and complete water-colours of Mauve date from Laren, a village near Amsterdam and Utrecht, celebrated among painters for the homely interiors of its weavers and peasants. Valkenburg, Neuhuys, Kever, Bastert, and, more recently, the not less famous Frenchman, Lhermitte, have made it their residence for a time. Mauve, too, loved the primitive old place for its commons and its flocks and folds, its graceful birches, black firs, and its silver skies. The first picture of this series was bought at the rather big price, for Holland, of £200, by Mr. Servatius, Overyssel. We give a reproduction of it on the opposite page. A flock of sheep is moving towards the groups of birches and firs in the background of the landscape. A softly resplendent grey sky hangs over the heathery expanse. It is said that a well-known collector was much taken with the drawing, but objected to what he considered the helpless tripping of the little lamb. Perhaps there may be some anatomical incongruity in the way the lamb manages its legs, but to my taste the natural characteristics of the little animal are excellently expressed, and full of gentle feeling and quiet humour.

It should here be mentioned, that among Dutch artists a

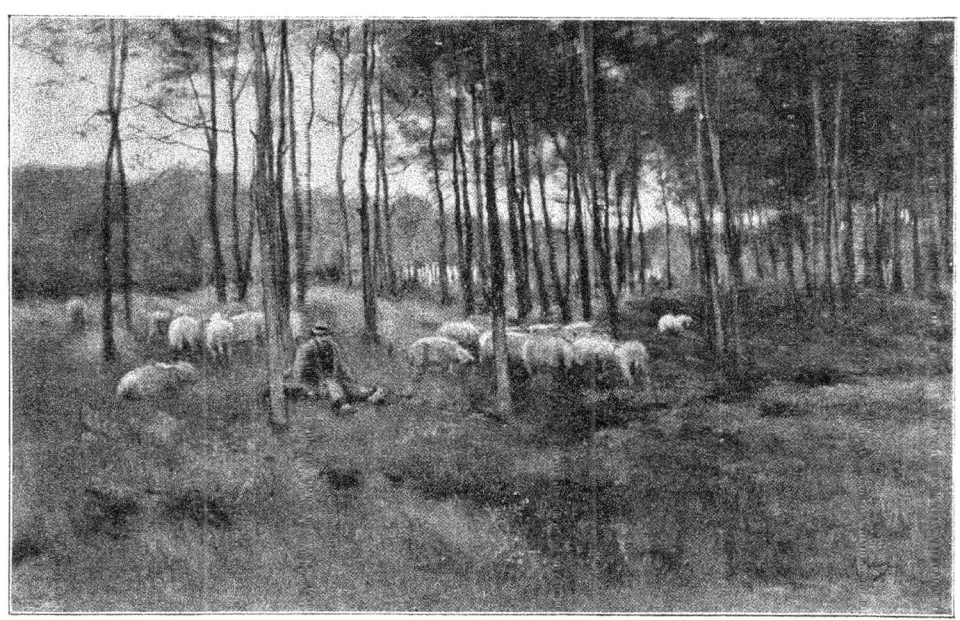

UNDER THE TREES. FROM THE DRAWING BY ANTON MAUVE, IN THE COLLECTION OF J. S. FORBES, ESQ.

photographic reproductions, of which he possessed towards the end a very rich collection. I remember one evening, about a year before he left The Hague, he invited one of our most talented young landscape painters, Bastert, and myself, to look over his little treasures.

few of Mauve's great admirers prefer the naive ways of his earliest manner, but the best-known British collectors, such as Mr. J. S. Forbes, Sir John Day, and Mr. Alexander Young, prefer the more mature and individual work.

Mauve had produced during the thirty years of his working

period an immense quantity of pictures, drawings in water-colour and some in black-and-white, mostly in a very genial and sympathetic art, of which a very small part only is to be found in Holland. His popularity in Great Britain and America may be ascribed to his eminently Anglo-Saxon character, the Dutch for the most part being of the same origin as the British. The poetry of Mauve's art, its tenderness, the unobtrusive, quiet sadness of the scenery and people which attracted him most; the homeliness, humour and domestic happiness which he interpreted in his interiors and scenes of country and village life, can only be fully appreciated by people of the same descent.

In 1881, at an evening exhibition ("Kunstbeschouwing") of the "Pulchri Studio," I saw for the first time an eminently characteristic water-colour, representing a timber auction in a wood-growing part of the country. The notary, the auctioneer, the farmers, labourers, village carpenters, and tradesmen inspect with seemingly indifferent but critical attitudes the lots and single trunks for sale. Most of the actors and spectators are seen from behind, but the drawing is so expressive that the quiet characteristic scene conveys to the full a significance of rustic shrewdness and diplomacy. Every type of character is expressed with the most delightful accuracy, with that rich fund of humour of which Mauve was the happy possessor.

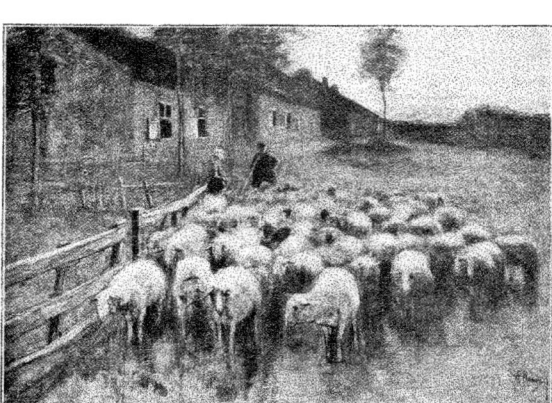

WINTER. BY ANTON MAUVE.

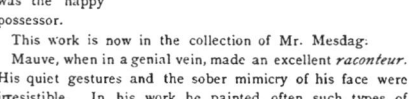

EVENING. BY ANTON MAUVE.

This work is now in the collection of Mr. Mesdag.

Mauve, when in a genial vein, made an excellent *raconteur*. His quiet gestures and the sober mimicry of his face were irresistible. In his work he painted often such types of personality of which he thought a little fun could be made in a quiet, harmless way. So the painter had a great deal of the actor in him. His gardeners, wood-cutters, labourers, shepherds were always remarkable for their complete individuality. Mauve rarely introduced a human figure merely to exhibit some plastic beauty in the ordinary acceptation of the expression. I can only recall one instance, where a country girl in light blue dress is gathering beans in a kitchen garden. Here our artist attained that ideal beauty of line and attitude in the expression of which Albert Neuhuys excels. The drawing was simply exquisite in the harmony of light blue, green and grey tints which it revealed.

I think the painter is best known all over the world by his flocks of sheep, depicted at all seasons and in every kind of weather, and under every condition of light and air; by his sheep in the folds and by his cows in "de Melkbocht";* also by his horses ploughing or at rest. Remarkable, too, are some of his coast scenes, showing the "pinks," or Dutch fishing-boats, about to be pulled over the sands by long teams of ill-fed looking horses.

Of Mauve's sheep pictures, the one which made the most lasting impression on my mind among many others belonging to the same style, was his magnificent painting first shown at The Hague Exhibition of 1881, depicting a small flock of sheep in the downs nibbling the scanty grass of the sandhills. The sheep were about eight inches long on the canvas and beautifully modelled and

* The paddock or reserved spot in the meadow where the cows are gathered for milking.

drawn. One could almost "pluck the wool from the fleeces," as the old amateurs are wont to say. Above the imposing downs there was only to be seen a small streak of light bluish-grey, silky sky; the rest of the picture was the silvery downs with their light-coloured vegetation, and "white woolly sea," as the Dutch poet Vandal described a flock of sheep.

Mauve was a great painter and poet of light in his sunny and glowing "melk-bochten." How beautiful is the glitter of the checkered light on the emerald grass—how splendid the sun's reflections upon the sleek hides of his black-and-white times seems covered by an almost imperceptible silken veil of the tenderest grey colour. A short time ago I was shown among the collection of an amateur a work by Mauve, representing a sheepfold on a snow-covered heath. The sheep are being quietly driven into the fold by the shepherd and his dog. But Mauve rarely chose snow effects for a subject. In this case the white tones of the snow were wonderfully true.

The painter always took a delight in drawing and painting birch-trees in his landscapes; the birch with its graceful and silvery stem was his favourite tree.

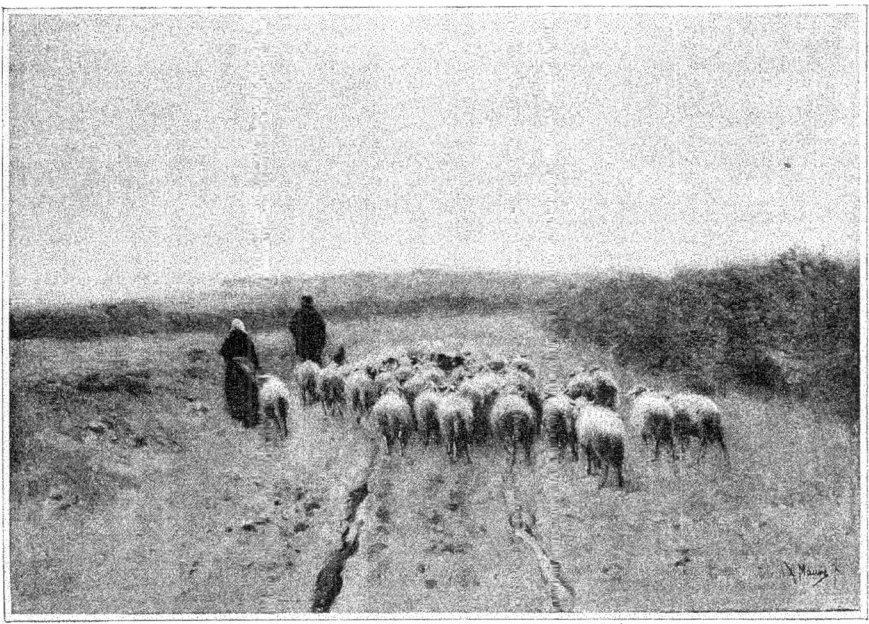

THE FLOCK RETURNING. FROM THE PAINTING BY ANTON MAUVE, IN THE COLLECTION OF ALEXANDER YOUNG, ESQ.

cow! The robe of an empress could not be more resplendent than the hides of Dutch cattle in the sunlight.

Our artist also delighted to represent in his works the richness and fertility of arable land, with the plough at work, drawn by black or white horses. He loved to paint some white powerful horse, contrasting its silvery reflections with the dark violet clods and the grey, hazy atmosphere. It seemed when he painted it as if the vapour were actually rising from the fertile land, and from the steaming hide and nostrils of the ploughing beast.

Other favourite themes of Mauve's were pretty country lanes enlivened, perhaps, by a wood cart, or a man on horseback, or, it might be, by a peasant woman on the way to market or collecting fuel, or a wood cutter at work.

Over these scenes he would spread that transparent and delicate haze, which is so characteristic of the fruitful days of March and April. For at that time of the year nature some-

It was quite a public ceremony when, early in February, 1888, the mortal remains of the painter were received by his relations, friends and brother artists, at the Rhenish railway station of The Hague, where it had arrived from Arnhem. Deputations of the principal Art societies and clubs in our country, and innumerable artists and friends from all parts of Holland, had assembled; and when the coffin was hearsed and covered with flowers, wreaths, and palms, the imposing tones of Beethoven's funeral march were heard from the Royal Military Band, which accompanied the funeral train. His brother artists, Mesdag, Bart van Hove, Sadee, Artz, Gabriel, and Weissenbruch were pall-bearers, either in the capacity of deputies of their respective societies, or as the dead man's oldest friends. When the procession passed the Art Academy, all the pupils were ranged before the portico to do homage to the dead master.

Anton Mauve was born September 18th, 1838, at Zaandam, the small town in North Holland which has become well known in history by Czar Peter the Great's sojourn there to learn the craft of shipbuilding. Mauve's father was a Protestant clergyman in this thriving little place ; chiefly known now for its oil and paper-mills, and extensive timber trade. Anton was still very young when the worthy pastor was nominated clergyman at Haarlem, the capital of North Holland. When a boy, the future painter manifested a strong taste for drawing, but his father objected to his becoming an artist. A compromise, however, was effected between youthful ambition and parental prudence. If the son would consent to study for a diploma as drawing-master, which would insure him a livelihood in case he should fail as an artist, his father undertook to withdraw his opposition, and Anton would be permitted to follow his bent. This proved rather a bitter pill for the youngster, as he possessed certain personal opinions on the art of drawing, which were not at all those generally accepted by the brotherhood of the pencil. The young artist, almost in despair, once burst into tears, asserting that he would never learn to draw in the manner his masters thought it should be done. He entered the studio of the cattle painter, Van Os, but the master was by no means pleased with his young pupil, complaining that Mauve could never finish a subject. Not long after this apprenticeship Anton set himself to painting little pictures, which are sometimes met with at auctions. They show mostly the neat manner and conventional style of the period and of his former master. The original genius that was to come can scarcely be discerned.

Mauve's family was not rich, and when on a fine day the youth packed his knapsack to go to Oosterbeek for some time, it was with a purse as light as his heart. But the painter never was of the modern Bohemian type, who spends a fortune in luxurious eating and drinking and collecting *bric-à-brac*. So he felt quite happy in beautiful Oosterbeek (near Arnhem), at that time the Barbizon of Holland.

During the winter season Mauve settled in Amsterdam, where he worked hard and made a little money. But, of course, his art was not yet well paid. A favourite resort of the painter in summer-time was The Hague with Scheveningen. He once brought his luggage to a farmhouse near Dekkersdinn, in the neighbourhood of Loosduiner, and lived there for a considerable time.

This is a fine spot with silvery downs bordered with bright grass, where small cows and sheep nibble their scanty pasture.

Here Mauve found some of his most important and favourite themes, such as poor cots built in or near the downs, where slender, poorly-nurtured women tended a few sheep or a goat, or occupied themselves in bleaching linen. His painting had not yet gained that transparency, and brilliancy of tone, which the artist acquired in subsequent years. At this time his work was grey but not always pellucid or silvery. Thus it came to pass that critics and public began to talk of "The Grey School," for a few other artists painted in the same neutral scale of tints. The farm, called "Kronenburg," still exists, but the quiet and picturesque environs of the rustic spot have been spoiled and desecrated by a steam tramway. The splendid downs have been levelled by all-encroaching "civilisation." At The Hague Mauve first met his wife, a gentle-minded, tender-hearted woman, belonging to a family very proficient in music. She was just the wife to be an angel in the home of an artist like Mauve, who at times could be moody and irritable, when under the influence of nervous troubles. He loved the naïve ways of children, and his marriage was happily blessed with them. Artz, the brothers Maris, Ter Meulen, Tholen, Bastert and Tersteeg, were, amongst others, good friends of the family. He lived in a roomy house with fine garden on the "Zwarteweg," near the Wood, almost opposite the "Gebouw voor Kunsten en Wetenschappen" (Hall for Arts and Sciences), where he frequently attended the fine concerts given during the season. In 1873, when Mauve was suffering from one of his fits of dejection, he spent some weeks at Godesberg, on the German Rhine. It was very amusing to hear him talk about his residence there: "One could be so lazy and tranquil at Godesberg," he would say ; "there was absolutely nothing to be seen or to be admired in nature, only a lot of *chromos*. What a treat it was to live on a hill, to walk, to eat, to drink a glass of hock, to be lazy and get better!" Mauve was no admirer of nature in Germany, as few will be if accustomed to the more delicate and poetic tones of our Dutch landscape.

The beloved and admired artist is not dead. As we walk in the rural lanes beneath the slender birches wrapped in their mantle of silver-grey haze, or watch the chequered sunlight dancing into the secluded nooks of some emerald meadow, when we hear the echoes of the tinkling sheep bells on the moors, we think, "There lives Mauve !"

A. C. LOFFELT.

The Hague, *February*, 1894.

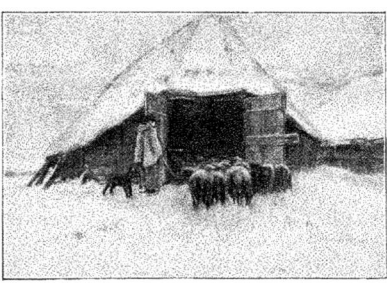

SHEEP ENTERING A BARN. BY ANTON MAUVE.

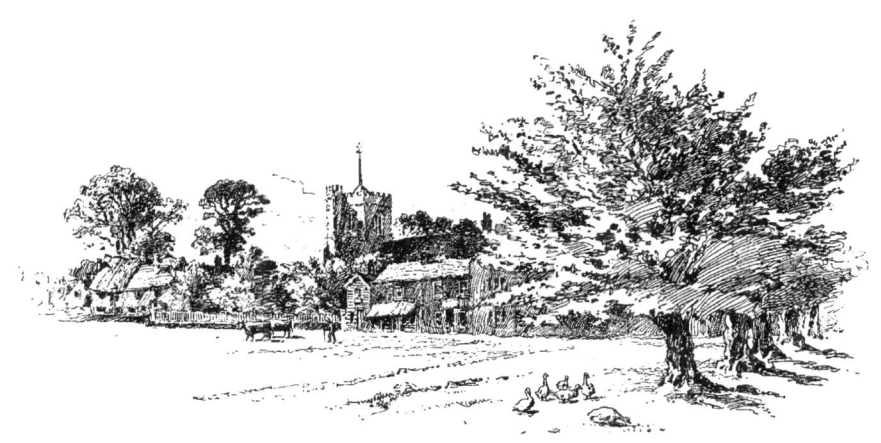

HARPENDEN CHURCH. FROM A DRAWING BY F. G. KITTON.

A PRETTY HERTFORDSHIRE VILLAGE:
HARPENDEN.

IT would be difficult to discover in the county of Hertford, or in any other English county, a more delightfully-rural locality than that where peaceful little Harpenden is situated. Though not so remarkable for the general primitiveness characteristic of smaller villages more remote from the Great Metropolis, it still retains many of the features of English rural life which exercise a fascinating influence over the minds of those dwellers in large towns who appreciate quiet seclusion and a temporary freedom from business worry and anxiety.

When we remember that Harpenden is barely five-and-twenty miles from London, that it is contiguous to the main line of the Midland Railway, and that, after a forty minutes' run from St. Pancras, we can be transferred from the busy hum of commercial activity to this eminently tranquil and picturesque spot, it seems remarkable that it should continue to be free from the intrusion of that utilitarian element which so frequently causes the "sentimentalist" to groan with despair. It must, however, be admitted, that the rural advantages to which I have just alluded are beginning to be recognised, for, unfortunately, the speculative builder has already made his presence felt, and the rows of suburban looking dwellings that are springing up here and there certainly do not tend to enhance the beauty of the neighbourhood. Nevertheless, there are, "within easy distance of the railway-station" (to use a familiar advertising phrase), residences of a superior class, the architects of which have rightly considered the desirability of imparting to their conceptions a sense of what is structurally pictorial. An excellent illustration of this is to be found in the attractive, homely dwelling known by the somewhat original appellation, "Pigeonswick," for the design of which (as well as of the quaint entrance-gate) Mr. E. W. Godwin is responsible; it is interesting to add that this charming house was formerly tenanted by that most delightful exponent of the dramatic art, Miss Ellen Terry, and that it is (so I am told) the birthplace of her son, Mr. Gordon Craig.

Harpenden (or 'Arden, as the rustics call it) derives its name from a valley close by, which (as geologists affirm) was

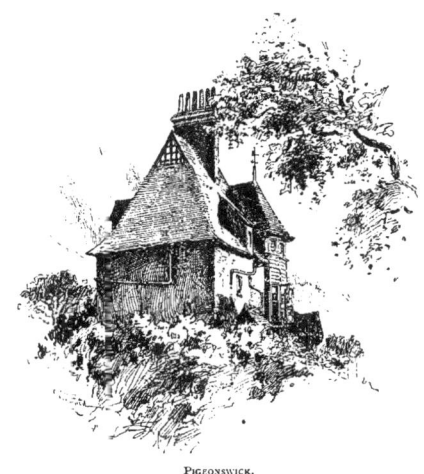

PIGEONSWICK.

scooped out by a great stream many ages ago; we are further informed that "Harpenden" (i.e. "Haerpendene) means "the valley of nightingales," and therefore it is fair to conjecture that, in Anglo-Saxon times, these sweet songsters were here so numerous as to justify the nomenclature. The village and locality, however, can probably boast a still greater antiquity than the period just referred to, for Mr. Cussans, the latest historian of Hertfordshire, opines that a Roman road ran from Verulam (near St. Albans) through Harpenden to Luton, while, in a field in the same locality, a Roman sarcophagus was discovered in the centre of a large tumulus about sixty years since, a relic that may now be seen in the British Museum. Other objects have also been found in the neighbourhood, demonstrating that the Conquerors of the World had a small station or settlement in this vicinity.

In approaching the village from the south, those who travel by road must first traverse that immense open space, Harpenden Common. This beautiful stretch of heath-land, surrounded by luxuriant trees and plentifully besprinkled with gorse (whose golden bloom so gladdened the heart of Linnæus), is undoubtedly the principal charm, the crowning glory of the district, and the great attraction for those who make Harpenden their favourite summer resort. By those who frequent race-courses the Common is remembered chiefly as the scene of mental excitement and equine endurance (and, possibly, of empty pockets), for here annual horse-races are held in the merry month of May, just before the Derby Day, which are followed, about a month later, by the Herts Yeomanry races. It is unnecessary to say that, on such occasions, the Common is *not* seen at its best; indeed, it is difficult to conceive a greater contrast than that presented by it during race-days and as viewed under normal conditions, for these annual meetings (I refer principally to the first of the two) bring in their train vast crowds of what may be justly termed the "seamy side" of humanity, while the consequent turmoil and bustling activity may be compared only to Derby Day itself. Fortunately for the peaceably-disposed persons who reside in the district, the irruption and disturbance are brief;

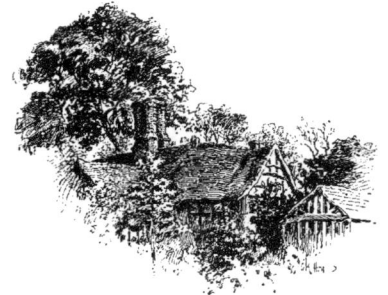

THE BULL, HARPENDEN.

itself to all lovers of natural scenery and effects. On a bright, sunny day in May or June the golden gorse, enriched by a background of verdant grass, delights the eye, and the scene is enhanced by the lights and shadows which chase each other over the breezy expanse as the fleecy clouds overhead are wafted across the sky; while in the autumn a more sombre effect is presented, when the tall heads of dry grass sway to and fro above the green furze-bushes, "like the sea under the caresses of a gentle breeze." This furze is a useful as well as an ornamental adjunct, for the neighbouring cottagers convert it into fuel during the winter; it serves them for warming and cooking, and in many other ways, being not only the poor man's door-mat, but is made available as thatch for the little shed in which he keeps his tools and his rabbits. So it is not an uncommon sight to see a stolid-looking native, armed with a pickaxe, cutting away the prickly shrubs and tying them in faggots, ready for carrying them to a farmhouse close by, where, as likely as not, they will soon be heating the oven, from whence will presently emerge some delicious home-made bread.

Mr. A. E. Gibbs speaks with authority when he says that Harpenden Common is the home of many species of birds and insects. Sometimes one may catch sight of a lizard or harmless snake sunning itself by the wayside, but which, directly it hears the approach of footsteps, is soon lost to view in a clump of ling or wild thyme. "Occasionally, a flight of goldfinches will visit the Common, and may be seen balancing themselves on the thistle-heads, pecking away at the fluffy seeds of which they are so fond. Linnets, bullfinches, wrens, tits, and a host of more familiar members of the feathered tribe, flit from bush to bush, and the common wagtail (or, as the country-folk call it, the 'dish-washer') struts along the ground just ahead

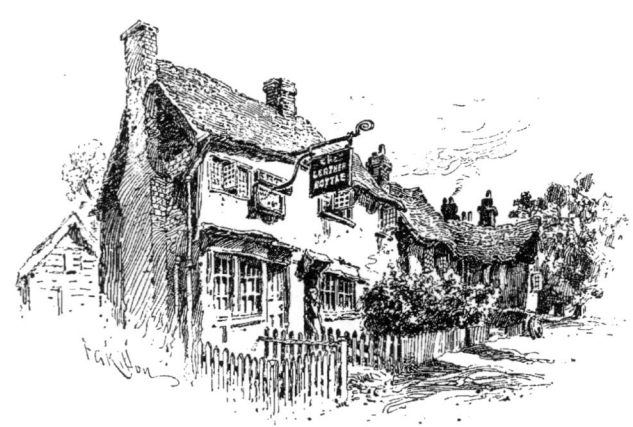

THE LEATHER BOTTLE, HARPENDEN.

the disfiguring traces which such festive revelry leaves behind soon vanish, and Nature rapidly recovers herself.

In all seasons of the year this splendid Common commends

of one, occasionally rising, and, with a short, jerky flight, providing for its safety by increasing the distance between itself and the too-inquisitive biped who it sees is watching its movements."

Perhaps the best (that is, the most comprehensive) view of the Common is to be obtained from a slightly elevated spot near the erstwhile picturesque dwelling known as "Lines's Cottages," recently rebuilt with the usual effect of red-brick modernity. Looking northward one may obtain a distant glimpse of the village, of the new red-tiled houses that cluster on the hill which is now the fashionable part of the place, and of the excellently conducted St. George's School. Prominent in the middle distance is a large pond, behind which stands a clump of foliage called by the juveniles the "baa-lamb trees," while just beyond will be seen the village cricket-ground, where sturdy urchins vigorously disport themselves whenever opportunity permits.

The village itself has attractions besides those afforded by that "rural paradise" which I have endeavoured to describe. Its old and quaintly-gabled houses, its shaded pond (a favourite haunt of ducks), and its little greens which, in bygone days, were used as rope-walks, tend to give the place a unique and pleasing appearance. Here and there we may get a peep of the old Church-tower,—the only portion of the venerable structure worthy of attention. The Church, dedicated to St. Nicholas, was formerly a chapel-of-ease to the neighbouring village of Wheathamstead, from which it was ecclesiastically separated in 1859. It is of the Early Decorated style of architecture, and constructed of flint and stone; but the massive tower, which dates from the fifteenth century, is the only portion of the original structure now remaining, for the building was enlarged in 1826, and then underwent such a thorough transformation that (except the tower aforesaid) nothing remains to enlist the attention of the archæologist. With few exceptions the mural tablets and other ancient memorials of the dead have been removed to the inner walls of the tower, so that the initial words of the inscriptions, "Under this spot lye the remains," have no longer any significance. In another part of the Church, however, may still be seen a tablet in memory of Sir John Wittewronge, and a couple of interesting brasses; one of the latter perpetuates the names of the Cresseys and Anabals, who held the manor about four centuries ago, and the other (dating from Elizabeth's time) represents two kneeling figures, with escutcheons above. There is another relic worthy of inspection, viz., the bowl of a Purbeck-marble font of the Saxon period; but even this has undergone the ordeal of "restoration."

Harpenden has reason to be proud of the fact that Sir John Bennet Lawes, the eminent scientific agriculturist, resides in the neighbourhood. It was here, on his Rothamsted estate,

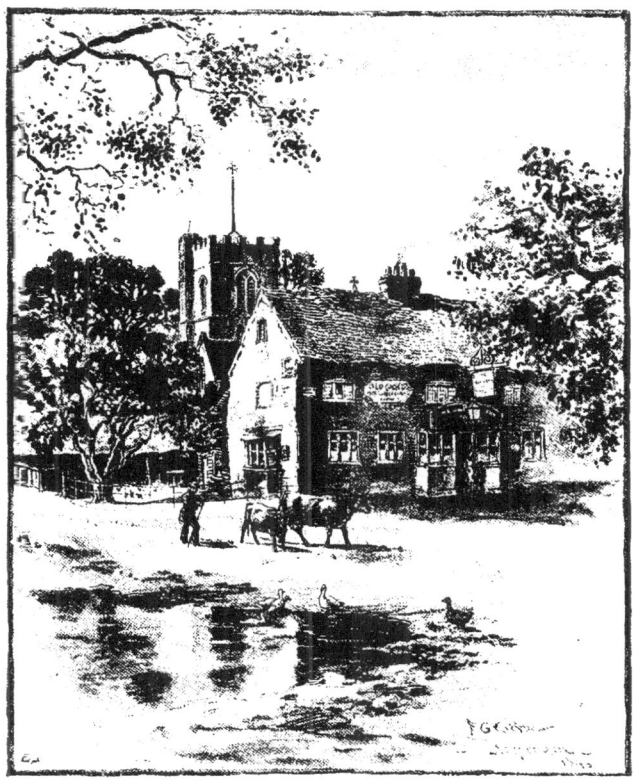

HARPENDEN, HERTS. FROM A DRAWING BY F. G. KITTON.

that the experiments which the venerable baronet inaugurated fifty years ago have been carried on with so much energy and practical success that his name has become world-famous. Sir J. B. Lawes is lord of the manor of Harpenden, and his ancient and historic mansion, situated in the very heart of Rothamsted Park, is wonderfully picturesque. It is an interesting example of Early-English architecture, and is constructed of red brick with stone facings, to which time has imparted a richness and mellowness of tone, this effect of age being enhanced by the ever-green growths upon the exterior of the structure. It was originally built about 1470, when the principal front (facing the lawn) had four pointed gables with a lower central tower; its present appearance is much the same, with the exception of the principal gables, which were rounded into the Elizabethan form by Sir John Wittewronge (a former owner), who enlarged the mansion in 1650, and also erected the quaint octagonal clock-turret.

This charming retreat, more attractive in its way than the regal home of the Salisburys a few miles distant, has been in the family of Sir John Lawes since 1622. Much of its beauty is doubtless due to the admirable taste of Lady Lawes, who, being an accomplished amateur artist, naturally appreciates and encourages all that tends to create pictorial effect, such as is produced by the tangled masses of magnolia and Irish ivy which we see clinging to the ruddy gables, and by the fragrant honeysuckle that, in due season,

small towns and villages, one is struck by the curious fact that the inns form the most picturesque feature; such, for example, as the modest little tenement bearing the familiar sign of "The Leather Bottle." "The Red Lion" inn, near the Church, is generally considered to be the site of the old Manor-house of Wheathampsted-cum-Harpenden; while another old hostelry—formerly known as "The Bull," but now a private residence—situated near the park gates, probably dates from mediæval times, and is said to contain good examples of fifteenth-century mouldings and carvings. The village, however, is marked by other interesting specimens of domestic architecture besides its inns, for there are timbered cottages with plaster fronts and thatched roofs, and more imposing structures of brick, with here and there a chimney of the Elizabethan period. Here we also find an unpretentious butcher's shop (not the only one in the place) having a window measuring about a yard square and a door to

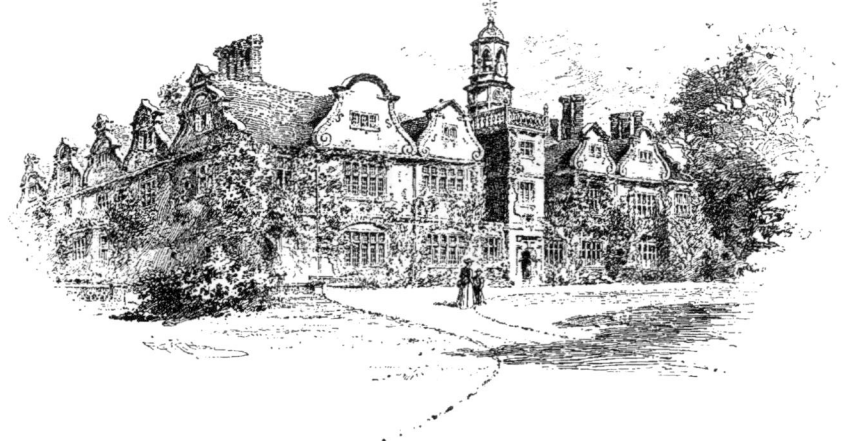

ROTHAMSTED MANOR-HOUSE, HARPENDEN. FROM A DRAWING BY F. G. KITTON.

grows luxuriantly about the entrance-porch. In wintry weather one may observe, swaying like pendulums, several cocoanuts with large holes through them, which are suspended in front of the stone-mullioned windows. These, it may be necessary to explain, are thoughtfully placed there as food for the tomtits and other diminutive birds, whose constant visits to the welcome store thus provided sufficiently testify to their thorough appreciation of the kindly act.

But let us return to the village with its quaint tenements fronted by an attractive green-sward where children delight to gambol, and which makes a happy hunting-ground for the domestic fowl, a roadside pond being available for the web-footed birds. One cannot help noticing the hoary old trees bordering the roadway, with their knotted and gnarled trunks; some of them have been vigorously lopped and are strongly bound with bands of hoop-iron to prevent premature collapse, while one older than its fellows has a huge gap in its massive hollow trunk, and is actually fenced in with props, similarly bound with hoop-iron. Here, as is not unusual in most

match, while near by may be noticed a solicitor's office of similarly unassuming proportions. Harpenden Lodge, at the "Old Bell" end of the village, dates from about the middle of the fourteenth century.

Around the Common are several substantial residences, with an occasional group of tenements of a poorer sort; the latter are embowered in foliage, and are made exceedingly picturesque by their thatched roofs, plaster fronts, and leaded casements. On the west side, adjoining one of the park lodges, is the home of Sir Joseph Gilbert, the enthusiastic colleague of Sir John Lawes; and appropriately near we find the Laboratory, where so much of their useful and valuable work is carried on—work requiring a considerable staff of scientific experts, such as chemists, botanists, analysts, and a host of other assistants, all of whom have received careful and skilled training. In front of the Laboratory, and facing the Common, stands a massive granite boulder, recently placed there by public subscription to commemorate the Jubilee of the Rothamsted Experiments; this huge monolith was brought "from the

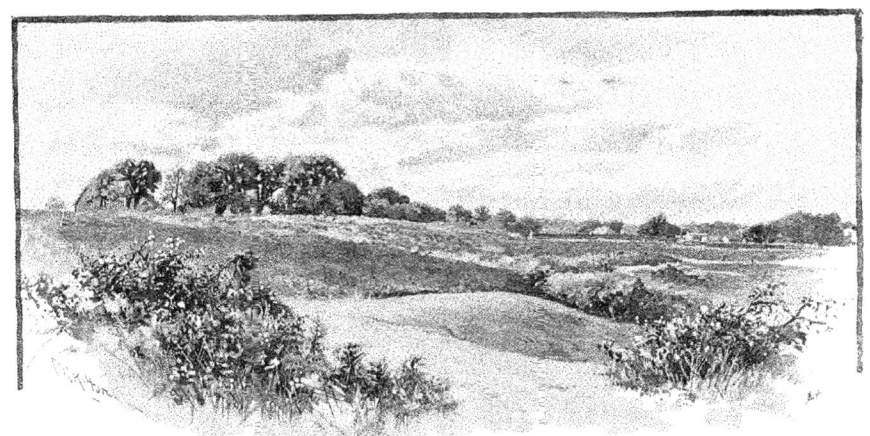

HARPENDEN COMMON. FROM A DRAWING BY F. C. KITTON.

silent solitudes of the everlasting hills" to where it now stands, there to remain as an outward and visible sign to present and future generations of the manner in which the splendid lifework of Sir John Lawes and Sir Joseph Gilbert had been appreciated by their contemporaries.

On the east side of the Common stands Harpenden Hall, now used as a private asylum; it is an old-fashioned house with wainscoted rooms, and is believed to be the original of Dickens's "Bleak House" by some of the villagers, but what foundation there is for the tradition it is difficult to discover. Speaking of the great novelist reminds me that he really did once associate himself with this particular locality, for in Forster's "Life of Dickens" we read that the Rev. T. B. Lawes, of Rothamsted, had, in conjunction with the novelist's brother-in-law, been interested in a sanitary commission having regard to all matters of sanitation in the houses of the poor, and this connection led to Dickens's knowledge of a club that Mr. Lawes had established at Rothamsted, which he visited and became eager to recommend as an example to other country neighbourhoods. The club had been set on foot to enable agricultural labourers of the parish to have their beer and pipes independent of the public-house; and, although the scheme was originated over thirty years ago, it is pleasant to know that the Rothamsted Club for Working Men still flourishes, and continues to prove a great attraction to the members, who undertake its management themselves.

There are many delightful rambles around Harpenden, and several interesting old houses worthy of a visit. Among the latter may be mentioned the ancient manor-house of Annables, about two and a-half miles west of the village, the residence of the Siblers, one of the oldest yeoman families of Hertfordshire, and located in the parish for at least three hundred years. In this house may be seen an old well, where, in a similar way to one at Carisbrooke, a donkey drives an immense wheel to raise water. This wheel, larger than the one in the Isle of Wight, is probably the most perfect of its kind; and there are not, it is confidently asserted, half a dozen such wheels in all England. Turner's Hall, an old farm-house which takes its name from its owner in the fourteenth century, dates from about 1640.

F. G. KITTON.

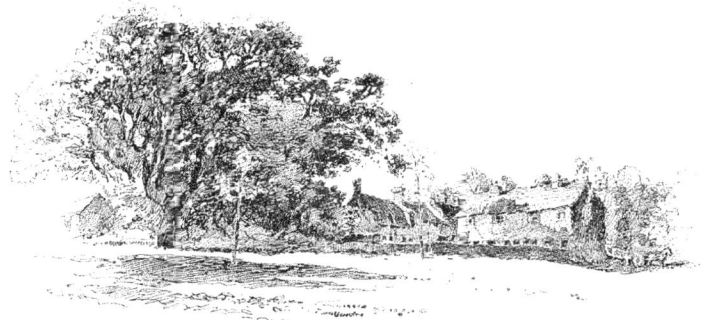

HARPENDEN. THE EDGE OF THE COMMON.

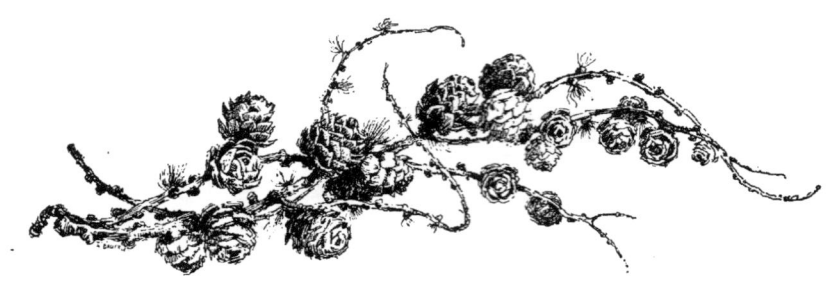

THE WORK OF BIRMINGHAM JEWELLERS.

EDMUND BURKE'S saying, "Birmingham is the toy-shop of Europe," is true to a greater extent to-day than it was in his time. As we find that in Birmingham *toys* originally meant buttons, buckles, clasps, and various trinkets, we begin to have a glimpse of how—if we cannot say exactly when—the making of jewelry began to develop into a distinctly recognised trade, now become so peculiarly identified with that centre of all kinds of human industry. There is nothing really definite in Hutton, or in any of the old writers on Birmingham, as to when the toy trades first made their appearance there; so we may as well be satisfied in the knowledge that the dress of the seventeenth to the middle of last century necessitated the almost general use of fancy buttons, buckles, and clasps, which for the greater part of that time were made, mostly of steel, in Wolverhampton and Birmingham, and also of the precious metals to some extent in the latter place, although Derby, Dublin, and Edinburgh were then particularly identified with the more costly work outside the metropolis. Ornamental and often really artistic steel examples of these, and chains and chatelaines, had at that time become a great industry of Wolverhampton. Wedgwood blue and white jasper imitation camei were in due course set in this work, and painted enamels, of a sort, from Bilston and Battersea. But really excellent enamels done in Paris were mounted in sword hilts and sent back there. The trade with Paris ended at the scattering and thinning down of the *noblesse* during the Revolution. Intaglio heads and entire figure work sunk in steel were done at both Wolverhampton and Birmingham many years before then; but with the establishment of the famous Soho Works under Boulton (Watts did not join him in partnership until eleven years after the works were started) Birmingham was in the ascendant with this superior class of production, including medals, coins, general steel toy manufacture, and the allied trades. As most of her industrial success has resulted from the "World of Soho," some reference to it is due to the proper consideration of our subject, and we think it will at the same time interest the reader.

Matthew Boulton was a toy maker of Snow Hill, Birmingham, which is about a mile and a half from "the barren heath and rabbit warren" of Soho, whereon he first erected workshops for one thousand pair of hands. A fair idea may be gathered of the multiform kinds of articles made there, by quoting from a letter written by Dr. Darwin to a friend in 1768, five years after the works were built. "Here are toys and utensils of various kinds in gold, copper and tortoiseshell, enamels, and many vitreous and metallic compositions, with gilt, plated, and inlaid works, all wrought up to the highest elegance of taste and perfection of execution." The faculty of invention seemed ever awake at Soho. It was there the "bloodless revolutionist," the steam-engine,* was perfected; there that gas was first used, and there were discovered and first put into working completeness numerous mechanical appliances in use at the present time, all more or less intended for the allying of Art with productiveness.

The growth of the jewelry industry of Birmingham may be best indicated by a few figures showing the quantities of silver and gold assayed there since the beginning of the century: Silver, 1801, less than 30,000 oz.; 1839-40, 103,869 oz.; 1891-92, 1,347,275 oz. Gold, during the two latter periods, 1839-40, 1,997 oz.; 1891-92, 228,008 oz. The quantities of metal and other materials used in the common jewelry and similar trades during the corresponding periods are much in excess of our means of reckoning.

Before and during Boulton's reign toy-making, and particularly button-making, meant, as it yet means but in a more marked degree, production of large quantities at a given price in a given time. Metal of all kinds, from the most precious† to the common, and even softer materials, were used in the stamp and press. Hand labour was reduced to a minimum when hundreds of grosses became the order of the day. The constant handling of such quantities naturally resulted in the habit of quickness and deftness of touch in every branch of the general business. From the making of the toy or button to the making of the brooch or locket, or such similar articles, was not a very difficult task. The mechanical appliances for each and all of these were to a great extent identical. Hence we may reasonably infer that the early inception of what was required of the skilled maker of toys, when directing his attention to jewelry proper, has carried with it, to the

---

* The steam-engine, however revolutionary in other manufactures, never became of general necessity in the production of jewelry.
† The term *metal*, in the trade, is seldom applied to silver or gold.

THE WORK OF BIRMINGHAM JEWELLERS.

present hour, the idea of rapidity of production—the cause of comparative cheapness, no doubt, but that which through good odour and bad has given Birmingham her commercial advantage in the markets of the world. To die-sinking and stamping above any other mechanical contrivances or inventions this advantage is due. It was to the recognition of material gain, to be derived from adapting the principle of the die, and its necessary auxiliaries the stamp and press, that machinery was cunningly contrived for rapidly producing varieties of patterns, and twistings of links of chains in gold, silver, and metal, the trade in which is now so much identified with Birmingham's jewelry quarter. The study of metallurgy and kindred subjects, and more particularly the division of labour throughout the trade as a whole, helped onwards this commercial advantage, but the die and the stamp were the real master-powers.

The die, as a rule, is made of steel which the forger has purposely left soft for the die-sinker to cut more easily. He has had some training in Art; occasionally is really clever, but too frequently the cleverness is merely imitative. He cuts into the die with his own make of sharp chisel or punch, which he strikes repeatedly with a hammer and deepens the pattern he intends to produce. When the detail is put in with finer tools of the kind, and the graver, and the work clean finished, the die is hardened ready for stamping from. In special, or in larger work generally, it has two or more blows; and to avoid cracking it is annealed between each of them. The clipping away of the superfluous metal from around the edges of the pattern, or, as the case may be, from its interior also, is effected at one blow. For this operation the "tools" are made specially, sometimes by the tool maker, but often by the die-sinker himself. Not only are the parts cut out to a nicety from the stamping, but the imitation of chasing, engraving, the making of the ground for enamelling, and the preparing of the ground for stone-setting of the commoner kind are done in this way from the die. Cups to take the different sizes of stones and pastes are stamped by the thousand gross at the press. Brooch backs and fronts are also done in great numbers in the ordinary way of stamping, but like the cups the small parts for soldering on the plainer brooch stampings are produced at the press. By means of these small decorative parts a single stamping can be made to lose its original outline and the design varied in many ways. The stamping process we have described as for large articles of a general kind, takes in those of the silversmith and the electro-plate worker, when not hand-made or spun. Stamping, of course, is simplicity itself compared with die-sinking. The stamper in love with his work, and seeing the magical result of a stroke of his hammer, should perhaps be excused if he forgets for the moment, as we have seen him do, that the effect he so proudly appreciates is not entirely a result of his own superior genius.

The manufacture of jewelry and other similar goods may claim a few words of description. Hand-made work under the old system involved, to start with, the hammering out of the gold or silver to the required thickness; now this is sent out to be rolled at the mill to the proper gauge. The workman, whether engaged on wrought work or in the making up of stamped work, sits at a bench which is scooped out to receive him, and has attached to it a leather apron for catching the lemel and particles of precious material he manipulates. Within his easy reach are files, punches, drills, shears, a hammer or two, some solder, a gas jet, and the inevitable blowpipe. The wrought work is hammered on a miniature anvil, the "sparrow-hawk," which while so doing he holds between his knees. Bezels, round and oval, are done on this tool. All the parts of a design are separately cut out of the metal and put together as required with solder. The "swage" is one of his most useful tools, as it is ornamented with different shapes and devices which are transferred to the work —a kind of stamp in its way. The "bull-and-butcher," or "snarling-iron," is used for "belchering" or doming parts of a pattern, and for shaping cups and the like where that is not done at the lathe by the metal spinner. Nearly everything in jewelry and small silversmithing can be made with these tools. Some jewellers confine themselves strictly to the production of one or two kinds of goods, such as gem and fancy rings, or wedding-rings, for which the die is seldom brought into use. But it is indispensable to the ordinary run of gold, silver or metal brooches, earrings, sleeve-links, bracelets, and many other suchlike things. Real stones and gems are, of course, the leading feature of the most costly but not the most artistic class of jewelry. The gold is simply used as a means of fixing or arranging them. Occasionally, enamel and engraving is very effectively made use of in this work. The bulk of the trade in jewelry is, however, in goods where the display of gold alone is the chief aim of the manufacturer; then the services of the chaser and engraver are most required. The gold may be of different colours, according to the alloy used in it, copper giving a deep, and silver or zinc a light, hue, and gradations of these according to the mixture, the effects of which can easily be distinguished from the surface-tints of the gilder. The gold that gives the most trouble in working is fifteen carat. Hall-marking is done on gold so low as nine carat; but for best goods eighteen, and sometimes twenty-two carat is used, the last being, of course, our sovereign standard.

The style of design generally is meretricious, although improvement is here and there becoming manifest since the School of Art and Technical schools have been giving more earnest attention to the subject. Still, we have not yet, by a long way, outlived the reign of banjos, fiddles, bats and balls, field-glasses, and horse-shoes, which, however realistic, are without any symbolic or spiritual meaning, so characteristic of pre-Christian as well as early Christian jewelry.

Many jewellers of late include the smaller goldsmithing and silversmithing in their manufacture. The trade in this way, and in similar goods in electro-plate is rapidly passing over to them from the goldsmith and silversmith proper and maker of electro-plate, as they, in the habit of doing their work more substantially, cannot compete with them in price. Thus we have—but mostly in silver—caskets, jewel-cases and trays mirrors, clocks, inkstands, candlesticks, and other articles too numerous to mention here, nine-tenths of which have at first passed through the stampers' hands. The assistance of the chaser is often brought into requisition ; sometimes to undercut and enliven a pattern after leaving the die, sometimes to designedly alter it ; and the engraver has also his share in beautifying the work. But the craft that is relied on most for finishing goods of the kind, and jewelry —especially metal jewelry—is that of the gilder and plater. It is curious to watch how defective making-up is seemingly improved away under the operations of the gilder and plater. The practised eye can, however, detect at a glance faulty putting-together and bad soldering. Like putty applied before paint, solder is pressed into service to hide itself and all imperfections under the gilding or plating. The number of patterns produced in the year at any average establishment is very great. "Something new" is always wanted. The "factor" and the shopkeeper will have it so, or they will not buy. At one time the factors, or middlemen, were indispensable to the Birmingham makers, but for the last few years the latter have been finding their way direct to the shopkeepers and wholesale houses; so the factors, wishing to equalise matters, are getting their hand in and becoming manufacturers themselves. New patterns in such goods as we have referred to, can be charged extra for under the name of "fashion."

The precious stones mounted in Birmingham may not, as a rule, be separately so valuable as those that are mounted in Clerkenwell and the West-end of London, but the quality is often quite as good, while the quantity used is very much greater. Well-to-do purchasers of jewels, who through early imbibed prejudice or other cause, don't like *Brummagem* and go to Bond Street, Regent Street, or elsewhere in London to satisfy their taste, would be surprised to learn that more than half the jewelry and other valuable goods they see in the shops and windows there are made in Birmingham. The Midland manufacturer is not often found openly alluding to this fact; he thinks he cannot afford to do so and risk giving offence to those on whom he depends most for his trade. What is true of the goods seen in London applies also, but in a greater degree, to such as are displayed for purchase in other parts of England, and in Ireland, Scotland, and the Colonies.

The lessons taught by the museums and Art and Technical schools are most difficult to put into practice, because there is no rational conception among the employers of what machinery and mechanical agencies are going to do for them, and for genuine Art and happy work and workers. In the realising of a new conception industrial Art requires that the designer and the workman shall be one person. Machinery, division of labour, and the capitalist are set against this. The workman cannot, even in wages, benefit by machinery which is the cause of the product of his labour being multiplied a hundredfold. The jobbing jeweller working for himself in the by-street, makes as much money as the factory hand who produces by the hundred with every facility for so doing. While the chief object of the manufacturer is to economise labour and yet produce quantities, bad finish and bad design must ensue. "Well, it sells!" you may hear him say; and he feels, no doubt, virtuously proud of himself, on the way to prosperity, not knowing that it only *seems* to sell, even though he may have received his quarterly, six-monthly, or yearly payments; he can, perhaps, calculate correctly temporary gains, but he never knows how to reason with over-supply, a glutted market, unpaid accounts, bills not met, short time, or no work for his hands; all which things, when not worse, are traceable to his devil-may-care competition and mad desire to become rich at any cost.

Natural expression of face or make, or the general personal appearance and dress, are scarcely ever thought of in connection with the wearer of jewelry. What is wanted is more educated beauty of form and detail in a piece of work; a better trained and clearer judgment in the arrangement of its colour-effect as a whole; such as shall more effectively complement and harmonize with the inner story of our lives, and the circumstances that have us thinking and acting high, and middle, and low class.

J. M. O'FALLON.

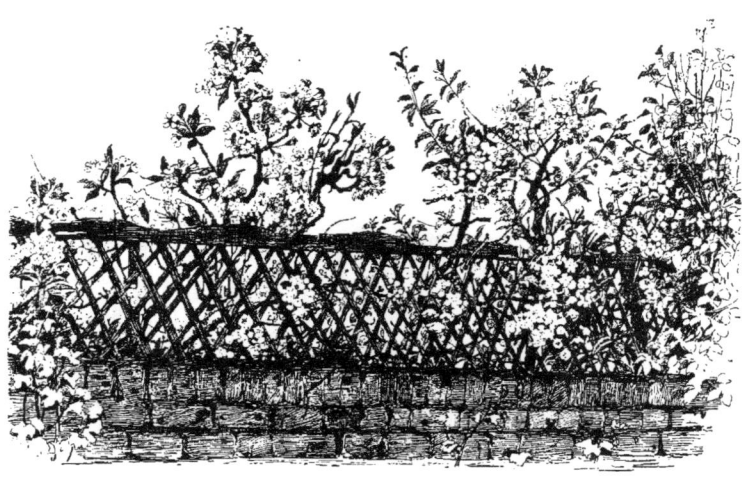

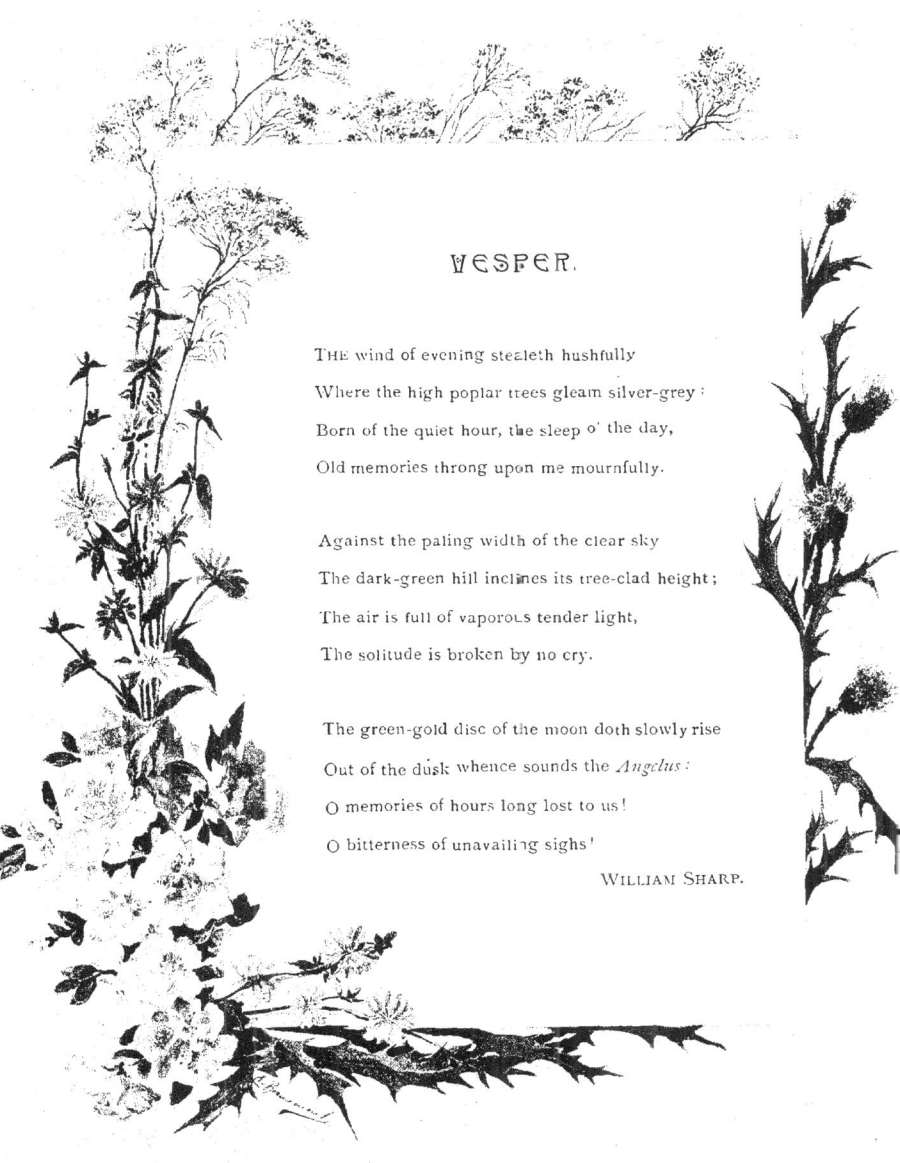

VESPER.

The wind of evening stealeth hushfully
Where the high poplar trees gleam silver-grey:
Born of the quiet hour, the sleep o' the day,
Old memories throng upon me mournfully.

Against the paling width of the clear sky
The dark-green hill inclines its tree-clad height;
The air is full of vaporous tender light,
The solitude is broken by no cry.

The green-gold disc of the moon doth slowly rise
Out of the dusk whence sounds the *Angelus:*
O memories of hours long lost to us!
O bitterness of unavailing sighs!

WILLIAM SHARP.

THE FIRST KNOWN AUTOGRAPH OF CATERINA SFORZA.

A VIRAGO OF THE RENAISSANCE.*

AMONG the illustrious women of the Italian Renaissance, there is no more striking figure than that of Caterina Sforza, Lady of Forli and Imola. In her we see one of the most remarkable instances of that development of individual character which was so marked a feature of the revival, "a product," in Bishop Creighton's words, "of the emancipation of ideas produced by the new learnings."

As Isabella d'Este and Elizabeth Gonzaga represent the refined culture and artistic feeling of the movement, as the deeper yearnings and religious aspirations of the age find a voice in Vittoria Colonna and Duchess Renée, so Caterina Sforza is the living type of that martial ardour and heroic spirit which was the theme of Ariosto and Tasso's song. She is the true *virago*, the *donna uomo* in whose person the beauty and courage of Clorinda are combined. On the lips of Machiavelli or Marino Sanuto, the term, as Burckhardt points out, implied no reproach. It was, on the contrary, the spontaneous expression of the universal admiration aroused by a courage and energy seldom seen in any of her sex. Such a title might well be applied to the woman who, alone among Italian princes, dared resist the triumphant march of a Borgia, and who, deserted by friends and allies, held the citadel of Forli against the combined armies of the Pope and King of France, until the walls were literally battered to the ground.

Thirty years ago, Adolphus Trollope introduced her to English readers in a lively chapter of his "Decade of Italian Women." And now an accomplished Italian scholar, Count Pasolini, has given us a full and admirable biography of this famous Madonna of Forli. Himself a native of Romagna, the descendant of a noble mediæval family, Count Pasolini has spared no pains to make his work as complete as possible. He has ransacked the public and private archives of Italian cities, and has discovered manuscripts relating to the Sforzas and Riarios in the Bibliothèque Nationale and in the British Museum. No less than five hundred letters from Caterina herself have thus been brought to light, besides a vast number of scarcely less valuable missives from foreign envoys at her court. Some idea of the magnitude of the task may be obtained from the author's Appendix, a volume of eight hundred and fifty pages, containing a complete register of the unpublished documents of which he has availed himself in the course of his work.

Thus seen for the first time in the light of modern research, Caterina Sforza is a more interesting figure than ever before. The halo of legendary romance with which the admiration of her contemporaries invested her, made her appear in the character of an armed Amazon. *fiera è crudele*, at once the wonder and terror of all Italy. But her latest biographer reveals a new and different aspect of her character. He lifts the veil and shows us Caterina as the true woman that she was, with the faults and weaknesses, the passions and virtues of her sex. No part of his carefully planned work is more interesting than the pages which he devotes to her private and domestic affairs, and brings her before us in the different relations of family life as daughter, wife, and mother. Many are the precious details he has to give concerning her tastes and habits, her love for dogs and horses, the delight she took in building splendid palaces, and laying out parks and gardens, her interest in alchemy and medicine. A true child of her age, Caterina's character presents a curious mixture of manly courage and capacity, womanly superstition on the one hand and of vanity on the other. Though she rode out in all weathers and appeared habitually in public wearing a man's belt and dagger at her side, she took the greatest care of her complexion, which was remarkable

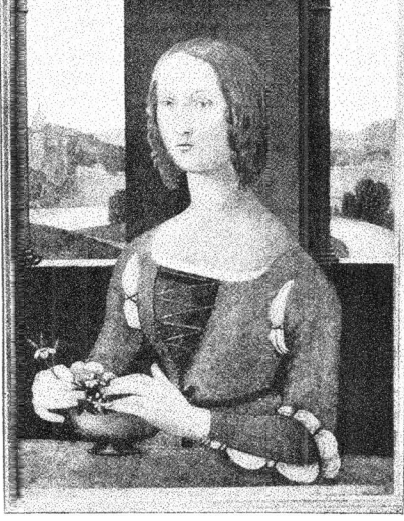

CATERINA SFORZA AT EIGHTEEN.

* "Caterina Sforza." By Count Pier Desiderio Pasolini. Roma: Ermanno Loescher & Co., 1893.

for its brilliant colouring, and made an elaborate collection of cosmetics and washes for the face.

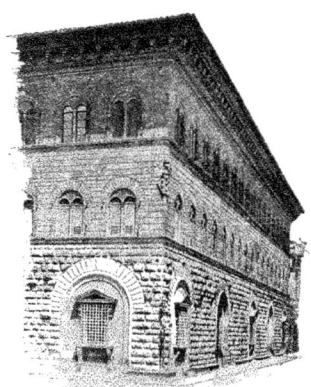

THE PALAZZO MEDICI, AT FLORENCE.

Count Pasolini has further enriched his volumes by a number of excellent illustrations, including portraits of Caterina herself, of her husbands and children, views of the castles and palaces which she built, of the churches and convents which she founded, as well as reproductions of medals and majolica plates bearing her effigy, and coats-of-arms belonging to the different noble families with which she was connected by birth or marriage. All this helps to make this new life of Caterina Sforza not only a pleasant and attractive book, but a valuable contribution to the history of the Renaissance, which cannot fail to be read with the deepest interest by every student of that memorable period.

An illegitimate daughter of Galeazzo, Duke of Milan, Caterina sprang from a race of fighting heroes, "men," as she said herself, "who had never known fear." Her grandfather was the famous soldier Francesco Sforza, the greatest and most fortunate of *condottieri*, who, by his boldness as much as by his marriage with the daughter of the last Visconti, won possession of Milan, and entering the Duomo on horseback, was crowned Duke amidst the acclamations of the people. Her own father, Galeazzo Maria, was a reckless and dissolute, but able and powerful prince, who ruled his duchy with a strong hand. Caterina was his first child, born in 1463, when he was only seventeen. Her mother, Lucrezia Landriani, was a beautiful Milanese lady, whom Caterina received in after years as a loved and honoured guest at her own court. But from her birth the child was entrusted to the care of her grandmother, Bianca Maria, widow of the great Sforza, and the first mention of Caterina we have is in the year 1468 in a letter addressed by the Duke to his mother from his camp near Bologna asking anxiously for news of his little daughter, whom he had left at Milan dangerously ill. So pressing were his inquiries that Duchess Bianca sent off two messengers to Bologna the same day to give her son the latest news. Fortunately the child recovered, and on the death of her grandmother a few months later she was adopted by the Duke's wife, Bona of Savoy, who brought her up with her own children, and loved her as dearly as if she had been her eldest daughter. At the age of ten Caterina, now a clever and beautiful child, was formally betrothed to Count Girolamo Riario, the nephew of Pope Sixtus IV. By the marriage treaty then drawn up, the Duke of Milan gave up the province of Imola to the Pope, who bestowed it upon his nephew, saying it was not fitting that the daughter of so great a prince should live as a simple gentlewoman. It was the old Pope's favourite dream to exalt his family and to found a dynasty, while Galeazzo, on his part, cherished wild schemes of sovereignty over the whole of Italy, and was eager to secure the help of Sixtus IV. in his ambitious designs. But before his daughter's marriage was consummated Galeazzo had fallen a victim to the hatred of his subjects, and on St. Stephen's Feast, 1476, he was murdered by two Milanese knights. The tragic event made a deep and lasting impression on Caterina's mind, and in after days she often recalled this princely father who had died at thirty-two, and who, with all his faults, was so fondly beloved by his wife and children.

The widowed Duchess held the punctual fulfilment of her husband's promises to be a sacred duty, and in the following April Caterina was married by proxy to Girolamo Riario, and immediately after the ceremony the youthful bride started for Rome attended by a brilliant escort of cavaliers and ladies.

Fortunately Caterina was too young to realise the vice and wickedness of that Roman world to which she had come. As radiant in the first flush of youth and beauty, she sat at the festive board in Count Girolamo's stately palazzo of the Lungara, or rode out, clad in scarlet, to entertain princely guests under the ilex groves of the Campagna, this unconscious child could not guess how deeply their hands were dyed with blood. It is hard to believe that Count Girolamo, cowardly and violent as he was by turns, could have won the affections of the high-spirited girl; but she bore him six children, and made him a true and loyal wife. But this at

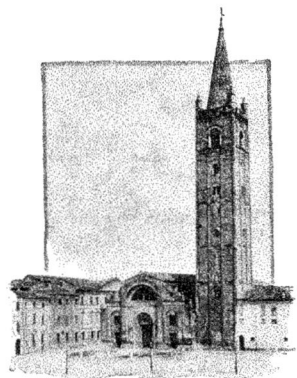

THE CHURCH OF S. MERCURIALE, AT FORLI.

least Caterina had in common with her husband: she was as ambitious as he was to reign over a state of her own, and when in 1480 the old Pope invested his nephew with the principality of Forli, she gladly accompanied her lord on a visit to his new subjects.

It was then that a native artist, Marco Palmeggiani, the favourite pupil of Melozzo di Forli, painted the charming portrait of Caterina which now hangs in the gallery of Forli. At first sight it is hard to believe that this gentle maiden of eighteen, with the frank eyes and pleasant face, holding the flowers in her hand and simply clad in square-cut bodice with slashed sleeves, can be the famous Madonna of Forli, who for twelve years held the people of Romagna *in virga ferrea* and dared resist the dreaded Borgia himself. Yet there is plenty of character in the broad forehead, and no less unmistakable are the marks of courage and determination we notice in the firm, well-shaped chin.

After a series of splendid festivities at Forli and Venice, the increasing age and infirmities of Sixtus IV. recalled them to Rome. There Girolamo rapidly assumed the supreme power, when suddenly the old Pope died, and the whole aspect of affairs was changed. When this event happened Girolamo was camping without the walls of Rome with his troops, but in this emergency his wife acted with a courage and spirit which took every one by surprise. Without a moment's delay she took possession of the Castle of St. Angelo and boldly announced her intention of holding this fortress until a new Pope had been elected. Meanwhile, Rome was in a state of anarchy; and the Cardinals thought it wisest to come to terms with the late Pope's nephew. They agreed to pay down the arrears due to his troops and to confirm him in the office of Captain of the Church, and in the independent possession of Forli and Imola, on condition that he would disband his army and surrender the Castle of St. Angelo. Even then Caterina would not yield, until her own uncle, Cardinal Sforza, and seven other members of the Sacred College presented themselves at the castle gates, and courteously entreated her in her husband's name to take her departure.

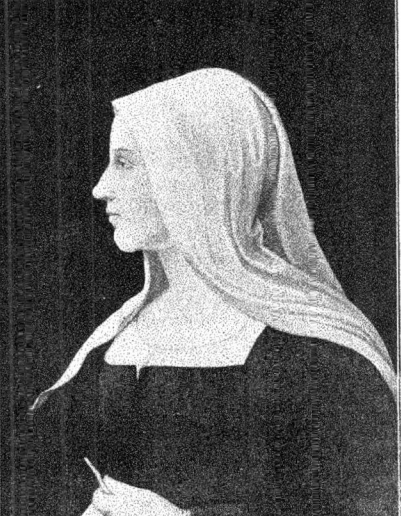

CATERINA SFORZA IN OLD AGE.

Caterina now accompanied her lord to Forli, and held a brilliant Court there during the next three years. When Girolamo fell ill, she took an active part in the Government, and repressed sedition with a stern hand. Her courage and vigour were amazing. One day, when she was nursing her husband at Imola, and hourly expecting the birth of her sixth child, news reached her of an act of treachery on the part of the governor of Forli; she rode off at once, summoned the Castellan to surrender, and installed a new governor in his place. Then riding back, ten miles over the Apennines to Imola, she reached home safely at two o'clock the next 1894.

morning and gave birth to another son. Girolamo recovered from his illness, but only to die a year later by the hand of one of his own favourites, as he sat at his palace window after supper, on the 14th of April, 1488. His death became the signal for a general rioting, and Caterina herself and her children became the prisoners of her husband's murderers. On that occasion the Countess showed her character. Amid all the horrors and darkness of that awful night she alone retained her presence of mind, soothing the weeping women and frightened children who clung to her skirts by the calm tones of her voice, and rocking her youngest babe to sleep in her arms. She reminded her little sons of the race from which they sprang, of her father and grandfather, who had never known what it was to fear, and told them the story of Duke Galeazzo's end. And at the same time she found means to send messengers to her uncle Lodovico Sforza, begging him to come to her help, and to Tommaso Feo, the governor of the citadel, telling him to hold the Rocca for herself and her son. On the 15th of April, Savelli, the governor of Cesena, who had taken possession of Forli in the Pope's name, and was anxious to obtain the surrender of the citadel, allowed Caterina to enter the Rocca, on pretence of persuading the governor to yield. But no sooner had the Countess set foot within the walls, than she laughed her foes to scorn, and announced her intention of holding the citadel until the arrival of the Milanese troops. Even the tears and prayers of her children, who were brought to the foot of the walls by their captors, were of no avail, and Caterina remained unmoved. All manner of legends grew out of this Spartan act, and Caterina has been represented by some writers as the most unnatural of mothers. But Count Pasolini points out that she had left her children in the charge of two of her most devoted adherents, and that, in all probability, the conspirators stood in too much fear of the Duke of Milan to dare to injure these innocent captives. In any case, the mother's bold act saved the state for her son. Before the month was over, twelve thousand Milanese troops appeared at the gates of Forli, and demanded the restoration of the rightful princes. Once more shouts of "Madonna!" were heard in the streets, the Orsi fled in terror, and on the 30th of April the citizens of Forli proclaimed Ottaviano Riario Lord of Forli and Imola, and Caterina Regent during her son's minority. Laying aside her mourning for a splendid robe of state, the Countess came out to receive the magistrates, who solemnly restored her children to their mother's arms. Between the intrigues of her uncle Lodovico il Moro, and the presence of the French army at her gates, Caterina had a difficult part to play, but she steered her path prudently and managed to keep her little state in peace and safety. Unfortunately a second marriage which she contracted with Giacomo Feo, a younger brother of the brave Castellan of Forli, involved her in fresh troubles.

As early as 1490, Caterina seems to have contracted a secret union with this boy of twenty, whose youthful beauty and pink-and-white complexion had so strange a fascination for her. The secret of the marriage was carefully kept, since by the law of the land its recognition would have cost Caterina the regency of Forli and the guardianship of her children. But she had Giacomo constantly at her side and loaded him with honours, and soon afterwards bore him a son named Carlo. A Florentine envoy, writing home in May, 1493, described how he found the Countess with Messer Giacomo, splendidly attired and seated in her presence, and reports that Madonna has declared she will rather sell her soul to the devil and her state to the Turk than give up her lover. But this sudden exaltation proved fatal to the foolish youth. He became haughty and arrogant, and when Charles VIII., wishing to gratify Caterina, made him a Baron of France, his insolence knew no bounds. Ottaviano Riario, Caterina's eldest son, now a boy of sixteen, began to resent the lordly airs assumed by his mother's favourite, and when Giacomo one day forgot himself so far as to strike the boy, the old servants of the Riario family vowed to avenge the wrong. One hot summer evening in August, 1495, when Caterina and her favourite were returning from a hunting expedition, singing joyous songs as they rode through the gates of the city, three armed men attacked Giacomo Feo, ran him through with their swords and dragged him from his horse.

When Caterina realised that her lover had been murdered, she gave way to a perfect frenzy of grief and rage. She buried Giacomo with royal honours, owned the dead man to have been her lawful husband, while her son Ottaviano was shut up in the citadel and kept in close confinement for some months. By her orders, not only were the murderers themselves savagely tortured and put to death, but whole families shared their doom. Innocent women and children in arms were not spared, and the streets of Forli literally flowed with blood. Even in these barbarous times, a shudder ran through Italy, and it is said that in after years Caterina bitterly repented her cruelty, and was perpetually haunted by the memory of the hapless victims whom she had sacrificed to her passion for revenge. "All Romagna cries out to heaven, and execrates the Madonna's name," wrote the Milanese ambassador to his master. "This grieves me truly, because she is of Sforza blood." And her latest biographer remarks truly that if after her first husband's murder she behaved as a heroine, after that of her second husband she became little better than a tigress.

The violent end which had overtaken both of Caterina's husbands did not prevent her from taking to herself a third. With all her courage and independent spirit, she was not a woman who could long stand alone. She had never forgotten the old ties which bound her to the Medici, and all her uncle's efforts had been unable to detach her from the Florentine alliance. The best hopes of safety for her state, she was wont to say, lay in the walls of Florence, and when Lorenzo de Medici died, she told an ambassador that the world would never see his like again. So when, in the autumn of 1496, a cousin of the Magnifico's came to Forli as ambassador from the republic, she welcomed him gladly, and received him as a guest in her palace. Giovanni de Medici was a gallant soldier just thirty years of age, and had, moreover, the reputation of being the handsomest man in Florence. Caterina herself was but a few years older and still in the prime of beauty. Giovanni remained in Forli acting as Caterina's lieutenant, and occupying Giacomo Feo's rooms in the castle, and on the 6th April, 1498, Caterina gave birth to a son, afterwards the famous soldier, *Giovanni dalle Bande Nere*. After that her secret became generally known; "only this time," says Cobelli, who had himself been sent to prison for daring to speak too freely of his mistress and her lovers, "every one held his peace."

One interesting result of Caterina's third marriage was the correspondence to which it led between her and Savonarola. Hearing from her husband of the great Frate whose wonderful preaching had worked a revolution in Florence, and seized with admiration for his zeal and eloquence, Caterina wrote to the Dominican friar, asking him for his blessing, and begging him to come to Forli. Her letter has perished, but Savonarola's answer may still be read, and is characteristic both of the man and of his teaching.

Caterina's new ties naturally drew her closer to the Republic. In July, 1498, the Signory passed a decree making the Madonna of Forli and all her children, born or yet unborn, citizens of Florence. At the same time her son, Ottaviano, entered the Republic's service, and with his stepfather's help defeated the Pisans in his first battle. The proud mother, filled with delight at the news, struck a medal to commemorate the event. But Ottaviano soon abandoned the career of arms to become a priest, and was made Bishop of Viterbo, while his brother Cæsar became Archbishop of Pisa. In the midst of Caterina's rejoicings over her son's feat of arms, her gallant husband fell suddenly ill, and he died in her arms on the 14th September.

Caterina wept bitter tears over the husband she had loved, and his death at that critical moment was a grievous calamity. Never had she needed a strong arm at her side more sorely than she did now. For all around her the horizon was thick with clouds, and the tempest she had long dreaded was about to break and overwhelm her in ruin. She had offended her old friend and her son's godfather, Pope Alexander VI., by refusing to accept his daughter Lucrezia for her son's wife. But the refusal was to cost her dear. Cæsar Borgia made no secret of his ambitious designs on Romagna, and on the 9th March, 1499, a papal bull was issued, solemnly deposing that "daughter of iniquity," Caterina Sforza and her children, and investing the Pope's son with their dominions.

After a fruitless appeal to Louis XII., whose arms had just conquered Milan, Caterina rode over the Apennines and pleaded her cause before the Signoria of Florence, who, however, offered her no help; so she rode back again to Forli and made preparations for a vigorous defence. She sent her children to Florence that they at least might be safe from harm, collected vast stores of arms and ammunition, and told her people that by the grace of God she would yet die Lady of Forli and Imola. Yet she was fully aware of her desperate condition, and in a touching little letter, addressed to the Abbess of the Murate at Florence, she begs the good nuns, who had sent her some pomegranates from their garden, to ask God very earnestly for his protection and guidance in her extremity. "Verily," wrote the Venetian chronicler, Marino Sanuto, "this woman deserves the title of Virago, and has proved herself worthy of her race." The eyes of all Italy were now fixed upon the little state of Forli, as Cæsar Borgia advanced at the head of the papal forces, supported by fifteen thousand French and Swiss troops which Louis XII. had sent to his help. On the 11th of December Imola fell, after a gallant defence. On the 19th, the citizens of Forli, panic-stricken at the victor's approach, opened their gates to Borgia, who entered in triumph. But Caterina was ready for him, and on Christmas Day the castle guns opened fire upon the foe. Upon this Borgia, impatient of delay and eager to pursue his victorious march, rode up to the castle wall and, cap in hand, courteously entreated Madonna di Forli to surrender, promising her safe and honourable terms. "My lord Duke," replied Caterina, "fortune aids the brave and abandons cowards. I am the daughter of a man who never knew fear, and whatever happens I mean to follow in his steps until I die. Italy knows how little the word of a Borgia is worth, and if it comes to the worst I know that I had rather die fighting with my comrades than accept your terms." Furious at finding himself foiled by a woman, Borgia gave orders for the bombardment to begin, and promised one hundred thousand ducats to the man who should bring him the Madonna alive or dead. "And so," writes Count Pasolini, "from the top of the central tower, where she stood to watch her own city and the camp of the enemy, on the plains already white with snow, Caterina Sforza saw the dawn of the new century and the sun rise on the first of January, 1500."

Twenty days the siege lasted, and during all that time Caterina's courage and energy never once failed. From early morning till late at night she was indefatigable in surveying the walls, giving orders, or taking counsel with her chief captains. But by the 12th of January, a breach was made in the walls. In spite of all Caterina's efforts at resistance, the enemy forced an entrance into the outer court, and a panic set in among the defenders. Then, ordering the powder magazines to be blown up, the heroic woman herself led a last charge against the foe. Clad in a steel cuirass she fought desperately in the thick of the battle until night fell, and exhausted, and some writers tell us wounded, she surrendered to the victor, and was led out among the dead bodies which strewed the ground, a prisoner into Borgia's house.

On the 23rd of January the victor left Forli, and a month later he entered Rome in triumph with his captive in his train. So Caterina once more saw the city which she had entered as the bride of the Pope's nephew three-and-twenty years before,

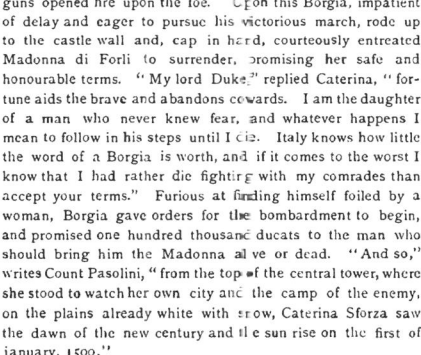

MEDAL OF CATERINA SFORZA.

and was lodged a prisoner in the Belvedere of the Vatican. A few months later she was removed to the Castle of St. Angelo, where she languished in close confinement, during a whole year, with the constant fear of death before her eyes. It is hardly likely that Caterina would have issued alive from her prison had it not been for the intervention of the French general, who demanded her release, as the King of France's prisoner of war. Neither the Pope nor his son dared offend this powerful ally, and on the 30th of June Caterina Sforza, sadly changed in appearance by the sufferings she had undergone, at length issued from her dungeon.

A fortnight later she went to Florence, where a warm reception awaited her. All her children came out to meet her, and the three-year-old boy whom she had parted from with tears, was once more clasped to her heart. Citizens of every rank and faction crowded to her doors and rejoiced to welcome her among them. Nowhere else had her fortunes been followed with keener sympathy, and the entries in the diary of Luca Landucci show with how much interest the fate of Forli and its Madonna had been watched by private individuals. The remaining eight years of Caterina Sforza's life were spent in retirement at Florence, partly at her husband's town house, partly at the beautiful Medici villa of Castello.

A fine portrait in the Uffizi, by the hand of an unknown painter, gives us some idea of Caterina's appearance in these last years of her life. She is represented wearing a black robe with white frills and a yellow veil over her head, and holding an orange-leaf in her hand. Her face is thin and worn, the expression is sadder and sweeter than of old, but traces of her once-remarkable beauty still remain, and there is a marked likeness between herself and her son Giovanni, whose well-known portrait by Titian hangs in the same gallery. The storms and changes of her troubled life had told upon Caterina's vigorous frame, and she did not live to be old. She died on the 28th of May, 1509, and was buried according to her orders, in the convent of Santa Maria delle Murate, with the poor nuns, among whom in these last years she had often sought refuge from the world. The blood of Caterina Sforza still flows in the veins of many illustrious houses. Bourbons and Stuarts, kings of France and England, of Spain and Sardinia, were alike descended from the great Madonna of Forli, and at the present time the line of Caterina Sforza has still one representative among crowned heads in the person of his youthful majesty, King Alfonso XIII., of Spain.

JULIA CARTWRIGHT.

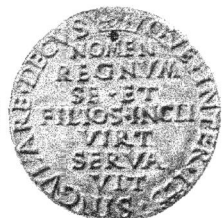

THE LAST AUTOGRAPH OF CATERINA SFORZA.

EARLY ITALIAN ART.

IF the British public care in the slightest degree about early Italian Art the Winter Exhibition at the New Gallery should be crowded from morning to night. The pictures alone form a collection which, if it were in any continental gallery, we should make a pilgrimage to see; and the objects of miscellaneous art, though rather bewildering in their variety, are a feast which those who best know their Italy and their South Kensington Museum can best enjoy. It is with these we have here to do.

Notable in the Central Hall (which has never been seen to better advantage) are the arms and armour, casques, swords, shields, daggers, and whole suits of steel from the collections of Messrs. G. F. Laking, Durlacher Brothers, W. H. Spiller, J. Gurney, and D. M. Currie, who lends, among other perhaps much more important things, the back of a gorget (1191), extraordinarily delicate in shape and quite perfect in workmanship.

In the Hall again we find quite a show of sculpture and modelling; quite a show, one might say, of Madonnas. One has the opportunity of comparing Donatello's 'Virgin and Child' in marble (1293) surrounded by angels and cherubim, with the silver plaque of the same subject after him (1294), and the terra cotta ascribed to Verrocchio (1283) with the coloured group of Luca della Robbia (1277). Of the several Madonnas in tinted gesso the most beautiful are the one sent by Sir F. Leighton (1279), reproduced on this page, and that belonging to Earl Brownlow (1289), both of which are charming alike in feeling and in colour. There is material enough here on which to form some opinion as to the possibilities in the way of painted panels in relief: of the decorative value of such work as this there is no doubt. The famous St. Cecilia in dark grey slate (1305) is here, and a juvenile St. John the Baptist in high relief (1305), also by Donatello.

VIRGIN AND CHILD IN GESSO DURO.
IN THE POSSESSION OF SIR FREDERIC LEIGHTON, BART., P.R.A.

In the South Gallery, where are the paintings of Giotto, Fra Angelico, and the rest of the "primitives," are placed the illuminated manuscripts. Some of these contain miniatures which may or may not be by Andrea Mantegna and other artists of repute. They are certainly very beautifully executed; but they are almost invariably out of scale, and out of keeping, with the ornament of which they pretend to form part, as are the quasi-natural birds and animals so frequently introduced among purely conventional scrollwork. The impression one had of the general crudity of the colour of illuminated MSS., even when the illuminators were Italians, is not here dispersed. A very interesting series of early printed books is displayed in the Balcony, where are also the greater part of the magnificent drawings of Raphael, Lionardo, Michelangelo, and other great masters, contributed chiefly by her Majesty and Mr. Fairfax Murray.

The gold and silversmith's work is very remarkable, especially the portable altar (303), a slab of oriental jasper, mounted in silver and richly ornamented in the style of the twelfth century, lent by the Bishop of Southwark. Another masculine piece of work is the casket of elaborately embossed leather, bearing the arms of the Medici, and bound with wrought-iron bands (317), contributed by Mrs. P. C. Hardwick. Mr. A. de Rothschild sends a severely designed casket of crystal (323), and Mr. Boore a gilt cup stem by Cellini (417). The personal ornaments are on the whole more wonderful than strictly beautiful; one can see here how early something of the spirit of the Rococo developed itself. Already we have misshapen pearls to form the body of a seahorse, a triton, and suchlike; almost one might fancy oneself in the Green Vaults at Dresden; a pendant à la Cellini (411) hangs from a necklace which is distinctly baroque. Quite the most tasteful piece of goldsmith's work is the enamelled reliquary in the form of a pendant, lent by Mr.

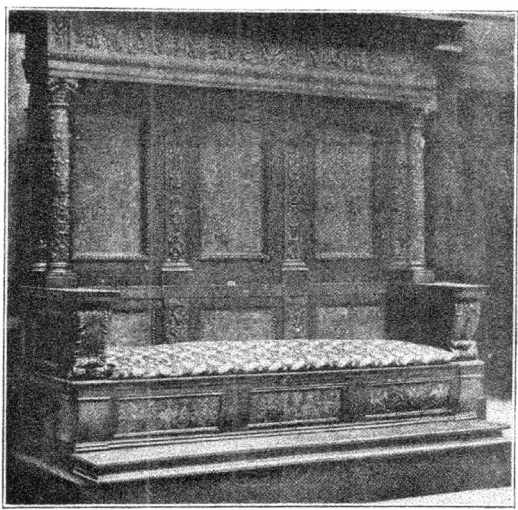

THE CEREMONIAL THRONE OF JULIANO DE' MEDICI. CARVED BY BACCIO D'AGNOLO.

Boore (407) ; the back of it in particular is exquisitely delicate.

In the way of furniture there is not very much—some cassoni, interesting chiefly on account of their painted panels, some bellows carved with more sense of style than refinement, a chair or two, an inlaid table, a spinet, and a cabinet of marvellous Milanese work (1258) belonging to Mr. Gurney—but the most superb thing in furniture is Baccio d'Agnolo's Ceremonial Throne, executed for Juliano de' Medici, which was formerly part of the Demidoff collection, and belongs now to Mr. G. Donaldson. The proportion and design of this work (illustrated above) speak for themselves ; the carving of the columns is the work of a master, and there is a charm in the perhaps somewhat accidental colour of the thing, which puts the finishing touch to our delight in it.

In the North Gallery are some fine ivories, and among them a writing-desk of ebony (776) inlaid with ornament in ivory so delicate it might almost be damascening. In the same case is a very interesting piece of tooled leatherwork, a medicine chest, which belonged once to Cosimo de' Medici (801), lent by Mr. H. H. Willett the little box belonging to it, which is supposed to have contained the antidotes to poisons, is in the form of a book. The greatest masters of bronzes and medals are represented by works in small not unworthy of their reputation. There is one case which should on no account be overlooked (case M), that which contains the works acquired by Mr. G. Salting at the Spitzer sale, luxuries in the way of knives and forks, and leather cases to contain them, keys, plaques, and an inkstand damascened in gold, in the elaborate manner the Italians learnt from the East.

There is a fair show of *faience* and majolica—lustre from Gubbio, at its best not perhaps below the average of Maestro Giorgio, but scarcely above it ; ceramic painting in the expected key of colour, but not superlatively beautiful, and in the matter 1894.

of design not on the whole particularly interesting. The display of needlework is poor, and it is not well placed in the hall. There are examples of embroidery and darning, of work in silk and linen, and an instance or two of lace, which will not be without interest to needleworkers, but there is scarcely anything in the way of textiles which one might not hope to find in the collection of a first-rate dealer. It is worth noting, perhaps, that many of the pictures on the walls are in their original, or at all events old, frames, carved, inlaid, painted, it may be, but in any case themselves works of Art. Within the frame of Lady Hervey's 'Annunciation' is again a framework of ornamental arabesque, connecting the medallions in which the figures of Mary and the Angel are enclosed (see below). One is disposed to doubt whether Raphael ever painted ornamental detail at all, and even whether, if he had so far condescended, he could have done it as well as some of his assistants— say Giovanni da Udine ; but, in any case, this is an excellent example of the kind of ornament commonly known by the name of Raphaelesque.

The Victorian, Guelph, and Stuart exhibitions of past years had mainly an historic interest ; to the Tudor Exhibition of 1890 there was added the interest of a period when art was

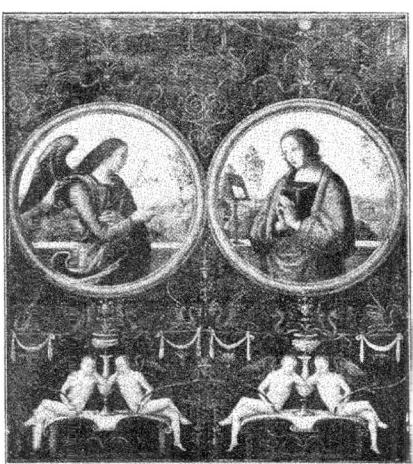

THE ANNUNCIATION. IN THE POSSESSION OF LADY SELINA HERVEY.

thriving among us. This is essentially an exhibition of Art, yet (for those who care most for such things) it lacks nothing of the human or historic interest which made its predecessors so popular.   LEWIS F. DAY.

ON THE SACRO MONTE AT VARALLO.*

ON Varallo's Sacro Monte, 'neath the chestnuts' balmy shade,
There I lay and dreamed at leisure, let the world around me fade.

I bethought me of the legend, how of old the chapels grew,
How the spirit of the ages lived in faithful hearts and true;

Of the story of the founder—how he roamed from sea to sea,
Forsaking friends and fortune, through the vales of Lombardy.

For once, when he was sleeping, God's own angel came to him,
What time o'er Monte Rosa's snows the dawn flushed faint and dim :

And told him of a chosen mount whereon to build a shrine,
That pilgrims might assemble there, to praise the Light Divine.

For years and years he wandered, till his hair was streaked with grey;
But the Sign was long in coming, and the Mountain far away.

Yet all his toil and trouble, and his closely-garnered hoard,
He gave them, nothing doubting, for the love he bare his Lord.

And at last in one bright summer-time, he stayed his weary feet
On the spot in Sesia's Valley where the branching torrents meet—

Where the mountain air comes fragrant from the Mastalone glen,
And the rocky boulders tufted with the scented cyclamen :—

(It may have been the Christ Himself who led him by the hand),
For he saw the green hills circling, and he knew the chosen land.

And they say a bird's sweet singing called him up the mountain stair,
Till he stood upon a terrace-lawn with prospect wide and fair :

"'Tis here, the place I dreamed of! here hath touched His garment's hem !
This shall be my sacred mountain! this my New Jerusalem!"

And he sent for many painters, and for noted men of lore,
For a nobler shrine should stand there than was ever built before ;

And the sculptors all flocked round him ; not for glory or for gold,
But for life and love and duty, worked those artist-folk of old.

So, crowned by many chapels, builded there by faithful hands,
Above the Sesia Valley still the Sacro Monte stands.

" Art is long, but time is fleeting :" those who moulded them are dust,
But the silent figures still withstand the mildew and the rust.

As sweet Ferrari painted and great Tabachetti planned,
To the living faith that raised them constant witnesses they stand.

Now sometimes at the grating prays a pilgrim 'mid the weeds,
Or a little black-eyed peasant-girl who kneels there with her beads;

But the Sacro Monte to our days seems Bernardino's whim,
Though 'twas said in those dark ages that the Lord had called him

To a work of His own choosing ; but the years since then have rolled ;
Gone are now the childlike spirit, and the simple faith of old.

E. C. C.

* The Sacro Monte, or " New Jerusalem," at Varallo, in the Val Sesia, one of the most remarkable remains extant of mediæval Art, was founded in the end of the fifteenth century by Bernardino Caimi, who came of a noble and illustrious Milanese family. The hill is covered with a series of fifty chapels, containing groups of painted figures modelled in terra-cotta, and placed behind iron gratings ; the best of these were designed by Tabachetti, whilst the walls and ceilings of many of the chapels are painted by Gaudenzio Ferrari.

NOTE ON MR. J. H. HENSHALL'S "ADAM BEDE.'

MR. HENSHALL has taken for his subject one of the most interesting and pathetic scenes in modern English fiction. It is from George Eliot's novel "Adam Bede." Hetty Sorrel is condemned to die for the murder of her child. On the eve of the execution Dinah Morris, the Methodist female preacher, comes to the cell where, in the dim evening light, she sees the convict "sitting on a straw pallet, with her face buried in her knees." She watches with her through the dark and silent hours ; the meanwhile, by kind and yet solemn words, softening her heart till she makes confession of the crime. In the early morning, Adam, in happier times—ere the young squire came as tempter—betrothed to Hetty, goes from his lodging to the prison, where he lingers in the court-yard, scarce able to face the ordeal of her presence. "The cart is to set off at half-past seven," he hears. And now he must go forward. The door of the cell grates open, and he is with the two women. Bright summer morning though it be, the thick window-bars hinder the clear light, and not till his eyes are tempered to the gloom and his agitation a little fallen, that he sees Hetty's marble face, the sweet lips pallid and half open, and her eyes " looking at him with that mournful gaze as if she had come back to him from the dead to tell him of her misery." She is on her knees close to Dinah, whose touch alone gives her strength, " for the pity and love that shone out from Dinah's face looked like a visible pledge of the Invisible Mercy." And then comes the passage which one must write under the picture—" And the sad eyes met—when Hetty and Adam looked at each other, she felt the change in *him* too, and it seemed to strike her with fresh fear. . . . She trembled more as she looked at him." They solemnly kiss

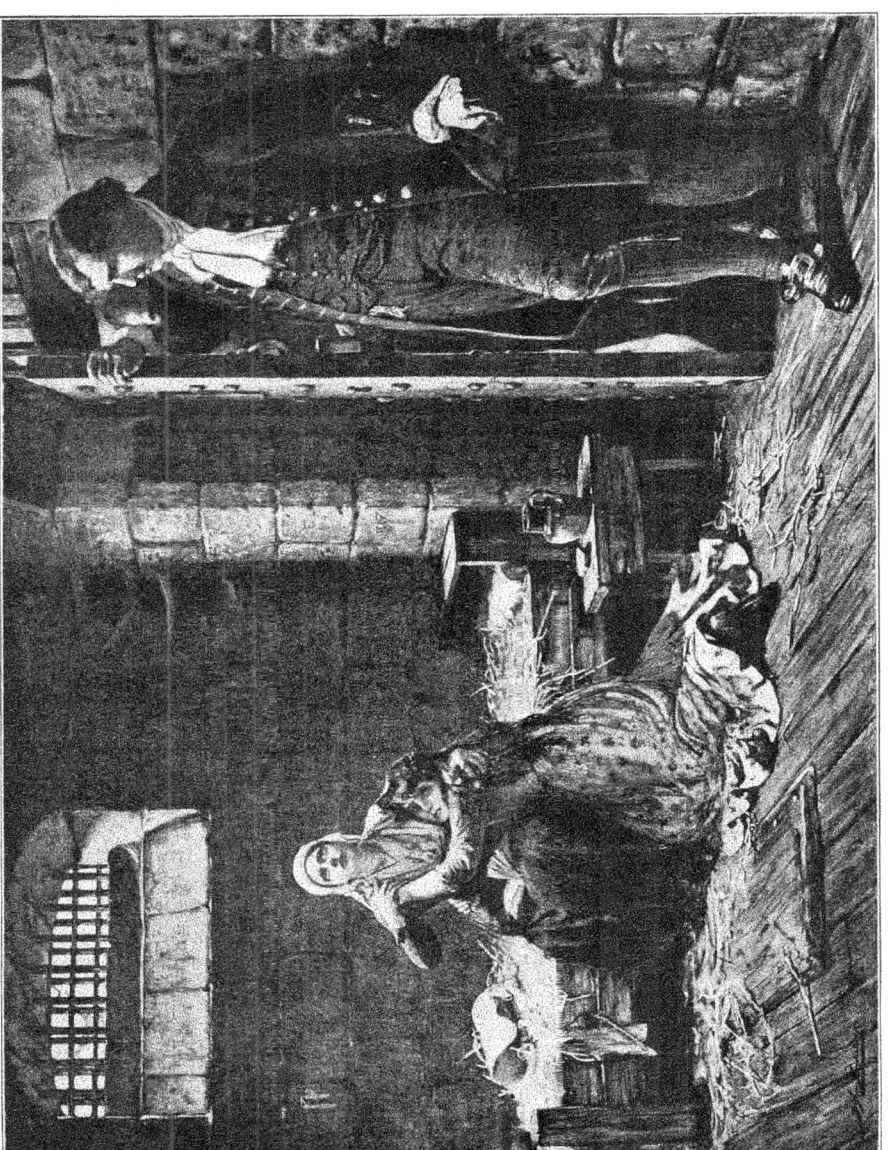

"Adam Bede." From the Water-Colour Painting by J. Henry Henshall.

one another as a sign of forgiveness and farewell. And so Adam departs as the last preparations are beginning. Need we tell how, at the very moment of execution, the reprieve arrives, and Hetty is carried back to await another destiny? For the reader of some thirty years ago these details were superfluous, but George Eliot is for the moment scarce in vogue, and certain critics would condemn the pathetic scene as "bleat." From another hand, they might call it "rant" or "pious twaddle," but for the fact that George Eliot was not of the Faith, so that her portrait of Dinah Morris is but the artistic presentment of a form of belief and certain phases of human life and character.

Maybe, her work was once lauded beyond its desert. She had a trick of half-wise and but half-true reflection that seems shallow enough now, and it maybe that here as elsewhere, the idol was worshipped rather for its clay than for its gold. But her thorough understanding of English provincial life, her power to make an ordinary character interesting, her large-hearted humanity, her insight into the pathos and tragic interest hid in the most common life, and her gift of vivid description—are these so common in current literature? Much of her work may be rubbish, but much of it is classic and enduring, and among her best passages must be ranked the one which the artist has wisely chosen.

We will only add that the original is a large water-colour, and very powerfully painted in that medium. F. W.

ART NOTES.

IT is satisfactory to know that the British Section of the Fine Arts at the Chicago Exhibition was, by far, the most popular of any of the sections in the Fine Art Building during the last two months of the World's Fair, and that Great Britain had her full share of what sales were effected, though these were, from several causes, disappointing throughout. It is thought by those most likely to know, that the result of the Exhibition will be to awaken a fresh interest in British Art in the minds of a large proportion of people who visited the Galleries.

The decision in Hanfstaengl v. The Empire Theatre is a very serious matter for artists and for publishers. To the artist, as the producer, the decision is one that will bring injury to his artistic reputation, and grave loss to his monetary returns. The law appears to be that any picture, however recent, may be reproduced for the delectation of the motley audiences of the music-hall, to come, mayhap, after a "turn" of the coster, and before an "exhibition" of tight-rope dancing. As soon as a picture is the talk of the town, like 'The Doctor,' 'The Roll Call,' or a dozen others, this work may be represented on the stage in exact reproduction with living figures, or parodied as to be only a "colourable imitation." In any case the work is rendered valueless for serious publication, and where several hundred pounds could before be safely paid for the copyright, the publisher in future will hesitate to give more than a nominal price for what can so easily be reproduced The decision seems to be a correct interpretation of the law, and the only remedy can be by Act of Parliament. For a long time the publishing section of the London Chamber of Commerce has been considering a new Copyright Act, but there seems to be some fatality connected with British copyright, and no attempt to make the law simple and workable appears to be possible.

The collection of Japanese Lacquer and Metal Work brought together in March by the Burlington Fine Arts Club was one of the very highest artistic excellence. The elaborate catalogue contains the fullest details of the pieces exhibited, preceded by a complete account of the Metal and Lacquer Work of Japan, written by experts.

THE ROYAL SCOTTISH ACADEMY EXHIBITION.—This exhibition, the sixty-eighth, was opened on February 16th. Adopting Alfred Stevens' words, *Un peintre a tort d'abandonner le pays où il est né et où il a passé sa jeunesse*, the Academy has drawn the line more strictly even than before, at Scottish Art, the main exceptions being a few of the Scotsmen who have made London their home. The President sends four portraits—including Lord Mountstephen and Dr. Walter C. Smith; the latter a very striking work—and a large 'Highland Pastoral' full of tender feeling. Mr. W. E. Lockhart exhibits his portrait of Mr. Speaker Peel, considerably altered since first seen in London. The most important original work is shown by Mr. Robert Macgregor. In 'Returning from the Market,' a sandy plain with excellent distance is occupied by two figures, a woman and girl accompanied by a donkey laden with vegetables and other purchases. If the canvas be a little empty, this fault is atoned for by the brilliant light that fills the scene, setting out the figures in fine relief. From Mr. C. M. Hardie comes the historic incident in Sciennes House where Burns met Scott, then a boy of fifteen. The persons present are Adam Smith, John Home (of "Douglas"), and other prominent men. The representation of Burns, as he turns from the picture on the wall to ask whose words they were which so moved him, is very satisfactory; while Scott is less so, the boy being a trifle saucy in manner. Mr. George O. Reid exhibits an animated group, the Jacobites in Smyrna Coffee House, London, receiving the news of Prestonpans. The agitated group is well conceived, and the costume painting merits praise, but the flesh tints are rather chalky. Mr. Allan Stewart gives an Armada incident, a Spanish commander seeking shelter from Maclean of Duart. The artist has realised the distinctions of race and differences of costume, and sets the distant vessel in a good atmosphere. Mr. J. D. Adam in 'Summer—Loch Ard,' cattle resting amongst trees, with the water and hills palpitating in the hot air, contributes one of the best landscapes. The contributions of Mr. MacTaggart are strong in tone and handling, but not quite so successful as we could have wished, and Mr. Robert Noble shows five works in his accustomed rich tone and suave manner. Amongst the water-colour drawings those of Mr. Thomas Scott and Mr. R. B. Nisbet deserve recognition; and Mr. Arthur Melville contributes a brilliant work, 'Moorish Procession—Tangier.' Sculpture embraces Burns panels, by Mr. W. G. Stevenson, for Chicago; a highly imaginative 'Rhythm,' by Mr. Pittendreich MacGillivray; and Mr. Birnie Rhind's two accepted statues with adorned pedestals—in model—of Sir Peter and Mr. Thomas Coats for Paisley. The recently deceased artists commemorated are John Pettie, Gourlay Steell, and Clark Stanton.

In the thirty-third Exhibition of the Glasgow Institute we have strong evidence, if any be needed, of the vitality of Art north of the Tweed. This Exhibition stands altogether apart from similar shows in other provincial centres, for in Glasgow, the strength of the Exhibition lies in the work that has been contributed by local men. The chief fault to be found with the present show is that it contains too many pictures, and that throughout the hanging is not quite satisfactory.

One of the finest portraits in the gallery is that by John Lavery, of a lady and child. It is dignified and simple, and its scheme of colour is most harmonious. James Guthrie's 'Archbishop Eyre,' and Joseph Henderson's 'Sir John Muir' are important contributions, each in its own way. A. Roche's 'Idyll' is one of the most beautiful and restful pictures in the gallery. Its colour is pleasant to the eye; its general composition shows the work of a thoughtful and accomplished painter. 'Solitude,' by A. K. Brown, is a view of the Arran hills from Skipness, exceedingly good and one of the pictures of the Glasgow Art-year. Stott's 'Summer's Day,' Millie Dow's 'Herald of Winter,' J. E. Christie's 'Red Fisherman,' E. A Walton's 'Miss Aitken,' and Tom MacEwan's 'Tarry O'o' are among the attractions of the galleries.

The pictures by "the Glasgow School" show distinctly that the best men are learning wisdom. They are modifying some of their eccentricities, and developing most steadily the power that is certainly theirs.

Art in the West Country has been represented, at Mr. Eland's gallery, at Exeter, by a series of water-colours in Devon and Cornwall by Mr. H. Wimbush and Mr. John White.

Mr. C. E. Johnson, the well-known landscape painter, has joined hands with Mr. Frank Calderon, already established as a teacher of animal painting, and together they propose to carry on, during the summer months, a school of animal and landscape painting in Baker Street, London, with a number of Royal Academicians as visitors.

OBITUARY.

By the death, on the 27th December last, of Mrs. Martha Combe, of Oxford, there has been removed, at the age of eighty-seven, one who was associated in no unimportant degree with the career of the more distinguished members of the pre-Raphaelite movement nearly fifty years ago. Her late husband, Mr. Thomas Combe, M.A., was the manager of the Clarendon Press at Oxford, and was among the first to discern and appreciate the originality and earnestness of the new workers. The then unpopular pictures, such as Millais' 'Return of the Dove to the Ark,' and Holman Hunt's 'Christian Priests and Druids,' found in Mr. Combe an encouraging sympathiser and a kind and ready purchaser. To him the first offer was made of 'The Light of the World,' and he at once secured it. At his death, some twenty years since, Mrs. Combe became the possessor of a truly interesting collection, which she has now bequeathed to the University. The only condition is that they are kept together for twenty years after the death of her last surviving executor. Several of the pictures are by Mr. Holman Hunt, notably 'The Early Missionaries,' dated 1850, 'The 1894.

After-glow in Egypt,' 'London Bridge on the Night of the Marriage of the Prince of Wales,' and 'Festival of St. Swithin.' The collection also includes early pictures of Sir John Millais, 'The Return of the Dove to the Ark'; two oil paintings and a drawing by Bonington, sketches by David Cox and W. Hunt, and Rossetti's 'Dante's Celebration of Beatrice's Birthday.'

Gourlay Steell, R.S.A., died in Edinburgh on 31st January, aged seventy-four. This well-known animal painter was a son of Mr. John Steell, a wood-carver of note in Edinburgh, whose elder son, the late Sir John Steell, R.S.A., sculptor to the Queen for Scotland, also attained to eminence in Art. Gourlay Steell's artistic tendencies were early developed, for at thirteen he showed the model of a greyhound at the R.S.A. exhibition. Although in later years the deceased preserved his love for the plastic art, acting for a number of years, in succession to his father, as teacher of modelling in the "School of Arts" in Edinburgh—the earliest of technical colleges—it was in painting he made his mark. From 1835 till the present year he exhibited at the R.S.A. exhibitions with almost unfailing regularity, securing election as Associate in 1846, and as Academician in 1859. In 1872, her Majesty appointed him her Animal Painter for Scotland, and ten years later he succeeded the late Sir William Fettes Douglas as Curator of the Scottish National Gallery. As an animal painter he produced in his best days some striking work, in which the character and expression of horses, cattle, and dogs were vividly caught. One of his notable pictures was 'Llewellyn and Gelert,' of which the Queen commissioned a replica; and his 'Highland Raid,' marauding Macgregors defending their spoils against the Royal troops, was a great success. In 1865 was produced "A Cottage Bedside at Osborne,' showing the Queen reading the Bible to an aged fisherman; and this picture secured a large popularity in its engraved form.

Miss Sarah Satchell, who died on the 8th of January at Sudbury, Harrow, aged eighty, was a water-colourist who made a hit as long ago as 1842 by a picture called 'The Momentous Question,' illustrating one of Crabbe's "Tales of the Hall." It was engraved by Samuel Bellin—who, by the way, also died in January, over eighty years of age—and attained a wide popularity. Her sudden unexpected success affected her health and even her sight, so that for a time she was unable to continue her artistic career.

Frederick Clive Newcombe, who died at Coniston, on the 10th of February, in his forty-eighth year, was a landscape painter of some merit and much modesty. His real name was Suker, but he adopted the name of Newcombe. He devoted himself to painting the Lake district, where he made his head quarters. He never sought distinctions or artistic honours, and though he sometimes exhibited his pictures, more often they were purchased by patrons direct from his easel.

John Chessel Buckler died at Oxford in January in his hundred and first year. He was the architect under whose direction the Houses of Parliament were restored in 1834.

The widow of Jean François Millet died in her sixty-sixth year, at Suresnes, near Paris, on the 31st of January. Madame Millet was fourteen years younger than her husband, and has survived him almost exactly nineteen years. She was buried by his side in the little cemetery at Chailly, near Barbizon.

K K

A NEW PIECE OF SCOTTISH ARCHITECTURE.

THE MacEwan University Hall, Edinburgh, designed by R. Rowand Anderson, LL.D., Architect, is a gift to the University of Edinburgh by Mr. William MacEwan, M.P., and virtually completes the large block of buildings erected ten years ago for the medical department of the University at a cost of some £250,000. The only feature still awaiting execution is the Campanile, 275 feet in height, the base of which is to the right of the illustration underneath.

The hall, which will cost, with the site, about £80,000, corresponds in style with the Early Renaissance design of the rest of the medical school, but is treated with great independence and boldness. In ground-plan like a theatre, it presents the rounded wall of the auditorium to the exterior, forming thereby the corner of the block of buildings abutting on the public streets. This wall is not opened with arcades, as in the Roman theatre, but holds the eye by its simple and vast expanse of masonry. Vertical divisions are given by two semicircular projections enclosing staircases, and by buttresses, but the horizontal stages are slightly marked, and a noble breadth of effect is thereby secured. The blind arcade, with statue-niches in the buttresses in the upper story, gives the needful enrichment, and, with the band of sharply cut Italian ornament below it, receives value from the plain wall of the middle story, upon which the eye dwells with a pleasing sense of repose.

The lowest story is less happy. The rustication in the form of "Channelled Ashlar," which girds the rest of the block, is here exchanged for a panelled treatment somewhat weak in light and shade, and carrying with it that suggestion of an origin in woodwork, which attaches to the panelled stone and marble surfaces so dear to the Renaissance architect.

Above this massively treated outer enceinte, measuring 64 feet to the top of the parapet, is seen the summit of an inner wall concentric with the last, which carries the domical roof constructed of steel. These concentric walls are connected above by flying buttresses, while on the ground story the space between them is utilised for a vaulted corridor, 12 feet wide, extending round the half-circle of the auditorium, and affording communication between the various staircases, entrances, and exits.

In the interior, the platform occupies the chord of the arc, with a clear floor space in front, bounded by tiers of seats following the sweep of the semicircle and extending back to the inner wall. The internal elevation above these floor-seats has not a little of the simplicity and greatness of the exterior. The inner wall here becomes an open arcade of round arches, twelve feet in span, supported on columns of red Corsehill stone with caps and bases of grey sandstone, measuring 26 ft. 6 in. in height, and behind this arcade are galleries in two tiers stretching back to the limits of the outer enceinte. The device of carrying the columns past both these two stages of the elevation is a happy one, and gives dignity to the whole interior.

Above the semicircle, the diameter of which is 106 feet, rises the low dome of the roof, pierced at its springing by a range of round windows. Its crown, where it is opened with a skylight 25 feet in diameter, is 90 feet above the floor.

The hall, when completed, will hold about three thousand people, and is destined to be used for Graduation and all other Academic ceremonies. It will also serve for concerts, for there will be a large organ behind the platform, while arrangements are made by which an orchestra to accommodate three hundred performers can be substituted for the platform. It will be by far the finest hall in Edinburgh, and will challenge comparison, in point of design, with any hall in the kingdom, or indeed in Europe. The architect, having large masses to deal with, has worked them into artistic harmony through his boldness in aiming at a grand general effect, instead of wasting his resources on details.

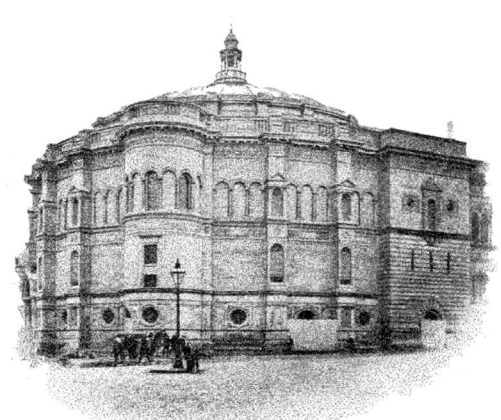

THE MACEWAN HALL, EDINBURGH.

G. BALDWIN BROWN.

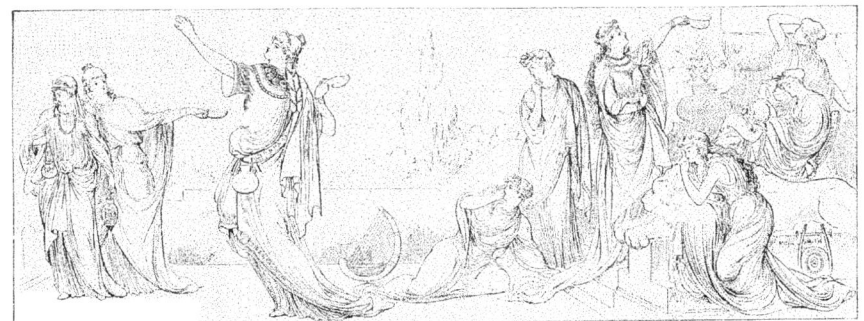

THE TEN VIRGINS. A HEADPIECE BY J. MOYR SMITH.

NEW BOOKS ON ART AND ARTISTS.

IN the concise and well-written volume, "SIR JOSHUA REYNOLDS" (Seeley), Mr. Claude Phillips has not added much to our previous knowledge of the first president and his time; but he has used his materials easily and with judgment, and the result is a study characterized—within its limits —by the charms of personal touch and independence of view. The growth—so rapid and luxuriant—of Reynolds's power is traced and exhibited from year to year, while the historical background and accessories, though they are sufficiently laboured to be intelligible, are nevertheless kept in due subordination to the principal figure. It is in purely artistic appreciation that Mr. Phillips is at his best; as, for instance, in the brilliant pages in which he contrasts the art of the two great rivals, Reynolds and Gainsborough; or when, differing from the traditional and popular view, he bases Reynolds's highest claim to distinction, not upon his renderings of childish innocence and female loveliness, fascinating as they are, but upon those profoundly studied male heads—the Johnson, the Hunter, the Gibbon—in which portraiture is raised to the dignity and endowed with the stability of history.

But, after all, these appreciations seem to lose something of their brilliancy when embedded here and there in a mass of material, which may be compressed indeed, but which is now far too familiar to be re-shaped. In fact, we cannot help regretting that Mr. Phillips did not either choose a much larger canvas, on which a man "of his literature"—if we may revive a phrase which would have sounded familiar to Reynolds —could not have failed to produce something solid and remarkable; or on the other hand, confine himself to the exploration of a single corner of this varied and fascinating field. For instance, Reynolds as a writer on Art has received rather scanty treatment at the hands of this his latest biographer, yet there is no theme upon which the minute knowledge, and wide sympathy of Mr. Phillips, could be brought to bear more usefully or more attractively.

"THE CONVERSATIONS OF JAMES NORTHCOTE, R.A.," by William Hazlitt (Bentley & Son) has been carefully edited by Mr. Edmund Gosse. It is a book for the artist and the amateur to read; for Northcote was a man of sense and sympathy, although blunt to a degree. Through Hazlitt's interpretation he becomes eminently entertaining. Mr. Gosse very judiciously confines himself to notes, and he introduces the writer in a short, but well-nigh perfect, essay on "Hazlitt as an Art Critic." He explains that the attitude of Hazlitt towards the leaders of artistic fashion in 1815, was similar to that of the young men of to-day who "cultivate the terrors of the initial signature." He compares Hazlitt to Mr. George Moore, and in no uncomplimentary way, for "each is perfectly honest, fearless, and unsympathetic." We are far from thinking Mr. Moore unsympathetic, but his style of criticism is not unlike that of Hazlitt.

"TENNYSON AND HIS PRE-RAPHAELITE ILLUSTRATORS" (Elliot Stock), by G. S. Layard, is a little book of gossip and pleasantly written information about the early days of the "P. R B." It gives a varied version of the origin of the Brotherhood; the author's sensible ideas on Millais, Holman Hunt and Rossetti; and it is illustrated by a sketch, by Rossetti, of Tennyson reading "Maud," and other plates.

"PICTORIAL EFFECT IN PHOTOGRAPHY," by that hero of the art, H. P. Robinson (Piper & Carter), has arrived at its fourth edition. "NEGATIVE MAKING," by Captain Abney from the same publisher, is a second edition of a practical "primer."—The "CATALOGUE OF FANS AND FAN LEAVES" (Longman), presented to the British Museum by Lady Charlotte Schreiber, is a simple list with no general interest attached.

"The first crime of the Revolution," said Chateaubriand, "was the death of the King; but the most frightful was the death of the Queen." Such is still the verdict of history on the horrors of the French Revolution, and Maxime de la Rocheterie's "LIFE OF MARIE ANTOINETTE" (Osgood, McIlvaine), paints the period with success. This work, translated by Cora H. Bell, is illustrated with a series of portraits of the personages involved. These plates are carefully selected, but the printing is done very indifferently, and no care has been taken to dry each impression flat. The text is well translated and readable, and the original work was "crowned" by the Académie Francaise.

In the preface to his handsome work on "ANCIENT ARMS AND ARMOUR" (Sampson Low, Marston & Co.), Mr. Edwin J. Brett sets forth his "passionate admiration of the marvellous skill of the armourer of the dark and the middle ages." "Most men," he proceeds, "have a hobby: this has been mine, and for twenty-five years it has engaged my unremitting attention." With such an introductory remark the reader of this volume, with its long series of full-page illustrations, willingly pardons any minor fault of style or setting, to examine with the author's enthusiasm the masterpieces of armour, shields, helmets, daggers, maces and axes in Mr. Brett's extensive collection. Before setting out on the minute description he gives of the uses in war, and in tournament, of the various pieces of armour, the author retells a considerable number of anecdotes of chivalry. After a portrait of the writer, successfully set in symbolical arms and armour, 133 plates follow, accompanied by most painstaking descriptions of their uses and designs; and the volume is closed with an intelligent index. If it should be felt that the continual heavy red line running round each page is a little unnecessary, and that the diagramatic effect of the illustrations is a trifle monotonous, the lover of arms and armour will leave such remarks to the hypercritical, and be satisfied in a more than ordinary degree with the loving care Mr. Brett displays throughout his well-bound and well-printed volume.

Mr. Aldam Heaton's "RECORD OF WORK" is a substantial catalogue or album of decorative work done by him, or under his direction, during the last few years. It contains some sixty or more plates, in photo-tint, of furniture, friezes, wall-papers, stuffs, stained glass, and painted decoration—all, one would say, rather out of the ordinary trade way, were it not that his furniture is for the most part deliberately in the manner of those last century cabinet-makers, whom it is now the fashion to imitate. Mr. Heaton's prefatory remarks on furnishing are to the point, and what he says is in the main true enough, but he takes rather higher ground than his actual performance, to judge by the selection under review, appears to warrant. After his triumphal celebration of the death of the "drawing-room" mirror, of "the handsome white marble chimney-piece," "the plaster ceiling rosette," and so on, one expects something more of him than the gilt over-mantel No. 2, the mirror frame No. 68, and the generally speaking meagre ceiling decoration which he illustrates. The illustrations on the whole show that Mr. Aldam Heaton is responsible for some very good work.

Under the title "JAPANESE ART" (Eyre & Spottiswoode), Mr. E. F. Strange has prepared a most useful list of all the Japanese books and albums of prints in colour in the National Art Library at South Kensington. Mr. Strange is one of the younger officials whose zeal and industry lend lustre to the administration. The "GRAPHIC ATLAS" (Walker & Co.) is marvellously complete, handy, cheap, and well printed. "LIST OF BOOKS ON FINE ARTS" (London: Gay & Bird) is compiled in Milwaukee, and only serves to show that it is not possible, so far from the centre of artistic affairs, to chronicle accurately works on the arts; at the same time there is a great deal of useful information not elsewhere to be found.

"HOME LIFE OF THE ANCIENT GREEKS" (Cassell) by its title touches a chord of human interest, and Miss Alice Zimmern's facile translation of Prof. Blümner's work is a complete story to be read from beginning to end. The Grecian home life is plainly depicted, the difficulties of telling the truth are grasped not evaded, yet the story is as free from any unpleasant flavour as it is free from cant. The illustrations are chosen with knowledge and reproduced with care. "IN A CORNISH TOWNSHIP," by Dolly Pentreath (Fisher Unwin), is not very interesting, and in any case the illustrations by P. R. Craft are decidedly unequal, and show a want of skill in producing work in black and white.

A debt of gratitude is due to those who bring us from time to time a genuine message straight from the heart of Nature, distracting our attention for a little from the world which is too much with us. Mr. H. S. Salt's "RICHARD JEFFERIES," a study (Swan, Sonnenschein & Co.), will interest all—and they are not a few—who have experienced the subtle charm of some of Jefferies' writings. If Mr. Salt's conclusions will not commend themselves always, we are at least free to admit that he is fair, lucid, and on the whole, discriminating. The large paper edition contains reproductions of four rather pretty drawings of scenery near Jefferies' home by Miss Bertha Newcombe.

It is seldom that the designer comes upon so useful a book as F. S. Meyer's "HANDBOOK OF ORNAMENT" (B. T. Batsford). Not that it answers in the least to its title of "handbook." It might much more properly be called an Encyclopædia of Ornamental Forms. A designer never knows what he may be called upon to design; and, however little he may be disposed to follow the beaten track, he often finds it convenient before he sets to work, to post himself up, as it were, in what has been done, if only that he may do something different. Accordingly the practical man gets together, by degrees, a collection of examples to which he may refer on occasion. Such a collection Mr. Meyer (whether for the purpose of practical design or of teaching) has made, and here publishes. It is not complete—no such collection could be, for there is no end to such an undertaking; but it contains in a compact and handy form much that even the experienced workman will be glad to have thus systematically arranged; whilst to the student, rightly used, it should be invaluable.

"THE TRANSACTIONS OF THE JAPAN SOCIETY" (Kegan Paul) forms a stirring record of probably the most quickly successful society ever instituted in London, and the office-bearers may be cordially congratulated on the appearance of this volume. "THE BOOK PLATE ANNUAL" (A. & C. Black) is the first yearly issue of a work which appeals to collectors of Book Plates and lovers of books generally. "SYLVIA'S ANNUAL" (Ward, Lock & Bowden), is a monthly magazine conducted on broadly sympathetic lines for ladies, and the illustrations are mostly very well done. The letterpress is almost entirely written by women and about women, but the manly element would lend variety to the publication. "THE STUDIO" (Bell) has successfully reached the end of its first volume, and the articles are chosen and illustrated with both skill and taste.

We strongly recommend Art-masters to obtain the series of reproductions of old Japanese prints, "DOCUMENTS DÉCORATIF JAPONAIS," published by *L'Art*, Paris, in eight pamphlets, at a very small price. For their own artistic enjoyment, and for the education of their older pupils, nothing could be better.

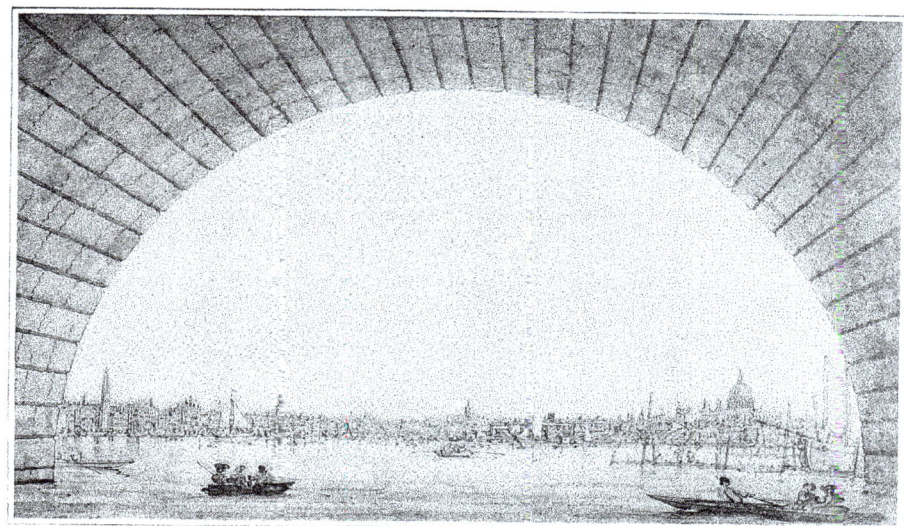

No. 1. LONDON FROM UNDER AN ARCH OF WESTMINSTER BRIDGE. CIRCA 1750.
FROM A DRAWING BY CANALETTO IN THE COLLECTION OF HER MAJESTY AT WINDSOR.

LONDON BY CANALETTO.

FROM DRAWINGS IN THE ROYAL COLLECTION AT WINDSOR.

THE collections of George III., in addition to the magnificent library of printed books which his successor various times by his Majesty's agents on the Continent, particularly in Italy. Of these priceless additions to the Art

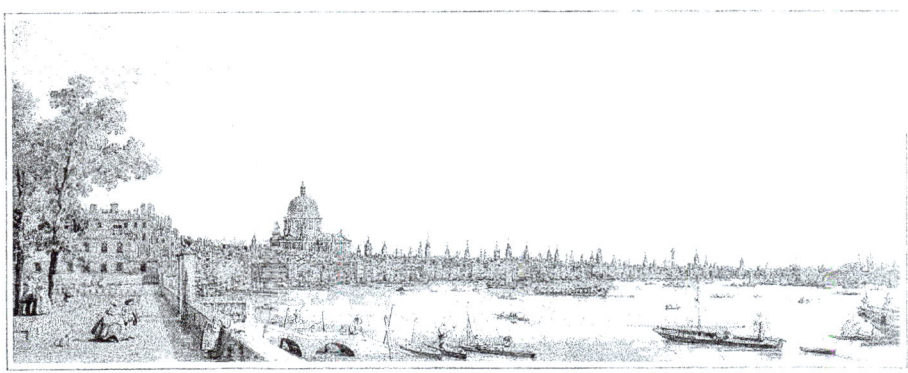

No. 2. LONDON FROM OLD SOMERSET HOUSE. FROM A DRAWING BY CANALETTO IN THE COLLECTION OF HER MAJESTY AT WINDSOR.

transferred to the British Museum, comprised a vast series of drawings, engravings, and other works of Fine Art acquired at MAY, 1894. wealth of the country, not the least noteworthy and important was the entire collection of Joseph Smith, Consul at Venice.

purchased from his executors. This collection was particularly rich in the works of Antonio Canal, or, as he was more frequently styled by others as well as by himself, Canaletto. By this purchase nearly fifty of his pictures came into the possession of the Crown, and, after having been for many years at Buckingham Palace, were removed to Windsor, where they form one of the special attractions of the great corridor which extends along the east and south sides of the quadrangle of the upper ward. Having remained so long in the private apartments of the Castle, they are comparatively unknown—and are not even mentioned in the last and most complete Dictionary of Painters—though it is hardly many views in the City and neighbourhood, and this drawing would be one of the last of his works, as Westminster Bridge was finished in 1750, and here only the two centre arches are incomplete. The Act for constructing this bridge, the second over the Thames in London, was passed in 1736. Great opposition to its erection was made by the citizens of London, who were very jealous of any interference with the stream of traffic which passed in and out of their city over London Bridge, but they were unsuccessful in their efforts to prevent this necessary addition to the public works of London, and the first stone of the bridge was laid in January, 1739. It was formally opened for traffic in

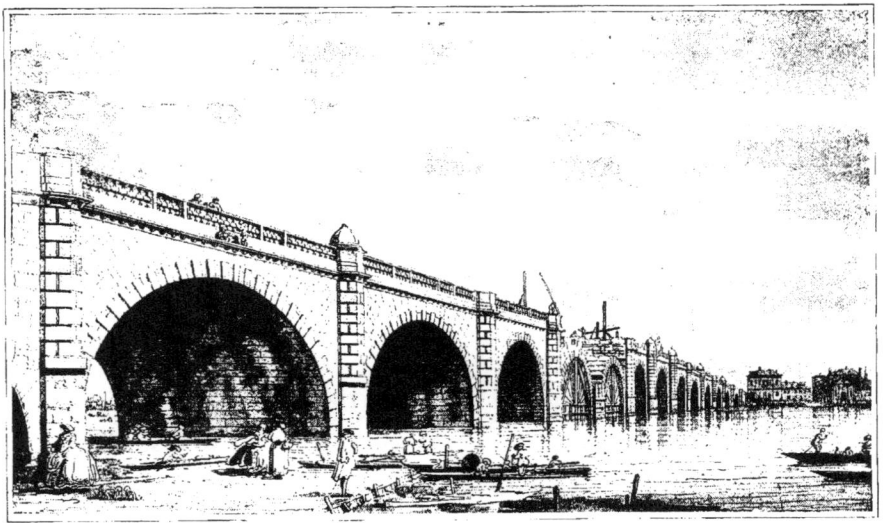

No. 3. WESTMINSTER BRIDGE BUILDING. CIRCA 1750. FROM A DRAWING BY CANALETTO IN THE COLLECTION OF HER MAJESTY AT WINDSOR.

an exaggeration to say that until they have been seen no adequate conception can be formed of the true power and excellence of the master—as his finest work, and the largest in style as well as size, is nearly all in this unequalled series. Besides the pictures, Consul Smith was also the fortunate possessor of a large volume containing no fewer than one hundred and fifty drawings by Canaletto, many of them sketches for the pictures he had obtained from the artist, and representing scenes, principally Venetian, with others from Padua, Rome, and Italian cities.

At the end of the volume are the drawings of London, six in number, hitherto unpublished, which have been specially reproduced by permission of Her Majesty for THE ART JOURNAL.

Four of these are of old Westminster Bridge. No. 3, illustrated above, must have been drawn during the artist's first visit to London, where he arrived in 1746, and where he stayed for about two years. During this visit he painted

November, 1750. Drawings Nos. 4 and 5 give a good idea of its thirteen fine arches, which were at this time considered triumphs of engineering and architecture.

These two drawings give with great clearness and accuracy the group of buildings which at that time was the principal ornament of the low land of Westminster, now overshadowed by the vast pile of the Houses of Parliament. Then the towers of Westminster formed the most conspicuous object, rising high over the long roof of Westminster Hall. Hard by is the tower of St. Margaret's with a standard flying from its tower; and the line is continued by the turrets and roof of St. Stephen's Chapel, destroyed by fire in 1834. To the left of these are the four curious turrets which surmount the corners of the church of St. John the Evangelist, Millbank, which are like the legs of an inverted dinner-table. In No. 5, the view extends to the other side of the river, where the towers of Lambeth rise among the trees of the Archbishop's gardens. The ferry from Lambeth to Westminster was the property of the See of

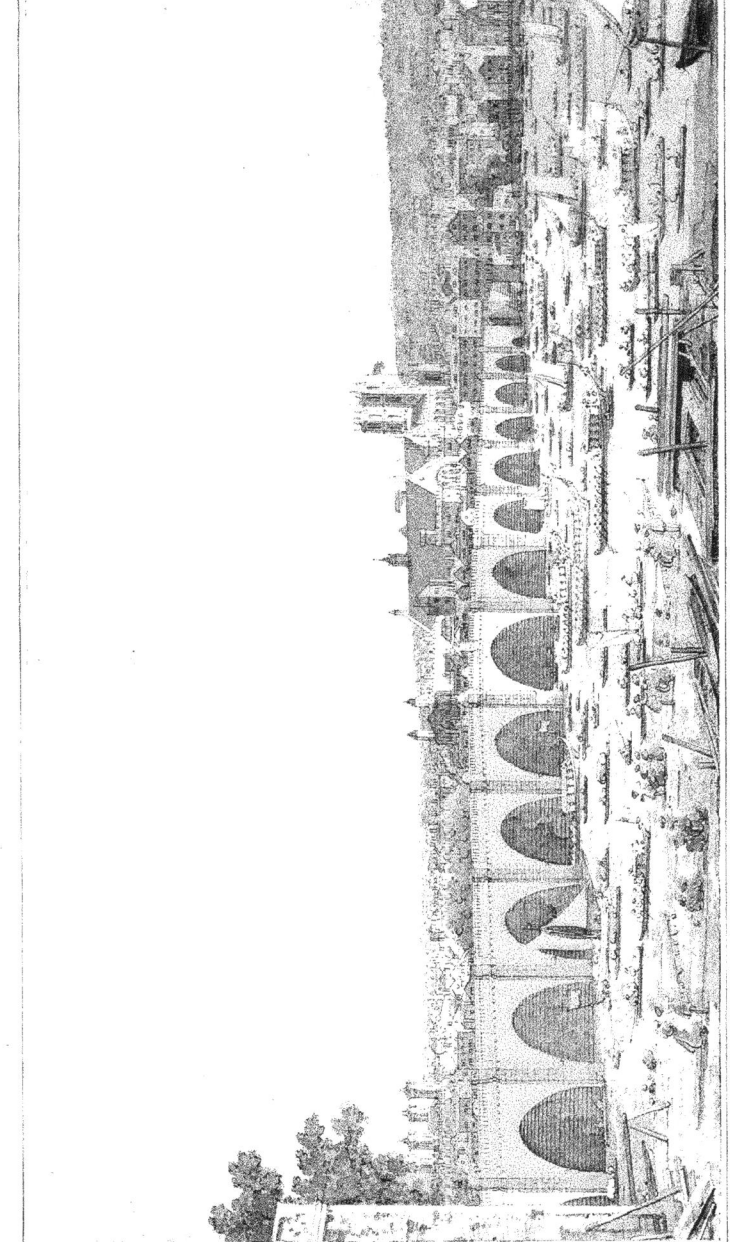

No. 1.—Westminster Bridge, showing Old Westminster Hall, the Abbey, and the Barges of the City Companies. From a Drawing by Canaletto in the Collection of Her Majesty at Windsor.

Canterbury, and on the opening of Westminster Bridge, a sum of £2,205 was granted as an equivalent for the destruction of the monopoly. The Watermen's Company received also a sum of much the same amount to compensate them for the loss in the reduction of the earnings of their members. In No. 4, the river may be seen crowded with barges of the City Companies, who at this time accompanied the new Lord Mayor in his procession to Westminster, a custom which a few still living may remember, but given up for the last fifty years or more.

Illustration 1 is a sketch from under one of the arches of Westminster Bridge, near the Surrey side, and gives a clear representation of the noble view from this spot; Somerset House and gardens can be seen just at the bend of the river, which must have presented nearly the same appearance when of old Somerset House. This, with its companion shown in illustration 2, are the original drawings for the two large pictures now hanging in Windsor Castle. Canaletto seems to have painted these views more than once, as they were engraved in 1750, the year the bridge was finished, as then being in Mr. West's collection. The pair at Windsor came over to this country with the rest of the pictures of Consul Smith. Canaletto was living in Silver Street, Golden Square, in 1752, whence he issued this advertisement: "Signor Canaletto gives notice that he has painted Chelsea College, Ranelagh House, and the River Thames, which if any gentleman or others are pleased to favour him with seeing the same, he will attend at his lodgings at Mr. Viggans, in Silver Street, Golden Square, for fifteen days from this day, July 31, from 8 to 1, and from 3 to 6 at night, each day."

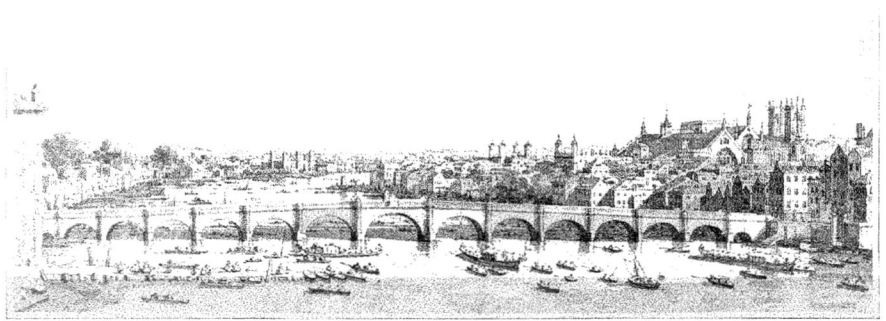

No. 5. WESTMINSTER BRIDGE, LOOKING UP THE RIVER. FROM A DRAWING BY CANALETTO IN THE COLLECTION OF HER MAJESTY AT WINDSOR.

Wordsworth wrote his splendid sonnet:—

COMPOSED UPON WESTMINSTER BRIDGE.
September 3rd, 1803.

Earth has not anything to show more fair:
Dull would he be of soul who could pass by
A sight so touching in its majesty:
The City now doth like a garment wear
The beauty of the morning. Silent, lone,
Ships, towers, domes, theatre and temples lie
Open unto the fields, and to the sky;
All bright and glittering in the smokeless air,
Never did sun more beautifully steep
In his first splendour valley, loch or hill;
Ne'er saw I, never felt, a calm so deep!
The river glideth at his own sweet will:
Dear God! the very houses seem asleep;
And all that mighty heart is lying still.

The bridge is also well shown in illustration 6 with the same group of buildings, but taken from a different point, the gardens At this time the site chosen for these views commanded the finest reaches of the river, and the Venetian artist seems to have enjoyed the opportunity of exercising his unrivalled skill in water painting, and the perfection of his delineation of boats and watermen. No hideous railway sheds or bridges broke the broad expanse of river and shore, and through the clear atmosphere the tower of Westminster and the spires of the City churches appear with the clearness of detail like that of an early summer morning. These gardens of Somerset House were the remains of the old Palace of the Protector Somerset, and were laid out by him when he built his house in the time of Edward the Sixth. On his attainder it reverted to the Crown. Elizabeth, Anne of Denmark, both resided here, and in 1626 it was settled for life on Henrietta Maria, whose Roman Catholic chapel and household were established here. After her time it was generally considered as the appanage of the Queens of England till 1775, when the Buckingham House, now enlarged and converted into Buckingham Palace, was settled on Queen Charlotte.

For a century before this, Somerset House had become a habitation for retainers of the Court and others to whom lodgings were assigned. The whole was pulled down in 1776, when the present pile of government offices was erected.

In the view looking West, up the river, illustration 6, will be noticed the wooden towers of the Water-works and the Banqueting House of Whitehall, the only portion of the stately palace, designed by Inigo Jones, to stretch thence to the river, which was ever created. Illustration 2 is the view looking Eastwards towards St. Paul's and its clustering city churches —further on the right may be seen the Monument, and the long series of small arches of old London Bridge, with the tower of St. Mary's, Southwark, close to the edge of the drawing.

RICHARD R. HOLMES.

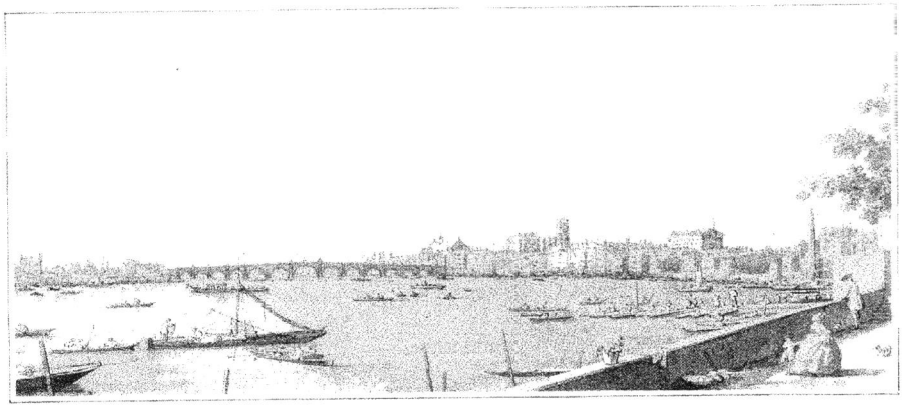

No. 6. WESTMINSTER BRIDGE FROM OLD SOMERSET HOUSE. FROM A DRAWING BY CANALETTO IN THE COLLECTION OF HER MAJESTY AT WINDSOR.

THE LOAN EXHIBITION OF PICTURES AT THE GUILDHALL.

IN this third effort of the Corporation of London to place before the people a collection worthy of their notice, the endeavour has been made to gather together, so far as they were obtainable, such a representation as would demonstrate in some measure the capacity of the British schools of painting. The representation is, of necessity, somewhat incomplete, by reason of the restricted wall space at disposal; but the Corporation, by the generosity of owners, have been able to include in the collection many exceptional productions which in themselves have been sufficient, by their artistic excellence, to mark certain epochs in the history of the country's art. Many distinguished works, which it was earnestly desired might appear in the exhibition, are, for unavoidable reasons, absent, and this is a matter for regret. The endeavour has been to secure what may be regarded as the chief work of each particular artist, and where this has failed his next in order of merit has in several instances been obtained. The difficulties of forming such a collection as has been attempted by a public body, which only in recent years has taken up seriously the question of Art at all, have been great; not the least obstacle being to convince those who lend their pictures, that the exhibition is an effort made in the interests of Art, and not solely for the entertainment of the populace.

Forming a section of the exhibition is a selection of works (many of them masterpieces) of the Dutch school, some forty in number. These we may notice later: for the present we propose to confine our observations to the British works in the Exhibition.

During the past fifty years men have come and gone who have left their impress upon the art of their country. Among these may be mentioned Rossetti, Windus, Lawless, Madox Brown, William Davis, Simeon Solomon, Mason, Walker—some of whom are apt to be forgotten, or remembered only by a few, but all of them are represented, in several cases at their best, in the Guildhall Exhibition. In Rossetti's 'Monna Vanna' and 'Pandora' we have perhaps two of his most striking three-quarter length impersonations of female beauty and character; the first-named—belonging to Mr. Rae, of Birkenhead—being in colour and expression singularly beautiful, and of a gentleness and dignity far removed from the strange morbidity of many of those comprised in this phase of his art; while in 'Pandora,' which we reproduce, and in which the sense of impending tragedy is near, the rich colouring is in fine harmony with the aspect of the face, thoughtful and farseeing, as she carries the mysterious casket from which issues the destroying flame, taking, as it rises, the form of crimson-winged messengers of evil. A smaller work of his is also seen, 'Joli Cœur,' a gem of colour and rich in sentiment. This was formerly, we believe, in the collection of the late Mr. W. A. Turner, of Macclesfield. In the works shown by Mr. W.

L. Windus, one wonders how men of such evident faculty should become so lost sight of, as to be scarcely known to many of the present generation. It is a matter of regret that his masterpiece, 'Burd Helen,' is not in the exhibition, to show of what the man at his best was capable; but failing that work, the three which have been secured are sufficient to indicate his power of design and his sense of the beautiful in colour. In 'The Young Duke' particularly these attributes are very conspicuous, and it is a pity that the large picture for which this was the sketch, and for which, we believe, the late Mr. Frederick Leyland offered the artist a considerable sum, was never carried out. In 'The Outlaw' (or 'The Fugitive,' as it was once called), a most delicate appreciation of nature is shown. It is said that this charming little work was observed by Rossetti in a pawnbroker's shop, and that although there was no direct indication upon it, such as his signature, he felt convinced it was Windus's work; and collecting the requisite sum among his small artistic coterie, the work was purchased. It subsequently passed into the hands of a Liverpool gentleman, and thence to the present owner. In Lawless's 'Sick Call' we see the work of a man who painted little, but painted well. His brief life was finished at the age of twenty-seven; but this, the last picture he executed, is sufficient to indicate his powers, and to enable us to realise in some measure the manner of man he was, and what might reasonably have been expected of him had he lived. Madox Brown is represented by the famous scene from 'Lear and Cordelia,' executed originally in water-colour, which Mr. Craven owns. In Mason's 'Evening Hymn' we have a picture rarely seen. Time was when the country children coming through the gloaming after evening service sang hymns on the way. Here is a group which, for natural grace

dimly seen against the golden light that still illumines the sky. Another work, smaller, but showing the artist again in his fervent love for nature, is 'The Gander.' Here the rich golden light left in the sky by the sunken sun, sheds sufficient radiance over the darkening landscape, to show the graceful form of a peasant child—in dark blue frock and light blue pinafore—stepping back with arms uplifted to keep off the sturdy gander that threatens her. In Walker's 'Sunny Thames,' lent by Sir Charles Tennant, the effect of full daylight is given, with the same sympathy with nature which distinguishes all his works. This is the one which was left incomplete, and which, we believe, was brought into its present satisfactory state by Mr. J. W. North, A.R.A.; a hazardous task, but none more able to accomplish it than he, his friend and fellow-worker. The works by Simeon Solomon are two in number, 'Love in Autumn,' and 'The Two Sleepers and one that Awaketh,' both of fine quality and finish, the first-named, painted in Florence in 1866, the property of Mr. Coltart of Birkenhead, being imbued throughout with poetic feeling, and showing the impersonation of 'Love,'—sad of aspect—taking his way along a leaf-strewn and rocky path, his crimson wings and raiment rudely blown by the chill winds of autumn.

Flourishing somewhat earlier than the foregoing, and of more practical vigour of mind, were John Phillip, Linnell, senior, Etty, Landseer, David Cox, Mulready, Turner, Constable, and Wilkie, whose work can be ably gauged by the examples at the Guildhall. Turner's 'Marriage of the Adriatic,' belonging to Mr. Ralph Brocklebank, of Tarporley—illustrative of the annual custom which for centuries prevailed in Venice, of the Doge (as the city's representative) dropping a ring with much gay ceremonial into the sea, and thus wedding the city

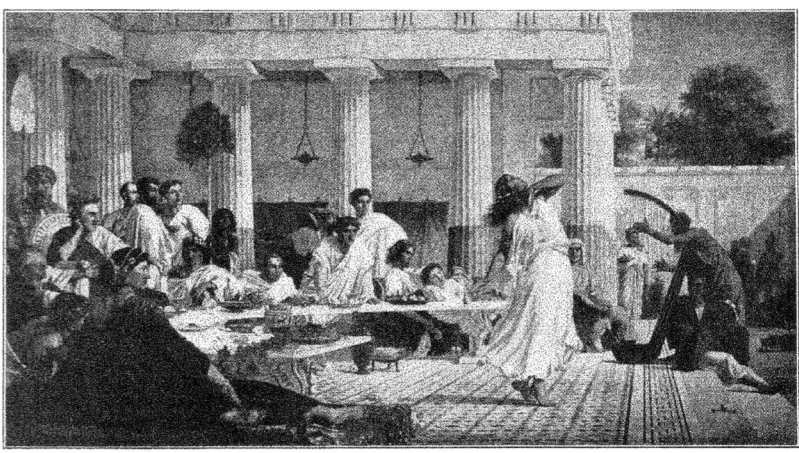

Herod's Birthday Feast. From the Picture by Edward Armitage, R.A., presented by the Artist to the Guildhall Permanent Collection.

and expression, harmonizes singularly with the calm of nature as it sinks into rest at the approach of night—slender girlish forms, coloured cotton frocks, and pretty granny bonnets, all

with the Adriatic—is a work of great brilliancy. Near to it hang John Linnell's 'Woodcutters,' and Constable's 'Salisbury Cathedral'; the latter, one of the painter's most celebrated works, executed in the prime of his career. It was said to have been his favourite production, and indeed it exhibits in the fullest manner the chief characteristics which distinguished him. Another favourite work of its master is Mulready's 'Train up a Child in the way it should go,' a picture over which Mulready is said to have bestowed more work than over any other of his compositions; fine in arrangement and of great finish, this picture has justly been greatly coveted, and it has been in the family of its present owner for very many years. It was once considerably injured by fire, but its painstaking author restored it —not, it is said, without further enriching the work as a composition. Delightful in theme is Sir David Wilkie's 'Letter of Introduction,' rivalling in depth and finish some of the best of the Dutch masters. Etty's 'Homeric Dance,' owned by Sir Charles Tennant, amply represents this fine colourist. It had been hoped to obtain the 'Benaiah slaying two lionlike men of Moab,' but this vigorous work, irreconcilable to the popular idea of Etty's compositions, could not be spared from the Scottish National Gallery, where it has been deposited by the Scottish Academy.

In John Phillip's 'Chat round the Brasero' is seen one of the every-day occurrences in Spanish life, the portrayal of which added so much to his fame as an artist. It is one of his most brilliant works. The 'Murillo' is larger, as also is 'La Gloria,' or 'The Spanish Wake,' which hangs in Sir John Pender's house in Arlington Street, but pictorially and in workmanship the present picture cannot well be surpassed. David Cox's 'Vale of Clydd' is in the same room as the Phillip, and is very rightly regarded as one of the highest achievements of this popular painter. It is now owned by Mr. T. J. Barratt, who also contributes the splendid performance by Landseer, which hangs next to it, 'The Monarch of the Glen,' intended by the painter to fill a panel (which accounts for its square form) in some apartment in the House of Lords. Landseer's price for the picture to the nation was £300. It was, however,

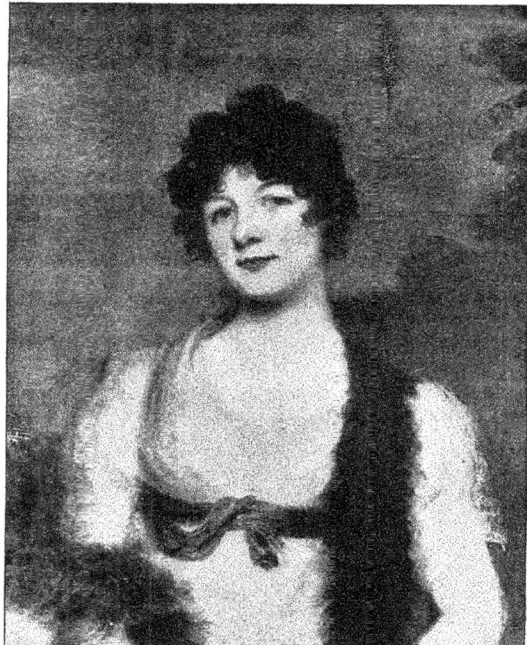

MISS MELLON. FROM THE PICTURE BY ROMNEY IN THE COLLECTION OF F. C. PAWLE, ESQ., J.P.

curiously enough, declined by the Committee of Fine Arts, and Landseer, it is said, who was furious, sold the picture to a ready customer for 800 guineas, and the copyright to Messrs. Graves for £500. The work appeared in the ensuing Royal Academy Exhibition (1851), where it evoked universal admiration. It afterwards passed to Lord Cheylesmore, and thence to its present owner, who gave nearly 7,000 guineas for it.

Going now still farther back we find a full-length portrait by Reynolds, of 'Isabella, Duchess of Rutland,' known as "The Beautiful Duchess," which comes to the Guildhall from Belvoir Castle, and is a splendid and graceful example of the famous painter; and four admirable examples of Romney appear in the collection. We have seen on former occasions at the Guildhall 'Lady Hamilton as "Euphrosyne,"' and 'Lady Hamilton as "Circe,"' and the chief of Romney's works in the present Collection shows that distinguished beauty seated at the spinning-wheel. It is a charming example and its owner, Lord Iveagh, could ill afford to spare it from his house in Grosvenor Place, but by his kindness it is in the Collection, and will prove a delight to all lovers of this favourite painter. Another Romney is a bust portrait, which is reproduced above, of the charming Miss Mellon, first Mrs. Thomas Coutts, and afterwards Duchess of St. Albans. Lowly born, the only education she had was that which she picked up in her wanderings with a strolling company of comedians, of which her mother was the wardrobe woman; but she obtained an introduction to Sheridan, and being by him allowed to play at Drury Lane, she soon made an impression by her beauty. Another of Romney's, the 'Sleeping Child,' lent by Mr. Humphry Ward, is a clever and pleasing production, rich in colour and refined in style.

Of the Norwich School, only three examples are in the present Exhibition, one by Alfred Stannard, another by his brother Joseph, and a third by John Crome. The two former are lent by Sir Charles Robinson, the Curator of the Queen's pictures, that by Alfred being a fine example, bearing a strong resemblance to Hobbema's work, excellent throughout and in perfect condition, while Joseph's, though small, indicates great capacity, and is full of light and vitality.

Coming now to the living British artists, at the head of the gallery is seen Sir Frederick Leighton's 'Idyll,' a large and beautiful work, painted in 1881, and showing two women, one in amber the other in white, listening to the piping of a shepherd, who sits at their feet. Two smaller examples of the President are also in the collection. 'Weaving the Wreath,' painted more than twenty years ago, and which we reproduce in our large plate, shows the figure of a young girl seated on an Oriental mat, amply clad in blue drapery, a piece of white showing, and wearing on her own head a wreath similar to that she is weaving. The other is the head of a Venetian girl, lent by Mr. Joseph Ruston, of Lincoln, and well known by the engraving. On an adjacent wall is seen two pictures, which, painted a quarter of a century ago, will be pleasing for the British public to again look upon : one is ' Jochebed,' one of the finest results of Mr. Goodall's visit to the East, the unfinished pyramid in the landscape being full of meaning, as suggestive of labour yet to be executed by the Israelitish people ; the other, hanging appropriately next to it, is Mr. Poynter's ' Israel in Egypt,' a work which, when it was exhibited in the Academy of 1867, gained for the artist approbation on all sides. In Mr. Marcus Stone's 'Edward II. and Piers Gaveston,' we have the weak monarch and the ingratiating courtier admirably portrayed ; and the groups on either side, with the royal park beyond, enables the observer to clearly realise this page of English history. The picture which first brought Mr. Herkomer into note, ' The Last Muster,' is also in the collection. Painted in 1874, it represents army pensioners in church, and is happily placed by the side of. Lady Butler's work, ' Scotland for Ever ! ' where the men in active service are facing the terrible chances of war. In this charge of the Scots Greys at Waterloo, more than ordinary artistic difficulties have been overcome, and the portrayal of the famous brigade tearing to the support of the 92nd Regiment has been splendidly achieved. By the courtesy of the proprietors, we give a reproduction of this on the opposite page. On the same wall hangs ' Herod's Birthday Feast,' by Mr. Edward Armitage, exhibited at the Academy in 1868. This is a picture which shows the artist at his best, admirably painted throughout, and the Corporation of London are to be congratulated that this picture is to remain at Guildhall to form, by the generosity of the painter, one of the most interesting gifts to the permanent collection : we reproduce it on a previous page.

The pre-Raphaelite brotherhood are represented in three works by Sir John Millais, and two by Mr. Holman Hunt. Of the former, the ' Sir Isumbras at the Ford,' which provoked so much hostile criticism in 1857, will be regarded with curious interest. Only recently the painter has worked on the trappings of the black horse with greatly improved effect, it having seemed in the eyes of many too much of a silhouette against the landscape, and needing relief of this character. Of Mr. Holman Hunt, the Exhibition is fortunate in securing his ' Finding of the Saviour in the Temple,' one of his most distinguished achievements, painted at Jerusalem under peculiar difficulties and occupying the painter for nearly six years. A smaller example by this painter is ' Strayed Sheep,' a widely popular example, also reproduced in THE ART ANNUAL for 1893. Of Sir Edward Burne-Jones there is only one example, but that one is of exceptional beauty and brilliancy. ' The Hesperides,'

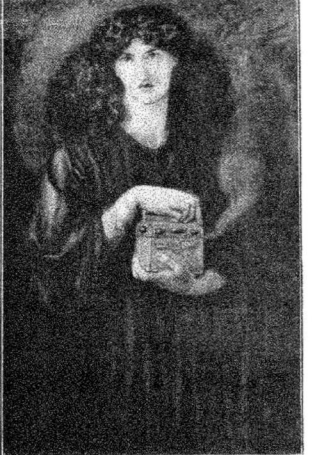

PANDORA. FROM THE PICTURE BY ROSSETTI, IN THE COLLECTION OF CHARLES BUTLER, ESQ.

lent by Mr. Craven, shows the beautiful guardians circling round the tree with the golden apples, clothed in rich bronze-coloured raiment, with the dragon Ladon in their midst. This work was not included in the exhibition of the artist's work last year at the New Gallery, and will therefore be very welcome to the lovers of this master.

Very poetical in sentiment too, is Mr. Waterhouse's ' La Belle Dame sans merci,' from Keats's charming ballad, which appears to advantage at the Guildhall. It will be a delight to many to see again Mr. Whistler's picture of Miss Alexander, while it is a matter of regret that the Corporation were unsuccessful in their efforts to induce the authorities of the Luxembourg to allow Mr. Sargent's brilliant example ' La Carmencita,' to appear in the collection. Mr. Orchardson is represented by ' Her Mother's Voice,' which comes from Mr. Tate's gallery, of which THE ART JOURNAL recently contained a reproduction ; Mr. Ouless by his vigorous portrait of Mr. Bancroft ; Mr. Tadema by the famous ' Roses of Heliogabalus,' kindly spared by its generous owner, Mr. John Aird ; while the newly elected Associate, Mr. Swan, is seen in his impressive picture of the Polar bears, bearing the quotation from " The Ancient Mariner "—" We were the first that ever burst, Into that silent sea." Mr. George Henry, of Glasgow, is represented by his ' Poppies,' which was reproduced in the March number of this journal. Examples also of Mr. Henry Woods, Miss Clara Montalba, Mr. J. W. North, Mr. David Murray, Mr. Gregory, Mr. East, Mr. Boughton, Mr. Leader, and other well-known painters, are also to be seen in the Exhibition, and it may be remarked that the aim has been to show comparatively few pictures, but to show them well.

A. G. TEMPLE.

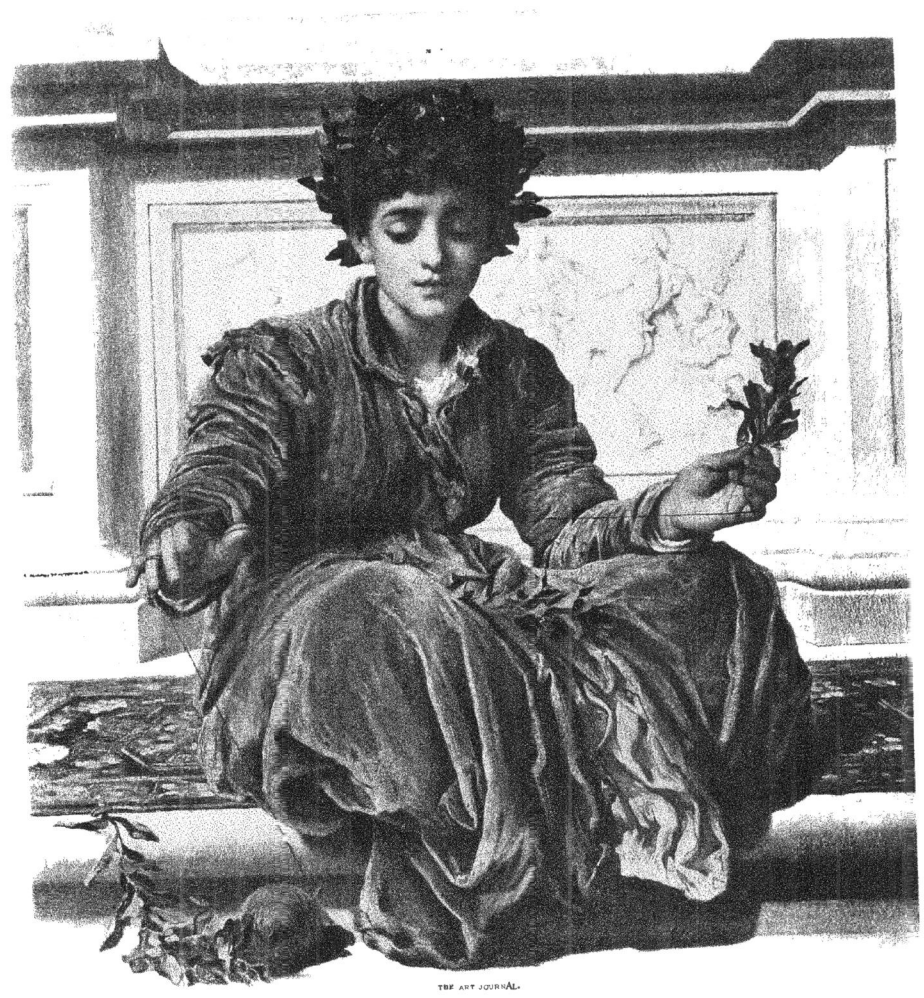

"WEAVING THE WREATH."

FROM THE PICTURE BY SR FREDERIC LEIGHTON, BART., P.R.A. IN THE COLLECTION OF GEORGE HOLT, ESQ. LIVERPOOL.

LONDON: J.S. VIRTUE & CO LIMITED.

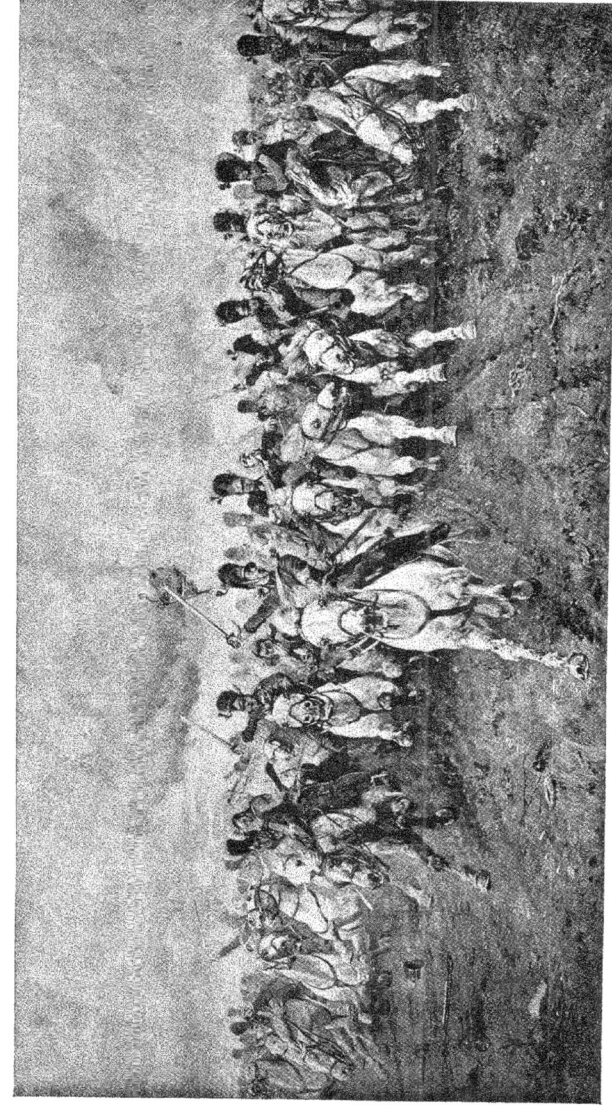

"SCOTLAND FOR EVER." FROM THE PICTURE BY LADY BUTLER BELONGING TO THE CORPORATION OF LEEDS.
BY PERMISSION OF MESSRS. HILDESHEIMER AND CO., LTD., LONDON AND MANCHESTER, OWNERS OF THE COPYRIGHT AND PUBLISHERS OF THE LARGE PLATE.

THE NEW SCULPTURE.
1879—1894.

OF all the artistic movements of our time in England, the most sharply defined and the most uniformly satisfactory is that which is identified with the reform of our national sculpture. In painting, the only really popular modern art, fashion has succeeded fashion, and the strong individuality of one man after another has grouped a school around him. With the disappearance of each founder, his school has been seen to decline, and another painter, of views diametrically opposed, has taken the place as a master. So the anarchy of our painting has proceeded, oscillating without any central principle of taste, from Mason to Rossetti, from Alma Tadema to Whistler. But in recent sculpture, and there alone, we have seen a highly vitalised art developed, not around the individuality of a single man, but around a theory of execution clearly perceived and consistently adhered to by a group of men of various talent, alike only in this, their loyalty to a common ideal.

The history of this school of sculptors has never been attempted, nor of the movements which culminated in its success. But some day the progress of these artists along their common path, and the singular good fortune which has attended them, must attract the close attention of the chronicler. All that the writer of these papers proposes to do is, firstly, to answer as well as he can the frequent question, "What is the New Sculpture?" and secondly, to give the results of notes which he has kept, as an ardent well-wisher to the cause, year by year, from the earliest dawning of the movement. He hopes that a somewhat bare statement of successive facts may not be wholly without value to the future historian. The moment seems to have arrived for closing the first volume of this history, and for reviewing the series of events which have culminated, by the election of Messrs. Frampton and Swan to be A.R.A.'s, in placing the whole academic prestige of this Art in England in the hands of the New Sculpture.

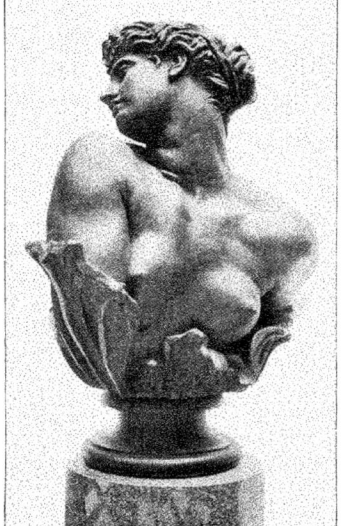

CLYTIE. BY G. F. WATTS, R.A.

I.

Twenty years ago sculpture had sunken in this country to the lowest depth of desuetude. The very thought of English statuary was ridiculous; every newspaper annually lifted a hoof and kicked the sculptors. About the year 1872 this began to be a *cliché*—"As usual, there is nothing of interest in the sculpture-rooms." To an intelligent and sympathetic observer this was an exaggeration. In those darkest seasons there was always something to arrest attention and to awaken enjoyment. But the fact had to be faced, that sculpture in England was practically dead. It had lived, with some briskness of vitality, at the beginning of the century, and all that still survived was a debased and sunken tradition of the Georgian age.

If we look closely at what English sculpture consisted of in the seventies, we see three streams of influence flowing from the 1800 period, three dying rivulets fast disappearing in the sand. The first was the purely conventional tradition of Canova, the Roman school; this had struggled to preserve its dignity and its polish in Gibson, it had descended to MacDowell, and when that artist died in 1870, it had passed to still feebler hands and emptier heads. More interesting, because more intellectual and more virile, had been the second influence, that which had descended through Behnes and Weekes from Chantrey. These men had dropped in some degree the Roman convention; they had dared to be slightly naturalistic; and in Foley, who died in 1874, and in the venerable Mr. John Bell, who still survives, the Chantreian school produced artists of high accomplishment and unquestionable talent. What characterized these men, however—as may be seen to excess in the great works of Foley—was presently to render them especially antagonistic to the New Sculptors. They thought nothing of surface, their sole anxiety was to obtain an effect by a strict study of form. Lastly, the delicate charm of Flaxman was still felt, like a fading perfume. It pervaded, with its love of the minuter forms of nature, its humble poetic grace, its touch of pre-Raphaelitism, the sculpture of Woodington and of Woolner. But all was sunken in convention, and where a real talent existed, as in the case of Mr. Armstead, with his strong Gothic feeling and sympathy with firmly-drawn sixteenth-century composition, the general air of dulness stifled and suppressed it. In 1877 the sculptor Royal

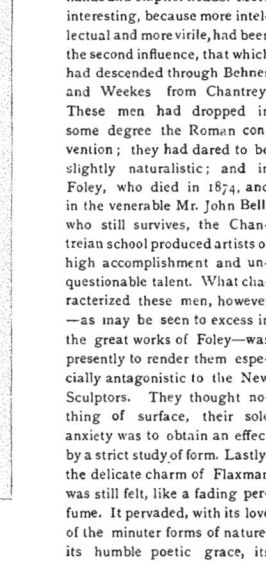

Academicians were Calder Marshall, Weekes, and Woolner;

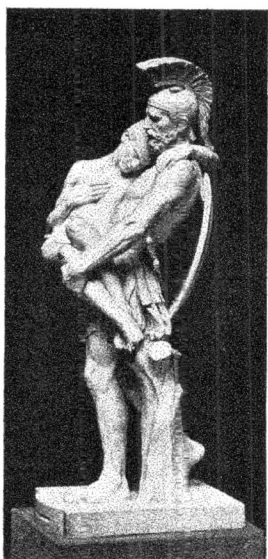

WARRIOR CARRYING WOUNDED YOUTH FROM BATTLE.
BY HAMO THORNYCROFT R.A.

the associates were Armstead, Durham, Stephens, and Woodington, while Boehm was immediately to take Durham's place. The Royal Academy seemed an absolutely impregnable fastness, barred against new light; yet this Jericho has so completely fallen that the only survivor of the old school remaining in it to-day is the one who, like Rahab, opened the doors of his sympathy to the new ideas. It is almost a romantic fact that Mr. Armstead, in whom the New Sculpture in its early days found its only influential friend in the profession, is now the solitary witness of its triumph.

It is usual to attribute the start of the New Sculpture to the example of Alfred Stevens. With the highest admiration for the genius of that great man, I cannot admit that this was the case. It may be said that, in the dearth of high talent, it encouraged young sculptors to know that a man of the dimensions of Stevens had been existing amongst them. Nor would I reject so sentimental a suggestion. But there, I think, the influence must have ended. Not only did Stevens live in isolation, little affecting the society of young men, but the character of his work was wholly out of sympathy with what was going to be produced five or six years after his death. Stevens was a disciple of Thorwaldsen, captured in his early maturity by the magnificent audacities of Michel Angelo, and determined to reproduce in modern work the heroic qualities of that master. The central principle of the New Sculpture has been a close and obedient following of nature. This was not a characteristic of Stevens, although he worked much from the model. He persistently bent the individuality of the model to a certain type which he kept before his imaginative eye. Alfred Stevens was a sort of pioneer for the new school; he was in no sense its founder or proposer. Far more truly might the 'Clytie' of Mr. Watts, that swallow of 1868 which brought no summer with it, be said, with the veracious texture of its flesh, its *aura* of un-exampled life and picturesqueness, to have been the true forerunner of the New Sculpture.

What the New Sculpture in England has really sprung from is unquestionably the French school of the last generation. Modern European sculpture, in fact, dates from 1833, when François Rude exhibited his 'Young Neapolitan Fisherman' in the Salon. This was the first attempt made anywhere to present, under an exact and individual form, the human body as it exists before our eyes. Criticism attacked this work and its successors as vulgar and ignoble; the old statuaries shuddered at the contemptuous reversal of all their rules and axioms. But the public saw an escape from the cold and lifeless apathy with which modern sculpture had hitherto overpowered the uninitiated, and Rude was welcomed as an innovator. From this moment, subjected though it might be to a variety of discouragements and retrogressions, sculpture was moving along the right road in France, and the astonishing thing is that, in spite of the close intercommunication between the two countries, no sort of influence from France penetrated our hide-bound conventions. Twenty years ago, when Italian sculpture had declined into a puerility and feebleness absolutely contemptible, and when Dubois and Chapu were producing masterpieces of incomparable beauty, it was a common thing to hear persons of assumed authority speak of French sculpture as of a thing of recognised absurdity, and regret that the conceit of the French prevented their young artists from imitating the clever Italians.

It was the more puzzling that no warmth from France should melt the ice of English conventionality, because the fall

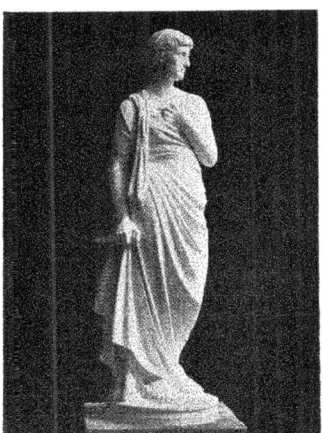

TRAGEDY. BY T. NELSON MACLEAN.

of the Second Empire sent several leading sculptors to this country. Loison had been an occasional exhibitor for years; in 1871 Carpeaux made a really remarkable show at the Royal

Academy; Carrier-Belleuse appeared there in 1873, and Dalou in 1874. Of these Frenchmen the one whose work was most copiously and favourably seen in London was Carpeaux, whose influence over the youngest generation must unquestionably have been great. Official criticism, however, ignored these French visitors altogether, and the exotic sculpture most admired at Burlington House in 1872 was a terrible 'Phryne' of the lowest and most lascivious Neapolitan trickiness. It was not in slight compositions and scattered busts that the real strength of the French naturalism could be seen, and the war had for the moment an extremely depressing influence upon the art in France itself. The new revival in Paris came to its height in 1876, and it is to the Salon of that year that we must look for the starting-force which set the New Sculpture moving in England.

The exhibition of sculpture in the Royal Academy for 1877 displayed the customary insipidities, the 'Cupids' and 'May Queens,' the 'Sleeping Babies' and the 'Bathing Venuses,' the simpering allegories and the waxen mythologies. But it contained one group of extraordinary novelty and vitality. Alone among the paintings in the Lecture Room, it seemed by that placing to suggest its solitary state in relation to the other statuary of the year. This was, of course, Sir Frederick Leighton's bronze group called, 'Athlete strangling a Python.' In this admirable composition, now so familiar as to render all description needless, a wholly new force made itself felt. Here was something far more vital and nervous than the soft following of Flaxman dreamed of; a series of surfaces, varied and appropriate, all closely studied from nature, and therefore abhorrent to the Chantreian tradition; attitudes and expressions so fresh and picturesque as to outrage the fondest principles of the Gibsonian Canovesques. This, in short, was something wholly new, propounded by a painter to the professional sculptors, and displaying a juster and a livelier sense of what their art should be than they themselves had ever dreamed of. 'The Athlete and the Python,' even with shortcomings which it may now not be difficult to point out, gave the start-word to the New Sculpture in England.

What had led Sir Frederick Leighton on the lines of his startling and revolutionising masterpiece? On that subject it is not my privilege to say anything with authority, since the secret has never been confided to me. But every one knows that the President (as it is natural to call him, and as he shortly afterwards became) was a close follower of all that was done in Paris, and an assiduous attendant on the show in the Salon. I cannot doubt for a moment that what he had seen there in the summer of 1876 had deeply impressed him, and that the character of the Parisian sculpture determined him to attempt to work on similar lines. It was in the year 1876 that the French sculptors, long scattered and depressed, drew themselves together and produced a show of models which took the light completely out of the pictures. Mr. Leighton (as he then was) would see in the Salon of that year the 'Courage Militaire' and the 'Charité' of Paul Dubois, the 'Tentation' of Allar, the 'St. Jean' of Hiolle, the 'Lamartine' of Falguière, the 'St. Sébastien' of Gautherin, the colossal 'Alexandre Dumas' of Chapu—in other words, the most accomplished, and at the same time most promising, collection of New Sculpture ever brought together anywhere in the modern world. When he left the Salon he would see, recently unveiled, in all its majestic virility, the 'Gloria Vinctis' of Mercié, in all its tender and radiant grace, the 'Education Maternelle' of Delaplanche. Let it never be doubted that this rich and sudden blossoming of the art of sculpture in France was not lost on the quick and sympathetic eyes of the English painter, nor that he wittingly broke off a rod of it to plant in England when he came back to his own people. Any sketch of the New Sculpture, however brief, would be incomplete if it took no note of the guidance and encouragement, the untiring fostering care, which it has met with from the President of the Royal Academy.

Nor was the opening of the Grosvenor Gallery in this same year, 1877, without its influence. Mr. J. Comyns Carr was at that time one of the very few Englishmen who realised what the French were doing in sculpture. At the first exhibition of this new gallery, which attracted an extraordinary amount of fashionable attention, a great group by Dubois was accorded a place of honour, while, if my memory does not fail me, a

CLEOPATRA. BY GEO. A. LAWSON.

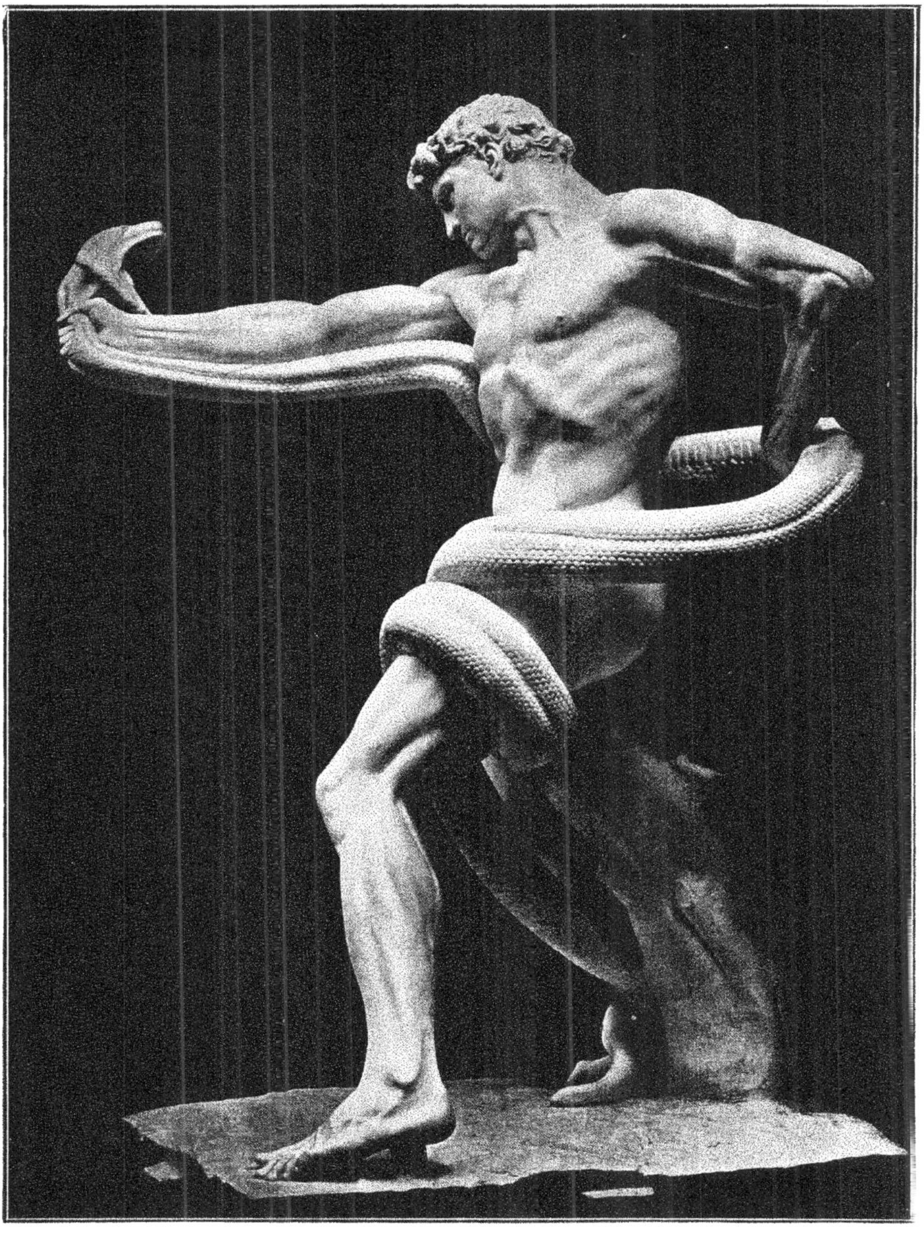

ATHLETE STRANGLING A PYTHON.
FROM THE STATUE BY SIR FRED. LEIGHTON, P.R.A.
Photographed by F. W. Birtwhistle.

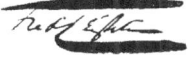

THE NEW SCULPTURE.

fine composition by Delaplanche, not recorded in the cata-

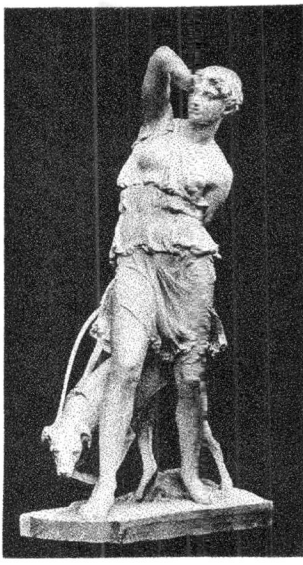

ARTEMIS. BY HAMO THORNYCROFT, R.A.

logue, confronted the visitor as he ascended the outer stairs. The severe picturesqueness, the noble vitality and suppleness, of these figures, and others which now began to be seen in London (I recall bits of Etex, of Oudiné, of Frémiet, seen about that date for the first time in England), filled the conventional Academic sculptors with indignation or contempt. Even in Paris the audacities of the young Falguière were shaken the head over by critics of position. But these objects were seen and hailed with perplexed delight by young men, students as yet of no status or accomplishment, the very men who so soon, with such almost theatrical ease, were to oust the old Chantreyans and Canovists from their arm-chairs.

The results of all this movement did not, however, display themselves immediately. No direct imitation of the central quality of the French was presently shown, no young sculptor at once repeated intelligently Sir Frederick Leighton's experiment. And here it is necessary, for historical purposes, to go back a little way to the competition for the gold medal in 1875. All along its course this movement of the New Sculpture has been marked by poetical proprieties and startling coincidences. Not the least of these is now seen to have been its obscure prologue or preface. In 1875 the gold medal for an imaginative competition in the round was competed for by two young students, neither until that day heard of, the merit of whose models, so it was then said, was so nearly equal, and so far beyond those of their fellow-students, that the prize long hung poised between them. The subject was, 'A Warrior carrying a Wounded Youth from Battle,' and the gold medal having been finally awarded to Hamo Thornycroft, 1894

Alfred Gilbert retired disappointed, and was for some years heard of no more. The collocation of these names at the very outset is truly remarkable, since these were the two men by whom, more than by any other, the New Sculpture was later on to be piloted into fame and universal recognition. These were to be, in their totally distinct manners, the standard-bearers of the two great wings of the army of conquest.

It is long since those juvenile works by the two future masters have been seen; the unsuccessful model, perhaps, is scarcely remembered. There was, in neither, yet apparent the qualities which were afterwards to shine in the work of each. Yet something of tenderness in the articulations of the joints, something in the freshness of the action and the harmony of lines in the one group, prophesied of the future of Mr. Thornycroft, still subdued by admiration of Flaxman; while in the equestrian composition of Boehm's pupil, with its wild Celtic or Gaulish warrior, with the youth flung across a hairy pony, the lance, and the rough accessories, something might be already guessed of Mr. Gilbert's pictorial use of detail. Mr. Thornycroft's model was seen in the Central Hall in 1876; Mr. Gilbert's, I think, was never exhibited again. Few critics or artists, it may be conjectured, gave much thought to either, and thus every day, under our careless eyes, great issues are started in unobserved publicity.

In spite of the example set by all the admirable French art seen in Paris and London, and in spite of the guiding note of 'The Athlete and the Python,' no decided improvement was

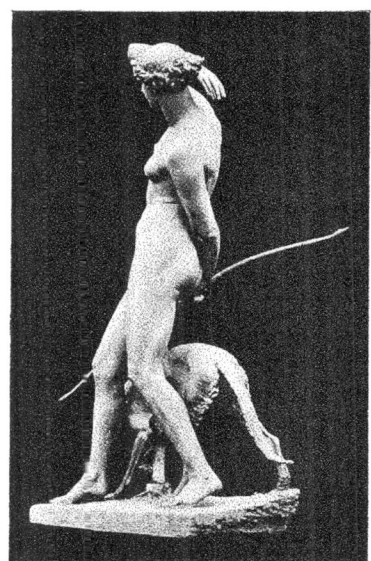

ARTEMIS (BEFORE DRAPERY). BY HAMO THORNYCROFT, R.A.

to be observed in the Royal Academy of 1878. Several of the future leaders of the new school were exhibitors that year, as they had been even in previous years—Mr. Thornycroft from 1872, Mr. Onslow Ford from 1875, Mr. Mullins from 1876, Mr. T. Stirling Lee from 1878,—but none of them had as yet any clear idea of what they wanted to do, or any perception of healthy Art. They were still, all of them, in the student stage. It was Mr. Hamo Thornycroft who earliest struggled up into something like a premonition of greatness. His 'Lot's Wife,' in the Royal Academy of 1878, had a rocky grandeur of conception, and something pyramidal and columnar in its arrangement, which gave freshness to its surface. The drapery was evidently inspired by the intricate treatment of the robes of the 'Fates,' at the British Museum.

There was nothing very satisfactory, perhaps, about this figure, nor much that prophesied of a happier time, but, in that dreary year, the 'Lot's Wife' was decidedly the most promising object to be found. Yet more accomplished and more graceful were one or two pieces by men whom we now look back to as holding a transitional position. Mr. George Lawson (born in 1832) had the misfortune to be introduced too soon into the world of sculpture. Of all the men prominent in the early seventies, he most readily and experimentally adopted the new views. It is not certain that his partial adoption of them did not, in those days, close the doors of the A.R.A.-ship against him, as, since the success of the movement, his incomplete adherence to them has kept it closed. His 'Dominie Sampson,' of 1868, was a marvel of humorous realism; his 'In the Arena,' of 1878, showed how closely Mr. Lawson had taken Sir Frederick Leighton's example to heart. This was a realisation of the struggle between a Roman captive and a panther—bold in design, a little raw in execution.

Other transitional figures of this, the dawn of the new school, were Mr. Percival Ball, Mr. T. Nelson MacLean, and Mr. Walter Ingram. If none of these has quite fulfilled the promise of those early times, all praise is at least due to them for their strenuous efforts to free themselves from conventionality and work upwards in the light of nature. The case of Mr. MacLean is peculiar. He was at that time the only English sculptor who had gone through the French schools, or had had any practical experience of French practice. He had been the companion of Falguière and of Mercié in their student-days, and had worked in the studio of Carrier-Belleuse. As early as 1875, at the very deadest hour of the night of our sculpture, Mr. MacLean, as a young man of thirty, had exhibited a cluster of models, all of which deserved notice and admiration. His statue of 'Ione,' in particular, became almost famous in numerous reproductions. It is certain that there was a moment in which Mr. MacLean might have won a great place as the leader of the new movement, but he allowed the psychological moment to pass, and the tide swept by him.

In the exhibition of 1879 these transitional figures were again present, although on the whole less prominent. Nor did the new school give any overt sign. But the old school made a last and most dangerous demonstration around the extremely clever and specious 'Dionysus' of Mr. George Simonds, which held the place of honour in the Lecture Room. Here all the qualities of the French were repudiated, and the traditions of Canova insisted upon. Here was the complete negation of colour and the picturesque, here the slurring over of all detail, of everything individual. The 'Dionysus' was surrounded all day long by admiring visitors, who declared it the only thing worth looking at in modern English sculpture. The vogue of this group among artists of the older generation was great. If a vacancy among the sculptors had occurred during the summer of 1879, it is unquestionable that Mr. Simonds would have been elected, so much were the Academicians pleased. But the opportunity failed, and it was the last time that the shadow of Gibson was to be cast over English sculpture.

We have led our readers to the very porch of the New Sculpture. In another article we shall invite them to enter the vestibule. EDMUND GOSSE.

[To be continued.]

[We have to thank all the sculptors for their kind and courteous help in preparing the illustration of these articles on the New Sculpture. The only exception has been that of Mr. Alfred Gilbert, who returned a bluff refusal to our request. —ED.]

THE PIANOFORTE: PAST, PRESENT, AND FUTURE.

IN these latter days a grand pianoforte is an ornament or useful machine, without which no drawing-room is complete. Like the patent medicines, you should always have it in the house. No self-respecting middle-class family is ever without it. Having bought one by Broadwood, Erard, Bechstein, or other eminent maker, with iron frame and the rest of it complete, the question arises, where shall you place it? If your drawing-room be sufficiently spacious, say not less than sixty by forty-five feet, it is a question easily answered. You need only hand over your instrument to your upholsterer: he will dump it in a convenient out-of-the-way spot, and so smother it under hangings and flowers and palms and statuettes, that it will never be seen until you have got near enough to break your shin on it. If, however, your drawing-room be anything under half the above-mentioned proportions and of the customary rectangular shape, the question of the placing of your piano will be a question indeed—a nearly, or quite, unanswerable one. Set it here and the light does not fall on the music; there, and it blocks one or more of your windows; there again, it stops your doorway; here, and it throws every other piece of furniture in the room out of harmony. In short, you will find that, place it where you will, cover it with elaborate trappings and ornaments as you please, it always remains an eyesore, an element of discord.

Then, and probably for the first time, you will look at the new possession and realise what an intractable leviathan it is. It stands there in the most helpless and ponderous manner on its four carved legs, without a beautiful line about it, possessing no sort of balance nor freedom nor self-supporting power. Part of one's pleasure in a noble piece of architecture comes from the sense that it is buoyant and needs not support —one is not oppressed by its weight. Here is this comparatively insignificant sound-producing machine: so long as it is in view you are painfully conscious that it rests heavily on its ugly legs, that only the legs keep the ponderous bulk

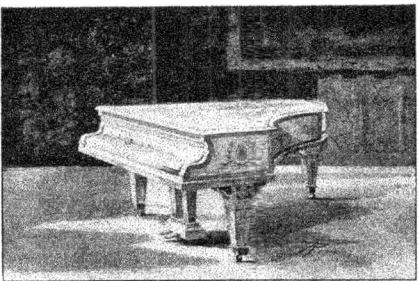

BECHSTEIN "ARTISTIC" GRAND PIANO.

from going to the floor with a mighty and destructive crash. Ascend—mentally, of course—to the ceiling: your piano looks like some misshapen hammer of Thor; it has five—sometimes six—sides; a long straight one, a short straight one, and a shorter straight one, the fourth either straight or a convex curve, the fifth a concave curve or divided into two straight lines, a short and a long. It has either five or six angles: three (probably) of ninety degrees, two of more than ninety degrees (but these two are not equal), and if there is a sixth angle it is of more than one hundred and eighty degrees. Was ever such a hotch-potch devised since Adam delved and Eve span! Of all forms of furniture invented by man it takes the palm for obtrusive lack of adaptability. In no circumstances will it adapt itself. The prevailing custom is to buy furniture to suit a room. But if your furniture include a piano you must buy a room to suit it. Until it has been sold second hand and third hand and many times more, and is worn out and finally converted into firewood, it remains the uncouth, unmanageable mass it left the maker's workshop.

That gradually this hideousness is becoming, if not intolerable, at least unpleasant to the inhabitants of the drawing-room, is shown by the attempts lately made by more or less eminent artists to beautify the piano—if, indeed it is not proved by the fact that the instrument is generally hidden in corners, when there are corners, or covered with ornaments and hangings. But so far, all the "artistic pianos" have been failures. Sir E. Burne-Jones painted a series of pictures on one exhibited at the New Gallery some time ago; Mr. William Morris covered one with a wall-paper design; and Mr. Alma Tadema did nothing in particular to his. Who is responsible for the Paderewski "thousand pounder" I do not know. But it—and the attempts of the above-named masters—failed, and were bound to fail, for they did not strike at the root of the evil—the form of the instrument. We know that no amount of detail beauty will save a badly-composed picture, no amount of gorgeous colour make a building of weak design beautiful. In the same way all Sir E. Burne-Jones's fancy, Mr. Morris's industry, and Mr.

Alma Tadema's striving have come to nought. The illustration of a Bechstein "artistic" short grand shows at once how much and how little may be done by ornament, so long as the form remains unaltered. The same may be said of the larger size Erard.

Is this ugliness of form a necessity? Well, it depends. Some makers say it is; but we must remember that few or none consider it an evil, and the reply may be a little too hasty and without due reflection. Some frankly state that a beautiful outline is not their aim: they are content with beauty and power—lately, I am afraid, more with power than beauty—of tone. After all, it is sound we chiefly want from a sound-making machine, and if great volume of sound be the chief end of a piano, it is to be feared that, in the present state of science, little can be done to improve its appearance. But is the volume of sound a necessity? In St. James's Hall it undoubtedly is; and it seems, therefore, that the concert-grand must remain a masterpiece of ugliness. But in the drawing-room the great volume of sound is no necessity. On the contrary, a concert-grand has no more business there than the organ of Westminster Abbey would have in the church of St. Mary-le-Strand. The genuine musician never avails himself of its full power: the amateur merely abuses it to the end that the beauty and happiness of life may be destroyed. And if the enormous proportions of the concert-grand can be dispensed with, it is possible to revert to an old form against which none of the many defects I have mentioned can be alleged—a form that in point of beauty can hold its own with the violin or harp.

As (I presume) many of my readers have small acquaintance with the "works" of a piano, as it is also necessary that the acquaintance shall be made, I propose (if a very mixed metaphor is permitted) to kill, not two, but several birds with one stone, by dragging them—my readers, not the birds—through the quagmire of a little musical history. This is sad, but necessary, and the shortest cut will be taken. My readers

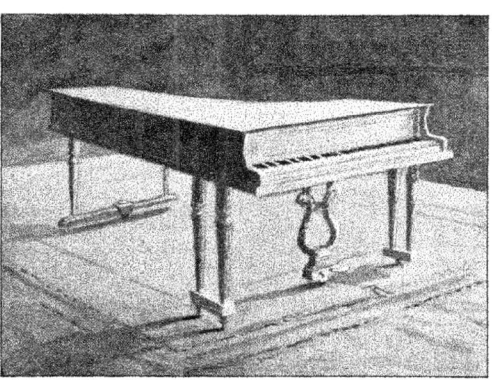

ERARD GRAND PIANO.

will thus get (1) a fairly-clear notion of the relation between the shape of the piano and its sound qualities; (2) a knowledge of the various prejudices and real necessities which have resulted in the evolution of the present form of the grand piano;

and (3) an idea of the advantages or shortcomings of the above-mentioned ideal form as it would be applied to the modern piano.

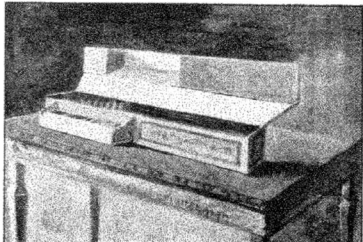

VIRGINAL.

It must first be understood that the harpsichord, clavichord and pianoforte are not variants of the same instrument. A writer in the *Magazine of Music* some time ago gave a "pedigree" showing clearly the radical differences between the various instruments, and this I venture to quote here:—

PEDIGREE.

The string plucked.	The string struck.	Movable bridge.
Psaltery.	Dulcimer.	Monochord.
Virginal.	Piano.	Clavichord.
Spinet.		
Harpsichord.		

With the third of these, the movable bridge species, we have nothing to do. The first keyed instrument we meet with is the "Virginalles." It was not lovely in form, being, in fact, merely an oblong box, "bearing," says the already mentioned writer, "a general resemblance to a badly-made coffin," as may be seen from the typical illustration above. But its ugliness is not intrusive, and the cases were frequently very beautifully painted. The sound was produced by a very simple expedient: when the key was pressed, the string was plucked by a *plectrum* of leather or crow-quill. The wire had to be very thin to be set in vibration at all by this means, and even unmusical readers will understand that the tones as well as the wires were thin. Further, the sound-board was small, and its shape did not permit of the requisite difference in length between the bass strings, which must, of course, be long, and those of the treble, which are short. With the object of securing greater length of string, greater size of sound-board, and greater difference between bass and treble, a new form, the spinet form, was devised. The oblong virginal shape might have served, but it would be very unwieldy in the larger size; and there are not wanting signs (such as elaborate decoration and painting) to show that the old makers were on the alert for any possible improvement in the appearance of their instruments. Such an improvement the spinet form decidedly was. It is the most satisfactory that has ever been used for a keyed string instrument. It has balance, buoyancy—the larger wedge-like portion compensating for the short solid mass of the key-board end. The moment that wedge-end is turned to the left, so that the side which is in the spinet an acute angle to the key-board becomes (as in the grand) a right angle, the balance and buoyancy are lost, for reasons that a practical designer can give more easily than I can. But the reader may compare the sketch of the beautiful Hitchcock spinet, now in the possession of Messrs. Broadwood, with that of a more than usually elegant harpsichord. We must remember that these instruments were small; the measurements of the illustration below is only 70 inches on the back and 48 inches on the keyboard end. But however large, they would be far superior in point of appearance to the modern grand; and if the latter is to be improved in that respect, it will be by making a return to the spinet—or, as it used to be called, the *flügel*, wing—form. But (to finish with history before discussing this) the spinet shape was soon left behind. Greater volume of tone and greater variety of tone-quality, *timbre*, were required, and to get these, greater length of string and elaborate apparatus at the key-board end.* And to bear the strain of larger strings, a stronger form of sound-board was needed. I have no doubt this might have been secured by the use of a stronger material, iron instead of wood—possibly without altering the form. But iron was not an easy metal to work last century, especially with the simple appliances to be found in a spinet-maker's workshop. Anyhow, the elaborate apparatus just spoken of, the elaborate

* "Harpsichords were constructed with more than twenty different modifications to imitate the sound of the harp, the lute, the mandoline, the bassoon, flageolet, oboe, violin, and other instruments. In order to produce these different effects new rows of jacks were added, which were furnished with materials of the softest kind and most conducive to expression; and yet, with all the complications of stops, springs, extra rows of keys, and Venetian swells over the strings, the grand secret—the real shading of the *piano* and *forte*—was still wanting.

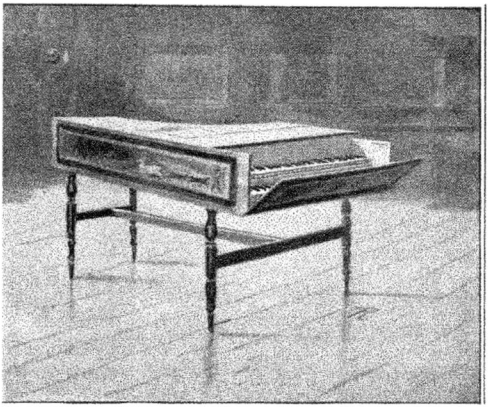

HARPSICHORD.

Nothing better was devised for augmenting or diminishing the sound than to put in motion different rows of jacks, so as to withdraw them from or approximate them to the strings at pleasure."—Fetis, "Sketch of the History of the Pianoforte."

THE PIANOFORTE: PAST, PRESENT, AND FUTURE.

arrangement of rows of "jacks,"* could not be got into the old form without immense complications arising. The wires of the spinet lay at an acute angle with the keyboard; the new machinery demanded that keyboard and wires should be at a right-angle. These two considerations, then, made it necessary to give the wedge-end that fatal pull to the left, and at once we have the characteristic harpsichord form. This is pretty much the same as that of the grand. It differs chiefly in two respects: (1) owing to the keyboard containing fewer octaves, the instrument is narrow in proportion to its length, and this slenderness somewhat saves its appearance; (2) being entirely made of wood, and therefore light, the thick legs of its modern successor were not required. Nevertheless, the harpsichord is not to be compared with the spinet in point of elegance of form; indeed, some specimens are nearly as awkward and intractable as the very finest pianos now turned out by the best European makers.

Having seen how the harpsichord was developed to the point of greatest possible ugliness, let us turn our attention to the pianoforte.

The first piano seems to have been made in or about 1710 by one Bartolommeo Christofali, or Christofori, an Italian. (We hear of one as early as 1598, but whether it was really a pianoforte or not is hard to ascertain.) That instrument I have never seen, but a drawing made by the late Mr. Bechstein shows that it resembled the harpsichord in form. The *pianoforte* or *forte-piano*, as it was then called, was not put "on the market" as a regular commodity until some years later, but when its time came it continued to be made in its first—the harpsichord—form. There were many reasons for this. Perhaps a sufficient one is the unwillingness of mankind, including buyers and makers of pianos, to change a custom, once it is formed. The musical public saw no reason for any change; they did not in the least mind the clumsiness of the harpsichord. Nor had the makers any reasons for change. In fact, they wanted the pianoforte to be as like the harpsichord as possible in all respects save one. They were quite satisfied with the quality of tone. The sweet snarl of the old instruments doubtless pleased them; they would turn up their noses at our modern fluty tones. All they desired was the power of getting gradation of tone by varying the pressure of the finger. This was impossible in the harpsichord. The new machinery of the piano made it possible. The second division of the pedigree shows the piano to be descended from the dulcimer. It is one of the class of instruments in which the string is struck and the strength of sound emitted varies

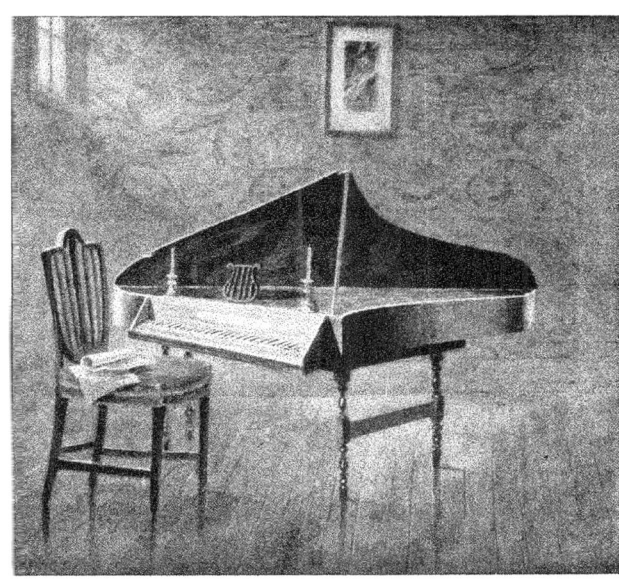

OLD HITCHCOCK SPINET. IN THE POSSESSION OF MESSRS. BROADWOOD.

with the strength of the blow. This power, then, of *crescendo* and *diminuendo* once gained, the makers were satisfied. The piano "action" was arranged in pretty much the same position as that of the harpsichord, and for some time, as has been said, the makers continued to turn out instruments of the harpsichord or grand shape.

These early pianos must have been somewhat unsatisfactory. The strings were of very thin wire, and capable of yielding only the feeblest tones. The hammer was a few pieces of leather pasted together: anything harder would have broken a string at every blow. It is not surprising, therefore, to read that for a long time the harpsichord, despite its monotonous tone, was preferred. Soon, however, a great improvement was made. A new shape—the "square," as the oblong was named—was adopted.* A stronger framework permitted a slightly—very slightly—thicker wire. Other improvements, which do not concern us here, were made; and soon a quite passable instrument was evolved, occupying only a fraction of the space of the harpsichord. One of the first made, a Zumpe, is in the possession of Messrs. Broadwood. It measures only 51 by 18 inches. It was at first intended to lie on a table, and closely resembled the early virginal. The illustration given overleaf of the Zumpe alluded to enables one to form a fair idea of the average specimen of its class. Soon, however, it was given legs of its own, and stood, looking exactly like a table—which, indeed, it was called—and possessing no more beauty, or the reverse, than a table.

So that here we have the piano starting from the same point

---

* The jack carried the plectrum that plucked the string.

* In 1758 or 1760.

1894   P P as the harpsichord did a century or more previous—namely, from the virginal form, or, rather, a form closely resembling it. Curiously enough, it went through a parallel history.

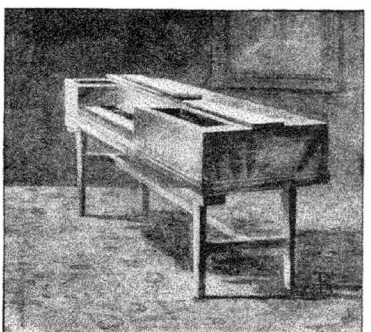

ZUMPE SQUARE PIANO. NOW IN THE POSSESSION OF MESSRS. BROADWOOD.

Longer strings were wanted, and stronger and better arrangements of the sound-board. The elaborate "actions" introduced by the later makers necessitated that the strings should run at right-angles to the keyboard instead of, as in the square piano, at right-angles to the keys. The introduction of iron for the material of the frame on which the strings are stretched hastened the return from the "square" to the old grand or harpsichord shape. But the early grands are not to be compared with the later ones for sublimity of ugliness. They were shorter than their successors. The compass was two octaves smaller, so that they were also much narrower. They were not so deep. Being wholly, or nearly wholly, made of wood, they were comparatively light and the modern dropsical legs were avoided. But pianists were incessant in their demands for louder instruments—instruments that could be heard in the largest halls. The strings were lengthened—and consequently the piano. The compass, and consequently the width, of the instrument was increased. Thicker strings at an enormous tension gradually came into use. To bear the strain a heavy and bulky cast-iron frame was needed—resulting in the increased depth of the body of the piano and the thick legs. So that by degrees the hideous hugeness already described was reached. The harpsichord form was retained because it permits of the strings lying at right-angles to the keyboard, which is convenient for the complicated modern action; also, it allows of the requisite difference in length between the short treble and long bass strings.

My readers now have a notion of the relation between the form of the instrument and its tone qualities. They have seen that the proportions, and in part the form, of the modern grand are due to the desire for excessive volume of tone. They know that the spinet-form entails certain disadvantages. But before recounting these let me describe a piano adapted to the drawing-room. The concert grand, I have already said, it seems impossible to remedy: so long as people wish to play and hear such an essentially chamber instrument in large halls, so long must they put up with its ugliness—which indeed, to do them justice, seems to give little annoyance.

A drawing-room piano, then, would be in the spinet form, about five feet on the longest side; the keyboard end, allowing for a compass of seven octaves, about four and a half feet, and the other parts in proportion. The legs would be replaced by a frame-stand similar to that already used by Sir E. Burne-Jones. Such a piano would yield a sweet, pure, full tone, equal to that of the best "cottage"; the touch could be easy and even as the best made now, the "staccato" or "cut off," and other requisites need be in no way inferior. Let us now consider and reply to the disadvantages that may be alleged. (1) It would not be so loud as the ordinary grand. It would not—and that (to me) seems no disadvantage. This excessive loudness is really a great evil which would be cured if my proposal were adopted. (2) The "action" would be more difficult to arrange. It would; and this I readily admit is a real disadvantage. But some South German makers still continue to turn out the otherwise obsolete square piano, and it was suggested to me by Mr. Rose (of the firm of Broadwood) that my ideal piano would really be a modification of that, rather than of the grand form. Perhaps so; and, in any case, an action analogous to that used in these German squares might easily be applied to the spinet shape. (3) The bass strings would be too short to yield a pure, full tone. They would be no shorter than in the "cottage" and in many "boudoir" grands now made. (4) The strings would lie obliquely, and therefore the hammers could not be arranged to strike them fairly. There seems no reason why the hammers should not be arranged, as in the "squares" just mentioned, to strike the strings fairly; but even if they could not, this is a disadvantage shared by the "overstrung" instruments of Messrs. Brinsmead and other makers, which yield really excellent tones.

Since writing the earlier part of this article I have taken counsel with practical pianoforte makers, and find that there is no solid objection raised to my proposal. That proposal is, in reality, two: I advocate, first, a smaller piano; second, one made in the spinet form, and most of the objections are directed against the former. Well, I frankly say that I actually prefer the smaller instrument for common use. Good results would follow its introduction, for makers would begin to aim at quality instead of, as at present, chiefly quantity of tone. It must be remembered that objections are always raised to any new plan. Here is an instance. The foreman of Messrs. Erard's Marlborough Street workshop is one of the cleverest men in the trade. His one objection was that were pianos to be made as I wished, new tools would be needed, new calculations for the strings and sound-board, and in short, that some little dislocation would ensue. Well, surely the end is worth the trouble.

The cottage piano has not been discussed here because there seems no more possibility of making it elegant than there is of making a household pet of an elephant. For purposes of study it will probably long be retained, being cheap, portable, and occupying little space. Were smaller and cheaper grands made it would soon disappear from the drawing-room, together with the unwieldy leviathan whose hideousness has provoked this article.

JOHN F. RUNCIMAN.

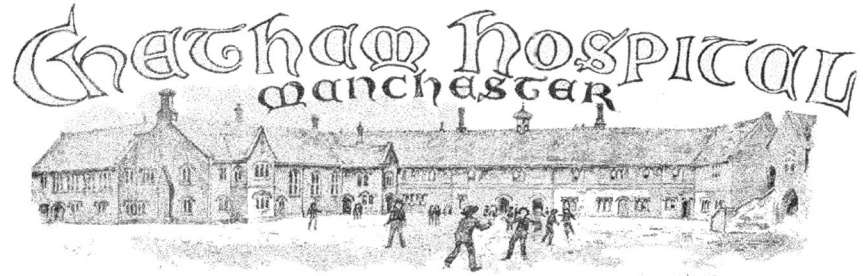

THE COURTYARD.

A LANCASHIRE CHARITY.

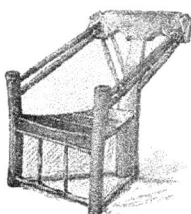

THE FOUNDER'S CHAIR.

THIS fine old Gothic structure, well known to Lancashire folk as "The College," and by others as Chetham's Hospital and Library, is a mediæval gem, sparkling with charming architectural bits and historic memories. Its beauties are intensified as soon as ever the visitor quits the garish and ugly surroundings of the place and enters into its quaint old-world influences. It stands on a site of great antiquity, at the confluence of the Irk and the Irwell. Dr. Whitaker, the historian of Manchester, speaks of it as "a Roman summer camp," and another eminent writer avers, "There is little doubt, however, that the Saxon Thegn fixed his abode there," while it is an historical fact that the Baron Greslet, Robert the Fifth, who lived about 1182-1230, was the first who kept his court here. In the Hull (i.e. Hill) Thomas, the eighth Baron, gave to the burgesses of Manchester their first charter, 14th May, 1301. Eight years afterwards, John la Warr succeeded to the barony, and his descendant Thomas, Rector of the parish, as well as Lord of the Manor, gave up the Baron's Hull, with other lands, for an endowment in 1421, when, with the consent of the parishioners, the church, now the Cathedral, was collegiated.

The then existing baronial hall was remodelled, and new parts erected as a residence for College of Priests, and fully set forth in the grant of 1 Henry VI. "Bluff King Hal" let it alone during the dissolution of religious houses, but it was disendowed on 1 Edward VI., and in 1549 transferred to Edward, third Earl of Derby, by whom it was used as the town house of the family. The Earl's son and successor, Henry, with other gentry of Manchester, obtained Queen Elizabeth's Charter of Re-foundation, and the building again became the residence of the Wardens of the College. Later, James, the seventh Earl, settled the property, with other estates, on his wife, the famous Charlotte de Tremouille. During the civil wars, it fell into the hands of the Parliamentary Sequestrators, who let it to one Joseph Werden. He sub-let the ancient Refectory to the Presbyterians for their meetings. A

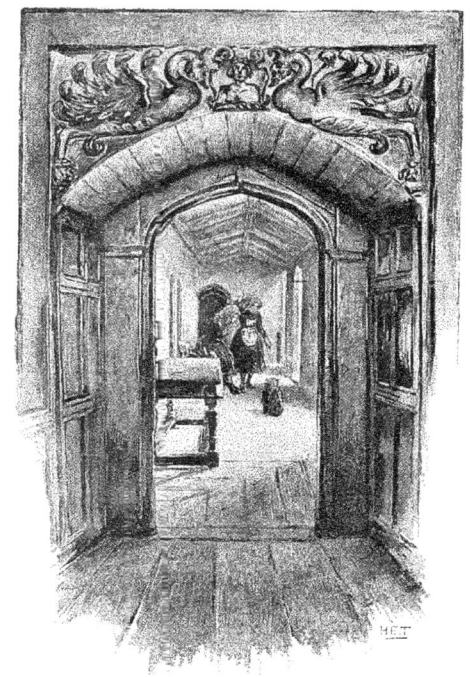

THE ENTRANCE TO THE UPPER CLOISTER.

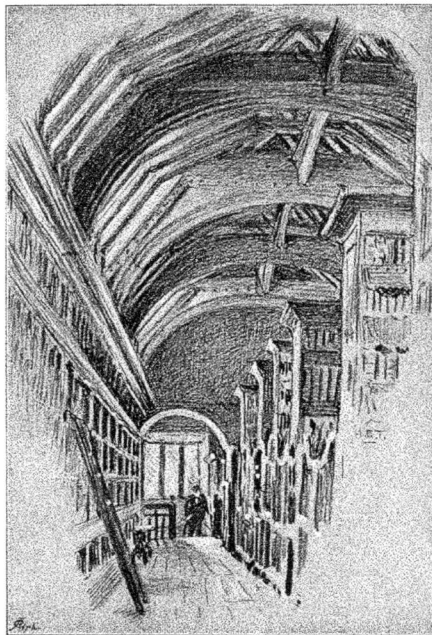

THE ENTRANCE TO THE LIBRARY.

large barn in the yard was used for a like purpose by the first Independent Church in Manchester. The head of this church, one Lieut-Col. the Rev. John Wigan, in conjunction with Capt. Ellison, contracted with the Committee in London for the reversion of the College, "parcel of ye estate of the late Earle of Derby, and part of ye jointure of ye Countesse Dowager already sequestrated."

At the same period, Humphrey Chetham desired to obtain it for his long-cherished scheme of an hospital for boys. The property was surveyed, and was said to consist of " Ye large building called ye College in Manchester, consisting of many rooms, with twoe barns, one gate house, verie much decay'd, one parcell of ground, formerly an orchard, and one garden, now in ye possession of Joseph Werden, gent., who pay for ye same for ye use of the Commonwealth tenn pounds yearly. There is likewise one other room in ye said College reserved and made use for publique meetings of X'sian conscientious people."

The trustees of Humphrey Chetham, under the provisions of his will, made three years before his death, 12th October, 1653, purchased " ye great house, with buildings, court gardens, and appurtenances called ye Colledge or the Colledge House," for £500. £7,500 was left for the use of the Hospital, and £1,000 was added to the buildings. The residue was spent in the purchase of books, and the founding of the " great Library," the first free library in the kingdom.

On Thursday, 5th August, 1658, a great meeting was held in the Refectory, to dedicate the building to its present uses. Hallworth, chief assistant to Warden Heyrick, in a brief speech recounted the history of the place, and finished by saying, " Henceforth the said house could fitly and justly be named by noe other name than by the name of Mr. Chetham's Hospital."

Since this important day the Hospital and Library have existed side by side, the one offering free board and education to a large number of boys, born anywhere, of "ye poor but ye painful parents," but resident, at the time of election, in certain townships; and the other ministering to the intellectual sustenance of " well-effected students," who come from all parts of the world to consult the precious contents of the 50,000 volumes on its shelves.

With this historical information in our hands, accompanied by our clever artist, we take our stand near the north porch of the Cathedral opposite. Here the eye can take in the entire range of buildings composing the Hospital and Library. The new school is a fine specimen of modern Gothic architecture, which our artist has, for æsthetic reasons, left out in the picture heading this article. The old-fashioned beauty of the view gives a desire to see further, and, passing through the mean gateway at the junction of Fennell Street and Hunt's Bank, we are at once conscious of the absence of the hurry-skurry and bustle of the nineteenth-century city. The change is restful and gratifying. Just now our ears are charmed by the sweet voicing of the quaint old Jacobean melody, " Farewell, Manchester," by the boys

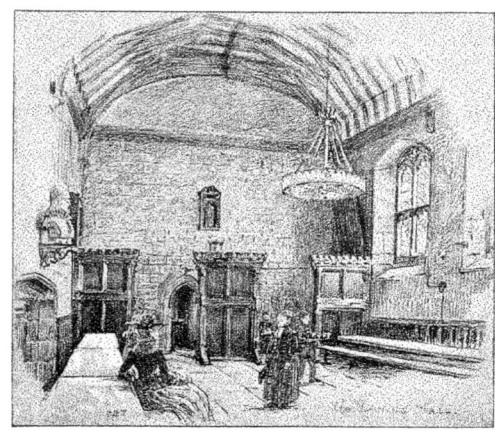

THE GRAND HALL OR REFECTORY.

in the schoolroom. The plaintive minor tones of the song

impel us to visit the singers. We find them assembled in the large, well-ventilated schoolroom. The sight affords us much pleasure, the discipline is splendid, and the bright fresh faces of the singers will live in the memory — for a hundred boys singing with the precision and quiet force of a well-trained choir, is not easily forgotten. On the black-boards are many indications that the teaching is thorough and up to date, fully meeting the requirements of the pious founder, "Ye boys shall be taught ye reading, ye writing, ye summes, and all kinds of ye ingenuitie."

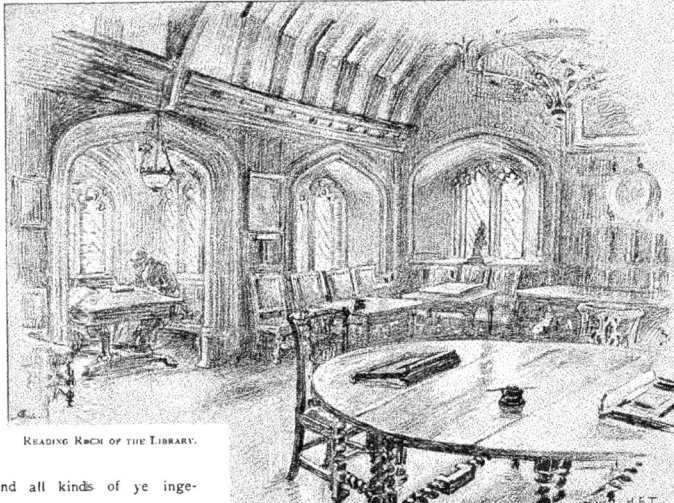

READING ROOM OF THE LIBRARY.

Here the educationist would like to linger, but our artist is in search of the picturesque to inspire his pencil. We leave the modern for the old. The first glimpse of the arched entry gives a foretaste of what is to come. Before us is a beautiful wrought-iron gate, with grille, on which is embossed in brass the arms of the founder. Below, in delicately worked tracery, is the motto, "Quod, Tuum Tene." It is so beautifully done, that a close inspection only reveals its presence. Beyond is seen the western stretch of the Lower Cloister, the quaint lamp at the end, the oak-timbered roof, the doors of the living cells, and the "Stone of Repentance." To our right is the old janitor's abode (now the Muniment Room, filled with antique and precious MSS.). Turning through a cell door at the left, we mount to "YE ENTRANCE TO YE LIBRARY."

The sun's rays are peeping through the diamond-paned windows, lighting up the fine open-timbered roof (beautifully drawn by the artist), and warming the sombre tomes in the long stretch of classes, protected by seventeenth-century rails, till they appear to vanish in the old coloured glass between the mullions of the north window. By sheer force of mediæval beauty Manchester is lost to view — yea, dead at this first glimpse of the Students' Paradise. No wonder our artist lingers to limn its fine proportions. Here on the right is a similar room of almost equal proportions and in some respects greater beauty. This is the "Old Mary Chapel," containing a beautiful oak altar rail, put in about 1549, and peculiar for its fine double spiral rails. The Jacobean door close by is open, and we enter Ye Warden's Room, now used as the Reading Room (see our illustration). It is artistically and faithfully depicted, and the picture does credit to the fine proportions of the room. Like the rest, it has an open timbered roof, and a cornice of date 1421. This is enriched with the portcullis and eagle's claw, part of the Stanley crest; the walls are panelled in dark Jacobean oak. The spandrel of the whole north wall over the fireplace is richly ornamented in honour of Humphrey Chetham, in 1594.

the coarse florid style which prevailed in the time of Charles II. Beside the south wall stands the famous fifteenth-century communion table, said to contain as many pieces as days in the year. The square bay in which the solitary occupant is reading has an elaborately vaulted plaster ceiling of late Gothic style, and is of great historic interest. Here sat the celebrated Sir Walter Raleigh, with other courtiers of "Good Queen Bess," as guests of the "Wizard Warden," Dr. John Dee. Close by is displayed an autograph letter of Raleigh's, which many curious eyes, from all quarters of the globe, have endeavoured to decipher. Near where our artist stands, busily sketching, is a finely carved oaken buffet. It is a "make-up" of the top of a bookcase presented by Chetham to Walmsley Church, Bolton-le-Moors; and a fourteenth-century bedstead, upon which the Pretender slept when staying at Hulton Park, Lancashire. It was presented to the Hospital by one of the Hulton family, a feoffee of the school. On the walls are some fine contemporary portraits of Lancashire worthies, among which are found John Bradford, the Manchester martyr, Dean Nowell, the author of the Church Catechism, and introducer of bottled ale. The furniture, too, is very old, and in keeping with the style of the room.

If we leave here without visiting the "Secret Chamber," at the west corner of the apartment, it will be an archæological loss. The entrance looks like a cupboard door in the panelling, but opening it a strong massive door of ancient make confronts us. Beyond this is another in the same style, which allows us to enter the chamber. Its original use, as "The Minstrel Gallery," is evident by the arrangement of the fine oaken arch on the side of the wall of the Refectory — walled up in 1421 — to convert it into "The College Scriptorium." In this wall are two quatrefoil "squints," through which the Warden could observe the revellers below.

Walking through the rare Upper Cloister, both sides of which are filled with valuable books, we stop to examine the grotesque carving above "Ye Entrance to ye Upper Cloister." This drawing is excellent, and helps to photograph the spot on the memory. To the right we get the best view of the Upper Cloister, with its low diamond-glazed windows and Gothic arched doors leading into the dormitories of the priests, and the original entrance into the "Mary Chapel." Walking towards the children playing with the Governor's dog, we admire the fine Tudor table on the left, look into the Librarian's

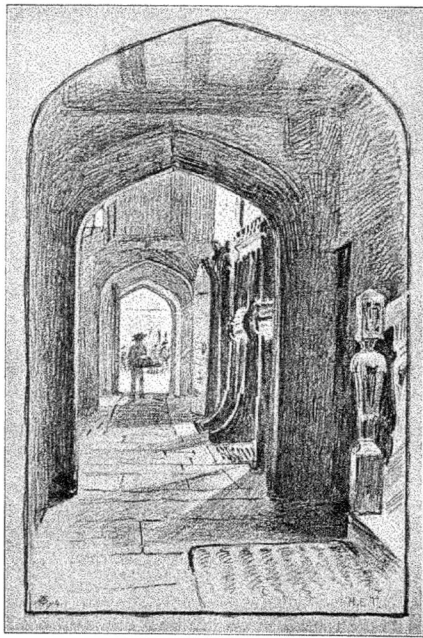

A Bit of the Lower Cloister, looking through the Dining Hall.

suite of rooms, inspect the illuminated deed of conveyance of the College to the Derby family; handle choice Caxtons, "Wynkyn de Wordes;" linger over the exquisite panelling on the door of the chief room; take a peep at the first draft of Byrom's famous hymn, "Christians, awake;" compare the monastic with the jacobean doors seen behind the figures on the picture; step into the Governor's rooms to see the fine pieces of contemporary oak, and scan with delight the noblest door in the place, evidently one of early date, and rich in the colour and polish of centuries.

Leaving here we go down the jacobean stairs, stop by the way to look into the "Priest Hole," thence to the point entitled "A Bit of Ye Lower Cloister." Standing here, no matter which way the eye is directed vistas open up of infinite charm. An artist of no mean repute said, in the writer's hearing, "The attempt to paint this spot decided me to become an artist." Mr. Tidmarsh is evidently under the same influence, for his facile pencil is at work. Gentle reader, it is before you, and in it you see the bottom of the Jacobean stairs, the beautiful ancient screens hiding the butteries from the grand hall.

To the south is "Ye Cloister Court." This is a charming spot, especially when "Old Sol" shows its face, then it is lit up with a glory all its own. It is sacred to calm and quietness, and always creates a dreamy influence in the mind. In the centre is the old well, to the right the windows of the "Scriptorium" are seen. Farther to the left is the outer part of the fine ingle nook, from the windows of which many a cowled monk has looked upon the fountains playing in the peaceful summer days. Next to this are the outer walls of the jacobean stairs, the windows of both cloisters, and the buttresses, all giving a true and beautiful idea of the prevailing architectural features of the court.

Continuing our perambulations of this cloister, we pass an array of quaint doors, the entrance to the cells, until we come to a dead stop before one of the finest arches in the building. Its many beautiful points are heightened by the artistic hand of time. By this we enter the Feoffees' or Audit Room. This is perfection: the fourteenth-century ceiling of oak is full of stern massive beauty, the enrichments of which tone down and produce a harmonious whole. It is wainscoted up to a certain height, above which is a floriated plaster frieze, done by the same hand which did the work at Haddon Hall. The other features of note are "Ye Founder's Chair" (see initial). It is monastic in character, and ascribed to the thirteenth century. Until lately it was considered unique, but another of the same kind has been unearthed at Warwick, and a fine specimen of Sussex fire-plate, upon which is found the arms of the Baron De la Warr. The other articles of furniture are in strict keeping with the character of the room; and here it is said Sir Walter Raleigh smoked the first pipe of tobacco in Manchester, and Dr. Dee held communication with the "Spirits of the vasty deep."

By a door at the western corner we gain admittance into "YE GRANDE HALL or REFECTORY" (see illustration), just at the point, "above the salt," where our artist is drawing. It is beautifully done, and in a sense he has transferred its fine proportions *en bloc* to paper. It is 43 feet long, 24 feet wide, 22 feet to the wall plates, and 35 feet from floor to the top of the open-timbered roof, which is divided into three bays by well-moulded principals. A fine panelled, battlemented canopy surmounts the dais, under which the high table was wont to stand. Before us we have a fine view of the grand old screens, and a glimpse of one of the buttery doors. At the back, where the ladies are seated, is the ingle nook, 11 feet wide and 12 feet deep. It is an irregular octagon in shape, and curiously twisted to the south. At the east corner of the dais is the "old Dole Window," and on the four walls are displayed some fine Scottish claymores and other weapons, while the bust of the Founder overlooks the little Bluecoat Boys at their prayers and meals, morning and evening. Just as we are making our exit, the boys come trooping in to dinner with a martial tread. Each and all take their places, the old-fashioned grace is sung, and a vigorous onslaught is made on the ample supply of viands. This is one of the sights of the Hospital, and few visitors fail in being present at the dinner.

The Kitchen is at the extreme eastern end of the Cloisters. It is a lofty apartment with open-timbered roof about 35 feet from the floor, 29 feet long and 17 feet wide. There is an old-time kitchen range, with spits and cooking appliances above. It is well lighted at the south side only, by windows arranged in two tiers.

Above the entrance is another "observation window," protected by iron bars of the character usually found in such places, affording a full view of the Kitchen from the "Lord's Solar." Below this is a small room, formerly used for the storage of the day's supply of wine and beer, with a buttery hatch opening into the kitchen. There is an air of substantial comfort, apart from antiquarian interest, about the place which attracts the onlooker, especially an Englishman.

It is but a step into the large playground seen in the picture heading this paper, where we get a full view of the most ancient part of the Hospital. The roof evidently is of a date prior to 1421. Here are found the old Brew House, Bakery, School, and Gate House. Above these is the ancient Hospitium, now the boys' dormitories. The open-timbered roof is very massive and striking, especially at the skew angle near the north-easterly corner, which is of ingenious construction, bringing to mind a similar piece of work in the old Cloth Hall at Ypres.

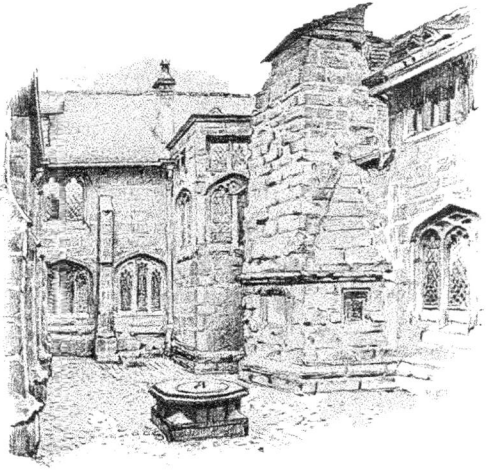

THE CLOISTER COURT.

Passing through the "Pump Court" to the river stairs leading to the Irk, now covered over, we watch the boys in the new manual training school, a model in its way, where some 75 boys are trained in daily sections to use their hands and eyes in working wood and metal work. Beyond this, at the extreme west, is a small court called the Governor's Garden, but 250 years ago it was named "Ye Scurvy Garden," for here the boys who had skin diseases were kept in isolation. From this point the picture entitled, 'A Peep from the North,' is taken. Though it is full of artistic feeling, at the same time it is photographic in its fidelity, and gives the reader a correct idea of the northern aspect of Good Old Humphrey Chetham's Hospital and Library, Manchester.

WALTER T. BROWNE.

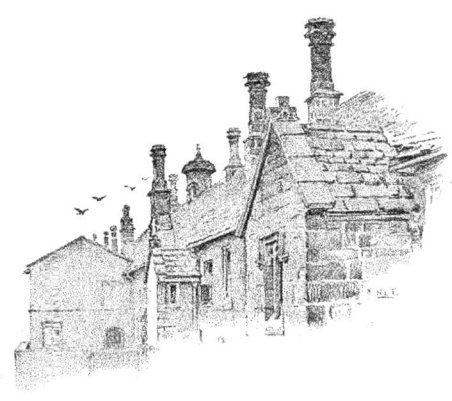

"A PEEP FROM THE NORTH."

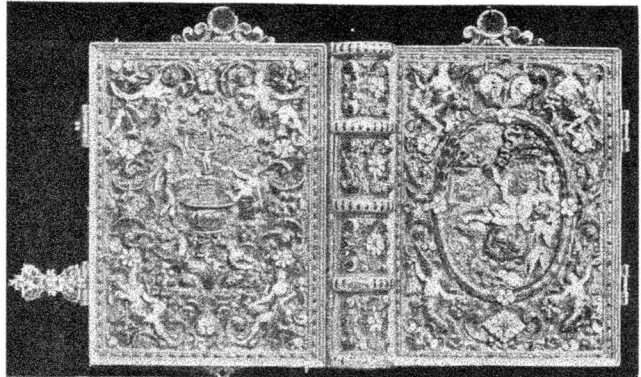

Book Cover, containing Chasing, Embossing, Engraving, Enamelling, Filigree, and Casting.

CINQUE-CENTO JEWELRY.

AS ILLUSTRATED BY THE "TRATTATI" OF BENVENUTO CELLINI.

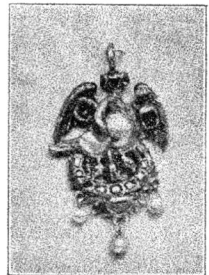

Pelican Drop.

I PROMISED in a previous article* to say a little about the methods of Cinque-cento jewelry as illustrated by the "Trattati" of Cellini. Methods without practical workshop recipes, however, are but sorry subjects, so I will confine myself rather to what I would call the point of view of the craftsman in designing and preparing jewelry for the market.

The leading theme of the "Trattati," if so clumsily constructed and at the same time so practical a work can be said to have a theme, is the intrinsic value of Works of Art however variously or diffusely expressed. We hear the craftsman tell of his workshop, and see the methods by which he and his apprentices have obtained their results; Caradosso, that marvellous master, ever among the first of goldsmiths in Cellini's estimation, stands at his shop door in terror at the irate Spanish nobleman to whom he has promised a job, that didn't get itself done in time; Piero di Nino, the octogenarian craftsman who specialised on filigree belts, trudging, after closing time one Saturday night, down the streets of Florence, and frightened to death by a small urchin who pretends to be the devil; Francis I. and his courtiers standing around Cellini and listening to his descriptions of how a filigree cup with translucent enamels is made; all the many touches of sixteenth-century life with which the book abounds help to reveal the

* The Art Journal, 1893, p. 247.

methods of the workshop. It is also characteristic of the "Trattati," and of the age, that Cellini in his introductory chapter, when recording the names of all the best goldsmiths of his generation, has among them not only names like those

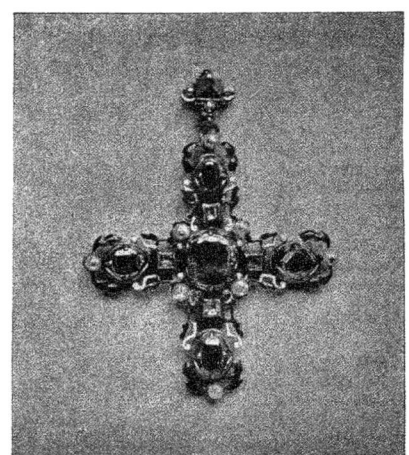

Red Cross, with Pearls.

of Amerigo, Maso Finiguerra, Michael Angelo da Pinzidimonte, Bastiano del Bernardetto Cennini, and Piero di Nino, such as were exclusively goldsmiths, but also Donatello, Brunelleschi, Ghiberti, Martin Schöngauer, and Albert Dürer;

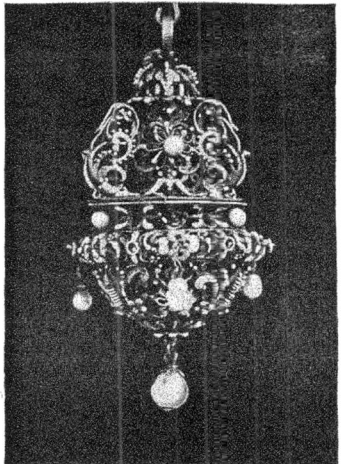

GOLD POMANDER—ENGLISH.

Cellini, in fact, finds it impossible to talk about goldsmithing without linking it to the other arts and crafts of Italy. The arts and crafts were one and indivisible.

"Perhaps never before, or, at least so rarely that it has never been recorded," he says, speaking according to his wont of himself, "has a man been found" (the inference, of course, being that Cellini is the man) "who was skilled in more than one, or at most two, of the eight different branches of the goodly art of goldsmithing, but when he is you may well imagine that he knows how to make a good thing of them. Of course, I don't intend to talk about those kind of muddlers who set themselves to ply all the eight branches at once, and who many and many a time are employed by such as either couldn't or wouldn't decide whether a piece of work was good or whether it wasn't" (a nasty one of Duke Cosimo, this!)—"men of that breed, methinks, may be likened to the sort of small shopkeeper who hangs out in the suburbs and slums of the town and does a little now in the bakery line, now in the grocery line, now a little in the apothecary line, now a little in general retailer's business—in fact, a little bit of everything, but nothing good in anything"—the right healthy contempt of the sixteenth-century workman for anything approaching to dilettantism.

It may be questioned whether the superlative assumption in his own favour, contained in the preface to the treatise on Goldsmith's Work, need altogether be trusted. Cellini's work varies greatly, and in many of the eight branches nothing remains that can be authenticated. Italian, French, even German Renaissance works, some of greater, the majority of less skill and beauty, are indiscriminately ascribed to his hand. These eight branches may respectively be cited as niello, enamel, filigree, grosserie (or large ware), minuterie (or small ware), jewelry, the treatment and manipulation of precious stones, and the founding and working of bronze statues; chasing, embossing, graving, etc., would come under one or the other of these various heads. As for the classification itself, it may have a certain general value in showing how far labour was subdivided in the workshops of the Cinque-cento goldsmith, and it is instructive as showing how all those divers ways of handling metals were the media of the artist in the time of Cellini, just as they had been in the time of the old monk Theophilus, whose treatise on the arts Herr Otto Brinckman has ably compared with the "Trattati."

For our purpose in considering workshop methods in their application to Cinque-cento jewelry as illustrated by the "Trattati," we need consider only certain methods and materials chosen from among different of the eight branches, and these might not unfitly embrace enamelling, melting, embossing, chasing, engraving, casting, filigree, and the cutting, polishing, foiling, and setting of stones. In the examples from the national collection here represented, almost all the processes are illustrated. What is especially noteworthy, moreover, is that in most cases nearly all the processes are illustrated together. It is not as at the present day of subdivision of labour, one workshop or group of men and machines producing one port on of a piece of work, and another, another. Even Cellini finds difficulty in keeping to his classifications, and when describing a piece of enamel in illustration of his recipe has parenthetically to hint at filigree or casting, with an "as I have just told you," or an "as I'm going to tell you directly, if you'll only have patience!"

Goethe, at the end of his translation of the Vita, gives an

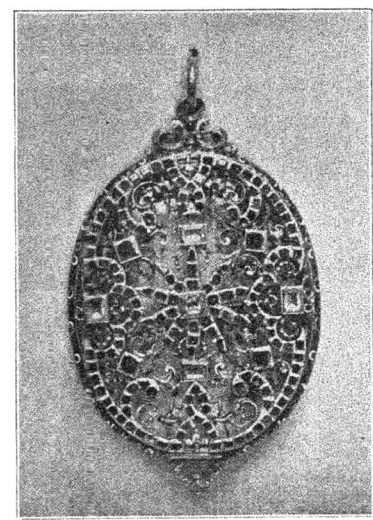

TRELLISED MINIATURE CASE—ENGLISH.

interesting analysis of the "Trattati," which those who propose studying the construction of the work from the point of view of the Renaissance classification of craft might profitably consult.

The well-known book cover which I give in the headpiece, from the national collection, illustrates this—it contains in it most of the methods of the art; chasing, embossing, engraving, enamelling, filigree, casting, all have their place. The piece has been ascribed to Cellini, and Plon reproduces it among the attributions; but it hardly has the entire chic of Cellini's work, and, indeed, cannot be authenticated; its chief interest is in the exquisite manipulation of the enamels.

With regard to jewelry and objects of personal adornment, the same applies; jewelry is a branch of goldsmith's work, and whether the artist be making "vasetti" or "pendente," silver-hammered ware cups or golden filigree earrings, if he would be a capable goldsmith, he must do either. Then, too, must he have a knowledge of the worth, intrinsic and pecuniary, of stones, but especially the intrinsic worth. This stone is a ruby, colour moderate, price so, so; we must foil it to increase its beauty, price increasing according to the artistic attractiveness we put into it. Not so the modern jeweller, he goes otherwise to work. This stone is a ruby, foil it? Oh dear no, the important thing to consider is its pecuniary value; to foil it would be to insinuate that the stone needs beautifying, or in other words is not so costly as it looks. Come, come, we are honest folk, and honesty is the best—! well, we need not mention that we sell our stones to the cut of our customers' coats, and that an amethyst which we buy in Clerkenwell for two shillings, we can sell in Bond Street for two guineas; but then the customer is as soaked with commercialism as we are, and may not one unlovely fool prey on another?

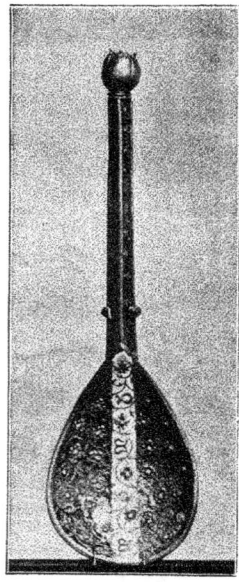

ENAMELLED SPOON—GERMAN.

There was great to-do once in Rome about the foiling of a ruby, and Cellini gives an amusing account of how he tricked the jewellers, and enhanced the beauty of the stone. "This ruby," he says, "had, when it came into my hands, been already set at different times by some of the best-known jewellers of the day. So I was incited to work at it with all possible care. Seeing that I could in no way satisfy myself with the result of my experiments, I locked myself up in a place where no one could see me; not so much because I wanted to keep my secret to myself, but because I did not want to be beaten and produce a feeble result with so goodly and wonderful a gem. I took a little piece of damask silk, stained with kermes, and with a pair of scissors cut it carefully, having previously spread a little wax over the bezel. Then I took the tiny bit of silk and pressed it firmly on the wax with the tip of a punch, and laid the ruby on it. So well did it make, and such virtue did it gain that all the jeweller folk who had seen it first, suspected me of having tinted it, a thing inadmissible in jewelry, except in the case of diamonds, of which more anon. But for this ruby some of the jewellers asked me to say what kind of a foil I had put beneath it, upon which I answered that I had not put any. At this reply of mine a jeweller who was with the gentleman to whom the ruby belonged, said, 'If the ruby has no foil, you can't have done anything else but tint it in some way or other, and that you know is inadmissible.' To which I replied again that I had neither given it a foil nor done anything inadmissible to it. At this the jeweller got a little nasty and used strong language, at which the gentleman who owned the ruby said, 'Benvenuto, I pray you be so good as to open your setting and show it to me only; I promise you I'll not tell anyone your secret.' Then said I to him I had worked on the job for several days, and had my living to earn, but that I would willingly do it if he paid me the price of the setting, and what was more, do it in the presence of all of them, because I should be much honoured in thus teaching my teachers. Having said this I opened the bezel and took out the stone in their presence. They were much obliged to me, we parted excellent friends, and I got well paid."

The same sentiment, i.e. the artistic grip of the craft, runs through all he tells us of the proper placing of stones in relation to design. You must put thought into where your stones are to go. Pope Clement has before him the array of competing goldsmiths, each with their sketch for a cope clasp; " but in all these designs," says Benvenuto, "their authors had devised that the big diamond was set in the middle of the breast of God the Father. The Pope himself had suggested the motto of the design, but when he saw how everybody alike had set so great a stone into the breast of so tiny a figure he said: 'Why can't the stone be set in some other manner except always in the breast?' Whereupon some of them replied that it could not be set otherwise if right value was to be given it in the design. The Pope, who was beginning to weary of so many designs, turned to me and asked if I had nothing to show. While I was still undoing my box the Pope turned to some of the older masters and said to them, ''Tis always well to look at everybody's rendering of a thing. Albeit Benvenuto is young, yet have I seen work of his which convinces me that he is in the right way.' Then, when I had uncovered my model and put it before him, he had scarce seen it when he turned to me and cried out, 'You've hit it! That's how I want it done!' Then he turned to the others and said, 'See you now how this diamond can perfectly well be applied in another manner. Mark how Benvenuto has made a stool of it and seated his figure thereon. A better way of rendering it I can't conceive.' Straightway he had me paid eight hundred golden scudi, and with most courteous words bade me God speed to my work."

The little pelican with the pearl body and the rubied drop of blood that I give at the beginning, well illustrates this. There is an infinite thoughtfulness in the placing of the stones towards the development of the subject or "incident" of the gem. Its neighbour, the red cross with the pearls, is also an admirably proportioned piece, and ought to be especially prized at the present moment of the fashion cycle, because it shows the sixteenth-century use of the uniform white pearl—the only pearl that the modern young lady, in her sublime unconsciousness of anything beyond the commercial value of stones, will wear. The more beautiful rugged grey pearl can be bought for a few pence, but then cheapness is damnatory, unless, haply, it *looks* expensive, and intrinsic beauty is not at ease in the West end.

The two specimens of English work next following—the gold pomander and the trellised miniature case, are as beautiful as anything Cellini is ever known to have produced. To make them the master would have to be cognisant of filigree, and all the subtlest methods of soldering and fitting together of slight pieces of metal work ; and what is more important still to note is, that it would be quite impossible for a working jeweller to construct a piece of the nature of the gold pomander without having great knowledge and mastery of design. To any one who is familiar with the making of drawings or wax models for the workshop, it will be evident at once that this pomander could only have been designed by the workman himself, since it would have been impossible to render its intricacies of form or delicacies of substance in a drawing on paper or a model in wax. It was undoubtedly made, as all the finest pieces were made, by the master designer himself, with the aid of his apprentices. The miniature case is simpler of execution, but in its way quite as subtle. It is a worthy setting of the stately portrait of "Good Queen Bess" that it contains, and to my mind its chiefest beauty is the slight irregularity in the setting of the little square garnets, a perfection of unevenness which the machine, strive it never so hardly, could not obtain.

The two remaining examples of work, the first an enamelled spoon, the second a bronze medal, German and French work respectively, again illustrate other methods of the craft. The spoon would be a hammered hollow-ware silver bowl, the stem cut or beaten into shape, the grooves cut for the enamel, and the pattern set on the silver by filigree process. Its colour is very rich and luminous. The medallion, not unlike in method to the one I described in my previous article, is modelled in wax, cast, and carefully chased. What is especially noticeable is the subordination of portraiture to the decorative effect, another thing in which nowadays we in our realistic ignorance sin Mrs. Smith, if she *does* attain to the artistic altitude of having her portrait done, insists upon having it "like"—she will tolerate no artistic "rendering:" flowers and love-knots for her—no fear!

Well, we live in an ugly time, and jewelry is not among the least of the lost children of Art ; if we seek to reform there we shall at all events begin near home. To this end let us look to the Cinque-cento. I will tell you more of it later ; or, better still, will have the "Trattati" translated for you to read.

C. R. ASHBEE.

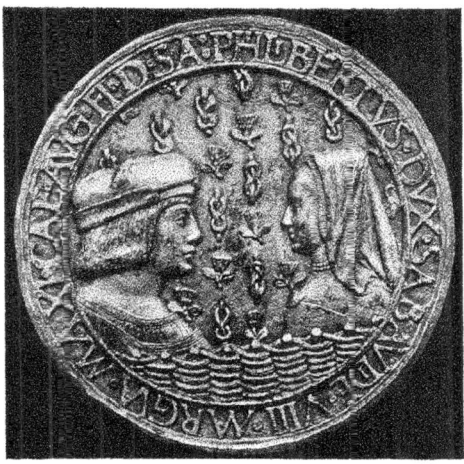

BRONZE MEDAL—FRENCH.

A PROPOSAL FOR THE PRESERVATION OF THE FEW REMAINING ANCIENT BUILDINGS OF GREATER LONDON AND ESSEX.

MUCH is done nowadays to satisfy our antiquarian and historical conscience with reference to London's old buildings, a little even is occasionally done to satisfy the æsthetic; but yet much remains for accomplishment, and what is done is mostly in that part of town where are the wealth and leisure.

A month or so ago the London School Board varied its religious discussions by a little vandalism in Greater London which might, with a little attention and thought, have been prevented. It destroyed one of the few remaining Elizabethan monuments, the old palace of Bromley-by-Bow. Fortunately some little of the old place has been saved to the nation, and the Board, as if ashamed of itself for its folly, subsequently bought back one mantelpiece in one of the state rooms for more than half the price for which it had bartered the whole palace away to its contractor.

Out of this action, however, has arisen a proposal for the prevention of such pieces of vandalism in the future.

It is proposed to form a Watch Committee, acting in conjunction with the Society for the Protection of Ancient Buildings, and to compile a register in which all work of an artistic and historic interest shall be catalogued and, in some cases, marked with a red star for possible preservation by local authorities. The details of the scheme are roughly as follows:

1. To undertake the work experimentally for one year; to systematically visit the old buildings of Greater London; to catalogue them in the register and on the map; to find out, if possible, who are their ground landlords and their leaseholders, and ascertain the length of the leases; and to discover whether the local public bodies in whose province they lie could be brought to preserve or utilise them for municipal purposes.

2. To confine the sphere of influence of the Watch to a radius of twenty miles, east and north of Aldgate, and bounded on the south by the Thames; this being the area into which Greater London has been and is rapidly extending, and comprising a great portion of Essex, one of the richest of English counties for old monuments.

3. To form, if possible, during the preliminary year, a Watch Committee, preferably of residents in the area suggested, who would undertake voluntary work in visiting and correspondence, and later, possibly, any financial liabilities in the continuing of the work.

4. To place the results of the year's work at the disposal of the Society for the Preservation of Ancient Buildings.

The scheme has already received the fullest support of the society, and out of the total minimum sum of £60 required for the first year's out-of-pocket and secretarial expenses, a guarantee of some £30 has already been provided from various sources, and by those who are interested in the idea of the work; a number of names have also been received of those who might be ready to act upon the "Watch."

The sphere of action has been limited to the Eastern district to begin with, but there is no reason why, when one year's work in the cataloguing and registering of the old buildings of one part of London has been thoroughly carried through, that other districts, for instance, the Chelsea, Battersea or Highgate districts, which also often need a little thoughtful and tactful care in the matter of the preservation of their historic monuments, should not be undertaken also. Indeed, I have already received a number of letters and communications from those who are anxious that the proposal should be extended to other parts besides the east, as the result of my appeal. These will be dealt with later.

When this number of THE ART JOURNAL reaches the people of Essex in particular, I should wish it to be to them as an appeal on behalf of their county which they shall but hardly set aside. It is in Essex that we propose to begin, that county into which the greater London of the artisan is spreading, and which every day sees some new ruin of an old piece of work that might with a little care and thought be utilised for the newer communal purposes that are daily shaping themselves for us. We need every old relic of a more beautiful past that we can save, we need everything that is beautiful in itself, and everything that will help to give that element of tradition which our democratic progress is too apt to thrust aside.

I venture also to appeal to the Archæological Societies and those bodies who profess to take any living interest in the work of the past, and for those whom it may interest I place here the letter received at the initiation of the scheme from Mr. Thackeray Turner, the Secretary of the Society for the Protection of Ancient Buildings, to many of whose members I am already indebted for promises of support:—

"9. BUCKINGHAM STREET, ADELPHI.

"Dear Sir,—I am directed to express the satisfaction with which my Committee regards your scheme for registering and watching buildings of interest in the East End of London and the adjoining parts of Essex, and your proposal to place the information you obtain at the disposal of the Society for the Protection of Ancient Buildings.

"The hands of the Society are at present so full that it could not itself inaugurate or work any such plan, but it will gladly make use of any trustworthy information you may be in a position to lay before it, and anticipates that it will thereby be enabled to do its work in the district under your charge with much greater efficiency.

"We feel sure that the document you propose to make will be of great archæological value, and no doubt the different Archæological Societies would be very glad to possess copies.

"26th January, 1894." "THACKERAY TURNER.

If those who read this are of a mind to render our young Committee any support, or would like to hear of our proposed methods, I shall be glad if they will put themselves into communication with me at Essex House, Bow, E.

C. R. ASHBEE.

ART AT BRADFORD.

THE opening of the ninth annual exhibition of the Arcadian Art Club at Bradford affords an opportunity of drawing attention to the good work which this club has done in that town to stimulate interest in artistic matters. Yorkshire folk, as a rule, have always taken a keen interest in everything which promotes individual culture and home decoration, but until the artists of Bradford combined themselves and held regular exhibitions it was difficult for their fellow-townsmen to realise the strength of the talent in their midst.

The rapid growth in influence and power of the Arcadian Art Club demonstrates that an appreciative *clientèle* exists in the town. The club owes its origin for the most part to the exertions of Mr. Arthur H. Rigg, in whose studio it was founded in 1886, in conjunction with eight or ten other local artists, and Mr. H. H. La Thangue accepted, and still holds, the position of president.

Readers of THE ART JOURNAL will be familiar with the work of Mr. La Thangue from the article devoted to his work published last year (p. 169), and we are enabled to give herewith a reproduction of the picture, 'Watering Cows,' which this rising artist has contributed to the present exhibition. We also reproduce Mr. F. Stead's 'Reverie,' and regret we have not here space for Mr. Rigg's 'Winter Fuel,' which we hope to illustrate later. Although the number of works exhibited this year is not much greater than that shown in the first

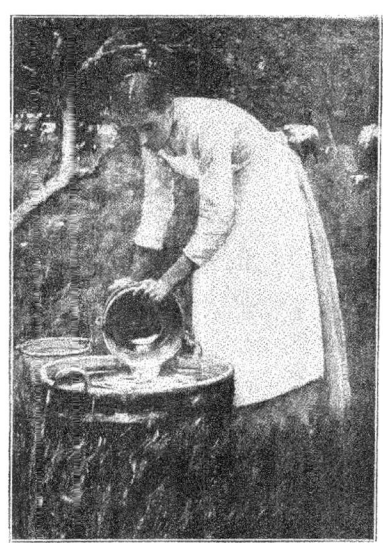

WATERING COWS. FROM THE PICTURE BY H. H. LA THANGUE.
EXHIBITED AT THE ARCADIAN ART CLUB, BRADFORD.

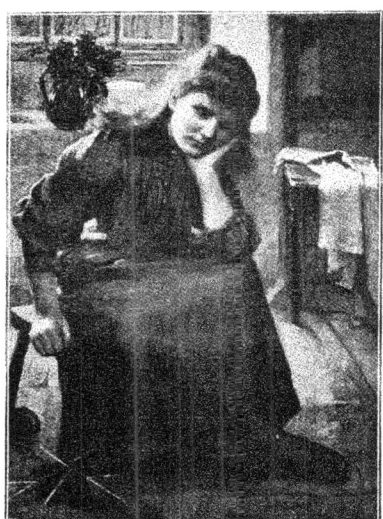

REVERIE. FROM THE PICTURE BY FREDERICK STEAD.
EXHIBITED AT THE ARCADIAN ART CLUB, BRADFORD.

exhibition, yet the quality has steadily increased from the beginning.

The methods of work and study most popular in the club are advanced and modern. It would seem to be full of life, and open to those great progressive influences which have well-nigh revolutionised Art within recent years. It claims to have had a great educating influence in its own sphere in developing and improving public taste as regards pictures, and to have brought much new artistic talent to public notice. The works of several Arcadians, such as Mr. Ernest Sichel, Mr. M. R. Jones, Mr. Arnold Priestman, Mr. Fred. Stead, Mr. H. J. Dobson and others are now welcomed and find honourable positions in metropolitan galleries.

A movement is now on foot to obtain a permanent Art Gallery in Bradford, and we wish it every success. Naturally, the Arcadian Club is in the van in endeavouring to promote the movement. Having done so much towards the Art education of its fellow-townsmen, it needs but a little more effort, we should think, to carry through the formation of a satisfactory Corporation Art Gallery, for it is impossible to believe that a town which numbers amongst its citizens so many wealthy Art connoisseurs, and possesses a club so full of wholesome vitality, will endure much longer the stigma of being without a public Art collection worthy of its reputation.

ART NOTES.

MR. G. F. WATTS, R.A., whose gift to the Luxembourg in Paris of one of his pictures, 'Love and Life,' we chronicled in a recent number (p. 60), has presented the version of the same subject, which he exhibited at Chicago, to the Government of the United States. The Act of Congress necessary for its acceptance was passed with enthusiasm, and the picture will be placed in the reception chamber at the White House, Washington. It must be understood that these pictures are in no sense replicas or copies, but were both carried on simultaneously with a view to experimenting with somewhat different arrangements. The one sent to America was first completed; the other was finished in accordance with the wishes of Monsieur Benedite, the Conservateur of the Luxembourg, who saw it after the other had been sent to Chicago, and asked Mr. Watts to finish it for that gallery. In reply to an inquiry as to the variations in these pictures, Mr. Watts writes with characteristic modesty:—"I regard my whole series of these works in the same direction of thought as so many monumental manuscripts not otherwise probably much to be valued. I have another version of the same subject—for I think the suggestion of especial value—which will go with the whole series that I have completed, and those I hope still to complete, to the nation here. I do not concern myself with the thought whether they will be cared for or not. The object is one I made for myself many years ago ; perhaps the intention and example may suggest to abler artists the carrying out of a similar intention with greater success."

ROYAL BIRMINGHAM SOCIETY OF ARTISTS.—This Society has for several years rendered much valuable service to Art-education, by getting together a loan collection of the works of an artist of eminence, and making it the special feature of each succeeding spring exhibition. In this way the Birmingham public have had opportunities of studying the works of Sir J. D. Linton, Sir John Gilbert, Carl Haag, T. Collier, Albert and Henry Moore, and Hubert Herkomer.

This, the twenty-ninth Spring Exhibition, is made memorable by a remarkably fine collection of the works of the late Frederick Walker, A.R.A., and of J. W. North, A.R.A. Through the self-denying kindness of the owners, choice examples of their work have been obtained, numbering forty-five by Walker and twenty-four by North. Such an opportunity for studying their work collectively is so rare that their many admirers will no doubt avail themselves of the privilege of studying it. They will delight to renew their acquaintance with such charming works as 'The Old Gate,' 'The Harbour of Refuge,' 'The Fishmonger's Shop,' 'The Plough,' 'Philip in Church,' 'Beehives,' 'Our Village,' 'Stobball Gardens,' and 'Mushroom-Gatherers.'

A local "Arts and Crafts" Guild has just been formed at Sheffield under promising auspices. The crafts represented are artists, chasers, designers, engravers, modellers, and saw-piecers. The officers are Mr. Charles Green, President; Mr. George Halliday, Treasurer; Mr. Charles W. Crowder, Arundel Place, Shoreham Street, Sheffield, Hon. Secretary. The Guild should become a valuable power for good with the important local industries.

The Society of Deaf and Dumb Artists, 113, Schellingstrasse, Munich, sends us a notice of its intention to hold this year an exhibition at Munich of the fine and decorative arts. It is proposed to confine the exhibits strictly to the work of deaf-mute artists, either living or dead, and the object of the exhibition is to raise funds to promote the organization of the education of the deaf and dumb. The Society is now inviting support for their project, and asks for the loan of works by deceased deaf and dumb artists.

OBITUARY.

Mr. John Miller Gray, the first Curator of the Scottish National Portrait Gallery, died after a very brief illness on March 22nd. Mr. Gray, whose writings are well known to the readers of THE ART JOURNAL, and whose work on the Tassie Medallions was noticed in the March issue, began life in the service of the Bank of Scotland at Edinburgh, under his uncle Mr. Robert Gray, well known as a leading authority on Scottish Ornithology. But his bent was towards Art, in the domain of criticism, and for twenty years past his somewhat effusive but strikingly subtle and searching analysis of works of Art, whether current or of bygone times, have been notable in the Edinburgh press. When through the liberality of Mr. Findlay, of Aberlour, proprietor of the *Scotsman*, the Scottish Portrait Gallery was founded, Mr. J. M. Gray's extensive knowledge and his fine literary and antiquarian taste, pointed him out as the fit man to organize and superintend the collection. Under his care, notwithstanding the narrow field and the narrower purse allotted to him, the Gallery has come to hold a valued place, not only in personal interest but in Art, and the illustrated catalogue *raisonné* he prepared is an admirable example of such a work, as well as evidencing the ripeness of Mr. Gray's judgment. Besides the work on Tassie, already named, Mr. Gray edited illustrated biographies of George Manson and P. W. Nicholson, two Scottish colourists of great promise who were cut off in early manhood. In the latter Mr. Gray collaborated with Mrs. H. Bellyse Baildon, of Edinburgh. For the Scottish History Society he edited the "Journal of Sir John Clerk, of Penicuick," and amongst his more recent contributions to the literature of art was a series of articles on Portraits of Burns. Mr. Gray, who was little over forty years of age, bequeaths his property to the furtherance of that aim in which he took so prominent a part, the extension of the Scottish National Portrait Gallery. In noticing his work on Tassie two months ago we spoke of Mr. Gray's conspicuous aptitude for still more important work, and it is with sincere regret that we learn that such expectations are shattered by his early death. Mr. Gray was of singularly gentle and modest demeanour. His capacity for grasping the inner meaning of the work of the age, combined with much suavity of expression, gave much value to his critiques.

In the article on Thomas Woolner, R.A. (page 86), his death was stated to have taken place in 1893, whereas the correct date was the 7th of October, 1892.

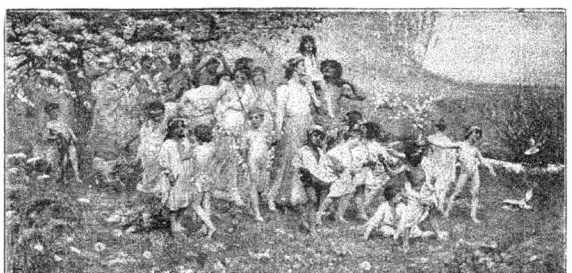

THE TRIUMPH OF SPRING. BY G. P. JACOMB-HOOD. IN THE NATIONAL ART GALLERY OF NEW SOUTH WALES, SYDNEY.

NEW ART PUBLICATIONS.

THE Illustrated Catalogue of the National Art Gallery of New South Wales (J. Sands, Sydney), gives an adequate idea of the brilliant collection of pictures formed there within the past twenty years. This collection now contains two hundred and thirty paintings in oil, one hundred and seventy-three in water-colours, and a large number of works in black-and-white, which, with about a hundred pieces of statuary, comes to a total estimated value of £100,000. This result has been obtained only by the continual efforts of the trustees, and especially of Mr. E. L. Montefiore, the director. In season and out of season, Mr. Montefiore has advocated the claims of his gallery, and when the Home Government is in search of some one to honour outside the usual political circles, we would recommend the powers that be to think favourably of this energetic gentleman. We give two illustrations from the catalogue of well-known pictures now in Sydney. Mr. E. J. Poynter's 'Meeting of Solomon and the Queen of Sheba' (1 Kings /ii-x); and Mr. Jacomb-Hood's charming picture of 'The Triumph of Spring.'

"SALOME," by Oscar Wilde, pictured by Aubrey Beardsley (Elkin Matthews and John Lane), is a book for the strong-minded

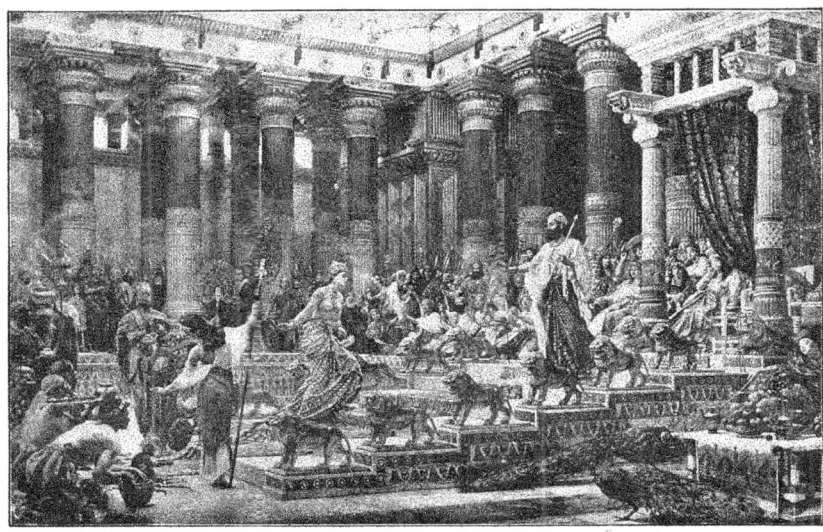

MEETING OF SOLOMON AND THE QUEEN OF SHEBA. BY E. J. POYNTER, R.A. IN THE NATIONAL ART GALLERY OF NEW SOUTH WALES, SYDNEY.
BY PERMISSION OF MR. T. MCLEAN, HAYMARKET, LONDON, OWNER OF THE COPYRIGHT, AND PUBLISHER OF THE LARGE ENGRAVING.

alone, for it is terrible in its weirdness and suggestions of horror and wickedness. Mr. Beardsley's drawings are thoroughly in harmony with the text, and give evidence of impressionism in illustrations not hitherto accomplished or even seriously attempted. Mr. Beardsley's artistic power is of a high order, and it is always worth while to examine his productions with care.

Although the volume has now been for some months before the public, it gives us much pleasure to notice Mr. T. B. Harbottle's translation of Baron J. de Baye's "INDUSTRIAL ARTS OF THE ANGLO-SAXONS" (Swan & Sonnenschein). The volume begins with an account of the invaders of Britain in the fifth century, and minutely describes the arms of the Anglo-Saxons, the fibulæ, chatelaines, necklaces, earrings, glass vases, and pottery. A large number of outline illustrations help the text, which is throughout well and clearly written.

Messrs. Hodges, Figgis & Co., of Dublin, have recently published several excellent reproductions of the books of Kells and Durrow, all first-rate examples of the typographic work of the Sister Isle. "Examples of Celtic ornament" from these books contain photographic reproductions of the design of the seventh century, which are more than ordinarily interesting to the connoisseur, as well as useful to the decorative artist.

We have received from La Librairie de l'Art, Paris, a proof of a new photogravure plate by Dujardin, from a picture by the Misses Desliens, entitled 'Un excellent pot-au-feu.' It represents the interior of a kitchen where a priest is watching with some intentness the operations of his housekeeper preparing a meal. There is evidence of skill in the arrangement of accessories, and the plate is not unpleasing and should prove popular, but in technical quality it is mediocre.

"THEORY AND ANALYSIS OF ORNAMENT," by F. L. Schauermann. "The study of ornament has made," says Mr. Schauermann, "such rapid progress during the last twelve years, that those books which were previously quite efficient have become obsolete." He has compiled, accordingly, what professes to be "a complete text-book upon the subject of Theory and Analysis of Ornament." Possibly Mr. Schauermann has something to say—his diagrams, some two hundred and sixty-three figures, would seem to indicate that he has—but they do not explain themselves. Much of what he says is absolutely unintelligible. It is not merely that he makes use of strange and awkward words, such as kinematic,

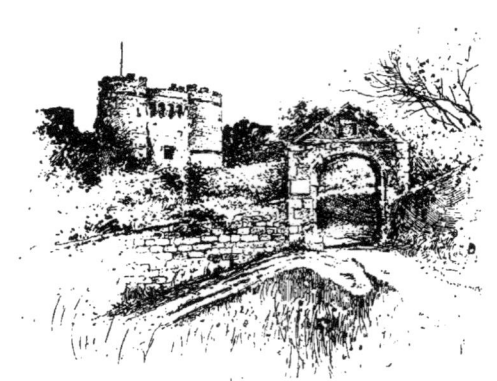

CARISBROOKE CASTLE. FROM "THE ISLE OF WIGHT."

ponderation, helicoidal, volubilial, euclidian, dimensive—all of which occur within the first twelve pages of the book—but that his definitions want defining. What is one to make of paragraphs like this:—"Permutation is an operation by which things of the same class can be arranged one with the other. Such are the rational foundations of the syntactic or science of order, i.e. exclusively logical and mathematical development. Order is Form in discontinuation. Form is Order in continuation." The pages teem with definitions to as little purpose as this, and with tables and classifications for which one sees no possible occasion. This "untutored production of the brain," to borrow a phrase of the author's, had better have been passed over without notice—but that a word of warning may be of use to the student. Mr. Schauermann has adopted the title of that very excellent work, the "Analysis of Ornament"; but the late R. N. Wornum's book is by no means superseded.

In a large portfolio the successors of F. Bruckmann, of Munich, publish a series of fifty reproductions of representative drawings by the best German masters under the title of "Zeichnungen Deutscher Kunstler." Beginning with Von Carstens (1754—1798), there are examples of the finished draughtsmanship of Cornelius, Overbeck, Schnorr von Carolsfeld (the author of the famous 'Bibel in Bildern,' one of the finest series of sacred designs ever made), Kaulbach, Richter, Preller, Rethel, to Mengel, who still lives, at a great age. The drawings which are reproduced in perfect fac-simile are described in full in the text by Dr. W. Von Seidlitz, and the whole work is dedicated to Mr. Richard Schone "dem Freunde Deutscher Kunst." This portfolio gives a good idea of the characteristics of the past German School.

Under the title "THE ISLE OF WIGHT: Picturesque Rambles and Views" (J. S. Virtue & Co.), the visitor will find an acceptable little souvenir of our sunny southern island. The chief attraction in this very moderately priced publication is the wealth of excellent illustrations, mostly executed by Mr. Percy Robertson, and suitably set in agreeable text.

Every one who cares for glimpses of nature and the gentle art of angling will be delighted with Mr. Edward Marston's "DAYS IN CLOVER" (S Low & Co.), a companion volume to his "Amateur Angler,' and "Fresh Woods and Pastures New." The writer discourses in a most unaffected way on his various experiences during brief holidays from London, and he never fails to strike the friendly note which is very acceptable to the angling reader.

FREDERIC HENRI KAEMMERER.

AT an epoch when the most extravagant eccentricity is accepted as originality and when it is sufficient to demolish without constructing, when to deny without exception everything that has gone before is to receive the stamp of a man of genius, it is soothing from time to time to cast an eye on productions that do not rely on the claptrap and staginess and the noisy music of a passing fashion, the work of a modest and hard-working individual, who has, nevertheless, obtained the favour of the public and the artists without resorting to scandal or eccentricity.

Such is Frédéric Henri Kaemmerer, and one who most deserves celebrity by reason of his conscientiousness stripped of vain pretensions, and his devotion to the past as regards everything that was beautiful, amiable, or alluring.

If certain reputations established on quicksands are fated to be extinguished with the lightning that has illumined their name, F. H. Kaemmerer, on the contrary, has constructed by steady work, as much as by continued effort directed to the one goal, a truthful monument that must ever remain a gallery of the finnicking costume, of the rustling, intangible *déshabillé* of that epoch of gallantry, the "Directoire," a regular link between the mincing affectations, the powder and patches of Louis XV.

Firstly, the connection has been naturally evoked by the artist, since side by side with the "Incroyables" and the "Merveilleuses," rendered still more attractive by the pointed wit and clearly demonstrated anecdote, Kaemmerer has equally paid his tribute to the soubrettes and seigneurs of the court of the "Well-Beloved," even as we like to picture them across the scenes of comic opera.

And, indeed, why should not our imaginations embellish the creatures and things of these bygone periods? Is it not a consolation in these prosaic days to dream of an epoch decorated with everything that is graceful and elegant—even were the reality inferior and possibly less seductive? And is it not the duty of the artist to give tangible expressions to our dreams?

F. H. Kaemmerer has assumed this task. He is an idealist, but an idealist that has not dazzled his vision in the mists and mirage of mysticism. Gifted with a robust temperament and a delicate wit, he has extracted the poetical quintessence of an epoch of heroism, and he has succeeded in making us forget, by the lightness of his brush and the dexterity of his execution, the terrible shocks that marked the end of the last century.

The strange part of the talent of Kaemmerer occurs in the fact that his origin was not such as would have obviously led to the task he imposed on himself. Dutch by nationality, he was born at The Hague. His father was a humble artisan, who in his condition of locksmith managed as best he could to bring up his seven children.

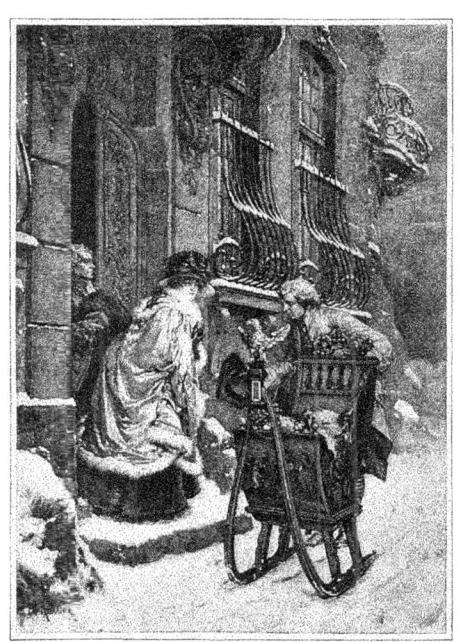

GOING TO CHURCH. BY F. H. KAEMMERER.

When in 1839 the young Frédéric first saw the light of day, the honest mechanic would certainly have been astounded had he been told that his son would one day develop into the painter of all the elegances of the most elegant age. It is even to be imagined that the simple workman might have said to himself, with an expressive shrug of the shoulders: "Let him be a good locksmith, and I shall be more than satisfied."

Whatever may have been, the young man was not thwarted in his vocation. Having exhibited from childhood a marked taste for drawing, the old Dutch professor Verveer was entrusted with the task of instructing him in the rudiments of his artistic education. The first attempts of Kaemmerer were landscapes—honest works showing much study, but in which his personality was not yet developed, but in which the qualities of drawing were already visible which were destined to bear fruit a little later.

The preceptor of the future artist, after having planted his feet on the right road, had the good sense (unlike many of his species) not to wish to monopolise the direction of his studies, thereby limiting the aspirations of his pupil. He advised him to leave for Paris, and to present himself at the Ecole des Beaux-Arts.

But the parental means, if not their sanction, had to be taken into consideration—and, in sooth, the Kaemmerer family was a large one! Nevertheless, thanks to the sale of some few canvases, and the small allowance his father could afford him, the young man was enabled to make his way to the great city. He left in company with Mauve and Maris, who are now world-renowned. Upon being admitted to follow the academical course of instruction, Kaemmerer entered Gérome's studio. This was in 1865.

M. Gérome at this period was omnipotent, and the Greek school dominated all artistic education. Kaemmerer had to pay his Hellenic tribute, and his first exhibit at the Salon in the Champs-Elysées in 1868 naturally expressed this influence.

This was a picture entitled, 'Ruse and Defiance,' altogether in the style of Gérome. It represented a young Greek girl, the torso nude, the head bent, holding in the raised hand a rod, and watching the arrival of a cat at the corner of an aviary door that was just ajar.

I understand that this picture brought the artist an honourable mention, but Kaemmerer has since portrayed a host of infinitely more personal impressions. In 1874, notably, Greece was very far from his thoughts when he exhibited 'La Plage de Scheveningen,' that was to bring him his first medal. This was already a step in the direction of genre painting in which he was to achieve success. In point of fact, nothing could be more amusing than this crowd of bathers and promenaders, the carefully studied position of the Rabelaisian curé who is chatting with his parishioners showing a real gift for observation. Further, the "top hat" of the Sunday "swell" is a miniature work of Art for truth and accuracy. How easily one realises the inhabitant of The Hague, who, tired out by his weekly occupations, comes to breathe the ozone whilst watching the continuous movement of the strollers.

Firstly, the care of the details of the composition is one of Kaemmerer's dominant qualities. In one of the pictures, entitled 'Une Ascension en l'An VIII' (Salon, 1880), this is particularly evident. Whilst the balloon ascends into the blue ether the eyes of the crowd are turned towards the object in question, and the whole hubbub is most amusingly treated.

To vary the monotony of the attitudes of the people in the foreground, naturally seen from the back, the artist has

THE HARP. BY F. H. KAEMMERER.

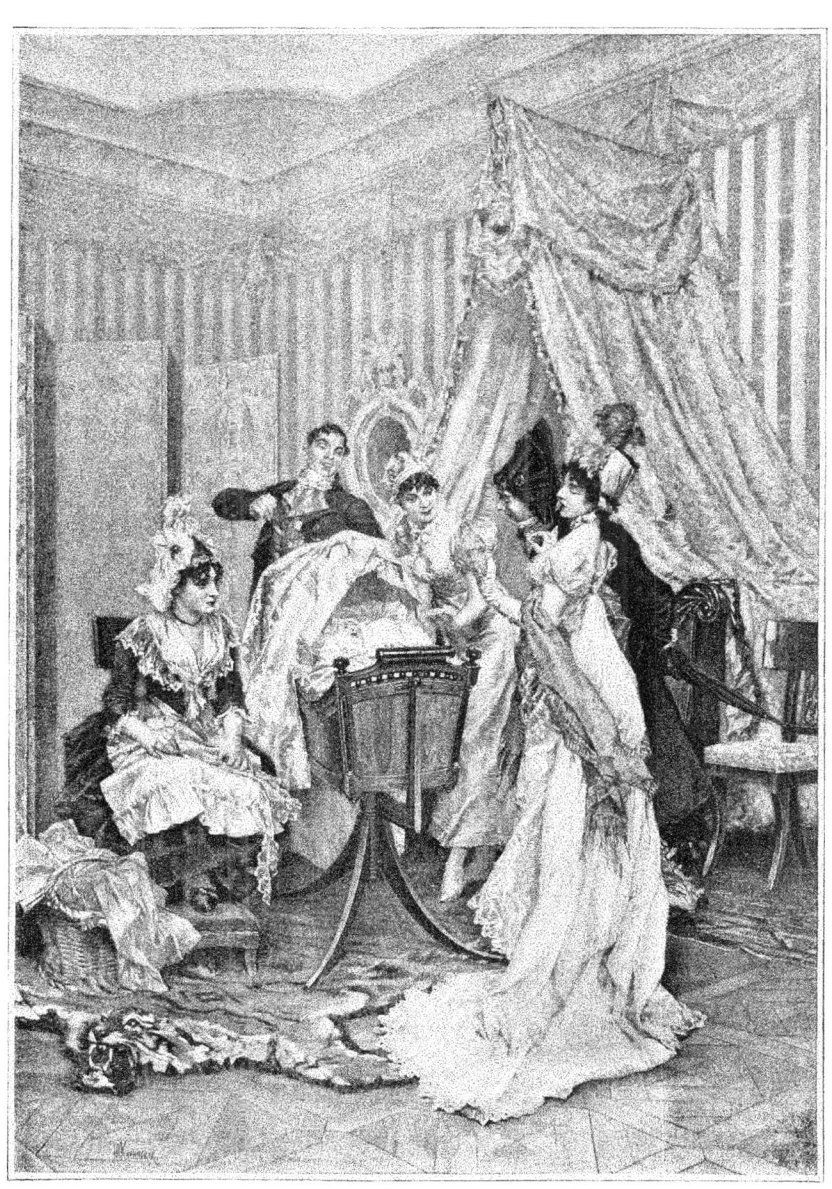

THE FIRST-BORN. BY FREDERIC HENRI KAEMMERER.

imagined the fall of a "petit maître," who in tumbling overthrows a pastrycook's apprentice, carrying refreshments, the noise of the broken glasses naturally making the spectators turn to look. Thus the trick to show the faces is accomplished. This ingenuity was in itself worthy of another medal, which was only awarded some years later.

If it were necessary to give descriptions of all the pictures of F. H. Kaemmerer the columns of this Journal would not suffice to contain them. His work is certainly of considerable proportions, as more than two hundred canvases have already been rapidly secured to take their places in many international collections and museums, without counting the water-colours and the illustrations reproduced in the artistic publications made popular by this means. Who is not familiar, by the means of the publishers' windows, with ' Le Portrait de la Marquise,' ' Le Baptême,' ' La Rupture,' and that exquisite subject ' The Revolutionist's Bride,' or, as it is known in France, ' Une Noce sous le Directoire,' full of grace, freshness, and ingenuity ? What an adorable costume, and what a delicious bride ! This sentiment is intensified by the young girl, still on the threshold of womanhood, who abandons herself, in an access of timid confidence, to the arm of her lord and master. By the side of her cavalier, filled with

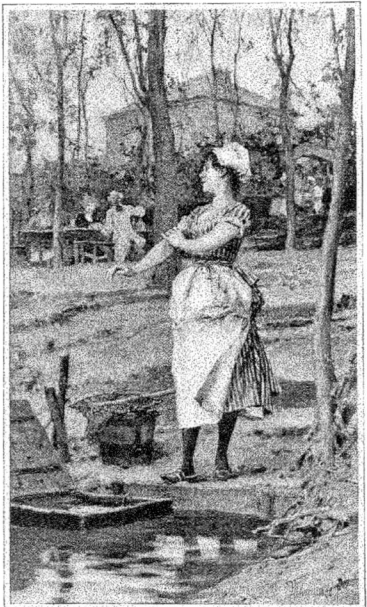

THE RIVERSIDE INN. BY F. H. KAEMMERER.

pride and happiness, the bride feels herself the object of all admiration, and she seems as if asking his protection from the attention which momentarily disconcerts her.

With a poetic touch the painter has scattered her passage with doves, which seem to guide her tender maidenhood into the smiling pathway of the idyllic honeymoon. Later in life, when years have powdered her sunny locks with the snow of time, she will behold in her turn, even as that lady in the background, other bridal couples displaying their glorified happiness in the heyday of their spring-time. And the past will come back to her, seeing the noisy hilarity of the wedding guests, remembering the touching sadness of her own mother, perhaps paying a tearful tribute to the reminiscence. But for the time being she loves and feels she is beloved, and philosophy is very far from her thoughts. Those who form part of the cortège are equally impressed by this touching confidence, and the procession continues through sallies of laughter. Never has the painter appeared more thoroughly himself than in this delightfully imaginative conception. It is all saturated with sunshine, health, and the joys of existence, and only the little group to the right breathes a note of subdued melancholy, which is but an added charm to the rest. This picture is one of Kaemmerer's best, and has excited much attention.

Physically F. H. Kaemmerer, with his eye-glasses and beard that is growing grey, his long face and ruddy complexion, has more the look of the city merchant than the commentator of the elegance of the past century and contemporaneous fashion. But if, as the proverb says, " It is not the cowl that makes the monk," the fact of producing worldly scenes does not imply a worldly nature, Kaemmerer has in point of fact preserved as his inheritance a tranquillity of existence that is entirely Flemish. His greatest pleasure consists in refreshing himself after his fatiguing work by breathing the fresh air of the fields, or smoking a pipe in the corner of his studio in company with some of his intimates.

No one who looked at him would believe himself in the presence of one of the painters who knows best how to delineate that part that should best represent the delicate whimsical Parisian—even were she of the Directoire.

Nevertheless, if one opens a drawer of the numerous chests of the studio, preserved with a care that is all Dutch, we discover brocaded satins, flowered stuffs and velvets of hues faded by time, watered silks of expiring lustre, that have served to guide the artist in the arrangement of his palette. Then there are old trimmed hats, the " ridicules," the cocked hat with tricolor cockades, hunted out from the nest of the collector, from the curiosity store-rooms, regular "leit motives" of the epoch that figures in the works.

In truth it was a Directoire costume, discovered among the flummery of a costumier, that originally turned the artist to the road on whose signposts he has written his name in large letters. The impression received by some tattered garments, the property of some bygone " merveilleuse," or, perhaps, even a simple grisette, who when the Sunday came round strutted about on the arm of some " Fanfan la Tulipe," determined the vocation of Kaemmerer.

In ' The First-born,' we find the care and finish of a Meissonier ; the mannered expression of physiognomy, and more manifold observations, are incorporated in the consistency of an expression.

Happy infant! happy father! The one sleeps, the other does not even try to dissimulate the satisfaction caused by the flattering expressions of the visitor—all of which goes to prove that if fashions change, human nature remains eternally the same.

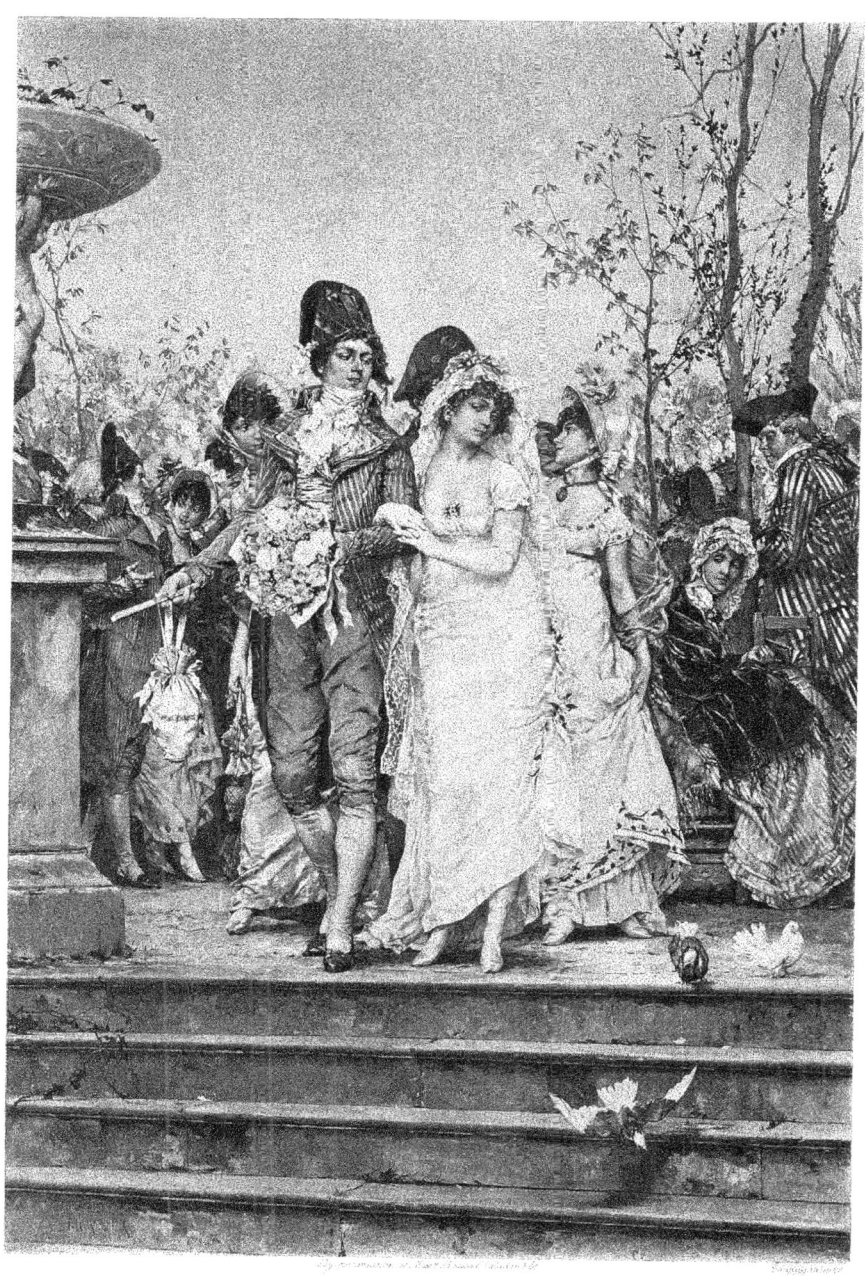

THE REVOLUTIONIST'S BRIDE, PARIS, 1799.
FROM THE PAINTING BY J. KAEMMERER.

Side by side with this tranquil page of family life is 'The Dispute,' the storm after the fine weather. Without wishing to interfere in the quarrel, we should instantly give that individual right that stands on the left, on account of the striking attitude and his firmly upright expression. It is a vigorous piece, treated with great breadth. The imploring pose of the first woman, and the protecting and frightened posture of the second, are most natural, and at the same time highly amusing. I do not allude to the picturesque disorder of tables overthrown and porcelain broken. For my part, the masterpiece of the artist is 'The Harp,' equally with regard to the grouping of the figures and the harmony of lines. Standing before her instrument, the performer in a luminous nimbus, whilst the rest of the room is in a half-light, seems, with her long, lithe, willowy body, to be the materialisation of those Christmas angels that accompany themselves on harps whilst singing hosannahs to the Most High. The young woman is lost in a reverie. What matter the whisperings murmured behind fans, or the flirtations lost in the twilight obscurity—she sings for herself. In the witchery of her song, doubtless some plaintive melody of Méhul or Garat, she thinks of the absent one, he who in leaving carried away a part of her life and her heart. The harp replies pathetically, and from this little scene a perfume arises, so delicate and tender that it resembles the faintness of those flowers dried in old books, that before yielding themselves finally to decay exhale their last fragrant breath redolent of their pristine perfection.

hale their last fragrant breath redolent of their pristine perfection.

The expression in this picture is intense and will remain

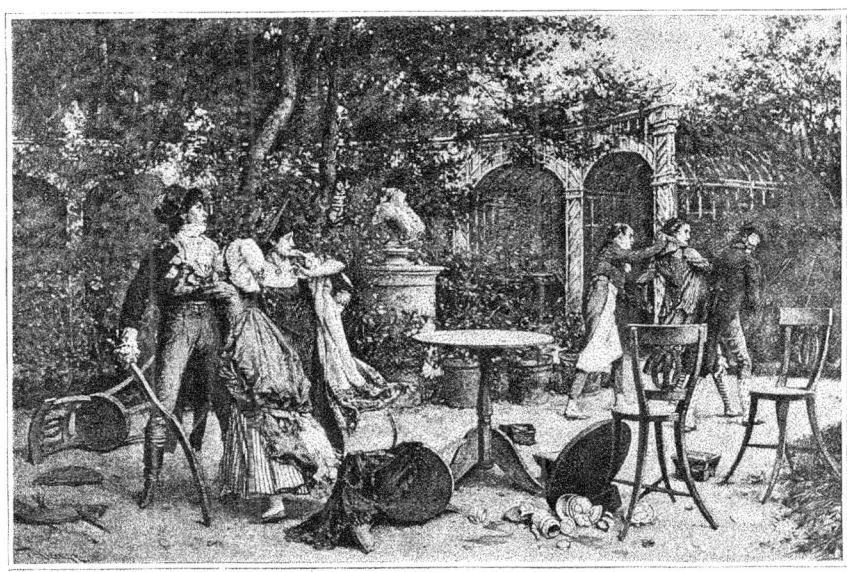

THE DISPUTE. BY F. H. KAEMMERER.

without doubt as the greatest work of the artist. In an utterly different conception, 'Going to Church' is another good canvas. In the snow we find, in the brisk cold of this Sunday morning, the bright little face of the pretty Parisian, half awake but most exuberant.

Finally, in 'The Riverside Inn,' a more jovial note, the painter has certainly remembered, despite the costume, the strong, hearty gossips that are certainly not one of the last attractions of his birthplace.

Nevertheless, Kaemmerer has become very French, and the truth of this is evident from the fact that a short time ago, at a party given at the Minister of the Netherlands, he found himself much embarrassed when it became necessary to answer a question put in Dutch. The excellent artist had entirely forgotten his mother tongue. The French government has for a long time considered him as one of their nation, and awarded him at the conclusion of the Universal Exhibition of 1889 the Cross of the Legion of Honour, whilst the Jury of Painting declared him "Hors concours," a worthy testimony to his merit and value in an artistic world. JEAN BERNAC.

*** We have to thank Messrs. BOUSSOD, VALADON & CO. for permission to reproduce the illustrations, most of which are published by them as large plates.

CRITICAL STUDIES ON PICTURES AT THE NATIONAL GALLERY.
I.—LEONARDO DA VINCI.

IT has often been remarked that both Leonardo da Vinci and Michelangelo, the two greatest artists of the Florentine school, painted only a very few pictures. Manifold causes contributed to bring about this result, and it is impossible to understand them without some inquiry into the circumstances and conditions under which the painters of the Renaissance lived—conditions which had little or nothing in common with those under which Art is cultivated at the present day. We can scarcely understand how it is that Michelangelo, who finished the paintings on the roof of the Sixtine chapel in the Vatican in twenty-two months— undoubtedly the boldest and most magnificent creation of modern painting—should in the course of his long life (for he died at the age of eighty-nine) only have painted three frescoes and two or three easel pictures besides. The case of Leonardo da Vinci is similar. Some thirty-five years of his life he spent in Florence, and about twenty-five in Milan. We possess only five pictures belonging to his Florentine period, and of these two were left unfinished, while of his Milanese period there remain not more than two. Since, however, both artists already enjoyed the highest reputation in their lifetime, so that the fame of their works was sung even by the poets of the period, and since posterity has made it its task still more to spread their appreciation and their fame, we cannot suppose that through negligence or indifference a great number of their works were destroyed. The same observation applies to only one other of the celebrated Italian painters, namely Giorgione; but in contrast to the Florentines just mentioned, the Venetian was only a painter, not an architect and sculptor besides. In addition Giorgione died young, at the age of thirty-three years. He seems to have painted not more than twenty pictures, of which about two-thirds are still preserved, all works of small dimensions. These three artists have this in common, that, in spite of the slender number of their works, an influence proceeded from them which altered the character of artistic production for whole generations, and directed taste into new channels. They obviously thought little about troubling themselves with numerous commissions. In fact, they were probably, all three, bad "men of business," as we should say nowadays; and if they did undertake commissions, what interested them in the execution of them was first and foremost the artistic problem. Both Michelangelo and Leonardo left several unfinished works behind them, works which were only completed so far as was necessary for the solution of the problem.

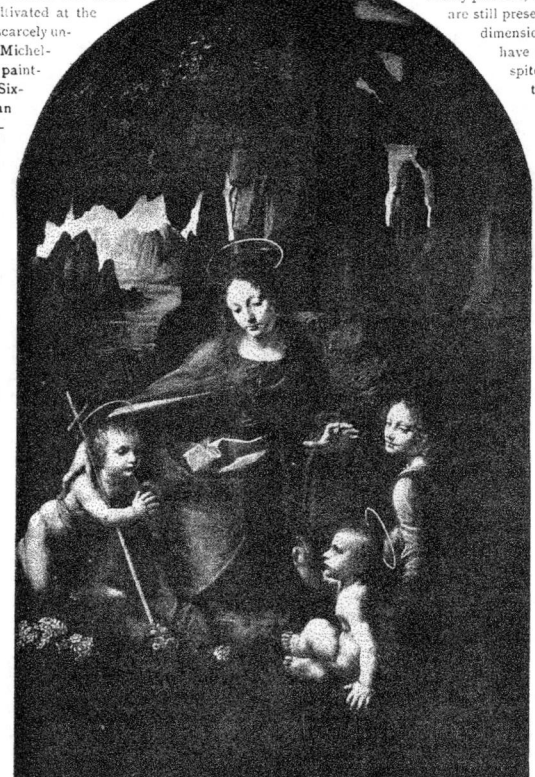

THE VIRGIN OF THE ROCKS. ASCRIBED TO LEONARDO DA VINCI. IN THE NATIONAL GALLERY, LONDON. No. 1.

The two best-known finished pictures of Leonardo are the portrait of 'Mona Lisa' and the 'Vierge aux Rochers,' both in the Louvre at Paris. They originally belonged to the collection of King Francis I., in whose service Leonardo spent the last years of his life. There is also in the National Gallery a picture called 'The Virgin of the Rocks,' which, as a pretended genuine work of Leonardo, was acquired some years ago from Lord Suffolk for £9,000. This latter work many critics have pronounced to be an original; without, however, furnishing the proof of the r assertion. They appeal to the fact that the Milanese writer, Lomazzo, sixty-five years after Leonardo's death, mentions the picture as a work of that master. It was then in the Capella della Concezione, in the church of St. Francesco at Milan. But whoever has taken the trouble to read the works of Lomazzo will perhaps admit that that most bombastic of writers must have possessed only very moderate qualifications as a critic. I suspect that the critics who so readily appeal to him are unaware of the fact that this Art-theorist and poet went blind at the age of three-and-thirty, and did not write his own works himself, but was

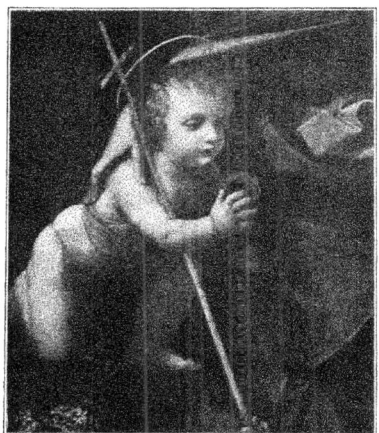

THE INFANT ST. JOHN IN THE PICTURE AT THE NATIONAL GALLERY. No. 2.

obliged to dictate them. Later Milanese writers, such as Bianconi, who is even quoted in the National Gallery catalogue, and Calvi, described the picture now in London as a school-piece, at a time when it was the custom to ascribe insignificant works to the greatest masters. They would hardly have expressed such an opinion if it had not been the universal one of their time. The picture was sold in the year 1777 to Gavin Hamilton, who was then collecting works of Art in Italy for the Marquis of Lansdowne. The price was thirty ducats! And this fact has more weight in my judgment than all the opinions about Leonardo from the pen of Lomazzo put together. Is it possible to believe that a picture from a public church in opulent Milan would have been sold for thirty ducats—and to an English collector too—if it had passed as an original by Leonardo? An inscription in the Ambrosian Library in the same town, of the year 1637, records that Charles I. in vain offered three hundred ducats for any one volume of Leonardo's manuscripts, and further light is thrown upon the question by Evelyn's statement that Lord A'rundel offered a thousand pounds to acquire Leonardo manuscripts in Milan.* These prices for manuscripts certainly afford a measure of the value which would have been put at that time upon a great genuine picture by Leonardo.

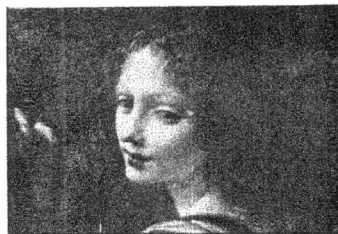

HEAD OF THE ANGEL IN LEONARDO'S PICTURE AT PARIS. No. 3.

The final judgment of the question whether the picture in the Louvre or that in the National Gallery be the unique original, can naturally be based only upon a detailed critical comparison of both of them. Apart from this, I wish to point out at the outset that the external evidence is by no means so decisively in favour of the genuineness of the London picture as might appear from the historical exposition in the official catalogue of the National Gallery, and before I enter upon a critical comparison of the two pictures, I must call attention to the fact that there has recently been discovered in the

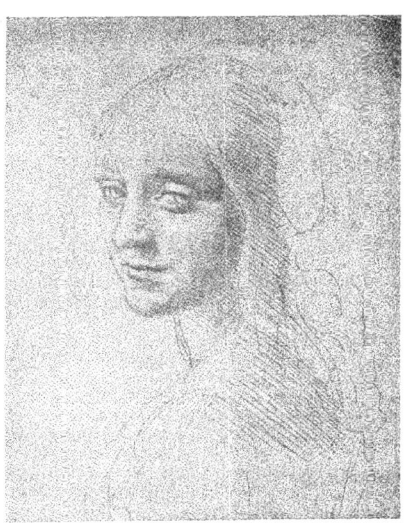

SILVER-POINT STUDY BY LEONARDO, IN THE ROYAL LIBRARY, TURIN. No. 4.

State archives at Milan a document calculated to throw light upon the origin of the London example. It is undated; but

* See the Literary Works of Leonardo da Vinci (J. P. Richter), Vol. II., p. 482.

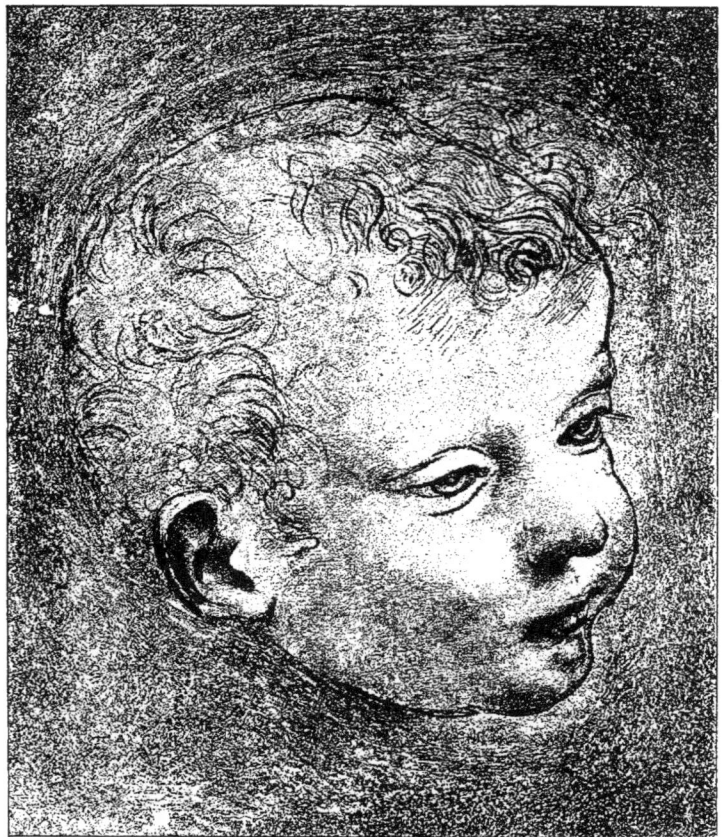

LEONARDO'S ORIGINAL DRAWING OF ST. JOHN. IN THE LOUVRE. NO. 5.

by the aforesaid Florentine (*la dicta nostra donna facta a olio per lo dicto florentino*) was valued at only twenty-five ducats, although it was worth a hundred, as is proved, not only by the accompanying calculation in detail, but by the fact that some one had been found ready to give a hundred ducats for the picture. Under these circumstances, and in consideration of the fact that the members of the brotherhood have no practical knowledge of these matters, for a blind man is no judge of colour (*et quod cechus non judicat de colore*), the Duke is petitioned to be graciously pleased

according to Emilio Motta in the *Archivio Storico Lombardo* (Anno xx., iv.), it belongs approximately to the years 1484—1494.

This document, which is too long to be inserted here in its entirety, is a petition addressed to the Duke of Milan, bearing the following signature: "Johannis de predis et Leonardi de vincijs florentini." In this petition the two painters set forth that the members of the Brotherhood "della Conceptione," in the church of San Francesco in Milan, commissioned them to execute an altar-piece in relief, to be overlaid with fine gold, and in addition a picture of the Madonna, to be painted in oil. The value of these works was to be fixed by two members of the brotherhood and Pater Fra Agostino, and they had fixed it at eight hundred imperial *lire* (*libre de' imperiali*); but, seeing that the expenses of the petitioners alone had amounted to that sum, the work itself would not be included at all. In the same estimate the Madonna picture painted in oil to direct either that the three arbitrators should immediately value the two works on oath, which they have hitherto declined to do, or that an expert should be chosen by either party for the valuation, and that the members of the brotherhood should then be compelled either to pay the price thus fixed forthwith, or to hand over the aforesaid oil painting of the Madonna to the petitioners, for the eight hundred imperial *lire* already paid to them amount to not more than the cost price of the altar-piece executed in relief.

We are not told how this dispute was settled by the Duke; but the nature of the decision is not difficult to guess, if we bear in mind that by the side of the one Madonna-picture a replica soon makes its appearance. The brotherhood had settled upon a fixed price for the works of Art which they had ordered, and they were by no means disposed to go beyond this sum for the decoration of their chapel. Moreover, the Duke will have had neither the means nor the inclination to compel them to do so. On the other hand, Leonardo was in a position to sell his Madonna for four times the price that the brotherhood were willing to give for it, nor could anybody have prevented him from doing this, as soon as he undertook to supply in its place a picture of the value of twenty-five ducats. The original was acquired by an agent of King Louis XII. of France, with whom Leonardo is known to have had personal relations; but before the despatch of the picture a copy with slight variations was prepared by an assistant in the master's atelier, and for this, on its delivery, the stipulated price of twenty-five ducats was paid.

It is hardly necessary to mention that at that time the value of money was higher than two hundred years later. In 1516, Fra Bartolomeo, who was then the most esteemed painter in Florence, received a hundred ducats for an altar-piece with five figures the size of life, which now hangs in the Pitti Gallery.

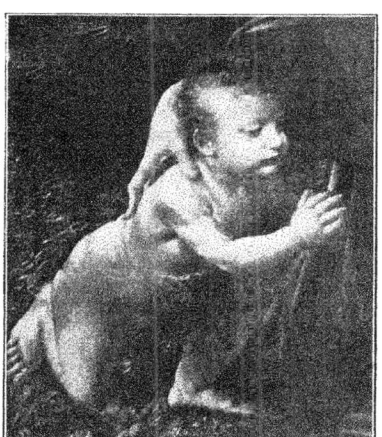

FIGURE OF ST. JOHN THE BAPTIST IN LEONARDO'S PICTURE IN PARIS. No. 6.

I will readily admit, then, that Gavin Hamilton did not do a bad stroke of business when he acquired the Leonardesque picture from San Francesco in Milan, though it seems very doubtful whether the responsible authorities of the National Gallery could say as much for themselves with regard to their own acquisition of the picture.

Excellent photographs, not only of the picture in the Louvre, but also of the National Gallery example have been taken by the well-known firm of Braun, and it seems to me that the mere comparison of the two reproductions would suffice to enable any one endowed with critical perception to recognise the enormous artistic superiority of the original from the cabinet of the old French kings. On the other hand I am far from wishing to deny that even in the picture at the National Gallery certain qualities of Leonardo's method are apparent. In fact, it stands to reason that even in schoolwork certain peculiarities of the master's way of conceiving and handling should recur, though in a weakened form, especially in a case like the present, in which the copy was possibly made in the master's own workshop. Yes, it is

possible that there also exist amateurs and critics whose conscience would be completely set at rest if there should still be found the receipt for the twenty-five ducats which the brotherhood once paid to Leonardo for the delivery of this copy in accordance with the estimate of the experts.

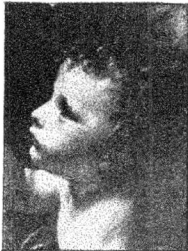

HEAD OF THE INFANT CHRIST IN LEONARDO'S PICTURE AT PARIS. No. 7.

In comparing the two pictures it will be useful to make a distinction between such variations as concern the design and those which are a matter of execution. Strictly speaking, it is the figure of the angel alone that comes within the former category. In the original in Paris the angel points with his right hand to the infant John, while the whole modelling of the left arm, with which he supports the infant Christ, is visible through the gauzy drapery. In the picture at the National Gallery both features are simplified. The sleeve of the drapery is here of some heavy untransparent stuff, and the right hand is completely hidden behind the head of the infant Christ. Moreover, the pose of the head is somewhat different in the two angels. In the London picture (No. 1) the angel has his eyes cast down, while in that at Paris he gazes straight at the spectator

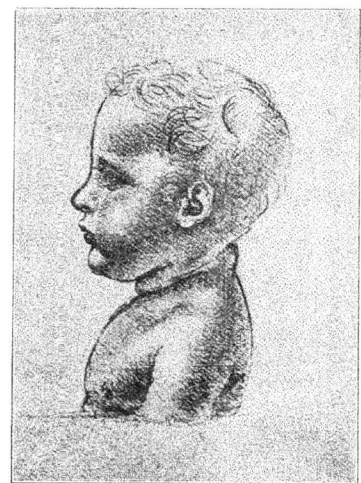

LEONARDO'S ORIGINAL DRAWING OF THE INFANT CHRIST IN THE ROYAL LIBRARY, WINDSOR. No. 8.

(No. 3). A silver-point study for this head by Leonardo is preserved in the Royal Library at Turin, and is here reproduced on a somewhat smaller scale than the original (No. 4). It is obviously a study from nature, in which the painter has taken the head of some young woman as the model upon which to form the type of his angel. Similar variations are noticeable in the treatment of the landscape in the foreground. In the Paris picture the flowers that adorn the foreground are worked out in all their details with an accuracy that makes it easy to determine them botanically. As is evident from his writings, Leonardo made a profound study of the forms and growths of plants; and just as his drawings of flowers, of which several are to be found in the Royal Library at Windsor, fulfil all the demands of scientific precision, so the flowers painted in this picture deserve the same praise, but in still higher measure. In the London picture, on the other hand, both flowers and leaves appear to have been executed with great carelessness and indifference.

The relatively insignificant artistic quality of the latter work is brought out in a strikingly disadvantageous light by a comparison of the figures of the children—the infant John and the infant Christ. In the Paris picture the hands exhibit a delicacy of mould which is almost unique in the history of Art. Michelangelo alone has been able to accomplish something similar in the marble group at Bruges and the reliefs in the National Museum at Florence and the Diploma Gallery at Burlington House. The right hand of the Virgin which rests on the shoulder of the infant St. John is in the picture at Paris (No. 6) of a slender shape, displaying well, in its anatomical structure, the firm grasp of its movement, whereas in the picture at the National Gallery (No. 2), that hand hangs down as in a purely academical performance. The difference of quality between the two pictures comes out most strikingly in the drawing of the children's heads. And here one should pay special attention to the treatment of the hair. Leonardo attached great importance to a light and flowing representation of it in undulating lines (Nos. 6 and 7)—in his manuscripts especially he lays stress upon this feature;* but the copyist who executed the London picture did not understand how even distinctly to reproduce the impression in this respect of the original. In his work the hair does not in the least look as if it had grown upon the head; it gives one exactly the impression of a peruke stuck on (No. 2). Leonardo's original drawings for both heads

* The Literary Works, Vol. I., p. 200.

are still preserved in the Royal Library at Windsor (for the infant Christ, No. 8), and in the Louvre (for the St. John, No. 5). In the former especially, a red chalk drawing in splendid preservation, the qualities of the master in point of modelling and the treatment of the hair are exhibited in an eminent degree, while as regards execution the original in Paris (Fig. 7) is well worthy to stand beside it. On the other hand, the London copy (No. 1) appears as an entirely wretched performance—a performance for which no one less deserves to be made responsible than Leonardo.

It will be sufficient to have pointed out the most striking points of difference between the two pictures—differences which may be observed by every one who studies the two pictures without prejudice. It must also be remembered that, as a matter of course, the differences in the execution of the two pictures appear in a minimised form, in the accompanying reproductions, on account of their great reduction in size. They are really such as to exclude the hypothesis which some have ventured to propound—that the same great artist had first executed the original picture now at Paris and afterwards its inferior copy in the National Gallery. Such an hypothesis becomes still more preposterous when we remember that the execution of paintings was infrequent in Leonardo's artistic career; and also when we consider how disappointing and annoying the conditions must have been to him which necessitated the production of this particular work—that is if the circumstances of the case were what I have endeavoured to explain in reviewing the newly-discovered document about the delivery and payment of the picture.

The rich collection of early Italian paintings in the National Gallery is pregnant with interesting problems about which, as far as I know, critical researches have not yet been published. Such studies are perhaps nowhere more needed than in the case of pictures which, like those in the national collection, claim the importance of being standard works for the guidance of the student as well as the amateur and the public. In a following issue I intend to discuss some pictures of the Venetian School.

J. P. RICHTER.

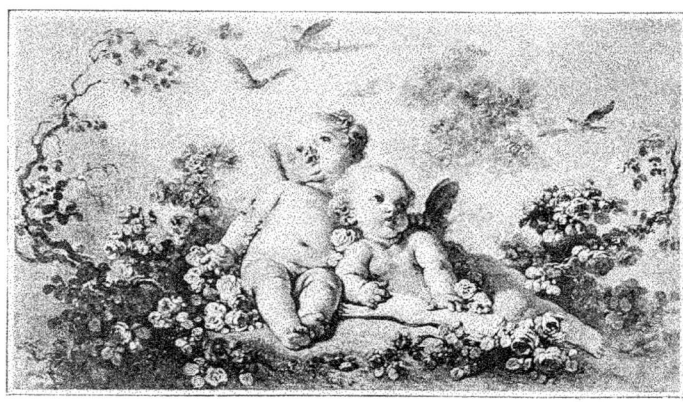

LE PRINTEMPS. FROM A PICTURE BY FRAGONARD.

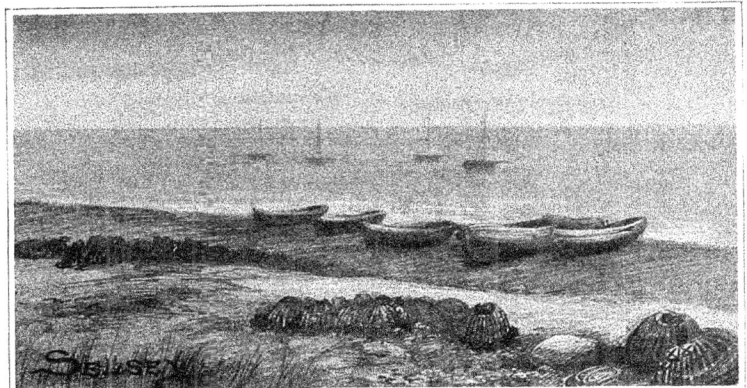

The Beach at Selsey. By G. Léon Little.

THE SELSEY PENINSULA.

THE country below Chichester, dropping a straight line south to Selsey Bill, and comprising the whole area east and west shut in by the Brighton Railway running from Littlehampton to Havant, I have made bold to designate, purely arbitrarily and for the sake of convenience, the Selsey Peninsula. The greater part of this country, and especially that part to which the term "Selsey Peninsula" may with some show of accuracy be applied, is comparatively little known; to the tourist of the baser sort it is almost entirely unknown, and may it ever remain so. One loves all mankind, of course; but there are men of a clearly-defined type one loves with far greater warmth at a distance, and I should consider myself a traitor to the inner brotherhood were I, in this article, to say anything which, spreading downwards, might entice the ordinary Cockney to come in his legions and drop his aspirates along the shores of Bracklesham Bay and among the junipers of Kingley Bottom.

But he will not come: there is nothing to attract him: no "niggers" on the sands, no grisettes along the esplanade—no esplanade, in fact. Here he will find himself face to face with nature, a kingdom in which his coinage has no currency. For the more objectionable visitor still, the merely vacuous and idle money-spender, to whatsoever class he may belong, Selsey Bill and its neighbourhood will have no allurements. Moreover, although I have visited this district in every season, perhaps in every month, I have elected to describe it in late autumn and early winter; in plain English, November—that much-abused month, though to me the most beautiful season of the year. It is the month of mysticism and suggestion, when colour reveals itself in softened reticence—none the less splendid for that.

The wise, in journeying from Chichester to Selsey, will choose that time-honoured means of conveyance—the carrier's cart, and keep company with all manner of comestibles destined for the shoremen's mouths; while from the said mouths—for he will be unfortunate if he does not find several shoremen among his fellow-passengers—many a racy story and old-world quip and phrase—coarse, brutal and direct maybe—will fall, bringing to the corners of his own, pleasant curves, that is if he be a true naturalist, and if the *malaise* of intellectuality, "religiosity," or other form of prudery have not curdled his paganism.

From the moment of leaving Chichester the country is uni-

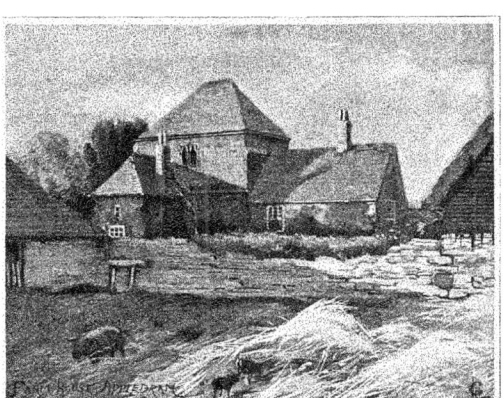

Farm-House, Appledram. By G. Léon Little.

formly flat; the road twists and turns a good deal, high hawthorns and quicks on each side of it, and elms and oaks studded about here and there. After passing Sidlesham the trees become sparser and sparser; indeed, save where a farmhouse or cottage springs from the plain, very little timber is to be seen, and it is with difficulty we imagine that this wide expanse, given over to the growing of corn and the grazing of sheep and cattle, was once a dense forest going by the name of the Main-wood or Manwood, a name which still survives in the "Manhood" by which the country between Selsey and Sidlesham is known.

Selsey itself consists of three or four straggling streets; the cottages, quaint and primitive, are largely in the occupation of fisher-folk, for the village is the seat of an important crab, lobster, and prawn fishery. The beach and foreshore are strewn everywhere with nets, lobster and crab pots, and fishing tackle generally. The lobsters and crabs are caught on the submerged rocks, but the prawn fishery is confined chiefly to the sands between the Bill and Bracklesham Bay. Beyond Bracklesham the sands are not especially attractive to the lay eye, though the artist will detect plenty of fine colour in them; they are not, properly speaking, sands at all, merely the detritus of chalk and clay mixed with a little silicious matter. Along the western coast from Pagham to Bognor the sands are firm and afford a pleasant foothold. One of the greatest natural attractions of this shore is the beautiful horned Sea-poppy (*glaucium luteum*). Its petals are of the purest yellow, its stamens golden; its leaves are of a delightful sea-green; the horn or seed-pod is a long thin bean, sometimes ten or even twelve inches in length. On the beach, or rather just above it, there are a boarding-house and a lifeboat station, the latter owing its existence largely to the energy of a former parish curate, now the Vicar of Rudgwick.

Selsey is full of historical association. In Saxon times it was the seat of the see of Chichester. It was here, in 680, St. Wilfred came with the remnant of his Northumbrian converts; it is said that he was wrecked off the coast, and received with every sign of favour by Ethelwealh, King of Sussex. Here he set about Christianising the South Saxons and he built a cathedral. Nothing remains of this building now; it has gone with the monastery he also founded. Throughout historic times, at various intervals the sea has played sad havoc along this coast, washing away acres and acres of land. Somewhere in the fourteenth century the tide made a violent inrush at Pagham, carrying away nearly three thousand acres of land and forming the so-called harbour. But it is scarcely known when St. Wilfred's abbey and cathedral disappeared. Certain it is that nothing of either remains, nor have I heard that the reclaimers, who have been busy within the last quarter of a century, have discovered in the course of their work anything of importance in the archæological sense, though they came one day upon a fine skeleton of the mastodon, of which one of the largest bones served, for some time, as a kerb-stone at the corner of the principal Selsey street.

The rectory grounds, surrounding a handsome Jacobean house, are among the pleasant places of Selsey. It is a fine old-world garden, with gillyflowers and hollyhocks, larkspurs, bergamot, red-hot pokers, arum-lilies, wall-flowers, lilac, Guelder-roses, and all the rest of them—the flowers our ancestors knew and loved. At the bottom of the garden there is a small wood, and here we have almost the only trees in the immediate neighbourhood. In the wood there are certain treacherous-looking holes, where the smugglers who used to be very active here, and about whom some finely crusted yarns are told, were wont to secrete their kegs of Schiedam and Cognac.

If we listen to ordinary chatter, we shall hear that Selsey is "a dull hole" possessing no kind of attraction. For me, I can only say the wide expansiveness of its wind-blown shores, the long swell of its almost treeless plain, have a peculiar message. If the enervation of so-called civilising agencies have gone very far, Selsey is certainly a place to be avoided; a little "roughing it" cannot be escaped; but for men and women of robuster mould, anxious to throw off for a while the husk of fashion, this farthermost point of Sussex can be confidently recommended; while without wishing to be guilty of the high presumption of suggesting to the painter, I should certainly be surprised if any artist, save the mere painter of the obviously pretty, who does not need to be reckoned with, should find Selsey altogether lacking in stimulus. Pagham, perhaps, is more essentially picturesque. The harbour is something of a myth, the "Hushing Well" very much so, but the cockle remains. "The Park" is a place of anchorage covering the site of the grounds of the ancient episcopal palace; it is asserted that even so late as the reign of Henry VIII. this park was still a chase for deer. Nytimber, hard by, is a pleasant little hamlet of which I have heard a painter speak with warmth; South Bersted is not without attraction; while the delights of Bognor are well known. It owed its existence to the ambition of Sir Richard Hotham, a London tradesman who ruined himself in the effort to make it a fashionable watering place; though it is true that at one of his villas the Queen, as Princess Victoria, lived with the Duchess of Kent during several summers. At Aldwick, Baron Albert Grant lives, while between Bognor and Felpham there are some fine Georgian houses which smell of the pages of Thackeray.

Felpham, the abode of that very tiresome poet Hayley, was also the home for a while of William Blake, whose friend Hayley was. One is tempted to ask one's self how the ethereal Blake could have tolerated the presumably pompous author of "Triumphs of Temper." The very name, however, of this superfluous work causes us in justice to reflect, that Blake could not have been at all times a very tranquillising companion. It may well be that Hayley has done a great deal to merit the love of posterity, in virtue of the toleration which may be reasonably supposed he had to exercise, in order to live in amity with a man so far removed from the normal as Blake. His cottage hard by the Fox Inn, a picturesque thatched-roofed, buff-faced hostelry, is called Rose Cottage. It is a tumble-down looking place; thatched, and with a cream-coloured external, which in the summer is more or less embedded in creeping plants.

It is fruitless to hope to receive assistance from the good people of Felpham, in the effort to discover this cottage; the only Blakes of whom the inn-keeper and his neighbours had heard were a certain coast-guardsman and a carpenter bearing the poet's name. As to Hayley's house, which I have heard spoken of as "a delightful villa," it is in reality as commonplace as the villas of the period were wont to be. It must be remembered, however, that as the friend of Cowper, and above all of Romney and Blake, Hayley had some claim to consideration. But among the many associations of Felpham, Rossetti was often there; Blake's sojourn stands out conspicuously. James Smetham, writing from Felpham, says:—"Here is the shore where dear old Blake, the painter, in four years' residence used to wander, seeing Moses and the Prophets." Apart from its associations, however, Felpham is delightful, and in its neighbourhood is many another inviting little village: Climping, the last village on the Arun before it reaches the sea; Yapton with its interesting church —the font, said to be Saxon, is one of the oldest in the county—and many another. But Felpham, whatever way it be approached, conveys a pleasing first impression. Coming upon it from Yapton one passes through a smiling country, chiefly arable land, rich and loamy. Some little way outside the village we arrive at an ancient English home, sentinelled by poplars and standing well back from the road. Here in the afternoon of a typical December day, the early lambs were skipping, while the trees, stripped by the rinders, made a delightful foreground to the massive form and russet colourings of the farm-house and its lichened-covered outbuildings: the effect was really big and romantic.

With these notes upon the eastern side of the peninsula, it will be convenient, in describing the western and more central districts, to shift my position, and I shall make Bosham my base instead of Selsey.

Bosham is a fishing village on the northern shore of Chichester Harbour; the branch of the estuary on which it is situated is called Bosham Creek. The parish includes the tongue or spit of land which, bounded by this creek on the one hand, is washed on the other by the most easterly part of the harbour which runs up to Appledram Sluice. The whole of this harbour is noted for its fish—at one time the Chichester oysters ranked next to Whitstable natives in the market. These fisheries have experienced strange fortunes and varied vicissitudes, which told would make an interesting narrative; but the threatened introduction of Chichester sewage matter, even in its purified and filtrated condition, is likely to prove the most serious blow, should it actually take place, that the Bosham fisheries have sustained; and indeed the fortunes of the village generally cannot but be seriously affected by it, though if the Hermite system of purifying sewage filth by an electrical current, which has proved so successful at Havre, be adopted, the fisher-folk may perhaps rest in peace.

St. Wilfred, of whom I have written in connection with Selsey, extended his proselytising zeal to Bosham, and a monastery was founded here. In later years, Earl Godwin, probably using covert threats to gain his end, induced the Archbishop of Canterbury to convey to him the manor of Bosham, which until then was an archiepiscopal appendage. The story of the wily Earl's method of acquiring the manor, though it has a suspicious flavour of monkish inventiveness about it, is so excellent that it is quite worth repeating. Godwin on the occasion of a ceremonial presentation to the Archbishop, is said to have substituted for the customary formula " Da mihi basium," by which the kiss of peace was bespoken, the words " Da mihi Boseam." The Archbishop, unsuspecting, answered " Do tibi basium," and Godwin and his retainers affecting to have heard " Boseam " where " basium " was uttered, proceeded forthwith to Bosham and took possession of it.

Harold had a residence here; the present Manor House probably marks its site. In the Bayeux tapestry Harold is shown on horseback, as he is about to set out from Bosham for

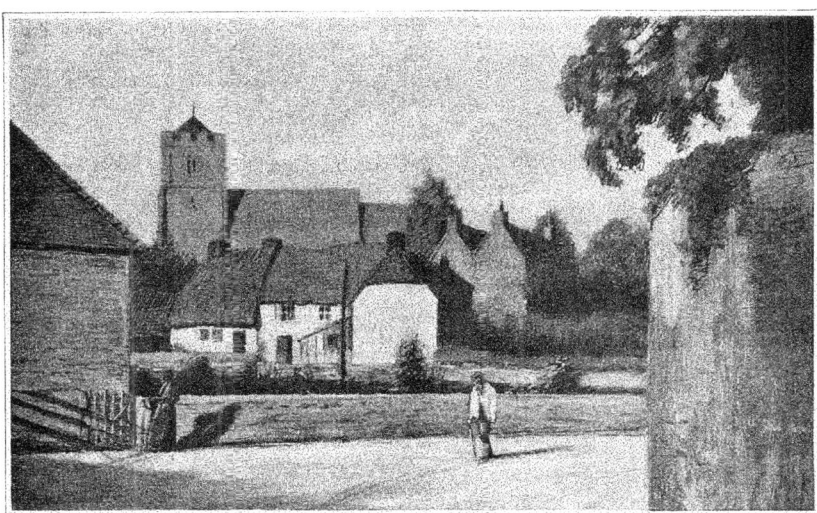

FELPHAM. BY G. LÉON LITTLE.

Normandy. Above is the legend: " Harold dux Anglor et sui milites equitant ad Bosham." This visit was to prove a memorable one for Harold. It was then that he made the unhappy compact, whereby he promised to hold England in fee for William—the first act in the drama which culminated in the battle near Hastings. A little more than a century later tragedy was again associated with Bosham: Herbert de Bosham, Thomas-à-Becket's private secretary, being forced to witness the murder of his master at Canterbury Cathedral.

That Bosham to-day has high claims to picturesque beauty is evidently the opinion of a noble army of painters; for apart from the well-known men who either live and work there, or have lived and worked there, painters of all sorts and conditions have hugged its shores during the last few years. It may be taken almost for granted, that any large exhibition of paintings held in London will contain one or more pictures of the harbour. Unfortunately these pictures—those, that is to say, by painters who imagine fondly that they can extract the sentiment of a place by pouncing down upon it hawk-like and carrying away *motifs* in their talons—are of a stereotyped character. There is a favourite spot from which to paint Bosham; it is situated somewhere above Gosport in the direction of Southwood farmhouse. The village comes as a fine line, the buildings mass effectively, though it is certain the spot so often selected is not the best that could be chosen. Moreover this view has greater possibilities for the painter when the tide is low and the creek is a mass of green "slob" and goldy-brown "wrack"; or when blocks of ice covered with snow float or stand exposed in it.

Bosham, however, is -like Melrose: if you would view it aright, you must view it by the pale moonlight. I have not yet seen an entirely successful moonlight picture of the village; nor do I think such a picture would touch the highest expression of romantic and poetic art. The soul of this beautiful district, æsthetically considered, lies elsewhere. A Rousseau or a Daubigny would not have rested content, had fate sent him to Bosham, until he had given pictorial interpretation to certain subtile, though scarcely obviously beautiful effects, which have so far evaded all the painters who have worked in and about the village. It is no disparagement to the local distinguished painters, to whose high attainments I have frequently testified, to say this. They put such effects religiously behind them; they know full well that they are too fleeting and depend too much upon the memory to be interpreted by any method save that of the romanticist.

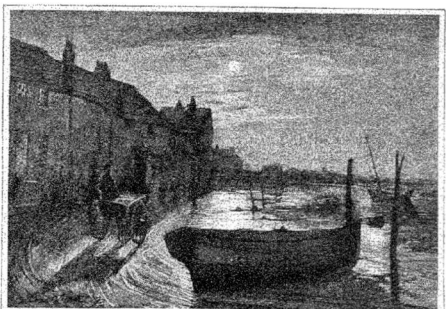

BOSHAM BY MOONLIGHT. BY G. LÉON LITTLE.

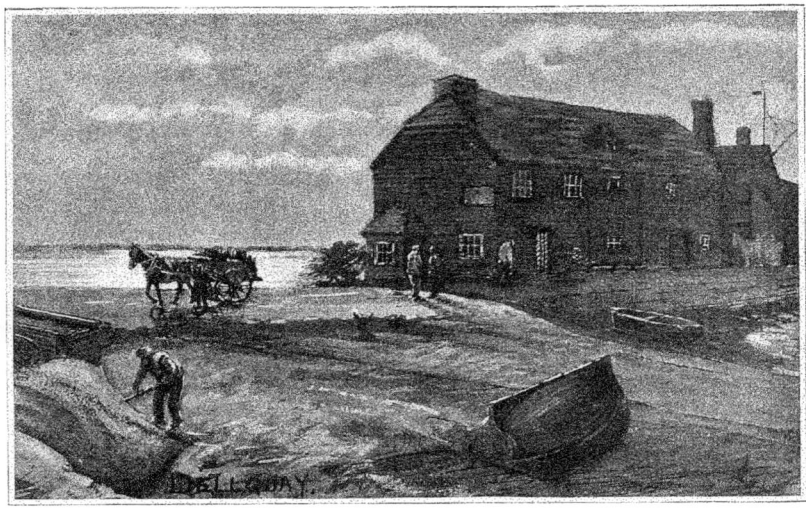

DELLQUAY. BY G. LÉON LITTLE.

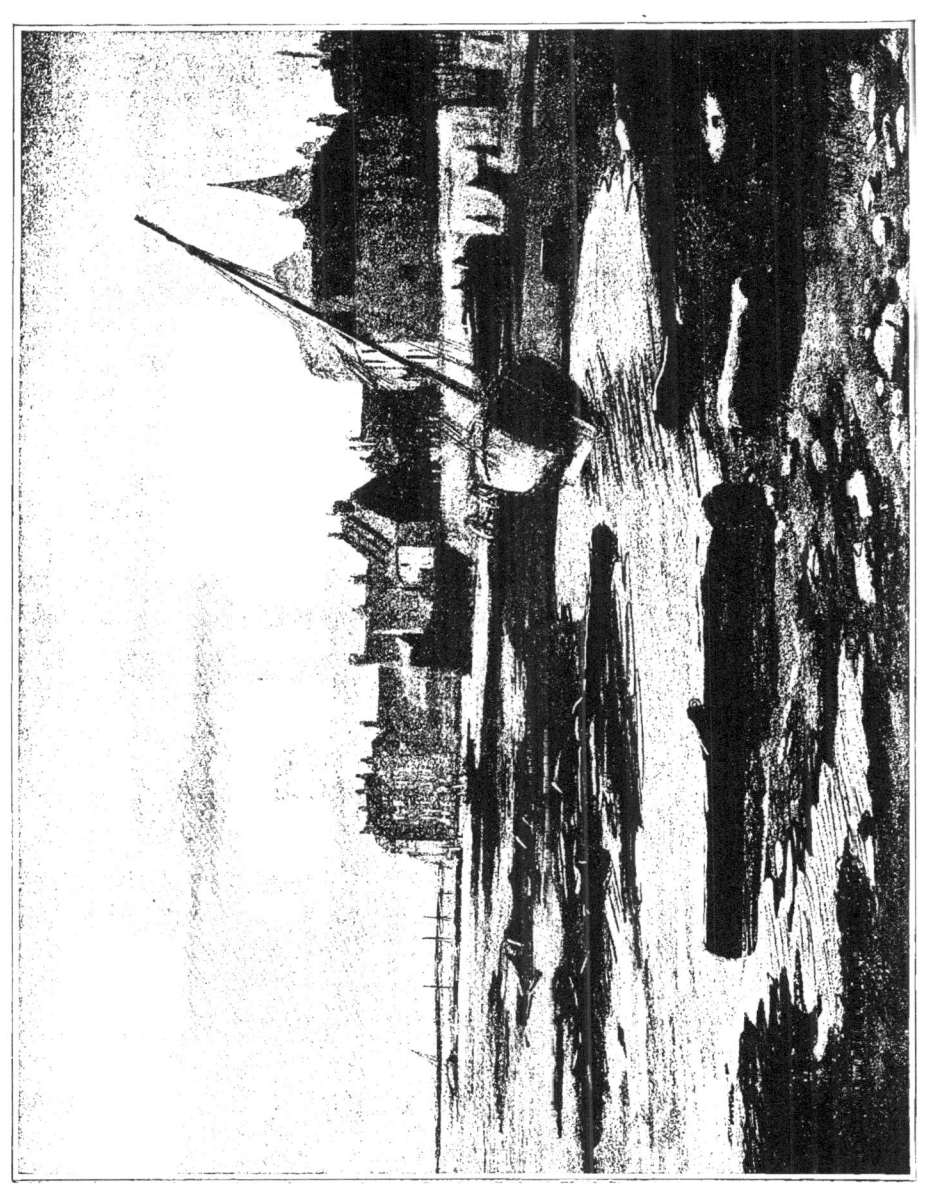

Bosham Harbour. From a Drawing by G. Léon Little.

THE SELSEY PENINSULA.

Several of these effects are burnt into the tablets of my mind. Of these none were more beautiful than those which I saw along the foreshore of the estuary which faces Itchenor, and upon the marge of the water from Itchenor itself round the coast in the direction of Birdham. On the Itchenor side there is an oak copse, the trees coming down to the shore, when the tide is high the waves break on the sandy soil about their roots, crumbling the earth away. Twisted into all manner of grotesque shapes, bleached by the sea and sun, these roots bring faint suggestions of the bones of a giant race.

Further afield is Fishbourne mill-pond. Here the yellowing reeds fringe the salt marshes on the other side of the dam, and a low embankment faced with chalk cubes takes one to Dellquay, to Appledram, and Birdham; to Donington with its Early English church, approached by an avenue of trees with a fine vista beyond; Hunston, unattractive as to its church, but with a suggestive house and pond by way of redemption; North Mundham, prosperous-looking, and in the churchyard some of those artistic grave-stones of the last century in which the burial-grounds of this district are so rich: Bosham, Puntington, Thorney Island, have some especially handsome ones. Rumboldswyke, with its pleasant Georgian houses and quaint inn; Prinstead, which also preserves some ancient dwellings— I must pass them all rapidly in survey. At Chidham traditions of the Tichbornes, who once owned the manor, still linger. The Manor House, a delightful elm-embowered place, boasts a ghost of nearly three centuries standing, while there is a family of fruit-growers, the Hacketts, in the parish, which family has held on to the same orchards for six centuries. Chidham is as lovely a hamlet as any in the county. It has an old-world inn, presided over by a jovial giant, somewhat deaf, but not too deaf to appreciate a joke, for on occasion he can be full of boisterous good-humour. He would make an excellent model for the gentleman whose knees Jack of the fairy tale loosened; while his wife, as handsome an old dame as ever wore a sun-bonnet, looks as if she had stepped out of one of Randolph Caldicott's pictures. Lordington, the home of a well-known naval hero, is redolent of the Poles and of the unhappy Countess of Salisbury. The Cardinal's fine house still stands, though shorn of its fair proportions. The oak staircase, ornamented with the floral emblem of the Tudors, the wainscoted walls, and the remains of the elm avenue, which once stretched up to Marden, suggest melancholy reflections. So, indeed, does Racton hard by, the quondam home of the Counters. Their mansion has entirely disappeared. The family were ardent adherents of the Stuarts, and within a few yards of the church, in a labourer's cottage, the royal arms are still to be seen in an upper room. It was here, on the 13th of October, 1651, Charles II. slept, on his way to the coast, after his defeat at Worcester.

All this county watered by the Ems is very beautiful; though toward the Downs at Kingley Bottom the villages are less attractive. . Kingley Bottom, with its British camp, brings us to Funtington, the home of the grand old Admiral of the Fleet, Sir Provo W. Parry Wallis, who died here on February the 13th, 1892, in his 101st year. And that recalls to me that, although I leave this district with the tantilising feeling that I have only been able to hint at its attractions, still everything must come to an end. The country I have covered is full of beauty, but this beauty must be sought out. It is the country for a good pedestrian and a patient investigator. To him it will disclose all manner of beautiful scenes. And if he arrive at Bosham in the early winter, let him take his way at sundown to the embankments along the back beach. This is "flight time," and here he will find the wily sportsmen crouching behind chalk wall and long grass, watching for the birds to fly over from the fields to forage for food among the wrack and slob left by the tide. Cormorants, locally called shags, sitting on stones dodge for the eels; ospreys, terns, sand-pipers, plovers, wild duck, and wild geese, land-birds and sea-birds, in great variety, congregate to make their evening meal; and the newcomer, having made acquaintance with a scene of exquisite loveliness, will find, if he be at all emotional, exhaustion has set in, and for that day will not pursue his investigations further.

JAMES STANLEY LITTLE.

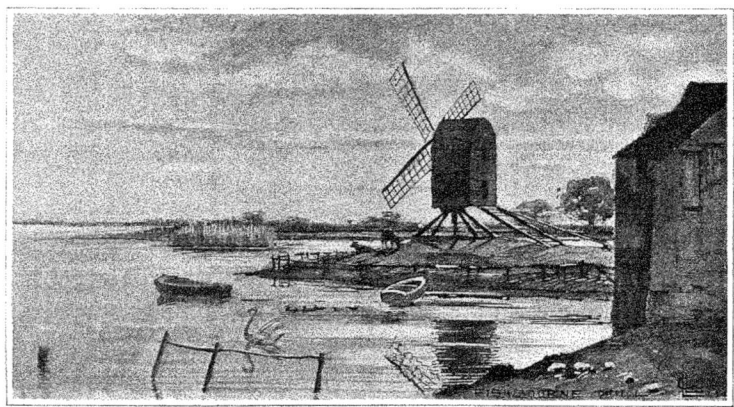

FISHBOURNE MILL. BY G. LÉON LITTLE.

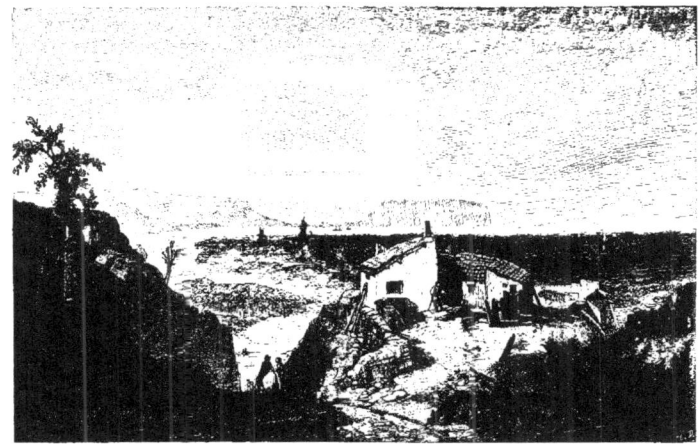

ALUM BAY. BY J. B. PYNE. ENGRAVED BY C. DIETRICH.

THE HENRY TATE COLLECTION.*

SOME years ago I saw at the Salon a picture called 'Le Vieux Monde qui s'en va.' I have forgotten who it was by, and its interest lay rather in conception than execution. A weary, weather-beaten old church stood in its over-crowded *cimetière*. Its long roof undulated like the sea, its walls and tower sloped this way and that, the cross upon the gable hung far out of the perpendicular, and the signs that man had long ceased to cherish and renew the structure were repeated in the

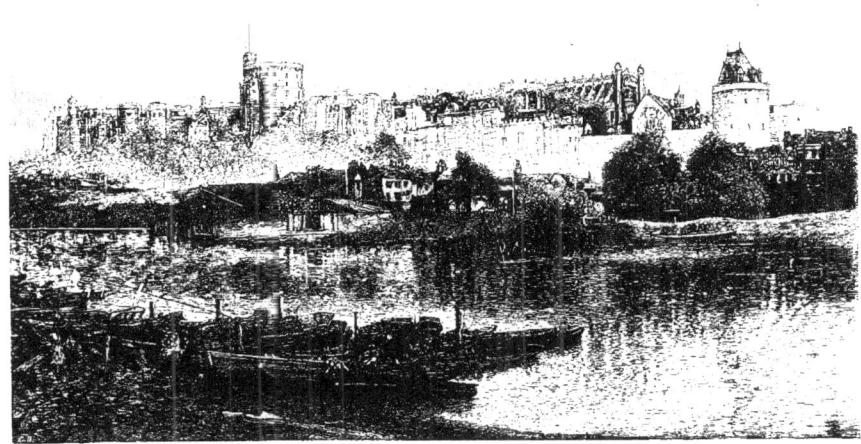

WINDSOR. BY ALFRED HUNT, R.W.S. ENGRAVED BY C. DIETRICH.

* Continued from page 4 and page 34.
1894.

tombs decaying in its shadow. The generations which had worshipped and been carried to their rest within its precinct had disappeared, and their children had simply turned their backs upon it, and gone off elsewhere to crowd round some more up-to-date symbol.

If you look at Mr. Alfred Hunt's drawing of Windsor Castle you may feel inclined to exclaim, "Le Vieux Monde," but, unless you are a very cynical person, you will not add "qui s'en va." It would be difficult to think of any other palace which can rival Windsor for the expression of utility, in its noblest sense, into which it has grown. Human life, with its various needs, peeps out all over it, and its mere outline proclaims the ease with which some five-and-twenty successive generations have grafted their wants upon each other. No revolutions have left their mark upon it. It has been the victim of no *volte face* in ideas. No clean sweep has left it bare. One accretion has succeeded another, and if those in authority have not always shown the finest taste—that would be a great deal too much to expect—they have at least been imbued with the *genius loci*, with the instinctive, half-conscious sense, that the continuity of English history should be reflected in the home of the English Sovereign. Many of us have learnt only lately that the Queen lives at Windsor not as Queen of England, but as head of the Order of the Garter. Even that would give her tenure the very respectable age of five hundred years, and would illustrate the peculiar conservatism which distinguishes certain sides of English life.

An interesting essay might be written on the way in which the conservative and the revolutionary spirits alternate, as it were, in the national ideas of France and England. As a rule, I fancy, the Frenchman is conservative where the Englishman is prone to experiment, and *vice versâ*. Where will you find anything that changes less than life in Paris? Not only does it preserve its ways from year to year, it has little contemporary variety. Go into the restaurant most in vogue on the Boulevard, and then work your way down through them all until you get to a half-franc dinner in Belleville—you will have travelled from spotless linen to none at all, from silver to pewter, from a dozen dishes to two, from a deferential civility which four revolutions have done little to impair, to a mere natural *bonhomie;* but you will have had no violent transitions on the way. The two *dames du comptoir* will have become fused into one; the *maître d'hôtel*, the *sommelier*, and the *garçon*, will have shrunk into a single specimen of the last-named animal, but the *cadre* of the whole thing is on the Rue St. Antoine what it is on the Boulevard des Italiens, or in the Place Favart. And so with time. It takes an old man to remember any real change in Parisian habits. The theatres, the restaurants, the domestic fashions are much what they were fifty years ago. Putting aside purely material developments (like the electric light), the only conspicuous domestic change I can remember—which means, in thirty years—is the adoption of the English fashion of dressing for dinner. That came about suddenly enough. In 1870 it was confined to the upper classes at home. In 1875 it was universal on the Boulevard. London, on the other hand, changes like a weather-cock. Any one who has been away from it ten years would scarcely know it to-day. The ways of society live on change. In the churches, the theatres, the hotels, the restaurants, as well as in private houses, fashion supersedes fashion with the rapidity of the patterns in a kaleidoscope. It is just the same when you come to decorative art. A French interior of to-day—putting aside the vagaries of a few very rich men—shows practically no change from one of half a century ago. It is marked by the same tasteful use of rather tasteless things, by the same curious commingling of audacity with cowardice, of skill in disposition with poverty of invention. In England we have passed through all sorts of stages since the Mother of Exhibitions closed her doors in 1851. An average London drawing-room has been half-a-dozen things since that date, her Paris sister has remained what she was.

What, in the name of relevance, you may ask, has all this to do with Mr. Tate's benefaction? Well, what I want to point out is that one of the sudden transpositions of character between the Anglo-Saxon and the Gaul occurs at the point of junction between decorative and expressive Art, between the Art which has to be applied, and the Art which obeys no conditions except those carried in its own bosom. As a decorator, the French painter is conservative to the backbone; as an expresser, he is a revolutionist, admiring the new for its newness, and insulting the old for its age. The phases in French picture-painting are like the stripes in a Neapolitan ice, and just as you forget the strawberry stripe when you get to the vanilla, so David has no purchase on a palate occupied with Degas. In England it is not so in anything like the same degree. To those who paid their shillings at the Academy in 1850 it seemed, no doubt, as if the 'Childhood of Mary Virgin' and the 'Carpenter's Shop' marked a wiping of the dish, a wiping it and turning it upside down. But to us, who enjoy a better perspective, it is not difficult to see that the operation was not so drastic as its authors believed. Practically, pre-Raphaelism amounted to nothing more than a new theory as to the age at which an artist should give himself his head. The outcome of it was not a new Art, but better foundations for the old. English painting had merely recoiled to get a better spring. The consequence of all this is that our development has had a peculiar continuity. The somersaults which the schools of Italy, Germany, the Low Countries, and even Spain, have learnt from the French, have only been repeated here by individuals, or at best by small coteries. Our way of doing things does not lend itself to audacity, does not lead to exciting exhibitions, but perhaps the one artistic virtue which outlasts all fashions—the virtue of sincerity in expressing æsthetic emotion—is better served.

The illustrations to this article are mainly landscapes, and landscapes of the school founded rather on the early practice of Turner than on Constable's more selective dealings with nature.

The earliest in date is, I suppose, Linnell's 'Anglers.' It belongs to a time in his career before predilections had crystallised into mannerisms. Linnell's art was never great enough to justify extravagance in speaking of it. At his best he handled inherited conventions with some skill and much force. At his worst he was a hot and hasty mannerist, only redeemed from insignificance by his fanatical sincerity. Judged by any objective test, nothing could be much worse than most of the pictures he painted during the last twenty years of his life. They are disagreeable in colour and texture, and conventional in design. It is by the force of character, the power of concentration in the man behind them, that our interest is roused. On the other hand, John Baker Pyne, a cleverer mannerist than Linnell, sinks far below his level through want of sincerity. His manner is a pose, without root in conviction. The example of his work engraved on the previous page, 'Alum Bay,' is not characteristic, however. It must have been painted on a day when his belief in himself had run very low. The second Linnell, 'Contemplation,' is injured by the figure from which it takes

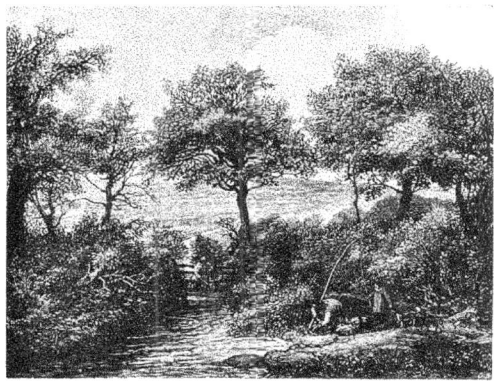

THE ANGLERS. BY JOHN LINNELL. ENGRAVED BY C. DIETRICH.

its title. This is in the wrong place, and *looks* out of scale. I once was present in the studio of a landscape painter when another painter, much higher in the artistic hierarchy, came in to see his picture for the Academy. It was a woodland scene, with an important figure in the foreground. The great man stood before the canvas, and praised the figure. "It's the best I ever saw of yours, well drawn, good in movement, a capital figure; *I should take it out if I were you!*" How often ought the same advice to be given in similar circumstances?

That seems a cruel question to ask when the next picture to be talked about is a landscape full of figures, but in Mr. Peter Graham's 'Rainy Day' they are so numerous that, if it came to "taking out," the thing to decide would be whether the figures or the landscape should go. How grateful we should be if some one would paint Scottish scenery *dry*. We laugh at the French because they make every Englishman lanky, long-toothed, long-whiskered, and yellow-headed, but they are only doing what our painters always do with the scenery of London and Scotland. London has the reputation of its fogs and smoke, Scotland of its mists and rain. And so, on canvas, we are allowed to see them under no other aspect. In the Western Highlands I have enjoyed, for weeks together, weather as brilliant, as blazing with colour, as that of Egypt. London has an unrivalled spell of glory from about the middle of May to the middle of June—the May, in fact, of the unreformed Calendar—when you may spend a morning in a walk from Hampstead Heath to Westminster, going by Primrose Hill, Regent's Park, Hyde Park, the Green Park, and St. James's Park, through a succession of beauties which, so far as I know, no city in the world can beat. Brilliance is an "effect" just as much as another. It demands more equipment, of course, than smoke or mist, but all the more should it have its turn. It would be unfair, however, to find fault with Mr. Graham for painting what he wants to. He has as much right to be faithful to mists and rain as De Hooch or Cuyp had to see things only in sunlight. So that what we must wish for is a painter who will make the brilliant side of things in our various island his speciality.

Mr. Alfred Hunt's 'Windsor' and the late Mr. Vicat Cole's 'Surrey Landscape' belong entirely to the old little-selective, non-impressionistic school of landscape. Painting of this sort makes a comparatively slight demand upon the faculties of observation and æsthetic organization. Its aim is to put down on canvas as many of the facts which contribute to the objective beauty of any chosen scene as the conditions will allow. It bears much the same relation to the dominant style of the day as the old-fashioned novel, which followed the hero from his birth to his wedding day, does to the short story. One feels before a picture by Mr. Hunt or Mr. Cole that their impulse came, not from a prevision of what they were going to *make*, but from a desire to *reproduce*. The distinction may appear over-subtle, but it embodies the whole difference, in principle, between such work as theirs and that, for instance, of Corot.

In writing of a collection of pictures formed by an amateur

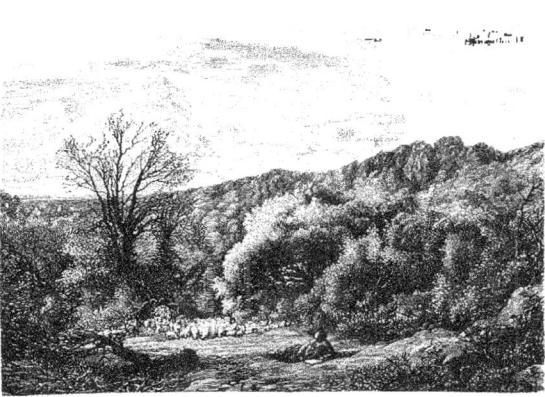

CONTEMPLATION. BY JOHN LINNELL. ENGRAVED BY C. DIETRICH.

and presented by him to the State, the critic is at a great disadvantage; at so great a disadvantage, perhaps, that many would say he should not do it at all. When I began these papers* I intended to confine myself as far as possible to

* See THE ART JOURNAL for 1893.

description, leaving readers to form their own conclusions as to the value of Mr. Tate's benefaction. It has been impossible, however, to avoid overstepping this boundary now and then. One thing that has induced a certain amount of criticism is the conviction, unhappily forced on all Writers upon Art, that whenever they leave what they have to say in the least degree indefinite, the Art-practitioner will read all the nonsense into it he can. The whole attitude of the studio to the study is unreasonable. The average painter has two articles of belief about the critic. They may be fairly summed up thus :—

1. The painter paints. The critic studies Art.

be tarred with one stick. But just as there are painters who take their Art seriously, who live rather to create than to enjoy the loaves and fishes that creation brings in, so there are critics who live to accumulate knowledge about Art, to educate their eyes and to develop the catholicity of their appreciations. Take two individuals of equal powers and set them to study Art, one as a painter, the other as a critic; the one as trainer of eye and hand together in a narrow field, the other as trainer of eye alone in a field as wide as Art itself; how will they stand after a given time? The obvious answer to the question is the true answer, and the one borne out by experience. Put

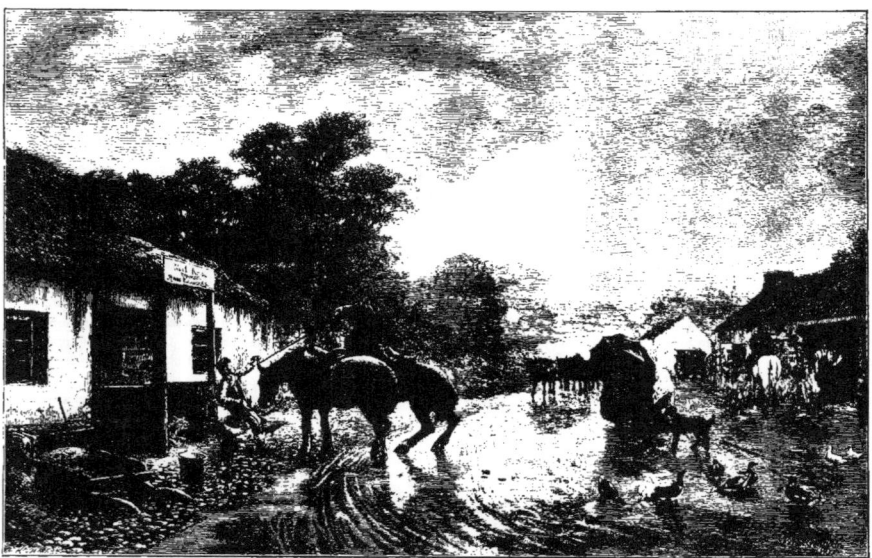

A RAINY DAY. BY PETER GRAHAM, R.A. ENGRAVED BY W. & J. R. CHESHIRE.

Ergo, the painter knows more about Art than the critic.

2. All Art critics are born duffers.

We have lately seen an artist for whom we all have a real affection, repeat with a more savage gusto the old libel that the critics are those who have failed in literature and Art. Every one knows that it is not true. Every one knows, or would know if he gave himself the smallest trouble to think, that the hack scribbler about the exhibitions writes on pictures simply because he can get money for doing it; that is for precisely the same reason as the hack painter paints. Both alike are hangers-on to the legitimate Art army, and both deserve to

these two men before a picture; the first will give you the better answer to the question, "Is the author of that a thoroughly trained painter?" the second to the question, "Is he an artist?" With equal powers it is all a matter of experience, unless we are to accept the vulgar fallacy that Art is a feat, and that the value of an artistic result depends on the difficulty with which it is brought about. In that case you must go on and declare that only poets can appreciate poems or novelists novels, or dancers dancing, or cooks a dinner. I must reserve Mr. Riviere's picture, 'Running the Gauntlet,' for discussion in the next article.

WALTER ARMSTRONG.

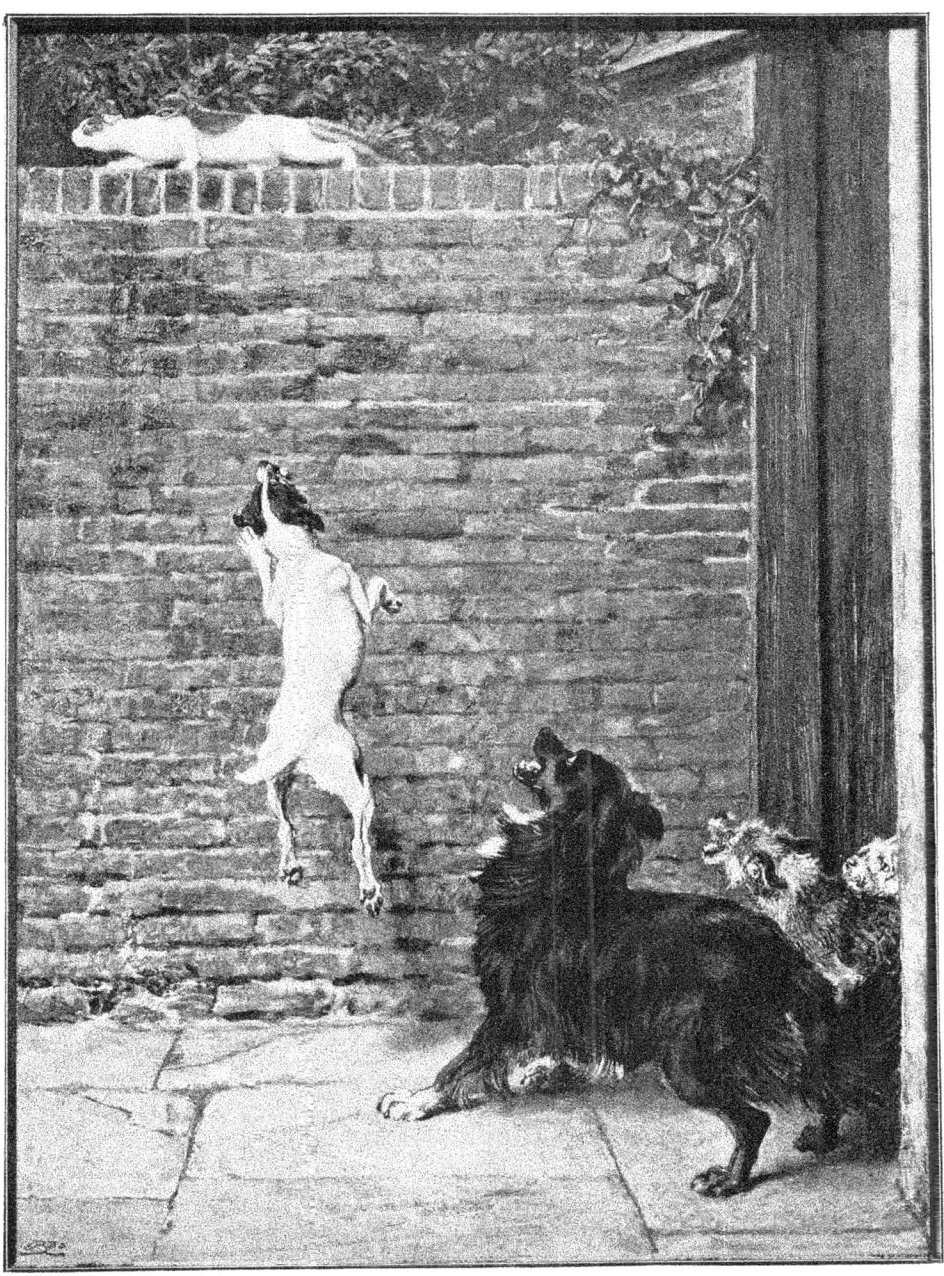

RUNNING THE BLOCKADE.
FROM THE PICTURE BY BRITON RIVIERE, R.A.
In the Henry Tate Collection.

"FANS OF JAPAN."

FANS play a part in the social life, the symbolism, the industries and the arts of Japan which has little parallel in the history or the uses of the fan in Europe. They were the instruments of industry used for winnowing and for blowing the forge; the baton of the general and of the umpire in the great athletic and wrestling contests; the insignia of priests, the indispensable accessory of the temple dancer, as of the Geisha. They were used to distinguish the rank of emperor and of empress, and were carried in various set forms and designs by nobles, physicians, courtiers, court ladies, and by men and women of every degree. They had not originally, as indeed few things if any had which were in use in Japan, a purely decorative origin or object. For in the far East, pure ornament, constructed for ornament's sake, hardly existed; and in this, as in the whole range of decorative Art objects in Japan, use and construction were the initial objects held in view, while decoration was applied as a natural and unforced sequence or corollary. Mrs. Salwey has done well, therefore, to treat this fertile and interesting subject in an extensive monograph.*

Her work is marked by adequate research, and it is careful and correct; it has been revised by so excellent an authority as Professor Anderson, and is liberally illustrated by examples selected from many of the best English collections.

Fans were introduced into Japan about the sixth century, together with many other products of Chinese civilisation, from the Korea. These early Chinese fans were hand screens of the oblong or semicircular shape, or of the well-known fiddle shape traversed by a midrib extending downwards to form the stem. This is still a common pattern in China.

Many centuries afterwards the Japanese invented the folding-paper fan, an invention which was speedily re-exported to China, and has spread thence to the Western world. The warrior carried into battle his fan of iron, either made screen-shaped in one piece or with folding ribs. The common soldier's fan was a folding ribbed weapon, decorated always with the blood-red setting sun upon a black background. The general's baton was an oblong fan in hard-hammered iron, a formidable weapon of offence or defence, and used as such, in case of need, as more than one tradition tells.

Fans carried by gentlemen, especially those of serious occupation, were very plain in material, mounted on delicate ribs of fine hard cedar or pine wood, uncoloured. The fan face was of ivory-coloured strong paper, often painted by the most celebrated artists of the courtly or religious schools of Tosa and Kano, with heroes, dignitaries, and classical persons, displaying scenes celebrated in history or song. The greatest artists did not disdain to decorate these fans: Korin, Kenzan, Kano-Masanobu, and Motonobu—names to conjure with in the history of Japanese pictorial art—ranked themselves among fan painters. There are some beautiful specimens extant of the work of Hokusai as a fan painter. This, the artistic side

* "Fans of Japan." Charlotte M. Salwey. Kegan Paul, Trench & Co. 1894.

of the question, is not very fully treated in Mrs. Salwey's monograph; the best specimen illustrated is a slight but delicately touched fan face by Kano Sanroku, but we should have gladly seen among the illustrations many of the beautiful fan designs and paintings by Hokusai, by Korin, and by Kano artists from private collections, such as were exhibited at the Japan Society's rooms last year, and some of which have since been illustrated elsewhere.

One of the most interesting fan forms is that of the ceremonial fan of the priests and of the dancers of the Nô dramas. Such fans were so constructed that when closed the ribs were in contact, but the fan face remained slightly open; this is known as the *tchuki*. The Geisha's, or public dancer's fan, was always a very showy affair, generally with rich gold or scarlet background and boldly-outlined decoration of flowers or birds, so that it could be well seen from a distance during its profuse and graceful use in the pantomimic posturing which constitutes a Japanese dance.

It is impossible within a limited space to illustrate or even to enumerate the still-existing uses of the fan in Japan. When a gentleman pays his visit he carries a small but elegant fan in his girdle, and makes his first salutation as he kneels on the floor by laying his fan in front of him; any little present is handed wrapped in the present paper, tied with its emblematic threads, on the half-opened fan. The fan covers a cough or hides a sneeze; the innkeeper presents his parting guest with a fan, often bearing either a view of his house and the surrounding scenery or a prettily-worded verse of compliment and thanks, or just an ornamental writing of his name and address. The Geisha presents her fan to her friend and admirer as the final proof of her favour; one such fan, a present from the leading dancer of Tokio to an English connoisseur, was shown on the occasion of Mrs. Salwey's paper at the Japan Society, and is mentioned but not illustrated in the text. It is described as a gorgeously-coloured maple fan. Autograph fans have of course long been in use in a country where writing is performed with a paint-brush, and where high accomplishment in caligraphy is as much esteemed as painting itself. To ask a lady to inscribe a verse upon a fan has for centuries been a highly-esteemed compliment, as it is now a common politeness; esteemed in England, however, chiefly for the purposes of fancy fairs.

Advertisement fans have a long historic lineage. When an artist changed his name, as he frequently did at various periods of his career, and on slight provocation, the change was announced to his friends by the presentation of inscribed and autographic fans. Actors and singers took the like means of making known their occupation of a new theatre, their adopt on of a new patronymic, or their latest triumph in the histrionic art. So that "Fans of Japan" may be seen to furnish a subject of no little interest for artistic as for historic research, and Mrs. Salwey's monograph does excellent justice to it.

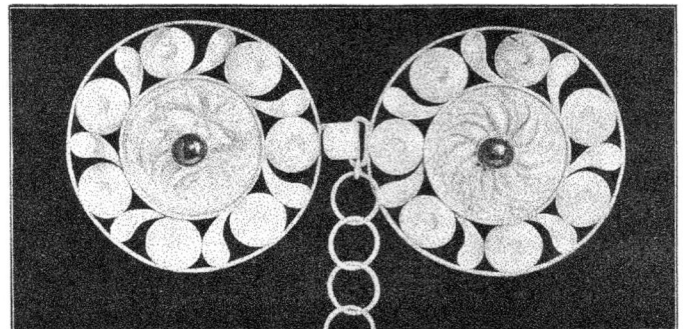

No. 1. Cloak Clasp in Hammered Silver, set with Carbuncles. (Under full-size.)

A LITTLE TALK ON THE SETTING OF STONES.

IN considering the question as to what one is to do in the setting of stones, I think the safest rule to be observed is that one must not bother much about their setting. The treatment of stones in metals should be a matter of feeling, of personal taste, of character. Apart from the technical, and I think less important, question as to whether a stone should be set in a band turned over or in a beaded rim, a clip or a branched cusping, there are a number of matters, more important really, which resolve themselves into artistic predilection. That rose topaz goes well with gold, especially grey gold; that a carbuncle should be polished *en cabochen* and foiled, not faceted and set *à jour*; that amethyst looks vulgar with gold, more particularly coloured gold; that rubies should not be placed by themselves—these and a number of other matters in the setting of stones are not to be reasoned about. Circumstances may come in which they may be reversed, all one can do is to shrug one's shoulders and say—so at least think I. Jewelry is a personal art in more ways than one.

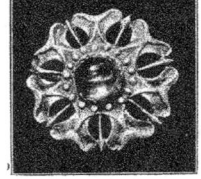

No. 2. Brooch with pale Amethyst set in Silver. (Full-size.)

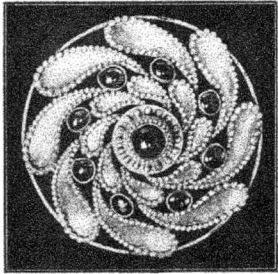

No. 3. Carbuncle Brooch in Silver. (Full-size.)

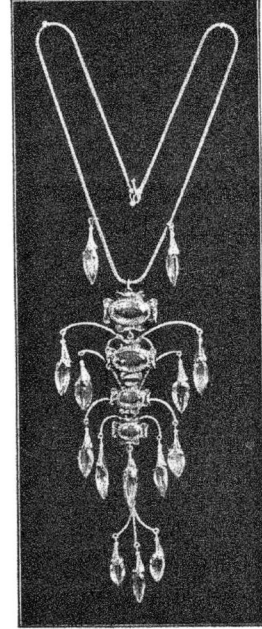

No. 4. Pendant Topaz and Gold Necklace. (Reduced size.)

In the accompanying plates—which of course can give no idea of what is the most important thing of all, *colour*—I give some experiments of work executed from my designs at Essex House, in these different treatments. No. 4 is a pendant topaz necklace, shown reduced size; No. 2, a little amethyst brooch set in silver; No. 1 and No. 3, two treatments of carbuncles, polished *en cabochen*, the one a brooch, the other a cloak clasp. No. 7, two spoons, both under full size, the one set with carbuncles in ivory, the other with a finial in malachite.

As to the arrangement of your setting, you should have your stone or group of stones before you and plan it out. I like to work in one of three ways—either with the pencil, painting curves in plan, section, and elevation

ON THE SETTING OF STONES.

on a piece of paper till I feel the lines I want, the main curves and the big central stone shot forward into prominence; or with a piece of wire shaping curves that flow from one plane into another, and object to paper renderings; or with a piece of wax that will let itself be lovably pinched and petted, and holds the stones affectionately as you develop your work.

No. 5 shows a setting of moonstones and a star sapphire set in wired silver—under full size—and no reproduction can give the beauty of the central stone,—as of a white spider creeping round a world of its own, always revolving and never coming to an end, resting sometimes, but, as soon as you with your moving light start in pursuit, hurrying on again. No. 6 a little medallion portrait in silver, with a border of eighteenth-century grey paste. No. 9 a simple treatment of chrysoprase in silver chains and as a pin. No. 8 a treatment of pearl in hammered silver, and No. 10 a necklace of gold, with blue enamelled violets, and grey pearls of varying sizes in their centres.

One might say, therefore, that in dealing with the setting of stones one should look for three things: *Spontaneity of treatment, good colour arrangement, and intrinsic beauty in the whole scheme without regard to commercial value.*

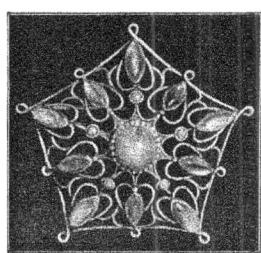

No. 5. STAR SAPPHIRE AND MOONSTONES WITH GREY BLUE ENAMEL, SET IN SILVER WIRE. THE PROPERTY OF MR. R. RATCLIFFE WHITEHEAD.

You must be entirely free and unfettered; you are dealing with the most conventional of all arts, go any way you like to work, twist your material about in any shape you like, use cast, hammered, or wired metal indifferently; and as construction is so slight a matter in jewelry, don't bother much about the "Lamp of Truth," it might put out the fire of your rubies. Be yourself, be spontaneous.

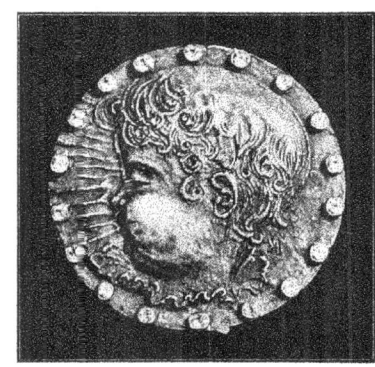

No. 6. SILVER MEDALLION BROOCH. PORTRAIT OF MASTER CECIL LANGHAM, SET WITH EIGHTEENTH-CENTURY GREY PASTE. (UNDER FULL-SIZE.)

As to my second demand, *good colour arrangement.* Get to love your stones, handle them, finger them, play with them, dip them in the water, get to know them intimately in various lights, carry them about in your pocket, look at them at odd moments, look at them on Friday evenings, come and peep at them again on Saturdays, have them out once more on Sundays after dinner, loose one every now and then,—but be an æsthetic miser as regards their colour. I like to think of my stones in the dark, and construct my colour compositions mentally; indeed, make little *mariages de covenance* for them without their knowledge—the fiery ruby with the passionate blue sapphire; the pale amethyst with the twinkling crystal; the dreamy moonstone on its bed of dark grey silver, the milky obsidine in its trembling cup of hammered metal; the fairy carbuncle, which nobody will wear because it is so cheap—the dear good parsons, kind, innocent men, preferring

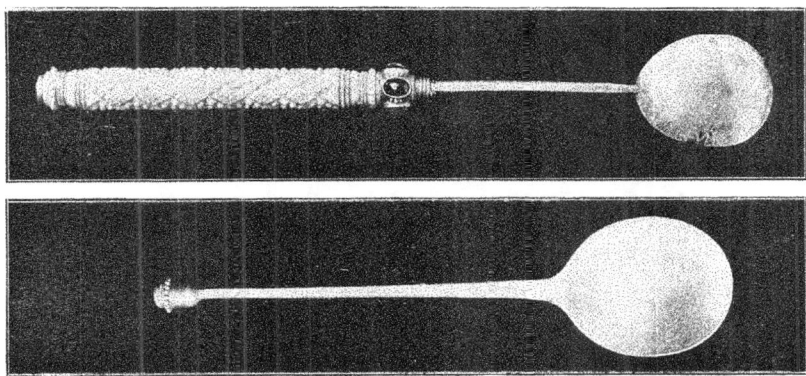

No. 7. SILVER SPOON, WITH POLISHED CARBUNCLES, SET IN IVORY. THE PROPERTY OF MRS. ARTHUR DIXON.
SILVER SPOON, WITH MALACHITE FINIAL. THE PROPERTY OF MRS H. S. ASHBEE.

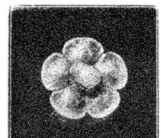

No. 8. TREATMENT OF SMALL GREY PEARL IN HAMMERED SILVER. (FULL-SIZE).

the imitation glass carbuncle, at four times the price—the green prismatic olivine, with the rainbow lights in it on its field of blue enamel, and the glorious opal of a thousand tints.

I have a blue opal (in my collection) that is a perfect fairy tale of beauty. It is deep with all the colours of the sea at mid-day, with the summer sky upon it, and one of my impressionist friends is going to borrow it to paint a seascape on. You've heard of music in a stone? I have thought for a long time how I shall set this glory of colours, and I've modelled two little mænads, with breasts and streaming hair, to go about the bezel of a ring. They have been cast in bronze, and when worked up will be re-cast in silver, then when the ring is finished I shall probably break them up and do them over again. You must be very generous to your stones, and no skinflint of labour, though as chary as you like of showy metal.

No, it is no use. You will not see the beauty of this opal all at once. You must come to it again—it is like an atmospheric effect—new English or otherwise—it needs focussing. You will not understand it for one shilling only, and no catalogue will help you to its colours. Mr. Abraham Booth, from whom most of my best stones come, sits, I believe, for hours in the sun, looking into the infinite abysses of his opals with a magnifying glass, and unless they are on a beautiful woman's neck, I have no doubt but that is the next best place and manner of getting the full enjoyment from them.

You know, I suppose, that there are spirits in stónes—colour demons that mesmerize you; pay them respect enough and they'll speak to you—they will begin to move, to twinkle,

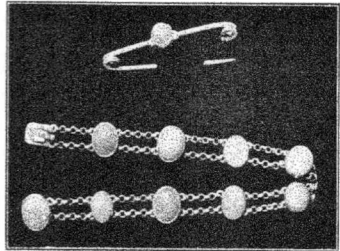

No. 9. CHRYSOPRASE BRACELET AND PIN.

to gesticulate, sometimes even they come out; only beware that you conjure them back again. Every jewel you set must have its colour scheme, every jewel must be treated as a painter would treat his picture.

C. R. ASHBEE.

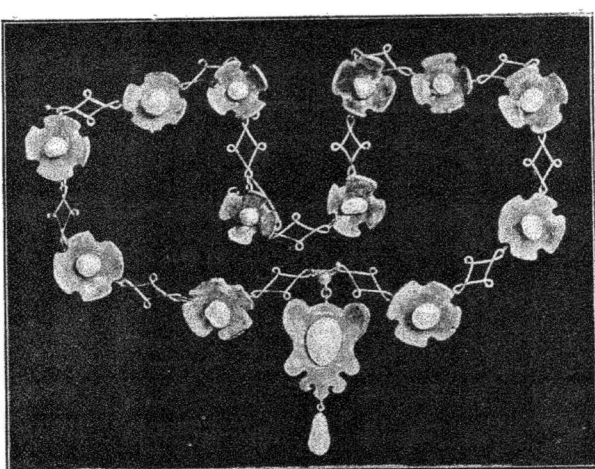

No. 10. NECKLACE OF GOLD, WITH BLUE ENAMEL, SET WITH VARYING GREY PEARLS. THE PROPERTY OF MRS. DAL YOUNG. (HALF FULL-SIZE).

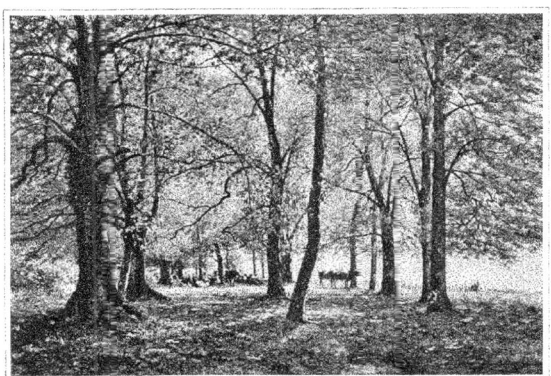

UNDER THE LIME TREES. BY BERNIER. AT THE CHAMPS-ELYSÉES.

THE PARIS SALONS.

AFTER all, the split has not been healed. Less than a twelvemonth ago things promised well; by Christmastide there was a definite prospect of union. But now there is one huge Salon at the Champ de Mars, and another still larger Exposition at the Palais des Champs-Elysées. It would be needless to go into a matter which can have little concern for most English readers; particularly as, like the famous mediæval controversy between the professors of the University of Paris and the monks of the Chapter concerning the actuality of one of two heads produced as the genuine article belonging to S. Denis, there is no end to the claims and counterclaims of the Champ de Marsiens and their rivals of

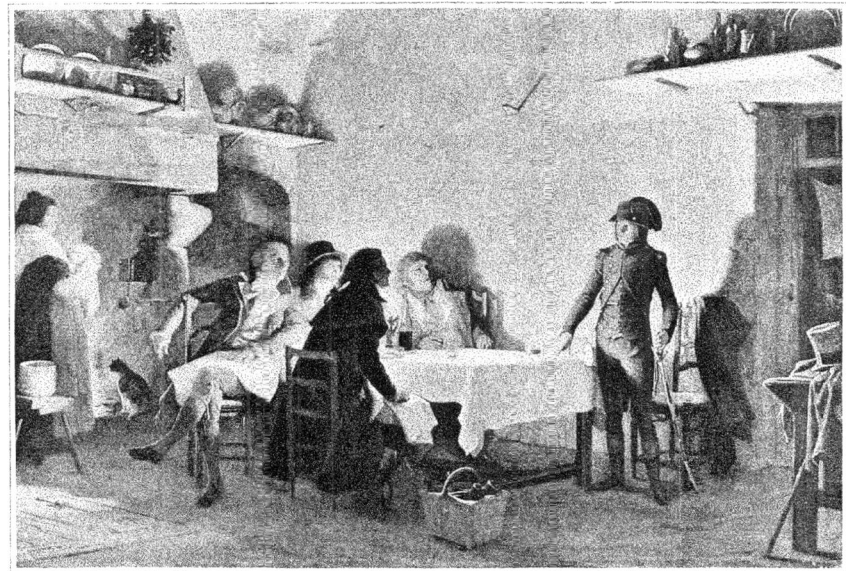

LE SOUPER DE BEAUCAIRE. BY LECOMTE DU NOUY. AT THE CHAMPS-ELYSÉES. (Copyright, 1894, by Lecomte du Nouy.)

the Champs-Elysées, save that which was reached by the puzzled arbiters in the St. Denis dispute, namely that, after all, the saint could have only one head—in other words, one Salon must be right and one wrong, but as neither will admit the possibility of its being wrong, the puzzled outsider may decide for himself at haphazard. It is regretable, however, that the schismatics prevailed. Never has French Art stood more in need of union. Everywhere the stranger is knocking at the doors, knocking as insistently and confidently as Ibsen's Younger Generation, and, moreover, steadily coming nearer and nearer, so that soon even the inner chambers will be inviolate no longer. Every year the contingent of foreigners is greater. This year there is an immigration *en masse* of British, American, Scandinavian, Dutch, Germanic, Slavic, Italian, and Spanish artists in all *genres;* an invasion which is really a serious matter, for already French painting is undergoing something of that decomposing process which has been induced in French literature by alien and Franco-foreign influences. "We haven't got a contemporary literature," wrote an eminent Parisian *littérateur* recently; "what we have is a mass of nondescript books, *c'est un mélange*." "French Art" at the Salons, if not in so dire a strait, is more than ever *un mélange*. Not only is the foreign element conspicuous in a very marked degree, but the influence of certain foreign painters upon their French confrères is unmistakable. I wonder how many pictures, for instance, have appeared at the Salons of the last few years, and now at the two present Expositions, which would never have been painted but for a certain famous canvas which Von Uhde sent from Germany some years ago? From Von Uhde to Jean Béraud is a wide leap : but the pictorial acrobats have achieved the feat. A few who have accepted the spirit, and not acted merely upon the letter, of the "message" of the Saxon painter, have produced good and even notable work : others, who have just stopped short of the insincere and ignoble displays of the painter who is at present so popular with a large section of Salon visitors, have merely expended in a futile quest powers that otherwise utilised might have won them worthier and more sustainable repute. This year we are spared "religious" grotesqueries. Herr Von Uhde himself is represented by a 'Flight into Egypt,' which will attract notice as much by its too assiduous modernity as by its intrinsic æsthetic value ; and his extreme, M. Béraud, has 'On the Way to Calvary' (to be illustrated later), which is sufficiently vulgar and claptrap to impress many people, all the more so that it is undeniably clever and dexterous. But this kind of dexterity in Art is kin to that effort in poetry which is called *tour de force*. In a sense all artistic achievement is a *tour de force;* commonly, the phrase simply indicates that a person has tried to jump beyond his own shadow. The only really fine, austerely simple, and convincing example of what is called religious Art that I can recall at either Salon is a small picture of Christ, by Dagnan Bouveret, at the Champ de Mars, wherein the Saviour is portrayed with absolutely no extraneous aids to sanctity, but is simply and convincingly what in the beautiful old-world phrase He is called, the Brother of Sorrow.

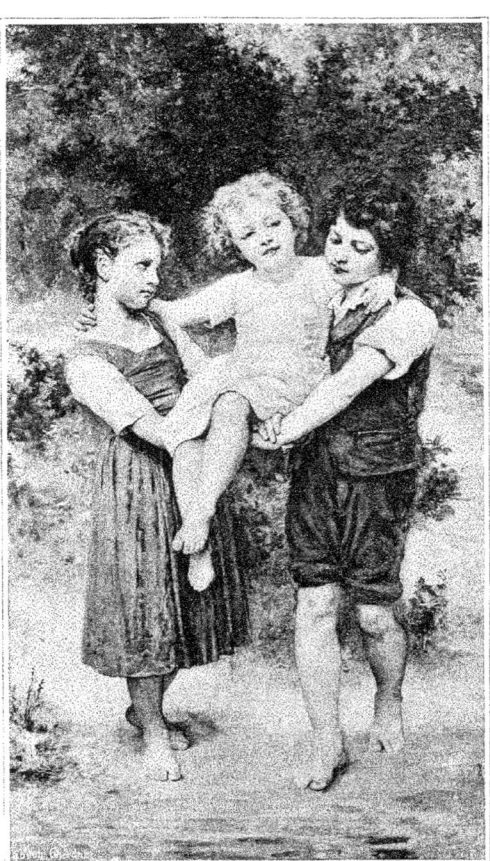

CROSSING THE BROOK. BY ELIZABETH GARDNER. AT THE CHAMPS-ELYSÉES.
(*Copyright, 1894, by Elizabeth Gardner.*)

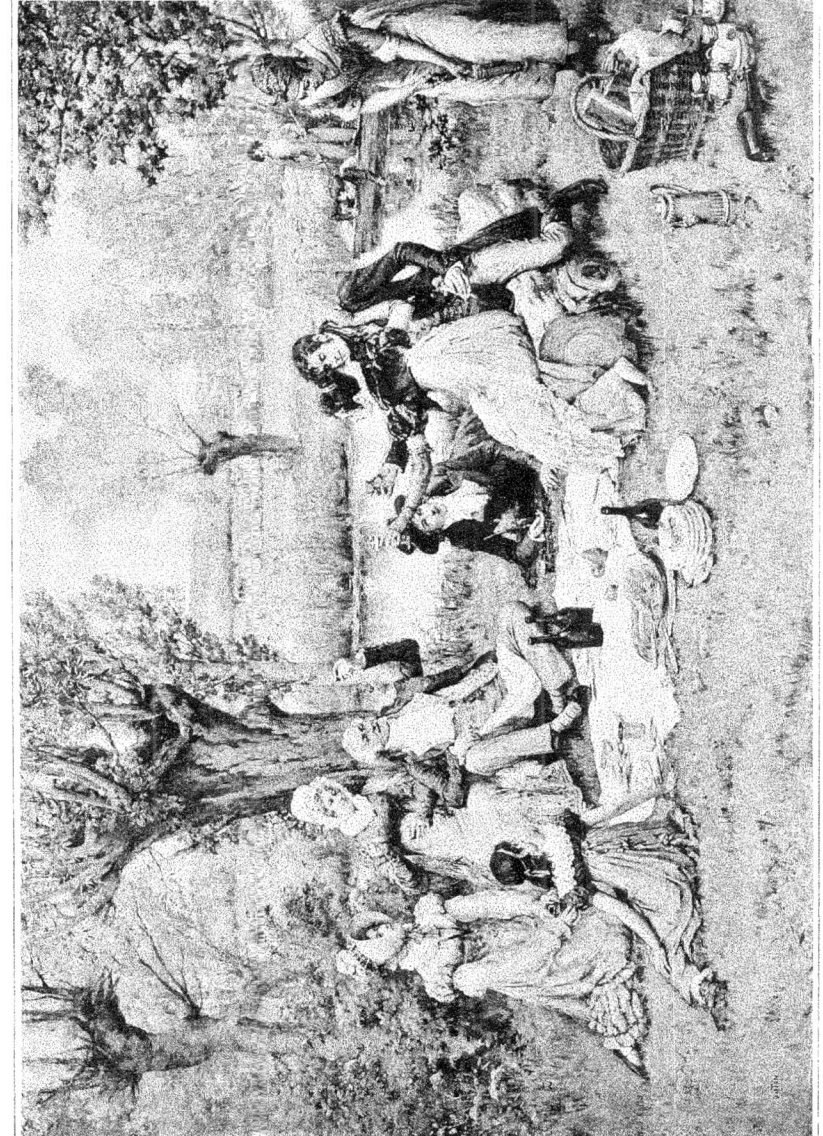

Déjeuner sur l'Herbe. By Pierre Outin. At the Champs-Élysées. (Copyright, 1894, by Pierre Outin.)

Leaving aside for the moment landscape and seascape, the *genres* which we anticipate to see most numerously represented at the Salon are religious pictures, military pictures, sanguinary pictures, and nude pictures. This year expectations will be disappointed. Imagine a Salon—a dual Salon, let us say—without a single notable nude painting, and not very many of a secondary or still inferior quality; with almost as few military as "religious" canvases; with no horrors, and fewer "sanguinosities" than nudities at Burlington House in a Horsleyan year; and Edouard Detaille become a civic illustrator, Bridgman changed into a decorative-designer, and Rochegrosse converted from his passion for bloody feuds to themes of idyllic symbolism, and a manner directly inspired by Claude Monet. It is as though in the year's literature we were to discover scarce a Baudelairien, hardly one Satanique, a few disheartened décadents; as though M. Zola were to emulate Jane Austen, or M. Huysmans to pursue the method of Bulwer Lytton, or M. Jean Richepin to change his skin for a Lewis-Morrisian felt!

There are few scenes of military life at the New Salon. At its rival there are a score or more of pictures which are good. The largest and most ambitious is Rouffet's 'Charge of the Cuirassiers of the Guard at Rézonville,' a highly creditable of this Republican hour (now that the Czar is being regarded somewhat askance, and the several Russian-visit pictures being looked at with suggestive smiles and furtive asides), is painted as Colonel, as General, as Commander of the Army of Italy, as a sentimental friend weeping because one out of a million Frenchmen happened to have his leg shot away, as a braggart trying to impress Pope Pius VI., as victor on the field of battle, as First Consul, as Emperor undergoing coronation, as the little corporal, the little general, the little emperor, the little hero, the little demi-god, till finally he becomes pictorially the little nuisance. But even in number there are not so many Napoleonic pictures as prophesied; in quality they are for the most part quite unnoteworthy. There is not one that remains in the memory as a work of creative power; all have, as it were, been made to order. It is a repetition of the Boulanger boom of a few years ago. Mr. Orchardson's 'Napoleon on the *Bellerophon*' will live longer than the best French picture of the kind either at the Champ de Mars or at the Champs-Elysées. P. Grolleron's dignified, pathetic, and most ably painted 'Saving the Flag' is a large canvas, of which we give an illustration, daringly composed on broad and simple lines, wherein we see a French infantry soldier, known to fame as Sergeant Tanviray, lingering

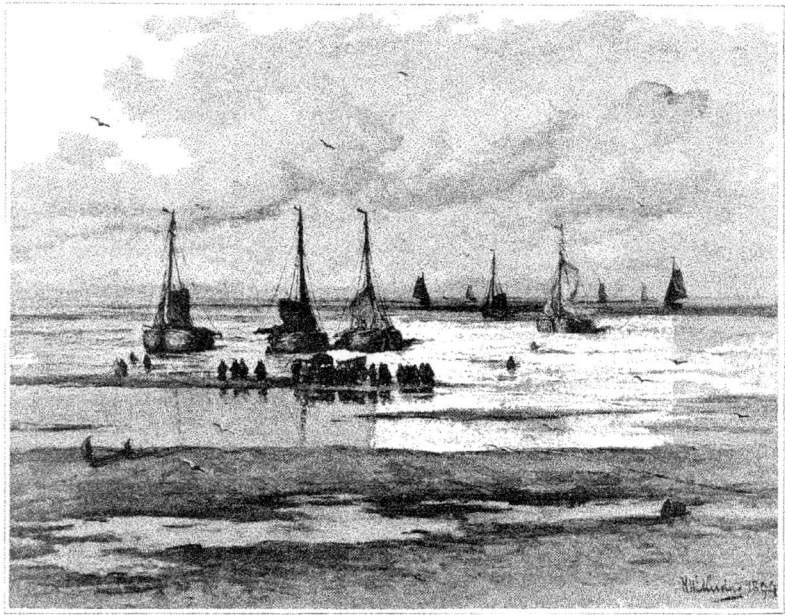

Low Tide. By H. W. Mesdag. At the Champ de Mars.

work of its kind, though surpassed by kindred pictures by Detaille and other war painters in previous Salons. The rumour that a Napoleon boom was to be a feature of the 1894 Salons has been only partially realised. The popular idol among his dead comrades in order to snatch the flag from the death-grip of the standard-bearer, although a score or more of Prussians are rapidly advancing and making him their target as they come, and though his doom is obviously

THE PARIS SALONS.

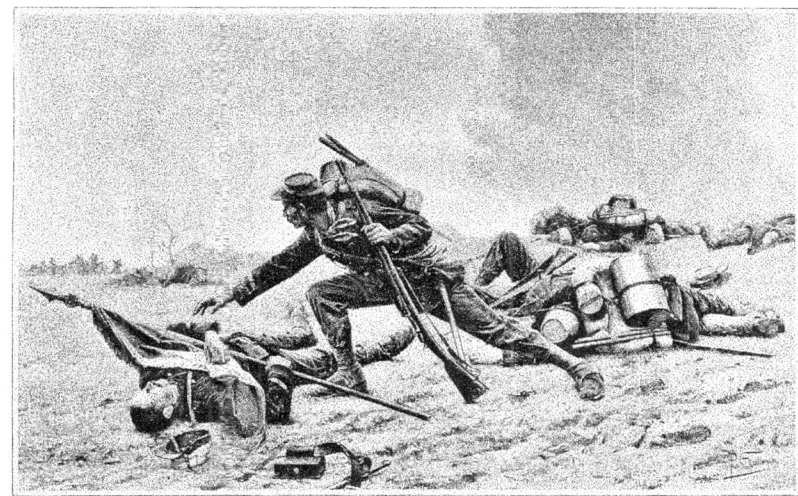

SERGEANT TANVIRAY SAVING THE FLAG. BY P. GROLLERON. AT THE CHAMPS-ELYSÉES. (*Copyright, 1894, by P. Grolleron.*)

almost inevitable. This I should rank as the finest picture of the year in its *genre*.

Besides landscape and seascape and decorative designs, there are the *genres* of "the subject picture," still - life, domestic interiors, and so forth. There is nothing very notable here. Let me mention, therefore, only one or two about which I made a note in connection with their reproduction in this article—M. Lecomte du Nouy's admirably clever 'Souper de Beaucaire,' which depicts an incident in the life of Napoleon that occurred on the 14th of March, 1794, six years before the passage of the Alps. The future Emperor, scarcely twenty-eight years old, is at present a young artillery officer in garrison in the Midi. One evening he finds himself at table with some citizens, who fall into an excited political discussion upon the troublous times, and the terrible crises which the nation has just gone through. Bonaparte has taken his part in the conversation in his haughty and reserved way, and at the moment of leaving the table, as if piercing the veil of the future and foreshadowing his own career, he takes his leave and lets fall these words: "At the right time someone will arise who will unite in his own person all the nation's hopes, and *then* . . . . ." I must also refer to Mdlle. E. Gardner's daintily pretty 'Crossing the Brook' (where the leafy and natural background is painted with delightful delicacy and grace); and a quaint old-fashioned *plein-air* canvas, Outin's 'Déjeuner sur l'Herbe,' where a happy family party are seated on the grass by a stream-side, met to celebrate the return from the honeymoon of the young couple in the middle foreground.

In decorative design we have, however, some of the finest things of the year. M. Puvis de Chavannes displays one of his ablest, if not perhaps most characteristic, mural paintings in his great scheme of decoration for the stairway of the Prefecture at the Hôtel de Ville. After Puvis de Chavannes, special mention must be made of Ecnnat, Bridgman, and

Chartrar, at the Champs - Elysées Salon. Léon Bonnat's ceiling design (for the Hôtel de Ville) will not enhance his reputation. It is meant to signify 'The Triumph of Art.' The lumpy white horse that caracoles under a triumphant youth has the effect upon one of a too great expanse of whitewash in a limited garden-vista. I may add that the work shows much better in reproduction, particularly in the case of the extremely decorative and flamboyant horse. Perhaps the distance at which it will hereafter have to be viewed will soften its crude colouration and enhance all the good and indeed masterly composition and drawing which undoubtedly are there. Mr. Bridgman among the Puvis de Chavannes following! It is unexpected. Turkish interiors, festas on the Bosphorus, Moslem episodes—these are what we look for from the clever Franco-American painter. But no one will grumble at the change, who sees his exceedingly graceful and charming mural design at the Old Salon—'The Music of the Past.' M. Chartran's noble canvas of St. Francis singing his chant to the sun, while he guides his two oxen and his rude plough across the sun-swept uplands of barren Monte Subasio, is not a decorative work in the same sense as the productions to which I have just alluded, but in the wider sense it—in common with M. Rochegrosse's beautiful, if fantastic, 'Chevalier aux Fleurs,' and François Gorguet's lovely modern rendering of the Garden of the Hesperides, and other canvases of highly creditable achievement and of real though less distinctive charm—certainly comes under this loosely-used designation.

Of animal painting there is not more than usual, and the average is certainly not higher than of recent years. The two canvases I recall with most pleasure are Bisbing's spirited 'Combat of Bulls' in the old Salon, and Besnard's fantastically impressionistic but brilliantly clever and vigorous 'Chevaux' at the Champ de Mars. In portraiture there is great range from good to distinctly poor. Some of the ablest work is foreign, such as Mr. Orchardson's 'Mr. Gilbey,' Mr. Sargent's 'Mrs. Hammersley.' 'The Comte de Montesquiou-Fezensac' is Whistlerian, perhaps, rather than convincingly Mr. Whistler's; but this will be dealt with later. In portraiture, speaking broadly, I find that the older French painters of the year are in no way noteworthy. The convention of Carolus Duran lies like a blight upon most of them. Among the younger men M. Aman Jean must be specially mentioned. His portraits of the sculptor Dampt and of the novelist Jules Case are excellent. Of portrait pictures, as distinct from portraits pure and simple, the honours lie with Benjamin Constant, with Henner, and with Agache. The last-named holds an unique place. He belongs to no school, and though he has masters, he imitates no one. His imagination moves on a high plane, and we discern this whether he paints a subject with a fanciful or a realistic motive.

In seascape there is some able work, but nothing, I fancy, to make the season of 1894 memorable. By far the best is Mr. Henry Moore's 'Fine Weather in the Channel,' which looks even better at the Champ de Mars than it did in London last year. There are some very unconvincing, but occasionally clever, seascapes in the convention beloved of certain of the "New English," and there are many painstaking and creditable, if not particularly noteworthy examples in the convention of Mr. Brett, who has his recent 'Dead Calm' in one of the "hintersalles" at the Old Salon. Mr. Alexander Harrison, who has been wont to refresh us annually with wide and lucent expanses of sea, is very disappointing this year. On the other hand, at the Champs-Elysées, M. Auguste Flameng has one of the most luminous sea-pieces he has ever painted, and M. Max Bouvet will enhance his reputation by a beautiful 'Ocean Calm.' At the Champ de Mars, MM. A. Stevens and Henry Moore have first honours, and next to them, some visitors will say with them must be classed Hagborg and Mesdag, both to be seen this year at their own high-water level, so to say. The reproductions here given are both from the New Salon collection.

It is strange to note that while landscape is becoming more and more the vogue with us, it is becoming rarer and rarer at the Salons. Of course there are many examples of landscape art, but fewer than last year, fewer than the year before, fewer than a decade, than two decades ago. The great race of the romanticists has all but passed away. Corot, Daubigny, Rousseau, Diaz, how little of what they once inspired would be found this year either at the Champ de Mars or at the Champs-Elysées. Out of a score that are at least worthy of praise I may name three of particular charm: M. Jules Breton's 'Last of the Crop,' a dignified and gracious picture of field labourers at sundown on the last day of the potato harvest; the 'Lovers' of Gaston la Touche, two half-seen lovers among a dense growth of wild parsley suffused with sunlight and dappled with green shadows innumerable; and an admirable forest landscape by Bernier at the Champs-Elysées (see our headpiece), with the woodland perspectives full of soft and exquisitely graduated light, the ground warm with dappled sunglow, and cattle lying under the tall trees, or standing looking vaguely across the calm, pale blue expanse of the waters of the "Baie des Tilleuls."

WILLIAM SHARP.

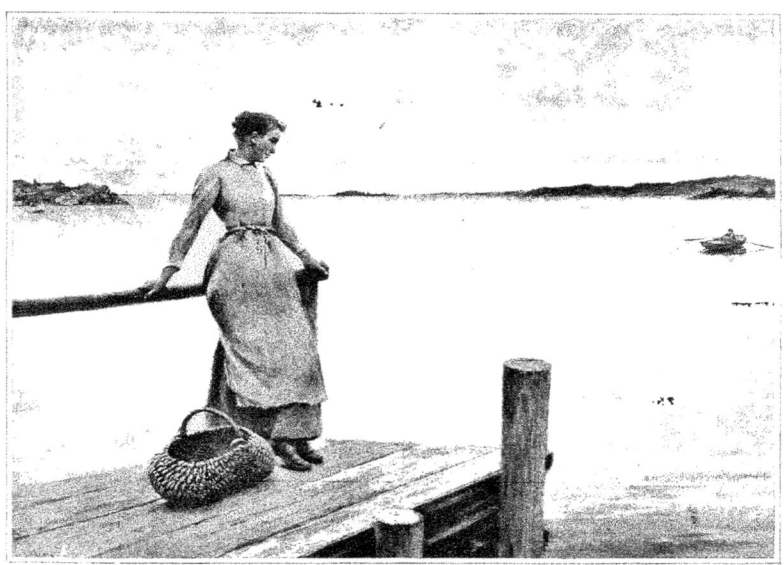

WAITING TO CROSS. BY A. HAGBORG AT THE CHAMP DE MARS.

ART NOTES AND REVIEWS.

THE exhibition of the Royal Academy will probably prove the most popular and profitable of recent years. There is small likelihood of any further drop in the shillings, for there are many subject pictures certain to interest the ordinary public. The anecdote is indeed supreme, and it must be reckoned with in all considerations of the Art of this country. Later, we shall discuss the collection in detail. Every branch of art and literature was represented at the banquet except Art-criticism.

The New Gallery is far below the level of interest of the Royal Academy. The only really fine picture is Sir E. Burne-Jones's superb portrait of Miss Amy Gaskell, which, without doubt, is one of the most masterly works produced by this artist, whose powers of obtaining fine colour seem to increase every year. There is also a strong landscape by Mr. A. D. Peppercorn.

The pictures purchased from the Royal Academy under the Chantrey Bequest are Mr. Briton Riviere's 'Beyond Man's Footsteps,' Mr. H. S. Tuke's 'August Blue,' and Mr. H. C. Fehr's bronze group, 'Perseus rescuing Andromeda.'

Of the smaller collections now open the most interesting is that of the Royal Water-Colour Society. Fresh life is gradually bringing out all that is best in the older men, and with one or two exceptions there is a feeling of gaiety and living power in the exhibition which is encouraging. The English Art Club is also the home of much good work, and from this small body emanates nearly all that is hopeful in the Art world of England. No doubt a good deal is lost in attempts, unwisely carried out, to command attention by eccentricity, but these young artists dare something, and are content frequently to lose in order occasionally to make solid progress in the newer developments of Art. The Lady Artists' Exhibition was rather higher in class than usual, and Miss Grant's picture of 'Baby' carried off all the artistic honours.

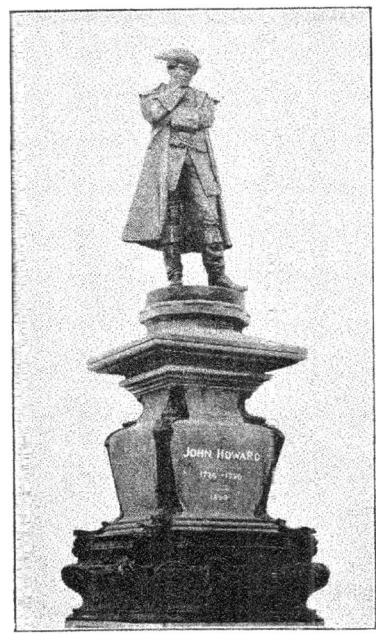

Les Aquarellistes Français have sent over from Paris their complete yearly exhibition to the Hanover Gallery in Bond Street. There is a very great deal to admire in this collection. Français, one of the older painters, is represented by several early drawings. Boutet de Monvel has many refined works. Vibert attracts attention with his figures in red garments and careful finish, and Luigi's drawings of the streets of Paris are strong and good. We reproduce one of these works.

We publish a representation of the memorial to the philanthropist, John Howard, unveiled in Bedford Market-place on March 28th by the Duke of Bedford. It has been erected by public subscription at a cost of £2,000. The work is one of the most successful of the recent productions of Mr. Gilbert, R.A.

Mr. E. J. Poynter has been appointed Director of the National Gallery in succession to Sir F. Burton. We commend to his notice Dr. Richter's remarks about certain pictures in the Gallery on a previous page.

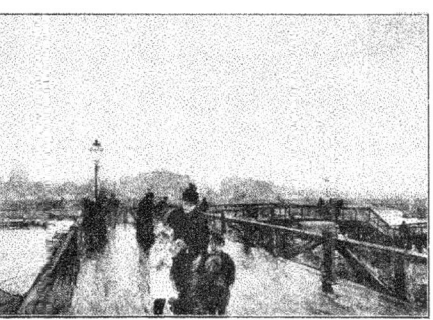

'Le Pont de l'Estacade.' From the Water-Colour Drawing by Loir Luigi exhibited at the Hanover Gallery.

A great deal of stir has been caused in the artistic world through the action of the Chief Constable of Glasgow, with reference to the public exhibition of certain nude pictures in shop-windows in the commercial capital of the north. A very respectable printseller, member of the Printsellers' Association, exhibited in his window a series of engravings and photogravures from celebrated pictures of the nude: 'The Bath of Psyche,' by Sir Frederick Leighton, P.R.A., 'The Visit to Æsculapius,' by E. J. Poynter, R.A. (engraved in THE ART JOURNAL in 1885), 'Syrinx,' by Arthur Hacker, A.R.A., and various others. It very soon became known that this collection was in the window, and in consequence crowds were attracted. The police heard of the matter, and the printseller was asked to remove the engravings, and, on his declining to do so, the Chief Constable of the City, supported by all the powers that be, insisted they should be removed, and of course the law-abiding citizen gave way. That it should have been deemed necessary for the Constable to interfere in this way is, at this time of day, deplorable, and much abuse has been heaped on that functionary's head. Sir Frederick Leighton, Mr. Poynter, and Mr. Hacker have made public protest against municipal interference in artistic matters, and the police have been soundly rated.

At the same time, there is something to be said on the behalf of the municipal servants. It is silly to speak as if it were Scottish prudery that dictated the action, for an almost exactly parallel case occurred less than ten years ago in the City of London. A printseller, then opposite King William's Monument, was compelled by the City authorities to remove from his window Mr. Palero's 'Faust,' and he quietly acquiesced. The Scottish officials, therefore, did not act without English precedent. But the point is that a collection of nude pictures in a street window, open to all the world, does not attract because of its art, but because of its representation of nudity. Had there been one single print, or even a couple, with other things, no objection would probably have been made, but a window filled with nude figures, and nude figures alone, points to another object of attraction besides an artistic one, and is too apt to be so understood by the unreflecting multitude. On the principle that while one man may walk in the city in any direction he pleases, twenty men cannot be permitted to walk arm-in-arm, so in a street window one print or two representing such subjects may be displayed, but it is not good form to show a dozen, which attract a rowdy mob necessitating the interference of the police.

Mr. J. A. Raemakers, the sculptor whose bust of Sir John Monckton was unveiled at the Mansion House on April 17th, met with a fatal accident owing to a fall at his residence on April 19th, and died during the night from his injuries, having fractured an arm and a shoulder. He was in his sixty-third year, and exhibited for many years at the Royal Academy and the Salons.

Lucy Rossetti, the wife of W. M. Rossetti, brother and biographer of Dante Gabriel Rossetti, died, after a long and painful illness, in April last. The daughter of the late Ford Madox Brown, she was herself an artist of talent, exhibiting from time to time both at the Royal Academy and the Dudley Gallery.

Mr. Harry Furniss, whose new periodical we hope speedily to welcome, diverts the public with his "Grand Old Mystery unravelled" (Simpkin). This is a pamphlet fully illustrated with humorous drawings of Mr. Gladstone, and the sketch of the late Prime Minister 'Laughing at Labby,' which we reproduce, is one of the best portraits "Lika Joko" has ever done.

Miss Kingsley has arranged to deliver a weekly course of six lectures, commencing May 25th, in the Queen's Hall, on 19th-century French Pictures and Painters.

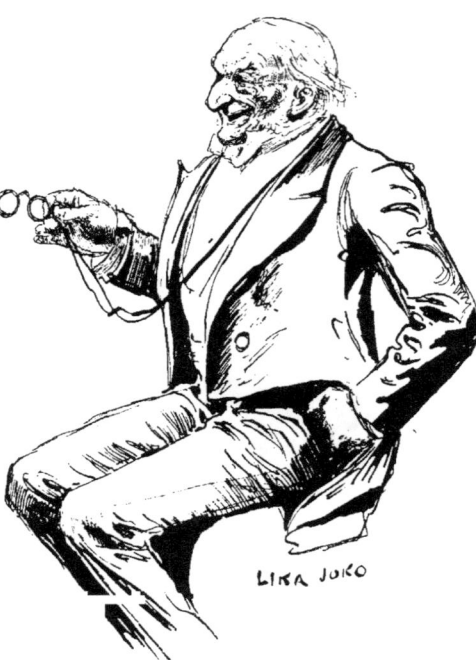

'LAUGHING AT LABBY.' BY HARRY FURNISS.

We give a very warm welcome to a new departure in wood engraving. Mr. W. Biscombe Gardner has engraved on wood a portrait of Mr. George Meredith, by Mr. G. F. Watts. This engraving is published by Messrs. Elkin Mathews and John Lane, as a proof signed by the artist, and besides being the only published portrait of the candidate for the Poet Laureateship, it is one of the most important wood blocks published in England. It recalls the finest engraving of Mr. W. J. Linton, and we heartily congratulate the engraver on the artistic success of his work.

Architects and trade decorators, as well as the Art-loving public, would do well to visit, before it closes, the varied show of really good things in the way of wall decoration still for a short time on view at the works of Messrs. Jeffrey & Co. (64, Essex Road, Islington). They will see there how much better things are to be had than are just now in fashion.

THE HENRY TATE COLLECTION.*

THOSE of Mr. Tate's pictures which still have to be noticed all belong to the more insular section of the British school. They are free from Continental influence, and show in a very marked degree the individualism which so struck the French when our school, as a school, made its *début* in Paris in 1855. The changes of the last few years have mostly been in the direction of breaking down this individualism, and of assimilating English ideals to those of the French; a remark which applies not only to men taught at the least partly in Parisian studios, but also to those who have been content with the London schools. The rival Salons which are now open in Paris afford a very striking illustration of the change which has come about. The English pictures are numerous, and they are still English enough to be recognised at one glance as English. Mr. Stanhope Forbes's 'Forging the Anchor,' for instance, in spite of those external forces which, pressing on the artist's personality, have compelled him, as it were, to think in French, proclaims itself unmistakably as the outcome of an English mind and English prepossessions; and so it is all through.

Mr. Lavery, Mr. Guthrie, Mr. Lorimer, Mr. William Carter, some with, some without, a French interlude in their training, all combine English ambitions with the broad, simple, and organic methods of which the French have been the apostles for the last thirty years at least. If we, on this side of the Channel, were to copy the proceedings of those French critics who set themselves to discover a Gallic origin for all that is good in painting, we might set up Sir Henry Raeburn as the father of the style now most in vogue. The fact that no one had ever heard of Georges Michel, and that his pictures were all stacked away in a broker's shop at Montmartre until about twenty years ago, has not prevented some of his fellow-countrymen from awarding him that place in the creation of modern landscape which belongs rightly to Constable. Acting on the same principle, we might say that, although Raeburn spent his life in Edinburgh, and although his pictures were almost unknown in England, to say nothing of France, until the "Old Masters'" Exhibitions began to bring them southwards, still he was the first to practise the methods now insisted on in all the great studios, and must, therefore, be accepted as the inventor of the square touch and of modelling in planes. It would be

MIND AND MUSCLE. BY H. STACY MARKS, R.A.

* Continued from page 130.

JULY, 1894.

wandering too far afield to point out how curiously, in some Raeburns, the latest fashions, both in handling and in the management of colour, have been anticipated. One of the best pictures at the Salon des Champs Elysées is a lady's portrait by M. Paul Chabas; the best, perhaps, at the Salon du Champ de Mars is Mr. Sargent's 'Mrs. Hammersley.' In both of these the system invented by Raeburn for himself is simply carried farther than he carried it. In Mr. Sargent's case it comes, of course, by way of Carolus Duran; M. Chabas too has probably formed himself on Carolus and Sargent. Both, no doubt, like Carolus himself, would point to Velazquez as their master, but the Scottish painter comes between the Spaniard and the moderns, and supplies a link in the chain.

But all this will seem not a little fantastic, and I have only ventured upon it to show what a wide field will have to be embraced by any one who may try to follow modern development in the same way as the growth of Italian painting, from the Renaissance to the decline of Art, has been followed. Even in the fifteenth and sixteenth centuries, when intercourse between nations flowed in such narrow and sluggish channels, the influence of some particular artist is found cropping up in most unexpected places. Channels of communication between Nuremberg and Venice, Naples and Bruges, Florence and Basle, to name only these, carried ideas from one place to another, and gave rise to similarities which are occasionally puzzling enough.

With the facilities for intercourse which modern Europe has now possessed for some two generations, it says a great deal for the robust individuality of Englishmen that their Art has preserved its local characteristics so long as it has. Nearly forty years have passed since our painters first found themselves, as a school, hung beside the schools of the Continent, and yet even now they have not made the full surrender to French system which was made by the Latins of the south, the Teutons of central Europe, the Scandinavians of the north, and the Americans, as soon as they found themselves face to face with its results. One British characteristic is an *inquisitive* emotion. Putting aside the great artist, who is synthetic and a creator wherever born, the Briton's delight is to make a sort of pictorial analysis of his feelings, to register every fact that takes his fancy, and to leave the required harmony to be brought about by the mere circumstance that a single personality has been behind them all. He is saved by sincerity. He selects neither emotionally nor intellectually, but incoherence is avoided by fidelity to his own predilections. The pictures reproduced in this article would, one and all, look a little queer if isolated among things contrived according to the ideas which are uppermost just now, but when looked at together, they save themselves and make good their claim to be to some extent representative of a not unwelcome phase of Art, by their transparent good faith and by the simplicity with which they display their authors' pleasure in the facts of life. Mr. Erskine Nicol's 'Paddy's Love-Letter'; Mr. Faed's 'In Silk Attire,' Mr. Dendy Sadler's 'A Good Story,' and Mr. Stacy Marks's 'Mind and Muscle,' have all certain pleasantnesses of design; they tell their stories well and simply; and in the years to come their quiet merits may give them a more serious place in English Art than most of us would venture to predict for them now. They are, of course, of the stock of Wilkie, and for the moment must share his loss of consideration. In saying this I am not thinking so much of the particular examples of these men's work which

"AND YE SHALL WALK IN SILK ATTIRE." BY THOMAS FAED, R.A. ENGRAVED BY R. PATERSON.

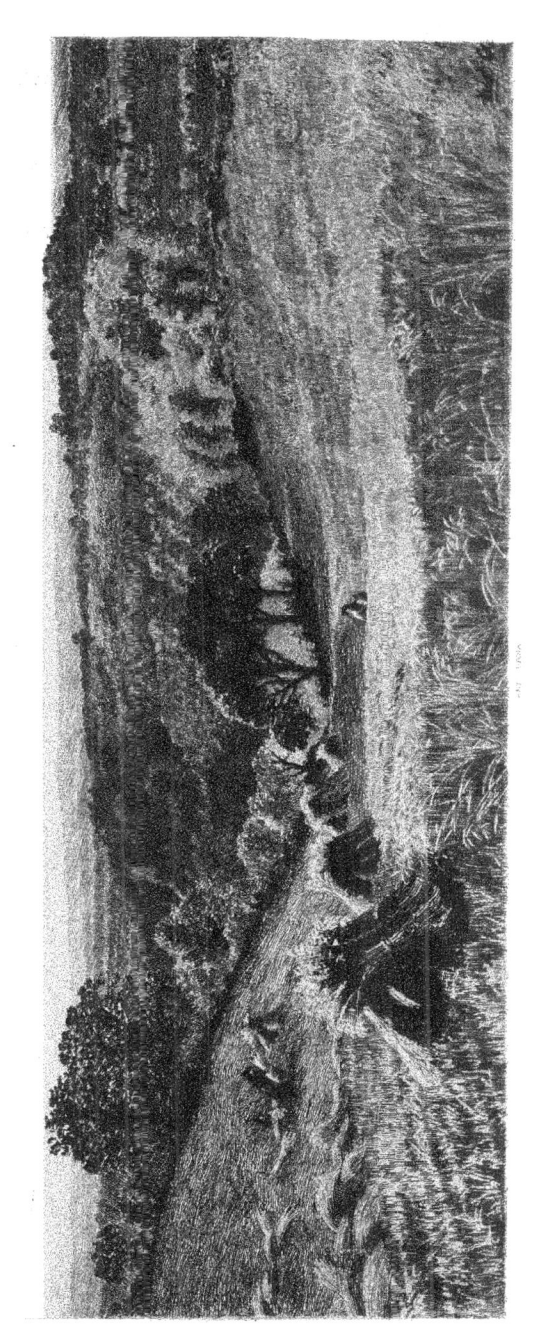

A SURREY AND CA F

TCHED BY OUR HOM FROM 1 PAI O B / C COL RA

Mr. Tate happens to possess, as of the group as a whole. Mr. Faed and Mr. Nicol have, moreover, both painted better pic-

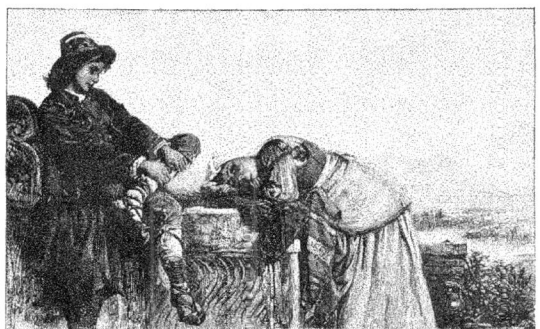

SUNNY HOURS. BY KEELEY HALSWELLE. ENGRAVED BY M. STAINFORTH.

tures than these; which, it must be confessed, are not among the things which cause impatience for the definite fruition of Mr. Tate's generosity. The late Mr. Keeley Halswelle's 'Sunny Hours' is a Faed translated into Italian, with the faults and virtues of its model, but with a diminished sincerity.

The other day in Paris, as I crossed the courtyard of the Ecole des Beaux-Arts, I met a young Italian model coming out. She was good-looking, and her dress was beautiful—an old, but not too old, green velveteen petticoat with embroideries in many reds, a bodice of the same colours, and the usual linen arrangements. Her arms hung down beside her, her lips were twitching, and tears were rolling down her cheeks. Twenty, nay ten, years ago she would have been thought an ideal model. Now, perhaps, she had been looking in vain for sittings, and had to go home empty-handed to the colony behind the Jardin des Plantes. She might have sat for the girl in Keeley Halswelle's picture, but it is a good many years now since he had to give up *contadine* for showery skies, and the piazza before the Pantheon for the heaths of the New Forest and the leafy banks of the upper Thames.

Halswelle's landscapes were often cold and false in colour, with a tendency sometimes to blackness, sometimes to the kind of lurid tone which nature puts on just before a thunderstorm. But they had personality. They embodied, almost always, a really pictorial idea, and they showed power both to select and to express. Of Vicat Cole's work pretty exactly the reverse of all this might be said. The impressions he received from nature were much more probable, on the whole, than those of Halswelle.

Allowing for his inability to suggest the pitch of nature, his colour was pleasing and, so far as it went, truthful, and his drawing good. Unhappily his landscapes scarcely ever have any pictorial *raison d'être*. They are simply pretty places reproduced with much skill and a certain show of affection, but they embody no idea; they display some power to arrange, but none to select; and they betray an almost complete incapacity to express. Such a picture as the 'Surrey Landscape,' etched in our plate by Mr. Clough Bromley, pleases the average spectator because he finds there exactly what he would see were he before the scene itself. The special gift of the landscape painter, the power to extract from any given scene those tints, lines, and effects of light and shadow, which can be welded into the coherent expression of a subjective idea or emotion, is quite absent from Mr. Cole's work. His pictures are not so literal as those of Mr. Brett, for instance, but they would be so if they could. They show a similar tendency towards the irrelevant, but the individuality behind them is infinitely less robust and positive than that of the painter of 'Britannia's Realm' and 'Mussels,' and the picture called 'Pearly Summer' in the present Salon.

All theorising about the true limits of any branch of Art is stultified, to some extent, by the undeniable fact that when a strong man contrives to express himself with the paint-brush or the modelling-tool, his work lives, no matter how improper the lines may be on which it travels. Nature never meant either Mantegna, or Ingres, or Albert Dürer, to meddle with a palette. What she gave them to say would have been

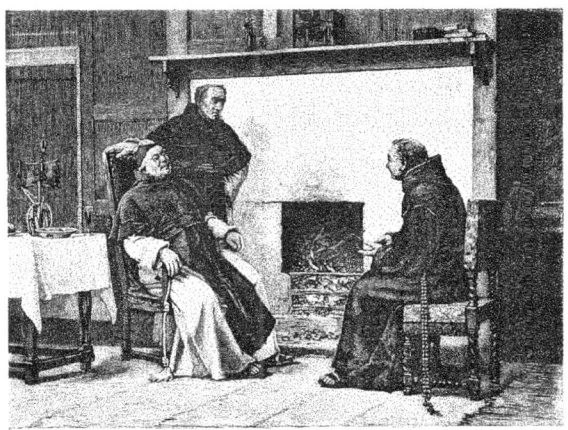

A GOOD STORY. BY W. DENDY SADLER. ENGRAVED BY C. DIETRICH.

better said with the help of a totally different instrument. And yet their pictures will always hang in good places in museums, their lives will always be written and read, their sayings on Art discussed. And so, in his degree, is it with Mr. Brett. His work, perverse as it seems, is alive with self-will, with pugnacity, with a personal insistence on his own standpoint. It is not so, however, with most of those who take what may be called the encyclopædic view of a subject. Mr. Brett puts in all the markings on a rock, all the crinkles in a rippling sea, all the engine-turnings on sand just left by the tide, for the same reason as Albert Durer would have done so. There is no difference in principle between one of his better pictures and the portrait of Holzschuher at Berlin. In this most remarkable performance you will see every hair set carefully in its place, every sign of age mapped out on the blonde skin, every streak elaborated in the blue Bavarian iris. Durer did all this because he wished to, because he felt a consuming interest in every detail, and meant the spectator to feel it also. We may call such methods perverse, but we should never look upon them as signs of weakness. Neither should we do so before a good Brett. It may leave us angry or perplexed, but never with a sense of weakness in the artist. Before too many landscape painters of the school which is now so rapidly dying out, we get a diametrically opposite impression. We feel that they put as much as they can into their pictures, not because they take any violent interest in the minor details of nature, but simply because they don't know what to leave out. We can see them opening their camp-stools, planting their easels, and setting their palettes, with a feeling in their hearts that can only be described as courage, courage to

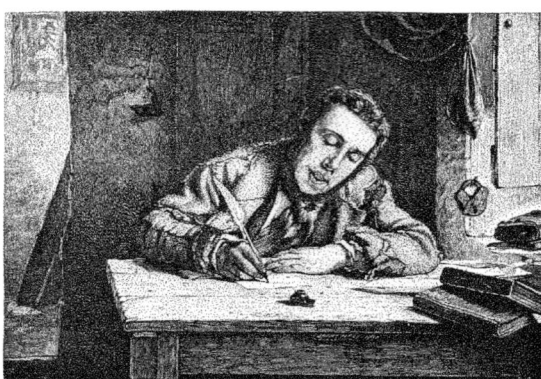

PADDY'S LOVE-LETTER. BY E. NICOL, A.R.A. ENGRAVED BY C. DIETRICH.

face all the facts before them and to grasp them all, in the hope that when the work is done, the charm which has drawn them to the spot may have got itself on to their canvas, and may be ready to seduce a buyer. But *qui trop embrasse, mal étreint*. This sort of comprehensiveness comes from weakness, from inability to perceive salient features, to decompose an object into things relevant and things irrelevant ; to, in fact, know what you want. It has, I fancy, become one of the characteristics of English exhibitions for a reason which has little enough to do with Art. England differs from other countries in its possession of a vast public buying pictures without either knowing or caring anything about Art. In France the comparatively small number of people who collect pictures buy them for their own sake, as pictures, or as notes to be used in a scheme of decoration. The small *commerçant* or *rentier* does not buy them at all ; in England he does. But what induces him to so expend his money? Not Art, but the desire to have about him imitations of things or scenes with which he is familiar. It is the real pump on the stage in another form. Design, colour, chiaroscuro, all that has nothing to say to him. What he wants is a reminiscence of his summer holiday, or a field of beans in which he can weigh the crop, or a cow whose yield of milk he can guess. Many an English picture-maker would have become an artist but for the temptation put in his way by a public like this, and the middlemen who cater for it.

WALTER ARMSTRONG.

'SOUTH KENSINGTON,'

AND ITS EXPENDITURE ON INSTRUCTION IN ART: A DEFENCE.

THERE is no medicine more wholesome for a public institution, than constant and intelligent criticism from outside. The mere necessity of working always from one point of view—generally that of the purse-holder—and the ever-present fear of creating dangerous, perhaps disastrous, precedents by departing from paths of proved safety, have an inevitable tendency to limit the scope of official action, in such wise as to sometimes give individuals *primâ-facie* cause for outcry against regulations framed in the interests of the many rather than of the few; and it often happens that in the

course of discussions raised on such questions, new and valuable considerations arise ; which tend to modify or expand official ideas, to the advantage of every one concerned. If, however, this criticism is to be of any value, it should not only be impersonal, free from the jealousy of school or party, but especially *grounded on accurate knowledge*. When it does not fill these conditions, it is not worth serious examination: always providing that the facts are sufficiently patent to speak for themselves. But official returns are not yet of such popularity, as to always make the results of the work of a great government department so well known as they might be ; and in the case of the Department of Science and Art, advantage has been taken of popular ignorance to float a number of fallacies and misrepresentations, many of which it would be complimentary to term spiteful. Recent events have shown that even a few men of standing, instead of inquiring for themselves, have weakly adopted some of the current scandal (to give it its real name) of the casual and irresponsible paragraphist ; and, for this reason, before the evil spreads farther, it has seemed worth while to place the matter on a more substantial basis, by setting down shortly some actual facts, derived from published material attainable by every one.

The most widely known portion of the Department's work is undoubtedly that connected with the various Schools of Art and Art Classes (excluding the National Art Training School, which is treated separately, and does not receive " payments on results "). The Estimates tell us that " direct payments, to encourage instruction in Art," will absorb in 1894 the sum of £69,000 ; and the Report for the same year states that in 1893 the number of individuals under instruction was, in round numbers, 180,000, and the papers worked at the annual examination, over 200,000 ; figures which should give a good idea of the sheer mass of labour involved ; and of the difficulty of that close inspection, and attention to detail, which are necessitated by a painstaking control exercised over the expenditure—in multitudinous driblets, be it remembered—of the tax-payers' money.

Now this distribution of grants is by no means to be taken as a State guarantee of the Schools of Art *en bloc:* the fact of a school participating therein, simply means that a proportionate amount of good work has been, unquestionably, performed by its students. The schools are not Departmental schools ; they are entirely local, and the Department has little absolute power, although certainly much influence, in the direction of controlling teachers. Its requirements are based upon the recommendations of the many independent painters, sculptors, designers—artists of every kind, in short—who have given in the past, or still give it, their assistance. If a school under the authority of its local committee chooses to adopt these conditions, it can easily supplement its private income by a government grant ; in which case certain information is required as to the status of pupils, number of attendances, etc., which may seem onerous to an unbusinesslike man, but which are undoubtedly essential to an efficient use of public moneys ; and are, at all events, insisted on by the Audit Office, whose business it is to check all expenditure thereof. .

If, again, a locality wishes to start a new school, it is furnished with the best advice that experience can provide ; and, subject once more to compliance with a few simple conditions, a sum of money not exceeding one-half the total cost, with a maximum of £500, will be granted in aid of the expense of the building, provided that the latter be used exclusively for the purpose of Art instruction. For the present year £4,600 is taken for this purpose. Finally, books and Art objects are lent freely for the use of students, and grants have been made to a large extent for the purchase of casts and school accessories. Since the allocation of portions of the Imperial Revenue to the purposes of technical education, these grants have very properly been reduced to a minimum ; but the fact remains that much of the apparatus now in use was acquired in this manner.

In connection with these Schools of Art and their annual examination, is the well-known National Competition, in which medals and prizes are awarded in various classes, for finished work sent in and examined, as has been already pointed out, by admittedly able and accomplished men *from outside* the Department, whose names appear in most of the official publications. In addition, a selection of examples actually worked in advanced "personal examinations" under very strict conditions, is, at the same time, shown for public criticism : and the payments on those form a considerable portion of the grant earned. . Now the aim of all this is very obvious, and is plainly and concisely enough stated in the estimate already quoted, viz. : *To Encourage Instruction in Art.* It is not sought to teach this, that, or the other system. If local managers like, they can fill the r schools with their female relations, and set them to make alleged copies of cheap chromos all day long. And it cannot be denied—or, for the matter of that, avoided— that many schools have derived a considerable income from fees paid by individuals belonging to the upper and middle classes in search of mere amusement ; to the detriment of the genuine artisan-student. But this is consistently discouraged ; the whole tendency of the course of instruction offered—*and on which only grants are paid*—being to provide such preparatory discipline, as shall enable its recipient to turn his attention to whatever branch of the Arts may prove to be most to his advantage. The experiment of direct interference with trade was tried in the infancy of the Department ; and owing to the impossibility of keeping abreast with fashion—to name one cause only—proved a complete failure.

It is found better to put a tool into a young man's hand, teach him to use it, and then leave him to his own resources, to apply it as he best may.

It cannot be too clearly stated that the general responsibility for the schools lies on the local managers. If they conceive that their moral obligations are limited to the attendance of a minimum of committee meetings, the Department should not be held accountable, and is powerless to drag a school out of the inefficiency into which it may sink.

Now as regards what may be called direct Art teaching— that which is carried out at headquarters in the Training Schools—there has been a most ludicrous diversity of criticism. The Department has been blamed for attempting to teach Art—meaning Fine Art—and reprobated because it is said not to have succeeded. It has been accused of wasting all its money and energies in a futile attempt to produce painters and sculptors ; and yet in due season there goes up a wild shriek because the school is not to be compared with one of the Paris studios ; and the annual exhibitions of works contain nothing of more importance than the tentative designs of students, whose education is not yet completed.

The facts in this case are again at variance with such statements as generally accompany these diatribes. In the first place, the Department does not exist for the purpose of manufacturing artists, either according to the so-called South Kensington 'System' (in this use of the word, a vain creation of the critics' brains, by the way), or any other. It very rightly leaves that process to the schools of the Royal Academy, and to hose artists whose studios are commodious enough, and whose time is sufficiently at liberty to undertake it. Neither does it pretend to fabricate either design or designers. Its duty is to afford facilities for the higher education of a certain number of students from all parts of the country, who have distinguished themselves in more elementary Art work, and who propose to devote themselves in after life to teaching that work ; and to a much larger number of designers who wish to study for a short time and then return to their trades. For both these classes are provided commodious studios, lectures by some of the best men of the day, and all the necessary models and other paraphernalia, which are available to every one, subject of course to the discipline indispensable to the regulation of a large establishment. The course of instruction here again has been drawn up, not by the permanent officials, but on the advice of consultative committees, composed of men against whom, in these days of the worship of the successful, scarcely a single Art critic can be found to raise his voice. And it is deliberately made sufficiently elastic to allow both teachers in training, and designers, to utilise to the full the admittedly unrivalled collections of Decorative Art in the Museum; and an excellent Art Library—advantages which are possessed by no other body of Art students in the world.

It is the veriest truism to say that no one can teach a man to be talented; but if a pupil has anything in him, and cannot develop it under these circumstances, he has only himself to blame.

The two foregoing branches of Art instruction are the best known—and most criticised—of the Department's duties; but there remains a third, of which so much ignorance is apparent as to demand a somewhat detailed explanation.

By far the largest portion of the State expenditure on Art is devoted to an important branch of public education, the nature of which is again so frankly and concisely manifested by the title under which the money is voted, as to leave, one would imagine, no possible room for misunderstanding. And yet, quite lately, an attempt was made, almost publicly, to include the whole amount apportioned for "instruction (Art)" and "manual training in public elementary schools," £180,250 (1893), in the alleged expenditure of "South Kensington," in an abortive attempt to train artists by "system."

Now it is not suggested for a moment that there was any deliberate *suppressio veri* in the position taken up by the gentlemen referred to; their names, if it were possible to give them, would be the amplest guarantee to the contrary. But their carelessness and neglect to avail themselves of the full, even profuse information in official publications open to the inspection, and within the reach of every one, argue an almost culpable readiness to seize upon any excuse to attack an institution to which they owe more than they would possibly care to acknowledge, or even, perhaps, than they are aware of.

But since these fallacious ideas have been put in circulation, it becomes valuable to draw attention to the actual fact; taking, for the sake of convenience, figures supplied by the estimates for the year 1894-5.

In the first place it will be as well to note that the Department of Science and Art is, in this matter, merely the examining and inspecting instrument of the Education Office, under whose direction "drawing and manual instruction" has become a subject to be compulsorily taught in every "elementary school for boys in England and Wales." To this is to be added the number of girls in schools which elect to take drawing as an optional subject; and also the number of children of both sexes, to whom it is taught in Scotland and Ireland. An estimate of two millions for the whole number of pupils is within the mark. For this purpose the sum voted is, excluding a small expenditure for Science teaching in training colleges, £208,000.

These two millions of children receive, every week, a lesson of stated minimum duration, in freehand and model drawing, and the use of simple geometrical instruments; passing through a regular course, under teachers whose capability to conduct it has been severely tested by a thorough examination in which a high standard of efficiency has to be, and is, attained. The whole of their work is inspected, examined, and reported on, by qualified inspectors with a large measure of independent power. And, since this enormous machinery has hitherto been simply ignored by the critics, it is reasonable to suppose that at least no flagrant causes of complaint have arisen. That being so, we may venture to point out some of its advantages.

To begin—it gives all these children, of artisans for the most part, an idea of form and proportion; it teaches them to use their eyes and brains; and, before their fingers are stiffened with age and toil, to master the use of instruments sufficiently to set out a simple plan, or make a rough measurement drawing or sketch—an acquirement, trivial as it may seem to some more highly cultured minds, which must be invaluable in after.life, to the man in his household as well as the craftsman in his shop.

And there is this further consideration for those who, with perhaps too much, but pardonable ideality, look at the whole question from the standpoint of the Fine Arts. If among all these children there are any with genius, the Department provides not only a means of discovering it, but a succession of disciplinary stages by which a student, assisted by the liberal scheme of scholarships already dealt with, can rise as high as his talent and perseverance entitle him.

That the instruction in these schools is on the whole mechanically carried out or unintelligently received, will never be credited by any one who will take the trouble to visit South Kensington Museum on a free night or holiday, and watch the industry of the small students sketching with their scanty materials whatever strikes their fancy; or who, as the writer of this paper had recently an opportunity of doing, will give himself a pleasant hour by explaining to an eager, intelligent, and appreciative class some of the elements of historic art.

All this the critics have hitherto chosen to ignore; it having suited them better to treat the expenditure involved as so much sheer waste, for which the public got no return whatever; with what fairness, or even common honesty, can now be judged.

In conclusion it may be shortly reiterated that the Department of Science and Art does not exist for the purpose of directly producing painters and sculptors, although the list of those living who are indebted to it would be unexpectedly comprehensive. Its great duty is not to manufacture the taste of the nation, but to initiate and aid a general training which is bound in the long run to influence and develop that hitherto doubtful quantity—scarcely, as widening the market for their productions, to the detriment of artists or craftsmen. From a mere experiment, it has grown, in spite of the bitterest opposition, to be one of the great factors of National Education; and on those who would hamper or limit its work lies the heavy responsibility of suggesting an efficient substitute—a responsibility they have not as yet been too ready to face.

CONQUERORS. BY E. ROSCOE MULLINS.

THE NEW SCULPTURE.*
SECOND ARTICLE.

IN the last days of 1879 Mr. Armstead was elected a full R.A., and towards the end of April, 1880—a month in which of late years no other election has taken place at the Academy—the members met to select an outsider to take his place. What made the date a curiously inconvenient one was that by that time the exhibition of the year was placed, although not yet seen by the public, and that the minds of the electors were therefore disturbed by fresh and yet unsettled impressions of the new work. The choice of the members fell upon Mr. Charles B. Birch (1833—93), a sculptor who combined the influences of Rauch, whose pupil he had been in Berlin, and of Foley, with whom he had afterwards worked. After having long attempted, not wholly without distinction, smooth, idyllic figures of rustic girls, Birch had suddenly been seduced by the popular successes of Boehm back again into a sort of rough and violent German realism. He had sent to the exhibition of 1880 a group of a young British soldier, in a very truculent attitude, striding across a fallen Afghan soldier. Boots, leathern straps, pistols, helmet—all the accoutrements of war were rendered in the most realistic way in this martial composition, which held the place of honour in the Central Hall.

This group, and perhaps a statuette called 'Retaliation,' a mountaineer defying an unseen eagle, attracted many of the

* Continued from page 142.

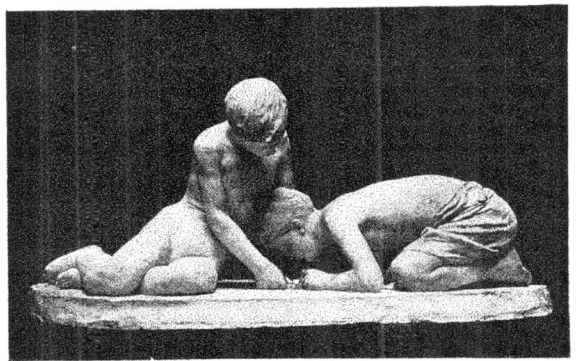

TEUCER. BY HAMO THORNYCROFT, R.A.

elder Academicians, who did not perhaps recollect how much the latter owed to the 'Eagle-Slayer' of Mr. John Bell. Birch was elected A.R.A., and continued to be a typical sculptor of the old, stranded school, wholly unaffected by the new ideas. One of the Academicians, an eminent architect, wrote to me next day: "Well, Birch is in! But I cannot help thinking that a good many of us, as we came back out of the council-room, and passed Thornycroft's 'Artemis,' wondered whether we had done the right thing!" But the name of Mr. Hamo Thornycroft was that of a modest and promising student, whom the members were not prepared, early in 1880, to accept as a master.

Yet when the exhibition opened a week later, there was a *furore* around his statue, and such a universal chorus of praise from outsiders as must have considerably startled the Royal Academy. A painstaking and intelligent student had suddenly risen to the topmost place in the profession. Born in 1850, Mr. Thornycroft was no longer very young, and it is rather difficult to conjecture the cause of a change so radical as that between his work of 1879 and his work of 1880. His 'Artemis' (see page 141) and his 'Putting the Stone' of that year were the two statues with which the New Sculpture started on its course in England. Each deserves from the historical critic sustained consideration.

The 'Artemis' of Mr. Thornycroft is an athletic figure of a girl, moving rapidly along in the woodland. Her hound has strayed on to the right side of her, and by his movement drags back her left hand, so compressing her light draperies. With the right hand she takes an arrow from her quiver. An element of great originality was the delicacy of the translucent draperies, through which the values of the flesh were seen. In order to prepare for this, the sculptor went through the labour of finishing the whole figure more highly in the nude than was usual, although nearly all its surface was presently to be obliterated by the muslin dainty robe. Fortunately a photograph was taken of the nudity, when finished in the clay, and of this, as well as of the completed statue, I gave engravings on page 141. The model was quite a fresh idea, and characteristic of the superior science and conscientiousness which were to animate the new men, to give this degree of finish to work which was presently to be concealed.

If delicacy, style, and dignified grace were highly characteristic qualities of the beautiful 'Artemis' of 1880, for the technical student almost a greater interest attached to that remarkable bronze, 'Putting the Stone.' The critics, bewildered at the naturalism of the surface, the modelling of the thin, but muscular legs of the youth, the absence of anything like Canovesque daintiness or plumpness, called out upon this figure as harshly realistic and wanting in "classic reserve." The 'Artemis' was so full of elevated beauty that it was impossible to fail to admire it. 'Putting the Stone' was more caviare to the general, and required an eye more learnedly trained than that of most artists to appreciate its value. This bronze, reproduced above, has constantly grown in the estimation of students of sculpture, and is now a sort of classic of the English school.

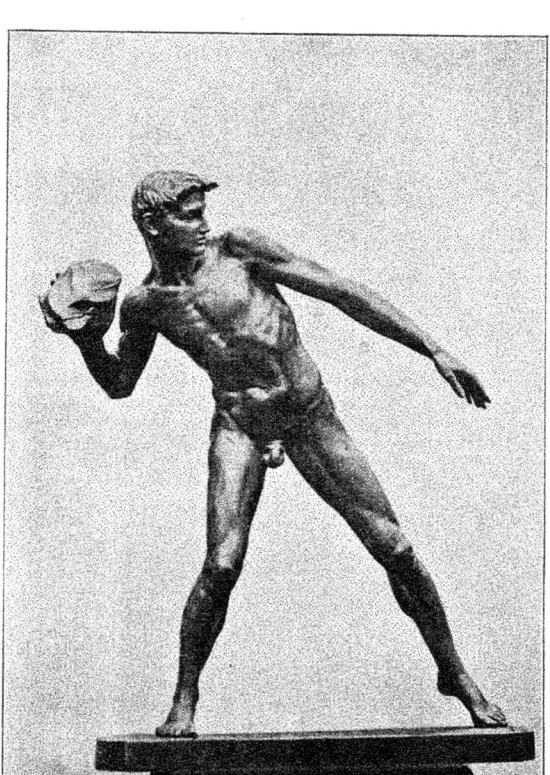

ATHLETE PUTTING THE STONE. HAMO THORNYCROFT, R.A.

There was little else in the exhibition of 1880 which we should now identify with the new sculpture, but much that showed increase of vitality and intelligence. At this period Boehm was prominent, with qualities which sometimes deceived the very elect. This year he exhibited casts of several iconic statues which were much admired, even by artists. Born in Vienna in 1834, Joseph Edgar Boehm had arrived in London when he was almost thirty, and in spite of a brief period of Parisian training, had preserved, and would persist in preserving, his German proclivities. In 1880 he was an A.R.A. of three years' standing, and by far the most successful and popular sculptor in the country. That Boehm possessed great skill as a modeller is what no competent critic would ever deny. Some of his busts, the best of his animal work, were truly excellent. But he was radically prosaic without distinction or style, and much that was admired in him was simply a differentiation in textures, which had been omitted by other men in England, and which gave a certain pleasant pictorial effect to the eye. This was a survival of his Austrian training. In Germany, through the worst period of its decline, the art of sculpture had always clung in an awkward fashion to a sort of realism in detail. It owed it, no doubt, to the national practice of wood-carving. Boehm had more than this, of course. He had unusual learning and dexterity. But he was not a great artist, he was never an English artist, and his place in the history of English sculpture is insignificant. What he had he owed largely, without question, to the influence of Dalou, a Frenchman settled like himself in London.

Mr. Armstead's work in 1880 showed a revival of a more important kind, and indeed of a highly significant character.

He was now carving and exhibiting certain marble panels in low relief of an imaginative kind in which the singular qualities of his art, due to no modern influence, but borrowed directly from the French Renaissance of the sixteenth century, were seen in great force. These plaques had, too, a curiously Assyrian look of intentional mannerism, the planes being flattened, without gradation, to catch all the high lights at the same angle. Somewhat barbaric, not at all in sympathy with modern modes, these panels, of which several are now in the Guards' Chapel in Birdcage Walk, are worthy of close attention.

If the new sculpture, in its technical sense, was to be discovered anywhere else in the Royal Academy, it was in two pieces, in the graceful and refined 'Daphnis' of Mr. George Lawson, and in the rough and still imperfect group of ' The Death of Abel,' by Mr. T. Stirling Lee, a young artist of whom we shall presently have much to say. In each of these the infiltration of the French methods of work was clearly apparent, although as yet accepted with timidity in the one instance and clumsiness in the other. In Mr. Lawson's case the recurrence of the types of Flaxman and the pure Greek, for some time extinguished under bad Scotch influences, was an interesting sign of a better and freer age dawning for British sculpture. Mr. Lee, it was plain, had been captivated, even to excess, by modern French work.

In 1881 Mr. Thornycroft had by far the most prominent name. On the 20th of January, in spite of the fact that no fresh vacancy had occurred among the sculptor Academicians, he was elected A.R.A. by a very large majority. His contributions to the annual show were eagerly awaited, and when his magnificent 'Teucer' was discovered at the entrance to the Lecture Room, it shared, with the most remarkable of the pictures, an attention from the public which sculpture had long ceased to awaken. This virile and slightly archaic statue was a direct answer to those who had prophesied that the elements

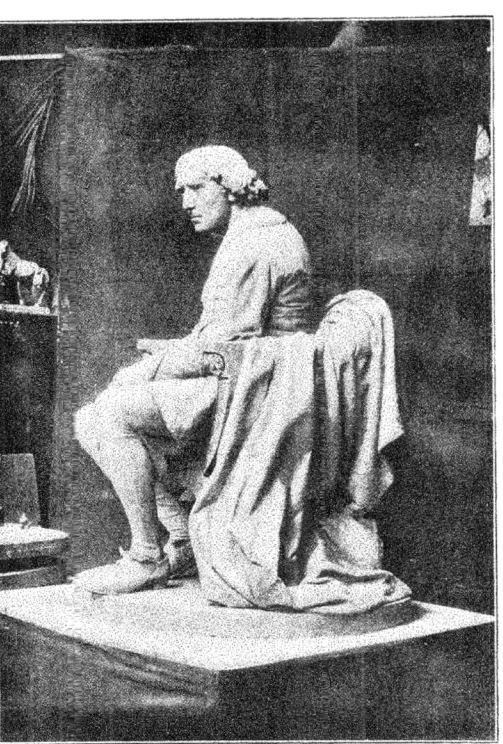

IRVING AS HAMLET. E. ONSLOW FORD, A.R.A.

of lyric grace and delicate refinement would alone prove to be at the command of the young artist. In the 'Teucer,' of which we give a small block, he proved himself master of the most masculine parts of workmanship.

Certain reforms undertaken in 1881 in the arrangement of the sculpture deserve to be recorded here, so great was the encouragement which they gave to the sculptors. Hitherto an absurd pyramid of shrubs and flowering plants had blocked up the middle of the Central Hall, and, what was worse, the busts were exhibited in a long row on a shelf running round what was then called the Sculpture Gallery, a small room now given up to pictures. In 1881 two large works, the 'Cleopatra' of Mr. Lawson and Mr. Brock's 'A Moment of Peril,' were placed where the centrepiece of shrubs had been, and by a most merciful providence, the busts were drawn away from the wall, and exhibited each on its own pedestal. Meanwhile the 'Teucer' and another statue were placed in the Lecture Room. In 1882 reform went still further: the pictures were turned out of the Lecture Room, a gallery specially well suited for sculpture, and the Vestibule, a room most improper for the exhibition of this art, on account of its raking perpendicular light, was relieved from the works which used to be shown there. At the same time the busts were drawn still farther from the wall. These were great reforms, the benefit of which is still enjoyed by the sculptors.

In other respects the exhibition of sculpture at the Royal Academy in 1881 was principally interesting as emphasising the features of the preceding year. Mr. Armstead displayed more of his curious panels in low relief, carved with unusual sensitiveness but somewhat experimental in the treatment of planes. Mr. Lawson surpassed himself in a dignified 'Cleopatra,' which, it is to be feared, has never been executed in a durable substance. Mr. T. Stirling Lee, in a statue of ' Cain,' showed great progress, and this was, no doubt, the work of the year in which the healthy French sentiment of the new school was most strongly felt. One new artist may be said to have made his appearance in 1881, Mr. Roscoe Mullins, for although work of his had been exhibited before, it had never shown the learning and accomplishment of his busts at the Royal Academy, or of his group of mother and child at the Grosvenor Gallery. His 'Conquerors,' though a little later in date, is reproduced in the headpiece as a typical specimen of his work. Meanwhile, the recognition of the new sculpture by the President and Council of the Academy did not go far, for the two works which were selected for purchase under the terms of the Chantrey Bequest were an old-fashioned group by an elderly sculptor who had known more skilful days, and 'A Moment of Peril' by Mr. Thomas Brock (b. 1847). This latter artist was presently to "find salvation," but at that time he was still in bondage to the practice of Foley, whose favourite pupil and accredited successor he was. In this his great bronze of a Red Indian fighting a snake he had followed Sir Frederick Leighton's 'Athlete' closely, and, at the same time, the equestrian statue of Outram by his late master, Foley. When we think of what Mr. Brock was eventually to do, the clumsiness of his work of this period is extraordinary.

In 1882 the critics and the general public woke up to the fact that English sculpture was revolutionised. For the first time in our artistic history, the sculpture at the Royal Academy could be inspected, and for the first time it was really worth inspection. But most of all, an *aura* of revival seemed to pass over all this art, hitherto so cold, so artificial, so spasmodically vitalised. Mr. Thornycroft was still the most prominent representative, as he had been the organizer, of the new school. His 'Artemis,' now executed in marble for the Duke of Westminster, and his 'Teucer,' cast in bronze, and presently purchased for the Chantrey collection, stood in the places of honour at the two ends of the Lecture Room, then first dedicated to sculpture. Both were presented with increased éclat; the marble having been worked up to the highest pitch of delicacy, and the bronze showing the effects of modifications made in the plaster after it returned to the artist's studio the autumn before. It was of the 'Teucer,' it is understood, that Sir John Millais spoke when he said that a certain work of a modern English sculptor was so fine "that were it dug up from under oyster-shells in Rome or out of Athenian sands, with the *cachet* of partial dismemberment about it, all Europe would straightway fall into ecstasy, and give forth the plaintive wail, 'We can do nothing like that now.'"

In 1882, Mr. Armstead, fired by a generous emulation with the younger men whose work he admired so much, rose to a culminating height. His little statue of 'Ariel' (above), not absolutely beautiful perhaps in arrangement, had a perfection of chiselled surface, full of individual detail, such as, it is safe to say, had not been seen equalled in England in the memory of man. In other work of his, a fine recumbent effigy, an unfinished panel of David wrestling with a Lion (see opposite page), Mr. Armstead displayed those qualities which make him so difficult to place in the criticism of our sculpture, and which affiliate him, without closer links, now to the French sculptors of the Renaissance, and now to the German.

Throughout the exhibition of 1882 signs might be discovered which led directly to satisfaction and to hope. As one eagerly passed round the walls one noted the name of Mr. Pinker as that of a careful and thoughtful young iconic artist, who had manifestly cast in his lot with the new ideals. Mr. Onslow Ford (although still showing but little of the peculiar brilliancy to be shortly developed) was working on, each year more skilful than the last. He was already at work on his fine iconic statue of 'Mr. Henry Irving,' the most important production of his first period. In the Salon of 1881, that powerful and eccentric genius, M. Auguste Rodin, had startled the amateurs of sculpture by the extreme cleverness of his 'St. John preaching in the Wilderness': the head of this dry and tortured composition was seen in the Royal Academy of 1882, and attracted much notice from the artists; while a mask by the same hand, strongly accentuating the element of picturesque or even of grotesque in sculpture, was to be seen at the Grosvenor Gallery.

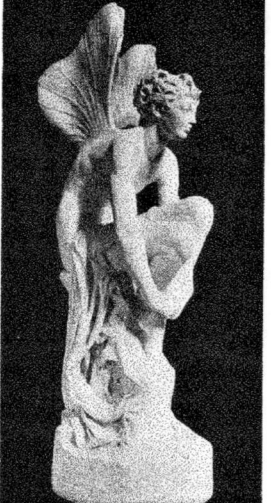

ARIEL. BY H. H. ARMSTEAD, R.A.
IN THE POSSESSION OF E. GOTTO, ESQ., J.P.

The great event, however, of 1882, was the appearance on the English horizon of a very eminent and shining star. There was so much to be seen in the Lecture Room that it was not, perhaps, every visitor who noticed a tenderly wrought and gracefully conceived marble group called 'The Kiss of Victory,' signed by a new name, that of Mr. Alfred Gilbert (b. 1854). Those who did so, however, must have felt that, here at least, was a wholly indubitable talent revealed. After the competition for the gold medal in 1874, Mr. Gilbert had gone to Paris, where, in the studio of Cavelier, he gained exactly the knowledge he required for the development of his genius. 'The Kiss of Victory,' I believe, was executed in Rome, but it showed not a trace of the bad Italian tradition. All that was not essential to the young artist himself, he owed to France. In particular, it cannot be rash to believe, that the author of this distinguished group of a young warrior dying under the shadow of the uplifted wings of a solemn Victory, had been greatly moved during his stay in Paris by that noble and tender monument, so rich in the purest and most sculptural dignity, the 'Gloria Victis' of Mercié. Curious as it may now seem, in the fuller development of Mr. Gilbert's talent, it was as an admirer and almost as an imitator of Mercié that this great original artist was first revealed to us.

Two other productions, each found in the Grosvenor Gallery, an 'Astronomy' and a 'Perseus Arming,' were, perhaps, more characteristic of what Mr. Gilbert has since become than the 'Kiss of Victory.' They were more picturesque, odd and unusual. The group in the Royal Academy revealed more plainly than they did what the training of Mr. Gilbert had been, and how completely he had learned the technical lessons which it was the privilege of Paris to teach him. But the 'Perseus Arming,' with its close study of natural forms, and its combination of virility and grace, showed the influence of Mercié's 'David' upon its author.

At the close of 1882 a lawsuit was tried, and decided on the 28th of December in favour of the plaintiff, which awakened the greatest possible public curiosity in the procedures and the habits of the sculptors. The once-famous Belt case was a trial of one not very distinguished artist on a charge of having libelled another by saying that he did not himself model the work he issued and sold as his own. The circumstances of the case itself are no longer of the slightest interest to anyone, but the issues of the trial were remarkably important in the development of the new school. In the first place, this picturesque and absurd tradition of the "ghost," the unseen Italian who entered the studio at night when the foppish and incompetent pseudo-artist had shown his clients into the street, and now carried on the real work—this tradition was fairly coped with and exposed. Whether in one or two dingy instances such a "ghost" was not employed was left uncertain. Perhaps in the light of subsequent revelations it may be admitted that he was employed. But at all events, it was very clearly propounded, and rubbed by a hundred newspapers into the stupidity of the ordinary citizen, that it was not the case that all sculpture was done by somebody else, that all sculpture presented exactly the same features and might have been done by one man or a firm of men, and that there was recognised among artists an individuality of touch.

In short, though it was impressed upon a jury that some sculptors might be rogues, it was also impressed that most sculptors were honest men.

The Belt trial, miserable and lamentable washing of dirty linen as it was, came at the right time. It attracted strong public attention to the art just at the moment when there was something for the world to look at. It enlightened a vast number of people, superficially, no doubt, but effectively, in the mysteries of sculpture. It emphasised the facts that the sculptor does not dash, in poetic frenzy, on a mass of marble and cut out the limbs of his statue as if he were slicing cheese. It modified the presentation of scenes in sculptors' studios on the stage and the imagery in the sonnets of minor poets. It did more, it united the jealous and suspicious confraternity of sculptors into closer and kinder relations against the common enemy, against the fashionable imposter and his "ghost." The year 1882 closed in melancholy for the sculptors; the case seemed to have been decided against them; the horrible "Pagliati bust" had been rolled round and round the court of Baron Huddlestone, and no one in that strange academy had seemed able to perceive in it high artistic merit. There was a sense of wretched disappointment throughout every branch of the profession, from the studios of the famous artists to the upper rooms where young and still unknown students were modelling on a piece of stick. The amateur and the "person of quality" seemed to have conquered all along the line. But we take such short views. After twelve years we can look back to that miserable episode, and see that it was all working out to the betterment of the status of our sculpture.

EDMUND GOSSE.

(*To be continued.*)

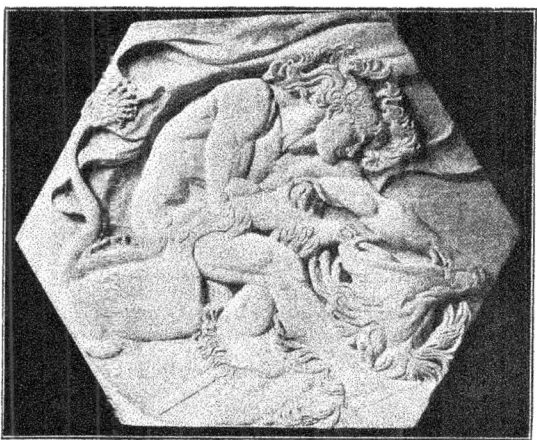

COURAGE. (DAVID WRESTLING WITH THE LION.) BAS-RELIEF BY H. H. ARMSTEAD, R.A. IN THE GUARDS' CHAPEL, NEAR BUCKINGHAM PALACE.

THE REHEARSAL. FROM THE PASTEL BY DEGAS.

DEGAS.

THE chief work that calls for mention of the studies of Degas's youth is his copy of a famous work by Poussin, 'The Rape of the Sabine Women,' in the Louvre Collection. In it he has followed the original with the greatest fidelity, reproducing so admirably Poussin's vigorous drawing and firm outlines, that if by some mischance his picture should be destroyed, one could almost say that this copy would make good the loss. Thus, at the very outset, Degas, led by instinct, as it were, to feel what was to be the chief characteristic of his own art, was drawn to the study of a master of exact form and learned technique.

In fact Degas has revived among the French school of painters a peculiarly national phase of Art, such as had previously been manifested by painters like Poussin and Ingres. For, in

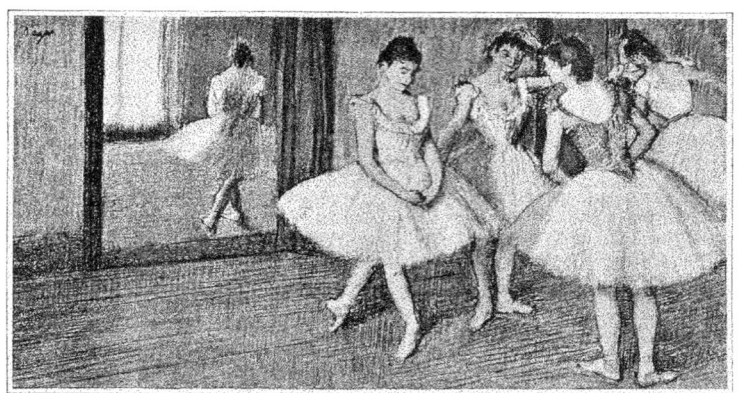

LA BLANCHISSEUSE. FROM THE PAINTING BY DEGAS.

spite of an apparent dissimilarity of conception in these two masters, they were actuated by the same strength of will, and subjected their themes to similar analytical and cerebral processes, so to speak; exhibiting a like sense of exact form and fixed methods of drawing, and a common logical concise disposition of parts in the balance of the whole. Poussin drew his inspiration from the antique, which he almost re-clothed with life, and Ingres studied Raphael, whose style he all but caught; but judging the two at this distance of time, one perceives, notwithstanding the distinct individuality of the art of each, that they possessed a resemblance caused by their common nationality, and amidst a crowd of masters of other schools, struck a note absolutely French, such as only Frenchmen can sound. Degas, allowing for different times and other surroundings, sounds at heart the same note as they, and must be ranked as their legitimate historical successor. He and they possess a common tendency to lead everything up to the drawing. That feast for the eye which masters of other schools seek in brilliant colour, "in the poetry of the palette," is foreign to them. Drawing, treated as an abstract beauty, is the aim of their achievements. They have given that attention to drawing which others of their nation have given to the medium of writing. The drawing of their subjects which gave their work its value to them, had to be absolutely perfect, in the same way that writers, like La Bruyère and Flaubert, would be satisfied with nothing short of the perfection of literary form.

To grasp the kinship of Degas with Poussin and Ingres, however, it is necessary to go much deeper than the mere surface of their respective works, for in respect of his choice of subjects, and of the point of view in depicting his scenes, he differs widely enough from the two old masters. The cause of this apparent difference lies in the fact that, notwithstanding the adherence to traditions shown by his prolonged studies, and by his love and knowledge of drawing, Degas is one of those artists who live in the closest contact with contemporary life, penetrating to the very heart of their own time. Thus it can be said of him that he is essentially not only a Frenchman, but a Parisian *fin de siècle*. No one has been more open than he to the various influences which have moulded the face of the time in which we live, and are giving it the distinctive character by which it will be known in the future. Finding himself at the commencemen of his career a contemporary of Manet, he has been, as it were, whetted by him to attempt to render modern life. Differing widely from the Impressionists in his methods of composition and work, Degas has none the less been brought into contact with them, and has profited by their scale of bright colour. The influence which the Japanese have exerted upon Art by the originality of their perspective and by their methods of placing the figure and accessories, has also left abiding traces in his style. Thus Degas' drawing, which is equivalent to saying the whole basis of his art, derives its inspiration from the sources of national tradition, tempered and modified by what has been given him of modern peculiarities by the surroundings in which he finds himself. This is the explanation of the novel aspect of his works.

In his choice of subject Degas has occupied himself with the female figure, generally ballet-dancers, and with race-horses. Besides his numerous renderings of these themes he has also devoted much work to the study of the nude. Portrait-painting and landscape he has practised more as accessories, as means to an end, or merely as studies. He works in three methods, oils, pastel, and drawing. Important oil paintings from his brush are comparatively few, and are already sufficiently rare to be eagerly competed for by collectors. Although in the majority of his oil pictures the composition is pleasing and gives with great perfection the effect aimed at, yet it must be confessed that in some of them there is a certain dryness and wiriness, allowing us to see the mechanism by means of which the effect has been obtained. Once again we are reminded that our artist's strong point, his predominating faculty, is his draughtsmanship, while the feeling for colour, strongest in such men as Manet, occupies with him only the second place. This is why he has preferred to work in the medium of pastel or crayon. He has been able to *draw* with it throughout, while at the same time giving his subject a soft-coloured envelope. It would be a mistake, therefore, in estimating the works of Degas to place his pastels after his paintings in oil, for they embody so completely the salient characteristics of his style that it is necessary to put them in the same rank. In fact one cannot be said to have grasped the whole of the man's art until one considers his oils and his pastels together. One could indeed almost go a step farther, and say that to comprehend his genius in its entirety it would be necessary to consider his drawings together with his oils and pastels; for drawings with him are never preliminary studies for paintings in oil, as with other artists, but have been carried to such perfection and raised to such importance that quite often they contain certain qualities not even to be found in his pictures.

When he first gave his attention to rendering scenes from the ballet he was content to depict simply certain slim and elegant beings in graceful motion. But from being merely a delicate and original painter of *genre* he has gradually raised his point of view to something infinitely more powerful. By incessant study of his subject and indefatigable perseverance

LA 'REMIÈRE DANSEUSE. (THE ENCORE.) FROM THE PASTEL BY DEGAS.
IN THE COLLECTION OF WILLIAM BURRELL, ESQ., GLASGOW.

he has succeeded in drawing out of a subject, which might have appeared at first sight both frivolous and unprofitable, all those elements of strength and pathos which he needed to express his perfect vision of woman herself. He has proved once more that, with genius, subject is a secondary matter, merely its opportunity, so to speak. It is out of itself, out of its inner consciousness, that the poetry and the beauty discovered in its productions are drawn.

It was caprice, a certain liking for dainty effect, and a love of elegant and nervous form, which drew Degas towards the ballet in the first place; but, studying more and more closely the *being* apart from the ballet dancer, he has ended by making his studies of "danseuses," convey a world of meaning to which at first they were strangers; penetrating behind the mere "danseuse," a particular class, he has caught and depicted the "*eternal feminine*" underlying every class. At first his "danseuses" were just what they seem to the ordinary observer—young women in a particular costume who appeared all smiles upon the stage, and conveyed to the eye, by means of graceful movements and studied poses, an effect of lightness, charm, and pleasure; but, as time went on, they were represented behind the curtain or in the flies as creatures agonised by their work, racked by the incessant effort to keep limbs and body supple. He gives their form the movements of female athletes, become so after a terrible strain, which has drawn from their frail bodies an enormous sum of strength and energy. With these works must be classed his studies of "danseuses" practising on the horizontal bar, with lightly contracted hands grasping the rigid bar placed just above their height, or hanging by the legs to obtain a serpentine flexibility of the body and a lengthening of the limbs.

From scant-clad ballet dancers to the study of the nude is but a short step. In commencing the study of the nude the conventional forms of tradition, handed down from the antique, and known as classic, are those which as a rule meet and seize the artist. But Degas' method of treating the nude has been quite original, for in depicting it he has simply developed farther the character which he had already formed and given of the modern Parisian woman. He has found new situations for the nude, in interiors, among rich fabrics and cushioned furniture. He has no goddesses to offer, none of the unveiled, legendary heroines of tradition, but woman as she is, occupied with her ordinary habits of life or of the toilette, exhibiting all the peculiarities—and one could often say even the defects—of a body unhealthily paled by town life; with wrinkled face, and bones too visible beneath the stretched skin, thin arms, short legs, and other obvious deformities. At first sight this looks like a breaking away from the past, and some have even gone so far as to call it a wilful pursuit of the repulsive; but such a powerful anatomy of the living body, rendered by so vigorous a method and by so precise a touch, and placed in environments so skilful and correct, leaves one at the end filled with admiration at a creation so absolutely masterly. And here it should be said that in the art of Degas there is to be found no speck of lubricity, no subtle taint of the unclean, such as might be found in the work of almost all treating like subjects; but, on the contrary, there runs through it rather a note of pain, a vein of pessimism, going almost to the length of downright cynicism.

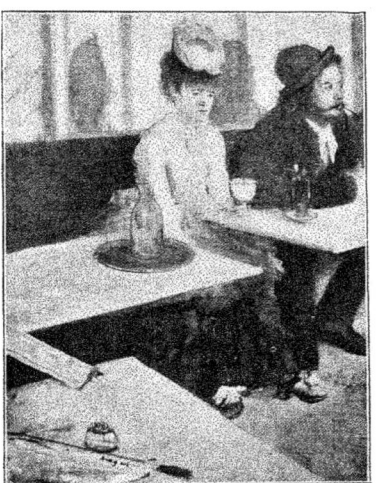

L'ABSINTHE. FROM THE PAINTING BY DEGAS.

It is in his studies and drawings from the nude that he has sounded with most vehemence this note of bitterness, which has to be reckoned with as an ingredient both of his art and of his personality. For a while he forsook his work in this direction, returning to the more refined side of Parisian life. Then we had a series of studies of *modistes* and millinery. In the greater part of these, even the *modiste* was put in the background, and hats of the last fashion, displayed upon stands in a shop window or on a table, became the principal persons in the compositions; persons is not too much to call them, for they have a personal character and an existence all their own.

Portrait-painting with Degas, as has already been said, holds but a secondary place. He has, however, indulged himself occasionally by recording a few typical characters. He has also given us—less frequently than we could wish—some few of those interiors in the style of the best Dutch painters, which perpetuate types of the people of a period. The masterpiece of his works of this kind is 'L'Absinthe.' Here a man and a woman are seated at a table in a café. The man is lounging over the table, smoking a pipe, with a glass of absinthe before him, while the woman that chance has placed next to him is staring straight before her with dull eyes in vacant thought. The foreshortened view of the tables, and the prominent shadows of the two, projected upon the clear depths of the window behind, contribute to complete the effect of the whole. This composition is one of the most vigorous that the artist has accomplished, and, as a study of contemporary manners, these two people form a perfect epitome of a class of shady individuals who spend their lives in the cafés of Paris, trifling away their days.

Racehorses have been treated and studied with as much attention as ballet dancers during the whole of our artist's career. They are in the animal world what the *danseuses* are

"LA LEÇON DE DANSE." FROM THE PAINTING BY DEGAS.

in the human, being trained for a special purpose, and full of nervous and graceful energy. And he has brought his racing scenes to as high a level of perfection as his representations of the ballet.

Degas's position among modern Frenchmen is, then, that of one who has revived the fixed drawing and exactness of form which others of his nation had manifested before him, and which may be said to be characteristics of the national art. At the same time, owing to his choice of subjects and the originality of his own genius, his art has had the appearance of being apart from current phases. In grasping the full breadth of his art one has to consider each of the stages through which it has passed—from the representation of charming creatures exhibiting elegance and coquetry, pictorial confections of refined woman, so to speak, to those lugubrious and fatal subjects which speak to us of lives misspent, of physical and moral health overdrawn. His work will thus remain as one of the most powerful, the most complex, and the most instinct with vitality amongst that of the masters of the nineteenth century.

Degas was born at Paris, and comes of an old bourgeois family. He is at the present time about sixty years of age. His personal appearance and manners are gentlemanly, quick, and direct; intellectually he is a keen—and often pitiless—observer of men and things. His conversation is incisive and full of sparkles of wit, often flashing out words and phrases which stick in the memory. His work and his studio absorb the whole of his life.

No one has carried to greater lengths than he a contempt for wealth, or a scorn for popularity and the publicity of the press; and no one has more utterly isolated and separated himself from others in order to create a work of genuine intrinsic value, apart from those things which bring mere ephemeral success—the superficial opinion and infatuation of the public.

In this respect, no man has shown a greater loyalty to Art, nor has maintained toward it a more inflexible attitude, and to our admiration of the man's work must be united our appreciation of the dignity of his life.

THÉODORE DURET.

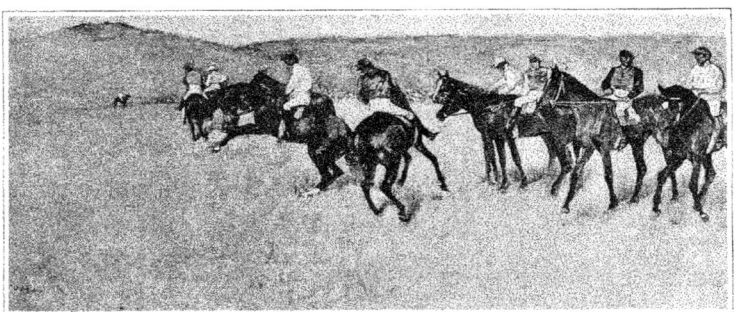

ON THE RACE-COURSE. FROM THE PAINTING BY DEGAS.

GREEK VASE PAINTING.*

IT was a happy idea which led Miss Jane Harrison to select examples of Greek Vase Painting, and to accompany them with descriptions and an introductory historical note. In the choice of illustrations she was aided by Mr. D. S. MacColl, who, moreover, contributes a preface explaining generally the origin of the plates, and offering acute critical remarks on the art of Greek Vase Painting. Speaking of these relics of Greek Art, Mr. MacColl, in the last sentence of his preface, gives the best reason for the publication of this book. "Tomb has delivered them to museum, and it is time that the book-worm should not be the only heir of his brother." If we judge rightly of its merits this volume will not remain in the hands of classical scholars and archæologists only; it appeals to a larger public, to artists and to all with a trace of taste for the fine arts, even to those whose curiosity is easily damped by dates and historical research. Mr. MacColl writes lightly and pictu-

* "Greek Vase Painting," a Selection of Examples with Preface, Introduction and Descriptions, by J. E. Harrison and D. S. MacColl. T. Fisher Unwin, London, 1894.

resquely in the preface, while Miss Harrison, in her part of the work, avoids superfluous erudition, all unnecessary matter, and any insistance on wearisome details. In writing her valuable essay, she has been careful so to sift the knowledge gained by many years of study, as to present her subject in the most compact, and the most lucid form.

Miss Harrison begins with an account of how vases were made and painted. A history of the black-figured masters, of the Transition period and of the red-figured masters is followed by an account of Athenian white funeral *Lekythoi*, after which Miss Harrison proceeds to examine the relation of the vase-painter to literature and to artistic tradition. She holds that his subjects were taken from mythology and daily life, and adds, "That borderland between fact and fiction, which we call history, the vase-painter would not suffer, or only when he had made mythology of it." He was no close illustrator of the written poem, but seemed rather to follow archaic types in his presentment of a subject than to seek a new composition by reading an epic poet for himself.

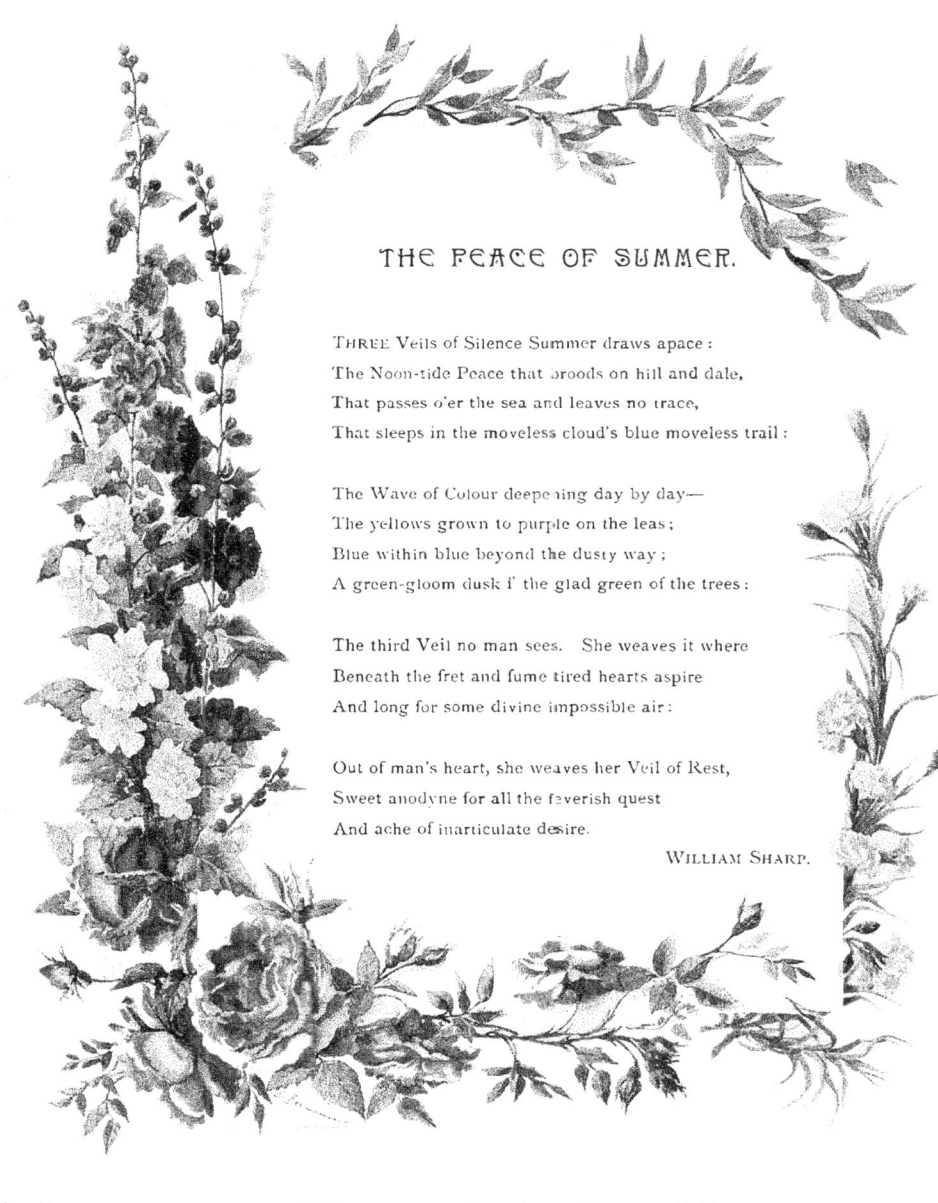

THE PEACE OF SUMMER.

THREE Veils of Silence Summer draws apace:
The Noon-tide Peace that broods on hill and dale,
That passes o'er the sea and leaves no trace,
That sleeps in the moveless cloud's blue moveless trail:

The Wave of Colour deepening day by day—
The yellows grown to purple on the leas;
Blue within blue beyond the dusty way;
A green-gloom dusk i' the glad green of the trees:

The third Veil no man sees.   She weaves it where
Beneath the fret and fume tired hearts aspire
And long for some divine impossible air:

Out of man's heart, she weaves her Veil of Rest,
Sweet anodyne for all the feverish quest
And ache of inarticulate desire.

WILLIAM SHARP.

The plates in "Greek Vase Painting" are arranged more or less in chronological order, and are constantly referred to in the Historical Note. The first example, of course in the earlier black-figured style, is signed Exekias, and illustrates the myth of Dionysius at Sea. Miss Harrison considers 'Heracles wrestling with Triton' the best example of black-figured work. Naturally, a decorative style, at once more involved and more flowing, is to be seen in the work of the red-figure men; 'The Revel' by Brygos, 'A Dance of Mænads' by Hieron, and 'Herakles and Geryones' by Euphronios, are only one or two out of many examples of a beautiful use of line and a wonderful sense of space-filling.

R. A. M. STEVENSON.

"AMONG THE MOORS."*

THIS book is an account of a journey through a good part of Morocco by a few friends, able—such influence had they—to go everywhere worth the going, and see everything worth the seeing. The style is a trifle turgid, but the author is a careful, honest, and good-humoured reporter as well as observer, so these scattered scenes effect a very exact and lifelike impression of Morocco as it is to-day. That impression is of a delightful climate, enchanting days, still more enchanting nights, a fascinating and varied landscape, now long stretches of barren desert, again luxuriant richness of hill and vale, an odd jumble of human figures clad in gaudy and varied dresses, artistic and impressive architecture everywhere falling into decay, incredible laziness and incredible filth. If one were to sum up Morocco in two words, these would be "picturesque" and "dirty." Take a street in Tangier ('tis the same at Mesquinez and Fez): "Dark narrow passages between high walls, with barred windows, parts of wall crumbling away at the base, and threatening every moment to tumble down. Through half-open doors thick vapours of fœtid odours escape. The road, paved in some places, cut up in others, is a sink of liquid mud, in which float loathsome carcases, dead cats, putrid fowls." The travellers take refuge in a café, of itself a picture, and then again near the tomb of a saint they find a snake-charmer, who goes through the strangest evolutions with a cobra, while his fellow plays on a bamboo flute a slow, melancholy rhythm. Peeping through an open door, they see a courtyard round which are "horse-shoe arches, with pillars overlaid with tiles in exquisite taste, opening into profound recesses shrouded in semi-darkness." There is also a marble fountain, ornamented with mosaics, and Moorish and negro servants clad in red and white. They descend into a vaulted dungeon, a haunt of haschich smokers, their nostrils filled with unknown odours, their ears filled with fantastic melodies.

The book is copiously and admirably illustrated. We have culled some examples at random. 'Nasty weather' shows the

* By Geo. Montbard. Sampsor Low & Co.

land across a long, flat, gloomy plain, the horizon hid in mist, pools of water on the barren ground. A pelting rain pours steadily down. Another is a charming 'Woman of Mesquinez at Home,' touched with a certain barbaric splendour. The travellers visit the prison, and one guesses the misery and filth here are *quite* beyond description, though they are met by the stolid resignation of the chained victims.

From the roof of the house where they are lodged they see long stretches of terraces, circles of hills round the town, and Atlas with its snow in the far distance. The women are at

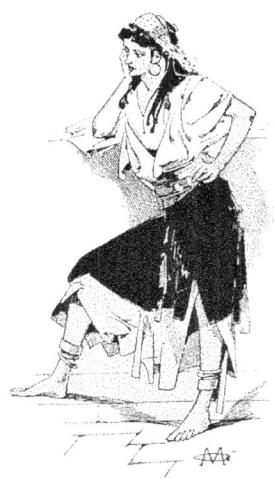

A WOMAN OF MESQUINEZ AT HOME.
BY G. MONTBARD.

least free of the house-tops; they sit on the edge with their feet dangling over, watching the people in the street, and chatting with their neighbours on the other side. Out of these higher levels ascend the minaret towers of the mosques, wherefrom, as the day falls, there rises the shrill droning voice that in strange accents calls all the Moslem world to prayer. By all means let us off to Morocco!

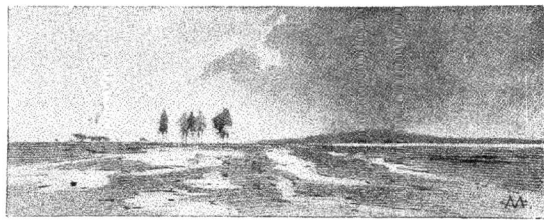

NASTY WEATHER. BY G. MONTBARD.

THE ROYAL ACADEMY, 1894.

NEW paint displeases the eye—especially when it occurs fortuitously on extensive walls or hoardings. This is the case of a large annual exhibition, for no one can pretend that the pattern of the walls is in any way designed. The object of the show is to give a general view of all the Art of the country —good, bad, and indifferent, æsthetic or commonplace, realistic or decorative, large or small, bright or sober—and this display, questionable from an artistic standpoint, seems necessary from a practical point of view of commerce. But it makes it extremely difficult for a person to feel sure of the intrinsic worth of any picture in the exhibition, or to judge confidently of what appearance it might make in other surroundings. At any rate, to form a sound conclusion about any one picture takes considerably more seeing than would be necessary if it were hung alone, and there are, let us say, a thousand pictures in the Academy. If one is in a humble mood the first glance at so much powerful fresh pigment, so many things drawn and coloured, inspires one with respect for such a monument of toil and accomplishment. Presently, when some more than usually decent canvas has kept one under a spell for a few minutes, one turns away to see the face of things changed, the glamour gone, and one realises that numbers of bad things do not make a good one, any more than many misdemeanours a crime. Indeed, one poor or mediocre canvas were better seen alone than staled by others and expounded by the light of worse than itself. It takes a very good man indeed to look well in a bank holiday crowd; but it is easy for a picture or a man to attract notice in a throng. Size, coarseness, and loud colours will win remark for either. Therefore, I do not mean to speak of all the conspicuous canvases in the Academy, nor do I pretend that those I mention are the only good ones. They are those that I shall speak of after a few words of general import.

Happily, the true gymnastic of art, working from the nude figure, continues to be practised or encouraged in England. Pictures with nudes come from Messrs. Bouguereau, Tadema, J. M. Swan, Herkomer, Tuke, Altson, Draper, B. E. Ward, G. Harcourt, Margetson, A. D. McCormick, and from Miss Henrietta Rae. Not all of these are really excellent, but the list of them contains one or two among the best pictures in the Academy. We have not mentioned with these that most prominent feature of this year's exhibition, Mr. J. S. Sargent's 'Lunette and Portion of Ceiling,' painted for the Public Library of Boston. It contains nude figures representing the persecuted children of Israel, but they obey a decorative law, and though a central point of the lunette they are merely a symbol, round which the warfare of higher powers is waged. On one side Pharaoh steps up to smite the Hebrews with a battle-axe; on the other, the Assyrian stands ready to strike, but from out of the rosy wings of the cherubim the hands of Jehovah are outstretched to stay the persecutor. The devices of the ceiling are interwoven over the dark formless body of primeval Night—in the centre, the sun and the signs of the Zodiac, from which rays shoot down to the left over the horned figure of Moloch, who faces Astarte, robed in blue diaphanous gauze, on the right. Description fails to give any idea of the novelty, wealth of invention, and barbaric beauty of this wonderful and original design. It blazes with gold moulded in relief on the handles of swords, on wings, head-dresses, and ornaments. It is astonishing to

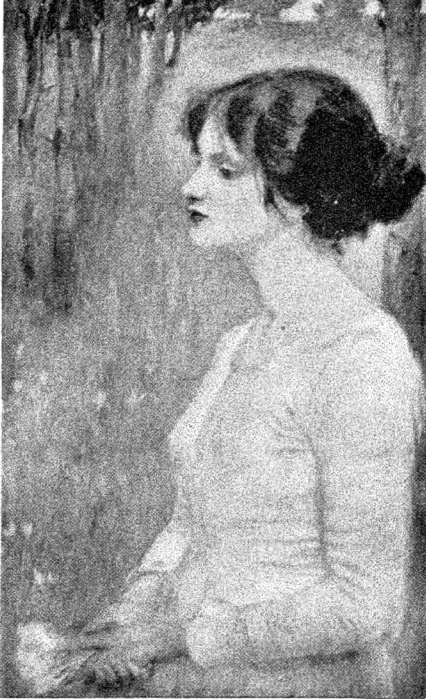

FIELD FLOWERS. BY J. W. WATERHOUSE, A.R.A.

see how this brilliant master of realistic style, this mirror of natural character, turns himself away from true light and living fact, and reflects a sort of mystic procession of archaic types and forgotten civilisations. But his magic of style and execution has not abandoned Mr. Sargent when he turns from nature to convention. The sacred emblems of Egypt, the bird and beast of Assyria, together with the dim Asian monsters that nurtured Greece, appear under the traditional form which would be recognisable by their ancient worshippers.

Some of the large nudes may strike you at first by their size and audacity, or may command your respect by their serious qualities of drawing and modelling; few of them, however, wear as well as less ambitious work, or possess to a satisfactory degree the insinuating virtue of an artistic *ensemble*. Here is a large baggy nymph of Mr. Herkomer's creation who inhabits a strange brown region bristling with white speckles of light. This is neither a quiet conventional background nor a landscape in acceptable relation to a figure. Were the figure cut out as an upright composition the treatment might appear more appropriate to the proportions of landscape and figure. Mr. Draper's 'Sea Maiden' caught in a fisher's net, grows daily more patently false to the visitor, and, as its unreality becomes apparent its febrile violence of colour becomes revolting. To a lesser extent this criticism holds good in the case of Mr. G. Harcourt's 'Psyche,' illumined by a setting sun. The figure in Mr. J. M. Swan's 'Orpheus' is full of grace and alive with movement. To see the masterly modelling you must stand fairly close to the canvas, but, unfortunately, to be freed from the importunity of surrounding accessories you must almost place yourself at the far end of the long gallery. I find Mr. Tuke's 'August Blue,' boys bathing from a boat, and Mr. Altson's 'Golden Age,' nude girls playing and dancing in the evening sun, about as good as any pictures of their class. In both cases the intention of the artist is to show things, where her fanciful or real, taking place as they might in nature. Too often weakness of imagination, incompetence in performance, or the mere delirium of the impossible, wraps itself in the mantle of decoration, defies criticism, and outrages with impunity that hereditary perception of reality from which alone our ideas of beauty can be derived. Beauty in Art comes from some side

of nature keenly felt and translated to best advantage on the flat. The two pictures in question make no claim to be judged on any more supernatural pretension to excellence. We may plead as much for some figure-pictures other than nudes, as well as for portraits and landscapes. In this connection we may quote the names of Messrs. J. H. Lorimer, Alma Tadema, John Collier, H. La Thangue, and H. H. Robinson; and I dare say that even Sir Frederick Leighton, Mr. Waterhouse, Mr. Boughton, and Mr. Dicksee would not object to be criticised on a point of large truth if one made fair allowance for the ideal or fanciful element in their work.

TURNING THE PLOUGH. BY GEO. CLAUSEN, R.W.S.

But I have not space to undertake so much, and I must speak of one or two pictures that have a peculiar interest for me. I will merely remark in passing that Mr. Lorimer's charming scheme of colour, 'The Eleventh Hour,' has the air of a young, sprightly, and less artificial Orchardson with its face washed. Like Mr. Orchardson, however, Mr. Lorimer takes in more width of view than he need. He might have concentrated his composition, or if not, he might have fused his subsidiary definitions after the manner of Corot. Not that he sins more than most men in this respect, but that his work is better worth improving.

Amongst the smaller pictures with a marked landscape interest you will find some canvases of exceptional charm. Mr. Clausen's 'Turning the Plough,' illustrated above, is one of the most fascinating things he has done. Whilst many large and showy pictures affecting poetry or loftiness of subject slowly reveal the secret of their trickiness and insincerity, this little poem of Mr. Clausen's remains fresh and interesting. It is composed naturally as it was felt, and not built up according to law or precedent. So the arrangement looks quaint but not eccentric, as of a thing seen in nature and shown with art. The canvas fits the group to perfection, and an intelligent treatment enforces the meaning of the main impression. The local tints of everything except the white horse and a few jewel-like flowers are brown and low, but they are steeped in an iridescent evening air in which both the shadow and the light are coloured. Too well one knows the usual renderings of such a scene; the bald nominal hues of fustian and ploughed land rudely streaked with cadmium and rose-madder, or else a visionary rainbow ghost without depth, body, or gloom. In

Mr. Clausen's picture one feels both sides of the truth as in nature: the underlying facts of solid shape and local tint, and also the luminous aërial robe shot with rosy light and blue and violet reflections.

Landscape and figure, since 1830, at least, appears to be a branch of Art in which many views of nature and many problems of style are worked out. Mr. Austen Brown, in 'Returning from Pasture,' seeks to add something like the quality we admire in lacquer or old furniture to a view of nature which might have been conceived by Mauve. We must grant him a colouring certainly agreeable, yet not finer than that of Sir John Day's 'Girl and Cows,' by Mauve. But in the interest of this decorative quality Mr. Austen Brown is content to forego all that subtlety of drawing, values and modelling, which in Mauve's picture so powerfully strikes the chords of association with nature. Though 'Returning from Pasture' inclines to be an object of vertu, rather than a representation of pictorial Art, it is one of the notably beautiful canvases of this year, and when we are tired of it and desire the more durable poetry of nature we can easily turn to Mr. Clausen, Mr. J. W. Waterhouse, Mr. A. Lemon, or other men of their turn of mind. 'Field Flowers,' by Mr. Waterhouse, of which we give a representation, is an exquisitely fresh and dainty upright of a girl gathering flowers in the silvery light of early morning. The head is charming and appropriately handled under the conditions of light; the greens are soft and naturally grey. In his picture 'Returning to Work,' Mr. Lemon has arranged, with the simplicity of science, two horses, a dog, a figure, a powdery path traversing a chalky down, and a great blue gap in grey clouds. His high silvery colour represents the dry dusty tones peculiar to such a country if you look broadly without decomposing the light. Mr. T. Griffiths

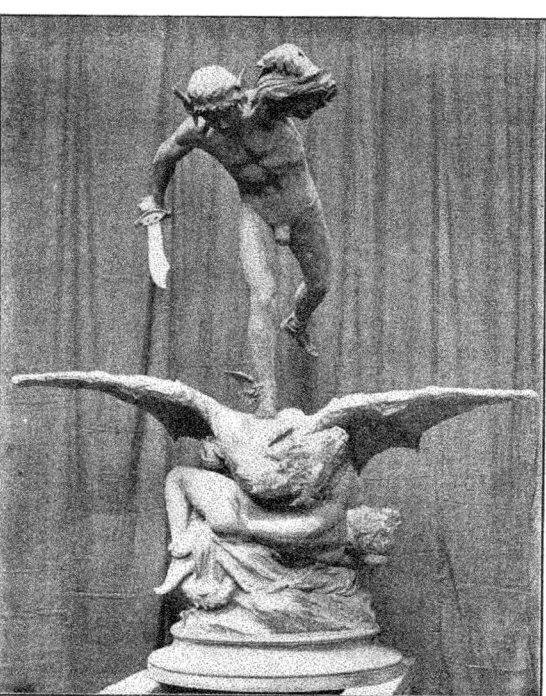

PERSEUS RESCUING ANDROMEDA. BY HENRY C. FEHR.

arranges a picture as well as any one; he chooses an evening scene and seeks to produce the effect of iridescence by means of the "pointilliste" manner of handling.

In portrait and in pure landscape there is nothing that I have space to discuss at length in this article, and there is perhaps little unlike the production of former years. Mr. Purse's portrait of Lord Roberts associates itself in some measure with the pictures we have just spoken of. It is, in fact, a reiteration of the once-popular equestrian portrait, conceived in proportions that are almost landscape with figure. Mr. Furse has not followed some of the moderns in the difficult enterprise of making a portrait on the lines of a realistic figure study out of doors. He aims at no closer naturalism than Van Dyck looked for in treating Charles I. on horseback. Mr. Furse is perhaps less realistic than Regnault was in 'Marshal Prim.' We cannot criticise the exhibit fully as it is a sketch for a larger picture, and for this reason doubtless the head appears a little over-studied and a little too fresh in colour. The colour-scheme of the foreground, trees and white horse, is much to be admired.

Of course, you may see finer and more complete portraits in the Academy. There is one, for instance, by Mr. Furse himself, as well as notable work by Sir G. Reid, Mr. Sargent, Mr. Orchardson, Mr. Lavery, Mr. Outram, Mr. Collier, Mr. Greiffenhagen, and others, but we shall speak of them no more than of interesting landscapes by Messrs. Hook, Parton, Davis, R. J. Leigh, P. W. Adam, A. Brownlie Docharty, W. MacBride, E. Waterlow, and ever so many more. Even if one cannot describe them or criticise them, it is well to mention a work or two that detained one in the melancholy journey round the water-colour room and the black-and-white room. There is not much to see there, but I remarked Mr. Garden Smith's solemn sunset, 'Borderers,' in the water-colour room, and Mr. Hole's translation of the 'Admiral,' by Velasquez, in the National Gallery, Mr. C. W. Sherborne's book plates, and Mr. H. M. Paget's 'Boxing Contest.' Amongst the sculpture one cannot avoid noting Mr. Gilbert's sketch for a monument to the Duke of Clarence. It is an ingenious scheme which can only be judged at present by the decorative effect of its general design. We give an illustration of a notable group, 'Perseus rescuing Andromeda,' by Mr. Henry C. Fehr. Andromeda and the Dragon, in a tumbled heap, serve as a kind of pedestal for the light, active figure of Perseus. His attitude shows lively movement, but not uncomfortably, and the bearing leg seems excellently modelled. This has been purchased by the Academy out of the Chantrey Fund.

R. A. M. STEVENSON.

ARCHITECTURE AT THE ROYAL ACADEMY.

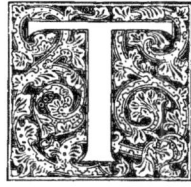

THE first impression received on entering the Architectural Room at the Royal Academy this year is one of confusion, amounting almost to chaos. Amidst a number of drawings of high excellence—though, truth to tell, the perspective has been unduly strained in several instances—executed in many different styles and in various media, it is at first difficult to appreciate the buildings which they represent and to grasp the meaning of their designers. Slowly, however, the buildings seem to appear one by one, and an array of modern architectural works presents itself which is hopeful in the extreme, especially when it is remembered that it represents but a very small proportion of the good work being done in our country in this great building age. It is not that there are any huge erections which stand out above all others, illustrating, possibly, the genius of a solitary man, but that the general spirit is so true, so national, so artist-like. Of schools there are many, of eccentricities there are not a few, and yet amidst it all the right Art feeling is constantly apparent.

Of course, there are exceptions to this rule. The strict revivalists, whether they work upon classic or on Gothic lines, have failed, as they must fail, presenting the precisely correct mouldings and exact proportions of their models and losing sight of the spirit of the ancient workers. It may safely be said that no one has shown himself imbued with the highly intellectual appreciation of the beautiful which actuated the Greeks in the best Grecian times; and yet, without it, to attempt buildings of strictly Grecian "pattern" is to court failure only. Similarly he who produces an "Early English" church, however exactly he may conform to precedent, if he be not possessed of the lofty purpose and poetic temperament of the Art-builders of the Middle Ages, can present nothing more in his finished building than a series of hard lines and curves.

The best efforts of the classic school are rather Renaissance than truly classic in their dress, with the exception, perhaps, of Mr. William Young's drawing of the marble staircase at the Glasgow Municipal Buildings. This is purely Roman in its treatment; but, beautiful as the drawing is, and excellent as is the work which it delineates, it may be questioned whether representations of different parts of this same building, long since completed, should be allowed to appear in the Academy year after year. A second exhibit by the same architect, a perspective view of Culford Hall, shows equally well the master-hand and the careful, thoughtful appreciation of what true dignity consists in.

Dignity and restraint are the most marked characteristics of the other Renaissance examples, generally without too marked formality. Mr. H. H. Statham's scheme for remodelling the front of the National Gallery is most noticeable in this respect, adding to the present uninteresting façade just that amount of dignity which it so sadly lacks. It is sorrowful to think how little chance the scheme has of realisation, while yet one is glad to have shown, if only upon paper, what it would be possible to do to render beautiful one of the great eye-sores of the Metropolis. We commend this scheme to the powers that be.

Some more of the best drawings in the room, in classic style, are those of Mr. John Belcher's works. The Institute of Chartered Accountants, with its deliberate lack of purity, redeemed by its great strength and the beauty of the sculpture with which it is adorned, is already well known through the monograph about it which has been published, and it is certainly one of the most remarkable buildings erected in London of recent years. In Mr. Belcher's design for the completion of South Kensington Museum, however, there is much greater purity, and a breadth of treatment which is rare. It is not to be carried out, another design having been preferred before it; and doubtless, putting convenience of plan aside—which the assessors in a competition cannot do —the design now under consideration would not harmonize well with the other huge erections which would be its neighbours at South Kensington, for it would show them off to disadvantage.

Edinburgh, always the home of a severe form of Renaissance, is represented at the Academy by 'St. Cuthbert's Church,' as recently altered by Mr. H. J. Blanc. The view chosen is a good one, the new turrets and the apsidal end reminding of Wren's school, in the simple lines of the latter and the dignified elaboration of the former. Insular as was this school, it has never had any great number of exponents since those men died, over whom Wren himself had exercised his personal influence; but it is worth reviving, and is suitable to the capitals of either of the sister kingdoms.

Turning our attention to the works of a different character, it is noticeable how almost universally our architects are now imbued with the Gothic feeling; how few works are of the hard and formal character of the revival period of a short time since, and how many show development and growth upon the true old lines. Of course, in works of reconstruction or repair, the ancient model has to be more closely followed than in entirely new buildings; yet even in such cases a certain amount of latitude of treatment is permissible, as it was certainly thought to be by the mediævalists. Even when buildings of the thirteenth century, left half completed then, were finished in the fourteenth or the fifteenth, according to the original design, the change of date is marked most clearly by differences of detail and of workmanship. In the same way, there can be no reason why the work of the nineteenth century should not be as readily distinguished—and, in fact, it may well appear to many to be ethically false to copy the work of other days so closely that those who come after us will not be able to discriminate between old and new. Thus it may be in times to come with the Church of St. Saviour, Southwark, of which a fine drawing is exhibited by Sir A. W. Blomfield. Looked upon as a piece of mediæval designing, the new south transept is beautiful, in keeping with the older portions of the church; but it would require an expert antiquary, in the course of a few centuries and in the absence of documentary evidence, to affirm that it was not part of the original fabric, and this in spite of eccentricity of tracery. This fault, if fault it be (and there are two opinions upon the point), is not so noticeable in the new stalls for the same church, in which there is a something, hardly to be described in words, which tells of the present day; and when dealing with a piece of furniture, the architect probably felt more free to do as he liked than when reconstructing a building which had been destroyed by an act of vandalism.

Possibly the strict following of precedent, so often seen, is largely due to the amount of measuring and sketching of old work which has been, and is still, indulged in by the younger men; and it is remarkable that many of the drawings hung this year in the Architectural Room at the Academy are studies of this kind—studies of ancient and existing works rather than the productions of living artists. Whether such should not be relegated to the Black and White Room is very questionable. The painter and the sculptor have to exhibit their own works, and, not being able to do this in actuality, architects are permitted to represent theirs by drawings of them; but it is quite doubtful whether these should be hung side by side with antiquarian studies, or with pretty sketches of old buildings, which in no way demonstrate that power of design and composition which it is necessary that the true architect should possess.

This careful study, which, in its right place, is absolutely necessary, even though it need hardly be in direct evidence at the Academy, has, however, in the last few years, been productive of something more than mere copyism—of a revival of the old spirit of development, so evident in other branches both of applied and of pictorial art. The first and most evident feature at present has been the engrafting of foreign ideas upon the strictly English form, and in some few instances of the production of buildings of almost completely foreign character, as, for example, in Mr. Fellowes Prynne's 'Church of All Saints,' at West Dulwich, which is exceedingly good, and as exceedingly German. The detail cannot be judged from the perspective drawing which is hung, but this is the impression conveyed by the general design and grouping. As a rule, however, it is in minor matters that the foreign influence is shown, while the general outline is English in character—the French flèche to the English church, near Preston, designed by Messrs. Clark & Hutchinson, for instance. Even in the more purely English designs which evidence this inclination towards development, as in the widely different churches of St. Augustine, at Sudbury, by Mr. Leonard Stokes, and that of St. Peter's, at Bushey Heath, by Mr. C. Neale, it is much to be doubted whether the great amount of foreign travel which is now undertaken, and the large number of sketches of foreign buildings which are annually published, have not greatly tended towards this advancement. A completely modern feature, this eclecticism, so long as it does not obliterate all national characteristics, is far from regrettable. As at present exercised, it seems to lead to a new life and a strong life, of which much good may be expected—and life of any sort, if healthy, is to be welcomed after a long dead period.

It is this same life which has been evidenced in our smaller municipal buildings, and in our domestic work, during the last decade—this same planting of the foreign upon English and the English upon foreign—until a new style has arisen, which future generations will recognise as that of the present day, though most of us are blind enough not to see what is going on around, and to give our works all sorts of fancy names. Nor is this much to be wondered at; for the work, while breathing the same spirit, whether it be applied to a town-hall, a school, or a farmhouse, is clothed in many a different dress, and adorned with details, often rich gems in themselves, brought from many a different country. Of half-timbered and tile-hung houses, with their simple grouping, so suitable for erection in wooded districts, and so distinctive of modern English architecture as to be the admiration of our foreign neighbours, there are many examples shown upon the Academy walls. Without exception these are good, and while in most instances they show the individuality of their designers, their family resemblance is striking, and this in spite of some being Renaissance, some Gothic, and several nondescript in style. Homeliness is perhaps the best word to describe what is here meant. It is as apparent in the broadly treated 'Summer Cottage for the Undercliffe,' by Mr. V. T. Jones, tile-hung and extremely simple, with turrets at the angles, as much as in Mr. T. W. Cutler's 'House at Enfield,' with its broken outline and rich timbering; these being instanced as examples only, for there is much more work of similar character displayed, and a great deal more is being erected all over England, by architects of different tastes and characters, but who have caught the spirit of the day, and are honestly meeting the demand for comfortable homes for English families.

It is the same, again, with the houses in brick and stone, the difference being in the material used and in the style adopted, and not in the desire for homeliness and comfort which underlies it all. It is equally the same with the essentially English work of Messrs. Gotch & Saunders, at Elm Bank, Kettering, and of Mr. L. J. Williams, at The Gables, Nightingale Lane, Balham, both of which buildings are examples of successful reproduction of the best domestic work of the Elizabethan period; and again, it is noticeable even in such an original production as the schools at Port Sunlight, by Messrs. Douglas & Fordham.

So also with larger works to meet various requirements, where the divergences of style are even more marked than in the small domestic buildings, there is a very general appreciation of the demands, from an æsthetic point of view, of buildings designed for different purposes and in different positions. So, equally admirable, are the Victorian Institute at Worcester, by Messrs. Simpson & Allen (like which there is much else now being put up in England and none elsewhere), the almost entirely German design by Messrs. Gibson & Russell for the County Council offices at Wakefield, and the suitable suggestion for new premises in Moorgate Court, by Mr. H. Huntly-Gordon.

There are many other drawings of really great excellence,

representing, as well as drawings can, the main features of designs which are intended to be carried out in solid substance; but enough has been said to show that there are hopeful signs in modern architecture, even as judged from such inadequate data as can be put before the public at the Royal Academy. The modern architect roams far afield, and gathers his ideas from many places, but those which he imbibes are good; and, possessed with the general conviction that he must suit his designs to their surroundings, and give an impression of comfort to domestic work and of dignity to such buildings of municipal and of national importance as may occasionally come his way, he does not as a rule go far astray. He does his best, and honestly, thus laying down in permanent materials the history of the inner thoughts and feelings of the people of his country and his day.

G. A. T. MIDDLETON.

HENRIETTA MONTALBA:—A REMINISCENCE.

IT is, I believe, one of the canons of the "new" criticism—or at least the chief creed of one of its more truculent mouthpieces—that women have been tried, and found finally wanting, as original artistic exponents. This is neither the time nor place to enter into the vexed question of sex in art, but were the question at issue, it is obvious that a pretty argument for the defence might be raised by the mention of the names of a dozen women who have of late gained little short of universal recognition. Amongst such a group Henrietta Montalba, no less than her famous sister Clara, holds a prominent place. In truth the sisters Montalba, like the brothers Maris, occupy, amid artistic families, something of an analogous position; analogous, I should say, to make my meaning clear, in sharing—as a family—a like bent joined to a like whole-hearted devotion.

Miss Henrietta Montalba, the youngest of the four well-known sisters, was born in London, and studied, to the credit of that much-abused department, at what is informally known as "South Kensington" and later, when the family migrated to Venice, exchanging fog and stucco for the laughing waters of the green lagoons, at the Belle Arti of that city. It was, however, if I mistake not, at the former institution, that is to say at South Kensington, that a friendship sprang up between Henrietta Montalba and another sculptor, Princess Louise, who not long after invited the sisters to Ottawa during the governor-generalship of the Marquis of Lorne in Canada. Here, it may be believed, that an orgy of work was indulged in by the enthusiastic fellow-students, who, falling on each other, painted and "busted" each other with a result now known to all the world. Princess Louise's oil-painting of Miss Montalba is still remembered by visitors to the Grosvenor Gallery, though the portrait, in which the sitter's picturesque—and no less striking than picturesque—face is outlined against a decorative background of azalias, is now, by the Princess's gift, a part of the Ottawa Academy collection. A probably no less well-known presentment by her sister Ellen, I may mention, was exhibited at Burlington House, and is reproduced on this page.

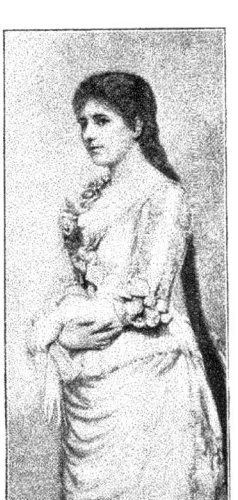

HENRIETTA MONTALBA.

Handsome and accomplished, a woman of parts, Henrietta Montalba had no less the modesty which is supposed to be the prerogative of the dull and plain. A linguist, a traveller, a student, yet instinct with a rare feminine sympathy, graciousness, and tact, one is tempted to stray from the study of Miss Montalba as a sculptor in order to dwell on her delightful personality as a woman. Not but what this personality is to be seen in her work. Art is the history of personalities, or rather a man's art is nothing but the visible record of himself. The inward and visible grace of Henrietta Montalba's personality had, then, its proper outward and visible sign. It was visible, now in the delicate modelling of a child's cheek, now in the suggestion of what of spirituality lay hidden in a poet's phlegmatic face. A small terra-cotta bust of a female child called, if I remember rightly, 'A Study,' is an excellent example of this quality of inwardness that I have in mind. There is realism in the study—more particularly in the spirited treatment of the hair; but added to the realism enough of that right kind of ideality to make the bust a type of childhood, rather than a mere portrait of some one and particular child. It may be urged, and with reason, that this inwardness must needs form an essential in the many component parts which go to make a work of art. Yet how many portraits in the plastic and other arts do we not see which give us the mere envelope or map of the subject?

Miss Montalba's chief essays were in portraiture, her medium being, for the most part, the somewhat treacherous and unsatisfactory one of terra-cotta. The artist worked, and worked with no little success, in Doulton's clay, but was, as we know by her later efforts, finally weaning herself of her allegiance to terra-cotta. Two of the sculptor's principal achievements, the head of Robert Browning, and the bust of Pallas illustrating Poe's masterpiece, "The Raven," were in what I am forced to call the "treacherous" medium, but the portrait of the Marquis of Lorne, and the full-length nude statue known as a 'Boy catching a Crab,' were seen translated into bronze; while a bust of Mr. George F. White was wrought in the sterner medium of marble.

venture in the round, one, in good sooth, held to be the finest work to which the artist put her hand, is the 'Raven,' already referred to. In the first work, spontaneity, largeness, which is yet not looseness of handling, is joined to a very individual sense of beauty, while in the second, much felicity of detail is married to a fine initial conception. Miss Montalba's bronze Raven, to use a somewhat venerable metaphor, "lives"; in its delicately caressed modelling is to be traced the sculptor's more than common understanding of birds.

Returning to portraiture, the artist attempted another child-study in 'Ethel'; a bust which, if suggesting something too much a Kate Greenaway in the round, has grace and decorative charm; while, happier in a more difficult subject, the year 1889 saw the birth of her original, comprehensive, and vigorous version of the poet, Robert Browning. The full length statue of a Venetian fisher-boy, called a 'Boy catching a Crab' (see illustration), was the artist's last serious essay in ideal composition, and, seen as it was a year ago in the Central Hall of the Royal Academy, needs neither comment nor praise in these pages. Briefly, what is notable in the work is its directness, its distinctiveness of conception. No over-accentuation, so common in common sculpture, no over-affectation of learning, so ordinary in ordinary sculptors, mars the modelling of the recumbent figure. The muscular structure of the torso and limbs is studied, and withal lovingly studied, but a masculine reticence, a certain rhythmical balance are marked characteristics of the work, and go a long way to make the unity as well as the naturalistic charm of the whole.

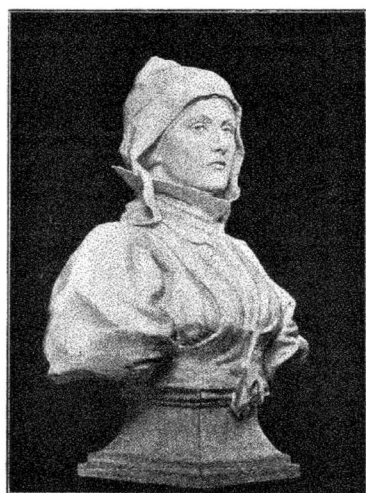

SWEDISH PEASANT. BY HENRIETTA MONTALBA.

To begin at the beginning and give even the briefest notion of the scope of Henrietta Montalba's output, we must go back to the year 1875, when the young student, then little more than a girl, exhibited a portrait of her father. The success of the attempt fortified the young sculptor for the ardours of the most wearing of all professions. 'Tito' and 'Romola,' companion busts in terra-cotta, and many really felicitous renderings of child life, followed. The bust of Lord Lorne, perhaps, more certainly proclaimed her powers. A glance at this portrait proves it to be informed with learning, distinction, and above all style, a quality without which a piece of sculpture is but sorry and cumbersome furniture. Happy as a likeness and as a work of art, it is no less happy in the treatment of its draperies. That bugbear of the modern sculptor, nineteenth-century dress, is tackled with skill and the uncommon sense called common. An open collar, a fur cap, and a befrogged fur-lined overcoat, an everyday winter dress in Canada, is a costume picturesque enough to satisfy the æsthetic sense without violating the probabilities; and it is in this garb that the late Governor-General of Canada is happily presented to us. Another dextrous piece of management of the drapery difficulty is to be found in the terra-cotta bust of Dr. Mezger. For here the well-known masseur of Amsterdam is depicted in a picturesque yet workman-like blouse, out of the loose sleeves of which garment the potent, yet almost femininely delicate hands, issue with what, we feel, must needs be a characteristic gesture.

In imaginative work—and it is by imaginative work that a sculptor must ultimately stand or fall—Miss Montalba's 'Swedish Peasant' of 1886, and her design inspired by Edgar Allan Poe's "Raven," exhibited in 1888, represent marked steps in her progress. The first essay (represented on this page) gives a spirited version of a Dalecarlian woman in the quaint dress of the Swedish province, while the more ambitious

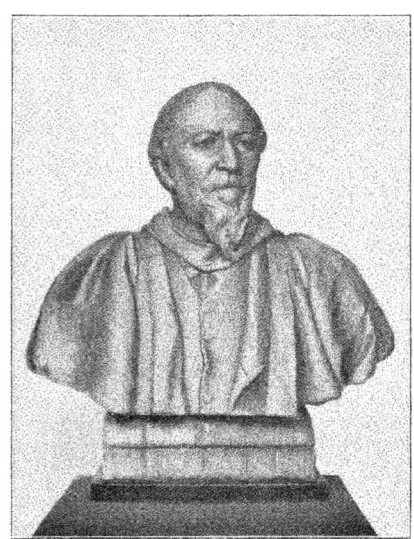

ROBERT BROWNING. BY HENRIETTA MONTALBA.

Little remains to be said. Death has written the ugly word "Finis" at the foot of the Venetian fisher-boy, and to lift the veil on the shadows cast by the artist's premature death would be little short of impertinence. What can we say, in sooth, but that lives of promise, of rare appreciation and worth, prove mutable at moments as those of ordinary clay? Mutable, alack! at the moment of achievement, of accomplishment, when the grim destroyer must even bid the artist "stand."

Passionately loved, Henrietta Montalba is no less passionately mourned. Her loss, a double one as an artist and a woman, is a loss to each and all of us. In the Belle Arti there is an empty place, in the long sunny *sala* of the Palazzo Trevisazz there is an emptiness which cannot be filled. For what is taken, what is removed by so rare a personality, even we, who stand far off, can almost gauge. "Unto me no second friend," says the poet, and though the secret of the stricken be sacred, must not a like cry go out from such as had a common purpose, a common purse, a common home—from such as were not merely sisters, but life-long companions, fellow-workers, and loyal friends?

M. HEPWORTH-DIXON.

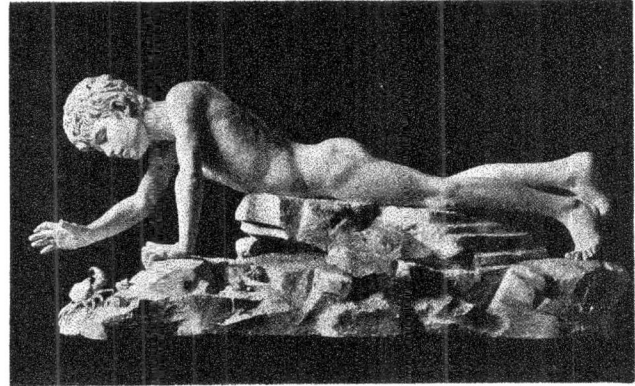

BOY CATCHING A CRAB. BY HENRIETTA MONTALBA.

THE WORK OF BIRMINGHAM SILVERSMITHS.

TO a greater extent than even the work of the jeweller, the productions of the silversmith and goldsmith have, in their own special way, throughout historic time, signalised advancement and civilisation. The results of man's best efforts would seem to have been devoted at first to the service of religion, and next to the beautifying and enrichment of his home. Gold, when wrought into such things, though of the greatest material worth, seldom reached the high value bestowed on silver by the loving labour of the handicraftsman. Perhaps nowhere in Europe has this been made more manifest, especially in secular work, and side by side with excellence of finish in silver ware for general use, than in Birmingham during the last fifty years. To secular work entirely we shall have to confine our observations in what follows.

It is a remarkable fact that in touching, however slightly, on the origin and growth of Birmingham trades, of almost any kind, one is confronted at every turn with the names of Boulton, Boulton & Watt, and the once-famous Soho works. No doubt, for at least a couple of centuries before their time, Birmingham had the curious power of attracting to herself workers in metals; yet the more easily definable rise and progress of her Art industries must always be associated most with the name of Boulton, at whose Soho Works, Watt after a time joined him in partnership, and brought the steam engine into practical use. There are many references to the silver work produced there; one of these will suffice to give some idea of it. "The silver plate shows that taste and design prevail here to a superior degree.... the plated work has the appearance of solid silver." (*Swinney's Birmingham Directory*, 1774.) It was by a medallist pupil of Boulton, named Edward Thomason—in after years knighted for his success in manufacture—that, towards the end of the last century, the first great silversmithing works proper was founded in the heart of Birmingham; although at that time, judging from the assay office entries of names, between forty and fifty gold and silversmiths—but each in a comparatively small way of business—were located there. At this works, as at Soho, Art products were executed in other metals besides silver, but in nothing like the variety that emanated from that extraordinary establishment. Thomason seems to have been the first in England, outside the metropolis, to succeed in the casting of life-size, and larger than life-size, statuary. This firm was, as time and change would have it, afterwards carried on by Coll s & Co., and now is in the hands of Smith & Co., but confined to silver and electro-plated goods. The names Prime, Wilkinson, Barker, Spurrier, Woodward, and Huken and Heath, have been identified for many years with the production of work of the kind of superior quality, but not, on the whole, claiming here special reference for Art merit—such as has lent so much attractiveness to international exhibitions, and gained highest honours for England—and Elkington & Co. The latter, since they started business, about sixty years ago, also paid close attention to simple useful designs in silversmithing and electro-plate manufacture. Two or three years after they procured their patent, in 1836, for electro-plating, they granted licences for the use of the process to the leading makers of such goods in Sheffield and Birmingham.

The means employed by the manufacturer of silver articles are nearly the same everywhere. Silver, like gold, is seldom used in the pure state, a little alloy of copper or other material being required in it for its more satisfactory working. Cups, goblets, tea and coffee pots, and hollow bodies of most kinds are now generally "raised" into form much more rapidly than by the old method, which necessitated the protracted application of wooden mallets and steel hammers; but this way of going about work in special things is yet, and must always be, necessary. Spinning forms in metal is now carried on in different trades; and electro-plate workers and silver-smiths avail themselves of it to a considerable extent. By this process the sheet silver, cut to size, is made to assume, at the lathe, a cylindrical shape, and gradually modified into the form required. Oval spinning is done when only one or two articles at a time are wanted, but stamping from the die is preferred for the goods in general demand. The die and stamp were described somewhat fully in a recent article in this journal (page 112), on the work of the Birmingham jewellers, so their principles need not now be enlarged upon.

The putting together by means of hard soldering, which is similar to brazing, has to be done with great care and watchfulness, because the solder used is a silver alloy of only slightly lower fusibility than the silver to be conjoined. The parts of an article about to be soldered are placed on a pumice-stone support, a borax compound is applied at the lines of juncture; the solder is then brought under the action of the flame of a blowpipe, and at the melting-point it unites with the silver. As the article is being advanced, other processes have then to be gone through, such as "scratch-brushing," or the sand-blast, before a good surface is effected and made fit for gilding or plating, as the case may be; or passed into the hands of the engraver or chaser. These arts require no particular description here; but repoussé, an important Art development of chasing, must have from us somewhat special reference presently. The enamelling of silver vases, tazzi, and dinner services has been a feature of the higher-class work done at Elkington's establishment — *cloisonné* and *champ-levé* principally. As it is not always, to the general observer, quite easy to distinguish one kind from the other, and although the separate processes have often been fully described, a brief glance at them here, while it seems due to our subject, may not be found altogether without interest. The *cloisonné* (partitioned) enamelling should have all the thin metal lines that confine the colours of one unvarying width. These lines are soldered on to the vessel, whereas in the *champ-levé* the field is cut out or incised by aid of the graver for the reception of the enamels, and the lines which mark them off may be varied in width and may taper away to nothing, according to the design; and portions of the area are sometimes left untouched for other treatment. Damascening, an old Syrian art, much encouraged by Messrs. Elkington, enhances the beauty and general effect of silver work in combination with steel. It is done on the steel. The designs are chiefly engraved or carved out to considerable depth, and the lines filled with gold or silver wire, or both, driven in by the hammer, the surface being then trimmed down and finished to a nicety. The Jasmine Vase here illustrated is an example of this art. Niello work, only occasionally practised on silver, is done by filling the engraved lines of an article with a powder compounded of silver, copper, and lead, fused and fixed by the heat of a muffle.

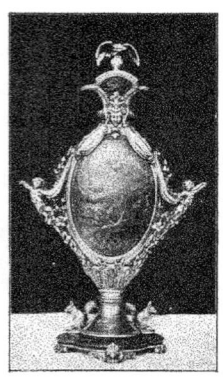

THE JASMINE VASE. DESIGN BY M. WILLMS.

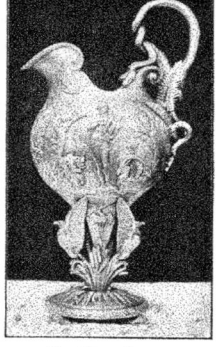

ROSE WATER EWER.
DESIGNED BY M. WILLMS. REPOUSSÉ BY
MR. SPALL.

The art of repoussé, whether one of the offspring fathered on Tubal Cain or not, is very ancient. A specimen of it—a half-length figure in the round, and belonging to a period at least six centuries B.C.—is preserved in the British Museum. With little practical difference the present method of repoussé working was known to the Greeks, and the mediæval craftsmen were proficients in it. After a long period of decadence, it was revived in France about the year 1838. It affords the greatest scope for the higher achievements of the silversmith. The process is simple: a few words will serve to describe it. On a vase, plaque, or shield, or any other article prepared to receive repoussé treatment, the design is arranged and traced in. Say it is a vase. The main convexities are hammered up from the inside. This done, it is filled with warm pitch, and, on cooling to stiffness, this has become a solid ground with resistance calculated to allow of the article being agreeably worked upon on the outside with the hammer and punches. Then small riffles, matting-tools and gravers are brought into service, and the details advanced. The texture and finish are given by these, and other—sometimes private—means and ways which the experience of the artist has found best. It is work that requires much application and true patience to accomplish well. A single masterpiece may take years to complete. The chief of the modern exponents of the art was Morel-Ladeuil, who spent the most of his life in the service of Messrs.

Elkington. His principal works are: the Helicon Vase, in possession of Her Majesty; the Milton Shield, which was purchased by the Government for the South Kensington Museum; the Bunyan Shield; and several remarkable plaques, the finest of them being the Pompeian Lady at her Toilet. It should be observed that only a selection of such things as have been executed within the last year or two are here illustrated. The special productions just referred to have already from time to time appeared in THE ART JOURNAL; and the like is true of some of the better designs of M. Willms, the able Art director of the firm. Besides Morel-Ladeuil and Willms, many true artists have worked for Elkington, among them Jeannest, Grant, Allen, and Beattie, and his son, who, for several years, did some of their best figure-modelling. Mr. Spall is their present chief repoussé-worker: he is following closely the style and manner of Morel-Ladeuil. The Lyre

succeed that the first really practical results were arrived at by the gentleman named. After many trials and continual difficulties in the factory, and discouragement outside from shopkeepers and opposition from manufacturers and others, lasting for nearly seven years, the old and tedious method of attaching a thin plate of silver to a foundation of copper at last gave way to the process of deposition by means of electricity. The invention of the dynamo for the generation of the electric force, in place of chemical action of the vats, before then in use, has greatly increased the rapidity, certainty, and perfection of manufacture. Electro-deposition differs in many respects from electro-plating, and is the most interesting and beautiful of the scientific applications of electricity to the work of the artist in metals, as well as to that of the sculptor-modeller. The method of reproduction by this process of the Milton Shield, for example, is as fol-

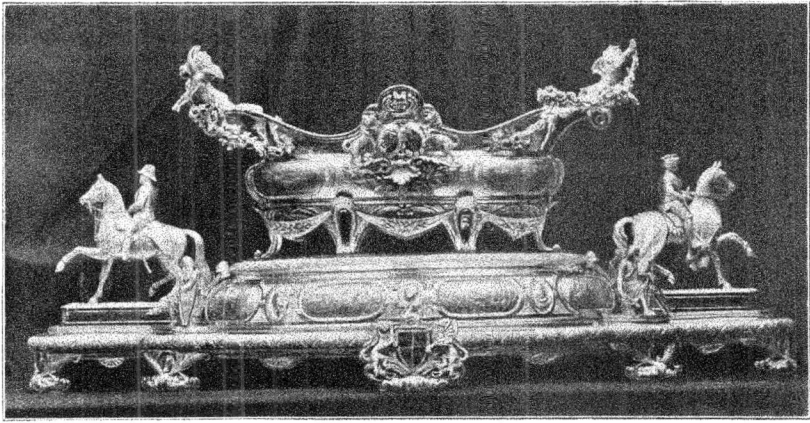

GOLD AND SILVER CENTRE-PIECE. THE WEDDING GIFT TO THE DUKE AND DUCHESS OF YORK FROM THE PEOPLE OF WALES.
THE GOLD AND SILVER FOUND IN WALES. DESIGNED BY M. WILLMS. PRODUCED BY MESSRS. ELKINGTON & CO.

Vase (overleaf) is his own design in the classical style, and is considered a feat of technical workmanship in repoussé. They have each helped to sustain the high reputation of this Birmingham atelier. As an educational school for the designer, modeller, and Art-workman it is ever proudly acknowledged, not only by those who at present belong to it, but by many who, having been trained in it, are now employed by other firms, or have become employers themselves in Birmingham, Sheffield, London, and elsewhere in the country, or in America and Australia.

It may now interest the reader if we say something about the method of reproducing works of Art such as we have been describing. So far back as 1836 the original patents in connection with electro-plating, which led the way to the reproduction by electro-deposition of some of the rarest specimens of ancient and modern repoussé, were taken out in England and France by Mr. G. R. Elkington, lately deceased. The process was foreshadowed by Volta, Dr. Wollaston, and others, at the beginning of the century; but it was owing to the intelligence, enterprise, and patient determination to

lows:—A mass of gutta-percha, or other plastic composition, is laid over the whole surface of the shield, which it reaches in crevice and detail; sometimes assisted in this way by hydraulic pressure; then, on being separated from the shield, it has formed a matrix, which is placed in the bath, where the metal, kept in solution by means of the dynamo supply of electricity, finds a way into every line and feature of it. According to the length of time of immersion, and the thickness of deposit required, a fac-simile of the original is obtained, in silver—in gold if need be—but, as is usual, in copper or bronze, which is surfaced in the like way that articles are plated or gilt, and it is then finished carefully by hand. Electro-deposition has not been confined to only such things as shields, plaques, and cups, for statuary of the larger kind are to be numbered among some of its most notable results. Statuary and large metallic productions seem, from times long before the days of Benvenuto Cellini's successes in that way for Francis I., to have come within the province of the worker in gold and silver; so it should be natural enough for the silversmith of our times, acted on by these historical precedents and exemplifications, to feel equal to such work, even apart from the productive and reproductive facilities of which the discovery of electricity has enabled him to take advantage. Rollers for impressing the patterns on special kinds of wall-decorations are now done in electro-deposition; and it is used in several other ways. While it is capable of giving birth to a colossal bronze statue, it can with the most tender touch revel in the naturalesque, and bring into light such a thing as a fragile basket with wealth of delicate grasses and ferns—a transmutation in this metal, which was presented to the Princess of Wales on her visit to the works in 1874.

The illustrations—which are all of the original and unduplicated kind—now require a few words devoted to them. The Welsh presentation to the Duke and Duchess of York to commemorate their recent marriage, is a centre-piece, one of the largest examples of silver and gold work produced in modern times. It consists of a jardinière resting upon a massive plateau, nearly 5 ft. 6 in. long, 3ft. wide, and 2 ft. 6 in. high, and is made of 18-carat gold, and sterling silver obtained from the Welsh mines; its weight exceeds 2¼ cwt. It was designed by Mr. Willms. There are eight gold panels around the plinth illustrating scenes in Welsh history; between the panels are portraits of famous Welshmen; on the ends of the plateau are equestrian statuettes of King Henry VII. and the Prince of Wales. The jardinière, in the form of an oval basket standing on six ornamental feet, is bold to a degree, in the stretch of its ends bearing Cupids emerging from a mass of flowers and garlands that fall from them over the sides, stopping short, in some unaccountable way, of the centre shields of the Royal arms and enamelled emblazonments of the arms of the Duke and Princess. The panels on the body are gold *repoussé*, each representing a famous Welsh castle. Orange blossoms, true-lover's knots, leeks, and Welsh bards and harps give the whole appropriate character. It is a remarkable piece of work, and most remarkable perhaps as having been designed, modelled, and carried through the different branches of silversmithing to completion in less than six months. The Lyre Vase is referred to above. The Jasmine Vase, designed by Willms, is a good example of combining silver with other metals. Its body, neck, and foot are formed of steel damascened with gold and silver. It is bordered with silver, the outer parts of which are wrought into Cupids and jasmine. The jasmine, though deftly done, does not entitle it to have the vase called after it. The Cupids at the sides, the eagle at the top, the mask on the neck, the squirrels on the foot, and the somewhat Japanese bird display on the front and back, overpower it, and arrest and absorb attention from the first look at the object as a whole. The

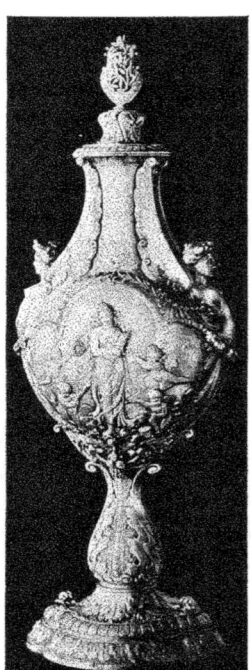

THE LYRE VASE. BY MR. SPALL.

mere misnaming of the vase does not, however, detract from the Art value of it, and the excellency of the work is beyond dispute. The repoussé Rose-water Ewer and Stand, designed by Willms, the repoussé by Spall, do much credit to the ability of both. The latter has carried out the design with feeling and finish that prove him to be endowed with qualifications of a high order. Were the gift of design, as possessed by Willms, and such as graced the genius of Morel-Ladeuil, equal to his manipulative skill, he would probably be unsurpassed at the present day. On one side of the ewer the subject is Orpheus, charming nature and the animal world with the music of his lyre. The other side (not among the illustrations) represents the story of Marsyas—a story that surely should be associated, not with Orpheus, but with Apollo, whose lyre music is said to have gained him the victory over Marsyas, who, in consequence, had to suffer the indignity of being flayed alive. The stand for the ewer exhibits animals of different kinds under the spell of the music, while the centre of it is intended to call to mind that "the waters stood still"—not an easy thing for any artist to express faultlessly; and in this case it seems suggestive most of the sea standing aside to look on at the light of conventionalism it has let in on the sands and its deposits.

The work of Birmingham silversmiths cannot of course be exhaustively treated in its ordinary, and especially in its higher grades, within the limits of this article. Many reflections occur to us, and some that would draw from the far past of industrial Art, and strengthened thereby make comparisons with what we find in the present. Viewed generally, the economic and other circumstances of our time are antagonistic to the cultivation of Art feeling as applied to industry. The master craftsmen of old were untrammelled by hard commercial considerations necessitating subdivision of labour and the consequent dwarfing of the growth of ability such as now commonly prevails: they therefore were individually capable of not only designing and modelling articles, but could make and carry them on to a finish—which often demanded much skill in casting, chasing, engraving, enamelling, damascening, and other processes, each one of which has been, for many years, a trade of itself, and as such in the old trade guilds had no really distinct and separate existence. The world-wide war of competition for profit is the bane of manufactures. All-trading Birmingham has been and is in the thick of the inglorious fight, in which workmen are often pitted against one another and squeezed to the last doit of a mere subsistence-wage for the sake of the captains of labour; yet it is refreshing to have to observe that the leading British firm of silversmiths —the leading firm of the world indeed, employing about 2,000

THE WORK OF BIRMINGHAM SILVERSMITHS.

workpeople—sees, as G. R. Elkington saw clearly from the first, that it bodes no good to be solely occupied in the accumulation of profits at the expense of Art and industry. Working under such favourable conditions as are here indicated, no wonder that their artists and handicraftsmen alike have been able to show exceptional ability. But it is the recognition of this that makes us feel, in so far as the designs may be considered, that they have yet to develop even more satisfactory results. Capable artists too frequently look up myth and ancient history for their motives and inspirations. They may of course treat the classical Olympos, and with something of the symbolism and imagery that arrests attention and commands respect; but that is not enough.

It is well and necessary that we study Art types and precedents, and, on occasions, render them as well as we may; they satisfied the old-time aspirations, and those who could best associate them with their thoughts and usages; but they should now have no greater hold upon us than respect, and our best acknowledgments for what they have taught us of the capabilities of man and Art. Art is the child of religious instinct; and because of that, will grow into the heart and soul only in proportion to the just interpretations it gives of nature and human wants. Art wins from the real what it shapes in the ideal. Whether to be painted in colours or wrought out of the stone, or done in the precious metals, the artist may find, if he wills to find, out-of-door or indoor, the surest and

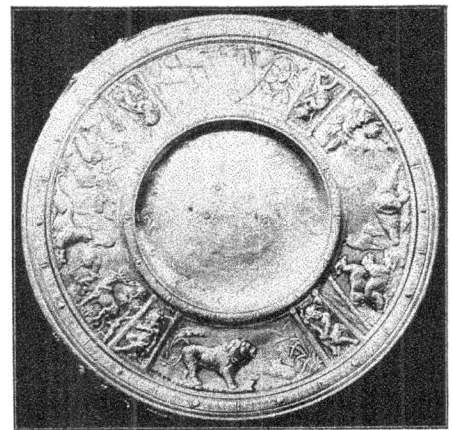

ROSE-WATER EWER STAND.
DESIGNED BY M. WILLMS.   REPOUSSÉ BY MR. SPALL.

freshest and best motives for his treatment. He can only hope to elevate the spirit of the time in which he lives by thinking and working in that spirit.

J. M. O'FALLON.

ART NOTES.

AT a General Assembly of the Royal Academy, held on the 28th of May to elect an Academician in the room of Mr. Edward Armitage, who has retired, the choice fell on Mr. Valentine Cameron Prinsep, who has been an Associate since 1879. It is said that the ballot was taken between Mr. Prinsep and Mr. Waterhouse. Mr. Prinsep has many friends, and is rich; and, besides his work as a painter, has written more than one novel. Mr. Prinsep being a good business man, it is likely that his services will be found useful on behalf of the Academy in the difficult business questions the Council has occasionally to arrange. We give a reproduction of his work in the present Academy, 'À Versailles.'

Having bought no pictures last year, the trustees of the Chantrey Bequest found themselves this year with some

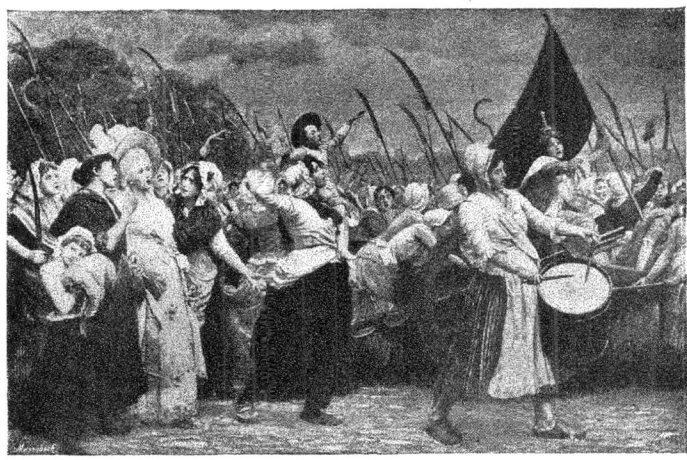

'A VERSAILLES!' BY VALENTINE CAMERON PRINSEP, R.A.

£3000 in hand, and in addition to the works by Mr. Briton Riviere, Mr. H. S. Tuke, and Mr. H. C. Fehr, announced last month (p. 191), they have purchased the following:—'Industry,' a water-colour, by Mr. H. S. Hopwood; 'Sunset at Sea, from Harlyn Bay, Cornwall,' by Mr. Edwin Hayes; and 'Morning Glory,' by Mr. Ridley Corbet.

We congratulate the President of the Royal Society of Painter-Etchers on the distinction of knighthood which he

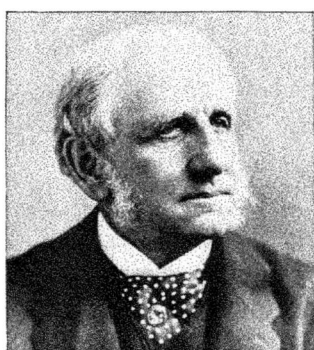

SIR FRANCIS SEYMOUR HADEN,
PRESIDENT OF THE ROYAL SOCIETY OF PAINTER-ETCHERS.

has received. Sir Francis Seymour Haden, whose portrait appears on this page, has been President of the Society since its formation in 1880. The sister of Mr. J. McNeill Whistler thus becomes Lady Seymour Haden.

The Royal Academy came up for discussion in the House of Commons in May, when £1,390 was voted for repairs of Burlington House and the London University. Before the money was voted Mr. T. G. Bowles said:—Burlington House was in the occupation of a close corporation, representing only one section of art. It was, moreover, an extremely rich corporation, and had at its command a huge annual revenue. If the corporation were really helping forward art by the exhibitions that were held there, then a grant of public money might be made them just as to the trustees of the National Gallery or other similar institutions. But the Royal Academy only fostered oil paintings—and that of a school which, he submitted, was founded on the Greek school of the worst period, while statuary, bronzes, water-colour painting, and other branches of art were practically ignored. He regretted "that government ministers gave their presence to the annual banquets, and condescended to crack bad jokes there, when all the time they must be aware that the cause of true art was hindered rather than advanced by the exhibitions held under their patronage. The corporation had, moreover, done all they could to ruin the appearance of Burlington House, and render a once-beautiful building unsightly." Curiously enough, this vote is not mentioned in *The Year's Art*. It will be news to many that the building of the Royal Academy is maintained by the State.

The remarks in THE ART JOURNAL last month on the "Nude in Glasgow" have given rise to much discussion. Consider-

able correspondence has ensued, one person asking sarcastically why should not the next collection at the Grafton Gallery be of the feminine form divine. If, as is contended, numbers of such pictures are not, by the fact of their quantity, somewhat objectionable, while one or two are absolutely otherwise, the suggestion of a nude collection in London should meet with some support. The president of the Glasgow Art Club sends the following:

"We should all feel indebted to you for your sensible and timely remarks about 'the nude in Art.' A deal of nonsense has been written about it, and a deal of fun made of Scottish prudery. The Glasgow magistrates, who had the courage of their convictions, afforded some sport for the papers, and were pelted with derision for not being up to date. But who, pray, are the Philistines? It is all very well for the painter of naked women to throw the trite maxim at us—that to the pure in mind all things are pure—but where are the pure in mind? We have to deal, not with exalted virtue, but with average humanity, and there can be no doubt that the ordinary man of normal virtue looks upon these pictures with very different eyes to the artist.   " I am, Yours faithfully,
"CHARLES BLATHERWICK."

Mr. Macaulay Stevenson, so long without honour in his own country, is fast earning a reputation in Germany. At Munich last year he received a gold medal, and his landscape, 'The Fairies' Pool,' has just been purchased by the State for the National Gallery of Germany. Mr. Macaulay Stevenson may soon expect to have his Glasgow compatriots selecting one of his poetic pieces for the gallery in his native place.

The Corporation of Glasgow have purchased 'Fir Faggots,' by Mr. David Murray, A.R.A., which was hung in the Glasgow Institute Annual Exhibition. The Glasgow Corporation have, so far, bought only two pictures by living artists, 'Fir Faggots' and the portrait of Carlyle by Mr. Whistler.

A plebiscite was lately taken in the Institute galleries to decide which in popular estimation were the best landscape, best figure picture, best seascape, best animal picture, best portrait, and best picture generally. Mr. Murray's picture proved to be in the popular estimation the best landscape and the best picture in the rooms; Sir Frederick Leighton's picture, 'Hit,' the best figure picture; Mr. J. M. Swan's 'Thirst,' the best animal picture; Mr. McTaggart's 'Ocean,' the best sea-picture; and Mr. Lavery's 'Portrait Group,' the best portrait. Popular opinion coincided very much with artistic criticism with regard to these judgments, and nearly all the pictures that received a large number of votes, in addition to those which were actually placed first, were works of outstanding merit. Artists such as Henry Moore, Colin Hunter, James Guthrie, J. E. Christie, George Pirie, and Alex. Roche, were strong favourites.

The show of English silks held recently at Stafford House, under the auspices of the Duchess of Teck, affords an opportunity of appreciating the progress made in the English silk industries since 1887, when, at the Jubilee Exhibition at Manchester, the National Silk Association of Great Britain and Ireland was first set on foot. The prime purpose of the display was to show what is being produced in England in the way of dress goods; but there was shown also a goodly array of curtain materials and upholstery silks. The Association has abundantly demonstrated that we can make here, and are making, dress and other silks which are all the heart of unprejudiced woman could desire. How far they can compete in price with foreign goods, it is not our business to inquire ; but it does seem as if, apart from feminine prejudice in favour of whatever comes from France, there is really no occasion to drive trade out of our own country. Under the promised patronage of Princesses, Duchesses, and Countesses galore, and of other ladies who have pledged themselves, it seems, to ask always for English silks, there should be a fair chance for the home industry. There would be a better chance still if English manufacturers were less content to copy French patterns—which is, so to speak, to play into the hands of their rivals.

Some really fine things were shown at Stafford House, but few exhibitors can be said to have made a fine display. Most of them showed, side by side with better things, designs and colourings which were very far from good; and most of them relied mainly upon the mere reproduction of old designs, not by any means invariably worthy of reproduction. In one case a design for poplin was directly inspired by a modern French silk shown at the last Paris Exhibition. The general level of taste displayed was distinctly below the level of the skill shown in manufacture. Apart from the personal work of Mr. Wm. Morris, and the distinctive productions of Mr. Thos. Wardle (to whom much of the success of the Exhibition, as of the Association, is due), and a few of the fabrics shown by Messrs. Liberty & Co., there was little that was fresh or living in design. In most cases it would be difficult, without the catalogue, to distinguish the work of one producer from that of another. Indeed it seems to be the policy of the producer to keep himself discreetly in the background ; his wares are more often than not shown in the name of the distributor, sometimes altogether without acknowledgment of the part he had in their production. The Association includes among its members some of the principal retailers. If these gentlemen wish us to believe that they really have at heart the interests of silk weaving in this country, they should be very careful to give full credit to the men who produce the wares they are good enough to sell. If trade jealousy is to prevail, the art of silk-weaving will inevitably suffer.

The opportunity of *réclame* has been seized by Messrs. H. & J. Cooper and Mr. F. B. Goodyer, who have been holding small exhibitions of English silks at their own shops. There is, however, no individual character about the sometimes very excellent stuffs they show—nothing to distinguish them from the general run of productions, or, rather, reproductions, made in Spitalfields, Macclesfield, or Braintree, as the case may be. Nevertheless, such subsidiary displays may help to impress upon the public mind the fact that silks are being woven in this country, and so, incidentally, do something towards the revival of English silk industries.

THE BLACKSMITH IN THE CITY.

CERTAIN of the City companies, spurred to action by the public demand that they should do something to justify their position, have of late years taken the industries which gave rise to them, more or less under their fostering care. Unfortunately, these companies have so long ceased to represent in the least the trades from which they get their names, that they seem scarcely to know how best to set about the business of encouraging them. This is exemplified in the Exhibition of Blacksmith's Work, recently held under the auspices of the Blacksmiths' Company in the Hall of the Ironmongers at Fenchurch Street.

The catalogue of the exhibition does not tell us the conditions of the competition in which the workmen contributing to it took part, and one is at a loss to understand the grounds on which many of the prizes were awarded. It cannot have been on grounds of workmanlike skill, for some of the most excellent and straightforward forging passed unrecognised. Still less can it have been on the score of artistic design, for several of the prize works were innocent of any such quality, and the work which was conspicuously the best in respect to design, a hammered grille by Charles Green, was merely "commended."

It is quite possible that such a show as this was may do more harm than good. Commendation has been bestowed by the judges upon the kind of fancy work young ladies are in the habit of twisting, upon ironmongery for the dinner-table, upon centrepieces in the form of naturalistic trees, upon iron flowers in iron pots, upon "japanned" lilies, extravagant mirror and photograph frames in iron ; an "extra prize" has even been awarded to a pretentious electrolier, distinguished only by its "expensiveness." In short, there has been little recognition of simple and subdued workmanship, still less of restrained and tasteful design. Most of the things premiated are such as appeal to the popular, not to say the vulgar, taste.

This is not the way to encourage smithing. As a matter of fact the blacksmith's craft is not in a very bad way. Our smiths are often quite excellent craftsmen ; and even journeymen and apprentices (as this exhibition goes to show) turn out some very creditable work.

If the Worshipful Company of Blacksmiths wants really to do good, let it another time set definite exercises in smithing which will test the capacities of boys and apprentices ; but let it also invite the solution of some of those practical problems with which every smith will in his vocation be called upon sooner or later to grapple ; let it ask him for designs appropriate to his craft, for invention indeed, but for restraint also, for some exercise of taste and common-sense.

Among the more commendable works at Ironmongers' Hall were the following :—an iron cross after a good old model, by L. Melior; an original, and in some respects tasteful, clock by C. Butler ; a fire-screen, by E. I. T. Lane ; a polished iron screen by James Cook, which gains the first prize, and a rather German-looking one by C. Steer, which gains the second — neither of them equal in originality and taste to Charles Green's unfinished grille. There were further some interesting examples of horse-shoes, and a few well-made implements. A small selection of ancient ironwork was also exhibited.

The good intentions of the promoters of the show are worthy of all praise. It is to be hoped that another year the success may be more in proportion to their well-meant efforts.

L. F. D.

RECENT BOOKS ABOUT ART.

A NEW edition of Fergusson's "HISTORY OF ARCHITECTURE" (Murray) is a serious event in the chronicles of Art. With the able and painstaking superintendence of Mr. R. Phené Spiers this third edition has been under revision for nearly three years. The labour involved in such a work is second only to the initial difficulty of compilation, for Mr. Phené Spiers has not been content simply to revise, but he has in all cases gone to the root of the matter in question; and in several notable instances he has largely augmented, by the light of later days, the learning of Dr. Fergusson. In Egyptian Architecture there are some very important changes made, and these have been necessitated by the accurate measurements of the pyramids and other information only recently obtained. Again, a new description is furnished of the Holy Sepulchre, for it was found that Dr. Fergusson's theories respecting it would not bear the test of later investigations. Forty new illustrations are added, one of the most notable being a view of the great mosque of Kerouan, in Tunis, the result of a French expedition in that quarter. Mr. Phené Spiers found several questions difficult to decide, such as whether he should give Dr. Fergusson's theories, which were sometimes exploded, and also to avoid the appearance of filling up serious omissions which the original writer would himself gladly have done. Altogether, Mr. Phené Spiers may be congratulated on the result of his lengthy task, which is in every way successful.

The fascination of Japanese Art is again making itself manifest in Europe in a prominent degree; although, for commonplace objects, the fashion is happily wearing away. For high-class Japanese work, however, the western mind is as eager as ever, and the new ideas conveyed in "LANDSCAPE GARDENING IN JAPAN," by Josiah Conder (Sampson Low, Marston & Co.), will be warmly received. In striking contrast to the formal Italian and French gardens of olden England and France, the Japanese idea of a garden, although governed by a scrupulous attention to æsthetic rules, is an adaptation of nature and something more. It is a poetic conception, and designed to suggest a suitable idea and arouse definite pleasurable associations. The finest garden is the Imperial grounds, of eighty-five acres, called "Fukiage Garden," in Yedo Castle, and Mr. Conder's second volume contains some excellent photographic views of it. The whole of the second volume is devoted to collotypes of the best gardens, which are of the greatest possible interest to the Japanese collector, and to the lover of gardening as an art.

"THE VENETIAN PAINTERS OF THE RENAISSANCE," by B. Berenson (Putnam), begins by stating the author's belief that Venetian painting is the most complete expression in Art of the Italian Renaissance, and that the Renaissance is like the rough model after which that of the nineteenth century is being fashioned. The author does not possess exceptional information, for he makes no mention in treating of Canaletto of that artist's fine series of masterpieces at Windsor.

"DRAWING-ROOM DUOLOGUES" (Fisher Unwin) is chiefly interesting for the fine series of illustrations by Mr. Maurice Greiffenhagen, while Mr. Fred. M. Simpson's text is very smart and really clever. The Duologues are so arranged that they can be played in a drawing-room without scenery. Next month we shall publish an article on Mr. Greiffenhagen's work in oil and in black-and-white.

Two new volumes of the series "LES ARTISTES CÉLÈBRES" have been published by *L'Art*. "Michiel Van Mierevelt" is a serious critical study by Henry Havard, on original lines. But "Antonio Canal," better known as Canaletto, by Adrien Moureau, is not so worthy of the series to which it belongs. There is little or no fresh matter, and the book is simply an adaptation of writers on Canaletto who have gone before. It is strange how ignorant Art writers continue to be of the really artistic treasures of Windsor Castle. M. Moureau incidentally mentions that Canaletto made some works for Windsor, but he has no independent idea of the fine series of paintings by this artist in our Royal collection.

"Genius originates, Art copies," is a very curious motto for the title-page of a book with some pretension to originality. Beautifully sent forth by its publisher, Mr. Iredale seems to know his business better than the writer. "GENIUS AND ART, AND COMMON-SENSE REMARKS ON BOOKMAKING AND PRINTING," by Henry Smith (Iredale, Torquay), is a strange combination of wisdom and weakness, and we should advise the writer to seek the aid of a faithful and fearless literary friend before he again ventures into print.

It is known to frequent travellers from England (when *mal de mer* is not in the question) that the most pleasant route to the northern Continent is by Queenborough and Flushing. The Dutch steamers are commodious and comfortable, and they start and return at convenient hours. To demonstrate this more strongly, Mr. H. Tiedman has prepared a comprehensive guide on the "Viâ Flushing" (Iliffe, St. Bride Street), with maps and information about the places served by this route.

The shilling illustrated catalogue of the City of Manchester Art Gallery is a beautiful specimen of local printing, and the whole work reflects the highest credit on Mr. Stanfield, the curator, and the Art Gallery committee. The Birmingham Catalogue of Drawings of Old Birmingham and Warwickshire is not quite so pretentious, but it is only one penny, and Mr. Whitworth Wallis may be trusted to have seen the best given for the money. The St. Louis Museum of Fine Arts publishes an additional catalogue showing all the recent acquisitions, many being of considerable artistic interest. "LIVING MEMORIES OF AN OCTOGENARIAN" (Elliot, Edinburgh), forms a most interesting series of notes by Mr. George Croal on Olden Edinburgh. Mr. Croal is now the only living person who was present when Sir Walter Scott revealed his identity with the author of "Waverley" in 1827.

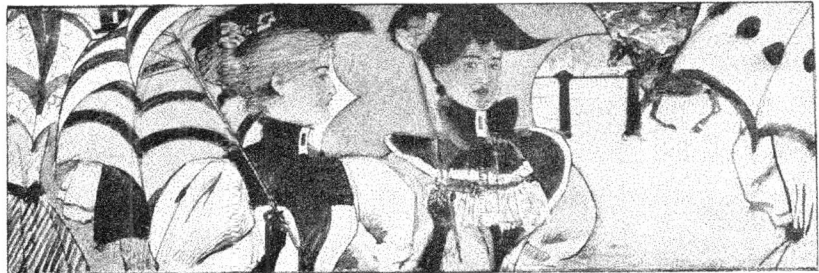

FROM AN ORIGINAL DRAWING BY MAURICE GREIFFENHAGEN.

MAURICE GREIFFENHAGEN.

TO inquire into the work of a man who, far from having completed his course, is scarcely, it may be said, on its threshold, is a task from which one is at first inclined to shrink. You look at the practical materials at your disposal and you find them meagre; you regard them closer, and you observe, it may be, the evidence of promise and the signs of originality, and these not unnaturally are apt to lead you away from the contemplation of his work hitherto, to the speculation (to adopt the language of the Chelsea sage) of "what he will grow to," and the individual capacity of the man assumes an attractiveness.

There must always be this speculation in the mind of any intelligent and observant man when he comes into contact with any work which, in a creative sense, differs from other works; and while large hopes may be formed and speculation be keen in regard to the development of its originator, such hopes, as all the world knows, are more often than otherwise destined never to be realised, and speculation transfers its enthusiasm to other on-coming men.

To the subject of this paper, he being, comparatively speaking, young, much appears to be possible, for the small amount of work, in the way of painting, which he has hitherto done, points in no undecided manner to uncommon characteristics and unusual aims. His own theory of what a painting should convey may probably be at variance, in some degree at any rate, with many well-accepted or popular theories; but in this age of "picture-making," when Art appears at times to be coming near to being confounded with some technical trade, would not caution suggest that a generous regard should be given to any signs of a separate growth, which in the putting forth of its leaves may to many be perplexing, and possibly to some

AUGUST, 1894.

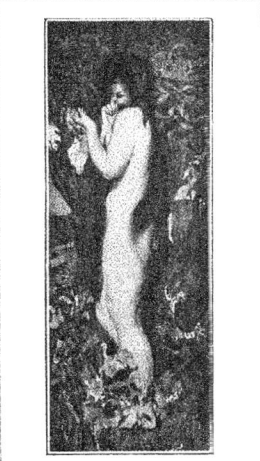

EVE. BY MAURICE GREIFFENHAGEN.

(whose range is limited to certain conventional standards) altogether unallowable, but which may nevertheless be to others, who at least discern in it that frequent absentee, honest endeavour, the precursor of unlooked-for and abundant fruit?

The first knowledge which we have of Maurice Greiffenhagen is at the age of fourteen, studying on his own account, and without supervision, from the marbles in the British Museum—a goodly beginning. He next appears as a student in the Royal Academy schools, carried thither by drawings from these same marbles; studying there intermittently and making no great effort for the competitive prizes awarded there, but gaining meanwhile some sort of competence by such black-and-white drawing as came to his hand, for humorous journals and others. We find then, in 1884, a work of his on the Academy walls (his first contribution) with the quotation, "Sweet lips murmuring, Find the low whispers like their own, most sweet;" and then appear two works at the new English Art Club, one in 1887, the other in 1889, entitled 'Ophelia' and 'Portrait of a Lady.' So at starting we encounter at least one encouraging characteristic: he does not appear to have poured forth his canvases pell-mell upon the world regardless of quality or legitimate aim.

It would appear to be about the year 1887 that it was suggested he should be selected to illustrate the remarkable story of "She," by Rider Haggard; and the specimen drawing, which it was requested he should submit, met at once with the approval of both author and publisher. In the series of drawings which he subsequently executed, a singular sympathy with the mind and ideas of the author is discerned by the apparent ease with which the scenes have been depicted; a degree of mysticism, apart from the originality of design

3 M

being imported into them in a manner which must have captivated the author of the book by their evident comprehension of his story. For it is not given to every man rightly to interpret pictorially such stories as "She," and, just as certain well-known men at starting have illustrated, with distinction, the works of some prominent living author, and developed subsequently into painters of a high order, so it is not uninteresting to contemplate the possibilities that lie before other men, similarly practising, in whom the creative faculty and the talent for design are united with adequate academical training. If in the "form of things" lies the picture, how more surely can this be attained with facility, than by the varied situations and scenes demanded of those who work rapidly in black and white? and if it be contended that the picture is dependent upon its colour, we touch then upon a rarer gift, unteachable—the semblance of it on all sides, but the thing itself marked but at rare intervals; and it is this union of the appreciation of form with the capacity of expression in colour which constitutes a true painter, and in contemplating the career of any artist it is well to inquire in what degree these two essential elements are associated.

To touch further, for a brief moment, on Mr. Greiffenhagen's work in black and white: other books by the author of "She" fell to him to illustrate— "Allan's Wife," "Cleopatra," "Montezuma's Daughter," while in a popular weekly journal, *The Lady's Pictorial*, upwards of a hundred illustrations of Mr. George Moore's story of "Vain Fortune" have, with other spirited designs, appeared from his pencil. One of his latest series for book illustration is for Mr. Simpson's "Drawing-Room Duologues."

Now in reference to what must be regarded as the more important phase of his art, his painted works, deficient in point of quantity as compared with his productions in black and white, we have already made brief allusion to three. Of these we reproduce the 'Ophelia,' certainly an original arrangement of an oft-painted subject, but dependent for pictorial merit chiefly, we should say, upon the sensitive relation of tones throughout the work. We have then 'The Mermaid,' certainly eccentric in design, and in colour more suggestive of an experiment than of a serious production, but the idea is fanciful. The long auburn air floating upward, and the coloured bubble rising to the surface, 'in the Purple Twilights under the Sea,' and we come then, in chronological order, to the particular work which brought to him considerable popularity, and the one by which his works

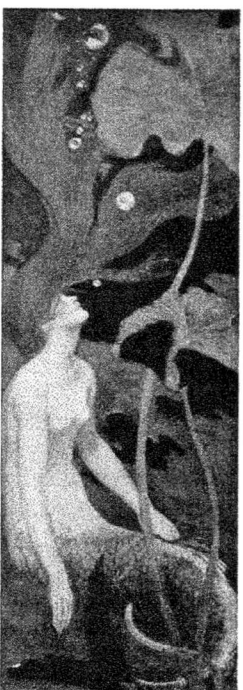

THE MERMAID. BY MAURICE GREIFFENHAGEN.

in colour are at present chiefly known, 'The Idyll.' Exhibited in the Royal Academy in 1891, and not there hung to great advantage, it subsequently appeared at Liverpool, where it was sagaciously purchased for the permanent collection of that city. Many times before had the refined touches in various phases of "la belle passion" been depicted on canvas, but seldom, if ever, had the passionate embrace been pictorially attempted; but to be attempted and achieved with such an absence of unseemliness, and with such accessories as to constitute it a refined work of Art, was to accomplish much. The first sketch for this work was made many years before the painting of it was dealt with, and a consensus of influences, which we need not detail, led up to the picture. Having succeeded in attaining in the face of the girl the degree of passion which it was his aim to express—

"My spirit soon,
Down-deepening from swoon to swoon,
Faints like a dazzled morning moon,"—

it would seem that his endeavour thereafter was toward the composition of graceful lines, and the combination of rich and brilliant colours, in order that, the emotion of the scene being secured, all that could be brought of the beautiful in line and colour should support and enhance it. To those who have seen the painting of 'The Idyll,' the etching in this number will readily recall its colour, but to those who are unfamiliar with it, it is necessary to speak of the auburn hair falling far down, till it is lost in the blues of the girl's raiment, and of the sharply coloured grassland abounding in scarlet poppies and white marguerites, illumined by a low red sun. In the Guildhall Loan Exhibition of 1892, this painting, lent by the Liverpool Corporation, occupied a conspicuous position. At that time the director of the gallery, upon whom devolved the selection of the pictures, had no personal knowledge of the artist, and included the picture in the loan collection solely on account of the independent and unconventional line assumed in the work, and certain other meritorious attributes it in other ways possessed. There appeared to be certainly the evidence of spontaneity in it, as of a man who must work off this final development of his idea at once, and be done with it. Quick to grasp, and quick to execute, relying less upon the outward forms around him than upon his inner vision of them, the work disclosed a striking measure of self-reliance, aided greatly, without doubt, by his efficiency in drawing—a solid advantage, and one without which he might fare ill in the particular walk which is his. But it would seem worth while, for a moment, to inquire by

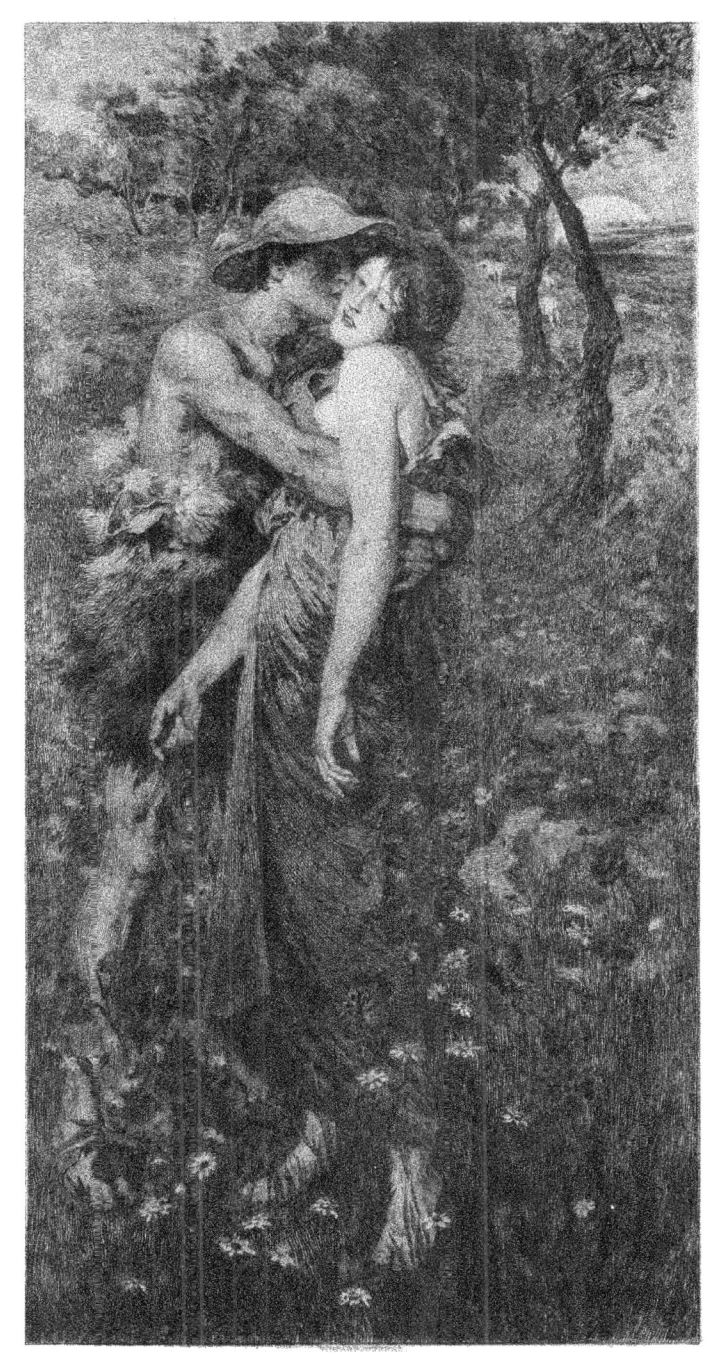

AN IDYLL.

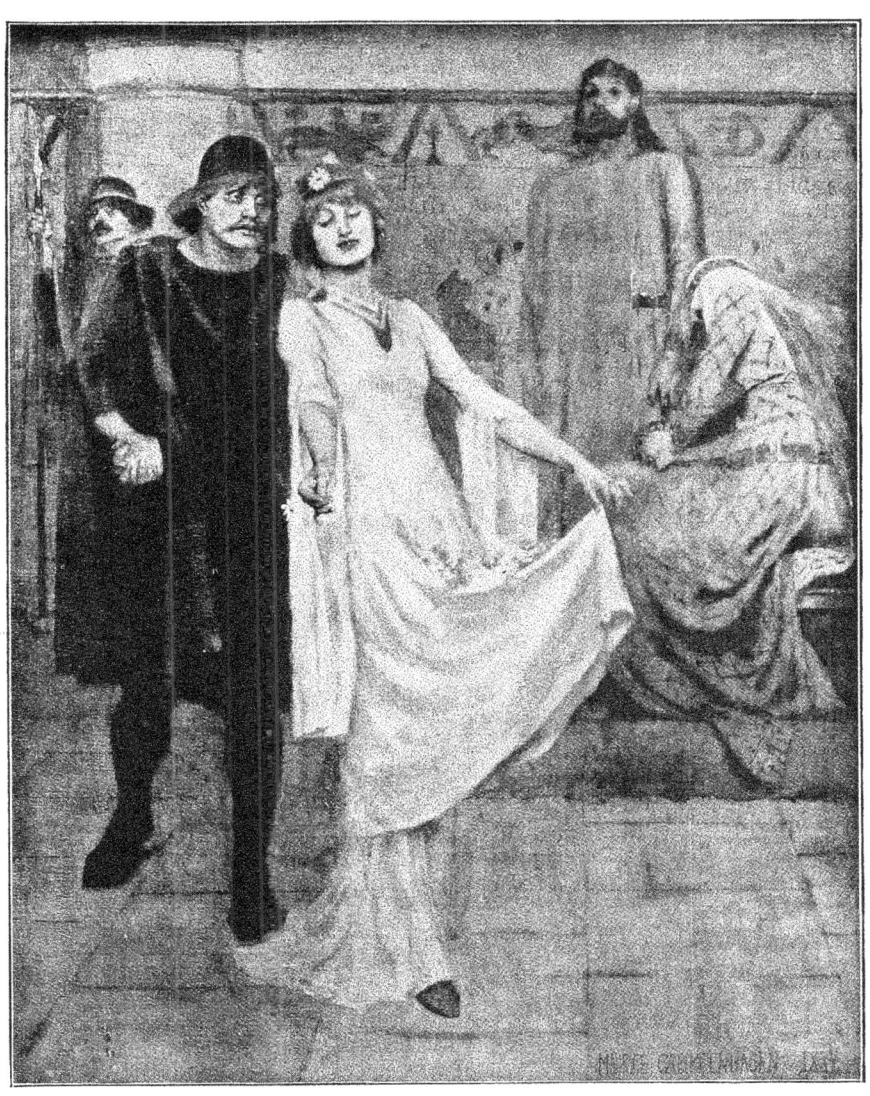

Ophelia. From the Painting, by Maurice Greiffenhagen, in the Walker Art Gallery, Liverpool.

what is he prompted in the subjects he takes. Is it by an historical incident, by a poem he has read, by a face or form which he has seen? These are the ordinary stimulants of modern art. Whence, for instance, came the first vision of 'The Idyll'? or (which we shall notice later) the 'Eve'? Due to no external sources, these two works may be said to be, in form and feeling, the offspring of the man's heart and temperament, starting with no well-defined idea at all, but receiving, curiously enough, only as they progress, those harmonies of colour, the production of which, in their completeness, is subject to no rule, and can only be accomplished by the exercise of an uncommon gift.

We pass now to his next important work, 'Eve,' exhibited in the Royal Academy of 1893, and again seen, after certain well-studied modifications, in the Guildhall Loan Exhibition of the present year. In the figure of 'Eve,' nude in the Garden of Eden, the absence of all high lights is impressive, and the soft gloom as of the inner woods falls with skilful uniformity on the limbs. Now what is very noticeable in this work is, that no slavish subservience to models or to any other outward thing can be detected. The artist has had his model, no doubt: he has diligently studied the serpents with their rich delineations of colour, he has gone to nature for the trees and large purple flags; but having thus, quite in the proper and orthodox way, secured his materials, he shows you only so much of each as will uphold, in its proper degree, the theme of the picture. Now this is Art; for while industry, great perseverance, and patience, with other high qualities, are required to paint, say as the pre-Raphaelite brotherhood painted nearly fifty years ago—every leaf and turn of drapery copied in its entirety of form, light, and shade with slavish and yet charming exactitude—here qualities of another kind are encountered, excellent also by reason of the results obtained by them. And the question becomes, not how much that the artistic eye can discern shall be put into the picture, but how much can be left out, always allowing sufficient to be retained to adequately express and enforce the purpose for which it is there. For illustration, what more seductive to the painter's eye than the brilliant form of a serpent? What more tempting than to paint all that one sees of it? and yet what more estimable than the discriminating eye that places so attractive an object for the most part in shade, leaving the onlooker to imagine for himself the beauty of the thing, amply indicated by the parts that catch the light? Here then, as has been said, is no narrow subjection to outward aids, but the operation of an artistic instinct upon material forms, for, standing before the picture, you are conscious of the purple flags although you scarcely see them; you can follow the entire form of the serpent, drawn with anatomical correctness, but only if you choose to look for it; and the ripe fruit, though intense in its richness, assumes, it will be observed, only its proper weight in the presence of the deep blues by which it is surrounded. And all this suggests the predominant aim and feeling of the artist, and it may well be conjectured that his theory of what a picture should convey is before all things a sense of beauty; it should be a beautiful work to look upon; and, whereas many pictures not wanting in beauty owe their charm in a great measure to the subjects they portray, from his outlook the picture should be a beautiful thing independent and apart from any subject. It should present itself to you as a harmonious richness—graceful in form, superb in colour.

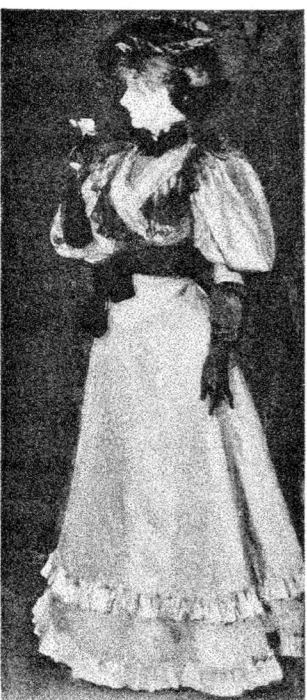

PORTRAIT. BY MAURICE GREIFFENHAGEN.

With this picture of 'Eve' there was also in the Academy of 1893 a full-length life-size 'Portrait of a Lady,' a work which, if we recollect aright, was a study in subdued tones, and a strong and pleasing harmony was obtained; while a portrait of the artist's wife, also under the title of 'Portrait of a Lady,' and here reproduced, was exhibited in the Winter Exhibition of 1893 at the Grafton Galleries. This portrait, also full-length, life-size, showed a lady in a green gown, passing to the left, large black hat, black gloves, and a Gloire de Dijon rose in her right hand, and dark background; while in the present year's Academy a further 'Portrait of a Lady' appears.

While demanding less in point of colour and arrangement than his subject pictures, these portraits are in many senses very agreeable compositions, conveying, in many successful instances, it would seem as if by a touch, the personality of the individual portrayed; much experience is evident in the painting of them, yet little sign of labour, unsuggestive altogether of the time bestowed upon them, or of the number of sittings which are demanded by the painter, a free and firm handling of the brush being clearly seen withal. Before him in this direction of portraiture would appear to lie a wide field, and if he would draw less and paint more, as he may one day be induced to do, something may reasonably be expected of him exceptional in character and distinguished in treatment; more especially if into these portraits he introduces or imports the varied harmonies of colour which mark his subject pictures. This, we may take it, has ere this occurred to him, though we are not by any means sure; but what we cannot help observing is that hitherto, so far as we know, the finer sense of rich colouring which distinguishes the two works upon which we have dwelt at some length, and which have been the means of drawing public attention to him as a painter, has not been allowed to display itself in his portraits. Presumably this will come later, and in all likelihood when it comes we shall find it has been worth waiting for.

But whether it be by portraiture or by subject pictures that he will hereafter be known, Maurice Greiffenhagen may be regarded as not ill-equipped for the path which is his.

Imagination, that deplorable want in so many of our painters whose technical accomplishments are great, is his in a marked degree. His sense of colour, as evidenced by the few paintings we have noticed, is obvious, and his capacity for design and arrangement has been abundantly shown by his drawings in black and white, ably illustrating, as we earlier stated, not merely the everyday stories of the society novelist, for which models and situations are at all times close at hand, but the weird and far-away tales that come from the imagination of such men as the author of "She."

A. G. T.

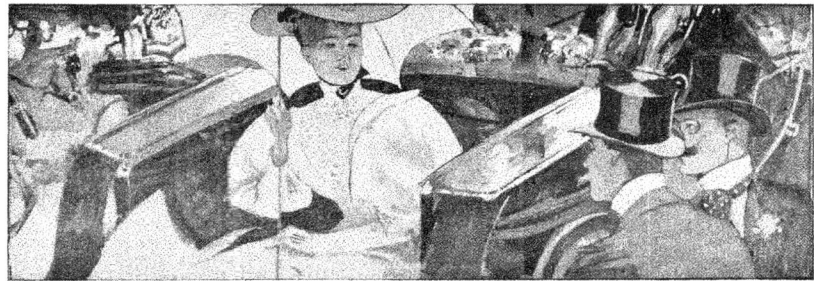

FROM AN ORIGINAL DRAWING BY MAURICE GREIFFENHAGEN.

OUR LADY OF THE ROCKS.

BY THE DIRECTOR OF THE NATIONAL GALLERY.

IN the June number of THE ART JOURNAL there appeared some critical remarks by Dr. Richter, founded on the document first published by Dr. Emilio Motta, and commented on by Signor Frizzoni in the *Archivio Storico dell'Arte* for January—February of this year.* These seem to require careful consideration before they can be accepted as disposing of a subject so much debated as the attribution of 'La Vierge aux Rochers' in our National Gallery to Lionardo da Vinci. I venture, therefore, to send to THE ART JOURNAL some reflections which occur to me on the various points raised in Dr. Richter's article.

Recently Signor Frizzoni required some more exact measurements of the panel on which the picture is painted than can be obtained on the wall, and it was necessary to take it down and remove it from the frame. I took the opportunity then afforded me to examine it carefully, and came to certain conclusions which will appear in the course of this paper.

But before coming to any considerations derived from this source or from the document referred to above, I must deal with an argument which Dr. Richter puts forward, and which I can hardly understand his having proposed seriously; as where he quotes, on the second page of his article,† a record

of the year 1637 to the effect that Charles I. was unable to purchase a volume of Lionardo's manuscripts for three hundred ducats, as evidence that in the year 1777, one hundred and forty years after, the picture sold to Gavin Hamilton for thirty ducats* could not be a genuine work of the master. This argument seems to me inconclusive. In the year 1777 taste ran in another direction, and to works of a different kind to Lionardo's. Raphael Mengs was the leading critic, and also, according to Winckelmann, "the greatest painter of this or perhaps of any age." Mengs hardly mentions Lionardo by name; the "*stilo secco*," as he called it, was not in vogue.

But this is not the main point of Dr. Richter's criticism. His arguments rest rather on the document recently discovered by Dr. Emilio Motta, and published in full in *Archivio Storico*, as mentioned above. This document is briefly a petition from the artists Ambrogio de' Predis and Lionardo the Florentine to the Duke Lodovico Sforza, begging him to require the Brotherhood of the Concezione of S. Francesco at Milan to pay Lionardo the sum of one hundred ducats, which they say the oil picture of the Madonna is worth over and above the eight hundred *lire imperiali*, which they were to receive for the whole altarpiece (which sum of eight hundred lire had been absorbed

* See editorial note at end of article.
† THE ART JOURNAL for June p. 167.

* I believe, however, that this thirty ducats story rests solely on Dr. Waagen's authority.

in the reliefs and gilding of the *ancona* alone), and which picture the valuers appointed by the fraternity estimate at twenty-five ducats only. They therefore pray that they may be paid the sum of one hundred ducats or have the picture returned to them. As Dr. Richter says, we are not told how this dispute was settled by the Duke, and one would be disposed to think that there is an end of the matter, and that this document does not do much to advance the solution of the question, which is, whether is the picture in the National Gallery, or the one in the Louvre, the picture painted by Lionardo for the Chapel of the Concezione in S. Francesco.

That the picture which Lomazzo saw there, and which he describes in ch. xvii. of the second book of his *Trattato*, is the picture which is now in the National Gallery, is, I believe, denied by any one. He describes it in detail, and so accurately, that there can, in fact, be no doubt about it. He writes of it as a man writes of a picture which is well known, and about the authorship of which there is no dispute, coupling it, for the qualities which it illustrates, with the cartoon of the Santa Anna (now in the Royal Academy), a work which I believe has never been doubted as a genuine work of Lionardo. And the fact that Dr. Richter puts forward that Lomazzo lost his sight at thirty-three years of age is no proof that he had not seen and studied the picture while he had the full use of his eyes; and that he did so is evident from the exact description which he gives of it, and of the movements and expressions of the various actors in the scene. If he wrote this description after he was blind it is a proof the more how deeply the qualities of the work had impressed themselves on his mind. Signor Frizzoni says that the remarks of a man so "ciarliero ed inconcludente"—garrulous and inconclusive—are not worthy of attention. An artist suddenly struck with blindness and condemned to inaction for the rest of his life, so that he has to take refuge in literary work, may easily become rather prolix, but it does not follow that when he had his sight he was incompetent to tell the difference between a copy and an original, and his subsequent blindness does not affect the case.

Nor is the description given above the only reference made by Lomazzo to the picture. In his chapter on "Light," ch. i. of the fourth book of the *Trattato*, he alludes to it as "mirabilissima e veramente singolare," citing it as the one example which will serve for all for its disposition of light and shade*; and here he only says what must strike every one in looking at the picture in the National Gallery, the luminosity of which is one of the principal characteristics. A third allusion to it is in a poem addressed to Pietro Martir Stresi, his pupil, in the third book of the *Grotteschi*, where he mentions it as one of the pictures which Stresi had copied full-size:—

". . . . . fra le quali v'è del Vinci
La rara Concettion ch'è in San Francesco."

Stresi being his pupil this copy was, no doubt, made at the suggestion of Lomazzo; if so, it would further show in what high estimation he held the picture.

Nor does it seem to me that his authority is to be dismissed so lightly on this point as Signor Frizzoni would have

* It is true that he here speaks of the picture as the "Concettione de la Madonna"; but the fact that he refers to it as being in San Francesco makes it pretty clear that it is the picture described in the second book; and if there were any doubt, it would be set at rest by his announcement that he shall refer to the picture again in his book on "Light"—"Della quali occorrerà ragionare anco nel libro de i lumi." Possibly from the picture being in the Chapel of the Concezione it was popularly known as "la Concezione."

it. The short life Lomazzo gives of himself shows that before he lost his sight * he was an artist of immense activity, with the keenest interest in all forms of art,† especially in that of the great men of the preceding century and of his own time, which he displayed in numerous sonnets addressed to them, forming the main part of the second book of his *Grotteschi*. Nor is it to be supposed, as Dr. Richter seems to suggest by his remarks on Lomazzo's blindness, that the *Trattato della Pittura*, any more than his book of *Rime*, was written entirely after he became blind; for he expressly mentions both these works as having been undertaken‡ before the accident which deprived him of sight. I must say that I do not think it possible that such a man as Lomazzo, himself an artist of renown, with a most active interest in all things connected with his profession, taught by a pupil of Gaudenzio Ferrari, and thus brought up in the traditions of Lionardo's school, should be so mistaken in his estimate of this work as to select it as a conspicuous example of the master if it were merely a copy.

Bianconi's evidence is also definite enough; he describes the two wings of the picture still existing in his time in the Church of San Francesco as of the "School of Lionardo." But he then goes on to say, "But there was indeed a picture, also on panel . . . by Lionardo's own hand" ("di mano di Lionardo") "which passed to a Luogo Pio, and then went away from us," thus making the distinction between what was known to be of the school (though, as he says, by some believed to be by the master), and what was known to be the master's own work. Dr. Richter must have hastily considered this passage, or he would hardly say that Bianconi describes the picture "as a school-piece."‖

These, with the exception of another passing reference to it by Lomazzo, are, I believe, all the existing written evidence pointing to the picture in the National Gallery as an original work of Lionardo da Vinci. But, says Dr. Richter, there is this newly discovered document, and he proceeds to found a theory upon it which he thinks goes far towards proving that the picture was returned to the artists, and by them sold to an agent of Louis XII. of France, and a copy substituted which is the picture now in the National Gallery; and he starts by saying that "the nature of the decision" (*i.e.* of the point submitted to the Duke) "is not difficult to guess if we bear in mind that by the side of the one Madonna picture a replica soon makes its appearance," meaning, no doubt,

* By an accident:—
"Doppo ciò non passaron molti giorni,
Che per grave accidente gli occhi miei
Chiusi, et perdei l'amata et cara luce."
Rime, Milan, 1587, p. 538.
† "Di virtù poi bramoso andai à Roma
Per veder le pitture et anticaglie.
Le qual mirar, et osservar giamai
Non furon gl'occhi e la mia mente satia."
Ib., p. 533.
‡ In his "lieta gioventude":—
". . . . . e Così scrissi
In rima i miei Grotteschi, dove espressi
Molti capricci c'havea in cor Concetti.
A quai poi cieco ancor molti n'aggiunsi.
Poco dapoi trattai de la pittura,
In molti libri, ch'or si veggon fuori."
Ib., p. 530.
I quote these passages merely to show that Dr. Richter does not put the whole case as regards Lomazzo's blindness, and that it would be to gather a false impression to assume that the *Trattato* was entirely the work of his later years.
‖ That there may be no mistake I give the whole passage:—"In certi comparti dell'ancona della Cappella . . . si vedeno due begli Angeli in piedi con istrumenti da suono sull'asse, della scuola di Lionardo, che molto sentendo del di lui stile sono stati creduti di sua mano. Eravi bene una pittura parimenti in asse con la Vergine, S. Giovanni putto, ed un Angelo adoranti il S. Bambino sopra fiorito praticello conformato da sassi ruvidissimi di mano di Lionardo, ma passata ad un Luogo Pio, e partita da noi."—*Nuova Guida di Milano*, 1787, page 280.

that, as we have two versions of the Vierge aux Rochers, one of them must be a replica made to fill the place of the original picture, which he assumes was restored to the artist. This, as a mere matter of argument, seems by no means sound; what is there to prove that the picture did not remain in its place, and that it was not Louis XI.'s agent who had the replica? It is as legitimate to guess one thing as to guess another. Dr. Richter goes on to say that "the Duke will have had neither the means nor the inclination" to compel the brotherhood to pay. How does he know that? Why should the artists have applied to the Duke unless they were fairly confident that he could satisfy them? It is quite conceivable that a powerful Duke may have been able to make his wishes respected by a religious body even if he had no legal jurisdiction. On the other hand, if he had no power to compel the payment of the money, neither had he power to compel the brotherhood to return the picture to the artist, as Dr. Richter assumes was done. And there is a third alternative at least as probable, which is that the brotherhood of the Conception neither paid the money nor returned the picture, but gave the artist the twenty-five ducats at which they had assessed its value, and kept it. Since, as Dr. Richter admits, we are not told how the dispute was settled by the Duke, this theory of the end of the negotiations is as probable as any other In any case, there is no definite conclusion to be drawn from the newly discovered document, nor does it in any way shake the evidence of Lomazzo or Biancони.

Further than this Dr. Richter criticises the picture in some detail, and illustrates his criticisms by photographic reproductions from Lionardo's own drawings and from the pictures themselves.

And first one cannot help asking why Dr. Richter all through his article speaks of our National Gallery picture as a copy, as when he refers to "the delivery of this copy in accordance with the estimate of the experts." The picture in the National Gallery, as a matter of fact, is far from being the same as the picture in the Louvre, and neither can be said to be a copy of the other; and so far from the variation between the two pictures being in the figure of the angel alone,* no single part of the groups is really alike. Nor are the differences such as would result from the inaccuracies of a copyist —the differences are essential, such, I mean, as an artist would make in working from different studies. The figure of the Infant Christ, for instance, though the action is the same in both pictures, is in a different perspective, being looked at more from above in the Louvre picture than in ours. And compare the left hand of the Virgin in the two pictures; here again the gesture is the same, but the point of view is different; in no sense is the one hand a copy of the other; they must have been made from different studies.

Again, supposing the London picture to be a copy of the one in Paris, why should the copyist have completely altered the action of the angel? not only leaving out the right hand with its "gesto intimamente Leonardesco," as Signor Frizzoni calls it, but omitting the very beautiful arrangement of the drapery over the sleeve, and also entirely changing the whole cast of the drapery. Again, the movement of the Infant St. John is quite different in the two

LA VIERGE AUX ROCHERS. BY LIONARDO DA VINCI. IN THE LOUVRE.

* Compare the reproduction of the National Gallery picture in the June number of THE ART JOURNAL (page 166), with that of the Louvre picture on this page. The two pictures are placed side by side as illustrations to Signor Frizzoni's article in the *Archivio*, and larger and much clearer reproductions are to be found also placed side by side between pp. 106 and 107 in Dr. Paul Müller Walde's 'Leonardo da Vinci,' München, 1889.

pictures, the whole figure in the Louvre picture having a more energetic leaning forward towards the Infant Christ. Still more marked is the difference in the folds of the yellow lining of the Virgin's drapery where it passes from under the right arm across the body. Here again separate studies must have been used. Does a copyist make fresh studies when he is repeating the work of a great master? But not only this loop of drapery, but the whole of the drapery of the Virgin differs in the two examples; the general intention and the principal forms are the same, showing that the artist had definitely made up his mind what the leading lines should be; but the details differ, and different studies must have been used throughout: for no one who has any experience can suppose that these highly finished and perfectly drawn draperies were done without careful studies from nature. Of the heads that of the Virgin is the only one which is in the same position in the two pictures; a comparison of the reproductions will show that the three other heads differ completely in their attitudes. The use of the word copy is, therefore, inaccurate, and makes an assumption which is unfounded on the document in question, seeing that there is in the document no mention of any delivery of a copy, or, indeed, of any copy at all; the only references being to "an *ancona* of figures in relief done all in fine gold," and to "a picture of Our Lady painted in oil," and "two pictures with two great angels likewise painted in oil," (which formed the wings of the altar-piece and with which we have nothing to do*). As regards the head of the Infant Christ, Dr. Richter has given us a reproduction of the study which Lionardo undoubtedly made, and it is odd that he should not see that this goes against his own view, for it is as certainly not the study for the head in the Louvre picture, as it certainly is that for the one in London, which corresponds with the study not only in position, being in direct profile, but in type and features, in all which respects it is *tale quale* the same.

Nor does the artistic superiority of the Louvre picture seem to me so obvious as it does to Dr. Richter. When, as I mentioned at the beginning of this article, I had our National Gallery picture out of the frame, the close examination which I was able to make† assured me of what, indeed, is obvious enough through the glass, that much of the picture has been disfigured by coarse repaintings by another and inferior hand; and such comparisons as Dr. Richter makes between such repainted parts and the picture in the Louvre cannot but be misleading. The left hand of the Virgin resting on St. John's shoulder, to which he draws special attention, is no possible test of comparison, for the hand in the London picture is obviously the mere daub of a picture-restorer.

It would be as fair to adduce the right arm and shoulder of the St. John in the Louvre picture, which even the photographic reproduction shows to be badly repainted, and to compare it with the beautiful modelling of the English example, as evidence against the general genuineness of that painting. The same may be said of the flowers in the fore-

* Except that it is clear from Bianconi having seen these wings in the chapel in S. Francesco that they at least were not returned to the artists.
† These are the notes I made on examining the picture:—
I consider the following to be the work of the original painter of the picture.
Figure of the Virgin.—Face; neck; hair except on top of the head; all the drapery; the left hand, but left unfinished (or subsequently injured), and coarsely touched with black by another painter; right hand somewhat repainted.
Angel on right.—The whole head and face and hair except some retouches on top and back; while left arm and hand, but left unfinished; and the whole figure seems original work not fully completed; the wings the same, but touched on.
St. John.—Probably the whole figure with the exception of the extremities which appear to have been left unfinished, and finished badly by an inferior artist; the hair also repainted in parts.
Infant Christ.—The head, but appears to have been injured and retouched, especially the eye and hair. All the figure also appears to be the original work except the right hand and arm, which look as if they had been left unfinished and painted in by an inferior hand.
Background.—Parts, especially about the angel's head, appear to be the original work, also the stones in the foreground to the right.
My impression of the picture generally is the same as I had when I first saw it in 1880, that it was left unfinished and completed by another hand.

ground and of the upper part of the background in the London picture, for they seem to be the work of a heavier hand than that which executed the figures, and I would not pretend that they are Lionardo's work. The flowers in the Louvre picture, on the other hand, have always seemed to me of beautiful workmanship.

I make no pretence in this paper of proving that the picture in our gallery is the work of Lionardo; in the absence of definite evidence this must always remain a matter of opinion; all that I have attempted is to show that there is no reason why it should not be. The document proves nothing on either side; we have as before only the internal evidence of the picture itself, with perhaps additional food for guessing. Although I have expressed no definite view, my opinion of the propriety of the attribution to Lionardo di Vinci may no doubt be gathered from what I have written; and while we are in the conjectural frame of mind, which the document discovered by Signor Motta seems to provoke, I would venture to hazard an opinion that the Madonna in the National Gallery is an earlier work of Lionardo's than the one in the Louvre; and to add that I am inclined to differ with Signor Frizzoni where he says that it is a "later edition of Lombard stamp," while he sees in the 'Vierge aux Rochers' in Paris the "sovrana finezza e perfezione d'indole tutta fiorentina." To me it seems just the contrary, and that our picture shows traces of his training in the school of Verocchio, and that it is the Louvre picture which has more of the idealized refinement of type on which Luini formed his style. The picture in the Louvre has so suffered from repainting that it is not quite fair, perhaps, to judge of its merits. The body of the angel especially, through the almost entire repainting of the red drapery, is now quite out of drawing, but it is to me certain that the addition of the right hand, and of the green drapery over the left shoulder, and *not* the omission of them, is the afterthought. To my mind the angel in our picture is by far the more beautiful of the two; the expression of the face has a profundity of reverential feeling which is wanting in the other, besides that it is more finely drawn. The Infant Christ in the Louvre picture, on the other hand, seems an improvement on ours: with the high horizon which Lionardo has chosen it is more truly in perspective; also it is the one part of the Louvre group which seems to me intact, with its beautiful primitive modelling. Again, although I consider the head of St. John finer in our work, and certainly the better drawn, the general movement of the Louvre St. John is more expressive and more momentary. Perhaps all painters are alike in finishing the heads in their pictures first and leaving the extremities to the last; there seems to be only one hand in our picture—that of the Infant Christ resting on the ground—which is original work; the rest of the extremities having been left incomplete, and finished by an inferior artist. Such are my views, derived from a careful consideration of both pictures: in my judgment ours is a work exhibiting, in its complete parts, those qualities of style—perfection of drawing, fulness of modelling with transparency of tone, exquisite and unlaboured finish, and above all, depth of expression—which characterize great and original work as distinguished from that of a copyist or a school. The difference between this view and the expression of Dr. Richter, "that the London copy appears as an entirely wretched performance," is so wide that I fear we must be content to agree to differ.

EDWARD J. POYNTER.

** We think it right to state that Dr. Richter's completed article was in our hands before the publication of Signor Frizzoni's paper. We received Dr. Richter's MS. in London on April 9th, whereas the *Archivio Storico dell'Arte* although dated for the beginning of the year, was not really issued at Rome until a few days later.—ED. A. J.

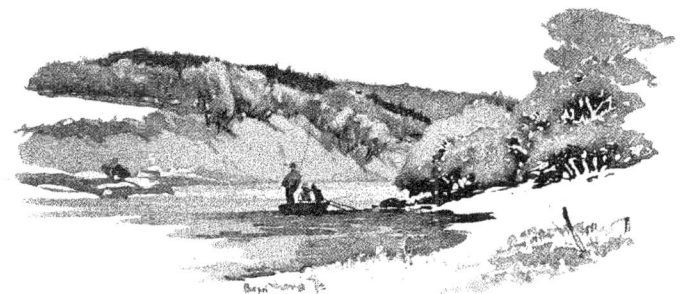

BENCHIL WATER. FROM THE DRAWING BY J. EDGAR MITCHELL.

BY THE SALMON POOLS O' TAY.

"I tell you more there was a fish ta en,
"A monstrous fish, with a sword by a side—a long sword;
"A pike in's neck, and a gun in's nose—a huge gun;
"And letters of mart in's mouth from the Duke of Florence.
Cleanthes.—" This is a monstrous lie!
Tony.—" I do confess it.
" Do you think I'll tell you truths?"
FLETCHER'S *Wife for a Month.*

WOULD it be paradox to assert a kinship betwixt Sport and Artistry? Many, if not, indeed, most of our landscape painters, handle the fisher's rod with an ever-fresh enthusiasm, it need hardly be said. But that sportsmen of higher game, followers of feather and fur, be it through forest, over heathery moor, or up in the mountains where stags " toss their beamed frontlets to the sky," do contrive to keep a little of their love for genuine works of art may be considered as evidence that they, too, share in the inspiration which artistry derives from the solitudes. In recalling the wild, natural joy of a springtime by stream or loch, or the maturer sweetness of autumn days spent on moor or hill, the painter, with his touches of nature strikes, as if by song, the tender chords in the hunter's heart of memory. Therefore, the paradox may stand.

The Tay has nought of the English meander about it. In spate, it comes down tremendously, pouring thrice the volume of the Thames into the sea. Not all Titan either, for the Sylph is there beside. Over the waters the ancient glamourie of Caledon still hangs, as they break forth of the misty glens, to sweep past hanging shaw and thickening wood.

There are four great bends in the river. The first, from Perth tidal waters to Isla-mouth at Meikleour, is the salmon-haunt in chief, and 1894,

where most fish are caught. Sometimes the tacksmen have the luck, sometimes the anglers, just as the spates run, provided there are fish to come; for should the spates be early and continued, the bulk of the salmon reach here frequently before the nets are off, and are (as one angler said) "lifted out for London." But, usually, it is not so, and *salmo salar* gets a chance to live his life, if hooks don't catch him. About the beginning of September, the rod-men cast their lures as the later, bigger fish come up. Being wary, nor always "on the feed," or keen to pluck the fly withal, these wise ones needs be tempted by all the skill of civilisation, vexed by angler's wiles with ardent longing for a gorgeous gnat, phantom-minnow, or what-not, as the weather and the humour is. There's the acme of the sport—its glorious uncertainty And when the pool-lurkers are stubborn, won't

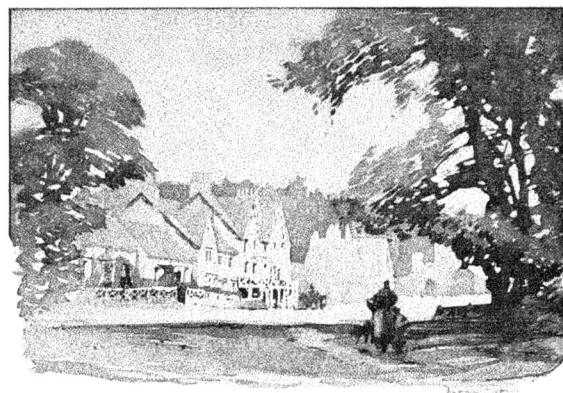

KENMORE VILLAGE. FROM THE DRAWING BY J. EDGAR MITCHELL.

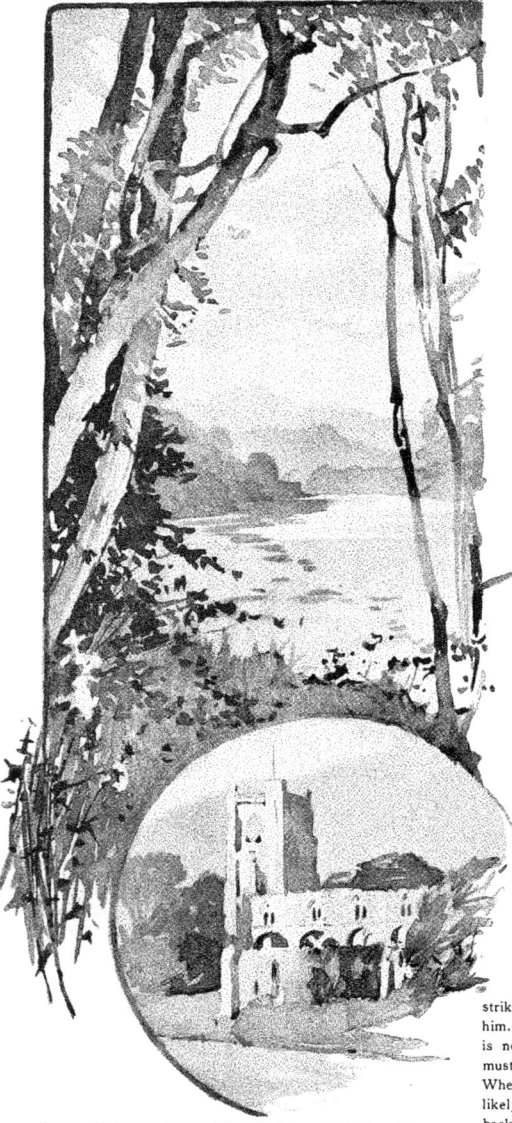

DUNKELD WATER AND CHURCH. FROM THE DRAWING BY J. EDGAR MITCHELL.

move, cast only an indolent eye, none of your Dr. Johnsons or kindred men of the chair can know the supreme glory of "a rise," nor ever felt the thrill along the nerves when a salmon is "struck," and the excitement that begins as

"Down the stream, like levin's gleam,
" The fleggit salmon flew."

The catches are smaller on the next great bend round to Dunkeld, though on the waters at Delvine, Murthly, Eastwood, and Birnam, many an ardent though patient angler is rewarded for his skill and fortitude. But there, the scenery, being finer, is a compensation to one who is not a mere killer of fish. It is less broken up into crag, and cataract, and swirl, and vehemence, than Stanley district. A deep, swift flow of waters, bubbling up in fast-receding rings, slides down past level haughs of pleasant open vale—a clean, silent spot of charming green, quaint and fresh, truly inspiring country.

What matter though salmon be chary of the fly and the "take" nothing to boast of? After all, what is the real magnet which draws men from the towns?

It is interesting to follow, in fancy, the wake of a Tay salmon. After a company of fry have donned the scaly armour, fallen down timidly to the sea and spent a few months there, they return as lusty silver grilse, soon to descend again (barring accidents) to the blue realm of Neptune, that Greek sea-god who is so old; thenceforth to live as rovers through the sea, wooing the furtive mermaids and eating sand-eels, crab and lobster, in the shallows of the German Ocean.

Sea-creatures fascinate us. Take the salmon: he loves not heat, nor cold; nor salt nor sweet; he takes each as it serves. Done with his savage roaming in what Browning calls "the green-dense, dim-delicious," through which the anemone, as it were a purple pansy of the sea, hangs, turns, and floats away, sport of the idle wave—the king of shore fish, surfeited with exhilaration, cleaves a royal way through rank and rank of very wondrous forms, *en route* for his silent inland-pool up in the recesses of a rocky grove. His unrest is almost human. A certain nobleness there is about him, too—which, in fact, attracts the fisher, forming an element in the sport. Fine sentiment, doubtless, it is to think a salmon loves; more, it is absurd. Probably, truth is strained even to say he has a pirate's joy, as "flying a black flag of Death high o'er the main," he fights. for life and scours the wavy plains for food. Salmo is but a fish, but watch his career homeward: full of power he cuts a gallant way up his parent stream and leaps —why so gay? Up he comes, a silver gallant, shining with brine; up he speeds with a bridegroom's air upon his marriage-jaunt. Frank Buckland says the fish *smells* his way. Suppose (says Buckland) a salmon, striking up the Bristol Channel, scents the waters meeting him. "I am a Wye salmon," he would say to himself, "this is not Wye water; it's the wrong tap; it's the Usk. I must go farther a few miles"—and he gets up-steam again. When he of the Tay arrives at the entrance to the Firth, likely he must run the gauntlet of the seals thereabout basking; then the nets of the canny fishermen hang athwart his nose, which, if wise enough, he may avoid, and race up by Perth's fair city with the impetuosity of a human soul on fire, on and on till, with the joy of return, he greets his home in the pools of upper Tay. Ah! but the tempter is even here! Lust of eye, hunger of belly, lures on our *salmo salar* till, presto! he snaps a pretty fly; but woe worth the day! for the angler, fresh from the far city, cries with an eager cry, "A birr! a whirr! a salmon's on! a goodly fish, a thumper!" (as in Stoddart's song). Salmo fights, sullens, fights again; he is played, gaffed, knocked on the head, and flung, not under cypress boughs, but into the bow of the boat, and strewn over with bracken fronds or twigs of fir. The victor draws his flask, and, in the company of his boatmen, libations to the Scottish Bacchus are duly poured. Than conquest what more dear to man? What villain he to cheat good fish!

And maybe (to use a figure) "the dance of the witches" is held by the waters of some quiet river-turn, or in a lonely far-up Highland glen, soundless save of wind and stream; a pool, perhaps, below a head of seething flood. "Hell's Hole," "Cat's Hole," Death's Throat, Kill Moo, Cradle Stone, The Garth, Campil Green, Beardie Willie's, Farneyhaughs, Tober-ma-veigh (pool of the spring of good health), are but a few names given to favourite pools, names descriptive enough. Did the capture happen on the sylvan cast of The Aldems at Taymount, adjoining the salmon-famous stretch of Stobhall; or in the vale of Athole, theme of song, scene of many a fray; or up that strath where Tay breaks from the cradled lake to sweep by the palace of Breadalbane, past the castle of the Menzies, under General Wade's celebrated bridge at Aberfeldy, winding between the hills to Grantully and Logie-rait (ancient haunt of hag and beldame), where the rapid Tummel joins—the scenery in any of these places is such as to give extra spark and piquancy, proper relish and abandon to the sport.

'Twere more dramatic in the non-angling but artistic eye

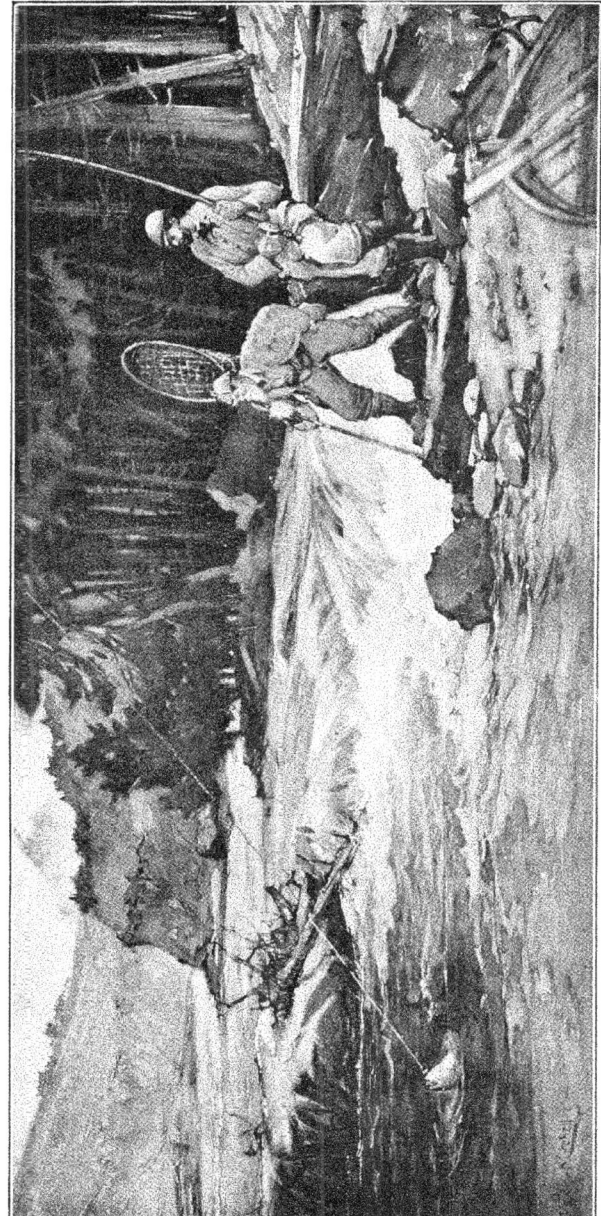

THE LAST OF THE STRUGGLE. FROM THE DRAWING BY J. EDGAR MITCHELL.

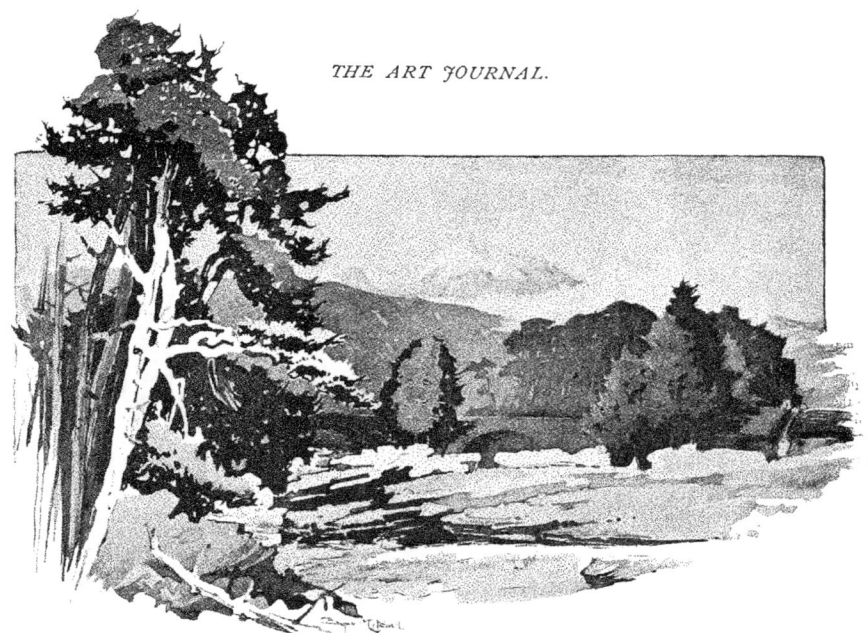

THE DOCHART. FROM THE DRAWING BY J. EDGAR MITCHELL.

had the affray fell out upon some wild night at Stanley, a tumult of a flood running. Then would the tragedy of the salmon have been set in savageness. Swift swirl, and plunge round a high, wood-crested cliff; loud acclaim from the white wave-tops breaking on boulder and sharp rock-edge; drumlie, growling torrents flinging madly down through dim-shadowed darkness, flecked with lurid light of sky, striking down strange shimmer on black pools below ridge on ridge of shaggy tree. That is the wild picture—din of waters, wind-clarions, trembling glamour round. But as the river would be out of ply, the incident is unlikely. Neither at such a time could John Leech's "Briggs" have landed in his arms his first fish at "Pitlochry Head" pool, just opposite.

Visitors familiar with the salmon parr controversy, in former days a very hot one, usually cross to the breeding ponds at Stormontfield, a mile below Stanley, on the other bank. As the keeper, in response to our hail, rowed us over the strong flood in his boat, no easy task in face of the rapids and swirls round covered rocks, we saw Sir John Millais, as well known on Tayside as in art-London, plying his rod on the Benchil stretch, while many another eager fisher was a-trolling farther down. The morning was one of those which, after a night of rain, are so lightsome and fresh, and the sun sends silver shafts through high masses of tumbling white and grey cloud. Each green blade held a tiny crystal drop; the leaves glanced with shimmer; and the red hips blazed on every bush where once the wild rose bloomed in the glory of summer. And out, with the buoyant morn, had come the cheerful angler. Words cannot re-echo the "aerial merriment." The ponds, just on the river's brink, in front of a row of keepers' pretty cottages, are quite open. There is slight meddling with the habits of the salmon-fry, save that in one pond they are fed thrice daily with grated liver; in the other, they are left with natural food. On the keeper throwing in a pinch or two of "feed," the fry rose up greedily, flashes of an inch or two. The ova are brought from Dupplin Hatcheries in autumn, and when the parr (it was here experiments proved that the parr *was* the young of salmon) are through their babyhood, a sluice is opened for the waters to carry them directly into the Tay. Some are taken higher up before they are turned in to fight life's battle amidst the pike, trout, and hungry eels.

The path from the ponds runs by the side of the lade which supplies them, through short vistas of tinted trees, above the pools of Aikenhead, Pitlochry Head, Hell's Hole to Burnmouth Ferry and the famous Campsie Linn, the scene of more than one romantic tragedy. For in the tempest of despair, the lack-love Gouacher or Bachin Maclan, young chieftain of Clan Kay, after his defeat at the combat on the North Inch of Perth, fled hence, and, taking a brief farewell of Catherine Glover at the monastery near, leaped from the crag into the whirlpool—as saith Sir Walter Scott—and was seen to rise no more. There is a huge rock in the centre, round which the waters swirl in a peculiar manner. Truly, from the throat of Atropos cometh the voice of the cataract. Within its hollow echo, bonnie Margaret Drummond of Stobhall was wooed "sae sweetly" by a gallant king. The way of a man with a woman puzzled Solomon, it is writ. Whether the lover-king was true in heart or faithless only in the head is not certainly known, but in the end the bonnie maid, with her two sisters, was dastardly poisoned.

But splash! a salmon leaped; the world is young again. Ho! our salmo has passed the falls, and shoots up the brown waters of the "Major's Cast," careless as a summer butterfly. Nothing in nature mourns. Up our fellow of the sea dashes through that element, his realm, off for the glens in the mist far away, miles and miles. At Cargill he will pass through waters which, years ago, drowned hapless Davie Drummond, of the ballad "The Wearie Coble," a victim of the lass he loved in vain.

Nearing Murthly, one discovers "Millais' Country"; the natives seem proud to have you made aware of that. All appear to know Sir John; his name to them is somewhat of a talisman. The *localité* of his famous pictures are pointed out to you, the prices whereof mingle with the gossip of the countryside. The region is fascinating, right up to Dunkeld. Naught bold or striking, strong or wild, the beauty of it is tender and exquisite, so that one's fanciful mood puts sylphids in the luminous atmosphere, and brings young Narcissus there to linger and gaze upon the strange sliding stream, crooning soft music to the winds. With a start, a heron rose near us, then came a rasp of a distant reel through the silence, another tetchy turn of the reel; a fish was on! and, looking ahead, we mark an angler, erect in a shallop's stern; a few more turns of the reel, and heigh!

> "The lengthening line extends,
> Above the lugging fish the arch'd rod bends
> Till forced, reluctant, from the deep
> He mounts; he bends, and with resilient leap
> Bounds into air; there gasping, struggling, twirls;
> Starts, dangles, flings, now curls and now uncurls.
> Fixt to the hook, the fluttering captive see!"

Dunkeld, away in the blue-wreathed hills—first touch of the Highlands! The twilight held its wondrous magic over the "bonnie" town as we stepped into the streets. Early stars sparkled in the sky; in the west, beyond the not far-distant hills, green mingled with the blue above, for it was long after sunset. A traveller who, frowsy with exposure, breaks from the solitudes into the medlied sounds of human voices of a town, finds therein new meanings as to life, feeling a strange impulse, like that from music, coming over him till words become eclipsed with tender thoughts. Such was our entry. Later, when the moon rose over Birnam Hill, and flooded the amphitheatre of wooded hills, hung with veils of haze, the sight from the bridge was superb.

But nature is just as savage as she is beautiful, and Perthshire is an evidence of the contrast, of which the Tay itself presents a variety. Wandering up the banks one finds the sylvan, the weird, the grim, the splendidly picturesque (of which the corner above Dunkeld, looking up "King's Seat," is unmatched, with terrace on terrace of fir and larch towering up against the sky), the magnificent and grandest types of nature, and but seldom the commonplace. Above the pool of "King's Ford" the first of a series of wide views reveals the classic vale of Athole, which recalls the sweet Scotch song connected with the "bonnie Prince Charlie." With Ben-y-gloe afar off, here begin the well-known mountain mist and cloud effects which make the Highlands so fascinating. Hence the salmon waters right up to Loch Tay are amid some of the finest scenery, more or less the acres—nay, the miles—of the Taysian potentates of Athole and Breadalbane.

At Kenmore, at the east end of the loch, another change is beheld. The idyllic has passed into the grand: nature assumes Titan majesty; the colossal hills strike the pretty woods to nothingness, they become the fringe that graces elemental power. This makes a sail up the loch for ever memorable. With the prow of the steam yacht heading for Ben More away in exquisite blue morning-effect, and crowned with a mighty cloud upon the cone, the passenger feels an exhilarating thrill. Ben Lawers rears up to the right, with snow a-top; mist and sunshine come and go on the breasts of many a hill around. Each moment brings some new beauty. White torrents gush down the corries of the hills and, struck by sunshine, radiant bows arch over. Hamlets, and crofters' cots, and small farms are dotted along the lower slopes. Stunted firs straggle up into the moving mists. The openness, the bluff-away of the breezy loch, makes one ejaculate "Romantic Perthshire!"

Land of dreams to him who loves nature with a deep, strong love! Wilder becomes the look-away as the little steamer speeds. It arrives at Killin. Up and around the hills push into the mist and the sky; down roars the furious Dochart past "Innis Buidhe" (The Yellow Isle), with its shaggy firs wailing in the wind. Ay, Killin, wild, picturesque Killin is rarest of all, as the most lustrous sapphirine that is set about a coronal. D. S. GRAHAM.

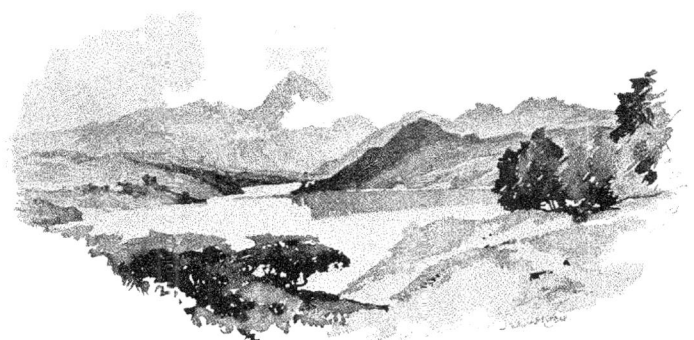

LOCH TAY. FROM THE DRAWING BY J. EDGAR MITCHELL.

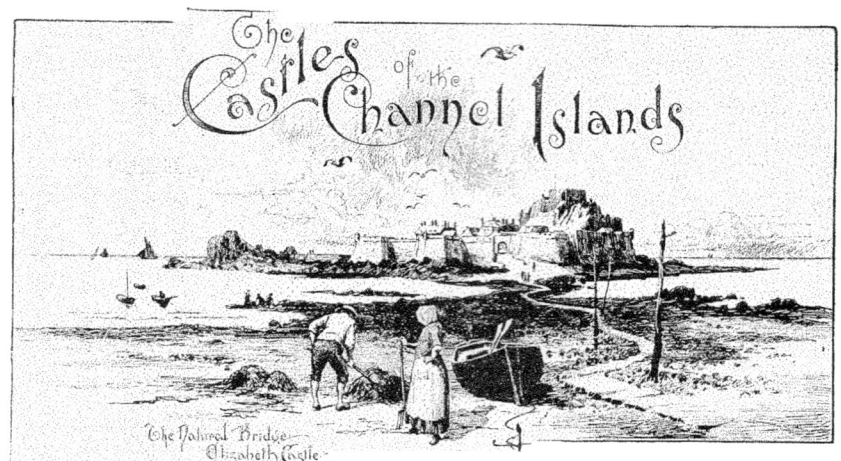

The Castles of the Channel Islands

The Natural Bridge, Elizabeth Castle

SINCE the days of William the Conqueror the Channel Islands have been under the dominion of the British Crown. But their laws, with which the British Parliament does not meddle, their racial peculiarities, and their situation, have kept them almost entirely aloof from the storm and stress of British history. The islanders have gone on quietly with their sowing, their reaping, and their fishing, contented with the charters given them by King John, who was quite popular and successful in Jersey, while the rest of Europe has been writing its history in slaughter and bloodshed. Once and again echoes of strife have reached their shores. Now and then an exiled king, as Charles II., a political prisoner, as Burton or Prynne, and a fugitive Frenchman, as Victor Hugo or Boulanger, has appeared among them. But they have taken small notice, and gone on peacefully as before, with their reaping, their sowing, and their fishing.

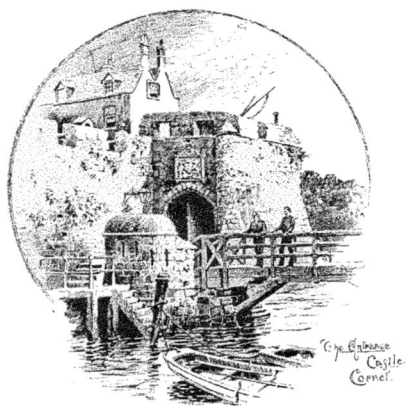

The Entrance, Castle Cornet.

Only the strongholds of the Channel Islands, planted on crags round the coasts, and garrisoned by English men-at-arms, have been washed by the surge of English strife, as the rocks at their base are battered by the waves of the English Channel.

The history of Castle Cornet, Guernsey, which stands upon a detached rock over against St. Peter Port, stretches back into the beginning of the Middle Ages, until it becomes a mere tradition. Whether or not the Romans fortified the rock, there is no trace of their architecture remaining. It is generally believed to have been founded by one Raoul de Valmont, a governor sent to Guernsey by Henry Plantagenet during his struggle against Stephen. It is clearly referred to in an order of Edward I., in relation to the building of a quay " between our castle there and our town of the Port of St. Peter." In all probability the order was never carried out; for down to recent times the castle was only open to approach or attack from the sea. At present it is reached by the more prosaic way of a breakwater—which runs out beyond it and bears a lighthouse—and a government pass.

There is very little grace about Castle Cornet. Around Mont Orgueil trees have grown, grass covers its slopes, and lichens spring from every nook and cranny. But there is nothing to soften the rugged age of Castle Cornet. It rises grim and brown from the rock, and the long marriage of rock and masonry has blended the two into a harmony of colour, so that it is hard to tell where the one ends and the other begins. The dull monotony of brown is only relieved by the fringe of yellow seaweed round the base of the rock—the vraic, which serves the Guernsey folk as fuel for their fires and manure for their fields—and the green seas which break continually into white foam below. The pride of Castle Cornet is in its strength; dogged strength is expressed in every line of it, whether one views it from the side of the shore, where the angles of the revetments are as sharp as the ram of an ironclad, or from the sea, where it rises gaunt and bare, without a break in its battlements. It was the very last stronghold in the whole British dominions to give up the cause of King Charles; and when at last its commander, Colonel Roger Burgess, could hold out no longer, he and his men were allowed to march out with drums beating and colours flying.

The oldest part of the castle is the entrance, which is reached from the breakwater by a curious little wooden bridge. But inside one is met at once by the evidence of modern life. A battery of artillery is stationed there, and the click of billiard balls from the sergeant's mess sounds oddly out of place among the time-worn walls. Modern guns look menacingly out from the patched embrasures, soldiers' wives dandle their babies on the ramparts, and the soldiers' children play marbles around the castle dungeon.

On entering the port of St. Helier's Jersey, from Guernsey, one rounds the mass of rock on which Fort Elizabeth is built. The first view is disappointing; for topping the ramparts and bastions of a former age is a row of barrack-like buildings, with gaunt expressionless windows, such as only the War Office knows how to devise. But beyond the main rock, and rising sheer out of the sea, is a lonely crag which is of some importance in the history of Jersey. The broken flight of stone steps which leads to the summit, and the little half-ruined cell above, are shown in the accompanying sketch. It was here that St. Helerius, the patron saint of Jersey, took up his quarters in the middle of the sixth century. Life, one might imagine, would be sufficiently vexatious in those unregenerate days, even under normal conditions; but the passion of St. Helerius for discomfort was insatiable, and he set to work to make his rock-dwelling as uneasy as possible. He spent the greater part of his time standing upon sharp stones laid in puddles of water, and guarded against the natural impulse to sit down by surrounding himself with boards studded with nails. When he did allow himself to rest, it was only on a rude couch which he had scooped out of the rock. The bed of the saint can still be seen—though not necessarily believed.

The reputation of St. Helerius for piety and discomfort spread far and wide, and many miraculous cures were reputed to have been wrought by him. But at length there came Northmen, men who lived by rapine and slaughter. The islanders fled in terror. Then St. Helerus stood up on his crag

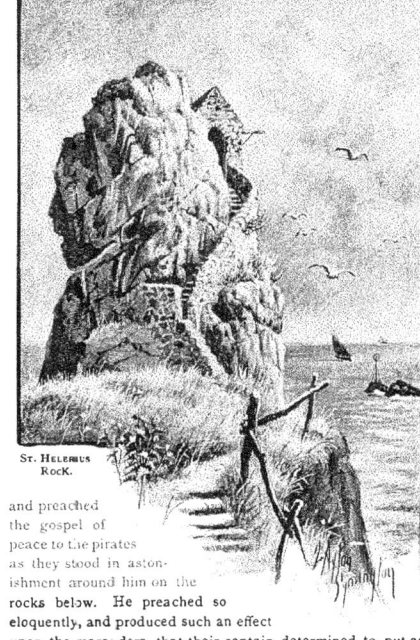

St. Helerius Rock.

and preached the gospel of peace to the pirates as they stood in astonishment around him on the rocks below. He preached so eloquently, and produced such an effect upon the marauders, that their captain determined to put an end once and for all to the subversive doctrine, and cut off the head of St. Helerius with his battle-axe.

For many hundred years nothing but the memory of the saint, and his cell, remained. But in the twelfth century Guillaume de Hamon, a Norman noble, who is supposed to have been a descendant of the nameless pirate chief, founded an abbey to expiate the crime of his ancestor.

Of the abbey and the church no trace survives. The abbey was suppressed by Henry V. The church, after becoming merged in the fort which was built in the reign of Elizabeth and named after her, was utilised for some time as a storehouse, and later on converted again into a chapel for the convenience of Charles II., who took refuge here during the Great Rebellion. It was finally destroyed by a shell thrown by the besieging Parliamentary forces in 1651. The same shell also laid in ruins the house in which the exiled king lived, and the room in which Lord Clarendon wrote the first part of his "History."

One may walk across to the rock from St. Helier's over the natural causeway which is left bare and dry at low tide, as shown in our headpiece. As soon as the sea ebbs, the tide of

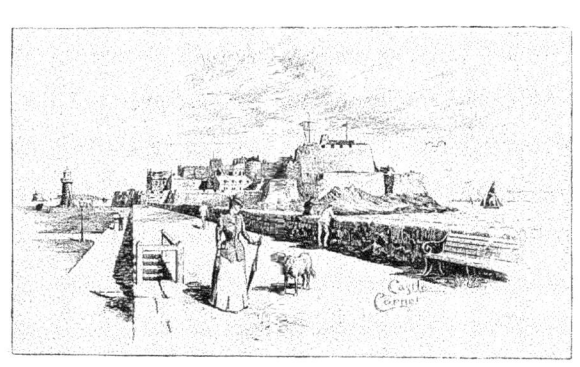

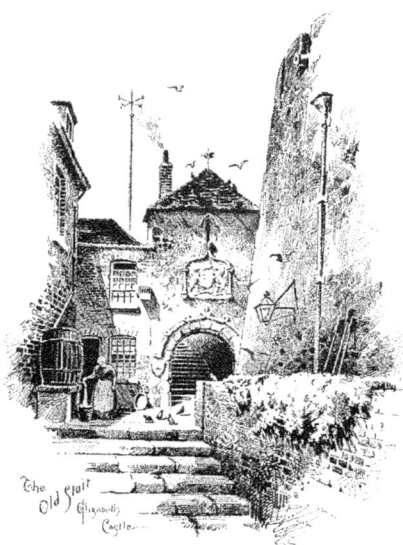

The Old Gate, Elizabeth Castle.

But the main tower still stands as it has stood since it was built; and if one can escape the attentions of the soldier showman who is intent on pointing out the position of the canteen, one can clamber to the summit and slide back to the days when Sir George Cartaret held the fortress for the King.

But if a close view of Fort Elizabeth falls somewhat short of one's expectations, its aspect from St. Aubyn's Bay will afford ample recompense. There is a hill behind St. Aubyn's from which one can overlook the whole sweep of coast with its fringe of white sands and green hills ; and the outermost point is the mighty rock, nearly a mile in circumference, crowned with its bulk of masonry. On a day when the sun is shining between showers, and the blue sea is swept by purple

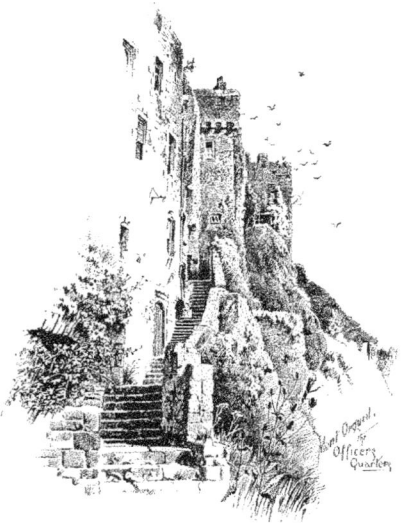

Mont Orgueil, Officers' Quarters.

human life begins to flow. Townsfolk troop across with stores for the garrison ; soldiers who are not on guard hurry to the delights of the town ; Jersey women, if it be evening, come over to the fort to visit their husbands ; for a large number of the artillery men, having been stationed there for some years, are married to Jersey women, who, not being "on the strength," earn their living in the town. Within the fort one cannot avoid a feeling of disappointment. The aged walls which frown upon St. Helier's are a hollow sham. They contain little but what can be seen in any barracks in the kingdom. The trail of the War Office is over all, and the picturesque angularities of the sixteenth century have been planed away to meet the demands of the nineteenth-century drill-sergeant.

shadows of clouds, the rock gleams out yellow in the sunshine, or sinks back into a weird mass of grey behind the rain. From St. Helier's the fort is scarcely noticed ; the rock stretching straight out to sea, is foreshortened and relatively insignificant. But from St. Aubyn's it can be seen in its true proportion. It seems to dominate the town, the island, and the sea.

There is, however, nothing in Guernsey or in Jersey, there are few things anywhere, to surpass the grandeur of Mont Orgueil, Jersey. Situated on the eastern point of the island, it rises sheer from the sea to a height—castle and all—of more than three hundred feet. Round the base of the cliff to the west, whence the accompanying sketch was taken, cluster the houses and shops of Gorey village. But the latter are in themselves not unpicturesque, and, being tinged with the vague blues and yellows commoner in French towns than in English, supply a valuable note of colour to the whole. They produce much the same effect as the houses and shops which surround the cathedral at Ghent, an effect of incongruity which is quaint and not unpleasing. One feels that they ought not to be there ;

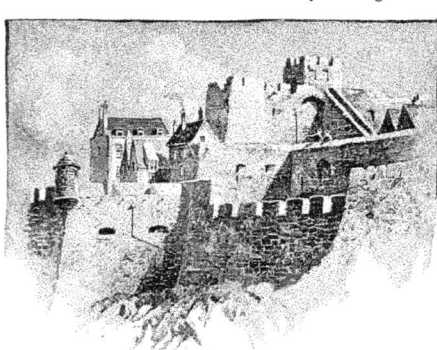

THE OLD PART, CASTLE CORNET.

that a café has nothing to do with a cathedral; but the café is so insignificant and the cathedral so supreme, that the absurdity of the one only serves to accentuate the grandeur of the other.

The Castle of Mont Orgueil has fortunately been left to grow old more or less in its own way, and has escaped the patching and pruning which have disfigured Fort Elizabeth. Only here and there its decrepitude has been propped and strengthened. For many years no soldiers have been quartered there. And its old age, like that of the gods, is fresh and green. Trees have sprung up around its lower plateaux, the slopes which lead up to the successive terraces are covered with turf, and over the face of the cliff and the walls, scarred by time and hard blows, lichens, grasses, and stonecrop have drawn a kindly veil.

The castle is old, so old that no one quite knows when it began to be a fortified place. There is a rampart to the north-east, hidden from view in the sketch, which is called Cæsar's foot. It is certain that the existence of these islands was known to Cæsar, and the discovery of buried Roman coins renders it probable that the Romans at least visited Jersey. But there is no evidence that Cæsar himself ever reached it. Parts of the main building of the castle date back to the tenth century. For Mont Orgueil was a fortress even before the Dukes of Normandy thought of becoming Kings of England. In the earliest records it is referred to as the Castellum de Gurrit. Its later and prouder title was bestowed upon it by the Duke of Clarence, the brother of Henry V. During the dark days before the death of the Back Prince, when the English king was weighed down by age and infirmities, the king of France, Charles, surnamed 'Le Sage,' decided to try the fortunes of war again. He sent Du Guesclin against Castle Gorey, with an army of ten thousand men. The siege lasted long, and it was finally agreed that if no help arrived by a certain date, the Castle should be surrendered. The succours arrived in time, and Du Guesclin retired, "having learnt" (to quote the mammoth phrases of a native chronicler) "that an army, however powerful, may yet be resisted, that arrogance, however haughty, may yet meet with humiliation, and that triumphs, however long uninterrupted, may yet find a period." It was in recognition of this successful resistance that the rock fortress was re-christened Mont Orgueil.

By the way, a list of the garrison stationed in the castle in the fifteenth year of Edward III.'s reign, together with their pay, is given by Falle, the early historian of Jersey. We find that the governor, Henry de la More, was provided with a salary of twelve pence a day.

The stairway which leads up along the sea-front of the castle (shown in the sketch entitled "Officers' Quarters") ends at the foot of the tower in which William Prynne dwelt for nearly three years. He had suffered many things, and worse things before this, having been twice fined five thousand pounds, and having left both his ears in the Star Chamber. But the energy of the indefatigable Puritan was undiminished. And indeed the quiet and seclusion of Mont Orgueil may well have been grateful after the turbulence and peril of English politics. From the three loopholes of his chamber in the tower he could view the rocks which skirt the Jersey coast, the sea which stretches away to a haze of land in the distance, and the turf and trees in the grounds below. The outcome of his confinement was a work of less incendiary nature than the famous and unlucky "Histriomastyx," namely "Mont Orgueil, or Divine and Profitable Meditations, raised from the contem-

Mont Orgueil Castle.

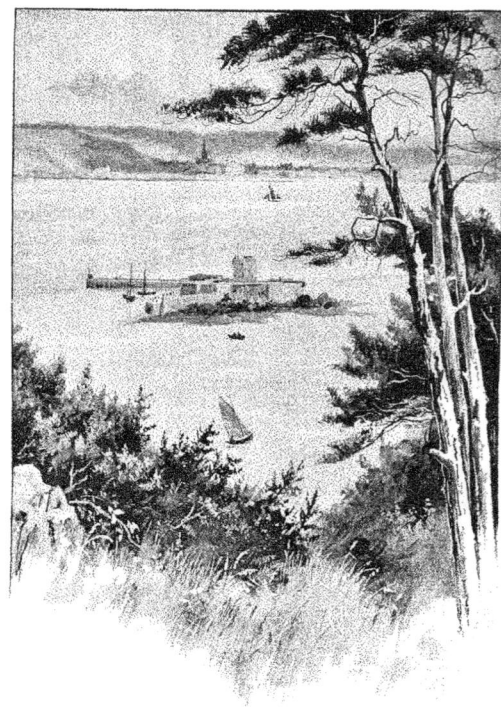

St. Aubyn's Castle, from Noirmont.

plation of these three leaves of Nature's Volume—1. Rocks. 2. Seas. 3. Gardens." The dedication of the poem to "Sweet Mistress, once fair, Margaret," a daughter of Sir Philip Cartaret, the governor, suggests that the author was treated rather as a guest than a prisoner.

One may absorb a lot of English history by conscientiously working through the annals of the castle. But at Mont Orgueil one rather resents history. In climbing the terraces and peering into the dim, cool chambers, haunted by the spirits of thirty generations, it is pleasanter to imagine than to know. For after all, what can one know but the bare date, the bald fact, that such a battle was fought, that this one gained the victory, and that one was killed? But the lives and thoughts of the men who have lived and fought and died upon this rock, the watching of the watchman, the suffering of the prisoner, the joy of the victor, all this we can only imagine. And it must be a dull imagination which is not stirred as one leans upon the lofty rampart, whither scarcely a sound reaches from the village below, on the spot where, century after century, English men-at-arms have stood, scanning the misty coast of France, to see the hostile ships, bristling with foemen, steal out across the blue sea. For Mont Orgueil is entirely restful, entirely satisfying. In the huge pile of stone, welded into the living rock, there is no jarring note of discord. Underneath the tides ebb and flow; the fishing boats glide in with dropping sails and anchor in the bay; the fisherfolk gossip and smoke upon the quay; the little railway-train which plies between Gorey and St. Helier's puffs and pants into the station; tourists, French and English, laugh and chatter through the village; men are born and men are buried; human life swirls and eddies around the feet of Mont Orgueil—but Mont Orgueil stands as it has stood for centuries, calm and grand; amid change an emblem of rest, in time a suggestion of eternity.

CLARENCE ROOK.

A NEW PHASE OF THE COPYRIGHT QUESTION.

COPYRIGHT in this country becomes more involved every day. It was recently decided that any picture may be reproduced as a tableau-vivant. It has now been decided (June 11th, Hanfstaengl v. Empire Theatre and *Daily Graphic*) that an illustrated newspaper may make sketches of these tableaux, without infringing the copyright of the original picture. In the face of the fact that Act 25 and 26 Vict., c. 68, confers on the artist "the sole and exclusive right of copying, engraving, reproducing, and multiplying his work," the Court of Appeal has held that the sketching of these tableaux by the *Daily Graphic* " are not copies of the pictures or reproductions of the designs thereof within the meaning of the statute." Justice Lindley held that no infringement had taken place because the pictures were not copied directly, but only through the medium of the tableaux. His Lordship in his judgment agreed, but apparently reluctantly, "that if the defendants had copied the plaintiff's pictures they would have infringed his rights, even although the use made of such copies could in no way compete with the sale of the pictures." Therefore if any enterprising illustrated paper wishes to publish a copyright picture, withheld from them otherwise, they have only to arrange a tableau-vivant and make a drawing from that.

The absurdity of this position is apparent, and with due respect to the Court of Appeal, we have to express our strong disapproval of this decision, which is alike unfair to artist and to publisher. It is probable the case will be taken to the House of Lords.

A SCOTTISH IMPRESSIONIST.

AT a time when impressionism is in the air, when criticism is dealing with the practice, and biography with its practitioners, it is not a little curious that one so seldom hears the name of William McTaggart mentioned. And yet, before the term had been imported from France, and ere Monet and the rest had formulated their creed, Mr. McTaggart had evolved for himself a method and a style, not unlike what they ultimately achieved, but exceeding it in suggestion, significance, and beauty. Impressionism, rightly understood, is the presentment of the essential elements of a scene, a character, or an incident, in the most expressive terms. In this sense, it includes the pictures of Mr. Whistler, Degas, and Mr. McTaggart, and of the "Glasgow School," as well as the exact and scientific realism of Moret and his followers.

The rigorous exclusion of all but what has to do with essentials should result in a rendering, striking in directness, and vividly suggestive to the imagination. Depending for result on selection of material, fine taste, and artistic perception of the rarest kind, a painter of this sort, by the very paucity of his statement, must, for success, possess the highest intelligence and sensibility. Of this kind is William McTaggart. That his work is not better known is possibly accounted for by the fact of his seldom exhibiting out of his own country, by his quiet and unobtrusive life, and his scorn of notoriety and advertisement. But among artists in Scotland he occupies the same unique position as Mr. Watts does in England. All his fellows, irrespective of school or set, respect him—the painters in the West regard him with as much admiration as his associates in the East; and although he has founded no cult, his influence has been wide and salutary.

Compared with much contemporary art-work, the one object of which seems to be to attract attention by vapid sentimentalism, or by eccentricity and startling cleverness of technique, Mr. McTaggart's work may seem simple and even ineffective; but if one is touched by beauty and sincerity, by charm of motive, grace of design, and expressive workmanship, he will turn from the "Pictures of the Year," as the expressive phrase has it—the pictures that people talk about this season, and forget long before the next—to the calm beauty and unforced poetry of McTaggart's pictures with a sense of satisfaction and refreshment. It is as if, on returning from the opera, you took up "Richard Peverel" and read the "Ferdinand and Miranda" chapter. The close, heated atmosphere of the theatre, the glare of the footlights, and brilliancy of the spectacle, are exchanged for the beauty of nature and the clear light of day; the artificiality of character, the tenor declaring his love on the top note, the heroine ending her swan-song in the falsetto, give place to the fervour of genuine passion and the ring of real emotion. It is not for a moment implied that Mr. McTaggart's work possesses the

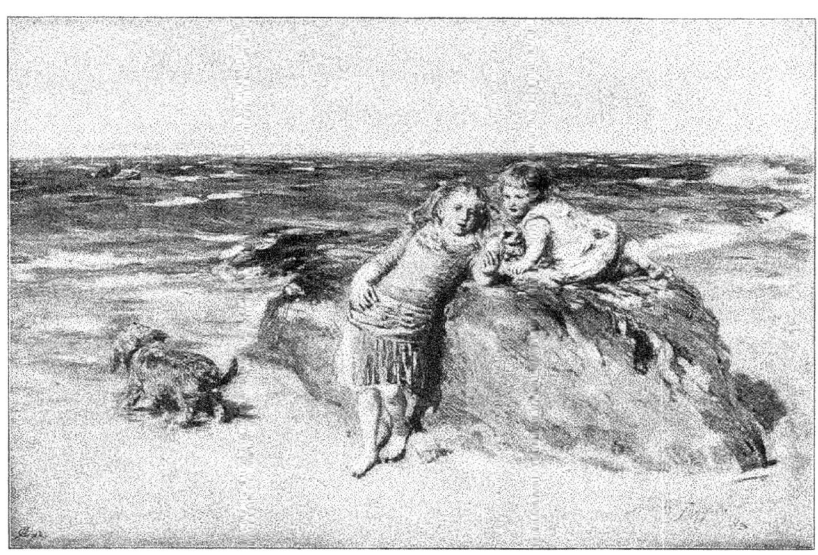

SUMMER BREEZES. BY WILLIAM MCTAGGART, R.S.A. IN THE POSSESSION OF PROFESSOR MCCALL ANDERSON, GLASGOW.

power of narrative and the wonderful insight into character that render Mr. Meredith's books so unique ; for the one is not the province of painting, the other but an attribute. The convention and atmosphere of make-believe are disconcerted by the freshness of nature interpreted by the painter-lover. Both of these forms of Art have their special spheres, but one is far more spontaneous and inevitable than the other.

At the beginning of his artistic career, like his friends and fellow-students, Mr. Orchardson and Mr. Pettie, he took subjects for many of his pictures from literature; but while they chose dramatic situations from the lives of lords and ladies for their themes, Mr. McTaggart found his subjects in the joys and sorrows of common people, as enshrined in old Scots ballads, and occasionally in contemporary poetry. Lord Tennyson's exquisite English Idylls, "Enoch Arden" and "Dora," were the inspiration of two of his most beautiful essays in this direction, but in them, as in nearly all his pictures of an illustrative nature, he has not striven to exactly realise the incidents as described by the poet, but used them as pictorial motives. They are, however, more than illustrations. Pictorial beauty justifies their existence as pictures, while the "literary element" is of a different kind from that which requires for explanation a page of catalogue, or the knowledge necessary for an honours degree. But gradually the conception that painting is in itself exquisitely fitted to express original ideas and visions of beauty grew upon him ; the germ, already visible in his free treatment of illustrative themes, broke into flower, and his work became freer, more beautiful, and expressive. He turned to Nature for inspiration, and found her fully responsive.

In his interest and appreciation of the visual aspects of nature, and the ever-varying phenomena of light and atmosphere, he is truly modern ; but he brings with him also the eye of the poet—a sympathetic insight into the significance of life and nature—which divides him from the mere recorders of fact, be they never so broadly expressive, and places him among creative artists. Even the slightest figure in a picture by Mr. McTaggart has its poetic, as well as its purely pictorial place in the conception; it is a dot of colour in the right place for the artistic effect, but it is also an integral part of the poetic motive. Quite alive to the necessity of an underlying idea in picture-making, his first concern is to make his work really and truly pictorially interesting.

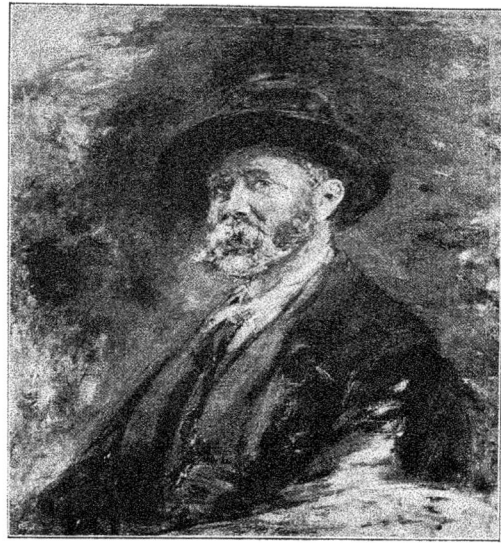

WILLIAM McTAGGART, R.S.A. BY HIMSELF.

No one has painted the heaving waters of the sundering sea, or given the joy of shimmering sun on pearly beach or country lea, so truthfully ; and in everything he does there is that personal note which is, after all, the very essence of Art. It is nature plus man, not in the conventional sense of the creation of the fanciful, but in that of the larger vision which comes of imagination. Mr. McTaggart has rarely given us a work of pure landscape, but on several occasions he has painted the sea in its utter loneliness. One of these, 'Machrihanish Bay,' comes back to me with peculiar vividness, and I remember how, standing before it, the keen, sweet smell of the sea, the roar of ocean thundering on the shore, even the taste of the briny on the lips, seemed to come from the painted canvas. It created an atmosphere through which one seemed in reality to contemplate the ever-changing sea.

But his great preoccupation is with man and his environment, or, as he would himself say, man at his work, and it is in such pictures as 'The Harbour Bar,' or 'Through Wind and Rain,' and above all in those dealing with children, such as 'Summer Breezes,' that he is most characteristic. In these latter the philosophic mind and the poetic spirit show, as they do in the work of Millet and Israels. His 'Harbour Bar' and 'Wind and Rain' are very different in conception and spirit from the theatrical realism we associate with the titles. Only boats coming in, in the grey of the morning, and yet the whole story of fisher life is there, not depicted, but certainly suggested. Reality has been dealt with so vividly and so sympathetically that association comes of itself. They come, safe and happy, a goodly haul of silver herring in the nets, and as the shore is neared, the boat is urged with oar and sail, for soon they will be home again. But one feels also the toil and weariness of the night, the uncertainty of the life, and the never far-off possibility of disaster. Something in the lift of the long green sea, full of air bubbles as it rolls over the shoaling bottom, in the frailness of the boat, as it rises buoyantly on the wave, gives one a poignant sense of the sorrow of the sea, and it requires little imagination to conceive it swamped,

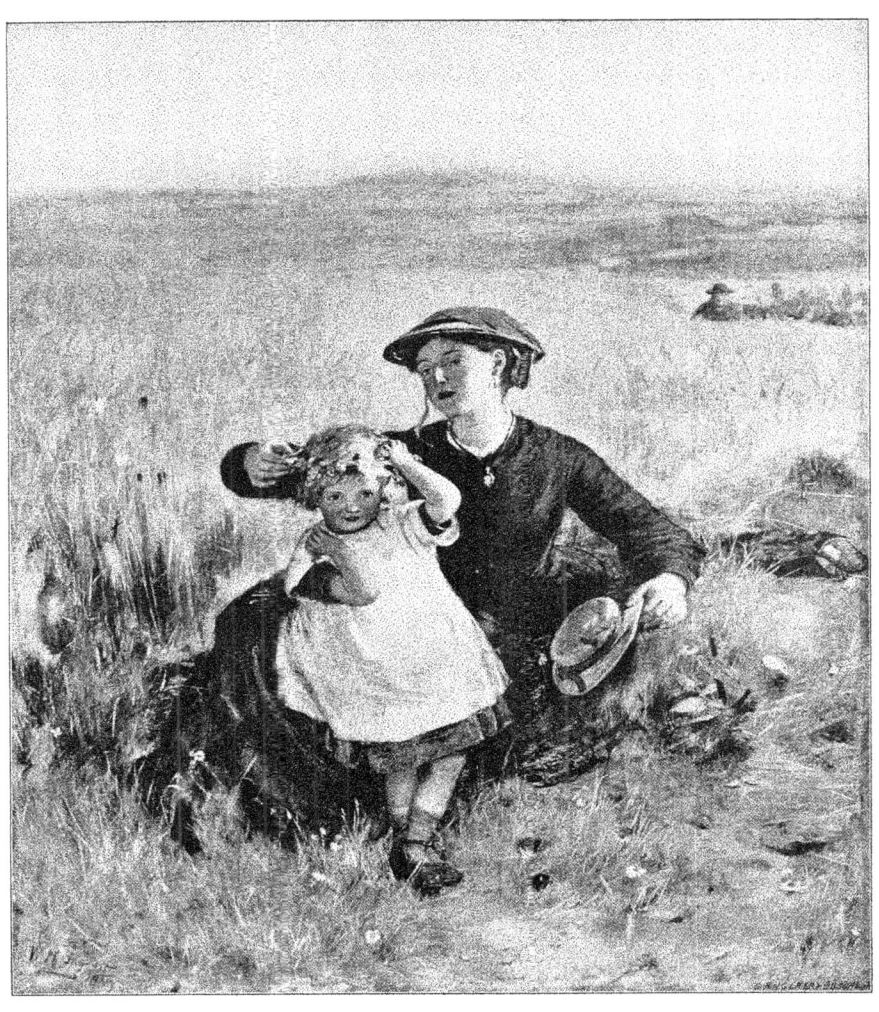

"DORA."
BY WILLIAM McTAGGART, R.S.A.
From the painting in the National Gallery of Scotland.
The Property of the Royal Scottish Academy.

the men beneath the bubbling water in the cold embrace of the long sea tangle, and the wail on shore. But his is usually a more gladsome mood; he has felt the weariness of life only that he might give fuller expression to the joy of living. But oftenest he turns to the happiness of childhood and the peacefulness of old age.

If you can imagine the "little boy full of joy, the little girl sweet and small," of Blake's "Songs of Innocence," set against a background of Shelley or Swinburne, you will have some idea of the tenderness and beauty in Mr. McTaggart's pictures of children. They shine as stars against the swimming blue of summer seas, or glow like wild-rose blooms amid the green of May. Now and then the frail, flower-like beauty of these happy children, amidst the rush and crash of stormy seas, sets one athinking that the irresponsible joy of youth will soon be over, and they, as men and women, be struggling in the iron grip of fitful circumstance. Far oftener, however, they leave a memory of pleasure unalloyed by pain, to cheer us in the dreary winter days. Some of his most beautiful pictures have been executed in water-colour, and one can recall drawings in which the material process that gave them being seemed non-existent—they seemed to have come upon the paper as frost-flowers on a window-pane, or to have grown like flowers, unconsciously. Exceedingly slight, the paper no more than delicately tinted here and there; but what of that?—how beautiful! He handles his water-colours lovingly, and one would not wonder if he prized them more highly than his oils.

Although Sir Henry Raeburn occasionally painted fine pictures of women, including the beautiful 'Mrs. Scott Moncrieff,' now one of the chiefest ornaments of the Gallery on the Mound, and Mr. Orchardson and Pettie have now and then done brilliantly in the same direction, Scottish portrait-painters have secured their greatest successes in delineating men. Mr. McTaggart, however, has achieved his in depicting the grace and beauty of women, and the charm and simplicity of children, and now that some of the younger artists are following so successfully in his footsteps, Scottish art may safely claim distinction on both sides. His portrait of a little girl—'The Belle'—dressed in red, and set against a background of ruddy brown, hung amongst Sir Joshuas and Gainsboroughs, would claim place as an equal. The delicate vigour and charm of handling, the naive grace of the pose, the beauty of composition and colour, and the distinguished style, proclaim it a masterpiece.

Keenly sensitive to the vibration of light and subtle influence of atmosphere on local colour, his handling is not "rough and chippy," nor his colour broken and detached, as in the pictures of Monet and his school. Exceeding them in material beauty, as in vividness of illusive effect, his work combines in a remarkable degree the charm of nature and the fascination of art. Judged by the standard of academic accomplishment, his technique may seem incomplete; but if expression be the end of art, and the finest painting that which conveys most vividly the artist's impression, then Mr. McTaggart's, for his matter and subject, is the apotheosis of expression. The seeming incompleteness contributes to the result, for the infinite cannot be expressed by the strictly finite. It is by concentration of material and suggestiveness of handling that Constable's landscapes are full of the life of nature, that

THE BELLE. BY WILLIAM MCTAGGART, R.S.A.

the myriad leaves of Corot's trees shake and quiver in the breeze of morn and eve, and the great white clouds for ever drift across Cecil Lawson's 'Barden Moor,' and it is by a similar process that Mr. McTaggart wins his results.

The freshness of handling, and the directness of touch in his pictures, are wonders to those who know the care and time expended in their execution. For his more important pictures he will often make a cartoon, and studies for different parts, but the scaffolding on which the whole has been raised is never traceable in the ultimate result. Perhaps the secret is that he seems never to place a touch on the canvas which is not to remain there, and take its place and meaning in relation to the whole. In his work the ordered beauty and harmonious proportion of parts that come of conscious art are added to the charm of perfect spontaneity. Highly dowered as a colourist, he uses colour with an audacity that, with one less gifted, might result in disaster. His clear colour, fresh and sparkling, has much of the fluency and limpidness which characterize Gainsborough's and Watteau's. To paint in the high key he usually chooses, and to preserve harmony, is indeed difficult, for in such work the slightest variation in tone or colour tells at once, and modulations which would never show in a low-tone picture instantly proclaim their presence to the destruction of the harmony; but as a rule Mr. McTaggart emerges from the test triumphant.

His is a kindred spirit to that of the Masters of the Barbizon school, and the great Dutchmen who followed them; there is something akin to Corot in his poetic realism, to Millet and Israels in his interest in humanity, and to Monticelli in the loose and delicate way in which the figures are wreathed into the composition. Although in the special phase—fisher life—with which he deals, he is a pioneer, he has not rejected the traditions of the past, but adapted them to suit the requirements of the new material. Whilst his pictures are essentially Scottish, and one would never mistake them for the work of a foreigner, or even of an Englishman, they are in no sense parochial. They have the universality that comes of the beautiful expression of beautiful things. An acute critic has remarked that it requires genius to paint wind. The same is true of sunshine, and Mr. McTaggart has done both. I know of no work which conveys so vividly as his, natural effect, particularly of the sea. Other men paint the form and colour of the sea, he its apparent life. Compared with the freshness and naturalness of his seas, those of Turner and Vandevelde seem but great conventions; contrasted with his pictorial conception the pictures of Henry Moore and Claude Monet only fine studies, and after the infinite variety of his moods even Hook's exquisite marines are monotonous. Mr. McTaggart's own phrase, "Like an attitude, a breaking wave is a conception," gives the secret of the vitality in his work. One may trace the shape of a thing with remorseless precision, and observe its characteristics with perfect accuracy, but except one also forms an emotional and mental conception of the thing observed, the life will leak out in the recording.

Of course Mr. McTaggart's art has its limitations, but, generally speaking, his range is wide, and within it he has done noble things. Sainte-Beuve has declared that freshness, energy, and masterly disposition are the marks of a genuine classic, and these Mr. McTaggart's work certainly possesses. A distinguished artist once expressed the opinion: "I wish McTaggart could be induced to exhibit eighty or a hundred of his finest pictures in Paris. I am certain they would create a perfect *furore*, that the French artists would hail him as a Master." Masters in any art are rare; too often their genius is unrecognised till they are dead. Let us give William McTaggart his due now.

JAMES L. CAW.

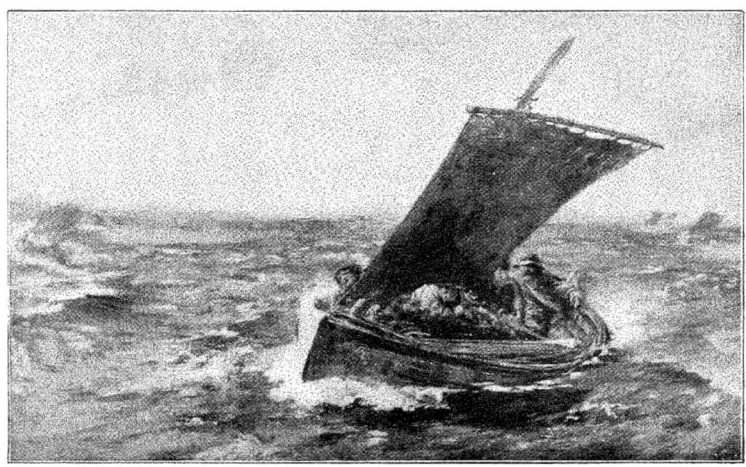

THROUGH WIND AND RAIN. BY WILLIAM McTAGGART, R.S.A.

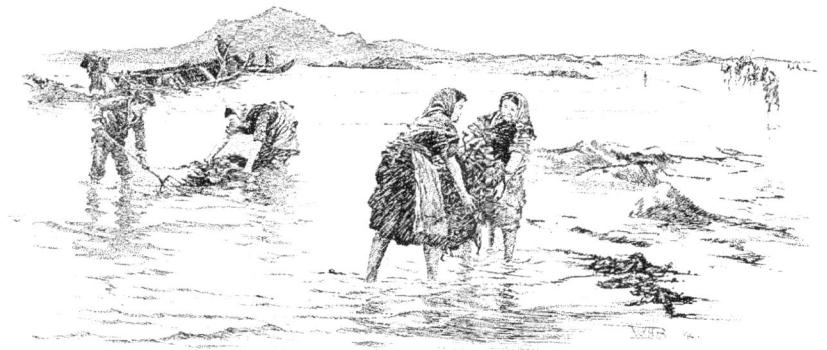

AFTER A STORM, GATHERING WRACK. FROM THE ORIGINAL DRAWING BY W. H. BARTLETT.

COAST LIFE IN CONNEMARA.

CONNEMARA is the name given to a district lying midway between the counties of Galway and Mayo, and is usually approached from the town of Galway. There is another route from Westport, in Mayo, but it is only during the summer months that there is any public conveyance running, although from a scenic point of view it is the more interesting of the two, passing as it does through Leenane, the pass of Kylemore, and Letterfrack. On the route from Galway to Clifden there is an all-the-year-round service with the long car, doing the journey in about seven hours, and if the weather be fine, this method of travelling offers a pleasurable novelty to those unused to this strange vehicle. But let that fifty odd miles be made in soaking rain—a very common experience in the West—then the discomforts of this elongated side car on four wheels become manifest.

To explore the interesting coast of Connemara is not by any means an easy matter, as communications are difficult, and one must be prepared to put up with a primitive accommodation. My headquarters for several summers were in a village on the coast about ten miles from Clifden, the capital of Connemara, and although the greater part of the time was necessarily occupied with my painting, opportunities were not lacking for explorations and excursions which I think enable me to form a good idea of the beauties and characteristics of the coast and coast life. About a mile from the village are a series of the most exquisite strands of the finest white sand, one of them being so landlocked that it forms an ideal bathing-place. I shall never forget the delight of seeing it for the first time. It was on one of those luminous grey days, so dear to the artist, when all the colours in nature are heightened by the moisture in the atmosphere. The combination of these beautiful "beaches" (as they are called locally), together with a background of the blue mountains known as the Twelve Pins, the sea a lovely green colour and exquisitely clear, gently rippling in over the pearly white sand, formed a scene of uncommon beauty. Among the sand-hills overlooking the bay is a small and primitive graveyard, in which it is still the custom to bury children. I chanced to see a funeral there, only once, and it was very striking. It took place in brilliant sunshine, and the general effect was very original, almost Oriental in character. The plain deal coffin, covered with a white sheet, was deposited on the sand, the mother sitting upon it, while two men made a grave, the custom being to dig it after the funeral party arrives on the ground.

Keening women with their picturesque cloaks were grouped around close beside the chief mourner, and their curious lamentations could be heard a considerable distance. The intense white sand, and the deep blue of the sky, and

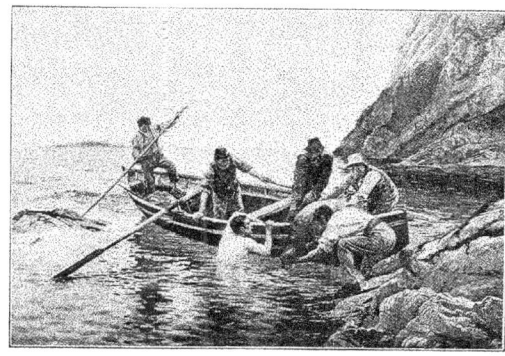

SEAL DIVING. FROM THE PAINTING BY W. H. BARTLETT.

deeper blue of the sea beyond, formed a fitting background to a strange and remarkable scene. With the exception of such an event as just described, or an occasional landing of turf or cattle from an adjacent island, towed as shown in the picture, these beautiful strands are quite deserted.

Fishing as a regular industry is, one may say, non-existent in Connemara, although from time to time government grants have been made to the peasants for the purchase of the necessary gear, but with little or no success as a result. I have never seen nets used at all, only lines, and the fish caught is for home consumption, either fresh or salted for the winter. Lobsters are, however, caught in fair quantities, and exported.

as "scarlet runners." One can easily imagine, in the event of friction between the guardians and the doctor, the former have the power of giving him many a needless trot across the bog.

The pattern (I believe the word to be a corruption of patron) is held in mid-July, and when the weather is fine all available kinds of craft are seen making for Macdara. There the object of the large number of excursionists is to do the various stations, which means the saying of so many prayers at the different shrines; the ruins of the saints' chapel (said to date from the sixth century) having generally the greatest number of devotees. A small force of the Royal Irish Con-

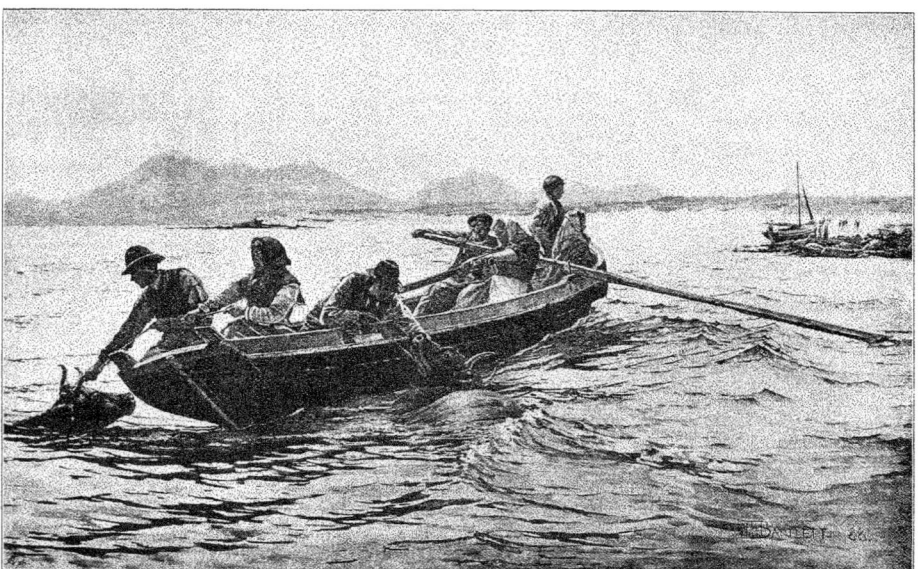

RETURNING FROM THE FAIR. FROM THE PAINTING BY W. H. BARTLETT.

One sees many examples of money woefully misspent on the badly placed piers, to which no access can be had, either by land or by water, for any but the smallest boats. Often, indeed, the only craft seen is the native corracle, which does not need the shelter of a pier, it being so light that two men can easily carry it.

Many of my most interesting excursions have been made with local doctors. As medical officers they are paid an annual sum (I believe by the Local Government Board) to attend to the community. The districts allotted to them are usually of immense extent, and were it not that the peasantry are a healthy lot, the work to be done would be out of all proportion to the remuneration. To prevent a doctor being summoned by a trivial case two kinds of tickets are issued by the poor-law guardians, a blue one for the patient who has to go to the doctor, and a red one when the doctor has to go to him, the latter kind humorously described to me by a local M.D.

stabulary is in attendance, but generally the proceedings pass off in orderly fashion enough; what scrimmages may occur are at a later stage, when the various parties have left the island to make a night of it somewhere. At all gatherings in the west, be it patterns or fairs, one cannot fail to be struck with the utter lack of any amusements for the people or power of amusing themselves beyond drinking.

Seals (the grey Atlantic species) were at one time very common all along the coast of Connemara, but to find them now it is necessary to go on to the small uninhabited islands a few miles from the mainland. Occasionally a stray family will find its way up the estuary of a river in search of the salmon they love so well; and if they are discovered, a seal hunt is immediately organized. The party is divided into two—a stalking party to get on to the rocks, and the remainder to go round by boat, having orders to lie "perdu" till they hear a shot.

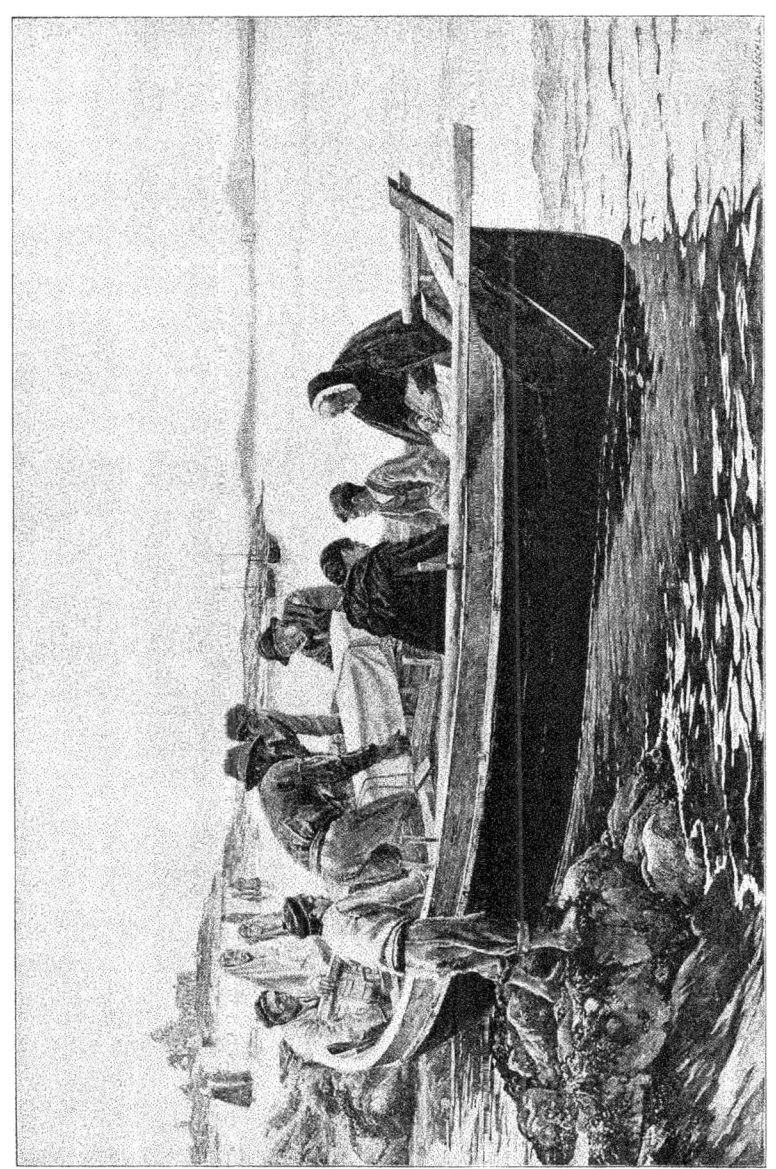

The Last Paddy Voyage. A Connemara Funeral. From the Painting by W. H. Bartlett.

A walk of about a mile brings us into the neighbourhood of the seals, and then comes a crawl over masses of seaweed, keeping as much as possible behind the rocks. Presently, a point is reached from which the seals can be seen lying on the rocks which have been partly uncovered by the tide. A flock of small sea-birds are hovering about them, and with their shrill cries seem to warn the seals of their approaching danger. A shot is fired, and the largest is seen to be hit, but all dive and disappear in the sea.

To get down to the water's edge as soon as possible and await the boat, which is already coming round the point, is the next step, and when we are all aboard, a chase of the wounded seal is commenced. At first it seems as if he had got clear away, but an excited "There he is!" and away we go, only to see him disappear when we come within a few boats' lengths of him. Then a wait ensues until a little black head is seen again, perhaps three hundred yards away. Again the rowers, straining every nerve, make another attempt to come to close quarters, only to see him dive once more, but not before we can see how he has been wounded. It is evident at last he is getting exhausted, and each time he remains up longer to get breath, and after perhaps an hour's excited chasing we succeed in gaffing him, and tow him back in triumph.

It frequently happens in shooting a seal in the water it is killed outright, and sinks forthwith to the bottom. If the water is not too deep, and clear enough at the bottom, it can be recovered by diving, as the body of the seal rises easily to the surface on being moved. The skin has little intrinsic value, but the peasants prize the oil, which is said to be "grand for rheumatics."

Seaweed, or "wrack," as it is called, plays an important part in Connemara life, both in the form of manure for the land and burnt for kelp. A most picturesque scene is after a storm in the spring, when all the available population make their way to the shore with their horses and donkeys and baskets of all sorts and sizes. Into the sea they all go, gathering wrack of every kind torn up by the rough Atlantic. It is an animated scene, and all appear to enjoy the work, joking and laughing with one another.

Great heaps of weed are put together, the horses with their side panniers loaded, and with great pieces trailing down, off they go up the steep beach and across the bog. It is the peasants' only manure, and many a mile have some to come to fetch the quantity necessary for their holding.

The making of kelp during the summer and early autumn employs a good many people, and a familiar sight all along the coast is the columns of white smoke arising from the burnings. Picturesque effects are seen, too, with the groups of workers half hidden by the wind-blown smoke; and at a later stage, when hammering the red-hot mass, the lurid glow lighting up their faces with, perhaps, a background of a wild, stormy sunset and a troubled sea—the whole effect forms a striking scene.

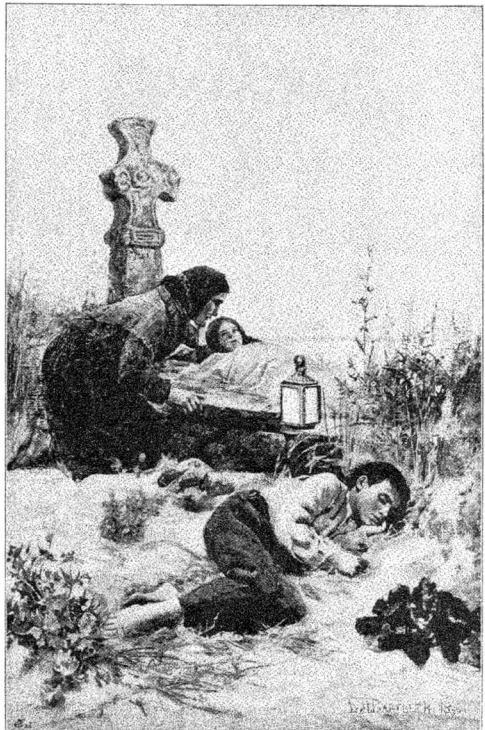

A CONNEMARA CUSTOM.—A HEALING SHRINE.
FROM THE PAINTING BY W. H. BARTLETT.

Among other disadvantages the inhabitants living on the island have to contend with, the difficulties of transport for their cattle are certainly not the least. Previous to the fairs, the cattle have to swim, in many cases, two and three miles in tow, and the greatest care has to be taken to prevent their swallowing large quantities of sea-water. Cords are strongly bound round the horns (see the illustration), and their heads are kept well up above the water by this means; but in spite of these precautions, if the weather be at all rough a beast will swallow so much water that it has no power left to disgorge it, and dies of suffocation on reaching the shore.

Healing shrines are not uncommon in the West of Ireland, both on the mainland and the adjacent islands, but the one of the large island of Aran is perhaps the most interesting. The custom is for the sick person to remain from sunset till dawn in the hope of being cured. Weird indeed is the scene during the night, with the pilgrims weary and anxious with watching the occupant of the shrine at their all night vigil.

Superstition against being sketched, especially among the old people, is by no means extinct. A common form of refusal is based on the idea that it would be considered "queer" by the other people. I have been enjoined to keep it a close secret that such and such a person had been sitting to me. Women of all ages are extremely shy, and it is always a matter of the greatest difficulty to get young girls as models. Many and many are the efforts I have made to get some particularly interesting-looking woman to give me a sitting, but without success. A really fine specimen of a Connemara peasant woman would be hard to beat. Tall, well-built, the face oval in shape, broad across the cheek bones, the deep-set eyes a fine blue-grey fringed with long dark lashes—in fact, beautiful eyes may be said to be a common heritage of the western Irish. The expression is usually a sad or pensive one, the not unnatural result of a melancholy climate and a continual struggle with a poor soil. I think many of the national characteristics are directly traceable to climatic influences. Englishmen, full of energy at the outset, settling in the wild west, have, in a few years, distinctly felt its deteriorating effects.

For clothes of both sexes homespun material is almost the general rule, and the well-worn madder-red woollen petticoat of the women of all ages is perhaps the most striking note in the peasant costume. The cloaks worn vary a little, according to the district. In the neighbourhood of Galway the rough-dyed dark blue cloaks with hoods are in general wear, and in a number of cases, doubtless heirlooms; also cloaks of smooth dark blue cloth, similar to those worn in the county Cork, are seen. The old red Claddagh cloak—which became, a good many years ago, quite fashionable among the well-to-do classes—is now very scarce. Shop-made shawls are unfortunately coming more and more into general use, although some of the thick heavy ones are not without a certain *cachet* of their own. Very frequently an ordinary flannel petticoat just slipped over the head and fastened round the neck instead of round the waist, is made to serve as a shawl. Only in one place did I see the homespun flannel dyed an indigo blue, but it was a pleasant change from the almost universal use of the white flannel by the men and boys, which soon becomes a somewhat monotonous yellow.

Their dress consists almost invariably of a "borneen," a sort of waistcoat with sleeves either worn loose or tucked into the trousers. The old knee-breeches and cut-away coat and tall hat of the traditional Irishman are still to be seen any market-day in Galway, but rarely worn except by the old men. I cannot remember to have ever seen any in Connemara. Boys very commonly wear petticoats up to the age of twelve or thirteen, being only distinguished by their cropped hair. The reason, I take it, is that where the family is a large one, the petticoat is the simplest garment to make.

It is to be hoped that with the light railways now in course of construction the West Coast of Ireland, now so little visited, may be opened up; and with the much-needed increase in the hotel accommodation, more and more visitors in search of something new, both from a human nature and scenic point of view, may be induced to pay it a visit. The Connemara coast, with its mountains and rocky shores, lovely sand bays, the glorious skies and clear green seas, possesses a charm which must be seen to be appreciated.

W. H. BARTLETT.

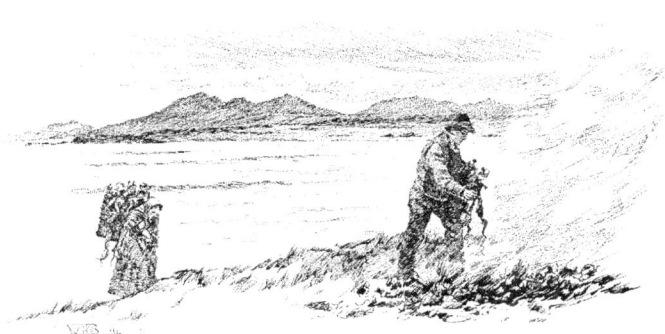

BURNING KELP. FROM THE ORIGINAL DRAWING BY W. H. BARTLETT.

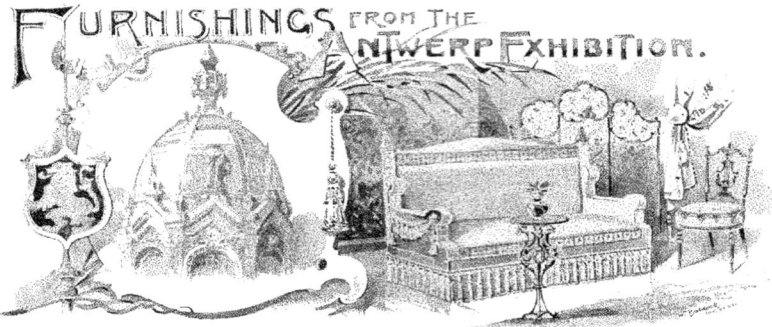

Furnishings from the Antwerp Exhibition.

IT was with the object of arriving at a correct estimate of the standard of the latest productions of our Continental neighbours, in those branches of industry immediately associated with the furnishing and decoration of the home, that I recently visited the Antwerp Exhibition, and, while so doing, the questions, "Need we go abroad for our furniture?" "Are nineteenth-century productions inferior to those of the much-vaunted 'good old days'?" and "What may we learn from the work of other countries?" were uppermost in my mind. The conclusions arrived at may be inferred from the brief comments which follow. The necessarily limited scope of a review of this description makes it imperative to confine the illustrations to just a few of those articles which may be considered as thoroughly characteristic, or which display exceptional novelty, and the task of selection from so great a variety has been somewhat difficult. However, the sketches accompanying these notes, though comparatively few in number, are fairly representative.

The upholsterers of this country must sit at the feet of their Continental *confrères* in the art of *portière* and window-draping. The rare taste and skill with which textiles are manipulated by the latter, especially in France; the choice harmonies of colour and skilful disposition of the materials, attained with but little apparent effort, are unexcelled the world over. It is a treat to watch the way in which a French

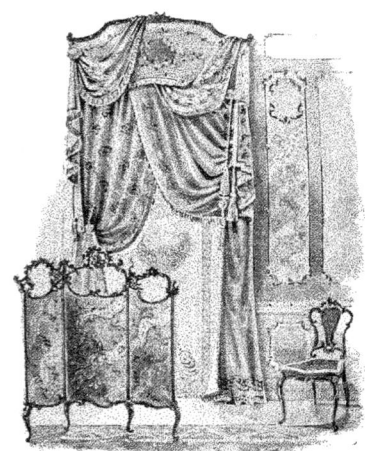

Window Drapery. Dementer fils & Cie., Brussels.

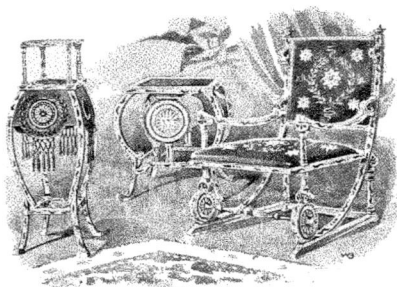

Oriental Group. Max Claire, Paris.

or Belgian upholsterer disposes even the simplest fabrics with an ease which reveals his perfect mastery of the art, and works them into a scheme which merits to be styled "a thing of beauty," if the nature of its composition precludes its being "a joy for ever."

Unfortunately, the effect of the window drapery, illustrated here, is almost entirely lost in reproduction by means of simple black and white. Clever as is the arrangement, the principal charm of the whole rests in the harmonizing of the subdued reds and delicate shades of green, which constitute the colouring of the silks employed. Messrs. Dementer fils et Cie., of Brussels, are responsible for this example, selected from many equally choice, as also for the Louis-Quinze screen

FURNISHINGS FROM THE ANTWERP EXHIBITION.

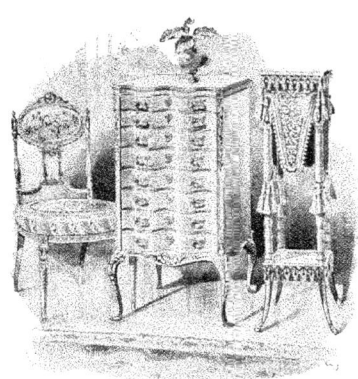

JARDINIÈRE, CABINET AND CHAIR.

and chair grouped with it. The walnut frame of this screen is gilded in parts, after the manner which finds so much favour in the country from whence it comes, and the panels are of silk of a thoroughly characteristic pattern. The chair —for this is the case with most Louis-Quinze seats—is of gilt, and, altogether, these two pieces are representative examples of a style which, by reason of its brilliant—if meretricious— effect, predominates in the salons and boudoirs of the French and Belgian aristocracy. Fortunately, the more refined and beautiful Louis-Seize shares the honours of those apartments; but that will be considered later.

The quaint Oriental group, by M. Max Claire, of Paris, embraces the most cultivated rendering of Eastern forms to be found in the exhibition. These pieces are of a dull ivory white, judiciously decorated with subdued reds and greens, and they stand in happy contrast to the gaudily coloured and bespangled atrocities which are not infrequently tolerated—nay, praised, because they are "Oriental." Many people do not seem to appreciate the fact that forms and colourings which accord with Eastern environments may not be used indiscriminately in our Western homes, and many an infraction of good taste is committed in consequence.

Continental furnishers are very fond of dressing up many small articles of cabinet work with trimmings and fabrics until the wood of which they are composed is almost entirely hidden, and the flower stand, or jardinière, illustrated above, is a good specimen of that practice. Upholstered, as it is, in silks and plushes, the sight of it extorts many exclamations of delight from members of the fair sex, but the manner of treatment is, in my opinion, more suited to the milliner than the cabinet-maker. The fact that it represents an important branch of the furnishing of the country of its production is the reason why it is illustrated here. It is, of course, true that an article of this kind lends colour to any apartment to which it 1894.

may be introduced, but that end may be attained in other and more legitimate ways. It must candidly be confessed that our own furnishers are not free from blame in this direction, and the cause of the popularity of this effeminate class of thing may undoubtedly be explained by the old advice, *cherchez la femme*. The Louis-Quatorze dwarf cabinet, in figured walnut, with gilt (ormolu) handles and mounts, is quite a type of its class, while the pretty Louis-Seize chair, with its dainty silk covering, is a good model of that style whose development the cultivated patronage of the ill-fated Marie Antionette did so much to foster.

Continental cabinet-makers do not employ so great a selection of woods as do their English competitors; walnut is their principal, and almost sole, medium. They rely, for variety of effect, upon gilding, painting, and the textiles used by the upholsterer, and they certainly know how to treat them to the best advantage. In contrast to this, the English cabinet-maker brings out the beauties of mahogany, oak, walnut, ash, maple, rosewood, satinwood, chestnut, and other woods with a skill in which he is unrivalled. In the matter of style, too, Louis-Quinze and Louis-Seize for drawing-room, and Flemish Renaissance and Henri-Deux—a phase of French Renaissance—for dining-room, almost entirely constitute the stock in trade of the Belgian furnisher, whereas, in this country, a far greater range of styles is cultivated. In discussing this feature of Continental furnishing, I may be excused for quoting a sentence from Mr. Armstrong's article in the June number of THE ART JOURNAL. That writer said: "A French interior of to-day"—and for "French," "Belgian" might be substituted, "putting aside the vagaries of a few very rich men, shows practically no change from one of half a century ago. It is marked by the same tasteful use of rather tasteless things, by the same curious commingling of audacity with cowardice, of skill in disposition with poverty

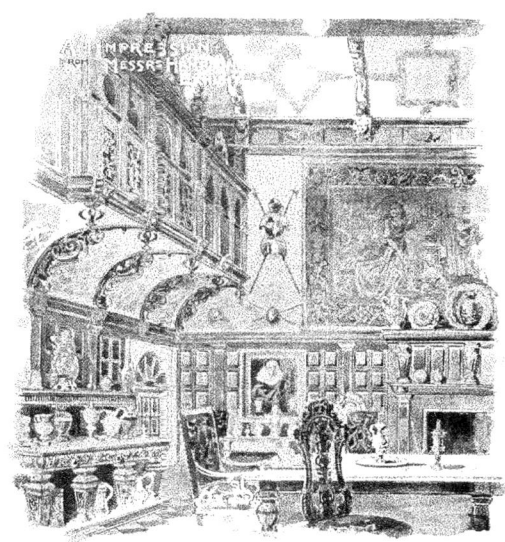

of invention. In England we have passed through all sorts of stages since the Mother of Exhibitions closed her doors in 1851. An average London drawing-room has been half-a-dozen things since that date, her Paris sister has remained what she was."

"What about the quality of construction?" some one may inquire. Well, in that respect we, as a nation, are second to none. And more! we undoubtedly display far greater fertility in the origination of new designs as far as cabinet work and chairs are concerned. In saying this I may lay myself open to the charge of prejudiced patriotism, but the opinion is an honest and impartial one. In the painted decoration of walls and the designing and carrying out of draperies, I reiterate that we cannot claim to be superior, nor even equal to those whose work has been under consideration, but in all other branches of furnishing we have no need to fear rivalry at present.

It was gratifying to discover that British cabinet work was represented at Antwerp by exhibits which could not do otherwise than enhance its reputation. Messrs. Hampton & Sons of Pall Mall are displaying their wonderful reproduction of the banqueting-hall, Hatfield House, there, and it is a specimen of craftsmanship which elicits unmixed admiration for its perfect workmanship and the beauty of its *ensemble*. This banqueting-hall, with its rich oak carvings, fine old tapestries and armour, plate and stately furniture, its minstrels' gallery and hospitable fire-place, represents a style which will never lose favour while there live Englishmen who have become endeared to the traditions handed down from the days of Shakespeare and Spenser.

Did space permit, I might with pleasure reproduce many things from the stand of Messrs. Howard & Sons, of Berners Street, but must be content with illustrating their choice inlaid Italian Renaissance Cabinet. It is a scholarly study in the Cinque-cento and is a pleasing illustration how rich an effect may be obtained by tastefully embellishing a comparatively simple constructive form with well-designed and perfectly executed marquetry. The applicability of the Cinque-cento to domestic uses, for drawing-room, dining-room, and bedroom alike, and the beauty and variety of its many phases,

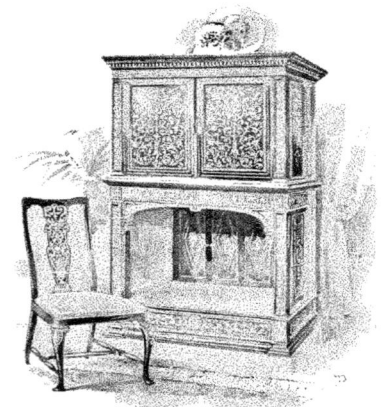

CABINET AND CHAIR. HOWARD & SONS.

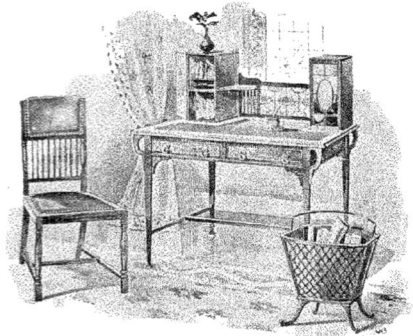

STAINED-GREEN WRITING TABLE AND CHAIR. ENGLISH.

leave little cause for wonder that it should have retained its hold on public favour for more than four centuries. The rest of Messrs. Howard's exhibit is intentionally English in every way, both as regards design and manufacture, and is powerful testimony as to what we can do in this country in the way of furnishing. The silks, carpets, wall decorations, and cabinet work are all of home production, and do not in any way suffer by comparison with the work to be found in other sections—to the contrary.

Stained-green furniture has found many admirers of late, and has been produced in many quaint and curious forms. If treated with taste and skill it certainly has a very pleasing effect, and, judiciously employed, lends helpful colour and variety to a furnishing scheme. The writing-table and chair are of this description, and are sketched from a selection of similarly attractive creations shown by an English wholesale manufacturer, which are rather a revelation to our foreign friends, whose furnishers have not yet cultivated the class of thing they represent.

It is time to bring these few cursory notes to a conclusion, but, before doing so, I feel bound to say a word with reference to the invidious comparisons which some people are fond of drawing between the work of contemporary craftsmen and that which has been handed down to us by our forefathers. The cheering critic who takes a delight in praising, "in enthusiastic tone, every century but this and every country but his own," seems to be oblivious of the fact that the "cheap and nasty" of centuries ago—for they had it—has been destroyed by time, and that, generally speaking, only the best work remains to us. Let there be no mistake! We have conscientious and highly gifted men to-day who, when opportunity favours, can turn out as excellent work as any of their ancestors. It is an injustice to place side by side a piece of furniture which was, say, produced in the Galleries of the Louvre, under the patronage of a monarch whose love of personal aggrandisement induced him to give his *ébénistes carte blanche*, and one put together—as is, alas! too often the case nowadays—at a competitive price, and say "Look at the difference!" The opportunity and encouragement to give their ideas and skill free play are all our workers require to refute the implication that they are intellectually, and practically, inferior to those who have gone before.

R. DAVIS BENN.

OLD FERRARESE AND BOLOGNESE PICTURES.

THE exhibition at the Burlington Fine Arts Club of pictures of the old Ferrarese-Bolognese School of the fifteenth and sixteenth centuries, should be welcome to those who take an interest in the development of Italian Art in its provincial branches. Special credit is due to the author of the descriptive catalogue for having at a considerable expense of time and trouble, got together as complete a collection as possible of photographs of all the works of this school scattered throughout Europe.

By Ercole Roberti, who may be called the Mantegna of the school, there are two small pictures; while a third from the Salting collection, representing a concert of three half-length figures—the only work in which the master can be seen in all his greatness—is most unexpectedly exhibited under the false name of Lorenzo Costa. However, in the case of the few other pictures from the second half of the Quattrocento, there is no lack of questionable attributions.

Interesting from the point of view of Art history are the three pictures, gorgeously coloured but of little originality in conception and design, by Marco Zoppo, who, with his expression of peevish hypochondria, follows, or rather limps in the wake sometimes of Squarcione of Padua, at others of Cosimo Tura; not, however, that he thereby in any way disgraces his title of 'Marcus the Lame.' Lorenzo Costa is, though insufficiently, nevertheless much better represented in the National Gallery and at Hampton Court, than by examples from English private collections. A considerable number of pictures are exhibited under Francia's name; but, with the single exception of the fine portrait of Bart. Bianchini from the Salting collection, they are of very doubtful value. Garofalo, too, is very unsatisfactorily represented. A Madonna with Saints from the collection of the Earl of Leicester, which was only recently exhibited at the New Gallery as a work of Ghirlandaio, appears again here with the equally improbable attribution to Aspertini. As a matter of fact, the picture is by Genga, an imitator of Signorelli, whose manner is clearly exhibited in the counterfeit bas-relief. Mazzolino is represented by several authentic examples, which afford a good general idea of his style.

The great master of the Ferrarese Cinquecentisti is undoubtedly Dosso Dossi, whose glowing colour vies with that of a Romanino, a Cavazzola or a Moretti; while his rich fancy endows his creations with a higher charm than any that breathes from the works of these colourists of the Veronese and Brescian schools. There are no genuine works by Dosso Dossi in the National Gallery; but he is much better represented at Hampton Court, whence several pictures have been incorporated in the present exhibition. Among the works by him from private collections, by far the most important are the mythological piece called 'Vertumnus and Pomona,' with its magnificent landscape, from the collection of Lord Northampton, and the 'Adoration of the Kings' from the Mond collection. A remarkable picture on a large scale by the little-known Ortolano is specially important from the fact that it affords a standard, as it were, by which we can estimate the pictures of a totally different character that have elsewhere been ascribed to him. Last of all, there are two genuine youthful works by Correggio here, one from Hampton Court, and the other from the collection of Mr. R. H. Benson. That Correggio himself was the outcome of the school of Ferrara, is a fact that Morelli alone so far has maintained and called attention to. It is therefore all the more gratifying to find this fact openly recognised in the present exhibition by a body so distinguished and enlightened as the Committee of the Burlington Fine Arts Club. On the other hand, that the introduction to the catalogue should have been converted into a tirade—as violent as it is unnecessary—against the method of that deserving inquirer is a circumstance that, to say the least of it, creates rather an odd effect. However, it may tend to explain—if not to excuse—the fact that several important Ferrarese pictures in English private collections are unknown to the Committee.

J. P. RICHTER.

THE "FAIR WOMEN" EXHIBITION.

IN a time prolific in temporary Art exhibitions of the first rank, such as the invaluable displays made at Burlington House in successive winters, the interesting "one-man" shows of the Grosvenor Gallery, the extraordinarily instructive collections that have, year after year since its foundation, been brought together at the New Gallery the "Fair Women" Exhibition has achieved an altogether exceptional and, indeed, phenomenal success, not less artistic than financial and popular.

What are the peculiar qualities which have caused it, while retaining the respect and admiration of the judicious, to win the popular fancy as no other retrospective collection has succeeded in doing of late years? No doubt there are to be found, at the Grafton Gallery, jewels of the first water among the Italian, Flemish, and French pictures of the fifteenth and sixteenth centuries; no doubt the French portraitists of the eighteenth century are better represented than they have been for a long time in any English picture-gallery; no doubt the English school of the corresponding period shines out with an unsurpassed charm, and is illustrated with a completeness such as has not often been attained in a modern exhibition. Still it would be rash to assert that the Italian, the Flemish, or the English pictures are finer than have been seen in many of the Old Masters' exhibitions of the Royal Academy; and these—it is an open secret—have rarely achieved more than a *succès d'estime*. The miniatures at the Grafton Gallery, though not invariably well chosen or well arranged, are, as a whole, a splendid series, well filling up such gaps as exist in the "Fair Women" show on panel and canvas. But then, it will hardly be said that they equal as a collection the great display made at Burlington House in 1879, or the equally remarkable series brought together some few seasons ago at the Burlington Fine Arts Club.

Something must be credited to the attraction exercised by an *ad captandum* title, which if distasteful to those who take the exhibition with the seriousness which it fully deserves, has proved an excellent catchword for the general public. Still the main attraction has evidently been the central idea itself, and the relative completeness, the absolute charm with which it has been realised. The magnetic power exercised by *Das ewig Weibliche* has never more completely asserted itself. And then the contemplation, and above all the criticism, of female loveliness is, as once more is here conclusively demonstrated, an unfailing source of pleasure to woman no less than to man; while it is by no means clear that, outside the narrow circle of painters and sculptors, the converse holds good in the same degree. Apart from the exquisite quality of a large portion of the works here brought together, there is a singular charm in tracing beauty, or what successive ages have accepted as beauty, through the centuries, and in the various and strongly contrasting schools of European Art. An added piquancy is obtained by the contrast between the group of fine modern works which bring "Fair Women" up to the present time, and the portraits of the eighteenth century which confront them, on the opposite wall of one and the same gallery, with results which this is not the place to appreciate.

The laces, the fans, the jewellery and goldsmith's work, though not in all cases of equal exquisiteness, happily complete the collection as a whole, and still further accentuate its unity. To the innumerable ladies who have made the Grafton Galleries their haunt during the summer months it has been almost as great a source of amusement to examine this armoury of feminine weapons, adornments, and appliances, as to gaze upon the counterfeit presentments of the fair dames themselves, to some of whom, or their sisters, they may well have belonged.

C. P.

A WORD WITH MY CRITICS.*

A DESIGNER and modeller, and worker in metals, having made art industries, their history, and their technicalities, his special study for more than a quarter of a century, the writer of the article in question had something to say to the general reader, as well as to the trade, and he said it. No one really familiar with jewelry manufacture could reasonably differ from him in any particular touched upon within the bounds of an article, not purposing therefore to be exhaustive of the subject, and it may be added that the more prominent members of the Jewellers' Association of Birmingham, and of its Vigilance Committee, have approved it. But two editors, of minor trade advertising papers mostly dealing in *réclames*, have had their fling at us. In a state of remarkable frenzy and self-inflation one of them rushes through his acrobatics. He publishes a penny monthly a fortnight in advance of his sixpenny brother rival, whose performance is tame by comparison.

Editor the second is good enough to quote correctly what editor the first misquotes. But he is supercilious; and while affecting to know all about things, considers details not worth notice. Since, however, THE ART JOURNAL article appeared, and his pasquinade critical in the May number of his publication, he has, according to his June record of labour done, reconnoitred the jewelry quarter of Birmingham.

One might now have some faith in his being thuswise able to trust himself had he, after quoting from THE ART JOURNAL nearly a column of what he calls "the best of the article," found something to say besides attempting to mislead his readers. For instance, he could have tried to point to the make and shape, and ordinary and exceptional use of the "bull-and-butcher," or the "snarling-iron"; names applied indifferently in *some* jewellers' workshops to one and the same tool, employed mostly by chasers. And as his means of illustrating are, it seems, at hand, he could have presented pictures to his subscribers in his June number. Better than bull-and-butcher or snarling-iron, he might have risked enlarging upon our statement that fifteen-carat gold—to nine-tenths of Birmingham jewellers and their stampers, engravers, and chasers—is harder than twenty-two, eighteen, or nine carat. He could, perhaps, have shown that fifteen parts of real gold and nine of copper and silver, the usual alloys, according to their respective proportions and the method of melting and pouring, and certain other observances of the jeweller in practice, make fifteen-carat gold comparatively hard. It would have been information to some, even of his technical students, if he could only have descended to trifles in teaching, that this hardness is not so likely to be noticed in London as it is in Birmingham, because, as a general thing, in the course of producing certain classes of goods distinct from its higher quality of hand-made work, more *delicate* rolling is demanded there; and this requires more annealing and care in the stamping, so peculiar to Birmingham, and more dexterity of touch under the graver, the chasing-tool and hammer—almost indispensable aids to finish—and in the course of making up. It is to be feared that, after all, London jewellers are unsophisticated, when we think of Birmingham and its proficiency in the mysteries of manufacture.

J. M. O'FALLON.

* Concerning "The Work of Birmingham Jewellers"—An Article in the April Number of THE ART JOURNAL.

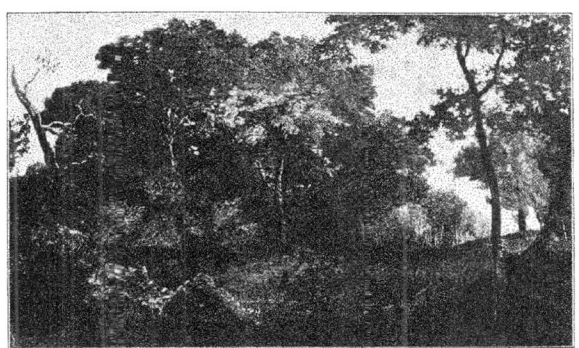

CLAIR-BOIS, IN THE FOREST OF FONTAINEBLEAU. BY THEODORE ROUSSEAU.

A REPRESENTATIVE SCOTTISH COLLECTION.

HER old intimacy with France endowed Scotland with many French terms and not a few French tastes, claret drinking amongst others; and, in the days of our forefathers, some of the best vintage of Bordeaux was shipped for the port of Leith. But of late France has found appreciation in Scotland, not only of its Bordeaux but of its Art. In this century Scotland has not been behind England in perceiving the importance of the work done by the French schools, and worthy private collections have been made in the North of an art that has influenced the whole world. Hitherto the work of the French schools of 1830 and kindred or derivative movements can be seen in no public gallery in Great Britain. If you would study this phase of Art you must visit a few private collections and one or two dealers' shops, or you must undertake a journey to France; and yet no one is bold enough to deny that for the last fifty years France has made or marred the Fine Arts. Few, indeed, are the painters who have escaped the influence of Paris; even unwillingly or unbeknown to themselves the majority have followed the prevailing tendency of their day. In vain, writers, archæologists, critics, faddists have turned the public mind on Italy, and have repeated the old cry "To Rome"; three-fourths at least of the younger practitioners of Art have turned to Paris for guidance and inspiration.

Mr. James Donald, of Glasgow, is one of those whose galleries of pictures have enabled the promoters of loan collections to show under these unfavourable circumstances something of the modern Art of Europe. As late as the Edinburgh Exhibition too many painters in Scotland were ignorant of the influence which had turned Europe upside down, and which was operating stealthily on them as well as on their neighbours.

Mr. Donald's collection is neither so large nor so homogeneous in composition as Sir John Day's, of which we spoke lately (THE ART JOURNAL, pages 261 and 309, 1893). It contains a few works of no meaning beyond an evident and anecdotic one, but these few works look particularly poor in the presence of pictures of a higher order of merit. If he has one or two ordinary things below the high general average of his collection, Mr. Donald atones for these lapses by one or two canvases quite above praise. I will mention those I think most notable, either as fine pictures or as particularly superb examples of their authors' work. These are a portrait of Philip IV. by Velasquez, a stately upright landscape by Corot, Millet's crayon drawing of the 'Sheepfold at Evening,'

GOING TO LABOUR. BY JEAN FRANÇOIS MILLET.

SEPTEMBER, 1894.

3 U

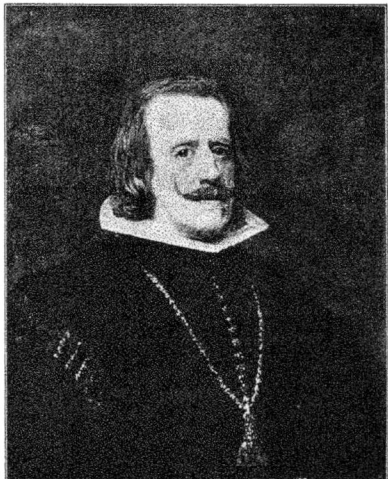

PHILIP IV. BY VELASQUEZ.

Rousseau's 'Clair-Bois, in the Forest of Fontainebleau,' and a large strong upright, with a figure and animals, by Troyon. The portrait is a good ordinary Velasquez of the middle period, but considering the painter this means much. It shows the King somewhere between the ages represented in the two portraits of the National Gallery. The other four pictures are not only remarkable in themselves but as illustrations of their authors in their most characteristic moods. Corot never more clearly showed than here the stateliness of natural tree forms when viewed under a broad impression. Millet never revealed with so fine an inspiration the weird dignity with which an unusual lighting can invest the most ordinary scenes. These pictures are all large, considering the usual size of works by the School of Barbizon. With them one might be inclined to take Decamps's 'St. Jérôme,' a small figure with a touch of red in his dress, set in the midst of a dark rocky landscape, out of which a knot of splendid trees rise into a blue sky streaked with bright orange clouds; Millet's well-known 'Going to Work'; a small grey Rousseau; one or two Corots, as well as other canvases. But good as they are, these pictures hardly deserve to be classed with the first five; nor can they be said to fill such important positions in the whole work of their respective authors.

In Mr. Donald's dining-room one enjoys good examples of Decamps, Daubigny, Corot, Dupré, Monticelli, Israels, Bosboom, Constable, Mauve, Artz, Blommers, Sam Bough, J. Holland, Cameron, J. Pettie, and, not least, Mr. William Hole's wonderful etching after Millet's 'Woodcutters,' which framed close up scarcely seems out of place among all these pictures, so powerfully does it render the texture of oil painting. But in spite of this formidable competition for your attention, nothing holds you more powerfully than the large upright by Constant Troyon. Its rich, mellow colour is disposed in such an ample pattern, and handled with so large and robust a touch, that the picture glows with a grave splendour even on the background of the romantic school by which it is surrounded. The composition (which we illustrate opposite) was in the recent Troyon collection in the Goupil Gallery, and shows cattle, sheep, and a figure beneath the overhanging branches of large trees. These objects are near at hand for the most part, but their textures and details are rendered in obedience to the position they occupy. For instance, the foliage is treated by just those masses which would become important to the eye when placed at a distance to embrace conveniently the whole view. This principle of treatment is necessary to convey with any sincerity the impressions we receive from nature in the present day, but it would be wrong to say that it is necessary to all kinds of painting. Some of the old men, notably Velasquez, felt a need of some such study to express their feelings, but others, even landscapists such as Claude and Hobbema, generally trusted to some law of decorative subordination in managing detail.

Like Crome, Theodore Rousseau took his first view of Art from the Dutch, and, like Crome, he often vied with his masters in

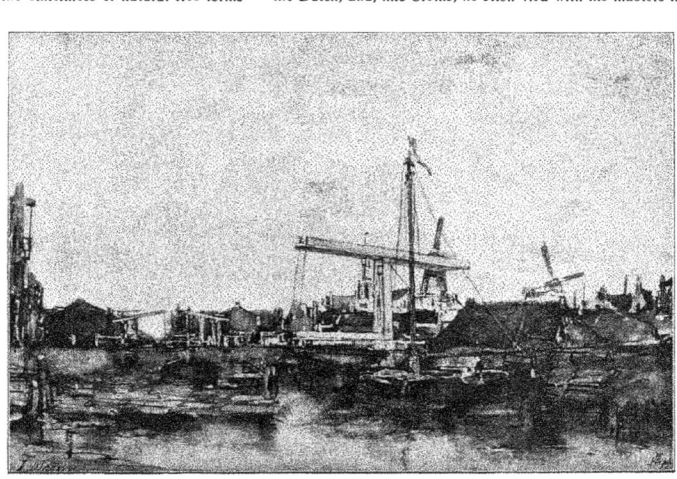

THE DRAWBRIDGE. BY JAMES MARIS.

elaborating each part of a picture with a treatment that would have been only suitable to it as a separate whole picture. This compilation of observations made at different focuses may be defended on the ground that, though contrary to the sentiments of true perceptive vision, it is conformable to the ordinary person's idea of what memory should tell us. But it is easy to see that such a habit of thought must blind one to the true poetry of large aspects of nature, and if proof is wanted we have it in the fact that Corot gave more of the essential poetry of natural appearances than any landscapist who came before him. But Rousseau, however closely he might burrow into particulars in his dull moments, always saw a tree as deep as it was broad, and never executed any of those pressed sea-weed patterns which painters of his time, Copley Fielding and others, elaborated from pencil drawings made at too-close quarters.

Rousseau's 'Clair-Bois, Fontainebleau' (see our headpiece), in Mr. Donald's drawing-room, is that broader, bolder kind of work, which made its author the centre figure of the Barbizon School of landscape. The execution throughout is of a kind that one might call tentative; of a kind, in fact, that may be taken up and left, and begun again, a kind that facilitates experiment and lends itself to study, and the consequent changes of purpose. A mixture of methods—a thin preparation worked into when wet, a frequent cragging of dry colour, and surface painting of a solid sort—continues to give the pigment quality and the charm of an accidental suggestion of detail. Rocks, bracken, juniper, furzes, and heathers make a soft, decorative, yet natural, confusion in the foreground. A wall of dark green trees rises behind, and, beyond that, a sunny sky. Several changes of composition are apparent in the work, and the canvas is evidently not quite finished. The rich low tone requires a strong light to

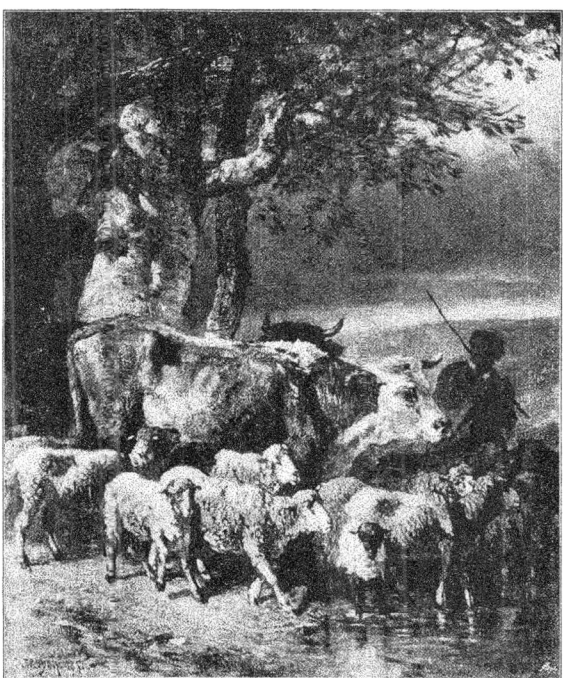

GOING TO MARKET. BY TROYON.

illuminate sufficiently its mellow various greens, for the work must have been at least begun out of doors. By its side hangs a small squarish Rousseau, showing the outside fringe of Fontainebleau Forest. The ground, dry and sandy, and the grey cloudy sky, a study of remarkable *finesse*, resemble the subsequent work of J. Maris and the modern Dutchmen.

Rousseau was an observer as original as any man of our century, but he never settled down to mature and polish his style to such purpose as Corot. For one reason, he was not so single-minded, and, judging by his variety of methods and his returns upon himself, he never seems to have fairly determined on a consistent attitude of mind in front of nature. If any man ever attained that consistency of view, that ravishing harmony between all parts of his art which constitutes beauty, it was Corot. No man knows what he may be going to see when he is about to look at a Rousseau; every one knows what a Corot will be like, but the fact is a surprise and a joy above the expectation. From the first true Corot one meets one knows the man by heart, whereas the mind of Rousseau remains a mystery. Which is the better sort of man I cannot presume to say, but I know which is the better artist. Corot's attitude is more difficult to keep up without cheapness, and to continue the interest demands consummate style and art.

We can easily follow these parallel lines amongst living men of our country. Sir Frederic Leighton, Sir Edward Burne-Jones, and Mr. Orchardson have made up their minds and their styles. Their effort is the purely artistic one of expressing what they have long wished to express, and they will never search any farther, because they know that nature will not reveal herself to them in a new dispensation. But all along such is the hope of Mr. Holman Hunt, who tries to look afresh each time, and proposes to himself no criterion, no theory of Art, and so has done many things and nothing well. The more he searches for what truth may come his way, the farther he gets from the expression of such beauty as may be in him.

Mr. Donald's finest Corot hangs in the drawing-room along with the Velasquez, the Rousseaus, and pictures by Millet, Turner, Diaz, Vollon, J. Maris, Jules Lessore, Orchardson, W. E. Lockhart, Wilkie, Linnell, Morland, Hamilton Maccallum, Clara Montalba, MacTaggart, and a few of the great Dutchmen, such as the three here illustrated—'The Toy,' by Josef Israels; 'Changing Pasture,' by Mauve; and the 'Drawbridge,' by J. Maris. This tall canvas, 'Le Pécheur d'Écrevisses,' of which we give a large reproduction, belongs to a fine class of evening Corots bathed in a mellow brownish medium —a brown fused with light and air neither hot nor unmeaning, but a literal decorative rendering of the gathering umbery shades of twilight. The upright composition emphasizes a noble bouquet of poplars, and somewhat recalls the arrangement of 'La Symphonie,' one of the best known of Corot's

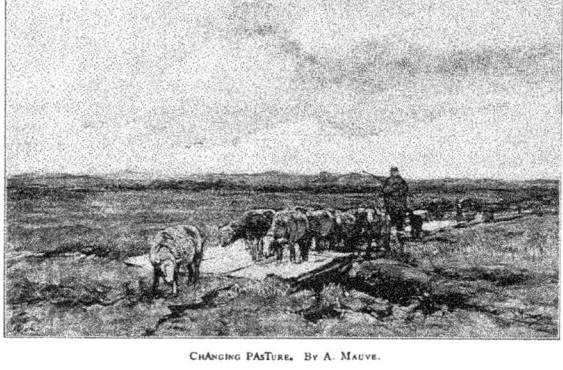

CHANGING PASTURE. BY A. MAUVE.

canvases. In Mr. Donald's picture, as may be observed, the group of trees stands a little farther off from you, so that you embrace its whole height in the field of vision. This tower of foliage fills the canvas with a decorative mass of quivering atmospheric colour infinitely varied, yet kept in the most solemn and imposing unity of plane and effect. The grey distance, like a moment prepared for in music, and foreshadowed by progressions, steals upon you by imperceptible gradations full of enfolded mystery. The grass at your feet, with a rare and deftly touched flower and a flicker or two of light on some pointed spear of reed or leaf attains the perfection of easy finish. This brush work is like the word à propos, which, in the pages of some classic writer, invokes a mood and stimulates imagination without laborious description. The canvas, some three feet high, is just the size to fetch out Corot's best quality of colour, and give full play to the magic of his handling. That enormous Lake Scene, hung under the central dome of the 1889 Paris Exhibition, appealed rather to ac-

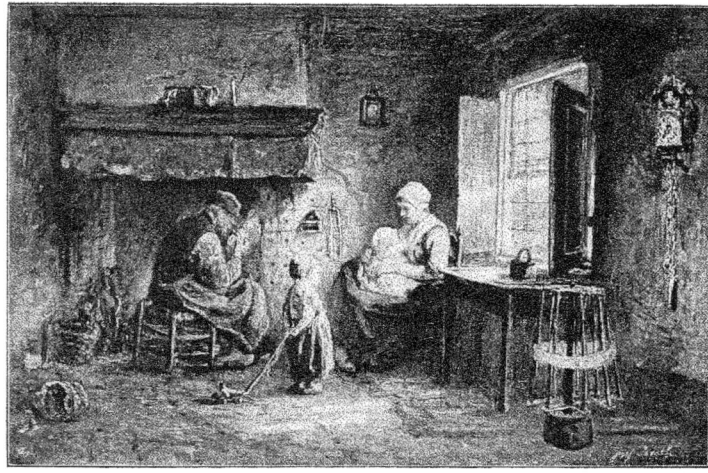

THE TOY. BY JOSEF ISRAELS.

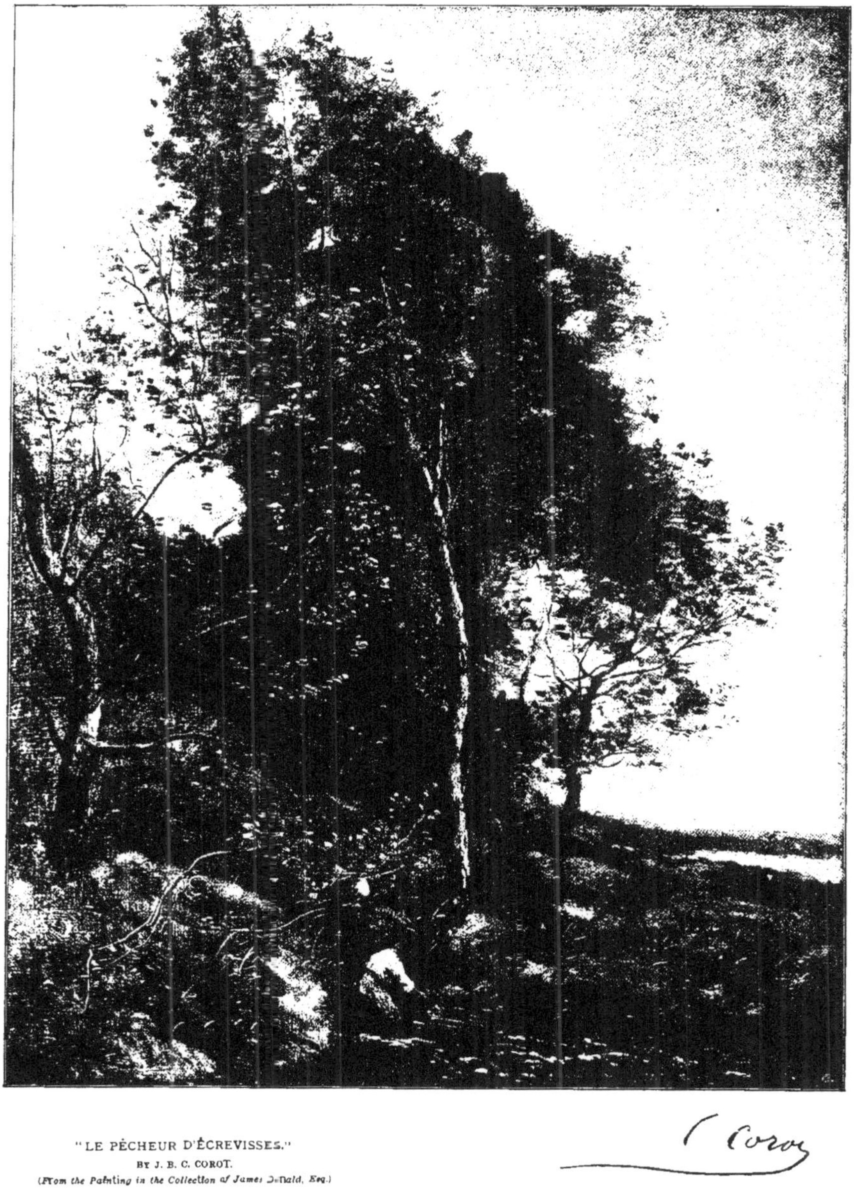

"LE PÊCHEUR D'ÉCREVISSES."
BY J. B. C. COROT.
(From the Painting in the Collection of James Donald, Esq.)

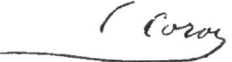

cepted traditions of decorative grandeur than to emotions due to the real mystery of nature. In its scheme the vein of brown colour dominated authoritatively all efforts of local colour to pierce the veil of enshrouding tonality; even the play of blue ripples, of cold reflected top-lights, was subdued to the close harmony of the key, the handling was stately, but formal and summary, and the view of nature, though grandiose, was far-fetched and abstract. Mr. Donald's Corot is large and broad enough to be dignified, true enough to touch the hidden strings of association, and yet delicate enough to be fairy-like and exquisite. This upright is not the only worthy example of Corot in Mr. Donald's collection. Another evening scene, smaller and darker, fascinates one by a still closer obedience to the ordinary habits of nature. Unlike the bigger canvas, it depends for its effect more on contrast than on subtle *nuances*; its weight of shadow is less interpenetrated by the magic soft-ness of atmospheric reflection. The diffused light of the larger picture is here replaced by strongly concentrated and con-trasted masses of brightness and darkness. Notwithstanding the beauties of this picture and of a small morning pastoral, there can be no hesitation of choice: Mr. Donald's large up-right Corot is the gem of his collection.

Yet is it so? You have but to turn your head to doubt, for near the Corot hangs Millet's wonderful 'Sheepfold on the plain of Chailly'; I mean the one executed in crayon with an extraordinary handling, like straws set in a stack. You will know it well from photographs; a gibbous moon is rising, and above the darkly shrouded earth the shepherd's uplifted arm shows against the sky with a menacing gesture. The sentiment, a novel one in Art, and the originality of the means used to convey it, make this a typical Millet, even more poetic than Mr. Donald's other example, 'Going to Work.' In this last picture, the noble effect got from the silhouettes on the sky of the boy's old felt hat and the basket on the girl's head, was undoubtedly something that only Millet could have seen, and that nothing less than Millet's style could have preserved from trivial finish or anecdotic trifling. Yet notwithstanding these grandiose and never-to-be-forgotten forms, the picture a little lacks charm, and to-day we feel its brown basis inconsistent with that fresh coolness of the hour and scene which Millet certainly intended to render.

But if we compare this picture with other work, with the ordinary English anecdotic idyll of the fields, how grand it appears, and with all its grandeur how true! The great masses of light and shade have been seized and held as the root of the impression, and so the figures seem made for the place. How well their rugged grandeur is now known, and how little attempted!—a grandeur fairly won from the most accustomed forms, and won by a noble preference of great truths to foolish picking out of features, cleaning up of edges, and all the other trivialities of school design. So the voice of night silences the idle whispers of detail, and reveals the character of big strange shapes to those who can understand.

R. A. M. STEVENSON.

ABOUT NORTH BERWICK.

NEAR its mouth, the opposite shores of the Firth of Forth shoot out into the water so as to narrow the entrance. Just in the middle of the southern projection there lies, on the Lothian shore, the ancient town of North Berwick. When or by whom it was first built is uncertain. Authorities quarrel as to the origin of the name. *Wick* is obviously Scandinavian for town or village, and the learned Chal-mers will have it as *Barewick*, from its open position, whilst others more reasonably infer that *Ber* is a contraction for *Aber*, a bay. The *North* is plainly to distinguish it from the city on the Tweed. This is sure enough: its founders took no thought of the tourist or the golfer, for as yet the watering-place was unknown in the land. Its site is, in one respect, like the sites of Edinburgh and Heidelberg. Were no town there you would scarce think there ought to be one; it is only the actual effect that proves how admirably human habitation fits into such surroundings.

The central piece in the combination of house and ground is that great hill "with cone of green," called the Law. It is steep, isolated, naked, strange. There is a little space of com-paratively flat plain between it and the beach. Here the town is built. The view is always sea-ward, for the lower slopes of the hill hide the broad inward swell of the East Lothian fields. Another great mass catches the view to the right: that is the Bass Rock, in the sea, over a mile from the nearest shore. In front of the town you have a row of rocky islets—Eyeborough, Craigleith, Fidra, The Lamb are their quaint names. Across is the Fife coast, and far beyond it, in clear weather, there loom —faint, mysterious, magical, even as shapes seen in a dream—shadows of great Highland mountains. Hills are to landscape what inspiration is to poetry, and style to prose. They lend it the ineffable touch that raises the whole thing out of the commonplace. You have them here, in ocean settings; you have to the west a glimpse of corn-land—taken from the finest rural scenery in all Scotland—to heighten the effect by way of contrast. See all this, in the pure light of a Northern summer's even, and you will say they did well who built here.

A few words must tell what sort of town it is. Of course, there is a High Street, and that runs east and west. Between it and the bay, of late years, a row of houses has grown up. To the east, at right angles to the sea, is Quality Street, fairly broad, and lined with plane trees, which give a grateful shade in the summer time, and form a pleasing, if unusual, feature: here are one or two picturesque bits of the old Scots architecture worth notice. All this is but the heart or kernel; round about is a great and ever-increasing number (for North Berwick is a rising place) of "desirable" villa residences. To the west they form a completely new quarter, and whilst the old parts are simply an improved version of the ordinary Scots fishing village, these later additions are so exactly like the Edinburgh suburbs that, were you set down where you could not see the bay, you might deem yourself in Merchiston. The road is the same, the houses are the same, the very passers-by are the same, for North Berwick is every whit as much Edinburgh-*super-mare* as Brighton is London-*super-mare*.

It was not connected with the capital by railway till 1848. In the "New Statistical Account" the parish minister tells how a stage-coach ran every lawful day. That worthy divine

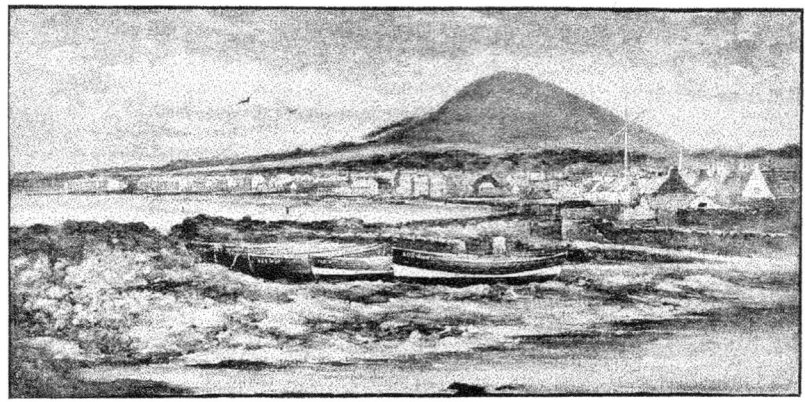

North Berwick and North Berwick Law.   Drawn by A. W. Henley.

solemnly and curiously commends the old-time vehicle as "conducted with great propriety," a laudation he does not extend to all the town institutions. He mournfully notes the existence of thirteen public-houses ("eight kept by widows"), and he computes that there was one for every fifty of the population. The consumption of whisky he estimates at three thousand gallons per annum, which gave an average of five gallons per head. It is, he moralises, "a melancholy source of impoverishment," but possibly the inhabitants were hard put to it to fleet the time, for the prosperity of the town is comparatively recent. Train communication with the Northern metropolis is easy and speedy, the distance is but twenty-two miles, and you can live in one place and work in the other with what would seem, to a Londoner, the greatest ease. Edinburgh has marked North Berwick with some of its mental, as well as physical, characteristics. There is an air of reserve, restraint, propriety, coldness, gentility—general superiority, in short—about the one as about the other. Of course, you do not expect the all-too-attractive casino of Dieppe or Trouville, where you may agreeably gamble away your spare cash; but the jetties and bands and short-trip yachts of Margate and Brighton are equally wanting, and any movement for their establishment would be sternly resisted. The cheap tripper is not encouraged; the very butcher and baker, you are assured, would repulse him from their door. It is good to have such places, and to many of its visitors North Berwick is, no doubt, as attractive for what it lacks as for what it possesses.

The two great employments of the visitor are bathing and golfing. The beach is excellent, but the slope is rapid and the currents in stormy weather dangerous. To the west of the town there is a long stretch of links, and here the royal game is so zealously prosecuted as to make North Berwick next to St. Andrews the most important *locus* in the golf world.

Golf has a great reputation at present. It is played all round London, and Mr. Andrew Lang, witty and graceful, sings its praises, and yet an outsider has some things against it. It seems playing at playing; the strenuous effort of football, the nice skill of cricket and tennis, are alike wanting. But then the outsider has a personal grudge against golf. Like a French duel, all danger is reserved for them who "assist." At North Berwick the links are superb, but if you do not play you walk there in danger of your life. You are between the golfer and the deep sea. One test of a great man is that he hesitates not to shed human blood, and they who play this royal game heed not the felicity of others. And here I must repeat a story I have told elsewhere. It is said that a wanderer over

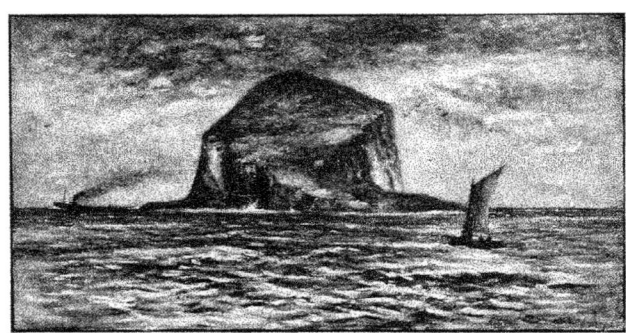

The Bass Rock.   Drawn by A. W. Henley.

TANTALLON CASTLE. DRAWN BY A. W. HENRY.

these links was smitten with a ball on the forehead. He dropped *come corpo morto cade*, and at the bottom of a bunker lay weltering in his gore. When consciousness returned he saw on the edge of the hollow the player looking down on him. Asked if he was hurt, he replied that he was killed. " Weel, it ser's ye right," said the golfer, stalking away, " for ye have spoilt the best stroke I ever made."

Two heaps of mouldering stone represent to-day the antiquities of North Berwick. One, near the station, was a prosperous Cistercian nunnery. It was pleasantly situated with charming prospects of that fair world which the inmates had renounced. And near the harbour are the ruins of the old church.

" Dryasdust " has much to say of both. He fills his page with obscure names and abstracts of mediæval charters, all as mouldy and disorderly as the fragments themselves. One incident, strangely grotesque and horrible, redeems the rubbish of his hoard.

Towards the end of 1590 a great witch trial began in Scotland. Gellie Duncan, a servant girl at Tranent, to-day a mining village in the same county, was gravely suspected by her master of the heinous crime of witchcraft. He applied the pilliewinks (screw for fingers). Under their gentle pressure she made a confession implicating others in the neighbourhood, on whom, as well as on herself, the devil's mark was found. Their confessions were full of strange details. " On All Hallow Even, to the number of two hundred, they went to sea, each one in a riddle or cive, and went into the same, very substantially with flaggons of wine, making merrie and drinking by the way in the same riddles or cives. They disembarked opposite the kirk of North Berwick in ' Lowthian,' and proceeded hither in great state. Gellie went before, dancing and playing on a Jew's harp with infernal skill whilst she sang :—

> " ' Kimmer goye ye before, kimmer goye ye,
> Gif ye will not goe before,
> Kimmer let me.' "

Three miles east of the town are antiquities more worthy of notice. On a precipitous cliff overlooking the sea there stands the still-imposing ruins of Tantallon Castle, once the chief seat in Scotland of the great house of Douglas. Scott's lines in " Marmion " are too well known for full quotation.

> " Broad, massive, high, and stretching far,
> And held impregnable in war,
> On a projecting rock it rose,
> And round three sides the ocean flows ;
> The fourth did battled walls enclose
> And double mound and fosse."

Hugh Miller hits it off in a sentence—" Three sides of walllike rock, and one side of rock-like wall." Some way off it seems perfect, its wall unbroken, but from the courtyard you see it is but a shell; staircases are wanting, its chambers rent open or inaccessible, and its gloomy dungeons alone wellnigh intact ; yet above the gateway you still trace the bloody heart of the great house of Douglas. Tantallon has had other foes than time alone, for its history is but wars and rumours of wars. When or who first built it, who can tell ? A ridiculous legend derives its name from a corruption of *Tam et Allon*, these being the names of its masons. Here old Bell-the-Cat had his lair, and here too was born Gawin Douglas, Bishop of Dunkeld, who " in a barren age, gave rude Scotland Virgil's page." The scenery around must have furnished many images enshrined in the sweet verse of those wonderful prologues. What place but Tantallon suggested the line—

> " Gousty schaddois of eild and grissly deed" ?—

of itself sufficient, as Hugh Miller says, to mark him a great poet. His gentle spirit was ill at ease in that iron time ; " he died in exile in London," as his memorial plate in St. Giles's, Edinburgh, states, far from those familiar scenes, and his bones lie in the very heart of London. Here the sixth Earl of Angus, in September, 1528, was attacked by King James V. His Majesty lustily battered the walls " with shot of thrawn-mouth'd Mag and her marrow"—so Lindsey of Pittscottie preserves the picturesque names of the two cannons. But to no purpose ; and so—

> " Ding doun Tantallon,
> Big a brig to the Bass,"

became common Scots for an impossibility. In 1639 the Covenanters seized it; a few years afterwards Monk forced his way in, and then it was left to go to ruin.

Opposite Tantallon, more than a mile right out at sea, is the Bass Rock. It is a full mile round, and rises on one side 313 feet sheer out of the water. On the south there is a slope from the summit to near the water's edge, but the one landing-place is only practicable in moderate weather. A wall thrown across a little way above this rendered the place impregnable to the rude guns of an earlier age. Much of the fortifications yet remain, and half-way between them and the top are the ruins of a chapel. Between the chapel and the summit was the garden of the place.

A vast multitude of sea-birds have nested in every hollow and crevice of the Bass. Their shrill cry and the flutter of their wings are heard all day long. What a coign of vantage when the storm-fiend is calling its loudest, when the mighty breakers from the German Ocean dash against its sides and thunder through its cavern till the huge bulk shakes and echoes, and the white spray clothes it as with a garment !

What an awe-inspiring scene, that tumultuous sea, revealed for a moment by the lightning flash, whilst the hoarse cry of the sea-bird fills up every lull in the storm ! And yet eerier still, as Mr. R. L. Stevenson has finely noted, in times of profound calm, when at sunset the shadow of the great rock stretches away vast and immeasurable across the sea. For even then the isle is full of noises " haunted and reverberated in the porches of the rock." In moonlight, again, how weird and unearthly Tantallon and it appear ! Every twist has its fantastic shadow ; the sea between " moans with memories," for it has an eventful history, this rock, and a page therefrom may here claim notice.

They made the Rock a prison for the Covenanters, and among the most eminent of the saints of the Covenant were the martyrs of the Bass. Chief were Alexander Peden, James Fraser, of Brea, John Blackadder, and Thomas Hogg, of Kiltearn. Of Peden the prophet, Patrick Walker has left us a full account, but Mr. R. L. Stevenson's description is almost terrible in its graphic force. " There was never the wale of him sinsyne, and it's a question wi' mony if there eyer was the like afore. He was wild's a peat-hag, fearsome to look at, fearsome to hear ; his face like the day of judgment. The voice of him was like a solan's, and dinnil'd in folks' lugs, and the words of him like coals of fire." And again : " Peden wi' his lang chafts an' hauntin een, the maud happed aboot his kist, and the hand o' him held oot wi' the black nails the fingernebs—for he had nae care o' the body." They sent him to the Bass in 1673, and there he was four years, " envying the birds their freedom." Walker tells some strange legends about him. Once a young woman, " mocking with loud laughter," interrupted his devotions, but the stern words with which he foretold "a sudden surprising judgment" sent her away with blanched cheek, and soor after a sudden blast of wind hurled her into the sea from the summit of the rock.

Fraser and Blackadder give us details of the daily life "in this melancholy place." The prisoners were almost obliged to support themselves. The victuals were bad; the water was but rain collected in crevices. They were obliged to drink, one complains the twopenny ale of the governor's brewing, scarce worth a halfpenny the pint. Hogg, of Kiltearn, was especially obnoxious to Archbishop Sharp, and had the worst treatment of any. A staircase led underground to the bastion, where was a place half cave, half cell, dripping with moisture, with an opening towards the sea, which broke on the rocks a few feet below. This was Hogg's dungeon. Though in weak health, he survived, and ended his days in peace at Kiltearn. Peden, too, was released, though he did not live to see the Revolution. Blackadder died on the rock, and was buried in North Berwick Churchyard, where you may still spell out the lines that tell his story.

The other party have also their romance of daring. In June, 1691, four Scots, Royalist officers, prisoners taken at Barrowdale, were confined on the Bass. On the 15th a boat came from the shore with coals and all the garrison save two or three went down to the landing-place to haul in the fuel. The officers simply shut the big gate and the garrison was outside! The Edinburgh Whigs were in a mighty pother. They stuck a company on the opposite shore, and every night boats cruised round the rock to intercept supplies, but during the winter 'twas easy to re-victual the place, and moreover a foreign vessel every now and again, quite unconscious of danger, came under their guns, and had to yield good part of its stores. Two ships sent against them peppered away in vain; nay, the garrison, collecting the spent cannon-balls, returned them with deadly effect. The war went on with many exciting and romantic episodes, till in April, 1694, the garrison was allowed to depart with all the honours of war.

1894.

They still pasture a few sheep on the Bass; their flesh—veritable *zigot de pré salé*—is delicious; and then there are the solan geese. A perfectly miraculous bird this. Among the wonders of the isle Hector Boece notes "great store of soland geese." The vulgar, he assures us, have a singularly erroneous idea of their conception, for "they believed that the geece grew upon trees, hanging by their nebs as apples and other fruit does by their stalks." The truth is that when a tree, or even a log, falls into the sea in these parts, it presently becomes food for an astonishing number of worms, which presently develop unto themselves wings and feathers and fly off to the Bass, where in due time they become solan geese. Later authorities are not far behind. The mode of hatching, says one naturalist, is well known. "The egg (for they produce only one) is fixed on its end, which the bird grasps with the sole of her foot, and rests upon it in that position. Hence some imagine they get their name, sole-on. Dr. Johnson derives it from *solea*, because they have but one egg. It is evidently, however, from 'sule,' the Norwegian name of a gannet." The old birds—again we dip into those fairy tales of science—are furnished with an elastic pouch capable, on occasion, of holding even five or six herrings, which "the young birds extract with their bills as with pincers. More incredible still is it that the old-time Caledonian *gourmet* licked his lips at the very thought thereof." Yet Ray the botanist (*temp.* 1661) affirms "the young ones are esteemed a choice dish in Scotland, and sold very dear—one shilling and eightpence plucked. We ate of them at Dunbar." I speak from experience, for I once partook of a solan goose; it was more than a quarter of a century ago, but nothing since has tasted quite equal to it. Its peculiar flavour once known is never forgotten, yet a strange hesitation possesses the mind; you know not

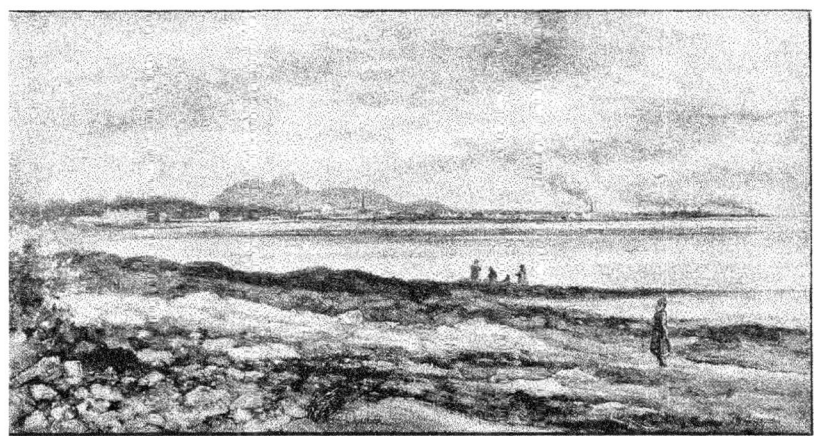

THE ROCKS AT WEST PANS. DRAWN BY A. W. HENLEY.

whether it be fish or fowl, or a combination of both, with something else—nay, the local guide-book assures us that an innkeeper at Canty Bay (which is a sort of port for the Bass Rock), "often made strangers believe it was a beefsteak, and they would go away perfectly satisfied; but he made them always aware, when they were on the point of leaving, of what they had partaken." The minister of North Berwick, as Vicar of the Bass, receives twelve solan geese per annum. The period of digestion would thus seem to be a month, but the schoolmaster is let off easily with two.

Time would fail to tell of the other wonders of the Bass—"that herb very pleasant and delicious for salad" which on another soil "either groweth not at all, or utterly giveth over the virtues with which it was erst endued;" of that stone "much like a water-sponge or pumice," through which salt water poured and became sweet and fresh.

Nor can we dwell on the other attractive spots on the coast —Dirleton, long ago esteemed "the pleasantest dwelling in Scotland," Gullane, Aberlady, and so on to Prestonpans, West Pans, and Edinburgh. Sweetest of all is it to climb the ridge due south and stroll over the *dulcia arva* of East Lothian. In the magic light of the Northern summer evenings, as the west wind blows with scented breath across the fields, how pleasant that ordered and cultured beauty, those marks of care expended on every fragment of soil till the dead earth seems almost a responsive living thing! And here is a land scarce touched by the tourist, though it borders one of his main routes. As yet you may have it all to yourself.

FRANCIS WATT.

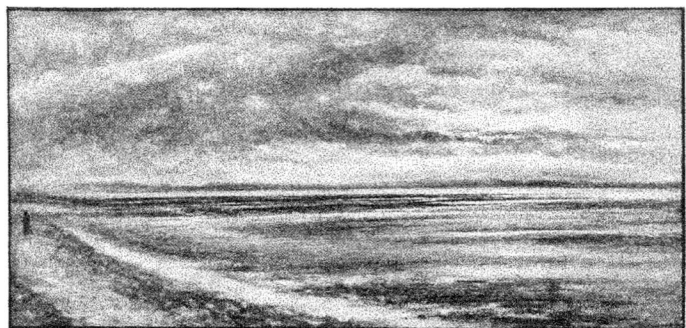

THE FIRTH OF FORTH NEAR NORTH BERWICK. DRAWN BY A. W. HENLEY.

'A SHEPHERD ON SALISBURY PLAIN.'

FEW of the Masters of the nineteenth century have exercised a more profound influence on contemporary Art than Jean François Millet. But we are growing so used to the work of artists who, either consciously or unconsciously, have been influenced by him—by his outlook on Art and on nature, as well as by his methods and treatment—that it is well at all times to pause and note how far-reaching the influence of this one man has been. On the walls of every exhibition in England and in France—in the work of the younger Americans, or of Constantin Meunier, the Belgian sculptor and painter—we see traces of Millet's ideal.

And the etching, by Mr. Edgar Barclay, of 'A Shepherd on Salisbury Plain,' is a case in point.

From whom has he caught the idea of the light horizon—the mass of feeding sheep—the serene and luminous sky—all accentuated and at the same time brought together by the dark figure of the shepherd in strong relief against the light background—but from the painter of that matchless series of shepherd pictures on the Barbizon plain? The very pose of the young Wiltshire shepherd reminds one of the famous 'Bergère,' now in M. Chauchard's collection.

Of course such effects are not new. They have existed since flocks were first herded

"On the sward of some sheep-trimmed down."

The point is, that such effects were not painted until J. F. Millet opened our eyes and taught us to see their poetry, their pathos, their beauty.

The etching in question is admirable, not only on account of its artistic merit, but of its truth to nature. Mr. Barclay is to be congratulated on his heroism in resisting the usual temptation of "Stonehenge in the distance"—and in relying solely on the simple, but ever-varying, ever-beautiful effects of those high-lying sheep-walks; the wide expanse of sky and plain; the flock of black-faced, black-legged Southdowns, whose neat, trim little forms when alive, and whose excellence when dead, are only to be matched on Welsh mountain or Exmoor forest—nibbling, after the fashion of all sheep at sunset, hurriedly and greedily at the aromatic turf of the Downs, fragrant with thymes and trefoils, chamomiles and bee orchises; the young shepherd leaning on his crook and watching the weather—who for weeks and months lives up alone with his flock on the plain, far away from his village, sleeping at night in his travelling hut—with no companion but the collie, who sits beside him, instead of standing to watch the flocks, as the French sheep-dogs do. Here are all the elements of a picture essentially English, and true to the life of those noble Downs that run from the Bristol Channel to Beachy Head.

ROSE G. KINGSLEY.

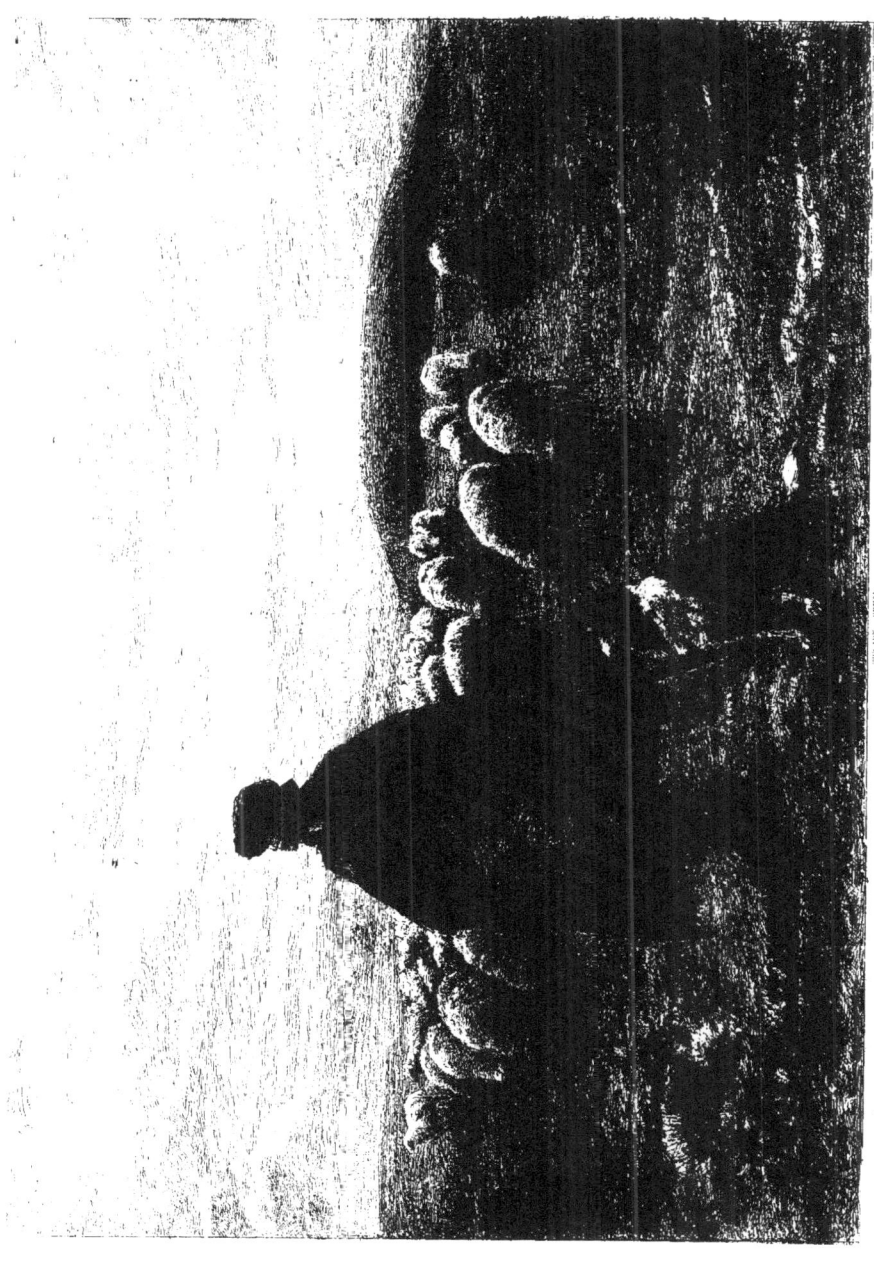

A SHEPHER ON SALISBURY PAIN

ORIGINAL ETCHING BY EDGAR BARCLAY.

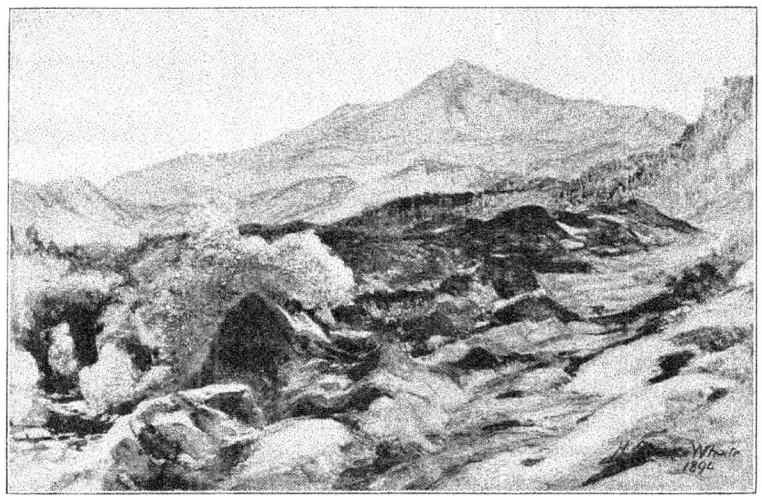

MOEL SIABOD FROM THE LLEDR VALLEY. DRAWN BY H. CLARENCE WHAITE, P.R.C.A.

BETTWS-Y-COED.

BETTWS-Y-COED is one of the resting-places for those of artistic temperament. At some time or another every artist and every art-lover has been there, if only for a single day. Since David Cox made it his chief resort, more than fifty years ago, Bettws-y-Coed has steadily increased in artistic fame. All the waterfalls have been painted, every valley has had its masterpiece, and almost every rock can be found in one picture or another.

Within recent years, Bettws— to give the simple name affectionately inscribed in the hearts of the whole Welsh world — has been considered too picturesque to be acceptable to the younger generation of advanced artists; but to those who do not care for scenery which is only pretty —and, therefore, probably namby-pamby—a morsel of special advice may be given. If fortune or fate leads you to Bettws, and you wish to draw the lesser known and unconventional, go up the hills behind the village and paint the moorlands a thousand feet above the houses. Lake Elsi, one of the calmest of placid

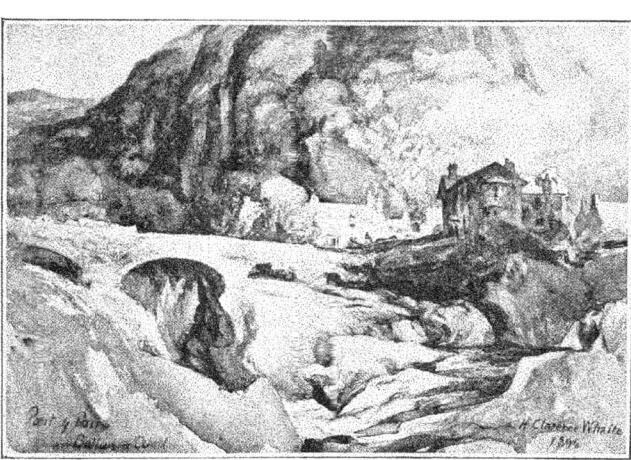

PONT-Y-PAIR, BETTWS-Y-COED. DRAWN BY H. CLARENCE WHAITE, P.R.C.A.

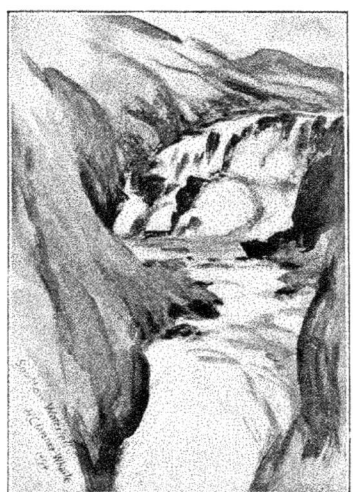

THE SWALLOW WATERFALL. DRAWN BY H. CLARENCE WHAITE, P.R.C.A.

lakes on a summer day, may be seen in storms to be one of the grandest sheets of small water in our islands. No pretty winding wavelets, no moss-grown rocks, not a habitation of any kind except a shelter for sheep; nothing but grand bold lines, straight, masterly, powerful, severe form and rocky masses, no trees, little herbage, and a nobility of composition directly impressionable to the true artist.

Below, amidst the cascades, the bridges and the cottages, Bettws-y-Coed nestles like a pretty child in its pretty mother's arms. So far as North Wales is concerned, it is the capital for the artist; easels and umbrellas and sketching stools stand at every corner, while cameras of all the oddest shapes and sizes seem part of the necessary impedimenta of every tourist.

At each dozen yards of the pathways, either below or above, the combinations of line and tint change their shape and colour. On the hills the wind roams freely, and sometimes fiercely, round the traveller; and in the valleys, ever green and shady, the rivers give forth their sweet sounds of rippling or rushing waters. Falls are so plentiful that only the greater cascades receive titles—the Swallow Falls, the Conway Falls, and the Falls of the Llugwy are the distinguished places, but at each hundred yards the declivity of the ground gives cause for water falling; and the showers, as they descend, alter each one so much that in a single afternoon the aspect of the river is entirely changed.

When the railway first came to Bettws, loud and long were the wails of the wrathful artists who looked to this locality for their laborious livelihood. Numerous navvies, new embankments, and rough railroads, were justly found execrably inartistic; but a score of years has made a wonderful difference, and at present the winding railway, overflowing with bracken and wild flowers, is itself an object of beauty, and no longer a point for discussion and dislike.

Forty or fifty years ago, to say a word in favour of a railroad track was considered a sign of artistic inability, but in our own no less exacting period no one dreams of cursing the railway any more. In all the London and North Western system no finer centre can be found than Bettws-y-Coed; and the ease with which one is taken from Imperial Euston to the wide and verdant valley of the Conway, renders the journey a matter of pleasant excitement. To the tired manufacturer of Yorkshire also, Bettws-y-Coed and North Wales are close at hand, and it must be owned that Yorkshire and Lancashire are not slow to take advantage of their geographical position in this respect.

From Bettws many four-in-hand coaches start for their perambulations of the higher lands along the mountain roadways: to Capel Curig, famed for its position amongst the hills, whence the pedestrian may walk to the summit of the larger mountains; to Snowdon, who sometimes hides his head for days together; to Moel Siabod, most shapely of mountains, as seen from the Conway Vale; to Carnedd Llewelyn, the Glyders and the three-peaked hill, the roughest of all the giants.

Or, passing Capel Curig on the box-seat of the whirling four-in-hand, the traveller may go forward to Beddgelert by the wonderful winding-road down the valley of the Gwynant, where the meadows shine like gems amidst the general gloom of the precipices of Snowdon and its supporters. Or up Cwm Dyli, where the monarch of these mountains seems to hold itself aloof from its scarcely less-exalted neighbours; to Cwm-y-Llan, where Snowdon shows himself with his lieutenants, like a general and his aides-de-camp on a day of Royal review. Or, again passing Capel Curig, a coach drives up the great glen of Llanberis to its lake and quarries, and the easiest ascent to the peak of Snowdon. Still another coach passes

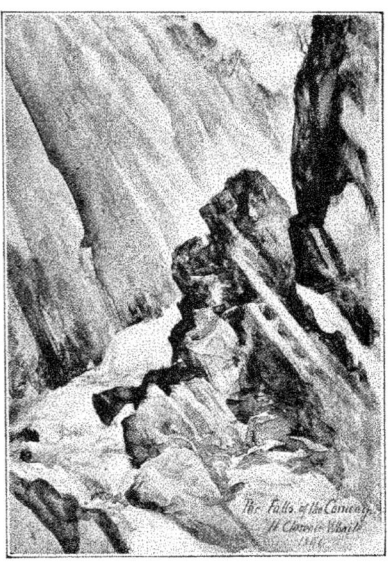

THE FALLS OF THE CONWAY. DRAWN BY H. CLARENCE WHAITE, P.R.C.A.

SNOWDON FROM CAPEL CURIG. FROM A WATER-COLOUR DRAWING BY H. CLARENCE WHAITE, PRESIDENT OF THE ROYAL CAMBRIAN ACADEMY.

Capel Curig from Bettws, going right on across-country, up hill, down dale, straight for the sea-coast at Bangor, by Telford's once much-lauded road, leading to Holyhead, for Ireland. At the present day this is an ordinary stage coach, and is one of the few survivors of the time, now becoming far-distant, when the Irish mails were carried along Telford's road, straight from London to Holyhead.

From Bettws-y-Coed the nearer walks are all as attractive as the longer journeys by four-in-hand or rail ; the falls of the Llugwy in Bettws itself never seem to fail to please. One cannot pass by, morning, noon, or night, without encountering half-a-dozen admirers on Pont-y-Pair overlooking the falls, with at least as many more on the rocks beside the water. Continuing the walk up the Llugwy, the river that joins the Conway a little below Bettws, every visitor goes to see what is called the Miner's Bridge, a few logs hung at high angle over a pretty torrent. Still farther, but within a couple of miles of Bettws, the famous Swallow Falls are located, amidst even prettier surroundings. It is not that the Swallow Falls are particularly high, or something very uncommon—the Falls of Clyde, for example, excel them both in volume and depth of fall—but they are the crowning point of a lovely walk, and are therefore unsurpassedly charming.

Again, in an opposite direction, and up the river Conway, there is, within walking distance, the Beaver Pool, quiet, restful, and singularly inviting to the fly-fisher ; with, farther on, the Fairy Glen, the favourite haunt of the cheap tripper, whose restlessness, however, seems quieted in the pathetic presence of the high hills. Still onward, but not too far for the same long afternoon's walk from Bettws, are Conway Falls, with high rocks and whirling eddies ; much spoiled artistically by a broken modern salmon ladder. While not far over are the Falls of Machno, where every artist makes a mental sacrifice if he does not return to paint a picture.

Amidst all this life-giving locality, the quiet soul who loves a day's fishing is frequently to be found, patiently waiting for the trout or salmon, which never in the summer months seem to jump to a fly. Ground bait is forbidden, but every holiday angler having flown his flies in days of disappointment, surreptitiously tries the worm ; his days of mourning are then over, unless unhappily the river bailiffs pounce upon him unawares, and wrathfully demand his name and residence. There are anglers, chiefly to be met in the hotels, who, after a hearty dinner, say they have often caught fish in August and September with the fly, but the records in this respect are not to be implicitly trusted.

At Elsi Lake, amidst the hill-tops, a mile or so above the village, the diligent fisher will whip the water until he strongly doubts the reputation of the Llyn for dozens of fishy prizes ; ground bait, he finds, is his only chance, for in summer the fly will not raise even the ripple of a fin.

Another well-known walk from Bettws is past the railway station—the centre of much activity in the summer-time—to the little parish church that David Cox so often drew and painted, past the churchyard with its many mounds and monuments, over a stile and along Conway's edge towards the stepping-stones. From this point, looking backwards to the river, is a ready-formed picture which tempts the tyro in sketching, and brings the amateur photographer much simple joy. The stepping-stones are not always easily passable ; after prolonged rain some of them are covered with water, and an ugly gap near the centre where the water is deep and almost dark, is the terror of feminine passengers who seek to cross. It is not often, but it once happened in our case, that an amiable salmon fisher, standing nearly waist deep in water, offers his services to lift the ladies across.

The road on the other side of the Conway is in Denbighshire, Bettws itself being in Carnarvonshire. Nearly three miles along this road, down the river, lies Llanrwst, a prosperous Welsh village, whose little ones are ignorant of English and whose men and women seem to translate their words from the Welsh. The unexpectedness of the enormous use of the language of consonants brings forth characteristic expressions of surprise from every English-speaking visitor; theoretically we all know that Welsh is a living language, but it is only in a village like Llanrwst that one realises the hold Welsh has on the ordinary people. When railway notices are headed "Rhybdd," followed by various unpronounceable words, when shop-signs and window-tickets are incomprehensible save when they carry a numeral, and when, most astonishing of all, lengthy advertisements appear in newspapers in Welsh, then the British traveller begins to feel like a stranger in his own island. This holding to hereditary language is only a sentiment, for sooner or later the young folks are compelled to master English ; but it is a pretty sentiment, and one we would not willingly let die.

Near Llanrwst and on the way back to Bettws, by side of rail and river, is Gwydir Castle, a fine example of olden opulence, and filled with furniture strong but very artistic ; to view which easy access is generously given. At this point the traveller is near Tal-y-Bont, an artist's club on the hillside, and half-way to Conway. Every autumn, an exhibition of pictures is open, the works being contributed by the forty enterprising members who form its constituency. Some day, perhaps, they will take their exhibition to Bettws, for it is no easy matter to induce visitors to spend time and money in driving so far as Tal-y-Bont is from a railway station. During the winter life, classes are said to be held in the club, and certain it is, that in their mountain loneliness, these excellent artists must have plenty of time for study.

Space permits not to tell of the many places which can comfortably be visited in a single day from Bettws. Llandudno and Great Ormes Head fill in a full day with pleasure and profit, another may be spent at Penmaenmawr and Conway Castle. At Conway in the autumn, Plas-mawr, a romantic old residence, is full of the fruit of the year's work of the Royal Cambrian Academy's members. Under the prosperous presidency of Mr. H. Clarence Whaite, this annual exhibition attracts general attention. The illustrations to this article are from the pencil of the president, whose amiable personality and devoted attention to the wants of the academy has deservedly placed him on the proudest pinnacle Welsh Art can provide.

Still farther round the coast Bangor and Carnarvon are easily visited within twelve hours, and energetic visitors to Bettws are sometimes known to take train right round the coast to Llanberis, ascend Snowdon on foot, spend an hour or more on the summit, and descend in time to reach Bettws again by train soon after nightfall.

From Bettws, going southwards, single-day journeys are almost as interesting. Blaenau-Festiniog, through a tunnel over two miles long, is nearly as famous as Penrhyn for its slate quarries. From thence descends the first of mountain railroads, locally called the "Toy Railway," to Port Madoc, on the southern edge of Carnarvonshire. Along the coast is Harlech Castle, remembered for its martial music ; and still farther is Barmouth, poised on a p rnacle, and within short distance of Cader Idris. All these are well-known places to hundreds of tourists, but there are still great numbers of travellers who know nothing of the many pleasures to be obtained from a month's visit to Bettws-y-Coed.

D. C. T.

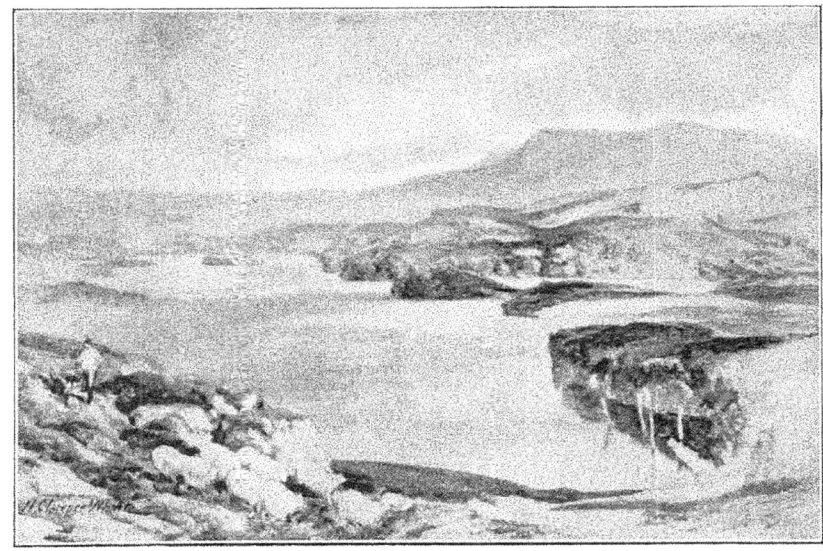

LAKE ELSI. DRAWN BY H. CLARENCE WHAITE, P.R.C.A.

THE UPS AND DOWNS OF A PICTURE.

A CURIOUS CHAPTER IN ART FIFTY YEARS AGO.

WHEN one visits the National Gallery of Scotland, or the annual exhibition of the Royal Scottish Academy in the adjoining suite of rooms, he is interested to learn the fact that the existence of the elegant building in which these exhibitions are housed to a large extent can be traced to the hanging and deposition of one bad picture in the Scottish Academy exhibition of fifty years ago. Most persons who care to know are aware of the somewhat stormy period through which the Scottish artists had to pass before they asserted their independence and finally attained a corporate character. Of that early struggle we are not now to speak. It has been fully told in the little volume on "Scottish Art and National Encouragement," published anonymously in 1846 by Sheriff Munro, and in the "Notes on the Early History of the Royal Scottish Academy," by the late Sir George Harvey, published twenty years ago. But the special incident of the rejected picture is not so fully known, and it, with the principal actors in it, forms the subject of this brief paper.

In 1844 the exhibitions of the Scottish Academy were held in the building still called "The Royal Institution," in a series of galleries subsequently used for the Scottish National Museum of Antiquities, and now used, under the joint management of the "Board of Manufactures" and the Edinburgh Architectural Association, as a School of Applied Art. The course of events which placed the interests of Art in Scotland in the control of a Board of "Manufactures" cannot now be told, but incidentally it may be stated that this somewhat anomalous condition of affairs had a very direct bearing on the occurrence we now relate. Amongst the pictures sent in for exhibition was a picture by Mr. George Dick-Lauder, entitled 'Scene after a Wreck—Twilight after a Storm,' and valued by the artist at £35. The picture is described by Sir George Harvey as "a large and certainly a most inferior work," and Sheriff Munro says, "the only question put by the public was, how it happened to be in the exhibition at all." We had hoped on entering into the story of this "powerful" picture—powerful we mean in its results—to have been able to present an illustration showing its merits. After passing through the experience to be immediately described, Mr. Dick-Lauder's picture was purchased as a prize by the Royal Association for

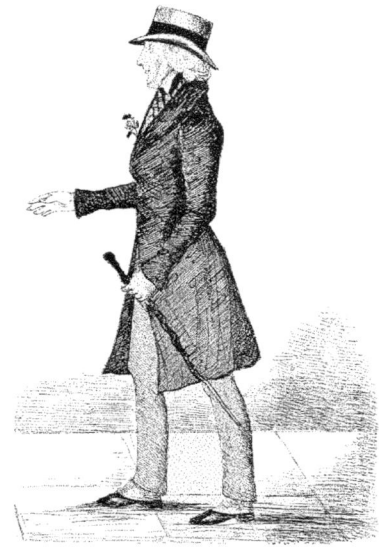

SIR THOMAS DICK-LAUDER. BY R. W. CROMBIE.

the Promotion of the Fine Arts in Scotland. The price paid was £25—for a large and inferior picture—and at the distribution it was won by a professional gentleman in Edinburgh, Mr. Watson, of the Scottish Provident Institution, now recently dead, who occupied a prominent position in the insurance world, from whom we hoped to get permission to engrave it. But this work of Art had its euthanasia in another way, having some years ago suffered destruction by a fire in some of the upper bedrooms of the house—to which it had been relegated in appreciation of its merit!

Here Mr. George Dick-Lauder and his picture practically leave the scene. But the artist's father was Sir Thomas Dick-Lauder, a gentleman of both literary and social fame, who held, at the time of the incident, the position of secretary to the Board of Manufactures. We may at once say that apart from this occurrence we have nothing but praise and appreciation of Sir Thomas Dick-Lauder to express. In the likeness we present, reproduced from a large series of semi-caricatures of Edinburgh celebrities of fifty to sixty years ago, drawn by Mr. Benjamin W. Crombie, we see a very gentlemanly man, suave, good-looking and intelligent. In the memoir accompanying the recent re-issue of Crombie's portraits, Lord Cockburn's words are quoted. "His powers in literature, the arts, and in science, are apt to be lost sight of by his friends amidst their enjoyment of his worth and amiable gaiety. . . . A flow of rambling natural talk, ready jokes, the twinkle of a mild laughing eye, a profusion of light yellow locks tossed over his head, face, and throat. . . . A tall gentleman-like Quixotic figure and a general picturesqueness of appearance." Sir Thomas Dick-Lauder's story of the "Moray Floods" of 1829 is a classic. Thus much as to the general character of the leading actor in the picture brawl.

The other combatant—though only in his official capacity—was Mr. David Octavus Hill, secretary to the Royal Scottish Academy at the time. Mr. Hill, who died in 1870, held a high reputation in his day as a landscape painter, and even yet, with the changes of taste and method which forty years have brought, the engravings of his Windsor Castle and Edinburgh Castle pictures hold a high rank. The portrait of Mr. D. O. Hill, by himself, which we are enabled to present, possesses great interest. It is reproduced from a "Calotype" photograph of date 1848, taken from life and now printed from the paper negative, with the permission of Mr. Andrew Elliot, publisher in Edinburgh, who owns a large number of these negatives of contemporary portraiture. Mr. D. O. Hill, in conjunction with Mr. R. Adamson, early took an interest in Mr. Fox Talbot's photographic discoveries, and the portraits and groups then taken are full of interest as a very early and very successful application of artistic treatment to photographic work.

From the powerful position held by Sir Thomas Dick-Lauder, we may infer that the hanging committee of the Scottish Academy in 1844 were not averse to giving his son's picture a good place. It was accordingly hung as No. 189—a central position in the centre room—and there the council saw it, and allowed it to remain. But when touching-up day came sixteen of the Academicians wrote a protest against the position given to such a work, and "in consequence of their request a more suitable place was found for it" (*Harvey*). This was in the south room, No. 348, and a painting by J. Coleman, 'Fountain near Terracina' (valued at £180), was given the space first occupied by Mr. George Lauder's large and low-priced work. But in the meantime Sir Thomas Dick-Lauder had been in the rooms, had seen his son's picture in the good place, and had learnt of its removal, and

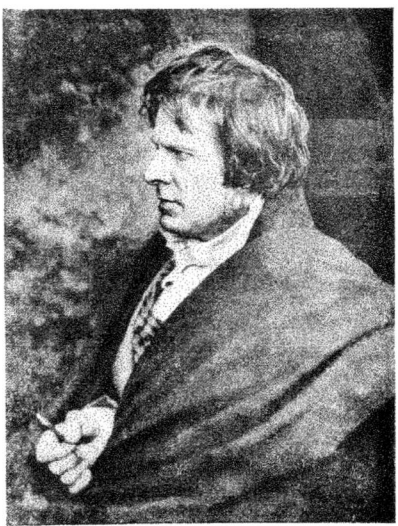

D. O. HILL, R.S.A. FROM AN EARLY CALOTYPE.

then the trouble began. His first act showed great want of temper. It had been the practice of the Academy to give him five complimentary season tickets, and he sent them back and bought others! He wrote to Mr. D. O. Hill a decidedly insolent letter in doing so. The protesting artists were described as " certain individuals," and public confidence was said to be destroyed in any body (the council) which could allow "not only the judgment of the hanging committee, but its own determination corroborative thereof, to be swayed and overturned by every unworthy intrigue that may be originated by selfish individuals in the body which it ought to govern." He was glad, he said, that so great a piece of injustice was done to his son rather than to one " more humbly connected," and pointed out that the "jealous intrigue " ought to be extremely flattering to so young an artist. And so with many hot words the indignant father poured out his wrath on the Academy, and all this was done on the official paper of the Board of which he was secretary. The Academy was not slow to resent the very offensive letter, and especially its official character. It turned out that objection had actually arisen within the council as to the hanging of the picture while the artist was as yet unknown to the objectors, but the rather weak admission was made that effect had not been given to this objection when it was found who the artist was, and that Sir Thomas had been in the rooms and seen where it had been placed. But it was shown that the protest of the sixteen artists was in full accordance with the rights and usages of the Academy, and that as the change was made two days before the public opening, it was quite within the powers of the council to make the removal. The rather equivocal remark was also made that the place eventually given to the picture was "a better position than others that might have been assigned to it." Apart from justifying its conduct, the council pronounced the Board secretary's letter "a deliberate insult to the Academy" and demanded its retractation, explaining at the same time that their only fault, if fault was imputable, was in having been induced to acquiesce at first in an undesirable arrangement from a desire to save Sir Thomas and his son from disappointment. Sir Thomas Dick-Lauder speedily disclaimed any insult or imputation of unworthy motives either to the council (who he had declared had been swayed by " unworthy intrigues ") or the members who carried on these intrigues. But the words remained, and when, after a great deal of discussion, the council of the Academy aimed a Parthian shaft by reminding him that his official position imposed "a duty of circumspection and restraint," the incident so far terminated.

But far-reaching consequences followed on the Board supporting their secretary in his claim of right to enter the rooms at all times. The example of the Royal Academy, and the imperative rule in the charter of the Scottish Academy, were pleaded in justification of the right of excluding " all persons except those officially engaged " during the selection and hanging of the pictures. In a lengthy minute the Board of Manufactures declared it impossible to accede to this view. The Academy might, it was said, make a regulation for its own members, and the example of other bodies could not be heard of. " If the conservators of that National Gallery leave that valuable collection without supervision or inspection by their own confidential officers in whom they have confidence, and expose it to hazard either of the Royal Academicians or of their tradesmen, which is entirely incredible, those gentlemen would incur a responsibility highly blameable, and from which were it known here can be no doubt they would be speedily relieved and more careful guardians substituted in their place." We give this gem of composition in full.

The position their Secretary assumed was fully supported and the Academy found itself in this position, that officials who knew nothing of their charter rights, and who might themselves be interested in the pictures, claimed to walk in and out during the hanging without let or hindrance. Lengthy and at times bitter correspondence and negotiation arose, which in the end resulted in the construction of the present building, and gave to the Royal Scottish Academy an independent suite of rooms for its exhibitions. Sir Thomas Dick-Lauder did not survive to witness the outcome of the conflict, for he died in May, 1848, aged sixty-four. Mr. D. O. Hill saw the Academy in its new rooms, ten years before his death, at sixty-eight, in May, 1870.

T. A. C.

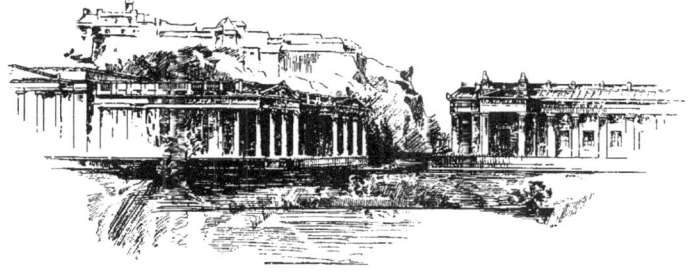

THE ROYAL SCOTTISH ACADEMY, EDINBURGH.

DOMESTIC ARCHITECTURE IN NORFOLK.

THE Domestic Architecture of the Eastern Counties dates partly from the days of the Plantagenets, but for the most part appear to have arisen with the influx of wealth

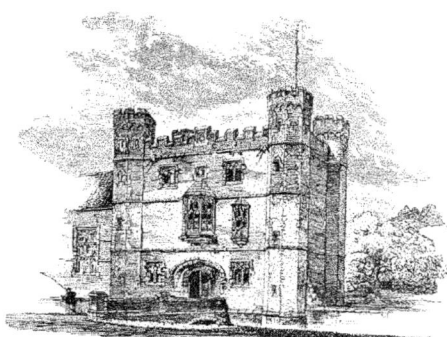

MIDDLETON TOWERS.

occasioned by the spread of the woollen and other industries introduced by the Flemings and other foreign settlers. Churches of unexampled size and splendour attest the magnificence of these prosperous merchants, and to them we owe a series of sumptuous dwelling-houses which were almost without a rival in the land. Their builders were limited as to materials. Stone was scarce, and therefore costly. Even in ecclesiastical works it was used parsimoniously, and in secular buildings it was sometimes altogether dispensed with. Bricks made from local clays, and terra-cotta from the finer sorts, with flints, and native timber in small quantities, were the only building materials easily obtainable. These our forefathers—guided by artistic instincts, and helped perhaps by foreign suggestions or reminiscences—turned to the utmost account.

One of the earliest and best instances of the employment of brick and terra-cotta in domestic architecture is to be found at the seat of Sir Henry Bedingfield, Bart., at Oxburgh. Hitherto this exquisite example of English Art lay a little out of the beaten track, being some eight miles from the nearest railway. Now, however, it may be reached from Stoke Ferry by an easy walk of two or three miles. It should be attentively studied by every lover of our native architecture, and it has an equal charm for the architect and the painter.

The original design is marked by an almost Grecian refinement of detail; but it has suffered both by destruction and attention—by "cruel hate and still more cruel love." Two or three generations ago the great hall, which occupied the southern front, was demolished to make way for some modern rooms and windows. Its removal has never ceased to be a subject of unavailing regret. The only considerable portion now remaining as its builders left it forms the subject of the sketch below. The bricks of which it is built are of a brownish red, and only two inches in thickness, the mortar joints being very thick and varying from three-quarters of an inch to an inch. Thus when new the whole must have been of a reddish grey rather than red, and very different in effect from the unmitigated red of much of our modern work. The "bond," moreover, is not so aggravatingly and mechanically regular as in our modern work. The value of these small matters, from a painter's point of view, cannot be overstated. An example of the effect of the old manner contrasted with the new can be seen at Hampton Court, where all the earlier brickwork has the wide joint. Time has spread over it a veil of ashen grey, through the interstices of which the ruddy tints of the old brickwork are felt rather than seen. One of the towers—the "Dove Tower"—in days gone by appears to have resisted at its summit this lichenous growth, and the effect is not unpleasant. It is nature adopting a painter's artifice, as when he throws the shadow of a passing cloud across one corner of a group.

An interesting feature in the composition is the frankness with which the windows are arranged to suit the internal requirements, and are not duplicated for the sake of symmetry,

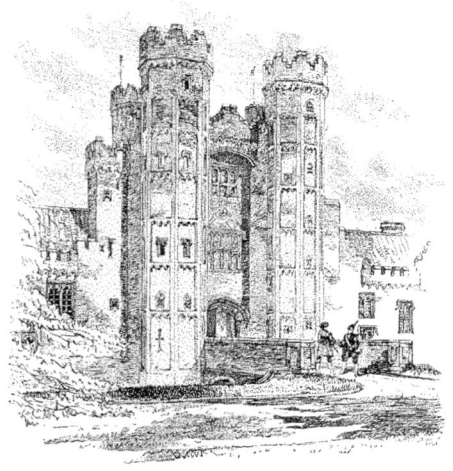

OXBURGH HALL.

The house, in fact, marks a turning-point in the history of architectural design, before the Gothic traditions had suc-

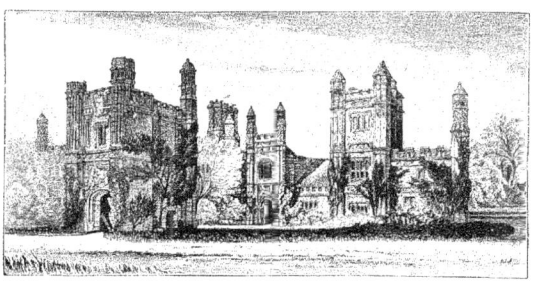

REMAINS AT EAST BARSHAM.

cumbed to the advancing tide of pseudo-classicalism. At some unknown date it suffered a grievous loss in the substitution of pantiles for the old plain tiles which covered its roofs. This destroyed, in a measure, the scale and harmony of the whole design, and robbed the building of a source of lovely colour, which must have been not the least beautiful passage in the composition.

A second example of nearly the same date is found at Middleton Towers, where the entrance gateway and its guard-rooms and flanking turrets, on a larger scale than those at Oxburgh, are in a very perfect condition. Although the little oriels above the gateway are more elaborate than anything at Oxburgh—stone having been used with a liberal hand—the Art displayed is certainly inferior. The corbel course under the battlements is clumsy and commonplace beside the exquisite delicacy of those at Oxburgh, and nowhere do we see the same evidence of a discriminating taste and a refined mind. The original house, of which only the entrance tower remains, was on a grand scale ; its size is marked by the existing moat, and it was further defended by an outwork, which can be easily traced on the ground.

The present owner has, by careful and judicious repairs and additions, converted a neglected ruin into an agreeable residence. The room over the gateway, with its two oriels and corner towers, makes a charming drawing-room, and from the leads the little angle turrets, fitted up daintily, make the most pleasant of boudoirs, commanding on every side delightful views over a charming country. The lover of old English architecture should be grateful to one who has preserved with so much care every fragment of the old work, which, but for him, would long ago have been a heap of undistinguishable ruin.

Of a somewhat later date, but of rare beauty, are the very considerable domestic remains at East Barsham. A portion is occupied as a farm-house, but by far the greater part is falling fast to "cureless ruin." The buildings were almost wholly constructed of brick and terra-cotta, although a little stone is used, and in one instance in combination with flint, after the local manner of church building. There are everywhere evidences of a tentative procedure on the part of the builders, as if experimenting with the various materials at command. A final effort appears to have been made to adapt the design to those which lay nearest at hand, viz., brick and terra-cotta.

The terra-cotta has not resisted the weather well, but has flaked off, showing up bright scarlet patches here and there. The ornament is skilfully modelled, and the pinnacles and chimney-stacks, many of which are partly modern, were in their original state of boldness and beauty. The large stack to the hall, consisting of ten shafts, is perhaps the noblest mass of chimneys in England, and displays the utmost skill and versatility in its design. Above all, the freedom and vigour of the heraldry over the entrances must strike every one. It is difficult to say whether it has been carved *in situ* or not, but the masterly manner in which it has been struck out is beyond all praise, and shows what strength was left in our native Art on the very eve of its extinction.

The picturesque farm-house at Great Hautbois, of which a sketch is given below, will explain some of the features common to nearly all the houses of the period in these districts.

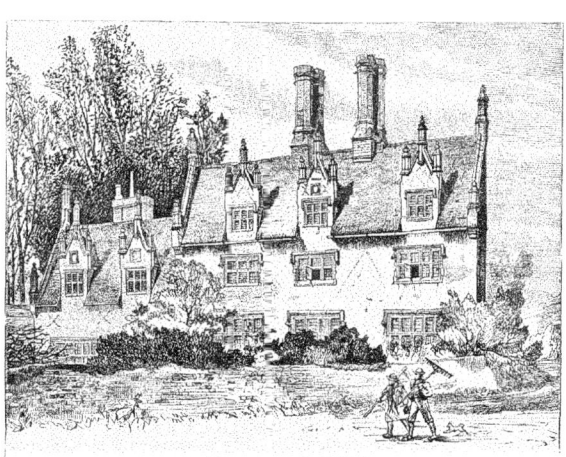

THE FARM-HOUSE OF GREAT HAUTBOIS.

No architect, eminent or otherwise, was probably engaged upon this work ; the detail and workmanship are of the rudest kind, and yet there is a character about the whole which is by no means unsatisfactory. The steep roofs and plain tiles alone go far to make it picturesque, and the introduction of the traditional dormers, with their octagonal pinnacles, are certainly architecturally effective. The chimney-stacks are not only of elegant plan and proportions, but, what is more

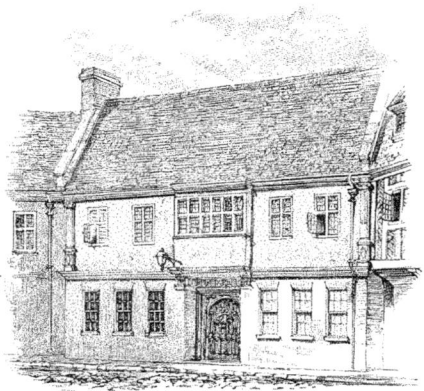

KING'S LYNN VICARAGE.

to the purpose, they fulfil perfectly the object of their construction. It is not necessary for me to add that the stack showing above the ridge of the low out-building is modern. It bears the marks of the century which lays no claim to artistic excellence, but which is, we are told, before all things scientific.

The retention of the high roofs and bold dormer windows down to a very late date has given to otherwise quite commonplace houses something of architectural character, and in looking down the narrow streets in Norwich one is constantly deluded into the notion that at last one has come upon an example of really old work.

The sketch on p. 275 will explain the matter, and show how a little liberality in the treatment of these features improves the general aspect of the meanest building. Without resorting to the use of ornament, and setting aside all attempts to be picturesque, the instinct of their builders succeeded in imparting to the simplest works an artistic value which is not always attained nowadays with the most lavish outlay.

The vicarage at King's Lynn, of which a little sketch is here printed, shows a perfectly unpretending front severely simple in its lines and arrangements. The lower windows are of course quite modern. At each extremity, on the principal floor, a very delicately designed Ionic pilaster marks the party wall, and a really rich and handsome entrance door with the elaborate tracery and carving of the Late Perpendicular period, stamps the whole as the work of an artist. You see, moreover, that he was working well within his strength. There is nothing fussy or obtrusive, no straining after effect, and if you want to realise the true value of this piece of good, quiet, domestic work, a walk in the suburbs of the town where the modern villas are rising will bring it home to you.

As you approach this interesting old town by the railway you see a long low roof and a few plain chimney stacks, and you are able to say at once with certainty, "there's an old building."

On strolling out in quest of it you come upon it and find it to be a block of Almshouses. Here is the quaint inscription over the porch:—

> THIS HOSPITAL WAS
> BVRN DOWN AT LIN
> SEGE AND REBVLT
> 1649 NATH MAXEY
> MAYOR AND EDW
> ROBINSON ALDMAN
> TREASVRER PROTEM

There is no special architectural character about this work of NATH MAXEY, MAYOR, and his friend the ALDMAN, and it is pretty evident that a rigid economy governed their operations. The buildings form a hollow square—a simple chapel opposite the entrance. High-pitched tile-roofs—the gables a little curved; the chimney-stacks thrown well up, and like those at Hautbois, innocent of the smoke doctor; a few simple casement windows painted white and glazed with small squares—and that is all. It scarcely ranks as architecture at all, so simple is it—so void of anything like artifice. Still there is something about it eminently satisfactory, something in the long level lines of its roof and the quiet inartificial look of the whole clearly expressive of its use and object, and entirely in harmony with the serene and uneventful lives of its inmates, who find in these humble dwellings a shelter from the storms of life and a haven of rest after its troublous voyage.

Z.

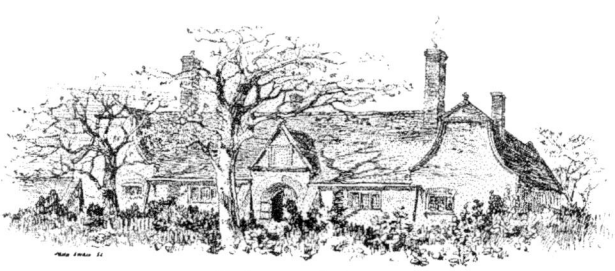

THE ALMSHOUSES, KING'S LYNN.

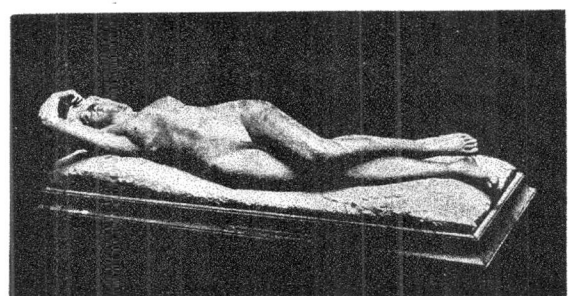

The Dawn of Womanhood. By T. Stirling Lee.

THE NEW SCULPTURE, 1879-1894.*
THIRD ARTICLE.

ON the 16th January, 1883, Mr. Thomas Brock was elected an A.R.A. in the room of Mr. Edward B. Stephens. Mr. Brock was thus the second man to enter the Royal Academy under the banner of the New Sculpture. He had had much to unlearn. He had been the cleverest and the most persistent of the pupils of Foley, and when that eminent sculptor died, he left his monuments, and mainly his great memorial to O'Connell in Dublin, to be executed by Mr. Brock. These important commissions burdened him, and in his desire to be loyal to the memory of Foley, he hesitated in adopting the new methods. During this early period he had occasionally shown, in ideal works, a style of his own, displaying a sweetness, —gained, however, in great measure by what would be called "softness" and "breadth." But now, in the face of all the fine things seen in London, and with cousiderable courage in a man approaching his fortieth year, Mr. Brock threw all these traditions aside, and joined the younger artists without any compromise with his past. Now, if any trace of his Foley training clings about his excellent work, it is in the direction of a certain hankering after "breadth."

* Continued from page 203.

1894

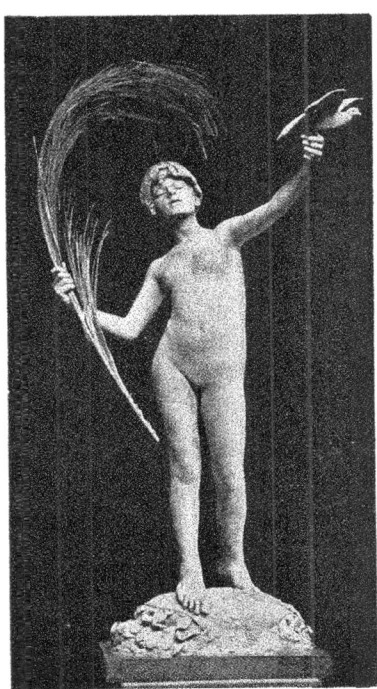

Peace. By E. Onslow Ford, A.R.A.

A step forward was taken in 1883 by Mr. T. Stirling Lee, in his 'Dawn of Womanhood,' a recumbent nude statue which attracted a great deal of somewhat bewildered attention in the Lecture Room. Never had anything of the kind been seen in England in which crude realism had been carried so far. Of this figure an engraving has been given, but no photograph does justice to this strange work, to which we look back with interest and amusement. The sculptor had, it is impossible to doubt, seen the "Byblis changée en Source," by which Suchetet had, the preceding year, awakened a *furore* in Paris. Mr. Lee had perceived, with an artist's instinct, how delightful and fresh that minute study of nature was. But he had missed the tact which so bold an experiment demanded. His 'Dawn of Womanhood' was like an absolute cast from the flesh. There was no selection of type, no striving after beauty of line; the figure was a literal copy of an ugly naked woman. Mr. Lee had not realised that, without style, Art does not exist. His experiment was interesting, and it distinctly marked a step in the progress of the school, but its influence was slight.

It was in 1883, too, that there was first revealed, unquestionably and without any

4 B

reserve, a talent of the highest order, one of the two or three which have since done most to illuminate and distinguish the art of sculpture amongst us. Mr. E. Onslow Ford (b. 1852), was, as he himself has recorded, "in the peculiar position of never having studied sculpture in any Art school," but had been trained as a painter at Antwerp and Munich. When he began to take up sculpture, then, as a profession, his touch was timid and uncertain, his eye irregularly guided, and his notions of design unsettled and undeveloped. For eight or nine years he devoted himself to iconic work without ever doing more than suggesting a possible promise. But in 1883 he exhibited a robed figure of 'Henry Irving as Hamlet' (see page 201), which raised the highest anticiparions—anticipations, it is needless to say, which were fully and promptly realised. But, even yet, the time had hardly been reached for a discussion of the style which Mr. Ford was presently to make his own.

For the rest, the year 1883 was mainly notable for a higher average of merit in busts than had been seen in any previous show at Burlington House; Mr. Gilbert leading the way with a 'Head of a Boy,' which was a veritable jewel, and for which,

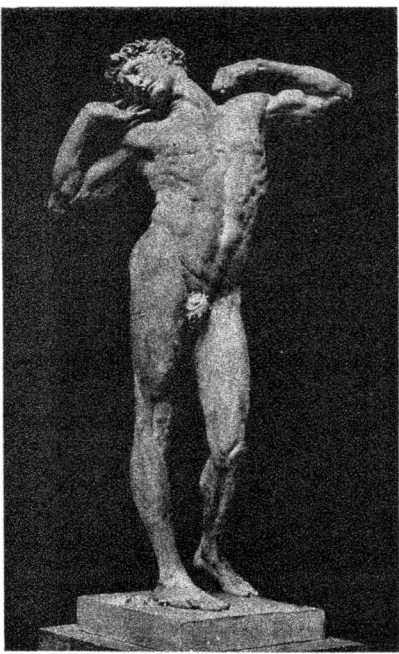

THE SLUGGARD. BY SIR FREDERIC LEIGHTON, BART. P.R.A.

on its first appearance, there was an amiable contest among would-be purchasers. Mr. Thornycroft enlarged the field of practicable domestic sculpture with his bronze medallion portraits, and a curious statuette of a lady singing. Throughout the iconic work of the year, there was a tendency to such fleshiness of form and incisiveness of line as had not been seen for a century in English sculpture.

An exceedingly important year for the art, perhaps the most brilliant single season that sculpture has ever had in this country, was that of 1884. At the close of the preceding year, at the biennial contest for the gold medal of the Royal Academy, a great sensation had been created by the exhibition of one model which then was, and still remains, by far the best relief ever done by a student in the schools. This excitement was, no doubt, fortuitously increased by the whisper which ran around to the effect that this marvellously beautiful and accomplished panel was the work of a boy in his teens. This was not the case, and no one who noted the ripeness and high technical science of the 'Socrates teaching the People in the Agora' could believe it to be the work of an untrained student. It proved to be modelled by a student,

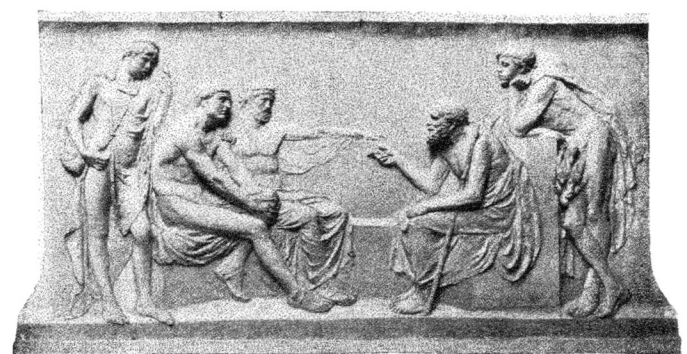

SOCRATES IN THE AGORA. BY HARRY BATES. A.R.A.

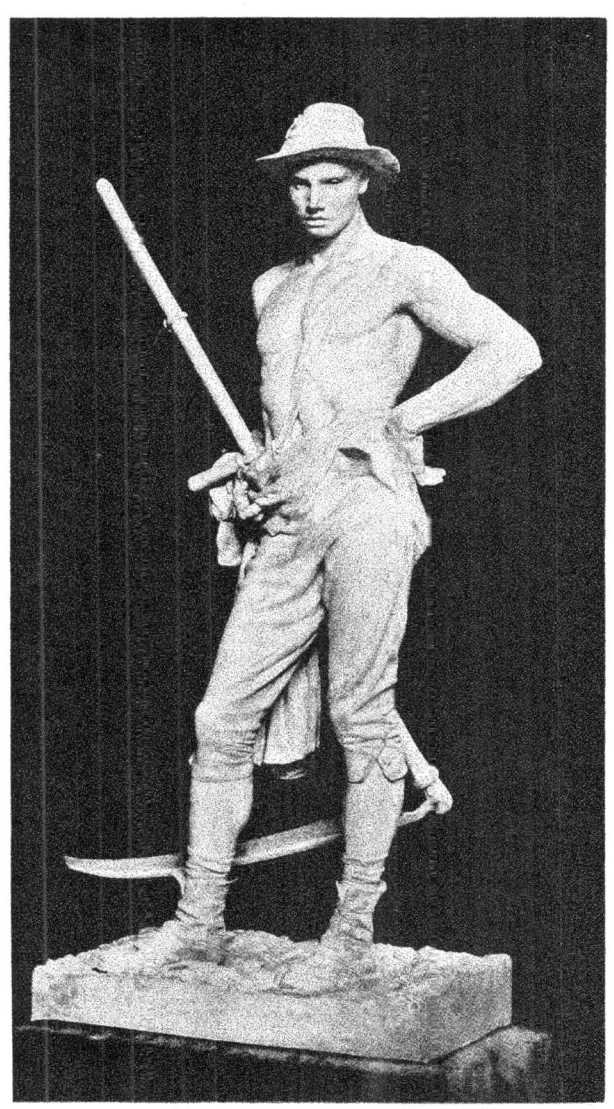

The Mower. By Hamo Thornycroft R.A.

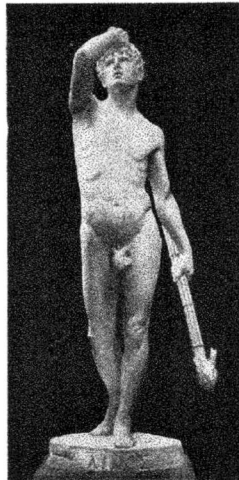

LINOS. BY E. ONSLOW FORD, A.R.A.

indeed, but not a very young one, Mr. Harry Bates, who became famous from this his first appearance.

This original work has never been surpassed by its author, who presently executed it in marble for Owens College, Manchester. It revealed gifts which had long been maturing, but which do not seem to have advanced. The great value of the 'Socrates,' as of later works of this kind, lies in the fact that they are founded on the best traditions of Greek relief, such as those of the Parthenon, and yet are instinct with the vitality of modern feeling. While perfectly slab-like and Parthenaic, the reliefs of Mr. Bates have a charming picturesqueness which delights the eye; he is as severe as a fine taste demands, but never more so. He avoids, with a most delicate tact, the errors of archaism and studied oddity which betray Mr. Armstead when he attacks the same difficult province of the art.

It was in 1884 that Mr. Thornycroft made an entirely new departure with his virile modern statue of 'The Mower.' Here was a figure of the life of to-day, seized in a position of perfectly natural grace, treated in the costume of his class. Something of the sentiment of Fred. Walker, and something, too, of the ideal realism of such young French sculptors as Coutan and Albert Lefeuvre, inspired this very noble statue, in which the beauty of the every-day life of to-day was heroically captured for the art which had seemed most definitely to decline to touch it. Progress in technical perfection was manifest in every part of 'The Mower,' a work which has not wanted admirers who have preferred it to any other of the master's productions. Whether we take so high a view of it or not, it is indisputable that it was the pioneer of a whole class of statuary of a modern and "actual" kind. That danger lies in this direction, where style is not jealously kept paramount, no one can know better than Mr. Thornycroft. 'The Mower' was seen in bronze at the Royal Academy of the present year.

Another epoch-making work of 1884 was the 'Icarus' of Mr. Alfred Gilbert. This was a small statue, scarcely more than a statuette, but it exercised an influence which has hardly been equalled. It may be well to remind the reader that this was a bronze figure of a young athlete, whose shoulders are bowed with the weight of heavy artificial wings, bound to his arms with leathern straps. Throughout, the bony structure of the body was thoroughly understood; without pedantic insistence, indeed, but with the most delightful and complete science. The type selected was that lank and thin-skinned adolescence in which Mr. Gilbert specially delights, and which no one has transferred to marble and bronze more skilfully than he. A strange poetic novelty was given to the languorous head of 'Icarus' by its being heavily swathed in folded cloths, so heavily that a shadow fell over the face. This was not quite a new idea in sculpture, but it was freshly treated, and we shall see that it was readily imitated.

Something must be said, too, of the execution of the 'Icarus.' It was, unless I am much mistaken, the first example of *cire perdue*, of any importance, made in this country. As a specimen of that ingenious contrivance it was not perfectly successful; the black patina was not beautiful, and in more than one place the process had slightly failed. But it was a most interesting experiment, and all the New Sculptors were keen to proceed with it. It did away with the unsightly seams which are inevitable in ordinary casting, and which cannot be so skilfully cut away as not to leave raw places where the patina has been destroyed. The *cire perdue* process, when it succeeds, presents us with a copy, which defies extinction, of the smallest touch made by the sculptor on the clay. The chaser is absolutely dispensed with and the bronze cast accurately repeats or mirrors the artist's finished clay or wax model.

A word must here be given to two appearances in 1884. Mr. Roscoe Mullins had been in previous years a frequent

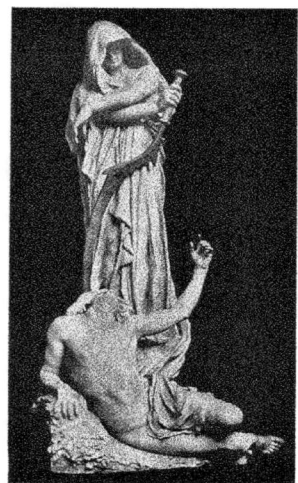

DEATH AND THE PRISONER. BY HENRY A. PEGRAM.

exhibitor, but he had never reached the level of his ' Bless me, even me also, O my father,' a group which was greatly admired in the Central Hall of the Royal Academy. He has never gone further than this, and his work, though always interesting, lacks something to give it a foremost rank. Mr. Mullins studied with Wagmüller, whose rocky, rough style has always affected him. Perhaps a close examination of Mr. Mullins' many accomplished productions will lead us to the conviction that where he falls a little below the highest excellence is in structure. His figures rarely suggest sufficient attention to anatomy. Mr. Henry A. Pegram first came to the front in 1884, and a relief of his, 'Ignis Fatuus,' was bought for the Chantrey Collection. Mr. Pegram was one of the earliest to come forward of those who were young enough to have worked from the very first on the new principles. We shall have to return to his name. Suffice it for the present to commend his large and imaginative style, and to note his acknowledged following of Mr. Alfred Gilbert.

It is difficult to leave 1884, that *annus mirabilis* of English sculpture, and we have yet to speak of the ' Linos' of Mr. Onslow Ford, a solemn mortuary torchbearer; Mr. Brock's large—even too large— ' Longfellow,' destined to be set up in Westminster Abbey ; and of the sensation caused among the extreme members of the school by the exhibition at the Royal Academy of M. Rodin's powerful, but eccentric, 'Age d'Airain.' This year, too, Boehm was roused by the competition of the younger men to put forward all his powers, and in his busts — especially his ' Lord Wolseley ' and his ' Herbert Spencer'—reached a very high excellence in his simple and prosaic way.

In 1885 the natural reaction took place. The show of sculpture at the Royal Academy was disconcertingly dull, and there were not Job's comforters wanting to announce immediately that the new school was already in decadence. As a matter of fact sculpture is an art which cannot be kept blazing before the public like painting. So much of the work by which a sculptor gains fame is of a kind that is wholly unremunerative, that he is forced to give himself breathing space for busts and portrait statues. The new process of *cire perdue* was responsible for a certain flatness in the show, the English craftsman being still so little proficient in it that there was a calamitous sacrifice of works by Messrs. Ford, Gilbert, and Lee, if by no others. Mr. Mullins sent to the Grosvenor his delightful group of boys playing, called ' Conquerors,' and Mr. Bates continued his series of admirable Virgilian panels in relief. In this very dead year, 1885, the principal event lay outside the Academy, and was the unveiling, at Pembroke College, Cambridge, of Mr. Thornycroft's exquisite marble bust of Gray, and appended bronze panel from the "Elegy in a Country Churchyard." This was a definite artistic addition to a university which boasts among its admirable busts, the 'Ray' and the 'Willoughby' of Roubiliac.

There was full proof, if proof were wanted, of the vitality of the New Sculpture, in the splendid show made in the following year, 1886. It was seen that the forces of the art had but been reserved, to make a more vigorous display. This was not a year in which fresh talent made itself prominent, but almost all of those men whose successive appearances have been recorded in the previous pages strengthened their claims and emphasised the individuality of their talent. It was in 1886 that Sir Frederic Leighton, after so long a silence, came forward once more among the sculptors. His ' Sluggard' held the place of honour in the Lecture Room, and by its side a small bronze called ' Needless Alarms ' testified still further to the versatility of the president. In comparison with the ' Athlete and Python,' these works—and particularly ' The ' Sluggard,' for ' Needless Alarms ' was, perhaps, a little frivolous — showed very distinct progress in the sculptor's conception of his art. The nature of that progress may be defined by saying that he had passed from hardness into suppleness and flexibility, that the forms of flesh and bone were far more under his control than they had formerly been. No one could doubt, in examining ' The Sluggard,' that the influence of the French had been strong on Sir Frederic Leighton, nor that he had greatly admired the ' Teucer ' of his own youthful colleague, Mr. Thornycroft. If it be not too technical to say so, one felt the thumb-touch in this splendid study of a powerful lad yawning and stretching; nothing could be modelled more closely in accordance with the principles of the new school.

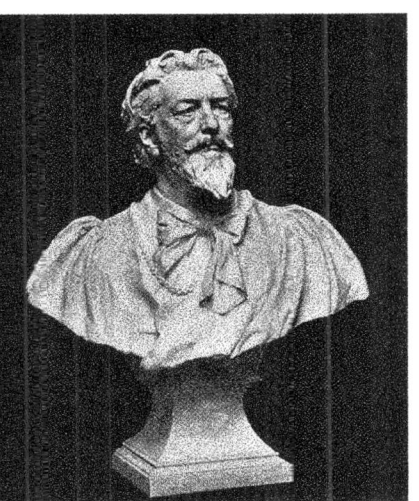

SIR FREDERIC LEIGHTON, BART, P.R.A. BY T. BROCK, R.A.

Another very important work of 1886 was ' The Enchanted Chair,' by Mr. Alfred Gilbert. It is said that this model, from which no durable work was executed, has been broken up, either through accident or caprice. If this be so, the loss to English art is a serious one, for this was a composition of very unusual importance. It may be well, in case of its complete destruction, to remind our readers of the design, and I will employ the words in which at the time I noted its features. A nude female figure of mature proportions lies drowned in a deep sleep in a magic chair. Her attitude expresses the extremity of lassitude, her muscles are lax with profound slumber. The chair has wings for arms, the feet of the woman rest on the outspread wings of doves, amoretti support the sides of the chair, a huge eagle overshadows it and the sleeper with vast pendent pinions, the very hair of the figure is feathery. What gave to this statue an historical importance in the progression of the New Sculpture, was the fact that in it was pushed to the last extreme that research after "colour" which had been Mr. Gilbert's great aim. Farther than this it has not been possible to push this characteristic. The wings, the draperies, the symbolic ornaments of the chair, were all arranged so as to relieve and illuminate, as in a richly lacquered jewel-box a diamond is enshrined, the soft and luscious flesh of the central animating figure. With this pursuit of colour and style was combined a realism pushed to an almost equal extreme, and testifying to the careful study of the type. It is needless to do more than point to a single instance of this, the toes were laxly inverted, exactly as they may be seen to be in deep sleep. If this work be indeed destroyed, the fact is much to be regretted.

Mr. Thornycroft proceeded with his bucolic experiments, in 1886, by the exhibition of a fine statue of a 'Sower,' striding along the damp furrows of the field. This was an eminently successful study of the beauty of modern rustic life, but it displayed no fresh characteristics which 'The Mower' of 1884 had not illustrated. On the other hand, the admirers of Mr. Onslow Ford were rewarded this year by the exhibition of a statuette which for the first time fully justified, and more than justified, the hopes which the slowly-developing work of this artist had awakened. The 'Folly' of 1886 was a bronze of exquisite delicacy and originality, and it displayed a quality in which, as it appears to me, Mr. Ford at his best excels all his contemporaries—the extreme finish of the surface of the flesh. Until this year his work, often exceedingly interesting, had been tainted by inexperience and even timidity; he had hardly known what effect it was he wished to produce, nor how to produce it. But in the 'Folly' the master stood revealed; this was absolute nature, translated in the purest and most select medium. It was a sort of paradox, that this giddy creature, waving and oscillating in her foolish nudity from the top of her rock, should represent the apex of sanity and health in the artistic career of her creator, who henceforth took his place among the leading sculptors of Europe.

It is difficult to trace to the influence of any particular foreign sculptor the singular line taken by Mr. Ford. We may roughly, but not inaccurately, say that Mr. Thornycroft started from Dubois and Mr. Gilbert from Mercié. Perhaps Dubois's work was not without its effect on Mr. Ford, but the relation is not so evident in his case as in those of the two English masters with whom alone he can be compared. It may here be noted that it was in 1886 that Mr. F. W. Pomeroy, with a group of 'The Family of Cain,' first attracted the attention of artists; but it will be more convenient on a later occasion to characterize the work of this sculptor.

On the 8th of January, 1887, the genius of Mr. Alfred Gilbert received the recognition of the Royal Academy, by his being elected an A.R.A., although no vacancy occurred among the sculptors. It was impossible any longer to keep outside a talent so impressive and so learned. The qualities of Mr. Gilbert were, during these years, spreading on every hand, and widening in a very marked degree the domain of practicable sculpture. Something of an epoch was marked in 1887 by the unveiling, in Westminster Abbey, of the memorial to Henry Fawcett, badly placed under a small window, in a remote corner of the Baptistry. Hitherto, and especially in work intended for the Abbey, the sculptors had been in the habit of ignoring the exigencies of the architecture. When, for instance, a generation earlier, a gigantic production by Gibson had to be placed, a portion of the original pillar, against which it was to stand, had positively to be hewn out. This was in the darkest age of the art, and such vandalism was entirely in disfavour with the New Sculpture; but it was Mr. Gilbert who first in England showed how the architect and the sculptor might work together in unity.

In the Fawcett Memorial, Mr. Gilbert went beyond suggesting colour by texture and shadow, he dared to introduce positive hues, and with brilliant effect. The monument consists of a frieze of seven bronze figures flanking the bust of the statesman, and is further adorned with corbels, heraldic designs and faces in relief. All these are in bronze, but of various tones of patina from silver to dark liver colour, while gold is very freely employed to vary the impression. Even vermilion is not disdained, and the effect of the whole composition is gorgeons and vivid to the highest degree. It is easy to feel that in the lavish and fanciful invention which vitalises the whole monument, the sculptor has been in intimate sympathy with the traditions and history of the Gothic fane in which it was to be placed. It was at once very intelligent and very artistic to insist in this way, against the whole weight of the tradition of three centuries, on harmonizing the jewel of sculpture with the great and ancient coffer in which it was to be hidden.

True to the curious biennial reduction of force, the retreating wave of each alternate year, to which I have already drawn attention, the public shows of 1887 were of inferior interest. Mr. Ford's 'Peace' was the most delightful contribution of the year. A new name, that of Mr. George Frampton, was observed. The principles of the New Sculpture were exemplified in 'Dawn,' a group by Miss Edith Gwyn Jeffreys, the only lady who has shown a serious aptitude for modelling during the progress of the movement; it is to be regretted that she does not seem to have persevered in what is, no doubt, a difficult path for a woman. The principal feature of 1887, however, was the remarkable recognition of the school at Manchester in the autumn of that year. Here for the first time the young men were seen to advantage, the work of their elders being almost entirely absent. Almost every one of the works to which attention has been drawn in the preceding pages was visible at Manchester on that occasion, and in particular such a set of ideal statuettes, including the work of Leighton, Thornycroft, Gilbert, Ford, Lee, and the younger men, such as had never been seen together before, and may never be seen again. Under whose intelligent auspices this remarkable collection was made, I do not know, but that it was of great service in concentrating and emphasising the contributions of the New Sculpture there can be no question. After this exhibition, it might be said that only two living sources of the art existed in this country, Sir Edgar Boehm's fashionable and extensive factory of iconic monuments on the one hand, and the studios of the new men on the other.

EDMUND GOSSE.

(*To be continued.*)

IN TEMPTATION.
FROM THE PICTURE BY MR. BRIGHT-MORRIS.

MR. BRIGHT-MORRIS is *par excellence* the painter of the *patio*. He understands the value of every accidental charm—an oleander, a pink in its pot, the hanging up of a handful of maize stalks, the hollows in a building that hold cool shadows, and those that glow with the secondary or reflected light—the filling of the shade with the spirit of sun-

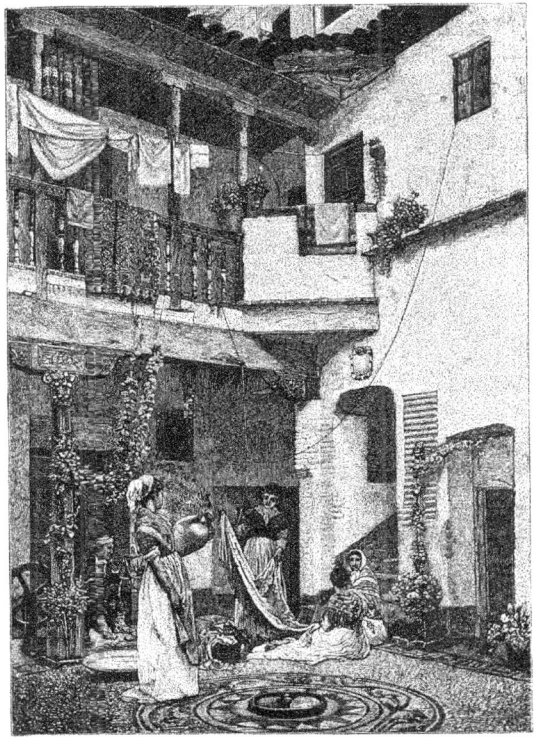

IN TEMPTATION. BY BRIGHT-MORRIS.

of ancient dignity, mingled with the odds and ends of present poverty, and the corner balcony, blank wall, little blind, unexplained window with its cord, the heavily-tiled eaves, and the garlanded trailers,—all things easy to recognise and admire, but not to be imagined beforehand; that is, time and local habit, and the way of the daily life of a Spanish family,

shine. All these things are essentially southern. They are appropriate to Italy, more appropriate to Spain, most appropriate to Algiers. In Tuscany many a *cortile*, seen through the arch of a *fattoria* gateway, shows the pictorial simplicity of whitewash and white oxen, while the Florentine palace, too, has its enclosed garden with fountain and some much-prized vine, bearing the famous *uva salamanna* for the table of the still-princely owner. But the Spanish courtyard is more full of careless and incidental beauty. In the picture engraved, there are all the fragments

and the way of the sun and climate produce results all their own. Mr. Bright-Morris has for many years delighted the lovers of character and charm of subject—those who hold a delicate appreciation of architecture, vegetation, custom, and climate to be no small part of a real painter's technique. For there is a technique of thought and vision, of judgment and apprehension, which is at least as valuable as the technique of the brush. To desire intelligently appreciated subjects in painting is not, therefore, to slight virtuosity but to desire virtuosity in its completeness.

AN IMPORTANT ARTISTIC DISCOVERY.

THE artistic world of Rome has of late been greatly impressed by the discovery of an important work of the Roman artist Bartolomeo Pinelli, which had remained entirely unknown. It is composed of two hundred and fifty-three pen-and-ink drawings shaded with sepia, retracing as many scenes from the Greek mythology. It is a whole pantheon of gods and demi-gods, where one assists by turn at their heroic exploits and at their adventures of a more tender kind. The gallantries and the not very exemplary amours of the master of Olympus, of his sons and his court, are rendered with great delicacy. The athletic wrestlings of Hercules, Achilles, Ajax, and Theseus furnish many noble attitudes. Certain dramatic subjects — for instance, Andromache weeping over Hector's tomb, the death of Alcyone — are pages of true beauty, where feeling rises to the height of the sublime.

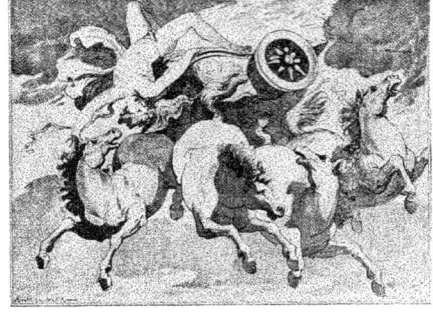

ONE OF THE PINELLI DRAWINGS.

It is to be noted that the artist, in the characters he puts in action, follows the alphabetic order from A to Z, beginning by Apollo and ending with Zephyrus.

The whole "gallery" was composed in the short space of a year. This is marvellous when we consider the fertility of conception, the effort of imagination that such a work called forth, as well as the perfection of the work itself.

The discovery of this important collection, worthy of being placed in a Royal Gallery side by side with the drawings of the old masters, is due to an amateur of Rome, M. F. O. Maruca, who has purchased it. The two hundred and fifty-three sketches, bound in three volumes, had remained in a family whose chief member, now dead, had been the editor of *Meo Patacca*, and of those numerous engravings representing scenes of the Roman people and robbers, that have made Pinelli's name known throughout Europe and principally in England. These drawings were to have been reproduced by the burin with a view to their publication, but, owing to the artist not having had time to execute the plates, or from some other cause, the collection, deposited at the editor's, remained there entirely forgotten. This publication is now in due course of execution, thanks to M. Maruca, who is seconded by a Committee of artists, having the Minister of Public Instruction for their honorary president.

Pinelli was born in 1781 in Trastevere, one of the quarters of Rome that has best retained its character and its traditional customs. His father was a poor door-keeper. From his childhood the young Trasteverian showed a great taste for drawing. His aptitude was noticed; but as his talent developed itself his manner improved more by a persevering study of the antique marbles, than by the fact of following any regular lessons of the academies. By so doing he acquired that great facility in rendering academical figures with the Attic elegance of form, the nobleness of movement of demi-gods and heroes. Even in the characters of his popular scenes, one finds the accent, the classical note that was the very essence of his talent.

He opened his first studio in a small coffee-house situated in Piazza Sciarra, on the Corso. Eating and sleeping there and while helping the waiters in their work, Bartolomeo copied pictures, and made drawings, which the waiters sold for a few francs, or even pence, to the foreigners who frequented the establishment. This meagre pittance, however, was sufficient in helping him to subsist; miserably, it is true, but permitted him also to follow the lessons at the academy of the capital.

The coffee-house no longer exists; but twenty years ago the proprietor still showed with pride the table where Bartolomeo was wont to sit surrounded by a small circle of artists. He was in the habit of pencilling some well-drawn and boldly-designed figure on the marble table, talking and drinking all the while. Very often while his friend Pistrucci, poet and engraver, was repeating some verses he had recently composed, he himself reproduced the subject.

Like the true and jovial Roman he was, Pinelli passed the greater part of his life at the *osteria*. He had made it both his home and his studio. I will give one trait of the life of this strange but genial Bohemian of Art, which will make him better known than a long description.

Having sketched a band with the greatest possible accuracy he sent it to Canova, then at the height of his celebrity. Canova admired the work, and, knowing how precarious his countryman's position was, sent him twenty-five *scudi* (five pounds), an enormous sum for that time. Of course Pinelli was at the *osteria* when they brought him the money. He was greatly offended that his colleague in Art should act as a Mæcenas towards him, and wanted to send back the money immediately. His friends, however, having dissuaded him from so doing, he called the *oste* (landlord) and ordered wine to be brought. Then Pinelli invited all the passers-by to come and drink, and drink they did all night long, until the last penny was gone.

London and Paris both made generous offers to the Roman engraver, but he could neither be induced to leave Rome nor to abandon his mode of living, where he died in 1835.

EUG. AUBER.

ART NOTES.

MR. HENRY TATE'S COLLECTION.—We are authorised to make the important announcement that the Trustees of the National Gallery have acceded to the request of the Government to undertake the management and control of the New Gallery of British Art, which is to be erected at Westminster. The fact that the new gallery will be managed jointly with the National Gallery cannot fail to increase the usefulness of Mr. Tate's gift. The first act of the Trustees of the National Gallery under the new arrangement has been to visit Mr. Tate's Collection, in order to select the pictures which they consider worthy to form the nucleus of the Gallery of British Art; a selection made, of course, entirely upon their independent judgment. Mr. Tate finally placed sixty-six pictures at their disposal from which to choose, with the result that the following sixty-one were chosen, a fact which supplies significant testimony—if any be needed—of the value of his offer.

John Crome.—1. Near Hingham, Norfolk.
John Hoppner, R.A.—2. Portrait of a Lady.
Sir John E. Millais, Bart., R.A.—3. Ophelia. 4. The Vale of Rest. 5. The Knight Errant. 6. The North-West Passage. 7. St. Bartholomew's Day. 8. The Stoning of St. Stephen. 9. Resignation.
Sir Frederic Leighton, Bart., P.R.A.—10. "And the Sea gave up the dead that were in it."
J. C. Hook, R.A.—11. Home with the Tide. 12. Love's Young Dream. 13. The Seaweed Gatherer.
Briton Riviere, R.A.—14. The Herd of Swine. 15. Giants at Play. 16. The Poacher. 17. Running the Blockade.
W. Q. Orchardson, R.A.—18. Her First Dance. 19. The First Cloud. 20. Her Mother's Voice.
Luke Fildes, R.A.—21. The Doctor.
L. Alma Tadema, R.A.—22. A Silent Greeting.
Peter Graham, R.A.—23. A Rainy Day.
T. Faed, R.A.—24. The Silken Gown. 25. Faults on Both Sides. 26. The Highland Mother.
H. W. B. Davis, R.A.—27. Mother and Son.
A. C. Gow, R.A.—28. Incident in the Early Life of Chopin. 29. The Flight of James II.
Henry Woods, R.A.—30. Cupid's Spell.
Sir Edwin Landseer, R.A.—31. A Scene at Abbotsford. 32. Uncle Tom and His Wife for Sale.
John Phillip, R.A.—33. The Promenade.
Frank Holl, R.A.—34. Hush! 35. Hushed.
Erskine Nicol, A.R.A.—36. Ways de Prayer. 37. The Emigrants.
G. H. Boughton, A.R.A.—38. Weeding the Pavement.
B. W. Leader, A.R.A.—39. The Valley of the Llugwy.
J. W. Waterhouse, A.R.A.—40. Consulting the Oracle. 41. St. Eulalia's Crucifixion. 42. The Lady of Shalott.
Stanhope Forbes, A.R.A.—43. The Health of the Bride.
J. P. Pyne.—44. Alum Bay.
John Linnell.—45. Noonday Rest. 46. Contemplation.
Keeley Halswelle.—47. Pangbourne.
Albert Moore.—48. Blossoms.
Albert Goodwin.—49. Sinbad the Sailor.
S. E. Waller.—50. Success. 51. Sweethearts and Wives.
Lady Butler.—52. The Remnants of an Army.
J. Haynes Williams.—53. The Dying Artist.
Dendy Sadler.—54. Thursday. 55. A Good Story.
J. R. Reid.—56. A Country Cricket Match.
E. Douglas.—57. Mother and Daughter.
S. Carter.—58. Morning with the wild Red Deer.
1891.
T. B. Kennington.—59. The Orphans.
Alfred Hunt.—60. Windsor Castle.
E. J. Gregory, A.R.A.—61. Marooned.

Among the many semi-public exhibitions held recently in London the following collections were the most successful: Mr. Mortimer Menpes and Mr. Theodore Roussel at the Dowdeswell Galleries, these exhibitions being productive of much discussion in artistic circles, the general opinion deciding that both painters have recently made satisfactory progress in colour and style. Sir John Millais's three paintings of children, at The Fine Art Society's, show that the hand of this master, notwithstanding recent ill-health, remains as strong as ever; and the collection of masterpieces and studies by Troyon at the new Goupil Gallery, in Regent Street, is a testimony to the continuing attraction of thoroughly good artistic work. In the St. George's Gallery, in Grafton Street, a new candidate for public patronage offered a most excellent series of pictures by the modern French painters.

The exhibition of the Home Art and Industries Association in the upper galleries of the Albert Hall was a magnificent testimony to the success of the movement. Any lady or gentleman with leisure will find real pleasure in starting a class for village home-workers in connection with this Association. Already a very large number of branches are in operation, but there are many quarters still unrepresented.

The Liverpool Exhibition comprised nearly five hundred pictures in oil and water-colours by local artists, and a good display of decorative and applied Art, which included examples of wall-papers, metal work, carvings, Japanese ivories, pottery and bookbinding. There was also a large collection of photographs, and a number of French pictorial posters. The exhibition was a pronounced success.

The administration of the Beaux-Arts in Paris is at present being carried on most energetically and successfully. The last idea is to gather together all the very latest acquisitions—purchases and gifts—in a Salon in Versailles Palace. This gallery has just been opened, and it now contains:— Bosio's silver statuette of Henri IV. in his infancy, and a bronze bust of Louis XII. unsigned, 1508. Two large paintings by Carrey represent the reception of the Marquis de Nointel, the Roi Soleil's Ambassador, by the Grand Vizier and the Grand Signor respectively. Among the portraits are those of General Bertrand, by Paul Delaroche; of Bernadotte, by Gros; and of Napoleon I., by Gérard. There is a study of Marat after death by David, and Carpeau's original sketch of Napoleon III., as he lay in his coffin. Also Kokarski's well-known picture of 'Marie-Antoinette in the Conciergerie,' and a drawing of Joséphine, by David.

More than eighty thousand pounds have been raised in Germany for a monument to Prince Bismarck, to be erected in Berlin. In view of the large sum at their disposal, the committee who have charge of the matter have endeavoured to obtain permission to erect an equestrian statue of the Prince, but so far without success. It is forbidden in Berlin

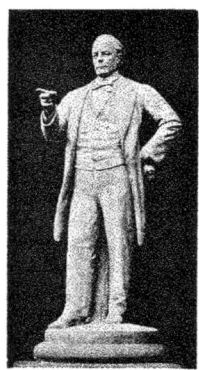

CHARLES BRADLAUGH, M.P.
FROM THE STATUE IN TERRA-COTTA
BY GEORGE TINWORTH.

to erect statues on horseback to persons not members of the Royal Family.

The widow of the late Frederick L. Ames, of Boston, U.S.A., has presented to the gallery of that city two paintings by Rembrandt, dated 1634, believed to be the portraits of Dr. Tulp and his wife. Mrs. Ames has also presented various objects of Persian and Japanese Art.

The statue of Mr. Bradlaugh, M.P., of which we give a small illustration, has just been erected in Northampton. The figure is by Mr. George Tinworth, carried out by Messrs. Doulton, of Lambeth, and is in that artist's favourite medium of terra-cotta. It is seven feet high, and with its pedestal reaches nearly sixteen feet in all. Mr. Bradlaugh is represented as he stood while addressing the House of Commons, and the likeness is excellent.

OBITUARY.

The death occurred on the 16th of June of Mr. William Calder Marshall, retired Royal Academician. Born at Edinburgh in 1813, he came to London at an early age, and studied sculpture under Bailey and Chantrey. He was elected Academician in 1852, and retired in 1890. The statues of Somers and Clarendon in the Houses of Parliament, and that of Dr. Jenner in Trafalgar Square, were executed by him.

The Director of the Academy of Fine Arts and of the Royal Museum of Painting in Madrid, Don Frederico Madrazo, died in June, at the age of seventy-nine. The deceased was court painter at Madrid, and studied under his father. He was a frequent exhibitor at the Paris Salons, where he received two first-class medals and the distinction of Commander of the Legion of Honour, and he occasionally sent pictures to our Royal Academy. His works are very numerous, many of them representing historical subjects, but his chief strength was in portrait painting. He is represented at Versailles by 'Godfrey de Bouillon proclaimed King of Jerusalem,' and other paintings. He was born at Rome, and is the father of the better-known Raimundo Madrazo, whose works are frequently to be seen in London at Messrs. Tooth's gallery.

One of the oldest of French artists, Jacques Léopold Loustau, died suddenly at Chevreuse on June 4th. He was a deaf mute, yet for many years exhibited at the Salon.

By the death of Mr. William Hart, on June 17th, at New York, aged seventy-one, America has lost a painter of some prominence.

The Paris painter, P. J. Mousset, died suddenly on the 30th of May, of congestion of the brain, whilst taking a Turkish bath at the well-known establishment in the Rue Auber.

An extraordinary report has been circulated in Paris that M. Henri Garnier, a well-known *marchand de tableaux*, has committed suicide. M. Garnier had acted as an agent for M. Chauchard, whose collection embraces Millet's 'Angelus.' His suicide is doubted, but in any case he has disappeared from Paris.

The death is announced, at Rome, on the 21st of May, of Scipio Vannutelli, Professor at the Institute of Fine Arts at Rome. Signor Vannutelli's works represent historical subjects, and have been exhibited in Germany, France, England, and America.

We give an illustration of a novel church decoration recently completed at Christ Church, Turnham Green. It is an altarpiece, of three trefoils, painted in monochrome on copper, representing the Entombment, Ascension, and Resurrection; and four pairs of quatrefoils which are painted in colour on canvas, and cemented to the wall. The subjects of these latter are appropriate Biblical parallels. The work has been executed by a parishioner, Captain E. H. Alleyne. There is a little tendency to angularity and stiffness in some of the figures, but the work deserves encouragement as a refined contribution to ecclesiastical decorative art.

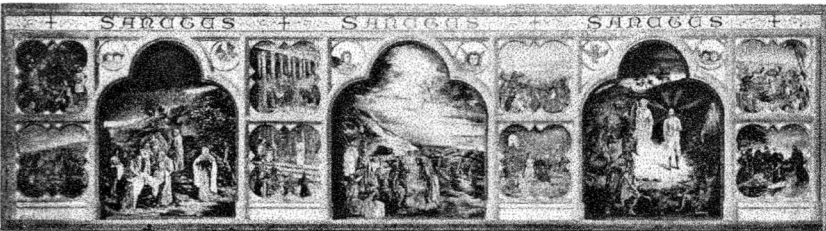

ALTAR-PIECE AT CHRIST CHURCH, TURNHAM GREEN. PAINTED BY CAPTAIN E. H. ALLEYNE.

RECENT ART PUBLICATIONS.

THE practice of the art of making drawings in black and white having so enormously increased, it was inevitable that books and handbooks on the best methods to produce such works should be published. First in the field is Mr. Henry Blackburn's well-printed "ART OF ILLUSTRATION" (W. H. Allen), wherein the compiler gives his views and opinions concerning black-and-white drawing when specially prepared for "process" reproduction. Mr. Blackburn does not take too exalted an aim, and in some cases he is content with the baldest facts, but he knows from experience what is best for ' process" work designed for illustrations, and he is willing to give his reader the full benefit of all he knows.

Mr. Blackburn thinks the early artists in monochrome worked in such a way that their productions are "misleading as to the principles on which modern process work is based." But we venture to point out that if an artist of the power of Holbein, Menzel, or Fortuny appeared now in England, process work would very soon conform to his requirements, and no one would dream of asking such an artist to change his technique. So far as Mr. Blackburn goes in this book he is an entirely safe guide. His volume is illustrated with nearly one hundred drawings, and the most of these are good examples of what is being done. One of the best is here given ' A Son of Pan,' by William Padgett. Doubtless Mr. Padgett would acknowledge his indebtedness to J. F. Millett, but the design is quite original, and the dignity and beauty of line are remarkable for a modern artist.

"THE THEORY AND PRACTICE OF DESIGN," by Frank G. Jackson (Chapman & Hall), " does not pretend," its author tells us, "to be a book *of* designs, but a book *on* design—not a picture book but a school text-book." Nevertheless, we expect in the illustrations of a book on Art something like artistic treatment and, failing it, we lose confidence in the taste of the writer. The various subjects to which Mr. Jackson devotes a brief chapter deserve each a separate text-book to itself; and to condense what has already been said on any one of them into a few pages, would tax the powers of a master of concise expression. Mr. Jackson, for all the enormous scope of his subject, finds occasion to tell us, *apropos* of the dragon, that " by some writers it is thought that the root from which the name is derived points to the probability of the term having been applied to meteors or shooting stars, which in early times were regarded as portents of disaster and evil," and otherwise to dwell upon subjects which have nothing to do with either the theory or the practice of design.

A portfolio of " Etchings of Biarritz " under the title of " Souvenirs du Pays Basque," is published " chez l'auteur à Biarritz," by M. Marcel D'Aubépine. They are very delicate little plates, etched with considerable success by an artist well known in France and in Spain. M. D'Aubépine exhibited in this year's Salon at Paris. Last year at Madrid, much admiration was testified in the interests of the etchings there

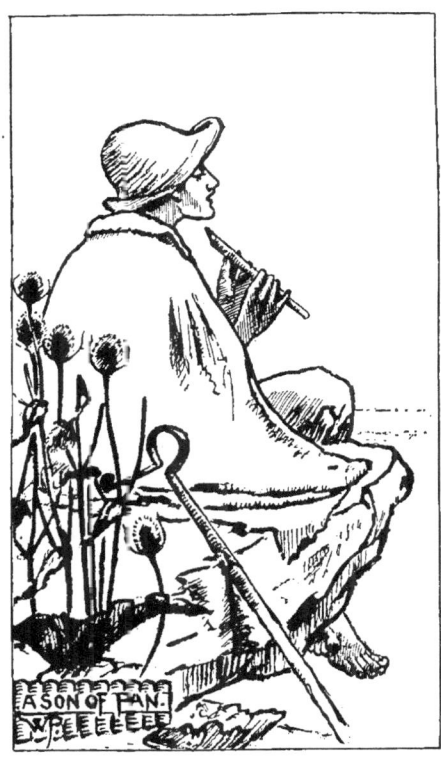

A SON OF PAN. BY WILLIAM PADGETT.

exhibited by this artist. M. D'Aubépine is decorated with various orders of merit in Spain and Portugal, and is President of some artistic French National Societies.

A good dictionary is as necessary in the studio as in the household, and for those who wish to possess a really excellent work of this kind we recommend " FUNK AND WAGNALL'S STANDARD DICTIONARY" (London : 44, Fleet Street). In two volumes, not over large in size, yet moderate in price, the editors have contrived to give not only the meanings of 280,000 words, but also their synonyms, and autonyms, with copious explanations by means of satisfactory engraved illustrations.

AT THE BRIDGE. BY J. MARIS.
FROM AN ETCHING BY ZILCHEN, PUBLISHED BY J. M. SCHALEKAMP, AMSTERDAM.

"WILD FLOWERS IN ART AND NATURE" (Edward Arnold) forms a series of artistic coloured reproductions, published under the superintendence of Mr. J. C. L. Sparks, of the National Art Training School. They are the best reproductions of their kind executed in England, and are well suited for use in advanced schools.

Under the title, 'The Old Strad,' Messrs. Jeffreys, of Newman Street, publish a reproduction of Mr. Lionel J. Cowen's picture, which represents a mender of violins carefully surveying a famous old fiddle. The subject is very well suited to reproduction in black and white, and being by the English firm, the Swan Electric Engraving Company, it is of special interest to those who watch the reproductive arts grouped under the term Photogravure.

Among the novelties for the sketching season brought in by Messrs. Reeves and Sons, is a clever combination of a sketching easel and oil colour box, which will be found useful for sketching out of doors, with canvases up to about 2 feet by 3 feet. It contains all that is required, arranged in the most convenient way, and the whole folds up rapidly and neatly into a portable size.

Appreciation of the great poet-artists of the modern Dutch School has been steadily growing during the last few years amongst the collectors in this country. The well-known publisher, J. M. Schalekamp, of Amsterdam, sends us the illustrated catalogue of his Art publications, etchings, photogravures, and photographs, which comprise reproductions of works by all the most important contemporary Dutch masters, such as Israëls, Jacob Maris, Anton Mauve, Bosboom, Apol, Mesdag, and Neuhuys. We are enabled to give a reproduction of an etching by Zilchen after a picture by J. Maris.

The attention of archæologists is called to a pamphlet on "THE CHRONOLOGY OF THE CATHEDRAL CHURCHES OF FRANCE," by Barr Ferree (New York, 231, Broadway). The author gives a table showing all the works executed in connection with French cathedrals during each century, and he specially asks for aid in correcting any errors that may be discovered. It is possible this table might be greatly enlarged, and profitably; but we do not think the compiler has made many mistakes.

The public are warned against George Williams, 292, Glyn Road, London, N.E., who circulates drawings, copies in black and white of newspaper illustrations. He sends a pitiful letter, with a drawing, which he leaves at houses in London suburbs. He avers he has been patronised by Sir Frederic Leighton. The Charity Organization Society have known him for seventeen years, and place him on their cautionary list.

Admirers of Bewick's "Birds" and "Quadrupeds" not already possessing copies ought to note that at present the market value of these charming books is very small. The low prices, however, are not likely to last, and the opportunity to acquire the *chefs d'œuvre* of the master of English wood engraving for a comparatively trifling sum will not probably occur again for many years.

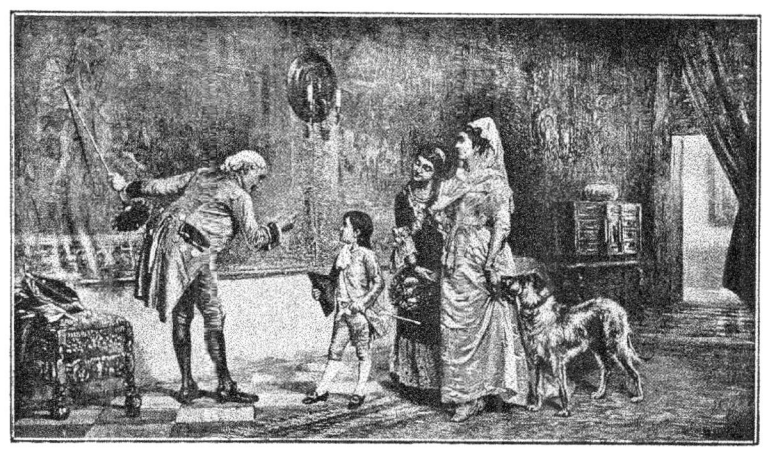

THE ANCESTOR ON THE TAPESTRY. BY J. HAYNES-WILLIAMS. THE PROPERTY OF THE CORPORATION OF LIVERPOOL.

THE WORK OF HAYNES-WILLIAMS.

THE ingenious and interesting, the industrious and gifted painter, to some slight study of whose work we address ourselves in the lines that are to follow, must be, I know, in the eyes of the cock-sure young man, who paints a little and dictates about Art, one of the most culpable of modern criminals. He tells tales upon canvas. The youths who, having no literary education, ask that pictorial Art shall be barren of all literary and of all human interest, have little tolerance, and absolutely no tenderness, for the painter or the critic who, with a wider vision than theirs, sees in Painting something beyond Decoration. But Mr. Haynes-Williams, like all his fellows in the past and in the present time, can afford to ignore the too boisterous and blatant presentation of the pedantic theory that claims to be "modern." Time is on his side. The fashions of the cock-sure young man, his sapient scorn for all pictorial story, will pass and be forgotten. "Art," so proclaims that inspired youth, "can only be concerned with the problems of colour and line." As well say that Literature can only be concerned with the dexterous formation of a sentence! Hogarth is against him; Rembrandt is against him; Raphael, whose "line" at least was irreproachable, and his contours the most soothing, is against him equally; and so are Tintoret and Veronese—colourists indeed; and all that wonderful family of seventeenth-century Dutchmen—Metsu and Terburg, Jan Steen and Van der Meer, whose brushwork, whose manipulation, whose sense of colour, illumination, tone, exacts, in his least bigoted moments, the admiration even of the "modern" himself. The cock-sure young man, who began by amusing, ends by simply boring us. Let him beware, lest we should listen no longer to his ineffectual sharpnesses. One suspects almost that the theory he espouses was invented by a greater than himself to excuse the limitations of a one-sided genius, like the fascinating genius of the late Albert Moore. It has all but had its day. It is consigned to a back seat— relapses into the dulness of the last fashion but one. The painter—as intelligent, unprejudiced folk now concede on every hand—the painter may tell a story. Nay, more—I

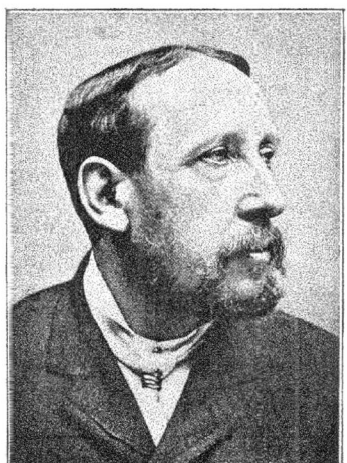

J. HAYNES-WILLIAMS.

OCTOBER, 1894

only fear that the next move in Art may recall the story-teller too absolutely to favour. The "advanced" of that moment will then be wanting, above all things, drama; the "modern" Williams can hold us by his masterly delineation of the long gallery; he can touch caressingly the fabrics of Marie-Antoinette's chamber; he can, without servile imitation, de-

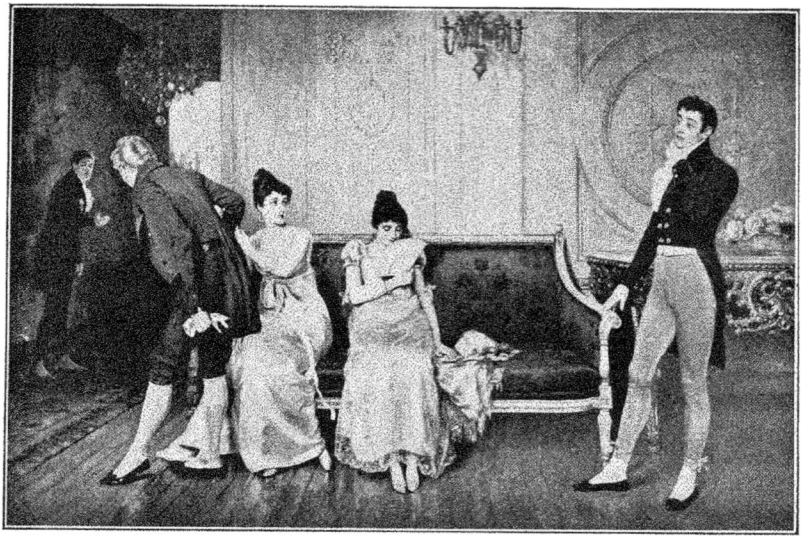

NOBLESSE OBLIGE. FROM THE PICTURE BY J. HAYNES-WILLIAMS. BY PERMISSION OF C. KLACKNER, ESQ.

of that particular day will rail only at the absence of narrative. That, as I greatly apprehend, may be the state of things to be brought about by the wheel's next turn. Meantime, I claim only for the painter, not Story's predominance, but the permission to be concerned with Story.

Mr. Haynes-Williams, in his different periods, has worked with somewhat different, but never incompatible aims; and though, as the illustrations that accompany this article sufficiently attest, he has treated Story with ability, it is true likewise that, if judged fairly, he must take high rank as a dexterous painter of beautiful objects, interiors that are exquisite, fabrics that are a luxury—as a painter, indeed, of that which in the widest sense may be called "still-life." Indeed, if Mr. Haynes-Williams could do nothing but tell us upon canvas humorous or emotional stories with ill-governed brush, he would not, we may be very certain, hold the place he now holds. I, for one, should never ask attention of any kind to his work. He deserves, and receives, no small degree of popularity, not because he tells stories, but because he tells them ably—with greater point than Mr. Marcus Stone, say, if sometimes with a little less than his distinction. He deserves a respect that is better than popularity, because, when he dispenses with stories altogether—as in his great Fontainebleau period—he can be occupied quite charmingly with the painter's craft by itself. Here, against him, Mr. Marcus Stone—whom I have chosen to take as a comparison—is not "in it" at all. With no incident passing, Mr. Haynes-

lightfully suggest the beauty of a vase of rock-crystal—one can look at it, even after the etchings of Jacquemart and the marvellous Desgoffe in the Luxembourg. An adroit twirl, with bits of colour snatched knowingly from the palette, and there shines the surface of satin, or, in the shadow, glows soberly the richness of tapestry. The treatment of these things results, moreover, not in "studies," but in pictures.

And here—with respect to Mr. Haynes-Williams's Fontainebleau subjects, and to his temporary residence in central France—I may be allowed a reminiscence, which to me personally attests, at all events, the success of that most happy episode in Mr. Haynes-Williams's artistic life. The Fontainebleau interiors—Mr. Haynes-Williams's series, exhibited at Goupil's—had always delighted me, and, gradually, looking at them and at the reproductions of them somewhat often, I had got to confuse, in a measure, the charm of the themes themselves with the charm of artistry with which Mr. Haynes-Williams had known how to endow them. Fontainebleau, as the most brilliant of its interpreters had represented it, had seemed to me quite an enchanted palace. Last spring—in the spring of last year, I mean—I was disillusioned. A stranger to that part of France for several years, I went down thither on a golden day, last April twelvemonth, from the white flare of Paris streets. The little town I found charming. The forest, green, romantic, rocky, *accidenté*, now bare with heath and fern, now rich and shadowy with oak trees, now silent in its leagues of waste land, its long roads now alive with the

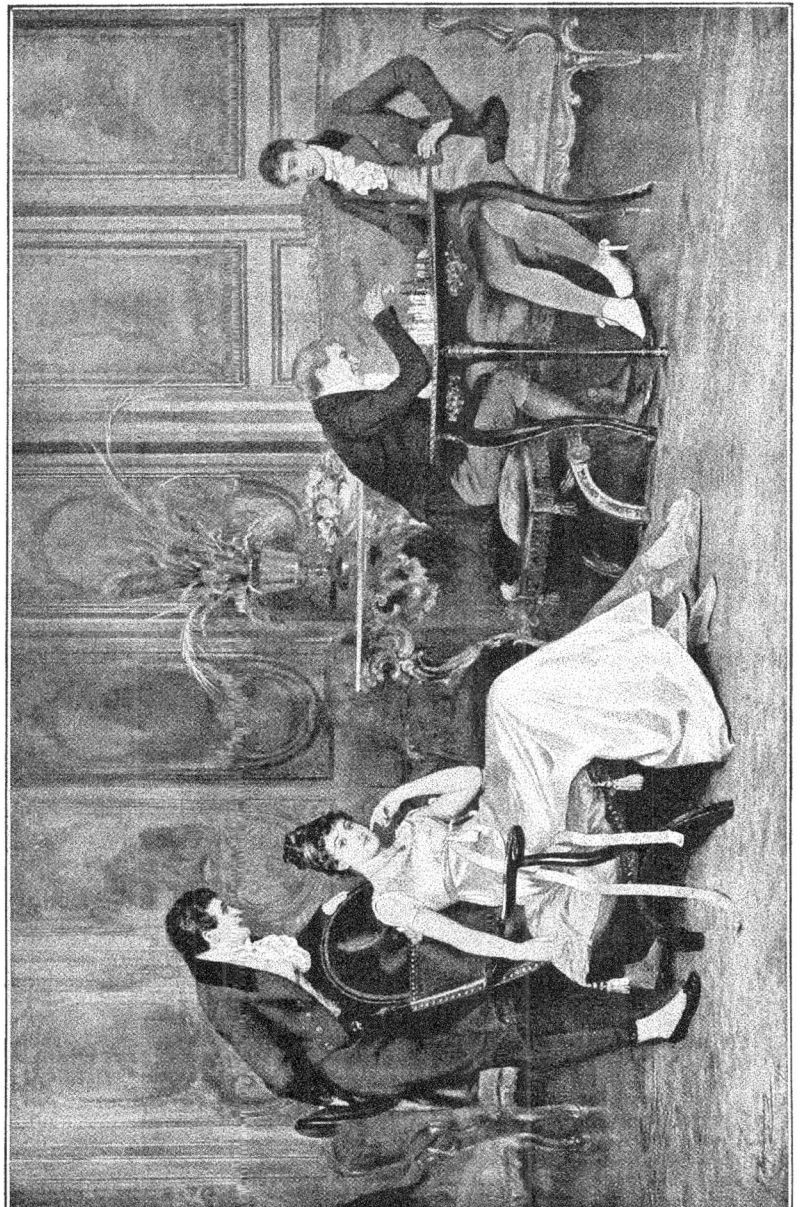

Losing. From the Picture by J. Haynes-Williams. In the possession of A. H. Harman, Esq.

march of cattle—so many Rousseaus, so many Troyons. And then, after the walk, the return to that pleasant hotel, where the people were so civil, and the weather so brilliant, that an extravagant *addition* for a modest breakfast seemed only a further courtesy no one could conceivably resent. And then, the visit to the Castle. How the charm was gone! The chambers so magnificent, but so material—dead matter, after all—with what a carnal attractiveness! The soul was somehow gone—the soul that had been caught, arrested, or infused, in Mr. Haynes-Williams's pictures. He had known—that experience showed me—he had known how to see, as well as how to pourtray. Like Fulleylove with Hampton Court, like James Holland with Venice, like Whistler with grey London, Mr. Haynes-Williams—faithful chronicler all the while—had known how to give as well as how to receive. He had fulfilled, how thoroughly! an artist's function—he had "put colour, poetising," in Mr. Browning's phrase. From the time that I saw Fontainebleau, last year, I had a higher opinion than before of Mr. Haynes-Williams's pictures.

From the Fontainebleau sojourn—I shall speak a little later of his earlier work—from the Fontainebleau sojourn dates, and is derived, Mr. Haynes-Williams's treatment of the Empire period. Familiar with those wonderful Fontainebleau interiors—in one of which, in his own pictorial dream, the Emperor himself sits by the fireplace—Mr. Haynes-Williams felt, doubtless, how rich, how varied, and how dignified was the background they afforded; and why not use them, or the like of them, with all their evidence of gentle life and of refined taste—this one or that as the occasion might require—as the appropriate background of some scene of blameless coquetry, of charming love-making, where, as in a picture by Orchardson, as in a drawing by Charles Green, the hero of romance is blameless and young, and is not endowed, after the literary fashion of these times of ours, with a wide experience and with fifty years, and where the heroine, whose soul Political Economy has never troubled, whose brains the insoluble and stupid social problems have never fretted or unhinged, who has never read Mr. Ibsen, and is too healthy to be plunged into the fanatic vulgarity of "Heavenly Twins," may blamelessly and naïvely accept the joys of a first fascination. This sort of scene, this sort of sentiment—now passing wholly from us, as the learned in such matters inform me—Mr. Haynes-Williams paints with real and restful appreciation of its elegance, of its grace—dare I add, of its naturalness?

A friend of this painter informs me that Haynes-Williams has been called "the novelist upon canvas." That is a title that many have sought for—before the days when it became quite wicked to be "literary"—and that few have earned. Well, I think Mr. Haynes-Williams *has* earned it. But his novel, be it understood, is not the sensation novel—Miss Braddon is as far from him as Charlotte Brontë, who invented the method in "Jane Eyre." Nor is his novel the psychological novel, in which, with Paul Bourget as the modern master of it, some neurotic Parisienne, over whom no wind of country life has ever refreshingly passed, dies in a stifling *salon*—of a rose in aromatic pain. Nor is his novel, like Mr. Henry James's, the novel of minutest analysis; nor is it big with romance, nor rich in Scottish character, nor burdened with an amateur theology that settles everything in Heaven and Earth to the satisfaction of the semi-educated. No; it recalls rather, when it is at its best, the wit of Peacock, the gentle satire of Jane Austen. Its affinities are with light

and graceful comedy. Look at 'Noblesse Oblige,' for instance,—how well-bred the people are, and yet the heart a little unruly, you see, under the pretty manners and the social obligations!

'Noblesse Oblige' was shown in 1891. 'Losing' was exhibited in 1893. It, too, is exceedingly effective. It is, indeed, highly ingenious, even if, as is possible, it may be in its expression a shade more obvious than the 'Noblesse Oblige' and other engaging canvases. These years, and several other recent ones, saw, too, the production of certain portraits, such as that of a robed and chain-wearing official, at the New Gallery of this present season; and that of the late Mr. George Critchett, the ophthalmic surgeon, and that, indeed, of Lord Lathom, portraits in which Mr. Haynes-Williams, not losing count of the likeness, has also aimed at very clearly, and has unaffectedly obtained, a result that is reasonably picturesque. Breadth of manner, richness of colour, and no little attention to *ensemble*, characterize such of the portraits by this painter as chance to have come under my eye.

But even in a more or less critical and "literary" notice of Mr. Haynes-Williams—a notice which leaves unsaid much of what the biographer would chronicle, and, I hope, absolutely everything that the interviewer would pounce upon—mention must be made of the existence of a group of quite important works more strictly dramatic, or pathetic, less at all events in the vein of comedy than those which —portraiture apart, and 'Fontainebleau' apart—have chiefly been mentioned; and that is the series of Spanish scenes, of which the exhibition, as far at least as the Royal Academy is concerned, dates from 1870. But eight years earlier than 1870 Mr. Haynes-Williams had first travelled to Spain, having gone there almost straight from a residence in the Midlands, in the earliest days in which he was devoted to painting. But before 1870 much of the work which he had executed had been of the nature of domestic *genre*, *genre* inspired by English theme, and Haynes-Williams was thirty-four years old before the Academy accepted his first Spanish subject. This, as I have said a moment since, was in 1870. Almost steadily from that time—practically without intermission save in the Fontainebleau period of 1887 and 1888—has the artist sent to Burlington House the more important of his works. Not least among them certainly was 'A los Toros,' exhibited in 1873, a picture very considerable in size and crowded with figures. In 1876 came 'The Ancestor on the Tapestry,' a telling popular invention bought by the Corporation of Liverpool, and in 1878 came 'Foundlings, Spain,' bought for the City of Melbourne. Here Mr. Haynes-Williams, having in previous pictures of Spanish and of old-world life been dramatic, pathetic, or vivid, allowed himself to be, perhaps above all things, piquant; for the Spanish foundlings presented to us in his picture are those who, under conditions of the very strictest propriety, engage in the unusual business of seeking for themselves husbands—a "marriage market" not comparable with any of Mayfair or of Bayswater, and not exactly to be thought of along with Mr. Edwin Long's. 'The Sermon' is another picture which with a great deal of seriousness cannot but admit a mixture of gentle humour. The preacher is not visible, but we see two or three rows of his listeners, and as we look upon the youthful cheek and the bronzed, upon young and old, upon peasant and soldier, and at the various receptions that are accorded—now of earnestness and now of indifference—to the word from the pulpit, it becomes evident that some indeed of the seed sown falls upon good ground and some upon "stony places, where they had not much earth.' Pictures like these, in which the observation of character, of foreign scene, of a world in part familiar, yet in part novel, enriches the purely pictorial interest, justify, of course if t ever required to be justified, the treatment of incident — the selection of the medium of paint, instead of the med um of writing, for the exposition of a given theme. It is not said for a moment that the medium of paint is the better one ; but that it is a permissible alternative.

In the Grosvenor Gallery, not many years ago, Mr. Haynes-Williams, in a simple, Paed-like subject, called 'Motherless,' boldly laid himself open to those shafts of ridicule which are directed from time to time by very "superior" people at the painter, perhaps even at the writer, who concerns himself with the record of earliest childhood. To these exalted beings the human infant appears ever in the light of a somewhat comic incident, a creature eccentric, abnormal, with whom only tolerant nurse or foolish parent can properly be concerned.

I have not been careful to inquire what they thought of Mr. Haynes-Williams's treatment of the sleeping child. Presumably it did not interest them, and I have myself forgotten—let the weakness be confessed—I have myself forgotten the actual picture. But any acquaintance with it that I may have previously enjoyed and then ignored, was renewed the other morning by means of a large photograph. Not "responding" for the colour, not occupied for the time with the brushwork, unable to assert whether or no the "touch" was "square," fashionable, and up-to-date, I may yet confidently utter an opinion on the goodness of the simple composition, on the naturalness of the "pose," on the likeness to sleeping childhood and solicitous girlhood which is conveyed so engagingly in 'Motherless.' The little deputy mother—an elder sister, one cannot doubt—grave, thoughtful, healthy, blonde, and sixteen, is surely one of the most charming of Mr. Haynes-Williams's figures. And to depict her so unfalteringly and so well, in her naïveté, her considerateness, and yet her inexperience, attests, at all events, the range of an artist's sympathies and of his observations, when it is remembered that that sympathy and observation had been wont to be directed to the portraiture of men of affairs, to the depicting of Southern comedy, almost of Southern vehemence, to the realisation—the idealisation even, as we have seen already—of noble interiors, in which History has been made, in which the lives of the great have been passed ; and, latterly, to the delicate seizure of the social comedy, to the fixing upon canvas of every episode of the discreet flirtation, of the sincere but fleeting *amour*. In 'Motherless,' with all its charm of constancy and abnegation, comes, after the smartness, say, of Peacock, and the elegance of Miss Austen, the homely Wordsworthian note.

FREDERICK WEDMORE.

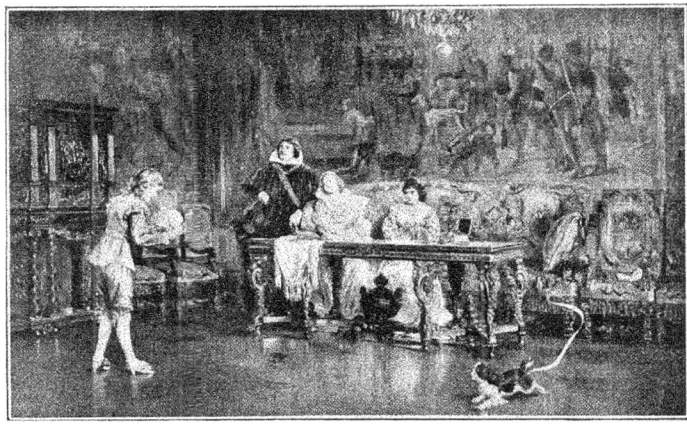

'FOR WHOM AND FROM WHOM?' BY J. HAYNES-WILLIAMS. IN THE POSSESSION OF SIR JOHN BLUNDELL MAPLE, M.P.

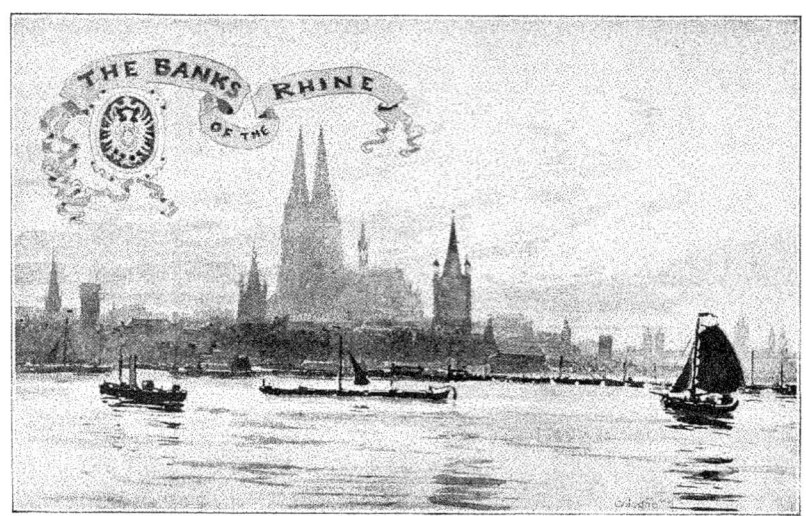

COLOGNE. DRAWN BY F. WILLIAMSON.

IN a quaint little handbook giving an account of a Continental ramble, the passage up the Rhine from Cologne to Mayence is delightfully compressed into the following:— "After leaving Bonn there is a constant succession of objects of interest, old castles, quaint towns, curious churches, terraced vine-clad hills, the whole region saturated with legend, and an excellent dinner on board the steamer for three marks." This, perhaps, fairly well epitomises the general idea that the steamboat traveller gets of the varied scenery through which he passes, perhaps too quickly, and with but an occasional chance of stopping and quietly enjoying any particular spot if he should desire so to do.

To the pedestrian, however, carrying the smallest possible impedimenta, a ramble along the river banks and country roads, following the river's many windings, and wandering at will through the curious old towns and villages studding its banks, offers a most delightful way of spending a week or two. The distances from town to town are for the most part but easy walks, and there is always the pleasurable certainty of a dinner and a "zimmer" at any place one may happen to reach.

Perhaps the greatest charm of the Rhine is in the notable variety and changes of the scenery along its banks. To start with, there are the grand architectural subjects given by the finely grouped buildings and skilfully designed towers of such cities as Cologne, Coblenz, and Mayence; the river spanned by the curious, but very useful, boat bridges, and the varied character of the boats continually passing up and down—from the broad, heavily built and elaborately decorated Dutch barges, with their great red or white sails and slow movements, harmonizing beautifully with the mediæval buildings; and the mellow air of antiquity which seems to pervade some of the old towns and villages, and pleasantly contrasting with the hurry and bustle of the numerous steam-tugs and passenger steamers, which seem now to consider the river their own. A little less in interest than the large cities are the smaller towns that stud the banks at intervals, on both sides of the river; for the most part very ancient and, in many instances, still partially enclosed by their mediæval walls and towers, surrounded by vine-clad hills, and generally with a ruined castle perched on the highest point in the neighbourhood. In some districts these castles form the most conspicuous features in the landscape, nearly every prominent hill seeming to have one upon it; they appear almost to be dotted about a little too liberally, for perchance you feel that you would like to take a closer interest in one of the old ruins, and you climb the hill to investigate, when, on nearly reaching the object of your ambition, you see perhaps two or even three more coming into view in the distance, and the spell is broken, and desire for investigation fails, and you go back once more to the fields and roads. These country roads are far from being uninteresting, for, besides the continually changing character of the landscape, every now and then you come across interesting little old shrines by the roadside, some containing perhaps the figure of a saint and a few faded flowers, others of a more pretentious character, with interiors painted like little chapels and with an altar and candles, and more rarely, one desecrated by dust and cobwebs. Now and then you may find, set up by the side of the road, a fine sculptured stone cross, as in our sketch near Niederbreisig, and in at least one of the villages is a crucifix, life-size, and painted most realistically.

On leaving Cologne on our ramble up the river, the first

stopping place is Königswinter, a little town lying at the foot of the Drachenfels, perhaps more noted for its comfortable hotels, than for its antiquity or picturesqueness. Crossing the ferry and taking the footpath along the river bank, several very fine views are obtained of the castled Drachenfels, and of the long range of what are called the Seven Mountains, but of which the peaks number at least thirty, stretching one after another for some eight or nine miles, nearly parallel with the Rhine. In about half an hour, we come to the beautifully wooded island of Nonnenwerth, with the turret and roof of the twelfth-century nunnery showing above the trees; and on our right are the steep wooded heights of Rolandseck.

A pleasant walk of a few miles along the bank and we reach the small town of Remagen, lying low in a bend of the river, its picturesque church-tower rising conspicuously above the town. In the distance, on the other side of the river, lies the town of Linz, partly surrounded by walls and towers, with beautifully wooded hills forming a background to the scene. For several miles beyond Remagen the ground near the river is rather flat. After crossing the bridge over the little stream of the Ahr, we are soon clattering through the streets of the little old town of Sinsig, which leaves on the memory a recollection chiefly of narrow streets, paved with large, uncomfortable

ruins of Hammerstein, we reach Andernach, one of the most ancient of the smaller towns. The mediæval walls and towers remaining nearly complete in places, the narrow streets and old houses, the late Romanesque church with its four towers, and the fine old watch-tower near the river, make the town one of considerable interest.

Beyond Andernach, the ground near the river is fairly flat and with not a great deal of interest until Coblenz is reached, and this, for beauty of surroundings, can vie with any other town on the Rhine; lying at the junction of the Moselle and the Rhine, the fortress of Ehrenbreitstein crowns the heights on the opposite side of the Rhine, which is crossed by the bridge of boats. The place has many interesting old houses and churches; of the latter, the basilican church of St. Castor, lying on the point of land at the junction of the two rivers, with its two rather flat western towers, is perhaps the most interesting. The grandly simple lines of its interior are finely enhanced with frescoes on the walls. The older parts of the town lie along the Moselle, spanned by a fine old fourteenth-century bridge of fourteen arches.

Near this bridge is the ancient Burg, a delightful building of yellowish stone, steep grey-slated roof, with rows of dormers, formerly the Archiepiscopal Palace, but now turned to more

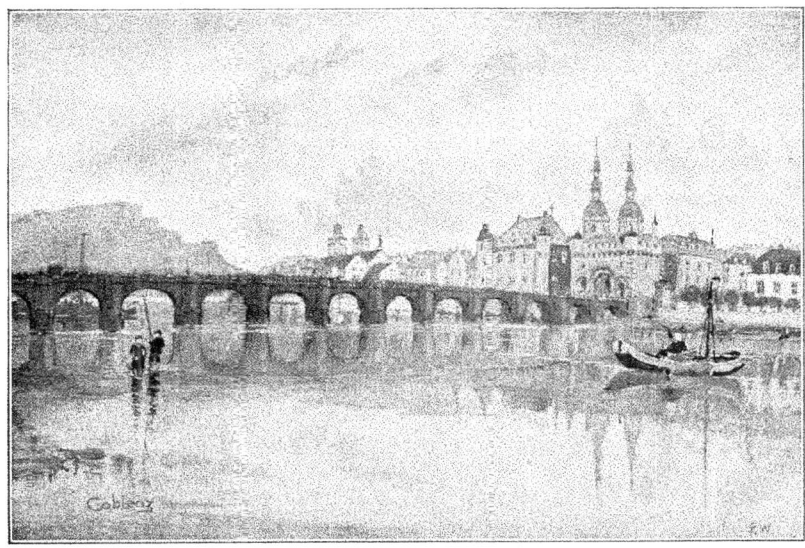

COBLENZ. DRAWN BY F. WILLIAMSON.

pebbles; it has, however, a beautiful late Romanesque church. A long straight road, fringed with apple-trees, leads through the fields, and passing the old wayside cross, we reach the village of Niederbreisig, and beyond this, on a finely wooded hill, stands the castle of Rheineck.

After a long walk through the fields lying low, between the hills and the river, and getting a passing glimpse of the grey

prosaic uses. Crossing the Rhine by the boat bridge, we continue our journey up the river by a footpath along the left bank. A little way after passing the second railway bridge, which crosses the river at a high level, the view becomes very romantic. The grassy path wanders under a row of tall poplars, growing by the side of the water, and we soon come to a very curious battering wall, with huge buttresses at intervals,

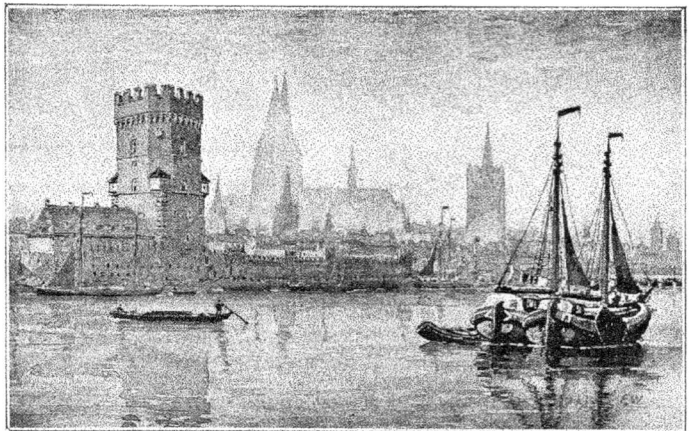

THE BAYERNTHURM, COLOGNE. DRAWN BY F. WILLIAMSON.

very ancient-looking and grey, seeming like the enclosing wall of the grounds of some old monastery. The scene, shut in by steep wooded hills on the opposite side of the river, gives quite an old-world impression; there are no sounds to be heard but the rippling of the stream and the quivering of the aspens, and no signs of human labour but this grey old wall, looking centuries old. But the scene quickly changes as we approach the mouth of the little river Lahn, passing the Romanesque church with tall square tower and grey pointed roof, standing quite alone among the trees at the bend of the river, a short distance from the quaint old-fashioned village of Niederlahnstein. Looking across the river we obtain a view of the royal castle of Stolzenfels, on the beautifully wooded heights above Capellan.

Crossing the Lahn, we soon pass through Oberlahnstein, some of its old walls and towers still standing, but rather ruthlessly cut through by the railway. Still following the path at the river's edge, a short walk brings us to the fine old castle of Marksburg, perched on a hill nearly five hundred feet above the river. At its base, nestling amidst trees and gardens, lies the little town of Braubach, of which the church has a quaintly designed tower. Beyond Marksburg, the road for several miles follows the many windings of the river, hemmed in on both sides by long ranges of undulating hills forming perhaps some of the wildest scenery on the Rhine.

After crossing the river by the ferry at Boppard, our road follows the right bank until St. Goar is reached. A little way, however, before reaching St. Goar, there is quite a Turneresque view, across the river, of a small town lying at the foot of a ravine between high hills, the church, with its typical Rhenish tower, and a few tall poplars by the water-side; a ruined castle crowns one of the hills above the town.

St. Goar itself is a curious little place, lying low on the river's bank and surrounded by hills, and on one stand the extensive ruins of Rheinfels. Across the river on the opposite hill is another castle, and at its foot the village of St. Goarhausen, consisting mainly of hotels and boarding-houses. There are several fine views from the neighbouring heights, but perhaps the most impressive scene is from the railway bank, a short distance below the town. On the wild rocky heights to the right are the Rheinfels ruins, and low

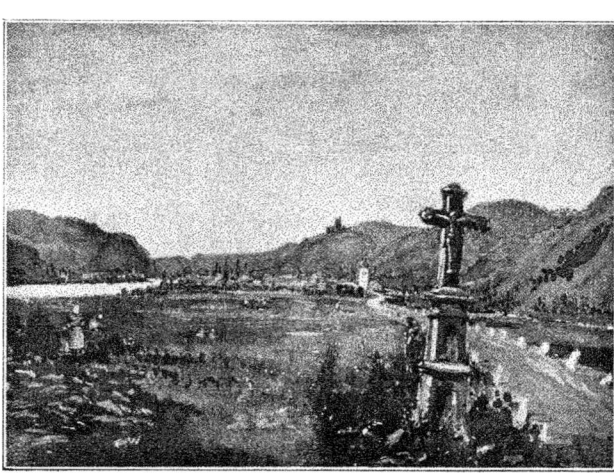

NEAR NIEDERBREISIG. DRAWN BY F. WILLIAMSON.

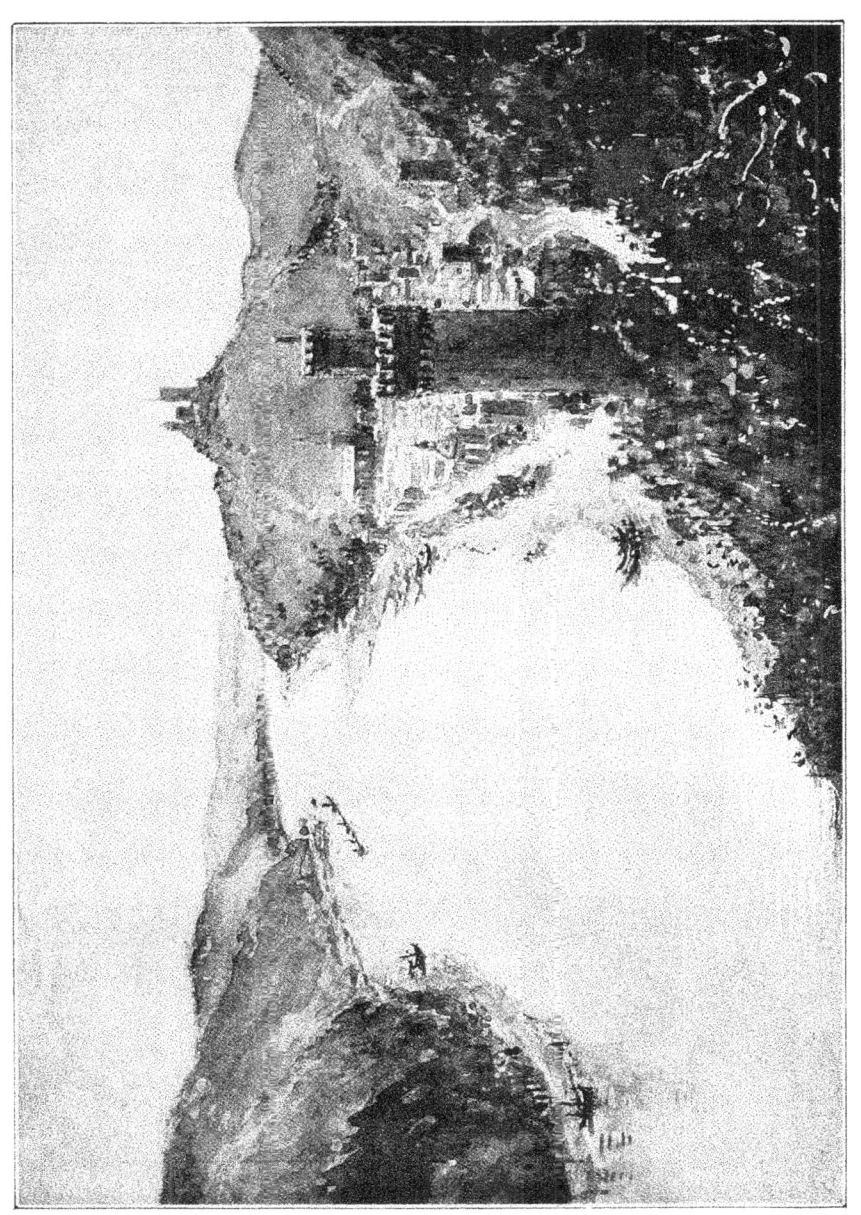

OBERWESEL ON THE RHINE. FROM A WATER-COLOUR DRAWING BY F. WILLIAMSON.

down in the hollow lies the little town, its church and tower standing well above the houses. Beyond is a fine series of receding hills, the river winding in serpentine curves between, St. Goarhausen and the Katz Castle forming a distant echo to St. Goar and the Rheinfels, for the foreground the winding road leading into the town, and a glorious group of poplars between it and the river.

A short distance above St. Goar, on the opposite side of the river, rises the legendary Lurlei rocks, and a couple of miles farther we reach Oberwesel, one of the loveliest spots on the Rhine.

Looking down upon it from the vineyards on the hill slopes in the bright early morning, it seems almost like a dream. The old town, delightful in the varied colours of its mellow walls and quaintly-shaped towers, its stately Frauenkirche, and the little chapel on the walls next the river, lies in one of the pleasantest spots imaginable, shut in and surrounded by beautiful hills covered with vineyards. On a wooded hill beyond the town rises the castle of Schonburg, its circular keep standing well above everything, and the broad-bosomed Rhine seeming almost to sleep as it glides along, so silent is it.

An hour's walk along the road, which is parallel with the river, brings us opposite Caub, another village with mediæval walls and towers. On a vine-clad hill at the back of the town rises the castle of Gutenfels, surrounded by battlemented walls and turrets, picturesquely following the rise and fall of the hill on which it stands.

On a reef of rocks, rising out of the middle of the river, nearly opposite Caub, stands the Pfalz, a mediæval river tollhouse, with its curious grey-turreted roofs. Still following the river banks for about a couple of miles, Bacharach is reached, a place full of interesting old work; beyond is the Templars' church, with its round choir next the street, the beautiful ruins of the church of St. Werner on a hill above the town, the tall pointed windows and arches looking, as seen from below, like a wonderful piece of lacework—these, with the old walls and towers, complete a scene which requires but a little imagination to realise the fifteenth century.

Leaving Bacharach it is a long afternoon's walk along the road by the river to Bingen. The scenery becomes less interesting; the lower hills are still covered with vineyards; one or two castles and the little Clemens-kapelle on the riverbank give variety to the scene. Just before reaching Bingen, however, the scenery gets wilder and more picturesque, and the river narrower and more rapid. Crossing the bridge over the river Nahe, which here joins the Rhine, nearly opposite being the ruins of Ehrenfels, we enter the little Hessian town of Bingen. The view from the quay at Bingen, looking across the river to Rudesheim, late in the afternoon, is very fine; its old towers and bright modern buildings of varied colours, with its background of low hills, lying bathed in the light of the setting sun, and being reflected in the shimmering waters of the Rhine, form a lovely gem-like picture. Between Bingen and Mayence the river wanders through a wide and fertile valley, the long, low hills on the left bank being mainly devoted to the wine industry, the success of which evidently accounts for the general air of prosperity and comfort of the several little towns, and the many well-groomed mansions and villas which are passed ere the city of Mayence is reached. F. WILLIAMSON.

THE CAPE OF GOOD HOPE ART GALLERY.

THE English school of painting stands marked out from the Continental school by its aversion to very large canvases, and (which is more regrettable) its distaste for great subjects. Once there was a third great school, Continental in its origin, but possessing many latent affinities with the coming English work—among them an intense nationality amounting (if one may use the word) to insularity. This was the school of Holland.

When the Dutch colonized South Africa, the school of Holland was in the zenith of its splendour; and it would have been no more than natural that the distinguished Dutch families who formed the early settlement, and whose descendants are the aristocracy of Africa at the present day, should have carried into their new homes not a few Wynants or Wouvermans, Mieris, Teniers, or Ruysdaels. Rumour says that this was, in fact, the case; and that numerous imported works of Art were carried up country, and hung for generations on the walls of farm-

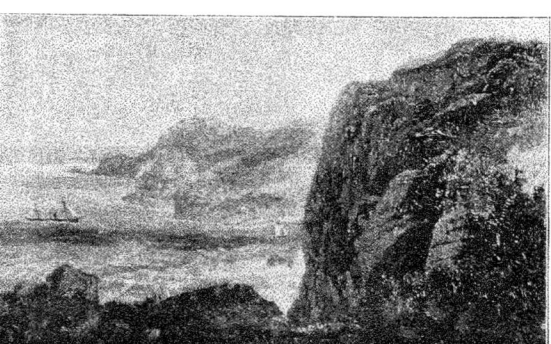

KNYSNA HEADS. BY A. DE SMIDT.

houses. Unfortunately, they are no longer to be found, either there or in the public collection of pictures. Exasperating stories are still told of how their undiscerning owners have, at different times, parted with them for an old song to travellers from Europe.

From one cause or another surprisingly few specimens of Dutch Art have found their way by gift or bequest to the Gallery of the Cape of Good Hope. In South Africa, as we must further remember, the gallery receives but little help from public funds. A Government Grant of £100 was received in 1880, which has since been increased to £200. By generous grants of public money there has been brought together at Sydney (under Mr. Montefiore's supervision) a very remarkable collection of drawings and pictures; and Melbourne has been as lavish as Sydney, although she has not as yet found a Montefiore. The more credit is due to Hobart and Capetown for the determination with which they have made their beginning unaided by large public funds.

Since the year 1871 an Association for the Promotion of the Fine Arts has existed at Cape Colony, which at the commencement occupied itself with holding loan exhibitions of works belonging to private owners with considerable success.

The origin of the present Art Gallery was a bequest in 1872, under the will of the late Mr. T. Butterworth Charles Bayley, of Cape Town, of his private collection of about thirty paintings. He appointed Mr. A. De Smidt (whose painting of the Knysna Heads is reproduced opposite) his trustee, and provided that a sum of £500 should be paid out of his estate towards the erection of a suitable building for housing the pictures, on the condition that a further sum of £1,500 should be raised by the Association for the Promotion of the Fine Arts within eighteen months of his decease. This amount, largely through the exertions of Mr. De Smidt, was duly raised, and a building formerly used as a school was purchased and fitted up as a Gallery, possessing class-rooms and a hall for an Educational Museum, at a cost of about £3,500.

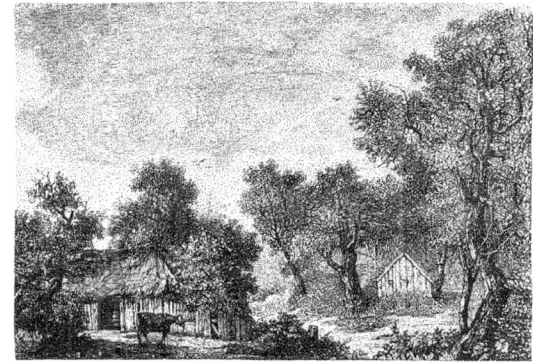

IN THE NEW FOREST. BY PATRICK NASMYTH.

The small collection bequeathed by Mr. Bayley has gradually increased by purchases and gifts. The Rev. G. Fisk was one of the largest donors. The Association has chiefly and successfully directed its efforts to the encouragement of the teaching of drawing; and the maintenance of the Art School and the expenses connected with Art examinations and exhibitions have absorbed the greater part of the funds

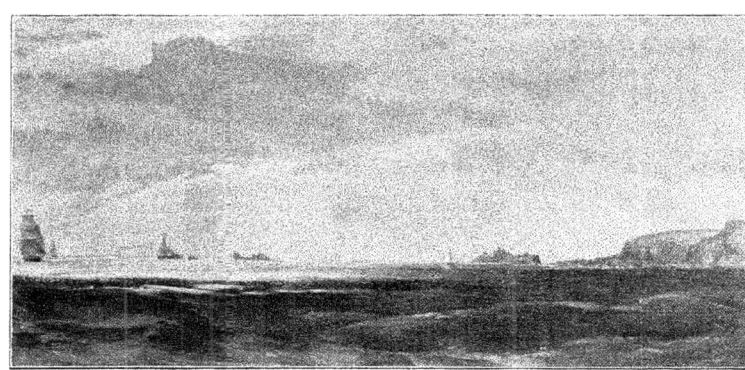

THE LAND'S END AND LONGSHIPS LIGHTHOUSE. BY E. R. LEE, R.A.

which might have been available for the purchase of pictures.

The collection consists of about three hundred drawings and paintings, with some signed photogravures of Mr. Alma Tadema's work. Funds have not permitted the Association to purchase as they could wish. The Customs' duty of twelve and-a-half per cent. *ad valorem* upon all works of Art admitted into the Colony is quite prohibitive so far as the purchase of valuable works from abroad is concerned; and it

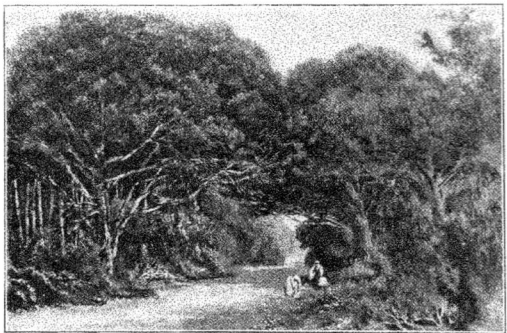

AVENUE AT NEWLANDS, NEAR CAPE TOWN. BY C. ROLANDO.

seems hard that the Government cannot make the concession of admitting, duty free, works of Art for the Colony's Public Gallery. The rooms are pleasant, and lighted from above, the pictures well hung and arranged. One passes an hour agreeably enough among them; and if the general effect is at first something like the day before a sale at Christie's when the season is not in full swing, there are many bits that one returns to with pleasure. Among these are two little Dutch interiors by Cornelius Bega dated 1664, and a 'Game of Cards' described as by Isaac van Ostade; but the latter ascription must not unprofitably be verified. The landscape modestly classed as "unknown" might pass muster as a Swaneveldt, and the portrait of himself by Van Strij, painted in 1770, is a very graceful and interesting piece of work.

A name once very familiar to visitors to the Royal Academy is that of F. R. Lee, R.A. It is not until one visits the Cape that one remembers that this once-popular Academician died there. Although Lee was born in the last century his collaborator, Mr. T. Sidney-Cooper, R.A: (the artist by association with whom Lee is best remembered in England), is still living. The last picture that Lee exhibited—'The Land's End and Longships Lighthouse,' illustrated overleaf—is in the possession of the Cape Gallery. It was painted in 1872 by Lee, working alone, and is a charming sea-piece with the pale familiar sunlight gleaming on the tumbling Channel sea. 'Youlstone,' near Lee's native town of Barnstaple, is the other specimen of his work here. There is also a capital example of H. Woods, A.R.A., purchased under the direction of Mr. Stirling Dyce.

In the anteroom are some welcome watercolours. Among them, in particular, are three which, if slight, are very characteristic. These are a blue Prout ('The Old Pier at Dover') —a brown Prout ('Bridge and Boats')—and a 'View of Eton' by Varley. The 'Scene in the New Forest,' with the proud signature "Patk. Nasmyth, 1827," is the most interesting of the British paintings; but (although it is comparatively a large canvas) it is by no means the most conspicuous picture in the Gallery. It is, in fact, overshadowed by a vast and appalling representation of the murder of Giuliano de Medici, which took the Heywood Gold Medal at Manchester. This picture has been accorded the further distinction of a commanding position in the Cape Gallery, and might now retire on its honours. 'A Beggar-boy' by Mulready is good for those who like beggar-boys by Mulready, and there is a small 'Ecce Homo' distressed and anæmic enough to be what it pretends to be, an Ary Scheffer.

But, after all, since there are no unrevealed glories of the Dutch school to be discovered at Cape Town, the most interesting works for an Englishman are those which render the varied and brilliant scenery of the Cape. There are many of these, the most successful being by Mr. De Smidt and an Italian of the name of Rolando. The latter was at his best in simple scenes like the 'Avenue at Newlands,' illustrated above, where he was not tempted to indulge his imagination. Mr. De Smidt did better, and in his 'Knysna Heads' and similar drawings has done a good deal towards enabling us to realise the possibilities of Cape scenery. It is a rich field, and almost a virgin field. Hardly anybody except Miss North (who chiefly painted flowers) has attempted to open it up. The fat loamy meadows where in winter time the arum lilies blow in the ditches, the broad red roads plunging from dazzling sunlight into coolest shadow, the heath that reminds one of Shere, the glen that recalls Fairlight, the turquoise sky, the thicket of masts in the Roads, the wondrous Table and Tablecloth—all these await their interpreter.

F. L.

'THE VIRGIN OF THE ROCKS' IN THE NATIONAL GALLERY.

"CORRUPTIO OPTIMI PESSIMA."

MY critical researches concerning 'The Virgin of the Rocks' in the June number of this Journal, dealt with questions that have been discussed and decided in a nearly contemporary Italian publication in an exactly similar sense. Signor Gustavo Frizzoni, the Milanese critic, well known as a thorough connoisseur of the Art of the Italian Renaissance, has in the *Archivio Storico dell' Arte* (Anno VII. fasc. 1), expressed himself to the effect that both external and internal evidence combine to place it beyond a doubt that the original picture painted by Leonardo is in the Louvre, while the 'Replica' in the National Gallery in London can only be regarded as a school-piece: " Come non riconoscere infatti nell' esemplare del Louvre la sovrana finezza e perfezione d'indole tutta Toscana, nell' altro invece una edizione posteriore d'impronta Lombarda, eseguita quindi da qualche allievo in Milano?"

In my explanation of the recently discovered document, of which the point is that Leonardo refused to deliver the original picture because the price offered for it was much too small, and did not even rest upon a valuation, I had assumed that Leonardo's petition succeeded, and that in return for the delivery of a copy of inferior value, he had not been deprived of the liberty to dispose of the original on more favourable terms in another quarter. On the other hand, Signor Frizzoni supposes that the original now in Paris may quite possibly at the outset have been placed in the church of S. Francesco at Milan, and that Francis I. acquired i from the church itself about twenty years later, on which occasion the copy now in London would have been made. The two pictures measured without the frame agree pretty closely in their dimensions. The Louvre example is about three inches higher and one inch broader than the one in London. Both pictures are painted on panel; but that in the Louvre was later transferred to canvas, which easily explains the slight difference in the dimensions. It is, therefore, perfectly possible that the London copy may have been put into the frame of the original, until the latter passed from the church of S. Francesco into the collection of Francis I. The close agreement in the dimensions is certainly remarkable, and, indeed, can only be explained on some such hypothesis as my own or that of Signor Frizzoni.

The sudden appearance of the duplicate copy recalls a similar case which also gave rise to minute and searching discussion. In the Dresden Gallery there is a picture, much admired and long attributed to Holbein, known as the 'Madonna of the Burgomaster Meyer.' The former keeper of the National Gallery, Mr. R. Wornum, was, so far as I know, the first to produce the proof that the Dresden picture is a copy, while the original is to be found in possession of the Grand Duke of Hesse in Darmstadt. This is now plainly stated even in the official catalogue of the Dresden Gallery, where the remark is made that in the case of a votive picture of this kind the assumption of a repetition from the master's own hand is antecedently improbable. I can only repeat what Eug. Müntz says in the conclusion of his "Studj Leonardeschi" (*Archivio Storico dell'Arte*, Anno V. [1892], fasc. 1):—"The differences between the example of the Vierge aux Rochers' in Paris and that in London are precisely the same as those between the two Madonna pictures by Holbein in Darmstadt and Dresden. The former picture, the original, is more archaic, more severe, but at the same time more expressive; the latter, the copy, is freer and more elegant."

In the latest edition of the Louvre Catalogue by Lafenestre and Richtenberger, it is said (p. 96): " Une excellente copie, avec quelques variantes, qu'on a regardée quelquefois comme un original, se trouve, depuis 1880, à la National Gallery de Londres. Cette dernière toile, qui ornait la chapelle des Franciscains à Milan, était déjà considérée comme une copie en 1796, lorsqu'elle fut achetée 30 ducats par le peintre Hamilton, qui la revendit au Comte de Suffolk."

If, then, it is permitted to such writers as Frizzoni, E. Müntz, Lafenestre, and others, to call the Leonardesque picture in the National Gallery a copy, I venture to think that I may do the same, although neither Sir Frederick Burton, the former director of the National Gallery, in his reply in the *Nineteenth Century*, nor Mr. Poynter, the present director, in his article on the picture in the August number of THE ART JOURNAL, thinks it right.

In the whole range of Italian Art I have never yet met with two pictures from the hand of the same master which resembled one another so closely in composition as the two under discussion in London and Paris, and were yet universally recognised as by the same hand. The same holds good of German, Dutch, Flemish, and of every other great Art in the pre-Academic period. Moreover, I believe I am correct in stating that at that time copies reproducing all the details of the original were rarely, if ever, made. It is true that

1894

artists of small imagination repeated their motives, and even their compositions; nevertheless, in all such cases they entirely altered certain details—such, for instance, as the landscape background. In this connection I will only recall the Madonna-pictures of Cesare da Sesto, in possession of the Marquis of Bute, and in the Brera, which closely resemble one another with the exception of their entirely different landscape backgrounds. Cases of this sort occur frequently in the work of painters of the second and third rank. It is perfectly possible, therefore, that from the point of view of a modern painter I may have been wrong to call—as I still call —the 'Vierge aux Rochers' in the National Gallery a copy or a replica of the original in the Louvre; nevertheless, seeing that my critical inquiries were from the first to last confined to the older or historical art, I think that I may be allowed to employ the terms in use at that period, without incurring any special reproach. From this standpoint it seems arbitrary to lay stress upon such a detail as the turn of the head in the angel—who in the Louvre picture looks round at the spectators, while in the London example he gazes straight in front with a certain silliness of expression—and to assert that it " entirely recasts the original (!) scheme," and " involves a profound change in the meaning of the whole."

My opinion of Lomazzo as an authority in favour of the London picture I am unable to alter, in spite of everything that has been said in his praise, when I again take up the works of his well-meaning but limited gossip. As a matter of fact, Vasari, whose works appeared before Lomazzo, managed to bring together in the few weeks which he spent in Lombardy incomparably more valuable material for the history of Lombard art than the contemplative Lomazzo in the course of his whole life. Lomazzo is a first-rate example of the *spirito di campanile* in history. On the other hand, I must here acknowledge that I did the worthy Bianconi— who a hundred and seven years ago wrote an indifferent "Nuova Guida di Milano"—an injustice when I stated that he referred to the picture in S. Francesco as a copy. I was misled by E. Motta's short and not easily intelligible quotation from this rare book. However, the utterances of such late scribblers have no importance for art criticism, whether in one sense or in the other. In cases like the present it is upon *internal evidence* that the decision must rest. It was a great pleasure and surprise to me to observe in Mr. Poynter's essay upon the picture ascribed to Leonardo in the National Gallery, that it is precisely those parts where I most miss the master's characteristic style that he describes as " obviously the mere daub of a picture-restorer." "The flowers in the foreground and of the upper part of the background" appear to him too to be " the work of a heavier hand," and he " would not pretend that they are Leonardo's work." He even goes so far as to assert: " My impression of the picture generally is . . . . that it was left unfinished and completed by another hand." The figure of S. John he describes as "finished badly by an inferior artist; the hair also repainted in parts."

If then he really thinks so, I maintain that it is the duty of the authorities to see that all the ugly repaints are removed. For artists and laymen alike could not be in doubt for a single instant as to its being unjustifiable to allow the original painting from the hand of such a master as Leonardo, and in such a valuable work, to lie concealed behind the disfiguring mask of a restorer, and thus hidden from sight in a public gallery.

J. P. RICHTER.

ART AT GUILDHALL.

UNTIL about the middle of the seventeenth century the Corporation of London had associated itself, so far as the records show, in no degree with Art. Not that Art was unknown within the precincts of the City before that time, for two of the Livery Companies of London — the Barbers and the Surgeons — had looked to Art to commemorate their combination as a single body, and had engaged Hans Holbein, the younger, to portray the granting to them of their new charter by Henry VIII. This was about the year 1541, and the picture being, it is said, the largest the artist ever painted — six feet in height and over ten feet in length — hangs now in the Company's banqueting-hall in Monkwell Street, City, a noble example of the master, and a lasting testimony of the taste and sagacity of the Companies' representatives of that time.

It may be said to have been more by accident than by deliberate intention that pictures were first seen at the Guildhall of the City. The fire of London in 1666 so obliterated the landmarks of property, and led consequently to so many difficulties between landlord and tenant, that the work of adjusting the various claims and contentions was naturally of great magnitude; and to this work the judges of the land, in association with the Corporation, addressed themselves, and accomplished their task so much to the satisfaction of the citizens that the Corporation put on lasting record its sense of their work, by ordering their portraits to "be taken by a skilful hand and be kept in some public place of the City for a grateful memorial of their good offices." The phrase, " by a skilful hand," is sufficient to show that it was not so much works of art which were desired, as faithful representations of the men, and this is more than ever apparent in the selection of the artist. Sir Peter Lely was the painter originally intended, but this distinguished artist was either too independent, or too deeply occupied, to take the trouble of waiting on the judges at their respective chambers for the purpose. There appears to be no evidence that any particular pressure was put upon this painter or any exceptional inducement offered to him to undertake the work, and the matter was soon determined in a curiously commercial manner by several of the better-known portrait painters of the day being invited to tender for the work, and, in the end, one J. Michael Wright was selected, and he executed most of the twenty-two portraits at a cost of £36 each. Framed in dark wooden frames, with the armorial bearings of each judge thereon, these historical portraits, deficient in quality, but fair work according to the standard of the day, are now at Guildhall in the old council chamber of the Corporation, having formerly adorned, with much solemnity, the old courts of Queen's Bench and Common Pleas when these courts sat at the Guildhall, and earlier still been ranged, according to old pictures of the time, on the stately walls of the great hall itself.

Some fifteen years later, in 1682, Jan Van der Vaart, who had recently come to England from Haarlem, and who ultimately became a mezzotint engraver, was commissioned by the Corporation to paint the portraits of William III. and Mary, which now hang in the library of the Guildhall. It appears that some fanatical person had seriously damaged a portrait of the then Duke of York by cutting off the legs. This portrait was then hanging in the great hall, but has since entirely disappeared. The Lord Mayor and aldermen offered a reward of £500 for the detection of the offender, and by way of retaliation the above-named portrait of William was defaced, the crown, globe, and sceptre being cut away. Although records show that a certain John Fletcher was committed to Newgate for boasting at Hertford that "he did mangle and cut King William's picture in

BANQUET IN GUILDHALL, 1814. BY WILLIAM DANIELL, R.A.

Guildhall," there is nothing to show that he was the actual offender. At the commencement of the eighteenth century,

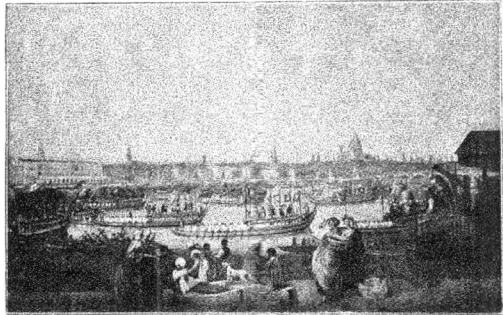

THE LORD MAYOR GOING BY WATER TO WESTMINSTER. BY F. WHEATLEY, R.A., AND R. PATON

portraits of George I. and George II. and of Queen Caroline were added, the first named being by Sir Godfrey Kneller, and a curious record exists, date 1723, of permission being given by the Corporation for the two last-named portraits to be put in a better frame than usual, the extraordinary charge thereof to be repaid the artist out of the Chamber of London.

At this time the first of our great English painters, William Hogarth, born in the city of London, was rapidly making his reputation, and during the next succeeding years Reynolds and Gainsborough were developing their brilliant powers in portraiture. In desiring the portrait of a great man it is not surprising that the Corporation are seen to be conscious of the growing interest in Art to which the country was becoming awakened by the achievements of these talented painters, nor is it unreasonable to assume that many individual members of that body took personal interest in the study and beauty of the works of these men, for evidence of this is apparent in the Corporation's next step in regard to Art. It desired to preserve the memory of a notable man of the time, Sir Charles Pratt, who, in his capacity of Chief Justice of the Common Pleas, decided against the legality of the general warrants directed by the Government against John Wilkes. The Corporation requested Sir Charles Pratt to sit for his portrait, and commissioned Sir Joshua Reynolds to paint it; and as illustrating the formality of the time, the famous painter attended at the bar of the Court of Common Council to receive the commission in 1764. The portrait is a vigorous and dignified composition, full-length, life-size, in a judge's red gown and ermine trimming, and hangs now in the Guildhall Art Gallery, having formerly occupied a place opposite the judge's bench in the old Court of Exchequer, now pulled down.

Some twenty years later the country was moved in its concern for the safety of the fortress of Gibraltar, which for four years had been laid in siege by France and Spain. Floating batteries were directed against the rock by the Spaniards, and these were finally defeated, 13th September, 1782, with immense loss of life. In the course of the repulse a detachment of British seamen at enormous risk rescued many of their enemies from the burning batteries. This scene the Corporation, for the honour of their country, resolved to place on record, and it commissioned John Singleton Copley to execute a large painting illustrative of the scene. The finished study for this is now in the National Gallery, and various sketches for it are in the South Kensington Museum, while the picture itself, measuring eighteen feet in height by twenty-four feet in width, hangs in the Guildhall Art Gallery, a splendid example of the painter's power of design, and of his grasp of a momentous scene composed of many moving figures. £1,543 was paid for the picture. It occupied for nearly a century the entire eastern wall of the old council chamber.

In 1790, two years before Reynolds's death, the Corporation became possessed, in an interesting way, of one of the finest examples of his male portraits, and of this we give an illustration. There was employed in the Chamber of London one Thomas Tomkins, a noted caligrapher, whose beautiful productions in ornamental penmanship, with its accessories of emblazoned heraldry, are seen in many of the honorary freedoms and addresses voted by the Corporation to illustrious personages. Tomkins was personally attached to the then Chamberlain John Wilkes, and to show his regard for Tomkins, Wilkes had his portrait painted for the Chamberlain's office, paying Reynolds £50 for it; the record in the artist's ledger being "February, 1790, Mr. Tomkins, writing master, £50." On the establishment of the Art Gallery it was removed thither, where it constitutes one of the chief

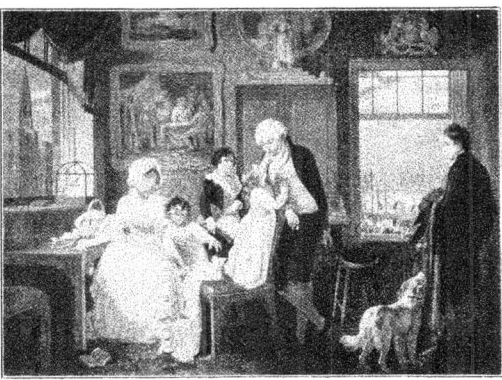

INDUSTRY AND PRUDENCE. BY ROBERT SMIRKE, R.A.

works of the collection. We now come to 1793, when a liberal gift of twenty-four oil paintings was made to the Corporation by John Boydell, an engraver and a publisher of engravings. He was a man whose liberality to artists gained for him a high reputation as an Art patron. He was the founder of the firm of Henry Graves & Co., of Pall Mall, and was Lord Mayor in 1790. Eight of the canvases comprised in the gift were three-quarter-length portraits, painted by the chief painters of the day, of the illustrious military and naval commanders of the time, Lords Heathfield, Rodney, Cornwallis, Nelson, Duncan, Howe, Hood and St. Vincent, all of whom, with the exception of the first-named, had attended at Guildhall, at one time or another, and received the Honorary Freedom of the City, either in a gold box or with a sword of honour. Nelson attended twice, once after Santa Cruz, when he received the freedom and a gold box, and secondly after the Battle of the Nile, when a sword of honour was presented to him. The best of these portraits—all, be it said, in full military or naval uniform—

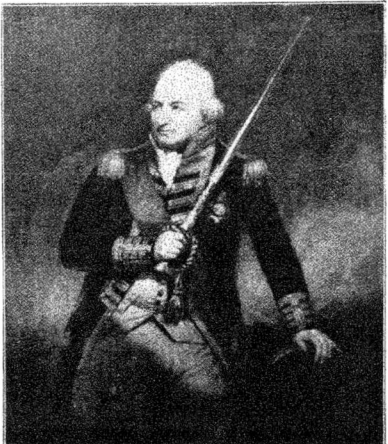

LORD ST. VINCENT. BY SIR WILLIAM BEECHEY, R.A.

are those of Lord St. Vincent, by Sir William Beechey, which we illustrate, and Lord Cornwallis by Copley; both are spirited in expression and rich in colour. It seems that the original of Lord Howe by Northcote was allowed, curiously enough, to go to decay, and the present portrait is a copy, the best that could be made of it by George Kirtland. The portrait of Lord Heathfield is also a copy, but a very excellent one, the original by Sir Joshua Reynolds being in the National collection.

Of the subject pictures given by Boydell, the most notable in point of art are the 'Murder of Rizzio,' and the 'Assassination of James I. of Scotland,' by John Opie, and the 'Death of Wat Tyler,' by Northcote; while an interesting picture of the Lord Mayor going in procession by water to Westminster (illustrated on the previous page), preserves a record of one of the old city customs, now discontinued. 'The Mayoralty Oath being administered to Lord Mayor Newnham in 1782,' is also an interesting work, artistically, showing a faculty for skilful grouping. It is ascribed to William Miller, who flourished at the end of the last century, but by some it is deemed to be by Copley; without doubt the composition is

worthy of that distinguished artist, but the technique of the painting lays it open to doubt as to its being a work of his. The picture by Robert Smirke of 'Industry and Prudence' (of which we give a small reproduction), was probably a commission by Boydell. A successful London merchant is in the presence of his family; the evidence of his success is suggested by the alderman's scarlet robe which a servant is holding for him; through the open window is seen the Thames with its busy shipping, and beyond it the city of a century ago.

In acknowledgment of this gift of Boydell's, the City commissioned Sir William Beechey to paint his portrait, and this, a full-length, life-size, now hangs in the Corporation gallery.

A few years later (1808), that painter of colossal pictures, Sir Robert Ker Porter, presented to the Corporation his large painting of 'The Battle of Agincourt.' This canvas, some 50 feet in length by 20 in height, has long since been in a state of decay, and now lies rolled up, beyond renovation, in the crypt of the Guildhall.

In 1814 the Czar Nicholas of Russia and the King of Prussia dined in the Guildhall, and a picture of the banquet was painted by William Daniell, R.A., and purchased by the Corporation. While the work itself, as may be seen in our reproduction, possesses no great artistic value, the painting has placed on record that which is of an extremely interesting character, viz., the hall as it was, with its flat roof, its red-draped galleries occupied by ladies, its large chandeliers of wax candles, and its series of flags and banners standing out horizontally from the walls; nineteen standards and forty-six colours which were presented to the City by Queen Anne to commemorate the victory of the Duke of Marlborough over the French and Bavarians at Ramilies, in Flanders. No other representation in colour is known of a scene such as this.

In 1820, the City was the recipient of two portraits, the gift of Queen Caroline—one of herself, the other of the Princess Charlotte, both by James Lonsdale, an old student of Romney and one of the founders of the Royal Society of British Artists. The frames of both are surmounted by a crown, but the portraits themselves, although not unpleasant in colour, cannot rank as important works of Art, either in composition or technique, although that of the Princess presents a certain degree of grace.

Other portraits soon after were added to the Corporation collection, notably among them being that of Richard Clark in 1825, by Sir Thomas Lawrence, a three-quarter-length, carefully painted throughout. This was a commission from the Corporation, the cost being £400.

In 1839, Royalty appeared once again on the scene in our present Queen, who being then at the age of twenty, presented a full-length portrait of herself seated on the throne in the House of Lords, by Sir George Hayter, who at the date of the portrait held the appointment of portrait painter to her Majesty. Five years later Louis Philippe of France commemorated the presentation of an Address to him by the Corporation, by having the ceremony painted. The work was entrusted to Jean Alaux, an old pupil of Ary Scheffer and Delacroix and the painter of several frescoes in the Louvre and Luxembourg. The picture was presented to the Corporation by the King. It is a composition of many figures and is thirteen feet in height by eighteen in width, and was for some time in the Art gallery, but now hangs in the lobby of the council chamber.

The Great Exhibition of 1851 proved a stimulus to Art throughout the country, and the Corporation, with a view of

ART AT GUILDHALL

encouraging Art, voted the sum of £10,000 for the purchase of seventeen pieces of statuary by the leading sculptors of this country. These now adorn the banqueting-hall of the Mansion House, and rank among them some of the masterpieces of Weekes, Foley, Theed, Westmacott, Bailey, and McDowell, all eminent men in their day. The most imposing piece is perhaps the figure of Sardanapalus, by Weekes, the cup high in his uplifted hand—

> "I've not forgot the custom ; and although alone
> Will drain one draught in memory of many
> A joyous banquet past."

While speaking of sculpture it should be observed that the Corporation has recognised this branch of the Fine Arts in a wider degree than it has done the sister art of painting. The great hall has been embellished from time to time since the middle of the last century by imposing groups in marble as monuments to Nelson, Wellington, William Pitt and others. In 1811 it commissioned Sir Francis Chantrey to execute a full-length statue of George III., which now stands in the council chamber, and paid him £3,000 for the work, while over a score of busts of distinguished public men have been executed for the Corporation during the last forty years, Woolner, Noble, Behnes and other prominent men ranking among the sculptors employed. For work in marble the Corporation have expended over £50,000. The latest commission, which has been executed by Mr. F. J. Williamson, of Esher; is that of a bust of Tennyson.

To return to the paintings. In 1865, at a time when the great philanthropist George Peabody was bestowing large sums of money for the benefit of the poor, a Mr. Philip Cazenove presented a full-length portrait of Mr. Peabody by H. W. Pickersgill, R.A., and a year or two later Sir David Salomons gave some seventy pencil drawings by E. W. Cooke, R.A., of old London Bridge, and the rebuilding of the present bridge. These are all very carefully executed with a truthfulness that makes them valuable as records of the past and delightful as finished works of Art. Similar in subject, but differing in treatment, are two large water-colour drawings of the new bridge under construction, painted by George Scharf. These also are interesting works at this date, and valuable topographically, apart from their artistic qualities, which are excellent. In 1877, two good examples of David Roberts were added to the Corporation's collection, 'Antwerp Cathedral,' and 'The Interior of the Church of St. Stephen, Vienna'; both are fine examples of architectural drawing, and in the case of the last-named, while the architectural details in all their intricacy are firmly dealt with, one is conscious less of the labour and application which their execution must have demanded than of the sense of space and the solemnity which the painter has conveyed. Following these came ten miniatures by John S. Stump, bequeathed by Mr. F. W. Daniels, interesting both historically and as works of Art, for they included portraits of Edmund Kean and his son Charles, Mesdames Pasta and Grisi, and Maria Foote, Countess of Harrington. All of the abovementioned works, many of them meritorious as works of Art, and many lacking in merit, were at this time scattered about in the various apartments in the Guildhall, and the time was arriving when a selection of them was to be brought together to constitute a gallery, to which the public, who hitherto had had very restricted access to them, should find the best of them freely accessible.

This gallery was established in 1886, and its career from that date to the present time we propose to deal with in a subsequent chapter.

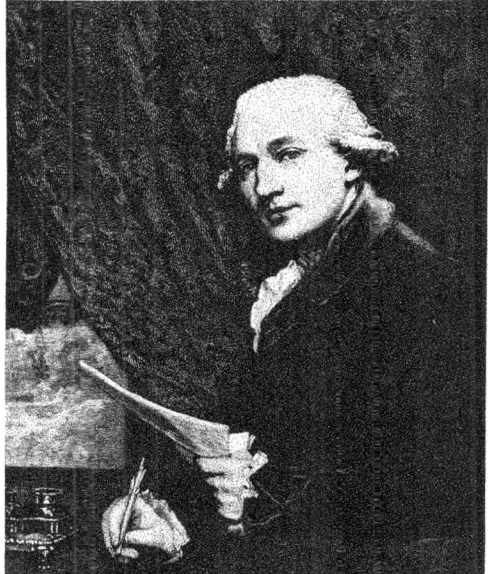

THOMAS TOMKINS, WRITING MASTER. BY SIR JOSHUA REYNOLDS, P.R.A.

A. G. TEMPLE,
Director of the Corporation of London Art Gallery.

THE NEW SCULPTURE, 1879-1894.*

FOURTH AND CONCLUDING ARTICLE.

IN the year 1888 the influence of the New Sculpture inside the Royal Academy was much strengthened by the election of Mr. Onslow Ford, on the 17th of January, to be an A.R.A. A few months later, Mr. Thornycroft received his promotion, and was the first member of the younger school who formed part of the governing section of the body. This was an exceedingly interesting year, too, from the point of view of the exhibitions, nor, indeed, have we seen one so stimulating since. The sculpture was charmingly arranged, and was found, even by the indifferent public, by no means an unattractive part of the show. Mr. Gilbert's 'Queen' dominated the Central Hall. This splendid regal figure, in voluminous draperies, was intended for the city of Winchester; but a hundred stories were afloat of insults and injuries to its surface, winked at by the local authorities, of a golden victory wrenched from its hand and discovered in the mud of the Itchen. I know not what truth there was in these tales, which indicated some inabilities in the people of Winchester to rate a great statue at its proper value. Mr. Thornycroft sent a poetic 'Medea,' and Mr. Ford some lovely iconic work. But the interest of 1888 centred around certain new men.

The word "new" is relative, and neither Mr. Frampton nor Mr. John made by any means their first appearances as exhibitors in 1888, yet we may consider them as acquisitions of that year, since it was then that their talent first made itself felt. Mr. George J. Frampton had in 1884 been an unsuccessful candidate for the gold medal which Mr. Bates won with a relief of 'Socrates in the Agora'; in 1888 he was still a student, and still striving for the gold medal. Great persistence and unwearied energy appear to be personal characteristics of Mr. Frampton, who has risen to the top of his profession—not at a single bound, like Mr. Thornycroft; not with a succession of brilliant short leaps, like Mr. Ford; but at a slow, earnest, pedestrian pace. In 1888 he gained the medal he had so long been working for,

* Continued from page 282.

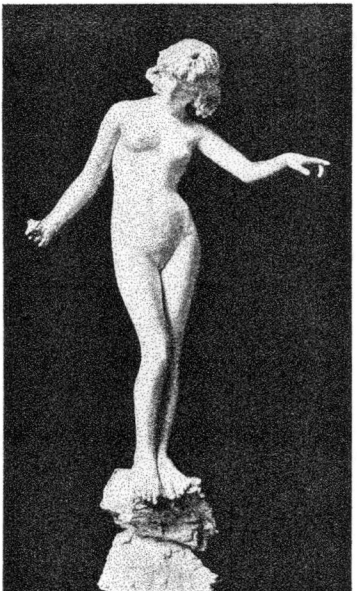

FOLLY. BY E. ONSLOW FORD, A.R.A.

with a delicate, subtly-laboured, pathetic little group called 'An Act of Mercy.'

At the same time a student named Mr. W. Goscombe John competed. He was younger, I suppose, and evidently then less accomplished, but a group of his also exhibited in 1888, and still more a head of a lady, modelled with an enchanting sweetness of touch, pointed out to all who had not observed his busts in 1886 and 1887 that here was another new talent of very high technical attainment. If I may speak for others, it may, perhaps, be admitted that the discovery of Messrs. Frampton and John in 1888 was the latest of those successive revelations of something like genius which had delighted the eyes of close observers since 1879. With them, I confess, the list seems ended.

Since 1888 talent has revealed itself, but not more than talent. Mr. John still seems to me to be the youngest of the important sculptors of the new school, the latest of the little band by whom the ninth decade of our century will be famous in the Art-history of the future.

In Mr. Frampton and Mr. Goscombe John we see the results of the Royal Academy schools at their best. These were students taught by the young masters of the New Sculpture in the first flush of their enthusiasm. In those years, as it has been described to me, a spirit of fire seemed to breathe through the modelling classes. To the damage of health and eyesight, the students would prolong their fascinating work from daybreak to midnight. Dreams of gigantic enterprises, walls and corridors clustered with bronze statues and lined with long marble friezes, passed across the brains of these poor lads, intoxicated with beauty and the desire for creating beauty. These schemes were of course never realised; to bad times worse times followed, and the enthusiasm of youthful genius sank in disappointment.

Mr. Frampton and Mr. John present in their work—which has steadily diverged, from a certain initial resemblance, into complete individuality of style—something of that composite character which often marks the production of the close of a school. Mr. Frampton has made his own a kind of pastiche of Donatello, both in the round and in very low relief. These last Madonna-like compositions of his, treated in the spirit of the fifteenth century, with excessive tenderness and the most adroit adjustment of planes, have secured his reputation with the public. But he is scarcely less skilful, though less attractive, in his heroic work in the round, of which his strange, phantasmal Angel of Death' (illustrated overleaf), in 1890, was a very capital example. In this he shows himself of the school of Mr. Gilbert, whose work has frequently affected him, although only by fits and starts. After going to Paris, Mr. Frampton exhibited, in 1891, a 'Caprice,' nude save for her sandals, waving gilded teazles in the air; parts of this statue were modelled with extraordinary closeness to nature. What attracts in Mr. Frampton is not his perfection, for he is seldom without a fault, but his versatility, his energy, and his persistent vitality.

In Mr. John it is the absolute mastery of technique which delights the eye. His historic forbears are difficult to trace, because of the faultless observation of nature which now marks almost all his work; but it would not be unsafe to conjecture that of artists older than himself, Mercié in France and Mr. Onslow Ford in England are those which have exercised the strongest enchantment over him. It would be hardly possible to carry modelling to a higher pitch of perfection than it has occasionally been carried by Mr. John, and he had none of the painful struggles of some of his fellows in this respect; the composition of his work was at first rather feeble, the modelling was always consummate. In 1888 his portrait of a lady took its place at once as the most admirable bust of the year.

Acknowledging this, it is a subject of some relative disappointment that Mr. John has not, in the course of these six years, shown quite the vigour that was expected of him. He has none of Mr. Frampton's elastic self-confidence; his hand seems to be slightly checked by a too-conscientious anxiety. His statues

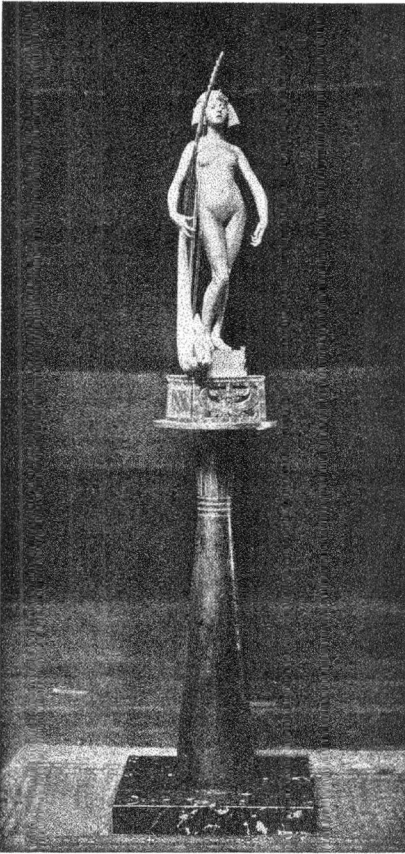

THE SINGER. BY E. ONSLOW FORD, A.R.A.

of 'Morpheus' in 1891, and of 'St. John' in 1894, show a maintenance of the great qualities with which he started. The last-mentioned even shows some advance upon them. But Mr. Goscombe John has yet to assert himself. His high value is admitted by artists, but it has not yet taken hold of the public. He is pointed out by his skill and his extraordinary learning as, without a rival, the most distinguished English sculptor now outside the Royal Academy, and the world at large will probably discover him for the first time the morning after his election to the A.R.A.ship.

In the Royal Academy of 1889, Mr. Brock came to the front as he had never done before with a noble statue of 'The Genius of Poetry.' Here, for the first time, Mr. Brock may be said to have bidden final farewell to his old " broad " Foley tradition. The modelling of the flesh was learned, without any loss of freshness and delicacy; not Barrias nor Dubois could have produced a more workmanlike pair of legs than those of this beautiful work, of which we give a full-page illustration; in 1891 Mr. Brock presented it to us again, executed in marble, and it had lost nothing of its distinction. To this male figure, meanwhile, the sculptor had appended a female counterpart, and called it 'Song,' but this had not quite the charm of 'The Genius of Poetry.' Meanwhile, in 1889, Mr. Ford's 'The Singer' (here illustrated), a nude Egyptian girl standing beside a harp, had created quite a sensation; and a more limited audience of artists and sportsmen had recognised the merits of a virile group of a naked man holding ' Hounds in Leash,' by Mr. Harry Bates.

This was, in fact, a year of good animal-sculpture, and connoisseurs had an opportunity of comparing two excellent but diametrically opposed styles. Mr. Robert Stark had long been advancing into notice for the careful studies of animals, which, since 1882, he had constantly contributed to the exhibition. In particular, he had shown a ' Bison ' in 1887, and a ' Rhinoceros ' in 1888 (see illustration, page 311),

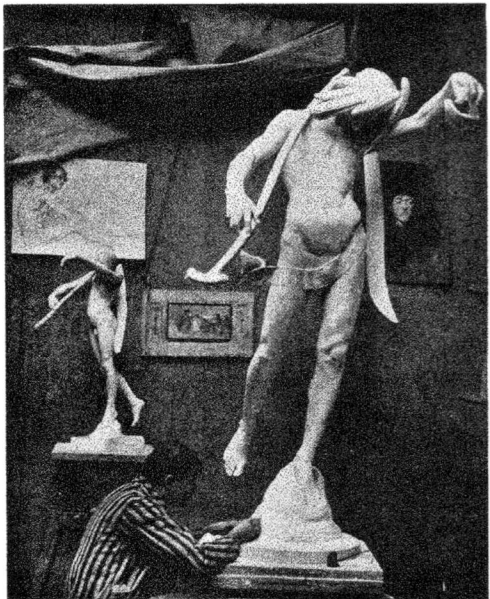

THE ANGEL OF DEATH. BY GEORGE J. FRAMPTON, A.R.A.

which were, from their own point of view, of absolute excellence. They were, that is to say, solid and true, they observed all matters of fact directly from the living model, and they showed evidences of intelligent and serious study. Mr. Stark is prosaic, he gives a faithful rendering of what he sees in nature. He reminds us of the Saxon *animalier*, Julius Haehnel, with even less of what we call style.

But, in 1889, Mr. Stark's prose found a very serious rival in the poetry of an artist who was already known as a painter, and who now gathered laurels in the groves of sculpture, Mr. John M. Swan. His ' Young Himalayan Tiger,' with arched neck and extended paws, tossing a ball (see page 21), was a work of high imagination, in which less of the detail of life was given than we had been accustomed to in Mr. Stark, but more imagination, more of the elasticity and essential charm of life. Since then Mr. Swan, constantly diverted to the art of painting, has given us fewer than we could wish of his delicious feline bronzes, full of the best spirit of Barye and Frémiet.

In reviewing the exhibition of 1890, the principal landmark to the memory is the reappearance of Mr. Frederick Pomeroy, who had, mainly perhaps for want of opportunity, failed to carry out before his early promise. That year, in an exquisite ' Dionysius ' (which we reproduce, not without a regret that in the bronze the sculptor should have added a sprawling ivy costume which breaks up the simple grace of the original forms), Mr. Pomeroy attracted wide admiration. The talent of this artist, who has not even yet, I am convinced, done full justice to his powers, has something very fresh about it. Whereas most of his colleagues seem even obtrusively French in their tastes, there is in Mr. Pomeroy I know not what that seems radically English. He has a touch of Foley, but it is evident that Mr. Thornycroft rather than Mr. Gilbert has been his master-influence. The same blithe and serene spirit, "tasting of Flora and the country green," was manifest in his ' Vintage Song ' of 1891 and his ' Love the Conqueror' of 1893, but I confess that his ' Dionysius ' is still my first favourite. No one among the younger men understands the conduct of a statuette better than Mr. Pomeroy.

A melancholy event, and one of grave significance, was the sudden death of Sir Edgar Boehm on the 12th of December, 1890. A man of great activity and vigour, still in the prime of life, no departure could less have been expected. It is scarcely needful in this place to say much that has not been suggested in previous pages of this history with regard to the art of Boehm. He was a prominent and living artist in this country during many dead years of English sculpture, and his work always showed a certain feeling for copying the colour of nature. Perhaps that was the best that could be said of it, since its boasted realism in form was excessive and since it was small in its tendency and without style. Boehm learned much, for a time, from Dalou, and, late in life, his works occasionally showed a rather close and unexpected imitation of Mr. Gilbert. Boehm was at his height about 1875 ; he never surpassed his really excellent 'Carlyle.' He saw the value of securing by undercutting the deep shadows which make life so picturesque, and he swept away the "broad" treatment of the tongue-licked Chantreyesque school. These were his gifts to sculpture, and for these we would be

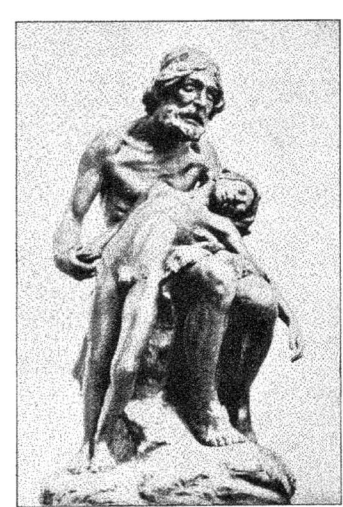

THE PARTING. BY W. GOSCOMBE JOHN.

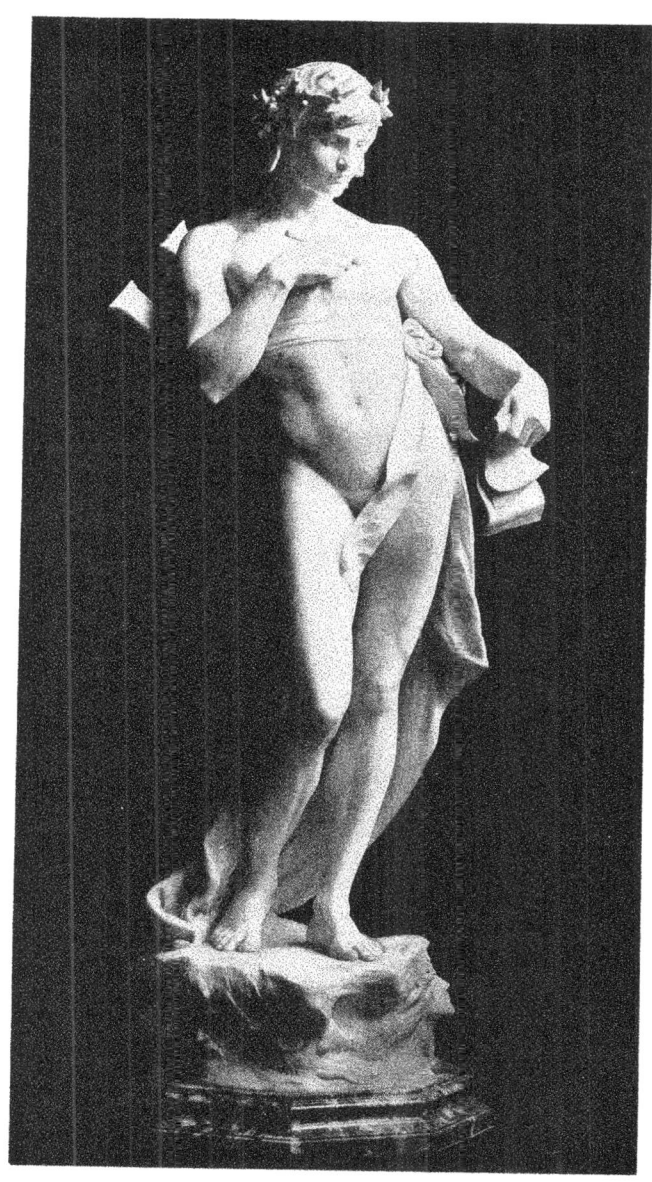

The Genius of Poetry. By Thomas Brock, R.A.

grateful. But the New Sculpture would have been more than mortal if it had appreciated very highly the value of a man who stood at the head of the profession, and resolutely, so far as in him lay, barred the road to "the young man knocking at the door." That Boehm should combine with so much power and so much prestige an absolute inability to see what the new sculptors were driving at, this was discouraging in a high degree. It was discouraging to others, who might have been inclined to come to him for guidance. I shall never forget the shock that it gave myself when, in 1883—the year of Mr. Ford's ' Irving,' and of Mr. Lee's ' Dawn of Womanhood,' and of Mr. Alfred Gilbert's 'Head of a Boy'—I asked Boehm, in his own studio, what had struck him most in the newly-opened exhibition, and he replied, "Nothing has struck me! I look around and I see, among the sculpture by Englishmen, nothing to admire. There is no accomplishment, no power, no promise! I look eagerly and wistfully, but I find—nothing!" His sincerity could not be doubted, but what melancholy blindness of prejudice, what inability to read the signs of the times!

It was inevitable, therefore, that in the courtly and popular Sir Edgar Boehm the New Sculpture possessed its most powerful enemy, and it was no small proof of its convincing internal force that in so few years it should succeed in pushing so far ahead in his despite. Boehm saw no necessity for individual studios of sculpture in this country. He thought—as that excellent modeller, John Bacon, thought a hundred years ago—that the practice of sculpture might very conveniently be centred around one man, who should direct it and preside at it. Boehm would gladly have employed the young men to produce work for him in some such universal emporium of monuments, of which he himself should be president and manager. It is said that at one time he hoped, with the help of the Court, to carry through some such scheme. Probably the public, supplied with capable sculpture at a reasonable figure, would not have complained. But this was scarcely to reckon upon the temperament of the young artist, or to do justice to his talent. The day is past for employing, on the most handsome terms, anonymous gangs of unambitious sculptors.

The death of Boehm and the retirement of Calder Marshall (who died in June, 1894) left the Royal Academy practically in the hands of the New Sculpture. Mr. Brock took the place of the former, and made room for the election of Mr. Bates to be made an A.R.A. on the 27th of January, 1892. Mr. Gilbert was promoted, and in January, 1894, Messrs. Frampton and Swan became associates. The death of Birch, then, as has already been pointed out, left the first and long the only friend of the New Sculpture, Mr. Armstead, the sole survivor of a condition of things previous to the revival. This record of changes in the composition of the Royal Academy is not a trifling matter. Painting, the broader and more popular art, is largely independent of the corporate body; it can create and extend its schools without encouragement or help from the Academy. But it is not so, and never has been so, with sculpture. From the very foundation of the body, whose earliest act was the recognition of Nollekens, Banks, and Bacon, the Royal Academy has been the home of English statuary and the mainstay of this costly and unpopular art. Again and again, the only bar to the complete success of some charlatan of a sculptor has been the quiet resistance to his claims by Burlington House. If it was so in the past, it is more so than ever in this generation, when the President, although so delightful a painter, is, above all things, in skill and in temperament a sculptor.

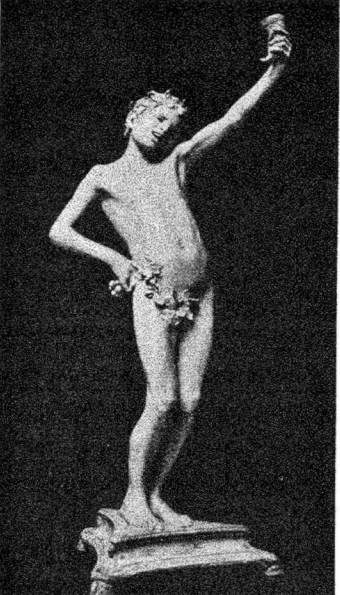

DIONYSIUS. BY FREDERICK POMEROY.

In looking round the field of sculpture in this country one gains the impression that the great movement begun in 1879 has now worked itself into an almost quiescent state. We cannot—and we should not—look for revolutions every twenty years. It will be to the advantage of the art that the lesson which now seems to have been learned by the English modeller should be practised in silence for a while. I am not able to say that since Mr. John's appearance, there has come forward any man whose talents seem to be of an extraordinary class. Every year the general level of accomplishment seems to grow higher and higher. Academy students produce solid, careful work, honest and capable, a little poor in idea, a little empty in imagination. Among the best of these are Mr. Fehr and Mr. Allen, from Burlington House, and Mr. Drury, a mannered Kensington student, somewhat under the influence of Dalou. No very young man seems to be carrying the New Sculpture on any further than its founder brought it. If one among them more than another has awakened hopes in myself, as I have wandered around the galleries, it is Mr. David McGill. I know nothing of his personal history, but his ' St. Sebastian ' of this year had qualities of high sculpturesque merit, and I recommend those who are interested in the art to look out for his signature in the future.

No one, I hope, can have read these successive pages, and still less have examined the illustrations which accompany them, without forming some impression of what we mean by the New Sculpture. But, having drawn its rapid history down to the close of its first period, and having witnessed its successful progress and complete recognition, it may be well to summarise very briefly the qualities which distinguish it from what it superseded. What the conventional elements were which it was necessary to sweep away, I endeavoured to suggest at the opening of this inquiry. It now remains to depict in a summary way what the features of the New Sculpture itself have been, and what it introduced. Vaguely, it might be defined as a fresh concentration of the intellectual powers on a branch of art which had been permitted to grow dull and inanimate; another, that is to say, of those periodical revivals in all branches of mental activity, by means of which the stream of life is kept wholesome and limpid in its various currents.

Less figuratively, it may be said that the bold introduction of the picturesque into that art of sculpture, from which it had so rigidly been excluded, was the most salient feature of the new school. Ample recognition was made of the effect of colour on the eye of the spectator. In connection with this element, the treatment of surface came to demand a very special attention from the sculptors, since it was perceived that colour and picturesqueness could only be secured by peculiar care in this direction. The odd phenomena of surface, those accidents which tend to remove the sense of absolute regularity, all the individualities of the model, which by the Old Sculpture had been considered inadmissible, were now accepted, and the minute forms closely adhered to—it being a matter of instinct for style, and of character in the personality of the artist, how far this pursuit of the accidental should be carried. But all the New Sculptors were at one in this—that detail which exists in nature must be represented more or less in the work. This eminently distinguished them from their predecessors, from those followers of Chantrey whose one aim was "breadth," and who sought for the typical rather than the individual characteristics. The final word about the New Sculpture may be that its vital impulse and the ambition which has led it so far, have been centred in carrying out with careful, sensitive modelling a close and reverent observation of nature. EDMUND GOSSE.

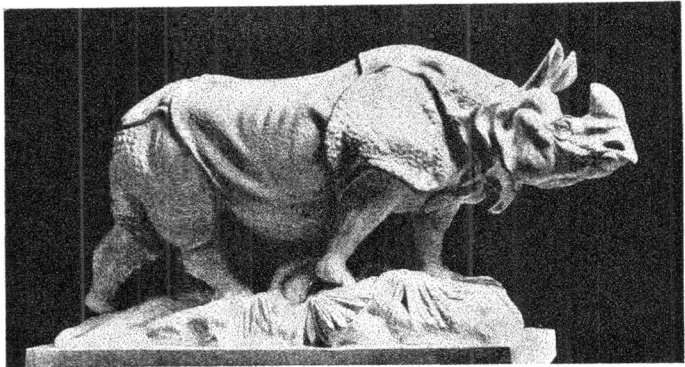

RHINOCEROS. BY ROBERT STARK.

PICTURE SALES OF 1894.

THE picture sale season of 1894 has not been marked by the dispersal of any collections of an exceptional character, but many important works by British and foreign masters have changed hands and some satisfactory prices have been realised. Last year's season was characterized by several important sales of collections whose owners had been hit by the prevailing commercial depression, but this year— with one exception, the important Adrian Hope Collection —the business seems to have resumed its normal character, and consists almost wholly of sales of collections which the decease of the owner has brought under the hammer.

The following are a few of the most important totals of sales at Christie's. The Adrian Hope Collection (pictures) nearly £50,000; the Fontaine, £14,311 (pictures £6,921); Sir H. H. Campbell's, £13,206 (pictures £8,000); the Brand, £12,246 (pictures £6,573); the Joseph (objects of Art), £12,000; the Dennistoun pictures, £11,029; the Delmé pictures, £10,975; Miss Romney's pictures, £9,745; Lady Eastlake's pictures, £9,030; the Duchess of Montrose's pictures, £8,249; the Medwin pictures, £6,000; and the Farquhar pictures, £4,703. The remainder of the Murrieta Collection of last season was also dispersed in February for £4,518, bringing the total up to £28,000, but it must be remembered that by far the larger portion of the Murrieta pictures was previously sold by private contract.

In the following account of some of the principal pictures which have changed hands this season, we give the previous prices so far as they are ascertainable; but of several important examples there is no previous record of auction prices.

Of the British masters Sir Joshua Reynolds heads the list, and the first President of the Academy is evidently still a prime favourite. His picture 'Lady Betty Delmé and Children' sold for £11,550, the largest sum paid for any picture— either British or foreign—this season, and the highest price ever paid at auction for a Reynolds. This was purchased for the private collection of Mr. Charles Wertheimer. It was bought from Sir Joshua for about £200. A 'Portrait of Miss Monckton' brought £7,875.

Gainsborough's 'Market Cart' and 'View near King's Bromley' fetched £4,725 and £3,780 respectively. Landseer may be said to be a waning star. His 'Chevy' was knocked down for £3,937, and it is thought doubtful whether such prices as that of £7,245, reached by the 'Monarch of the Glen' last year, will be maintained. 'Yarmouth Water,' by Crome, obtained the unprecedented auction price, for this master, of £2,730.

'The White Horse,' by Constable, was sold for £6,510, one of the largest auction sums paid for this master. It has since been purchased for a new collector in Philadelphia. It was bought in 1855 for £630. 'Hampstead Heath' fetched £1,837, the previous price on record being £150. Hoppner's 'Mrs. Gordon as Rosalind' brought the respectable sum of £1,155.

No remarkable Turners have come into the auction market this year. The most important, a sea piece, brought £1,260. Several very fine examples of Turner have, however, passed from England to America for large sums this season.

Romney's popularity seems to be steadily maintained, and £1,207 was given for his 'Head of Mrs. Tickle.' The largest sum paid at auction for a Callcott for many years, £892, was brought by the 'Shrimpers.' Wilkie seems to decline year by year as the change in public taste becomes more marked. His 'Sheep Washing,' however, fetched £745, which was a not unsatisfactory price. An Opie, the 'Lady in White Dress,' was sold for £588.

W. Muller has been declining of late years, but his L'Ariccia,' and a 'Mediterranean Coast Scene,' were knocked down for £755 and £598 respectively, and it is almost certain his work will some day be more sought after.

Two of Etty's pictures brought fair prices, £525 and £430, being different versions of the 'Choice of Paris.' D. G. Rossetti's 'Venus Verticordia,' sold for £525. Previous price (1886) £325. J. Linnell is a master who has fluctuated somewhat in recent years. His 'Timber Waggon' went for £651. A portrait by Sir Thomas Lawrence, 'Mrs. Whittington,' brought £750.

Of living British painters, Mr. Fildes, R.A., heads this year's list with 'An Al Fresco Toilette,' which fetched £1,365. Others that may be mentioned are:—Mr. J. C. Hook, R.A., 'Little to Earn and Many to Keep,' £798 ; Mr. Alma-Tadema, R.A., 'Water Pets,' £651 ; Sir E. Burne-Jones, 'Music,' £598; and a series of seven, 'St. George and the Dragon,' £2,100.

In referring to the foreign masters we can only repeat that the worthy appreciation of the avowedly great masters, and especially of the old Dutchmen, no new school, craze, or affectation can apparently reduce. First, stands the 'Portrait of Nicholas Ruts,' by Rembrandt, which went for £4,935 to a Yorkshire collector. Its previous known price was £283, for which sum it was bought from the King of Holland's collection. There can be no question as to the ever-growing admiration for the 'King of Shadows.' His 'Jonckeu Petronella Buys,' and the 'Girl in Brown Dress,' were sold for £1,365 and £703 respectively. The latter was bought in 1889 for £299.

The unprecedented auction price of £3,675 for a Gerard Dow was obtained by the 'Flute Player.' The previous records of this picture are £451 in 1841 and £425 in 1846.

The interest in Hobbema is as keen and strong as ever. A small landscape with cottage and figures obtained £3,150. The sum of £3,003 for the picture representing a woman pumping is probably the largest ever paid for a Maas. This work was bought in 1824 for £84. An 'Interior with Woman and Child,' by Pieter de Hoogh, went for £2,257. Previous prices, 1826, £73 10s .; 1861, £441. A 'Grand Landscape with Lady and Gentleman on Horseback,' by Cuyp, was sold for £2,100. In 1850 it was £577 10s.

Rubens' 'Grand Boar Hunt,' an unsatisfactory picture not likely to keep its price, produced £1,743. It was bought from the King of Holland's collection for £1,666. His 'Prodigal Son' fetched £840, having been bought from the collection of W. Wilkins, architect of the National Gallery, for £246 15s.

We drew attention last year to the prices that are being realised by pictures by Ruysdael, and this year they have been well maintained. A 'Waterfall' sold for £1,680. Its records are, in 1841, £672 ; and in 1851, £372. The present price well compensates for the previous fall. The following are the prices of some other examples of this master :—' An old Fort,' £640; previous prices, 1835, £120 ; 1857, £132. 'View on the Brill River,' £1,207 ; 'Lake of Haarlem,' £982 ; 'Forest Scene with Brook,' £1,312.

The largest price obtained at auction for a work by Hondekœter, at least for many years, was the sum of £1,575 paid for his 'Long live the King!' Its price in 1857 was £158.

Metsu's 'Lady seated, with Book and Spaniel,' sold in 1851 for £120 15s., realised £1,260. Terburg's 'Drinking the King's Health' brought £1,113.

The record of Paul Potter's 'Oxen in a Meadow,' shows that this master more than maintains his hold on popularity, a fact very difficult to explain. In 1750 its price was £25 ; in 1787, £160 ; in 1801, £194 ; in 1812, £320; in 1894, £997.

Jan Steen's 'Lady and Gentleman, with Musicians, on a Terrace,' and 'A Merry-making,' brought the satisfactory prices of £819 and £567 respectively. Van der Helst's 'Portrait of an Officer' obtained £819.

Pictures by A. Both continually rise in value. A 'Landscape with Horsemen, Figures, and Dogs,' sold for £787, and a 'Hilly Landscape—Peasant and Mules,' for £609. Price of the latter in 1807, £304 10s.

A picture by Van de Velde, 'Calm, with Frigate at Anchor,' was purchased at £735. The sum obtained by A. Wouwermans' 'Les Quartiers des Vivandiers' was £735. Price in 1801, £120 ; in 1817, £376. Hals' 'Boy with Dog,' a circle, sold for £682. It was bought in 1875 for £189. The following items are also of interest. Van der Heyden, two views of a Dutch town, £630 and £498 15s. ; P. de Koning, 'Bird's-eye View of Village and River,' £619 ; K. du Jardin, 'Mother amusing her Child,' £504 ; price in 1832, £134.

Of works by masters of other schools may be noted a 'Madonna with Infant Saviour,' by Ghirlandajo, which realised £1,228. Very few of this master's works have come under the hammer within recent years.

Canaletto, 'View on the Grand Canal, looking towards the Doge's Palace,' £934 ; 'A Madonna and Child enthroned,' by Bellini, £682; and a 'Madonna and Child holding Pomegranate,' by Botticelli, £756 ; Guido, 'Il Diamente— Venus stealing Cupid's Bow,' £1,000 ; F. Francia, 'St. Roch,' £997 ; J. B. Greuze, 'Young Girl with Hands on Windowsill,' £3,045, bought in 1857 for £157 10s. ; Joanowitz, 'Sword and Dagger Fight,' £787 ; Karl Müller (died August 15, 1893), 'Almée's Admirers,' £640.

In conclusion we may refer all who require fuller particulars of the Art Sales of the year to "The Year's Art" for 1895, which will contain in due course the usual classified lists and tables showing the chief movements of the picture market.

AFTERMATH.

THE herald-redbreast sings his winter lays,
    The fieldfares drift in flocks adown the weald;
    The turbulent rooks gather on every field,
And clamorous starlings dare our garden-ways:

O beautiful garden-ways, not grown less dear
    Because the rose has gone, and briony waves
    Where lily and purple iris have their graves,
Or that, where violets were, tall asters rear.

Lo, what a sheen of colour lingers still,
    Though the autumnal rains and frosts be come!
The tall, o'erheavy sunflowers seem to spill
Lost rays of sunshine o'er the tangled mould,
While everywhere, touched with a glory of gold,
    Flaunts the imperial chrysanthemum.

WILLIAM SHARP.

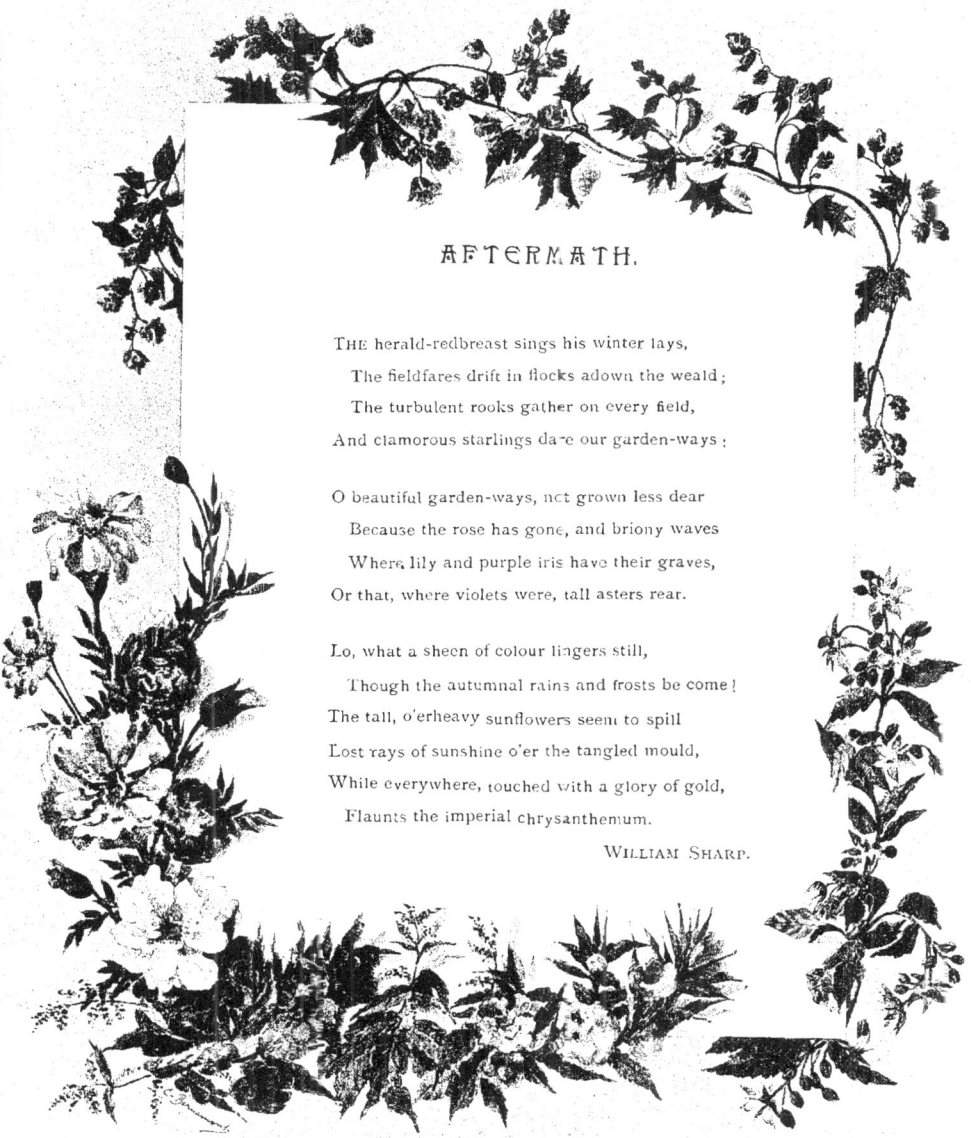

BIRMINGHAM BRASS WORK.

BRASS is to be found everywhere ; and chiefly of Birmingham manufacture. Forty thousand people are engaged producing it in Birmingham and its immediate vicinity. Though the supply of ordinary goods undoubtedly forms a great part of its trade, the best brass work in the world has been and is made there.

The first "brass house" in Birmingham was established in Coleshill Street about 1740; but fifty or sixty years earlier she had entered into the manufacture of brass. The calamine stone for her brass making was obtained from Bristol, and from Cheadle in Staffordshire. It was not at any time found in or close to Birmingham; yet, even with that disadvantage, she seriously undertook to compete with Bristol, whose trade from that and other causes began to decline.

Early in the eighteenth century a water-power mill was laid down at Hockley Brook (there were two or three others, but of less note, within a mile or so at the time), and then it was that, so it would seem in Birmingham at least, the old system of obtaining sheet metal by "battery" began to give way to the rolling process. In due course of time the astute Matthew Boulton on business bent visited Hockley Brook. His visit resulted in the erecting of the world-famed Soho Works by its side. When Watt joined him in partnership a few years afterwards, and his steam-power began to supplant water-mill power, the industrial prosperity of Birmingham was assured, and the world of trade revolutionized. But it was when Murdoch, a Scotsman in the employ of Boulton, brought gas-light into practical working at Soho Works, that the brass trade of Birmingham began to look forward to the commanding position it soon held. No doubt the canal system which before then had been vitalizing the heart of England and had reduced the price of coal to one-third of its former cost, helped much to bring this about. Steam-power transit by land and sea, and the inherited metal-working ability of the natives of Birmingham, did the rest. So it was that in 1838 when Welby Pugin joined with John Hardman, Birmingham was ready to receive their teaching and produce art metal-work not to be excelled. But more of this presently. Over a hundred years ago the better patterns in Birmingham brass work indicated a desire to satisfy the then prevailing taste for the classic and semi-classic, introduced to a great extent by the brothers Adam, who were much influenced by the statues, vases, bronzes, and domestic implements disinterred from the ruins of Pompeii and Herculaneum. The pattern-sheets of the time literally speak volumes of this style of brass work; some of which may yet be seen at Messenger's establishment. Such constructive adaptations, it is almost needless to say, were altogether wrong in principle; but they, all the same, now serve well to indicate the unconscious striving after the genuine in art that then obtained. Reproductions of the sort, occasionally expressing more or less originality, were introduced by Flaxman, Francis Chantrey, and Wyon—a progenitor of the mint medallist associated with Boulton at Soho works. Each of these famous men designed and modelled at times for the then remarkably enterprising Messenger firm. The spirit of enterprise, however, still remains in it, under the able supervision of its now principal, Albert Jones. The electrolier in the style of the Renaissance, No. 8 of the illustrations to this article, excellently modelled and cast, and in part hammered, proves that the firm is quite alive to modern requirements in that way. It is not possible in our limited space to do justice to the other centenarian, and almost centenarian, Birmingham brass-foundry establishments. Pemberton and Sons, and Winfield, both afford, almost in themselves, a history of the highest

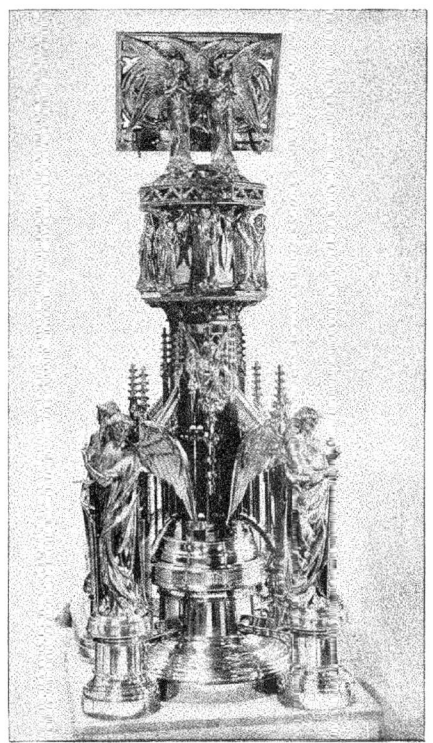

LECTERN. MESSRS. HARDMAN. DESIGNED BY JOHN POWELL. (NO. 1.)

efforts in secular brass work; the latter also having, to some extent, identified itself with church furnishings, but not in such a special manner as Jones and Willis, Hart Son and Peard, and Thomason.

The names of Birmingham manufacturers in brass are legion—there are over six hundred of them. From this number let us try to select about a dozen of the best known, not inclusive of those whose names accompany our illustrations; for in so trying we are seeking to emphasize the fact that brass making and fashioning is, through long years of striving firms, now numerically the chief among the industrial arts of Birmingham: Blews, Martineau and Smith, Collins, Barwell, Clark and Timmins, Harcourt, Evered, Phipson and Warden, James Hinks, Ingram and Kemp, Benton and Stone, Souter—and here we must stop, and in another way go farther into our subject.

The processes of making brass and manufacturing it into articles of utility and ornament are many, and technical enough to warn us that only the briefest reference to them can be indulged in here. Brass, like glass or gold, is of varied quality and colour according to the quality and quantity of ingredients contained in it, and the methods of working it. Best brass may be composed of three parts of copper to one part of zinc; and good ordinary brass of two parts of copper to one of zinc. Designing and modelling, for casting from, are often done on the brassfounder's premises, but more frequently supplied from without. So likewise is the designing for die and stamp work, inclusive of press and pierced work as distinct from cast, and all hammered patterns which require the services of the chaser or "repairer." The *repairers* or chasers chop out, chase, sharpen, and bring up the details' of patterns that often come blurred and indistinct from the mould. What is called *fine casting* requires little or no tooling, but much precaution is necessary for this, not only while the pattern is in the hands of the modeller and the chaser, but when passed on to the caster, whose sand or loam must be of the proper granulation to take its minute markings. For special undercut work *coring* has to be done, so that the molten metal shall flow into every part of the object being cast. Shadow and depth

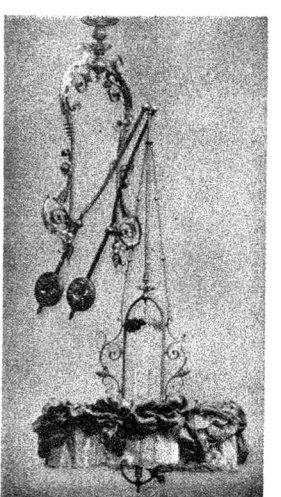

THE SURPRISE PENDANT.
MESSRS. R. H. BEST AND LLOYD. (No. 2.)

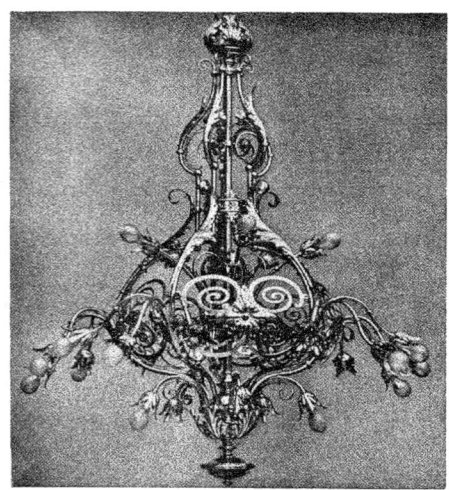

ELECTROLIER FOR 25 LIGHTS. MESSRS. BEST AND LLOYD. (No. 3.)

in figures and draperies are thus obtained. All patterns are made a little larger than the size required, so as to allow for shrinkage of the metal in cooling. In order to perfectly clean articles so far advanced it is necessary to dip them in a mixture of nitric and sulphuric acids. The result may be a bright or a dead surface, all over, or in part only, according to what effect is wanted, and the strength and temperature of the acids. When bright they are finished by burnishing or polishing, and a protecting coat of lacquer is then given to them. The lacquer is a solution of shell-lac in spirits of wine. *Kristiline*, which approaches nearer to a transparent enamel, is now frequently employed for this purpose. Lacquer protects brass from oxidation and tarnish.

To enumerate the different kinds of brass articles made in Birmingham is unnecessary. So it is that while brass may be said to lend its cheerful presence to the palaces and mansions of the rich, it contributes a ray of brightness to the poorest home, and finds fitting place some way or other in churches, theatres, offices, factories, and in the ocean-going steamers that carry it also as merchandise to the distant parts of the earth. Many tribes of Africa, referred to by Burton, Livingstone, Stanley, and others, adorn themselves with it in forms of bangles, bracelets, anklets, and coils for the waist; and some use it made into "Manilla money" (when that is not composed of only lead and copper alloy, hardened with arsenic), and such-like tokens and signs of well-being that "please the natives."

We have now to refer to craftsmanship in brass with a little more particularization; and, to do so, it is necessary to go back for a moment to the era of Pugin and the revival of art metal-work in Birmingham. Pugin and Hardman first met in 1838; and they soon agreed to co-operate and strive to renew the purer art principles that actuated the workmen of the Middle Ages. Their difficulties at first were almost unsurmountable. Three centuries of ignorant neglect of the spirit and methods of working in metals had to be faced;

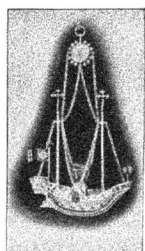

SANCTUARY LAMP.
MESSRS. HARDMAN. (No. 4.)

and the whole of that dark time traversed anew, as it were, in order to regain possession of the secrets of the crafts. While almost despairing of securing any one in England capable of *raising* metal shapes, a ray of hope came through the darkness but, to be quite precise and matter-of-fact on the point, Pugin's own words will be best to quote here: "We were compelled, for the first altar-lamp ever produced by us, to employ an old German workman who made jelly moulds for pastry-cooks as the only one who understood beating up copper to the old forms!" It seems singular that in France the repoussé, or *beating up*, process, was revived in 1838, the year when, as we have said, Pugin and Hardman first met. Pugin advocated the practice of repoussé with all the enthusiasm of his nature, and had journeyed

natural, and accounts for much of his logical sequence of thought that found such vehement expression at a time when he denounced the corrupters of Gothic who would treat metal as if it were stone or wood. It was this same *beating up* idea that, carried out in iron more than in brass, because of its greater ductility and tenacity—so well known to the Mediæval ironsmiths—caused him to point out its capability of taking all manner of curves, twists, and foliations, bespeaking lightness, and at the same time strength in beauty.

The revival of metal work had far-reaching effects: besides Hardman's, other firms in London and elsewhere soon began to rise and prosper by its production. But the house of Hardman has always held the lead. It has ever excelled in design and manipulation. Its handiwork is to be found adorning the principal churches, public buildings, and mansions of Great Britain and Ireland; among these may be mentioned the Houses of Parliament at Westminster, Alton Towers, and Lismore Castle. Gold, silver, tapestries, and stained glass attest the extent and variety of the manufacture of this truly epoch-making firm. The Lectern, No. 1 of our illustrations, is intended to represent in tangible shape some

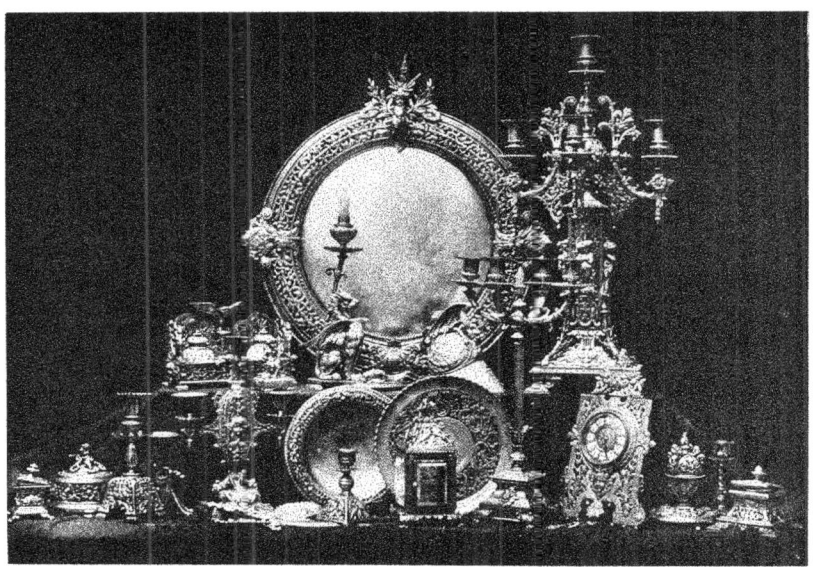

BIRMINGHAM BRASS WORK. DESIGNED BY MR. HERBERT MASON. MESSRS. JAMES CARTLAND AND SON. (No. 5.)

frequently on the Continent, making close study of its architectural features, and particularly of its metal work. So the coincidence of repoussé revival in England and France about the same time may be attributable in some way to him. His central idea, inspired by his keen sense of the beautiful, and kept alive by travel throughout England as well as the Continent, was, that all decoration is futile unless it subserves construction and grows out of it. The connection between this idea, then, and his liking for repoussé was quite

of the angelic visions of St. John, and is probably the finest ever produced in this country. It was designed by John Powell, the gifted pupil and son-in-law of Pugin, since whose death he, as art director, has well maintained the reputation of the firm. Fixed in position in St. Paul's Church, Brighton, it cost about £1,000. We must leave, for want of space, the fascinating subject of symbolism which this beautiful work of art so well represents to the initiated. The Sanctuary lamp (No. 4), in brass, copper, and oxidized metal, is, in its way, almost as full of symbolism; and for the reason just given, let us hope it may silently speak for itself.

The electrolier (No. 3) for twenty-five lights, is by Best and Lloyd, one of the foremost firms in the kingdom as makers of brass in all its varieties for lighting purposes. The bold artistic effect of its curved lines, and its hammered leaf work and petal arrangement around the pendent glass bulbs, from which the lights radiate, give it a character much in advance of ordinary productions of the kind. The other illustration (No. 2) represents a rather striking novelty, the invention of R. H. Best of the same firm, and patented by him. It is called the "Surprise Pendant," and has already been adopted by the incandescent companies of England, France, Germany, and Austria. It is so constructed that it can be with ease balanced safely in almost any position over the table, and raised or lowered at will to the extent of four feet. It gives an even, soft, and agreeable light, which may be made to extend, if desired, all over the room, or concentrated on any part of the table. Literary men and artists must find it a very desirable aid to them in their pursuits. Its pleasant appearance and proved economical advantages recommend it even more

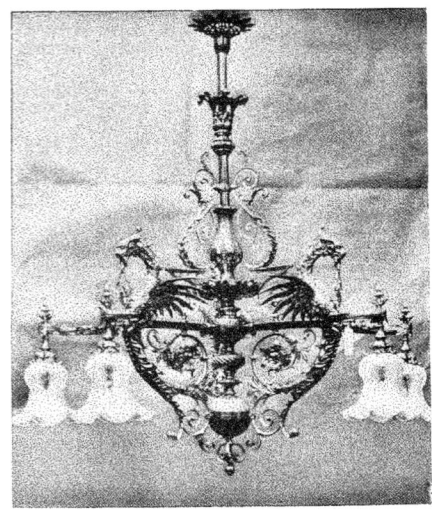

ELECTROLIER. MESSRS. MESSENGER. (No. 8.)

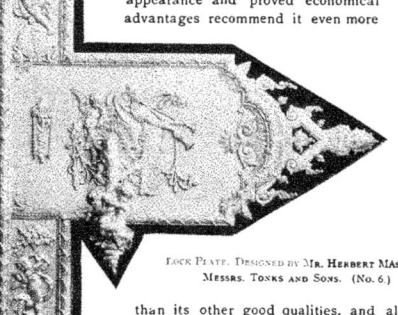

LOCK PLATE. DESIGNED BY MR. HERBERT MASON. MESSRS. TONKS AND SONS. (No. 6.)

than its other good qualities, and altogether, it may not have been misnamed the *Surprise Pendant*.

The group (No. 5) introduces us to a class of goods that, during the last quarter of a century or so, has, in purely secular work, done much for the high reputation of Birmingham's industrial art. They are from the designs and models of Mr. Herbert Mason, an artist of rare ability, whose restless energy and desire to see his work finished to his liking led him some time ago into manufacturing on his own account. For a few years he was very successful, but the artistic faculty is difficult to satisfy, and seldom is equal to the task of sustaining itself without permanent injury in contention with the hard and too frequently un-

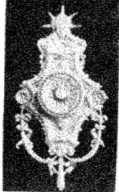

ELECTRIC PUSH. DESIGNED BY MR. HERBERT MASON. (No. 7.) MESSRS. TONKS AND SONS.

scrupulous spirit of trading for profit; so he returned for a while to designing and modelling for the trade. He has again, quite recently, become his own manufacturer. Messrs. Cartland and Son, one of the larger of the enterprising Birmingham firms, some time ago entered into arrangements and purchased the right to make such articles as are represented in the group. The lock-plate (No. 6) and electric push (No. 7) are also from the designs of Herbert Mason. This lock-plate is one of the best things of the kind done in brass. The electric push, as may be observed, is in the same style—a treatment of Renaissance having characteristics sometimes called "First Empire." It is made by Tonks and Sons, probably at the present moment not surpassed for ornamental brass-work of excellent finish by any establishment in Birmingham. The Burmese gong (No. 9) is an example of Townshend & Co.'s decorative iron and brass for domestic purposes. This house has succeeded well of late in catering for the general taste in such goods. The clock (No. 10) is another specimen

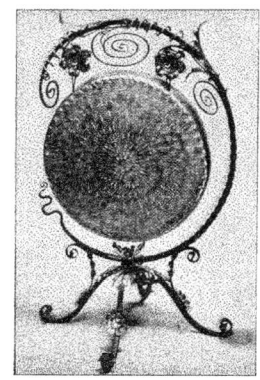

GONG IN THE BURMESE STYLE. MESSRS. TOWNSHEND AND CO. (No. 9.)

of Mr. Mason's work, made originally with silver mountings by him for Messrs. Howell and James, of Regent Street, London. It is also executed with copper and with brass mountings, and oxidized silver discs. It is worth noting here that Mr. William Furness, the directing spirit of this celebrated London house, perceiving the exceptional ability of Herbert Mason, was the first to induce him to try his hand at brass work. The acumen of Mr. Furness was well rewarded by the superior class of work Mason was in a short time able to supply him with. Thenceforward the name and fame of Mason was secured. The group (No. 11) in which the clock in the Japanese style (also by Mason) appears, is representative of Birmingham brass and metal gilt work, such as is on show at Messrs. Howell and James's establishment.

Mason may fairly claim to be the revivalist of Renaissance as applied to Birmingham brass work. He was, at any rate, the first to seriously entertain and bring out a succession of patterns in it all bearing the stamp of his own individuality. But it is because Mason is capable of yet better work that he should take warning in time and escape from a mannerism that, if persevered in, must limit the duration of his artistic success. The artists of the Renaissance periods, those who lived in them, were too frequently only revivalists of ancient classic and ornamental details. Their modern imitators are in danger when they become the bond-slaves of precedents—the precedents themselves being imitative and lacking the spirituality that actuates all truly

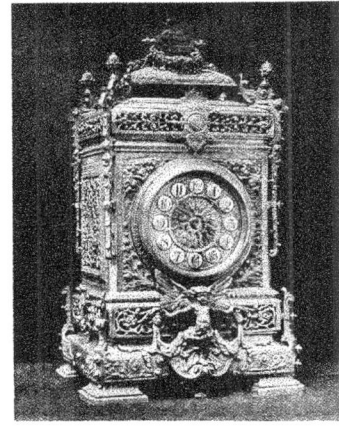

CLOCK DESIGNED BY MR. HERBERT MASON (No. 10.)

original design. Far better for the artist to leave the academic thraldom and take vigorous licence to produce even his own barbarisms, so long as the chances are that they will come out at times fresh with surprises that delight us. If improbability and eccentricity of structure and ornament would to some extent necessarily follow such experiment, there might not be any permanent harm done, for they would be eliminated by degrees under the censorship of modern aspirations after the new and the beautiful. The dead level of imitative sameness must not be so much traversed, or constructive shams and falsities will be sure to follow. The growing commercial spirit is too strong for conscientious work. Competition, in the better and even the best class of goods, asserts its baneful rule more and more. Accepted types of articles, whether for home, civil, or church uses, are too obviously and mechanically imitative. Flimsiness and falsehood in manufacture come of pretension to merit and truth ; and, notwithstanding the great and honourable achievements of the Birmingham art and technical schools, whose influences have been so beneficial to her industries, and to workers in brass perhaps more than all, the hope of the future is assured, made certain, only as the adjustment of the economic conditions of Capital and Labour become fully understood and practised. True life-enjoyment and satisfaction will not till then be the result of work done honestly and well.

J. M. O'FALLON.

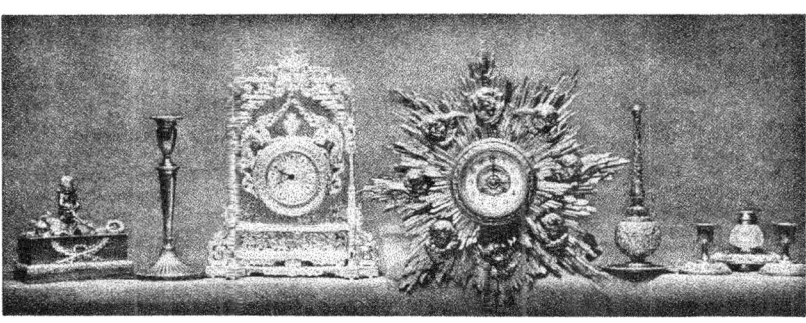

EXAMPLE OF BIRMINGHAM BRASS WORK. EXHIBITED BY MESSRS. HOWELL AND JAMES. (No. 11.)

'HOME WITH THE TIDE.'

BY JAMES CLARKE HOOK, R.A. ETCHED BY R. SPINELLI.

OUT of the sixty-six pictures offered by Mr. Henry Tate to the trustees of the National Gallery for inclusion in the projected gallery of British Art, sixty-one have been chosen, and few can have given rise to less debate than Mr. Hook's 'Home with the Tide.' It is an excellent example of his best time, of the time when knowledge was complete and the delight in it not yet beginning to pall. Some people find fault with Mr. Hook for his monotony of subject, for the fidelity with which he clings to the sea-coast and to one aspect of that. But, as the writer of this note has often had occasion to point out, that is the way in which nearly all painters of realistic landscape, or natural phenomena generally, have arrived at perfection. Cuyp painted sunlight in the fields, De Hooch sunlight in a house, unapproachably, because they were doing it always. It was the same with Constable and a showery June, and it is the same now with Mr. Hook and the breezy, bracing brininess of a fishing coast. He has watched the humours of his favourite subject so long that none of their constituents escape him, and before such a canvas as 'Home with the Tide,' we feel as we do when after a long day's walk we come suddenly upon the sea through some gate in the controlling cliffs. It would be interesting to *know* why Mr. Hook places his figures so curiously. Has he put his fisherman's wife down in the corner of the canvas, with her back to his subject, out of perversity, and the mere determination to be different from other people, or because he felt that his scheme required this eccentric note? It is undeniable that if this had been the first picture ever painted, it would have been improved if the said lady and her daughter (or son) had been pulled a little out of her corner and turned to face a little more into the gleaming vista which gives the conception its charm. The arrangement would, of course, have been more commonplace, but it would also have been more coherent. Is novelty with a touch of discord more desirable than a harmony we have enjoyed before, when the elements are as new and personal as they are in all the works of Mr. Hook? This question becomes very difficult to answer.

W. A.

ART NOTES.

A LEGACY, consisting of pictures, bronzes, china, ivories, enamels, jade and lacquers, is announced as having been made to the South Kensington Museum by the late Mr. John Hill, of Streatham, as "a token of gratitude for the pleasure and profit" derived by the testator from visits to the collections there. We understand that the bequest has not yet been inspected or formally accepted by the authorities, and the various conditions laid down by the testator will necessitate careful consideration before a decision can be made.

In the list we published last month of works of Art presented to the trustees of the National Gallery by Mr. Henry Tate to be placed in the New National Gallery of British Art, we omitted the beautiful bronze statue, 'The Egyptian Singer,' by Onslow Ford, A.R.A., a reproduction of which appears in this number.

The Dresden Gallery has bought from Lord Dudley, through the agency of Dr. Richter, 'The Death of St. Clara,' one of the finest and largest pictures by Murillo in this country. It is an early work of the master and very attractive by the fanciful treatment of the subject. The well-known 'Cuisine des Anges' in the Louvre formed originally a pendant to it at Seville. The price paid is stated to have been £3,000, whereas Lord Dudley had paid for it 95,000 francs at the Salamanca sale.

The unfortunate dispute between the heirs of Meissonier over his estate, prevented the realisation of the great painter's dream that his fine house in Paris should be turned into a national museum after his death. This mansion, situated at the corner of the Boulevard Malesherbes and the Rue Legendre, was furnished with the most perfect taste upon models at Venice and elsewhere, and is now in course of demolition.

Mr. H. S. Tuke has been awarded a medal of honour at the Munich Exhibition, together with a similar honour to Benlliure, the Spanish artist, living in Rome. The chief medal has fallen to Arnold Böcklin, of Florence, an artist almost unknown in London. Mr. C. W. Furse also receives a medal of the second class, and Mr. Alexander Koch, of London, one for Architecture.

A small private exhibition of oil and water-colour sketches of Warwick and the district is now on view at the studio of Mr. Trevor Haddon, in Great George Street, Westminster.

Pen draughtsmen, professional and amateur, are always glad to know of any improvement in the materials which they employ. The carton prepared by F. & S. Turnbull & Co., of which we have received some samples, seems to answer admirably the purpose for which it is prepared, being faced with a hard-surfaced hand-made paper which is not liable to become fluffy under the finest crow-quill pen.

Woodburning, or poker work, is one of those genteel hobbies of a more or less artistic character which the exigencies of decoration seem to demand in many suburban homes. It is an alternative to the inevitable *machramé* and crewel work. With a special eye to the requirements of this domestic 'Art,' Moeller & Condrup, of Fore Street, have produced a book of designs, but they are not very remarkable either for originality or correct drawing.

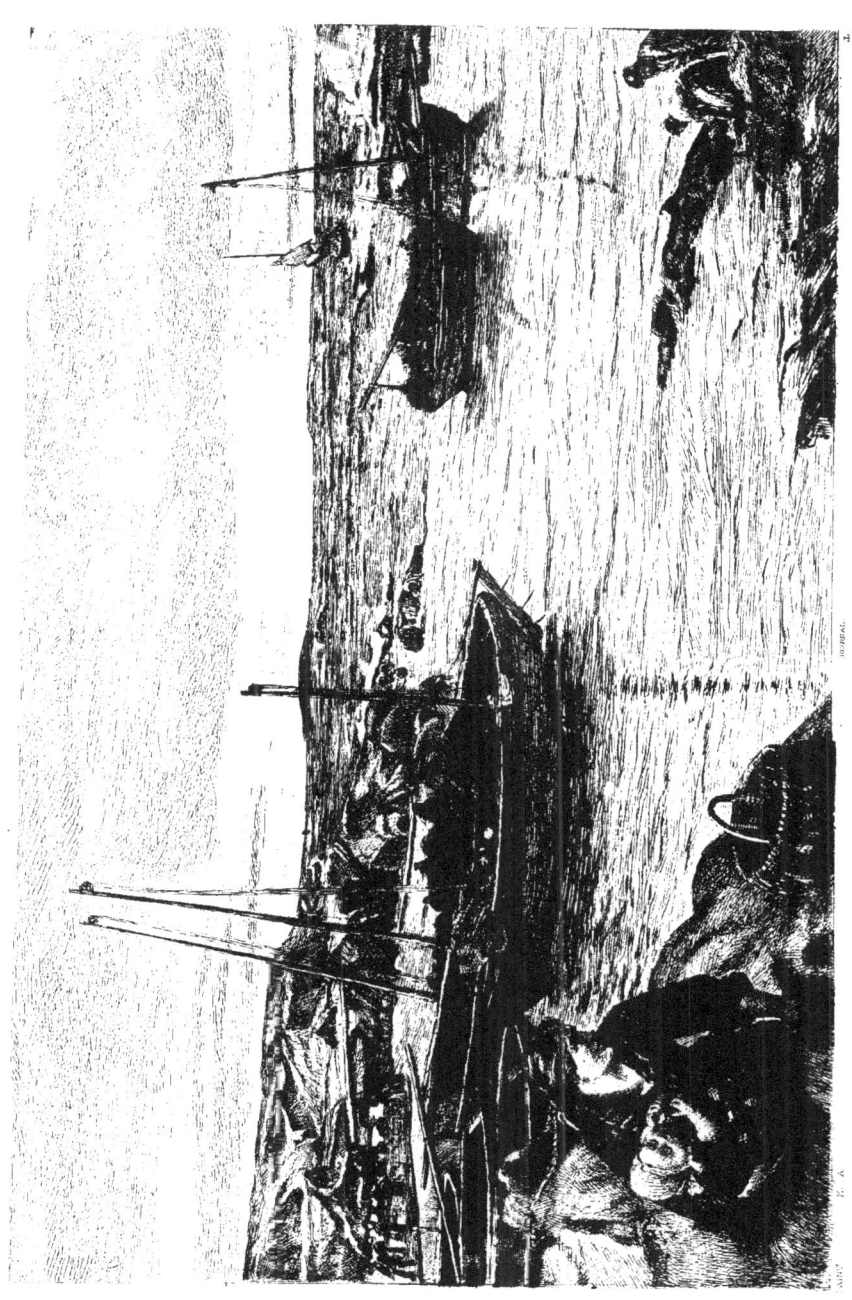

NOTES ON ART BOOKS.

MR. W. Robinson is the best authority in England on landscape gardening, and by long practice he has added to his unquestioned knowledge a graceful style of setting forth all he has to say. Twenty years ago Mr. Robinson published his first edition of "THE WILD GARDEN," and now he has superintended the issue of a fourth enlarged edition (Murray) with a brilliant series of illustrations by Mr. Alfred Parsons. This book ought to be studied by every possessor of an ordinary garden, however small. The author's main theory is that the foolish old laws of landscape gardeners, that a garden is "a work of art, and in it we must not attempt to imitate nature," ought to be abandoned; and that the plants of other countries as hardy as our hardiest wild flowers ought to be placed in our English gardens, "where they will flourish without further care or cost." Another theory fully developed in the book is the placing of bulbs in meadows, lawns, and grass plots, where they will flourish early in the spring without interfering with the grass. We print one of Mr. Parson's beautiful drawings, from Mr. Robinson's book.

A most important work has been commenced in "THE CHURCHES OF SHROPSHIRE," an architectural and archæological account of the many beautiful and interesting ecclesiastical edifices in that locality (Hobson, Wellington, Shropshire). The author, Mr. D. H. S. Cranage, M.A., of Cambridge, is an enthusiast in his labours, and nothing escapes his notice. He is ably seconded by Mr. M. J. Harding, who has taken all the photographs reproduced to illustrate the volume, and by Mr. W. A. Webb, who has prepared plans of the more important churches. The work will be issued in parts, and the first is an account of the Hundred of Brimstree. Later we hope to notice this undertaking more in the detail it deserves.

The Manchester Whitworth Institute is very fortunate in its officers and council. Taking a large-minded view of their duties, these gentlemen have caused an "HISTORICAL CATALOGUE OF THE WATER-COLOUR DRAWINGS" (Cornish, and Palmer and Howe, Manchester) to be prepared, illustrated by twenty-four clearly printed and excellent illustrations. Mr. Cosmo Monkhouse has written a readable, if somewhat diffuse, introduction, and each drawing is fully annotated. As it was only in 1889 that the Institute was incorporated, the Council has

THE BLACK POPLAR IN THE KENNET VALLEY.
BY ALFRED PARSONS. FROM ROBINSON'S "WILD GARDEN."

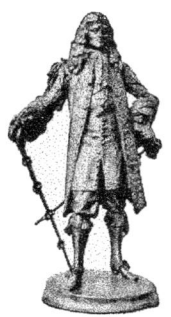

LOUIS XIV.
BRONZE STATUETTE BY CHAPU.

been singularly active in pursuing its plans, and already gifts from the magnates of the locality help to swell the original fund, Mr. William Agnew, Mr. J. E. Taylor, Mr. C. E. Lees, and others having made important presentations.

The Chicago Exhibition brought little grist directly to the mill of the British artist, but it is likely that the satisfactory collection gathered together there will ultimately bear fruit. One of the best means to help the desire of American purchasers to form collections of modern British works of Art is the splendid publication, "THE ART OF THE WORLD," published by Messrs. Appleton, of New York (also Sampson Low & Co., London). This work has been issued in thirty parts, each containing magnificent reproductions, some in black and some in colour, of the chief pictures exhibited, and it forms one of the most imposing publications of recent years. The text is edited by Mr. Charles Yriarte, who writes with due appreciation and knowledge. The notice of each artist is accompanied by an excellent portrait of the painter.

Another publication connected with Chicago has been published under the title of "HISTORY OF THE WORLD'S COLUMBIAN EXPOSITION" (Columbian History Company, Chicago; and Simpkin, Marshall, London). It is entirely different from Messrs. Appleton's great work, but it is almost worthy to stand beside it. This is the complete history of the Chicago World's Fair, compiled from the most reliable sources. The illustrations are very numerous, and are composed chiefly of really splendid photographic reproductions of views of the buildings and their surroundings. As it is allowed on every side that the artistic aspects of the World's Fair showed more architectural beauty than any previous exhibition in any part of the world, the publishers have wisely made superb views of these, the chief portion of the work. It is a beautiful souvenir of the Chicago Exposition.

The new and picturesque West Highland Railway is illustrated and described in a well-written and well-printed book under the title of "MOUNTAIN, MOOR AND LOCH" (Causton). It is a pity the artists' names are not given to some at least of the two hundred and thirty illustrations, for many of them are instinct with artistic appreciation.

"PIERRES GRAVÉES DÉCRITES" (Spoleto, Premiata Tip. dell' Umbria) is a catalogue of the small but interesting collection of nearly two hundred ancient Intaglios, mostly found in the excavations of Dalmatia, now in the collection of S. Meneghelli at Zara, on the Adriatic coast.

One of those beautiful souls who happily are not uncommon in the artistic world, passed away on April 21st, 1891, by the death of Henri Chapu, the sculptor *bien connu* in France. From 1833 until his death fifty-eight years later, Chapu was loved by every one he met. As the winner of the Prix de Rome in 1855, he came prominently before the French public, and in later years he carved many fine monuments, which now decorate the Ecole des Beaux-Arts, Père Lachaise, the Luxembourg, and several provincial museums in France. He was the sculptor of the 'Figure tombale' of the Duchess of Nemours, at Weybridge, in Surrey; of the colossal bronze medallion of Millet and Rousseau at Barbizon; and of the bust of the Princess of Wales at Copenhagen. Chapu's 'Death of Clyte,' in the Dijon museum, is one of his most elegant compositions, and, together with two other designs, we give a reproduction of the artist's study for this work. M. O. Fidière has written his biography, "CHAPU, SA VIE ET SON ŒUVRE" (Plon, Paris), in a sympathetic gathering together of the sculptor's memorials, well illustrated with plates and blocks, and printed with care. Chapu's life is worth reading and also worth studying.

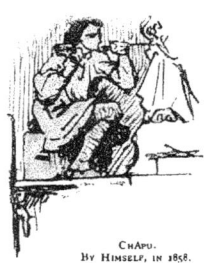

CHAPU.
BY HIMSELF, IN 1858.

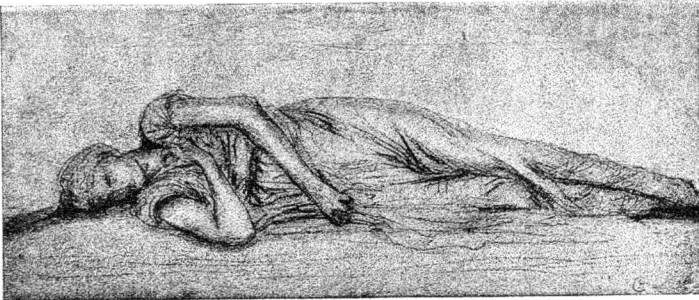

SKETCH FOR 'CLYTE.' BY CHAPU.

TONY ROBERT-FLEURY.

In 1845 one of the commentators of David wrote the following lines on the subject of the painter of the 'Sabines': "Equally republican at the Convention as he was at the studio, the painter of 'Brutus' was the judge of Louis XVI.; in the midst of a revolutionary Paris, at a moment when France was palpitating with questions of life and death, David was calling to mind the examples of other ancient republics; he experienced a genial warmth from the remembrance of their virtues, even as at the contemplation of their bas-reliefs, and he sallied forth from the Jacobin club, or the meetings of the Convention, with his head filled with the designs of ancient liberty; then when he was face to face with his canvas, in the silence of his studio, the enthusiasm that the cries of Danton or St. Just had evoked in him, slowly burnt out, his calmness reasserted itself. . . . . ."

Taking into consideration the characteristics of the epoch and the personality of the painter, one part of these observations might equally well apply to the artist who is the subject of this article.

It actually seems, in carefully considering the work of M. Tony Robert-Fleury, that the enthusiasm of the first movement, roused by the sight of some classic work of Art, or the perusal of an historical event which has made every generous fibre in his being vibrate, has gradually given place to a well-thought-out scheme, a renewed grasp on his own identity. In every case where M. Robert-Fleury was about to take a right step in letting his fancy take the reins, he has grasped a second conclusion, perhaps more reasonable, that seemed to him a happier thought. In the face of the practical results that accrue therefrom, he may well be said to have made no error. M. Tony Robert-Fleury has, in point of fact, run through the scale of official distinctions that have fallen to his share, let us say as a result of work conscientiously performed, and an incontestable artistic sense of honesty. Nevertheless we should be glad to discover more frequently in the *ensemble* of his pictures the initial spark a little more to the fore, less hidden by the ashes of a laborious method to which the first impression seems invariably to have been sacrificed. Far be it from me to allege that M. Robert-Fleury lacks sincerity. I do not think it by any means, but it may be said that almost always the forethought for form, decoration, and the *mise-en-scène* have come detrimentally to his inspiration to evict his primary intentions.

Take, for example, 'Le Dernier Jour de Corinthe,' the principal work of the artist (illustrated on page 325), now hung in the Luxembourg, having gained the *médaille d' honneur* for him in 1870. The troubles of that terrible year, the apprehensions of war in which nobody yet really believed, had no influence on the thoughts of the painter for the elaboration of his work. The young man's mind was absolutely free from exterior considerations, when the idea occurred to him to depict this page of Grecian history. Here and there, where a Delacroix would have insisted upon savage episodes, such as mutilated women wallowing in bloodshed, children with their throats gashed by the side of overturned altars, a devastated village illuminated by the crimson blaze of fire, M. Robert-Fleury, who must have been suffering all this agony and misery whilst thinking of the episode, only remembered in the presence of his picture how best to depict beautiful creations, to compose

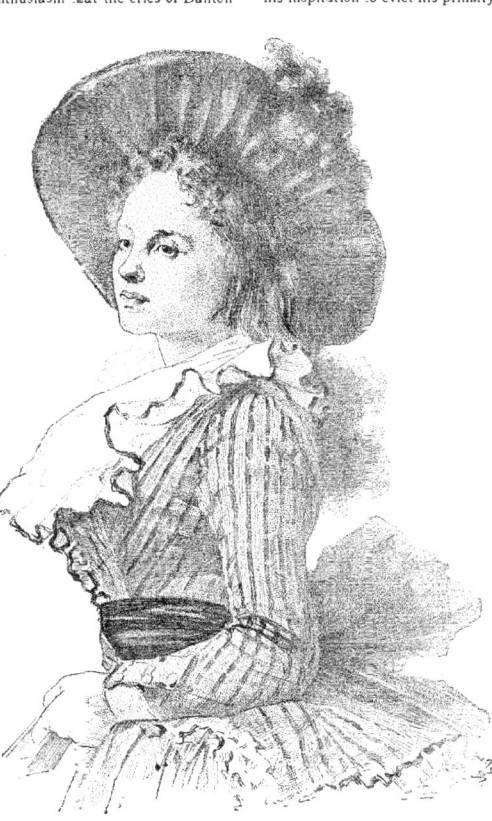

'1789.' BY TONY ROBERT-FLEURY.

noble attitudes, without feeling within his soul any of those disturbing currents which instil the very essence of life to human beings and inanimate nature.

At the foot of the statue of Minerva women in tears glide around in studied attitudes; in the background a column of smoke that might have issued from a picture of Ingres rises upwards, whilst a chariot yoked to a pair of classic and stationary oxen appear to have been conducted to this spot solely for the exigencies of the composition. Whilst to the right soldiers incidentally indicated massacre prisoners, to the left the Consul Mummius, astride his martial steed, and followed by Roman legions, enters the town.

Not a trace of emotion is visible in this picture, so elegantly composed, that might equally well be called 'The Victor's Portion,' or 'The Beautiful Captives,' as 'Le Dernier Jour de Corinthe.' In sooth, it is not the painter that is at fault but the school whose faults M. Robert-Fleury, then making his début, annexed. Still, what emotions could have been portrayed at this eventful date, the close of an epoch of civilisation! Fear, hatred, suffering on the one side; on the other brutality, licentiousness, and the lust of triumph; and what a figure to depict would have been that Roman general that the painter so unconcernedly ignored, that might so well have represented the coarseness of the soldier—the ignorance of might have to be replaced at their own expense should they be lost or injured in the transit. But of what use were such documents as these? The school of David that still reigned supreme at this time cared less for reality than the principles of decoration. "Fo-orm" as Brid'oison says in the "Noces de Figaro"—everything lay in that nutshell!

The first painting exhibited by M. Tony Robert-Fleury takes us back to 1866. It was entitled 'Varsovie, Scène de l'Insurrection polonaise' (illustrated below), an event that took place in the Polish capital on the 8th April, 1861. An article in the *Moniteur* relating the fact of the fusillade of four thousand Poles by Russian troops, caught the eye of the young man, and, moved by painful indignation and noble ardour, he hastened to call in his brushes to pay his tribute to the unfortunate victims.

By a rather ingenious procedure, more dramatic than conclusive, M. Robert-Fleury shows successively groups falling beneath the Muscovite artillery. Here a father supports the head of his son, who has just been struck with a bullet; in the foreground two monks elevate the cross before the charge of the enemy, whilst one of them raises his hand to his chest, where he, too, has received his deathblow; there, women wait their death in various attitudes, and by the side three men, standing one by the other, bravely behold the rain of shot without exhibiting any visible emotion. The ground is

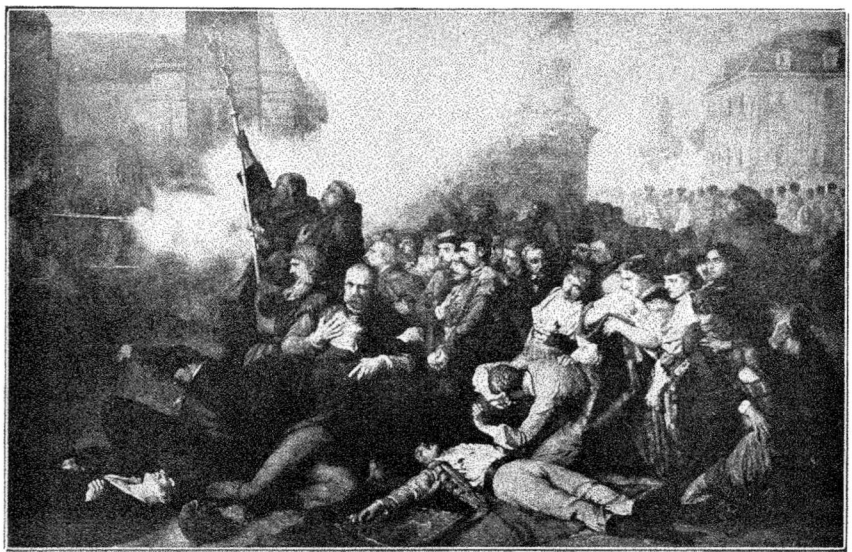

'VARSOVIE.' INCIDENT OF THE POLISH REBELLION. BY TONY ROBERT-FLEURY.
Photo by Braun & Co., Dornach, Alsace.

Mummius in all that concerned Art was proverbial. The canvas of 'Bacchus,' so celebrated at Corinth, was given by this consul to his men, who used it as a gaming-table, although this did not prevent him very seriously attending to the transport of certain works of Art from Corinth to Rome, which covered with corpses, from here, there and everywhere. It is the moment previous to the final extinction of everything by the fire of the conquerors. Finally, to the right, towards the background, a battalion of Cossacks bars the place so as to completely shut out the egress.

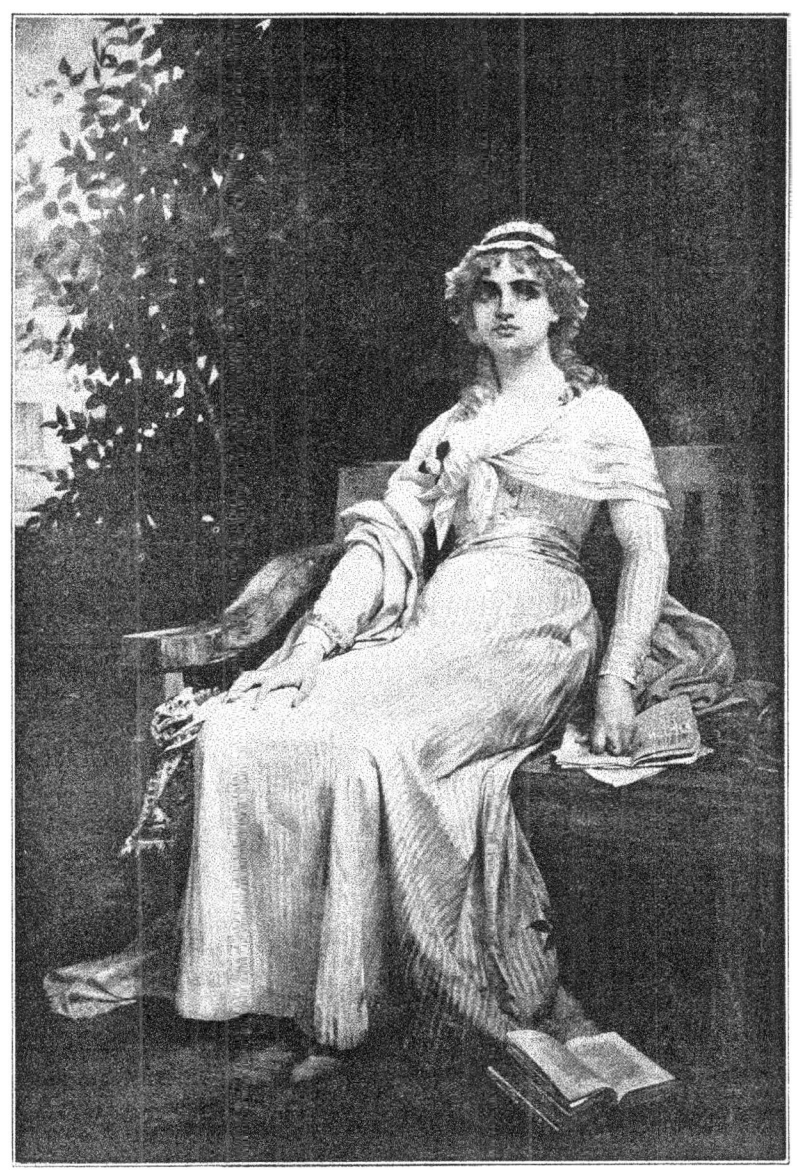

CHARLOTTE CORDAY AT CAEN. BY TONY ROBERT-FLEURY.
(Photo by Braun & Co., Dornach, Alsace.)

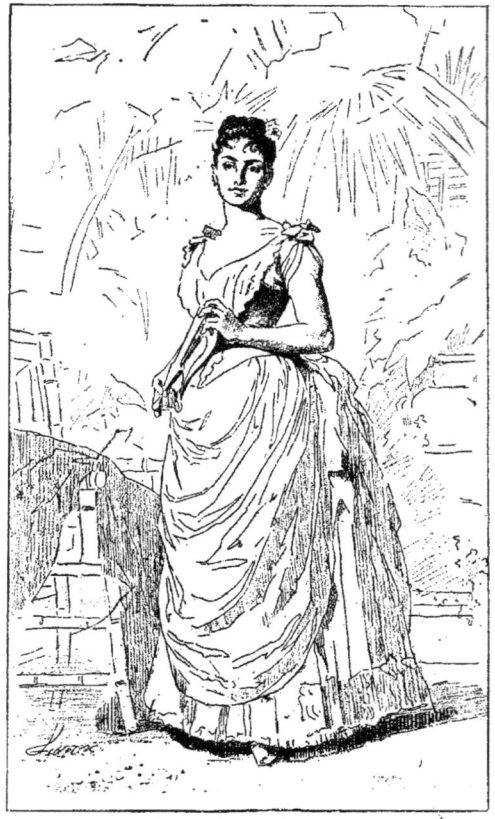

SKETCH BY TONY ROBERT-FLEURY.

At the moment of the appearance of this canvas all the younger generation at the schools was infatuated with Poland, and a year later M. Floquet made the famous ejaculation concerning the passage of the Emperor Alexander, upon which his political career was built. The press went equally far and dissimulated nothing, not even their sympathy for the Poles, therefore the appearance of 'Varsovie' was the occasion of a manifestation in which politics played at least as great a part as Art.

Edmond About wrote on this subject: "'Varsovie' is one of the events of the year. It is not only the sympathy for a great nation that is oppressed that attracts the public round this picture—the young artist owes the better part of his success to his own efforts. The composition is powerful, the thought is expressed with energy linked to simplicity. The work says plainly what it wants to say, which is by no means a commonplace merit. Without explanations, without commentaries, we understand the sombre heroism of this unarmed crowd which stands ready to receive its death-warrant.

These old men, these women, these children go bare-chested into the fire, filled with hope at the thought of being massacred, that the death-roll would be a mighty one, that at the sight of this carnage the whole of Europe should rise in pity. The patriotic martyrs, animated by this divine fire that the despotism of the Czars has ever been powerless to extinguish, compose this group. The picture speaks, it cries aloud, and woe be to the heart that shall not hearken to its sobs!"

Beyond the medal which M. Tony Robert-Fleury obtained for 'Varsovie' the Polish colony in Paris offered the artist an ebony casket, on the cover of which was reproduced the picture with a dedication of "gratitude" inscribed beneath it. Dramatic, historical, and tragic scenes seem, moreover, to have exercised a powerful influence over M. Robert-Fleury during the major part of his career.

In 1876 he sent to the Salon 'Pinel à la Salpêtrière,' which is perhaps one of the best works produced by his brush. After having become known by a translation of a "Treatise of Practical Medicine," by Culley, Pinel, in 1795, was named chief doctor at the Salpêtrière. Before his advent, lunatics were treated as regular pariahs. Abandoned to themselves, chained like convicts, the unfortunate maniacs dragged on a wretched, hopeless existence to which death was the only release possible. It is easy to picture a corner of Dante's "Inferno" in reading these descriptions of such shelters. Pinel came upon the scene, and for this barbarous and inhuman régime he substituted a treatment of gentleness, and his first care on taking possession of his post was to completely abolish the chains with which the prisoners were loaded.

It is this scene that M. Tony Robert-Fleury wanted to fix indelibly. Despite the rather scattered order of the subject, the whole thing is very striking. The picture is placed now in one of the sections of the Salpêtrière, thereby commemorating, at a few steps from where it happened, an event that entirely changed the established usages of the treatment of lunacy.

After having attacked large historical subjects M. Robert-Fleury did not immediately renounce his favourite style. He exhibited again, in 1875, 'Charlotte Corday at Caen,' a work we illustrate and where keen expression is shown to advantage; and in 1882 a 'Vauban donnant le plan des fortifications de Belfort,' where the celebrated engineer is represented in Louis XIV costume beside three personages leaning over a map, while in the background labourers are engaged on building work. The canvas, without representing much interest, had nevertheless better luck than the 'Glorification de la Sculpture Française,' destined originally in 1880 for the Luxembourg. Some time later, when the ceiling was finished, the Senate reclaimed as its personal property the palace that the State had hitherto considered its own.

After much talk and discussion the Upper House was definitively considered the property of the "immeuble national," but the State having defrayed the cost of the decoration of

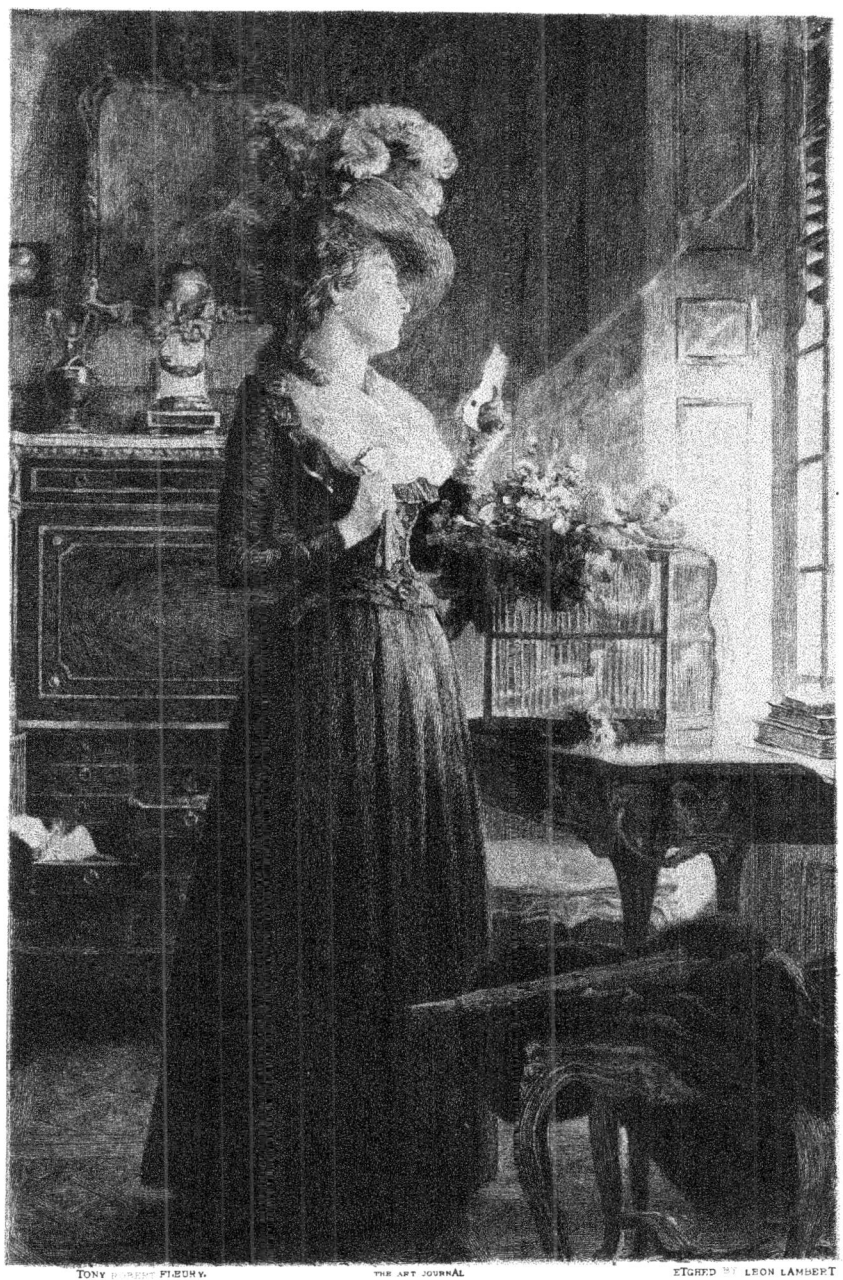

TONY ROBERT FLEURY.   THE ART JOURNAL   ETCHED BY LEON LAMBERT

THE BILLET-DOUX.

LONDON: J.S. VIRTUE & CO LIMITED.

the ceiling ordered from the artist, would not give it up to the Senate, and for want of a proper place to instal it the 'Glorification de la Sculpture' has been wheeled (where it now is) into the loft of the lumber-room, where the mice alone keep it company.

M. Robert-Fleury had still to reveal himself as a painter of genre subjects connected with myths and anecdotes. 'Ophélie,' in 1887, 'Magdelena,' in 1889, '1789,' reproduced here, which appeared in the year 1890, 'Le Billet Doux,' in 1891, all mark evolution in his style. In the 'Billet Doux,' of which we give an etching by Léon Lambert, the painter has truthfully described, by an episode, the particular style of the period. The love letter read by this "Parisienne," of the Directoire, must evidently be filled with those sweet words Parisian ladies, even contemporaneous, are always delighted to peruse!

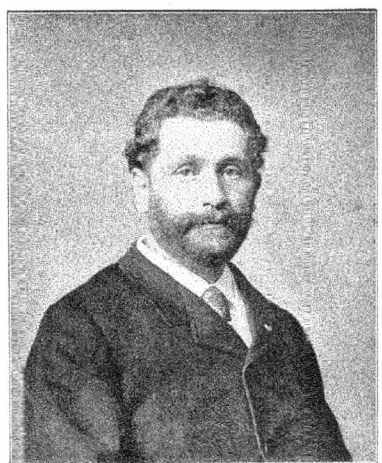

TONY ROBERT-FLEURY.
PRESIDENT OF THE JURY OF PAINTING AT THE PARIS SALON FOR 1894.

The author of 'Corinthe' has obtained all the rewards of the Salon and many others, so he would be fully entitled to rest on his laurels. He obtained the medals in 1866—67 and '70, became Chevalier of the Légion d'Honneur in '73, again received a first-class medal at the Universal Exhibition in 1878, was further promoted to Officer of the National Order in 1884, he then received the gold medal at the Universal Exhibitiou, 1889. He has been " hors-concours" for a long time, and after having taken part in the juries of the Exhibitions of the Champs-Elysées, M. Tony Robert-Fleury has been finally named President of the hanging committee. His courtesy and affability, concealed by a slight crust of coldness, at which nobody could possibly take offence, well fit him for his position.

JEAN BERNAC.

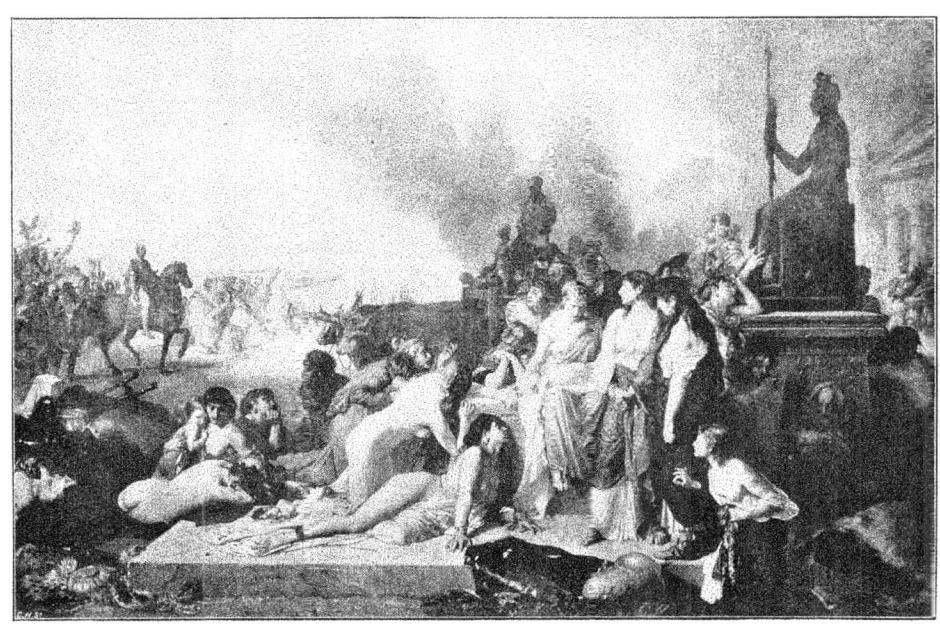

'THE LAST DAY OF CORINTH.' FROM THE PAINTING BY TONY ROBERT-FLEURY.

SIR J. C. ROBINSON ON BITUMEN AND VARNISH.

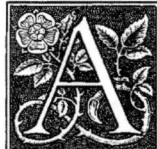 LENGTHY letter by Sir J. C. Robinson, who worthily holds the position of Inspector of Her Majesty's pictures, was recently published,* giving a carefully prepared opinion on the present state of English pictures painted with bitumen or asphaltum, or laden with varnish. The occasion for the letter was the severe strictures of Sir James Linton and Mr. Orrock on the condition of certain English pictures in the National Gallery; a condition we are glad to know that is receiving the attention of our energetic new director. It may be added that Sir J. C. Robinson's views are the outcome of most varied experience and special knowledge. He writes:—" The nature of the evil has been distinctly pointed out, and it has been shown to be one almost exclusively inherent in English pictures of the last, and early part of the present century. Its worst development is to be seen in the works of two of our greatest national painters, those of Sir Joshua Reynolds and Sir David Wilkie; and, unfortunately, so completely is the matter illustrated in these admirable pictures that, in further discussion, reference need scarcely be made to the productions of any other of our national artists.

Unquestionably the pictures of these world-famous masters are, as a rule, in an unsound and unstable state, for although time has conferred upon them certain ripened graces, it has developed more than counterbalancing drawbacks.

As this subject cannot be put in too clear a light, the use, or rather the abuse, of bituminous pigments, which has been the main and patent cause of the mischief, may, I think with public advantage, be discussed in somewhat fuller detail. It has been noticed that the evil in question is not manifest in the works of the great Dutch painters, who were the precursors and real masters of Sir Joshua and Wilkie.

It might, nevertheless, have been pointed out that Rembrandt and Ostade, whose works were familiar to, and always respectively held in view by, the two English artists, made in their time as free and unrestricted a use of the obnoxious pigments as did their modern followers; but with this saving difference, that their methods of mixing and applying them were evidently sounder and more scientific, that the oils, varnishes, and essences with which they tempered the colours in question were such as from long experience they knew would safely unite with them, and, indeed, counteract the deleterious tendencies which they were well aware were inherent in the pigments; whilst their methods of making use of the resultant colours were at the same time more deliberate and well reasoned.

In the time of Sir Joshua Reynolds, who was obviously the chief sinner, if not the real originator of the bad bituminous English technique, no such care was taken. Incongruous vehicles and pigments were used in a careless, haphazard fashion, and so, indeed, it has in great measure continued down even to our own time.

The inherent evils of the *régime* of bitumen and asphaltum

* *The Times*, August 23, 1894.

were at the same time aggravated by the universal use of a thoroughly bad and deceptive, though very alluring vehicle. The reign of 'McGilp' was concurrent, and it is to the lavish use of this incongruous diluent with bituminous pigments that some of the most fatal effects are due.

The fluid vehicle known by the cant name of McGilp, probably from that of the inventor of the odious compound, was a mixture of drying linseed oil and mastic varnish, and it possessed the properties, so greatly desired by Sir Joshua and his school, of enabling colours mixed with it to be applied in thick unctuous impasto and of apparently causing them to dry quickly.

But bitumen and asphaltum were of very different natures. Although in this vehicle they apparently very soon became dry, the solidity was only on the surface, and when applied in any volume they remained, and often for a century or more have remained, practically in a semi-fluid state within. The discordant properties of the vehicle and these particular pigments were then entirely opposed to all conditions of natural equilibrium and stability. Both were liable to shrink and contract greatly in their partial drying, and hence, sooner or later, the occurrence of the cracks, corrugations, and numerous changes of other kinds which have often so greatly disfigured the works of the English masters. There can be little doubt that in some of Sir Joshua's pictures these defects must have been manifested in his own time, very shortly, indeed, after their completion. Doubtless these evils have been accelerated or retarded by accidental and modifying circumstances, but it is the fact that parts of some of Sir Joshua's pictures have to this day never become dry, and, indeed, never will do so.

Another and almost universal aggravation of the evil has ensued from the too-frequent and profuse application of surface varnishes—very necessary in due measure and season for the preservation of oil pictures, but sometimes and in some cases most deleterious. The longer newly-painted pictures can, with due regard to their preservation in other respects, be left without varnish the better. If varnish is applied to such pictures, consequently, before the pigments have thoroughly dried, the inevitable result is to cause the paint beneath to crack; the reason being that the varnish closely adherent to the paint dries quickly and thoroughly, and at the same time contracts in volume, and in so doing tears asunder the tender film of pigment beneath. Naturally this action on the thickly-loaded bituminous passages of Sir Joshua's pictures, which have never really become dry, has been marked and considerable. It was an evil, moreover, which tended to perpetuate itself in an aggravated degree, inasmuch as unreasoning possessors of such pictures and their unskilled advisers more frequently than not, as the works in course of time became dull, irregular, and patchy in appearance, endeavoured to remedy the matter by simply applying successive coats of varnish—needless to repeat, thereby only intensifying the evil.

One of the principal ill-effects of this over-varnishing has been to render it most difficult to apply any safe cleansing process to Sir Joshua's pictures. Friction, the only really reliable method, is often quite inapplicable to the irregular, soft, and loaded bituminous surfaces in question; and the use of solvents, even in the hands of the ablest and most experienced practitioners, is dangerous and not unfrequently destructive.

To make this matter clearer, if any one will examine an average portrait picture by Sir Joshua Reynolds, he will note that the surface is in a very irregular and varied state of conservation. The high lights, usually the head, hands, and other portions in which a solid white pigment (white lead) has been the chief component, will be found in a smooth, compact, lustrous condition, as if enamelled; in the other parts, mainly in the half tints, cracks fissures, and slight corrugations, more or less abundant and disturbing, will be seen; but in the extreme darks, usually in the background and the draperies, there will be found heavy, opaque, rugose passages of loaded colour, cracked, shrivelled, and distorted in the most extraordinary manner. Again, in the dark parts which have been more thinly painted, he will sometimes see passages showing a curious network of dark clots of opaque colour—little islands, as it were, more or less regularly disposed in a sort of transparent sea. This is simply the result of the gradual contraction and clotting together of the too-fluid bituminous pigments floating in the incongruous medium before described.

There are no natural or mechanical means of bringing back these altered passages to their original condition. The picture-restorer's remedy, that of bodily repainting them or of stippling into the cracks, is but a clumsy and fallacious one, in nine cases out of ten best let alone.

Even the most skilful hands can do little to restore to Sir Joshua's pictures their pristine hues and keeping. Minor accidents and blemishes can, of course, in some cases be successfully remedied; but before the slightest touch is put upon any valuable picture in the condition described the careful consideration and advice of the most eminent professional experts should be sought. Such persons, though they will usually be able, in a measure, to remedy mishaps, caused it may be by the action of unskilled predecessors, will in most cases advise that the ills that are should be endured rather than that by doubtful efforts to remedy them further mischief should sooner or later be made to ensue."

CRITICS AND CRITICISM.

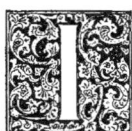

IT is amusing to see with what constant recurrence the epidemic of discussion on the subject of Art criticism breaks out every now and again. Opinion on this matter is like a spring that overflows at irregular intervals, and that makes up for long periods of quiescence by occasional displays of violent energy. There is no foretelling when the outburst may come, nor how long it may continue; it begins as a rule with hardly a warning, and all at once drowns the world with a muddy torrent, that carries along all sorts of incongruous mental wreckage, and intellectual odds and ends. Yet these alarming manifestations are only so much force wasted. It is surely obvious that, so long as the artist who possesses and uses technical knowledge is confronted with a public that neither has nor desires anything of the sort, the critic must find occupation—as a go-between. This indeed, however it may be disguised, is the real mission of all who write about Art. The public knows nothing about pictures and takes no interest in them except as illustrations of well-known stories. Watch the average person as he goes round a picture gallery. He reads the labels on the frames; if the label interests him he looks at the picture, if it does not he passes on to the next—label. And the function of the critics is to write these labels to explain what the artist meant when he painted the picture. The extent of the artist's success may be gauged by the length of the explanation that the critics find necessary. Some painters put things so simply and lucidly that the critic's task is quite an easy one, and only a few explanatory words are wanted to tell the whole story. Others, usually at the higher end of the scale, wrap up their meaning in such mysterious circumlocutions, that even the critics are perplexed, and have to make wild shots at the subject matter of the label. As often as not these shots are very wrong, and serve only to increase the bewilderment of the already puzzled public. Then critics and public combine to abuse the unhappy artist who has bewildered them, and to say that he does not know his business, that he does not understand the necessity for all art to be intelligible to the weakest comprehension that he is a fraud, delusion, and snare. This is unkind perhaps, and illogical; but, after all, for the critics to try and shift the blame for their own mistakes on to other shoulders is only human nature—and the artist is such a convenient scapegoat. It is a mistake, however, for them to leave off appealing to the public, and to say things to the artist himself about his work. He is apt to remember who it was started the mud-throwing, and is now and then rather rude to the critics in consequence. At all events he refuses to accept their suggestions in quite the same ready way that the public do the labels; and this the critics generally call rudeness.

The fact is that from the artist's point of view very little criticism is necessary. Any one who spends a lifetime in learning complicated technicalities, is not unnaturally impatient of dogmatism from people whose technical knowledge is only theoretical, and altogether superficial. When the whole thing is reduced to a question of one opinion against another, the convictions that come from experimental practice are, he feels, more likely to be right than those which have been formed merely by comparison of results. So long as the critics speak as mouthpieces of the public, and argue just as they are prompted by the absolutely untechnical, they are to a limited extent interesting, because they reflect that outside opinion which fascinates the artist even while he scorns it; but if once they cut themselves off from their base of support, and pit themselves in single combat against the Art-practitioner, they cease to have for him even a second-hand interest, and become instead hindrances, and sources of annoyance. It is safest for the critics to disabuse themselves of the idea that they can persuade anybody. Even the public will not be induced to change its beliefs against its own inclination. It is by the persistence of the artist, not by the guidance of the critics, that popular opinion is modified. All that criticism can do is to assist with its label writing the progress of a movement that has originated in the studios.

To properly fulfil this function of description, the critics must of course try to discriminate between good work and bad, between progress and retrogression. Fanaticism in criticism is a contradiction in terms; the first essential is impartiality. Every sincere artist who is trying to keep art alive, and to aid in its development, must be encouraged. Sincerity is the foremost thing that should be recognised, the first thing that people should be led to appreciate; and this sincerity must be not mere intenseness of subject or story, but the earnest expression of æsthetic belief, and of real study of nature. Good workmanship, important though it always is, concerns the critics less than evidences of observation and taste, than proofs of artistic balance and discreet selection. These may be found in the productions of very divergent schools. It is the man who would so far forget his artistic mission as to fall under the yoke of convention who should be exhibited as an impostor, as an impudent usurper of an artist's privileges; and yet, by a curious satire upon critical common-sense, it has hitherto been the innovators, the sturdy protestants against the limiting of æsthetic practice by hard-and-fast rules, upon whom the abuse of those who expound has been heaped most lavishly. Art is not a fixed and immutable thing; and the forms in which it may be expressed are subject to changes and variations. There is not for all time a particular pattern to which all pictures must conform. This is a point for critics to note; it may perhaps help them to understand much that is at present hidden from them, and it may be of assistance in the composition of labels for the next century. The old ones have been in use a long time; it is surely time that the public should set its servants to work upon a new set. There is plenty to describe.

A. L. BALDRY.

THEORY OF SENSATION OF COLOUR.

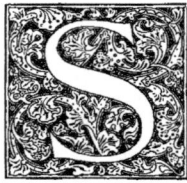

SOLID objects, under Newton's theory of vision, which are illuminated by any light, reflects this light in all directions, so that the light received upon the crystalline lens of the eye is brought to focus upon the nervous layer of the retina at the back of the eye, and by this means an exact picture of external objects is produced thereon. The form and colour of an object, Newton says, is perceived in the sensorium by being "propagated by the motion of the optic-nerves to the brain." * This theory presents no difficulty as regards the definite form of monochromatic objects, and was accepted as a sufficient theory until it was analysed by Thomas Young, early in the present century,† at which time the crystalline lens of the eye had been discovered to be non-achromatic. Therefore, to correctly specialise colour by refraction upon the retina, this organ must possess some distinctive nerve-functions for this purpose, as colours wide apart upon the spectrum, say red and blue, could not be brought simultaneously to focus upon the retinal-plane by a non-achromatic lens. To meet this difficulty Young proposed as a theory that there are three sets of nerves equally distributed over the retina. One set of which are specialised to pick up one colour only, red, green, or blue. Impressions from which colours, the brain by combination perceives all colours and tints. This theory has obtained the able support of the late great German physicist Helmholtz,‡ and is generally accepted by scientists. The non-achromatism of the eye upon the three-nerve theory is its greatest defect. Helmholtz said of the eye, "that if an optician had made an instrument so imperfect for him, he would have returned it to the maker for correction with severe censure." ||

In a paper recently read before the Physical Society of London, Mr. W. F. Stanley suggests that if the nervous system of the eye is adapted to pick up colours *refracted to different depths within the retina*, the non-achromatic lens of the eye would be specially adapted to this purpose, therefore certainly not defective. In fact, the eye would analyse colour exactly by the same method as the physicist analyses colour by the spectroscope. Therefore this new theory only demands what is quite consistent with the structure of the retina, where the single nerve is thirty times the depth that it presents upon the retinal surface, that the eye *makes use of its property of dispersion of light into colours* for perception, by separation, just as we analyse coloured lights by the prism for the same end. Mr. Stanley's objections to Helmholtz's theory are:—

"1. That we are sure that the intense crowding of the nerves in the retina is necessary for the recognition of the clear outline of form by the image passing through separate focal points, as if it were not so crowded the outline would be imperfect. In Helmholtz's theory for a coloured object,—say red, green, or violet—only *one-third* of the nerves covered by the image can be active at one time. If this is the actual case, it indicates indeed a poor though complex natural arrangement, and deserves the censure Helmholtz gave it.

"2. That with a non-achromatic eye the images of mixed colours could not be picked up on the plane of the retina in focus *at all*, as Helmholtz's theory demands. The violet would focus towards the front surface nearest the lens, the green central, and the red far back, so that the nerves, which are all transparent, would, for simultaneous vision of these colours, if tricolour nerve arrangement is necessary, be much better arranged in planes at different distances from the lens. We find them actually placed upon a definite smooth limiting plane, with the thickness of the sensitive retinal layer only to accommodate this difference of focus."

This adaptability of the eye to functions of recognition of dispersion of colour by depth of focus here proposed is not greater than that the naturalist finds in the specialised organization of every living creature, and it meets all the difficulties proposed by Young necessary for ensuring distinct colour vision.

* Newton's "Opticks," p. 13. † "Phil. Trans.," 1802, p. 12.
‡ "Encyclopadie der Physic," vol. iX. p. 127.
|| Quoted, Tyndall on "Light," page 8.

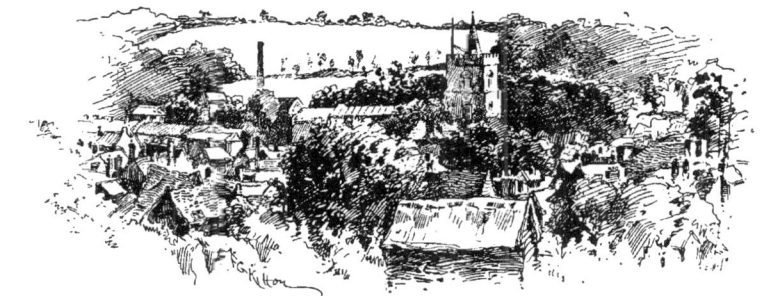

RICKMANSWORTH, AS SEEN FROM THE PARK. FROM THE DRAWING BY F. G. KITTON.

RICKMANSWORTH.

THE parish of Rickmansworth, called "Rychemareworde" in Domesday Book, stands on the borders of three counties — Hertfordshire, Buckinghamshire, and Middlesex. Although barely a dozen miles from London, the town still retains many of those rural features which are so rarely to be found within that distance from the Great Metropolis; indeed, the easy means of access thereto afforded by the "iron roads" makes this fact still more surprising. It should, of course, be said that Rickmansworth, like other small towns so near the centre of civilisation, "goes with the times" to a certain extent, and in its own quiet way; but we do not find there such strong evidence of the "jerry-builder" as we might, under the circumstances, expect to discover. And the simple explanation, I believe, is this:—The land in and around this unobtrusive Hertfordshire town is owned by two or three distinguished residents who do not favour any proposals for purchasing it for building purposes, deeming it inexpedient, or, at any rate, undesirable, to enter into any negotiations that might possibly tend to depreciate the natural attractions of the locality.

Rickmansworth is decidedly a town with a history. It is mentioned, as I have already stated in Domesday Book, where it is described as having land for twenty ploughs, and containing four Frenchmen, and forty-one labourers and bondmen of different grades; allusion being also made to certain fishing-rights, pasture for cattle, pannage or woods for 1,200 hogs—the entire value being £20 10s. by the year. In the reign of Henry III., however, the village assumed the rank of a town by being granted a charter to hold a market, and since those early days it has increased in importance and prosperity.

For Londoners, the most convenient approach to Rickmansworth is by the Metropolitan Railway; but until the recent extension of this system the only way of reaching it (apart from road-travelling) was by the little branch line from Watford, some three miles distant. From the typical country station of the London and North-Western Railway at Rickmansworth the visitor soon finds himself in the heart of the town, entering it on this side by the public thoroughfare through the churchyard, which renders this God's Acre less quiet and secluded than it otherwise would be. The well-kept burial-ground, however, is made really attractive by the luxuriant foliage of ancient chestnuts and lofty pines, these casting pleasant shadows over the gravestones, while the many shrubs that flourish amid the turfy mounds enhance the pictotial effect.

The flint embattled tower of the old Church, surmounted by a short spire or "spike," is, of course, a conspicuous object from almost every point around the town. The sacred edifice, dedicated to St. Mary, is the most ancient building in the parish; or, rather only the tower can be so described, for the body of the Church has been practically rebuilt within recent years, and in a manner compared with which the restoration that took place during the beginning of the present century is justly described as hideous, and altogether unworthy of so interesting a fabric.

There is an earlier instance of even a greater act of vandalism on the part of the inhabitants, when, in Cardinal Wolsey's time, they indicated their zeal in the Protestant cause by burning the images above the altar; unfortunately, the conflagration spread, and finally consumed the chancel, organ, and rood-

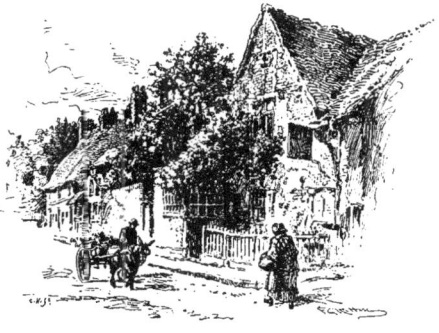

OLD COTTAGE IN THE HIGH STREET. FROM THE DRAWING BY F. G. KITTON.

screen. There remain, however, some remarkable monuments and brasses perpetuating the memory of local worthies, the finest probably being that of Sir Thomas Fotherley and his son, the former of whom was "one of the gentlemen of the Privy Chamber to Charles I. of *glorious* memory, and one of the Privy Council to his son, Prince Charles, afterwards King of England, of *immortal* memory." The arms that appear on the panels of a family tomb are those of the Earls of Monmouth and Middlesex; the black marble slab of this tomb was, until quite recently, used as an altar-top. The Earl of Monmouth here referred to had ten children, and his eldest son (so runs the inscription) "was slain A.D. 1644 at Marston Moore fight, in his Majestie's servise." One who played an important part in the history of the Church was Mr. George Swinnock, a Puritan clergyman and a voluminous writer, who was appointed vicar in the seventeenth century. He was succeeded by a still more eminent literary divine, Dr. Edmund Staunton, "who," says his biographer, "preferred work before wages," and successfully laboured here for twenty years, but amid much domestic sorrow, for he buried in one vault no fewer than ten children. In 1662 he was ejected from the Church for conscience' sake, and died nine years afterwards. It is interesting, also, to know that the famous ecclesiastic, Richard Baxter, used to preach in the town and neighbourhood, where he received quite an enthusiastic reception. Baxter even held a public controversy with the Quakers, who then abounded in this locality.

The latter statement is not surprising when we remember that Rickmansworth has for many years the home of the most distinguished of that sect, William Penn, afterwards the founder of Pennsylvania; it was here that he laid the basis of that colony which, it is said, was at the time the largest and freest ever formed by the British. In 1672, Penn married a pretty little quakeress whom he had met at Chalfont, near by,—a highly accomplished girl, who frequently entertained Milton with music in his Buckinghamshire home.* The youthful couple took a house in Rickmansworth — now called "Basing House"—where they lived happily for several years. A gentleman lately residing in the town (one of whose ancestors accompanied Penn across the Atlantic) remembered going to school in this house, and seeing a pane

* The cottage at Chalfont St. Giles, where Milton resided during the Plague, and where he wrote his immortal poem, is still intact.

of glass on which Penn had written with a diamond his name and the date, 1676—a relic which, unfortunately, has not been preserved. This enterprising Quaker, of whom it is said that he refused to move his hat even in the presence of royalty, left Rickmansworth for America in 1677; subsequently returning to this country, he died at his seat in Ruscombe, Berks, in 1718, and was interred (among other "Friends") in the little green burial-ground at Jordans, Chorley Wood, where his first wife and six children lay beside him.

Basing House is now in the occupation of Mr. R. W. Henderson, who, naturally enough, fully appreciates the interesting associations of the place. He informs me that the earliest deed in his possession relating to it is dated 1420; no doubt a large mansion originally stood somewhere on the site of the present structure, and was surrounded by its own grounds, as many of the neighbouring plots bear names such as Basing Meadow, the Basing Barn, etc., the original cognomen having apparently been "Baison," since converted into "Basing." Mr. Henderson is the fortunate owner of Penn's chair, which, however, is not considered as affording a particularly comfortable seat.

Apart from the Church, the most important building (by reason of its historical qualifications) is undoubtedly that known as "The Bury," the approach to which, from the fine wrought-iron entrance-gates and ancient ivy-covered lodge, is by a beautiful avenue of limes. On arriving at the end of the avenue, and turning sharply to the right, we see before us this fine old manor-house, which was apparently built about the time of Henry VIII. upon the foundations of a still older structure, some brickwork of that period being still visible. Dating from the Conquest, when the manor belonged to the Abbey of St. Albans, it passed subsequently to the Crown, in whose possession it remained until the time of Charles I.; it was then presented by the King to that staunch Royalist, Sir Thomas Fotherley. The worthy knight's equally loyal son, Sir John, entertained his sovereign, the Second Charles, at this very mansion, and local tradition says that on the southern side of the house (which eventually lapsed into decay) is a room in which that unfortunate monarch lay concealed for some days. Sir John Fotherley also assisted the King considerably when abroad, contributing largely to his restoration, and afterwards he is said to have been honoured with a visit from his royal master.

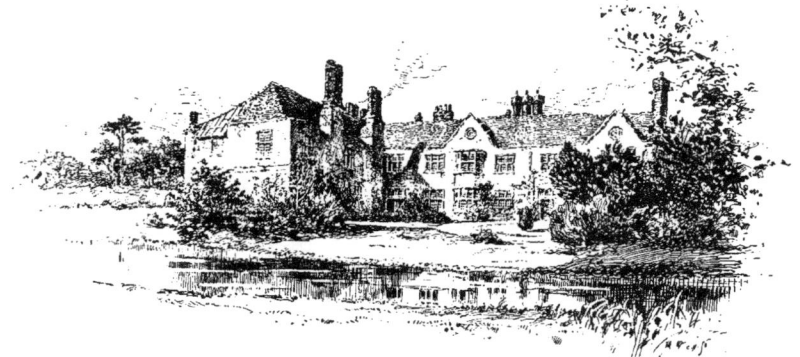

THE BURY. FROM THE DRAWING BY F. G. KITTON.

RICKMANSWORTH.

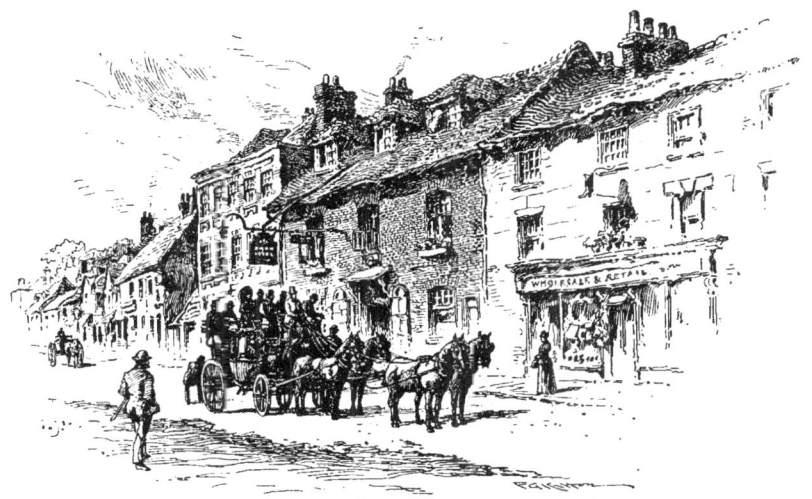

THE "SWAN" HOTEL, HIGH STREET. FROM THE DRAWING BY F. G. KITTON.

Having changed hands several times, The Bury was purchased in 1884 by Mr. John Taylor, who, however, had no respect for historical associations or archæological beauty, preferring to avail himself of the commercial value of the position, and other similar advantages which this beautiful mansion offered; so he converted it into what was practically a store-house for goods, and erected in the grounds a factory with a lofty chimney-shaft, both structures (although, happily, much disguised in foliage) being still visible. At Mr. Taylor's death the property was purchased by Lord Ebury, and the mansion then fell into the hands of the present tenant, Mr. T. W. Bevan, a gentleman of refined artistic tastes and capabilities, who may honestly be credited with having saved so fine an example of Tudor architecture from absolute ruin. Originally the house had two wings, thus forming three sides of a square; it also possessed a private chapel, but it, together with the north wing, disappeared many years since. The large and lofty rooms are enriched with oak panelling; the fireplaces are mainly Tudor-arched ones, that in the dining-room measuring eight feet across, and is surmounted by a splendid overmantel of the early Jacobean period. In the east front the casements are the original Tudor leaded ones; the two staircases are handsomely carved in chestnut, the second, or subsidiary, one being beautifully designed. In the drawing-room there still remain some quaint Elizabethan latches and hinges, which probably suffice to indicate the date of the building. The south wing of The Bury was in an almost hopeless state of dilapidation when Mr. Bevan rented the property; so much so, indeed, that it seemed desirable that this part of the house should be entirely demolished. It was, however, restored under the efficient superintendence of the present tenant, who reproduced, as far as possible, the original character of the structure, and designed some overmantels, adapting the details of those already existing. The suite of rooms in this wing now presents a charming and picturesque appearance; and here Mr. Bevan has made his study, in which one observes, among other artistic treasures, a portrait of his father, sketched in chalk from the life by that much-neglected painter, B. R. Haydon. On an exterior wall of this wing, protected by a glass conservatory, are traces of mural decoration. At one time a bell-turret surmounted the roof, but this was demolished, and the bell removed to Seth Taylor's Flour Mill, over Waterloo Bridge, where it still serves its purpose in commercial life.

There is another old manor-house just outside the town, at Croxley Green. The manor came into the possession of Dr. Caius, physician in ordinary to Edward VI., Mary, and Elizabeth, and the co-founder of the college in Cambridge bearing his name. The manor-house, known as Croxley Hall, is now a farm-house, but it yet contains certain architectural features which, together with the huge tithe-barn close by, proclaim them to have once been important adjuncts of this mediæval manor.

The principal street in Rickmansworth is, of course, the High Street. It retains much of its old-world character in its tiled roofs, plastered gables, leaded windows, and antiquated hostelries. Prominent among the latter is the "Swan," conspicuous by reason of the swinging sign projecting from its front, and which, apart from modern innovations, still has an old-fashioned look, with its high-pitched roof of red tiles and its massive dormers; the yard at the rear is well worth inspection, and the same may be said of the interior of this posting-house, with its comfortable oak-panelled rooms, so suggestive of prosperous coaching-days. It is not improbable that the "Swan" was established by some retired servant of the Monmouth family, who took for a sign his late master's crest, for over the coach entrance may be seen a bas-relief of this graceful bird, with a last-century date. There is another ancient hostelry in High Street that cannot fail to attract notice; I allude to the "Bell," at one time an important coaching-inn, which, with its plaster front, projecting gables, and massive window-frames, is really picturesque. Proceed-

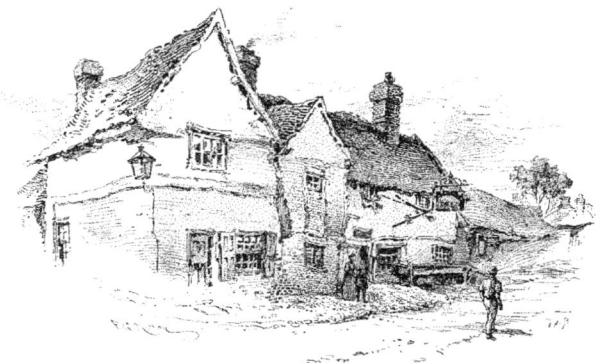

The "Bear" Inn. From the Drawing by F. G. Kitton.

ing westwards, one observes here and there a remnant of the old town, as, for instance, the row of dingy red-brick tenements to which scarlet geraniums in the leaded windows add a desirable touch of colour, these being the almshouses "given by John Fotherley, Esq., Lord of the Manor of Rickmersworth,* Anno Domi. 1682," for so reads the inscription on the time-worn tablet of stone affixed to the brickwork. What a contrast is presented by such quiet, unpretentious dwellings and the new, up-to-date Fire Brigade Station nearly opposite, or the recently-erected premises of the London and County Bank hard by! Such commodious structures as those just mentioned are, doubtless, requirements of the age, but their presence in our country towns easily explains the reason of the gradual disappearance of the picturesque bits of architecture that once adorned our streets and delighted the eye of the artist. After so much modernity it is a relief to look upon a cosy, old-fashioned cottage over which a climbing rose-tree flourishes; or upon a quaint, weather-boarded structure left stranded between nineteenth-century cottages, with a projecting wooden canopy, shading, as well as sheltering, the modest window of a taxidermist, whose stock-in-trade is here displayed to the public gaze.

Besides the High Street, there is a noticeable air of antiquity about Church Street. Running under it is a rivulet called the "Town Stream," and in close proximity thereto we find the Vicarage—an old house without a history. The "Chequers" Inn,

* This spelling of the name may still occasionally be seen on country carts in the locality.

near by, has been so much modernised that its antique appearance, externally at all events, has entirely vanished, together with a watchman's box that, until recently, was visible in a recess in the wall. Another place of refreshment, the "Feathers," still bears evidence of its weight of years in the massive oaken door under the primitive porch; besides this, its little pendent sign is decidedly curious. The Church tower, as seen from this part of the street, surmounting the dense foliage of a chestnut tree, the Tudor timbered house at the corner of the churchyard, and the quaint little "Feathers" Inn itself, combine to make a picture which will prove irresistible to an artist.

It would be difficult to find a mansion richer in associations than Moor Park, the Hertfordshire residence of Lord Ebury. This remarkable house is not more than half-a-mile from the town, and to reach it we cross the river, leaving Batchworth Mill on our left and that old-fashioned hostelry, the "Bear," on our right, presently arriving at the Park gates, opposite which the visitor cannot fail to observe the pretty little thatched dwelling adjoining the entrance to the Cottage Gardens. Once within this pleasant demesne, we soon realise the beauty of the natural scenery around us, the gracefully-undulating grassland, the lofty trees, and the charming glimpses of town and distant country obtainable here and there through the umbrageous foliage. Here one may see groves of magnificent oaks, some of them from three to four centuries old, and from twenty-five to thirty feet in girth, which tradition avers were pollarded by command of the sorrowing Duchess of Monmouth after the decapitation of her unfortunate husband—to unfit

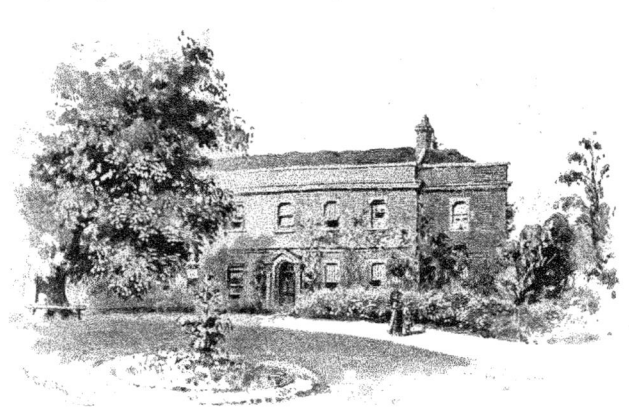

Basing House, formerly the Residence of William Penn. From the Drawing by F. G. Kitton.

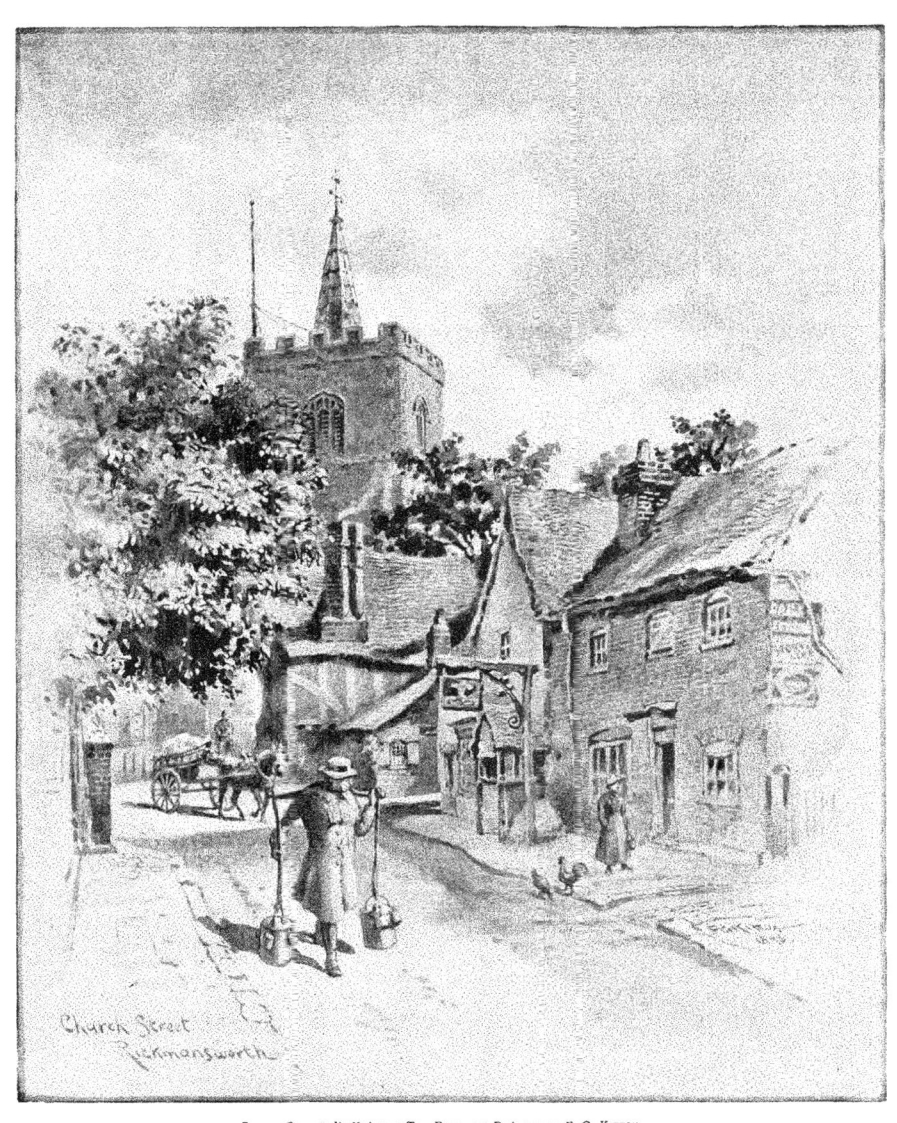

Church Street, Rickmansworth. From the Drawing by F. G. Kitton.

them (it is said) for being used in building ships for the Royal Navy. There once flourished in the Park an unrivalled lime-tree, which grew to a height of ninety-five feet, and whose branches extended to a diameter of a hundred-and-forty feet; this splendid tree was destroyed by a gale in 1860, and, curious to relate, some of the branches that were embedded in the earth have taken root and shot up afresh. Here, also, are two ancient oaks—mere skeletons, dwarfed and dead—which have borne the brunt of all weathers for centuries past, and are now known as "The Aged Couple." The gardens have been famous for centuries; they were laid out by Lucy, Countess of Bedford, in the old formal style, with fountains, terraces, and parterres, but afterwards altered by "Capability" Brown, as he was called. Of these private grounds, Sir William Temple, in his essays, says, "The perfectest figure of a garden I ever saw, either at home or abroad, was that of Moor Park, in Hertfordshire, when I knew it about thirty years ago. It was made by the Countess of Bedford, esteemed among the greatest wits of her time."

The mansion itself has an eventful history. The original house (where resided George Nevil, who became Bishop of Exeter in 1459, at the early age of twenty-four) was built much lower down the hill and nearer the river Colne than the present structure, and, although all traces of it have disappeared, there may yet be discerned the remains of ancient fish-ponds and gardens, these indicating approximately the original site. The estate was originally held under the Abbots of St. Albans, and having come into the possession of Edward IV., that monarch granted it to Neville, Archbishop of York, brother to the King-making Earl of Warwick, after whose death, in 1476, it reverted to the Crown and was granted by Henry VII. to the Earl of Oxford. Of the distinguished owners of this property, the most interesting personage is Cardinal Wolsey, who lived here in a remarkably sumptuous style, and who, in 1529, here entertained Henry VIII. and Queen Catherine of Aragon for a whole month with royal magnificence. On the occasion of this visit, both the King and the Cardinal endeavoured to persuade the Queen to consent to a divorce, but in vain; the Queen refused to yield, and shortly afterwards Wolsey became anxious and depressed, sometimes throwing himself into an arm-chair and burying his face in his hands in silent reverie, at others rushing out of doors to throw himself into the saddle, in order to "drive away the vapours that gathered around him." It is worthy of remark that both the chair and the saddle are still preserved in the mansion; while in the Park there is another relic of the famous Cardinal, in the form of a stately but weather-beaten tree called "Wolsey's Oak." After his death it passed into the hands of several eminent people, including the unhappy Duke of Monmouth already referred to, who built the present mansion, and whose widow sold it to a rich citizen, Mr. Benjamin Hoskins Styles, he having amassed his large fortune by that infamous scheme known as the "South-Sea Bubble," which involved so many persons in ruin. It was Mr. Styles who practically gave to the edifice its present appearance, both externally and internally, and had it decorated under the superintendence of a celebrated Italian architect, Leoni. His successor, Lord Anson, the great circumnavigator, also laid out large sums of money upon the house when he purchased it for his residence. After this it passed into the hands of Sir Lawrence Dundas, and soon to Robert, Marquis of Westminster, second Earl Grosvenor, eventually becoming the property of Lord Ebury. The mansion is an exceedingly fine example of the classic style of architecture, the west front having a magnificent portico consisting of a richly-embellished pediment supported by four lofty Corinthian columns. Passing under this, we find ourselves in the noble entrance hall—without doubt the finest apartment in the mansion— the interior of which is adorned on every side with enormous paintings by Amiconi, a clever Venetian artist, of subjects inspired by Heathen Mythology; massive doorways of white marble (also in the Corinthian style), crowned with sculptured allegory, lead into different rooms, while above is seen a golden gallery surmounted by a flat ceiling, the latter ingeniously painted so as to represent the dome of St. Peter's at Rome. The grand staircase is crowded with paintings of mythological scenes, and the dining-room contains a fireplace beautifully carved in marble, which is said to have cost more than £3,000, while a similar sum was paid to Sir James Thornhill for the decoration of the saloon.

In the immediate neighbourhood of Rickmansworth there is another park, which, though not so attractive as Lord Ebury's charming demesne, possesses much to please the eye. This is named after the town, although it used to be called Bury Park, as at one time it formed part of the extensive possessions of the Bury estate, to which reference has already been made. It is well wooded, and commands beautiful prospects, although it must be confessed that the sense of seclusion which one expects to enjoy in so rural a spot is somewhat marred by the occasional passing of trains on the Metropolitan Railway adjoining it.

Rickmansworth Park is situated upon elevated ground; the approach thereto, from the High Street, is by means of a steep incline, leading to a bridge crossing the railway. A narrow path, running parallel with the line, brings us to a little wooden gate, opening into the Park, whence a very pretty and extensive view can be obtained. From this point of vantage we can see the Church with its castellated tower, surrounded by the red roofs so deservedly eulogised by Richard Jeffries; here and there this accumulation of tenements, ancient and modern, is relieved by a rich mass of foliage, glimpses of old-fashioned gardens and orchards, with fruit-laden trees. Around are seen verdant meadows, well watered below by a network of clear, fresh streams—the Colne, the Gade, and the Chep—while beyond, uprising from the valley, are pastures which overlook the habitations of men. Indeed, it would be difficult to find in this part of the country a more picturesque scene than is here presented by the pretty and historical town of Rickmansworth.

F. G. KITTON.

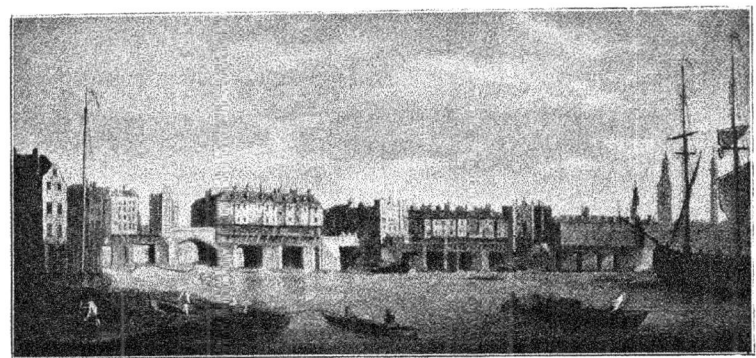

OLD LONDON BRIDGE. BY SAMUEL SCOTT.

ART AT GUILDHALL.

PART II.*

IN 1886 an important departure was taken by the chief municipal body in this country by the establishment of a permanent public gallery at the Guildhall for the exhibition of their pictures. The demand for such a gallery in the City of London had not hitherto been so acknowledged as in the case of other municipalities in provincial towns, owing to the National collection itself being not very distant, but it soon became apparent that the public appreciated its establishment and that many were disposed to seek a brief respite from the busy affairs of city life in the quiet gallery provided by the Corporation; something over 50,000 persons visiting it during the first year of its existence. Although no sum was set aside for the purchase of works of Art as additions to the collection, it should be borne in mind that the Corporation provided the gallery and defrayed all administrative expenses, not out of rates levied for that purpose as in other cities in the kingdom, but from their own privy purse. At its outset the gallery received some interesting gifts,—'Phillimore Island, Shiplake,' by A. de Breanski; 'Flirtation' (which we reproduce), a firm but free example of Seymour Lucas, purchased and presented to the Gallery by Mr. Henry Clarke, who had taken a leading part in the establishment of the Gallery; 'Dutch Schuyts beating out

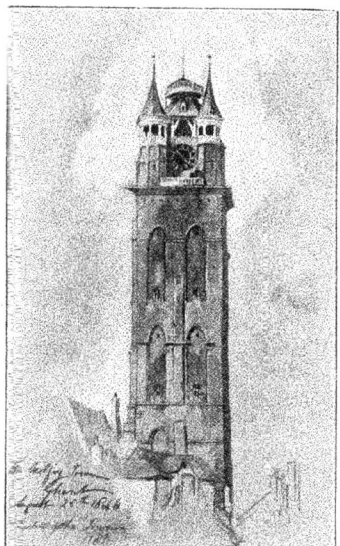

THE BELFRY TOWER, GHENT. FROM A DRAWING BY SIR JOHN GILBERT, R.A., P.R.W.S.
PRESENTED TO THE CORPORATION ART GALLERY BY THE ARTIST.

of the Scheldt,' by R. Beavis; and a very finished example of Edward Bird, entitled 'The Poacher,' one we presume of the series of six, illustrative of a poacher's career, painted we believe about 1812. These were quickly followed by the purchase and presentation by the Drapers' Company of 'The Stream in Summertime,' by B. W. Leader, A.R.A.; by the Salters' Company of 'A Storm on Albion's Coast,' by Phil Morris, A.R.A.; by the Vintners' Company of 'The Thames at Bray,' by Walter Goldsmith; and by the Goldsmiths' Company of 'The Violinist,' by G. A. Storey, A.R.A., reproduced in our large illustration, an accomplished piece of technique, showing a young lady seated to the right with her face turned to the spectator and in the act of turning over a leaf of the music. The blue figured dress, rich in colour, being admirably suited to the fair complexion and light hair; in ease and posture and quiet tone, a very excellent example of this Associate.

In 1888 there died at Villa Franca, near Florence, an old inhabitant of the city of London, William Dunnett, who, after many years of business life, had retired and taken up his residence in Italy. He appears to have found a pleasant occupation abroad in collecting pictures—some of them meritorious, and

* Continued from p. 305.

others deficient in merit. He bequeathed this collection to the Corporation in its entirety, and it was in due course brought to England. While the paintings were in all ways suitable for the embellishment of a private house, as appealing to the individual taste and learning of their possessor, it became necessary, when considered in relation to a public gallery, and more especially to the fact that many of the pictures were undoubtedly copies, that a careful selection should be made; and this having been done, some thirty-seven of the pictures were placed, and are now seen, on the walls of the Corporation gallery, the remainder being suitably hung in the various official apartments of the Guildhall. Among the more interesting of those which found a place in the gallery are Hubert Van de Venne's 'Vase and Flowers'; a small 'Annunciation,' on panel, by Franz Francken; 'A River Scene,' School of Van Goyen, which is here reproduced, — 'Vase and Flowers,' by Baptiste, and, coming to a later date, a charming example of William Shayer, entitled 'Harvest Time,' and a well-finished watercolour of 'Landscape and Cattle,' by T. Sidney Cooper, painted in 1832.

In 1889 the Corporation considered that the time had arrived to enlarge their gallery, and a commodious adjunct was built with the latest improvements in lighting, and with wall space more than doubling that which had previously been at its disposal, and the enlargement was inaugurated by a Loan Exhibition of Pictures, which remained open free to the public for three months. It had been urged in many quarters that an exhibition would not be likely to succeed in the city, the public mind having become so accustomed to associate the western district of London with matters relating to Art, especially Art of a high character, but the Corporation were enabled, by the kindness of noble and distinguished collectors, to place before the public a selection of works which, in the brief period above-mentioned, attracted, without any direct advertisement, over a hundred thousand persons. The attraction lay undoubtedly in the pictures themselves, some of the first examples of modern English Art, which had certainly never been freely seen before, finding a place upon the walls. Among these were several which in past years had been counted as high achievements in Art, but which were new to the rising generation. Millais' 'Chill October,' painted in 1870; Holman Hunt's 'Two Gentlemen of Verona,' exhibited at the Academy in 1851, and the subject of much discussion then in the first years of the pre-Raphaelite movement, and now in the possession of the Corporation of Birmingham, and permanently on view in its public gallery; Leighton's 'Hercules and Alcestis,' and 'Summer Moon,' painted in 1870 and 1872 respectively; Sir Noel Paton's 'Fairy Raid,'

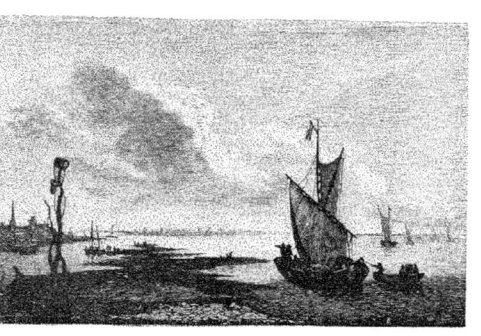

RIVER SCENE. SCHOOL OF VAN GOYEN.
BEQUEATHED TO THE CORPORATION ART GALLERY BY WILLIAM DUNNETT, ESQ.

one of his most elaborate fairy pieces, unsurpassed, we believe, even by the examples of a similar character in the Scottish National Gallery; Maclise's 'Earls of Desmond and Ormond' and Faed's 'Worn Out,' in relation to which a poor working-girl was heard to make the telling comment that "It's not always the clothes that shows the heart." Then there reappeared that little-known and remarkable work of high finish, 'The Cavalier and the Puritan,' by W. S. Burton, exhibited at the Academy in 1856; and, coming nearer to the present time, one of the most beautiful of the works of Burne-Jones, 'Le Chant d'Amour,' reproduced in the ART ANNUAL for 1894. The general public understood these pictures and appreciated them; for such as were familiar with and found delight in the earlier masters, ample opportunity for study was found in the newly constructed gallery, where were gathered together some seventy examples. Of these Lord Northbrook generously contributed from his town house in Hamilton Place some of the choicest specimens in his collection. There are few finer instances of Van der Heyden's work, either in this country or on the Continent, than the one entitled 'View in a Town.' This was one which his lordship lent, and was regarded as one of the gems of the Dutch pictures in the collection. Then Ruysdael's famous sea-piece, 'A Fresh Breeze,' was another, with brilliant specimens of the work of Van der Hagen, Gerard Dow, Backhuisen, and Teniers; and going back to earlier times, two marvellously finished small works by Mabuse of 'The Virgin and Child Enthroned,' and the remarkable Antonella da Messina of 'St. Jerome in his Study,' since added to the National Gallery. Many of these have been well reproduced in the printed catalogue of the Northbrook collection. Other notable examples of early masters were also contributed which we have not space to enumerate. The examples of Reynolds were conspicuous ones; two half-length portraits—Mrs. Robinson, 'Perdita,' and Miss Jacobs, known as 'The Blue Lady,' were lent by the Marquess of Hertford, and the famous 'Ladies Waldegrave' was shown, for which the painter received from Horace Walpole, their grand-uncle, eight hundred guineas, representing not a twentieth part of its value at the present day.

On the reopening of the permanent collection in the autumn of 1890 a gift was made to the gallery of twenty-three drawings, small but of great finish, by artists who some half a century ago employed a portion of their time in work of this kind for book illustration—Henry Corbould, Burney, Uwins, Westall, and Thurston. The donor of these (the late Mr. Felix Joseph) had previously made large gifts of a similar character to the towns of Derby and Nottingham, with valuable collections of old china (more especially Wedgwood),

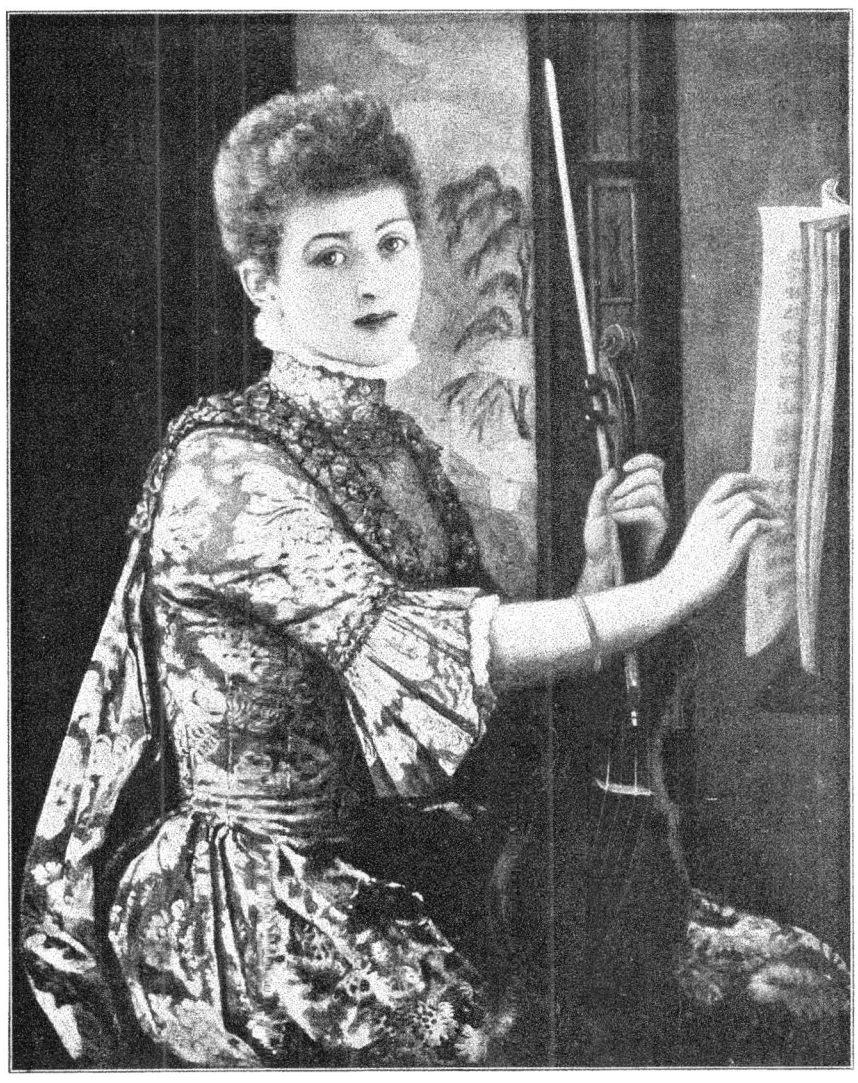

A VIOLINIST.
FROM THE PICTURE BY G. A. STOREY, A.R.A.
By permission of the Art Committee of the Corporation of the City of London.

of which he was for many years a very ardent collector. A bequest followed from Mr. John Kirchner, an engraver by profession, of an important water-colour painting, 'The Shepherd's Meal,' by F. W. Topham; and several oil paintings were presented, among the more important being 'The Wife of Jeroboam and the Blind Prophet,' by G. Manton, given by Mr. George Shaw, a member of the Corporation, and one of the chief promoters of the Corporation Art Gallery. A marble statue of Mr. Henry Irving in the character of Hamlet, by E. Onslow Ford, A.R.A., was also added as a gift from the sculptor, and is reproduced at page 201. The embellishment of the inner lobby of the new Council Chamber with

and the small Van Eyck, 'Madonna and Child,' four and a-half centuries old, and exquisite in design, both from Ince Hall, Lancashire; the last-named picture bearing, with singular humility for so eminent a master, the inscription, " Als ikh Kan," the first words of an old Flemish proverb, " As I can, but not as I would;" and it is worthy of remembering the reverence with which the inhabitants of his native city of Bruges regarded him, in their celebrating yearly, for upwards of three hundred years after his death, funeral masses for the repose of his soul, which brought thirty-four gros annually to the church revenue. Works by Fra Angelico, Luini, and Durer were also in this exhibition, as well as fine examples of the Dutch

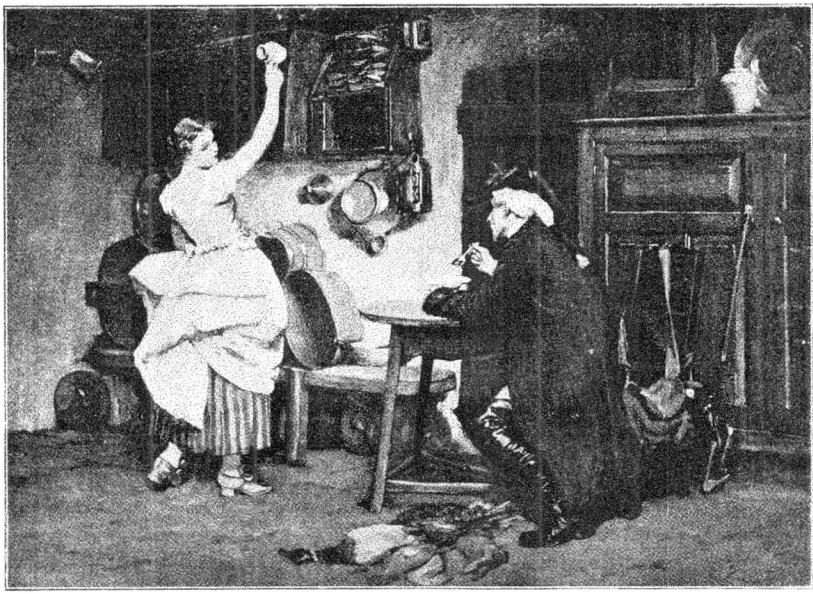

FLIRTATION. BY SEYMOUR LUCAS, A.R.A.
PRESENTED TO THE CORPORATION ART GALLERY BY HENRY CLARKE, ESQ., C.C., L.C.C.

mural decoration was undertaken in 189 , by Sir Stuart Knill, the late Lord Mayor, at his own expense commissioning Mr. Powell to execute the work at a cost approaching £2,000. A superficial area of about seven hundred and fifty feet was covered, and the design was peculiarly suitable for the interior of a municipal institution.

The Corporation at this time, 1892, resolved to hold a second Loan Exhibition, the success attending its first venture in this direction inducing them to again afford the public the opportunity of seeing and studying a further selection of masterpieces. The Corporation was again greatly helped in its enterprise by the co-operation of many distinguished owners, who in many instances spared the gems of their collections for the time required. Among the early masters was the brilliant 'Madonna with the Cherries,' by the Master of Cologne, 1894

School, the most distinguished being, perhaps, the ' View on the Maas,' by Cuyp, in which the delicacy of the aerial gradation showed the astonishing height which the art of painting in general had attained in Holland in the seventeenth century.

The most interesting of the modern works embraced some of the best of the pre-Raphaelite school, including the famous 'Huguenot' by Millais; and this feature of the exhibition proved invaluable to Art students of the present day, it being now over forty years s nce this remarkable movement made its impress on the Art of this country. Another painting rarely seen— never, we believe, in England since the International Exhibition of 1862—was Delaroche's 'Christian Martyr,' lent from Paris by M. D'Eichthal.

In the course of three months the Exhibition was attended

by nearly a quarter of a million of people, who were admitted without charge, the Corporation defraying the entire expenses. The Gallery was thus further popularised, and in the spring of 1893 evidence of this was manifested by Sir John Gilbert determining that the new gallery of the Corporation should be offered to participate, with certain other municipal cities in the kingdom, in the distribution of his accumulated works. Five oil-pictures, thirteen water-colour paintings, and thirty drawings were comprehended in the City of London's share in this gift, and may fairly be said to include some of the artist's best work, ranging over à variety of subjects, fanciful and historical, chivalrous and romantic, conceived in a spirit peculiarly his own and executed with a command of detail that left no part of the composition incomplete. A special article dealing with the paintings appeared in THE ART JOURNAL of July, 1893 (page 199), and we give now a reproduction of one of the drawings, 'The Belfry Tower, Ghent,' executed in 1846.

The Corporation testified its appreciation of so generous a public gift by presenting Sir John Gilbert with the Honorary Freedom of the City in a gold box—a distinction bestowed on many illustrious men in war, statesmanship, and philanthropy during past centuries, but now conferred for the first time on a member of the artistic profession. His brief and dignified reply at the formal ceremony of presentation which took place in the following September in the presence of some four hundred persons, was in its simplicity characteristic of the man: "I cannot, I fear, offer you my thanks in a proper manner. The honour which you have been pleased to confer upon me is one which I shall hold second only to that which I have received from the Queen. I trust that the works which I have presented to the Corporation—which were the works, perhaps, of the best years of my life—may prove to be a nucleus for the formation of a gallery of Art which will be worthy of this great and illustrious Corporation, and of this great City – the capital of the world."

Among other gifts to the Gallery during 1893 were 'Clytemnestra,' by the Hon. John Collier, presented by Mrs. Harrison, of Wolverhampton; 'The Haunted Mill,' by Mr. Murphy Grimshaw, exhibited in the Royal Academy of 1893, and presented by the artist; and a portrait of the late James Anderton, presented by Mr. Commissioner Kerr; while early in the present year Mr. Edward Armitage, R.A., presented one of his most important works, 'Herod's Birthday Feast,' a gift which has greatly enhanced the Corporation's collection of modern works.

· The latest event in relation to the Gallery has been the third Loan Exhibition, which opened on the 2nd April and closed 1st July of the present year. It consisted of a collection of Dutch examples, and of representative works of the British School, which latter section was dealt with at some length in the May number of this journal (page 133). Among the Dutch examples appeared three works of remarkable quality by Cuyp, including the famous 'Landscape and River' lent by the Marquess of Bute, a much-envied work and of great value; and Terburg, De Hoogh, Rembrandt, Jacob Van Ruisdael, Jan Steen, Hobbema, Franz Van Mieris, Metsu, Sorgh, Moreelse, Molinaer, and Adrian Van Ostade were strongly represented by contributions from the chief collections of the country, while the inclusion in the collection of the celebrated canvas by Vandyke from Althorp of the portraits of the Second Earl of Bristol and the First Duke of Bedford, lent by Earl Spencer, gave particular satisfaction. The exhibition was visited by upwards of 300,000 persons, showing an average per day of 3,580, against 1,500 per day on the occasion of the first exhibition in 1890, further proving to the Corporation's satisfaction the increased appreciation of their efforts by the public.

A. G. TEMPLE, F.S.A.,
Director of the Corporation of London Art Gallery.

ANCIENT AND MODERN DANCING.—I. GREEK DANCES.

FOR many years we have been made familiar with Greek life as portrayed by the President of the Academy and Mr. Alma Tadema. They have shown us Greek girls dancing, bathing, playing with knucklebones, sitting on marble terraces in the sunshine and in the shade. It is little wonder that they have been attracted by a subject so full of interest, that they never weary of representing these lithe forms which seem to adapt themselves so readily to every conceivable attitude. If we want, however, to study Greek life and Greek art, we will see it in fuller perfection when coming from the hands of the Greeks themselves. Their portraiture is purely artistic; they do not always select the rosy tint of sunshine nor the balcony with trellises of grapes and vines; their art does not need these accessories. An aged woman drawing water, a worn and emaciated slave, whose pathetic expression tells a story of degraded misery, are in their hands beautified. So, too, with the domestic groups which ornamented the walls of every household, sometimes painted but more often in plaster. These were the records of the family: their marriages, their burials, their daily life were represented here. Each figure is instinct with grace and animation, every limb is in its right place; each fold of the garments hangs as it should do; the hands join in an almost living clasp of friend to friend; the arms of lovers intertwine tenderly, as they would have done in life. You see their story in every motion of the figures, and if the mouth is perforce silent, the lips seem almost to breathe forth words of love. It is this sense of harmony and fidelity to truth in nature which gives the spectator such intense satisfaction, although it may be that he is quite ignorant of the cause from which his content springs.

This beautiful harmony attended the inner life of the Athenians. Vulgar objects, even in common use, were unknown to them. From earliest infancy they were surrounded with artistic things, for they held the theory that the eye enlightens the mind; and even the commonest jug or cooking utensil was shaped in accordance with this idea, without in the least interfering with its usefulness. What can be more artistic than their amphoræ or vases? The shape is perfect, so is the colouring; and here we have the record of their amusements. We see the chariots rushing round in the giddy

ANCIENT AND MODERN DANCING.—I. GREEK DANCES.

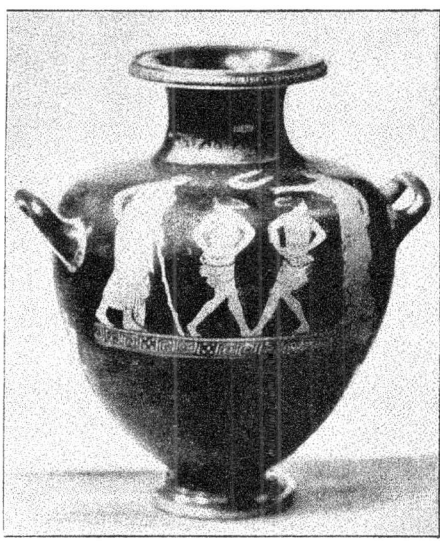

A DANCING LESSON. FROM A GREEK VASE IN THE BRITISH MUSEUM.

race; youths and maidens dancing; actors with their masks in their hands, performing their satiric burlesques, groups of Mænades, Satyrs, Bacchantes, maidens, and youths dancing. The Greeks, and in particular the Lacedæmonians and Athenians, loved music, dancing, acting. In these arts they found expression for their artistic feelings, and the Government wisely fostered this taste by building large gymnasia where the people could exercise themselves in such amusements. Here the artists and sculptors of Athens came to study the delineations and attitudes of these youths, so perfect were they; it seemed impossible for an Athenian to fall into an ungraceful attitude. The girls drawing water at the fountain, the young Greek driving his chariot, the mother nursing her infant, all took poetical forms, for a love of the elegant and harmonious inspires with grace the most homely actions.

It was only natural that this grace should lend itself to making the dancing of the Greeks the true poetry of motion. Unconsciously they fell into charming positions, arranged themselves in chains and circles, and infused a romantic element into the figures of the dance. The Cretans were considered the best dancers. The story went that the goddess Rhea had been their teacher. Perhaps the soft air of the island gave to its inhabitants a more dreamy temperament which accompanied all their actions, and imparted to their dancing more languor and grace.

Dancing and music have ever gone hand in hand, they are complements to one another, the rhythm of the one falling in with the cadence of the other, and adding harmony to motion. A child feels this, and when it hears its mother's voice singing, tries to move its infant limbs in some sort of dance. The savages make a noise with their kettles and tom-toms to accompany their war dances. At first the Greeks supplied music by the voices of a chorus, but later a Sicilian flute-player introduced dancing to the sound of an instrument, and from this time we find flute-players appearing in all representations of domestic life. Socrates is represented as practising his steps with the flute-boy in attendance; on which occasion Charmid, the Senator, calling to consult him on affairs of State, found him thus engaged.

Hermann, a German professor who has written largely on Greek Art, ranks the Greek dances under three specific

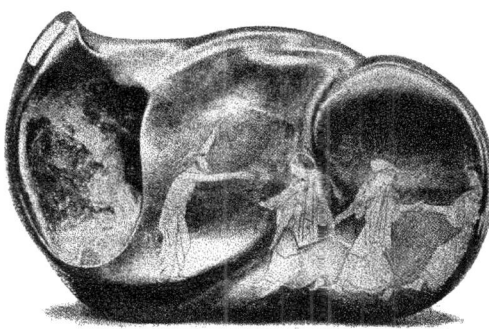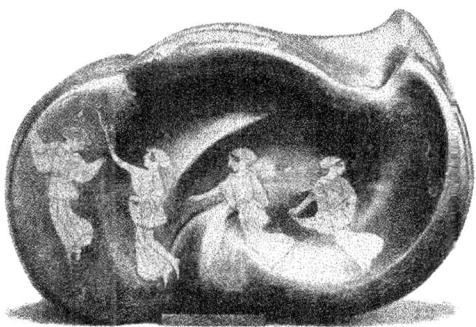

WOMEN DANCING IN IMITATION OF THE FLIGHT OF BIRDS. FROM THE KNUCKLEBONE VASE IN THE BRITISH MUSEUM.
(Photographed by the London Stereoscopic Company.)

heads. (1) The Tragic dance, which gave expression to all elegant and benevolent sentiments. It was of a serious character, each movement being marked with dignity. (2) The

Comic; a wild, loose dance, divided into the Emmileia and the Cordax. Theophrastus, the pupil and heir of Aristotle, says that to dance the Cordax unless a man were drunk proved him to have lost all shame; and Demosthenes marks the three steps towards degradation thus: dissipation, drunkenness, and the Cordax. There was a variation of the Cordax called the Hyporchema, which was a mimic dance, executed by men and women, and very popular in the Island of Delos. (3) The Satiric dance, a wild, tumultuous, violent dance, not without pathos. The comedy consisted in imitating the serious movements of the Tragic dance, and making them laughable. The performers were oftentimes disguised as Satyrs, Silenes, Mænades; sometimes as animals. They wore masks of extraordinary ugliness, which they are occasionally represented as carrying in their hands. The word Satiric means "put together," and the Satiric dances took their rise from the festival of Ceres and Bacchus, when a homogeneous offering was made of flowers, fruit, etc. Hermann says the chorus always accompanied these dancers, and that there were a number of figures which are difficult, if not impossible, to trace. The pantomime dance united the characters of the Tragic, Comic, and Satiric dances, and was seen only on the stage. It required exceptional gifts to be a pantomime dancer. Music, poetry, geometry and philosophy, rhetoric, painting and sculpture were in the course of study for the profession of a pantomime dancer or Baladine. He should likewise possess a wonderful memory, a thorough mastery of gesture, and a power of imitation so perfect that he never made a gesture which did not exactly fit the personage whom he represented. In fact, upon the stage, these dancers absorbed all the attention of the spectators, and, as is often the case in our own day, diverted their minds from the legitimate drama.

Homer, in the eighteenth canto of the Iliad, says that Vulcan represented on a shield a dance similar to the one composed by Didales for the beautiful Ariané; there were young men and maidens holding one another's hands while they danced; the maidens had very tight dresses, and crowns upon their heads; the youths wore tunics of spangled cloth and their swords were in silver scabbards. With wonderful lightness and grace they danced in a round with a movement similar to that a potter gives to his wheel. Sometimes they divided into circles, which again mixed with one another and met again; a crowd of spectators surrounded the dancers, and in the middle of the circle were placed two *palestri* or acrobats, who sang the music and occasionally varied the performance by feats of extraordinary agility.

" A figured dance succeeds: such once was seen
In lofty Gnossus, for the Cretan queen,
Formed by Dædalian art: a comely band
Of youths and maidens, bounding hand in hand.
* * * * *
Now all at once they rise, at once descend,
With well-taught feet: now shape, in oblique ways,
Confusedly regular, the moving maze."—*Iliad*, canto 18.

This constant movement and dispersion was meant to represent the labyrinth of Crete, and traces of this dance, as also of the Romēcla, are to be found in the more modern dance of the Brawl or Thread-the-needle. So too with the Grega, or Hornpipe, which comes to us from the Greek dance Mouscharos and had a chorus of old men, or Tarracomos, who sang—

" We once were young and gay as you;
Valiant, bold, and active too."

This was succeeded by a chorus of young men, singing—

" 'Tis now our turn, and you shall see
You ne'er deserved it more than we."

And these in their turn were followed by a group of boys—

" The day will come when we shall show
Feats that surpass all you can do."

Another dance was for women only, a number of girls imitating the flight of birds, most graceful and charming. The illustration of this, given on the previous page, is from an amphora or vase in the British Museum in the shape of a knucklebone. It is an exquisite specimen, and Mr. A. S. Murray, the keeper of the Greek and Roman Antiquities, says it is the best he has ever met with. The dancing-master or teacher, in his Athenian robe, directs the troupe of dancers, and with his finger uplifted in command, has the dignified appearance of one who is fully alive to the importance of his profession.

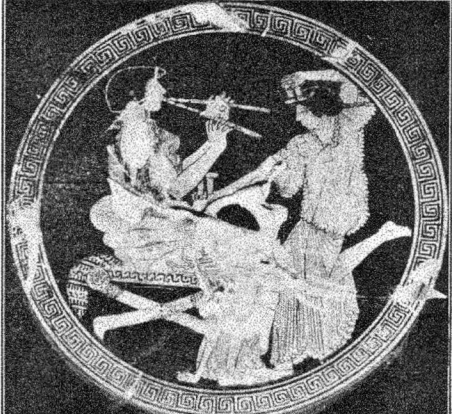

GIRL DANCING TO A FLUTE-PLAYER.
FROM THE INTERIOR OF A GREEK VASE IN THE BRITISH MUSEUM.

In addition to these character and national dances there were other dances for times of rejoicing, such as marriages, vintages, and harvestings. Here is an account given by Longus, a Greek writer, of a vintage dance.

"Dryas," he says, "having risen, commanded a Bacchanalian air to be sung, and then commenced to dance 'The Wine-Pressers' Dance.' As he danced, he imitated the different actions of the vintagers; those who carried the basket, those who trampled with their feet upon the fruit to press out the juice, those who filled the tuns, and those who drank the wine. Of each of these different processes, Dryas gave a faithful representation."*

---
* This was the dance taught by Cythera to her handmaidens on the marriage feast of her son to Psyche.

ANCIENT AND MODERN DANCING.—I. GREEK DANCES.

Xenophon, who was a strong advocate for dancing, describes a feast given by himself. "After the table was cleared, the libations had been made, and hymns had been sung, a Syracusan was brought in, accompanied by a flute-player, who was well to look at.* The girl dancer was one of those who take perilous leaps in the air. There was a boy also, who danced and played on the flute perfectly. The dancing girl having entered the hall, the flute girl began to play upon her instrument. The dancing girl then took up twelve 'circeaux.' As she danced, she threw these in the air, catching them with great dexterity, the sound as they fell marking the cadence. Then they made a large circle with swords, the points being on the inner side ; but she managed to dance through these without giving herself any injury." Finally, she executed a sort of tableau or character dance, representing Bacchus and Ariadné, which Xenophon much commends.

It is to be noted, however, that at these feasts and entertainments where pantomime dancing was the amusement, the performers were altogether Baladines, i.e. professional artists. It would have been deemed a disgrace for any one of position to join in these dances. Nevertheless, some of the Athenian young men did break over the fence, and became Baladines. A well-known instance is that of Hippoclides, who sought in marriage the daughter and heiress of Clisthenes, Prince of Sicyon. Clisthenes was very particular in the choice of a son-in-law, but Hippoclides had so far satisfied him that he fixed a certain day for the announcement of the approaching marriage. Grand preparations were made, two hundred oxen were killed, and a royal feast given, at the end of which Hippoclides, having got royally drunk, called for the flute girl and set to dancing the Cordax, to the disgust of his father-in-law elect. But worse was to come. The young Athenian,

* The flute girls were chosen for their beauty.

intoxicated with the applause he had received, wound up with standing on his head on a table, and in this posture cutting capers with his legs. Upon which the Prince of Sicyon rose and said with much dignity : "Young man, you have danced away your bride"; and then withdrew with all his courtiers.

This action on the part of Sicyon shows how the feeling of society ran counter to non-professional display of dancing. It was, however, usual in private houses to engage dancers to amuse the invited guests. In Lord Lytton's well-known novel, "The Last Days of Pompeii," mention is made of a dinner party given by the hero Glaucus to some of his fashionable friends, and we will conclude this paper by quoting the passage which describes it.

"It was the last course. Slaves brought round water and hyssop for the finishing lavations ; at the same time a small circular table, which had been placed in the space opposite the guests, suddenly opened in the centre ; an awning which had concealed the ceiling was drawn aside, and the guests perceived that a rope had been stretched across the ceiling, and that one of the nimble dancers, for which Pompeii was so celebrated, was treading his airy measures right over their heads. This apparition, removed from them by only a cord, was somewhat alarming. The Pompeians, who were accustomed to the spectacle, were filled with delighted curiosity, and applauded in proportion as the dancer appeared to have the more difficulty in keeping himself from falling. Suddenly a strain of music was heard without ; the dancer paused, the air changed, he danced on more wildly ; the air changed again and again ; he listened, then began as one who by some strange disorder is compelled to dance, and whom only a certain air of music can cure. As the right tune came, the dancer gave one leap, swung himself down from the roof, and alighted on the floor."

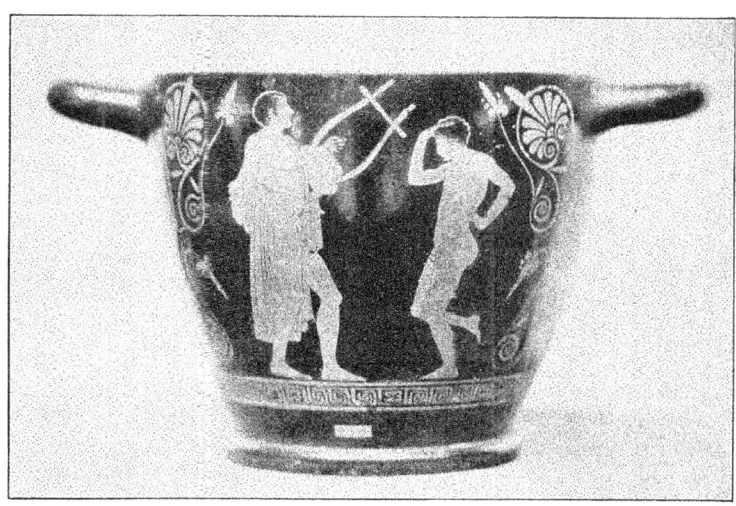

A CITHARIST ACCOMPANYING A DANCING YOUTH. FROM A GREEK VASE IN THE BRITISH MUSEUM.

A NOTE ON JAPANESE COLOURED PRINTS.

WITH ILLUSTRATIONS FROM A SERIES IN THE POSSESSION OF J. S. FORBES, ESQ.

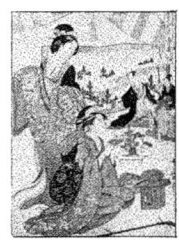

COLOURED engravings were first made in Japan about the year 1730. They appeared as a natural outcome and new branch of the ordinary engravings in black, which had been produced in Japan from the end of the sixteenth century; and the art from the time of Moronobu, at the end of the seventeenth century, had become a very important one. At first coloured engravings were confined to the representations of scenes from the theatre or pictures of actors. It would be a pity for this class of subject ever to be abandoned; and, indeed, it has continued to occupy the attention of Japanese artists right up to the opening of Japan to Europeans. But in the latter half of the eighteenth century the range widened, and to the theatrical scenes were added representations of every characteristic of the national life, pictures of women of every class in their everyday occupations and dress, and finally landscape and views of the world and things about us. The development of engraving in colour is due to many celebrated artists, Harunobu, Kyonaga, Toyokuni, and finally Utamaro.

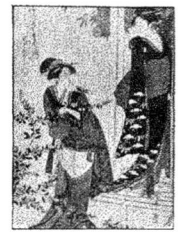

Utamaro was first amongst the men who drew and painted the Japanese woman. From what is known of him we learn that he was a man of refinement, but of easy morals and greatly addicted to pleasure. He died of constitutional exhaustion at Yedo, in 1806, at the age of fifty years.

In studying the productions of Utamaro one makes the acquaintance of the Japanese of every rank and condition.

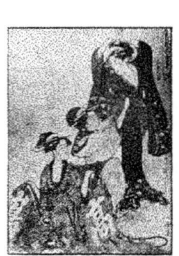

One part of his work, full of profound feeling, is devoted to the representation of mothers with their children. The scenes are of the most varied description, in which the artist has put on record the thousand delightful pictures of affection which occur between mothers and their offspring. It is necessary to say, however, that the greatest number of the women whom Utamaro depicts are the courtesans amongst whom he spent his life. But it is reassuring to add that representations of this class are almost always quite unobjectionable. Courtesans in Japanese prints, unless one were informed, might be taken for princesses or for ordinary women of the world at least.

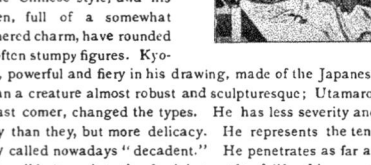

Harunobu approached the classic Chinese style, and his women, full of a somewhat mannered charm, have rounded and often stumpy figures. Kyonaga, powerful and fiery in his drawing, made of the Japanese woman a creature almost robust and sculpturesque; Utamaro, the last comer, changed the types. He has less severity and purity than they, but more delicacy. He represents the tendency called nowadays "decadent." He penetrates as far as it is possible to go into the feminine mode of life; his women are tall, full of grace and *abandon*.

The artists of the end of the eighteenth century were not content with the representation of figures and scenes in single engravings, each complete in itself; they produced compositions spreading over three or five leaves, or series of subjects consisting of chapters, so to speak, of seven, ten, or twelve prints. The productions of Utamaro are very numerous, and his triptychs especially so. He has also made many famous series, especially that of the 'Silkworms,' and that known under the name of 'The forty-seven Rônin represented by the most beautiful women,' of which we reproduce several examples.

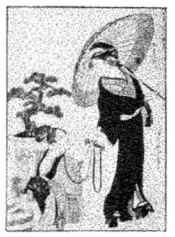

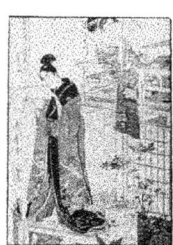

This series of prints represents scenes from the celebrated historical drama *Chiushin-Gura* (the Storehouse of Loyalty), the most popular play on the Japanese stage. This drama appeals strongly to the national instincts of the Japanese, being a faithful representation of the famous Conspiracy of the Forty-seven Rônin, who avenged their feudal lord. Various versions of this play are performed, the one selected for illustration by Utamaro dealing with the life of feigned dissipation led by

A NOTE ON JAPANESE COLOURED PRINTS.

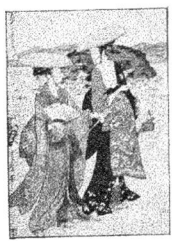

the chief of the Rônin, to disarm the suspicion of the authorities. This phase of the celebrated story was performed, until about eighty years ago, by a company consisting exclusively of actresses, contrary to the general custom of the Japanese stage, by which all characters, both men and women, are impersonated by men. Utamaro was probably intimately associated with the leading ladies of this troupe, and portrayed them in the chief scenes of the play.

In this series we have the most varied scenes of life and character possible—women at the toilet adorning themselves, women at their private gatherings, where they sing and play on the *shamisen* or Japanese guitar, drinking *saké;* women in town dress preparing to go out with open sunshade; and women occupied in trimming and tending the shrubs of flowering plants which ornament the interiors of the houses.

The upper print on the right on this page should be noticed. It shows us a very busy lady engaged in conversation with tradespeople who have brought various articles for the toilet in their boxes. This will serve to teach those who do not know it, that things are much the same in Japan as in Europe, that the women there, as elsewhere, spend money freely in adorning themselves. Indeed, there is an engraving of Hokusai's representing a woman who was famous for her beauty and unbridled extravagance, bathing in liquid gold, which an attendant is pouring out upon her in an uninterrupted stream.

We reproduce also the last of this series in the centre of this page, and it gives us the portrait of the artist Utamaro himself. It is a somewhat singular thing, that the Japanese, who have so faithfully and so constantly depicted for us the natural characteristics of their country, the streets, the bridges, the temples of Yedo and Kiôto, the Fuji-yama—of which they have given us the exact structure, a genuine likeness of every aspect—have not cultivated in the least the art of portraiture, strictly so called, and it is only as quite an exceptional thing that we possess a likeness of some artists in certain of their compositions, where they have been by chance introduced. This print of the 'Rônin represented by Women' is in the highest degree interesting as giving us the likeness of Utamaro. He is represented in the company of three women, at evening in a *maison de plaisir* on the banks of the Sumida. One of the three holds up a lantern, which sheds light on the group. Another prepares to pour out the *saké* into a cup which the artist holds to receive it. On each side of the garment which he wears are figured the characters

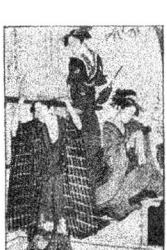

of his name—Utamaro. And to make it more certain, on the wooden pillar which supports the roof he has written these words:—"Surune asks Utamaro to draw his own 'elegant likeness.'" The details of the portrait answer the inscription well: the man is gentlemanly, of agreeable countenance, and one can understand that he was likely to please the women whom he spent his life in depicting.

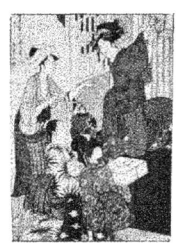

Utamaro is the last of the great artists who have especially devoted themselves to representing, with exquisite lines and skilful composition, the women of Japan. After him the art changes. Hokusai applied himself to other subjects. Hiroshigé devoted himself to landscape; Kuniyoshi to battles and soldiers and crowds of people. Utamaro, by his own genius and the charm of his subjects, wields a veritable fascination over the Europeans who learn to appreciate him. The engravings which we owe to him are at the present time in the very first rank of the possessions a collector covets. It may be as well, however, to utter a word of warning to connoisseurs, to put them on their guard against imitations and copies. Utamaro himself was a very prolific artist, but as he enjoyed a great reputation in his own lifetime, in order to increase his production he employed a certain number of pupils to work with him, whose works were signed with his name. Moreover, after his death his widow married one of his pupils, who signed the name of the dead man to his own work; and in addition, the publishers themselves appear to have long continued to employ others of his pupils who always made use of his name. The number of Japanese prints signed with the name of Utamaro is simply enormous. But all of these are very far from possessing the charm, the elegance, and the high qualities of those which are really due to the master. The collector must make it his business to sift the tares from the wheat, and to recognise in each case whether the engraving which comes before him is Utamaro's genuine personal work, or only that of some pupil or imitator.

THÉODORE DURET.

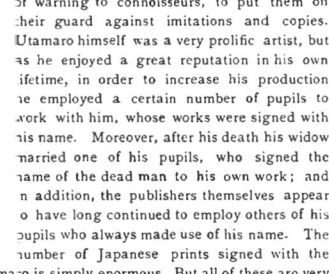

PORTRAIT OF UTAMARO.

₊ The subject dealt with by Monsieur Duret is one of such extensive interest that it is not possible to do more than suggest its outline. Ample justice will, no doubt, be done to it by Professor Anderson when he reads his paper on "The Popular School of Japanese Pictorial Art," at a forthcoming meeting of the Japan Society, to whose Vice-Chairman, Mr. Diósy, we are indebted for interesting particulars on the subject of this article.

ED. *A.J.*

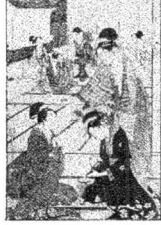

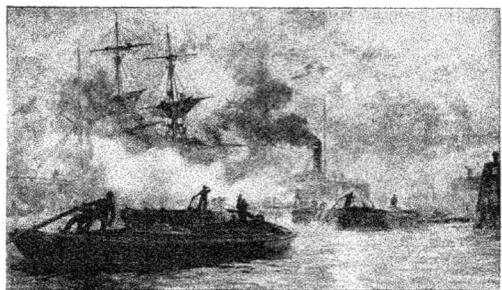

OUR RIVER. BY W. L. WYLLIE, A.R.A.

THE ART GALLERY AT ADELAIDE, SOUTH AUSTRALIA.

SOUTH AUSTRALIA has made more than a beginning, and now possesses a collection of pictures housed, for the present, in the Exhibition building at Adelaide. Here they are seen to advantage; although, in some instances, not to the best advantage. This is notably the case with J. V. Krämer's 'Descent from the Cross,' a large altar-piece which there would be a difficulty in hanging in most galleries. It happens, however, that the Adelaide Gallery consists of an entrance hall and two large rooms along the same front of the building, opening the one into the other by lofty openings without doors. The obvious place for the 'Descent from the Cross' is that wall of the second room, which will allow the picture to be viewed from the entrance hall through the two doors. This would give a perspective of about one hundred and twenty feet. Hung where the picture is, on a side wall, one cannot get farther from it than about fifteen feet.

This is not the only case in which the Adelaide Gallery has done itself an injustice. In particular, it ought certainly to possess a catalogue.

In the end room, where the 'Descent from the Cross' hangs, there is first of all a picture by Mr. Gotch, which has been christened 'Destiny.' It occupies the place of honour, and its rather meagre effect is helped on by a spotty 'Venice by Moonlight,' hung just over it; the two together fill the space that would have so well suited the 'Descent from the Cross.' To the right hangs a sea-piece of Mr. Colin Hunter, 'Waiting for the Homeward Bound off Ailsa Craig,' an even better specimen of Mr. Hunter's work than the 'Salmon Fishers' of the Sydney Gallery. It is instructive, but a little severe, to turn from Mr. Colin Hunter to Mr. H. J. Johnstone, who is here represented by 'Evening Shadows,' which we illustrate. Mr. Johnstone's abiding merit is his power of composition. There are those who impeach the accuracy of his detail, who reproach his colouring with being hard, and who see no effect of breadth in his treatment. The fact remains that his pictures are always interesting; but it is better for him that 'Evening Shadows' is hung next to Van Pochinger's 'Evening' and not next to 'Waiting for the Homeward Bound.' 'Titian's Niece' is the only specimen of Mr. Val Prinsep's work in Australia, and it is a very fair specimen.

In this room hangs also 'Noarlunga Headland,' a view of coast scenery in New South Wales. Australian scenery painted by an Australian artist must always be interesting; this particular gem is the more so in that it is the work of the curator of the Gallery, Mr. H. P. Gill.

Returning towards the entrance hall the most conspicuous canvas in the first room is Mr. Schmalz's 'Zenobia's Last Look on Palmyra'; but one of the most interesting, if not the most interesting, is 'On the Conway,' the gift of the Chief Justice of South Australia. This is a picture that tells a story; not, indeed, a story of some personal bereavement, or of some historical incident that twenty lines of text hardly elucidate, but the much more interesting story of the develop-

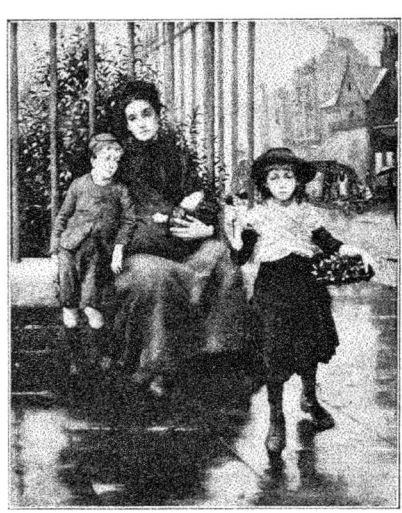

THE PINCH OF POVERTY. BY T. B. KENNINGTON.

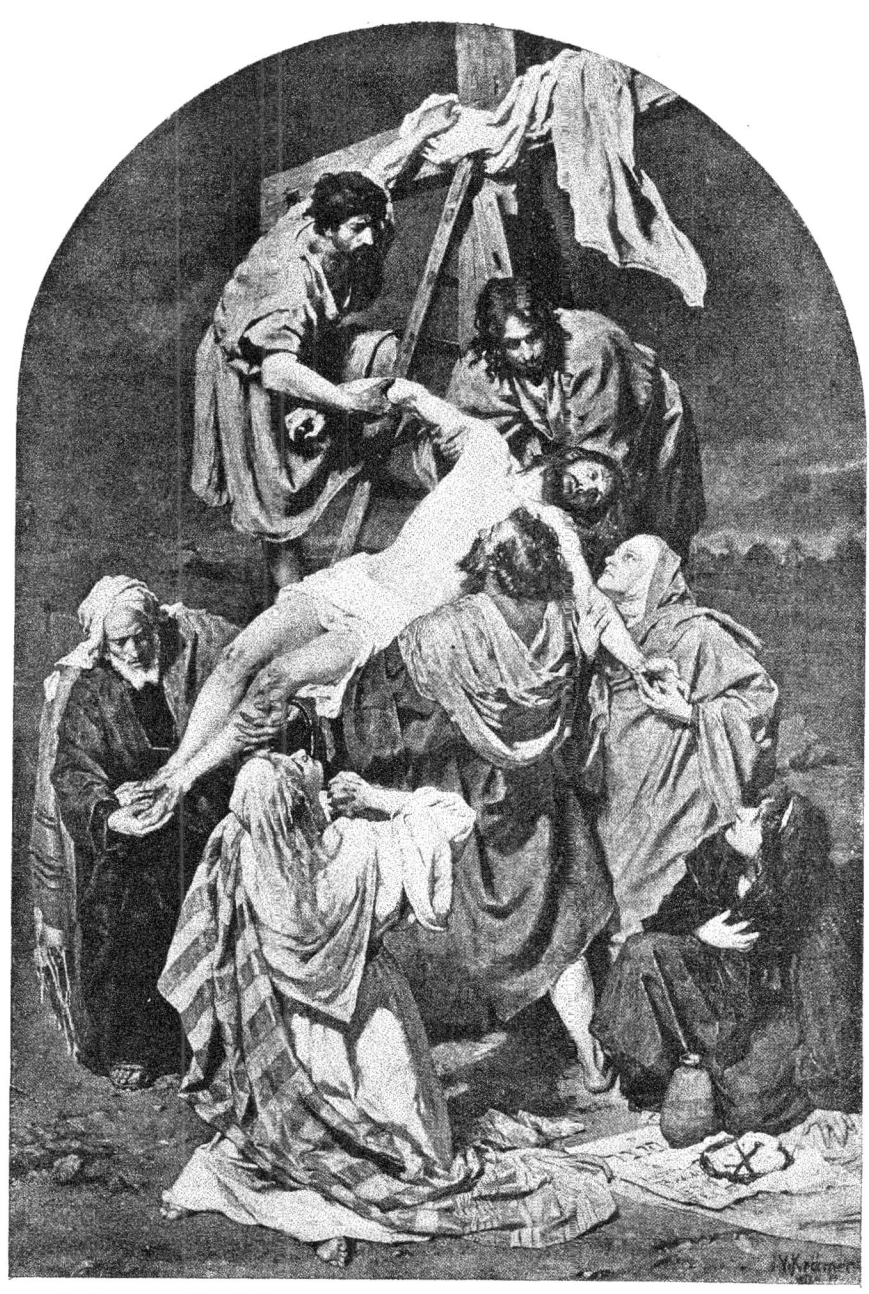

The Descent from the Cross. By J. V. Krämer. By Permission of Messrs. T. Wallis & Son, the Publishers of the Large Plate.

ment of an artist's genius. It is an early picture of Mr. Leader's, and the Gallery only wants a good late picture to

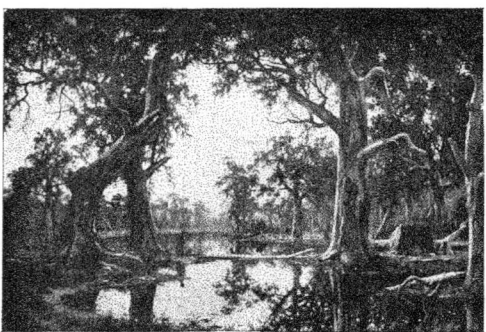

EVENING SHADOWS. BY H. J. JOHNSTONE.

have a representative pair. 'On the Conway' was painted when the artist was soaked in the style of Linnell, and the glow over the whole canvas is a beautiful echo of the earlier master.

Mr. Wyllie's 'Our River' (see the headpiece) is like meat and drink to a traveller long separated from London. The eternal din, the dusky sun, the vast clouds of smoke, rolling skywards like the incense of some awful sacrifice, all these things that—strangely enough, perhaps—a Londoner longs for when he cannot get them, make Mr. Wyllie's picture very welcome. A man would not, perhaps, sigh for the Thames if he only knew it through Mr. Wyllie, but when he has been under the spell of the mighty city, more ideal painters move him less.

The air of quiet distinction that Mr. Waterhouse throws round his work can be well studied in the 'Favourites of the Emperor Honorius,' of which we give an illustration. It was engraved on steel in THE ART JOURNAL for 1886. The Emperor Honorius is as uninteresting a figure as history is burdened with. We should pass him in a crowd if he were now living, and his occupation, if amiable, is trivial enough in a man of his position. And yet, for all that, or rather, perhaps, in consequence of the direct admission of all that on the face of the picture, the Emperor and his pigeons hold our attention as much as any picture in the gallery. "The favourite picture in the Gallery" must always have a certain melancholy interest. We give a representation of it—'The Pinch of Poverty.' It is painted by Mr. T. B. Kennington, of whom great things may be expected some day.

There are a number of genre pictures, large and small, of which 'Before the Procession,' by Chevilliard (see below), is a good example, and there are many interpretations of English country life and scenery. Mr. Bromley's 'Where Clouds touch Earth' is conspicuous among these as a picture full of rich colour, and not aggressively green. A very graceful pastoral by Mr. Yeend King called 'His Road Home' ought to be a more favourite picture than it is. Mr. Nettleship is represented by 'Seeking his Meat before God'—a leopard prowling on a rocky pathway.

There is only one conspicuously good interior in the Adelaide Gallery—Mr. Wyke-Bayliss's 'Strasburg.' In the entrance-hall there is a good deal of sculpture by Mr. Marshall Wood, the chief pieces being a replica of the 'Song of a Shirt' in the Sydney Gallery, and a 'Daphne,'—and with 'Daphne' our notice must close.

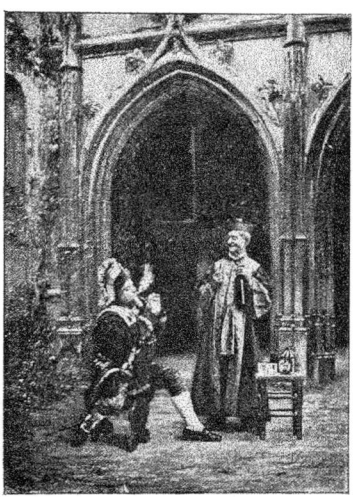

BEFORE THE PROCESSION. BY V. CHEVILLIARD.

It is not the fault of the Adelaide Gallery that a number of exceptionally trying bequests and gifts have to be displayed on its walls. These blows of adversity will fall on the most distinguished institutions, and must often be borne unresistingly and even welcomed. Time and the judgment of the hanging committee must be relied on to mitigate their effects.

FREWEN LORD.

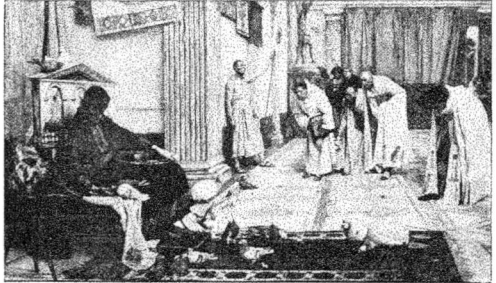

THE FAVOURITES OF THE EMPEROR HONORIUS. BY J. W. WATERHOUSE, A.R.A.

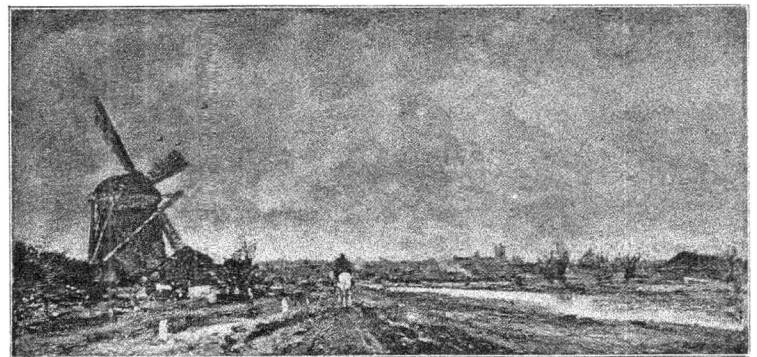

THE MILL AT THE CANAL. BY JAMES MARIS

FORTHCOMING SALES IN FRANCE AND HOLLAND.

THE auction sale-rooms on the Continent begin to be alive again with business, and it is probable that the winter season will be a very good one. Several sales of more than ordinary importance are announced, and the dispersal of the collection of the late M. Post, of The Hague, and also of the late Charles Jacques' atelier, in Paris, are likely to be well attended.

The Post collection, as befits a gallery in Holland, has been formed chiefly from the best modern Dutch painters, and it embraces several very fine specimens by Josef Israels, James Maris, William Maris, and Albert Neuhuys, and a few studies by Mauve. The sale takes place in the well-known rooms called the Pulchri Studio at The Hague, and the pictures will be on view some days before the auction, which will be held on November 13th.

An illustrated catalogue has been published, and we give reproductions of several of the chief pictures. Josef Israels

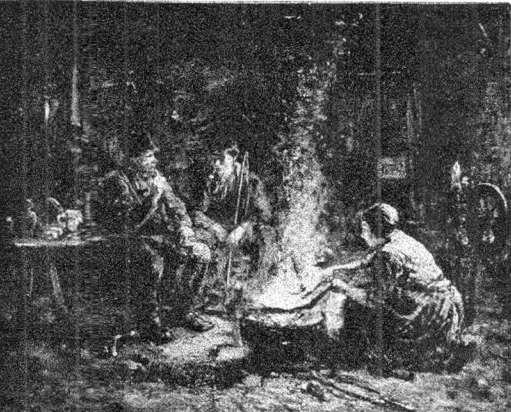

GOOD NEIGHBOURS. BY JOSEF ISRAELS.

is represented by his rich and powerful 'Good Neighbours,' where, in a typical dusky Dutch cottage, the cronies converse. The wife prepares the supper over the open fire, placed, as in Ireland, in the centre of the apartment, whence the smoke rises to the roof. A spinning wheel shows the *eident* hand of the helpmate. The colour of this picture is remarkably masterful in quality. It will interest this artist's many admirers to learn that since his wife's sad death about a year ago he has kept in good health, although his pencil has not been quite so busy as of old.

James Maris, the master *par excellence* of the sky, is represented by five or six magnificent canvases. The one illustrated, 'The Mill at the Canal,' is a typical composition of this artist. The great windmill against a cloudy sky, the man on horseback moving slowly along by the somewhat *triste* canal, make up a subject which gives the painter plenty of

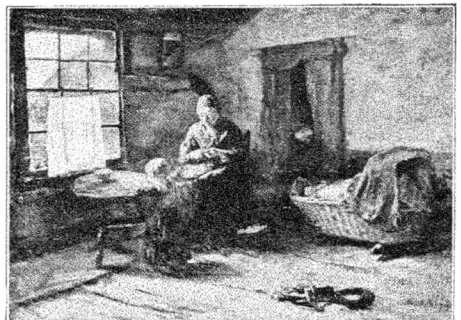

THE HOUSEKEEPER. BY ALBERT NEUHUYS.

scope for his strong schemes of colour. James Maris, it is well known, considers that a picture is not ready to be looked at until it has been painted about a dozen years. At first his colours look raw and cold, but as they ripen on the canvas a wonderful charm of subtle tone spreads over the work, until, in about the time named, the pictures are so perfect in harmony and quality as to justify the opinion of many of our best connoisseurs, who look on James Maris as one of the greatest living landscape painters.

Albert Neuhuys, friend and follower of the revered Josef Israels, is one of the most promising of the younger generation of modern Dutch artists. His 'Housekeeper' shows his treatment of the interiors of Holland cottages. His colour is clearer than Israels', and his power of definition greater, but it is only when he will have still further developed, and, in fact, left these qualities behind, that he will be as great an artist as his master. His reputation is already high and the future is entirely his own.

William Maris is the younger brother of James and Matthew Maris, the only family of really first-rate artists living and painting in our own day. Matthew Maris still works, but, it is to be greatly regretted, produces little or nothing. He spends his time in his studio in St. John's Wood, fastidiously dissatisfied with his own productions, but exercising a powerful influence over certain prominent English artists who cherish his friendship. William Maris paints the open fields with cattle grazing. Willow-trees and brilliant sunshine are his greatest favourites, and in his own way there is no one can surpass him. 'Milking Time' is a pleasant example of his work, one of several which will be at the Post sale.

The Charles Jacques' sale will take place on November 12th and 13th, and in the Galerie Petit, Rue de Sèze, Paris. It will consist of the pictures, sketches, and studies left by Jacques at his death a few months ago. As the last of the really great men of the Barbizon School, his atelier will certainly attract immense attention. There will be over fifty pictures and several hundred sketches and original

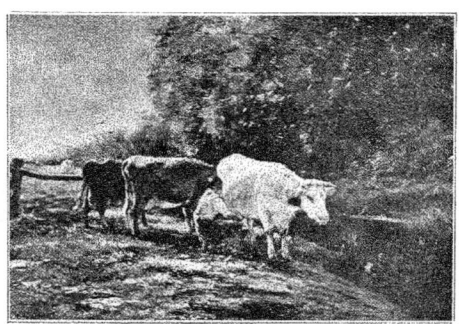

MILKING TIME. BY WILLIAM MARIS.

etchings, and the illustrated catalogue is both interesting and beautiful.

THE NEW TRUSTEES OF THE NATIONAL GALLERY.

THAT any question concerning the management of the National Gallery should provoke keen, often irritated interest, is really a tribute to its past record. For the National Gallery is a very legitimate object for pride: despite a few sins, more of omission than commission, it not merely holds its own with any gallery in the world, but comes first in point of quality. Hence, when the choice of a successor to Sir Frederick Burton was yet undecided, the battle raged fiercely enough. Now that Mr. E. J. Poynter, R.A., is established in his place, it would appear as if the British love of fair-play had silenced all hostile criticism, and that both critics and the public are content to wait and see what the new director will do before championing, or objecting to, his appointment. Certainly the first list of acquisitions since he took office—for which, however, he is probably not entirely responsible—would disarm opposition, if only by reason of the catholicity of appreciation it shows. Two new portraits by Lawrence help towards strengthening the British school, which is still sadly incomplete in many directions, as the briefest study of the catalogue will show. A Mantegna, 'The Agony in the Garden' (1417), is another distinct gain. Even now, five pictures are all that represent a master who has influenced recent English painting to a remarkable extent, as every fresh study of the 'Triumph of Cæsar' at Hampton Court proves more and more. The later pre-Raphaelites, Burne-Jones and his school, seem as if they must have been actual pupils of this master, when standing before it you note certain tricks of drapery and composition in that superb procession. Each visit to the original but leaves an abiding regret that so great a work is not hung at Trafalgar Square. Surely a good copy would suffice to carry on the traditions of the old palace

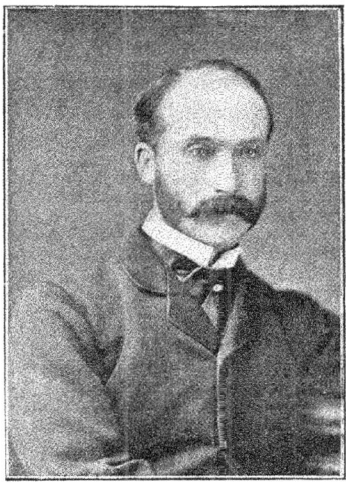

THE MARQUIS OF LANSDOWNE.
(From a Photo by the London Stereoscopic Company.)

where the paintings are almost invisible owing to the glass, necessary to protect them, reflecting the windows immediately opposite. But the Lawrences and the Mantegna are only three items upon a list which includes a 'Holy Family' by Le Sueur, a 'St. Jerome' (1466) by Antonelli da Messina, a fine work by Cordelle Agii, and 'A View in Haarlem' by Berkheyden, and other paintings by Jan Steen, Van Ravesteyn, etc. The obvious regret that at present our National Gallery yet waits a single example of later French painting is tempered by remembering that, until a few years since, the Louvre itself knew little or nought of Barbizon and the Romanticists.

Regarding certain changes in the administration lately made by the Treasury, it is as well to point out that they are more formal than real. The position of the Board of Trustees and the Director has but received official sanction for what, in recent years, at least, has been the practice in the conduct of the business, viz., that the Director shall consult the Trustees, whenever possible, before deciding on the purchase of a picture, or on other matters relating to the management of the Gallery. Formerly the Director was not bound to consult the Trustees, nor to act on their advice; and, as the minute of April 26th of this year puts it, "under this arrangement, the Trustees, while apparently occupying a position of authority and responsibility, are debarred from the exercise of any real power." This anomaly is removed, and the authority is now real, the Board as a whole being responsible for the management of the Gallery and the purchase of pictures, instead of, as hitherto, the Director alone. Yet this apparent change is but continuing the same course as hitherto. The Director

invariably, whenever possible, did consult the Trustees, and monthly meetings were held for the management of business during the season. Under the new Treasury minute no alteration has been made in either procedure.

The vacancies caused by the deaths of Sir Henry Layard and Viscount Hardinge have been filled by the appointment of the Marquis of Lansdowne and Sir Charles Tennant. The former, if better known as an administrator than as a patron of Art, is the second holder of his title who has been a Trustee of the Gallery. His name is not unfamiliar as a contributor in the catalogues of Winter Exhibitions at the Royal Academy. His country seat, Bowood Park, near Calne, Wiltshire, contains a fine collection of paintings. Sir Charles Tennant is so obviously the right man for the position that it is needless to dilate upon the fact, or to refer to his peculiarly fine collection of pictures, chosen with such marked discretion and appreciation.

One can but hope that the new blood infused into the administration may be able to bring the requisite power to bear for the enlargement of the building. Many chapters of the history of this country, which are definitely recorded in the annals of Art, yet wait illustration in their collection, and in this respect London is behind New York and other cities of far less pretension. That the private collections of Great Britain are full of treasures, the records of a quarter of a century at the "Old Masters" at Burlington House suffice to prove; to obtain the best of these by bequest or purchase, is not so easy to accomplish as to suggest; yet now that America is bent on acquiring treasures of the past, and the rivalry at auction rooms will probably be intensified as she enters the lists of buyers in earnest, it is of the utmost importance that the National Gallery should not rest content with its well-won

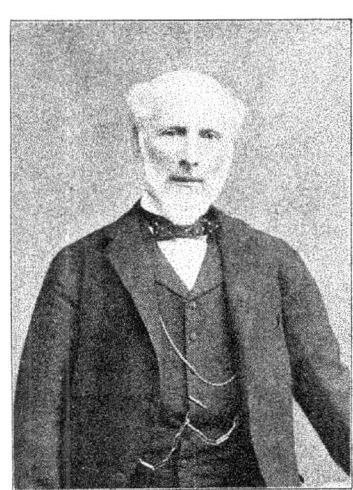

SIR CHARLES TENNANT, BART.
(From a Photo by Elliott & Fry.)

laurels, but regard its present collection only as a good start towards one still more complete.

NATIONAL COMPETITION AWARDS, 1894.

THE awards of the examiners are slightly in excess of those made last year—786 as against 748. The number of works sent in for competition increases annually in greater proportion than that; but the standard of the examiners also advances year by year—as may be seen at South Kensington, where the prize works certainly make a very good show. A vast amount of originality there is not. But originality is a very rare thing; and, after all, it is not the business of the Department to produce it. All that the schools can do is to turn out good workmen, and give invention a chance of expressing itself with full effect. It is not so much to be regretted, therefore, from the educational point of view, that the gold medallists are this year rather less in number than last. A gold medallist is a sort of *rara avis*, hatched perhaps in the scholastic nest, but hardly belonging to it, reflecting it may be more credit on a particular school than it strictly deserves. But for the winning of the lesser rewards, silver and especially bronze medals, and books, the school and the master of the school are certainly very largely responsible; and they may congratulate themselves this year upon their success. Against a decrease of two gold medals they can show an increase of six silver and twenty-five bronze medals and thirteen book-prizes.

The honorary awards to students of the training class at South Kensington show rather a falling off in number; but one student at least, Lilian Simpson, has distinguished herself by carrying off three gold medals, one silver and two bronze medals. Florence Steele and Jane M. Twiss of South Kensington, Eleanor L. Mercer of Sheffield, and Evelyn G. Thompson of Southport, also make their mark. Robert Spence of Newcastle has a very clever Rethel-like design for book illustration, and Harry Kershaw of Heywood has a design for a panel in monochrome, which, as the work of a lad of fifteen, is remarkable.

Some who gained last year small prizes obtain this year higher awards: this is as it should be. Some, on the other hand, who distinguished themselves last year take now a lower place. This may mark (as it does in some instances) a falling off on the part of the student; but it goes in the main to substantiate what was said about the higher standard of 1894. It suggests, however, a reflection. How is it that a student who has gained the highest award is allowed to compete a second time for the same prize? It is hardly fair to expect a student to compete with a past gold medallist.

Another question also arises. Some of the works rewarded are obviously the work of men already experienced in their *trade*; they may have been educated in the Government schools or they may not—they must attend classes in these schools or they would not be allowed to compete—but their work is hardly a test of Departmental teaching. It might not be just, it might not be possible, to exclude such work; but, clearly, it should be judged in a class apart, and not by the side of work done by *bonâ-fide* students, who owe their training entirely to the schools. If that is for some reason or another impracticable, there might be at least some limit of age: there comes a time in his life when, if a student has not taken honours, he scarcely deserves them.

L. F. D.

ART NOTES.

THE discussion in the House of Commons on August 20th as to the various votes for the support of the native artistic institutions was somewhat perfunctory. A gleam of humour was introduced into the consideration of the estimate for the Irish National Gallery. Mr. John Morley stated he wished to recognise the excellent work accomplished by the directors of the National Gallery in Dublin. With a modest allowance of £1,000 a year they had got together a most interesting and valuable collection. The gallery was, in fact, a model and a most democratic picture gallery. Colonel Nolan said he preferred an artistic to a democratic picture gallery—the allowance of £1,000 was a ridiculously small sum, and he wished the forms of the House permitted him to move to increase it.

A little later Mr. J. H. Lewis, member for the Flint Boroughs, said that no museums grant was made to Wales, which had as great a claim as England and Ireland. The people of Wales highly appreciated all that had been done for Welsh education, but gratitude did not preclude them from claiming their share of the grant for museums. There were many antiquities in Wales which would be attracted to a central national museum. A national gallery in Wales would do a great deal to encourage Art in the Principality, and also to promote trade and industry. The Chancellor of the Exchequer, however, did not think it could be said that the claims of Wales had been neglected by him. He had received this session three deputations from Wales asking for pecuniary assistance from the Treasury, and acceded to them all. The Government would always be ready to consider in a liberal spirit the claims of Wales, and of all parts of the country as far as possible, and he submitted that the Government had some right to claim that they had not neglected the interests of Wales.

The votes for the National Gallery were not permitted to pass until the Chancellor of the Exchequer gave a pledge that the present condition of many of the British pictures in the Gallery should be examined, Mr. Tomlinson having pointed out that some of the pictures in the National Gallery were getting into a deplorable state. No doubt it was partly due to the pigments the artists had used, but judging from the correspondence on the subject in the newspapers the dry condition of the atmosphere in the rooms had a good deal to do with it. He hoped, therefore, that the authorities would carefully consider the question, and see what could be done to remedy the evil. The estimates for the South Kensington Museum and the National Portrait Gallery were passed without discussion.

The Earl's Court Industrial Exhibition sustains its reputation as a place of entertainment. The Art Section has one or two interesting pictures and several excellent bits of sculpture. The gardens, with the geometrical beds, "Fernery," and Welcome Club, brilliantly illuminated by thousands of Cremorne gas and electric coloured lights, together with music from the orchestra and the bands, make the Exhibition a charming promenade in the evening. There are "Tableaux Vivants" in the Theatre, Organ Recitals frequently, Military Tournaments, The World's Water Show, where one can "shoot the Chutes," and be mystified in the Haunted Swing, which furnishes a novel yet harmless excitement as much to the onlooker as to the performer.

The American Tariff Bill came into operation at the end of August, having passed through Congress on August 13th. Under the new regulations the works of modern artists of all nations enter the United States duty free. Hitherto Oil Paintings, Water-colours, and Statuary paid an *ad valorem* duty of fifteen per cent. Curiously enough, opinion is divided as to the result of this total abolition of duty, for it has been considered by many competent to judge, that a small duty—say 10 per cent.—would prevent the importation of the least meritorious kinds of works of Art. With a duty to pay, American purchasers of low-priced pictures were careful to select something with some pretensions to merit, but now all duty being removed, the United States will probably be flooded by furniture dealers with all the rubbish of Europe. With the acquisition of high-priced pictures, the duty of fifteen per cent. has never practically interfered, since the reduction to that percentage from the thirty per cent. duty of half-a-dozen years ago.

It is quite possible that another Congress may re-impose a duty, and should it be found advisable to do so, we would suggest that the amount realised by the Customs on works of Art should be ear-marked. The sums thus collected should be utilised for the purpose of purchasing really fine pictures or statues to be gifted to the various public Art galleries throughout the United States.

Artist's proof engravings will also be admitted duty free, but it appears that consignments of ordinary prints and proofs will have to pay the same duty as hitherto, namely, 25 per cent. It is difficult to discover why a guinea print should pay a heavy duty, and an artist's proof—usually the purchase of a wealthy person—should escape. It must also be noted that the new tariff does not render pastels exempt from duty, and these presumably remain at 15 per cent.

MEISSONIER'S LAST WISHES.—Letters of administration of the personal estate in the United Kingdom of Jean Louis Ernest Meissonier, of 131, Boulevard Malesherbes, Paris, artist, who died on January 31, 1891, have been granted to his son, Jean Charles Emanuel Claudius Meissonier, of Poissy, artist, administration having been renounced by Mme. Elizabeth Meissonier, the widow. *The Times* gives some interesting details regarding the circumstances :—M. Meissonier did not appoint any executor of his will or any residuary legatee. On March 23rd, 1889, he wrote :—"I feel this morning a slight discomfort which I cannot account for. I am just going out to visit the Exhibition. If a misfortune should happen to me I have no dispositions to make with regard to my children, my natural heirs. I embrace them only. But for Miss Elizabeth Bezanson, whom I love tenderly, who has always shown me an unchangeable love, and to whom I intend in a very short time to unite myself should God grant it to me, I leave the life interest in all my pictures, studies, drawings, and sketch-books which she may choose. All the manuscripts in her writing shall be returned to her, and she shall take from amongst my letters and papers those which she may desire as a souvenir of my unchangeable affection. May the name of God be blessed." On November 5th, 1889, M. Meissonier, having given to Miss Elizabeth Bezanson the portrait painted at Venice for which she was good enough to sit to him as 'The Woman in Trouble,' exhibited and known as the 'Madonna dell' Baccio,' gave to her also his portrait, exhibited at the Champ de Mars under No. 1,014, and the view of Venice under No. 1,012. He added :—"At the time of the death of their mother I cancelled in favour of my children an act of donation of the disposable portion which my wife and I mutually entered into in favour of the survivor. They are now entitled, as I am married without a marriage contract, to half of everything I have gained by my work, and I can only dispose of the disposable portion from my share at the time of the death of my first wife. I wish to dispose thereof in favour of her who now bears my name, and whose every thought is for me, and who is now endeavouring to soothe the bitter grief which overwhelms me. I cause her very great trouble—I who love her with all my strength—but should God grant me strength to hold out I will cause her to forget it." On October 13th, 1890, he ordered that his wife should not be molested in her enjoyment of his house on the Boulevard. By a memorandum dated April 4th, 1879, he asked the Louvre to be good enough to accept the small picture 'L'Attente,' exhibited at the Exhibition of 1867 (which picture he had never thought proper to part with, whatever price might have been offered for it), and an unfinished picture which he had never cared to complete. On January 1st, 1884, he wrote :—"In the secret cupboard in the wainscoting of the large studio there may be some money which my children will necessarily take, and I conjure them, if they wish to avoid remorse for having failed to respect the wishes of their father, to place all the letters and all the papers which they may find shut up there, without reading them, in a box which they will seal with a seal, and which they will convey in my name to the library of the Institute, only to be opened thirty years after my death. Let them believe that I have ever loved them tenderly."

OBITUARY.

In the ART JOURNAL last year we gave a short account of the late Mr. James W. Wild, Curator of Sir John Soane's Museum, and we have now to record the death of his successor, Mr. Wyatt Papworth, which took place on the 19th of August, in his seventy-third year. Mr. Papworth was principally known for his literary work in connection with architecture, such as his contributions to the "Transactions of the

Royal Institute of British Architects," and his great work—the "Dictionary of Architecture"—issued by the Architectural Publication Society, which was commenced in 1852 by his late brother, Mr. J. W. Papworth, and himself, and was carried on, until its completion in 1892, under his own sole editorship. Mr. Papworth possessed an exhaustive knowledge of the dates and history of the various London buildings, and he was always ready to help others from the vast stores of his learning. He was a Past Master of the Clothworkers' Company.

The well-known animal sculptor, Auguste Cain, died at Paris on the 10th of August. He was born there on the 16th of November, 1822, and was the son of a veteran in the 'Grande Armée,' who had served for twenty years under the great Napoleon. The sculptor's early life was one of much hardship, and he commenced to earn his bread at an early age in the shop of a Havre decorator. He entered the studio of the sculptor Rude, and afterwards of Barye, and made his first appearance at the Salon in 1846, and received his first medal in 1851. The works which he executed for the beautification of his native city are well known to all visitors to Paris. At the garden of the Luxembourg is the 'Lion à l'Autruche'; at the gardens of the Tuileries are the 'Tigre étouffant un Crocodile,' the 'Rhinocéros attaqué par les Tigres,' and the 'Sleeping Lionesses'; and at the Hôtel de Ville, the Château de Chantilly, and the garden of the Elysée, he is also represented by fine groups and figures of animals. His work is characterized by fine decorative quality, and much feeling of movement and life. He leaves a widow and two sons, who are both painters.

RECENT BOOKS ON ART.

An excellent translation of M. Lafenestre's work on the Louvre has been published by Dean & Son. This is an authoritative volume largely illustrated by the keeper of the paintings in the Louvre, assisted by M. Richtenberger. The illustrations serve chiefly as reminders, for in a moderately priced book it is impossible to give really successful plates. The fourth edition of "TURNING LATHES" (Britannia Company, Colchester), edited by J. Lukin, B.A., is considerably enlarged. Although more or less of a trade *réclame*, it is thoroughly satisfactory, discussing technical details intelligently and in a reliable way. The new portions of the book deal with ornamental lathe work and the endless variety of "chucks" specially attractive to the amateur.

The publications of the Science and Art Department are happily becoming more artistic in outward appearance. "BOOKBINDINGS AND RUBBINGS OF BINDINGS IN THE NATIONAL ART LIBRARY" (Eyre & Spottiswoode) is the latest, and as a catalogue of some of the hidden treasures in South Kensington, it will be useful to every binder of books. "ARCHÆOLOGIA OXONIENSIS" (Frowde) has now reached its fourth quarterly part, and as its advertisement says, "Future issues will depend on the amount of support Part V. receives." This is a well-conducted publication of great interest to every one connected with the Oxford Colleges, and as it fills a distinct place of its own, it is likely the wishes of the promoters will be realised.

In Germany the custom of publishing studies for the use of artists has been steadily developing. These studies, which are taken direct from nature, are mostly interesting and useful, and on the Continent many artists study and select portions from these publications for their pictures. A new series of "TWENTY-FIVE HELIOGRAVURES," by M. Otto Schmidt, of Vienna, is published by Erdmann and Schanz, Salcott Road, Clapham, as a guinea portfolio. Many of these are interesting—Tyrolese cottage interiors, and others of landscape and river "bits" likely to be useful to the painter.

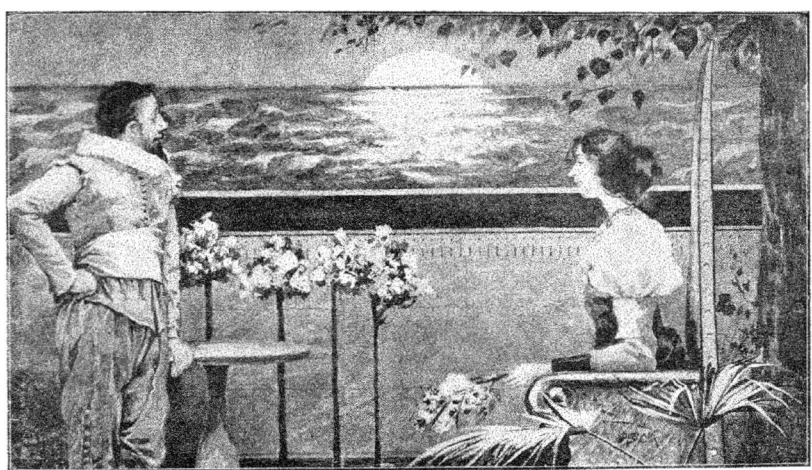

'SUNSET.' FROM A DRAWING BY MICHAEL DIGNAM.

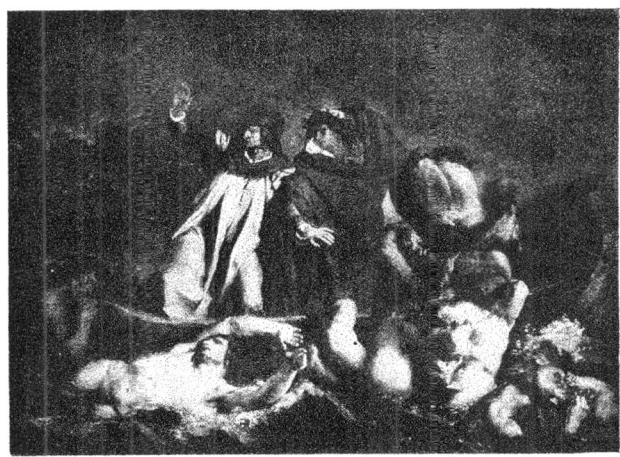

DANTE AND VIRGIL CONDUCTED BY PHLEGYAS ACROSS THE STYGIAN LAKE. BY EUGÈNE DELACROIX.
(Photo, Braun & Co., Dornach.)

EUGÈNE DELACROIX.

THERE must inevitably come a period after the death of a great artist, be he poet or painter when the immortality of his fame is placed in doubt : when posterity, if it still knows him, either refuses to repeat, or repeats in half-hearted fashion, the praise of a former generation.

The bolder, those undeterred by the authority of tradition, or perversely stimulated to run counter to it, then cast stones at the idol, striving to show that it is of clay, or even to overturn and shatter it. This period of reaction, this descent after the zenith has been reached, is perhaps inevitable. How far the star thus momentarily obscured will shine out again, and whether it will regain its former radiance, or even reappear with an intensified brightness, can, to the spectator of the intermediate, the transitional period, only be a matter of surmise.

Delacroix's whole career, from his début in 1822 with the 'Dante et Virgile' to his apotheosis, while he was yet among the living, at the International Exhibition of 1855, had been one of storm and combat. No man was ever more pas-

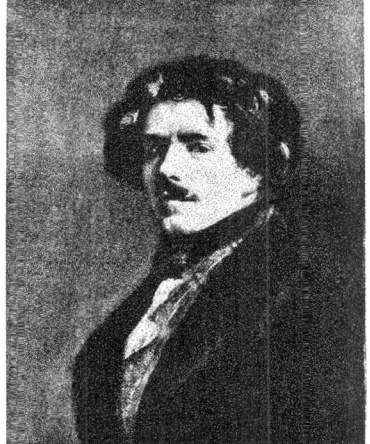

PORTRAIT OF EUGÈNE DELACROIX. PAINTED BY HIMSELF.

sionately worshipped on the one hand or more ruthlessly, more absolutely condemned on the other. Thenceforward, down to his death in 1863, and for some years afterwards, his fame stood at its highest point, and the scoffers, though they might not be convinced, were at any rate silent.

It is to the rise of Naturalism—that offspring of Romanticism which ended by devouring its parent—that the gradual decline, if not exactly of Delacroix's reputation, yet certainly of his popularity, may be traced. Now that the din of battle between the modified Raphaelesque classicism of Ingres and the passionate, imaginative romanticism of Delacroix has so long died out, critics of authority, in and outside France, are practically unanimous in acknowledging that the chief of the Romantics was and must remain a great figure in the art of the nineteenth century. They differ in their estimate of his technical accomplishment, and of the quality of his genius, but in this only.

It is the public that now stands aloof, in an attitude sufficiently respectful to a master who has been accepted as *une des gloires nationales de la France*, but still marked by some bewilderment and an unmistakable lack of sympathy. The constituted authorities of France have now accorded to the great colourist all the honours which can be accorded to a painter. From the museum of Versailles and from the Luxembourg his most famous works have been brought to the Louvre, where they occupy posts of honour in the great saloon devoted to the French art of this century. His noted canvases in so many of the provincial museums of France, the vast decorative works from his brush which adorn the Louvre, the Palais Bourbon, the Luxembourg, and the church of St. Sulpice, would alone suffice to establish and maintain his glory. Still, though it can hardly be doubted that Delacroix will stand forth hereafter as one of the greatest French masters—in many respects the greatest—of the nineteenth century, it may be questioned whether he will ever maintain a permanent hold on the affections of the larger public, whether he will ever in the .true sense of the word become popular. The latest and best of the artist's biographers, M. Ernest Chesneau, has furnished the following solution, which contains a part of, though not the whole truth :—

"Voilé par la vivante magie de la couleur, par l'emportement du dessin, par la suprême distinction du goût avec lequel le mélodrame est évité, sous l'enchanteresse parure le l'art, au fond de cet œuvre immense il coule un flot de sang. Le bourgeois n'aime pas cela." And he adds the comment, showing how accurately he appreciates English sympathies and antipathies in art : "Et c'est aussi pourquoi l'Angleterre ne l'acceptera jamais."

The last two or three generations of Frenchmen have pretty conclusively shown that scenes of blood and horror have rather a morbid attraction than a repulsion for them : so much so, indeed, that to reproach French artists of the latter half of this century with an excessive tendency in this direction has become almost a platitude.

All the same, it may well be that M. Chesneau is right, and that no lasting and unquestioned reputation has been or will be established, even in France, on a foundation of blood and horror only. The name which at once occurs to us, as that of an artist of distinction and apparently established fame, whose art has mainly taken this peculiar direction, is that of M. Jean-Paul Laurens. But then, notwithstanding the ultra-dramatic character which gives distinctiveness to all his most prominent works, the horror which they exhale is that of a drama of Victor Hugo, rather than that of reality ; its effect is momentarily to thrill, but not permanently to disquiet the beholder.

The disquietude produced by the contemplation of Delacroix's works is different. It is more than the mere clangour of combat, the flow of blood, the sound of lamentation, the ruthless overthrow of the weaker by the stronger, that are brought before us by his pictures, though these are his chief and most obvious themes. It is, in reality, all the restlessness, the storm, the change of the modern period following upon the Revolution, and set loose after the downfall of the Empire, that the master makes us feel. It is the reflection, in the shifting colours and with the transforming power of art, of the ever-restless, the deeply wounded spirit of the poet-painter, at war with the world as he found it, and aggressively disdainful of its outer aspects and inner conditions.

Yet another disadvantage weighs against Delacroix. He selected most of his subjects, when they were not of a purely decorative character, from the great poets of former times, or the romantic literature of his own—from Dante, Shakespeare, Ariosto, Tasso, Goethe, Byron, Walter Scott ; and he had thus against him from the beginning all those—and they must inevitably have been the majority—who came to him with preconceived notions, who had already conjured up their own visions of the scenes which the poet of the brush boldly undertook to paraphrase rather than to reproduce.

And yet the French master was not a painter of literary temperament, like our own pre-Raphaelites of the second generation, or like Mr. Watts in his later development. He was an artist who took inspiration and sustenance from literature, but saw his subjects, however imperfectly at times, with the true vision of the painter, content only when they flashed before him complete in every essential part, and willing to leave nothing to the laborious processes of conscious evolution and re-arrangement. What he did in the majority of instances—we say this remembering the unstinted admiration expressed by Goethe for the lithographed illustrations to his *Faust*—was to re-cast the literary subjects chosen, to re-create them from the plastic standpoint in his own mould, so that to do them justice they must be judged by themselves, and without *arrière-pensée*.

For the reasons now lightly touched upon the chief of the Romantic school may possibly never regain the now more than half-estranged love of the outer world. It is hardly probable either, that any Romanticist of these latter days, however enthusiastic may be his admiration, will be found to repeat those words of passionate yet not indiscriminate worship which fell from the lips and the pens of Théophile Gautier, Baudelaire, and the generation of those who were young in 1830. Still, when the artistic history of the nineteenth century comes to be written, it will be found that of the Romanticists proper —leaving out the great school of landscape to which the description *romantic* is sometimes, though not very appropriately, applied—Delacroix, with his precursor and friend Géricault, and his contemporary, the Orientalist, Decamps, will tower high above the other painters of their school, most of whom have been submerged and overwhelmed by the mere fashions, the outer *défroque* of the movement they represent. Leaving out of consideration for the moment the technical merits as well as the technical defects and mannerisms of Delacroix, the chief characteristics of his art are its intense vitality, the absolute sincerity of its passionate agitation, the unconscious truth with which, while dealing with scenes far removed, not only by reason of their *mise-en-scène* but in their essence, from those of his own time, it reflects the clouds and storms of that time and its passionate repudiation of accumulated tradition.

Strangely enough, it was in the studio of Guérin, the most ultra-classic of the classicists, that was prepared the great revolt from the frozen immobility to which the arbitrary principles of David in historic art had reduced his generation. Here Delacroix met Géricault (his elder by some seven years), besides Ary Scheffer, Sigalon, and Champmartin.

Born in 1799, the young student* was seventeen years old when he entered Guérin's studio. Left fatherless in 1805, and placed by his mother at the Lycée Louis-le-Grand, the ardent youth had during his school days had opportunities of visiting

---

* The latest and by far the most comprehensive work on the art of the Romantic master is "L'œuvre Complet d'Eugène Delacroix, catalogué et reproduit par Alfred Robaut, Commenté par Ernest Chesneau," published in 1885 ; the preface and accompanying notes by the last-named accomplished and sympathetic critic containing a remarkable exposition of the master's principles and style.

the Louvre, and studying the unparalleled collection of masterpieces then accumulated in its halls. These filled him with unbounded admiration, and aroused a spirit of emulation which caused him to decide upon the adoption of painting as the career of his life. Before he revealed himself, already individual and fully developed, if not yet technically perfect, in the 'Dante et Virgile,' Delacroix had had (1818—1822) like Ingres—the uncompromising rival and opponent whose art was in all respects the antithesis of his—a preliminary period of Raphaelism. He had studied and copied Sanzio in the Louvre,* had painted for the church of Orcemont, a 'Vierge des Moissons,' which M. Chesneau describes as "toute impregnée de Raphaëlisme," and a 'Vierge du Sacré Cœur,' for a convent at Nantes—this latter, a commission to the unfortunate Géricault, which his failing health prevented him from carrying out.

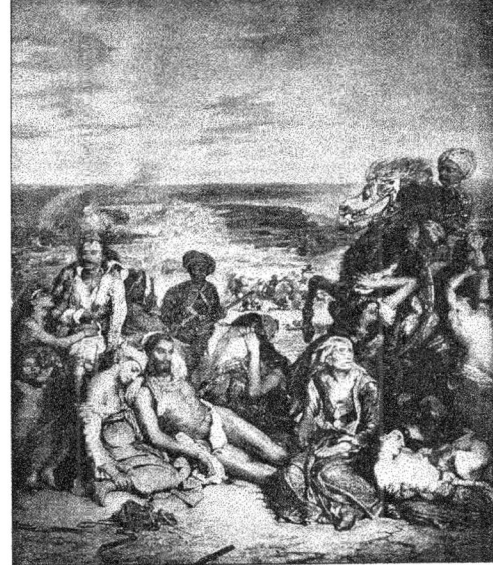

THE MASSACRE OF SCIO. BY EUGÈNE DELACROIX. (*Photo, Braun & Co., Dornach.*)

Still, the real beginning of Delacroix's serious career as an artist, the point of departure of his fiery course as the typical romanticist, is the exhibition of the 'Dante et Virgile' at the Salon of 1822. Every one knows Charles Blanc's pretty and true story, telling how the young artist of three-and-twenty, being too poor to afford an orthodox frame for his large canvas, had patched up what he hoped would be deemed a sufficient one out of four laths of common wood, gilt, or painted yellow. When the Salon opened—it was then held in the Louvre—Delacroix, rushing through the galleries, and failing to find the canvas on which he had built such high hopes, was reduced to despair. At last, to his amazement, he discovered it in the Salon Carré, ther as now the place of honour, in a handsome new frame. His own poor substitute had fallen to pieces, and Gros, enthusiastic in his admiration of the picture, though it answered to his former rather than to his actual style, had thus splendidly replaced it.

In some respects the artist rises higher in this work of his youth than he ever did again. Though drawing and modelling may in many respects be open to criticism, the picture which is reproduced at the head of this article is, what Gros recognised it to be, a masterpiece of its kind. It is a question whether any painter has realised with a power so

* A copy of the Infant Christ in the "Belle Jardinière," by Delacroix, fetched some years ago in a sale no less than 5,700 francs—£228.

closely akin to that of the poet the lurid yet perfectly plastic and precise imaginings of Dante.

The august, shadowy figure of Virgil, wonderfully significant in its contrast to the living fire of the Florentine bard and the frenzy of the damned striving to climb into the ferryman's barque, is unforgettable in its serene beauty. A subdued vibration of light permeates the sombre splendours of the canvas, and half reveals, half conceals the terrors of the Inferno. Already here the treatment of light, colour, and atmosphere is new, and personal to the artist; it is absolutely opposed to the cold classicalities of the David school then still accepted. The colour has not only a sombre beauty and already an audacity of its own, but a special fitness to express the theme chosen; it adds to it a significance, a poetic fire such as noble verse lends to a subject worthy of it. Baudelaire does not overmuch exaggerate—for a poet-critic—when he says much later, in relation to 'Le Sultan de Maroc entouré de sa Garde'—"Qu'on cite un tableau de grand coloriste où la couleur ait autant d'esprit que dans celui de M. Delacroix."

A still greater sensation was created at the Salon of 1824 by the 'Massacre de Scio' (here illustrated), upon which the young painter had been labouring since his first success. The lyrical quality of his genius finds full scope when he depicts *more suo* this contemporary event, so vast and tragic in its horror. There is in the expression of the subject that higher truth which gives by a kind of divination its essential character, though neither historical accuracy nor realistic adherence to fact has been attained, or indeed intended.

We have it on the authority of Frédéric Villot, once conservator of the pictures in the Louvre, and the author of an essay on Constable, that Delacroix, having sent in his picture, obtained access before the opening of the exhibition to the landscapes by Constable, which were then to make their first appearance in France. A new world opened itself before the eyes of the astonished and delighted artist, already at war with the over-smoothness, the lifelessness of the waning classic school. He saw for the first time Nature depicted without artifice or conventionality, with her wind-swept skies, her scintillations of light, her infinite reflections. Delacroix, by favour, obtained permission to remove his picture from the upper galleries and had it placed below in the Salle des Cariatides, where, before the opening of the Salon, he entirely retouched it, enriching the half-tones, giving added transparency to the shadows, and new life to the whole.

It was about this time, too, that he made acquaintance, in the galleries of the Louvre, with Bonington, "*le grand adolescent en veste courte,*" as he calls him in a letter to Théodore Thoré. The acquaintance ripened into an atelier friendship, and the two young artists worked for a considerable time together, the influence of Bonington on Delacroix being very noticeable in such paintings as, for instance, the 'Combat du Giaour,' exhibited in 1826. It was in the latter year that Delacroix, following in this the example of his luckless friend Géricault, made a journey to England, and there studied English art with an enthusiasm of which proof may be found in his published correspondence.

M. Paul Mantz sees in the vast 'Sardanapalus,' exhibited at the Salon of 1827, the influence of the English school; but it surely reveals still more strongly, in the brilliant, rosy flesh-tones and warm transparent shadows, that of Rubens.* The admiration of Delacroix for Byron was further proved at this same exhibition by the well-known 'Marino Faliero,' now in the Wallace Collection at Manchester House, London, and probably the most important example of our master to be found in England.

To this early time belong—although they were not published with the text until some few years later—the famous lithographic illustrations to Goethe's *Faust*, which are the very quintessence of 1830 romanticism. One hesitates to criticise these, remembering that the august poet himself ("Eckermann's Conversations with Goethe"), said of them: " I must confess that Monsieur Delacroix has surpassed my own

* We give an illustration of a later version of this subject.

conception of the scenes of which I am the creator; how much more then will they stand out and appear living to my readers." The lithographer's pencil is everywhere used with power and ease, the chiaroscuro is full of force and significance, but the mannerism of the ultra-romantic time is occasionally not a little difficult for the less lyrical mortal of to-day to swallow. The best pages are 'Mephistopheles in Mid-air' (Prologue in Heaven); the 'Duel between Valentine and Faust;' the 'Vision of Gretchen,' when she appears to Faust amid the mad turmoil of the *Walpurgisnacht;* and the 'Ride to the Abyss,' with its frantic horses treated in the fashion of Géricault.

Much inferior in every respect, and such, indeed, as the English student could not with any amount of explanation be made to accept, are the illustrations to *Hamlet* (1834 and 1843). Everything in these—general conception, gesture, expression—is open to criticism, nay almost to ridicule ; and yet one feels somehow that the mistake is the mistake of a big man.

At the Salon of 1831 appeared 'Le 28 Juillet, 1830: La Liberté guidant le Peuple' (now in the Louvre)—the only canvas not a portrait in which the master has depicted a contemporary scene with the intractable civilian costumes of his time. The Liberty is a robust, half-naked young virago, as furious as Théroigne de Méricourt, or her enemies, the terrible *Tricoteuses* of the Mountain. At the same Salon appeared one of the artist's masterpieces, the 'Massacre de l'Evêque de Liège,' painted, however, as far back as 1827. He depicts here, after Sir Walter Scott, the gruesome scene in which Guillaume de la Marck, the Wild Boar of the Ardennes, presiding over an unbridled orgie held in honour of his victory, profanes the holy vessels, and causes the venerable bishop to be dragged into his presence and there massacred. In the sombre splendours of the colouring, the chiaroscuro heightening by its significance the terrible drama, Delacroix for once almost rivals Rembrandt himself, while the passion, the physical and mental horror of the scene, are all his own.

The painter's expedition to Morocco in 1832 had a paramount influence in developing his system as a colourist and *luminariste*. The Africa he saw and painted was not, it must be borne in mind, the commonplace tourist's resort of to-day, but a land which from the artist's standpoint was still to be discovered. Moorish Africa must still count, notwithstanding its western position, as an offshoot of the East, and it is thence that Delacroix brought back those pages instinct with oriental life and poetry, among which the most notable are the 'Femmes d'Alger' of 1834 (Louvre), the 'Noce Juive

THE DEATH OF SARDANAPALUS. BY EUGÈNE DELACROIX

dans le Maroc' of 1839 (Salon of 1841—now in the Louvre), and the brilliant 'Muley Abd-el-Rhaman sortant de son Palais' of 1845 (Museum of Toulouse).

These are among the few examples in the life-work of Delacroix in which, captivated by the novel problems of light and colour, and by the strangeness of the *milieu* he was interpreting, he attained, if not to perfect peace, yet to a relative serenity.

There is some discrepancy among the authorities as to the date of the fine portrait of the painter by himself, bequeathed to the Louvre in 1872 by Mlle. Joséphine Leguillon. The official catalogue gives the date as 1837, while MM. Chesneau and Robant place it as much earlier as 1829. A study of the physiognomy itself tends to confirm the official date of the Louvre; but, it must be borne in mind that with men who lived their lives feverishly in this *Sturm und Drang* period this is not so absolutely safe a guide as might at first be imagined.

The portrait (of which we give a reproduction) shows with a power of self-analysis not common where great masters limn themselves, the restless, nervous temperament of the artist, and forcibly suggests that aristocratic disdain of the *profanum vulgus*, which was an essential characteristic of the man, little as it may seem to accord with the temperament of the pioneer, the revolutionist in art, whom his detractors were wont to accuse of painting with *un balai ivre*.

To the year 1840 belongs the 'Naufrage de Don Juan,' bequeathed to the Louvre by M. Ad. Moreau. The scene is one of concentrated horror, realistic for once rather than romantic, and to accentuate its note of gloom and despair the painter has not hesitated to depart from Byron's description by enframing his boat and crew in a deep-green, agitated sea and a cloudy sky.

The 'Prise de Constantinople par les Croisés' (1841), which some years ago was brought from Versailles and placed in the Louvre, is the definite expression of Delacroix's art in its later phase. In it, intensely dramatic as are some isolated passages, the dramatic standpoint, which was supreme in the earlier works, is now on the whole subordinated to the decorative. It is beyond doubt the sumptuous art of Paolo Veronese that has suggested this vast splendid canvas, in which against a background of azure sky and water, of grey-white architecture such as Veronese loved, stands out the troop of mounted Crusaders, making its way, still in battle-array, through scenes of prolonged struggle and massacre. The colour is a feast to the eye, and notwithstanding its family resemblance to the Venetian school, quite personal to Delacroix. But, perhaps because monumental splendour has been chiefly aimed at, the dramatic unity and intensity of expression which marked those early productions the 'Dante et Virgile' and the 'Massacre de Scio' are in some measure wanting.

Lack of space renders it impossible to continue here the enumeration of the works contributed year by year by our master to the exhibitions, or to enter into detail with regard to the hostile attitude which the Institute—now in virtue of the ordinances of Louis Philippe, supreme arbiter at the annual Salons—maintained both openly and covertly towards Delacroix and his works—a hostility culminating on more than one occasion in their actual exclusion from the exhibitions, to which in the days of his less firmly established celebrity he had always been made welcome.

Ingres, whose attitude of protest against the art of his revolutionary rival is so well summed up in his famous dictum, *Le dessin est la probité de l'art*, was his bitter and consistent opponent throughout, not from unworthy jealousy or personal enmity, but from a stern, unbending sense of his duty to Art.

We have already noted the triumph of the artist at the International Exhibition of 1855, where the world had the opportunity of pitting his thirty-five canvases against the forty of his detractor. The heads of the rival factions were in presence, as they are now again in the great new saloon of the Louvre, where the 'Apothéose d'Homère,' the 'Odalisque,' the 'Roger et Angélique,' the 'Chérubini,' are opposed to the 'Dante et Virgile,' the 'Massacre de Scio,' the 'Entrée des Croisés,' the '28 Juillet, 1830.' To neither great chief has the world, however, even now definitely conceded the *spolia opima*. Strange to say, for reasons not easy to define, there is just now a tendency in the more extreme factions of modern French Art to exalt the austere Ingres at the expense of their legitimate parent Delacroix.

This last triumph of the arch-romanticist forced open the doors of the enemy's stronghold, the very Institute itself, of which august body he became a member in 1856, filling the chair left vacant when Paul Delaroche died in that year. Our master's last Salon was that of 1859, in which he showed, among other things, a 'Montée au Calvaire,' 'Christ au Tombeau,' 'St. Sébastien,' and 'Ovide chez les Scythes.'

The last great gathering of Delacroix's works was that of the exhibition held at the École des Beaux-Arts in 1885, to obtain funds for the erection of a monument. This was, however, if taken by itself, unavoidably incomplete, although the provincial museums and the private collections of France contributed to it some of their choicest possessions. We have shown that Delacroix's power can be fairly estimated only by those who study him in the Louvre, or seek him out in the public monuments of Paris.

It is strange that the master whose life was one battle with the Græco-Roman school of David, with the Italianised classicism of Ingres, with the constituted authorities of the Institute, should have lived chiefly by official support and by official commissions. The French State possesses his chief masterpieces, and what is not to be found in the Louvre or in the public buildings of the French capital is chiefly to be sought for in the provincial galleries.

The monument erected by private subscription, but a few years since, to Delacroix in the Luxembourg Gardens is not unworthy of him. It is the work of Jules Dalou, one of the chiefs of the now popular school of revolt from classic tradition in sculpture, and it shows in the seemingly undisciplined but really calculated energy of the design, in its deliberate defiance of conventionality, certain affinities with the standpoint of Delacroix himself. The great bust which crowns it is developed from the portrait in the Louvre. It should, with its suggestion of haughty defiance, of the power and the desire to stand alone, have satisfied the master, little as—judging from his formally expressed wishes—he cared to have his features perpetuated in such fashion.

CLAUDE PHILLIPS.

ART AND MR. WHISTLER.

IT is odd to note how diligently men seek to set a fashion in Art as in dress. Nor need one look beyond the last half century for proof of this diligence. It is a far cry from pre-Raphaelite to Newlynite; and yet each, for a time, has been leader of the mode in England. In France *Pleinairiste* has been speedily followed by *Impressioniste*, who, in his turn, has given place to *Vibriste* and *Pointilliste*—and who can say how many more? and each has had his vogue for a day. In the Academy the painter's success will depend upon his skill in telling now a classical story, now a tale of death-bed sentiment; in the Salon he will triumph according to the degree of his eccentricity, now of colour, now of technique. A Frith or a Fildes, a Bastien or a Béraud, may supply the painter's fashion-plates for a season. But Art itself knows nothing of these vagaries and vulgarities. It does not change with the years; it accepts no distinction of nationality or of school. The artist's concern is not with passing fads and affectations, but ever with beauty, whether of colour, of form, or of line.

Fortunately these last fifty years, so prolific in devices to catch the fancy of a fickle public, have also produced a few artists who are not to be tempted into straying after false gods of notoriety and fortune. Mr. Whistler has been criticised for his refusal to believe in the special artistic periods, the special art-loving notions that have become favourite *clichés* with the critic. But the study of his own work helps to explain and establish the truth of his artistic creed. In his canvases you will look in vain for the subjects and tricks that happen at the moment to please patron and dealer; but, instead, you will find that "painter's poetry"—the phrase is his—which is the charm of all Art; of the frescoes in the lower church of Assisi, as of the masterpieces in the Prado, of Utamaro's Japanese beauties as of Titian's goddesses, of Rembrandt's old women. Artistic problems may vary, artistic knowledge may increase; the landscape painter to-day may be able to render light and atmosphere with a truth undreamt of by Salvator Rosa or Claude; until the coming of Velasquez it may be that no portrait painter made his people stand upon their legs within the frame. But whatever the problem, however great the knowledge, the end has ever been one and identical: to make form, or colour, or atmospheric effect, or light yield its loveliest harmony, its subtlest poetry. And it is because Mr. Whistler has never lost sight of this one and only end of the artist that his canvases have that dignity and serenity which distinguish the good work of all ages and all countries. The portrait of his Mother would not look amiss in the Prado, nor the Nocturnes out of place in the Louvre.

The consistency of his intention is still more apparent when you come to consider his pictures in relation, not to those of his fellow artists, but to each other. His art presents none of the phases or periods which critic or compiler loves, for the "copy" they inspire. His style is the same to-day, when the Champ de Mars Salon reserves its chief centre for his canvases, as it was in the beginning when, in London, for him to exhibit was to be covered with derision and abuse. There is no man who has had a more far-reaching influence upon the younger generation of painters; not one who has remained so entirely independent of contemporary fashions and tendencies. His subject or theme may call for different treatment, but this, with him, never means sacrifice of style or distinction. If you compare his early pictures with his latest, you cannot fail to be struck with their unity of aim, differ as they may in the result obtained. It is now many years since 'The Little White Girl' was painted; the portrait of the 'Comte de Montesquien' dates but from yesterday. In both these is the same simplicity of scheme, the same restraint in the treatment; in both there is the same dignity, the same grace of pose. The girl, in her flowing white gown, leans against the mantel, her fine head reflected in the mirror; the Count, in sober evening dress, stands holding languidly his long, light cane. For one, as for the other, the most limited palette has served the artist's purpose, and an arrangement as uncompromisingly severe as in those royal portraits by Velasquez, where a curtain, a chair, and a table alone enter into the composition. But in one, as in the other, he has "put form and colour into such perfect harmony, that exquisiteness is the result." It is impossible, here, not to use his own words, since not only do they express so well that subtle quality which delights in his work, but they show how admirably his practice accords with his theory of Art. In black and white reproductions it is inevitable that the refinement of his colour should be, in a measure, lost. But at least the excellence of pose and arrangement cannot disappear.

If in his paintings it is with colour and form he has been necessarily most preoccupied, his etchings have hitherto been his tribute to the loveliness of line, and he proves himself none the less the artist absorbed in the creation of the beautiful because he exchanges his brush for the needle, his pigments for acids. But, within the last few years, when he has sought to express himself in pure line, the lithographer's stone has appealed to him more forcibly than the etcher's copperplate. He heralded, as it were, the revival in the art of lithography, which has had such a marked influence upon artists in Paris, and which is virtually the expression of their revolt against the encroachments of the photographer. As the camera is developed and perfected, the artist, whose medium is black and white, is called upon to produce something more than the sham photograph which at one time delighted and astonished. His individuality must assert itself in his design; if a figure be his subject he cannot be content with the mere fidelity of the portrait, if a landscape, with the bare realism of the copy, for in both these respects the photographer could rival him. It is rather upon the nature of his personal impression, upon the manner in which he records it, that he must rely. Any one who saw the fine collection called L'Estampe Originale, exhibited first at the Champ de Mars and then at the Grafton Gallery, cannot but be grateful for the results to which the revival is now leading. Many of the prints were etchings and wood-engravings, but more were lithographs, painters as distinguished as M. Carrière and M. Besnard contributing. It is really Mr. Whistler, however, who has tested to greatest advantage the

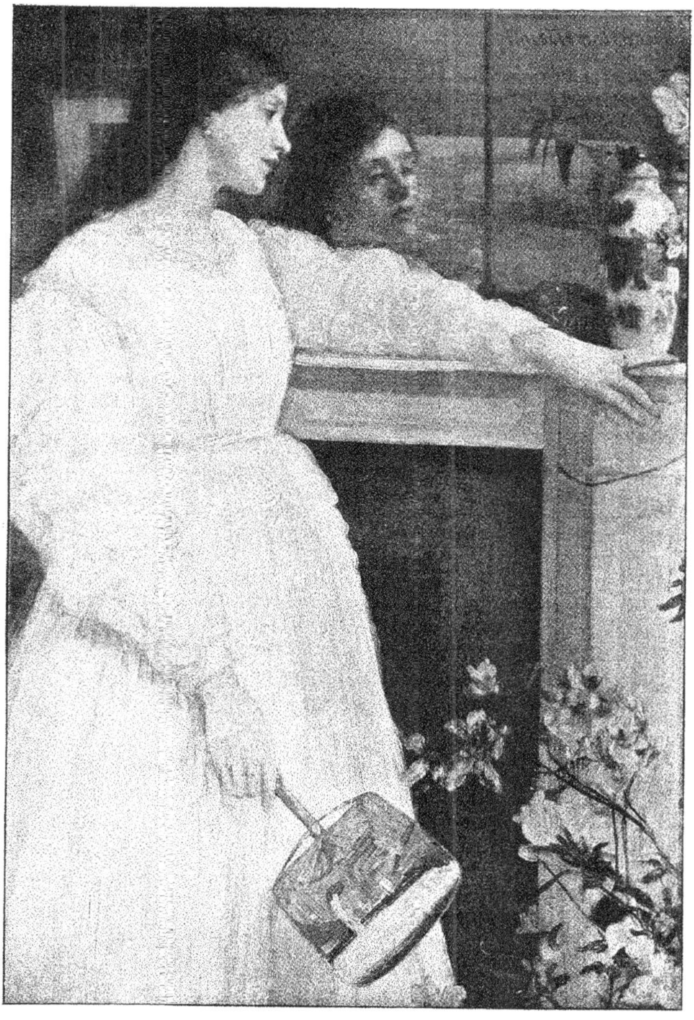

THE LITTLE WHITE GIRL.
FROM THE PICTURE BY J. MCNEILL WHISTLER.
In the possession of A. L. Studd, Esq.

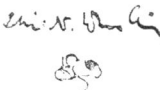

resources of the stone, and for lithography there is this much to be said, that it gives us his every line and touch, without the intervention of acids; even with the artist to superintend, the effect of a copperplate is somewhat due to chemical action. 'The Babies' playing in the Luxembourg Gardens show the daintiness and delicacy of lithography as an art in his hands. Some of his lithographs have been printed in colour. But in the greater number, as in this one, as in his etchings, it is upon line he depends. Is it not too late in the day to add that of line he is the master?

ANCIENT AND MODERN DANCING.*
THE MINUET AND OTHER DANCES.

AS we advance nearer to our own time, we find dancing taking a higher place, and growing more intimately connected with Art. Artists, to please their noble patrons, introduced a favourite dancer into a picture representing some court ceremonial. In the gallery at Munich there is a curious painting of the dance called the Volte or Sauteuse, a dance much in favour in the time of Henry IV. of France, who was a famous volte dancer, as was also Queen Marguerite of Valois, his sister. This volte was, however, a dangerous dance, requiring both strength and agility on the part of the male dancer. If this were wanting his partner, the Sauteuse, was likely to come off with perhaps a sprained ankle or broken knee-cap.

There was a time when the minuet was only one of many, being considered on an equal footing with the courante and sarabande, and other similar dances, which were all performed in the course of stage ballets and ceremonial balls. But gradually the noble dance (as it was called) was selected for especial favour (like the belle of a family destined for a brilliant match), and it became the favourite dance of the ballroom and the stage, long after its sister dances were faded and forgotten. No doubt this was partly on account of its intrinsic beauty, as well as for the influence it had upon the manners and carriage in a day when deportment meant much; and a man might lose or gain a good place about the Court by the way in which he took off his hat, or carried his cane. The minuet was the favourite dance during the Regency, and continued in favour throughout the reigns of Louis XV. and Louis XVI., but it is more especially associated with Louis Quatorze, the king who used to pride himself so much upon his dancing, and loved to appear in the ballet. It was owing to the patronage of *le Grand Monarque* that the art of dancing found its chief centre in France, whence, like fashions of other kinds, it spread to other parts of Europe.

Louis XIV. was stage-struck if ever a man was, and did all in his power to popularise theatrical performances. The minuet was his special pride, and he is said to have danced it with a very noble air. It seemed as though the king could not tear himself away from the stage; in fact he presents the single exception of a dancer who has made more than one "last appearance." Singers and actors return again and again to the scenes of their triumphs, dancers never. But to the amateur all things are possible, and after Louis had made his last appearance as the sun-god in the ballet of *Flora* in 1669, he reappeared after a year's "rest" more energetic than ever. The patronage accorded by the king to the ballet gave a tremendous impetus to the national love for dancing. The court ladies thought of nothing but of learning the minuet, and the ateliers of the dancing masters were besieged. The dancing masters were kings, they charged tremendous prices for their services, and treated their pupils with the utmost hauteur.

The minuet was danced at all court ceremonials, and the minuet was to the *débutante* what the court curtsey is now, only executed before a much larger audience. The graceful attitudes of the minuet have made their mark in the painting of the time, and we see them produced repeatedly in the pictures of Watteau and in groups of old china. So accurately are these attitudes given, that a dancing master looking at them would know at once what was the precise moment of the dance. We find the dance depicted over and over again, now in a sumptuous palace, as in our illustration, with courtiers looking on at the dancers, now at a *fête champêtre* with a couple of figures dancing on the grass, whilst some rural musician makes music on a mandoline or pipe. The dignity of the woman's figure is always enchanting, and the cavalier is often depicted as treading the measure awkwardly, so as to give additional point to the serenity of the woman who is so evidently sure of her steps. Watteau came to Paris at the moment when scenic and theatrical displays were organized on a scale of unexampled magnificence by the Chevalier Servandomi, the able manager of the Court theatre. The people might groan under unheard-of taxations, but the sensualist monarch, now growing old and petulant, must be amused. Novelty must be procured at any price. The happy thought came to one Baptiste Lulli, to present to the satiated appetite of Louis XIV. the intoxicating spectacle of beautiful women enacting a story by means of music and dancing combined. This was the first conception of the modern ballet. Lulli wrote the music; Beauchamp arranged the dances; Watteau painted the scenes; Servandomi directed the whole. The success of the spectacle was immense, and from this time ballets became the fashion at every Court in Europe. It was in this manner that the minuet made its first appearance. It was introduced by Lulli in a ballet, and at once secured its position in the front rank. Adam Smith says that it is of Moorish origin, and that it expresses in its different movements the passion of love. Hawkins ascribes it to the Poitevins, while other writers say it derived its graver measures from the Cushion dance, which found such favour during the reigns of Henry VIII. and Queen Elizabeth. Sir George Grove tells us in his pleasant dictionary that the Minuet took its name from the word *menu* (small), referring to the small steps of the dancers.

The orthodox minuet consisted of the minuet step, the hop in the minuet, the double bourrée, the two coulies, the step behind and before. The dancers could add to these if they wished, but the figures were always the same and were danced to the same measure. One of the greatest charms of the

* Continued from page 311.

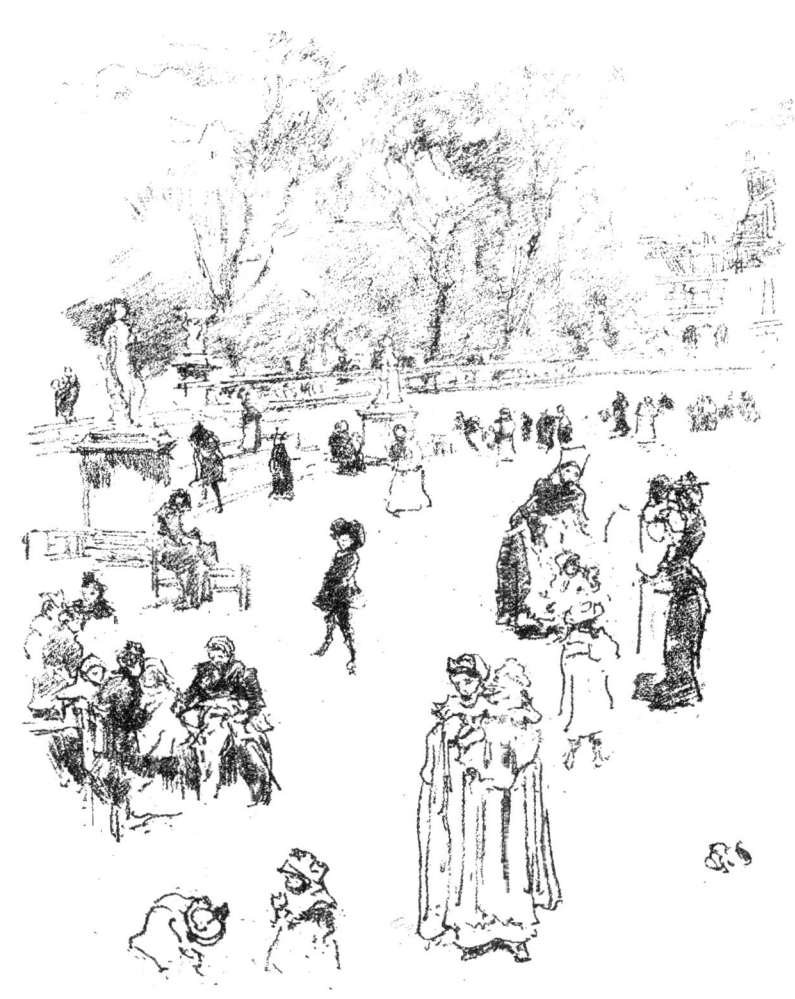

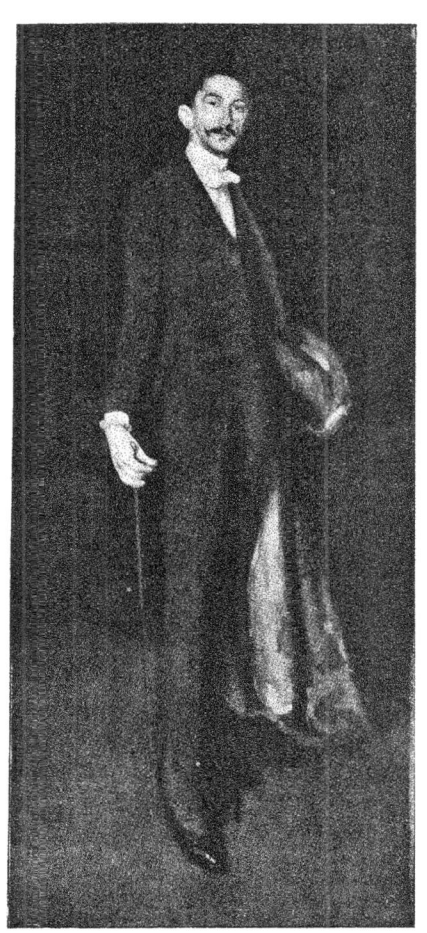

THE COMTE DE MONTESQUIEU.
FROM THE PICTURE BY J. MCNEILL WHISTLER.

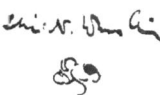

minuet being its *tempo*, which made it a favourite with composers, such as Haydn, Mozart, Bach and Beethoven. The well-known and always welcome minuet in *Don Giovanni* is a very faithful reproduction of the original form of the dance. As a complement to the short movement a second minuet was soon added, similar in form to the first, but contrasted in feeling. This was mostly written in three-part harmony, whence it received the name " trio." Beethoven is credited with transforming the minuet into a *scherzo*, and Bach composed some which were remarkable for their variety of form and character.

Affectation in the minuet was the danger most to be avoided. Gallini, the Italian ballet master, declares that "a mincing miss dancing the minuet would be a sight to *faire pleurer les Dieux;* a shade of affectation, or of anything not natural, free, and easy, having on the spectators the worst effect, and a very little matter has the power to make the dancer ridiculous. So, too, with the bow or curtsey, which should be free yet dignified."

All the movements of the minuet are graceful and calculated to set off the figure to good advantage. And every movement of the dance had its meaning, and must have taught gentle manners to the men and dignity to the women. The man makes a low reverence to the lady before he commences to dance with her, and he does not take her hand without preface and apology. There is a pretty figure towards the end of the dance in which the couple join hands and go round in the centre of the room, but they first walk the entire length of it extending the hand which is to be given. This performance is gone through with each hand in turn, and finally with both together, the gentleman joining his hands by the finger tips upon his breast before extending them, so as to signify the great affection he is supposed to entertain for the lady. All the movements are executed with deliberation, and the dancers should never be completely still, one step leading into another without cessation. The minuet commences and ends with salutations to the partner and to the company (who are supposed to represent the king and court). When the dance commences the couple stand facing the spectators at a slight distance from one another, the gentleman standing a little to the rear, so that the lady may be well seen, for though the gentleman must be graceful, he must never shine at her expense. Then a bar is played, during which the lady stands still and the gentleman takes off his hat. He does it exactly in the space of a bar, and puts it under his arm, being careful to turn his eyes upon the lady all the time. They now take a few steps and, facing each other, make a deep bow. They then turn to the audience and bow and curtsey to them, after which the minuet proper begins. If you draw a large square upon the floor, making each side twelve feet in length and draw two diagonal lines across it, you will get the space and lines in which the couples move. The steps are by no means easy, particularly the gentleman's, who has some very difficult movements to go through; with one part of the dance he has to execute a step called the corkscrew, the name of which will sufficiently indicate its appearance. It is done by bending one knee very low, and then throwing the balance on to the other foot and coming up in a kind of twist, very much the way in which a cork is drawn out of a bottle. This difficult step only occurs once during the minuet, but the elaborate curtseys of the ladies have to be executed several times.

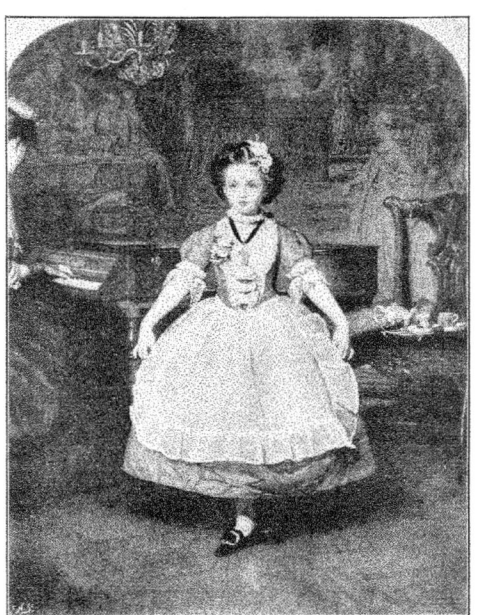

THE MINUET. BY SIR JOHN E. MILLAIS, BART., R.A.
By permission of Algernon Graves, Esq.

Learning the steps is a great effort of memory, but it is said that when it is once mastered it is impossible to forget it.

One is never tired looking at the representation in the works of Watteau, Lancret, and Boucher, of the frail but lovely creatures who graced the court of Louis XIV. We see them " pass, repass, curtsey, give one hand then the other, finally surrendering both." As they danced it the minuet is a story of coquetry and woman's weakness. They are quite present to us in these charming pictures. We see their white bosoms, their rounded arms, their glittering jewels, and painted faces; we catch the turn of the seductive eyes, the bend of the graceful heads; we almost hear the ripple of their laughter from the half-open lips. We see the shimmer on their brocaded trains; the light falls on the soft blues and yellows of their satin petticoats, and the loose sacques which

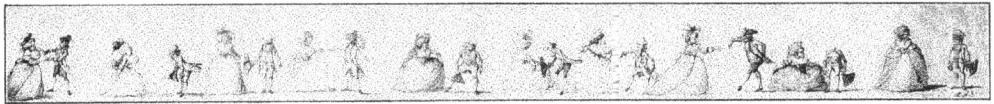

A LONG MINUET AS DANCED AT BATH. FROM AN OLD PRINT BY H. BUNBURY, 1787.

were then in fashion. In Watteau's picture, costume and colour played a most important part; he subjugated to it his personages, and it was said of him that the most lovely woman was put in merely to harmonize with a balcony or a shrubbery.

Lancret, his pupil, followed so closely in his footsteps as to be often mistaken for his master a subject of much annoyance to Watteau, and with some justice, for Lancret was wanting in that airy gracefulness which is such a distinguishing mark of Watteau's pictures. Lancret's work was more decorative; his screens and panels had a wonderful reputation.

From the court of the Grand Monarch the minuet travelled to England. When it got there is not quite certain, but we may suppose it came with the first of the Georges. In Hanover everything was French. The court well-nigh ruined itself and the country in its effort to imitate French fashion.

An important functionary was the Minutier, or teacher of the minuet; there was always one attached to the court. In Queen Charlotte's reign, Le Picque was the fashionable Minutier, he taught the princesses, and no young lady of fashion presented herself in the court circle, or at Mr. Almack's balls in King Street, without having taken lessons from Le Picque. Even with this advantage it was an ordeal for the *débutante*,

everything depended upon the verdict that would be passed upon her by the fops and dandies of White's and Boodle's, who judged her different points as they would have done those of a horse, and made her the subject of witticisms that circulated next day tarough the town. It is some such scene as this which is depicted by Mr. Orchardson in his well-known picture of 'Her First Dance,' illustrated in THE ART JOURNAL for 1893, page 300.

The minuet, and indeed dancing in general, have not often been subjects for the brush of the English school of painters. Sir John Millais' charming picture, 'The Minuet,' which we reproduce, and Mr. Orchardson's 'Her First Dance,' are two of the best-known instances of the treatment of the minuet by contemporary artists, but we have no men who followed in the footsteps of Watteau; Angelica Kauffmann and Cipriani, with their Cupids and ceiling decorations, were our nearest approach. But neither of these artists had the lightness of brush possessed by the Frenchman. Hayman in his Vauxhall pictures touched the fringe of the subject, and Collette's dancing lessons are humorous. Bunbury, the gentleman caricaturist, in his drawing of the Long Minuet, which appears or this page, shows great talent, and is very interesting.

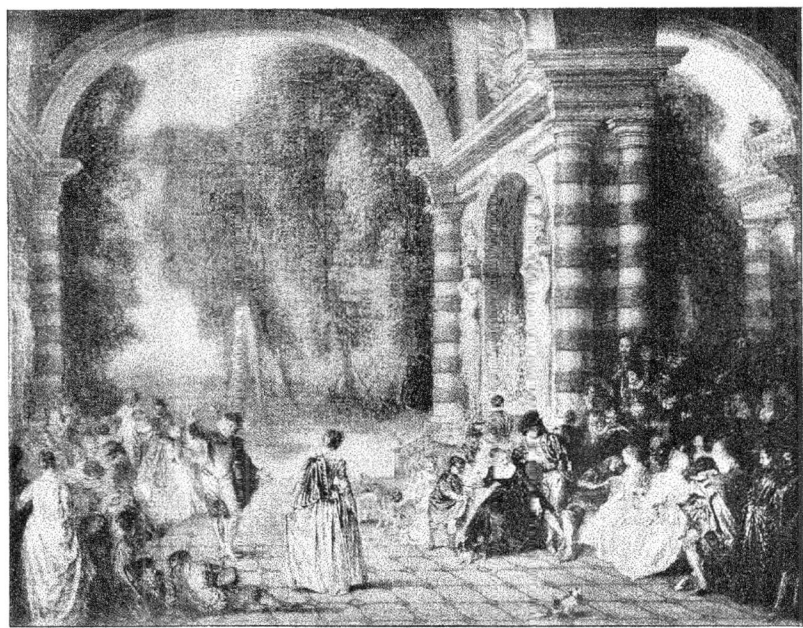

A BALL UNDER A COLONNADE. FROM THE PICTURE BY WATTEAU IN THE DULWICH GALLERY.

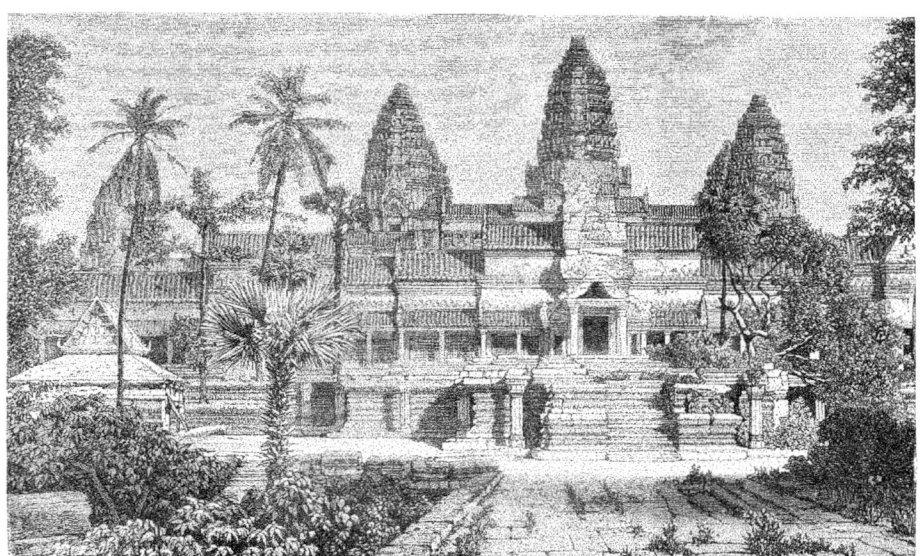

GENERAL VIEW OF THE PRINCIPAL FAÇADE OF THE TEMPLE OF NAKHON WAT, LOOKING WEST.

ANCIENT CAMBODIAN ART.

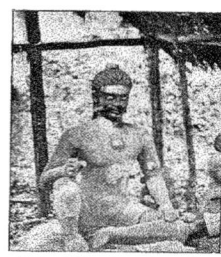

ANCIENT STATUE OF THE LEPER KING.

CAMBODIA is a small state situated on the eastern border of Siam, and until recently was tributary to that country, and is a remnant of a once populous and powerful empire.

The Siamese claim to have wrested the kingdom from the Cambodians in 1373 A.D. It again, after a struggle, reverted to its native owners, and eventually, about the close of last century, became subject to Siam. But one must go back to a much earlier period to trace the decay and downfall of a race so powerful and enlightened as the ancient Cambodians, the builders of stone cities, temples, and palaces; monuments having, in grandeur of conception and design, no equals in all Asia.

In examining these remains one has evidence of a sudden and disastrous onslaught by some powerful foe, in sculptured stone doorways hastily blocked or half built up to form barricades, and in the unfinished temple, Nakhon Wat. This, the crowning work of the ancient Cambodians, was destined never to be completed. In an outer pavilion of the temple one can trace the last touch of the sculptor's chisel on the capital of a pillar, where the flowers and stems of the lotus still await the vanished hand of the artist to give them form and grace. Very little is known about the builders whose works afford such evidence of enduring strength and constructive skill; their degenerate descendants, sheltering in huts under the shadow of the great stone structures, describe the ancients as a race of giants. They left no annals, or if they did, their history must have been written on perishable material which has succumbed to the humid heat of the climate. There are inscriptions in many of the temples, fortunately dated, and dedicating them to Brahminical divinities. These furnish some clue to the chronology of certain periods, giving lists of kings who built and endowed these religious edifices. None of the inscriptions, so far as is yet known, take us back to a period anterior to the beginning of the seventh century A.D.[*] The inscription found at Aug. Chumick, in the province of Ba Phnom, gives the year 667 A.D. as the date at which the temple was dedicated to the goddess Siva. In the Chinese annals Cambodia is noticed under the names Tchinla, Funan, Kan-pogee.[†] The Anamese also refer to the kingdom as Funan and as Chanlap. This name Chanlap occurs in the annals of the

[*] *Journal Asiatique*, p. 144.
[†] History of Tsin Dynasty A.D. 26 to 419; Sui Dynasty A.D. 560 to 618; Tang Dynasty A.D. 800; Sung Dynasty A.D. 1000.

ANCIENT CAMBODIAN ART.

Chinese Emperor Lung-King, 1565 to 1571: "The king of Siam made war against Chanlap, eethroned its king, and annexed his territory." The Cambodians are also noticed in Indian literature,* in the Ramayana, the Maharabata, and the Puranas. This brings me to the link Brahminism, the only one, I believe, which united India and Cambodia, found in the ancient temples, and notably in Nakhon Wat, the building I am now about to describe. This temple stands alone, as probably the greatest monument ever raised by the devotees of the Hindoo faith. Its designs and ornaments are symbolical, while its stone galleries contain, sculptured in low relief on the walls, a marvellous series of illustrations of the events described in the Hindoo Epics just named, the Ramayana and the Maharabata. I photographed many of the representations when I visited the temple in 1866, and was earnestly requested by the king of Siam to complete the series, a work which would have taken me months to accomplish, but this I had to forego for want of materials. The Cambodian antiquities are found shrouded in the heart of the dense tropical forests of the country, with the exception of Nakhon Wat, which is kept fairly clear. They consist of walled cities, stone causeways traversing the region uniting city to city, aqueducts, stone-faced tanks of vast extent, exquisitely built bridges, temples and palaces of the ancient kings.

The foundations of the buildings and retaining walls of the tanks consist of iron conglomerate, and the buildings themselves chiefly of blocks of polished freestone, fitted together without mortar, and with such accuracy as, in the finest

* "Garnier," vol. i., p. 106.

examples almost to defy a trace of joining.

Nakhon Wat, the subject of the illustrations, is situated fifteen miles north of the lake "Tale Sap," and distant about six miles from the ruined city of Nakhon Thom. This city is surrounded by a massive stone wall nine metres high, enclosing an area 3,800 metres by 3,400 metres, having gateways

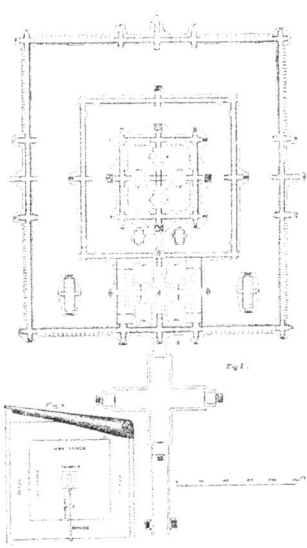

GROUND PLAN OF THE TEMPLE OF NAKHON WAT. BY J. THOMSON.

on each side surmounted by towers in the form of the four faces of the all-seeing Brahma.

In Nakhon Thom I found the termination of one of the great raised causeways of the country. Hunting scenes with elephants were portrayed in high relief on its walls, and most remarkable of all, on each side of a flight of steps I found the head and forelegs of an elephant projecting, the trunk in each case dropped vertically, having the end twisted into lotus flowers, so as to form an outstanding pillar, while the two forelegs served as pilasters supporting the heavy entablature, conveying the impression of great strength and stability. But I must revert to the temple outside the city, reluctantly leaving Nakhon Thom, where, within the walls, are a multitude of ruins which one cannot venture to notice in an article such as this.

This temple is perhaps more commonly known as Angkor Wat. But I have the written authority of the late first King of Siam, who was a distinguished Sanscrit scholar, for the name of Nakhon Wat. There is a note in the *Journal Asiatique* for 1883, to the effect that Angkor Wat is a corruption of Nagara Vata, "The Temple of Royalty."

The general design of this vast building will be gathered from my plan. Like the majority of the ancient buildings, it is constructed upon a solid stone platform, and rises in somewhat pyramidal form in three quadrangular tiers, the apex of the great central tower having an elevation of one hundred and eighty feet. The outer walls

SECTION OF AN OUTER GALLERY AT NAKHON WAT.

1894.

5 A

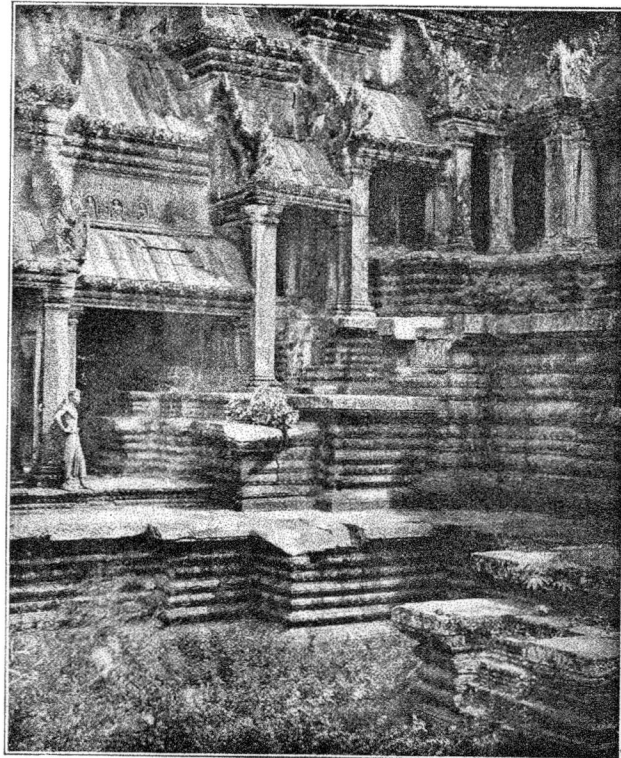

SCULPTURED STONE TANK AND STAIRCASE AT NAKHON WAT.

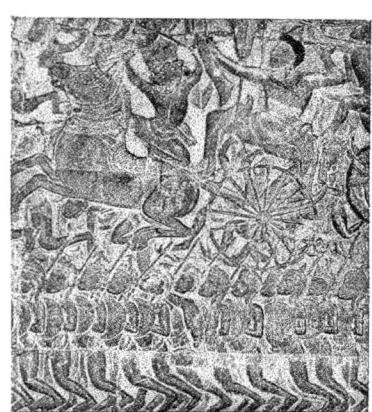

BAS-RELIEF OF BATTLE SCENE AT NAKHON WAT.

double screen of square pillars. These galleries are in form like a Gothic arch, and side aisle on one side, while on the other is a wall sculptured with bas-reliefs.

The mechanical arrangements of the galleries or colonnades are as perfect as the design is artistic. On the left is the wall of masonry, the stones fitted together in large blocks so closely and without cement as to render it difficult to trace the joints. It would appear that the blocks had been ground together. This solid, rock-like structure characterizes the entire building. The quarries from which supplies of stone were obtained are over thirty miles distant, and it speaks well for the appliances of the ancients which enabled them to transport the massive blocks, and raise them in the form of this stupendous monument.

The row of pillars on the right is ten feet six inches from the back wall. The pillars are without bases, and carry capitals of lotus design, beneath which in low relief are figures of Hindoo devotees in the attitude of worship. Above are and galleries enclose a nearly square space measuring about three-fourths of a mile each way, and surrounded by a ditch two hundred and thirty feet broad. This moat is crossed on the west by a raised stone causeway, having stone pillars on each side in form like bound reeds, and flights of sculptured steps communicating with the water. Facing the cardinal points of the compass, in the centre of each side of the outer wall, are long galleries with arched roofs and monolithic pillars. Entering the main approach on the west, the galleries on each side are pierced with similar gateways, and passing up a broad inner platform paved like the outer one with blocks of polished freestone, we reach the west front of the temple shown in the illustration at the head of this article. Ascending a cruciform terrace by a flight of steps, guarded on each side by colossal stone lions, we stand before the main entrance of this western front, which has a length of over six hundred feet. About a third of this space is walled and divided into compartments lighted by windows, each having seven ornamental stone bars. The lotus patterns composing these bars are as carefully repeated as if cast in one mould. The remaining two-thirds of the space are taken up by galleries having a architrave, deep frieze and cornice, and over the cornice the pointed arch formed by corbeling. This arch, I believe, was originally hidden by a richly carved wood ceiling. I discovered a fragment of such a ceiling in an obscure place in an upper part of the temple. Outside this gallery is a second with a screen of pillars each supporting a tie beam, which is inserted into the inner columns below the capitals.

Perhaps the most attractive features in the whole temple are the bas-reliefs, found in eight compartments, one on each side of the central groups of entrances. Each subject measures about three hundred feet in length, with a height of six and a half feet. In these there are about twenty thousand figures of men, animals, and mythological beings represented. A small section of one of these remarkable pictures is given on the opposite page, taken from a battle-scene in the western gallery. The characteristics of the contending forces are so similar, their chariots, horses, elephants, costumes, and weapons, that there is some difficulty in distinguishing between the combatants. This fragment is sufficient to convey a correct impression of the skill displayed in the execution of the whole. As a work of art it compares favourably with Assyrian bas-reliefs of a like nature. The whole subject is, indeed, a most graphic representation of a battle-scene. The advancing chariot and its wheels require special notice, showing as they do a masterly knowledge of the art of construction. A wheel to combine in a higher degree elements of strength and lightness would task the resources of the most accomplished modern craftsman. To withstand the rough usage of war it must have been made wholly or partly of metal.

We give an example of elaborate ornaments which are sculptured on the outer vaults. It is a fragment in which

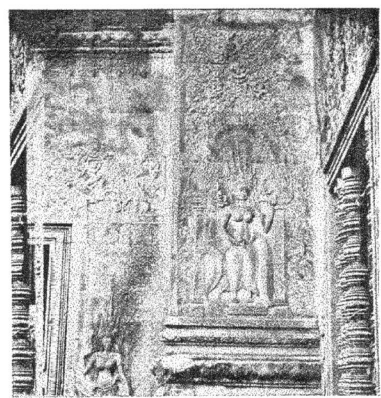

SCULPTURED DESIGN ON OUTER WALL.

the female form takes part, mingled with a conventional ornament in foliage. This occurs on the outer wall near the western entrance, above which a flowing floral design decorates the wall just below the eaves. This is made up of female dancing figures and an arching tracery of leaves in low relief.

Ascending to the next cross terrace by a flight of broad sculptured steps we find four tanks (see illustration on page 366), each surrounded by a peristyle of pillars, and at the inner angle of each tank a staircase by which the higher terraces are reached.

I was greatly charmed by the cool shade afforded by the staircases and colonnades. They are so designed as to admit light and air and to exclude heat. Fergusson, in his "History of Architecture," says that the ancient Cambodians solved this problem for the tropics, which puzzled India for ages, of admitting light and air and excluding heat. An upper terrace, with tanks and peristyle surrounding, carries four subordinate towers, one at each angle, and the great central tower dominates the structure.

It is impossible in so narrow limits to do more than give a general survey of this, the last and noblest effort of the ancient Cambodian builders —whose works proclaim the greatness, the wealth, and the resources of a highly civilised race that has passed away, leaving no record of its own save a few scattered inscriptions on its temples and palaces. The existence of these monuments was known before I visited the country, but no photographs had been taken before my arrival, and no survey made, and I have no doubt that the plan which accompanies this paper was the first one made since the time when the architect placed the design in the hands of the builders.

JOHN THOMSON.

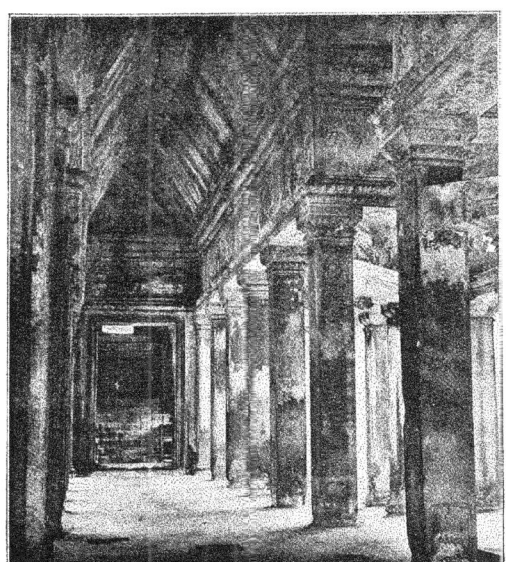

ELEVATED COLONNADE LEADING TO CENTRAL TOWER AT NAKHON WAT.

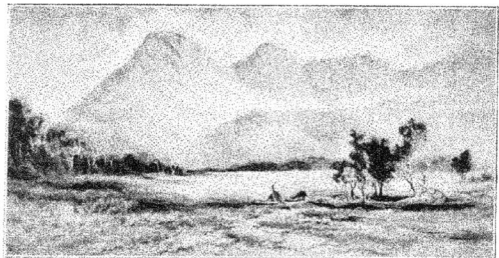

The King William Range. By W. C. Piguenit.

THE HOBART (TASMANIA) ART GALLERY.

PERHAPS the most interesting event that could happen in the world of Art would be the discovery of some English-speaking country where the deities that we worship in England have already their shrines and votaries. But, seeing how short a time it is since our own picture-loving public cared intensely, and almost exclusively, for a "picture that tells its story," and openly expressed its disdain for "pretty pictures"—as it called them—we must not be too exacting. Nor is our own devotion to Corot, to Whistler, Degas, and Monet, so firm that we can assume pontifical airs towards those whose minds are still nebulous on the question who are, and who are not, masters. The phrase "masters of the future" is over-diffident, and is something too often in our mouths. Our trumpet gives forth an uncertain sound; and it is, therefore, only in the spirit of indulgent compromise that we should approach and consider the galleries of the Colonies, and especially the gallery of Hobart. It will be admitted that it is something that Hobart should have a gallery at all; it is much that it has an enthusiastic curator who has not hesitated to demand £5,000 for a better building, although the present "Museum" is well enough. It is much also that the gallery is a popular institution, and all these advantages have brought their natural fruits in two handsome gifts which we shall notice later. But in sober truth, none of these various merits hold our attention so much as the work of a Tasmanian artist—Mr. W. C. Piguenit. Mr. Piguenit works at Tasmanian scenery, and he has a great field. An enchanting climate—a little too much like the Riviera to be quite favourable to English folk—has produced strange combinations of flora. A half-explored island of about the size of Ireland supplies endless possibilities for the adventurous and the nature-loving. If climate has any influence on race, the centuries may see Tasmania becoming a second Cadore. The human interest is lacking for the present, but the coming days will, perhaps, supply incidents more stirring than a dreary labour dispute or an anxious premier struggling with a refractory budget. In the meantime the scenery remains as it was when only greasy savages looked down the Derwent towards the South Pole, and Mr. Piguenit is its first considerable interpreter.

The first impression that we get of this South Hemisphere England is somewhat as if the scenery of our own country had been mounted with sub-tropical properties; it is dainty, but not broad or impressive, and it is in seizing broad effects—and especially gloomy effects—that Mr. Piguenit mostly excels. Colour is not his strong point; so he has, with great wisdom, left the gentle views of trimmer Hobart and devoted himself to the wilder interior. 'Mount Gell' (to pursue the parallel we just now hinted) is a very good example of the bent of his genius: it might almost be a view in the Upper Cadore. The parallel must not be pushed too far: but it hardly needs an excuse; for until the scenery of England beyond the seas is better known, it must be content to be introduced and god-fathered by association with scenes of established

Snowdon. By E. M. Wimperis.

fame. Canada is as yet the only one of our over-sea homes that stands on its own footing in this respect.

But as if to remind us where we are, and to insist on the individuality of his country, Mr. Piguenit has introduced into 'King William Range' a group of kangaroos in the middle distance : see our illustration. There is no use in hunting for parallels after that: this is Tasmania—we do not find kangaroos in Westmoreland.

mystery of Hebrew theology, we find the treatment to which Mr. Piguenit's work most nearly approaches. Nothing in particular breathes through these views of Tasmanian scenery; but that is not the artist's fault, for there is nothing particular to breathe as yet. Nevertheless, for his misfortune, though not for his fault, the artist can only take the rank of a consummate illustrator.

Mr. Poynter's 'Chloe' has found a home and a place of

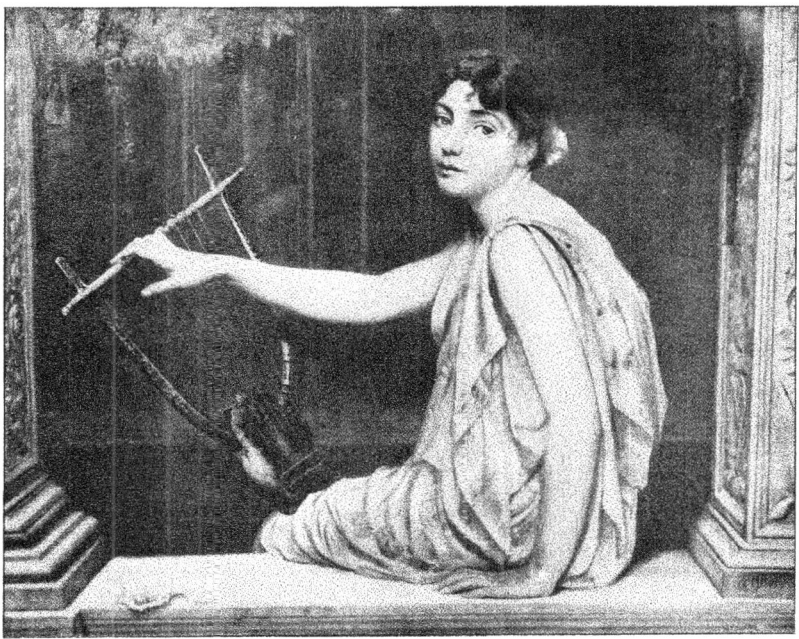

CHLOE. BY E. J. POYNTER, R.A.

I have ventured the position that the abiding strength of this artist is in broad and somewhat gloomy effects, and the next two illustrations are fair supports of that position. There are few scenes that would not be overweighted with the august associations of Olympos. Nevertheless, the explorers of Tasmania have dared to give that resplendent name to one of their inland mountains girt with clouds and waited on by a broad and placid lake. In truth, as Mr. Piguenit has given it to us, the hill might do for a sort of British Olympos—awful, regular, majestic—ideal home for the gods of a dour race born to rule. But the name is too tall as the hill to the lake. Walhalla might stand on that dread summit, high-towered and menacing, but not the Pantheon. Nevertheless, the name is not Mr. Piguenit's doing and the picture is.

In 'Hell's Gate' the artist is at his best; both name and scene are a little melodramatic and the treatment does not jar. It would be unfair to call Poole melodramatic, but in the windswept height of the 'Vision of Ezekiel,' breathing the

honour in the Hobart Gallery. It is the first picture of Mr. Poynter's to find its way to the Southern Hemisphere; and unless some other gallery has acquired one since last November, it is still the only specimen of his art there. It was purchased for six hundred guineas and presented to the Hobart Gallery. At the same time the same generous person presented a view in Wales, 'Snowdon,' by Mr. E. M. Wimperis. Hobart has not as yet afforded itself the luxury of a catalogue, which it well might do, for there are many other drawings and pictures in the museum rooms of which we can give no notice.

Money is not now so plentiful in Hobart as it might be, and it is at present unlikely that the curator will get the £5,000 that he has asked for. When he does, and the gallery expands as it ought to do, it is to be hoped that the judicious arrangements of the Sydney gallery will be studied, and not the much too Royal Academic methods of Melbourne; for there is a good prospect that Hobart will some day possess a collection worthy of the best setting.   FREWEN LORD.

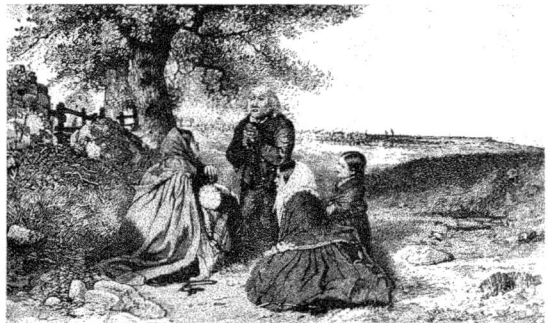

WAYSIDE PRAYER. BY ERSKINE NICOL, A.R.A.

THE HENRY TATE GALLERY.*
CONCLUDING ARTICLE.

SINCE these papers were begun the whole enterprise of Mr. Tate, so far, at least, as his offer to the nation is concerned, has taken definitive shape, so that we know exactly what we are to have through his beneficence. In the first place, the trustees of the National Gallery—to whom is to be confided a supervision of the new institution similar to that which they now exercise in Trafalgar Square—have selected from the sixty-six pictures offered by Mr. Tate sixty-one which they look upon as worthy to form the nucleus of an English Luxembourg. It was no part of my duty in writing these articles to attempt any forecast of what the selection might be. I confined myself to description of the pictures offered, tempered with as much criticism as seemed desirable in the case of a gift still—as it were—in a state of probation. But, nevertheless, those who have had the patience to read what I have written, and now and then to read a little between the lines, have found in them a pretty accurate forecast of the choice made by the trustees, acting, no doubt, on the advice of Mr. Poynter. It is proposed that the Tate collection should be kept together and hung in the chief room of the Gallery now well under weigh. This seems a very judicious proposal. In the case of old masters, especially when many schools are embraced in a single collection, it is most inconvenient to have to put up with restrictions which prevent pictures being classed according to date and place of origin. Such an objection, however, has little or no force when applied to a gathering of works all of one school, and, with but two exceptions, approximately of one date, while it leaves the responsibility for the quality of the collection on the right shoulders.

A full list of the pictures accepted has already appeared in THE ART JOURNAL for September (p. 285), so that all I need do here is to refer the reader to that page.

On a subsequent page will be found reproductions from the architect's final plans for the Gallery itself, together with particulars supplied by him as to the work; but there are one

* Continued from page 196.

or two historical and critical remarks which I should like to make here about the structure, and these will supply a fitting conclusion to what I have to say.

The central building at Milbank was erected about ninety years ago, on a site which until then had been little better than a swamp. The builders had great difficulty with the foundations, and thought of nothing better than perseverance in shooting what was little better than rubbish into the marsh, to form a bed on which to raise their structures. The consequence was that, long before the prison was pulled down, cracks and settlements began to ornament its walls. The area enclosed by the great outer fortification is about eight acres, of which one of them has been ceded to Mr. Tate. The rest of the space will be occupied by barracks, artisans' dwellings, and the necessary roads. At the back of the site, at the point farthest from the river, lies the Milbank graveyard. Here not only prisoners, but many warders and matrons were buried. Nothing could be more dreary than the present aspect of the place. The prisoners' graves are not marked in any way, but over the resting-places of turnkeys and matrons slabs record their names and the estimation in which they were held by their fellow-servants. The railings are rusting away; the graves are overgrown by weeds as tall as a man; the paths have been obliterated, and nothing seems conscious that here lie the remains of two or three prison generations, except the great wall, which hangs over the forsaken God's acre with what looks like a conscious guardianship. One of the first questions to be solved by those who will have the rearrangement of the ground will be put by this awkward relic of the past.

At present the whole site is hideous. In England we have invented many ugly things, but I don't know that we have ever shown more ingenuity in that direction than in the backs of our London houses; and the land at Milbank is surrounded by regiments of these backs. They are partly masked, no doubt, by the great wall, but when that goes they will stand out for a time in all their naked repulsiveness. It shows a confidence in the War Office and the London County Council which they have done little enough to merit, but we cannot help wishing that they would get on with their building, if only to shut out the sights revealed by the disappearance of the prison. On one side there is a little relief to the pervading squalor in a building used by Messrs. Mowlem, the contractors, as a sort of stone house and cart shed. Here, probably by accident, a really artistic effect has been won by the vigour with which the purpose of the building has been summed up in its design.

The land assigned to the Gallery is in the centre, facing the river. The first step leading up to the main entrance will be about sixty feet from the existing road, while round the sides and rear of the building, when complete, there will be a clear space not less that seventy feet wide, of which thirty feet will be within the gallery railings, the rest being taken up by a road. It will be seen, therefore, that the gallery will be quite isolated, and will have no external interference with its light. Reference will be found on page 373 to the great central dome, with domelets at the angles which the architect, Mr. Sidney Smith, proposed in his original plans, but has since abandoned. In proposing the domes he was following the example set by Wilkins in the National Gallery, and endorsed by the late E. M. Barry in the abortive design for Wilkins' supercession, which was accepted by the Government of some five-and-twenty years ago. A dome has nothing to do on a picture gallery. In expression it contradicts the purpose of the building, while it too often actively interferes with its light. Of all problems which can be put before the architect there is none, perhaps, which demands more skill and taste than the designing of a home for pictures. Unlike most other buildings it has no central point of interest. Concentration and subordination have in it to be exchanged for an appearance of even distribution.

A church has its sanctuary, a parliament house its chamber, a theatre its stage, to which other parts are subsidiary. But a picture gallery is all centre. One room should not be distinguished above another. Evenness of accent, impartiality of treatment should mark the whole. This being so, it is,

in the abstract, bad policy to choose such a building for the centre of a group at all. Perhaps the ideal arrangement is what you find at Vienna, where twin museums are put opposite to each other with an important object—the monument to Maria Theresa—between, to give a centre to the group. Picture galleries are too low, too, for commanding sites. They can seldom be more than two stories high, and they are spoilt by those external features which a conspicuous position demands, or at least suggests. So far, then, we must not expect the final aspect of the group of buildings now begun at Westminster to be entirely satisfactory, even supposing that each is a good piece of architecture in itself. So far as Mr. Sydney Smith's work is concerned, he has certainly improved it as a design since it was first put forth. All the architectural changes have been in the direction of simplicity; and have tended to make the building more truthful to its purpose as well as more practically convenient.

Mr. Smith's design has one merit which is very uncommon in London. His building sits comfortably on the earth. It has no sunk story. The robust basement rises some fourteen feet from the ground with a slight batter or inward slope. It is heavily rusticated. The only visible openings are arched windows (like the *cloaca maxima*) at wide intervals, which rather add to than take away from the apparent solidity of this part of the work. The height of a room for pictures, when the light comes from above, is more or less of a fixed quantity, and a width of forty feet is not in good proportion to it. The great Venetian room in Trafalgar Square is too wide for its height, with the result that the roof seems to come down on one's head, and to give a crushed appearance to the whole, and yet it could not be raised without making the lower part of the walls too dark. There is another great disadvantage in too wide a gallery. It tempts to the introduction of screens. By these the general effect of the National Gallery, as well as the individual effect of the pictures, is at present seriously diminished, and we may be pretty certain that, if the rooms were wide enough to allow of it, the same drawback would exist in the Westminster Gallery for many a long year before the Government would sanction any increase to the building.

FAULTS ON BOTH SIDES. BY THOMAS FAED, R.A.

At South Kensington, no doubt, where the rooms are, I think, even less than thirty feet wide, there is a plague of screens; but there the comparative paucity of visitors makes such an abuse more possible than it would be under similar conditions in Trafalgar Square, or will be, let us hope, at Westminster.

Even more important to a picture gallery than its length and width, is its method of lighting. Like other English architects, Mr. Sidney Smith has tabooed side lights altogether. The German system of small rooms with windows in the wall for small pictures, the system followed, too, by Cuypers, the architect of the new Rijks Museum at Amsterdam, has found but little favour in this country. Mr. Christian has been driven to its partial adoption in the New Portrait Gallery, just as Mr. Rowand Anderson was in Edinburgh; but, so far as I know, these are the only important instances of its deliberate adoption in the United Kingdom; and, in truth, it is neither a practical nor a logical system. In a side-lighted room a few pictures can be shown to better advantage than if the light came from the ceiling, but they profit at the expense of their companions. Those far from the window, and, still more, those which are opposite to it, are sacrificed to the rest. No one who has attempted to make anything like exhaustive studies in the galleries at Munich, Dresden, Amsterdam or even Berlin, where the system is used more intelligently than elsewhere, to say nothing of places like The Hague, where the gallery is merely a converted house, can forget the peering round reflections, the trying search into shade, the waiting for some shadow-casting neighbour to move, which diversifies enjoyment in such places. In London the system would be impossible in any popular gallery.

And now a few words as to the treatment of the walls. In the National Gallery the system followed has been to put on a cheap colour, good for the moment, and to think of nothing else. The practical dilemma, on one horn of which we must elect to sit, may be put thus: either you must have the best colour for the moment and consent to see it rapidly deteriorate into the worst; or you must put up with an inferior tint, consoling yourself with the prospect of permanence. The best background for pictures is crimson silk, but no crimson has yet been invented which will stand unless combined with the most costly materials. In my opinion the next best colour is a rather warm brown, like *café au lait* without too much *lait*, and, perhaps, the best way of using it has been hit upon in the Salon Carré in the Louvre. There the walls are covered with a strong coarse canvas, which has been painted brown, and then stencilled with a pattern in a rather lighter shade of the same colour. The effect is not as good as it would be with walls of crimson silk, but it is vastly better than anything you can get with a red distemper or even paint, which fades to a chilly grey purple in a year or two. It is rather expensive, no doubt, to begin with, but that is soon made up for by its durability. The walls of the Salon Carré have not been touched, except with a duster, for thirty years, and yet they are as satisfactory as they were at first.

Lastly, we come to the floor. Mr. Smith has resisted the temptation of pure utilitarianism, and will not succumb to the tile fallacy of South Kensington, or to the worse temptation of Italian *tesserœ*. The floors at Westminster are to be of oak, which, when properly treated, is the best of all materials for a picture-room; unfortunately it never is treated properly in this country, except in private houses. The tone of a polished oak floor is perfect; that of one unpolished, and trodden by thousands of dusty feet, is about as discordant and unpleasing as anything you can imagine. The cold grey drab to which the National Gallery floors are reduced within a few hours of their periodical washing, is absolutely painful to any eye which can really enjoy a Venetian picture. The practical difficulty is not great. Every Sunday thousands of men, women, and children tramp over the mile of oak floors in the Louvre. Every Tuesday the visitor finds them restored to their usual warm transparency, and ready to take their part in the general harmony. There seems to be no reason, beyond our insular slowness to take a hint, why the same thing should not be done in the National Gallery. Perhaps the Gallery at Westminster may set the example.

WALTER ARMSTRONG.

THE HIGHLAND MOTHER. BY ERSKINE NICOL, A.R.A.

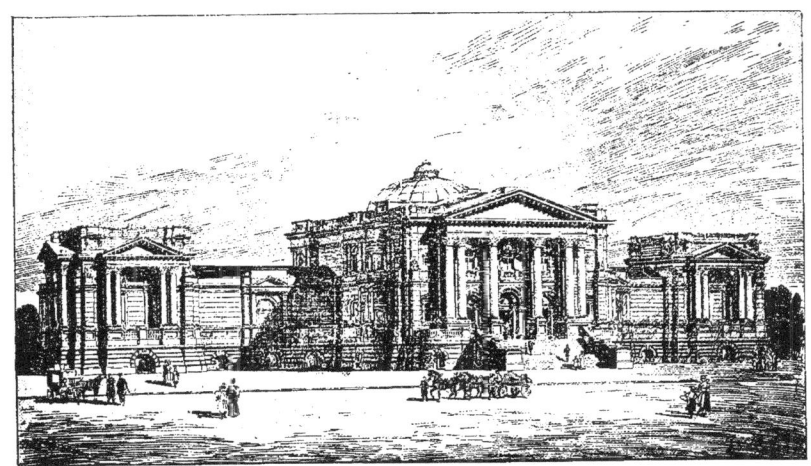

PERSPECTIVE VIEW OF THE NEW BRITISH ART GALLERY AT WESTMINSTER.
FROM THE DRAWING BY THE ARCHITECT, SIDNEY R. J. SMITH, F.R.I.B.A.

THE BRITISH ART GALLERY.
THE FINAL PLANS FOR THE HENRY TATE COLLECTION.

THE actual building of the gallery which Mr. Henry Tate is erecting at Westminster to receive the pictures and sculpture presented by him to the nation as the nucleus of a gallery of British Art, is now progressing rapidly. The foundations have all been laid, and already in places the work has been raised to about twelve feet above the pavement level. It is hoped to complete it some time in 1896.

The architect, Mr. Sidney R. J. Smith, of 14, York Buildings, Adelphi, has very considerably altered the original plans which he submitted, and the final and correct design, which is published herewith for the first time, is the sixth that he has prepared. An examination of the illustrations accompanying this article will show, we think, that in the alterations which have been made, such objections to the first scheme as intelligent and reasonable criticism had to make, have been fully met. At the suggestion of several leading Academicians and others, the domes and towers originally proposed have been omitted, the principal objection to them being that they might be likely to throw heavy shadows which would reduce the light of glass-roofed galleries. With them the somewhat towering and vast appearance—not perhaps wholly desirable—of the early designs also disappears. There were some other objections, which Mr. Armstrong refers to in the previous article.

From the perspective view of the gallery forming the headpiece of this article it will be seen that the style of architecture which has been adopted is that of the Italian Renaissance with Grecian motives. The building will be faced with Portland stone, and stand back some little distance from the roadway. The dimensions of the site which has been placed by the Government at Mr. Tate's disposal are: frontage 340 feet, depth 300 feet, being the largest site of any picture gallery in London. By means of the scale reproduced with the ground plan on the next page, the reader can see how much of this will be covered at present, and how much when the building is extended and completed in accordance with the full plans. Mr. Armstrong has already referred to the fact that the site has roads on three sides, and a large open space at the back, so that good light is ensured.

The main building is approached by a flight of steps surmounted by a portico of six columns supporting a pediment. Our reproduction of the architect's elevation, on p. 375, will enable the reader to see the detail of this handsome façade in a better way than is possible from its necessarily reduced size in the perspective view. Passing through the portico, the visitor enters a large vestibule with a vaulted ceiling, supported by groups of columns. On the first floor above the vestibule, and immediately under the pediment, is the chamber which is designed as a Council Saloon. Three doorways lead from the vestibule to the Central Sculpture Hall, from whence access to the picture galleries is obtained. This hall is arcaded, and has a low glass and iron-roofed dome, which is shown in the perspective view, but will not be visible from the street level. In the central hall are the staircases which lead to arcaded galleries on the first floor, intended for the exhibition of paintings and sculpture, and also give access to the corridor communicating with the Council Saloon. The basement contains rooms for students, picture-cleaning, and offices for the staff.

The ground-plan, which we reproduce, shows the seven picture galleries which are at present being erected. The future extension has been provided for with the greatest care, so that when carried out the scheme will be balanced and complete. The proposed extension is indicated by hatching, while the solid lines represent the work now in course of construction. The galleries will be all top-lighted, with a single roof, without the objectionable inner skylight, and they are ranged on central axes right and left of the central hall, so that anyone standing in the hall will be able to see to each end of the galleries. Moreover, they have been so arranged that the visitor may pass from gallery to gallery without the necessity of re-entering one which he has already seen. The general height of the ground floor will admit of a ceiling is elliptical, approaching the segmental. Above this there will be a ridge roof, and the skylights are introduced on either side of the ridge, at the points where the inner ceiling sinks into the outer roof. This means that each of the long galleries will be lighted by a pair of skylights running from end to end, and divided from each other by a space of ceiling approximately equal in width to the coves which separate them from the walls. Thus the lighting area will be about two-fifths of the whole roof. It is to be hoped that this will be found enough. For the lighting of oil pictures in London, and especially in the neighbourhood of the river, a skylight area of at least one-half of the ceiling is almost a necessity. In the summer it is easy enough to modify the light by blinds or *velaria*,

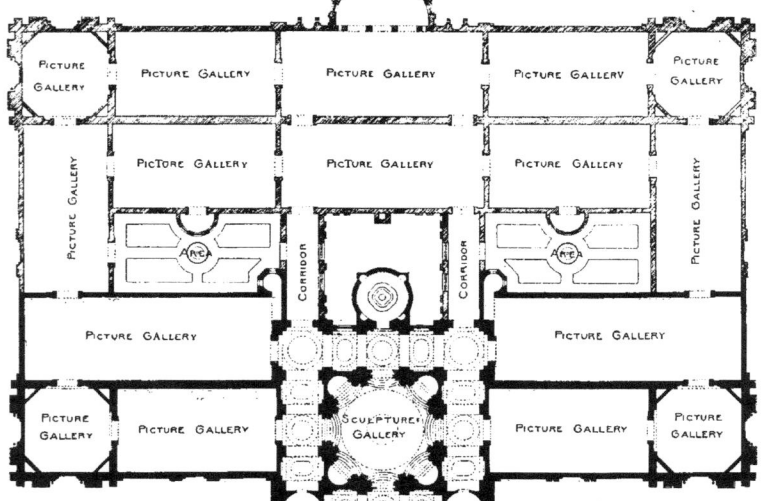

GROUND-FLOOR PLAN
OF THE BRITISH ART GALLERY.
FROM THE FINAL DESIGN OF THE ARCHITECT,
SIDNEY R. J. SMITH, F.R.I.B.A.

N.B.—The future extension is shown by hatching; the solid lines indicate the work actually in course of construction.

GROUND FLOOR PLAN

clear space, eighteen feet high, for hanging pictures, and the hanging space in the galleries (without the future extension and leaving out the Sculpture Hall and basement rooms) will be only 250 ft. less than the Royal Academy galleries, and considerably more than that of the New Gallery, and the Royal Institute of Painters in Oils, Piccadilly, added together.

In the National Gallery the skylights are in the centre. At the Grafton Gallery they form the cove between the walls and the ceiling. In the Gallery belonging to the Royal Society of Painters in Water-Colours—perhaps the most satisfactory picture-room in London — they, to some extent, combine the two ideas; and this Mr. Sidney Smith also proposes to do. The section he has chosen for his but the converse proceeding can scarcely be carried out in winter.

Art committees in other parts of the world, who may have on hand the erection of buildings of a similar character, will be glad to have some fuller particulars of the British Art Gallery, and for their benefit and that of others who may be interested we give the measurements in some detail. The Central Sculpture Hall (octagonal) is to be thirty-eight feet across. The corridor or arcade which runs round will have a width of twelve feet. The largest picture galleries will be ninety-three feet long. The next largest will be each sixty feet in length. The general width of the galleries will be thirty-two feet. Of the octagons at the corners of the wings two will be thirty-one feet six inches wide, and two will measure thirty-two feet across.

With reference to the important questions of ventilation and heating, we need only say that they have been settled on lines suggested by the best expert advice and embody the latest results of modern science. The "English Luxembourg" bids fair, when completed, to be a dignified and handsome building fully worthy of the position which its generous donor desires it to take.

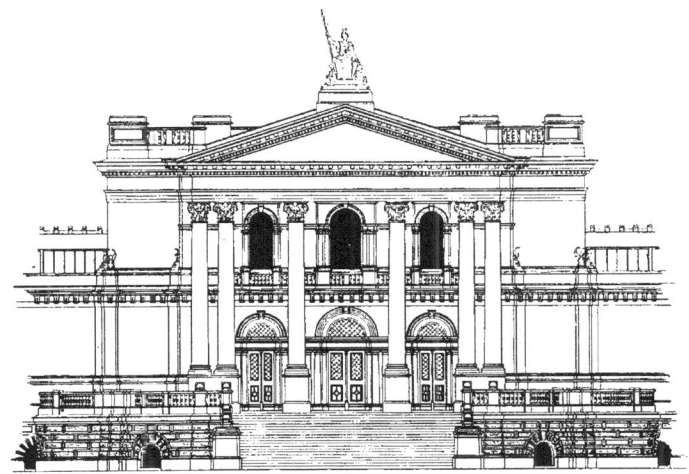

Central Part of Front Elevation. From the Design of the Architect, Sidney R. J. Smith, F.R.I.B.A.

'LITTLE MISS MUFFIT.'

FROM THE PAINTING BY SIR J. EVERETT MILLAIS, BART., R.A.

"IF he had never touched historical nor sacred art, if he were not supreme in portraiture and admirable in landscape, if nineteen-twentieths of his work were swept away by accident, his studies of the beauty and sweetness of childhood alone would still win for him a place beside the painter of 'Penelope Boothby.'" Thus wrote Mr. Andrew Lang of Sir John Millais in 1881, and if there was then no question as to this artist's claim to be ranked with Sir Joshua Reynolds as an interpreter of child life, there can be still less question now; seeing that in the intervening years many more superb pictures have appeared to add to his series of studies of children, a series already long enough at that time to establish a reputation.

It may be of interest to recall here a few of the most important of these subjects. One of the earliest is 'Autumn Leaves,' now in the Manchester City Art Gallery, in which are four little maidens, each of whose faces is an interesting study of typical childish character, while the composition, with its burning leaves and autumn twilight, conveys, by the painter's art, as Mr. Lang has said, a sentiment not consciously present in the minds of the actors in the scene. Then there are the two pretty children whom kind-hearted old Sir Isumbras, in his golden armour, is carrying across the ford in the picture of 1857—one of Sir John's own favourite pictures. And who is not familiar with 'My First Sermon,' which, by the way, represents the painter's eldest daughter, an awed little maiden sitting straightly on a straight bench looking up in awe and wondering at the preacher? Or 'My Second Sermon,' in which the novelty has already worn off, and she has incontinently gone to sleep? We must not forget, too, the 'Minuet,' illustrated in this number, the charming 'Souvenir of Velasquez' (now in the Diploma Gallery), the ' Boyhood of Raleigh,' 'Forbidden Fruit,' 'The Princes in the Tower,' and countless portraits, most of which at one time or another have been published in THE ART JOURNAL. But his later triumphs are, of course, fresher in the public mind, and they are certainly stronger in public favour. One of the most successful was 'Cinderella,' exhibited at the Royal Academy of 1881. That picture and the one before us both represent themes taken from the nursery, and to some extent invite consideration together.

It should be remembered that there are few keener critics than children of the representations of subjects which they know and understand. They are intense realists, and like to find every detail, and to find it correct. Who of us has been so long a "grown-up" that he cannot still recall the feeling of half-resentful indignation which he experienced as a child at some Christmas pantomime, on finding that a story with which he was familiar had all got jumbled, and was not performed " by the card"? How disappointed we were to find that Ali Baba (or Robinson Crusoe, as the case may be) was a person of feminine appearance, with a shrill, strident voice and a turn for topical songs! How keen was our disgust at Sinbad the Sailor's mother—of whom, by the way, we had never heard before—a wholly odious and vulgar individual with coarse manners and unshaven chin! There are no judges more acute or pertinacious than children, none more quick to detect and to resent liberties taken with subjects which they know by heart.

It may be that Sir John remembered to what an exacting class of little critics he was appealing when he painted these pictures of 'Cinderella' and 'Little Miss Muffit.' It certainly seems that the childish observer would be difficult to please who found either of them unsatisfying. There is Cinderella in her shabby clothes, broom and all, seated in the kitchen waiting for her fairy godmother; and here is Miss Muffit, with her curds and whey, and a most exquisitely comical expression of alarm on her face, caused by the imposing big spider who is just about to commit his great historical act of seating himself at her side. What more could the most exacting juvenile demand? The elders, of course, look for other qualities in these pictures than those which delight the children. Their old enthusiasm has faded, alas! for nursery rhymes and nursery games—save, perhaps, for the old game of " trying to pick up gold and silver on Tom Tiddler's ground," which, indeed, has an unpleasant knack of demanding attention after schooldays are over. They are drawn by the masterly technique, the faultless drawing, the exquisite colour and the felicitous arrangement of these fascinating creations of child character; qualities which, though the children cannot help unconsciously feeling, they shall not completely understand until the time arrives at which a man begins to analyse his pleasures.

And yet, while the painter has met all the possible objections of a juvenile audience, a study of these works of Sir John Millais seems to point to the fact that it was the artist's love of childish character, and not primarily the desire to illustrate any story, which prompted him to paint them. They only afforded an opportunity for depicting some charming phases of childhood in an original way. The accessories that complete the themes are all put in, and well put in, but they are carefully restrained and subordinated. The necessary accessories for Miss Muffit's story were not too distracting to be rendered *in toto*, so that she is not so apt an illustration of what we are saying as Cinderella, whose broom and bellows are kept well in the background, and only a faint glow betrays the kitchen fire behind. Other artists have represented Cinderella as a small figure in a large kitchen, Sir John gives us the figure and only suggests the situation. In the 'Little Princes in the Tower,' engraved in THE ART JOURNAL in 1884, the picture is obviously for the two fair English lads with their bonnie faces, expressive of terrified expectation, for the background is only a wall and a stone staircase.

We have no space to do more than allude in passing to such well-known pictures as ' Bubbles,' with its noble little fellow with the curly hair; 'Cherry Ripe,' the one of which Sir John is himself most proud ; 'Sweetest Eyes were ever seen,' and ' Une Grande Dame ' ; but they must be known to nearly every one. Several others which have not been engraved are equally fine in artistic quality, and the four delightful canvases recently exhibited at The Fine Art Society show us how strongly the delights of childhood still appeal to the painter.

Of the men of our generation to whom the power has been given to enter fully into childhood's feelings, to realise and record its happy innocence and unconscious charm, we can only think of one who is worthy to rank with Millais, and he is the creator of Little Nell, of Tiny Tim, of Paul Dombey, and David Copperfield. It is not too much to say that in the case of both artist and novelist the insight shown in their work proceeds from a genuine love of their little subjects. There can be few of us who have never felt the regret expressed in Tom Hood's pathetic lines—

"That now I'm farther off from Heaven
Than when I was a boy";

and does not the secret of the never-failing charm of these creations of Millais and Dickens lie in the fact that they bring back to us the recollection of the lost days of our buried youth—

" When the Heavens were closer to us,
And the Gods were more familiar"?

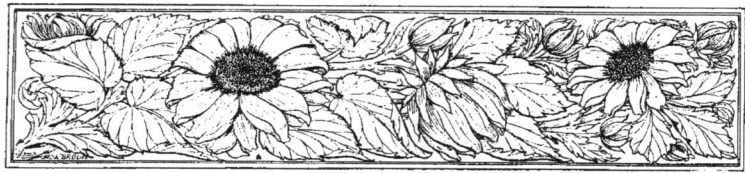

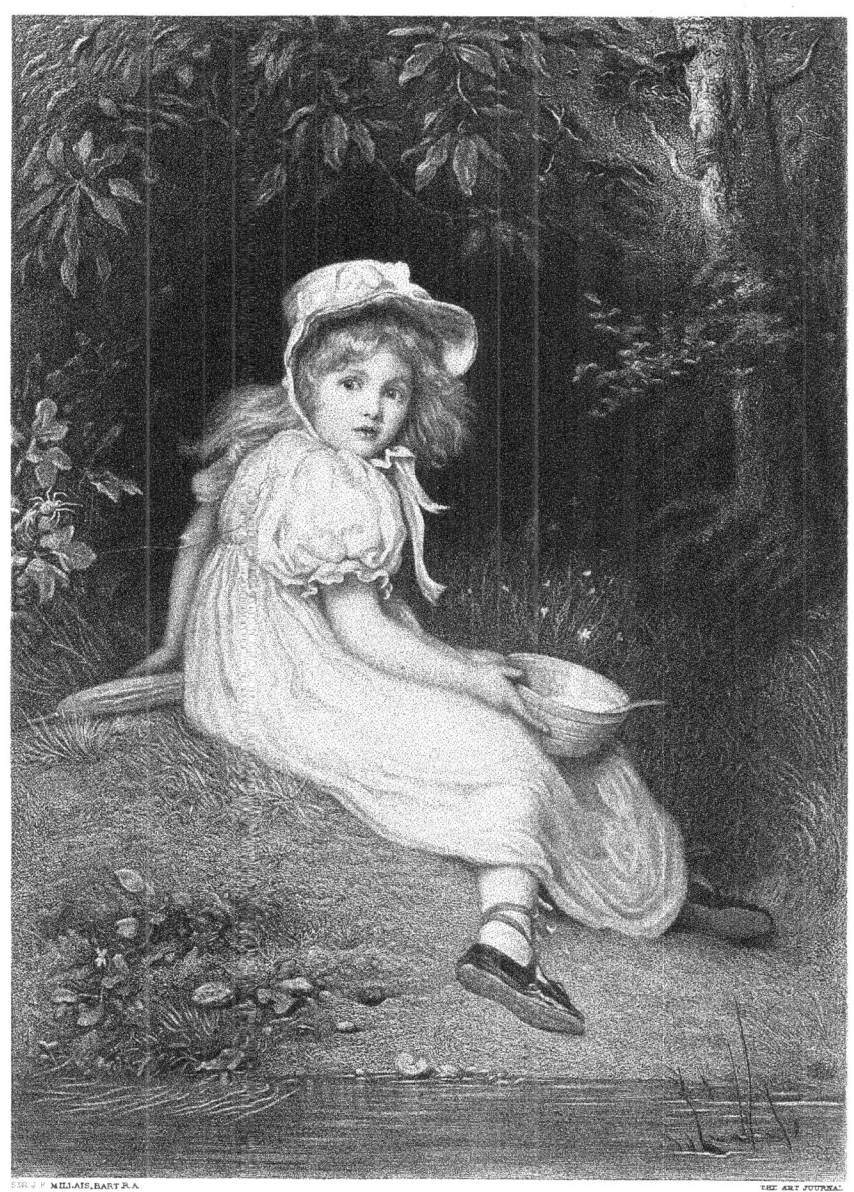

"LITTLE MISS MUFFIT."

BY PERMISSION OF MR T. MCLEAN, THE OWNER OF THE COPYRIGHT.

LONDON. J.S. VIRTUE & CO LIMITED.

ART NOTES.

THE death of Mr. Philip Gilbert Hamerton, editor of *The Portfolio*, removes the most prominent Art critic, next to Mr. Ruskin, of our time. Of a singularly retiring disposition, one to whom controversy was ever distasteful, Mr. Hamerton was not very well known to the general public; but to the connoisseur and lover of the Fine Arts his works were appreciated, and his opinions more widely accepted, than any other writer, not even excepting the eminent critic just mentioned.

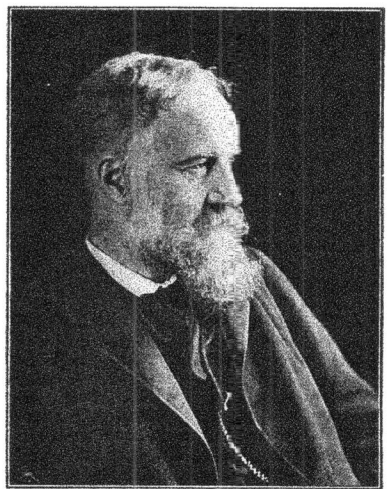

PHILIP GILBERT HAMERTON.
(*From a Photo. by F. Saterfield.*)

At the same time Mr. Hamerton was not without his limitations; and his estimate of the famous Barbizon painter was, that although Corot might be a poet, " it was only in a tame and limited way." He also failed to understand the best work of Mr. Whistler, and " The Gentle Art " contains a memorable passage devoted to the remarks of " a Mr. Hamerton."

Mr. Hamerton was born at Laneside, Shaw, Lancashire, on September 10th, 1834, and his experience was somewhat varied before he settled down as a writer on Art. At twenty-eight, however, he was selected by Woodward, the Queen's Librarian, who edited the publication, to contribute to the *Fine Arts Quarterly Review* an estimate of the Paris Salon of 1863, and from this time forward Mr. Hamerton was a recognised authority on Art questions. From 1866 to 1868 he was the Art critic of *The Saturday Review*, and in 1868 he published his most famous work, " Etching and Etchers." Ten years later his " Graphic Arts " appeared; in 1884 " Landscape," and only two years ago " Man in Art."
1894.

Besides these large volumes he also published a number of smaller works of great interest, and always charmingly written. Since its first number, in 1870, he has " conducted " *The Portfolio*, which throughout has been rendered attractive by his writings and illustrations, both in etching and block work. Mr. Hamerton spent most of his life in France, first at Sens, afterwards at Autun, and latterly near Paris, where he died on November 4. He was in active correspondence with artists and critics in Great Britain, and it is to be hoped that some day his delightful letters will be brought together in a memoir.

The exhibition of the Society of Portrait Painters in the New Gallery is the most successful which has been held. Professor Herkomer's large canvas of a skirt dancer is another evidence of the wonderful fertility and enterprise of this artist. The picture as a work of Art is far from being entirely successful, and it is unnecessarily cold in colour, but it gives evidence of a lively spirit, which does not hesitate to dare something, even although perfection is not achieved at one bound. Mr. Lavery makes a decided step forward in the ' Duchesse de Frias,' a Spanish aristocrat of elegant mien expressively painted. Bastien Lepage's full-length of a French dame is a wonderfully careful piece of technique, marking the full tide of a style of work which is not now so run after by young artists as it was ten years ago.

The autumn exhibition of the Royal Society of British Artists is marked by considerable advance in artistic quality, and some of the younger painters, notably Mr. Bernard Priestman, Mr. G. C. Haité, Mr. Snell, Mr. Fullwood, and Mr. Frank Dean, contribute canvases of great merit in tone and colour. The Institute of Painters in Oil Colours also moves on a little towards better quality, and the pictures of Mr. J. L. Pickering, Mr. Hope McLachlan, Mr. Leslie Thomson, Mr. R. W. Allan, and Mr. A. D. Reid are satisfactory examples of good artistic work.

The November exhibitions far exceeded in number the usual formidable array; unhappily quality of work was not so abundant. In Mr. McLean's exhibition, several early English pictures were of the highest quality. Messrs. Tooth contented themselves with a more florid display. Messrs. Graves opened with a collection of ' Picturesque Wales,' by W. W. Manning, and Mr. Dunthorne with a number of ' Wild Animals,' by J. T. Nettleship. Amongst the last a giraffe was remarkable for the fine quality obtained, by pastel, of its furry coat.

With reference to the Hill bequest to the South Kensington Museum announced in our October number (p. 314) we understand that there is no likelihood of its acceptance by the authorities of the Museum, as the conditions laid down by the testator's will are too onerous.

Special attention is directed to the important announcement respecting the Presentation Etching of ' HIT,' after Sir Frederic Leighton, P.R.A., which will be sent, under certain conditions, to all subscribers to THE ART JOURNAL for 1895.

5 D

With reference to the article on "The Cape of Good Hope Art Gallery," which appeared in our October number (p. 298),

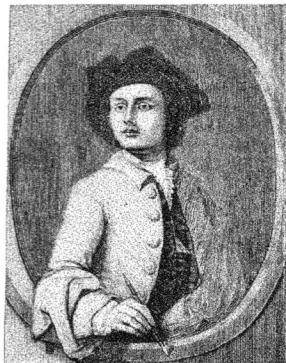

PORTRAIT OF VAN STRY. BY HIMSELF.
IN THE CAPE OF GOOD HOPE ART GALLERY.

we are asked by Mr. A. De Smidt, the Trustee of the Gallery, to state that the Cape Government contemplate taking over the property, in buildings, money, and pictures, of the Association for the Promotion of the Fine Arts in Cape Colony, as soon as the necessary arrangements can be completed. It is proposed to create a committee of management, elected in equal numbers by the Government and the Association. We are enabled to publish herewith an engraving of the portrait of Van Stry, painted by himself, one of the most important Dutch pictures in the collection.

THE SOCIETY OF ILLUSTRATORS.

To the Editor of the ART JOURNAL.

SIR,
May I hope that you will be able to spare space to answer some reflections upon the above Society (of the Committee of which I am a member) that have appeared in the November number of *The Magazine of Art*.

With the objects, aims, and possible action of the Society, I shall, by the request of my colleagues, deal with elsewhere, and at no distant date. But those objects and possible action may be, if indeed they be not already, seriously affected by the criticism I refer to. That such should be issued under the ægis of a firm employing so many of the craftsmen we have already enrolled as members, is in itself sufficient to excite regret, apart from the fact that these strictures were made from a point of view far from broadly editorial.

The opening remark that "*the prospectus issued by the Committee of this new Society is strange reading*" is possible, but infinitely preferable, methinks, to strange reasoning. The first cause of complaint appears to be that "it declares no distinct policy, but appeals for one to its members." To whom should it appeal? is the deduction from this objection. In such a society as that of the Illustrators we think it should be the function of the committee to as far as possible give force to the opinions of its members as a body, and not necessarily to any personal grievance.

It may be, that it will be found both desirable and necessary to formulate a new method of contract between artist and publisher, not *journalist and editor*; but why such should necessarily be "*with the result that an end would soon be put to all confidence between the parties*," is difficult to understand or accept. The deduction is, that a confidence exists. Unfortunately, no such general confidence exists, and we are anxious, amongst other things, by strict business observance to put an end to this *want* of confidence.

Now, in answer to the remarks which follow under the heading "The Cliché Question." Why should we be expected to supply *The Magazine of Art* with information or suggestion as to "*how the matter may be dealt with*," etc. As our Committee is composed of practical men, we are quite aware, from experience, of the difficulties; and as most of us have been sufferers from the present system, why is the question of "*wholesale reproduction of exhibited works*" wholly outside the field of a society of illustrators, since many of them are painters first and illustrators after, or merge from one to the other? Moreover, one of the distinct rules of the Society is more explicitly expressed in a note, thus:—

"*In consequence of enquiries as to the scope of Rule III., the Committee have, after due deliberation, agreed as follows:—Seeing that Rule V. provides that 'fifteen members of the Committee shall be workers in black and white,' it may be taken that the ten others need not be specially classifiable under that head, and the Rule, as agreed by the meeting of March 2nd, 1894, may be safely interpreted to mean that all artists whose work is or has been reproduced are eligible, thus admitting painters.*"

It does not prove that the present method of publishing pictures of the year is not a nuisance, "*because the public quickly buy them up and demand them.*" The public pay, and have a right to demand what they pay for. What we complain of is that the younger artists receive applications for permission to publish their pictures appearing in exhibitions (and generally when permission is granted reproduced and printed vilely) without *any payment*. It is true that Messrs. Cassell adopted a method of payment, but this has been confined to the works of Royal Academicians and a few well-known men, and has been by no means representative. Moreover, the issue of such was not considered a nuisance, but the *wholesale* issue reproduction. In answer to the query, "*Is the Society prepared to undertake the production?*" Yes! the Society would be so prepared, and bring it out to date, but the Society would not do all these things *without editorial, commercial, and publishing training*, which exists in more quarters than one. We are quite convinced of this —may in many cases be assured of it—that many of our leading painters would give the proceeds of the reproduction of their pictures in such form to benefit some society like this.

It is perfectly obvious that everything must depend upon the numerical strength of the Society and its financial resources. All societies and undertakings do. Moreover, we hold that we can only move in such matters, if and when we are a sufficiently representative body.

Further that "*The Society, in fact, aims at being a trade union, but without a trade union's power to establish a strike, and would dictate terms without the ability to enforce them.*" We have only the assertion of this anonymous writer; who having complained that we had not declared a policy, proceeds to make one for us, but we must be excused if we do not see our way to adopt it, especially as the writer seems to confuse his terms. We have the "ability" to dictate terms, though not the *power* to enforce them. At present we have attempted neither.

To the remark, "*We have every sympathy with the Society of Illustrators, the formation of which we have advocated for years; but we can confess little admiration for the admittedly commercial tone of its programme,*" it will be difficult to detect the sympathy from the way in which the Society has been commented upon before any action whatever has been taken; and why the *commercial* tone of our programme should be objected to, is difficult to imagine. Artists have for all time been twitted with want of business capacity. We *should* be grateful to learn from such an unquestionable authority upon this point, that our objects are commercial. As to the dignity of our art, it is that very point which alone should be sufficient to enrol all Art-workers, for now the dignity is at the mercy of those who have all to gain and nothing to lose by sowing discord in any combination attempted for mutual benefit. Finally, we have not asked any one to pay *one or two "annual subscriptions."* One annual subscription is enough, and we do not propose to interfere with a *couple of trades*. (What of the commercial instinct here?) Since we already number most of the leading artists of the day as members, from the reference to the *masquerading as an artistic society* we can only assume that the writer's knowledge, like his logic, is very deficient.

I am, sir, your obedient servant, GEO. C. HAITÉ.

BOOKS FOR CHRISTMAS.

THE recent discoveries in methods of reproductions are best employed in the making of plates from well-known pictures. Only a few years ago, to examine any of the older

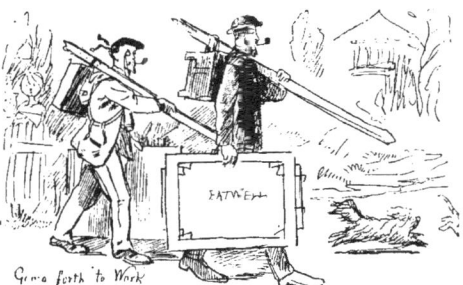

FROM PEN AND PENCIL SKETCHES. BY H. S. MARKS, R.A.

masters it was necessary not only to visit all the galleries of Europe, but also to be able to remember them in detail if comparisons were required, or to rely on engravings, which, though excellent works of Art, did not pretend to exhibit the technique of the painter. All this is changed now, and the whole work of a painter may be brought together in a volume for comparison and discussion. "RAPHAEL'S MADONNAS," by Karl Károly (Bell & Sons), contains excellent plates of all the chief pictures of the master, together with an unambitious but sufficient account of Raphael's life. Great care has been bestowed on the selection of the pictures, and the volume specially appeals to those who wish to continue the comparisons indicated in the text. A graceful design by Mr. Gleeson White adorns the cover.

The youthful admirers of Mr. Andrew Lang will be more than satisfied with the "YELLOW FAIRY BOOK" (Longmans), the fourth of the series, and full of delightful tales for children. Mr. H. J. Ford, who provides the illustrations, brings adequate artistic powers to the pictorial expression of the text, and it is interesting to observe the development of this talented artist since the publication, several years ago, of the renowned "Red Fairy Book." 'The Green Monkey in the Bath' is one of the more elaborate compositions.—Equally interesting to children, and even more artistic and satisfactory in its get-up, is the "BOOK OF FAIRY TALES," by Baring-Gould, illustrated by A. J. Gaskin (Methuen). The pictures give evidence of some haste in design, but their simple directness appeals strongly to the untraditional mind of youth, and the only regret is that there are not more of them. 'Red Riding Hood' is illustrated overleaf.

"THE PILGRIM'S PROGRESS" has probably been illustrated as often as the Bible, but we doubt if the majestic religious sentiment pervading the similitudes of the "Man of Bedford" has ever received so complete artistic expression as in Mr. William Strang's austere illustrations, published by J. C. Nimmo. With here and there a recollection of Rembrandt, Millet and Legros—perhaps too evidently the artistic gods worshipped by Mr. Strang — these etchings breathe the essence of the religion approved by John Bunyan. The "Slough of Despond" alone is enough to make the volume remarkable; and, in these days of the fleeting and the pretty, it is consoling to find a publisher with enough moral courage to prompt the publication.— Serious art is also represented in the two new volumes of "LES ARTISTES CÉLÈBRES" (L'Art), Saint-Aubin by Adrien Moreau, and Benveruto Cellini by E. Molinier, which space forbids us to more than mention. Cellini is the more interesting, and the illustrations much excel the average of the series.

The "genial" and almost "veteran" Academician, Mr. H. S. Marks, has published his "PEN AND PENCIL SKETCHES' (2 vols., Chatto & Windus), which are illustrated by many drawings by himself and by his friends. The book should be read by both painters and patrons, not to mention Art critics and Art historians. The young painter of to-day will find a forecast of his present-time aspirations and friendships in the "St. John's Wood Clique," the patron will learn how he is regarded by the artist and how precious his visits can be made by acting promptly and generously

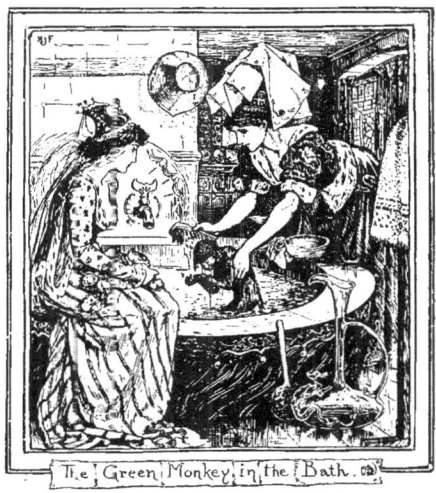

FROM THE YELLOW FAIRY BOOK. BY ANDREW LANG.

to a struggling painter; the Art critic will be surprised to find that Mr. Marks was the "somewhat rough and chippy" pen-slasher of the *Spectator* thirty years ago; and the historian will find many anecdotes and incidents likely to enliven the sombre pages of an artistic chronicle. Mr. Marks makes comments on the events of the past few years, but he has learned the art of praising the individual and never mentioning a name when he finds it necessary—and that is but seldom—to set forth a word of blame. On the previous page we give a sketch of Mr. Marks and Mr. G. D. Leslie "Going forth to Work," Mr. Leslie leading the way.

Following up the success of Mr. Spielmann's beautiful volume on "Cat Life and Cat Character," Messrs. Cassell have issued a companion folio on "CATS AND KITTENS," by Madame Henriette Ronner. The most exacting lover of our purring favourite could wish for no finer representations of the race. Madame Ronner has completed her mastery of the painting of fur, and having a remarkable gift for story-telling, the compositions are always interesting as well as satisfactory. The sketches interspersed add to the artistic value of the publication. As a handsome Christmas present, no better volume has been offered this season.

Another charming book, and of handier size, is Mrs. Fielde's "CORNER OF CATHAY" (Macmillan), with a dozen dainty reproductions in colours of Chinese drawings by masters of "Go-Leng," in Swatow. Their qualities in tone and delicacy are unsurpassed in modern work. The text is interesting, and what is not so common in works on the people of China, it is also trustworthy.—The illustrated Dryburgh Edition of Scott's Novels (A. & C. Black) is now complete in twenty-five well-printed volumes, with illustrations by many eminent artists.—Messrs. Jacques' Games in the character of "Quartettes" of pictures in the National Gallery and other subjects, are ingenious and instructive Christmas novelties.

"WILD FLOWERS IN ART AND NATURE," by J. C. L. Sparkes, of the National Art Training School, and F. W. Burbidge, of the Dublin Botanical Gardens (Edward Arnold), combines Art and Science in a happy way, each flower being

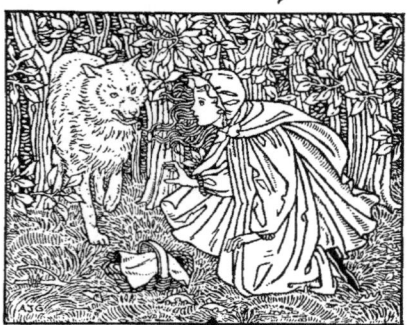

RED RIDING HOOD. BY A. J. GASKIN.
FROM BARING GOULD'S "BOOK OF FAIRY TALES."

described botanically, and then artistically in simple language. The flower is represented in a large coloured plate by H. G. Moon, and this is analysed and explained so that the Art student may easily follow the directions given.

It is regrettable that Archdeacon Farrar does not come forward frankly as a critic of Art, for then it would be possible to meet him on what is really his own ground. But as he continually takes care, in his excursions into the region of artistic criticism, to begin by disclaiming any desire "to intrude upon the functions of the Art critic," so no doubt he would consider criticism based on the contents of his recent works, to be unfair, if treated from what is the point he can most easily be attacked. But at Christmas time, and for Christmas books, one must be lenient, so we shall content ourselves by commending the illustrations in "THE LIFE OF CHRIST AS REPRESENTED IN ART" (A. & C. Black), which have been most carefully selected.

Waldstein's "WORK OF JOHN RUSKIN" (Methuen), is a guide to that writer's most varied literary labours, giving special attention to his volumes of artistic criticism. It is doubtful, perhaps, if such a work is necessary, but granting that it is, this series of essays is instructive to the beginner in the cult of Ruskin through which every one must pass. Due appreciation is given to Mr. Ruskin's splendid wealth of language, the most noteworthy gift possessed by the once anonymous "Graduate of Oxford." This brings us to "LETTERS ADDRESSED TO A COLLEGE FRIEND," by John Ruskin (Allen). These letters, written between 1840 and 1845, that is, when Mr. Ruskin was only twenty-one, are very suggestive reading for youths who seek to know the methods of our most discussed Art critic. They show the care he bestowed on trifles, and for this reason alone are worthy of preservation.

Amongst books which take their interest from local themes Geo. Milner's "STUDIES OF NATURE IN ARRAN" (Longmans) is likely to be a favourite. An unembellished—in fact, somewhat plain—narrative of the usual pleasure of a seaside party, the ordinary reader will probably find some reflection of the experiences of himself and his friends, and thus feel delicately flattered. The plates by Noel Johnson lose something in the reproduction, but they are suitable to the text, although the drawing is not always unimpeachable.

The Art Union of London subscription plate is an important etching by Mr. David Law, after the picture 'The Silver Dart,' by J. Clayton Adams. The subject of the etching is so beautiful that Mr. Law has had no difficulty in rendering his plate one of his most successful productions. Now that the recent trade depression is near its end, it is to be hoped that the Art Union will regain its former popularity.

'The Minister's Man' is an excellent reproduction from the picture by Henry Kerr, A.R.S.A., and published by Messrs. Dott of Edinburgh. Presbyterians in search of a present for their "minister" should see this publication, which has been appropriately dedicated to Mr. J. M. Barrie.

PRINTED BY J. S. VIRTUE AND CO., LIMITED, CITY ROAD, LONDON.